PLANNING AND URBAN DESIGN STANDARDS

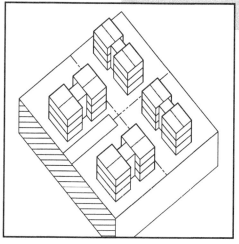

PLANNING AND URBAN DESIGN STANDARDS

STUDENT EDITION

FREDERICK STEINER
KENT BUTLER
University of Texas at Austin

AMERICAN PLANNING ASSOCIATION

EMINA SENDICH
Graphics Editor

BICENTENNIAL
1807
WILEY
2007
BICENTENNIAL

JOHN WILEY & SONS, INC.

This book is printed on acid-free paper. ∞

Copyright © 2007 by John Wiley & Sons, Inc. All rights reserved.

Published by John Wiley & Sons, Inc., Hoboken, New Jersey.
Published simultaneously in Canada

No part of this publication may be reproduced, stored in a retrieval system, or transmitted in any form or
by any means, electronic, mechanical, photocopying, recording, scanning, or otherwise, except as permitted
under Section 107 or 108 of the 1976 United States Copyright Act, without either the prior written
permission of the Publisher, or authorization through payment of the appropriate per-copy fee to the
Copyright Clearance Center, Inc., 222 Rosewood Drive, Danvers, MA 01923, (978) 750-8400, fax (978)
750-4470, or on the Web at www.copyright.com. Requests to the Publisher for permission should be
addressed to the Permissions Department, John Wiley & Sons, Inc., 111 River Street, Hoboken, NJ 07030,
(201) 748-6011, fax (201) 748-6008, e-mail: permcoordinator@wiley.com.

Limit of Liability/Disclaimer of Warranty: While the publisher and author have used their best efforts in
preparing this book, they make no representations or warranties with respect to the accuracy or
completeness of the contents of this book and specifically disclaim any implied warranties of
merchantability or fitness for a particular purpose. No warranty may be created or extended by sales
representatives or written sales materials. The advice and strategies contained herein may not be suitable
for your situation. You should consult with a professional where appropriate. Neither the publisher nor
author shall be liable for any loss of profit or any other commercial damages, including but not limited
to special, incidental, consequential, or other damages.

For general information on our other products and services or for technical support, please contact our
Customer Care Department, within the United States at (800) 762-2974, outside the United States at
(317) 572-3993 or fax (317) 572-4002.

Wiley also publishes its books in a variety of electronic formats. Some content that appears in print may not be
available in electronic books. For more information about Wiley products, visit our website at www.wiley.com.

Library of Congress Cataloging-in-Publication Data:
Planning and urban design standards / American Planning Association.— 1st ed.
          p. cm.
      Includes index.
        ISBN-13: 978-0-471-47581-1 (cloth)   ISBN-13: 978-0-471-76090-0 (student version)
        ISBN-10: 0-471-47581-5 (cloth)   ISBN-10: 0-471-76090-0 (student version)
   1. Building—Details—Drawings. 2. Building—Details—Drawings—Standards. I. American Planning
Association.
      TH2031.P55 2006
      711—dc22
                      2005016319

Printed in the United States of America

V10013141_082019

CONTENTS

Part 6

IMPLEMENTATION TECHNIQUES 345

FOREWORD

On behalf of the American Planning Association (APA) and our Planning Foundation, and along with our partners, John Wiley & Sons, Inc., and the University of Texas at Austin, we are delighted to see the publication of the first student edition of *Planning and Urban Design Standards*. This book, derived from the full edition of *Planning and Urban Design Standards,* published in January 2006, contains information from that volume determined to be especially suited for planning students.

What is a planning and urban design "standard"? Responding to this question was a serious challenge for the contributors, editors, and advisors developing the book. According to the Merriam-Webster dictionary, a standard can be "the ideal in terms of which something can be judged: 'they live by the standards of their community'"; or it can be "a basis for comparison; a reference point against which other things can be evaluated: 'they set the standard for all subsequent work.'" This book strives to do both—provide reference to the standards met by the profession and present the standards all should work to achieve. Moreover, the work embraces both standards that are widely used, as well as those that are emerging.

The full edition of *Planning and Urban Design Standards* was the result of a highly complex, three-year collaborative effort involving a broad array of planning and urban design disciplines. With contributions from leading experts in private planning and urban design firms, academia, and public planning agencies across the United States, this book is by the profession for its future professionals. We express our deep appreciation to these contributors, many of them APA members. They shared their wisdom and insights unselfishly for the benefit of all who will use this work to develop their planning and urban design knowledge and skills.

The structure and content of *Planning and Urban Design Standards* would not have been possible without the guidance of the gifted planners, designers, practitioners, and educators who served on our advisory board: Karen B. Alschuler, FAICP, SMWM, San Francisco; W. Paul Farmer, FAICP, Executive Director and CEO, American Planning Association, Chicago; Jerold S. Kayden, Harvard University, Cambridge, Massachusetts; M. David Lee, FAIA, Stull & Lee, Inc., Boston; Diana C. Mendes, AICP, DMJM + Harris Planning, Fairfax, Virginia; John S. Rahaim, Department of Planning and Development, Seattle, Washington; Brenda C. Scheer, AICP, AIA, University of Utah College of Architecture and Planning, Salt Lake City; and Frederick R. Steiner, FASLA, University of Texas at Austin.

APA is a nonprofit education organization and membership association committed to urban, suburban, regional, and rural planning. In 2003, APA celebrated the twenty-fifth anniversary of the consolidation of two predecessor organizations: the American Institute of Planners, founded in 1917, and the American Society of Planning Officials, established in 1934. Today, our 38,000-member organization has 46 geographically defined chapters and 19 divisions devoted to specialized planning interests. APA and its professional institute, the American Institute of Certified Planners (AICP), advance the art and science of planning to meet the needs of people and society. Our involvement in creating *Planning and Urban Design Standards* is the latest contribution to that goal. We hope you will find this volume, the full edition of *Planning and Urban Design Standards,* and the revised editions that follow over the years to be the most comprehensive and useful quick references on essential planning topics available.

MEGAN S. LEWIS, AICP
Managing Editor, *Planning and Urban Design Standards*
American Planning Association
Chicago, Illinois

WILLIAM R. KLEIN, AICP
Executive Editor, *Planning and Urban Design Standards*
American Planning Association
Chicago, Illinois

PREFACE

John Wiley & Sons, Inc., the American Planning Association (APA), and the Community and Regional Planning Program, School of Architecture, University of Texas at Austin, are pleased to present this first edition of *Planning and Urban Design Standards, Student Edition*. We hope that students in planning and related fields will find this book a companion for their education. The student edition is not intended to serve as the primary text for introductory planning courses. Rather, it serves as a reference for a broad range of planning courses required in accredited planning program curricula. In addition, the student edition is meant to be a useful reference for planning courses offered in architecture, landscape architecture, geography, civil engineering, environmental studies, and public administration programs.

To better understand the needs of planning curricula, we surveyed course materials from 30 accredited planning programs. Some 150 course syllabi were reviewed and analyzed for content. We used 65 planning course keyword categories, ranging from "architecture" to "urban form." Information about planning programs, course descriptions, and reading lists was collected and compiled in a database.

We found that planning programs offer a significant proportion of course curricula on environmental issues. These courses are not usually a part of the standard, required curriculum but do constitute a large share of types of courses offered. This could reflect theoretical shifts in the profession and/or trends across changes in primary concerns of society. We also found that required curricula tend to have similar lists of recommended readings whereas electives have a wider range of references.

The survey also indicated a need for more sources that address graphic communication. In addition, we found this need especially important for courses related to physical planning, urban design, environmental planning, and transportation.

This student edition is an abridgement of the first edition of *Planning and Urban Design Standards,* edited by Megan Lewis and William Klein of APA. The editors of *Planning and Urban Design Standards* made our task both easy and difficult. They produced such a thorough, excellent book with comprehensive, detailed information, which eased our undertaking. Our task proved to be a challenge for the same reason. With this rich resource base, we were challenged to identify material to cull. Our survey helped with this task, as did the Student Edition Advisory Board.

Although the student edition is an abridgement of the larger, more comprehensive volume produced by APA, it contains original pages whose content was guided by the Student Edition Advisory Board: Timothy Beatley, University of Virginia; Cheryl Contant, Georgia Institute of Technology; Ann Forsyth, University of Minnesota; Gary Hack, University of Pennsylvania; Jerold Kayden, Harvard University; G. Mathias Kondolf, University of California-Berkeley; Megan Lewis, APA; and Janice Cervelli Schach, Clemson University. In addition to planning educators, we included faculty involved in landscape architecture, architecture, and geography programs on this advisory board.

We would like to express our deep appreciation to Paul Farmer, William Klein, Megan Lewis, and their APA colleagues for setting the stage for the student edition. They spent three years preparing *Planning and Urban Design Standards*. Their work was built on Wiley's experience with the Graphic Standards series, which has been led for more than 70 years by *Architecture Graphic Standards,* currently in its tenth edition with more than 1 million copies sold. The architecture standards book has been joined by similar volumes for interior design, landscape architecture, and planning and urban design. Each of these larger volumes is accompanied by a student edition.

Planning is a profession and, even more, a way of thinking, which links the best possible information to choices facing communities and regions. As a result, planning is an academic discipline that overlaps with several other fields. Planning is also fundamental to democracy, involving many citizens and elected officials. Students and future citizens are at the beginning of a lifetime of making choices about the future of the built environment. Our hope is that *Planning and Urban Design Standards, Student Edition* will serve as both a launching pad and a touchstone for that journey.

FREDERICK STEINER, Ph.D. FASLA
KENT BUTLER, Ph.D.
Community and Regional Planning Program
School of Architecture
University of Texas at Austin

ACKNOWLEDGMENTS

JOHN WILEY & SONS, INC.

Amanda Miller
Vice President and Publisher

Kathryn Malm Bourgoine
Acquisitions Editor

Rosanne Koneval
Senior Editorial Assistant

Lauren Poplawski
Editorial Assistant

Fred Bernardi
Senior Production Manager

Jennifer Mazurkie
Senior Production Editor

Justin Mayhew
Senior Marketing Manager

Lucinda Geist
Designer

Janice Borzendowski
Copyeditor

STUDENT EDITION EDITORS

Frederick R. Steiner, Ph.D. FASLA
Executive Editor

Kent S. Butler, Ph.D. FASLA
Executive Editor

Kelly Beavers
Editorial Assistant

AMERICAN PLANNING ASSOCIATION

W. Paul Farmer, FAICP
Executive Director and CEO

William R. Klein, AICP
Executive Editor

Megan S. Lewis, AICP
Managing Editor

Lynn M. Ross, AICP
Assistant Editor

James A. Hecimovich
Editorial Advisor

Editorial Associates

Karen K. Lindblad, Associate AIA
Stuart Meck, FAICP
James C. Schwab, AICP
Stephen Sizemore, AICP
Suzanne Sutro Rhees, AICP

Interns

Kathleen Lacey
Courtney Owen
Sarah Wiebenson

Graphics Editor

InfoDesign, Staten Island, New York
Emina Sendich, Principal
Erin M. M. Conwell
Valerie E. Aymer

Illustration Support

URS Corporation, Minneapolis
SMWM, San Francisco

Student Edition Advisory Board

Ann Forsyth, Ph.D.
University of Minnesota Metropolitan Design Center
Minneapolis, Minnesota

Gary Hack, Ph.D.
University of Pennsylvania School of Design
Philadelphia, Pennsylvania

Jerold S. Kayden, J.D.
Harvard University
Cambridge, Massachusetts

Mathias Kondolf, Ph.D.
University of California
Berkeley, California

Megan Lewis, AICP
American Planning Association
Chicago, Illinois

Janice Cervelli Schach, M.L.A. FASLA
Clemson University
Clemson, South Carolina

Timothy Beatley, Ph.D.
University of Virginia
Charlottesville, Virginia

Cheryl Contant, Ph.D.
Georgia Tech University College of Architecture
Atlanta, Georgia

Text Contributors

Kheir Al-Kodmany, Ph.D.
Steven C. Ames
Americans for the Arts
Larz T. Anderson, AICP
Randall G. Arendt, FRTPI ASLA (Hon.)
Randall I. Atlas, Ph.D. AIA CPP

David L. Barth, ASLA AICP CPRP
Timothy Beatley, Ph.D.
Kelly A. Beavers
James F. Berry, J.D. Ph.D.
David C. Bier
Mia Birk
L. Carson Bise II, AICP
Brian W. Blaesser
Hendra Bong
Anthony J. Brazel
Jeanette Brown, P.E. DEE
Chris Burger
Andrea Burk
Kent S. Butler, Ph.D.
David M. Bush, Ph.D.

Robert J. Chaskin
Richard Claytor, PE
Elaine C. Cogan
Haven B. Cook
Donald G. Copper

Richard Dagenhart
Thomas L. Daniels, Ph.D.
Greg DiLoreto, P.E.
David Dixon, FAIA
Harry Dodson, ASLA
Donna Ducharme, AICP
James Duncan, FAICP
Teresa Durkin, ASLA

James D. Ebenhoh, AICP
Ann-Margaret Esnard, Ph.D.
Maurice G. Estes, Jr., AICP
Mary E. Eysenbach

Lee A. Fithian, AIA
Charles A. Flink, FASLA
Stephen B. Friedman, AICP CRE

Dale Glowa
Jay S. Golden
Michelle Gregory, AICP

William R. Haase IV, AICP
Julie Herman
Richard Herring, AIA LEED AP
Scott W. Horsley
Cynthia L. Hoyle, AICP
Christopher R. Hugo
Richard Hurwitz

Mark R. Johnson, AICP

Phillip R. Kemmerly, Ph.D.
Peter J. Kindel, AIA ASLA
William R. Klein, AICP
Gerrit J. Knaap, Ph.D.
G. Mathias Kondolf, Ph.D.
John P. Kretzmann, Ph.D.
Walter Kulash, P.E.

Megan S. Lewis, AICP
Karen K. Lindblad, Associate AIA
Michael K. Lindell, Ph.D.
Anne Locke, AIA
Thayer Long

Alan Mallach, FAICP
Richard D. Margerum, Ph.D.
Larry McClennan
John L. McKnight
Stuart Meck, FAICP
Diana C. Mendes, AICP
Roger M. Millar, PE FASCE AICP
Jennifer Morris, AICP
Marya Morris, AICP
John R. Mullin, Ph.D. FAICP

National Charrette Institute
Natural Lands Trust
William J. Neal, Ph.D.
Arthur C. Nelson, Ph.D. FAICP
Mark E. Nelson, LEP
Nancy I. Nishikawa, AICP

Robert B. Olshansky, Ph.D. AICP

Robert Paterson, Ph.D.
PICA — The Wireless Infrastructure Association

Bruce Ream, AIA Emeritus
Suzanne Sutro Rhees, AICP
Linda Cain Ruth, AIA

Maria Salvadori, SMWM
Henry Sanoff, AIA
Nancy Sappington
David Schellinger
Jeffrey Schoenbauer
James C. Schwab, AICP
Khaled Shammout, AICP

Geeti Silwal
Stephen G. Sizemore, AICP
Mary S. Smith, P.E.
Ken Snyder
Don Springhetti
Frederick R. Steiner, Ph.D. FASLA
Peter Swift, P.E.

Kenneth R. Tamminga
Stephen Tocknell, AICP

Sheila Vertino

William D. Wagoner, AICP PEM
Gregory A. Walker, AICP
Rachel N. Weber, Ph.D.
Alan C. Weinstein
Betty Jo White, Ph.D.
Jon D. Witten, AICP

Samuel Zimmerman
Paul Zykofsky, AICP

Illustration Sources

A. Nelessen Associates Inc.
Albany County (NY) Airport Authority
Alta Planning & Design
American Planning Association
Richard B. Andrews
Andropogon Associates, Ltd.
Donald Appleyard
ARI
Sherry Arnstein
ARUP

Jon Bell
Deborah Bowers
Brauer & Associates, Ltd.
Gary Brenniman
Andrew Brookes
Bucher Willis and Ratliff Corporation

California Air Resources Board
California Department of Transportation
California State Lands Commission
Camiros, Ltd.
Campbell Tui Campbell, Inc.
Center for Watershed Protection
CHANCE Management Advisors, Inc.
Chicago Metropolis 2020
City of Austin, TX
City of Burnsville, MN
City of Des Moines, WA
City of Miami Beach, FL
City of Navato (CA) Community Development
  Department
City of Pawtucket, RI
City of Phoenix, AZ
City of Platteville, WI
City of Portland, OR
City of San Francisco, CA
City of West Linn, OR
Collier County (FL) Emergency Management
Continuum Partners, LLC
CSO Architects
Cubellis, Inc.

Richard Dagenhart
Hemalata C. Dandekar, Ph.D.
Dane County, WI
Defenders of Wildlife
John J. Delaney
F.C. Dennis
Design Workshop
Dodson Associates
Constantinos Doxiades
Thomas Dunne

ECONorthwest Inc.
Bartholomew Elias
ESRI

Federal Emergency Management Agency
Federal Highway Administration
Federal Interagency Stream Restoration Working
  Group
Federal Transit Administration
Lawrence S. Finegold
FitzGerald Associates Architects
Florida Division of Forestry
E.C. Freund
Futurity, Inc.

Joel Garreau
Gas Technology Institute
Glatting Jackson
Goody Clancy
W.I. Goodman
Ronald Goodson
Greenways Incorporated

William Hallenbeck
Truman A. Hartshorn
Hillsborough County (Florida) City-County Planning
  Commission
Hoopa Valley Tribe
Horsley and Witten Group
Ebenezer Howard

Idaho Association of Soil Conservation Districts
Illinois Regional Transportation Authority
Indiana Department of Natural Resources
Institute of Transportation Engineers
Island Press

Carolyn Johnson
Bernie Jones

King County, Washington
David Knox Productions, Inc.

Landrum & Brown, Inc.
Luna Leopold
LMN Architects

Karl Manheim
Jerry Mitchell
Peter Musty
McGraw-Hill
Mead and Hunt, Inc.
Metcalf and Eddy
Metropolitan Design Center
Mid-America Regional Council
Montgomery County, MD

Napa County (CA) Board of Supervisors
National Agricultural Statistical Service
National Association of Home Builders
National Capital Planning Commission
National Charrette Institute
National Hurricane Center
National Interagency Fire Center
National Oceanic and Atmospheric Administration
National Oceanic and Atmospheric Administration
National Park Service
Naval Facilities Engineering Command
Noise Control Engineering Journal
North Carolina Division of Coastal Management
North Carolina Sea Grant

Gregory Ohlmacher
Oregon Department of Transportation
OWP/P Architects
Frederick Law Olmsted

Arthur Palmer
Patrick Engineering, Inc.
Perkins and Will
Phillips Swager Associates
Pima County (AZ) Clerk of the Board
Portland Metro

Rich Poirot
Steve Price

Reed Construction Data
Regional Plan Association

Mel Scott
Skidmore, Owings & Merrill LLP
Southeast Michigan Greenways
Southeastern Pennsylvania Transportation Authority
State of New Jersey Pinelands Commission
Paul Sullivan

The Consensus Building Handbook
Transportation Research Board
Tri-Met

U.S. Army Corps of Engineers
U.S. Census Bureau
U.S. Department of Agriculture
U.S. Department of Agriculture, Economic Research
    Service
U.S. Department of Commerce
U.S. Department of Energy
U.S. Department of Housing and Urban Development
U.S. Environmental Protection Agency

U.S. Fish and Wildlife Service
U.S. Forest Service
U.S. Geological Survey
U.S. Geological Survey, Northern Wildlife Prairie
    Research Center
U.S. Government Printing Office
U.S. Green Building Council
United Properties
Urban Design Associates

Vanasse Hangen Brustlin, Inc.
Calvert Vaux
Virginia Marine Resources Commission
VR Marketing, Inc.

Walker Parking Consultants
Washington Metropolitan Area Transit Authority
Water Environment Research Foundation
W.J. Weber
Williamson County, TN
Karen S. Williamson
Winston Associates
Wisconsin Department of Transportation

Xtra-Spatial Productions, LLC

Thomas R. Zahn and Associates

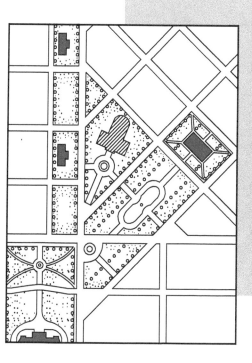

PLANS AND PLAN MAKING

Plan Making

Types of Plans

Participation

Part 1

PLAN MAKING

PLAN MAKING

A plan is an adopted statement of policy, in the form of text, maps, and graphics, used to guide public and private actions that affect the future. A plan provides decision makers with the information they need to make informed decisions affecting the long-range social, economic, and physical growth of a community. This section provides an overview of plan making as applied to a wide variety of plan types.

PURPOSES AND APPLICATIONS OF PLANS

Plans are used when making decisions concerning the future of an area or of a specific topic under consideration. For example, a plan may be used to identify:

- Housing needs—and recommend a program to meet them
- Transportation needs—and propose alternative systems and modes to meet them
- Open-space preservation areas—and present mechanisms to protect these areas permanently
- Priority investment areas—and recommend programs to stimulate growth
- Strategies for a specific area, such as a downtown, corridor, or neighborhood

Some specific applications of plans include:

- Providing residents, local officials, and others with an interest in the area with an overview and projection of development and conservation in the planning area, along with a summary of trends and forecasts.
- Serving as the basis for the local government enacting and administering regulatory measures, such as zoning and subdivision laws, and establishing urban growth boundaries.
- Serving as the basis for making budget allocations for capital improvements, such as parks, utility systems, and streets.
- Serving as the basis for many other public programs, such as those relating to growth management, historic preservation, economic development, transportation systems, and open-space preservation, for example.

PLAN AUTHORITY

Plans may be expressly authorized or required by statute or administrative rule, depending on the type of plan and the state in which the community is located. For example, every state has its own planning statutes, one part of which authorizes or requires communities to prepare a comprehensive plan, referred to in some states as general or master plans. The statute specifies which elements are included in the plan and the process required for developing and adopting it. States also often use their administrative rule-making powers to further specify, refine, and interpret the statute. In addition to state planning statutes, federal and state programs established by law sometimes require

EXAMPLES OF PLANS AUTHORIZED OR REQUIRED BY STATE OR FEDERAL STATUTE

PLAN TYPE	STATUTE	JURISDICTION
Conservation Element	Florida Statutes Sec. 163.3177(6)(d)	Florida
Economic Development Element	R.I. Gen. Laws Sec. 45-22.2-6(4)	Rhode Island
Hazard Mitigation Plan	42 U.S. Code Sec. 5133	Federal Emergency Management Agency (FEMA)
Housing Assistance Plan	Cal. Gov't. Code Secs. 65580 to 65589.8	California
Housing Element	N.J. Statutes Annotated Sec. 52:27D-310	New Jersey
Land Use Element	Kentucky Rev. Statutes Sec. 100.187(3)	Kentucky
Transit-Oriented Development Plan	Cal. Gov't Code Secs. 65460 to 65460.10	California
Transportation Improvement Program	49 U.S. Code Sec. 5304	U.S. Department of Transportation

Source: American Planning Association, 2004.

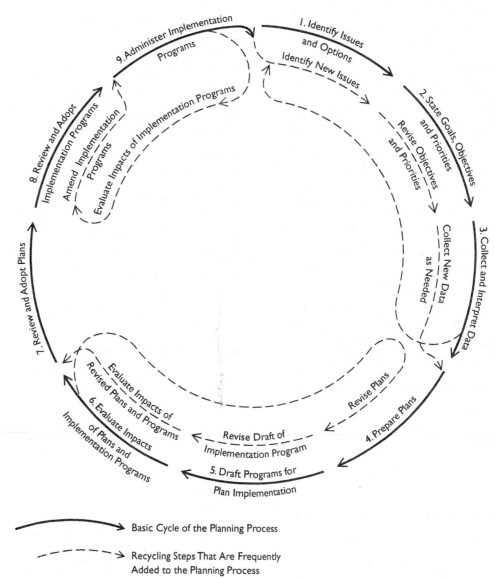

Basic Cycle of the Planning Process

Recycling Steps That Are Frequently Added to the Planning Process

The process of plan making should be viewed as a continuous cycle. There are interrelationships among the phases of the planning process. Information gained at a later phase can inform the outcome of an earlier phase. It is important to recognize the iterative nature of planning and to allow for continuous cycling to occur.

THE PLANNING PROCESS

Reprinted with permission from Guidelines for Preparing Urban Plans, copyright 1995 by the American Planning Association, Suite 1600, 122 South Michigan Avenue, Chicago, IL 60603-6107.

Larz T. Anderson, AICP, Santa Rosa, California
William R. Klein, AICP, American Planning Association, Chicago, Illinois
Stuart Meck, FAICP, American Planning Association, Chicago, Illinois

that plans of a certain kind be prepared as a condition for participation in the program. The table here includes examples of plans authorized or required by state or federal statute.

For the most part, however, many types of plans are not expressly authorized or required in state or federal statutes. Examples include many types of area plans, such as neighborhood plans, corridor plans, and downtown plans, and some types of functional plans, such as parks and open-space plans, bike route plans, and urban forest plans. The content and format of these plans, and many others like them, are guided primarily by professional planning practice. They also represent the kinds of plans for which there is a great deal of variation in form and content.

PLAN INNOVATION

Although state planning statutes and federal and state regulations provide general guidance about plan content and process for some plans, plans can vary greatly from the prescribed themes. In recent years, planners have begun to break away from tradition by reinventing what plans look like and do, shaping the form of plans to fit the unique content and process requirements of the community.

Moreover, some of the most exciting and effective plans in recent years take advantage of new ways of thinking about what a plan should contain and how it can be presented. Interactive electronic participation, benchmarking, Web-based plans, scenario analysis and modeling, and visualization techniques are a few of the new components and techniques found in plans today. Many of these innovations are featured in the plans described in the first part of this book.

An essential first step of any planning effort is to determine the plan's content, format, and process. The degree to which a planner crafts a plan to meet the unique needs of a situation, time, and place will determine whether a plan results in positive outcomes in the real world. An appendix to this book provides a list of award-winning plans to illustrate the breadth and scope of innovative plan making today.

SCOPING CONSIDERATIONS

The subsections to follow comprise a general checklist of some of the most basic considerations to keep in mind when determining the scope of any plan.

Time Frame

What is the time period covered by the plan? Plans almost always cover a time span of longer than a year, and usually address a period between 5 years and 20 years. The time period may be determined by statute or by the subject matter and process.

COMPREHENSIVE VERSUS STRATEGIC

Are all topics covered or just those important to the chosen strategy? Plans that employ a comprehensive approach consider a broad range of topics related to the area or function of the plan, even if some topics are only relevant in a minor way. Plans with a comprehensive orientation are sometimes more general in their treatment of a wide variety of subjects, providing depth only when needed. Alternatively, plans with a strategic approach consider only the topics

and relationships that appear to have a direct relevancy to the subject of the plan, hence to the strategy. Consequently, these plans are more focused and can usually be completed more quickly and with fewer resources.

Community Involvement

The issues, findings, and recommendations of a plan should take into account the knowledge and concerns of existing residents, businesses, and other interests in the planning area, and the anticipated concerns of those interests in the future. Issues to consider are those with a connection to local, regional, statewide, and even global matters. Consequently, an important scoping task is the creation of a legitimate and effective process for involving a wide variety of interests in the preparation of a plan. Successful public involvement processes are designed to fit the unique context of the plan.

In-House versus Outsourcing

Who should prepare a plan? Choices typically include in-house staff, outside consultants, community-based nongovernmental organizations (NGOs) or volunteers, or a combination. The best mix results from a realistic assessment of in-house staff capacity in terms of hours and expertise available, funds available for outside consultant services, and the capacity to train and lead an NGO or volunteer effort.

Binding

Plans are officially adopted or endorsed by a governmental body and thereby become a statement of its policies. Depending on the state and type of local or regional governance structure, the governmental body may be the local legislative body, the planning board or commission, a council of governments, or regional planning agency. Occasionally, plans are adopted by nonprofit regional planning organizations for the benefit of the public they serve, such as the regional plans prepared by the Regional Plan Association for the New York metropolitan area or Chicago Metropolis 2020 for the Chicago region.

BASIC PLAN STRUCTURE

The structure of a plan usually consists of two basic components: a core, followed by a number of elements. The specific contents of a plan depend upon numerous factors, such as the type of plan being prepared, the purpose of the plan, and the scope being addressed. Consult the chapter on types of plans for information on plan contents for specific types of plans.

The Plan Core

The core includes the following:

- A statement of authority to prepare and adopt plan
- Background data, including area history, existing conditions and trends, and data projections
- Documentation of stakeholder interests and stakeholder involvement process
- A vision statement or statement of goals and objectives for future conditions
- An evaluation of plan and design alternatives
- A program of implementation

The Plan Elements

The elements of a plan consider, specifically, the plan's various topics. The elements that must be included depend upon the plan's purpose. For a comprehensive plan, the land use, transportation, housing, and community facilities elements are considered essential—they form the foundation of the comprehensive plan. Other elements are added as considered to be appropriate, based on the plan's scope and as required by state law.

Elements frequently included in a comprehensive plan or often prepared as separate functional plans include the following:

- Economic development
- Historic preservation
- Natural hazards
- Farmland preservation
- Parks, recreation, and open space
- Urban design

GOALS, OBJECTIVES, AND ASSUMPTIONS

Universal to all plans is an identification of the goals, objectives, and assumptions of the plan. Reaching consensus on these three components is often quite difficult, if not impossible. Sometimes, agreement can be reached only in the broadest of terms; often, participants reach "incremental" agreement using negotiation and compromise. Intensive communication between those preparing the plan and the stakeholders is required here.

Goals

A goal is a statement that describes, usually in general terms, a desired future condition.

Objectives

A set of measurable objectives should accompany the goals established for the plan. An objective is a statement that describes a specific future condition to be attained within a stated period of time. Typically, these objectives are more numerous than the goals, and they are organized according to the topics in the goals statement.

Several questions can be asked at the outset of the planning process to determine the objectives of the community. Examples of such questions include:

- What type of development pattern do the stakeholders want?
- What type of transportation system and network does the community want?
- What forms of housing do stakeholders want in the community?
- What program of uses do stakeholders want for the downtown area?

The effort to create and evaluate objectives for each of the broader goals can be instructive for communities and planners, helping all to understand the implications of goal setting as applied in a planning and implementation process.

Assumptions

An assumption is a statement of present or future conditions describing the physical, social, or eco-

Larz T. Anderson, AICP, Santa Rosa, California
William R. Klein, AICP, American Planning Association, Chicago, Illinois
Stuart Meck, FAICP, American Planning Association, Chicago, Illinois

nomic setting within which the plan is to be used. At the outset of the process, it is necessary to identify the basic assumptions concerning the planning area.

On the local level, these can include the accepted boundaries of urban growth, the probable rate of growth, and the desired general character of the community, for example. At a larger scale, it is also usually desirable to state assumptions concerning national and regional economic trends. Where current research data are not available, it can be essential to state and obtain agreement on a set of working assumptions for the particular planning effort.

GOALS AND OBJECTIVES FOR BALANCED GROWTH: NANTUCKET, MASSACHUSETTS

Goal A: Open Space Acquisition

To establish and manage a communitywide network of publicly and privately held open spaces intended to protect critical land and water resources, habitat, and scenic vistas, while affording reasonable access consistent with a policy of wise stewardship.

Goal B: Protection of Water Resources

To protect the quality and quantity of the community's groundwater and surface water resources.

Goal C: Growth Management

To better manage the design, location, and rate of new residential and commercial development in a manner that: protects important natural and cultural resources; encourages development in or near village centers; promotes and preserves the vitality of the downtown; is compatible with the community's historic character; minimizes dependence on the automobile; and creates opportunities for affordable housing.

Goal D: Transportation

To provide a transportation system that will move people and goods to, from, and through the community in a way that is safe, convenient, economical, and consistent with the community's historic, scenic, and natural resources.

Goal E: Affordable Housing

To promote the development and retention of affordable housing for families, individuals, and the elderly.

Goal F: The Economy

To strengthen and diversify the local economy.

Goal G: Energy and Utilities

To provide energy and utility services to the community in a manner that is affordable, efficient, effective, and environmentally safe.

Goal H: Human Services

To facilitate, sustain, and improve the health, education, and well-being of all persons in the community by providing those public and private human services that will improve the quality of life for all age groups.

Source: Nantucket Planning and Economic Development Commission, 1990.

TYPICAL DATA NEEDS FOR PLAN PREPARATION

MAPS AND IMAGES
Base maps
Aerial photographs
GIS map layers

NATURAL ENVIRONMENT
Climate
Topography
Soils
Vegetation
Water features
Habitat areas
Natural hazards

EXISTING LAND USES
Residential
Commercial
Industrial
Institutional
Open-space lands
Vacant urban lands
Farmlands

HOUSING
Inventory of housing
Housing condition
Vacancy rate
Affordability

TRANSPORTATION
Street network
Street capacity
Traffic flow volumes
Parking supply and demand
Transit facilities by mode
Bicycle networks
Pedestrian networks

PUBLIC UTILITIES
Water supply
Wastewater disposal
Stormwater management
Solid waste management
Telecommunication services

COMMUNITY SERVICES
Administrative centers
Education facilities
Parks and recreation facilities
Health services
Public safety facilities

POPULATION AND EMPLOYMENT
Population size
Population characteristics
Vital statistics
Labor force characteristics

LOCAL ECONOMY
Employment
Retail sales
Cost of living

SPECIAL TOPICS
Historic sites and buildings
Archaeological sites
Urban design features
Existing zoning

DOCUMENT STRUCTURE

Whether published on paper, as a series of posters, or on the Web, it is important to create a clear, usable plan document. When creating a plan document, consider the reader's needs. The document should clearly reflect the planning process and serve as a useful tool for future users.

Name of the Plan

Identify a name for the plan that is simple, sensible, and incorporates the planning area or topic name.

Table of Contents

Provide a table of contents so that readers find the plan easy to use and can go directly to a topic of particular interest. Include tables and figures in the table of contents.

Time Frame

Provide the dates of all pertinent planning milestones, such as initiation of the planning process, completion of the first draft, and when certain benchmarks might be achieved. This information gives readers a sense of the plan's progression, shows investment in the planning process, and provides the plan's full time span. Include the plan adoption date on the front cover or title page.

Acknowledgments

Include an acknowledgments page that lists the names, titles, and affiliations of individuals who contributed to the production of the plan.

Glossary/Terminology Key

A glossary can explain technical or local jargon and acronyms, and describe unfamiliar places.

See also:
Analysis Techniques
Implementation Techniques
Participation
Types of Plans

Larz T. Anderson, AICP, Santa Rosa, California
William R. Klein, AICP, American Planning Association, Chicago, Illinois
Stuart Meck, FAICP, American Planning Association, Chicago, Illinois

TYPES OF PLANS

COMPREHENSIVE PLANS

The comprehensive plan is the adopted official statement of a local government's legislative body for future development and conservation. It sets forth goals; analyzes existing conditions and trends; describes and illustrates a vision for the physical, social, and economic characteristics of the community in the years ahead; and outlines policies and guidelines intended to implement that vision.

Comprehensive plans address a broad range of interrelated topics in a unified way. A comprehensive plan identifies and analyzes the important relationships among the economy, transportation, community facilities and services, housing, the environment, land use, human services, and other community components. It does so on a communitywide basis and in the context of a wider region. A comprehensive plan addresses the long-range future of a community, using a time horizon up to 20 years or more. The most important function of a comprehensive plan is to provide valuable guidance to those in the public and private sector as decisions are made affecting the future quality of life of existing and future residents and the natural and built environments in which they live, work, and play.

All states have enabling legislation that either allow, or require, local governments to adopt comprehensive plans. In some states, the enabling legislation refers to them as general plans (California, Maryland, and Arizona, for example), or master plans (Colorado). Most state-enabling legislation describes generally what should be included in a comprehensive plan. However, several states, including Oregon and Florida, detail the content of plans through administrative rules promulgated by a state agency.

REASONS TO PREPARE A COMPREHENSIVE PLAN

Local governments prepare comprehensive plans for a number of reasons, which are described in the following subsections.

View the "Big Picture"

The local comprehensive planning process provides a chance to look broadly at programs on housing, economic development, public infrastructure and services, environmental protection, and natural and human-made hazards, and how they relate to one another. A local comprehensive plan represents a "big picture" of the community related to trends and interests in the broader region and in the state in which the local government is located.

Coordinate Local Decision Making

Local comprehensive planning results in the adoption of a series of goals and policies that should guide the local government in its daily decisions. For instance, the plan should be referred to for decisions about locating, financing, and sequencing public improvements, devising and administering regulations such as zoning and subdivision controls, and redevelopment. In so doing, the plan provides a way to coordinate the actions of many different agencies within local government.

Give Guidance to Landowners and Developers

In making its decisions, the private sector can turn to a well-prepared comprehensive plan to get some sense of where the community is headed in terms of the physical, social, economic, and transportation future. Because comprehensive planning results in a statement of how local government intends to use public investment and land development controls, the plan can affect the decisions of private landowners.

Establish a Sound Basis in Fact for Decisions

A plan, through required information gathering and analysis, improves the factual basis for land-use decisions. Using the physical plan as a tool to inform and guide these decisions establishes a baseline for public policies. The plan thus provides a measure of consistency to governmental action, limiting the potential for arbitrariness.

Involve a Broad Array of Interests in a Discussion about the Long-Range Future

Local comprehensive planning involves the active participation of local elected and appointed officials, line departments of local government, citizens, the business community, nongovernmental organizations, and faith-based groups in a discussion about the community's major physical, environmental, social, or economic development problems and opportunities. The plan gives these varied interests an opportunity to clarify their ideas, better envisioning the community they are trying to create.

Build an Informed Constituency

The plan preparation process, with its related workshops, surveys, meetings, and public hearings, permits two-way communication between citizens and planners and officials regarding a vision of the community and how that vision is to be achieved. In this respect, the plan is a blueprint reflecting shared community values at specific points in time. This process creates an informed constituency that can be involved in planning initiatives, review of proposals for plan consistency, and collaborative implementation of the plan.

PLAN ELEMENTS

The scope and content of state planning legislation varies widely from state to state with respect to its treatment of the comprehensive plan. The American Planning Association has developed model state planning legislation in its *Growing Smart℠ Legislative Guidebook* (2002).

Required and Optional Elements

The guidebook suggests a series of required elements and optional elements. Required elements include:

- Land use
- Transportation
- Community facilities (includes utilities and parks and open space)
- Housing
- Economic development
- Critical and sensitive areas
- Natural hazards
- Agricultural lands

Optional elements addressing urban design, public safety, and cultural resources, for instance, may also be included. Moreover, the suggested functional elements are not intended to be rigid and inflexible. Participants in the plan process should tailor the format and content of the comprehensive plan to the specific needs and characteristics of their community.

According to the guidebook, comprehensive plans should include two "bookend" items: an issues and opportunities element at the beginning in order to set the stage for the preparation of other elements, and an implementation program at the end that proposes measures, assigns estimated costs (if feasible), and assigns responsibility for carrying out proposed measures of the plan. The level of detail in the implementation program will vary depending on whether such actions will be addressed in specific functional plans.

Issues and Opportunities Element

The issues and opportunities element articulates the values and needs of citizens and other affected interests about what the community should become. The local government then interprets and uses those values and needs as a basis and foundation for its planning efforts.

An issues and opportunities element should contain seven items:

- A vision or goals and objectives statement
- A description of existing conditions and characteristics
- Analyses of internal and external trends and forces
- A description of opportunities, problems, advantages, and disadvantages
- A narrative describing the public participation process
- The legal authority or mandate for the plan
- A narrative describing the connection to all the other plan elements

Vision or Goals and Objectives Statement

This statement is a formal description of what the community wants to become. It may consist solely of broad communitywide goals, may be enhanced by the addition of measurable objectives for each of the goals, or may be accompanied by a narrative or illus-

Stuart Meck, FAICP, American Planning Association, Chicago, Illinois

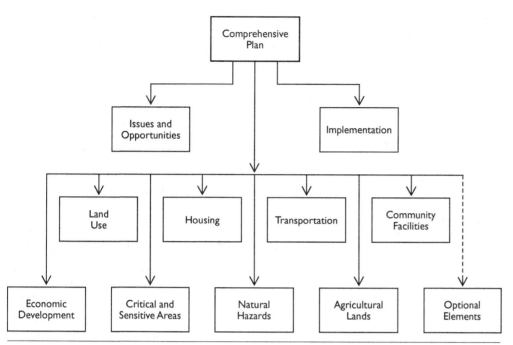

COMPREHENSIVE PLAN ELEMENTS

Source: American Planning Association.

tration that sets a vision of the community at the end of the plan period.

Existing Conditions and Characteristics Description

This description creates a profile of the community, including relevant demographic data, pertinent historical information, existing plans, regulatory framework, and other information that broadly informs the plan. Existing conditions information specific to a plan element may be included in that element's within the plan.

Trends and Forces Description

This description of major trends and forces is what the local government considered when creating the vision statement and considers the effect of changes forecast for the surrounding region during the planning period.

Opportunities, Problems, Advantages, and Disadvantages

The plan should include a statement of the major opportunities, problems, advantages, and disadvantages for growth and decline affecting the local government, including specific areas within its jurisdiction. This is often referred to as a *SWOT analysis*—a description of strengths, weaknesses, opportunities, and threats.

Public Participation

This summary of the public participation procedures describes how the public was involved in developing the comprehensive plan.

Legal Authority or Mandate

This brief statement describes the local government's legal authority for preparing the plan. It may include a reference to applicable state legislation or a munic-

ipal charter. Summaries of past planning activities may be included here (if not included in existing conditions discussion).

Connection to Other Elements

The implications of the local government's vision on other required and/or optional elements of the local

---

SAMPLE VISION STATEMENT: OAKLAND, CALIFORNIA

The Vision for Oakland

In the year 2015, Oakland will be a safe, healthy, and vital city offering a high quality of life through:

- a dynamic economy that taps into Oakland's great economic potential and capitalizes on its physical and cultural assets;
- clean and attractive neighborhoods rich in character and diversity, each with its own distinctive identity, yet well integrated into a cohesive urban fabric;
- a diverse and vibrant downtown with around-the-clock activity;
- an active and accessible waterfront that is linked to downtown and the neighborhoods, and that promotes Oakland's position as a leading United States port and a primary regional and international airport;
- an efficient transportation system that serves the needs of all its citizens and that promotes Oakland's primacy as a transportation hub connecting the Bay Area with the Pacific Rim and the rest of the United States; and
- awareness and enjoyment of Oakland's magnificent physical setting—hills, views, water, estuary—in every district and neighborhood.

---

comprehensive plan, including the potential changes in implementation measures, should be described in this concluding section.

The Land-Use Element

The land-use element shows the general distribution, location, and characteristics of current and future land uses and urban form. In the past, comprehensive plans included color-coded maps showing exclusive land-use categories, such as residential, commercial, industrial, institutional, community facilities, open space, recreational, and agricultural uses.

Many communities today use sophisticated land-use and land-cover inventories and mapping techniques, employing Geographic Information Systems (GIS) and new land-use and land-cover classification systems. These new systems are better able to accommodate the multidimensional realities of urban form, such as mixed-use and time-of-day/seasonal-use changes. Form and character are increasingly being used as important components of land-use planning, integrating the many separate components into an integrated land-use form.

One example of a process that can be used to create such multidimensional mapping is the system of Land-Based Classification Standards (LBCS), developed by the American Planning Association (APA). This system creates a current land-use map using a number of data sources, including orbital and suborbital remotely sensed data, tax assessor records, U.S. Geological Survey quadrangle maps, soils maps, and other county or state mapping data, which are field-checked on the ground.

Future Land-Use Map

Future land uses and their intensity and density are shown on a future land-use map. The land-use allocations shown on the map must be supported by land-use projections linked to population and economic forecasts for the surrounding region and tied to the assumptions in a regional plan, if one exists. Such coordination ensures that the plan is realistic. The assumptions used in the land-use forecasts, typically in terms of net density, intensity, other standards or ratios, or other spatial requirements or physical determinants, are a fundamental part of the land-use element. This element must also show lands that have development constraints, such as natural hazards.

Land-Use Projections

The land-use element should envision all land-use needs for a 20-year period (or the chosen time frame for the plan), and all these needs should be designated on the future land-use plan map. If this is not done, the local government may have problems carrying out the plan. For example, if the local government receives applications for zoning changes to accommodate uses the plan recognizes as needed, the locations where these changes are requested are consistent with what is shown on the land-use plan map.

The Transportation Element

The modern transportation element commonly addresses traffic circulation, transit, bicycle routes, ports, airports, railways, recreation routes, pedestrian movement, and parking. The exact content of a transportation element differs from community to community depending on the transportation context

Stuart Meck, FAICP, American Planning Association, Chicago, Illinois

of the community and region. Proposals for transportation facilities occur against a backdrop of federally required transportation planning at the state and regional levels.

The transportation element considers existing and committed facilities, and evaluates them against a set of service levels or performance standards to determine whether they will adequately serve future needs. Of the various transportation facilities, the traffic circulation component is the most common, and a major thoroughfare plan is an essential part of this. It contains the general locations and extent of existing and proposed streets and highways by type, function, and character of improvement.

Street Performance

In determining street performance and adequacy, planners are employing other approaches in addition to or instead of level-of-service standards that more fairly measure a street's performance in moving pedestrians, bikes, buses, trolleys, and light rail, and for driving retail trade, in addition to moving cars. This is especially true for urban centers, where several modes of travel share the public realm across the entire right-of-way, including adjacent privately owned "public" spaces. Urban design plans for the entire streetscape of key thoroughfares can augment the transportation element. In addition, it is becoming increasingly common for the traffic circulation component of a comprehensive plan to include a street connectivity analysis. The degree to which streets connect with each other affects pedestrian movement and traffic dispersal.

Thoroughfare Plan

The thoroughfare plan, which includes a plan map, is used as a framework for roadway rehabilitation, improvement, and signalization. It is a way of identifying general alignments for future circulation facilities, either as part of new private development or as new projects undertaken by local government. Other transportation modes should receive comparable review and analysis, with an emphasis on needs and systems of the particular jurisdiction and on meeting environmental standards and objectives for the community and region. Typically, surface and structured parking, bikeways, and pedestrian ways should also be covered in the transportation element.

Transit

A transit component takes into consideration bus and light rail facilities, water-based transit (if applicable), and intermodal facilities that allow transportation users to transfer from one mode to another. The types and capacities of future transit service should be linked to work commute and nonwork commute demands as well as to the applicable policies and regulations of the jurisdiction and its region.

The Transportation/Land-Use Relationship

The relationship between transportation and land use is better understood today and has become a dominant theme in the transportation element. For instance, where transit exists or is proposed, opportunities for transit-oriented development should be included; where increased densities are essential, transit services might need to be improved or introduced. This would also be covered in the land-use element.

The Community Facilities Element

The term "community facilities" includes the physical manifestations of governmental or quasi-governmental services on behalf of the public. These include buildings, equipment, land, interests in land, such as easements, and whole systems of activities. The community facilities element requires the local government to inventory and assess the condition and adequacy of existing facilities, and to propose a range of facilities that will support the land-use element's development pattern.

The element may include facilities operated by public agencies and those owned and operated by for-profit and not-for-profit private enterprises for the benefit of the community, such as privately owned water and gas facilities, or museums. Some community facilities have a direct impact on where development will occur and at what scale—water and sewer lines, water supply, and wastewater treatment facilities, for example. Other community facilities may address immediate consequences of development. For example, a stormwater management system handles changes in the runoff characteristics of land as a consequence of development.

Still other facilities are necessary for the public health, safety, and welfare, but are more supportive in nature. Examples in this category would include police and fire facilities, general governmental buildings, and elementary and secondary schools. A final group includes those facilities that contribute to the cultural life or physical and mental health and personal growth of a local government's residents. These include hospitals, clinics, libraries, and arts centers.

Operation by Other Public Agencies

Some community facilities may be operated by public agencies other than the local government. Such agencies may serve areas not coterminous with the local government's boundaries. Independent school districts, library districts, and water utilities are good examples. In some large communities, these agencies may have their own internal planning capabilities. In others, the local planning agency will need to assist or coordinate with the agency or even directly serve as its planner.

Parks, Open Space, and Cultural Resources

A community facilities element may include a parks and open-space component. Alternatively, parks and open space may be addressed in a separate element. The community facilities element will inventory existing parks by type of facility and may evaluate the condition of parks in terms of the population they are expected to serve and the functions they are intended to carry out. To determine whether additional parkland should be purchased, population forecasts are often used in connection with population-based needs criteria (such as a requirement of so many acres of a certain type of park within a certain distance from residents). Other criteria used to determine parkland need may include parkland as a percentage of land cover or a resident's proximity to a park.

Open-space preservation may sometimes be addressed alone or in connection with critical and sensitive areas protection and agricultural and forest preservation. Here the emphasis is on the ecological, scenic, and economic functions that open space provides. The element may also identify tracts of open

land with historic or cultural significance, such as a battlefield. The element will distinguish between publicly held land, land held in private ownership subject to conservation easements or other restrictions, and privately owned parcels subject to development.

The Housing Element

The housing element assesses local housing conditions and projects future housing needs by housing type and price to ensure that a wide variety of housing structure types, occupancy types, and prices (for rent or purchase) are available for a community's existing and future residents. There may currently be a need for rental units for large families or the disabled, or a disproportionate amount of income may be paid for rental properties, for example. Because demand for housing does not necessarily correspond with jurisdictional boundaries and the location of employment, a housing element provides for housing needs in the context of the region in which the local government is located. In some states, such as California, New Hampshire, and New Jersey, there may be state-level or regional housing plans that identify regional needs for affordable housing, and the local housing element must take these needs into account as part of a "fair-share" requirement.

Jobs/Housing Balance

The housing element can examine the relationship between where jobs are or will be located and where housing is or will be available. The jobs/housing balance is the ratio between the expected creation of jobs in a region or local government and the need for housing expressed as the number of housing units. The higher the jobs/housing ratio, the more jobs the region or local government is generating relative to housing. A high ratio may indicate to a community that it is not meeting the housing needs (in terms of either affordability or actual physical units) of people working in the community.

Housing Stock

The housing element typically identifies measures used to maintain a good inventory of quality housing stock, such as rehabilitation efforts, code enforcement, technical assistance to homeowners, and loan and grant programs. It will also identify barriers to producing and rehabilitating housing, including affordable housing. These barriers may include lack of adequate sites zoned for housing, complicated approval processes for building and other development permits, high permit fees, and excessive exactions or public improvement requirements.

The Economic Development Element

An economic development element describes the local government's role in the region's economy; identifies categories or particular types of commercial, industrial, and institutional uses desired by the local government; and specifies suitable sites with supporting facilities for business and industry. It has one or more of the following purposes:

- Job creation and retention
- Increases in real wages (e.g., economic prosperity)
- Stabilization or increase of the local tax base
- Job diversification (making the community less dependent on a few employers)

Stuart Meck, FAICP, American Planning Association, Chicago, Illinois

A number of factors typically prompt a local economic development program. They include loss or attraction of a major employer, competition from surrounding communities or nearby states, the belief that economic development yields a higher quality of life, the desire to provide employment for existing residents who would otherwise leave the area, economic stagnation or decline in a community or part of it, or the need for new tax revenues.

An economic development element typically begins with an analysis of job composition and growth or decline by industry sector on a national, statewide, or regional basis, including an identification of categories of commercial, industrial, and institutional activities that could reasonably be expected to locate within the jurisdiction. It will also examine existing labor force characteristics and future labor force requirements of existing and potential commercial and industrial enterprises and institutions in the state and the region in which the local government is located. It will include assessments of the jurisdiction's and the region's access to transportation to markets for its goods and services, and its natural, technological, educational, and human resources. Often, an economic development element will have targets for growth, which may be defined as number of jobs or wages, or in terms of targeted industries and their land use, transportation, and labor force requirements.

The local government may also survey owners or operators of commercial and industrial enterprises, and inventory commercial, industrial, and institutional lands within the jurisdiction that are vacant or significantly underused. An economic development element may also address organizational issues, including the creation of entities, such as nonprofit organizations, that could carry out economic development activities.

The Critical and Sensitive Areas Element

Some comprehensive plans address the protection of critical and sensitive areas. These areas include land and water bodies that provide habitat for plants and wildlife, such as wetlands, riparian corridors, and floodplains; serve as groundwater recharge areas for aquifers; and areas with steep slopes that are easily eroded or unstable, for example. They also can include visually, culturally, and historically sensitive

areas. By identifying such areas, the local government can safeguard them through regulation, incentives, purchase of land or interests in land, modification of public and private development projects, or other measures.

The Natural Hazards Element

Natural hazards elements document the physical characteristics, magnitude, severity, frequency, causative factors, and geographic extent of all natural hazards. Hazards include flooding; seismic activity; wildfires; wind-related hazards such as tornadoes, coastal storms, winter storms, and hurricanes; and landslides or subsidence resulting from the instability of geological features.

A natural hazards element characterizes the hazard; maps its extent, if possible; assesses the community's vulnerability; and develops an appropriate set of mitigation measures, which may include land-use policies and building code requirements. The natural hazards element may also determine the adequacy of existing transportation facilities and public buildings to accommodate disaster response and early recovery needs such as evacuation and emergency shelter. Since most communities have more than one type of hazard, planners should consider addressing them jointly through a multihazards approach.

The Agriculture Element

Some comprehensive plans contain agriculture and forest preservation elements. This element focuses on the value of agriculture and forestlands to the local economy, although it can also include open space, habitat, and scenic preservation. For such an element, the local government typically inventories agriculture and forestland, and ranks the land using a variety of approaches, such as the U.S. Department of Agriculture's Land Evaluation and Site Assessment (LESA) system. It then identifies conflicts between the use of such lands and other proposed uses as contained in other comprehensive plan elements.

For example, if an area were to be preserved for agricultural purposes, but the community facilities element proposed a sewer trunk line to the area, that would be a conflict, which if not corrected would result in development pressure to the future agricultural area. Implementation measures might include agricultural use valuation coupled with extremely

large lot requirements (40 acres or more), transfer of development rights, purchase of development rights, conservation easements, marketing programs to promote the viability of local agricultural land, and programs for agricultural-based tourism.

IMPLEMENTATION

A local comprehensive plan must contain an implementation program to ensure that the proposals advanced in the plan are realized. Sometimes referred to as an "action plan," the implementation program includes a list of specific public or private actions organized by their scheduled execution date—short-term (1 to 3 years), medium-term (4 to 10 years), and long-term (11 to 20 years) actions. Typical actions include capital projects, changes to land development regulations and incentives, new programs or procedures, financing initiatives, and similar measures. Each listed action should assign responsibility for the task and include an estimate of cost and a source of funding.

Some communities produce comprehensive plans that are more broadly based and policy-driven. These plans will require a less detailed implementation program. The individual functional plans produced as a result of the comprehensive plan address the assignment of costs or specific tasks.

REFERENCE

Meck, Stuart (gen. ed.). 2002. *Growing Smart℠ Legislative Guidebook: Model Statutes for Planning and Management of Change,* 2 vols. Chicago: American Planning Association.

See also:
Critical and Sensitive Areas Plans
Economic Development Plans
Housing Plans
Mapping
Parks and Open-Space Plans
Participation
Plan Making
Projections and Demand Analysis
Regional Plans
Transportation Plans
Urban Design Plans

Stuart Meck, FAICP, American Planning Association, Chicago, Illinois

URBAN DESIGN PLANS

Urban design is the discipline between planning and architecture. It gives three-dimensional physical form to policies described in a comprehensive plan. It focuses on design of the public realm, which is created by both public spaces and the buildings that define them. Urban design views these spaces holistically and is concerned with bringing together the different disciplines responsible for the components of cities into a unified vision. Compared to comprehensive plans, urban design plans generally have a short time horizon and are typically area or project specific.

Key elements of an urban design plan include the plan itself, the preparation of design guidelines for buildings, the design of the public realm—the open space, streets, sidewalks, and plazas between and around buildings—and the "public interest" issues of buildings. These include massing, placement, and sun, shadow, and wind issues.

Urban design plans are prepared for various areas, including downtowns, waterfronts, campuses, corridors, neighborhoods, mixed-use developments, and special districts. Issues to be considered include existing development, proposed development, utility infrastructure, streets framework, open space framework, environmental framework, and sustainable development principles. Urban design plans require interdisciplinary collaboration among urban designers, architects, landscape architects, planners, civil and environmental engineers, and market analysts. The central role of the urban designer is to serve as the one who can often integrate the work of a diverse range of specialists.

REASONS TO PREPARE AN URBAN DESIGN PLAN

An urban design plan must respond to the circumstances under which the project will be conducted, including the goals of the sponsors of the plan, the political or social climate in the community, and financial and marketing realities. Below are a few examples of reasons to prepare an urban design plan.

Forging Visions

Urban designers are often asked to provide a vision for communities to attract investment and coordinate many disparate and even discordant interests. By providing such a vision, urban designers can bring individual efforts together to create a whole that is greater than the sum of its parts. Creating such a vision needs to be a public process, to cultivate widespread enthusiasm for the vision and build a "bandwagon" of support.

Devising Strategies

In addition to an overall vision, an urban design plan must also include a strategic implementation plan, with both short- and long-range initiatives. To keep the momentum going, it is also important to assign specific tasks or projects to groups conducting implementation.

Creating Good Locations

Many projects begin with sites that are compromised or deteriorated. An urban design plan illustrates how a site is linked to surrounding strengths, and it can show how the site can become a great location.

Marketing Sites or Areas

Urban design plans often work to transform an area, creating a new image for an area once overlooked or blighted. Urban design documents, illustrations, and publicity around the process all become part of the overall marketing effort to attract development and residents.

Forming "Treaties"

Urban design plans are sometimes born as a result of a conflict; for example, a proposed redevelopment project may result in displacing existing businesses or residents. An urban design document can serve as a "treaty," to bring about a truce among warring parties. By focusing on the issues, presenting thoughtful analysis, and urging parties to come forward with their concerns and ideas, urban designers can use an urban design plan to help resolve problems in a nonconfrontational way.

THE URBAN DESIGN PLANNING PROCESS

An urban design planning process has much in common with a comprehensive planning process; both include basic elements such as data collection and analysis, public participation, and involvement of other disciplines. However, urban design differs in the use of three-dimensional design tools to explore alternatives and communicate ideas. Below are the essential attributes of an urban design planning process.

Public Outreach

Because urban design plans usually involve multiple stakeholders, public participation in the planning process is essential. A representative steering committee is one mechanism to ensure involvement of a cross section of interests. Among the various public outreach techniques used are focus groups and public meetings. Input from the public informs the urban design team about assets, liabilities, and visions for the project area.

Involvement of Major Stakeholders

In addition to the public outreach process, one-on-one meetings with key representatives of the major stakeholders, such as elected officials, community leaders, and major institutions, are important for both sides—the urban design team gains insight into the stakeholders' concerns and goals, and the major stakeholders develop confidence in the team and the planning process.

Features such as waterways and adjacent land features influence street grid orientation.

EXISTING STREET PATTERNS

Source: Urban Design Associates.

Don Carter, AICP FAIA, Urban Design Associates, Pittsburgh, Pennsylvania; Raymond L. Gindroz, FAIA, Urban Design Associates, Pittsburgh, Pennsylvania

Multi-Disciplinary Team

Urban design is a collaborative process involving urban designers, architects, planners, and landscape architects. However, other disciplines are usually required, such as transportation planners and engineers, civil and environmental engineers, residential and commercial market analysts, construction cost consultants, and public/private finance consultants. When such a team has been assembled, the individual consultants should be coordinated so that their expertise permeates the planning process from beginning to end.

Focus on Implementation

Urban design projects are often complicated plans with multiple projects and participants. Implementation can be difficult, even when all the forces are aligned properly. The process should begin with implementation in mind. Develop a plan that is tied to the realities of receiving funding, obtaining approval, and getting the project built.

Design as a Tool for Decision-Making

By exploring alternatives—the "what ifs" of a site or district—the design process allows for speculation, brainstorming, and innovative thinking. Alternatives can be tested against various factors, including physical constraints, regulatory controls, the market, overall costs and benefits, economic feasibility, property valuation, phasing, public input, and experience elsewhere. The consensus vision will then reflect those realities.

COMPONENTS OF AN URBAN DESIGN PLAN REPORT

As a general rule, an urban design report should be light on text and heavy on graphics. Diagrams, charts, rendered plans and sections, and perspective drawings are often the most effective communicators of the plan's elements. Below are brief descriptions of the typical sections of an urban design plan report.

Executive Summary

Key images from the body of the report and summary text can convey the "big ideas" of the plan in just a few pages.

Existing Conditions

Assemble all existing conditions data related to the project area, including streets, building coverage, land use, topography, vacant buildings and land, and environmental constraints. This information is documented in the report as the existing conditions "portrait" of the area.

Analysis Drawings

Analysis drawings can be some of the most influential materials of an urban design initiative. Creating these drawings involves professional review of existing conditions data and mapping, to translate this information into findings that will influence the plan. More information on analysis drawings can be found in *The Urban Design Handbook* (2003).

Summary of Issues

During the planning process, involve citizens and stakeholders in focus groups and public meetings to

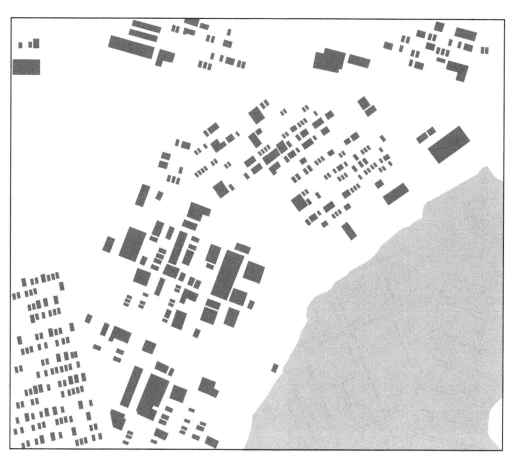

Block patterns of an area, presented here as a figure ground map, show the building coverage of a site.

BUILDING COVERAGE

Source: Urban Design Associates.

learn about the strengths and weaknesses of the project area and the community's vision for the future. The issues and opportunities that arise from these meetings are summarized in the report, in both narrative and diagrams.

Development Program

Market studies, forecasting demand for residential and commercial development, are frequently done concurrently with the urban design planning process. These studies are summarized in the urban design plan. If such studies were not commissioned, the client's development program is described in the development program.

Urban Design Plan

The urban design plan is a color rendered plan showing existing and new buildings, parking, streets, trails, and landscape planting. The urban design plan presents a two-dimensional vision of the final project build-out.

Streets Framework Plan and Street Sections

The streets framework plan identifies existing and new streets. It includes cross sections of streets indicating sidewalks, parking, travel lanes, and medians.

Open Space Framework Plan

The open space framework plan illustrates parks; trails; "green streets," which are streets designated for enhanced landscape planting and pedestrian amenities; plazas; public space; and the connections between them.

Perspective Drawings

Three-dimensional perspective drawings are essential in conveying the sense of place of an urban design plan. Often the general public cannot easily interpret plan drawings; however, eye level and bird's eye view perspectives are often more readily understandable.

Design Guidelines

Urban design plan reports often contain a section on design guidelines, including massing, height, building setbacks, architectural style, parking, streetscapes, signage, materials, and sustainable design.

Implementation and Phasing Plan

The implementation section details the mechanisms to make the plan a reality. Among the tools typically included are public and private partnerships, funding sources, regulatory issues, conceptual budgets, and a phasing plan with early action and long-range projects described.

Don Carter, AICP, FAIA, Urban Design Associates, Pittsburgh, Pennsylvania; Raymond L. Gindroz, FAIA, Urban Design Associates, Pittsburgh, Pennsylvania

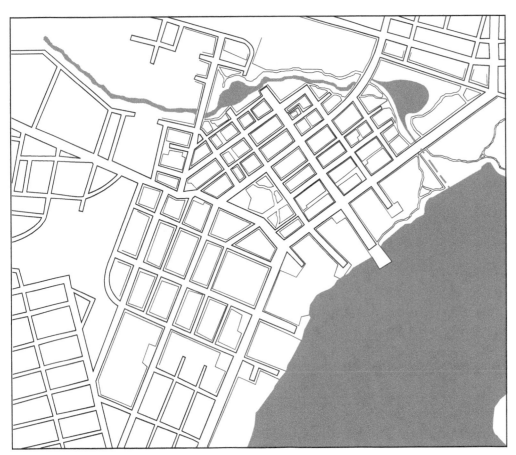

The street framework is upgraded to follow the patterns that the existing street patterns, building coverage, and open space framework define for the place.

STREET FRAMEWORK

Source: Urban Design Associates.

THE ROLE OF URBAN DESIGN IN IMPLEMENTATION

By translating general planning policies into three-dimensional form, urban design makes the connection between planning and architecture, this makes it possible to test the feasability of projects through a variety of mechanisms, described below.

Public Support

If the community perceives the various images and three-dimensional form of a development to be consistent with its goals and policies, then gaining support for the various public approvals needed for the development will be strengthened. Developing the urban design for a project in an open public forum helps to facilitate this outcome.

Zoning Enforcement and Regulatory Approvals

Use vivid and explicit representations of the proposed development to assist the various agencies responsible for zoning enforcement and regulatory approvals to support implementation. In many communities there are a number of agencies, with different mindsets, involved in administering the approval and implementation process The urban design plan, especially if

developed in a process that engaged the approval agencies as a group, can provide a common framework within which governmental decisions can be made.

Investment and Finance

Urban designs are often developed to a level of detail sufficient to determine the amount of space being built and to develop conceptual cost estimates for buildings and public improvements. Therefore, the economic feasability and fiscal impact of developments can be effectively evaluated.

Marketing

A project's feasibility is directly related to the effectiveness of its marketing program. The character and quality of its address is one factor in how successfully a development can capture the market potential of an area. The products of an urban design project are often used in marketing programs to communicate the new image of the place and to promote the development.

Framework for Implementing Agencies

An urban design project often serves as a "road map" for the implementing agencies. It becomes a standard reference for developing budgets, setting priorities, funding projects, and granting regulatory approvals.

EXAMPLES OF URBAN DESIGN PLANS

Described below are three of the most commonly produced urban design plans: neighborhoods, downtowns, and mixed-use developments.

Neighborhood Plans

On the neighborhood scale, urban design plans often address the location and design of infill housing, new parks, and community institutions; main street revitalization; housing rehabilitation guidelines; and street reconfiguration. Sponsors of neighborhood plans include cities, community development organizations, foundations, and private developers.

Downtown Plans

Downtown urban design plans are usually part of a larger economic development strategy focused on attracting jobs, residents, and visitors to a downtown. The development scale is relatively dense and multistory, which requires sensitive treatment of the public realm for pedestrians. Topics covered in downtown urban design plans include mixed-use buildings, historic preservation, adaptive reuse, height and density, setbacks, views, parking strategies, transit corridors and nodes, streetscapes, waterfronts, street networks, highway access, redevelopment policies, zoning overlays, incentive districts, new stadiums and convention centers, and entertainment and cultural districts.

Cities, downtown organizations, business improvement districts, and regional agencies all may sponsor downtown urban design plans.

Mixed-Use Developments

Mixed-use developments are typically one-owner, site-specific projects. Among the various types are infill projects in downtowns, brownfield reclamation projects, lifestyle centers (also called specialty retail centers), and office/technology developments. Office, retail, and housing are among the typical uses in mixed-use developments. Project sizes can range widely, from a few acres to hundreds of acres. A central goal is to develop a pedestrian-friendly place to live, work, and play. Sponsors of mixed-use developments are often private developers, redevelopment agencies, and large institutions, such as universities and medical centers.

KEY AND EMERGING ISSUES

Housing Density

As the smart growth movement and rising housing costs have become determining forces in residential planning and development, density has emerged as a major issue. While there is still the great American desire for the single family home and the cul-de-sac subdivision, regulatory controls and environmental restrictions have begun to limit available land for such development. Smaller lot sizes, attached housing, and multi-family housing have become contentious issues in many communities. Urban design planning processes can help test different residential densities in the context of a holistic solution that includes housing, amenities, and place making.

Recognizing the Value of Urban Design

Urban design is a strong strategic planning tool. However, many cities and developers approach

Don Carter, AICP FAIA, Urban Design Associates, Pittsburgh, Pennsylvania; Raymond L. Gindroz, FAIA, Urban Design Associates, Pittsburgh, Pennsylvania

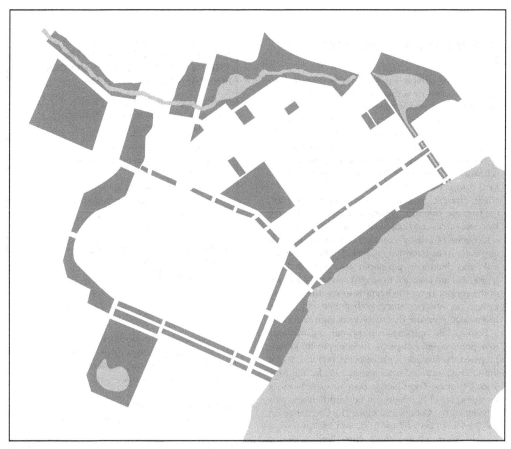

The open space of a site shows the green network that helps define a place.

OPEN SPACE FRAMEWORK

Source: Urban Design Associates

development on a project-by-project basis, often in isolation from adjacent uses and without a comprehensive view of all the forces impacting or impacted by the project. While urban design plans are not always regarded as essential pre-development projects, experience in the field has demonstrated that the new ideas and approaches that emerge from an urban design planning process can add significant value to a development and appreciably ease and shorten the public approval process.

Urban Design Education

Because of the three-dimensional building design and the physical transformation of the public realm aspect of urban design practice, an urban designer should have an architecture degree. Ideally, an urban designer has either received a master of architecture degree in urban design or has completed an internship in an urban design firm.

RESOURCE

Urban Design Associates. 2003. *The Urban Design Handbook: Techniques and Working Methods*. New York: W.W. Norton and Co.

See also:
Places and Placemaking
Viewshed Protection

Don Carter, AICP, FAIA, Urban Design Associates, Pittsburgh, Pennsylvania; Raymond L. Gindroz, FAIA, Urban Design Associates, Pittsburgh, Pennsylvania

REGIONAL PLANS

Regional plans cover geographic areas transcending the boundaries of individual governmental units but sharing common characteristics that may be social, economic, political, cultural, natural-resource-based, or defined by transportation. They often serve as the skeleton or framework for local government plans and special district plans, supplying unifying assumptions, forecasts, and strategies. The information that follows is adapted from the American Planning Association's *Growing Smart℠ Legislative Guidebook* (2002).

DEFINING THE REGION

The following factors may define a region:

- Geographic and topographic features, especially watersheds
- Political boundaries, especially county boundaries
- Transportation patterns, especially those related to the journey to work
- Region-serving facilities, such as hospitals, airports, trail terminals, and wastewater treatment plants
- Interrelated social, economic, and environmental problems
- Population distribution
- Existing intergovernmental relationships, usually expressed in the form of written agreements
- Metropolitan area or urbanized area boundaries as identified by the U.S. Census Bureau
- Boundaries of existing regional or multijurisdictional planning or service provision organizations, such as regional sewer districts

REGIONAL FUNCTIONAL PLANS

Regional planning agencies may prepare regional functional plans to cover specific topics such as parks and open space, bikeways, water, sanitary sewerage and sewage treatment, water supply and distribution, solid waste management, airports, libraries, communications, and others. For example, a regional sewer plan is a device used to ensure that disputes can be resolved over which jurisdiction will provide sewers and sewage treatment facilities to developing areas. The most typical regional functional plan is a regional transportation plan; see Transportation Plans in this chapter for more information.

The Regional Housing Plan

A number of states, including California and New Hampshire, require the preparation of regional housing plans. In general, regional planning agencies prepare these plans to assess present and prospective need for housing at the regional level, particularly affordable housing. Typically, they establish numerical housing goals to be included in local government plans.

In New Jersey, regional housing planning is the responsibility of a state agency, the Council on Affordable Housing, which prepares "fair-share" housing allocations for affordable housing for each local government. Under New Jersey law, local governments then have an obligation to identify sites for affordable housing and take necessary steps to remove barriers in order to provide a realistic opportunity that such housing can be built or rehabilitated.

THE REGIONAL COMPREHENSIVE PLAN

The regional comprehensive plan is intended to address facilities or resources that affect more than one jurisdiction and to provide economic, population, and land-use forecasts to guide local planning, so that local plans and planning decisions are made with a set of common assumptions. Consequently, a regional comprehensive plan will propose a more schematic pattern of development than provided in a local comprehensive plan.

For example, in a regional comprehensive plan, the land-use pattern is generally simple, demarcating land into urban and rural, with a general indication of a hierarchy of activity centers. Such centers may be targets for more intensive residential, office, commercial, and industrial developments, supported by transit, that are intended to serve a substantial portion of the region. Here, the intent is to use the regional plan as an device to direct both public and private investment to ensure that such development occurs.

Both public agencies and private organizations may prepare regional plans. Indeed, private groups prepared the first true regional plans, one in 1909 for the Chicago area and a second in 1929 for the New York City area. The Chicago plan was the work of planners Daniel Burnham and Edward Bennett, with funding by the Commercial Club. The Committee for the Regional Plan of New York and Its Environs, a private group whose efforts were funded by the Russell Sage Foundation, produced a multivolume regional plan for the New York metropolitan area, beginning in 1929.

Regional Comprehensive Plan Elements

Typical Plan Elements

State statutes usually define which elements are required in a regional comprehensive plan. The following list is for guidance only; to determine which elements are required, consult state legislation.

- A narrative of planning assumptions, and their relationship to state and local plans
- Population trends and projections
- Regional economy
- Existing land use
- A transportation system overview
- Regional housing trends and needs
- Community facilities and services
- Natural features and cultural assets
- Agricultural lands
- Natural hazards
- Regional density study
- Public involvement
- Urban growth areas
- Regional growth policy statements
- Implementation recommendations

Urban Growth Areas

Some regional plans delineate urban growth areas, which are land areas sufficient to accommodate population and economic growth for a certain period, typically 20 years, and which will be supported by urban-level services. The purpose of an urban growth area is to ensure a compact and contiguous development pattern that can be efficiently served by public services while preserving open space, agricultural land, and environmentally sensitive areas not suitable for intensive development.

Special Resource Areas

A regional comprehensive plan also identifies special resources areas, such as farmland, aquifers, and major wetlands. It may propose strategies for a particular watershed or basin to ensure that groundwater and watercourses are protected as supplies of potable water. The plan can also include actions to protect areas of biodiversity. Depending on the nature of the region, it may also identify the general location of natural hazard areas, such as earthquake zones or areas prone to wildfires.

Regional Facilities

The plan may contain proposals for new or upgraded regional facilities, such as multimodal transportation centers, new highways, transit, airports, hospitals, and regional parks or open space systems that link together. Functional plan elements may examine details of such proposals, such as road widening, highway safety improvements, and operational changes to mass transit systems, or the exact locations of regional wastewater facilities and major trunk lines.

Descriptive and Analytical Studies

In order to prepare a regional comprehensive plan, the regional planning authority or other suitable authority must undertake a series of descriptive and analytical studies. Such studies may cover the following topics:

- The economy of the region, which may include amount, type, general location, and distribution of commerce and industry within the region; the location of regional employment centers; and trends and projection of economic activity, both in terms of income growth and changes in the number and composition of jobs
- Population and population distribution within the

Stuart Meck, FAICP, American Planning Association, Chicago, Illinois

region, as well as its local governments, including projections and analyses by age, education level, income, employment, or similar characteristics

- Natural resources, including air, water, forests and other vegetation, and minerals
- Amount, type, quality, affordability, and geographic distribution of housing among local governments in the region correlated with projected job and population change
- Identification of features of significant statewide or regional architectural, scenic, cultural, historic, or architectural interest, as well as scenic corridors and viewsheds
- Amount, type, location, and quality of agricultural lands
- Amount, type, intensity or density, general location of industrial, commercial, residential, and other land uses, and projections of changes in land use, correlated with projected job and population change

MAP COMPONENTS

The regional comprehensive plan provides a visual representation of the plan's objectives. The components of the map may include the following:

- Location of urban growth area boundaries
- Existing and proposed transportation facilities
- Other public facilities and utilities of extrajurisdictional or regionwide significance
- Potential areas of critical state concern (such as areas of significant biodiversity, scenic beauty, historic significance, or archaeological value, or areas around major facilities, such as military bases, airports, or national or state parks)
- Natural hazard areas
- Urban and rural growth centers

- Any other matters of regional significance that can be graphically represented.

THE IMPLEMENTATION PROGRAM

A long-range implementation program for the regional comprehensive plan may include the following components.

An Implementation Schedule

The implementation program may include a schedule of development for proposed transportation and other public facilities and utilities of extrajurisdictional or regionwide significance. The schedule may include a description of the proposed public facility or utility, an identification of the governmental unit to be responsible for the facility or utility, the year(s) the facility or utility is proposed for construction or installation, an estimate of costs, and sources of public and private revenue for covering such costs.

Development Criteria

The program may include development criteria for use in local government and special district plans. Performance benchmarks may be defined to measure the achievement of the regional comprehensive plan by local governments and special districts.

Monitoring and Evaluation

A statement may be included to describe the criteria and procedures the agency creating the plan will use in monitoring and evaluating the plan's implementation by local governments, special districts, and the state.

Coordination

There may also be a statement of measures describing the ways in which state and/or local programs

may best be coordinated to promote the goals and policies of the regional comprehensive plan

Legislative Changes

The program may also include proposals for changes in state laws to achieve regional objectives, such as regional tax-base sharing or procedures to review large-scale developments with multijurisdictional impacts or to consolidate existing planning organizations to improve services and coordination. Regional planning agencies may also propose interjurisdictional agreements to clarify responsibility for the provision of urban services.

REFERENCES

Burnham, Daniel H., and Edward H. Bennett. [1909] 1970. *Plan of Chicago*. Reprint, New York: DaCapo Press.

Chicago Metropolis 2020. 2003. *The Metropolis Plan: Choices for the Chicago Region*. Chicago: Chicago Metropolis 2020.

Committee for the Regional Plan of New York and Its Environs. 1929. *The Regional Plan of New York and Its Environs. The Graphic Plan*. Vol. 1. New York: The Committee.

Meck, Stuart (gen. ed). 2002. *Growing Smart[SM] Legislative Guidebook: Model Statutes for Planning and Management of Change*. 2 vols. Chicago: American Planning Association.

See also:
Housing Plans
Population Projections
Regions
Transportation Plans
Watersheds

Stuart Meck, FAICP, American Planning Association, Chicago, Illinois

NEIGHBORHOOD PLANS

A neighborhood plan focuses on a specific geographic area of a local jurisdiction that typically includes substantial residential development, associated commercial uses, and institutional services such as recreation and education. Many of the same topics covered in a local comprehensive plan are covered in a neighborhood plan.

REASONS TO PREPARE A NEIGHBORHOOD PLAN

The neighborhood plan is intended to provide more detailed goals, policies, and guidelines than those in the local comprehensive plan. Neighborhood plans often emphasize potential partnerships among government agencies, community groups, school boards, and the private sector—partnerships that can act to achieve neighborhood goals. These plans are often developed through highly collaborative processes involving citizens, business, nongovernmental organizations (NGOs), and the local government of the neighborhood.

Neighborhood plans describe land-use patterns in more detail than do comprehensive plans. They may even approach the specificity required for amendments to a zoning district map or street classification system. These descriptions and maps can be used for greenfield or developing areas in a manner similar to that used in sector or specific plans, an approach used in Florida and California.

These plans also often propose a program of implementation shorter in duration than is proposed in a comprehensive plan. For an established neighborhood, the plan may emphasize issues that can be addressed in one to two years. They may include actions to be taken by the local government, other governmental agencies, school boards, nonprofit organizations, or for-profit groups. In many respects, this reflects the nature of the neighborhood planning process itself, which often focuses on visible and politicized problems that can be resolved quickly, such as trash cleanup, park improvements, or specific code enforcement issues. For newer neighborhoods, the plan's content may be more far-reaching and functional.

Neighborhood planning succeeds when the process is cyclical, small successes are emphasized, and the issue of identifying neighborhood leaders and legitimacy is addressed at the onset.

PLAN ELEMENTS

The American Planning Association conducted research in the mid-1990s that identified more than 36 elements in neighborhood plans. This group of elements, which appeared in various combinations, suggests a realm of possibilities for a particular neighborhood plan. While no definitive recommendation can be made about which specific elements a neighborhood plan should contain, the plan's content should result from a process that assesses the neighborhood's specific needs, resources, and ideals.

While there is no definitive list of required elements for neighborhood plans, certain elements appear to be common and essential. They can be grouped into five categories, based on their relative purpose and sequence in the planning process:

- *General housekeeping:* Organizational items that make the plan readable and usable, and serve to encourage further involvement in the planning process
- *Planning process validation:* Elements that demonstrate the legitimacy of the research and consensus-building processes that led to the development of the plan
- *Neighborhood establishment:* Elements that serve to create a community image or identity distinct from the jurisdiction as a whole
- Functional elements: Substantive items that may vary widely from plan to plan (e.g., safety element, housing element)
- *Implementation Framework:* The goals, programs, actions, or schedules used to implement the plan

General Housekeeping

The elements in this category are used to create a clear, usable plan document. Because neighborhood residents may not be familiar with planning, this element is particularly important to include. More information on this element is covered in the Plan Making section of this book.

Planning Process Validation

Stakeholder participation is critical at the neighborhood planning level. Planning information must be accessible and comprehensible to all involved parties. Certain information should be made public throughout the planning process. In addition, placing some of that information directly in the plan allows other citizens to participate in the planning process more intelligently at a later time. This makes the plan a working reference document and validates the process that culminated in the plan.

The Neighborhood Organizational Structure and Planning Process

An important part of plan validation is how the planning process is initiated and carried out. Flow charts are often used to illustrate the sequence of events. This section may also reference the ordinance that adopts the plan, the community feedback that supported it, or the background information about why the process was initiated. Many jurisdictions require a formal neighborhood organization to be in place as a condition for planning assistance or plan adoption. Neighborhood leadership should be made clear in a plan or at least emerge out of the planning process. A legitimate, publicly accessible power structure gives the neighborhood-city relationship credibility, encourages neighbors to act responsibly with public resources, and facilitates a leadership development mechanism within the community.

The Mission/Purpose Statement

The mission/purpose statement establishes the importance of the neighborhood planning process. It should convey that the process is all-inclusive and in accordance with policies set forth in the jurisdiction's comprehensive plan, if one exists. The statement can also be linked to the municipal code or city charter.

The Participation Proclamation

This section documents the participation process as it actually happened for the plan. It should be located at the beginning of the plan, setting the stage for the policies and recommendations that follow. Local ownership of the planning process must be evident. Both positive and negative feedback is important to include. Meeting minutes, survey results, or local newspaper articles can document feedback.

Needs Assessment

A needs assessment for services and facilities is a fundamental component of neighborhood planning, especially when it identifies underserved neighborhood groups. Needs assessments can measure social services, physical conditions, commercial resources, and cultural amenities. When assessing needs, it is important to take stock of existing community resources. Evaluating the positive aspects of a neighborhood can reveal unexpected opportunities for dealing with the negatives.

Defining the Neighborhood

In addition to securing the future, neighborhood plans fortify the present by defining the neighborhood.

Boundary Delineation

The neighborhood and the city departments should agree to, or at least accommodate, each party's perception of neighborhood boundaries. Boundary identification should involve representatives from the community, pertinent city departments, and, if possi-

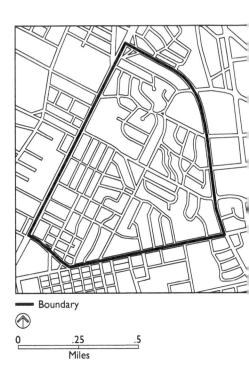

— Boundary

0   .25   .5
        Miles

NEIGHBORHOOD BOUNDARY DELINEATION

Source: Adapted from Upper Boggy Creek Neighborhood Plan, City of Austin, TX, 2002.

Michelle Gregory, AICP, Soapbox Enterprises, Portland, Oregon

ble, social service providers. One method of determining boundaries is to have participants draw lines on maps to define their own boundaries. Combining the maps can reveal the most common perception of the area that constitutes the neighborhood. The walkable distances to key community services, such as elementary schools, public transportation, local grocers, and health care resources, often define neighborhood boundaries. Neighborhood definition is also sometimes related to historic district designation.

The Functional Elements

Most neighborhood plans address functional elements, such as housing, safety, land use, and recreation as separate topics. Plans may treat these topics from start to finish, beginning with a description of existing conditions and concluding with recommendations, or they may simply list policy recommendations and the implementation strategies for those recommendations. Some neighborhood plans have required that elements be consistent with those in the community's comprehensive plan or, sometimes, with the regional plan. These might include density targets or impact and mitigation requirements for new development.

Residential

Residential development policies can include promoting owner-occupied housing or rental housing, code enforcement, and amending zoning and other land-use controls to encourage more housing development and vacant property rehabilitation. Issues pertaining to private property maintenance, housing stock, affordability and demand, building conditions, safety, property values, infill, abandonment, and design standards can also be included.

Transportation/Circulation/Pedestrian Access

Transportation elements in neighborhood plans often identify specific circulation problems at intersections and street corners. Plans can include recommendations for improving sidewalks, reducing vehicles or vehicle speed, creating bicycle lanes, and improving access to transit. Transportation elements and policies should promote the connection and flow of all transportation forms to serve people of all ages and abilities.

Land Use/Zoning

Current land-use patterns and zoning classifications are frequently presented in neighborhood plans, often as part of a needs assessment. To help residents understand the information, land-use and zoning data should be provided simply and clearly. Growth projections and areas where growth is expected to happen should be identified.

Infrastructure/Utilities

Infrastructure quality is important to neighborhood residents and businesses. It is also perhaps the least

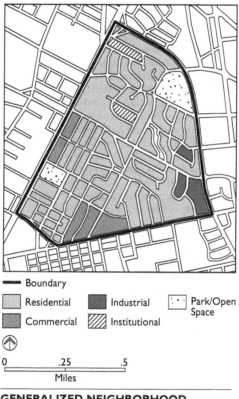

Boundary

Residential   Industrial   Park/Open Space

Commercial   Institutional

0   .25   .5

Miles

GENERALIZED NEIGHBORHOOD LAND-USE MAP

Source: Adapted from Upper Boggy Creek Neighborhood Plan, City of Austin, TX, 2002.

controllable aspect of neighborhood development, particularly where city officials have not been involved in the neighborhood planning process. Public works departments and private utility companies are not always directly responsive to neighborhoods because their agendas are usually tied to citywide capital improvement programs rather than to each neighborhood's planning process. Plans may include actions such as petitioning public works departments and the city council as a method of obtaining needed infrastructure improvements.

Implementation Framework

Once a neighborhood plan has evaluated the existing conditions, the needs assessment, and the community's desires for the future, generally the plan frames a set of goals and objectives. An implementation program sometimes follows the goals and objectives.

Goals, Objectives, and Other Resolutions

The goals and objectives of the neighborhood plan represent the community's vision and values. They may be presented as vision statements or policy recommendations.

Implementation Program

The schedule for achieving goals and objectives must be set, commitments must be made, and responsibility for actually accomplishing them has to be assigned. Neighborhood plans should include an implementation element, either woven into the functional plan elements or at the end of the document, shown as a chart or matrix.

Funding

City capital improvements funds, special assessments, transportation funds, tax increment funds, community development block grant (CDBG) funds, special state or federal program grants (such as historic preservation or urban forestry), donations, fund-raisers, private investors, and community development loans are viable funding sources to use in the implementation of neighborhood plans.

See also:
Neighborhoods
Participation
Plan Making

Michelle Gregory, AICP, Soapbox Enterprises, Portland, Oregon

TRANSPORTATION PLANS

Effective transportation systems are central to maintaining the productivity, health, and safety of communities and regions. A transportation plan guides the investment in, and timing of, improvements to the transportation network to meet community mobility, accessibility, safety, economic, and quality-of-life needs.

REASONS TO PREPARE A TRANSPORTATION PLAN

Transportation plans are typically prepared to address the following items in a systematic, coordinated, and comprehensive manner:

- Management of existing systems
- Maintenance of previous investment
- Realignment of existing services
- Introduction of new services
- Construction of new facilities
- Identification of ways to finance system maintenance and improvements

The process of preparing various transportation plans gives government agencies, elected officials, and the public the opportunity to assess the adequacy of the existing system and to plan to meet future needs while maintaining local and regional transportation systems in good condition. The outcome of the process should be a transportation plan that defines existing problems and issues, predicts future deficiencies and problems, defines solutions, and identifies where to find the resources needed to manage and implement plan recommendations.

The goals of a particular transportation plan are usually determined by comparing existing transportation system performance to projected future demands and by considering the particular social, economic, and environmental circumstances of the community. Given the importance of effective transportation systems to the health and vitality of a community, transportation plans often provide a "blueprint" for future development and redevelopment in support of regional and comprehensive land-use plans.

TRANSPORTATION PLANNING ROLES AND RESPONSIBILITIES

The development of a successful transportation plan requires the insights of those entities responsible for various components of the transportation system, working in concert with those who will use and be affected by the transportation service and improvements, to develop solutions responsive to diverse considerations. Those responsible for plan development must create an effective forum for evaluating system deficiencies, assessing alternatives, and selecting the most effective course of action. Development of some plans is a highly structured process, complete with formal committees. Others are less structured and rely more heavily on exiting committees or informal communication networks to solicit participation.

Whether structured or informal, because transportation plans affect so many interests and a wide range of people, broad and meaningful participation

in plan development is essential. The development stage of transportation planning should include representatives from the following constituencies:

- U.S. Department of Transportation
- State departments of transportation
- Metropolitan planning organizations
- Local governments
- Public transit providers
- Resource and regulatory agencies
- Citizens and communities

U.S. Department of Transportation

The modal administrations of the U.S. Department of Transportation, including the Federal Highway Administration, the Federal Transit Administration, and the Federal Railroad Administration, administer, grant, and oversee funds for the planning, development, implementation, and operation of transportation services and infrastructure. In transportation planning efforts funded by the federal government, such as corridor plans, direct involvement of the federal agency is advisable during key decision points, at a minimum. In the development of a local transportation plan where there is no clear federal interest, there may be no involvement of the federal government, or the involvement might be limited to consultation regarding the availability and applicability of federal programs and funding.

State Departments of Transportation

Through their departments of transportation, states are responsible for the construction, maintenance, and operation of designated state highways. As part of this responsibility, state departments of transportation (DOTs) are responsible for provision and administration of funds for construction, maintenance, and operation of transportation facilities and services. State DOTs are also responsible for leading the preparation of statewide plans. Like metropolitan planning organizations (MPOs), they may have responsibility in the development and maintenance of regional travel demand forecasting models. State DOTs provide technical assistance and support to a wide range of transportation plans. They are the repositories for much of the data required to assess existing transportation systems.

Metropolitan Planning Organizations

The federal government charges MPOs to prepare metropolitan area long-range plans for urbanized areas. In some instances, MPOs will also lead the preparation of corridor plans. In addition, MPOs are often in charge of developing and maintaining the regional travel demand forecasting models used as a basis to support many transportation planning functions, including the development of employment and population forecasts and administration and disbursement of transportation funds. Consequently, in addition to their leadership role in preparing metropolitan regional long-range transportation plans, MPOs also provide technical assistance in support of other transportation planning efforts.

Local Governments

Local governments play a major role in constructing, operating, and maintaining surface transportation net-

works, often including transit service and roadways. Consequently, their involvement in the development of transportation plans is essential. In some cases, such as for a local transportation plan, the city, county, or town public works departments or transportation divisions might take the lead in preparing the transportation plan or the transportation element of a comprehensive plan. For other plan types, such as metropolitan area long-range transportation plans, local governments might provide technical support and knowledge specific to their jurisdictions. In either case, the insights of those engaged in the day-to-day operations of the system are an invaluable asset to any plan. In addition, since local government might be charged with implementing particular recommendations of the plans, it is essential that there be consensus for action and an understanding of the basic needs and technical analysis supporting the action.

Public Transit Providers

With respect to public transportation services, the role and responsibilities of public transit providers is similar to that described for local governments. However, because transit providers may not have a dedicated funding source for operations and may be dependent upon local governments for funding, early consultation regarding the availability of resources is even more critical.

Resource and Regulatory Agencies

Transportation plan recommendations can affect a broad range of natural and social resources. Consequently, early involvement of resource and regulatory agencies in transportation plan development can help identify constraints that could potentially prohibit implementation of future projects because of regulatory requirements, schedule impacts, or financial requirements.

Citizens and Communities

Citizens and communities are an important resource in the development of transportation plans, as both the "customers" of the system and those who might be affected by proposed changes. Statewide plans, metropolitan area long-range transportation plans, and corridor plans specifically require public involvement to inform plan development. Involvement should range from the average resident to neighborhood or civic associations, community leaders, and business community representation, such as chambers of commerce. For larger transportation plans, it is advisable to establish a formal citizens advisory group.

TYPES OF TRANSPORTATION PLANS

Transportation plans vary widely in approach, content, and scope as determined by geographic coverage, scale, and time frame. There are four basic types of transportation plans:

- Statewide transportation plans
- Metropolitan area long-range transportation plans
- Local transportation plans
- Corridor plans

Diana C. Mendes, AICP, DMJM+Harris Planning, Fairfax, Virginia

Statewide Transportation Plans

Statewide transportation plans, which are prepared by state DOTs, provide the basis for coordinating data collection and analyses to support planning, programming, and project development decisions. A basic requirement of plan development is coordination with the public and other entities with jurisdiction. The extent of coordination required with other transportation planning entities in developing the plan is based on the scale and complexity of many issues, including transportation problems; safety concerns; and land use, employment, economic, environmental, and housing and community development objectives within the state. The plans typically reference, summarize, or contain information about the availability of financial and other resources needed to implement the plan, although state plans, unlike metropolitan area long-range transportation plans, are not required to determine the likely availability of funding and the sources of funding to carry out the plan. State plans are evaluated on a regular basis and updated periodically to reflect changing statewide priorities and needs.

Statewide plans are intermodal in nature. They address passenger, goods, and freight movement for a minimum 20-year planning horizon. These plans are federally mandated to consider the following issues:

- Economic vitality
- Safety and security
- Accessibility and mobility
- Environmental quality
- Quality of life
- System connectivity
- System efficiency
- System preservation

In addition, state DOTs are all obligated to consider the opinions of elected officials representing local governments and the concerns of Native American tribal governments and federal land management agencies that have jurisdiction over land within the boundaries of the state. The plan is coordinated with adjacent states and counties and, where appropriate, international borders. It is conducted in a manner consistent with the metropolitan area planning process conducted by MPOs. By federal mandate, statewide plans are coordinated with air quality planning, and provide for appropriate conformity analyses as required by the Clean Air Act.

Metropolitan Area Long-Range Transportation Plans

Metropolitan area long-range transportation plans focus on evaluating alternative transportation and land-use scenarios to identify major travel corridors, assess potential problems, and provide a basis for planning and programming major improvements. These plans cover multiple jurisdictions and are therefore "regional" in emphasis. Prepared under the direction of a federally designated MPO, they typically cover a 20-year planning horizon. Under federal requirements, the adopted plans must be "fiscally constrained." In other words, the plan must demonstrate the likely availability of funding sources needed to implement proposed programs and projects.

Local Transportation Plans

Local transportation plans are prepared either as stand-alone documents or as an element of a com-prehensive plan. Local governments or regional transit providers typically prepare these plans, but they are coordinated closely with MPOs and state DOTs. The plans provide the basis for the programming and implementation of local transportation actions. They address small-scale improvements and projects requiring major capital investments. The typical plan consists of an inventory of existing facilities and a description of existing conditions, an assessment of system deficiencies, a projection of future needs, a description of the proposed plan, discussion of cost implications, and a summary of actions required for plan implementation. These plans usually address some short-range early action items (1 to 5 years), some midrange actions (5 to 10 years), and longer-term activities in a 20-year time horizon. In addition, the land-use implications of the plan are addressed. As with the other plans discussed, public and agency coordination during plan development is essential to successful plan implementation.

Corridor Plans

Corridor plans that focus on transportation are prepared for high-priority areas showing signs of congestion or predicted for significant future travel volume, or for transportation facilities of historical or natural significance. The entity responsible for implementing the improvements most frequently prepares these plans; therefore, state DOTs and transit providers often undertake them, although MPOs, local governments, and resource agencies such as the National Park Service also conduct such studies. Coordination of corridor plans with the general public is required, as well as with federal, state, and local agencies with an interest in the plan's outcome. Corridor plans usually have a 20-year planning horizon. The degree of federal or state DOT participation is often governed by the proposed funding for the plan's implementation.

Corridor plans involve the definition of the corridor to be studied, along with a clear presentation of the problem to be solved, both of which form the basis of the purpose and need for action. Consideration of a wide range of alternative means to solve the identified transportation problem or resource management objectives should be at the core of plan development. These alternatives can involve different levels of investment or different types of corridor improvements. They are systematically evaluated using a set of stakeholder-developed evaluation crite-

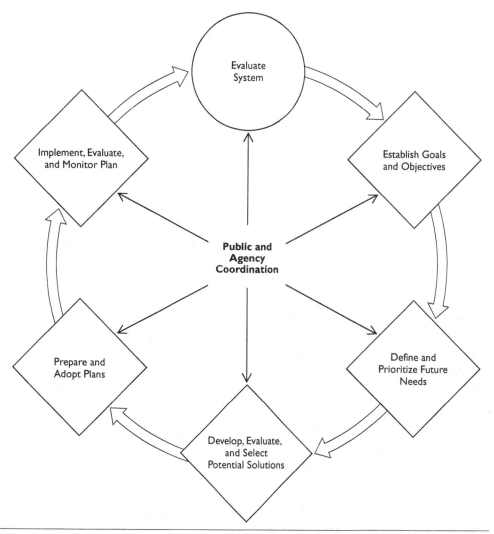

TRANSPORTATION PLAN DEVELOPMENT CYCLE

Source: Diana C. Mendes, AICP.

Diana C. Mendes, AICP, DMJM+Harris Planning, Fairfax, Virginia

ria. These criteria typically include land use, environmental effects, community concerns, cost, capacity, and effectiveness. The analysis results are shared and discussed publicly prior to making a decision on a preferred course of action. The final plan document summarizes both the planning process and the results, explaining how the decision was made, and the actions necessary to implement the plan and recommended improvements.

PLAN COMPONENTS

Transportation plans should include the following elements:

- An overview of the planning process
- A description of existing conditions (transportation network and land use)
- A forecast of future conditions (transportation network and land use)
- A summary of transportation needs
- Goals and objectives
- An assessment of transportation system capacity
- A series of alternative scenarios for future and proposed improvements
- A description of cost implications and funding sources
- Guidelines for implementation and performance monitoring
- A program for ensuring public involvement

TRANSPORTATION PLAN DEVELOPMENT

There are six basic steps in the development of a transportation plan:

1. Evaluate system capacity, deficiencies, and needs.
2. Establish goals and objectives.
3. Define and prioritize future needs.
4. Develop, evaluate, and select potential solutions.
5. Prepare and adopt the plan, including public review and comment.
6. Implement, monitor, and evaluate plan performance.

The development of responsive and effective plans is predicated on the active involvement of the public and appropriate federal, state, and local agencies in transportation decision making at each step of transportation plan development.

Evaluate System Capacity, Deficiencies, and Need

Evaluation of the current system begins with an inventory of the existing facilities and services and their capacity, including the roadway network, transit systems, freight systems, as well as the interrelationships to air and waterborne transportation. This evaluation should establish where the transportation network is performing well and where deficiencies currently exist or are predicted to exist in terms of accessibility, mobility, and efficiency relative to community aspirations. Both quantitative and qualitative measures, including evaluation of population and employment characteristics, land-use trends, travel markets and patterns, and user surveys, are often used in the plans to describe the trans-

portation problems to be solved and to establish a need for action.

Establish Goals and Objectives

The goals and objectives, which are developed in response to the analysis of system capacity, deficiencies, and needs, form the foundation upon which different alternative transportation scenarios and investments are evaluated during plan development. The goals and objectives vary and are dependent upon context (rural, suburban, and urban), trends in population and employment, and planning horizon (short term or long term). Transportation plans are increasingly becoming more context-sensitive, incorporating more goals related to land-use compatibility, economic considerations, energy, environmental management, and community quality. Criteria by which the performance of different potential actions can be measured against these goals and objectives should be clearly articulated to facilitate public understanding of the decision-making process.

Define and Rank Future Needs

Once planners have established the plan's goals and objectives, the next step involves defining and

ranking future needs. This analysis uses the information gained during the initial system evaluation in combination with population and employment projections, regional and local land-use plans, and the results of public and agency coordination.

Transportation Models

Planners employ transportation models to conduct regional travel demand forecasting and to simulate traffic impacts to assess and evaluate the capacity of existing and future transportation networks to accommodate projected demand. Regional models are focused on the large-scale "macro" travel movements in aggregate, while traffic simulation is focused on the smaller-scale, or "micro," travel movements on an individual basis.

The regional travel demand forecasting models are developed, maintained, and operated by MPOs and state DOTs, and can vary in size and scope dependent upon the area they are designed to serve. These regional models characterize the transportation system networks, as well as the demand for the system in terms of its users, travel patterns, and how changes to the system might affect demand. These regional models provide insights

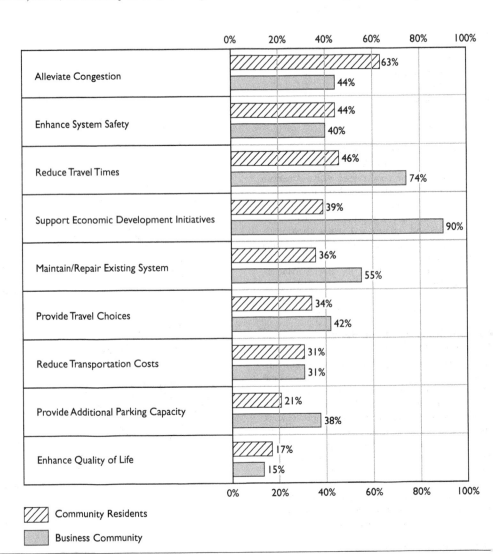

TRANSPORTATION GOALS BY PARTICIPANT PREFERENCE

Source: Diana C. Mendes, AICP.

Diana C. Mendes, AICP, DMJM+Harris Planning, Fairfax, Virginia

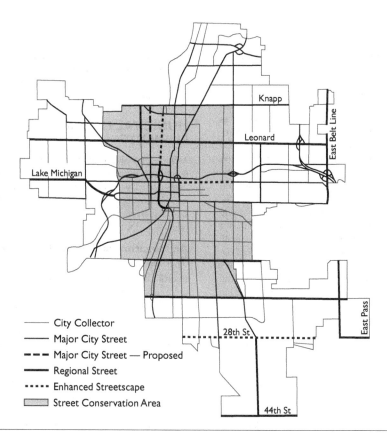

TRANSPORTATION FRAMEWORK PLAN: STREETS

Source: Adapted from City of Grand Rapids, Michigan, 2002, Plan for Grand Rapids.

about where trips are generated and attracted, how trips are distributed, the likely choice of modes, and the routes to be traveled in order to predict the future volume of use.

In cases when regional models either are not available or may not be appropriate, such as when small changes in the transportation network need to be analyzed for a specific site, traffic simulation models are used. Traffic simulation models can be valuable not only in determining future conditions and level of service, but also in identifying appropriate mitigation

measures such as changes in signal timing or additional street improvements to address degradation of capacity. A number of software packages are commercially available, and the models are typically developed and applied by the project sponsor on a case-by-case basis to address specific project needs. Irrespective of the type of modeling tools and processes applied, priorities should be based upon the results of the technical analysis, overlaid with the opinions of the public and agencies participating in plan development.

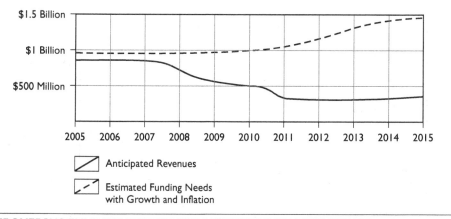

NEEDS VERSUS FUNDING FOR TRANSPORTATION INFRASTRUCTURE

Source: Diana C. Mendes, AICP.

Develop, Evaluate, and Select Potential Solutions

Following a clear understanding of and agreement on priorities, alternative scenarios or solutions can be defined and developed. These scenarios consist of adjustments to the transportation system based on changes to services or investments in new programs or infrastructure. While planners may evaluate each of the transportation modes (e.g., rail, air, auto) addressed in the plan independently, the results of this initial assessment can be used ultimately to develop and to test potential combinations of investment among different modes to best meet needs.

It is during this iterative process that alternative solutions can be evaluated and compared based upon their performance and effectiveness in achieving stated goals and objectives and meeting needs. To assist elected officials, community leaders, and the public in making decisions among alternatives, planners need to explain and document the potential benefits and impacts, and the trade-offs of each alternative. They need to pay special attention to which populations benefit from a particular set of actions versus which may experience adverse impacts to anticipate support for and resistance to the plan.

Prepare and Adopt the Plan

The plan should document the public decision-making process and provide the technical rationale for its conclusions. It should also describe future implementation of proposed programs and improvements, including a clear delineation of action to be taken, the sequencing of improvements, responsibility for implementation, and cost.

A brief executive summary of the plan should be prepared for the public. Because transportation plans can be quite technical, the summary should be written for the lay reader. Adoption of the plan should follow a public review process that includes a number of public outreach activities, including formal hearings. During the project review process, it may be necessary to revise the plan. Particular attention should be paid to the financial element of the plan in terms of cost, revenues, shortfalls, and options for using current and potential new sources.

Implement, Monitor, and Evaluate Plan Performance

Plan implementation requires clear direction on responsibilities, schedule, and funding. Successful plan implementation also depends on ongoing monitoring and performance evaluation. This systematic, regular assessment of the effectiveness of implemented actions should provide the foundation for the evaluation phase of the next planning cycle. The performance measures should be the same as or a subset of the evaluation criteria used to assess and select the adopted plan.

See also:
Air Quality
Comprehensive Plans
Environmental Impact Assessment
Federal Legislation
Participation
Transportation

Diana C. Mendes, AICP, DMJM+Harris Planning, Fairfax, Virginia

HOUSING PLANS

More than 70 years ago planning pioneer Patrick Abercrombie (1933) wrote, "The subject of housing enters into planning continuously, whether under the heading of density, of the living conditions of the population, of slum clearance or suburban growth." Those same issues remain central to the planning process today. To address them, jurisdictions with the authority to prepare and implement housing plans are increasingly likely to prepare and adopt housing plans or housing strategies, either as a part of their comprehensive plan, or as a separate freestanding document.

REASONS TO PREPARE A HOUSING PLAN

Municipalities have many different reasons for preparing housing plans.

To Address Legal Requirements

Some states require a housing plan as part of the municipal comprehensive plan or master plan. Washington State, for example, mandates a housing element, which must "make adequate provision for existing and projected needs of all economic segments of the community" (Laws of State of Washington, RCW 36.70A.070(2)). Other states, including California and New Jersey, require that the municipality address its fair share of regional housing need, as defined by a state or regional agency. Municipalities that receive HUD Community Development Block Grant or HOME funds must prepare a Consolidated Plan, which delineates the municipality's overall housing needs and strategy and shows how their federal funds will be used.

To Address Affordable Housing Needs

Even with no formal legal requirement, many municipalities undertake housing plans when they recognize that rising housing costs or loss of existing housing units is making the community unaffordable to many of its present and prospective residents. As described in the Cary, North Carolina, affordable housing plan, when the town realized that the "escalating price of housing was excluding many people from living within the city limits...including Town staff, policemen, teachers, retail clerks, and service people," it adopted an affordable housing plan, which included a detailed action-oriented "affordable housing tool kit."

To Encourage Economic and Social Integration, and to Build Stronger Neighborhoods

Affluent suburbs may develop affordable housing plans to ensure that less affluent people can continue to live in, or move into, the community. At the same time, many older urban centers—for example, Baltimore and Norfolk—have begun to develop housing strategies designed to expand their economic diversity by attracting middle- and upper-income residents into their neighborhoods and downtowns. Such strategies can be citywide or can focus on creating economic diversity in a specific neighborhood, such as Fall Creek Place in Indianapolis. HUD's HOPE VI and Homeownership Zone programs have funded effective neighborhood-oriented housing strategies.

FORMS OF MUNICIPAL HOUSING PLANS

The form that a municipal housing plan takes flows from the reason it is being prepared. Where a housing element is part of a comprehensive plan, its features will usually be spelled out in the state planning statute. These typically include inventories, need assessments, and goal statements, as well as action plans. The New Jersey Fair Housing Act describes the contents of a fair-share plan, including "a consideration of the lands that are most appropriate for construction of low and moderate income housing and of the existing structures most appropriate for conversion to, or rehabilitation for, low and moderate income housing..." (New Jersey Statutes 52:27D-310(f)). Washington State requires each city or county to identify "sufficient land for housing, including but not limited to government-assisted housing, housing for low-income families, manufactured housing, multifamily housing, and group homes and foster care facilities."

A municipality is driven to prepare a plan for internal reasons, such as the need for more affordable housing, but the scope of the plan may vary widely. Recognizing that housing needs far exceeded the community's ability to address them, the Stamford, Connecticut, Affordable Housing Strategy concentrated on a detailed strategy to assemble land and financial resources for affordable housing.

Housing strategies in communities seeking to attract middle- and upper-income residents tend to focus much more on the real estate *market*, rather than on housing *needs*. These plans may include identifying potential target markets, such as empty-nesters or young professionals, focusing on how to attract them into the city's housing market, whether by developing new housing oriented to their preferences or by highlighting particular features of the city's existing housing stock.

A housing plan is fundamentally a *strategic action* plan, which emphasizes those parts of the housing market unlikely to be adequately reached by the private market unaided by public intervention. The assessment of conditions and analysis of trends is not an end in itself but should be designed to lead to specific strategies and programs designed to achieve the community's housing goals.

MUNICIPAL HOUSING PLAN ELEMENTS

Although housing plans vary widely, a series of elements are common to most plans. As noted, in some cases, state law will mandate that certain elements be included, while in others local officials and community stakeholders must determine which are most relevant to local concerns.

An Inventory of Existing Conditions and Trends

In order to understand existing housing conditions in the municipality, most plans begin with an inventory, including the distribution of housing in the community by cost and by type (for example, single-family, two-family, or multifamily housing), for both owner-occupied and rental housing. It should also identify specialized housing types, such as manufactured housing or single-room occupancy (SRO) housing. It should both provide a profile of current housing conditions and analyze trends to determine how those conditions are changing—increases in house prices, for example, or movement from ownership or rental, or vice versa, in the housing stock.

Regional conditions and trends should also be presented, to show how the municipality relates to the larger regional context. Job growth trends, important as an indicator of potential housing needs, should also be measured. Information on substandard or abandoned housing should be included where sound data is available. Census data should be used as a starting point, but, particularly as the end of each decade approaches, it must be supplemented by other data sources. A property information system, as has been developed in many cities (e.g., Los Angeles or Minneapolis), can be used to identify buildings at risk of abandonment by tracking code violations, tax arrearages, and crime complaints.

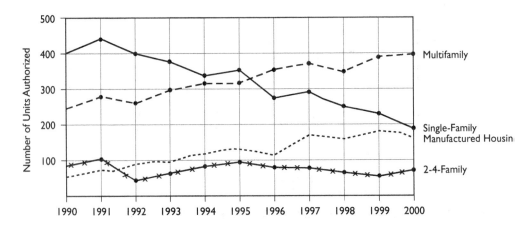

HOUSING PRODUCTION TRENDS BY TYPE, 1990–2000

Source: Alan Mallach.

Alan Mallach, FAICP, National Housing Institute, Montclair, New Jersey

Housing Need Analysis

Most housing plans are designed to focus primarily on affordable housing. Affordable housing is defined differently in different jurisdictions. In New Jersey, it refers to households earning no more than 80 percent of the regional median income, while elsewhere it may include households earning as much as 120 percent of regional median or as little as 50 percent. At present, households earning less than 50 percent of regional median income are most likely to have deficient housing conditions and are least likely to see their housing needs addressed by the private market.

The housing plan should attempt to quantify housing needs wherever possible, using census data to identify the number of households living in overcrowded housing or suffering undue cost burdens in the community. Where feasible, a community survey should be used to identify households living in substandard housing. The sum of these needs is often referred to as the community's present, or indigenous, housing need.

Prospective affordable housing needs are those of low- and moderate-income households who should have the opportunity to move into the community in the future. This is where the fair-share principle becomes most relevant since, by definition, a substantial percentage of all new households are low and moderate income. Since "low and moderate income" is defined relative to regional median income rather than as a set dollar amount, it will represent a consistent share of all households over time, with the share depending on where the cutoff is placed. Where low and moderate income is defined as 80 percent of regional median, roughly 40 percent of all households will fall below that line. Where it is defined as 50 percent of regional median, it will include roughly 25 percent of all households. (See table.) A fair-share plan, or regional fair-share allocation, identifies the share of the region's household growth that should appropriately be accommodated within the municipality and defines how housing for those households will be provided.

See *Housing Needs Assessment* elsewhere in this book for more detail on conducting such a study.

Market Analysis

Understanding the workings of the housing market, at the regional level and within the municipality—and in large municipalities, within individual neighborhoods—is a critical step toward framing effective, achievable goals and strategies, and determining realistic targets. Enacting a successful inclusionary program, for example, requires an understanding of

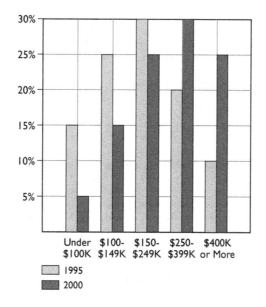

DISTRIBUTION OF HOUSE SALE PRICES, 1995 AND 2000

Source: Alan Mallach.

how the market will respond to incentives, such as density bonuses, or the extent to which market prices will support internal subsidies. In an older city, the market analysis may be used to identify those households that may be attracted to redeveloping neighborhoods or downtown loft districts.

Goals and Targets

A strategic plan must be grounded in a body of clear goals and, to the extent feasible, realizable targets. Goals should be well focused, such as those in Denver's 1999 housing plan, listed here:

- Reduce the regulatory costs of housing.
- Expand the resources available for housing programs and services.
- Preserve the existing housing stock.
- Address the needs of low-income and special-needs populations.
- Attract and retain middle-income families.
- Undertake housing efforts to support economic development strategies.

Each of these goals is expressed in a way that can easily be translated into specific strategies and action programs.

Strategy Analysis

A vast number of potential housing strategies are available. Before settling on the specific strategies to pursue, a valuable part of the planning process is to conduct a strategy analysis to evaluate the available options to determine which are most likely to respond effectively to the community's conditions. The strategy analysis should look at removing impediments and establishing affirmative steps to reach affordable or other housing goals. Systems—including barriers created by the town's own regulations and administrative procedures—that affect the affordability or availability of housing should be examined, as should the means and resources the town can use to affirmatively promote its housing goals. Each strategy should be assessed with respect to its potential impact if implemented and the relative ease or difficulty of implementing the strategy.

Implementation Plan

The worth of a housing plan ultimately depends on its implementation. The implementation plan should begin with a description of the strategies and programs the town has selected to carry its goals forward. It should follow with specific information about how each strategy will be carried out, including:

- the financial resources that will be assembled;
- the sites, buildings, or target areas that will be the focus of the strategy;
- the design and planning standards to be followed;
- the key players or participants in implementing the strategy;
- identification of entities responsible for implementing each part of the strategy; and
- specific targets and timetables for each strategy or program.

The implementation plan should be *specific*. It should identify both specific areas to be rezoned and the specific standards that will ensure that the sites will be used as intended. It should include an assessment of the municipal, state, federal and private funds realistically available to carry out the plan.

Some productive implementation strategies municipalities use include:

- rezoning of areas for higher density;
- inclusionary zoning;
- creating infill opportunities;
- creating opportunities for specialized housing types, such as accessory apartments, SRO housing, or group homes;
- incentives for housing preservation and rehabilitation, including adaptive reuse projects;
- assembly strategies and land banking;
- removing regulatory barriers, including creating simpler and expedited approval procedures;
- financial assistance to developers of affordable housing; and
- housing trust funds.

Some housing strategies can be carried out within the existing structure of town or city government, but others will entail new responsibilities and may require new managerial entities or partnerships to carry them out. Partnerships with community development corporations, developers, employers, and others are critical. Few, if any, towns or cities are capable of implementing a housing strategy without strong private sector partners.

DISTRIBUTION OF HOUSEHOLDS AND RENTAL UNITS BY INCOME AND AFFORDABILITY

CATEGORY	MAXIMUM INCOME	MAXIMUM AFFORDABLE RENT	PERCENT OF ALL HOUSEHOLDS IN COUNTY	PERCENT OF RENTAL UNITS AT/BELOW AFFORDABLE RENT
Low income (<50% of median)	$25,000	$625/month	25%	3%
Moderate income (<80% of median)	$40,000	$1,000/month	40%	32%
Middle income (<120% of median)	$60,000	$1,500/month	60%	74%
Countywide Median Income	$50,000			
Countywide Median Rent		$1,200/month		

Source: Alan Mallach.

Alan Mallach, FAICP, National Housing Institute, Montclair, New Jersey

KEY AND EMERGING ISSUES

Housing is a complex, multidimensional subject, both in itself and in its relationship to other planning and development issues. Changes in economic conditions and housing needs, as well as new thinking about how best to plan towns and cities, have led to the emergence of a series of important issues, many arising from smart growth principles, that a community's housing plan should address.

Integrating Housing with Other Planning Activities

As planning moves away from a history of separated uses and disconnected plans to a more holistic view of a community, the importance of linking housing with other uses and other planning processes has become apparent. The recognition of the advantages of mixed-use development, in which housing and nonresidential uses complement each other, as well as recognition of the links between housing and open-space or major community facilities, such as schools, are important considerations for building stronger, healthier communities. The creation of transit-oriented development, for example, which combines housing and other uses around transit hubs, is but one of many such available strategies.

Housing and Jobs

The extent to which a community provides housing opportunities for a diverse workforce is not just a matter of creating a more balanced community; it is essential for the community's economic vitality. Housing plans should not only evaluate the community's economic base and job growth as a basis for planning future housing, but should also actively explore opportunities for direct linkages between major employers and workforce housing strategies.

Preservation

Housing plans are not only about what should be built in the future, but also about how to preserve what already exists. Housing strategies are a key element in preserving the fabric of existing neighborhoods and historic areas, particularly with respect to affordable housing. As the loss of the affordable housing stock, either through disinvestment or through price appreciation, becomes a critical issue in many communities, housing strategies must incorporate activities to preserve that stock as well as produce new affordable housing.

Downtown and Neighborhood Revitalization

Housing development grounded in market-building strategies has turned out to be one of the most powerful tools available to urban centers to spur reinvestment and revitalization in their downtowns and older residential neighborhoods. Cities such as Cleveland and Baltimore have reinvented their downtowns by drawing upon the regional pool of young professionals and empty-nesters, while attracting a diverse body of homebuyers to buy and rehabilitate homes in the city's neighborhoods. Strategies designed to maximize private sector reinvestment and revitalization activities are important parts of the housing plans of the many cities and towns seeking to rebuild.

Resolving Conflicts over Affordable Housing

Certainly, any development is potentially controversial, but few areas are as likely to trigger conflict as affordable housing. Despite widespread public support for meeting housing needs in general, a specific affordable housing proposal will often become a lightning rod for a variety of community concerns. Indeed, even the term "affordable housing" can become a matter of contention, prompting some advocates to refer to their efforts as "workforce housing" or "affordable home-ownership." The framers of an affordable housing plan must recognize the reality and depth of community concerns, and incorporate into the planning process a method for building support and, to the extent possible, consensus around the plan's specific strategies, beginning well before the plans are finalized.

REFERENCE

Abercrombie, Patrick. 1933. *Town and Country Planning*. New York, NY: Henry Holt & Co.

See also:
Federal Legislation
Housing Needs Assessment
Neighborhoods
Residential Types

Alan Mallach, FAICP, National Housing Institute, Montclair, New Jersey

ECONOMIC DEVELOPMENT PLANS

An economic development plan guides a local or regional effort to stimulate economic growth and to preserve existing jobs. Economic development may also be aimed at ensuring increases in real wages, stabilization or increase of the local tax base, and job diversification—making the community or region less dependent on a few employers and thus insulating it from economic downturns in specific industries.

In most places economic development has broadened from job creation and retention and provision of land and infrastructure for business to promotion of prosperity and quality of life—the idea that with economic growth should come broader societal well-being. Thus, economic development is increasingly linked with education, culture, affordable housing, and preservation of the environment.

REASONS TO PREPARE AN ECONOMIC DEVELOPMENT PLAN

A number of factors typically prompt a local or regional economic planning effort. They include the following:

- Loss of a major employer or the attraction of a new employer
- Competition from surrounding communities or regions
- Belief that the community should take an active role in promoting itself
- A desire to provide employment for existing residents
- Economic stagnation or decline in a community, or part of it
- Need for new tax revenues, especially to finance the concurrent costs of residential growth

Economic development efforts may also simply reflect an innate entrepreneurial spirit, a desire to experiment and to grow.

APPROACHES TO THE PLAN

All economic development plans should include a series of background studies intended to identify the strengths and weaknesses of the community or the region and make some assessments about the type and extent of desired economic growth. If the analysis is for a community, the larger frame of reference should be the region. If the analysis is for the region, the state or a substantial subregion of it should be the context. Trends that dominate the larger unit of analysis will in some way affect the subunit.

The planners preparing the plan should seek out or conduct background studies of a number of economic factors, especially the following:

- Economic base and shift-and-share analyses
- Job composition and growth or decline by industry sector on a national, statewide, or regional basis
- Tax structure of the community
- Existing labor force characteristics and future labor force requirements of existing and potential commercial and industrial enterprises in the state or region
- Locational characteristics of the community or

region from the standpoint of access to markets for its goods and services

- Patterns of private investment or disinvestments
- Commercial, industrial, and institutional lands within the community that are vacant, significantly unused, or environmentally contaminated
- Projected employment growth by industrial sector for the state or region
- Regulations and permitting procedures imposed by the local government on commercial and industrial enterprises and their effects on the costs of doing business
- Existing businesses
- Quality of life and lifestyle

PLAN COMPONENTS

An economic development plan will use these background studies and data to draw inferences about the strengths and weaknesses of the regional economy of which the community is part. From that analysis the local government can begin to define goals, policies, and guidelines for economic development. This analysis should, at a minimum, reveal the following:

- The community's role and responsibilities in the region's economy
- Categories or particular types of commercial, industrial, and institutional uses desired by the community

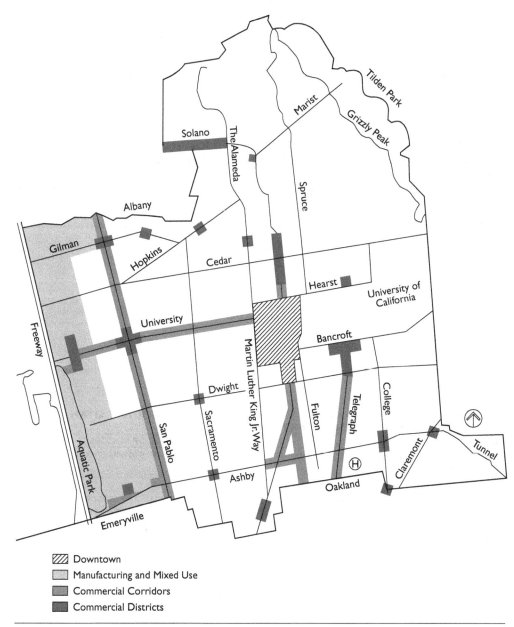

Downtown
Manufacturing and Mixed Use
Commercial Corridors
Commercial Districts

COMMERCIAL AND INDUSTRIAL EMPLOYMENT AREAS, BERKELEY, CALIFORNIA

Source: Berkeley, California, General Plan, 2003.

Stuart Meck, FAICP, American Planning Association, Chicago, Illinois

- The adequate number of sites of suitable sizes, types, and locations for such uses
- The community facilities that should be included in the community facilities element of the local comprehensive plan to support the economic development plan

The economic development plan may also include goals, policies, and guidelines to maintain existing categories, types, or levels of commercial, industrial, and institutional uses.

RELATED ACTIONS

Housing for Employees

Providing housing to accommodate new employees is an important part of economic development. The economic development plan must be closely coordi-nated with the housing plan and its implementation to provide reasonable opportunities for new employees to obtain housing. If that is not done, the local government will effectively export the need for housing and its associated costs to other nearby communities. The local government should take aggressive steps to ensure that sufficient housing is available for the expected or desired type of businesses and job growth.

Public/Private Coordination

In some cases, the economic development plan will involve the orchestration of a number of public and private actors to bring about economic change in a certain part of the local jurisdiction. For example, a community may decide to attract conventions. Thus, a convention and tourism authority may need to be established and funded, a convention center built, hotels and restaurants enticed to locate nearby, and transportation improvements of various types (some the responsibility of the state, others of the county) built.

IMPLEMENTATION

Implementation of the goals and objectives of an economic development plan can involve several actions:

- Setting aside or making available, through clearance and land assembly, land for business and industry through zoning, environmental remediation of contaminated sites, urban renewal, and other techniques for land assembly
- Underwriting risks though grants, loans, and tax abatement
- Providing amenities and infrastructure through a variety of capital investments
- Creating an ongoing economic development financing, attraction, and promotion entity
- Focusing attention on other quality-of-life factors such as colleges and universities, local schools, and environmental, recreational, and cultural amenities
- Attracting "creatives"—painters, writers, sculptors, musicians—to encourage a diverse cultural scene
- Establishing a joint economic development zone
- Instituting job training and placement
- Refining local, regional, or state permitting procedures and regulations to make them friendlier to business
- Establishing programs that monitor the needs of existing businesses and institutions, to ensure their retention
- Adopting design guidelines for commercial, industrial, and institutional areas

Implementing actions or strategies will be scheduled, with responsibility assigned to different actors or institutions, and costs estimated. An economic development plan should assume the private sector may need to take certain actions, either on its own or through formal public-private partnerships. Moreover, such a plan may contain measurable benchmarks in terms of job growth or retention, desired levels of private investment, and changes in real wages.

See also:
Housing Plans

ECONOMIC DEVELOPMENT STRATEGIES: DIRECT BUSINESS ASSISTANCE—PROJECTS

PROJECTS	LOCATION FACTOR ADDRESSED	PROS	CONS
Land or building purchase and assembly	• Land availability and cost	• Puts ownership of key property in hands of public job-creating authority. • Overcomes fragmented ownership and scarcity of large developable sites.	• Risk of holding undesirable property • Expensive
Industrial park creation	• Land availability and cost • Access to markets	• Prepares land for development. • Designed for multiple users and many jobs.	• Land can remain vacant and underused while waiting for desired firms.
Business accelerator (incubator)	• Land availability and cost • Workforce • Business formation	• Focuses on job creation. • Nurtures companies of the future.	• High initial costs for space and program management. • Need to have management expertise to provide technical assistance. • Small businesses do not lead to employment and tax base growth immediately.

Evaluation of the pros and cons of a discrete set of strategies and the locational factors they address as a way of sorting through actions for an economic development plan.

Source: ECONorthwest, Eugene, Oregon, 2003.

EXCERPT FROM WASHINGTON COUNTY, UTAH, STRATEGIC PLAN

I. RETAIN AND EXPAND BUSINESS

Goals	Measure of Success	Critical Strategies	Implementation Agent
Retain and expand existing businesses with the County that are consistent with the core economic values.	Employment in existing County businesses will expand by 5% per year.	1.1 Facilitate incentive program for existing businesses equivalent to what is offered to new businesses. 1.2 Increase the education and training opportunities of the existing workforce to prepare employees to better meet customer needs. 1.3 Provide an outreach effort to directly contact and assist existing businesses. 1.4 Develop and provide financing packages to assist in financing growth of existing businesses. 1.5 Facilitate conflict resolution between businesses and government.	[Omitted]

A series of goals and strategies that Washington County, Utah, has established for ensuring the retention and expansion of local businesses.

Source: Washington County, Utah, 2003.

SELECTED GOALS AND BENCHMARKS IN THE WASHINGTON COUNTY, UTAH, STRATEGIC ECONOMIC DEVELOPMENT PLAN

GOALS	MEASURE OF SUCCESS
Diversify and strengthen our economy and increase our wage scale by attracting value-added business.	Locate 750 new value-added jobs within the next five years. Increase the per capita wage of the county to the level of the Utah State average.
Develop improved industrial sites, which are affordable and attractive to new and expanding value-added businesses.	Monitor the industrial market to ensure that at least 100,000 square feet of industrial high cube inventory is available.
Encourage the construction of spec buildings for use by value-added companies.	Maintain sufficient fully developed land and available building space to service existing and new value-added business.
Expand existing infrastructure to maintain and improve service levels.	Increase private and public funding for key infrastructure and services by 25% over the next five years.
Increase the county's economic development capability such that it fully utilizes the strengths and resources of both the public and private sectors.	Fully fund economic development organization with sufficient cash reserves.
Increase the advanced degree, technical, and professional skills training provided within the county through Dixie State College of Utah and Dixie Applied Technology Center.	Annually increase the number of courses available for advanced technical skills training.

Benchmarks that Washington County has set for monitoring success for the plan's goals.

Source: Washington County, Utah, 2003.

Stuart Meck, FAICP, American Planning Association, Chicago, Illinois

PARKS AND OPEN-SPACE PLANS

A parks and open-space plan outlines a systematic approach to providing parks and recreation services to a community. Parks and open-space resources within a community include environmental, recreational, scenic, cultural, historic, and urban design elements. Planning for parks and open space takes place at national, state, and local levels.

REASONS TO PREPARE A PARKS AND OPEN-SPACE PLAN

Jan Gehl (1987), the Danish urbanist and architect, states, "The proper hierarchy of planning is life, space, and buildings, not buildings, space, life." Therefore, communities need to plan for open spaces that provide a multitude of public functions before development occurs. These functions are numerous and may include:

- protection of natural resources and biodiversity;
- creation of places for recreation;
- support for economic development opportunities;
- development of neighborhood gathering places;
- promotion of public health benefits;
- creation of civic and cultural infrastructure; and
- shaping patterns of development through open spaces.

APPROACHES TO THE PLAN

Many forms of park and open-space systems exist. Some communities have an interconnected system, linked by green corridors, while others have a disconnected system scattered throughout the neighborhoods of a community. Communities that are largely built out have new parks and open-space opportunities created primarily from redevelopment; communities with available land should concentrate on identifying and protecting park space in areas *before* development occurs.

Whatever the park system configuration, park and open-space plans are influenced by the following factors:

- Agency or departmental mandate and mission
- Parks and open-space definition
- Park classifications
- Parks standards
- Development and management policies

Agency or Departmental Mandate and Mission

The organization with authority over parks planning may need to meet the statutory requirements for the plan's contents. The mission should be reaffirmed at the beginning of the planning process and explicitly stated in the beginning of the plan document.

Definition of Parks and Open Space

Communities often have different definitions of what constitutes a park. The definition may list specific resources, such as plazas, greenways, and even cemeteries. Some communities may use a broader approach, defining open space as "any land that is free of residential, institutional, commercial, or industrial use"; and others may restrict the definition to include only conservation areas protected by law. Planners should define terms at the outset because they will influence demand and supply inventories.

Park Classifications

A park classification system is a way of creating order to and providing a common language for the park and open-space system. Park types are often arranged by service area, size, population served, and typical facilities. Park classifications may also address functions, such as serving recreation, social gathering, and green infrastructure functions.

Parks Standards

To quantify their demand for park space and facilities, in addition to a variety of public participation activities, many communities use a set of national park standards developed in the 1970s and 1980s by the National Recreation and Park Association (NRPA). However, in 1996, NRPA replaced those standards with a locally determined set of facility guidelines, following its publication, *Park, Recreation, Open Space and Greenway Guidelines.* Communities should complete a level-of-service (LOS) study to quantify the number of necessary recreational facilities to meet specific community needs as well as the minimum acreage to support those facilities. The LOS study and the standards that it produces are important tools in projecting the effect of residential growth on necessary facilities and space. This study is critical for both sound park planning and for addressing the rational nexus test in mandatory dedication and impact fee programs should there be legal challenge to those programs.

That said, LOS and assessment studies results reflect only the recreational facility function of the park spaces. They do not include other functions, such as resource conservation, cultural enrichment, or urban design. And though no LOS formula currently exists for those functions, it is important that a plan address them.

Policies

Both development and management policies can shape the park and open-space plan. For instance, if the department normally pursues nongovernmental organization partnerships for service delivery, the plan inventories and implementation strategies should reflect that.

PLAN COMPONENTS

The majority of parks and open-space plans include the following elements. Consult applicable statutes and agency mandates to determine required plan components.

Goals and Objectives

Typical expressions of parks and open space goals and objectives consider the following:

- *Quantity:* Targeting a total percentage of the jurisdiction's acreage to be set aside for parks, or protecting a total percentage of the land in any new development as open space

- *Proximity:* Locating a park within a certain number of blocks of every resident, or providing a facility within a specific driving time of every resident
- *Accessibility:* Assuring that parks are located to be physically accessible by foot, bicycle, or public transit, and visually accessible for the greater public
- *Distribution:* Arranging park locations to ensure balanced service across geographic areas
- *Equity:* Providing facilities and programs evenly across socioeconomic populations
- *Environmental protection:* Assuring the protection of specific natural resources
- *Coordination:* Combining park objectives with other functional or jurisdictional plans
- *Balance:* Offering a mix of places and activities throughout the system
- *Shaping:* Identifying ways that the open space will promote or contain growth
- *Sustainability:* Determining physical and financial methods to support the park and open-space system
- *Urban design:* Addressing the way the park or space relates to the structures around it
- *Connections:* Identifying places and ways to link parklands and associated resources

Legal Requirements

The plan should include a review of laws that might be applicable to the lands or facilities included in the plan. These typically include:

- federal, state, and local environmental protection regulations;
- federal, state, and local parkland preservation regulations;
- historic buildings and landscapes regulations; and
- the Americans with Disabilities Act (ADA) regulations

Supply Inventory

A park and open-space plan contains a set of inventories related to the park plan elements and functions. This includes a list of park sites, their size, the facilities and equipment at each site, the function each site serves, site photos, and an assessment of the condition of the site. In addition to sites typically considered part of the parks inventory, the following may be included:

- Endangered species habitats
- School sites with playgrounds
- Public and private golf courses
- Waterways and floodplains
- Vacant lots
- Trails
- Private recreational facilities (e.g., ice rinks, tennis clubs)
- Bike lanes on highways
- Historical sites
- Cemeteries
- Gravel mines
- Private campgrounds
- Scenic viewsheds
- Country clubs
- Boulevards

Mary E. Eysenbach, American Planning Association, Chicago, Illinois

- Parks in concurrent and adjacent jurisdictions (including county, state, and national)
- Industrial park open space

Demand Assessment

Most demand assessments are a combination of general data, such as demographic trends or physiographic resources, and specific community information gleaned from public participation mechanisms. The needs assessment for parks and open spaces can be initially organized by function:

- Recreation function
- Conservation function
- Community shaping function

- Additional functions, such as public health, economic development, and green infrastructure.

See Parks, Recreation, and Open-Space Needs Assessment elsewhere in this book for more detail.

Surpluses and Deficiencies Analysis

A comparison of the demand and supply data yields a surpluses and deficiencies analysis. The results may be expressed in terms of acreage, facilities, or other forms dictated by the various functions of the system.

The analysis should also consider how other plans affect the park and open-space plan goals Planners

should consult the comprehensive plan, other functional plans, neighborhood plans, and those of partner stakeholders to determine those effects.

Alternatives and Draft Plan

After completion of the surpluses and deficiencies analysis, planners should generate a number of plan alternatives to correct the deficiencies identified by the analysis. The scenarios should address the creation of new park areas, the renovation of existing park areas, the linking together of parks, and the required connections to other plans to achieve park and open-space goals.

Following further review and revision, the adopted plan should include:

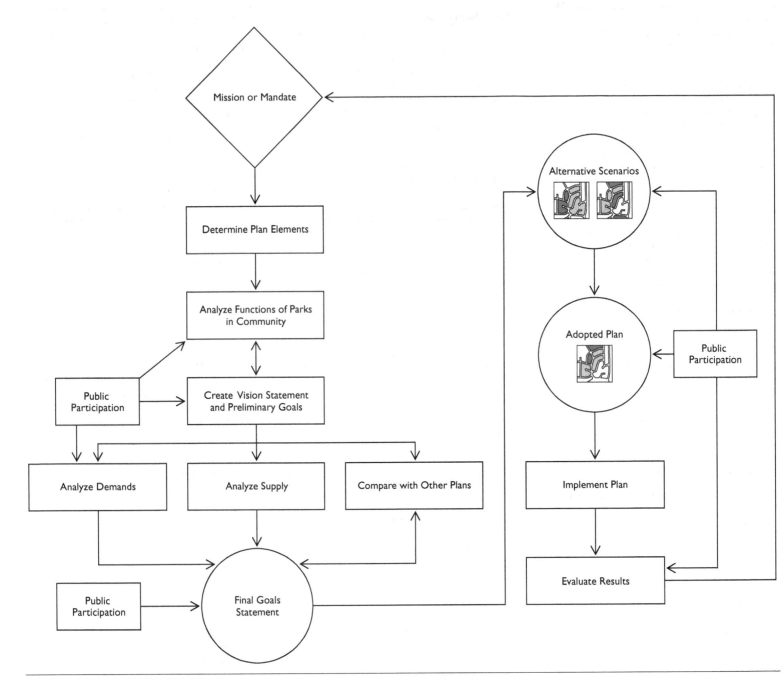

PARK PLANNING FLOWCHART

Source: Mary Eysenbach.

Mary E. Eysenbach, American Planning Association, Chicago, Illinois

PART I   PLANS AND PLAN MAKING

- a prioritized list of land protection areas (future parks, green infrastructure);
- a prioritized list of improvements for existing park areas;
- a rioritized list of opportunities for linkages;
- a list of site selection and acquisition criteria;
- the identification of opportunities for integration with other plans and processes; and
- a map summarizing these items.

IMPLEMENTATION

For each objective in the plan, a park and open-space plan should have an implementation strategy that takes the following actions.

1. Identify what will be accomplished.

2. Identify the party responsible for accomplishing the goal.
3. Identify any partners involved in implementation.
4. Establish timing or phasing for achieving the goal.
5. Set cost estimates and identify funding sources for the goal.
6. Prepare maintenance and operational impact statements for new land or facilities.
7. Define methods for evaluating success and set a schedule for conducting the evaluation.

The parks and recreation plan should be updated at a regular time interval, preferably every five years. Although that frequency may outpace the schedule for the comprehensive plan, the need for identifying and preserving parks and open space is an urgent business, especially in rapidly urbanizing areas.

EMERGING ISSUES

Green Infrastructure

Green infrastructure is a green space network of natural ecosystem functions. Instead of investing in man-made "gray" infrastructure, some communities are using their existing system or creating new parks as way to manage stormwater, reduce the urban heat island effect, and create wildlife habitat.

Design Guidelines for Park Systems

Some jurisdictions are producing design guidelines for parks. The guidelines help create an aesthetic and natural resource management standard for park development while visually connecting the park with its surroundings. They may address:

- park siting;
- pedestrian, vehicular, and transit access;
- utilities;
- site furnishings such as fencing, seating, and playground equipment;
- landscaping;
- building materials;
- signage; and
- environmental sustainability.

Linkages

Much like the park and parkway systems designed in the late nineteenth and early twentieth centuries, there is growing recognition that a good parks system is one where individual park nodes are connected by linear green corridors. Linkages may be achieved through riparian buffers, street design, transit paths, utility rights-of-way, or any other linear corridor.

Special Use Parks

A number of recent cultural and technological trends have created new demands on today's park systems. These can include dog parks, skateboard parks, off-road vehicle (ORV) parks, mountain bike trails, water trails, parks designed to meet the needs of an aging population, and wireless technology availability in parks. Planners should conduct specific research to determine the planning needs of these types of parks and park functions.

Partnerships

An increasing number of communities are working with other governmental agencies, nonprofit agencies, and even private providers to create interconnected parks systems within their communities.

REFERENCES

Gehl, Jan. 1987. *Life Between Buildings: Using Public Space.* New York: Van Nostrand Reinhold.

Mertes, James D., and James R. Hall. 1996. *Park, Recreation, Open Space and Greenway Guidelines.* Washington, DC: National Recreation and Park Association.

See also:
Parks and Open-Space Plans
Parks, Recreation, and Open-Space Needs Assessment
Types of Parks

Railroad Link
Riparian Link
Streetscape Link

Railroad — - - River
Parks Links

Open-space connections can be created with a variety of linear corridors.

OPEN-SPACE CONNECTIONS

Source: Mary Eysenbach.

Mary E. Eysenbach, American Planning Association, Chicago, Illinois

CRITICAL AND SENSITIVE AREAS PLANS

Critical and sensitive areas are generally defined as lands or water bodies that provide protection to or habitat for natural resources, living and nonliving, or are themselves natural resources that require identification and protection from inappropriate or excessive development. In some communities, critical and sensitive areas may also include historic structures or archaeological features. These latter elements are often protected by state and federal regulations.

REASONS TO PREPARE A CRITICAL AND SENSITIVE AREAS PLAN

When acting to protect critical and sensitive areas, planners often have to make choices as to which resources should be protected and to what degree. These choices often include deeming some natural resources more or less "critical" and "sensitive" than others. The process of preparing a critical and sensitive areas plan or an element for a comprehensive plan provides a framework for identifying the resources, determining what will be protected, and identifying mechanisms for protecting them.

PLAN COMPONENTS

The components of critical and sensitive areas plans typically include the following:

- Descriptions of the identified critical and sensitive resource areas
- GIS maps of critical and sensitive resource areas, based on field surveys
- An analysis of the carrying capacity of the resources identified or, if not known, mechanisms for determining the carrying capacity of each resource
- A description of the public involvement used to determine which resources are critical and sensitive and the level of degradation deemed acceptable for each
- Policies to protect the resources
- Implementation strategies

APPROACHES TO THE PLAN

Whether you are preparing an element of a comprehensive plan or a separate plan, the same overall process applies, namely:

1. identify the resources;
2. evaluate their value;
3. determine their carrying capacity;
4. map the location of resources;
5. create policy to protect the resources; and
6. identify regulatory and nonregulatory tools to implement the plan and help ensure protection.

Identification of Resources

The first step in the analysis of critical and sensitive areas is the identification of these resources. APA's *Growing Smart*^{SM} *Legislative Guidebook* identifies the following as resources that should be considered:

- Aquifers
- Watersheds
- Wellhead protection areas

- Inland and coastal wetlands
- Other wildlife habitats, including animals, birds, fish, and plants, along with habitats for federal- and state-listed endangered and threatened species
- Hillsides and steep slopes
- Any other areas considered to be critical or sensitive areas, including built resources such as historic structures, and, where relevant, the open spaces that accompany these built resources

Federal, state, and local government agencies, nonprofit organizations, and the private sector preparing development applications for public review have also created sources that can be used to identify critical and sensitive areas.

For example, the U.S. Environmental Protection Agency (U.S. EPA) has mapped major aquifer systems throughout the nation. State agencies have mapped significant wildlife habitats and wellhead protection areas throughout their respective states. Local governments have often mapped wetlands, watersheds, and historic structures throughout their corporate boundaries. Developers seeking permits from federal, state, and local agencies often provide these agencies with details relating to critical and sensitive areas in pursuit of development permits.

Evaluation

After planners have identified these resources, they often evaluate the critical and sensitive areas according to the value they have to the community. There are three types of value:

- *Utility value*: How the resource is used by the community
- *Economic value*: How much dollar value the resource provides
- *Aesthetic value*: How the resource is valued for its qualitative importance, notwithstanding its economic value

For example, aquifers provide a utility value—drinking water for the community (if that is the drinking water source); an economic value—the price imposed by the water utility on water usage; and an aesthetic value—providing recharge to wetlands, surface water bodies, or coastal embayments (if a coastal community).

This placement of value on a resource, which may be difficult in some circumstances—how do you "value" a wildlife habitat?—nevertheless is an important step to undertake in determining what should be protected.

The protection of critical and sensitive areas has additional, obvious (albeit not always quantifiable) benefits. For instance, the regulations prohibiting construction within floodplains can benefit landowners by minimizing threats of flooding to real property; regulations limiting impervious coverage within watersheds can protect waters used for shellfishing; and regulations limiting the clear-cutting of forested lands can also protect abutting properties from erosion.

Carrying Capacity

Carrying capacity analysis determines the point at which a resource's function will be reduced to an

unacceptable level. (A resource's carrying capacity is often also referred to as its "assimilative capacity.") Establishing the carrying capacity of a resource requires an objective analysis. The goal is to establish the point at which the resource ceases to function as nature "intended" or the point at which the resource be used as intended by the community (its utility value is undermined).

Carrying capacity analysis provides a factual basis for a community's comprehensive plan provisions that promote resource protection. In other words, through this analysis the community gives itself a rational and logical basis for the adoption of management controls designed to limit development to the assimilative capacity of a resource.

Federal and state environmental protection agencies (e.g., U.S. EPA and state counterparts), the U.S. Geological Survey, state and local universities, and nongovernmental environmental organizations are all reliable sources of information for completing a carrying capacity analysis.

Thresholds

Identifying carrying capacity first requires establishing thresholds for the resource (e.g., a coastal water body's assimilative capacity for nitrogen) and, second, the carrying capacity of the specific resource (e.g., the carrying capacity of the specific water body in California or Maine).

General Resource Thresholds. The federal government regulates many critical resources, and local governments can use these regulations as a basis for determining the resources' carrying capacity. For example, the federal Clean Air Act establishes maximum pollutant levels for air quality; the Safe Drinking Water Act establishes maximum contaminant levels for drinking water quality; and the Clean Water Act establishes maximum contaminant levels for coastal water quality. Similar thresholds are defined in state law.

Specific Resource Thresholds. Federal and state carrying capacity thresholds define the point at which the carrying capacity of the air, land, or water resources is threatened. They do not establish *if* the particular air, land, or water resource in the community will reach or exceed its assimilative capacity. A specific calculation for the specific resource at issue needs to be determined.

For example, while the quality of coastal water bodies begin to decline as nitrogen inputs increase—a result of the acceleration of the natural aging process (eutrophication)—the carrying capacity of such a water body in California can vary greatly compared to a coastal water body in Maine. This variation is a result of differences in water and air temperature, flushing cycles, depth of water, extent of the respective watersheds, and the presence of other contaminants in the water.

Maps

Planners should identify critical and sensitive areas on maps. Map makers should prepare these maps as overlays so that all resource areas can be identified individually (e.g., separate maps for watersheds, well-

Jon D. Witten, AICP, Daley and Witten LLC, Duxbury, Massachusetts

SAMPLE CARRYING CAPACITY THRESHOLD ASSESSMENT

Nitrogen is a common water pollutant that can degrade water resources significantly. A carrying capacity threshold assessment can be used to determine the amount of nitrogen a water body can assimilate, thereby establishing a water quality standard. Data needed for this assessment include the surface area, volume, and flushing rate of the water body. A sample calculation follows:

$$L = \text{Critical loading rate (lbs/yr)} = (TN \times V \times f)/454{,}000 \text{ mg/lb}$$

where:

A = Area
d = Water depth (mean low water, or MLW)
r = Average tidal range
V = Bay volume at mean tide = $(A)(d+r/2)$
f = Flushing rate (time per year)
TN = Total nitrogen standard or threshold (mg/m³/R).

The equation can also be rearranged to calculate what the loading will be under a given development scenario:

$$TN \text{ (mg/m}^3\text{/yr)} = (L \times 454{,}000 \text{ mg/lb})/(V \times f).$$

head protection areas, wetlands resources, and historic structures) and cumulatively (by overlaying the separate maps) as the aggregate critical and sensitive areas. Maps should be based on field surveys and prepared with a geographic information system (GIS). While there is no required scale for the maps, it is strongly recommended that the scale chosen be practical and useful. For example, a scale of 1 inch = 100 feet is far more useful than a scale of 1 inch = 2,000 feet, but will require a greater level of precision and cost more.

Policies

The plan should contain a statement of the local government's goals, policies, and guidelines with respect to the protection of critical and sensitive areas. This portion of the plan may also include a map or maps showing the areas to be protected.

IMPLEMENTATION

Regulatory Tools

Zoning, subdivision controls, health regulations, and wetland regulations can all be used to protect critical and sensitive areas. Traditional regulatory tools include adopting overlay zoning districts for critical areas, requiring permits for uses that may negatively affect critical resource areas, adopting appropriate setbacks from resource areas, and employing related regulatory controls on private property. More innovative regulatory tools include transfer of development rights, impact fees, development agreements, and mandates that development not exceed defined carrying capacity thresholds set for critical and sensitive resource areas.

Nonregulatory Tools

Nonregulatory tools include fee and less-than-fee acquisition of critical and sensitive resource areas; public education programs, to inform the general public about the importance of the resources; and related programs, such as citizen monitoring of water and air resources and consistent attendance at local municipal board meetings to act as "watchdogs" and advocates for critical and sensitive resource areas. Nonregulatory tools have the advantage of avoiding the regulation of private property and the attendant potential negative political and legal consequences.

A community's capital improvement program provides an additional nonregulatory means to protect critical and sensitive resource areas. The outlay of local dollars to expand public water, sewer, and road access is a catalyst to new growth, and often conflicts with preserving these areas. Public improvements should not be built in critical and sensitive areas. The capital improvements plan and the comprehensive plan should both address such restrictions.

REFERENCE

Meck, Stuart ed. 2002. *Growing Smart*ᴹ *Legislative Guidebook: Model Statutes for Planning and Management of Change,* 2 vols. Chicago: American Planning Association.

See also:

Environmental Planning and Management

Jon D. Witten, AICP, Daley and Witten LLC, Duxbury, Massachusetts

PARTICIPATION

ROLE OF PARTICIPATION

Community participation is the involvement of people in the creation and management of their built and natural environments. Its strength is that it cuts across traditional professional boundaries and cultures. The activity of community participation is based on the principle that the built and natural environments work better if citizens are active and involved in its creation and management instead of being treated as passive consumers (Sanoff 2000).

The main purposes of participation are:

- to involve citizens in planning and design decision-making processes and, as a result, make it more likely they will work within established systems when seeking solutions to problems;
- to provide citizens with a voice in planning and decision making in order to improve plans, decisions, service delivery, and overall quality of the environment; and
- to promote a sense of community by bringing together people who share common goals.

Participation should be active and directed; those who become involved should experience a sense of achievement. Traditional planning procedures should be reexamined to ensure that participation achieves more than simply affirmation of the designer's or planner's intentions.

CHARACTERISTICS OF PARTICIPATION

Although any given participation process does not automatically ensure success, it can be claimed that the process will minimize failure. Four essential characteristics of participation can be identified:

- Participation is inherently good.
- It is a source of wisdom and information about local conditions, needs, and attitudes, and thus improves the effectiveness of decision making.
- It is an inclusive and pluralistic approach by which fundamental human needs are fulfilled and user values reflected.
- It is a means of defending the interests of groups of people and of individuals, and a tool for satisfying their needs, which are often ignored and dominated by large organizations, institutions, and their bureaucracies.

Experiences in the participation process show that the main source of user satisfaction is not the degree to which a person's needs have been met, but the feeling of having influenced the decisions.

CATEGORIES OF PARTICIPATION

Participation can be classified into four categories, or "experiences," with the goal of achieving agreement about what the future should bring (Burns 1979):

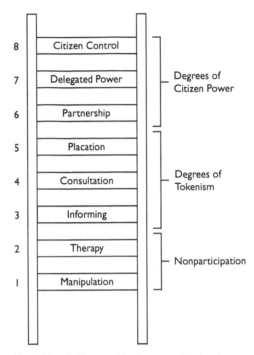

The ladder of citizen participation presents a typology of eight levels of participation. Each rung of the ladder corresponds to the degree to which stakeholders had power in determining the outcome. The gradations represented go from nonparticipation to token participation to various degrees of citizen power. While the ladder was conceived in the context of federal programs of the late 1960s, planners and urban designers today still should strive to ensure that they are working near the top of the ladder in their public participation activities.

LADDER OF CITIZEN PARTICIPATION

Source: Reprinted with permission from Journal of the American Planning Association, copyright July 1969 by the American Planning Association, Suite 1600, 122 South Michigan Avenue, Chicago, IL 60603-6107.

- *Awareness.* This experience involves discovering or rediscovering the realities of a given situation so that everyone who takes part in the process speaks the same language, which is based on their experiences in the field where change is proposed.
- *Perception.* This entails going from awareness of the situation to understanding it and its physical, social, cultural, and economic ramifications. It means sharing with each other so that the understanding, goals, and expectations of all participants become resources for planning and design.
- *Decision making.* This experience concentrates on working from awareness and perception to a plan for the situation under consideration. Here participants propose plans, based on their priorities, for professionals to use as resources to synthesize alternative and final plans.

- *Implementation.* Many community-based planning processes stop with awareness, perception, and decision making. This can have significant detrimental effects on a project because it ends people's responsibilities when the "how-to, where-to, when-to, and who-will-do-it" must be added to what people want and how it will look. People must stay involved throughout the processes and take responsibility with their professionals to see that there are results (Hurwitz 1975).

DETERMINATION OF GOALS AND OBJECTIVES

The planning that accompanies the design of any participation program should first include a determination of participation goals and objectives. Participation goals will differ from time to time and from issue to issue. In addition, participation is likely to be perceived differently depending on the type of issue, people involved, and political setting in which it takes place. If differences in expectations and perception are not identified at the outset, and realistic goals are not made clear, the expectations of those involved in the participation program will likely not be met, and people will become disenchanted.

Related to this, to address participation effectively, the task should conceptualize what the objective is for involving citizens. For example, is the participation intended to:

- generate ideas?;
- identify attitudes?;
- disseminate information?;
- resolve some identified conflict?;
- measure opinions?;
- review a proposal?; or
- provide a forum to express general feelings?

PLANNING FOR PARTICIPATION

Once planners have identified the overall goals and objectives for the participation process, planning for participation requires the following steps (Rosner 1978):

- Identify the individuals or groups that should be involved in the participation activity being planned.
- Decide where in the process the participants should be involved, from development to implementation to evaluation.
- Articulate the participation objectives in relation to all participants who will be involved.
- Identify and match alternative participation methods to objectives in terms of the resources available.
- Select an appropriate method to be used to achieve specific objectives.
- Implement chosen participation activities.
- Evaluate the implemented methods to see to what extent they achieved the desired goals and objectives.

Henry Sanoff, AIA, North Carolina State University, Raleigh, North Carolina

THEORY AND PRACTICE

The theories and practices of participation can be synthesized into the following five statements:

There is no "best" solution to design and planning problems.

Each problem can have a number of solutions, based traditionally on two sets of criteria:

- *Facts.* The empirical data concerning material strengths, economics, building codes, and so forth
- *Attitudes.* Interpretation of the facts, the state of the art in any particular area, traditional and customary approaches, and value judgments.

"Expert" decisions are not necessarily better than "lay" decisions.

Given the facts with which to make decisions, citizens can examine the available alternatives and choose among them. In a participation process, planners and designers should work along with citizens to identify possible alternatives, discuss consequences of various alternatives, and state opinions about the alternatives (not decide among them).

A planning task can be made transparent.

Professionals often consider alternatives that are frameworks in their minds. They should be presented for users to discuss. After understanding the components of planning decisions and exploring alternatives, citizens in effect can generate their own plan rather than react to one provided for them. The product is more likely to succeed because it is more responsive to the needs of the people who will use it.

All individuals and interest groups should come together in an open forum.

In this setting, people can openly express their opinions, make necessary compromises, and arrive at decisions acceptable to all concerned. By involving as many interests as possible, the product is strengthened by the wealth of input. In turn, learning more about itself strengthens the citizens' group.

The process is continuous and ever changing.

The product is not the end of the process. It must be managed, reevaluated, and adapted to changing needs. Those most directly involved with the product, the users, are best able to assume those tasks.

The professional's role is to facilitate the citizen group's ability to reach decisions through an easily understood process. Most often this will take the form of making people aware of alternatives. This role also includes helping people develop their resources in ways that will benefit themselves and others.

INDICATORS OF THE VALUE OF PARTICIPATION

A review of the public involvement literature, conducted by Lach and Hixson (1998), revealed that participants valued such issues as public acceptability, accessibility, good decision making, education and learning, time commitments, and trust. To identify value and cost indicators of public involvement, they conducted interviews with people who had been involved in participatory projects. Combining the literature review, interviews, and expert judgment, they identified these key indicators of the value of participation:

- Opening the process to stakeholders
- Diversity of viewpoints
- Meaningful participation
- Integrating stakeholder concerns
- Information exchange
- Saving time
- Saving and avoiding costs
- Enhanced project acceptability
- Mutual learning
- Mutual respect

Lach and Hixson also developed direct and indirect cost indicators of the public involvement effort. Certain costs can be linked to traditional accounting practice, such as preparation and participation time, facilities, materials, and services. Other indirect costs, such as participants' time commitment, lack of opportunity to participate in other projects, and heavy emotional demands on participation, cannot be easily measured. The intent of their research was to develop prototype indicators to be tested in ongoing and completed public involvement programs. Results from project participants indicated that the positive aspects of their involvement were twofold: (1) a diversity of viewpoints in the participation process

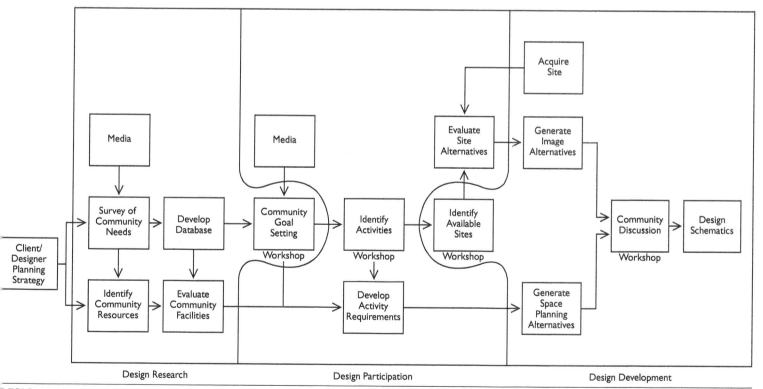

DESIGN RESEARCH, PARTICIPATION, AND DEVELOPMENT PROCESS

Source: Henry Sanoff.

Henry Sanoff, AIA, North Carolina State University, Raleigh, North Carolina

was valuable; (2) project savings occurred in the form of saving and of avoiding costs.

Informing a large audience about proposals, generating interest, or securing approval can take the form of a community meeting, also referred to as a public hearing or a public forum. Public meetings allow community leaders to present project information at any time during the process. The tight structure of such meetings does not, however, permit ample time for discussion. Although referred to as community participation, only the most aggressive personalities tend to participate and often dominate the discussion (Creighton 1994). Public reactions in open meetings are often taken by a vote through a show of hands. The key to making community design work effectively is to incorporate a range of techniques for enabling professionals and citizens to creatively collaborate, where voting is replaced by consensus decision making.

A wide range of techniques is available to designers and planners. Some of these techniques have become standard for use in participatory processes, such as interactive group decision-making techniques that take place in workshops. At the same time, designers and planners have effectively used field techniques, such as questionnaires, interviewing, focus groups, and group mapping, to acquire information. In general, many of the techniques facilitate citizens' awareness of environmental situations and help activate their creative thinking. The techniques can be classified as *awareness methods*, *group interaction methods*, and *indirect methods*.

REFERENCES

Arnstein, Sherry R. 1969. "A Ladder of Citizen Participation." *Journal of the American Institute of Planners.* 35, no. 4:216-224.

Burns, J. 1979. *Connections: Ways to Discover and Realize Community Potentials.* New York: McGraw-Hill.

Creighton, J.L. 1994. *Involving Citizens in Community Decision Making: A Guidebook.*

Washington, DC: Program for Community Problem Solving.

Hurwitz, J.G. 1975. "Participatory Planning in an Urban Neighborhood. Soulard, St. Louis, MO: A Case Study." *DMG Journal.* 9, no. 4:348-357.

Lach, D., and P. Hixson. 1996. "Developing Indicators to Measure Values and Costs of Public Involvement Activities." *Interact: The Journal of Public Participation.* 2, no.1:51-63.

Rosner, J. 1978. "Matching Method to Purpose: The Challenges of Planning Citizen Participation Activities." In *Citizen Participation in America,* edited by S. Langton. New York: Lexington Books.

Sanoff, Henry. 2000. *Community Participation Methods in Design and Planning.* Hoboken, NJ: John Wiley & Sons, Inc.

See also:

Plan Making

Henry Sanoff, AIA, North Carolina State University, Raleigh, North Carolina

STAKEHOLDER IDENTIFICATION

Stakeholder is a term commonly used in planning and public policy. A stakeholder is defined as someone with a "stake," or interest, in the issues being addressed. In practice, this means anyone could be a stakeholder because a resident, taxpayer, and concerned citizen could all have an interest. Because the distinction between the public and stakeholders can be confusing, it is important to consider why stakeholders should be involved, and how they should be selected. People who convene a collaborative planning effort—conveners—need to plan this step carefully.

CATEGORIES OF STAKEHOLDERS

Stakeholders can be broadly classified into four categories. First, there are people who are representative of a certain sector of society. This sector may be a broad category, such as farmers or homeowners, or it may be a specific category, such as "Orchard Street residents" and park users. These stakeholders usually speak for themselves. Conveners choose them because their views may be "typical" of other people in their sector or because they have personal knowledge. However, because these people cannot be asked to speak on behalf of people they do not formally represent, the involvement of this category of stakeholder is not a substitute for public involvement.

Second, there are individuals who represent organized interests, which can range from an informally organized neighborhood coalition to a formally organized nonprofit interest group. Such an individual is expected to represent the views of the organization. However, this requires the person to confer with others in his or her organization. This is often referred to as the "two-table" problem because the individual may have to negotiate at the stakeholder table and the decision-making table within his or her organization.

Third, there are those who represent government organizations, such as city departments and state agencies. They must also work with both the stakeholder process and their organization's process, but they tend to operate under more specific administrative rules and policies. Individuals higher in the organization may have more discretion, but they also tend to have more demands on their schedule.

LIST OF POTENTIAL STAKEHOLDERS
SECTORS OF SOCIETY

People living adjacent to a proposed activity
Neighborhood residents
Residents
Landowners
Renters
Minorities
Users (park users, boaters, etc.)
Neighborhood business owners

INTEREST GROUPS

Chamber of commerce
Environmental groups
Racial or ethnic groups
Industry organizations
Religious organizations
Civic groups
Social groups (Kiwanis, Optimists)
Neighborhood associations

AGENCIES

Special districts (water, sewer, park, etc.)
School districts
Planning commission members
Local government (city manager, department head, staff)
Council of government
State agencies
Federal agencies

ELECTED OFFICIALS

City and county councilors
Mayors
School board members
State representatives and senators

Finally, there are elected officials who are formally voted upon as representatives. Their elected position gives them a unique status because they are accountable to the public for their decisions. However, like staff in government organizations, they often have many demands on their time. Furthermore, members of local government councils and legislatures cannot speak for the entire legislative body.

REASONS FOR SELECTING STAKEHOLDERS

Before starting a stakeholder selection process, a convener needs to consider the reasons for selecting stakeholders, to determine the potential pool of participants.

Jurisdiction over an Issue

One common reason is to include people or organizations that have jurisdiction over an issue. This includes organizations with the power to make decisions as well as individuals with the power to veto decisions. For example, an open-space plan that involves city land, county parks, and state forests should include a representative from each jurisdiction.

Particular Information or Knowledge Base

Another reason for selecting a stakeholder is because he or she has information or knowledge that will lead to a comprehensive understanding of a problem or issue. A group composed of people with different training, different data, and different perspectives can develop a much more complete picture of an issue than if they each considered the issue individually. For example, information about watershed health may be spread among a range of different state agencies, local governments, and landowners.

Party to an Actual or Potential Conflict

A stakeholder process offers an informal and flexible forum for bringing participants together to try to resolve their differences. For example, a city proposal to annex land could involve county officials, landowners, and local residents in an effort to come to a mutually agreeable solution.

Connected to Community Networks

A fourth reason for choosing a stakeholder is because he or she is connected to community networks. Such people are important because of their informal networks of influence and the respect that they garner in the community. For example, an influential landowner who participates in an ecosystem management process could help convince other landowners to help protect critical habitat.

DETERMINING GROUP SIZE

Because a collaborative planning process may need stakeholders for many of the reasons listed above, the list of potential stakeholders could be lengthy. There are different views about the optimum size of a stakeholder group. Some facilitators argue that groups should not be larger than 10 to 12, but some multiparty collaboration processes have successfully involved 20 or 30 stakeholders.

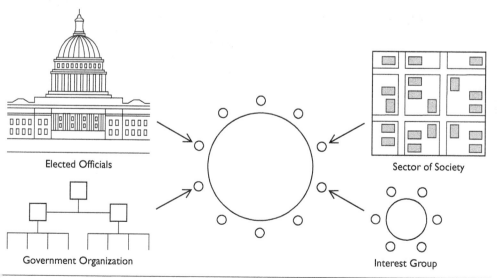

Elected Officials

Government Organization

Sector of Society

Interest Group

TYPES OF STAKEHOLDERS

Source: Richard Margerum.

Richard Margerum, Ph.D., University of Oregon, Eugene, Oregon

REASONS FOR STAKEHOLDER INVOLVEMENT

REASON	DESCRIPTION	EXAMPLES OF STAKEHOLDERS
Jurisdiction	An organization or individual has jurisdiction over an issue.	Local government State and federal agencies Private landowner
Information	An organization or individual has information and knowledge.	Technical experts People with first-hand knowledge Agencies with data
Conflict	An organization or individual is party to an actual or . potential conflict	People with legal standing Existing parties to a dispute Decision makers
Networks	An individual is connected in the community or has local influence.	People involved in community groups People in social groups and clubs Long-term residents

One way to reduce this number is to consider additional personal criteria in the selection process:

- Does the person work well in groups?
- Is the person interested in being involved?
- Does the person have the time to participate?
- Will the person help provide gender, racial, or ethnic balance?
- Does the person have additional skills that will help the group?

A process involving a large number of stakeholders may need to be broken into smaller groups. This increases the complexity of the process and increases the need for communication between groups, but it may be appropriate for large, complex, or controversial issues.

Some of the common categories include the following:

- Steering committee (to make the primary decisions)
- Technical advisory committee (to respond to technical questions)
- Citizens advisory committee (to provide broader public access)
- Geographic-based committees (to obtain input from different parts of a region)

Specific Selection Strategies

With these background issues in mind, a convener will have a better idea of the types of stakeholders to involve in a collaborative process. The next step is to determine the specific strategy for choosing a group of stakeholders. The perception of how the stakeholders are chosen can be just as important as who is chosen.

Collaborative processes that involve organizations add an additional level of complexity to the selection process. Some organizations want to appoint their own representatives, rather than have an external party choose one. In this case, the convener may simply designate a seat at the stakeholder table to a specific organization. This strategy may also be used to ensure that certain types of organizations are represented. For example, a group may have stakeholder slots designated for an environmental interest group, an industry organization, and a landowner.

Convener-Picked

There is no one correct way to select stakeholders, but different strategies are better suited for certain situations than others. One approach is for the convener to handpick the participants. This approach tends to work well if the convener is viewed as being

neutral and if it is relatively clear who should be selected. It is an efficient strategy that also allows the convener to add other criteria for selection, such as group composition, group skills, and working relationships. That said, there will be some bias in this process because it will be defined by the knowledge of the convener.

Selection Committee

Another approach is to use a selection committee to choose the stakeholders. This approach tends to work well if the issues are politically charged or involve conflict. Each step of the collaboration process will be scrutinized. Any concerns about bias in stakeholder selection could lead people to question the decisions of the group. As with the handpicked approach, a committee can also incorporate additional criteria into the selection process. The primary disadvantages to this process relate to the additional time, resources, and participants required.

Self-Nomination

A third approach is to form a committee through self-nomination. This approach works well when the composition of the committee is not critical and when it is important to involve motivated stakeholders. Self-nomination is often linked to a public participation process. People are mailed newsletters, surveyed, or invited to public meetings; those who are interested are invited to participate in a stakeholder group. There is less opportunity or potential perception for bias with this process; however, the resulting group may lack diversity, may not include key stakeholders, or may overrepresent certain interests or organizations.

Snowball

A final strategy for stakeholder selection is the "snowball" strategy. This is an important strategy for all stakeholder selection efforts, regardless of how it is initially established. The strategy involves asking those involved, Who is not at the table that should be? As the list of people expands, the new people are asked the same question, until a full set of participants is involved. This can improve the breadth of participants and ensure that stakeholder membership is adjusted as new issues arise. The disadvantage of this process is that stakeholders coming late to the process may have less ability to influence outcomes and therefore may be less inclined to support the effort. Furthermore, if not done carefully, it could lead to an ever-expanding list of stakeholders.

See also:
Plan Making
Types of Plans

STAKEHOLDER SELECTION STRATEGIES

STRATEGY	POSSIBLE ADVANTAGES	POSSIBLE DISADVANTAGES
Convener-picked	Compatible personalities Can meet expertise needs	Perception of bias Limited range of participants
Selection committee	Diverse committee can reduce bias Can choose for expertise and personalities	More time-consuming Requires additional participants
Self-nominating	Motivated participants Open process	Representation problems May only attract strongly opinionated
Snowball	Flexible Allows participants to expand with issues	Initial participants have more power Later participants may have concerns about earlier decisions

Richard Margerum, Ph.D., University of Oregon, Eugene, Oregon

SURVEYS

Planners looking to make good decisions need solid, reliable information. The survey is a widely accepted tool for gathering information from the people involved in any planning action. Good-quality surveys are doable even for the novice. The basic concepts and steps needed to plan and execute a survey are introduced here.

The particular advantages of the survey are that it allows planners to obtain quantitative results, to anticipate and address many of the sources of error before the data are collected, and ultimately to generalize findings from a relatively small number of respondents (the sample) to a larger group (the population). With increasing emphasis on *representative* citizen participation, surveys offer a useful method both to reach a broad public and to gather input from people who typically are not consulted on planning issues.

REASONS TO USE A SURVEY

Consider a survey when the data needed are not available from secondary sources. The existing data may be outdated and no longer reflect current conditions or may describe a geography that does not coincide with your needs, such as state-level data that cannot be disaggregated into local units.

Surveys are conducted to find out the characteristics, behaviors, opinions, and knowledge of a particular population. Before embarking on a survey, clearly establish your objectives. Determine who is to be sampled and what you want to learn about the sample. Your questionnaire should flow directly from your information objectives.

TYPES OF SURVEYS

At the core of all surveys is either a questionnaire or an interview—these are the instruments for gathering information.

Questionnaires

Questionnaires are self-administered instruments. They generally enable respondents to complete the survey at their convenience and to proceed at their own pace. Respondents often have a greater sense of anonymity, which leads to greater honesty. Respondents can also verify their responses against other records and documents.

Interviews

Interviews involve human interaction, even though it is scripted to some degree. In an interview, respondents can ask for clarification, thereby reducing the potential for error. The interviewer can control the sequence of questions by following a skip pattern according to previous responses—a feature now possible with self-administered, computerized questionnaires. Depending on the study objectives, a skilled interviewer can also pursue certain subjects by using probes and follow-up questions. In a face-to-face situation, interviewers have the advantage of being able to observe nonverbal cues. To a lesser degree, even telephone interviewers can detect and respond to changes in the respondent's tone of voice and speech.

	Interviewer-Administered		Self-Administered	
	Face-to-Face	Telephone	Mail	Web-Based
Resource Constraints				
Inadequate Sampling Frame (e.g., Incomplete Mailing List or Directory)	++	++	--	--
Quick Turnaround to Complete Survey	--	++	--	++
Limited Skilled Staff	--	--	++	++
Limited Budget	--	+	++	++
Special Needs				
Multiple Languages	-	-	+	++
Maps or Other Visual Materials	++	--	++	++
Complex Instructions or Need to Follow Precise Order	++	++	--	+
Need to Probe, Explain Unclear Questions	++	++	--	--
Some Items Require Additional Research	-	--	++	++
Anonymity Needed for Sensitive Responses	--	++	+	++
Respondent Characteristics				
Large Sample Size	--	-	++	++
Geographically Dispersed	--	+	++	++
Survey Must Be Conducted at Specific Location	++	--	--	--
Target Population Is Difficult to Contact	++	-	-	--

The matrix compares four major survey methods under varying conditions of resource constraints, survey needs, and respondent characteristics.

SELECTING A SURVEY METHOD

Reprinted with permission from The Planner's Use of Information, 2nd Edition, copyright 2003 by the American Planning Association, Suite 1600, 122 South Michigan Avenue, Chicago, IL 60603-6107.

MODES OF DISTRIBUTION

Surveys are further differentiated by their modes of distribution. They cover the entire range of communication technologies currently in use—face-to-face (both intercept/"street corner" interviews and in-depth interviews), posted mail, fax, telephone, email, and the Web—and combinations of these modes. The most appropriate survey method will depend on your resources, survey objectives, and characteristics of the sample. Increasingly, survey software is being used to gather data, reaching survey takers through email. The advantages of this approach include drawing upon an existing database of survey recipients and quickly creating reports, graphs, and tables from the data.

POPULATION SELECTION AND SIZE

Sampling

Sampling refers to a plan for randomly choosing a sample. Determining the correct sample size used to be one of the most daunting steps in survey preparation. Today this challenge is easily met by going online and typing "sample size calculator" or "random sample calculator" into a search engine. Several Web sites provide a utility that allows you to find out instantly how many people you need to survey. All require you to establish three parameters: population size, error level, and confidence level.

- *Population size* refers to the total number of people within the study area. For any given level of accuracy, the larger the population, the smaller the sample needed (percentage of people to be surveyed).

- *Error level* (or margin of error) is expressed as "plus or minus times percentage points" and refers to the difference between the estimated value (derived from the sample) and the true value (from the population).

- *Confidence level* is also expressed as a percentage and refers to the number of times similar results are expected if the study were replicated 100 times.

Error and confidence go hand in hand. Say a survey found that 59 percent of households in the city own one or more bicycles. If the survey were designed with an error level of ±3 percentage points and a 95 percent confidence level, it would mean that household bicycle ownership rates could actually range from 56 percent to 62 percent, and this finding would occur 95 out of 100 times if the survey were conducted over and over. If your survey does not have an acceptable level of confidence, it will be difficult to know what to make of the results.

In a city with a population of 50,000, the following sample sizes are needed:

Confidence Level	Margin of Error ± 3 %	Margin of Error ± 5 %
90 percent	745	271
95 percent	1,045	381
99 percent	1,778	655

Response Rate

Sample size refers to the number of completed surveys. Therefore, the actual number of surveys distributed must be adjusted to account for the response rate—a function of contact (reaching

Nancy I. Nishikawa, AICP

PARTICIPATION

respondents at viable addresses or working phone numbers) and cooperation (getting people to complete the survey). The formula to calculate the total number of surveys that must be distributed is:

Sample ÷ response rate = total surveys to be distributed

Therefore, if one estimates a 20 percent response rate for a mail survey with a sample size of 381, one would need to send out 1,905 questionnaires. However, if there are indications that a higher estimate of a 40 percent response rate is warranted, one could reduce the mailing to 953 questionnaires.

Some of the common techniques to improve cooperation include:

- sending out prenotification letters, then following the questionnaire with reminder cards;
- developing persuasive introductory language;
- ensuring that the questionnaire is attractive and easy to complete; and
- training interviewers for more effective "first contact."

Response rates are an important and challenging component of surveys. That said, noncontact and noncooperation should not seriously affect data quality to the extent that they occur randomly (Langer 2003). Addressing sources of bias is still paramount.

ALTERNATIVE SAMPLING DESIGNS

In addition to simple random sampling, planners should be familiar with two alternative sampling designs: stratified sample and clustered sample.

Stratified Sample

In a stratified sample, the population is divided into subgroups (strata) before sampling. For example, if the survey is about a city's bike paths and it is known that households with school-aged children are more likely to own bicycles, one might select separate samples for households with school-aged children and those without. Each subgroup is a separate sample, and the respective sample sizes would reflect the subgroup's size relative to the overall population. Within subgroups, individuals are selected at random.

Clustered Sample

In a clustered sample, the population is divided into smaller geographic units (clusters), such as neighborhoods within a city or blocks within a district. The sample consists of a random selection of clusters and all individuals within those clusters are surveyed.

TIPS FOR SUCCESSFUL DATA COLLECTION

The survey is a way of creating an area-specific, customized database. Even a hurriedly put-together survey can fill a critical information gap. Designed properly, the survey can be a rigorous tool. The following tips can maximize your data-gathering efforts:

- Start with a brief, compelling introduction that clearly states the purpose of your study and its potential value to the respondent.
- Use plain language that is easy to understand; avoid jargon and acronyms.
- Organize questions in logical groups; provide transitions when shifting topics.
- Ask important questions first, profile questions last.
- Proofread to eliminate typographic and grammatical errors; make the layout crisp and legible.
- Include graphics (maps, plans, diagrams, renderings, and photos), as appropriate.
- Keep the survey short and simple.
- Pretest with a few people (ideally representing a cross section of the sample), then debrief and ask for candid feedback.

DESIGNING A QUESTIONNAIRE

Researchers have several options in designing a questionnaire, primarily in constructing and sequencing items. Two basic categories of questions are the closed- versus open-ended inquiries.

Close-Ended Questions

In close-ended questions, respondents are asked to select from a list provided by the researcher, with instructions either to select a single answer (one that "best fits") or multiple answers (all that apply). A variation of the closed-ended question is one that asks respondents to evaluate on a scale or rank in order of preference, such as one of the following:

- *Rating scale* is an ordinal measurement of degree, which asks respondents to indicate a position between opposite word pairs (e.g., noisy-quiet or frequently-never, etc.).
- *Likert scale* asks respondents to indicate the extent to which they agree with a statement (e.g., strongly agree, agree, disagree, strongly disagree, don't know).
- *Numerical scale* asks respondents to correlate their position to a numerical rating (e.g., satisfaction level rated on a scale of 1 to 5, with 1 being least satisfied and 5 being most satisfied).

In close-ended questions, the choices do not have to be words. Many planning-oriented issues are amenable to choices presented in drawings, plans, and photos. Another possibility is to ask respondents to indicate their preferences by allocating a "theoretical budget"—$1 and $100 are easiest to work with.

Open-Ended Questions

Open-ended questions give respondents an opportunity for self-expression and spontaneity that can lead researchers to new insights. Their disadvantage is that they can be difficult to summarize without postcoding. A compromise is to offer a list of what are expected to be the most popular choices, based on prior knowledge of the subject, then include an "Other" category that allows respondents to provide answers outside the predetermined categories.

The importance of sequencing questionnaire items in a clear, logical order should not be overlooked. Respondents are more likely to find an instrument credible if it is readily apparent that questions are relevant to the overall purpose of the study and are connected in a way that makes sense. The most basic patterns are the *funnel sequence*, which begins with the most general question and works down to detailed points, and the *inverted funnel sequence*, which begins with specific questions and then moves to more general issues. Transitional questions, brief explanations, or headings can be inserted to signal a change of topic or to show how the new topic relates to what had been asked previously.

ADDITIONAL CONSIDERATIONS

Despite the tremendous usefulness of surveys for researchers, they are not met with the same level of enthusiasm among the survey-taking public. Many factors have contributed to the survey's diminished reputation; however, it is possible to avoid further tarnish by observing a few common-sense practices. Foremost, respect the privacy of respondents. Do not release names and addresses of respondents. Codes are typically assigned to questionnaires, in which case, secure the name-to-code assignments. Results can be reported confidentially by tabulating data so that individual responses cannot be singled out. And, whenever possible, provide respondents with a copy of your findings—prompt feedback will demonstrate how the study has contributed to a better understanding of important community issues.

REFERENCES

Dandekar, Hemalata C. 2003. *Planner's Use of Information*, 2nd ed. Chicago: Planners Press.

Langer, Gary. 2003. "About Response Rates: Some Unresolved Questions." *Public Perspective*, May/June, 16-18. www.ropercenter.uconn.edu/pubper/pdf/pp14_3c.pdf

See also:
Analysis Techniques
Plan Making

Nancy I. Nishikawa, AICP

COMMUNITY VISIONING

Community visioning offers local communities new ways to think about and plan for the long-term future. The visioning process was inspired in part by the concept of "anticipatory democracy," an approach to governance that blends futures research, grassroots public participation, and long-range strategic planning.

Visioning has caught on quickly around the country in communities undergoing rapid growth and development as well as those experiencing economic decline. As an adjunct to traditional community planning, visioning promotes greater awareness of societal change and deepened citizen involvement. It also gives communities a stronger sense of control over their destinies.

WHAT IS VISIONING?

In the simplest terms, visioning is a planning process through which a community creates a shared vision for its future and begins to make it a reality. Such a vision provides an overlay for other community plans, policies, and decisions, as well as a guide to actions in the wider community. While a significant number of communities employing a wide range of approaches and techniques have undertaken community visioning, the most successful efforts seem to share these five key characteristics:

- *Understanding the whole community.* The visioning process promotes an understanding of the whole community and the full range of issues shaping its future. It also attempts to engage the participation of the entire community and its key stakeholder groups.
- *Reflecting core community values.* The visioning process seeks to identify the community's core values—those deeply held community beliefs and ideals shared by its members. Such values inform the idealistic nature of the community's vision.
- *Addressing emerging trends and issues.* The visioning process explores the emerging trends driving the community's future and the strategic issues they portend. Addressing such trends promotes greater foresight, adding rigor and realism to the community's vision.
- *Envisioning a preferred future.* The visioning process produces a statement articulating the community's preferred future. The vision statement represents the community's desired "destination"—a shared image of where it would like to be in the long-term future.
- *Promoting local action.* The visioning process also produces a strategic action plan. The action plan serves as the community's "road map": to move it in the direction of its vision in the near-term future.

BENEFITS OF VISIONING

For communities that successfully engage in visioning, the process offers clear benefits. Visioning:

- brings community members together in a uniquely different context to consider their common future;
- encourages the community to explore new ideas and possibilities;

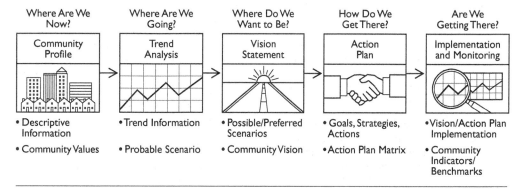

THE NEW OREGON MODEL

Source: Steven Ames Planning.

- creates a shared sense of direction and a framework for future community decisions; and
- produces a process that results in concrete goals and strategies for action

Additionally, there can be second-order benefits that may not be immediately apparent in undertaking the process, such as:

- enriching public involvement by expanding the terms and scope of civic engagement;
- fostering new leadership in citizens who have not been previously active in public life;
- promoting active partnerships among government, business, civic, and nonprofit organizations; and
- strengthening community cohesion and "social capital."

In other words, engaging in the *process* of visioning can be as rewarding as its *products*.

Finally, there can be significant visioning benefits for the function of planning itself. For example, strong consensus on community goals can provide an informed and supportive context for the development of other plans and policies. This, in turn, can facilitate and even streamline public involvement.

At the same time, visioning can place new demands on planning. It stretches the traditional role of planners, calling upon new skills and competencies. It demands increased levels of dialogue and trust with the public. Ultimately, to the degree that visioning extends beyond the traditional domain of planning, it requires more effective cross-sector communication and collaboration.

THE OREGON MODEL

Oregon was one of the first places in the United States to experience the proliferation of community-based visioning. In a state widely recognized for its land-use planning and growth management policies, visioning was seen as an overlay for local land-use plans and a tool to help communities manage change.

Based on Oregon's early community visioning successes and similar state-level efforts, the Oregon Model represents a comprehensive approach to visioning that has since gained widespread acceptance around the country. The model is framed by four simple questions, which collectively form the basis of the visioning process:

1. Where are we now?
2. Where are we going?
3. Where do we want to be?
4. How do we get there?

Answering each question implies a discrete step in the process, with different activities, outcomes, and products. Step one involves profiling the present community's current conditions and core values. Step two involves analyzing emerging trends and their probable impact on the community's future. Step three is geared to the creation of a vision, and step four involves developing an action plan.

Some communities have added a fifth step promoting action plan implementation:

5. Are we getting there?

This addition to the Oregon Model responds to criticism that the visioning process does not always produce real results. The fifth step may also incorporate the development of indicators or benchmarks to monitor and measure the community's success in achieving its vision over time.

Visioning is designed to be iterative and ongoing. Benchmarking provides an important feedback loop for the eventual update of the community's vision and action plan. The action plan, having a much shorter planning horizon than its companion vision, requires more frequent updates.

Applying the Model

The Oregon Model is a flexible approach that can be adapted to a wide variety of settings and can be scaled up or down depending on the nature of the community, its needs, and its resources. The key to its success is to shape the process to fit the place.

Establishing a vision framework—timeframe, overall focus, and specific focus areas—provides a strategic starting point. Most communities set their vision timeframe at 20 to 25 years into the future. They also adopt a broad overall focus, encompassing the full spectrum of community concerns. Focus areas may range beyond traditional planning to

Steven C. Ames, Steven Ames Planning, Portland, Oregon

encompass such topics as education, arts and culture, health, and public safety. Building on this framework, the design of every visioning process will vary widely.

As a relatively new approach to planning, community visioning can have a steep learning curve; it may employ nontraditional planning techniques such as "environmental scanning" or alternative scenarios. Managing diverse stakeholder groups or alleviating public skepticism regarding the process can prove daunting. Midprocess course corrections are necessary.

Fortunately, none of these challenges are insurmountable. Moreover, the ability of visioning to provide strategic input for such perennial planning concerns as growth management, urban design, transportation, housing, community development, and sustainability justifies the up-front investment. Indeed, planners often use the outcomes of visioning to frame and legitimize other major planning initiatives.

Involving the Public in Visioning

True to visioning's roots in anticipatory democracy, public involvement is a critical element of the visioning process. Engaging the public is essential in creating a shared community vision and action plan, as well as in promoting their eventual achievement. This implies an inclusive, participatory process capable of forging broad public consensus on key community goals.

To some planners, such a dialogue may seem increasingly difficult in today's society, given the numerous urgent issues on the public agenda, shrinking local government budgets, the busy lives of citizens, and the ever-present distractions of the media and pop culture. For these reasons, public out-

reach and strong "branding" of the visioning process are absolutely critical to successful public involvement.

Fortunately, for many people, there remains a fundamental appeal in talking about the future of their community. The reason is probably the abiding importance of "place." People relate to and care about where they live; it's one of the fundamental

---

SUCCESSFUL COMMUNITY VISIONING

Visioning works when:

- The community is concerned about its future and is eager for dialogue.
- The process is well designed, managed, and adequately resourced.
- Key community institutions and opinion leaders are involved in the process.
- Elected officials and city managers are supportive of the process.
- The public is authentically engaged in the process.

Visioning doesn't work when:

- The community is too polarized to engage in a civil dialogue.
- The process is poorly designed or managed or inadequately resourced.
- Key community institutions or opinion leaders are not involved in the process.
- Elected officials or city managers are unsupportive of the process.
- There is no follow-through in implementing the vision and action plan.

---

ways through which we continue to connect as human beings.

There is also an array of tools and techniques to stimulate and facilitate the visioning dialogue. These include participatory techniques, such as public workshops and open houses, as well as more representative techniques, such as citizen task forces, scientific surveys, and focus groups. The former help ensure broad public input, allow for open dialogue, and promote public awareness; the latter help capture diverse viewpoints, promote in-depth discussions, and facilitate the development of specific visioning products.

Additionally, computer-mediated communications are increasingly integral to the visioning process. While "electronic town meetings" have yet to realize their original promise, other tools have stepped in to fill the gap. Visioning today would be inconceivable without the Internet, search engines, and community Web sites, with their respective capacities for disseminating and gathering information. Graphical computer simulations have also increased our ability to actually *see* aspects of preferred—or not-so-preferred—futures.

Undoubtedly, evolving forms of electronic communication will continue to add new dimensions to community visioning, just as the process itself continues to evolve as an integral part of community planning.

See also:
Places and Place Making
Public Meetings
Surveys
Visualization

Steven C. Ames, Steven Ames Planning, Portland, Oregon

CHARRETTES

A charrette involves a multidisciplinary team of professionals developing all elements of a plan. The team works closely with stakeholders through a series of feedback loops, during which alternative concepts are developed, reviewed by stakeholders, and revised accordingly. The charrette is a sophisticated process that best serves controversial and complicated urban design and planning problems. Its capacity to bring all the decision makers together for a discrete amount of time to create a solution makes it one of the most powerful techniques in a planner's toolkit.

Charrettes are not a substitute for a standard planning process, which is executed over several months. They are conducted to address specific problematic situations and should complement the overall planning process. The charrette process works best for situations such as:

- high-stakes projects;
- volatile yet workable political environments;
- complex design problems; and
- projects that include imminent development.

The combination of the sophistication of the process with the complexity of the situations in which it is most often used means charrette practitioners *must* be well trained.

DYNAMIC PLANNING

A charrette is the central event of a larger process that the National Charrette Institute calls *Dynamic Planning*, a multiday, collaborative planning and design effort with the goal of arriving at a comprehensive, feasible plan.

Dynamic Planning has three governing values:

- Anyone affected by the project has the right to provide input with potential impact on the outcome.
- Each participant has a unique contribution that is heard and respected.
- Many hands make the best plans.

BENEFITS OF THE CHARRETTE PROCESS

The benefits of the charrette process are numerous. When done correctly, the charrette promotes trust between citizens and government through meaningful public involvement and education. It fosters a shared community vision by turning opposition into support. It continuously strives for the creation of a feasible plan, which increases the likelihood of the project getting built by gaining broad support from citizens, professionals, and staff. Identifying the stakeholders early and often, and encouraging public participation creates a better plan through diverse input and involvement. Finally, the charrette makes economic sense. Because all parties are collaborating from the start, no voice is overlooked, which allows the project to avoid costly rework. Also, the charrette allows for fewer and more highly productive work sessions, making it less time-consuming than traditional processes.

THE NINE STRATEGIES OF THE CHARRETTE PROCESS

The term "charrette" is overused and often misused. Although "charrette" refers specifically to a holistic plan to bring transformative change to a neighborhood, some use the word to refer to an afternoon meeting or a marathon planning workshop. The following nine strategies are what differentiate a charrette from other planning processes.

1. *Work collaboratively.* All interested parties must be involved from the beginning. Having contributed to the planning, participants are in a position both to understand and to support a project's rationale.
2. *Design cross-functionally.* A multidisciplinary team method results in decisions that are realistic every step of the way. The cross-functional process eliminates the need for rework because the design work continually reflects the wisdom of each specialty.
3. *Compress work sessions.* The charrette itself, usually lasting two to seven days, is a series of meetings and design sessions that would traditionally take months to complete. This time compression facilitates creative problem solving by accelerating decision making and reducing unconstructive negotiation tactics. It also encourages people to abandon their usual working patterns and "think outside the box."
4. *Communicate in short feedback loops.* During the charrette, design ideas are created based upon a public vision and presented within hours for further review, critique, and refinement. Regular stakeholder input and reviews quickly build trust in the process and foster true understanding and support of the product.
5. *Study the details and the whole.* Lasting agreement is based on a fully informed dialogue, which can be accomplished only by looking at the details and the big picture concurrently. Studies at these two scales also inform each other and reduce the likelihood that a fatal flaw will be overlooked in the plan.
6. *Produce a feasible plan.* The charrette differs from other workshops in its expressed goal to create a feasible plan. In other words, every decision point

must be fully informed, especially by the legal, financial, and engineering disciplines.
7. *Use design to achieve a shared vision and create holistic solutions.* Design is a powerful tool for establishing a shared vision. Drawings illustrate the complexity of the problem and can be used to resolve conflict by proposing previously unexplored solutions that represent win-win outcomes.
8. *Include a multiday charrette.* Most charrettes require between two and seven days, allowing for three feedback loops. The more difficult the problem is, the longer the charrette should be.
9. *Hold the charrette on site.* Working on site fosters the design team's understanding of local values and traditions, and provides the necessary easy access to stakeholders and information. Therefore, the studio should be located in a place where it is easily accessible to all stakeholders and where the designers have quick access to the project site.

THE THREE PHASES OF DYNAMIC PLANNING

As discussed above, the charrette is the central element of a larger comprehensive process called Dynamic Planning. There are three phases in Dynamic Planning: *research, education, and charrette preparation; the charrette; and plan implementation.* The most common cause of project failure is not a poorly run charrette; rather, it is usually due to incomplete preparation and/or inadequate follow-through during the implementation phase.

Research, Education, and Charrette Preparation

During this phase, all the necessary base information is gathered and all the necessary people are identified and engaged. A complexity analysis of the project is completed, so that the charrette manager can decide how much time is needed for the charrette. During this time initial stakeholder meetings are held and feasibility studies are completed. Finally, the charrette logistics are arranged. The studio setup is planned, the design team is formed, and the charrette is scheduled step by step. This step can typically take around four months.

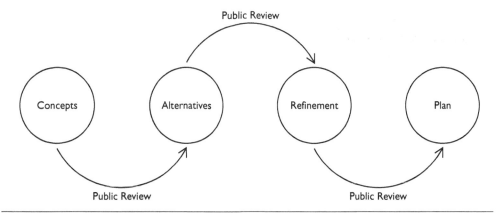

CHARRETTE FEEDBACK LOOPS

Source: National Charrette Institute, 2003.

National Charrette Institute, Portland, Oregon

PARTICIPATION

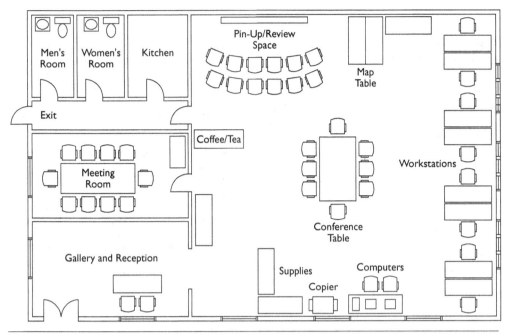

CHARRETTE STUDIO LAYOUT

Source: National Charrette Institute, 2003.

The Charrette

The charrette brings all the right people and all the right information to a series of highly focused and productive work sessions. Before the first public meeting is held, the design team takes a tour of the area and holds meetings with key stakeholder groups. The first public meeting is held to determine the direction in which the public would like to take their community. Based on public input, gathered through a number of different participatory methods employed during the first public meeting, the design team begins to work on the development of alternative concepts. The next evening, another public meeting is held to display the alternative concepts

and gather another round of public feedback. After this second public meeting, the design team meets to discuss the best way to synthesize the different concepts into one preferred plan. This new plan is then presented to the public in an open house. Following the open house, the preferred plan is developed further, and the design is refined. Additional stakeholder input is gathered. The preferred plan is then presented to the public again during the final charrette public meeting.

Plan Implementation

Dynamic Planning does not end with the charrette. It is critical that the preferred plan undergo further feasibility testing and public review. Each team member is in charge of his or her element of the charrette plan and performs feasibility tests and then refines the element as necessary. These revisions to the plan are then presented to the public again, usually about a month after the charrette. The final product of the Dynamic Planning process is a full set of documents that represent the complete record of the Dynamic Planning and charrette processes, including records of the meetings, who was involved, and the evolution of the plan.

WHERE CHARRETTES SUCCEED

The key to a successful charrette is in its preparation. Because a successful charrette requires all the right people and all the right information, most mistakes are made by not identifying and involving the right people early and throughout the process and/or not planning enough time to produce the documents necessary for implementation. The importance of stakeholder reviews and soliciting public feedback cannot be overemphasized.

NEXT EVOLUTION OF CHARRETTES

Traditionally, charrettes have been "high-touch," relying on low-tech elements, such as hand drawings. High-tech modeling tools are increasingly being incorporated into traditionally high-touch charrettes. They include keypad polling, environmental impact analysis programs, and vision scenario development. These tools are helping to increase public involvement, execute design, and perform feasibility analysis. As high-tech tools are refined, they will provide the design team with an increased capability to give quick feedback during a charrette.

See also:

Visualization

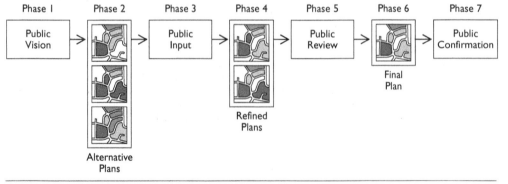

CHARRETTE WORK CYCLE

Source: National Charrette Institute, 2003.

PUBLIC MEETINGS

Public meetings are among the most common forms of citizen participation for planners and urban designers. They can be used to ascertain public opinion generally or to reach consensus on a recommended action. When they are successful, it is due to careful planning and follow-through. Well-organized and executed public meetings can be valuable opportunities for planners to provide information on important issues to the citizenry and obtain meaningful input.

There are three primary purposes for holding a public meeting: share information, seek advice, or solve problems. Though any issue can be the subject of this form of public dialogue, planners most frequently deal with matters such as zoning, comprehensive planning, parks and open space, environmental protection, and transportation. The meetings themselves may take a variety of forms. They differ substantially from public hearings, which generally follow formal rules and procedures. In fact, it can be said that governmental bodies usually are required to hold public hearings, whereas they have a choice about whether and how to hold public meetings.

At an effective public meeting, planners can enlist citizens as partners or at the least give them important information. By listening and responding respectfully, they can help diffuse opposition and build trust and confidence. The most successful public meetings are designed and executed very carefully, with attention paid to myriad details and nothing left to chance.

THE PURPOSE OF A PUBLIC MEETING

Before developing the agenda or any other part of the public meeting, the first matter to be agreed upon is its purpose: Is the meeting being convened primarily to share information, to seek advice, or to solve problems? Once that is decided, planners then should choose the appropriate structure and organization that best carries out this objective. To avoid misunderstandings, it is important that all notices indicate clearly the nature of the meeting and the expected outcomes. This also should be emphasized during introductory remarks. For example, citizens can be upset if they come to a public meeting ready to vote on options or alternatives, only to find that the purpose of the gathering is only to ask for their opinions.

Informational Meetings

Informational meetings are held to convey information or data to the public and to receive their comments. Public hearings are the most common, but not the only, form of informational meetings. At public hearings, staff presents information to the decision makers or hearing officers, followed by testimony from citizens, all within strict constraints. Other informational meetings are more informal, with planners making reports to neighborhood, civic, or other interested groups, and then answering questions. Although time for short presentations from the attendees may be permitted, prolonged dialogue and interaction are discouraged.

Advisory Meetings

While advisory public meetings also provide information, the public is given meaningful opportunities at these meetings to interact with staff or decision makers. Similar to the structure of informational meetings, advisory meetings begin with a presentation of basic information, possibly followed by a summary of the advantages and disadvantages of various alternatives. After the presentations at an advisory meeting, however, the public engages in an open but structured dialogue.

Workshops

The most common form of dialogue session is the workshop, where 8 to 10 participants discuss issues pertinent to the subject, led by a facilitator. Notes are taken, with the assurance that feedback from the attendees will be shared with the decision makers. No promises are made that the results from the workshop will be the final decision; the only assurances given are that decision makers will consider citizen concerns in their final deliberations.

Open House

Another form of advisory meeting becoming popular among planners is the community open house. While informational or advisory meetings should be no more than three hours long, an open house is typically longer, from 3:00 to 8:00 P.M., for example. A busy public appreciates the flexible hours. For example, seniors or others may prefer not being out after dark, and working people can drop by on the way home or after supper.

To hold an open house requires a large room that can hold many people milling about, such as a school gymnasium or cafeteria, senior or community center, or church basement. As people enter, they are given information packets that include a small map or room layout, agenda, and background materials. Well-placed

signs mark the different areas of activity or stations. Planners and others who can answer questions and engage people in a dialogue about a particular segment of the issue staff each station. For example, if the open house is being held about a draft comprehensive plan, the people at the various stations can address elements of the plan, such as transportation, parks, and housing. Speakers may provide formal presentations in a screened-off part of the room at specific times. Citizens are encouraged to stay as long as they like, moving at their own pace between stations and other informational displays. Short written questionnaires give attendees additional opportunities to comment and express their opinions. This open format, with staff and decision makers committed to listening and actively engaging the public, can generate much community goodwill as well as provide valuable information.

Problem-Solving Meetings

The purpose of the third, and least common, form of public meeting is to solve problems. In this case, the results of citizen input will directly influence the decision-making process. The workshop format discussed above, consisting of a presentation of technical material followed by facilitated discussion, is also a useful technique for problem-solving meetings. However, in this case, the public is asked to reach conclusions or make recommendations. If there are more than a dozen attendees, people should be divided into small discussion units. Group consensus or agreement is more likely to emerge if participants are randomly dispersed at small discussion tables. This will produce results more reflective of the group process than of any particular advocate or dissenter. The successful problem-solving meeting requires an informed citizenry, skilled discussion leaders following an agenda with specific questions and discussion topics, well-trained recorders, and decision makers who commit themselves to following the results.

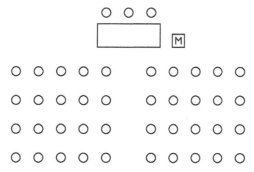

With this arrangement, all eyes are on the speaker. There is minimal interaction with the audience, typically limited to questions and answers. To be heard, one must generally go to the front.

TYPICAL INFORMATIONAL SEATING ARRANGEMENT

Reprinted with permission from Successful Public Meetings, *copyright 2000 by the American Planning Association, Suite 1600, 122 South Michigan Avenue, Chicago, IL 60603-6107.*

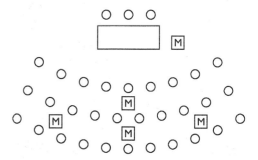

The curved shape of the arrangement creates fewer perceived barriers between the speakers and the audience. It also allows the audience to have views of each other. The placement of microphones invites questions and comments.

IMPROVED INFORMATIONAL SEATING ARRANGEMENT

Reprinted with permission from Successful Public Meetings, *copyright 2000 by the American Planning Association, Suite 1600, 122 South Michigan Avenue, Chicago, IL 60603-6107.*

Elaine C. Cogan, Cogan Owens Cogan, LLC, Portland, Oregon

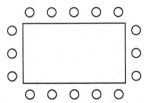

The rectangular table is typical for conference room meetings. It encourages face-to-face interaction, but those on the ends may talk more and receive more attention. Substituting an oval or round table allows participants to see each other easily.

BOARDROOM SEATING ARRANGEMENT

Reprinted with permission from Neighborhood Planning, *copyright 1990 by the American Planning Association, Suite 1600, 122 South Michigan Avenue, Chicago, IL 60603-6107.*

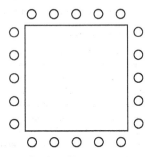

(with or without table)

This arrangement is similar to the boardroom seating arrangement. It makes the role of "leader" less obvious. Corners may be "dead" areas, however.

CLOSED-SQUARE SEATING ARRANGEMENT

Reprinted with permission from Neighborhood Planning, *copyright 1990 by the American Planning Association, Suite 1600, 122 South Michigan Avenue, Chicago, IL 60603-6107.*

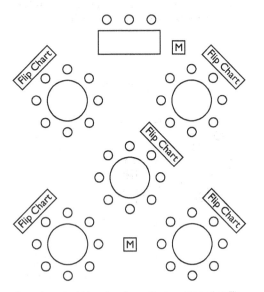

Several smaller tables allow for small-group interaction. Flip charts and microphones allow for breakout exercises and reporting back to the group.

WORKSHOP SEATING ARRANGEMENT

Reprinted with permission from Neighborhood Planning, *copyright 1990 by the American Planning Association, Suite 1600, 122 South Michigan Avenue, Chicago, IL 60603-6107.*

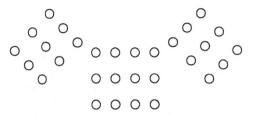

This arrangement is similar to the improved informational seating arrangement. It allows for interaction when a circle arrangement is not possible. A main speaker may have to turn to view certain audience members.

THEATER SEATING ARRANGEMENT

Reprinted with permission from Neighborhood Planning, *copyright 1990 by the American Planning Association, Suite 1600, 122 South Michigan Avenue, Chicago, IL 60603-6107.*

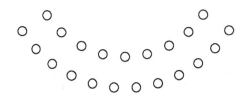

When a circle is not possible, a semicircle gives most of the same advantages. Use an even number of rows, as the odd, middle row is often left vacant.

SEMICIRCLE SEATING ARRANGEMENT

Reprinted with permission from Neighborhood Planning, *copyright 1990 by the American Planning Association, Suite 1600, 122 South Michigan Avenue, Chicago, IL 60603-6107.*

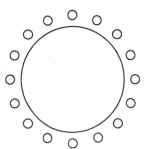

A circle arrangement allows everyone to see everything and creates a more equal setting. Including a table allows participants to take notes.

CIRCLE SEATING ARRANGEMENT

Reprinted with permission from Neighborhood Planning, *copyright 1990 by the American Planning Association, Suite 1600, 122 South Michigan Avenue, Chicago, IL 60603-6107.*

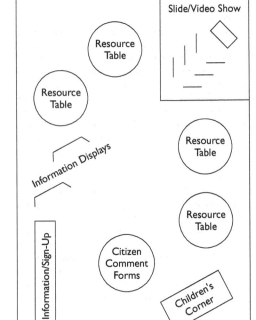

The community fair arrangement allows for many informal opportunities to receive information, discuss issues, and give opinions.

COMMUNITY FAIR ARRANGEMENT

Reprinted with permission from Neighborhood Planning, *copyright 1990 by the American Planning Association, Suite 1600, 122 South Michigan Avenue, Chicago, IL 60603-6107.*

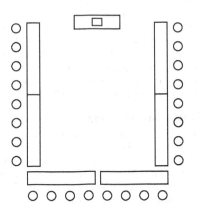

This room arrangement is commonly used for group meetings. The "U" allows a speaker to move around within the group. However, it creates open space between participants. Moving the tables closer together encourages interaction across the "U."

U-SHAPE SEATING ARRANGEMENT

Source: © 1995 David Knox Productions, Inc.

Elaine C. Cogan, Cogan Owens Cogan, LLC, Portland, Oregon

PART 1   PLANS AND PLAN MAKING

UNDERREPRESENTED POPULATIONS

In an increasingly diverse society, planners should be sensitive about how to involve people who may not generally come to public meetings. One successful technique is to contact representatives of minority, non-English speaking, or other underrepresented communities to ask them to help you reach their constituents, friends, and neighbors. Take their advice seriously. They may suggest several approaches, such as:

- advertising in local newspapers or radio stations;
- printing notices in languages other than English;
- using interpreters at meetings;
- providing child care; and
- meeting at unconventional times, such as weekends;

PRESENTATION SKILLS

In deciding the amount and kind of information to provide at all public meetings, consider the needs of your audience. What do they need or want to know in order to be conversant with the subject and provide useful feedback? By asking this question and answering it honestly, planners will avoid making the common mistake of writing technical papers instead of simple handouts or speaking in jargon or language well beyond citizens' understanding. Recognize also that not all good planners are good presenters. Some professionals relate well to people at informal neighborhood meetings but are not able to speak to a great number in a big hall. Others have just the opposite skills. Either obtain training to increase your abilities in different settings or recognize your limitations and deploy the people best able to handle specific situations.

Likewise, remember that one type of presentation does not fit all situations. While computer presentations are popular with planners and designers, they can backfire if done poorly, using too many words and confusing images. Computers also are prone to malfunction so it is important always to have a backup, such as a written handout. With some audiences, simple charts or drawings may be more effective than flashy graphics.

KEYS TO SUCCESSFUL PUBLIC MEETINGS

Successful public meetings are characterized by a number of considerations:

- Set aside sufficient time and resources to plan each event, agreeing first on the basic purpose and primary audience.
- Choose the best format to meet your objectives.
- Provide notice well in advance and in the language(s) understood by your target audiences.
- Hold the meeting at a time and in a place convenient to the people you want to attend.
- Agree on roles and responsibilities for hosts, presenters, discussion leaders, and recorders.
- Develop clear, appropriate, and readable written materials and graphics.
- Be well prepared so that you can deal with any last-minute crises or challenges.

See also:
Public Hearings

Elaine C. Cogan, Cogan Owens Cogan, LLC, Portland, Oregon

PARTICIPATION

PUBLIC HEARINGS

The law requires that most public agencies and elected bodies hold public hearings before making important decisions. These hearings follow specific rules and procedures legally prescribed by state statutes and local ordinances. Generally, public hearings are held near the end of the planning and development process, just before the authority in charge votes about or decides the final disposition of the matter at hand. Notification of the hearing is sent to those parties legally required to receive them or inserted in advertisements in the local newspaper.

The hearing body usually sits on a raised dais with staff close by. The public is seated auditorium-style. Public comments are limited, and they may be recorded on audio or videotape, or by professional stenographers.

Planners participate as staff or consultants, reporting to the hearing body and answering questions. Public testimony follows. To maintain a sense of fairness, proponents and opponents may be given alternate turns to speak. Decision makers listen and rarely ask questions. If an issue is contentious, the hearing may go on for hours.

THE ELEMENTS OF A GOOD PUBLIC HEARING

Planners, who must follow the legally prescribed rules for public hearings, can ensure that the hearings achieve their desired ends (receiving and documenting comments from the public about the nature of the matter at hand). Beyond that, however, they should also ensure that the actions they take meet the letter of the law, the spirit of the law, and the standards for effective and fair planning. The following sections offer some guidelines for effective public hearings. These actions should constitute a standard for the way in which public hearings are arranged and conducted.

Notification and Other Informational Materials

1. Write all notices in plain language, with translations as needed for non-English-speaking people. Disseminate as widely as your budget will allow, using community newspapers, Web pages, and other electronic means of communicating. If legal text is required, have it accompany the plainly written notice.
2. Hand out written agendas and summaries so attendees can follow along with the presentations. Make sure to have a sufficient quantity for all, and arrange to duplicate extras if needed.
3. Present technical material in as nontechnical a manner as possible. Remember that the public and some of the decision makers are not likely to be as well versed on the subject as the planners.

Room Arrangements

1. Hold the hearing in a room where all can see and hear with ease. If the dais is a fixed platform, set up chairs and tables for the public officials and staff at the same level as the audience.
2. Arrange charts or screens for slides or video presentations so the public as well as the officials can see them. If the room is large, position several screens so that everyone can see.
3. Have a sufficient number of working microphones for presenters, hearing personnel, and the public, and place them strategically to give citizens easy access.
4. Combine the hearing with an "open house" or similar opportunity for the public to receive and provide information in a more informal setting.

Interaction and Involvement

1. Station one or two staff at the door to greet the public, give them the handouts, and show them to empty seats. It is especially important to make latecomers welcome.
2. Have a sign-in sheet for all who want to comment, and call upon them in order.
3. Divide a long agenda into manageable portions. Instead of programming all the technical reports at one time, seek public comments after each section or portion under consideration. This decreases the likelihood that large groups of angry or restless people will remain throughout, as most will leave after the matters in which they are interested have been discussed.

4. Announce beforehand and throughout if the public's comments are being recorded.
5. Provide alternative ways to give public testimony. Deploy a stenographer in another room to take down, verbatim, comments; have a tape recorder and staff person available; or hand out written comment forms.

See also:
Public Meetings

"USER-FRIENDLY" NOTIFICATION FORM

The key elements of a successful public hearing notification are:

- Clear statement of purpose is included at the top of the notice.
- Purpose of the meeting and the public action being taken are described in plain language.
- Date, time, and location of the public hearing are included near the top of the notice.
- Potential financial implications of the project, of interest to citizens, are included.
- Ways that citizens can provide comments, at the hearing or in other ways, are provided.
- More detailed contact information is included.
- Legal references, if needed, are cited at the end of the notice.

The user-friendly version of a notification form follows.

Proposal to Change Use of Residential Property to Allow Senior or Community Center

Thomas McIntire, living at 2900 Elm Street, is asking the city to rezone his property from residential use (RS-2) to PS-1, to allow construction of a senior or community center.

The city's Planning and Zoning Commission may either allow or deny this request and is holding two public hearings to obtain citizen comments. Both hearings will be held in the third-floor city hall auditorium, February 28 and March 9, at 6:30 p.m.

If the property is approved as proposed, it will be used by a nonprofit corporation, which will not pay property taxes. The remaining property taxpayers in the city will be required to make up the difference. The current property taxes paid by the owner are approximately $1,500 per year.

All citizens who own property within 400 feet of this property are invited to testify in person or write to the Department of Planning and Zoning before midnight of the second hearing, March 9. Any other interested parties also may speak at the hearing or write a letter.

For more information, contact Hortense Allen, project planner, Department of Planning and Zoning, City Hall, Room 725, or call Ms. Allen at 811-555-5656.

Please refer to accompanying map for specific site information. The legal petition for this case is on file as #1789222 PB and #5589167 PB.

#   #   #   #   #

Source: Elaine Cogan, 2000.

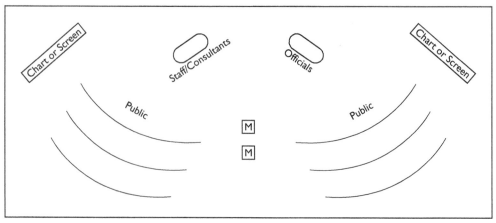

Hearing room arrangements should have public officials and staff seated at the same level as the audience. More than one screen often is provided for presentations, and they are positioned so the public and the officials can see them. Several microphones should be placed strategically so citizens have easy access.

HEARING ARRANGEMENT

Source: Elaine Cogan.

Elaine C. Cogan, Cogan Owens Cogan, LLC, Portland, Oregon

COMPUTER-BASED PUBLIC PARTICIPATION

Planners are increasingly recognizing the potential of computer-based participation as a key element in developing appropriate and effective solutions to community design and planning problems. As computer and Internet technology becomes more mainstream, planners should develop ways to harness these technologies to work more effectively with the public.

Computerized tools represent a paradigm shift in the planning and design process that may fundamentally change the way planners communicate ideas to the public. These computer-based participation tools presently consist of the following:

- *Electronic sketchboard.* This simulates traditional pen and paper sketching and provides additional capabilities of layering, tracing, and coloring.
- *Geographic information systems (GIS).* Use of GIS represents a move from a paper map to a digital one empowered with spatial analysis, navigation, and visualization capabilities.
- *Imaging software.* This software provides new ways of editing, manipulating, and animating traditional photographs.
- *Virtual reality (VR).* VR represents a move from 3-D physical models to digital ones that provide participants a degree of freedom in "experiencing" proposed projects before construction.
- *Urban simulation.* Building on virtual reality, urban simulation shows simulations of dynamic changes of the environment, including seasons, weather, landscape, pollution, and movement of people and automobile.
- *Hypermedia.* Also called *multimedia*, this is a new computerized environment that integrates multiple media, such as maps, photographs, videos, and sounds on a stand-alone PC.
- *Internet.* The Internet can provide a virtual setting of traditional same-place and same-time participation that integrates multiple tools, such as GIS, drawings, photographs, and virtual reality.

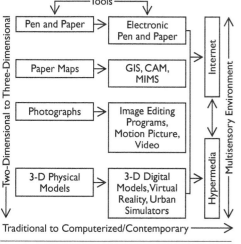

THE PROGRESSION FROM TRADITIONAL TO COMPUTERIZED VISUALIZATION TOOLS

Source: Kheir Al-Kodmany, 2004.

ADVANTAGES OF COMPUTERIZED TOOLS

Represent Contextual Data

Computerized tools can illustrate abstract concepts, such as environmental impacts, in a way that would be impossible with traditional tools, such as paper, photographs, or physical models. For example, with GIS, one can layer maps derived from different data on top of one another, query the database that is the source of the map information to highlight correlations between data, and visualize those correlations through the use of patterns and colors on the maps. Such tools also allow the user to extrude data into 3-D models and to simulate a fly- and walk-through experience. In a planning process that employs GIS, hypermedia, and virtual reality, average citizens are granted unprecedented access to a rich array of data presented in an easy-to-understand format. Computerized tools may enhance the public's interaction in the decision-making process because the tools provide so much more specific information that can be provided on the spot, thus enabling the public to explore alternatives quickly and with more competence.

Selective Display of Information

One key advantage of computerized tools is that they provide the capacity to selectively display information. When working on paper, even a relatively small amount of information can quickly become overwhelming and appear cluttered. The amount of detail displayed in computerized programs can be adjusted interactively as the scale is changed. Also, participants can easily overlay data by turning layers on and off as needed. In systems that incorporate hypermedia, different types of information can be queried and complex information displayed simply. Different types of data, such as sound, movies, animations, maps, and texts, can also be used selectively to enrich the study and analysis.

However, in a complex computerized data environment, citizens may not be able to freely participate because they will need "expert" assistance to manipulate data.

Geographic Scale

Another clear advantage of computerized tools is the ability to navigate geographic scale. With traditional tools, multiple maps are needed for each geographic scale: region, city, community, neighborhood, and individual lots. Computerized mapping allows for zooming in on a region, city, neighborhood, or even a specific house on a single map. As a result, computerized tools may increase interactivity, accessibility, and selectivity of information concerning issues at various geographic scales and therefore enhance discussion about contextual and spatial issues.

CONCERNS ABOUT COMPUTER-BASED PARTICIPATION

Believability

One drawback of computerized tools is that the images can be so realistic and persuasive that they mislead people. It has been found that computer visu-

alization can lead to false conclusions by the public. Some critics have suggested that the use of impressive video and graphics will cause decisions to be made on the strength of visual images alone. Further, with the capability of creating very concrete, realistic images, there is the danger that audiences may see a generated image as constituting reality. The more realistic the maps and images appear, the more danger there is they will be accepted as "truthful."

Similarly, computerized images can erroneously appear to be value-neutral. Just as these tools can be used to create compelling representations of future urban development, they can create compelling misrepresentations as well. Computer visualization must combat this by explicitly demonstrating the accuracy of the data being used and by providing accessibility to metadata (Obermeyer 1998).

Affordability

The hardware and software needed for computer visualization require a large capital outlay; thus the question of whether to implement advanced visualization technology often comes down to a question of resources. Depending on the scale of implementation and the richness of the data, these systems can vary widely in development and maintenance costs. Low-tech tools can provide an alternative when it is necessary to respond to a tight timeline or cost control that are a reality in many local planning arenas (Pietsch 2000).

Engagement

A prime consideration in any public participation-planning scheme is how well the tools engage the targeted participants. In general, traditional noncomputerized public participation methods are more participatory, experiential, and interactive. They provide more social interaction among participants. These approaches are particularly effective when the audience involves varied interest groups and stakeholders with opposing interests. They are also useful for conflict resolution when face-to-face interaction is needed to facilitate discussions. Practical experience asserts that the added value of real-time social interaction among neighbors, while using a physical simulation game, for example, surpasses computer simulations even when they have user-friendly computer interfaces. Computerized methods lose their advantages when people have to "work" the computer. Findings indicate that traditional methods of manipulating physical objects facilitate comprehension and retention more than working on a computer screen (Moughtin 2003).

Access to Institutions

In public participation, whether computerized or traditional, access to institutions and people remains the most challenging issue. Are citizens willing to participate? What are the motivating factors and incentives? Will their participation be taken seriously? Will their opinions make a difference in the decision-making process and ultimate outcome? How open are the planning processes? Are the powerful players willing to open up and allow others to participate through information sharing? Institutional challenges may continue regardless of technological advancement.

Kheir Al-Kodmany, Ph.D., University of Illinois at Chicago, Chicago, Illinois

The foremost advantage of computerized participation is access to accurate representation and presentation of complex contextual information. That said, while computerized tools usually impress participants and help them attain a comprehensive understanding of the spatial relationships, these tools often fall short in allowing the participants to design and alter the representation; computerized tools must do a better job of allowing the public to "get their hands on" something. The real need is not to force a choice between the social benefits of low-tech methods and the efficiency and power of high-tech methods; rather, we need tools that support the integration of real worlds and virtual worlds by providing users with the flexibility to move along the continuum.

REFERENCES

Moughtin, J.C., Rafael Cuesta, Christine Sarris, and Paola Signoretta. 2003. *Urban Design: Methods and Techniques*. 2nd ed. Oxford: Elsevier Press.

Obermeyer, Nancy J. 1998. "The Evolution of Public Participation GIS." *Cartography and Geographic Information Systems*. 25, no.2:65–66.

Pietsch, Susan M. 2000. "Computer Visualization in the Design Control of Urban Environments: A Literature Review." *Environment and Planning B: Planning and Design*, 27, no. 4:521–536.

See also:
Charrettes
Geographic Information Systems
Visualization

Kheir Al-Kodmany, Ph.D., University of Illinois at Chicago, Chicago, Illinois

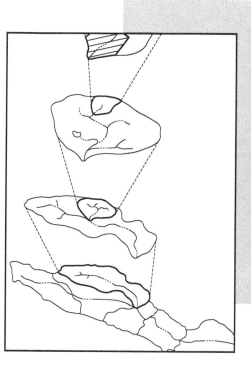

ENVIRONMENTAL PLANNING AND MANAGEMENT

Part 2

ENVIRONMENTAL MANAGEMENT OVERVIEW

ENVIRONMENTAL PLANNING CONSIDERATIONS

"Environment" refers to our surroundings. Its meaning is closely related to two other terms used in planning and urban design, "ecology" and "landscape." Ecology involves the study of the reciprocal relationships of all organisms to each other and to their biological and physical environments. Landscapes comprise the sum of natural and cultural elements seen in a single view. When we add "planning" to each of these terms, the combined term refers to developing future options for our surroundings, for the interrelationships among biological and physical processes, and for the visual manifestation of those relationships.

Because our surroundings contain physical, biological, and built elements, environmental planning involves using knowledge about those elements to provide options for decision making. The typical components that need to be considered include physical phenomena, such as air, climate, rocks, terrain, and water; biological elements, such as plants and animals; and the built environment, which

encompasses buildings, streets, yards, and parks. Soils are an especially important element because they occur at the interface between physical and biological processes. Some surroundings may appear natural, such as farmlands, but are actually part of the built environment.

COMPONENTS OF THE ENVIRONMENT

The elements and processes involved in environmental planning are complex, hence the ordering of various components is important. Planning theorist Ian McHarg suggested a layer-cake model for such ordering. In this approach, time and ecology were used as organizing devices. Older environmental layers were used to understand younger phenomena. For example, regional climatic and geology processes result in specific physiographic, groundwater, and surface water characteristics. These physical processes create the parent material for soils, which

allow specific plants to grow. Animals and people use these plants to live.

These layers can be overlaid in order to understand ecological relationships and to determine suitable land-use possibilities. The concept of layering environmental information provides the theoretical underpinnings for geographic information systems (GIS). Planners and urban designers use GIS maps to explore relationships and patterns, and to determine the possibility of suitability with greater speed and efficiency.

The components of the natural environment can be viewed as both sources and sinks for human activity. The environment is a source when it provides resources for people, such as productive soils, drinking water, clean air, timber, and minerals for energy and building. Environments are sinks when they are used as disposals for our wastes.

Natural environments can also pose hazards to human health, safety, and welfare. Some hazards, such as floods, are relatively easy to forecast, while others are more difficult to predict, such as earthquakes, hurricanes, and tornadoes. Even though difficult to predict, areas susceptible to earthquakes, hurricanes, and tornadoes are well defined by geologists and climatologists. As a result, emergency plans can be prepared and building modifications can be made to minimize the loss of life and property. Even well-defined areas might change as a result of human activities, shifting hazard areas or creating new ones, such as when new built-up areas change flooding regimes or when developments move into woodlands, thereby increasing wildfire potential. Certain hazards are quite cataclysmic, such as the eruption of a volcano. Others may occur more gradually but also result in deleterious consequences, such as soil erosion.

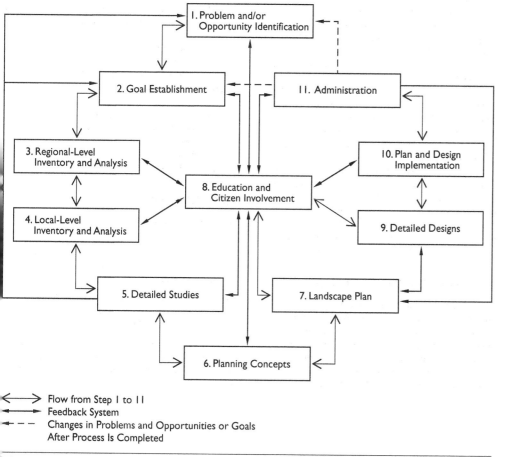

Flow from Step 1 to 11
Feedback System
Changes in Problems and Opportunities or Goals
After Process Is Completed

ECOLOGICAL PLANNING MODEL

Source: Steiner 2000.

LAYER-CAKE MODEL

Human	People	Community Needs Economics Community Organization Demographics Land Uses Human History
Biotic	Wildlife	Mammals Birds Reptiles Fishes
	Vegetation	Habitats Plant Types
Abiotic	Soils	Soil Erosion Soil Drainage
	Hydrology	Surface Water Groundwater
	Physiography	Slope Elevation
	Geology	Surficial Geology Bedrock Geology
	Climate	Microclimate Macroclimate

Source: Steiner 2000.

Frederick R. Steiner, Ph.D. FASLA, University of Texas at Austin

THE LEGAL BASIS FOR ENVIRONMENTAL PLANNING

With the passage of the National Environmental Policy Act (NEPA) in late 1969, the U.S. Congress put into motion the machinery for protecting the environment. NEPA required all federal agencies to "initiate and utilize ecological information in the planning and development of resource oriented projects." Furthermore, agencies were required to use "a systematic, interdisciplinary approach which will insure the integrated use of the natural and the social sciences and environmental design arts in planning and in decision making which may have an impact on [the human] environment." NEPA instructs all federal agencies to include an impact statement as part of future reports or recommendations on actions significantly affecting the quality of the human environment.

Several states and many other nations adopted similar environmental protection measures. So many environmentally oriented laws were enacted during the 1970s that it was dubbed the "environmental decade." These laws sought to protect water quality and quantity, clean air, coastal zones, floodplains, wetlands, historical areas, rare and endangered animal and plant species, and prime agricultural lands. The laws originating from the 1970s to the present provide the basis for environmental planning in the United States and other nations.

In the United States, environmental planning laws rely on three general approaches: *regulatory, financial incentives,* and *voluntary.* Regulatory approaches control activities that result in environmental degradation. For example, the amount of pollution that can be dumped by a factory into a water body can be regulated. If the factory managers fail to comply with regulatory limits or standards, they can be fined or forced to close operations. Financial incentives can involve direct grants, such as providing funds to purchase lands for wildlife habitat conservation, or tax benefits, such as reductions in taxes for dedicating property for conservation. Voluntary activities can be encouraged through environmental education designed to convince an individual to do the right

ENVIRONMENTALLY SENSITIVE AREA CLASSIFICATION SYSTEM

CLASS	SUBCLASS
Ecologically critical areas	Natural wildlife habitat areas Natural ecological areas Scientific areas
Perceptually and culturally critical areas	Scenic areas Wilderness recreation areas Historic, archaeological, and cultural areas
Resource-production critical areas	Agricultural lands Water quality areas Mineral extraction areas
Natural-hazard critical areas	Flood-prone areas Fire hazard areas Geologic hazard areas Air pollution areas

thing, such as not to litter. Voluntary programs also involve nonprofit organizations engaged in conservation, cleanup, and protection activities.

Federal environmental laws significantly influence regional and community planning. For instance, the federal Clean Air Act requires the regional control of ozone, carbon monoxide, nitrogen dioxide, sulfur dioxide, lead, and particulate matter. These pollutants have serious health and welfare consequences. If an air quality control region fails to comply with federal air quality standards, then state and local transportation funding and plans can be affected. Federal flood control laws provide another example. Federal law requires local governments to adopt flood zones in order for buildings to qualify for federal flood insurance. Without such floodplain zoning, it becomes extremely difficult to build in a flood-prone area.

Environmental laws encompass many similar issues to air quality and flood protection that planners and urban designers need to address on a regular basis. This approach to environmental planning has a strong rule-making orientation. As planning educator Paul Niebanck (1993) noted, "Rules are everywhere and seem to cover everything: rules for disaggregating an issue; rules for selecting priorities; rules for measuring impacts; substantive rules; procedural rules; rules for discourse; rules for appeal; and so on." Critics observe that this approach contains a strong reliance on analysis that might lead to "analysis paralysis."

A contrary approach to environmental planning is based in *place making.* Whereas rule making has a strong legal and scientific orientation, place making has a stronger grounding in the environmental design arts. To achieve its maximum potential, environmental planning first needs rules to prevent harmful actions and to direct positive changes, and then creative interventions that result in healthier, more sustainable places.

A guiding principle for both rule making and place making is: first, do no harm. Understanding environmentally sensitive or critical areas is useful in preventing harmful actions. Environmentally sensitive areas can be defined as places vulnerable to negative environmental impact. These could include areas such as unstable soils, steep slopes, floodplains, wetlands, and vulnerable habitat. Areas can be defined as ecologically critical, perceptually and culturally critical, resource-production critical, and natural-hazard critical. On the local level, such an area may be used as a basis for a zoning district or an overlay zone that employs regulations specifically designed to protect that district.

SUSTAINABLE DEVELOPMENT

An emerging issue in environmental planning is sustainable development; that is, development that meets the needs of the present without compromising the ability of future generations to meet their own needs. Advocates of sustainable development argue that environmental concerns need to be balanced with social equity and economics. The intersection of these

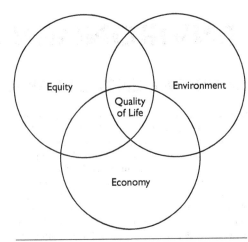

THREE-E DIAGRAM

Source: From A Region at Risk by Robert D. Yaro and Tony Hiss. Copyright © 1996 by Regional Plan Association. Reproduced with permission of Island Press, Washington, D.C.

three Es—equity, economics, and environment—is suggested to be where the quality of human life can be best obtained. Some planners include a fourth E. In the case of Burlington, Vermont, it is education; for others, it is ethics. In urban design, it might be esthetics because of the visual relationship of built form to equity, environmental, and economic concerns.

The concept that we should leave the planet a better place for subsequent generations provides one ethical argument for environmental planning. And there are other ethical and practical reasons:

- We depend on the environment for our survival, so we better take good care of it.
- We are not the only species on the planet, and we have a responsibility to protect the habitats of other creatures.
- We can reduce costs and enhance benefits by using resources effectively and through environmental protection.
- We will improve our health by ensuring that air, water, and soils are not polluted.

REFERENCES

McHarg, Ian. 1969. *Design with Nature.* Garden City, NY: Natural History Press. Inc.

Niebanck, Paul. 1993. "The Shape of Environmental Planning Education." *Environment and Planning B: Planning and Design.* 20:511–518.

Steiner, Frederick. 2000. *The Living Landscape: An Ecological Approach to Landscape Planning.* 2nd ed. New York:McGraw Hill.

Yaro, Robert and Tony Hiss. 1996. *Region at Risk: The Third Regional Plan for the New York-New Jersey-Connecticut Metropolitan Area.* Washington, DC: Island Press.

Frederick R. Steiner, Ph.D. FASLA, University of Texas at Austin

AIR

AIR QUALITY

NATIONAL AMBIENT AIR QUALITY STANDARDS CRITERIA POLLUTANTS

Air quality in the United States is measured by whether a region is in compliance with the National Ambient Air Quality Standards (NAAQS) for the six criteria area pollutants initially designated in the Clear Air Act Amendments of 1970: carbon monoxide, lead, nitrogen oxides, particulate matter, ozone, and sulfur dioxide.

Carbon Monoxide

Poisonous to humans, carbon monoxide (CO) is a colorless, odorless gas. Approximately 90 percent of it in the atmosphere is a by-product of vehicle emissions from internal combustion engines. Fatal in large enough doses where ventilation is lacking, carbon monoxide reduces the ability of the body's circulatory system to deliver oxygen. CO emissions increase when conditions are poor for combustion; thus, the highest CO levels tend to occur when the weather is very cold or at high elevations where there is less oxygen in the air to burn the fuel.

Lead

Lead (Pb) is a heavy metal. In the past, it came primarily from automotive emissions as an airborne pollutant, but since lead was phased out of U.S. fuels starting in 1973, atmospheric lead has been greatly reduced. Instead, stationary sources, such as lead smelters, peeling paint, and the production of storage batteries, have become the main sources. Lead poisoning of the bloodstream can result in development disabilities among children as well as cause cancer and neurological damage. In some urban areas, lead remains an issue due to remaining lead-based paint on older structures and past lead deposits in soils along highway corridors.

Nitrogen Oxides

Nitrogen oxides are a group of highly reactive gases that contain nitrogen and oxygen in varying amounts. Nitrogen dioxide (NO_2), the most common, can often be seen as a reddish-brown layer over many urban areas. It is a main ingredient in smog. When combined with water vapor, it forms nitric acid, which as precipitation is known as acid rain. Nitrogen oxides form when oxygen and nitrogen in the air react with each other during combustion. Primary sources are motor vehicles, electric utilities, and other industrial, commercial, and residential sources that burn fuels.

Particulate Matter

Particulates are microscopic particles that comprise dust, soot, smoke, and other airborne debris. PM-10 refers to particulate matter no more than 10 micrometers in diameter. PM-2.5 is particulate matter less than 2.5 microns in diameter and is referred to as PM-fine. Sources for particulate matter include smokestacks, fireplaces, open fires, blown dust on dirt roads, various manufacturing plants, and almost

all motor vehicles. Particulates produce haze, reducing visibility. Health threats include various respiratory ailments and nose and throat irritation. Particulates are a particular threat to those with existing respiratory ailments such as asthma.

Ozone

One of the most familiar criteria pollutants is ozone (O_3). Ground-level ozone is also commonly known as smog. This is different from stratospheric-level ozone, also known as the ozone layer, which serves to protect the planet from ultraviolet radiation from the sun. At ground level, ozone is produced by a combination of pollutants. Sources include cars, smokestacks, and various volatile organic chemicals from paints, solvents, and other industrial materials. The process of smog formation is accelerated by certain weather factors, such as heat and temperature inversions (where warm air is trapped near the ground instead of rising).

Sulfur Dioxide

Like nitrogen dioxide, sulfur dioxide (SO_2) is a component of acid precipitation when sulfur dioxide combines with airborne water vapor. The resulting mix can, over time, erode stone, metal, rubber, and plastic materials and structures. Sources include coal-fired electric generating plants, paper and metal factories, and gasoline-powered vehicles. Sulfur dioxide as a gas can also harm lungs and destroy plants by inhibiting photosynthesis.

AIR QUALITY STANDARDS

Criteria air pollutants are regulated based on health-based criteria (science-based guidelines), which are used as the basis for setting permissible levels. For each of these pollutants, the U.S. Environmental Protection Agency (U.S. EPA) has established primary standards to protect health and secondary standards to prevent environmental and property damage.

Attainment and Nonattainment Areas

An attainment area is a geographic area whose air has been determined through monitoring and modeling to have criteria pollutant levels below the primary standard. A nonattainment area is one whose air exceeds the primary standard for one or more criteria pollutants.

In the *Green Book,* maintained by the U.S. EPA's Office of Air and Radiation, Air Quality Planning and Standards Division, there are current data about areas of the United States that are in nonattainment for which criteria pollutants and the criteria behind current NAAQS standards. This publication also provides data on the areas of the country where air pollution levels persistently exceed the national ambient air quality standards.

Of the six criteria pollutants, ozone has been particularly important to monitor because it is the main component of smog and contributes to lung damage and respiratory problems.

Air Quality Index

The Air Quality Index (AQI) also provides information on pollution concentrations for the six criteria pollutants.

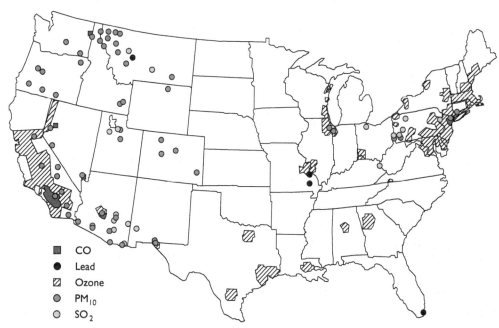

■ CO
● Lead
▨ Ozone
◉ PM-10
○ SO₂

Note: Incomplete data, not classified, and Section 185(A) areas are not shown. Ozone nonattainment areas are based on the one-hour ozone standard. PM-10 nonattainment areas on map are based on the existing PM-10 standards.

LOCATION OF NONATTAINMENT AREAS FOR CRITERIA POLLUTANTS, 2002

Source: U.S. EPA 2002.

Anthony J. Brazel, Arizona State University, Tempe, Arizona
Jay S. Golden, Arizona State University, Tempe, Arizona
James C. Schwab, American Planning Association, Chicago, Illinois

State and local agencies use the AQI for reporting daily air quality to the public. The AQI may be found in national print and broadcast media. It also serves as a basis for community-based programs that encourage the public to take action to reduce air pollution on days when levels are projected to be of concern.

AQI values for each of the pollutants are based on the concentration of that pollutant. The index is "normalized" across each pollutant so that, generally, an index value of 100 is set at the level of the short-term, health-based standard for that pollutant. The higher the index value, the greater the level of air pollution and health risk. The U.S. EPA has established six general AQI categories corresponding to different levels of health concern and index value ranges:

Good (0–50): Air quality is considered satisfactory. Air pollution poses little or no risk.

Moderate (51–100): Air quality is acceptable; however, for some pollutants, there may be a moderate health concern for a very small number of individuals. For example, people who are unusually sensitive to ozone may experience respiratory symptoms.

Unhealthy for Sensitive Groups (101–150): Certain groups of people may be particularly sensitive to the harmful effects of certain air pollutants, but the general public is not likely to be affected. For example, people with respiratory disease are at greater risk from exposure to ozone, while people with respiratory disease or heart disease are at greater risk from particulate matter.

Unhealthy (151–200): Everyone may begin to experience health effects. Members of sensitive groups may experience more serious health effects.

Very Unhealthy (201–300): Air quality in this range triggers a health alert, meaning everyone may experience more serious health effects.

Hazardous (over 300): Air quality in this range triggers health warnings of emergency conditions. The entire population is more likely to be affected.

TOXIC AIR POLLUTANTS

The 1990 Clean Air Act Amendments established a list of 189 toxic air pollutants for which the U.S. EPA must establish categories of sources for their release, such as auto body shops or coal-burning electric generation plants. The difference between these 189 toxic air pollutants and criteria pollutants is that the latter were targeted because they are the most common pollutants, while many of the toxic air pollutants are specific to certain industrial processes, such as various types of chemical plants, and thus are not common. They may still pose important public health issues, in particular local areas affected by sources emitting such hazardous air pollutants.

SOURCES OF AIR POLLUTION

Mobile Sources

Motor vehicles, engines, and equipment that moves or that can be moved from place to place, including cars, trucks, buses, earth-moving equipment, lawn and garden power tools, ships, railroad locomotives, and airplanes, are considered mobile sources of air pollution.

TYPES OF AIR POLLUTION EMISSION SOURCES

Source: U.S. EPA 2004.

Stationary Sources

Stationary sources include any place or object from which pollutants are released that does not move around. Stationary sources can be further defined as point, biogenic, and area sources. Point sources include factories and electric power plants; biogenic sources include trees and vegetation, gas seeps, and microbial activity; area sources consist of smaller stationary sources, such as dry cleaners and degreasing operations.

PLANNING ISSUES

Planning decisions routinely affect air quality in metropolitan areas. Traffic patterns resulting from the routing of highways and the development of transit systems that help to relieve congestion affect air quality by influencing the level of vehicle emissions. Decisions about the location and permitting of various stationary sources, such as industrial plants, also affect air quality. Increasing vegetative and forest cover through land-use regulations, incentives, and other means may help to mitigate regional air pollution problems.

More broadly, urban form dictates the shape of many transportation and other decisions that can affect air quality. The Washington State Department of Ecology has identified five characteristics of urban form that help reduce driving distances, increase use of alternative modes of transportation, and, as a result, positively influence air quality:

- Increasing neighborhood, development, or regional density
- Incorporating different land uses within a development or neighborhood
- Locating transit near high-density locations
- Encouraging pedestrian-friendly designs
- Centralizing or clustering activities within a metropolitan area and in relation to transit development

Metropolitan Planning Organizations

Metropolitan planning organizations (MPOs) are responsible for planning transportation projects meant to maintain their region's air quality or move toward attainment of federal air quality standards over time. There are 341 MPOs, and each has to develop a transportation plan containing three elements:

Regional Transportation Plan (RTP): RTPs have a 20-year planning horizon, and must be consistent with the state transportation plan and the state air quality improvement plan.

Transportation Improvement Plan (TIP): TIPs, which are updated at varying intervals, depending upon state requirements (typically between two to three years), and for varying planning horizons (typically six to seven years), must also be consistent with the state transportation plan and air quality plan. These plans include specific techniques and implementation actions to address air quality.

Individual Transportation Projects: Individual transportation projects include specific projects to be undertaken, such as roads, rail lines, and bus routes. To be considered for federal funding, these projects must be consistent with the state transportation plan, TIP, and air quality improvement plan. They also have to be listed in both the RTP and TIP.

State Implementation Plans

The U.S. EPA also requires states to submit State Implementation Plans (SIPs). These plans describe a state's strategy for achieving and maintaining the National Ambient Air Quality Standards. States with areas that do not meet the standards are required by the Clean Air Act to develop a written SIP outlining the steps they will take to reduce air pollution.

The purpose of a SIP is to ensure the implementation of programs that will reduce emissions. State environmental agencies prepare and submit a proposed SIP to the U.S. EPA that describes their plan, outlines air pollution reduction programs, contains projections of emission reductions from these programs, and commits to implement and enforce these programs. The SIP must also explain how funding and resources will be provided, and it must provide supporting technical information.

TOXICS RELEASE INVENTORY

An urban area's industrial base has potential impacts on local air quality. The Toxics Release Inventory (TRI) is a publicly available U.S. EPA database containing information on toxic chemical releases and other waste management activities reported annually by certain industry groups and federal facilities. This information is also available at the state and local levels.

REFERENCES

U.S. Environmental Protection Agency, Office of Air and Radiation, Air Quality Planning and Standards Division. *Green Book Nonattainment Areas for Criteria Pollutants.* http://www.epa.gov/oar/oaqps/greenbk/

Washington State Department of Ecology. 2003. *Focus on Linking Land Use, Air Quality, and Transportation Planning.*

See also:
Air Sheds
Federal Legislation
Transportation Plans

Anthony J. Brazel, Arizona State University, Tempe, Arizona
Jay S. Golden, Arizona State University, Tempe, Arizona
James C. Schwab, American Planning Association, Chicago, Illinois

AIR SHEDS

An air shed is a specified volume of air with similarities in climate, weather, and topography. Typically, it also shares issues of development, planning, or problems of air quality related to emissions, meteorology, and terrain. Air sheds are dynamic in geographic extent and volume; the volume of air that constitutes an air shed for any given period greatly depends on emissions, local/regional meteorology, and accepted regulations of health related to pollutants of concern to the community located within the air shed.

An air basin is often defined as a large land area containing one or more individually distinctive air sheds that generally has within it similar meteorological and geographical conditions. To the extent possible, an air basin is also defined along political boundary lines, including both the source and receptor areas of pollutants. For example, California is divided into 15 air basins, which contain many smaller individual air sheds.

In many ways, an air shed is similar to a watershed. It contains a "fluid," which in this case is the atmosphere; its geographical extent may be confined to a specific area; it may contain air contaminants concentrated more frequently in lower elevations due to inversions and air drainage; and, without major external weather effects from outside the air shed, it may be well identified through the analysis of digital terrain mapping, vertical profiling of the atmosphere, and local emission inventories.

However, unlike water, air can move upvalley or upslope in the terrain and spill into another nearby topographic basin. As a result, air shed dimensions and boundaries may be highly variable geographically and over time of day, year, and from year to year.

CONDITIONS WITHIN AN AIR SHED

The vertical mixing potential of air over a day varies considerably. As the sun heats the Earth's surface and causes air to rise over an increasing volume of air above the surface, the volume of air carrying pollutants expands accordingly. This expanded volume may cause the pollutants to be diffused over a larger zone than may occur at night when the Earth cools, the lower atmosphere contracts, inversions set in, and more local diffusion or confinement of pollutants occurs over a smaller zone both vertically and horizontally. Thus, the air shed relative to a particular pollutant may expand and contract even within a day's time.

Movement of air within an air shed is often characterized from weather stations with the aid of wind "roses," which describe the frequency of wind direction at any location for any time of day or year and the speeds associated with those directions.

Air shed analysts keep close tabs on the vertical mixing potential by using air-sampling devices to measure the vertical dimension of the atmosphere, which includes factors such as temperature, wind velocity, wind speed, humidity, and pressure. Models and monitoring systems are used to predict diffusion and concentration, and to monitor air quality.

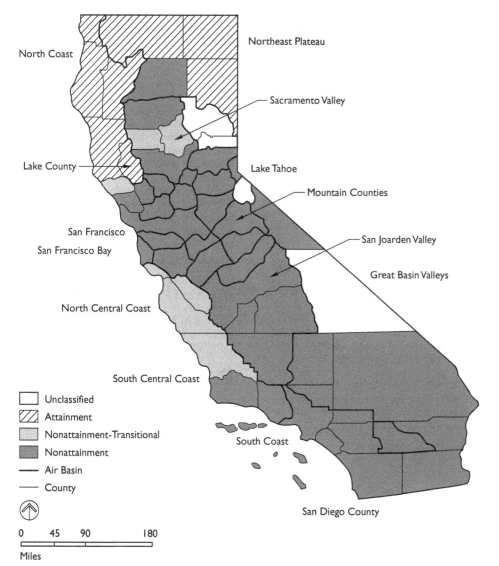

The area designations for ambient air quality standards are a combination of local air sheds and political boundaries.

AREA DESIGNATIONS FOR CALIFORNIA AMBIENT AIR QUALITY STANDARDS FOR OZONE

Source: California Air Resources Board.

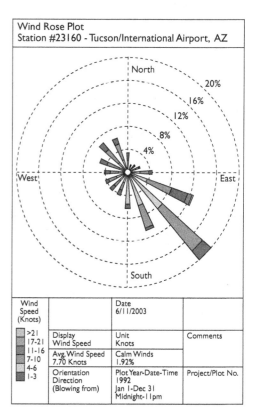

Wind rose was created using WRPLOT View 5.5, by Lakes Environmental Software, for the Tucson area. Wind speeds are classified in knots (nautical miles per hour) intervals, which are colored-coded, and by 16 wind direction categories. Length of partial and whole bar segments indicate percent frequency of wind from that direction.

SAMPLE WIND ROSE, TUCSON, ARIZONA

Source: U.S. Department of Energy 2003.

Anthony J. Brazel, Arizona State University, Tempe, Arizona
Jay S. Golden, Arizona State University, Tempe, Arizona

SCALE OF AN AIR SHED

The penultimate air shed is the entire three-dimensional spherical shell of air surrounding the Earth. It is essential to analyze this dimension to facilitate the understanding and mitigation of gases, such as carbon dioxide (CO_2), major continental emissions of sulfur dioxide (SO_2), diffusion into the upper atmosphere of chlorofluorocarbons (CFCs) that affect global ozone (O_3), and massive emissions of particulates from continents to oceans or to other continents from dust emissions and industrialization processes. These global-to-regional interconnections must be kept in mind when addressing certain environmental problems, such as how long-range transport of pollutants might explain local pollutant events. Modeling of global and regional atmospheric processes over geographical areas larger than the immediate confines of any particular air shed may be required. These scales and levels of air sheds/air basins are common across countries, hence protocols for modeling these processes, such as the Kyoto Protocol, have to be developed at high governmental levels.

AIR TRAJECTORY ANALYSIS

Although at first glance an area demarked initially by terrain characteristics (e.g., a small valley) may provide a definition of an air shed, on a regional-to-local scale, a planner or analyst may also have to consider external forces that can affect the local area, thus often accepting an expanded view of the local air shed in air quality assessments. One way this is done is with an "air trajectory analysis," whereby the analyst tries to determine where the air and its concentrations of various pollutants came from over many days preceding an important period of concern about pollutant levels exceeding a standard or a series of such excesses.

An excellent example is the air trajectory pollution climatology of the Lake Champlain Basin of eastern Canada and the United States. The local air shed does not necessarily have fixed geographical boundaries. In fact, those boundaries can vary over the seasons and years. The local air shed also may be characterized by upwind meteorology, meaning that it can suffer pollution from regional sources that affect the basin downwind. Thus, regional air sheds of varying sizes are determined for SO_2, volatile organic compounds (VOCs), and nitrogen oxide (NOx) emissions, based on probabilities of occurrence, in a more holistic view of regional-to-local variability of source regions, emissions, and regional-to-local meteorology.

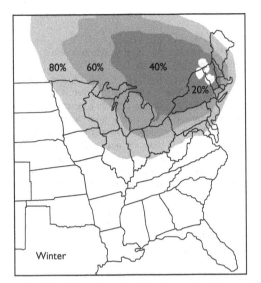
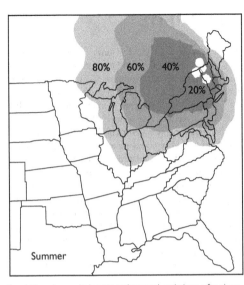

Regional air sheds are based on air trajectory climatology analysis of variations in upwind meteorology and emissions of various selected pollutants. Local data should be collected and analyzed to define local air sheds.

SEASONAL VARIATIONS IN PROBABILISTIC LAKE CHAMPLAIN, NEW YORK, AIR SHED

Reprinted courtesy of American Geophysical Union.

PLANNING AND AIR SHEDS

When considering a particular air shed, planners, air quality analysts, and policy makers, among others, often face many methodological, scientific, and managerial issues, which typically require the formation of local alliances or stakeholder affiliations in order to fully comprehend them. For example, Our Airshed is a partnership covering approximately 2,700 square miles (4,500 square kilometers), including various communities and a park, near Edmonton, Alberta. Such alliances assist in developing management plans, focusing on problems, and ultimately identifying possible air quality and sustainability solutions.

From the planning perspective, considerations often range from producing fast-track fixes to preventing deleterious possibilities of air quality in a proactive way so as to carefully address the future quality of life and health of the populace. The focus must become the "nonattainment" area, other critical parts of the area, or the whole air shed. Environmentally related management plans for communities and regions are multifaceted, often comprising many issues that have to be considered together to produce solutions, such as factors related to biological, land resource, recreation, water, and, certainly, air resources. Each of these areas is challenging, and conflicts often arise among planners in attempting to find solutions.

In addressing air issues, each area plan should attempt to identify those of local and regional concern that affect health, while considering, to as great a degree as possible, the larger regional issues, such as greenhouse gas impacts on the local region and long-range transport of pollutants that affect the local area. These plans must also develop an appreciation for future development scenarios in the region and account for them in the plan.

REFERENCE

Poirot, Rich, et al. 1999. "Air Trajectory Pollution Climatology for Lake Champlain Basin," in *Lake Champlain in Transition: From Research Toward Restoration*. Thomas O. Manley and Patricia L. Manley, eds. Washington, DC: American Geophysical Union.

See also:
Air Quality
Federal Legislation
Heat Islands

Anthony J. Brazel, Arizona State University, Tempe, Arizona
Jay S. Golden, Arizona State University, Tempe, Arizona

HEAT ISLANDS

Dark roofs and paving materials absorb more of the sun's rays than vegetation, causing both surface temperature and overall ambient air temperature in urban areas to rise. This phenomenon is called the *urban heat island effect.* Trees and other vegetation naturally process solar radiation and help reduce ambient air temperatures through evapotranspiration—when water absorbed by vegetation evaporates from leaves and surrounding soil, naturally cooling the surrounding air. When vegetation is removed and replaced by urban development, temperatures can increase noticeably. Areas of the United States with a hot, arid microclimate, such as Phoenix, Arizona, are particularly affected adversely by the heat island effect. Annual temperatures, rainfall, and wind regimes all are factors in urban heat island formation.

REASONS HEAT ISLAND OCCUR

Most urban building materials are watertight, so moisture is not readily available to dissipate the sun's heat through evaporation. Temperatures of unshaded, impermeable surfaces can reach up to 190°F (88°C) during the day, while vegetated surfaces with moist soil might reach only 70°F (18°C). Also, urban areas trap more of the sun's energy due to the use of dark materials and the canyonlike configurations of buildings and pavement. Anthropogenic (human-produced) heat, slower wind speeds, and air pollution in urban areas can also contribute to heat island formation.

The increased surface temperatures in the urban environment lead to increased air temperatures, especially at night, as urban surfaces cool slowly and warm the air around them. The warming effects of the heat island are most pronounced during calm, clear weather conditions, and are most conspicuous during summer and winter. In most communities, the negative effects of the summer heat island include increased discomfort, a rise in the incidence of human health problems, higher energy bills, and stress on vegetation. In contrast, in colder areas at higher latitudes and elevations, the winter warming effects of the heat island can be somewhat beneficial.

HEALTH AND COST IMPLICATIONS

Research by the Lawrence Berkeley National Laboratory (LBNL) in Berkeley, California, indicates that on summer days in Los Angeles, a one-degree Fahrenheit temperature increase boosts the risk of smog formation by 3 percent. Smog, or ground-level ozone (as opposed to the atmospheric ozone that protects the Earth from ultraviolet radiation) is an invisible pollutant that can permanently damage lungs. Chronic bronchitis, asthma, and other cardiopulmonary disorders may be caused or exacerbated by ground-level ozone.

There are also noticeable cost implications. The same one-degree increase in Los Angeles is estimated to increase the demand for cooling power by 2 percent, which translates to about $25 million worth of electricity every year over the entire city. In addition, metropolitan areas can lose federal transportation dollars if their states do not provide the U.S. Environmental Protection Agency (U.S. EPA) with an acceptable State Implementation Plan (SIP) to ensure compliance with U.S. EPA air quality standards for ozone.

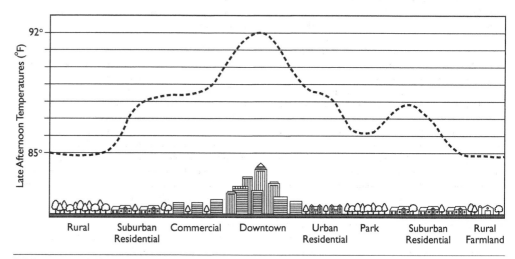

URBAN HEAT ISLAND PROFILE

Source: U.S. EPA.

LAND COVER ANALYSIS

To develop a heat island mitigation strategy, it is important to understand the relationship between land cover types and the formation of urban heat islands. Remote sensing data from satellites and aircraft can provide infrared images from which surface temperatures can be derived and associated with land cover and land-use classes.

In infrared images, warmer areas appear bright or white, and cooler areas appear dark, from gray to black. Brighter areas are often roofs and paved surfaces. Darker areas are primarily vegetation and highly reflective light roofs. Infrared satellite data at approximately 100-foot (30-meter) and coarser resolutions are available for all areas of the United States. By using these data, urban areas can be analyzed for hot spots in terms of their land cover or whatever elements exist on the land (e.g., forest, grass, concrete, asphalt, buildings and water). The spatial and temporal resolution of the imagery will influence the depth of possible analysis.

Based on a preliminary analysis of major land cover types in four cities—Atlanta, Georgia; Baton Rouge, Louisiana; Salt Lake City, Utah; and Sacramento, California—that were part of the joint NASA and U.S. EPA Urban Heat Island Pilot Project, conducted in 1998, surface temperatures by land cover type may be generalized from hottest to coldest, as follows:

- Dark roofs
- Roads and parking areas (dark asphalt is warmer than concrete, and aged asphalt is similar to concrete)
- Grass and other vegetation
- Forest
- Water

Planners, urban designers, urban foresters, and others can use remotely sensed data to identify hot spot areas and then develop appropriate urban heat island mitigation strategies.

MITIGATION STRATEGIES

Successful urban heat island mitigation strategies require community participation and acceptance. The identification of stakeholders and partners as early as possible will facilitate development and implementation of strategies.

As the connection between higher temperatures in urban areas and poor air quality continues to be realized, strategies such as using more reflective building materials and tree planting designs to reduce surface temperatures are becoming more popular. Continuing research indicates such strategies can improve air quality, promote energy savings, and produce the added benefit of increasing the livability of urban environments.

Local climate has a significant connection to the overall benefits that can be expected from urban heat island mitigation strategies. For example, areas with cooler mean temperatures and more cloudy days, as in the Pacific Northwest, would likely have less energy savings compared to the southwestern United States with its reduced cloud cover and rain and higher summertime temperatures. Also, the effect of sea breezes in dispersing pollutants may affect potential air quality benefits. Finally, trade-offs between roofing types and insulation may also be influenced by the local climate.

Reflective Roofs

When the sun shines on buildings with dark-colored roofs, most of the heat absorbed by the roof is transferred inside, which causes a number of adverse impacts: the demand for air conditioning increases; energy usage and costs are higher; and the roof materials deteriorate more rapidly. More than 90 percent of the roofs in the United States reach summer peak temperatures of 150°F (66° C) to 190°F (88° C). Materials commonly used in commercial property roofing include ethylene propylene diene monomer (EPDM), a type of rubber, and asphalt and tar with a gravel base.

Roofs with these materials have been found to be hot spots of surface heating in all four cities studied

Maury G. Estes, Jr., AICP, USRA, Huntsville, Alabama

in the Urban Heat Island Pilot Project. By putting a lighter-colored material on the roof, such as river rock, the roof becomes cooler, primarily because it is more reflective. The insulating capability depends upon the thermal conductivity of the rock material; that is, the amount of energy absorbed by the rock that is then conducted to the roof.

Depending on the slope of a building's roof, two categories of roofing materials are available for use. Low-sloped roofs, with slopes of 2:12 or less (less than 2 inches of rise over 12 inches of run), are most commonly found on commercial and industrial buildings and can be covered with cool roof coatings or single-ply materials. Many cool, low-slope products are available, primarily white; however, manufacturers are working toward providing highly reflective, colored products for low-slope roofs.

Sloped roofs with more than 2 inches of rise per 12 inches of run are found mostly on houses and small commercial buildings. They are generally covered with clay or concrete tiles, metal roofing, shingles, or shakes. Cool roof products available for sloped roofs are much more limited, which includes the majority of the residential market, where aesthetic considerations become more important as well. The U.S. EPA's Energy Star Program and the Cool Roof Rating Council are two sources of additional information on cool roofing products.

Green Roofs

Cooler roofs can also be achieved by innovative rooftop design, which can also provide aesthetically pleasing and functional places. One design alternative is the so-called green roof, a combination of vegetation, hydrology, and architecture. Originally conceived in Iceland, where sod roofs and walls have been used for centuries, modern green roof technology was developed more than 30 years ago in Germany, and today it is a popular approach throughout Europe. Such roofs consist of several layers of protective materials, including a waterproof membrane at the base, a root barrier, an optional insulation layer, drainage layers, a filter fabric for fine soils, the growing medium, and the plant material. These systems are not designed for the weight of people or trees. However, they can be installed on roofs with slopes up to 33 percent.

Rooftop Gardens

In contrast to green roofs, rooftop gardens are more elaborately designed landscapes intended for human interaction and are engineered to conform to heavier load requirements. The City of Chicago, for example, has installed a rooftop garden on top of City Hall. The city also has plans to install gardens on other city ward buildings and buildings along elevated public transit routes.

Trees and Shading

Planting trees to shield buildings from the sun's rays can reduce the amount of heat buildings absorb. Within 10 to 15 years—the time it takes a tree to grow to a significant size—strategically placed trees can reduce heating and cooling costs for a typical home or office by an average of 10 to 20 percent.

Trees and vegetation are most useful when planted in strategic locations around buildings. Researchers have found that planting deciduous species to the west and east is typically most effective for cooling buildings, especially if these trees shade windows and part of the building's roof. Planting deciduous trees to the south may reap the benefits of solar energy in the winter, when the sun is low in the sky, because these trees shed their leaves in winter, allowing sunlight and warmth through. Conversely, planting evergreen species to the north is one approach to impede winter winds (Nowak and Dwyer 2000).

Shading pavements in parking lots and streets is also an effective way to cool and beautify urban areas. Trees can be planted around the perimeters or in medians inside parking lots or along streets. Some communities have enacted ordinances requiring street and parking lot planting. Generally, increased shading will make urban areas more comfortable and healthy for people.

Additional benefits from trees include reductions in stormwater runoff, erosion, and urban noise.

Paving Materials

Roads, parking lots, and driveways paved with dark impervious materials contribute to the urban heat island effect. Most paved surfaces in an urban area are asphalt or concrete. While dark new asphalt has a lower reflectivity and higher surface temperature than new concrete, as both surfaces age, the differences in reflectivity become significantly smaller. Additives can also be used with either surface to increase reflectivity and give planners a range of potential heat island mitigation options.

One technique, Ultra-Thin Whitetopping, can be used on roads and parking lots to reduce maintenance costs and cool surfaces. This process removes the outer several inches of deteriorated asphalt and tops the remaining asphalt with a concrete mold 2 to 4 inches thick. Key design elements include adequate pavement thickness, concrete strength, drainage, and jointing.

Porous pavement, an alternative for parking areas, tennis courts, pool decks, greenhouse floors, and patios, both reduces runoff and cools surfaces. It allows airflow and moisture to penetrate the paved surface, producing a cooler surface than impervious paving materials. Porous pavements can consist of concrete, asphalt, open-celled stones, and gravel mixed to create an open-cell structure allowing for the passage of air and water. Water is allowed to filter through the concrete layer and recharge groundwater sources, thereby reducing runoff volume and velocity.

Development Patterns

A study by Stone and Rodgers (2001) focused on the relationship between residential development patterns and urban heat island formation in the Atlanta, Georgia, area. While acknowledging that further work must be done to establish the significance between urban design decisions and heat island formation in different climactic areas, the authors found for the Atlanta area that lower-density housing patterns contribute more radiant heat to surface heat island formation than higher-density development. The amount of land dedicated to residential lawns and landscape planting in areas of one-half- to three-acre lots emitted higher net thermal emissions than areas with one-eighth- to one-half-acre lots. Compact moderate to high-density new construction, along with area-based tree ordinances, are recommended as policy strategies to mitigate the effects of development on regional climate change.

REFERENCES

Nowak, D. J., and J. F. Dwyer. 2000. "Understanding the Benefits and Costs of Urban Forest Ecosystems." In *Handbook of Urban and Community Forestry in the Northeast.* J. E. Kuser, ed. New York: Kluwer Academic/Plenum Publishers.

Stone, Brian Jr., and Michael O. Rodgers. 2001. "Urban Form and Thermal Efficiency: How the Design of Cities Influences the Urban Heat Island Effect." *Journal of the American Planning Association.* 67, no. 2: 186-198.

See also:
Air Quality
Remote Sensing and Satellite Image Classification

Maury G. Estes, Jr., AICP, USRA, Huntsville, Alabama

WATER

HYDROLOGIC CYCLE

The hydrologic cycle describes the movement of water about the Earth. Its components include precipitation, evapotranspiration, surface runoff, recharge, groundwater flow, and discharge back into lakes and oceans.

Precipitation

Precipitation includes rainfall, snowfall, and hail. The annual amounts, temporal distribution, and intensity of precipitation vary geographically. A significant portion of annual precipitation returns to the atmosphere through evaporation and transpiration.

Evapotranspiration

Evaporation occurs on land and water surfaces. Transpiration, from plants, also returns water to the atmosphere. Together these phenomena are called evapotranspiration. Evapotranspiration may recycle as much as 50 percent of precipitation back to the atmosphere and—more in arid environments. The water not recycled, the net precipitation, replenishes streams, lakes, wetlands, groundwater supplies, and, ultimately, the ocean.

Surface Runoff

Surface runoff is precipitation that runs off the land's surface and flows downhill. Precipitation, soil type, slope, and vegetation all influence the amount of surface runoff. Areas with low-permeability soils, steep slopes, and sparse vegetation may have more than 90 percent of net precipitation flow as surface runoff.

Recharge

Recharge refers to water that infiltrates the lands' surface and percolates downward to the underlying water table, the upper surface of groundwater. Areas with high-permeability soils, minimal slope, and sparse vegetation have the highest recharge rates.

Groundwater

Groundwater is water present in saturated ground, where all the pore spaces are completely filled with water. Groundwater moves slowly, commonly less than one foot per day, and moves down-gradient from higher to lower water table elevations. Ultimately, groundwater discharges to streams, lakes, wetlands, or the ocean. This discharge is called base flow, and it is important to many ecosystems.

POTENTIAL IMPACT FROM DEVELOPMENT

Planners and urban designers must incorporate their knowledge of the hydrologic cycle into their work to protect the wide range of water resources that depend upon the cycle. Land development commonly disrupts the hydrologic cycle and can result in significant environmental damage.

Impervious Surfaces

Impervious surfaces, such as parking lots, roads, and rooftops, preclude the infiltration of precipitation into soils and can significantly reduce groundwater recharge, subsequently lowering the water table, depleting groundwater supplies, and reducing ecologically important base flow to streams and wetlands. Some commercial land uses, such as shopping malls, can render 90 percent or more of the lands' surface impervious through structures and paving for parking, causing a notable reduction in recharge rates.

Impervious surfaces increase surface runoff rates, sometimes causing flooding to down-gradient properties and inhabitants. Flood control structures, such as detention basins, attempt to mitigate this problem by slowing the flow of surface runoff. These structures do not commonly restore natural recharge rates, however. Better methods to manage stormwater include constructed wetlands and infiltration basins, which replenish the underlying groundwater system.

Water Extraction

Water extraction from both groundwater and surface water supplies also can disrupt the hydrologic cycle,

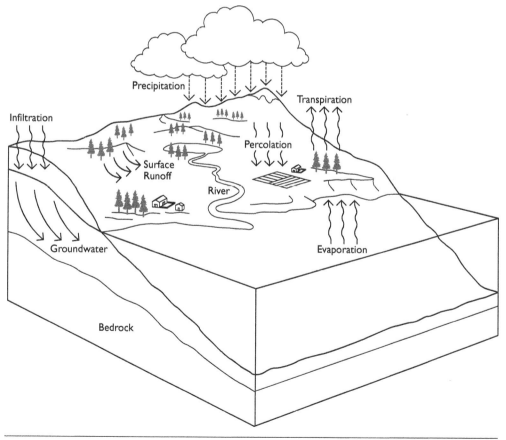

HYDROLOGIC CYCLE
Source: Horsley Witten Group.

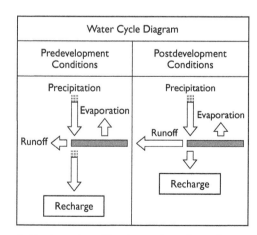

Postdevelopment conditions increase impervious surfaces and surface runoff while decreasing infiltration and recharge.

WATER CYCLE DIAGRAM
Source: Horsley Witten Group.

Scott W. Horsley, Horsley Witten Group, Sandwich, Massachusetts

causing environmental impacts. For example, pumping a water supply or irrigation well will cause both short-term and long-term declines in the water table. Unless the water is returned back to the groundwater system, long-term negative effects, including wetland losses, diminished stream flows, and depleted aquifers, will result.

MANAGEMENT TECHNIQUES

Guidelines have been developed to minimize and, in some cases, eliminate impacts to the hydrologic cycle. Flood control is the most common technique applied to land-use plans and development. Many local regulations require that postdevelopment peak flow of surface runoff be managed so that it will not exceed predevelopment peak flow runoff rates. This reduces the potential of negative effects of flooding to downstream properties. The 10-, 25-, and 100-year storm events are commonly used as benchmarks for this. Peak flows are typically managed using detention basins, which temporarily store the stormwater and slowly release it following the storm event.

A less commonly applied technique is to require that predevelopment or natural recharge rates be maintained in postdevelopment. This technique maintains groundwater reserves and base flows to downgrade streams, ponds, and wetlands. Recharge is accomplished through minimizing impervious surfaces and stormwater infiltration. Pretreatment of stormwater should be required prior to infiltration to protect water quality.

Integrated Water Management

Integrated water management is an evolving approach for integrating three infrastructure elements that historically have been addressed through independent planning processes: wastewater, stormwater, and water supply. Wastewater projects have traditionally focused on collecting wastewater in sewers, treating it, and disposing of it. This results in a hydrologic shift, where water is transferred to another watershed basin. This can result in a loss of water in aquifers and watersheds. Integrated water management seeks to balance the hydrologic cycle before returning the traded wastewater to the on-site basin, thereby replenishing water supplies. In this way, wastewater management can also be used to manage and maintain water supplies.

Innovative stormwater programs replenish water supply by collecting surface runoff, treating it, and infiltrating it back into aquifers. In some cases, stormwater infiltration systems can be designed to enhance natural recharge rates to compensate for other consumption losses in the aquifer or basin.

See also:
Aquifers
Stormwater Runoff and Recharge
Wastewater
Water Supply
Watersheds

Scott W. Horsley, Horsley Witten Group, Sandwich, Massachusetts

WATERSHEDS

A watershed is the land area that contributes surface water to given location. A watershed is defined and delineated by surface topography. Water that falls on one side of a given ridge ultimately drains to a given location; this process defines the watershed boundary.

Although no standard watershed size exists, watershed management programs are often designed and implemented in direct response to the size of a watershed. Regulatory agencies, environmental organizations, and planners increasingly are evaluating and integrating water resources planning at the "watershed scale."

WATERSHED SCALE TERMS

Defining what constitutes the watershed scale depends upon various factors, such as geographic location and overall planning objectives. Five common terms are used to help planners describe watershed scale and adjust management programs accordingly. (Note: These terms are all based upon U.S. practice; watersheds may be defined by a different set of terms in different countries.)

Basin. A basin typically defines a major river, estuary, or lake drainage area that covers several thousand square miles. It may cover major portions of a state or group of states.

Subbasin. A subbasin is smaller in area than a basin, ranging from several hundred square miles in area.

Watershed. A subbasin is composed of a set of even smaller watersheds, usually in the range of tens to a few hundred square miles.

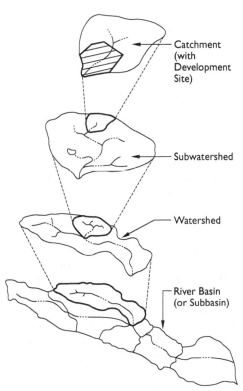

Catchment (with Development Site)

Subwatershed

Watershed

River Basin (or Subbasin)

A local watershed may have dozens of individual subwatersheds within its boundaries. A watershed plan tracks the planning and management within individual subwatersheds.

WATERSHED MANAGEMENT UNITS

Source: Adapted from Clements, et al. 1996 with permission from the Water Environment Research Foundation.

Richard Claytor, PE, Horsley Witten Group, Sandwich, Massachusetts

Subwatersheds. A watershed is composed of subwatersheds typically ranging in size from a few to several square miles. They are often defined as the land area above the confluence of two second-order streams.

Catchment area. Subwatersheds are composed of a group of catchment areas. They are usually measured in acres and can be defined as the land area above a given point that drains to the first intersection of a stream.

WATERSHED CHARACTERIZATION

Watershed planning involves a characterization of baseline conditions to establish the foundation of the plan development.

Impervious Cover Characterization

Urbanization has a measurable and quantifiable impact on surface water hydrology, morphology, quality, and ecology (Horner et al. 1996). This impact can be used to help develop watershed protection and restoration plans. A simple model that depicts current and future water resource quality as a function of increasing impervious cover can predict the relationship between impervious cover and watershed quality.

Impervious cover evaluation is typically used to help define the intensity of land uses and provide an overall estimate of water resource health. Three broad classifications—low, moderate, and high—can be used to assess the potential for watershed restoration and provide a baseline for watershed protection.

At relatively low levels of impervious cover, receiving water characteristics are typically of the highest quality and support the most sensitive aquatic species, with the presence of abundant species indicating diversity. Watershed plans should strive to protect these conditions. At moderate levels of impervious cover, receiving water characteristics begin to exhibit measurable and quantifiable degradation, but

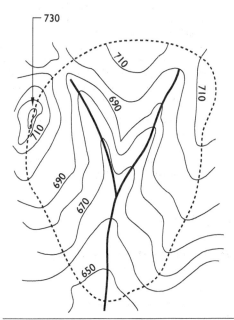

SIMPLISTIC MANAGEMENT DEFINITION

Source: U.S. EPA, 1994.

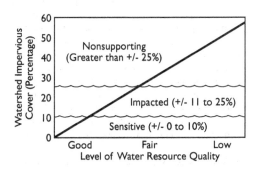

RELATIONSHIP BETWEEN IMPERVIOUS COVER AND WATERSHED QUALITY

Source: Center for Watershed Protection, 2003.

still maintain some of the beneficial uses. At relatively high levels of development, where impervious cover begins to exceed approximately a quarter of the watershed, receiving water characteristics show few beneficial uses and exhibit many of the effects of water runoff from impervious surfaces, including increased flooding, extremely poor water quality, highly altered morphology, and little aquatic habitat.

Although the impervious cover model is a powerful tool, there are assumptions and limitations that must be clearly understood. Prior human activities may have caused severe, long-term impacts on streams with relative low levels of impervious cover. Unusual geologic conditions may allow some streams to maintain unique aquatic diversity, even with modest impervious cover. The impacts of impervious cover are generally most noticeable on small streams and rivers. As watersheds grow in size to the subbasin level, the effects of other land uses, pollution sources and disturbances, and unique geologic settings may dominate the quality and dynamics of these systems.

Alternative Receiving Waters

Receiving waters include rivers, streams, lakes, oceans, reservoirs, aquifers, or other watercourses that receive water input. The type of receiving water to which a watershed drains dictates many aspects of a watershed plan. For streams, channel morphology, water quality, riparian cover, and temperature are generally the variables most notable in the watershed planning process. For freshwater lakes and reservoirs, phosphorus loading, sediment inputs, bacterial loading, and shoreline erosion dominate the variables list. In coastal systems, nitrogen, pathogens, and viruses are key parameters to assess and manage. Finally, where groundwater aquifer protection is a concern, recharge rates, soluble pollutants, pathogen inputs, and the connection between surface activities and groundwater, particularly where groundwater is the primary source for potable drinking water supplies, are all important factors.

WATERSHED MAPPING AND MODELING METHODS

Many complex tools exist to allow planners to develop watershed maps. These include the latest GIS technologies, many of which are available online. The key is to know how to integrate data, models, and mapping with watershed plan objectives.

Skill and experience are valuable in integrating data accuracy, ease of adaptation, and data collection time with key variables needed for watershed planning and protection. For example, if a municipality does not maintain updated maps of the storm drainage network, the planner must evaluate the cost of securing that information, including the cost of data manipulation and conversion, with the need to know where storm drainage outfalls exist and which land uses drain to which locations. In most watershed plan scenarios, storm drainpipe locations are vital to developing an effective plan, so the planner must weigh the techniques and costs of accurate, somewhat accurate, or general information. General accuracy levels include:

- detailed surveys: accuracy to within centimeters;
- global positioning systems (GPS) data: accuracy to within a meter;
- aerial photogrammetry: accuracy depends on several factors; and
- compilation of paper maps: accuracy depends on several factors.

Models are valuable watershed planning tools. A model has been developed for almost every situation. The keys to a model's success are the resources, skills, budget, and audience of the watershed plan. Sometimes complex models are warranted, particularly to defend a regulation that might be subject to legal challenges. The complexity of the model depends on the situation. The most important rules of modeling are verification of results, usually through the collection of monitoring data, and calibration of variables where predictive results are needed. One resource for evaluating the different models typically used in watershed planning is in Shoemaker (1997).

WATERSHED MANAGEMENT STRATEGIES

Watershed planning and management applies an integrated approach that involves people with a wide range of skills, interests, backgrounds, and experience from a broad cross section of professions. The most successful watershed management programs are implemented with both public and private involvement. Many view the watershed approach as the most comprehensive way to solve complex problems that affect receiving water resources.

An extremely wide array of watershed management strategies and techniques have been employed in watershed planning activities across the country. A detailed examination of these techniques is beyond the scope of this text, but planners and watershed managers should know these techniques exist and that adaptations have been applied in the broad spectrum of watershed planning in both protection and restoration plans and in the vast array of receiving waters.

Watershed plans are often developed as either protective plans, to maintain the current qualities of a watershed, or as restorative plans that planners need to implement to correct past abuses and to attain an improvement in water resource quality. In many cases, and particularly in coastal areas, watershed plans must tackle both protection of existing resources and restoration.

Watershed Protection

The Center for Watershed Protection, a national nonprofit watershed research organization, has advanced eight tools for use in the watershed protection arena (Center for Watershed Protection 1998). This broad classification system identifies eight major management areas that roughly correspond to the stages of the development cycle, from land-use planning and zoning and site design to construction and ownership.

Watershed planning. This is broadly defined as a suite of zoning and land-use management techniques applied to help align compatible land uses with resource quality.

Land conservation. This encompasses the choices and methods for preserving land in its natural condition.

Aquatic buffer. Establishing an aquatic buffer involves alternative approaches to protecting stream, shoreline, and wetland riparian corridor areas.

Site design. Lower-impact development techniques can minimize runoff and maximize on-site infiltration of precipitation.

Erosion and sedimentation control. This involves a suite of practices and construction behaviors oriented toward minimizing erosion and maximizing capture of sediment on-site.

Stormwater best management practices (BMPs). Stormwater BMPs involves a suite of practices and behaviors that manage and treat runoff after the construction cycle is complete.

Nonstormwater discharges. Also called *illicit discharge management*, this encompasses the identification, control, and management of pollutants entering the environment from failed wastewater systems (both on-site and municipal), inappropriate or illicit connections to the drainage system, and control of pollutants from household and industrial products.

Watershed stewardship. Identifies the myriad programs, outreach, and involvement of citizens and watershed activists who participate in "green-up" days, tree planting events, and habitat-enhancement workshops.

Watershed Restoration

Watershed restoration involves adapting watershed protection tools to address the often unique situation in restoration areas. Many of the watershed protection tools will serve as restoration tools with specific modifications, most notably the last four listed above. Four prominent restoration strategies are listed here:

Environmental site assessments and remediation. Many existing sites have prior contamination of soils and groundwater. This tool describes the approaches and methods to identify both natural systems and synthetic contamination remediation methods.

Preservation of natural area remnants. Unlike new development areas, restoration watersheds often have only fragmented remnants of natural systems. Planners must balance preservation or restoration with other competing uses, such as infill and redevelopment near existing infrastructure and transit, which are often linked to smart growth initiatives.

Restoration of impaired aquatic systems. Such restoration encompasses the broad spectrum of management techniques in the stream restoration arena, including habitat restoration, natural stream geomorphic design, stream daylighting, aquatic corridor replanting and revitalization, and wetlands restoration.

Reuse and adaptation of existing buildings and infrastructure. Reuse and adaptation are key components of watershed restoration, where existing buildings, parking lots, and other infrastructure are reused, improved, and updated to provide a net improvement beyond existing conditions.

REFERENCES

Center for Watershed Protection. 1998. *Rapid Watershed Planning Handbook: A Comprehensive Guide for Managing Urbanizing Watersheds.* Ellicott City, MD: Center for Watershed Protection.

Center for Watershed Protection. 2003. *Impacts of Impervious Cover on Aquatic Systems.* Ellicott City, MD: Center for Watershed Protection.

Clements, et al. 1996. *Framework for a Watershed Management Program.* Alexandria, VA: Water Environment Research Foundation.

Horner, Richard R., Derek B. Booth, Amanda Azous, and Christopher W. May. 1996. "Watershed Determinants of Freshwater Ecosystem Character and Functioning: Results of 10 Years of Research in the Puget Sound Region." In *Effects of Watershed Development and Management on Aquatic Ecosystems.* L.A. Roesner, ed. Snowbird, UT: ASCE Engineering Foundation.

Shoemaker, L., M. Lahlou, M. Bryer, D. Kumar, and K. Kratt. 1997. *Compendium of Tools for Watershed Assessment and TMDL Development.* EPA 841-B-97-006. Washington, DC: Tetra Tech, Inc. and U.S. EPA Office of Wetlands, Oceans, and Watersheds.

See also:
Erosion and Sedimentation
Flood Hazards
Floodplains and Riparian Corridors
Mapping
Regions

WATERSHED SCALE AND TYPICAL MANAGEMENT PRIORITIES

WATERSHED MANAGEMENT UNIT	TYPICAL DRAINAGE AREA (SQUARE MILES)	TYPICAL MANAGEMENT STRATEGIES
Basin	1,000–10,000	Basin planning—broad nutrient reduction goals
Subbasin	100–1,000	Basin planning—broad goal refined based on unique geologic or terrain characteristics
Watershed	10–100	Watershed planning—specific goals based on intensity of development and current water resource health
Subwatershed	1–10	Stream/water body classification and specific management strategies
Catchment	.05–.5	Specific criteria for site designs, including best management practices

Source: Center for Watershed Protection, Rapid Watershed Planning Handbook, 1998.

Richard Claytor, PE, Horsley Witten Group, Sandwich, Massachusetts

AQUIFERS

Aquifers are subsurface areas that hold groundwater and from which significant quantities of groundwater can be extracted. There are three main types of aquifers: sand and gravel, fractured rock, and limestone or karst formations.

CONFINED AND UNCONFINED AQUIFERS

Aquifers can be either unconfined or confined. Unconfined aquifers occur where the groundwater system is contained in permeable materials that extend to the land's surface and therefore are at atmospheric pressure. Water levels in wells in an unconfined aquifer define the water table, the upper surface of the saturated zone.

Confined aquifers exist where a low-permeability geologic deposit, such as clay, overlies the groundwater system. In these settings, groundwater may be under a greater-than-atmospheric pressure. In some cases "artesian" conditions may occur, where free-flowing wells discharge groundwater at the land's surface. The pressure in an aquifer, called the head, can be determined by measuring the water level within a well. A piezometer is installed in the well to measure the pressure. In a confined aquifer, the water level can lie above the top of the aquifer. This elevation is commonly known as the pressure surface but is more appropriately called either the piezometric or potentiometric surface.

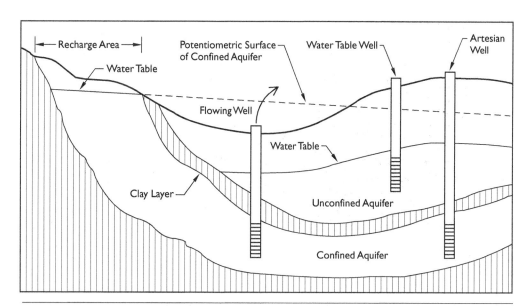

CONFINED AND UNCONFINED AQUIFERS

Source: Horsley Witten Group.

Precipitation or surface water that percolates downward into the aquifer recharges groundwater. Subsurface wastewater discharge and infiltration of stormwater runoff may also recharge groundwater.

This is known as artificial recharge because the water is infiltrated as a result of land-use activity.

EFFECTS ON WATER QUALITY

Aquifers are important water supply sources. They serve as underground drinking water reservoirs, irrigation sources, and as a source of industrial water supplies. Aquifers are also potentially important for wastewater disposal. Because they are highly permeable, they are commonly used to receive wastewater infiltrated to the subsurface. These two types of uses can cause conflicts.

Land uses that overlay aquifers or their recharge areas can have effects on hydrologic and water quality. Impervious surfaces preclude direct aquifer infiltration and recharge, thereby reducing available water supply. Land uses that demand large quantities of water, such as golf courses, can also deplete groundwater supplies within the aquifer. Dewatering of aquifers can also cause land subsidence.

If land uses are located in aquifer recharge areas, water quality can be affected. . For example, septic systems can discharge wastewater into the subsurface, introducing nitrogen, bacteria, and viruses into the aquifer.

AQUIFER PROTECTION TECHNIQUES

To protect aquifers and groundwater supplies, the recharge areas need to be identified clearly. This may be the land area directly overlying the aquifer; or, in the case of some confined aquifers, it may be remote from the aquifer. U.S. Geological Survey (USGS) hydrogeologic maps are excellent sources for locating aquifers and their recharge areas.

Regulatory and nonregulatory techniques are available to protect aquifers. Zoning and subdivision ordinances and health regulations can all be devel-

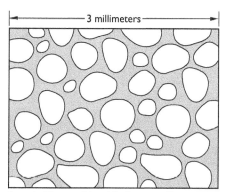

Pores in Unconsolidated Sedimentary Deposits

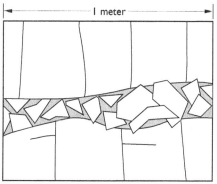

Rubble Zone and Cooling Fractures in Extrusive Igneous Rocks

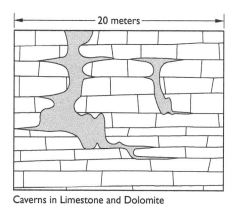

Caverns in Limestone and Dolomite

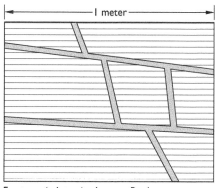

Fractures in Intrusive Igneous Rocks

TYPES OF OPENINGS IN SELECTED WATER-BEARING ROCKS

Source: U.S. Geological Survey 1984.

Scott W. Horsley, Horsley Witten Group, Sandwich, Massachusetts

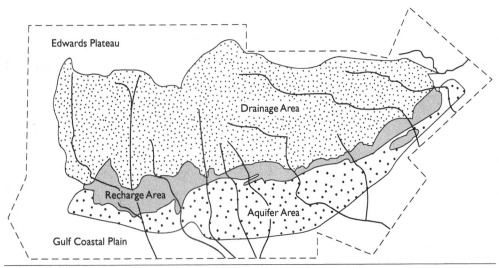

AQUIFER AREA

Source: U.S. EPA 1988.

oped to prohibit or limit certain land uses deemed to present unacceptable risks to underlying aquifers. For example, zoning may be used to preclude high-risk uses, such as chemical manufacturing, automotive service stations, and high-density residential development, from critical aquifer recharge areas. Wellhead protection areas can be mapped for actual wellfields.

They are the areas that contribute water (and potentially contaminants) to drinking-water wells.

Nonregulatory techniques include land acquisition within identified aquifer areas. Public education programs, which include posting signs stating, for example, "Entering Aquifer Protection Area," have also been used successfully.

SAFE YIELDS

Managing water withdrawals from aquifers so as to not exceed "safe yields" is an emerging water supply issue. Safe yield is the amount of water that can be withdrawn from an aquifer without significant ecological impacts. Water withdrawals can be balanced with return flows to the aquifer, which can include wastewater returns, after appropriate treatment, and collecting and infiltrating treated stormwater.

Determining safe yield limits is an evolving discipline. It requires a clear understanding of climate, hydrogeology, and ecological thresholds, especially where streams and wetlands are hydrologically connected to the aquifer. Land-use planners are beginning to try to control growth in sensitive aquifer areas by considering the cumulative inputs of all potential development within a resource area, known as a build-out analysis, and allocating water consumption demands accordingly. This requires careful integration between groundwater science and land-use policy. The Ipswich River Water Association in Massachusetts is attempting to restore natural flow conditions in the river by managing its safe yield.

See also:
Hydrologic Cycle
Water Supply

Scott W. Horsley, Horsley Witten Group, Sandwich, Massachusetts

RIVERS AND STREAMS

Rivers and streams arise in the landscape because the atmosphere brings water evaporated from the oceans over the land, with the result that more rain and snow fall on the continents than evaporates from them. Rivers and streams carry from land to sea excess water, sediments, nutrients, and organic material. Along their course, they support diverse habitats, adjacent riparian forests, and floodplains. Surface flow in streams also interacts strongly with groundwater in the subsurface.

Where the water table slopes from the adjacent land toward the stream, groundwater flows into the stream, creating a gaining stream. By contrast, along a losing stream, water flows from the stream into the groundwater, often maintaining bands of riparian vegetation in semiarid areas. The hyporheic zone comprises the shallow groundwater below and adjacent to the channel with frequent interchange with the surface water. It supports a variety of organisms. The land area draining to a particular river is its drainage basin, also termed the catchment or watershed of the river.

FLOW MEASUREMENT

Flow is the volume per unit time of water passing a point.

U.S. Measurement Units

In the United States, stream flow is usually expressed in cubic feet per second (cfs). Flow from wells is usually expressed as gallons per minute. Annual flow or runoff is sometimes reported in millions of gallons, more commonly in acre-feet. An acre foot is the volume of water covering 1 acre to a depth of 1 foot, which is equal to 43,560 cubic feet or approximately 326,000 gallons. Flow records for many rivers and streams in the United States can be accessed on the U.S. Geological Survey website (Kondolf and Piégay 2003).

International Measurement Units

Outside of the United States, the majority of other countries report flow in liters per second or cubic meters per second. Annual flow is expressed as thousands or millions of cubic meters per year.

Hydrographs

The plot of daily flows over a year is the annual hydrograph. The seasonal patterns shown in hydrographs can vary widely, reflecting differences in geology and climate among watersheds. Both the base flow during dry months and high flows are important, the former mostly for water supply and maintaining ecological values, the latter for analyzing flood risk.

THE EFFECTS OF URBANIZATION ON BASE FLOW AND FLOOD FLOW

Flood flows and base flows are both affected by urbanization. Because pavement prevents rain from infiltrating into the soil, more rain runs off during storms. For the same rainfall, peak flows in urban areas may increase 5 times over predam conditions.

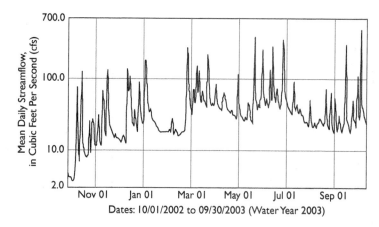

Mid-Atlantic Region

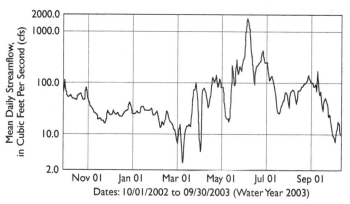

Rocky Mountain Region

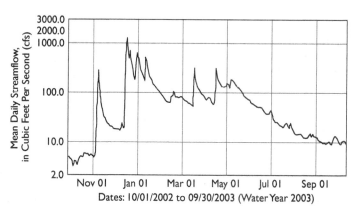

Pacific Coast Region

The hydrographs reflect annual patterns of runoff from: humid Atlantic climate with rainfall distributed throughout the year (Jones Falls, Maryland); snowmelt runoff, with the highest flow concentrated in May and June (Boulder Creek, Colorado); and a Mediterranean-climate stream, whose runoff is concentrated in the winter rainy season, with flow trailing off in to the rainless summer and fall (Carmel River, California). Jones Falls experiences moderate flood peaks nearly all year long, while high flows in Boulder Creek and Carmel River are confined to the snowmelt and winter rainy seasons, respectively. These hydrographs show flow over the water year, which is from October 1 to September 30. Note that the y-axis (flow) is logarithmic.

HYDROGRAPHS FROM THREE DISTINCT CLIMATIC REGIONS IN NORTH AMERICA

Source: U.S. Geological Survey.

G. Mathias Kondolf, Ph.D., University of California at Berkeley

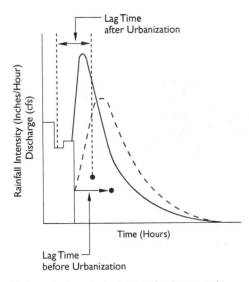

Hydrograph of an urbanized stream, showing pre- and posturban patterns.

HYDROGRAPH OF URBANIZED STREAM

Source: Dunne and Leopold 1978.

Base flows can be affected in different ways: less infiltration means less recharge of the water table, and thus less groundwater seeping into the stream to maintain flow during the dry season, so streams may dry up during summer and fall in urban areas. However, some streams that naturally dried up during the dry months now run year-round. These streams are fed by "urban slobber," which is water that comes from sources such as excess landscape irrigation and leaking pipes. It may be of poor quality due to high concentrations of nutrients and other constituents.

SEDIMENT LOADS

Streams and rivers also carry sediment, thereby shaping the landscape, eroding highlands, and depositing valley bottoms and deltas. The sediment load of a river consists of the bed load, which is sand and gravel transported along the bed; the suspended load, which is the clay, silt, and sand held aloft in the water column by turbulence; and the dissolved load, which comprises the soluble constituents.

CHANNEL TYPES AND RUNOFF RATES

It is important to distinguish between river channels that flow through bedrock and those whose bed and banks are composed of river-borne sediments or alluvium. Bedrock channels are relatively resistant to change because the bedrock resists erosion. Alluvial channels can self-adjust to the flow regime and sediment load supplied to them from the drainage basin. If the independent variables of runoff and sediment load change, the shape and dimensions of an alluvial channel will usually change in response.

Human activities, such as clearing for agriculture or urbanization, commonly increase runoff rates, leading to larger floods, which in turn may cause alluvial channels to erode and widen. Increased sediment loads from activities, such as land clearing, timber harvesting, or road building, can increase sediment loads, leading to deposition of fine sediment in gravels, which affects aquatic habitat. A larger buildup of sed-

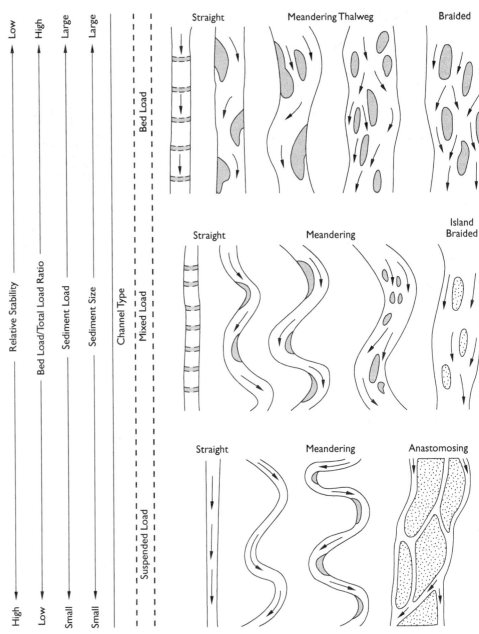

Channel patterns in relation to channel stability and type of sediment load.

CHANNEL PATTERNS

Source: Schumm 1985 and Knighton 1998.

iment in the channel can induce channel instability. Dams trap sediment, so the areas downstream may be sediment-starved, often causing erosion of the stream bed, lowering its elevation. This is called channel downcutting, and loss of aquatic habitat. Gravel and sand are mined from many rivers, causing sediment deficit and also resulting in channel downcutting.

Channel Patterns

Though often thought of as separate entities, the channel and floodplain function as a unit; the floodplain accommodates overflow from the channel. Natural channel patterns range across a broad spectrum, including straight, meandering, braided, multichannel (anastomosing), and wandering, which is a transitional pattern between braided and mean-

dering. Sinuosity, the channel length divided by the straight-line valley length, a ratio of channel length over valley length, is a useful indicator of channel pattern.

Channel Cross Sections

Cross sections across the channel transverse to the flow direction are commonly used to illustrate channel form. Monitoring programs use level surveys of cross sections to document channel changes over time. They are also important data for computer models and are used to predict flow through river channels and estimate flood capacity. Natural channel cross sections are usually asymmetric, with the deepest point in the channel cross section, known as the thalweg, on the outside of bends and a shallow depositional area on the inside of the bends.

G. Mathias Kondolf, Ph.D., University of California at Berkeley

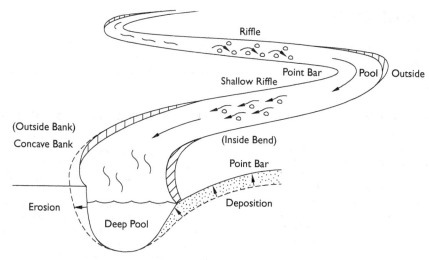

Characteristics of a meander bend, showing direction of migration.

MEANDER BEND MIGRATION

Source: Adapted from California State Lands Commission 1993.

Meandering Channels

Channels naturally migrate and change their course. Meandering channels do so by eroding the outsides of meander bends, while building up the point bars on the inside of the bends. Understanding the dynamic nature of river channels can help in predicting areas at high risk of channel erosion.

Bankfull Flow

Most of the time, river and stream channels are only partly filled with water. Many streams in humid climates and those carrying runoff from melting snow commonly experience flows reaching the tops of banks, called the bankfull flow, with a return interval of every 1.5 to 2 years (Leopold et al. 1964). The bankfull flow is widely considered to be the channel-forming discharge, and the 1.5- to 2-year flow is often referred to as the bankfull flow. However, the actual return intervals for bankfull vary widely (Williams 1978). In drier regions, the flows responsible for shaping channels are likely to be larger and less frequent events (Wolman and Gerson 1978).

HABITAT PROVISIONS AND HUMAN USE

Organisms, including fish, amphibians, birds, and invertebrates, require good water quality and depend on the habitats that result from overhanging vegetation, large pieces of wood, and complex channels, which have deep pools, shallow riffles, and irregular banks. Salmon and trout require clean gravel to spawn. In general, complex, irregular channels provide the best habitat, especially if riparian forests abut them and the channels are free to flood, erode, and deposit.

Unfortunately, the characteristics most favorable to the aquatic ecosystem are often in conflict with human uses. For example, bank erosion, even if natural, can threaten human settlement adjacent to streams, so bank protection is common. Large concentrations of wood in channels play important ecological functions, but they are commonly removed to reduce the risk of debris jams and flooding. Where settlements and infrastructure are located on the floodplain and vulnerable to flooding, channel capacity is commonly increased by channelization (dredging and straightening activities) and construction of concrete trapezoidal channels and culverts, eliminating habitat values and often creating a perpetual maintenance problem as communities chronically fight against natural processes.

Alternatives to Channelization

Where channel capacity must be increased, there are many alternatives to channelization (Williams 1990). Environmentally sensitive flood control approaches include disturbing only one bank and carving out an artificial floodplain to accommodate flood flows, thereby creating a compound, or multistage, channel, and creating a bypass channel for flood flows while allowing the natural channel to remain intact (Brookes 1988).

STANDARDS AND GUIDELINES

Established standards and guidelines vary widely from state to state. Activities that alter or disturb the channel bed often fall under the jurisdiction of the U.S. Army Corps of Engineers in its enforcement of Section 404 of the Clean Water Act (CWA), which regulates the discharge of fill into wetlands. In many states, such activities require permits from state agencies, such as the Department of Fish and Game (which in California requires a streambed alteration agreement for activities disturbing the bed). Under CWA, states set water quality standards (for temperature, turbidity) and do most of the enforcement. Recent amendments to the CWA now require municipalities to have permits to discharge their stormwater.

REFERENCES

Brookes, A. 1988. *Channelized Rivers*. Chichester, England: John Wiley & Sons, Inc.

California State Lands Commission. 1993. *California's Rivers: A Public Trust Report*. California State Lands Commission, Sacramento.

Dunne, Thomas and Luna B. Leopold. 1978. *Water in Environmental Planning*. New York: W.H. Freeman.

Knighton, D. 1998. *Fluvial Forms and Processes: A New Perspective*. London: Arnold.

Kondolf, G.M., and H. Piégay, eds. 2003. *Tools in Fluvial Geomorphology*. Chichester, England: John Wiley & Sons.

Leopold, L.B., M.G. Wolman, and J.P. Miller. 1964. *Fluvial Processes in Geomorphology*. San Francisco: W.H. Freeman and Company.

Schumm, S.A. 1985. "Patterns of Alluvial Rivers." *Annual Review of Earth and Planetary Sciences*. 13: 527.

Williams, G.W. 1978. "Bankfull Discharge of Rivers." *Water Resources Research* 14: 1141-1154.

Williams, P.B. 1990. "Rethinking Flood Control Channel Design." *Civil Engineering*. 60, no. 1:57–59.

Wolman, M.G., and R. Gerson. 1978. "Relative Scales of Time and Effectiveness of Climate in Watershed Geomorphology." *Earth Surface Processes* 3:189–208.

See also:
Flood Hazards
Floodplains and Riparian Corridors
Watersheds

. Mathias Kondolf, Ph.D., University of California at Berkeley

FLOODPLAINS AND RIPARIAN CORRIDORS

FLOODPLAINS

Floodplains are the flat bottomlands adjacent to river channels. They are important to planners because they are prone to flooding, thereby posing a risk to human settlements. Perhaps less commonly understood are the roles of the floodplain in river ecology and water quality, and the consequences of cutting the connection between channel and floodplain.

Floodplains accommodate floodwaters in excess of channel capacity, store floodwater, and thereby attenuate peak flows downstream. By acting as a "pressure-relief valve" for the channel, floodplains moderate the increase in stream energy in the channel, expressed as force-per-unit area on the bed, or shear stress, during floods. Silts suspended in fast-moving floodwaters settle out from the slower-moving waters on the floodplain, leaving behind highly fertile soils that constitute the best agricultural land in many regions.

RIPARIAN CORRIDORS

Floodplains naturally support riparian corridors, which are the bands of vegetation that flank a channel or lake. Riparian corridors provide important habitats, filter suspended sediments from floodwaters, and uptake nutrients from shallow groundwater, leading to better water quality. Distinct riparian vegetation zones can be identified, defined by hydrology and substrate materials. Each offers habitats to a distinctive suite of species. Floodplain water bodies, such as side channels and oxbow lakes, are commonly hot spots for biodiversity. During floods, floodplains are often important feeding or breeding areas for fish.

LEVEES AND BANK PROTECTION

When levees cut off the floodplain from the channel, flood flows are concentrated in the channel and are funneled downstream more quickly, producing higher peak flows downstream. The hydrologic "sponge" effect is lost, and the floodplain no longer absorbs flood flows, increasing downstream flooding, as occurred along the Mississippi River in 1993. Because flows are concentrated in the channel between levees, there is increased shear stress on the channel bed, which commonly leads to erosion of the stream bed, lowering its elevation. This is called channel downcutting or incision. Moreover, the riparian forest is no longer sustained by flooding, fish no longer have access to feeding and breeding areas, and floodplain water bodies lose their seasonal connection to the channel.

Developing right up to the stream bank has negative effects:

- The loss of riparian corridor
- Runoff from buildings and other developed areas going directly into the stream
- Roads and buildings on banks being threatened by bank erosion

Bank erosion often is an impetus for bank protection using traditional "hard" engineering structures, such as riprap. These commonly deflect stream energy elsewhere, typically toward the opposite bank downstream, which then experiences increased erosion.

An alternative approach is to use live plants and plant material to stabilize banks, thereby slowing near-bank velocities and providing some habitat value (Gray and Leiser 1982). Even if rocks and similar structural elements are used in the design, riparian cuttings can be planted within them to permit the growth of vegetation over the artificial protection, thereby allowing the benefits of slower velocities along the bank, shading, cover, and food production to develop, improving habitat even along artificially modified channels (Shields 1982, 1991).

BUFFERS

Vegetated buffer strips are required in many areas to: filter sediment from diffuse surface runoff; reduce nutrient concentrations through uptake by plants; contribute leaf litter and insects to the channel from riparian trees; provide wood to the channel as undercut trees fall in; and provide habitat for many species, notably (and best studied), birds, including neotropical migrants.

Buffer Strip Widths

The most common standards and guidelines are setbacks from banks for urban development and agricultural uses. The appropriate width of these buffer strips depends on objectives and can vary widely. Urban buffers typically require setbacks of 20

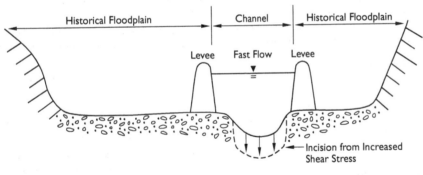

Water Flow during Floodwater Storage
During floods, flow in excess of channel capacity flows slowly across floodplain.

Water Flow with Levees
If levees prevent overflow onto the floodplain, flood flows are forced to stay within narrow channel between levees, causing deeper, faster flow with high shear stress on the bed.

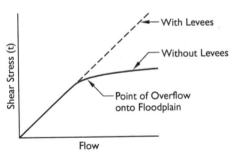

Shear Stress on Streambed
Shear stress in channel with increasing flow without levees and with levees.

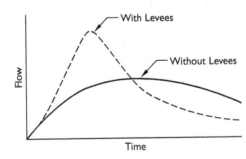

Downstream Flow
Peak flow downstream with attenuation by floodplain storage upstream (solid line) and without floodplain—that is, with levees (dashed line).

FLOODPLAIN-CHANNEL INTERACTIONS

Source: G. Mathias Kondolf.

G. Mathias Kondolf, Ph.D., University of California at Berkeley

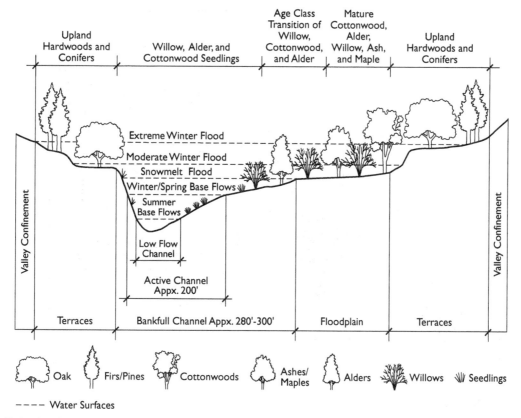

Zones of riparian vegetation with elevation above channel, showing areas inundated by different flood levels. Example is from the Trinity River, California (predam condition).

RIPARIAN VEGETATION ZONES

Source: Adapted from U.S. Fish and Wildlife Service and Hoopa Valley Tribe 1999.

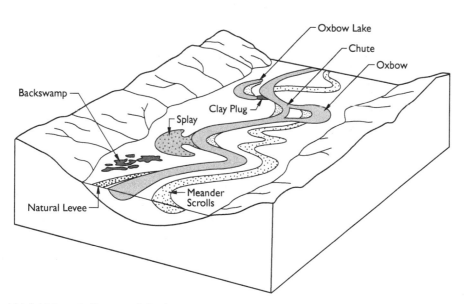

Topographic features and resulting floodplain habitats created by a meandering river.

MEANDERING RIVER

Source: Federal Interagency Stream Corridor Working Group 1998.

G. Mathias Kondolf, Ph.D., University of California at Berkeley

WATER

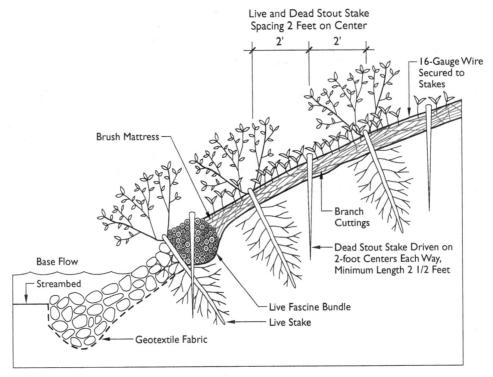

Live and Dead Stout Stake
Spacing 2 Feet on Center

16-Gauge Wire
Secured to
Stakes

Brush Mattress

Branch
Cuttings

Dead Stout Stake Driven on
2-foot Centers Each Way,
Minimum Length 2 1/2 Feet

Base Flow

Streambed

Live Fascine Bundle

Live Stake

Geotextile Fabric

An example of streambank protection using the brush mattress bioengineering technique.

STREAMBANK STABILIZATION USING PLANT MATERIAL

Source: Federal Interagency Stream Corridor Working Group 1998.

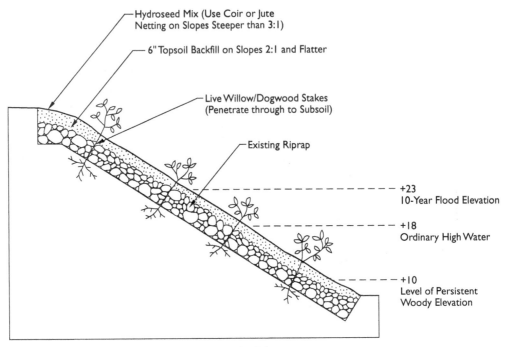

Hydroseed Mix (Use Coir or Jute
Netting on Slopes Steeper than 3:1)

6" Topsoil Backfill on Slopes 2:1 and Flatter

Live Willow/Dogwood Stakes
(Penetrate through to Subsoil)

Existing Riprap

+23
10-Year Flood Elevation

+18
Ordinary High Water

+10
Level of Persistent
Woody Elevation

Application requirements: (1) Stable, existing riprap; (2) 2:1 slopes or flatter; (3) Riprap depth less than 5 feet.

PLANTING EXISTING RIPRAP

Source: City of Portland, Oregon 2001.

G. Mathias Kondolf, Ph.D., University of California at Berkeley

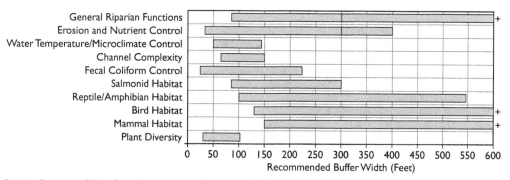

Results of a survey of 54 buffer strip requirements for a range of objectives.

RANGE OF BUFFER STRIP WIDTHS FOR VARIOUS OBJECTIVES

Source: Robins 2002.

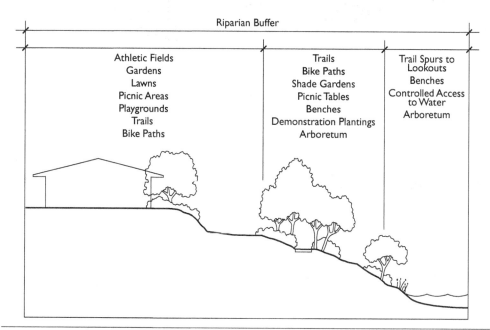

THREE URBAN STREAM BUFFER ZONES

Source: Schueler 1996.

to 200 feet. A 100-foot width is widely accepted as a minimum width to filter pollutants, and 300 feet as the minimum to protect wildlife habitat (Otto et al. 2004; MacBroom 1998). Buffer width can also vary depending on the slope of the ground surface adjacent to the channel, degree of urbanization, and ecological resources present. The optimal buffer strip width depends on the purpose of the setback.

Buffer Zones

For urban stream buffers, three zones can be identified (Schueler 1996; Otto et al. 2004).

The Streamside Zone

The streamside zone should be left intact where it has mature or developing native riparian forest and be restored elsewhere. Except for occasional points of access to the water, benches, and other viewpoints, this zone should be left as undisturbed as possible so it can provide a natural, complex edge to the channel, shading, and large woods to house complex habitats and leaves and insects, which are food inputs

to the aquatic ecosystem. At a minimum, it should cover the sloping riverbank and continue for a minimum of one tree width, measured at the dripline.

The Middle Zone

The middle zone can accommodate some clearing for trails, bike paths, picnic areas and other recreational uses, and stormwater detention, but should be mostly protected or restored native riparian forest. This zone should encompass the entire width of the 100-year floodplain and include floodplain water bodies and other protected wetlands.

The Outer Zone

The outer zone should be an additional setback of at least 25 feet before the first structures. It is suitable for athletic fields, gardens, playgrounds, picnic areas, trails, bike paths, and stormwater detention.

Channel Migration

The channel should ideally be allowed to migrate into the buffer zone. This dynamic channel behavior

is key to diverse, healthy river habitats. Such migration is feasible if infrastructure and structures are kept out of the bottomland. However, sewer lines and other utilities commonly are buried adjacent to the channel, so the expense of moving them may be prohibitive, resulting in a demand for bank protection.

DESIGNING STREAM BUFFERS

1. Designate uses based on inner, middle, and outer zones.
2. Restore buffers to native riparian vegetation.
3. Expand and contract buffers to cover 100-year floodplain, steep slopes (>2%), wetlands, and important wildlife habitat.
4. Delineate buffers, develop criteria for scale at which buffers are mapped, define edge of stream and beginning of buffer, specify permitted uses by zone.
5. Accommodate bridges and utility crossings with minimum disruption to channel and floodplain functions. Avoid embankment fill for bridge approaches, using causeways over floodplain wherever possible.
6. Use buffers to detain and treat stormwater where possible, but also augment by stormwater management elsewhere in watershed.
7. Make buffers visible, educate public about buffers, conduct stream walks, post interpretive signs, involve public in replanting efforts, and conduct annual buffer walks to check for encroachment of illegal uses into buffers.

Source: Adapted from Otto, McCormick, and Leccese 2004.

REFERENCES

Gray, D.H., and A.T. Leiser. 1982. *Biotechnical Slope Protection and Erosion Control.* New York: Van Nostrand Reinhold Company.

MacBroom, J. 1998. *The River Book: The Nature and Management of Streams in Glaciated Terrains.* Hartford, CT: Connecticut Department of Environmental Protection.

Otto, Betsy, Kathleen McCormick, and Michael Leccese. 2004. *Ecological Riverfront Design: Restoring Rivers, Connecting Communities.* Planning Advisory Service Report No. 518-519. Chicago: American Planning Association.

Robins, J.D. 2002. Stream setback technical memo 26. *Report to the Napa County Board of Supervisors.* Oakland, CA.: Jones & Stokes.

Schueler, T.R. 1996. "The Architecture of Urban Stream Buffers." *Watershed Protection Techniques* 1, no.4.

Shields, D.F. 1982. "Environmental Features for Flood Control Channels." *Water Resources Bulletin* 18:779-784.

———. 1991. "Woody Vegetation and Riprap Stability along the Sacramento River Mile 84.5-119." *Water Resources Bulletin* 27:527-536.

See also:

Flood Hazards
Rivers and Streams

G. Mathias Kondolf, Ph.D., University of California at Berkeley

WETLANDS

Wetlands have become a centerpiece of environmental planning efforts in the United States due to their limited protection under the federal Clean Water Act and many state laws. Historically, wetlands were considered sites of disease or as obstacles to human progress, but later studies showed that they have important purposes, such as providing wildlife habitat, serving as filters of groundwater, and aiding in flood control. Unfortunately, more than half of U.S. wetlands have been lost since colonial times, mainly due to agricultural conversion; many wetlands that remain have been seriously degraded.

Wetlands are difficult to define and to classify because they are highly variable. This variability is due to local and regional differences in hydrology, soils, vegetation, geology, topography, climate, and the relative degree of disturbance. The regulatory definition, however, requires that they generally meet three criteria. First, wetlands must have water (hydrology) covering the soil or present either at or near the surface of the soil during all or part of the year including the growing season. Second, wetland (hydric) soils must be present. Hydric soils develop under conditions of submergence and low oxygen. Third, wetland-adapted plants (hydrophytes) must be present during at least part of the growing season.

CLASSIFICATION OF WETLANDS

The following is a simplified classification of the major kinds of wetlands.

Marshes

Marshes are among the most easily identified wetlands. They are characterized by emergent soft-stemmed vegetation adapted to saturated soil conditions. There are many different kinds of marshes, ranging from prairie potholes to the Everglades, coastal to inland, freshwater to saltwater. All types receive most of their water from surface water, though many marshes are also fed by groundwater. Nutrients are plentiful, and the pH is usually neutral, leading to an abundance of plant and animal life.

Nontidal Marshes

Nontidal marshes are the most common and widely distributed wetlands in the United States. They frequently occur adjacent to lakes, ponds, rivers, and streams, but also appear in poorly drained areas where surface or groundwater can collect. Water levels in these wetlands generally vary from a few inches to a few feet and may occasionally become completely dry. These marshes include playa lakes, prairie potholes, wet meadows, vernal pools, and some fens.

Nontidal marshes are characterized by highly organic, mineral-rich soils of sand, silt, and clay, and by characteristic vegetation (cattails, bulrushes, and reeds, among others), and characteristic wildlife (red-winged blackbirds, herons, and muskrats). They serve to mitigate flooding, trap excess nutrients and pollutants from runoff, and provide habitat to thousands of species of plants and animals. The biodiversity of these marshes is generally high.

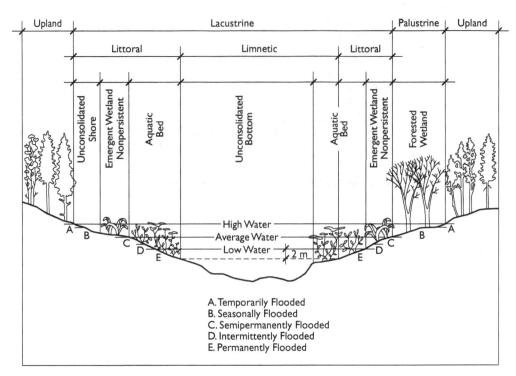

Shown are the distinguishing features and examples of habitats in wetlands adjacent to lakes, also known as lacustrine wetlands.

WETLAND ADJACENT TO A LAKE

Source: USGS Northern Wildlife Prairie Research Center 1998.

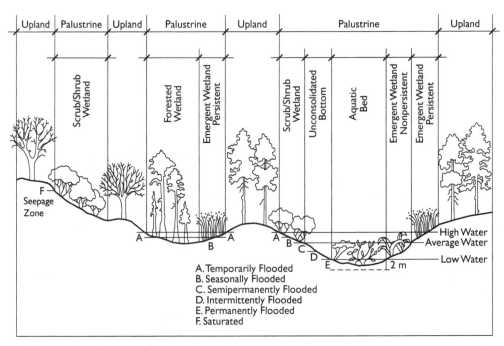

Shown are the distinguishing features and examples of marsh wetlands, also known as palustrine wetlands.

MARSH WETLAND

Source: USGS Northern Wildlife Prairie Research Center 1998.

James F. Berry, J.D., Ph.D., Elmhurst College, Elmhurst, Illinois

Tidal Marshes

Tidal marshes are influenced by ocean tides. They occur along most coastlines but are most abundant along the East Coast of the United States and the Gulf of Mexico. Tidal marshes are most often brackish but may be saline (salty) or even fresh. They are characterized by extremely high biological productivity. Tidal marshes help to reduce storm damage to coastlines; absorb excess nutrients and pollutants before they reach oceans and estuaries; and serve as important sources of food and habitat (for mollusks and crustaceans, among others), as breeding grounds for fishes and invertebrates, and as shelter and nesting sites for migratory waterfowl.

Swamps

Swamps include any wetland dominated by woody plants, such as trees or shrubs. Swamps are characterized by saturated soils or standing water during certain times of the year, highly organic soils, and dominance by woody plants, including both trees (e.g., cypress trees, white cedar, willow, or maple) and shrubs (e.g., buttonbush, alder, or dogwood). Pocosins are swamps in the southeastern United States generally dominated by evergreen shrubs.

Swamps are important in flood protection and nutrient removal, and riverine swamps are particularly high in productivity and species diversity. Lowland swamps are often an important source of food and serve as breeding grounds for birds and upland animals.

Bogs

Bogs are characterized by a thick covering of sphagnum moss, spongy peat deposits, and acidic waters. They receive all or most of their water from precipitation, rather than from runoff, groundwater, or surface water, and are low in nutrients.

Bogs can form when sphagnum moss blankets dry land and prevents water from leaving the surface (paludification) or when sphagnum moss grows over a lake or pond and gradually fills it in (terrestrialization). Either way, acidic peat is deposited, often many feet thick. The flora and fauna of bogs generally possess unique adaptations to low nutrients, saturated conditions, and acidic water (e.g., pitcher plants).

Like other wetlands, bogs help to mitigate flooding by absorbing precipitation. In addition, bogs support unique flora and fauna.

Fens

Fens are like bogs in that a spongy layer of peat is deposited, but fens receive their water from groundwater and surface water. Because they receive nutrients from sources other than precipitation, fens are less acidic and have higher nutrient levels than bogs, and support a more diverse flora and fauna. Like marshes, fens are characterized by emergent soft-stemmed vegetation (grasses, sedges, and rushes). Fens are most common in the northeastern United States, the Great Lakes region, and the Rocky Mountains, which are generally associated with low temperatures, short growing seasons, ample precipitation, and relatively high humidity.

Like other wetlands, fens help to mitigate flooding, to remove nutrients and pollutants from surface waters, and to provide habitat for unique flora and fauna.

JURISDICTIONAL WETLANDS AND PERMITTING

Section 404 of the federal Clean Water Act (CWA) authorizes the U.S. Army Corps of Engineers to issue permits for the discharge of "dredged or fill material" into the "waters of the United States." While the CWA does not mention wetlands, Army Corps regulations specifically discuss those wetlands over which the Army Corps may claim "jurisdiction" and may enforce the permit requirement. The Army Corps has primary jurisdiction over 404 permits, but the U.S. EPA has the authority to veto a 404 permit if it violates environmental standards.

Many legal battles have been fought over whether a specific wetland is jurisdictional and whether a 404 permit should (or should not) have been granted. Some plaintiffs have argued successfully that failure to issue a 404 permit amounted to an illegal regulatory "taking" of property without just compensation. In another issue, the U.S. Supreme Court held, in 2001, that "isolated" wetlands (i.e., those without a surface or groundwater connection to a navigable waterway) were generally not jurisdictional wetlands.

General Permits

Clean Water Act Section 404(e) authorizes the Army Corps to issue general permits on a nationwide, regional, or statewide basis for particular categories of activities that cause only minimal adverse environmental impacts. These activities do not require an individual 404 permit. Some nationwide categories require notifying the Army Corps prior to commencement of the activity in a wetland. Information about regional or state-level general permits may be obtained from Army Corps Division or district offices.

All activities allowed by nationwide permits must include the use of appropriate erosion and siltation controls. Activities may not disrupt the movement of indigenous aquatic species, and heavy equipment must be placed on mats.

Individual Permits

Any person discharging dredged or fill material into a wetland must apply for a 404 permit from the Regulatory Division of the local Army Corps of Engineers office. The permit form is available from the Army Corps, and the EPA (or their websites); in addition, many states provide the form through state agencies.

The application must describe the project "with particularity," including engineering drawings and descriptions. Also required is a "preliminary jurisdictional determination," which is usually done by consultants who follow the Army Corps' wetlands delineation manual. The applicant must describe all activities "reasonably related" to the project. The applicant may change the project without a new permit if the scope of wetlands fill and impacts are similar to those in the original project.

Applicants must demonstrate they have examined all available alternatives to the impact of the discharge of dredged or fill material and show no practicable alternative exists that would have less adverse impact on the aquatic ecosystem. In addition, no discharge can be permitted if it would violate other applicable laws (e.g., state water quality standards, toxic effluent standards, or the Endangered Species Act). Any wetland discharge cannot significantly degrade wetlands by adversely affecting wildlife, ecosystem integrity, recreation, aesthetics, or economic values.

Once all of these conditions are met, the applicant must then show that all appropriate and practicable steps will be taken to minimize adverse impacts of the discharge on wetlands. After avoidance and minimization criteria are satisfied, the Army Corps may consider compensatory mitigation of lost wetland values (a minimum of one-for-one functional replacement with an adequate margin of safety to reflect scientific uncertainty). The applicant must prepare an environmental assessment or Environmental Impact Statement (EIS) for each individual permit application.

Army Corps officials generally request written comments from the public. Public hearings may be held on the application for very controversial projects.

PLANNING AND DESIGN STANDARDS

Planners are likely to encounter wetland issues in at least three different situations. First, existing, natural wetlands are often an important part of a landscape, and planners must be aware of ways to design development to minimize impact. Second, existing wetlands may be degraded such that significant wetland restoration is an important part of development planning and design. Third, there may be a need to construct wetlands where none exist, requiring a careful balance of wetland standards with other design standards.

Planners and developers should, at a minimum, follow these practices when development will affect a wetland:

- Identify appropriate geology and soils. Healthy wetlands require a balance of surface and groundwater, as well as soils.
- Identify proper vegetation both within and around a wetland. Proper vegetation contributes both to healthy wetland design and to important visual characteristics. Proper vegetation provides shading moisture, contributes to soil conditions, and provides physical barriers.
- Pay proper attention to visual characteristics, which are an important part of wetland design. Designs should incorporate access to views of plants and animals by residents and visitors.
- Be aware of legal constraints on wetland development, such as private property boundaries, easements and rights of way, comprehensive plan provisions, zoning, and other limitations on use.

It is important to remember that proper planning and design will make wetlands important amenities benefiting an entire community.

See also:
Federal Legislation
Floodplains and Riparian Corridors
Watersheds

James F. Berry, J.D., Ph.D., Elmhurst College, Elmhurst, Illinois

BEACH AND DUNE SYSTEMS

Much of the world's coastline consists of sandy beach and dune systems. Beaches can be simply defined as "unconsolidated deposits of sand and gravel on the shore" (Bird 1996). Beaches are found along barrier islands and on mainland coasts. According to a recent study by the Heinz Center, sandy beaches comprise approximately 16 percent of the U.S. coastline, or 6,000 linear miles.

Healthy intact beach and dune systems provide extensive aesthetic and recreational benefits. They also serve as an important form of natural hazard mitigation. Dunes serve as natural seawalls, providing considerable protection to property located landward of them. Beach and dune systems are also major buffers to wave and storm activity.

Beach and dune systems can be defined as transitional ecosystems—lying at the interface of marine and terrestrial environments. These systems serve as important natural barriers to flooding. They are subject to a complex and dynamic sand transport system. They are constantly in flux, affected by the littoral sand "budget" (the long-shore current that moves sand along the beach), delivery of sand materials from fluvial and river sources, and human alteration of the shoreline (such as the construction of a seawall).

Beaches generally extend from low tide landward to the dune structure or the first line of vegetation. Dunes represent accumulated areas of windblown sand, typically stabilized through vegetation. Extensive systems of dunes exist along virtually every segment of U.S. coastline. For example, extensive dunefields exist along the Oregon coast and the Great Lakes shoreline. Along with offshore sand bars, dunes constitute sand reservoirs that accrete or erode depending on storms, wave action, and human alteration.

CHARACTERISTICS

Beaches can consist of many different kinds of materials, including sand, pebbles, and stone. Gravel and stone beaches are common in northern latitude shorelines, the result of glacial deposits. Sand, the common beach material along most of the U.S. coastline, is composed primarily of quartz. The size of the sand particles strongly influences beach slope—the coarser the grain size, the steeper the profile; the finer the sand, generally the flatter the beach. At any given time, beaches are stable, eroding, or accreting. In the longer term, most U.S. beaches are eroding and moving landward, primarily in response to long-term rise in sea level.

HABITATS

Dunes and dunefields provide important habitat for many species. Along the California coast, these include rare butterfly species like the Morro Blue butterfly, deer mice, and black legless lizards. Along the East Coast, they are important habitats for the piping plover and many other shore birds. Beaches, moreover, provide essential habitats for nesting sea turtles and a rich diversity of aquatic organisms.

ELEMENTS OF BEACH AND DUNE SYSTEMS

The beach zone generally extends from offshore, where source materials from sand bars are often located, to inland areas such as maritime forests and habitats lying beyond the dunes. The fore dune, or primary dune, marks the seaward extent of dune-stabilizing vegetation. The beach berm is the area of dry sand seaward of dunes and landward of the beach face. It is the portion of the beach most used and enjoyed by visitors (Rogers and Nash 2003). Dunes consist of a ridge of elevated sand lying parallel to the coast. The base of the primary dune is typically a distance of about 100 feet from mean high water. Secondary or tertiary dunes lie landward of the primary dune.

Beach and dune systems change with the seasons and in response to storm activity. Surge and wave action from hurricanes or storms erode and modify the dune face and beach profile, moving much sand offshore. Dunes are essentially sand storage mechanisms. Over time, much of this material will return to the dune and beach face, though some may be lost from the location entirely. Along the U.S. coast, beaches tend to erode extensively during the high wave-energy period of winter months, then accrete during the summer months.

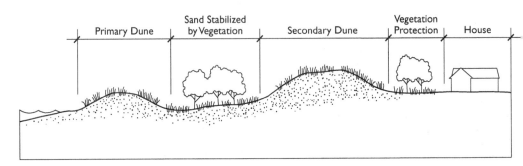

Preserving and stabilizing dune systems along the shore, and maintaining adequate setbacks for buildings, affords considerable natural protection against the power of winds and waves from coastal storms.

DUNE CROSS SECTION

Source: Schwab 1998.

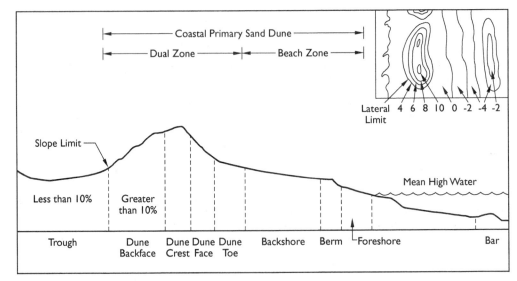

The main elements of beach and dune systems. The dune and beach system extends from a few feet offshore, including sand deposits and the beach profile that extends underwater, to landward of the primary dune. Other key elements include the beach face (extending to the beginning of the berm), the first line of vegetation, and the primary dune itself (including the tune toe, face, crest, and backface).

DETAILED BEACH AND DUNE ELEMENTS

Source: Virginia Marine Resources Commission 1993.

Timothy Beatley, Ph.D., University of Virginia, Charlottesville, Virginia

POLICY ISSUES

Federal

Federal policy toward beaches and dunes is primarily found in the Coastal Zone Management Act (CZMA), enacted in 1972. Under CZMA, coastal states have been encouraged to prepare coastal management programs, with extensive federal funding provided for their development, and, once approved, their implementation. While most beach and dune management and regulation happens at the state and local levels, many of these programs owe their existence directly to the encouragement and incentives of CZMA.

A related law, the Coastal Barrier Resources Act (CBRA), was enacted by Congress in 1982 (and substantially expanded in 1990). It restricts availability of federal flood insurance, nonemergency disaster assistance, and other federal funds for development projects and infrastructure on designated undeveloped barrier island units. (See Beatley, Brower, and Schwab (2002) for an extensive discussion of these and other federal coastal laws and programs.)

State and Local

A number of local planning and policy issues emerge with respect to beach and dune systems. In most coastal states, it is no longer permitted to destroy or otherwise negatively affect natural dunes. North Carolina and Florida, for example, impose erosion-based beachfront setbacks that mandate a minimum distance from the ocean for new construction.

Under North Carolina's Coastal Area Management Act (CAMA), new development along the oceanfront must be set back a minimum distance of 30 times the average annual rate of erosion for that particular stretch of coast, measured from the first line of vegetation (Beatley, Brower, and Schwab 2002). For larger structures, this distance is 60 times the rate of erosion. North Carolina's regulations also mandate that development be set back from primary and frontal dunes, and impose a minimum distance of 60 feet.

Florida implements a similar, but more complicated permitting system for construction along its oceanfront. Since the 1970s, the state has delineated and regulated activities seaward of its so-called Coastal Construction Control Lines (CCCL). These lines are intended to depict the landward extent of the wave action, winds, and flooding likely to be experienced from a 100-year storm. Construction seaward of the CCCL must be designed to withstand these forces, including, for instance, minimum 110 mph wind load (115 mph in the Florida Keys). Within the CCCL, Florida also enforces a 30-year erosion setback line, similar to North Carolina's. Calculated on a site-specific basis, development likely to be threatened by erosion within 30 years is not permitted. In addition, a special Coastal Building Zone was created in the mid-1980s, and imposes special construction standards for development within a zone that extends from mean high water to 1,500 feet landward of the CCCL.

In addition to these measures, there is a growing sentiment among coastal planners that more proactive and aggressive management standards ought to be applied. Among these measures are requiring a minimum 100-year shoreline setback (requiring new development to be landward of where the shoreline will be, and where erosion will occur, within a 100-year period) and taking into account future impacts of

Timothy Beatley, Ph.D., University of Virginia, Charlottesville, Virginia

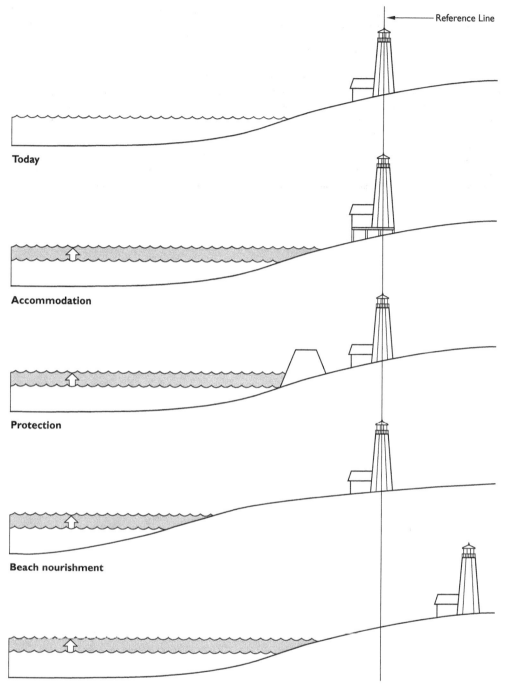

Today

Accommodation

Protection

Beach nourishment

Retreat

Reference Line

There are several major approaches to shore protection. Adaptive responses include accommodation, maintaining the physical location of development along the coast, but designing it in ways that minimize damage (e.g., flood elevation), or other strategies, such as evacuation, that acknowledge the hazardousness of these shoreline locations. Protection entails structurally armoring the shoreline, as through the construction of seawalls and revetments. Shoreline retreat suggests the need to adjust to coastal forces by gradually moving people and property back from the water's edge, as through coastal setback requirements or acquisition/relocation following a hurricane or storm.

ALTERNATIVES FOR STORM PROTECTION

Source: U.S. Army Corps of Engineers, Coastal Engineering Manual 2003.

sea-level rise on long-term coastal flooding and shoreline change (Beatley, Brower, and Schwab 2002).

Many communities have adopted dune protection ordinances and other building and land-use regulations that apply in beach and dune areas. Dune protection ordinances typically prohibit building on or major alter-ation of dunes and dune vegetation. Elevated walkover structures providing pedestrian access to beaches without damaging dunes are commonly required. In Oregon, under its Goal 18, "Beaches and Dunes," local governments must inventory and include in their comprehensive plans beach and dune areas. Most development in these areas is prohibited, and grading plans are required for any dune alteration. (Check local ordinances for specific requirements.)

Actions are also commonly taken to build dunes where they are meager or nonexistent, often along developed coastlines. Techniques include planting sea oats, beach grasses, and other native vegetation, and erecting sand fences, both relatively inexpensive methods for enhancing and restoring the beach. Where there is room, municipalities should also establish dune buffer zones; these are areas landward of existing dunes where dune migration can be permitted to occur over time. Dune building efforts must be cognizant of the potential impacts on the habitat values of the beach. Construction of continuous sand fences, for instance, is often not desirable because of the potential negative impact on nesting sea turtles.

REFERENCES

Beatley, Timothy, David J. Brower, and Anna K. Schwab. 2002. *An Introduction to Coastal Zone Management*. Washington, DC: Island Press.

Bird, Eric C.F. 1996. *Beach Management*. Hoboken, NJ: John Wiley & Sons, Inc.

Rogers, Spencer, and David Nash, 2003. *The Dune Book*. Raleigh, NC: North Carolina Sea Grant.

Schwab, Jim, et al. 1998. Planning for Post-Disaster Recovery and Reconstruction. Planning Advisory Service Report No. 483/484. Chicago: American Planning Association.

Virginia Marine Resources Commission. 1993. *Coastal Primary Sand Dunes/Beach Guidelines: Guidelines for the Permitting of Activities Which Encroach into Coastal Primary Sand Dunes/Beaches*. Newport News, VA.

See also:
Erosion and Sedimentation
Estuaries, Flats, and Marshes

Timothy Beatley, Ph.D., University of Virginia, Charlottesville, Virginia

ESTUARIES, FLATS, AND MARSHES

An estuary is a transitional aquatic zone, the area between freshwater river systems and open ocean. Estuaries generally involve the mixing of freshwater from rivers and river systems with saltwater from oceans. Of the more than 100 estuaries in the United States, major examples include the Chesapeake Bay, Galveston Bay, Albemarle-Pamlico Sound (in North Carolina), Narragansett Bay, and Puget Sound.

BENEFITS OF ESTUARIES

Estuaries are highly productive ecosystems. They provide important habitat for some 75 percent of the nation's commercial fish, as well as for migratory birds and other wildlife. Estuaries also filter pollutants and provide buffers to storms and flooding. According to Restore America's Estuaries, the economic value of commercial fish catch in estuaries is estimated at more than $100 billion per year, providing some 28 million jobs.

ESTUARY CLASSIFICATION BY GEOLOGIC FEATURES

Estuaries can be classified according to their geological features and origins. Four types of estuaries can be identified this way: flooded river valleys (or drowned river valleys), tectonic estuaries, fjords, and bar-built estuaries.

Flooded river valleys. Sea-level rise is the driving cause in creating flooded river valley estuaries. The Chesapeake Bay and Narragansett Bay are prominent examples.

Tectonic estuaries. In tectonic estuaries, tectonic forces cause land sinking or subsidence, as in the case of the San Francisco Bay.

Fjords. Fjords are deeply cut valleys formed through glacial movement. In the United States, they are found only in Alaska.

Bar-built estuaries. Bar-built estuaries, such as Albemarle-Pamlico Sound and Galveston Bay, are created through the formation of barrier islands that create protected aquatic systems behind them.

ESTUARY CLASSIFICATION BY MIXING AND CIRCULATION

Estuaries are also commonly classified according to the extent and nature of the mixing and circulation of freshwater and saline water. Three types of estuaries are commonly identified in this way: stratified, partially mixed, and fully mixed.

Stratified. In stratified estuaries, freshwater and saltwater layers remain largely separate, with heavier saltwater usually nearer the bottom. The presence of large rivers characterizes these estuaries.

Partially mixed. The Chesapeake Bay is a partially mixed estuary, where large areas of brackish water are found and where there is a range of water salinities.

Fully mixed. In fully mixed estuaries, salinity levels are constant throughout.

The precise mixing of freshwater and saltwater in an estuary is a function of many factors, including wave action and the extent of seasonal changes in river flows and wind patterns. Estuaries are highly affected by sediment transport and can also be classified according to the relative influence of river flow, wave action, and tidal action (river-dominated, tide-dominated, and wave-dominated estuaries; see Davis 1994).

ECOLOGICAL ZONES

Estuaries are composed of several important habitats or ecological zones. These include transitional lands on the margins of the estuary, which are often the most ecologically productive. Salt marshes and intertidal flats, especially, perform critical biological and environmental functions by filtering pollutants, reducing shoreline erosion, absorbing floodwaters, and providing critical habitat and food sources for birds and wildlife, among others. These are areas that generate high primary productivity from plant growth and serve as important exporters of organic matter.

Other important estuarine habitats include oyster reefs and sea grass meadows (submerged aquatic vegetation, or SAV). These habitats, which are always submerged, provide important nursery grounds for fish and aquatic life, refuge from predators, and nutrient banks, and help to oxygenate and stabilize estuarine sediments. Open bay waters and benthic (or sea floor) habitats are also important for many species, including flounder and shellfish, as well as a variety of invertebrate species.

Any estuarine ecosystem also consists of the critical upland areas of rivers and streams, riverine wetlands, and forests. Maintaining these habitats is essential for ensuring water quality downstream and for understanding that the ultimate health of estuaries depends on a complete watershed perspective.

PRESSURES AND THREATS

These highly productive ecosystems face numerous threats. Many U.S. estuaries have already been heavily altered. For example, more than 90 percent of the wetlands that originally existed along the San Francisco Bay are now gone. Galveston Bay has lost 70 percent of its sea grasses. In the Chesapeake Bay, some 90 percent of the sea grass meadows have been lost, and oyster harvests there have experienced a major decline, from 25 million pounds in 1959 to 1 million pounds in 1989.

Excessive nutrient loadings, especially nitrogen and phosphorous, are major problems in many estuaries. Major sources of these nutrients are runoff from

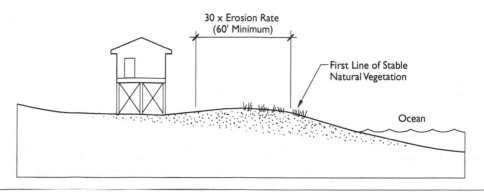

STRUCTURE SETBACK FROM EROSION SETBACK LINE

Source: North Carolina Division of Coastal Management 2004.

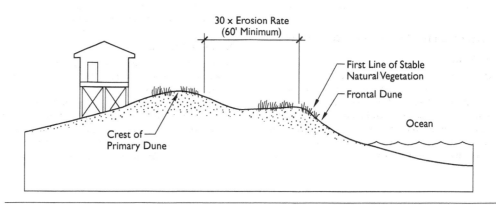

STRUCTURE SETBACK FROM CREST OF PRIMARY DUNE

Source: North Carolina Division of Coastal Management 2004.

Timothy Beatley, Ph.D., University of Virginia, Charlottesville, Virginia

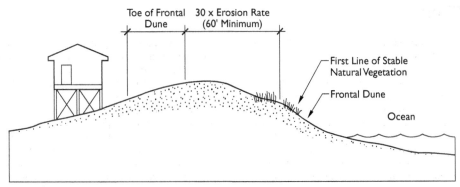

Under the North Carolina Coastal Area Management Act, all buildings being constructed in the area designated the Ocean Hazard Area of Environmental Concern (AEC) have to be set back as far from the ocean as possible. At a minimum, all buildings must be located behind the crest of the primary dune, the landward toe of the frontal dune, or the erosion setback line, whichever is farthest from the first line of stable natural vegetation.

STRUCTURE SETBACK FROM TOE OF FRONTAL DUNE

Source: North Carolina Division of Coastal Management 2004.

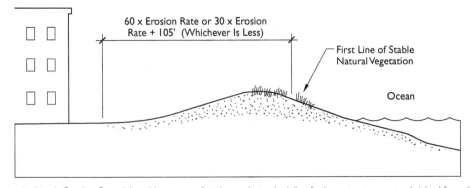

Under the North Carolina Coastal Area Management Act, the erosion setback line for large structures extends inland from the first line of stable natural vegetation a distance of 60 times the average annual erosion rate at the site. The minimum setback is 20 feet. In areas where the erosion rate is more than 3.5 feet per year, the setback line is set at a distance 30 times the annual erosion rate, plus 105 feet.

STRUCTURE SETBACK FOR LARGE STRUCTURES

Source: North Carolina Division of Coastal Management 2004.

farm fields, urbanization, airborne sources from car and truck emissions, and discharges from older municipal sewage treatment plants. Sea-level rise, which may especially raise winter water temperatures, is also likely to have significant ecological effects—shifting the range of certain aquatic species and making estuaries more subject to invasion by nonnative species (Bosch, Field, and Scavia 2000).

PROTECTION AND MANAGEMENT

Federal

The federal government has actively sought to conserve and protect the nation's estuaries. Under the federal Coastal Zone Management Act (CZMA), the National Estuarine Research Reserve System (NERRS) was created. Intended to protect representative samples of estuarine ecosystems, 26 reserves covering more than 1 million acres have been designated

(National Oceanic and Atmospheric Administration 2002). Another important initiative, the National Estuaries Program, has funded substantial estuarine research and the development of Comprehensive Conservation and Management Plans for 17 U.S. estuaries. These management plans, developed through extensive participation and work with stakeholder groups, serve as "blueprints," to guide future management policy and planning decisions.

State and Local

Under Oregon's planning system, Goal 16 ("Estuarine Resources") requires localities to prepare estuaries plans, consistent with overall development limits established by the state for each estuary. In North Carolina, the Coastal Area Management Act (CAMA) applies significant regulatory standards to estuarine resources, including restrictions on the alteration of coastal marshes, development setbacks along estuar-

ine shorelines, and limits on the size of docks, marinas, and other projects affecting estuaries.

Estuaries sometimes extend beyond state boundaries, requiring multistate strategies. The Chesapeake Bay drains a watershed of 64,000 square miles, for instance, and is affected by activities in four states and the District of Columbia. Consequently, a unique cooperative interstate compact—the Chesapeake Bay Agreement—was entered into in 1983 and has been reratified several times. It establishes a set of management and conservation targets for all parties. The most recent agreement, in 2000, lays out some ambitious goals—all to be met by 2010—including those with major land-use and community planning implications:

- Permanent protection of 20 percent of the land base of the watershed
- Cleanup and restoration of 1,050 brownfield sites
- Restoration of an additional 25,000 acres of wetlands
- Expansion of the riparian forest buffer by 2,010 miles

LAND USE AND DEVELOPMENT PRACTICES

Modifying land-use and development practices in the watersheds that drain into estuaries must be a key planning strategy in protecting estuaries. During the development process, planners and developers should take steps to reduce the extent of impervious surfaces and to use a variety of low-impact development techniques, such as rain gardens, bioswales, tree planting, and green rooftops. Conserving existing wetlands and natural habitat and encouraging new farming techniques that reduce organic and chemical runoff (e.g., agricultural buffers, planting of perennial crops, crop rotation) are also important steps. Because many estuaries have already been highly altered, restoration is an equally important goal. Converting farmland back to forests and wetlands, restoring upland fish passages, restoring sea grasses and oyster beds, and cleaning up contaminated port and industrial lands are all valid actions.

REFERENCES

Davis, Richard A. 1994. *The Evolving Coast*, New York: Henry Holt and Company.

National Oceanic and Atmospheric Administration. 2002. *Strategic Plan, National Estuaries Research Reserve System, 2003-2008*, Washington, DC: NOAA.

Boesch, Donald F., John C. Field , and Donald Scavia, eds. 2000. *The Potential Consequences of Climate Variability and Change: A Report of the National Coastal Assessment Group for the U.S. Global Change Research Program*. Washington, D.C.: National Oceanic and Atmospheric Administration.

See also:

Wetlands

Timothy Beatley, Ph.D., University of Virginia, Charlottesville, Virginia

LAND

SLOPE, RELIEF, AND ASPECT

Slope, relief, and aspect all relate to the topography of a land surface. Knowing how the land surface elevation varies across a site is useful for site design and land protection.

SLOPE

Slope is the rate of change in elevation between two points in a given area. Slope is measured by:

1. determining the difference in elevation between two points (the rise), and
2. dividing the elevation by the horizontal distance between the two points (the run).

The difference in height ("rise over run") can be determined from surveyed points or estimated from the contour lines on a topographic map. This calculation yields a number between 0 and 1, which is often converted to a percentage. A slope of 1 (or 100 percent) implies a vertical drop. A slope of zero (or 0 percent) implies a completely flat surface.

Slope must be known to properly design roads and structures and to evaluate the stability or extent of

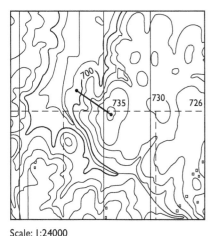

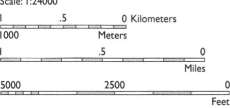

Scale: 1:24000

Contour Interval 10 Feet
National Geodetic Vertical Datum of 1929

Length of Measured Line = 0.5 Inches

Horizontal Distance = 0.5 Inches $\times \dfrac{2,000 \text{ Ft.}}{1 \text{ Inch}}$ = 1,000 Feet

Elevation Change = 40 Feet (from Contour Lines)

Percent Slope = $\dfrac{40 \text{ Ft.}}{1,000 \text{ Ft.}} \times 100$ = 4% Slope

CALCULATING SLOPE FROM A TOPOGRAPHIC MAP

Source: USGS 1999.

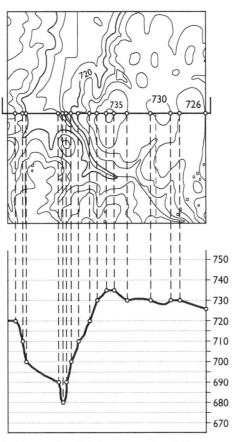

Drawing a section: (1) Indicate cutting plane. (2) Draw parallel lines according to contour internal and proposed vertical scale. (3) Project perpendicular lines from the intersection of the contour line with the current plane to the corresponding parallel line. (4) Connect the points to complete the section and delineate the ground line.

SLOPE IN SECTION VIEW

Source: USGS 1999.

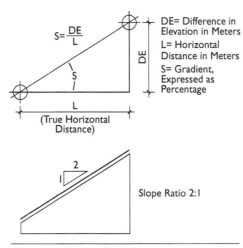

$S = \dfrac{DE}{L}$

DE= Difference in Elevation in Meters
L= Horizontal Distance in Meters
S= Gradient, Expressed as Percentage

(True Horizontal Distance)

Slope Ratio 2:1

CALCULATING SLOPE AS A PERCENTAGE AND A RATIO

Source: American Planning Association 2001.

potential erosion at a site. Roads need to be designed so that the slope is not too steep. Many state or town regulations specify a maximum slope. (Check local regulations for the maximum slope allowed.) The maximum slope is often between 5 percent and 10 percent. To achieve this, site grading may be required; this involves either removing or adding soil (cutting or filling) to create the proper slope.

It is also necessary to know a site's slope to design appropriate revegetation plans to hold soils in place after final grading is complete. In steeply sloped areas, an erosion control fabric is often used to retain soils until the vegetation takes hold.

RELIEF

Relief expands on the concept of slope. It refers to the overall changes in topography on a site or a particular region. Relief is defined as the vertical difference in elevation between highlands and lowlands in a given region. A relief map represents the changes in topography. They are often created by shading the areas between contours on a topographic map. The thinness or thickness of these shaded areas implies how quickly the topography is changing. The less distance between the contours, the faster the relief is changing, and the greater the slope of the land. Relief maps can be created in three dimensions to depict changes in topography as changes in height of the map surface

A geographic information system (GIS) software package can be used to readily develop a relief map. These maps are often created as digital elevation models, which are developed by creating a grid

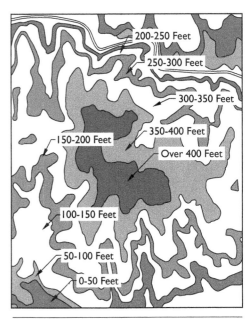

200-250 Feet
250-300 Feet
300-350 Feet
350-400 Feet
150-200 Feet
Over 400 Feet
100-150 Feet
50-100 Feet
0-50 Feet

RELIEF MAP

Source: USGS.

Mark E. Nelson, LEP, Horsley Witten Group, Sandwich, Massachusetts

across a particular area, designating an elevation for each cell in the grid, and calculating the change in elevation between grid cells. A digital elevation model can be used to calculate and remap changes in the land surface elevation caused by proposed site grading.

Relief maps are often used to evaluate the pathways for existing or proposed drainage through a watershed or across a site. As shown on a relief map, runoff flows downhill, perpendicular to the topographic contours. Runoff erosion is typically greatest in the steepest slope areas, where water will be traveling the fastest. Relief maps also depict the areas with the highest elevation. This information can be used to evaluate the view from a particular site and to determine how development along the top of a slope or ridge will affect the view from areas further downslope.

ASPECT

Aspect is the direction in which a sloping land surface faces relative to the cardinal points, such as southern aspect and northern aspect. It is measured in compass degrees. An aspect of 90 degrees means

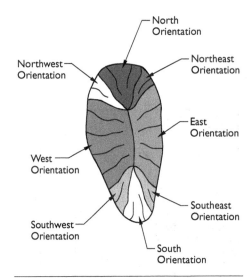

CONCEPT OF ASPECT

Source: Horsley Witten Group.

a sloping hillside faces due east. An aspect of 180 degrees describes a south-facing slope.

Aspect maps are maps of selected aspect categories, which are broken down further into southwest, southeast, northeast, northwest, and so on. When site topography data are available, aspect can be readily calculated and mapped in a GIS software package. Aspect maps are constructed on the basis of contour line data, not slope data. Aspect change is measured relative to the change in direction of contour lines.

The interaction between aspect, slope, and relief changes microclimate conditions. Aspect is useful in evaluating solar orientation for maximizing passive solar gain for building construction or for evaluating how solar illumination supports or restricts the agricultural use of a property. Knowledge of aspect is also useful for viewshed protection and, for ski-resort design, to understand how the sun or predominant wind patterns will affect the retention of snow on a ski slope, for example.

See also:

Erosion and Sedimentation
Landslides
Viewshed Protection

Mark E. Nelson, LEP, Horsley Witten Group, Sandwich, Massachusetts

SOILS CLASSIFICATION AND MECHANICS

Soils are unconsolidated sediments originating both from the breakdown of solid rock and from the decay of organic material. A soil must contain nutrients and trace minerals to be capable of supporting plant growth. The mineral component of soils originates from the underlying parent material, which can include rock in sedimentary, igneous, or metamorphic forms, or unconsolidated sediments previously created from rock through alluvial or glacial processes. The type of soil formed from the parent rock depends on how the rock weathers, which is a function of climate, topography, biologic activity, and time.

Soils information is used in a number of planning applications, including agricultural management, resource protection planning (such as for watersheds), site design, wastewater and stormwater management, erosion control, and building/foundation design.

SOIL HORIZONS

The soil formation process creates layers, called horizons, with depths that can be seen in a test hole dug into the ground. Soil horizon mapping is used to create a soil profile. A typical soil profile can have up to six layers extending into the ground, including:

O horizon. A thin organic-rich layer at the surface that consists of decaying plant material and humus.

A horizon. Also known as the topsoil layer, it consists of organic material mixed completely with the mineral soil particles.

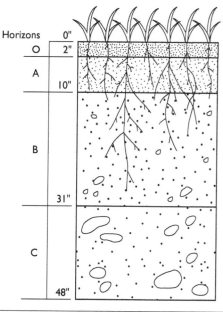

TYPICAL SOIL PROFILE
Source: USDA.

E horizon. A band of mineral soil with little organic material where infiltrating water has leached many of the trace minerals and metals further into the ground. The E horizon is not found in all soils.

B horizon. Also known as the subsoil, it is the next layer where materials leached from the overlying soil layers have been deposited.

C horizon. Represents the unconsolidated material that has not been affected by the soil formation processes.

Bedrock or ledge. If it exists near the surface, it is found below the C horizon. If rock has weathered in place, there may be no C horizon, and bedrock is found directly below the B horizon.

SOIL TEXTURE

Soil texture is the relative proportion of three particle sizes within a particular soil: sand, silt, and clay. Larger gravels or cobbles are also sometimes included. The U.S. Department of Agriculture, Natural Resources Conservation Service (NRCS), formerly the Soil Conservation Service, classifies the sand, silt, and clay particles by specific size ranges. Running a soil sample through a series of sieves and measuring the percentage of materials that passes through mesh of a sieve with a particular opening size can measure the particle sizes. Soil texture can also be identified in the field.

The NRCS has created a soil triangle to provide a standardized way of defining soil texture. A soil that is 100 percent sand, silt, or clay would be defined by one of the three points of the triangle. Mixtures of the three are then defined based on where they fall within the triangle. Clay soils contain a minimum of 40 percent clay particles. Loam is a relatively equal mixture of all three particle sizes. Loam soils are further defined by describing which of the three particle sizes is dominant (sandy loam, silt loam, or clay loam).

Soil texture is often used to determine the loading rate for wastewater effluent in the design of on-site

SIZE FRACTIONS OF SOIL PARTICLES

FRACTION NAME		DIAMETER (MM)
Sand		2.00–0.05
	Very coarse	2.00–1.00
	Coarse	1.00–0.50
	Medium	0.50–0.25
	Fine	0.25–0.10
	Very Fine	0.10–0.05
Silt		0.05–0.002
	Coarse	0.05–0.02
	Medium	0.02–0.01
	Fine	0.01–0.002
Clay		<0.002
	Coarse	0.002–0.0002
	Fine	<0.0002

Source: U.S. Department of Agriculture.

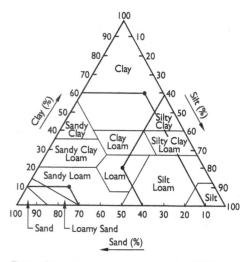

Three soil textures are shown on this standard USDA textural triangle: a sandy loam, loam, and clay. Also shown are the textural class names and range of allowable sand, silt, and clay values for each.

SOIL TRIANGLE
Source: USDA, NRCS 1993.

septic systems or larger wastewater disposal facilities. It is also commonly used to design stormwater infiltration facilities.

SOIL SURVEYS

Soils have been mapped for most, if not all, of the United States. The NRCS publishes soil surveys, containing maps and descriptions, for each county or a portion of a county.

Soil surveys provide maps on an aerial photo base map that shows the locations of general, or regional, soil map units. The general map units differentiate soils by major soil groups, created by evaluating the soil texture and grouping similar soils based on local topography and drainage patterns. A map unit contains one or more major soil units and may contain a few minor soil units, such as a small area of isolated wetland soils in an upland soil unit. The general map unit is named after the major soil within the unit.

General soil units are also broken down into more detailed soil map units that provide soils data on a more localized scale. These detailed map units are named, and a description of the soil is provided that explains soil composition, profile depth, and slope.

The NRCS soil surveys provide a wealth of data on the suitability of individual soils for a variety of uses, including agriculture, forestry, wildlife habitat, site development, wastewater disposal, landfill, use in construction materials, such as gravel mining and cement production, and water management. Therefore, the soil survey is worth reviewing for most planning studies, both at the watershed scale and site scale.

Mark E. Nelson, LEP, Horsley Witten Group, Sandwich, Massachusetts

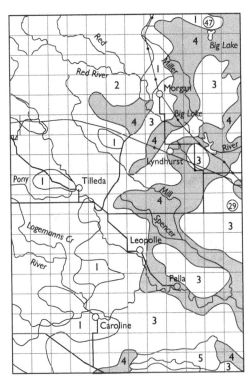

□ 1   Kennan-Rosholt: Nearly Level to Very Steep. Well Drained. Loamy Soils: on Uplands

□ 2   Rosholt-Seelyeville: Nearly Level to Very Steep. Well Drained and Very Poorly Drained. Loamy and Mucky Soils: on Uplands and in Depressions.

□ 3   Tilleda-Menominee: Nearly Level to Moderately Steep. Well Drained, Loamy and Sandy Soils: on Uplands.

■ 4   Menahga-Croswell-Mahtomedi: Nearly Level to Steep. Excessively Drained and Moderately Well Drained, Sandy Soils: on Uplands.

□ 5   Cormant-Markey-Wainola: Nearly Level and Gently Sloping. Somewhat Poorly Drained to Very Poorly Drained. Sandy and Mucky Soils: on Uplands and in Upland Drainageways and Depressions.

*Texture Terms in the Descriptive Headings Refer to Surface Layer of the Major Soils in the Map Units.

SOIL MAP WITH SOIL DESCRIPTION

Source: USGS 1981.

SOIL MECHANICS

An understanding of soil mechanics, the evaluation of the mechanical properties of soils, is needed for proper site design and construction. The soil survey provides a first cut at this information, but, often, detailed, site-specific information is needed because soil texture can vary over short distances or at depth. Testing can include on-site test pits to map soils and *in situ* or laboratory analysis of their mechanical properties.

The two main soil mechanics issues are the compaction, or settling, of soils and their shear strength. Both of these are affected in part by the percentage of water within the soil matrix. This is especially true for clay soils.

Compaction

The weight of a structure, such as a building, road, or dam, can cause the underlying soils to compact and settle. These changes need to be considered to properly design the building to avoid settling problems. Laboratory tests of undisturbed soil samples can be used to estimate the extent of compaction. In addition, soil borings and sampling techniques can be used to estimate the density of soils and the potential for additional compaction or settling.

Shear Strength

The shear strength of a soil is its capability to resist a force acting at right angles to the soil formation. Understanding the shear strength is important in understanding the stability of a slope and the potential for soils to erode or fail catastrophically, especially where cuts or fills are proposed to change the existing topography. It is also important for structure design where the land is sloped and where the weight of a building or other structure can cause the soils to fail, potentially undermining the structure.

Shear strength is a function of both frictional resistance and the cohesive strength of the soils. Soils consisting of round particles will have less frictional resistance than flat or angular particles, which tend to interlock with each other and have more friction between them; they will remain more stable on a steep slope when additional weight is placed on top of them. Also, clay particles are electrically charged, and a strong bond can form between them, making them more cohesive than sandy soils and therefore resistant to compaction or movement. However, as clay soils become wet, the presence of water reduces their cohesive strength.

Shear strength can be determined through laboratory tests, such as a direct shear or triaxial compression test. In these tests, an undisturbed sample of the soil is pressurized and the amount of pressure needed to cause the soil to fracture or break apart is determined.

OTHER SOIL QUALITIES

A soil can exhibit dry, plastic, or liquid qualities, depending on the extent of water present. If soils are moist, they are plastic, and if deformed will retain their new shape. If too much water is added, soils behave as a viscous liquid. The plastic limit forms the boundary between solid (dry) and plastic soils, and the liquid limit represents the point at which a soil begins to behave as a liquid. These limits have been named Atterberg limits for the Swedish scientist who created the classification process. Clay soils that exhibit plastic properties are difficult to use in construction materials. In addition, clay soils tend to shrink and swell based on the amount of water they contain, creating further problems for siting structures. Buildings, bridges, or dams built on clay soils often need deeper footings to offset the shrink/swell properties of the clay, or require other design features to control the amount of water within the clay.

The water retention capability of a soil is also important in cold climates, where frost heaves can be formed. These are areas where soils expand and shift as they freeze as a result of the expansion of water as it freezes within the soil. Roads are typically constructed over a gravel or sand base that will not retain water and will minimize the damage caused by frost heaves. Building foundations and footings are also set below the frost level to reduce shifting of the structure caused by soil expansion in the frost layer.

In arid regions of the country, soil surveys can provide information on the water retention of a soil useful for irrigation planning for agriculture or turf management. They provide data on a soil's capability to adsorb or leach salts, which can affect plant productivity, the infiltration rate of the soil that will control the rate of irrigation water application, and the slope of the land surface that will control the extent of erosion caused by the irrigation water.

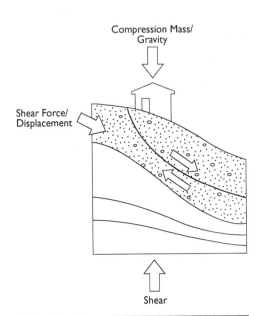

SHEAR STRENGTH

Source: Horsley Witten Group.

REFERENCES

Natural Resources Conservation Service, U.S. Department of Agriculture. Local soil surveys created for each county in the United States. http://soils.usda.gov/survey/online_surveys/.

See also:
Erosion and Sedimentation

Mark E. Nelson, LEP, Horsley Witten Group, Sandwich, Massachusetts

HABITAT PATCHES, CORRIDORS, AND MATRIX

An important cause of the loss of biodiversity in the United States and in the world is habitat fragmentation. Habitat fragmentation is the breaking up of a continuous habitat, ecosystem, or land-use type into smaller fragments.

Natural habitats are fragmented by topographic heterogeneity, such as hills and streams, as well as natural processes, such as fires, landslides, and floods. Natural habitat heterogeneity usually contributes to a rich biodiversity. Such mosaic patterns are found on all spatial scales and may be composed of patches, corridors, and matrix, which are the three basic spatial elements of any pattern on land. Patches of habitats with differing sizes and compositions and with merging borders and edges promote species richness and biodiversity.

Human activity can also create habitat fragmentation but usually results in a loss of biodiversity. Negative human activities include logging, conversion of forests into agricultural areas, urbanization, introduction of nonnative species, and road building. These activities create patches, corridors, boundaries, and mosaic patterns, but they can serve to break up natural habitat into smaller patches that no longer support many species. These changes affect natural dispersal and migration patterns. In addition, habitat changes often alter patterns of water and nutrient movement, species composition, and available vegetation cover such that habitats are no longer compatible with natural vegetation and wildlife.

PATCHES

Fragmented habitat consists of patches of habitat. Patches are spatial units at the landscape scale, which are surrounded by matrix and may be connected to other patches by corridors. These patches vary in size, with larger patches generally having greater diversity than similar but smaller patches. Some larger species require large home ranges for feeding or mating that may only occur in the largest patches.

Adjacent patches may share a common edge, with some "ecotonal" species adapted to these edges. Many interior species avoid edges, and these species are negatively affected when patches are very small with relatively larger edges.

Areas between patches are gaps and generally have little biodiversity. Patches with small gaps (closer together) are generally more valuable than patches with wide gaps because wider gaps present greater obstacles to migration and dispersal.

Nodes are patches with special conservation value because they have high diversity or because a target species of interest is abundant there.

WILDLIFE CORRIDORS

Corridors are elongated patches that connect other patches together. Corridors can vary from narrow to wide, high to low connectivity, and meandering to straight. Corridors often form interconnected networks across the landscape, such as road systems, lawns, and canals. The corridor's characteristics, such as width, connectivity, curvilinearity, and nodes, determine its importance as a conduit or a barrier.

Connectivity describes how patches are connected in the landscape by corridors. A spatial connection means either the patches are sufficiently close so that movement can occur among them or there is some other corridor along which the organisms can move. Several analytical methods are available to determine connectivity:

- Gamma Index: ratio of the number of links to the maximum possible number of links
- Alpha Index: a measure of "circuitry," or loops that provide alternative routes for flow
- Connectivity Matrix: identifies direct and indirect connections

RESERVE DESIGN

The best way to preserve biodiversity is to avoid activities that cause habitat loss or fragmentation. But this is rarely possible, so an alternative is to design developments in a way that protects biodiversity as much as possible using corridors to connect patches of habitat.

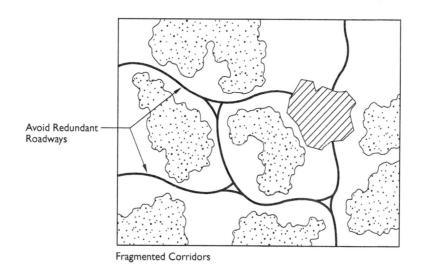

Avoid Redundant Roadways

Fragmented Corridors

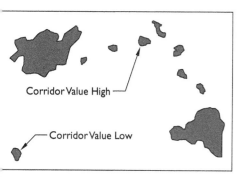

Corridor Value High

Corridor Value Low

STEPPING STONES
Source: American Planning Association.

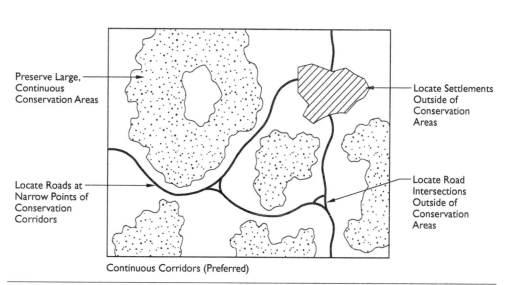

Preserve Large, Continuous Conservation Areas

Locate Roads at Narrow Points of Conservation Corridors

Locate Settlements Outside of Conservation Areas

Locate Road Intersections Outside of Conservation Areas

Continuous Corridors (Preferred)

CONTINUOUS CORRIDORS
Source: American Planning Association.

James F. Berry, J.D. Ph.D., Elmhurst College, Elmhurst, Illinois

In designing a reserve with interconnecting corridors, it is best to minimize the edge affect. The core area of one habitat (where human activity is minimized) is connected to the core area of another habitat by a corridor. This corridor must have sufficient habitat characteristics to sustain dispersing or migrating animals for the time they spend in the corridor. Ideally, buffer areas where human activity is minimized as much as possible surround both the patches and the corridors. The area beyond the buffer zone is open to human activity (and only human-tolerant wildlife species can be found there).

Several empirical techniques are available for reserve design. The best involve GIS technology and gap analysis, which is a scientific method for identifying the degree to which native animal species and natural communities are represented in conservation lands. Those species and communities not adequately represented in the existing network of conservation lands constitute conservation "gaps." The National Gap Analysis Program (GAP) provides broad geographic information on the status of ordinary species (those not threatened with extinction or naturally rare)

and their habitats in order to provide land managers, planners, scientists, and policymakers with the information they need to make better-informed decisions. However, planners should enter the field of reserve design very carefully. Even the most careful reserve design cannot protect all biodiversity.

SUCCESS OF CORRIDORS

The use of corridors in design reserves is controversial. For more than 20 years, conservation biologists have emphasized the potential benefits of connecting fragmented pieces of habitat with habitat corridors. However, a lack of empirical evidence regarding the success of corridors has prevented planners and land managers from recommending their use. Several studies now show that corridors work for certain species, but not all. As would be expected, species that tolerate human presence in general are the best suited for corridors.

Landscape ecologists and conservation biologists are split on the issue. Critics argue that reserves with elaborate corridors are expensive to construct and maintain, and probably do little to conserve biodiver-

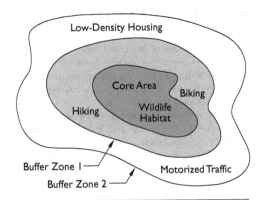

THE CORE/BUFFER CONCEPT

Source: American Planning Association.

sity. Supporters counter that they may be the last and best hope for preserving large areas of habitat in an increasingly fragmented world.

See also:
Biodiversity Protection

James F. Berry, J.D. Ph.D., Elmhurst College, Elmhurst, Illinois

BIODIVERSITY PROTECTION

The protection of biodiversity, or the total variety of life and its interactions, has become a major environmental challenge for planners. Conservation biologists emphasize that biodiversity must be protected at three levels: species diversity, genetic diversity, and ecological or ecosystem diversity.

THE VALUE OF BIODIVERSITY

Biodiversity is generally accorded high value because it benefits ecosystems in ways that positively affect human health and well being. For example, healthy natural ecosystems help to provide fresh air, clean water, and productive soils. Furthermore, natural products, such as foods and medicines, result from healthy biodiversity, which leads to benefits that maintain a healthy economy. The natural beauty of healthy ecosystems supports recreation and improves the quality of life.

Unfortunately, all indications suggest biodiversity is being rapidly lost, both in the United States and worldwide. Many factors probably contribute to dwindling biodiversity, but habitat loss and fragmentation due to human impact and introduction of nonnative species of plants and animals are among the most important.

EXISTING LEGAL REMEDIES TO THREATS TO BIODIVERSITY

Legal protection of biodiversity is limited. The federal Endangered Species Act (ESA) makes it unlawful for any person to "take" an endangered species or to damage the species' "critical habitat." Other federal laws, such as the Marine Mammal Protection Act, offer protection to specific groups of animals and plants. Most states have their own version of the ESA, which often provides protection to additional species.

A few states have developed biodiversity protection programs. For example, California's Natural Communities Conservation Planning Act provides a measure of protection for valuable ecosystems and their associated biodiversity. In addition, all state fish and wildlife agencies are now engaged in completing comprehensive wildlife conservation strategies under the new State Wildlife Grants program. Each state is charged with completing a strategy by October 2005. The intent of these plans is to address wildlife habitat needs before species require listing under the Endangered Species Act. Many statewide biodiversity planning efforts are being connected to these wildlife strategy efforts.

At the international level, the Convention on Biological Diversity (CBD) was designed for "the conservation of biological diversity, the sustainable use of its components, and the fair and equitable sharing of the benefits arising out of the utilization of genetic resources."

WILDLIFE INVENTORIES, WILDLIFE MAPPING, AND HABITAT ASSESSMENT

Before action can be taken to protect and enhance biodiversity, it is first necessary to evaluate the extent of the problem. Landscape ecologists have developed

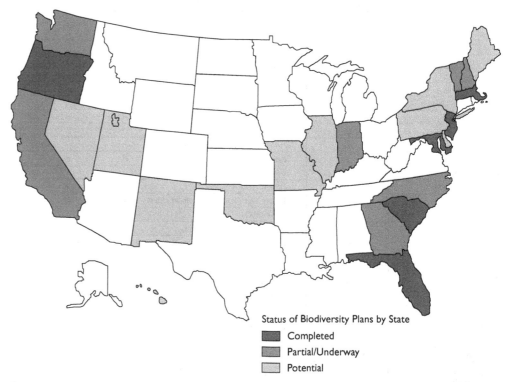

Status of Biodiversity Plans by State
- ■ Completed
- ■ Partial/Underway
- ▫ Potential

Several state agencies, local and regional governments, and conservation groups have started comprehensive biodiversity conservation planning processes. Florida, Massachusetts, Maryland, New Jersey, and Oregon have developed plans; seven other states have begun to draft plans; and other states have expressed interest in drafting plans in the near future. South Carolina has completed a statewide assessment.

STATEWIDE BIODIVERSITY PLANNING STATUS MAP, 2003

Source: Defenders of Wildlife 2003.

several useful tools for the purpose, but among the most useful is the wildlife inventory (WI).

A WI is a comprehensive listing of species of plants and animals in an area, which ideally also provides at least some information on relative abundance of each species. A WI can be a formidable undertaking because it requires a great deal of taxonomic expertise to identify plants and animals and a great deal of time and effort. Many successful WIs have enlisted the assistance of volunteers and community activists who are trained to identify certain kinds of species.

An ideal WI should account for all species of plants and animals in an area as well as for seasonal differences in abundance. Such an accounting is functionally impossible for large, topographically complex areas with many species. As an acceptable alternative, a modified WI may be performed in which only certain key species are identified, such as "keystone species" (i.e., those that are especially important to an ecosystem) or species that are simple to see and count.

Linear Transect

A common WI method uses a linear transect: Surveyors simply identify individual plants and/or animals and count them. Linear transects can be conducted on foot or by vehicle. They usually follow predetermined straight lines, roads, contours, or drainages. Species may be sampled continuously along the transect or at fixed points along it.

Mapping and Gap Analysis

An important part of a WI is the preparation of accurate mapping of the data derived from the transects. Accurate maps of wildlife and vegetation provide the habitat, species, topography, and land management information necessary to protect biodiversity. In many cases, wildlife maps allow examination of wildlife species currently protected by existing public reserves and identify "gaps" (that is, those species and habitats not found on public lands or preserves and therefore requiring protection). Maps can be verified in a variety of ways, including field observation, use of existing covertype maps, and airborne videography.

Gap analysis has become technologically sophisticated, and now can yield several important kinds of information:

- Land cover/land-use maps (including digital maps) based on Landsat or other satellite imagery
- Maps of predicted species distribution
- Land ownership, biodiversity protection on public land, and stewardship.

With appropriate wildlife inventories and maps, it becomes possible to identify and analyze the most effective means for protecting threatened habitats and species.

James F. Berry, J.D. Ph.D., Elmhurst College, Elmhurst, Illinois

WILDLIFE INVENTORY FOR WETLAND BIRD SPECIES

SPECIES	NUMBER OF DETECTIONS	HABITAT CLASS
Horned Grebe	2	Open Water/Emergent Vegetation
Canada Goose	119	Open Water/Emergent Vegetation
Mallard	16	Open Water/Emergent Vegetation
American Wigeon	1	Open Water/Emergent Vegetation
Ring-necked Duck	4	Open Water/Emergent Vegetation
Common Goldeneye	2	Open Water/Emergent Vegetation
Barrow's Goldeneye	5	Open Water/Emergent Vegetation
Goldeneye spp.	8	Open Water/Emergent Vegetation
Bufflehead	16	Open Water/Emergent Vegetation
Common Merganser	6	Open Water/Emergent Vegetation
Bald Eagle	1	Nutrient Rich—Mixed
Belted Kingfisher	1	Sand/Gravel/Cobble
Downy Woodpecker	1	Nutrient Rich—Mixed
Northern Flicker	2	Nutrient Rich—Deciduous, Upland Mesic-Coniferous
Steller's Jay	1	Nutrient Rich—Deciduous
Common Raven	2	Over Upland Mesic—Coniferous
Chestnut-backed Chickadee	16	Nutrient Rich—Mixed and Deciduous, Upland Mesic—Mixed and Coniferous
Red-breasted Nuthatch	12	Nutrient Rich—Mixed, Upland Mesic—Mixed and Coniferous
Brown Creeper	4	Nutrient Rich-Mixed and Deciduous Upland Mesic—Coniferous
Winter Wren	8	Nutrient Rich—Mixed and Deciduous Upland Mesic—Mixed
American Dipper	3	Sand/Gravel/Cobble
Golden-crowned Kinglet	12	Nutrient Rich—Mixed and Deciduous, Upland Mesic—Mixed
Varied Thrush	3	Nutrient Rich—Mixed
Dark-eyed Junco	3	Upland Mesic—Coniferous
Pine Siskin	57	Nutrient Rich—Mixed and Deciduous, Upland Mesic—Mixed
Evening Grosbeak	42	Nutrient Rich—Deciduous, Upland Mesic—Mixed
Total Number:	**347**	
Total Species: 25		

Note: Data are from four days of observations in the Stehekin River drainage area, Washington State, in January and February 1992.

Source: National Park Service 1992.

METHODS

A variety of techniques are now available to facilitate wildlife inventories and wildlife mapping.

PATN Pattern Analysis

The PATN Pattern Analysis software package, designed for ecological analysis, incorporates a range of algorithms to identify and interpret patterns in terms of variation of climatic and substrate variables, species, topography, or other characteristics of the environment.

USGS-NPS Vegetation Mapping Program

The U.S. Geological Survey and the National Park Service have created the USGS-NPS Vegetation Mapping Program to classify, describe, and map vegetation communities in more than 270 national park units across the United States. The program provides national-scale descriptions of vegetation and comprehensive vegetation information at national and regional levels. The spatially enabled digital products produced by the program are available on the World Wide Web. Data provided include spatial data, map classification, spatial database of vegetation communities, and metadata for spatial databases.

Geographic Information Systems

Geographic information system (GIS) information and environmental modeling allow analysis of multiscaled data, including an integration of climate modeling, terrain analysis, and vegetation cover at specified scales. Analytical procedures based on these concepts provide the basis for the quantification and prediction of biodiversity information.

See also:
Federal Legislation
Habitat Patches, Corridors, and Matrix
State Enabling Legislation

James F. Berry, J.D. Ph.D., Elmhurst College, Elmhurst, Illinois

HAZARDS

FLOOD HAZARDS

Flooding is the overflowing of water upon land not usually submerged. Understanding the probability of a flood is essential in understanding the phenomenon. Factors such as the normal water level for a particular stream or river, and the odds that the water may rise 10 feet, 20 feet, or higher, need to be determined. Terrain is also a critical factor because riverbanks can be high and steep, or there can be flatlands where the water easily spills out. Also, wetlands function as a critical middle ground between uplands and floodways. In addition, human-made obstructions, such as levees and dams, influence the direction of floodwater movement.

FLOODING PROBABILITIES

Probabilities and topography are at the core of mapping flood hazards. A 100-year flood is one that has, in any given year, a 1 percent chance of occurring. Even after it occurs, it has the same chance the following year. Depending on the location, the term refers to a specific level of inundation as measured by engineers, assuming certain conditions upstream that affect the flow of waters downstream.

However, when new development upstream reduces the amount of pervious surface that can absorb precipitation, more water is then forced downstream, and the probabilities change. A 100-year flood can become a 50-year or 25-year flood, with correspondingly higher chances (2 or 4 percent, respectively) of occurring. These measurements of risk are generally intended to be a means of determining how to regulate land use with flood safety in mind, but the National Flood Insurance Program (NFIP) and local ordinances use the 100-year flood as a regulatory device.

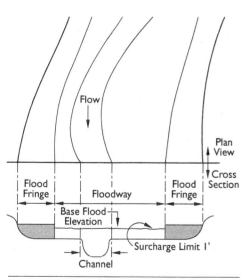

ELEMENTS OF THE 100-YEAR FLOODPLAIN

Source: Morris 1997.

TERMINOLOGY

In addition to the 100-year flood just described, the following floodplain management terms are some essential definitions for planners and urban designers to understand:

Base flood elevation (BFE). BFEs are rounded, whole-foot elevations of the 1 percent (100-year) annual chance flood at selected intervals that have been studied in detail. Communities issuing building permits for structures should refer to BFE, for example, so that living space in residential structures is elevated at or above that level by a specified amount, such as one foot.

Flood insurance rate map (FIRM). A FIRM is a map developed by the Federal Emergency Management Agency (FEMA) to illustrate the extent of flood hazards in the community. It may include risk zones for flood insurance, the 100-

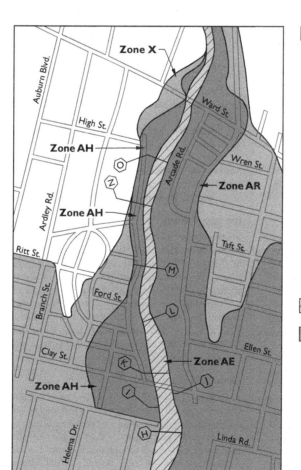

SAMPLE FLOOD INSURANCE RATE MAP

Source: FEMA National Flood Insurance Program 1998.

BASE FLOOD ELEVATION/FREEBOARD

Source: FEMA.

year and 500-year floodplains, floodways, base flood elevations, and the physical features of the floodplain.

Freeboard. Any additional height above a flood elevation is called the freeboard. A community may use this calculation to determine the

Special Flood Hazard Areas Inundated by 100-Year Flood

Zone A   No base flood elevations determined.

Zone AE   Base flood elevations determined.

Zone AH   Flood depths of 1 to 3 feet (usually areas of ponding). Base flood elevations determined.

Zone AR   Area of special flood hazard, which results from the decertification of a previously accredited flood protection system which is determined to be in the process of being restored to provide a 100-year or greater level of flood protection.

Floodway Areas in Zone AE

Other Flood Areas

Zone X   Areas of 500-year flood: areas of 100-year flood with average depths of less than 1 foot or with drainage areas less than 1 square mile, and areas protected by levees from 100-year flood.

James C. Schwab, AICP, American Planning Association, Chicago, Illinois

FLOOD INSURANCE MAP ZONES

ZONE SYMBOL	DEFINITION
A	Area of special flood hazard without water surface elevations determined
A1-30, AE	Area of special flood hazard with water surface elevations determined
A0	Area of special flood hazards having shallow water depths and/or unpredictable flow paths between (1) and (3) feet
A99	Area of special flood hazard where enough progress has been made on a protective system, such as dikes, dams, and levees, to consider it complete for insurance rating purposes
AH	Areas of special flood hazards having shallow water depths and/or unpredictable flow paths between (1) and (3) feet, and with water surface elevations determined
AR	Area of special flood hazard that results from the decertification of a previously accredited flood protection system that is determined to be in the process of being restored to provide base flood protection
V	Area of special flood hazards without water surface elevations determined, and with velocity, that is inundated by tidal floods (coastal high-hazard area)
V1-30, VE	Area of special flood hazards, with water surface elevations determined and with velocity, that is inundated by tidal floods (coastal high hazard area)
V0	Area of special flood hazards having shallow water depths and/or unpredictable flow paths between (1) and (3) feet and with velocity
B, X	Areas of moderate flood hazards or areas of future-conditions flood hazard
C, X	Areas of minimal hazards
D	Area of undetermined but possible flood hazards
M	Area of special mudslide (i.e., mudflow) hazards
N	Area of moderate mudslide (i.e., mudflow) hazards
P	Area of undetermined, but possible, mudslide hazards
E	Area of special flood-related erosion hazards

Source: 44 CFR §64.3, October 1, 2003.

required level of elevation for a structure's lowest floor in accordance with floodplain management regulations, for example.

Regulatory floodway. Also known simply as the floodway, shown on the FIRM, the regulatory floodway is the channel of a stream and any adjacent floodplain areas that must remain free of encroachment in order to allow the 100-year flood to move downstream without substantial increases in flood heights. Those increases are one foot by federal standards, but local standards can be more stringent.

Special flood hazard area (SFHA). An SFHA is the area included within the 100-year floodplain as shown on the flood insurance rate map.

TYPOLOGY OF FLOODS

Water is the primary factor in the overwhelming majority of natural disasters. Floods account for about 70 percent of presidentially declared disasters in the United States each year. That percentage is almost certainly higher for smaller, more localized disasters.

Flooding is the most ubiquitous and common hazard. Every state has floodplains; even many arid regions are at risk of damaging floods in the event of heavy rains on normally dry washes and hillsides. The NFIP was created in 1968 to respond to the loss of lives and property from flooding. These disasters continue to inspire amendments to the program.

Despite their ubiquitous nature, the characteristics of floods vary with regional climate and topography. In largely flat areas, such as the lower Mississippi Valley, vast areas of normally dry land can be submerged when floodwaters overflow their banks because the modest rise in elevation beyond the floodplain does little to restrain their lateral flow. This is fairly typical riverine flooding, in which the geographic extent of the flooding is largely a function of the increase in elevation away from the river, the

degree to which the river has been artificially constrained by such means as levees, and the absorptive capacity of the land itself.

There are, however, other specific types of floods whose prevalence varies with regional climate and topography. These variations in circumstances affect the duration of the inundation of the floodplain, with rapid water movement draining floodplains faster. The duration of storm patterns also affects the length of the period of inundation. Many storms unleash considerable amounts of rain within just hours, producing very short-term but damaging floods in localized areas. At the other end of the spectrum, the highly prolonged weather patterns affecting whole states in the relatively flat Midwest in 1993 left most communities inundated for weeks and, in many cases, for two or three months.

Ice Jam Floods

Ice jam floods merit some special consideration in communities with cold winters. They involve ice blocking the free flow of water downstream, causing a backup of water upstream. They often occur at particularly vulnerable locations in the river channel. Northward-flowing rivers in areas with freezing weather are especially vulnerable, as illustrated in 1997 along the Red River, which flows along the Minnesota-North Dakota border through Canada into the Hudson Bay.

Ground Saturation

A significant issue in the Midwest floods of 1993 was that heavy rainfall the previous fall and spring had left the ground largely saturated and therefore unable to absorb summer precipitation. Under such conditions, groundwater levels are so high that the earth has lost its absorption capacity and almost all rainfall becomes floodwater, at least in the sense that farm fields and lawns temporarily become shallow ponds and marshes. This is largely a problem in flatter terrain that drains slowly and in urban areas with large percentages of impervious surface.

Fluctuating Lake Levels

Inland lakes are always subject to minor variations in water level simply as a function of variations in seasonal temperatures and precipitation. For the most part, small variations can be accommodated in most human waterfront activities, but prolonged wet weather patterns can induce water-level rises that threaten lakeshore areas. A few lakes, most notably Devils Lake in North Dakota and the Great Salt Lake in Utah, because of flat shoreline topography and wide variations in seasonal weather, have expanded and contracted considerably within recent years, threatening or inundating near-shore development and infrastructure.

Alluvial Fans

In areas with wide valley floors beneath steep hills and mountains, particularly in regions with largely arid climates, rainfall can produce substantial erosion of rocks and other debris into fan-shaped deposits at the base of the incline. These formations are known as alluvial fans, and their presence, when they are obvious enough, is a signal that the area along the fan may be a dangerous location for development, particularly at the base. In a severe thunderstorm, the combination of rain and rocky debris pouring down the mountainside into the valley can produce considerable destruction, in large part because the material moves at high speeds, producing erosion and deposition at unpredictable locations.

Flash Floods

In mountainous areas with steep topography, rapid snowmelt or intense precipitation can produce a rapid, downhill flow of waters that overwhelm the riverbanks and sweep away most floodplain development in its path. Development within or near floodplains subject to flash floods, such as in areas in the Rocky Mountains or in much of Appalachia, is often extremely dangerous and problematic. In areas where mountains have been denuded of protective vegetation, such as those with surface mines or recent wildfires, mudslides can clog the floodway and increase the dangers and resulting damages.

NFIP STANDARDS AND FLOOD REGULATIONS

NFIP plays a special role in flood hazard identification and mitigation efforts. Property owners cannot obtain flood insurance through NFIP unless their community is in compliance with NFIP requirements.

The Community Rating System (CRS) is an incentive system to reward communities for going beyond the basic NFIP requirements in planning for and mitigating local flood hazards. It works on a point basis; communities that accomplish CRS goals earn reductions, in 5 percent increments (one 5 percent reduction for reaching specific goals), for flood insurance premiums.

State Involvement

Largely because of NFIP, state mandates or oversight of floodplain management regulation is more likely than it is in the case other hazards.. Every state has some type of floodplain program with a designated manager. According to a 2003 survey by the Association of State Floodplain Managers, 13 states

James C. Schwab, AICP, American Planning Association, Chicago, Illinois

COMMUNITY RATING SYSTEM*
CREDITED ACTIVITIES

Public Information Activities

Elevation Certificates

Map Determinations

Outreach Projects

Hazard Disclosure

Flood Protection Library

Flood Protection Assistance

Mapping and Regulatory Activities

Additional Flood Data

Open Space Preservation

Higher Regulatory Standards

Flood Data Maintenance

Stormwater Management

Flood Damage Reduction Activities

Repetitive Loss Projects

Floodplain Management Planning

Acquisition and Relocation

Retrofitting

Drainage System Maintenance

Flood Preparedness Activities

Flood Warning Program

Levee Safety

Dam Safety

FEMA's Community Rating System (CRS) allows participating communities to garner points by undertaking additional measures to reduce flood losses, which then translate into reductions in flood insurance premiums for local property owners, in 5 percent increments up to a potential total reduction of 45 percent. See FEMA's CRS Coordinator's Manual for details.

and the District of Columbia and Puerto Rico directly regulate floodplain development activity. The state role is largely that of intermediary and facilitator. FEMA administers the program, and local government retains control of floodplain management planning and permitting and must choose to apply for participation in NFIP.

HAZARD IDENTIFICATION

Some special types of flood hazards typically associated with, or triggered by, other hazard types are discussed elsewhere in this book (e.g., coastal storm surges, seiches, and tsunamis). The focus here is on those flood hazards resulting directly from high lake and river levels due to precipitation or melting snow and ice. One other related form of flooding discussed above, constituting a special hazard in western states, involves alluvial fans.

Mapping conducted according to NFIP is an overriding consideration in hazard identification. NFIP conducts the mapping of floodplains and produces and revises, as necessary, the FIRMs that provide the basis for establishing flood insurance premiums and local floodplain management requirements. Local governments may, however, apply to FEMA for map revisions based on locally developed or acquired data they feel may justify the request.

The key contributing factors in identifying the scope of the local flood hazard are:

- size of the watershed;
- development within the watershed affecting stormwater runoff;
- Soil characteristics;
- topographic characteristics affecting the direction and flow of flood waters; and
- regional climate.

FEMA's risk assessment software program, HAZUS-MH, can be used for analyzing potential losses from floods, hurricane winds, and earthquakes.

RISK ASSESSMENT

It is important to understand the risk assessment terminology. Planners and public officials should also know that the 100-year flood is used as a general regulatory standard and does not delineate the worst possible flood. The FIRM is the basic risk assessment device for floodplain management. In addition, an inventory of all vulnerable structures provides a means of quantifying the value of the built environment within the at-risk community at various potential flood levels.

MITIGATION OPPORTUNITIES

Opportunities for planners to mitigate flood hazards and prevent losses of life and property are extensive, in large part because flood risks are so much more clearly definable for land-use purposes than almost any other hazard. The mapping functions of NFIP provide an effective basis for establishing floodplain management regulations through zoning, subdivision controls, and other measures within clearly defined areas with readily quantifiable risk factors. For existing structures in the floodplain, the two most extensively used mitigation actions are relocation and elevation. Build-out analysis can be used to identify potential increases in floodplain boundaries in order to adapt zoning regulations for mitigation of future hazard threats.

ISSUES FOR PLANNING AND
URBAN DESIGN

Federal disaster legislation has steadily been pushing communities toward advance planning for various kinds of natural disasters, flooding included. FEMA now expects communities to develop flood mitigation plans as a condition for receiving federal hazard mitigation grants. Because flood contours can be clearly mapped beforehand, there is a growing awareness that communities can and should also prepare predisaster plans that facilitate postflood recovery. Federal and other disaster aid can be used to reduce vulnerability by elevating, relocating, or otherwise mitigating dangers to flood-prone proper-

---

CHECKLIST OF FLOOD MITIGATION STRATEGIES

This checklist, originally prepared by L.R. Johnston Associates, divides mitigation strategies into four categories:

1. Modify susceptibility to flood damage and disruption:
   - Acquisition and demolition, and relocation of properties in flood-prone areas
   - Floodplain regulations and building codes
   - Development and redevelopment policies
   - Floodproofing and elevation-in-place
   - Disaster preparedness and response plans
   - Flood forecasting and warning systems

2. Modify the impacts of flooding:
   - Information and education
   - Flood insurance
   - Tax adjustments
   - Flood emergency measures
   - Disaster assistance
   - Postflood recovery

3. Manage natural and cultural resources:
   - Preservation and restoration strategies
   - Regulations to protect floodplain natural and cultural resources
   - Development and redevelopment policies and programs
   - Information and education
   - Tax adjustments
   - Administrative measures

4. Modify flooding:
   - Construction of dams and reservoirs
   - Construction of dikes, levees, and flood walls
   - Channel alterations
   - High-flow diversions and spillways
   - Land treatment measures

---

ties. In determining whether they will permit rebuilding within designated floodplains, many communities exceed federal criteria for repetitive losses by looking at cumulative losses over a period of time rather than individual flood losses, for example. Multiobjective management involves local governments connecting flood mitigation objectives with plans for floodplain uses, such as greenways, bicycle trails, and other low-impact uses.

REFERENCE

Morris, Marya. 1997. *Subdivision Design in Flood Hazard Areas.* Planning Advisory Service Report No. 473. Chicago: American Planning Association.

See also:

Floodplains and Riparian Corridors

Rivers and Streams

Watersheds

James C. Schwab, AICP, American Planning Association, Chicago, Illinois

EROSION AND SEDIMENTATION

Erosion is any process by which sediment is entrained (eroded) and moved away from its original location by gradational agents, which include gravity, water, wind, ice, and humans. Sedimentation is the deposition and accumulation of transported sediment, or precipitation of deposits from water. Erosion and sedimentation can be considered in terms of their environments of occurrence, such as alluvial fan, river floodplain, delta, beach, dune, and desert.

The gradational processes become hazards when they negatively affect human health or development through land loss, site-specific destruction of or damage to buildings or infrastructure, dispersal of pollutants, burial of property or infrastructure, or other impacts. Generally, the highest rates of surface erosion and sediment yield are associated with agricultural land uses and all types of construction sites. The most serious erosion/sedimentation hazards are associated with riverine and coastal environments. Local government inspectors typically craft ordinances and laws to regulate these hazards.

AGRICULTURAL SOIL LOSS

Erosion on agricultural land can be significant because of soil disturbance by cultivation and exposure of bare soil during the growing season. Estimated average annual soil loss for U.S. farmlands is four to five tons per acre. Some of the world's highest erosion rates occur in Canada and the United States, but certain areas of China experience short-term rates that are many times higher. Agricultural land use tends to result in detrimental effects, such as stream channel degradation and impact on biota, shortening of flood recurrence intervals, loss of reservoir capacity due to infilling, and contamination of surface waters by sediments containing fertilizers, pesticides, and herbicides.

CONSTRUCTION SITE SEDIMENT

Construction sites, from a single-dwelling building site to extensive urban, highway, utility, and industrial developments, have sediment yields far in excess of those associated with agricultural lands. Soil erosion from bare, disturbed construction sites and from piled soil during the construction phase results in the same detrimental effects associated with agricultural runoff. Sediments accumulate in adjacent streams and topographic lows; stream water quality and biota are affected; and flood recurrence intervals are shortened.

Erosion control on construction sites involves two basic steps: minimizing the amount of land disturbed and limiting damage caused by change in water flow on the land. Basic steps can be taken to control erosion on most residential construction sites, as noted in *Erosion Control for Home Builders* (Johnson 1999):

1. Preserve existing grass and trees to the extent possible.
2. Replant the site as soon as possible.
3. Use best management practice techniques (described later) to trap sediment.
4. Locate soil piles away from waterways or roads.
5. Construct an access drive for all vehicles to use to limit tracking of mud onto streets.

6. Clean up sediment carried off-site by storms or vehicles.
7. Install downspout extenders to prevent erosion from roof runoff.

EROSION AND SEDIMENTATION PROCESSES AS HAZARDS

As with any geologic process, erosion and sedimentation are considered to be hazards only when they interact with humans or human development. This typically occurs when humans encroach into the pathways of erosion, transport, and deposition of sedimentary materials.

Riverine

Collectively, the greatest economic losses due to erosion and sedimentation occur in association with riverine systems. Erosional running-water processes include sheet wash, rill erosion, gullying, bank erosion, river channel migration, avulsion (breaching of levees or channel abandonment), and flooding. With major flooding, sedimentation formerly regarded as good and necessary to maintain the productivity of floodplains, such as mud, sand, and gravel accumulation, now causes economic loss to property developed on floodplains.

Coastal Erosion and Accretion

Coastal erosion and sedimentation also rank high in terms of annual economic impact, particularly because of extensive development in coastal areas subject to hurricanes, winter storms, and sea level rise. Coastal land loss is a major economic problem in terms of the impact on developed property, and sedimentation can be a hazard whenever sediments are deposited in unwanted locations, such as storm overwash fans, infilling of navigational channels, and formation of dunes.

Mass Wasting

Mass wasting, the downslope movement of soil and sediment, is a widespread phenomenon, from slow imperceptive downslope creep that may induce foundation cracking to massive debris flows and landslides that potentially erode or bury everything in their paths. Sites made too steep during construction are common failure sites due to slumping and mud flows.

Wind Gradation

Wind is an important agent of erosion and sedimentation, although not as significant volumetrically as flowing water and waves. Deserts and coasts are two areas where windblown transport is often considered to be the dominant sedimentation process. Deserts lack stabilizing vegetation, so loose material is exposed to wind for easy entrainment. Beaches and coasts have an abundance of loose material provided by the erosive power of waves, plus typically strong and frequent winds to move material. High winds in both inland and coastal regions are capable of considerable destruction but can generally be mitigated through construction techniques. Eliminating the nuisance of blowing sand in such areas, however, is difficult.

Other Processes

Other processes that may generate erosion or sedimentation hazards include groundwater solution/subsidence/collapse in areas underlain by soluble rocks, such as limestone or rock salt. Glacial advance and retreat in higher latitudes or high elevations is significant in eroding and depositing sediment; however, these areas usually are not subject to development. The exception would be the problems associated with permafrost, such as the downward flow of water-saturated soil (solifluction) and subsidence.

Construction of impervious surfaces, such as roofs, roads, and parking lots, results in changes to the hydrology, particularly the increased frequency and magnitude of flooding, causing increased erosion and sedimentation.

PLANNING AND MANAGEMENT

Planning and management strategies depend on the type of hazard encountered (e.g., runoff and stream erosion, coastal erosion, blowing sand). In any case, the best approach is avoidance—identify the areas affected by the hazard and do not develop such areas. A close alternative is relocation—move development out of the hazard zone in the postdisaster reconstruction phase. The most common approach, however, is some form of mitigation to reduce the impact of the hazard by either engineering the construction or the natural system.

Sediment Reduction Programs

A sediment reduction program is often implemented to control erosion due to surface runoff. For most locations, state, county, or local ordinances govern the means of erosion control at specified sites. Check with the appropriate regulatory agency to determine procedures and standards to use.

Sediment reduction programs include watershed-level planning and restrictions on construction, steep-slope development, and road building. A watershed management plan identifies sensitive areas, designates acceptable land uses, and specifies overall management goals. The protection of pervious surfaces allows precipitation to infiltrate into the ground, resulting in less stormwater runoff and erosion potential. Restrictions on steep-slope development and road building also result in less surface erosion, fewer landslides, and minimized land loss.

Best Management Practices

Three general management strategies are used to reduce erosion and sedimentation: minimize erosion from disturbed surfaces; control the erosive impacts of increased or concentrated runoff; and eliminate opportunities for sediments to be transported to streams and coastal waters. Specific best management practices address these sediment control approaches by preventing erosion at the source. These can be generalized into the following categories, which include some examples:

- Development practices: clearing only essential areas and minimizing road disturbances
- Surface stabilization: seeding, mulching, and matting
- Runoff diversion: perimeter dikes and swales

David M. Bush, Ph.D., University of West Georgia, Carrollton, Georgia
William J. Neal, Ph.D., Grand Valley State University, Allendale, Michigan

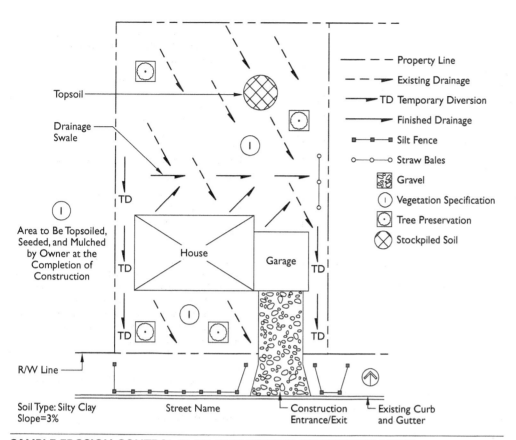

SAMPLE EROSION CONTROL PLAN: ONE- TO TWO-FAMILY DWELLINGS

Source: Johnson, C. 1999. Erosion Control for Homebuilders. University of Wisconsin-Extension, Division of Cooperative Extension in cooperation with the Wisconsin Department of Natural Resources.

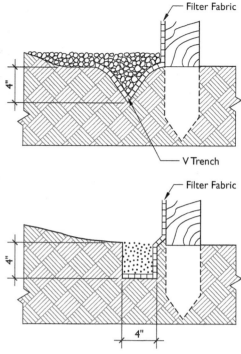

Silt fence installation: (1) Excavate a 4-inch by 4-inch trench along the contour. (2) Stake the silt fence on downslope side of trench. Extend 8 inches of fabric into the trench. (3) When joints are necessary, overlap ends for the distance between two stakes. (4) Backfill and compact the excavated soil.

SILT FENCES

Source: Johnson, C. 1999. Erosion Control for Homebuilders. University of Wisconsin-Extension, Division of Cooperative Extension in cooperation with the Wisconsin Department of Natural Resources.

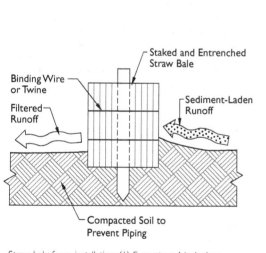

Straw bale fence installation: (1) Excavate a 4-inch-deep trench. (2) Place bales in trench with bindings around sides away from the ground. Leave no gaps between bales. (3) Anchor bales using two steel rebars or 2-inch by 2-inch wood stakes per bale. Drive stakes at least 8 inches into the ground. (4) Backfill and compact the excavated soil.

STRAW BALE FENCE

Source: Johnson, C. 1999. Erosion Control for Homebuilders. University of Wisconsin-Extension, Division of Cooperative Extension in cooperation with the Wisconsin Department of Natural Resources.

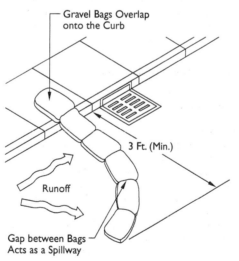

Protecting a Downslope Curb Inlet

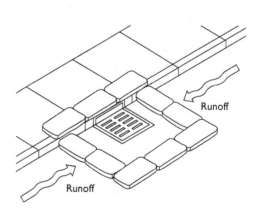

Protecting a Sump-Position Curb Inlet

Curb inlet installation: (1) Fill geotextile bags approximately half full with 2- to 3-inch stone or gravel. (2) Lay tightly in a row curving upslope from the curb and away from the inlet. (3) Overlap bags onto the curb and extend a minimum of 3 feet into the street. (4) If using more than one layer of bags, overlap the bags with the row beneath, and leave a one-bag gap in the middle of the top row to serve as a spillway. (5) Install downslope of the lot to keep sediment from washing down the street. (6) Place bags in an arc around curb inlets that are in a sump position. (7) Inspect and repair as needed, and remove any accumulated sediments after every storm.

CURB INLET PROTECTION

Source: Indiana Department of Natural Resources 2001.

David M. Bush, Ph.D., University of West Georgia, Carrollton, Georgia
William J. Neal, Ph.D., Grand Valley State University, Allendale, Michigan

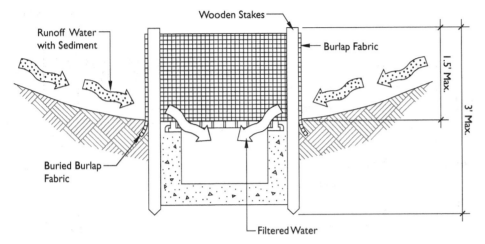

Drop inlet installation: (1) Construct a 6-inch dike on the downslope side to prevent bypass flow. (2) Dig a trench 12 inches deep and 4 inches wide. (3) Space support posts evenly against the inlet perimeter a maximum of 3 feet apart, and drive them about 1 1/2 feet into the ground. (4) Cut enough filter fabric from a single roll to eliminate joints. (5) Using lath and nails, fasten the fabric to the posts. (6) Bury the bottom of the fabric at least 1 foot deep; then backfill and compact the backfill. (7) Cross-brace the corners to prevent collapse. (8) Inspect and repair as needed, and remove accumulated sediments after every storm.

DROP INLET PROTECTION

Source: Indiana Department of Natural Resources 2001.

- Runoff conveyance: lined channels, temporary slope drains, and check dams
- Outlet protection, sediment traps, and barriers: sediment fence, brush barriers, straw bales, sediment basins, and sediment traps
- Stream protection: buffer strips and riprap

T Value

Another factor related to soil loss is the "tolerable soil loss," or "T" value. The T value is the maximum tolerable soil loss in tons per acre per year that, if exceeded, would remove soil faster than it is being formed, adversely affecting soil productivity. Tolerable soil loss rates vary among soil types; however, the majority of rates are from three to five tons per acre per year.

ENGINEERING APPROACHES

Sea level is known to be rising at a worldwide rate of about eight inches per century, and most of the world's shorelines are eroding. The typical approach to address this problem is to attempt to hold the shoreline in place. Historically, shore-hardening structures, such as seawalls, revetments, bulkheads, and groins, have been constructed to accomplish this. However, hard shoreline stabilization leads to degradation of the recreational beach, is costly in the short and long terms, destroys beach aesthetics, makes beach access difficult, and is dangerous.

Artificial beach and dune construction has been adopted as the solution of choice in combating coastal erosion. But beach nourishment is not a panacea. When artificial beaches are constructed, only the upper beach is covered with new sand, creating a steeper beach. This new steepened profile often increases the rate of erosion; in fact, nationally, replenished beaches almost always disappear at a faster rate than their natural predecessors. Also, the replacement sand's grain size is a factor in the success of a beach nourishment project. Beach dredge and fill projects are costly, and the environmental impacts of dredge and fill projects are poorly understood. Fragile habitats, such as turtle-nesting grounds, are altered; dredging and pumping may bury productive hard grounds; and turbidity may cause kills of invertebrates and fish or smother sea grasses. Such impacts must be evaluated before new replenishments are undertaken, and either avoided or mitigated.

RULES AND REGULATIONS

Aspects of erosion and sedimentation hazards fall under various federal, state, and local regulations.

Federal

Federal regulations that address erosion and sedimentation include the Clean Water Act of 1972; the National Flood Insurance Act of 1968, which established the National Flood Insurance Program (NFIP) and which was amended by the Flood Disaster Protection Act of 1973; the Rivers and Harbors Act of 1889; the Water Pollution Control Act of 1972; the Soil Conservation Act of 1935, which created the Soil Conservation Service (now called the Natural Resources Conservation Service) in the U.S. Department of Agriculture; and the Food Security Act of 1982, in particular its Swampbuster and Sodbuster programs. Federal legislation led to the requirement of Environmental Impact Statements (EISs) for major construction projects.

AGENCIES AND ORGANIZATIONS WITH EROSION AND SEDIMENTATION INFORMATION

U. S. Government Agencies
U.S. Environmental Protection Agency
U.S. Geological Survey
U.S. Department of Agriculture, Natural Resources Conservation Service
Federal Emergency Management Agency
National Oceanic and Atmospheric Administration

Private Agencies
Institute for Business and Home Safety
The Natural Hazards Center
American Society of Civil Engineers

Two key federal agencies that deal with erosion and sedimentation issues include the U.S. EPA and the U.S. Department of Agriculture. Other agencies that address this issue include the Federal Emergency Management Agency, including the National Flood Insurance Program (NFIP) under the Federal Insurance Administration, the U.S. Army Corps of Engineers, the Farm Services Agency, Cooperative Extension Service, Natural Resources Conservation Service, the Federal Energy Regulatory Commission, and the U.S. Fish and Wildlife Service.

State and Local

Most state- and local-level regulation is through state soil and water conservation commissions or departments of natural resources. Most states require local governments to establish erosion and sedimentation regulations for construction sites or other land-disturbing activities, specifically with regard to soils and sediment eroding off of such sites, and to control sedimentation in sensitive environments. States may have model ordinances or workshops to assist in ordinance and guidance development. The local (municipal or county) office in which the building inspector is located will have information on local regulations. Some states have a central agency website from which searches for pertinent information can be found. The American Society of Engineers is a private organization with extensive experience in construction and erosion control.

REFERENCE

Johnson, Carolyn. 1999. *Erosion Control for Home Builders*. Madison, WI: University of Wisconsin Extension Service and Wisconsin Department of Natural Resources.

See also:
Flood Hazards
Landslides
Sinkholes and Subsidence
Soils Classifications and Mechanics
Watersheds

David M. Bush, Ph.D., University of West Georgia, Carrollton, Georgia
William J. Neal, Ph.D., Grand Valley State University, Allendale, Michigan

HURRICANES AND COASTAL STORMS

Hurricanes are the most potent and damaging subset of coastal storms. They represent the extreme end of a spectrum of tropical storms that begin over the oceans and usually make landfall before dissipating their energy. Tropical storms, in turn, are the major but not the only category of coastal storms. In more northerly regions, gale-force winds ride along the Atlantic coast as northeasters, bringing wet, cold weather. In winter, such storms can produce devastating blizzards.

Virtually any coastal area in the United States can be struck by a coastal storm. A violent tropical storm becomes a hurricane as winds exceed approximately 75 miles (120 kilometers) per hour. Meteorologists view it as an intermediate storm, somewhere between large frontal cyclones and much smaller tornadoes, all of which share strong atmospheric vortices (i.e., whirlpools of air moving in circular patterns around a core). Meteorologists rate the severity of hurricanes according to five levels of wind speeds on the Saffir/Simpson scale. Unfortunately, hurricanes are the focus of a good deal of popular terminological confusion; for instance, the same type of storm is labeled a cyclone in the Indian Ocean and a typhoon in the Pacific.

Hurricanes generally do not form above 30 degrees latitude. They depend on tropical trade winds above warm ocean temperatures of at least 80°F (26°C) for their formation. They also depend on low central pressure in the eye, or core, of the hurricane, where downdrafting occurs. As they gain force over water, their wind speeds can build to nearly 200 miles (approximately 322 kilometers) per hour. Because they draw their strength from warm ocean waters, their power wanes as their path crosses land or cooler water.

HAZARD IDENTIFICATION

Satellites are used to identify and track hurricanes and tropical storms. Because hurricanes are weather-driven phenomena, they have a clear seasonal aspect. In northerly latitudes, this season generally runs from June through November. Once they are in motion, however, they can move far beyond their tropical origins. All the Caribbean islands, plus every coastal state and province along the Atlantic Ocean and the Gulf of Mexico, including all of New England and the Canadian Maritimes, are capable of being hit by a hurricane. Hawaii experiences the majority of landfalls among the Pacific states.

One specific area that deserves special attention in coastal storm hazard identification is the capacity of coastal areas for evacuation. Hurricanes provide predictable lead times before they make landfall. And in spite of skyrocketing coastal populations in recent decades, the advances made in meteorological science in identifying and tracking tropical storms account for the decline in their death toll. Communities that just a century ago were caught completely unaware now have anywhere from several hours to several days to prepare for the event. However, it is the responsibility of local emergency managers—and state and regional governments in some cases—to determine how a local population could and should be evacuated prior to a hurricane

SAFFIR/SIMPSON SCALE

CATEGORY	AIR PRESSURE (LBS/SQ IN)	WIND SPEED (MPH)	STORM SURGE (FEET)	POTENTIAL DAMAGE
1	⊒ 28.94	74–95	4–5	Minimal
2	28.5–28.91	96–110	6-8	Moderate
3	27.91–28.47	111–130	9–12	Extensive
4	27.17–27.88	131–155	13–18	Extreme
5	<27.17	155	>18	Catastrophic

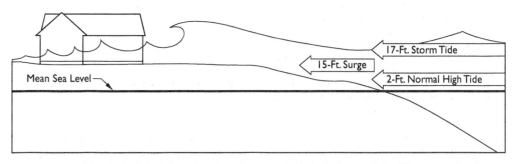

Storm surges result from high winds forcing water ashore above normal tide levels. The surge is the difference in water elevation between normal tide level and the storm tide.

STORM SURGE

Source: NOAA 2003.

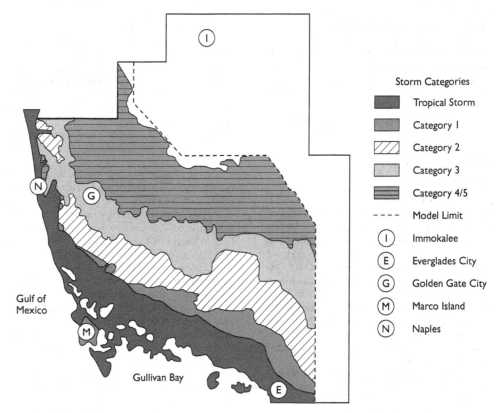

Storm Categories
- Tropical Storm
- Category 1
- Category 2
- Category 3
- Category 4/5
- - - - Model Limit
- (I) Immokalee
- (E) Everglades City
- (G) Golden Gate City
- (M) Marco Island
- (N) Naples

This map of Collier County, Florida, shows an application of the National Hurricane Center's SLOSH model for mapping storm surges from various hurricane categories.

STORM SURGE MAP

Source: Collier County, Florida 2003.

James C. Schwab, AICP, American Planning Association, Chicago, Illinois

and how long that process might take; it is the responsibility of planners to help determine what might be done to improve the situation.

The Sea Lake Overland Surge from Hurricanes (SLOSH) model is used by the U.S. Army Corps of Engineers and the National Hurricane Center to help the Federal Emergency Management Agency (FEMA) and coastal states develop evacuation plans for populated areas. The SLOSH model differs from the National Flood Insurance Program's (NFIP's) coastal hazard delineations, and inundation areas shown on SLOSH maps may be more extensive than the coastal hazards shown on flood insurance rate maps.

The specific hazard issues associated with hurricanes are deceptively simple: wind and water. It is obvious that coastal zones can invariably expect to bear the full brunt of a hurricane's winds wherever it makes landfall. Water damage is far easier to address through land-use planning. Knowing where water is and how it will move under storm conditions is the beginning of any hazard identification effort. Several areas deserve significant attention:

- Coastal high-hazard areas
- Coastal floodplains
- Inland bodies of water, such as lakes, rivers, and canals
- Wetland areas, such as the Everglades and tidal marshes
- Barrier islands and their associated inlets and sounds

Mapping storm surge zones is basically a process of showing how far inland ocean waves can be expected to reach, and with what force. The NFIP provides for mapping 100-year storm-surge zones just as it does 100-year floodplains. The demarcations are based on a combination of the local topographical factors noted above plus the expected frequency of severe storms based on past experience. The coasts of Florida and North Carolina, for instance, have much higher probabilities of hurricane landfall than others, and this enters into the calculation.

RISK ASSESSMENT

Wind

Identifying potential wind damage can be problematic for two reasons. One is that, as in the case of Hurricane Andrew, a hurricane can move across the low, flat Florida peninsula or some other strip of land with only moderately abated winds, destroying buildings, trees, and infrastructure almost at will. The useful land-use planning lessons to be drawn from such widespread destruction are of necessity somewhat more limited than those for water damage. For wind damage, hurricane-resistant building codes have been the primary answer. Risk assessment therefore consists largely in pinpointing substandard structures for mitigation efforts.

Difficult though the task may be, FEMA's National Hurricane Program and the National Weather Service have sought to improve our knowledge of wind patterns. FEMA's Region IV (Atlanta) released the Inland Hurricane Wind Display Model, designed to identify the degree of expected wind decay as a hurricane moves over land. Such information is likely to prove most valuable in the application of new construction methods and improved building codes.

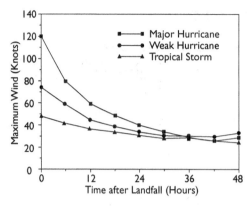

The National Hurricane Center has charted the decay of sustained hurricane wind speed once the storm makes landfall. This occurs because of the higher friction over land and the loss of heat and moisture sources from the ocean.

WIND SPEED DECAY

Source: National Hurricane Center.

Hurricane winds are most powerful as they make landfall; coastal communities, therefore, must pay the closest attention to wind-damage issues. Following landfall, from .5 miles (0.8 kilometers) to 1.5 miles (2.41 kilometers) inland, wind speeds decline to about 75 to 80 percent of those measured at stations with ocean exposure.

Water

Coastal geomorphology is crucial in defining storm hazards. Barrier islands have evolved as nature's way of buffering the mainland from the battering of coastal storms. These islands are inherently unstable, consisting largely of migrating sand dunes with only modest vegetative cover. Powerful storms move them back and forth by scores of yards over time and can actually destroy or sever them. Development on such islands can be the equivalent of building castles in the sand to the extent that such coastal development collapses or implodes under hurricane pressure. Moreover, the hazards are magnified by the danger of flying debris.

Offshore bathymetry also affects wave action. Deep water tends to absorb much of the wave energy below sea level. However, the steeper the shore, the closer large amounts of energy can come before dissipation occurs. In shallow water, the waves can build to heights well above normal sea level, making low-lying coastal areas highly vulnerable.

In a hurricane, the low central pressure creates a bulge in the water that causes its level to rise because less air pressure is being exerted downward. The swirling counterclockwise winds surrounding the core serve to push forward the water to the right of the storm's path. The result is a wall of water typically 15 to 20 feet (4.6 to 6.1 meters) high. How far that water reaches beyond the high-tide line depends largely on the coastal topography. Areas with high natural rock walls along the coast, which are relatively few in the southeastern United States, obviously afford better protection than most barrier islands. Even so, dunes tend to protect people and structures behind them by absorbing and breaking the force of the waves. They may not, however, survive the storm intact, so their protection is anything but permanent.

Near the shore, coastal waterways can amplify the impact of storm surges and add other dangers. Hurricane winds can move sizable walls of water upstream along coastal tributaries, adding flooding dangers to the ordinary floodplain worries along riverbanks. Because hurricanes often generate considerable precipitation ahead of the storm front, rivers can swell with rainwater just as a storm surge moves upstream, and these combined dangers must be accounted for in riverfront hazard identification. Likewise, large inland lakes, such as are present throughout much of Florida, can flood under storm conditions and produce considerable damage. In a historically infamous hurricane that struck Florida in 1927, killing more than 1,800 people, this is precisely what happened to Lake Okeechobee.

MITIGATION OPPORTUNITIES

Wind

Among the major wind hazard issues is the impact that inadequately constructed buildings and poorly secured property (trash cans, lawn furniture, or even trees) can have on neighboring properties. In the midst of the frontal impact of a hurricane, buildings and people suffer some of their worst damage not merely from the winds themselves but from the collateral impact of flying debris. The strength of buildings and infrastructure in high-hazard coastal zones thus becomes an essential focus of any worthwhile coastal storm hazard identification effort.

Construction on barrier islands and beaches tends to suffer the greatest threat from hurricane-borne winds. The combination of powerful winds and unstable soil necessitates strong countermeasures, such as:

- building design, such as hip roofs and avoidance of overhangs;
- tie-downs, especially for manufactured housing; and
- stabilizing measures for connections between building parts.

In assessing risks, land-use choices significantly influence the nature of the construction required to offset the threat. Building away from the shore on forested, vegetated upland, even on barrier islands, affords some greater stability and protection from wind-induced building failure. The vegetation indicates more stable soil, and the trees provide some friction and shelter to mitigate wind speed. Several states, such as North Carolina and South Carolina, have adopted and enforce required shoreline setbacks to mitigate against flooding and scour hazards from coastal storms. In short, effective coastal hazard mitigation results from considering both the quality of the built environment and its location.

Water

Mitigation efforts for water damage from hurricanes are essentially those described in "Flood Hazards" elsewhere in this book.

See also:

Beach and Dune Systems
Erosion and Sedimentation
Flood Hazards

James C. Schwab, AICP, American Planning Association, Chicago, Illinois

LANDSLIDES

Landslides are movements of large masses of soil and rock material under the force of gravity. They are an extreme form of erosion.

CAUSES OF LANDSLIDES

Landslides occur when external forces exceed resisting forces within the soil and rock of a hillside. The most frequent landslide-triggering mechanism is water from intense rainfall or human-introduced sources. Although earthquakes also cause a great number of landslides, heavy precipitation is a much more frequent event, hence, causes more landslides. The destruction of hillside vegetation from lightning or wildfires can also cause a landslide to occur.

Human alteration of land surfaces can contribute to slope destabilization by:

- placing fills on top of marginally stable slopes;
- cutting slopes at too steep an angle;
- redirecting storm runoff so as to concentrate flows artificially onto portions of the landscape not prepared to receive them;
- removing woody vegetation;
- adding water by means of hillside septic systems; and
- excessively irrigating hillside plantings.

Predicting the locations and establishing the probabilities of future landslides is difficult. At best, geologists can qualitatively identify zones of relative landslide hazard; the quantitative probabilities of landslides at specific sites, however, usually cannot be established. Slope stability of specific sites can only be understood after extensive exploration. By comparison, flood hazards can be quantitatively identified by generally accepted statistical methods.

LANDSLIDE COSTS

Landslides cause significant property damage and threaten public safety in more than half of the United States. Recent significant landslides have included huge, slow-moving slides that severely damaged entire subdivisions; avalanchelike debris flows that obliterated homes in their paths; and large, rapid slope failures that buried homes and residents.

Fortunately, loss of life in the United States from landsliding is relatively low. But landslides are a costly problem to public agencies and private property owners alike. Landslides can disrupt roads and infrastructure. Even a small landslide can take the entire economic value of a private parcel.

Perhaps one of the greatest cost problems with landslides in the United States is that earth movement insurance is unavailable. Consequently, landslide damages always result in complex litigation, as damaged parties search for financial relief from various other parties. Often, such litigation concludes with a private settlement, with public agencies usually paying a significant share, even if they are not at fault. Furthermore, this financial relief is expensive and inefficient, with much of it going to legal proceedings rather than engineering actions. Clearly, for both fiscal and safety reasons, local governments need to be more active in preventing landslides.

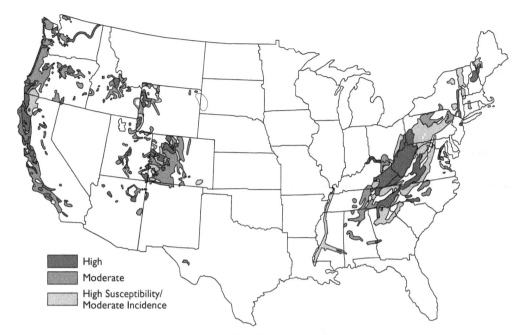

High
Moderate
High Susceptibility/
Moderate Incidence

Shaded areas are those of high to moderate incidence of landslides, plus areas of moderate incidence but high susceptibility to landsliding. Incidence of landslides is high when greater than 15 percent of the area is actually part of a landslide or other ground failure. Moderate incidence means that 1.5 to 15 percent of the area is involved in mappable landslides. Alaska and Hawaii are not depicted in part because equivalent detailed hazard maps do not yet exist.

MAP OF LANDSLIDE HAZARD AREAS IN THE UNITED STATES

Source: USGS 2002.

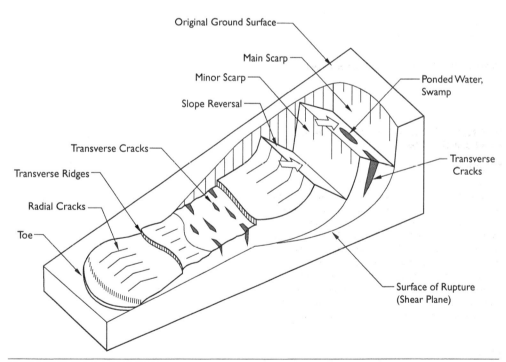

FEATURES OF A LANDSLIDE

Source: U.S. Geological Survey.

Robert B. Olshansky, Ph.D. AICP, University of Illinois at Urbana-Champaign

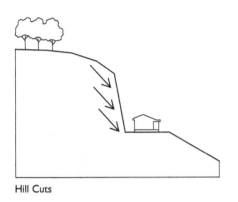

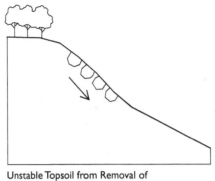

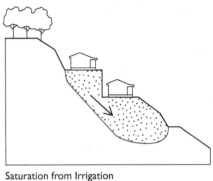

Hill Cuts

Unstable Topsoil from Removal of Deep-Rooted Trees

Saturation from Irrigation

POTENTIAL SOURCES OF LANDSLIDES

Source: American Planning Association.

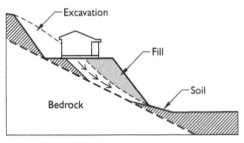

- - - Original Ground Surface

— — Potential Failure Surface

Diagram of a house built on a landslide-prone hillside, constructed with questionable practices. The soil upslope from the house was excavated, leaving a steep soil face. This soil was placed as fill on top of existing soil to create a building lot (pad). Vegetation was removed from the slope, and surface water might pond on the lot. A potential failure surface is shown below the house.

CONSTRUCTION PRACTICES THAT CAUSE LANDSLIDES

Source: Ohlmacher 1999.

PLANNING ACTIONS TO REDUCE LANDSLIDE DAMAGES

Mapping

In order to intelligently—and legally—regulate development for landslide hazard reduction, the first priority is to prepare landslide hazard maps. At a minimum, these should consist of slope maps and identification of previous landslide locations. Local governments in landslide-susceptible regions also should retain geologists to identify potentially unstable areas. These maps can be at a level of detail appropriate to the degree of hazard, geological understanding of the region, and resources of the jurisdiction. Such maps form an important foundation for subsequent actions.

Plans

Local comprehensive plans should include landslide hazard maps, identify appropriate policies, and present a comprehensive strategy for reducing present and future landslide hazards in the community, using some of the actions listed below. In potentially unstable areas, it is important to establish policies and regulations that clearly shift the burden of proof to

Scale: 1" = 4000'

State Highway 37

▨ Land with Landslides and Unstable Slopes

━ ━ City Limit Line

- - - Sphere of Influence

LANDSLIDE HAZARD MAP

Source: City of Novato, California Department of Community Development 1996.

the applicants to demonstrate the safety of their proposals. Owners of such property should have an expectation that they cannot develop unless they can convincingly prove otherwise.

Subdivision Review

Any proposed subdivision in a designated landslide-prone area should include a geologic study, reviewed

by a city-designated professional geologist. This should be in addition to normal civil engineering aspects of the subdivision review process. Because evaluating the stability of natural hillslopes depends upon a high degree of professional discretion, it is important that at least two independent, highly qualified geologic professionals be involved in this process. Subdivision approval should include specific

Robert B. Olshansky, Ph.D. AICP, University of Illinois at Urbana-Champaign

conditions for parcel layout, engineering details, and subsequent review and inspection processes. It might include additional requirements based on the jurisdiction's landslide hazard maps.

Grading Ordinance

A grading ordinance requires developers to obtain grading permits whenever placing cuts or fills. For hillside areas, it should include detailed engineering requirements and geologic reports prior to approval of grading, and these reports should be reviewed by city-designated professionals. The ordinance should include specific requirements for engineered slopes, fill quality, retaining walls, and hillside drainage, and might include additional requirements based on the jurisdiction's landslide hazard maps.

Hillside Development Ordinance

A hillside development ordinance can be a separate ordinance or a part of a grading, zoning, or subdivision ordinance. A broader hillside development ordinance can address other factors relevant to slope stability, such as wastewater, vegetation, and roads. It can also resolve the sometimes-conflicting issues of slope stability, fire safety, aesthetics, natural resources, natural habitats, and access.

Maintenance Requirements

Through one of the above ordinances, local governments can make specific requirements for long-term maintenance of developed parcels or common open spaces in potentially unstable areas. Maintenance can be accomplished via deed restrictions on individual properties or by covenants of homeowner associations.

Regulation of Land Use and Intensity

Although reducing intensity does not by itself ensure slope stability, it can make it easier to apply other tools, such as clustering, or specific engineering design requirements. Local governments may use their zoning ordinance to regulate types and intensities of land uses in hillside areas, based on either slope maps, general geologic maps, or slope stability maps. Land-use intensity can be regulated by means of maximum densities, minimum parcel sizes, minimum setbacks, or maximum lot coverage by buildings and/or pavement.

Clustering

Clustering is appropriate for large subdivisions in which only some areas are potentially unstable. Clustered subdivision designs allow the developer to cluster all the permitted units in the stable parts of the property.

Transfer of Development Rights

A transfer of development rights ordinance provides a means for a property owner to transfer development rights from unstable parcels to stable areas. Such schemes are legally complex, however, and are only appropriate in certain situations.

Public Purchase

A direct way to prevent development of potentially unstable land is to purchase it and retain it as a natural area. Alternatively, it may be possible to purchase only the development rights. Land trusts are often appropriate mechanisms for facilitating such transfers. Public or nonprofit entities owning such land, however, should also be sure that the land poses no threats to adjacent landowners.

Limiting Public Investment

Local governments can discourage development in potentially unstable areas by not funding roads or sewer services to these areas.

Management of Existing Unstable Areas

Landslide problems in existing urbanized areas pose particularly difficult problems for local governments. Local governments can provide technical assistance to property owners, especially by establishing hillside maintenance, monitoring, or repair programs, which allow all affected owners to share in the expenses. This can be done by means of voluntary organizations, by changing the covenants of homeowner associations, or through legal mechanisms such as special assessment districts. Local governments can also spend general funds for slope stabilization or for purchase of properties for permanent open space.

REFERENCES

Ohlmacher, Gregory. 1999. *Landslides in Kansas.* Lawrence, KS: Kansas Geological Survey.

Pipkin, Bernard W. 1994. *Geology and the Environment*, 2nd ed. Egan, MN: West Publishing Company. New York: Thompson Learning.

See also:
Earthquakes
Erosion and Sedimentation
Slope, Relief, and Aspect

Robert B. Olshansky, Ph.D. AICP, University of Illinois at Urbana-Champaign

SINKHOLES AND SUBSIDENCE

In the 19 percent of the United States underlain by soluble rocks, sinkholes can pose urban planning problems. Sinkholes typify the landscape category known as karst topography. Karst topography describes an environmentally delicate landscape underlain by soluble rock and characterized by sinkholes, disappearing streams, caves, numerous springs, poor surface drainage, and well-developed subsurface drainage. Sinkholes can be broadly defined as closed depressions, generally elliptical to circular in landscape view, resulting from the settlement or collapse of soil or rock into openings in bedrock beneath the surface, such as caves or enlarged fractures in the soluble bedrock. They are shown on topographic maps as closed contour lines with multiple crossing lines, called hachure marks.

Sinkhole development involves either bedrock or soil. Most sinkholes occur in soil overlying bedrock. The depth to bedrock in sinkhole areas varies on a magnitude not found in any other geologic terrain. Following intense and uneven weathering of bedrock, soil migrates downward into the subsurface through vertical openings in the bedrock, called joints, which are bedrock fractures found in groups that follow distinct directional trends in a given locality. Joints carry much of the groundwater that infiltrates through soil.

SINKHOLE TYPES BY ORIGIN

Two distinct types of sinkholes exist in karst terrains: collapse and subsidence. Collapse sinkholes are a dropout of the soil in a portion of the side or bottom of a depression, resulting in a nearly vertical, typically funnel-shaped opening extending deep into the subsurface. In cross-sectional view, it typically appears bowl-shaped. Subsidence sinkholes have no dropout of the soil into the subsurface; they typically do not experience collapse. In cross-sectional view, subsidence sinkholes resemble a pan shape.

Both types do pose problems for urban development, including:

- structural failure;
- chronic flooding;
- insect breeding in ponded water; and
- groundwater contamination from runoff.

FLOODING IN SINKHOLES

Planners, policy makers, and local governments often do not widely recognize flood hazards posed by sinkholes. Neither state nor federal statutes specifically address liability or compensation for sinkhole flood damages (Quinlan 1986). Because sinkholes are efficient collectors of surface runoff, urbanization of these areas increases the frequency of flooding, which results in both direct and indirect costs. When a sinkhole floods or collapses, direct losses are incurred by individual property owners; indirect losses come from depressed tax revenues on property (Kemmerly 1993).

Sinkholes can be classified into two types from the perspective of drainage: conduit and porous media. Conduit sinkholes typically drain more efficiently but have increased risks of further collapse episodes.

Each collapse event triggers slope failures in the wall of the sinkhole, enlarging the sinkhole and threatening adjacent properties.

Porous media sinkholes pond water more efficiently. They also have increased risks of flooding, whether or not fill has been placed in part of the depression. Because they do not show a history of collapse, porous media sinkholes tend to be backfilled for urban development. Development occurs in the sinkhole or immediately adjacent to it, and flood risk increases significantly. To reduce future collapses, flooding, and groundwater contamination, require a minimum setback from sinkholes and avoid disrupting surface drainage near the sinkhole.

If increased flood damage, drainage litigation, and bad public relations are to be minimized, planners, policy makers, developers, mortgage bankers, and federal underwriting agencies need to define and

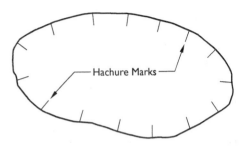

CONVENTIONAL TOPOGRAPHIC EXPRESSION FOR A SINKHOLE IN SOLUBLE ROCK

Reprinted with permission from Journal of the American Planning Association, copyright Spring 1993 by the American Planning Association, Suite 1600, 122 S. Michigan Ave., Chicago, IL 60603-6107.

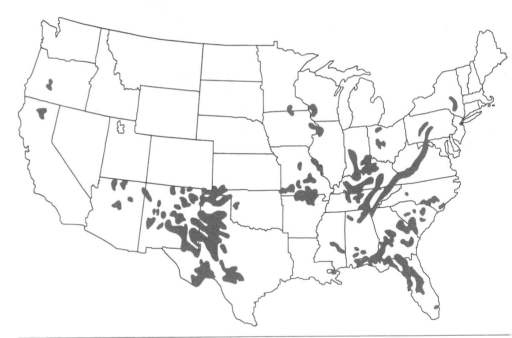

SOLUBLE ROCK TERRAINS

Source: Palmer, Arthur. 1989. "Recent Trends in Karst Geomorphology." Journal of Geological Education, 32:247–53.

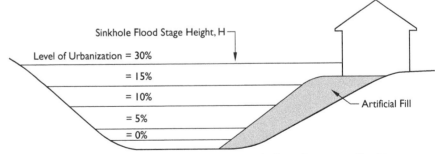

EFFECTS OF URBANIZATION ON SINKHOLE FLOODING

Source: Kemmerly, Phillip. 1981. "The Need for Recognition and Implementation of a Sinkhole-Floodplain Hazard Designation in Urban Karst Terrains." Environmental Geology and Water Sciences, 3:281–292. ©Springer-Verlag.

Phillip R. Kemmerly, Ph.D., Austin Peay State University, Clarksville, Tennessee

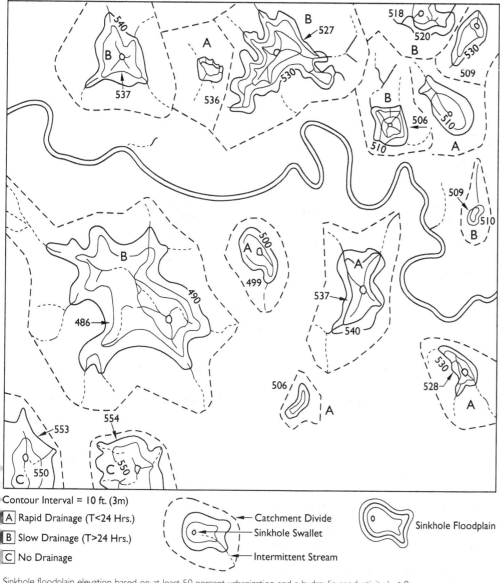

Contour Interval = 10 ft. (3m)

A Rapid Drainage (T<24 Hrs.)

B Slow Drainage (T>24 Hrs.)

C No Drainage

Catchment Divide
Sinkhole Swallet
Intermittent Stream

Sinkhole Floodplain

Sinkhole floodplain elevation based on at least 50 percent urbanization and a hydraulic conductivity, k ->0.

SINKHOLE FLOODPLAIN

Reprinted with permission from Journal of the American Planning Association, copyright Spring 1993 by the American Planning Association, Suite 1600, 122 S. Michigan Ave., Chicago, IL 60603-6107.

protect sinkhole floodplain areas. They should incorporate requirements for flood risk assessment into local subdivision and zoning regulations for development in karst terrains.

SINKHOLE COLLAPSE

Approximately two-thirds to three-fourths of sinkhole collapses that occur in the country result from human actions associated with urban development (Newton 1987). The primary reasons for this include excessive groundwater pumping and changes in surface drainage associated with urban development. Causes for sinkhole collapse include water that has ponded in surface depressions, artificial fill placed in a sinkhole, excavation in a sinkhole, disruption of surface drainage to accommodate development, excessive groundwater pumping, and dynamic loading (the rhythmic and variable frequency of vibrations produced by heavy construction

equipment or earthquake waves). Sinkhole collapses also can result from groundwater flooding into the fractures beneath the soil-bedrock contact.

In order to minimize property damage and the litigation that can follow, local planning policies and subdivision regulations should place restrictions on the filling of sinkholes, require the use of lining if they are to be used as retention ponds, and prohibit development within at least 300 feet from the edge of a sinkhole. Adopting these criteria will produce more environmentally sensitive public policy and yield cost savings to taxpayers, who indirectly support the cost of settling sinkhole-related litigation.

GROUNDWATER CONTAMINATION

Sinkholes efficiently connect the surface with the subsurface. Routing urban runoff into sinkholes produces a deterioration of groundwater quality because little if

any trapping or slowing of contaminated runoff occurs. Consequently, many states and the U.S. Environmental Protection Agency (U.S. EPA) have strict regulations concerning the construction of drainage wells in sinkholes and treatment of urban runoff in karst terrains. Planning officials in sinkhole areas should protect groundwater from contamination generated by urban development. Such risk assessment becomes particularly important in commercial development.

SINKHOLE HAZARD ZONING AND SUBDIVISION ORDINANCES

In the 1980s, several municipalities with sinkhole hazards implemented special ordinances. Three of the most promising ordinances were adopted in Allentown, Pennsylvania (Lehigh Valley Planning Commission) (Dougherty 1989); Clinton Township, New Jersey (Fischer and Lechner 1989); and Lexington, Kentucky (Dinger and Rebmann 1986). These ordinances can serve as workable examples for other communities grappling with sinkhole hazards, especially rapidly growing communities in sinkhole areas in the Sunbelt. A locally developed ordinance, based on input from affected constituencies, can effectively manage development within karst hazard areas.

REFERENCES

Dinger, James S., and James R. Rebmann. 1986. "Ordinance for the Control of Urban Development in Sinkhole Areas in the Bluegrass Karst Region, Lexington, Kentucky." In *Environmental Problems in Karst Terranes and Their Solutions.* Conference Proceedings. Dublin, OH: National Water Well Association.

Dougherty, Percy H. 1989. "Land Use Regulations in the Lehigh Valley: Zoning and Subdivision Ordinances in an Environmentally Sensitive Karst Region." In *Engineering and Environmental Impacts of Sinkholes and Karst*, edited by Barry Beck. Rotterdam, Netherlands: Balkema Press.

Fisher, Joseph A., and Hermia Lechner, 1989. "A Karst Ordinance-Clinton Township, New Jersey." In *Engineering and Environmental Impacts of Sinkholes and Karst*, edited by Barry Beck. Rotterdam, Netherlands: Balkema Press.

Kemmerly, Phillip R. 1993. "Sinkhole Hazards and Risk Assessment in a Planning Context." *Journal of the American Planning Association.* 59, 2:221-227. Chicago: American Planning Association.

Newton, John G. 1987. *Development of Sinkholes Resulting from Man's Activities in the Eastern United States:* U.S. Geological Survey Circular 968. Reston, VA: United States Geological Survey.

Quinlan, James F. 1986. Legal Aspects of Sinkhole Development and Flooding in Karst Terranes, 1; Review and Synthesis. *Environmental Geology and Water Sciences* 8, no. 1: 41-61.

See also:
Erosion and Sedimentation
Flood Hazards
Soils Classification and Mechanics

Phillip R. Kemmerly, Ph.D., Austin Peay State University, Clarksville, Tennessee

EARTHQUAKES

According to the Federal Emergency Management Agency (FEMA), an earthquake is a sudden, rapid shaking of the earth caused by the breaking and shifting of rock beneath the surface. Earthquakes pose a special challenge for emergency management, compared to weather-related hazards, in that they typically offer little warning before they strike. There is thus almost no opportunity for evacuation prior to the disaster.

While people in the United States tend to associate earthquake hazards primarily with California, in reality, many parts of the country are affected by seismic threats. The entire Pacific Coast faces such problems, with particularly potent threats existing in both Puget Sound, affecting metropolitan Seattle, and the southern coast of Alaska, affecting Anchorage.

Faults also stretch across the southeastern United States into Charleston, South Carolina, through the Wasatch Valley of Utah, and within New England. Perhaps the most worrisome of those east of the Rockies, however, is the New Madrid fault, centered in New Madrid, Missouri. It was the site of an estimated 8.0 magnitude earthquake in 1811–1812, which caused parts of the Mississippi River to run backwards, created lakes where none had existed, and even rang church bells in distant Boston. What was then a sparsely inhabited portion of the United States now contains Nashville and Memphis, Tennessee; Evansville, Indiana; and St. Louis, Missouri.

HAZARD IDENTIFICATION

Earthquakes result from the abrupt release of accumulated strain on the Earth's tectonic plates, causing trembling at the surface and for some distance below. Earthquake hazards thus arise in those areas where those plates are moving against each other, sometimes catching and arresting each other's motion until the tension is released in a sudden snapping motion. The resulting movement at the Earth's surface falls into four subcategories of seismic hazards, as detailed in the FEMA publication *Multi-Hazard Identification and Risk Assessment* (MIRA):

- Ground motion
- Seismic activity
- Surface faulting
- Ground failure

Ground Motion

The release of accumulated energy along an earthquake fault line sends off shock waves that travel varying distances depending on the power of the earthquake itself and the surrounding topography. These waves fall into three categories.

- *Primary (P) waves*, similar to sound waves, spread longitudinally at approximately 15,000 miles per hour and are the first to cause vibration.
- *Secondary (S) waves* cause sideways vibrations in structures and are slower. These cause more damage because they shake buildings horizontally, the main source of vulnerability for unreinforced buildings.
- *Surface waves* are the slowest and, as their name suggests, move along the surface. With low-frequency vibrations, these are more likely to cause tall buildings to vibrate.

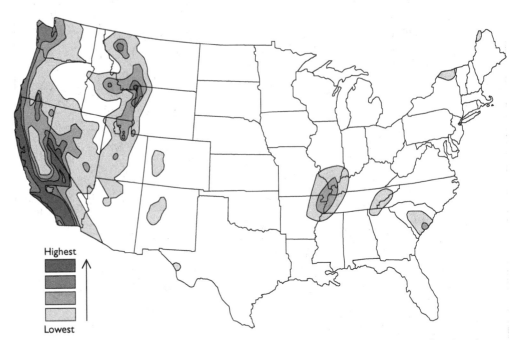

Highest

Lowest

The highest ground-shaking hazard areas in the continental United States are along the West Coast, but significant hazards occur in other areas as well.

GROUND-SHAKING HAZARDS FROM EARTHQUAKES IN THE CONTIGUOUS UNITED STATES

Source: USGS 2002.

Seismic Activity

It is worth understanding the basic technical meaning of two terms most popularly recognized in stories about earthquakes: "magnitude" and "intensity." The former, measured on the logarithmic Richter scale, characterizes the total energy released, while the latter, evaluated on the Modified Mercalli scale, subjectively describes effects at a particular place. These are two very different concepts: The first is a single number dealing with the entire event; the second varies with location, especially distance from the epicenter (a point directly above the true center of disturbance, from which the shock waves radiate). Knowing both the distance of a community from potential earthquake epicenters and the barriers to earthquake shock waves that would mitigate their impact thus has some value for estimating the degree of risk facing a community in terms of the intensity of impact. Earthquakes of the same magnitude produce varying intensities depending on their geographic locations.

Surface Faulting

While earthquake faults occur beneath the Earth's surface, they produce effects on the surface that create hazards for any structures built near or astride active faults. Planners can generally avoid the worst impacts on buildings by ensuring that structures are built away from known active fault lines, typically by using setbacks (e.g., the 50-foot buffer mandated in California's Alquist-Priolo Act). However, ground transportation facilities, such as railroads and highways, inevitably must cross fault lines and often suffer severe damage where surface faulting occurs. In those cases, engineering solutions are more appropriate.

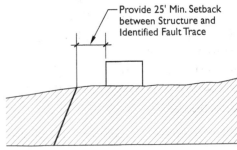

Site Section

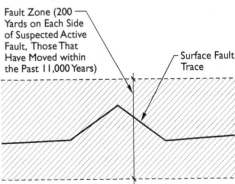

Site Plan

Within a fault zone, trench to determine the exact location of the fault trace. Development within a fault zone should be restricted to low-density land uses, open space, and other low-occupancy activities.

SURFACE FAULTING

Source: Architectural Graphic Standards, 10th edition, 2000.

James C. Schwab, AICP, American Planning Association, Chicago, Illinois

Ground Failure

Weak or unstable soils stressed by earthquake pressures can undergo liquefaction, which can lead to ground failure. Liquefaction occurs in certain types of clay-free soils, mostly sand and silt saturated by water, which become viscous fluids under the impact of ground vibrations from shear waves. MIRA indicates that the younger and looser the sediment and the higher the water table, the more susceptible a soil is to liquefaction. MIRA lists three types of ground failures that result:

- Lateral spreads develop on gentle slopes and involve the sideways movement of large blocks of soil.
- Flow failures, the most catastrophic, occur on slopes greater than three degrees and involve blocks of intact material riding on a layer of liquefied soil moving considerable distances.
- Loss of bearing strength entails the failure of liquefied soil that has been supporting a structure, which then settles or tilts.

Sources of earthquake hazard maps are local consultants or universities, state geological surveys, or the U.S. Geological Survey (USGS).

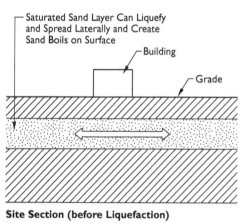

Site Section (before Liquefaction)

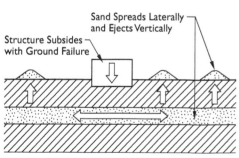

Site Section (after Earthquake and Liquefaction)

Avoid sites subject to liquefaction (water-saturated sandy soils), design foundation systems to withstand ground failure, drain water from the site, and change the composition of the soil and compact the site.

SUBSIDENCE OR LIQUEFACTION

Source: Architectural Graphic Standards, 10th edition, 2000.

RISK ASSESSMENT

The U.S. map provides some idea for planners of both the geographical distribution and level of severity of earthquake threats across the contiguous United States. Local maps need to be considerably more detailed and ought to make the best possible use of planning and development data and geographic information system (GIS) technologies to incorporate detailed information on building quality and infrastructure, among a variety of other data types.

Planners should be aware of a FEMA-developed resource, HAZUS, which has been designed as a GIS-based system in MapInfo and ArcView, both products of ESRI. The program uses mathematical formulas and information about building stock, local geology, and the location and size of potential earthquakes, economic data, and other information to estimate losses from a potential earthquake. HAZUS is capable of mapping and displaying ground shaking, the pattern of building damage, and demographic information about a community. Once the location and size of a hypothetical earthquake is identified, HAZUS estimates the violence of ground shaking, the number of buildings damaged, the number of casualties, the amount of damage to transportation systems, disruption to the electrical and water utilities, the number of people displaced from their homes, and the estimated cost of repairing projected damage and other effects.

MITIGATION OPPORTUNITIES

Good data on building construction are essential in effectively mapping earthquake risks at the local level. Most deaths and injuries from earthquakes result not from surface faulting or ground shaking itself, but from the damage to structures in which people may be working or residing, or from falling cornices and other debris. The structural integrity of infrastructure can affect the extent and nature of both monetary and human losses largely because of the potential for collapse, particularly in the case of bridges, tunnels, and rail lines. Thus, loss of both life and property can be significantly reduced with seismic strengthening of buildings and infrastructure. While planners are not generally involved in such design questions, it is important that they know where there are concentrations of buildings and infrastructure that require seismic upgrading.

The National Earthquake Hazards Reduction Program (NEHRP) was authorized through the National Earthquake Hazards Reduction Act of 1977, as amended (42 U.S.C. Section 7701 et. seq.). This program is charged with the development and enhancement of provisions to minimize structural

| Ground Rupture | Ground Shaking | Differential Subsidence | Liquefaction |

MAIN CAUSES OF FOUNDATION FAILURE

Source: Architectural Graphic Standards, 10th edition, 2000.

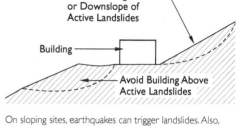

On sloping sites, earthquakes can trigger landslides. Also, alluvium and unconsolidated soils can increase the violence and duration of ground shaking. For example, during the 1989 Loma Prieta earthquake, ground shaking in San Francisco's marina district, on nonengineered fill, was more than twice as violent and lasted more than twice as long as ground shaking on adjacent bedrock sites.

UNSTABLE SITES

Source: Architectural Graphic Standards, 10th edition, 2000.

damage and hazard to life due to earthquakes. FEMA is responsible for managing NEHRP, whose participants also include USGS, the National Science Foundation, and the National Institute of Standards and Technology.

NEHRP Recommended Provisions for Seismic Regulations for New Buildings (FEMA 368 and 369) presents minimum criteria for the design and construction of new buildings. One of its intended uses is as a source document for use in various building regulatory applications. There is a great deal of compatibility between the Provisions and the Uniform Building Code's seismic safety criteria. *NEHRP Guidelines for the Seismic Rehabilitation of Buildings* (FEMA 273 and 274) presents minimum criteria for rehabilitating existing buildings.

Following the creation of NEHRP, FEMA worked with the National Science Foundation (NSF), the National Institute for Building Sciences (NIBS), the American Society of Civil Engineers, the Applied Technology Council (ATC), and the National Institute for Standards and Technology (NIST) to create, in 1979, the Building Seismic Safety Council (BSSC) under the auspices of NIBS. The purpose of BSSC is to address the various issues involved in developing and promulgating national regulations concerning seismic safety. For example, according to BSSC, the first step in pursuing mitigation opportunities for existing buildings is to develop an inventory of the buildings needing seismic rehabilitation. Because the financing of seismic rehabilitation projects is often a major issue in the private sector, financial incentives tend to play a major role in facilitating the accomplishment of mitigation objectives. Many California communities have been operating such incentive

James C. Schwab, AICP, American Planning Association, Chicago, Illinois

programs, in some cases for 20 years or more. Local capital improvements planning should include the seismic upgrading of public facilities where short-comings have been identified.

Areas in the immediate vicinity of mapped fault lines are generally best kept as open space. For instance, Salt Lake City established Faultline Park to avert planned apartment development along a known fault line on the Wasatch Front. For other areas, the strict application of seismic safety building codes is essential. Subdivision regulations and site plan review can be used to ensure adequate access and evacuation routes so that the failure of a single transportation facility, such as a bridge, does not isolate residents.

REFERENCES

Building Seismic Safety Council. 1997. *NEHRP Guidelines for the Seismic Rehabilitation of Buildings*. Washington, DC: FEMA.

Building Seismic Safety Council. 2000. *NEHRP Recommended Provisions for Seismic Regulations for New Buildings and Other Structures*. Washington, DC: FEMA.

Federal Emergency Management Agency. 1997. *Multi-Hazard Identification and Risk Assessment*. Washington, DC: FEMA.

See also:
Landslides
Tsunamis and Seiches

James C. Schwab, AICP, American Planning Association, Chicago, Illinois

WILDFIRES

Wildfires are uncontrolled fires that destroy life, property, or natural resources. They occur in wildland areas but can invade the Wildland/Urban Interface (WUI). Wildland areas are defined areas uninhabited by humans; for wildfires to occur, these areas must provide dry fuel in the form of brush, forests, or grasslands. The interface is an area lying between developed areas and wildlands or in which development is interspersed among wildland areas.

Wildfires can be triggered by natural causes, such as lightning strikes, or human causes, such as campfires, smoldering cigarettes, or even arson. The U.S. Forest Service indicates that about one-fourth of reported wildfires are caused by arson, and almost another one-fourth by debris burns. States such as Kansas, Mississippi, Louisiana, Georgia, Florida, the Carolinas, Tennessee, California, Massachusetts, and the national forests of the western United States contain significant areas of wooded, brush, and grassy areas, making them wildfire danger zones.

HOW WILDFIRES OCCUR

Wildfires tend to result from hot, dry weather patterns that create the conditions, in the form of dry fuel, for their occurrence. Actual occurrence then depends simply on the right spark in the right place. The three factors affecting the spread of the resulting fire are topography, fuel, and weather. Topography can slow or accelerate flames by affecting wind patterns and the connectivity of fuel supplies. A prolonged drought in areas abundant in natural fuels, such as Florida, where rain is typically abundant, can actually produce more vicious fires than in areas with typically thin vegetation because of an arid climate.

Wildfires are a part of nature and serve an ecological purpose regardless of their inconvenience for humans. In wildlands, they clear underbrush from the forest and facilitate the regeneration of certain species at the expense of others.

Twentieth-century attempts to suppress fire at all costs, coupled with the widespread deforestation and settlement of the landscape, combined to generate new and previously uncommon fire hazards affecting developed areas.

THE SIGNIFICANCE FOR PLANNERS

A basic understanding of the causes of, and means of mitigating, wildfires is essential for planners working in environments where the WUI is an established or growing part of the landscape. Numerous urban wildfires, such as those in Oakland, California (1991), Los Alamos, New Mexico (2000), and elsewhere, have demonstrated that a large number of lives and homes can be put at risk by not properly accounting for the effect of development in these areas. At the same time, it is also clear that design principles based on lessons learned from recent wildfires can be extremely useful in minimizing both the ecological impact of new development and the potential danger to new and existing development.

HAZARD IDENTIFICATION

Efforts to eliminate wildfires from the natural environment, rather than helping matters, have served to make such fires more severe when they occur. A practice of automatic suppression of all wildfires causes vegetative fuels to accumulate in the forest understory, resulting in fires even more severe and disastrous than they might be otherwise.. So-called prescribed burns have become one way of reducing that risk, but these must be undertaken with great care and a solid knowledge of the local ecosystem. It is equally important to incorporate new knowledge of wildfire mitigation techniques into the planning of any development in the WUI, as well as to avoid such development to the extent possible.

The pattern of American urban development has shifted wildfire management attention further west, but the problem is not simply a regional one. The upper Midwest, northern New England, and any other forested areas that may suffer prolonged drought also are potentially at risk from wildfires.

It is important to be aware of the interactivity of wildfire with other hazards that contribute to wildfires and are triggered or affected by wildfires themselves, such as winds (both exacerbating wildfires and being induced by them, particularly in firestorms), mudslides, and landslides (induced by the stripping of the vegetation from hillsides, followed by rainstorms).

RISK ASSESSMENT

Nan Johnson, a planner with the Colorado State Forest Service, lists the following factors, in order of importance, as items for consideration in identifying, mapping, and rating wildfire hazards in urban interface areas, based on Boulder County, Colorado's experience in tapping a variety of kinds of expertise to address the problem.

Site location and topography. What types of fuels are in the area of the buildings in question? Fuels include all vegetation in the surrounding area. What fuel model classes do they fall into? The National Fire Danger Rating System provides a list of 20 fuel types, with letter ratings for individual fuel models, each rated on the basis of the density and flammability of various kinds of living and dead biomass, such as pine, chaparral, grasses, and timber slash. Is there forest? If the area is mountainous, how stable is the slope?

Building construction and design. What materials have been used for existing buildings? How are the eaves built, and what are the overhang features? These features can produce significant updrafts that feed fires into houses and add to the severity of fire damage. Are there porches? Wooden decks add to the fuel base to prolong the fire. What materials were used for the roof and siding? Wood-shake roofs, for example, are notorious fuel extenders. How flammable are the materials overall?

Defensible space and landscaping. What sort of vegetation or other fuel exists in the immediate area around the structure? Tall pine trees and shrubs may be beautiful but deadly within a few feet of the house. Moreover, the composition of the transition zones away from the house leading into the wildlands also makes a difference, as far away as 200 feet from the structure. What is the nature of the landscaping that surrounds the house, and is it irrigated? Various types of vegetation are more or less fire-resistant than others. Find out what works locally.

Access. How are the lot structures set up? Are there power lines overhanging the property? Are there overhanging trees? Steep or tight curves leading to the property? How will fire and rescue vehicles reach the area?

Water. Where is it accessible? Streams, ponds, and springs may provide natural sources of water but also have inherent limitations during a drought or when frozen. Some rural communi

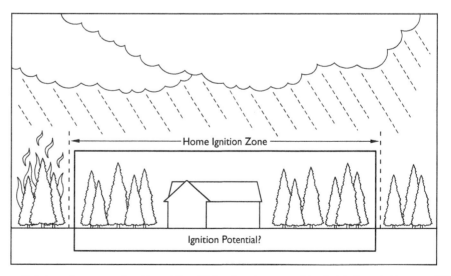

A home with its immediate surroundings (about 100 to 150 feet from the structure) is called the home ignition zone (HIZ). Many factors about the HIZ determine the potential for ignition during a wildland fire.

HOME IGNITION ZONE

Source: U.S. Forest Service.

James C. Schwab, AICP, American Planning Association, Chicago, Illinois

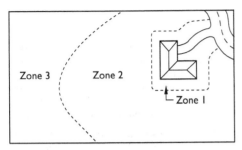

There are three fire-defensible zones around a home or other structure.

DEFENSIBLE SPACE ZONES

Source: Dennis 2003.

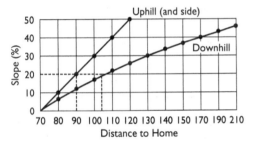

This chart indicates the minimum recommended dimensions for defensible space from the home to the outer edge of Zone 2. For example, if a home is situated on a 20 percent slope, the minimum defensible space dimensions would be 90 feet uphill and to the sides of the home, and 104 feet downhill from the home.

DEFENSIBLE SPACE DIMENSIONS

Source: Dennis 2003.

ties build cisterns to overcome these limitations, thus storing rainwater for future fire needs. Wells, swimming pools, and other devices are limited only by local planning ingenuity. Are there hydrants, and who maintains them? Dry hydrants, which consist of nonpressurized piping connected to a natural water source such as a pond, are an option in many areas. The National Fire Protection Association (n.d.) has a manual on planning for water supplies in the WUI that provides many of the basic details pertaining to such questions.

Fire protection. What is the nature of the fire protection available? What fire protection exists on site? Monitoring the conditions that can increase wildfire hazards in the short term is critical, even if not entirely relevant to long-term land-use planning decisions. Awareness of the potential for wildfire incidents puts planners on the alert for the potential need to implement all or part of a postdisaster plan and to allocate resources accordingly. The U.S. Forest Service tracks moisture patterns nationwide to spot areas that are potential tinderboxes. (Cohen et al. 2001)

MITIGATION OPPORTUNITIES

Quick and efficient access by a local, often volunteer, fire department to remote home sites located on steep, winding hills in the midst of a raging inferno can be highly problematic. The problems created in connection with the first five issues above make fire protection at best a secondary factor in the level of actual danger posed by wildfire hazards and puts mitigation at a premium.

The WUI is an area where development is coming to the hazard, and thus the natural and built context is important on a case-by-case basis in determining the level of hazard to which buildings are exposed. Hazard identification can become a vital first step in designing plans to engage property owners in a proactive program to mitigate hazards prior to a disaster and to seize opportunities to reduce future

vulnerability. For example, implementing plans for regular clearance of flammable underbrush in proximity to homes can be critical in reducing both a wildfire's fuel supply and chances for igniting homes in a rural subdivision.

Two major national standards exist for addressing and mitigating wildfire hazards, one produced by the National Fire Protection Association (NFPA) and the other by the International Code Council. Both are cited in the references for this book.

Computerized mapping and hazard identification models for wildfire hazards are increasingly available as mitigation tools. The Western Governors Association has released its own Hazard Assessment Methodology. Boulder County has been using its own Wildfire Hazard Identification and Mitigation System (WHIMS), a geographic information system (GIS) program allowing county planners to apply what they have learned as they review development proposals and seek mitigation before construction begins.

REFERENCES

Cohen, Jack, Nan Johnson, and Lincoln Walther. 2001. "Saving Homes from Wildfires: Regulating the Home Ignition Zone." *Zoning News* May.

Dennis, F.C. 2003. "Creating Wildfire-Defensible Zones." Fact Sheet no. 6.302. Fort Collins: Colorado State University Extension Service. As found on the Colorado State University Cooperative Extension website, www.ext.colorado.edu

International Code Council. 2003. *International Urban-Wildland Interface Code*. Country Club Hills, IL: International Code Council.

National Fire Protection Association. 2002. NFPA 1144: Standard for Protection of Life and Property from Wildfire. Quincy, MA: NFPA.

See also:
Forestry
Habitat Patches, Corridors, and Matrix

James C. Schwab, AICP, American Planning Association, Chicago, Illinois

HAZARDOUS MATERIALS

According to the U.S. Department of Transportation (DOT), hazardous materials are defined as substances "capable of posing unreasonable risk to health, safety, and property" (49 CFR 171.8). Hazardous materials (also known as *hazmat*) are regulated by a number of federal agencies, including the DOT, U.S. Environmental Protection Agency, U.S. Nuclear Regulatory Commission, and the Occupational Safety and Health Administration of the U.S. Department of Labor. In addition, the U.S. Coast Guard and Federal Emergency Management Agency (FEMA) of the U.S. Department of Homeland Security have responsibilities for emergency response to hazmat incidents. Because these agencies have different responsibilities, they have correspondingly different definitions of hazmat.

FIXED-SITE AND TRANSPORTATION SOURCES

Planners typically expect to find hazmat produced, stored, or used at fixed-site facilities, such as petrochemical and manufacturing plants, but these materials are also found in warehouses (e.g., agricultural fertilizers and pesticides), water treatment plants (chlorine is used to purify the water), and breweries (ammonia is used as a refrigerant).

Hazmat is transported from one location to another by a variety of modes—ship, barge, pipeline, rail, truck, and air. In general, the quantities of hazmat on ships, barges, and pipelines can be as large as at many-fixed site facilities, but usually are smaller when transported by rail, are smaller still when transported by truck, and are smallest when transported by air. Small to moderate-size releases of less hazardous materials at fixed-site facilities are occupational hazards but often pose little risk to public health and safety because the risk area lies within the facility boundary lines. However, releases of this size during hazmat transportation are frequently a public hazard because passersby can easily enter the risk area and become exposed. The amount actually released is often much smaller than the total quantity available in the container, but prudence dictates that the planning process assume the plausible worst case of complete release within a short period of time (e.g., 10 minutes in the case of toxic gases).

HAZARDOUS MATERIALS CLASSIFICATION

In addition to the quantity of the hazmat released, the size of the risk area depends on its chemical and physical properties. These properties form the basis for categorizing hazmat into nine classes described in the following sections.

Explosives

Explosives can cause casualties and property damage due to overpressure from atmospheric blast waves or flying debris. Destructive effects from quantities found in transportation can be felt as much as a mile or more away from the site of the explosion.

Flammable Gases

Flammable gases, such as liquefied petroleum gas (LPG), are of significant concern because they can travel downwind after release until they reach an ignition source, such as the pilot light in a water heater or the ignition system in a car. At distances of one-half mile (0.8 kilometers) or more, the gas cloud can erupt in a fireball that flashes back toward the release point. Rupture of gas containers can launch fragments as missiles up to a mile, so evacuation out to this distance is advised if there is a fire.

Flammable Liquids

Flammable liquids, such as gasoline, present a similar threat as flammable gases, in that a volatile liquid (one that rapidly produces much vapor) can travel toward an ignition source and erupt in flames when it is reached. When dispersed on land, there should be a downwind evacuation of at least 0.2 miles (0.3 kilometers). A flammable liquid that floats downstream on water could be dangerous at even greater distances, and one that is toxic requires special consideration (see "Toxic Materials and Infectious Substances," below). A fire should stimulate consideration of an evacuation of approximately 0.5 miles in all directions.

Flammable Solids

Flammable solids are somewhat less dangerous than flammable gases or liquids, because they do not disperse over wide areas as gases and liquids do. A large spill requires a downwind evacuation of 0.06 miles (0.1 kilometers), but a fire should stimulate consideration of an evacuation of a half mile (0.8 kilometers) in all directions.

Oxidizers and Organic Peroxides

Oxidizers and organic peroxides do not burn but are hazardous because they promote combustion. A large spill should prompt a downwind evacuation of 0.3 miles (0.48 kilometers), and a fire should initiate an evacuation of a half mile (0.8 kilometers) in all directions.

Toxic Materials and Infectious Substances

Toxic (poisonous) materials are a major hazard because of the effects they can produce when inhaled into the lungs, ingested into the stomach by means of contaminated water or food, or absorbed through the skin. Of these exposure pathways, inhalation hazard is typically the greatest concern, because high concentrations taken in during acute exposure can kill in a matter of seconds. Prolonged ingestion exposures can cause cancers in those exposed and genetic defects in their offspring. Moreover, chemical contamination of victims could pose problems for volunteers and professionals providing first aid and transporting victims to hospitals. These chemicals vary substantially in their volatility and toxicity, so evacuation distances following a spill or fire must be determined from the Table of Protective Action Distances in the DOT's *Emergency Response Guidebook*.

Infectious substances have rarely been a significant threat to date, but the potential for terrorist attacks should be of concern to planners.

Radioactive Materials

With the exception of nuclear power plants, the planning for which is supported by state and federal agencies and electric utilities, releases of radioactive materials are likely to involve small quantities. Nonetheless, even a few grams of a lost radiographic source for industrial or medical X-rays can generate a high level of public concern. Here also, the recently recognized threat of terrorist attack from a "dirty bomb" that uses a conventional explosive to scatter radioactive material over a wide area deserves planners' attention because of the potential for long-term contamination of central business districts. A large spill should prompt a downwind evacuation of approximately 0.06 miles (0.1 kilometers), and a fire should initiate an evacuation of approximately 0.2 miles (0.32 kilometers) in all directions.

Corrosive Materials

Corrosive materials, which can be either acidic or alkaline, cause chemical burns, but the substances in this class most frequently used and transported are not highly volatile. Thus, the geographical area affected by a spill is likely to be no greater than approximately 330 feet (approximately 100 meters), unless the container is involved in a fire or the hazmat enters a waterway (e.g., via storm sewers). These chemicals vary substantially in their volatility and toxicity, so evacuation distances following a spill or fire must be determined from the Table of Protective Action Distances in the *Emergency Response Guidebook*.

Miscellaneous Dangerous Goods

As the name of this category suggests, this class comprises a diverse set of materials such as air bags, certain vegetable oils, polychlorinated biphenyls (PCBs), and white asbestos. Materials in this category are low to moderate fire or health hazards to people within 33 to 82 feet (approximately 10 to 25 meters).

THREAT POTENTIAL

In almost all cases, hazmat becomes a threat when it is released either accidentally or deliberately from the tanks and pipes in which it is normally contained. The emergency response to such incidents has long been recognized to be a responsibility of first responders in public safety agencies, such as the fire and police departments.

In the 1980s, emergency management increasingly became a profession that attempted to conduct hazard and vulnerability analyses to identify the areas of the community exposed to hazmat hazards, as well as the more common meteorological (hurricane, tornado, and flood) and geophysical (earthquake, volcano, and landslide) hazards. Emergency managers are increasingly involved in working with community planners to identify hazard-prone areas, the vulnerable households and businesses located there, and the physical vulnerability of the structures in which these vulnerable populations are housed. In this regard, homes within the potential blast areas from explosions or under the plumes of toxic chemicals or radiological materials need to be identified.

Some of the sources available for this purpose include the *Technical Guidance for Hazards Analysis* (U.S. Environmental Protection Agency, Federal Emergency Management Agency, and U.S. Department of

Michael K. Lindell, Ph.D., Texas A&M University, College Station, Texas

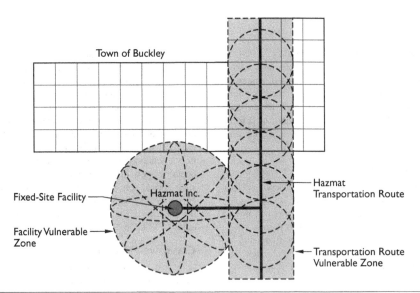

VULNERABLE ZONES AROUND FIXED-SITE FACILITY AND TRANSPORTATION ROUTE

Source: Michael Lindell.

Source: Adapted from Lindell and Perry 1992.

Transportation, 1987), the *Handbook of Chemical Hazard Analysis Procedures* (Federal Emergency Management Agency, U.S. Department of Transportation, and U.S. Environmental Protection Agency, n.d.), and the aforementioned *Emergency Response Guidebook* (U.S. Department of Transportation, Transport Canada, and Secretariat of Transport and Communications of Mexico, 2000), as well as more information on these agencies' websites.

VULNERABLE ZONE

The vulnerable zone around a fixed-site facility is a circle because a toxic chemical plume—which is roughly elliptical in shape—could travel in any direction from the plant depending upon wind direction. The vulnerable zone radius is a function of the quantity of the hazmat released, its release rate, its toxicity, wind speed, and atmospheric stability. A hazmat release can take place at any point along a transportation route, so its vulnerable zone is defined by a series of circles whose radius is calculated in the same way as for a fixed-site facility. Thus, the vulnerable zone for a transportation route forms a rectangle. These vulnerable zones can be overlaid onto local maps to identify those areas within the local jurisdiction that require hazard mitigation and emergency preparedness actions to protect the public health and safety, property, and the environment.

Planners can use the *Technical Guidance for Hazards Analysis* to calculate the size of the vulnerable zone for extremely hazardous substances (EHSs—members of a list of about 400 highly toxic gases or liquids) by identifying the number of pounds of EHS in a tank (obtained from the facility operators) and the level of concern (LOC—the minimum concentration at which adverse health effects could occur, which is listed in an appendix to the *Technical Guidance*). These data are used to enter one of four tables defined by the type of terrain (urban or rural) and atmospheric conditions at the time of the release (assumed to be either moderately stable or extremely stable). Thus, the release of 800 pounds of chlorine

(LOC = .0073) over a 10-minute period from a water treatment plant located in a rural area during extremely stable atmospheric conditions and a wind speed of 3.4 miles (5.4 kilometers) per hour would have a vulnerable zone radius of approximately 10 miles (16.09 kilometers). If the plant were located in an urban area, the same scenario would result in a vulnerable zone radius of only about 1 mile (1.6 kilometers) because the presence of buildings causes greater terrain roughness and, thus, more vertical atmospheric mixing of the toxic gas.

Emergencies in hazmat transportation usually involve much smaller quantities of hazmat than fixed-site facilities and, because they often occur in populated areas, emergency responders rarely have the time to perform the computations described in the previous example. Consequently, the *Emergency Response Guidebook* provides guidance on protective action distances (the equivalent of vulnerable zone radiuses) for small and large spills during daytime and nighttime conditions. For a nighttime release of chlorine, the protective action distances would be 0.5 miles for a small release and 1.9 miles for a large release.

ROLE OF PLANNERS

Planners should work with emergency managers, local emergency planning committees, and facility operators to promote safe land-use practices to ensure that high-density residential and commercial land uses are located outside the vulnerable zones for fixed-site facilities. Planners should also ensure that these uses are adequately separated from transportation routes where high volumes of hazmat may be carried. High priority should be given to facilities housing vulnerable population segments that lack physical mobility, ready access to evacuation vehicles, or weathertight buildings that provide on-site shelter.

Planners also should work with local energy utilities to ensure that residential and commercial structures are safe places for shelter in a hazmat emergency. This includes assessing air infiltration

rates in these structures to determine the speed at which toxic pollutants would enter during a chemical release. Assessment of air infiltration rates should be accompanied by programs to promote safe building construction practices that reduce this vulnerability. Such activities could include more stringent building codes for new construction; for existing structures, home weatherization retrofits will be needed to reduce their vulnerability.

Success of retrofit programs depends upon the quality of the risk communication programs used to make residents aware of these hazards as well as the technical support and financial incentives that are provided (Lindell and Perry 2004). In many jurisdictions, retrofit programs to protect residential and commercial structures from hazmat releases can be integrated with the corresponding programs designed to reduce vulnerability to meteorological (e.g., hurricanes, tornadoes, and floods) and geophysical (e.g., earthquakes and landslides) hazards.

REFERENCES

Federal Emergency Management Agency, U.S. Department of Transportation, and U.S. Environmental Protection Agency. No date. *Handbook of Chemical Hazard Analysis Procedures*. Washington, DC: U.S. Government Printing Office.

Lindell, M.K., and R.W. Perry. 2004. *Communicating Environmental Risk in Multiethnic Communities*. Thousand Oaks, CA: Sage Publications.

National Response Team. 1987. *Hazardous Materials Emergency Planning Guide*. Washington DC: U.S. Environmental Protection Agency, Federal Emergency Management Agency, and U.S. Department of Transportation.

Michael K. Lindell, Ph.D., Texas A&M University, College Station, Texas

U.S. Department of Transportation, Transport Canada, and Secretariat of Transport and Communications of Mexico. 2000. *Emergency Response Guidebook*. Washington DC: U.S. Department of Transportation, Transport Canada, and Secretariat of Transport and Communications of Mexico.

U.S. Environmental Protection Agency, Federal Emergency Management Agency, and U.S. Department of Transportation. 1987. *Technical Guidance for Hazards Analysis*. Washington DC: U.S. Environmental Protection Agency, Federal Emergency Management Agency, and U.S. Department of Transportation.

Michael K. Lindell, Ph.D., Texas A&M University, College Station, Texas

TSUNAMIS AND SEICHES

Seiches and tsunamis are both waterborne hazards that affect shoreline or coastal areas.

SEICHES

Seiches are large waves that resemble the rolling action of water in a bowl knocked off balance. They occur in inland lakes or other enclosed bodies of water when powerful waves are generated by some disturbance. The disturbance can take the form of strong winds, earthquake tremors, or landslides from a steep shoreline slope. As these causes are diverse, the important factor for hazard identification is to be aware of their potential occurrence and to map the shoreline zones that could be affected by wave run-up. Near-shore and low-lying property is most vulnerable. Shoreline mapping is virtually a necessity in predisaster planning for any seismically active region that contains inland lakes or even a large bay or inlet.

TSUNAMIS

Tsunamis are by nature a far more potent hazard than seiches, potentially gathering force across hundreds or even thousands of miles of ocean, where they may often be unnoticeable, to pile up walls of water towering up to 100 feet (30.48 meters) before they crash into narrow harbors and bays along the coast. Sometimes called tidal waves, they actually have no relationship to normal tides but result from seismic or volcanic disturbances on the ocean floor. Another less likely but potential generator is a mid-oceanic meteor strike. The word "tsunami" ("harbor wave" in Japanese) more accurately describes the phenomenon—the long oceanic wavelength concentrates its power in a confined body of water.

Remote-Source Tsunamis

Remote-source tsunamis travel long distances at high speeds for potentially an hour or more before hitting shore. Their great danger is that the high wave speed at sea slows down in shallow coastal waters, the wavelength shortens, and wave energy increases, magnifying waves to heights exceeding 50 feet (15.24 meters) during coastal run-up. This process of wave transformation at the shoreline is called reflection, and its impact largely depends on the nature of the shoreline.

Locally Generated Tsunamis

These result from tectonic plate subduction, landslides, and volcanic activity. In contrast to remote-source tsunamis, locally generated tsunamis involve events much closer to the affected shoreline and result in a much faster impact following the geologic event.

RISK ASSESSMENT

Relative to other potential hazards, tsunamis constitute a smaller risk, but in the most affected areas they still require attention. Most at risk are shallow inland bays that tend to magnify wave energy to dangerous levels, accompanied by developed, low-lying coastal regions where wave run-up can do substantial damage and endanger life. In contrast, areas with high coastal escarpments pose little if any risk.

Tsunami hazard mapping is advisable for coastal communities that fit the high-hazard profile. Tsunamis have been the object of new attention from federal, state, and local planners, with the Federal Emergency Management Agency (FEMA) and the National Oceanic and Atmospheric Administration's (NOAA) Pacific Marine Environmental Laboratory (PMEL) in the lead. The first local tsunami hazard mapping project, completed in early 1995 in Eureka, California, serves as the prototype for similar efforts elsewhere. The Oregon Department of Geology and Mineral Hazards has a program for mapping tsunami hazards.

MITIGATION OPPORTUNITIES

PMEL has conducted tsunami hazard mitigation workshops in West Coast communities. Warning systems can help local officials evacuate threatened shoreline areas to prevent loss of life. They are most effective when coupled over time with public education efforts. In some areas, shore-protection structures may limit damage from wave run-up, but the most important steps in affected coastal zones are elevating buildings above flood levels and keeping the area below the buildings free from obstruction. This allows for the passage of waves and water and reduces the amount of debris that can become projectiles during serious floods.

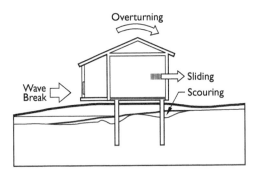

Tsunami waves breaking over a vulnerable near-shore structure can overturn the structure from below, or cause sliding of the structure or scouring of the soil beneath.

FORCES ON STRUCTURES CREATED BY TSUNAMIS

Source: National Tsunami Hazard Mitigation Program, 2001.

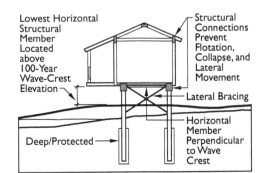

Design solutions for such structures include deep pilings and elevation of the living space, plus bracing of the structure.

DESIGN SOLUTIONS TO TSUNAMI EFFECTS

Source: National Tsunami Hazard Mitigation Program, 2001.

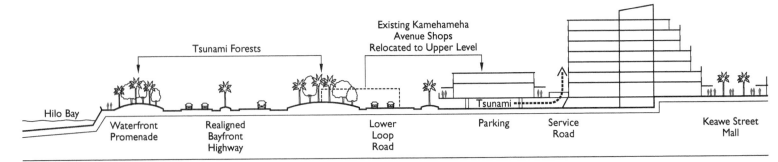

The Hilo Downtown Development Plan, adopted in 1974, required redevelopment in its Safety District to meet building design standards to withstand the impacts of a tsunami. That plan was later superseded by a 1985 plan.

DOWNTOWN CROSS SECTION FROM HILO DEVELOPMENT PLAN

Source: National Tsunami Hazard Mitigation Program, 2001.

James C. Schwab, AICP, American Planning Association, Chicago, Illinois

Relocating buildings out of the hazard zone and using land-use regulations to limit new development is also an effective way to reduce potential damage. The County of Hawaii has employed such regulations in Hilo, in its downtown redevelopment plans, creating a safety district and requiring buildings below the 20-foot elevation contour line to be built to withstand tsunami impacts. The FEMA publication *Multi-Hazard Identification and Risk Assessment* (MIRA) also suggests planting with vegetation capable of resisting and reflecting wave energy and locating streets and homes perpendicular to wave paths to allow penetration along a path of least resistance. FEMA has also provided guidance for architects and engineers in tsunami-resistant building design in its *Coastal Construction Manual*.

REFERENCES

Federal Emergency Management Agency. 2000. *Coastal Construction Manual: Principles and Practices of Planning, Siting, Designing, Constructing, and Maintaining Residential Buildings in Coastal Areas,* 3rd ed. FEMA 55. Washington, DC: FEMA.

Federal Emergency Management Agency. 1997. *Multi-Hazard Identification and Risk Assessment.* Washington, DC: FEMA.

See also:
Beach and Dune Systems
Erosion and Sedimentation
Estuaries, Flats, and Marshes

James C. Schwab, AICP, American Planning Association, Chicago, Illinois

HAZARDS

NOISE AND VIBRATION

Noise is simply unwanted sound. Sound level is measured by the difference between atmospheric pressure without the sound and total pressure with the sound. It is described using the logarithmic decibel (dB) scale.

The frequency (or pitch) of sound is measured in Hertz (Hz), which is the number of cycles, or waves, per second. Humans hear best at frequencies between 1,000 and 6,000 Hz. Sounds above 10,000 Hz (high-pitched hissing) and below 100 Hz (low rumble) are much more difficult to hear. The A-weighted decibel (dBA) scale, which gives more weight to the frequencies easily heard by people, is used to describe sound where audible noise is the focus of study.

The duration of sounds also influences human response. Sounds can be continuous (like a waterfall), impulsive (like a firecracker), or intermittent (like aircraft overflights).

Vibration is similar to sound, but it is primarily structure-borne rather than air-borne. Vibration can propagate through the ground to the foundations and walls of buildings, producing a rumbling noise from vibration of the structure or causing the rattling of objects.

NOISE DESCRIPTORS

Noise descriptors commonly used in environmental planning are summarized here.

Maximum Sound Level (L_{max})

L_{max} is the maximum sound level of an event, a common concern in noise studies. L_{max} provides no information, however, about the duration of the event or the total sound energy of the event.

Sound Exposure Level (SEL)

SEL describes the total sound energy of an individual event. The time-varying sound energy is mathematically compressed into an equivalent duration of one second, combining both loudness and duration in a single metric.

Equivalent Sound Level (L_{eq})

L_{eq} is the average sound level over a given period of time. The sound is logarithmically averaged over the number of seconds during the period. The result is equivalent to a steady sound of the same magnitude over the period.

Day-Night Average Sound Level (DNL)

DNL is the time-weighted average sound level over a 24-hour period. It is computed in the same way as L_{eq}, but an extra 10-decibel weight is added to all sounds after 10:00 p.m. and before 7:00 a.m.

Community Noise Equivalent Level (CNEL)

CNEL is substantially the same as DNL, with an additional 4.8-decibel weight added to sounds occurring between 7:00 p.m. and 10:00 p.m. California law requires the use of CNEL in noise studies.

Time Above a Given Level (TA)

The TA metric describes the amount of time, over a stated period, that sound exceeds a given level. Different threshold levels are established based on the study objective. For example, if the objective is to determine how often outdoor speech is likely to be interrupted, thresholds would be set at levels where noise could impair speech.

X Percentile Exceeded Sound Level (L_x)

The L_x metric describes the sound level that is exceeded X percent of the time over the observation period. Thus, L_{10} is the level that is exceeded 10 percent of the time, L_{50}, the level exceeded 50 percent of the time, and L_{90} the level exceeded 90 percent of the time. L_{50} and L_{90} are often used to describe the "ambient" or "background" sound level.

NOISE EFFECTS

Hearing loss is the most serious adverse effect of noise, but this risk is limited to certain high noise settings such as industrial or transportation-related work environments and entertainment venues where amplified music is played. In community settings, annoyance is the most common adverse effect of noise. Annoyance can be caused by speech interfer-

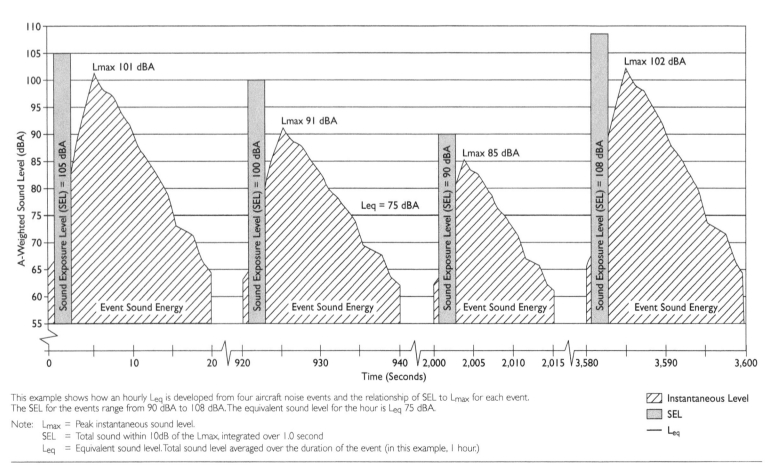

This example shows how an hourly L_{eq} is developed from four aircraft noise events and the relationship of SEL to L_{max} for each event. The SEL for the events range from 90 dBA to 108 dBA. The equivalent sound level for the hour is L_{eq} 75 dBA.

Note: L_{max} = Peak instantaneous sound level.
        SEL = Total sound within 10dB of the Lmax, integrated over 1.0 second
        L_{eq} = Equivalent sound level. Total sound level averaged over the duration of the event (in this example, 1 hour.)

RELATIONSHIP AMONG SOUND METRICS

Source: Landrum & Brown.

Mark R. Johnson, AICP, Landrum and Brown, Overland Park, Kansas

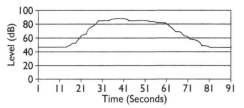

Lmax = 90 dB
Event Duration = 70 Seconds
SEL = 100 dB

Aircraft Flyover

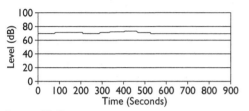

Lmax = 72 dB
Event Duration = 900 Seconds
SEL = 100 dB

Roadway Noise

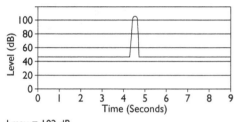

Lmax = 102 dB
Event Duration = 0.03 Seconds
SEL = 100 dB

Firecracker

COMPARISON OF DIFFERENT TYPES OF SOUND

Illustration shows the relationship of SEL to L_{max} for different kinds of noise events. As shown, three different sounds, all of which have the essentially the same SEL, can differ in loudness and duration.

Source: Landrum & Brown.

ence and sleep disturbance. Community noise may also disrupt classroom learning.

Speech Interference

Noise can interrupt conversations, radio listening, and television viewing. The degree of interference depends on the level, frequency, and duration of the noise.

People typically talk at 55 to 65 dBA (measured at a distance of three feet). At background sound levels below 55 dBA, speech can be carried on without substantial disruption. Disruption increases slightly as background sound increases to 65 dBA, then increases rapidly as background sound increases above 65 dBA. Communication becomes difficult if voices must be raised above 70 dBA. Unaided face-to-face communication becomes impossible if voices must be raised above 90 dBA.

SLEEP DISRUPTION

Transportation noise has a small but measurable effect on sleep disturbance in the home. Research shows that the potential for noise-induced awaken-

Mark R. Johnson, AICP, Landrum and Brown, Overland Park, Kansas

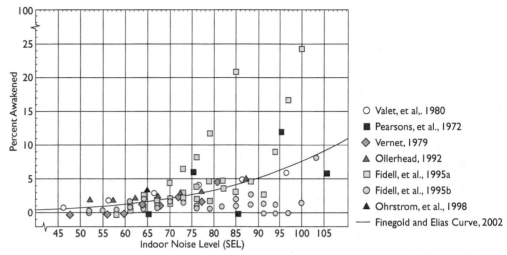

The composite awakenings curve shown here is based on the results of seven previous field studies. The equation for the curve is: $Y = 0.58 + (4.30 \times 10^{-8}) X^{4.11}$, where Y is the percent of people awakened and X is the indoor SEL in A-weighted decibels. At a SEL of 60 dBA, 1.5 percent of people would be awakened, at SEL 80 dBA, 3.4 percent would be awakened.

PREDICTED AWAKENINGS CAUSED BY TRANSPORTATION NOISE

Source: Finegold, L.S. and B. Elias. 2002. "A predictive model of noise induced awakenings from transportation noise sources." Inter-noise 2002. Proceedings of the 2002 International Congress and Exposition on Noise Control Engineering, Dearborn, Michigan.

ings is best explained by sound exposure levels (SEL). The composite awakenings curve shown here represents the relationship between awakenings and noise exposure.

Classroom Learning

Studies suggest that noise in the classroom may decrease the motivation and cognitive abilities of children. High noise levels can cause feelings of helplessness, which can occur when an individual cannot control or change a stressful event. This can reduce

the motivation to initiate new tasks or persist in ongoing tasks. Studies also suggest that children who grow up in noisy environments become inattentive to sound by tuning it out. When this leads to tuning out speech, it may cause reading and learning problems and may interfere with language acquisition.

VIBRATION

The most commonly used descriptor in the U.S. to quantify vibration is the vibration velocity level (L_v),

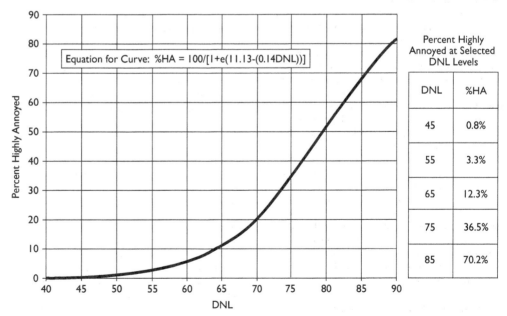

DNL	%HA
45	0.8%
55	3.3%
65	12.3%
75	36.5%
85	70.2%

Percent Highly Annoyed at Selected DNL Levels

Equation for Curve: %HA = 100/[1+e(11.13-(0.14DNL))]

This curve was derived from numerous studies of the effect of transportation noise on people at their residences. According to the equation for the curve, 0.8 percent of people are highly annoyed by noise of DNL 45 dBA, 3.1 percent by noise of DNL 55, 6.1 percent by noise of DNL 60, 11.6 percent by noise of DNL 65, 20.9 percent by noise of DNL 70, and 34.8 percent by noise of DNL 75.

REVISED SCHULTZ CURVE: PERCENTAGE OF A POPULATION HIGHLY ANNOYED BY TRANSPORTATION NOISE

Source: Finegold, L.S., et al. 1994. "Community annoyance and sleep disturbance: updated criteria for assessing the impacts of general transportation noise on people." Noise Control Engineering Journal, Vol. 42, No. 1.

expressed in VdB. Sound in the low frequency range is the cause of vibration.

Vibration may contribute to annoyance reported by residents near airports, construction sites, or heavy industrial areas. High-impulse sounds such as blasting, thunder, or sonic booms are more likely to induce vibration serious enough to cause damage than intermittent or continuous sounds such as aircraft or highway noise.

NOISE AND LAND-USE COMPATIBILITY

Community planning is most often concerned with noise as an annoyance to the public. Noise can be especially disturbing to people in residential, classroom, and contemplative settings.

In 1978, T.J. Schultz published a paper synthesizing the results of several studies of the sensitivity of people to transportation noise at their residences ("Synthesis of social surveys on noise annoyance." *Journal of the Acoustical Society of America*, Vol. 64, No. 2, p. 377-405). Annoyance was shown to increase along an S-shaped curve as noise increased. This work was updated in 1994 by adding more studies to the analysis, resulting in the revised "Schultz Curve."

The Schultz Curve (and its recent revision) have provided the basis for federal agencies and state governments to establish thresholds above which noise is presumed to constitute an adverse impact on residences and other sensitive land uses.

Federal Guidance and Regulations Relating to Noise

Several federal agencies have noise guidelines and standards related to planning and development.

Department of Defense

The Department of Defense administers the Air Installation Compatible Use Zone (AICUZ) program for Naval Air Stations and Air Force Bases, the Environmental Noise Management Program (ENMP) for the Army, and the Range Air Installation Compatible Use Zone (RAICUZ) program for Naval aerial firing ranges. These programs provide information for local governments considering land-use controls to promote compatible development in areas exposed to noise and potential safety hazards associated with military operations.

In 1985, the Department of Defense initiated the Joint Land Use Study (JLUS) program to promote greater application of the AICUZ, ENMP, and RAICUZ program recommendations. The JLUS program encourages cooperative planning among military installations and local governments so that future community growth can be made compatible with the missions of the military base. The DOD Office of Economic Adjustment provides matching grants to communities participating in Joint Land Use Studies.

Department of Housing and Urban Development

The U.S. Department of Housing and Urban Development (HUD) applies noise standards in its analysis of the acceptability of sites for federally supported housing projects. Three site classifications are defined based on the DNL level to which the sites are subjected, as shown in a table here.

HUD SITE ACCEPTABILITY STANDARDS

CLASSIFICATION	NOISE LEVEL (DNL)	SPECIAL APPROVALS AND REQUIREMENTS
Acceptable	DNL 65 dBA	None
Normally Unacceptable	DNL 65 to 75 dBA	Environmental clearance required. Sound attenuation: to achieve 5 to 10 dB more attenuation than standard construction.
Unacceptable	Above DNL 75 dBA	Environmental clearance required. Sound attenuation requires approval of Assistant Secretary.

Source: 24 CFR part 51, subpart B, Sec. 51.103.

NOISE ABATEMENT CRITERIA – HOURLY A-WEIGHTED SOUND LEVELS

ACTIVITY CATEGORY	$L_{eq, 1 hour}$ (dBA)	$L_{10, 1 hour}$ (dBA)	DESCRIPTION OF ACTIVITY CATEGORY
A	57 (exterior)	60 (exterior)	Lands on which serenity and quiet are of extraordinary significance and serve an important public need and where the preservation of those qualities is essential if the area is to continue to serve its intended purpose.
B	67 (exterior)	70 (exterior)	Picnic areas, recreational areas, playgrounds, active sports areas, parks, residences, motels, hotels, schools, churches, libraries, and hospitals.
C	72 (exterior)	75 (exterior)	Developed lands, properties, or activities not included in Categories A and B above.
D	—	—	Undeveloped lands.
E	52 (interior)	55 (interior)	Residences, motels, hotels, public meeting rooms, schools, churches, libraries, hospitals, and auditoriums.

Note: $L_{10, 1 hour}$ describes the A-weighted sound level that is exceeded 10 percent of the time during a one-hour period.

Source: USDOT/FHWA Highway traffic noise analysis and abatement policy and guidance.

LAND-USE CATEGORIES AND METRICS FOR TRANSIT NOISE IMPACT CRITERIA

DESCRIPTION OF LAND USE CATEGORIES	NOISE METRIC (dBA)
Category 1 Buildings and parks where quiet is an important element of their intended purpose. This category includes tracts of land set aside for serenity and quiet, and special uses such as outdoor concert pavilions.	Outdoor $L_{eq}(h)$*
Category 2 Residences and buildings where people normally sleep. This category includes homes, hospitals, and hotels where nighttime sensitivity to noise is assumed to be of utmost importance.	Outdoor DNL
Category 3 Institutional land uses with primarily daytime use. This category includes schools, libraries, churches, and active parks.	Outdoor $L_{eq}(h)$*

L_{eq} for the noisiest hour of transit-related activity during hours of noise sensitivity

Source: Transit Noise and Vibration Impact Assessment Guidance Manual (DOT-T-95-16; 1995).

Federal Aviation Administration

The Federal Aviation Administration (FAA) manages the Part 150 Noise Compatibility Planning program, a voluntary program that provides grants to airport operators to prepare Noise Compatibility Plans. (See 14 CFR Part 150.) After FAA approval of a Noise Compatibility Plan, the airport operator becomes eligible for funding assistance to implement the plan.

Federal Highway Administration

The current FHWA procedures for highway traffic noise analysis and abatement are outlined in 23 CFR Part 772. Planning and design of federal and federal-aid highways must conform with noise standards mandated by 23 USC 109(i). Traffic noise prediction must comply with the methodology in the FHWA Traffic Noise Prediction Model (TNM).

Traffic noise impacts occur when levels "approach or exceed" FHWA criteria, or when predicted levels "substantially exceed" existing noise levels. A table here presents the criteria for determining traffic noise impact where abatement must be considered.

Although FHWA noise regulations do not define the term "approach or exceed," all state highway agencies (SHA) must define "approach" as at least 1 dBA less than the noise abatement criteria presented in the table. Also the SHAs are given the flexibility to define the term "substantial noise increase," which ranges

from 10 to 15 dB, depending on the state. When impacts are identified, noise abatement measures should be designed to achieve a "substantial noise reduction," defined by most SHAs as 5 to 10 dB. Noise

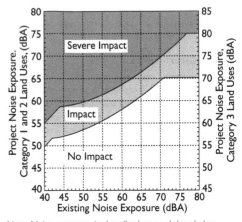

Note: Noise exposure is described as peak hourly Leq — Leq(h) for Category 1 and 3 land uses, DNL for Category 2 uses.

NOISE IMPACT CRITERIA FOR TRANSIT PROJECTS

Source: Federal Transit Administration. 1995. Transit Noise and Vibration Impact Assessment Guidance Manual, (DOT-T-95-16).

Mark R. Johnson, AICP, Landrum and Brown, Overland Park, Kansas

DESCRIPTION OF VIBRATION LAND-USE CATEGORIES

Category 1: Special noise- and vibration-sensitive building uses
Includes buildings in which vibration-sensitive research and manufacturing take place, hospital operating theaters, and laboratories that have work activities that cannot tolerate building vibration. Critical noise-sensitive building uses in this category are concert halls and radio or television studios. Ground-borne noise, in addition to vibration, can be a serious intrusion for activities in these buildings.

Category 2: Residential building use
Includes all residential building uses, with no differentiation among different types of residential areas, such as low or high density, urban or rural. Also includes hotels and motels.

Category 3: Institutional building use
Some institutional buildings have sensitivity to vibration, especially those in which people seek a quiet place for concentration, rest, or meditation, such as libraries, hospitals, and churches.

Source: Transit Noise and Vibration Impact Assessment Guidance Manual (DOT-T-95-16; 1995).

abatement measures, however, are not normally approved for land uses developed after May 14, 1976.

Federal Transit Administration (FTA)

The FTA has noise impact criteria for transit projects involving buses, heavy rail, light rail, and commuter rail. These criteria also apply to storage and maintenance yards, passenger stations, parking facilities, and sub stations. The criteria are based on the increase in noise with the project, described as either $L_{eq\text{-}1\ hour}$ or DNL, compared with noise without the project. The criteria are described in a table and illustration here. FTA uses FHWA noise abatement criteria in assessing the noise from bus ways on existing roads, high-occupancy vehicle lanes, and highways.

FTA also requires evaluation of ground-borne vibration and noise in noise assessments. The FTA defines three land-use/vibration categories: Category 1 includes the most sensitive uses, such as scientific, technical, certain health-related uses, and performing arts facilities. Category 2 involves all residential uses, including transient residences such as hotels. Category 3 includes institutional uses such as libraries, schools, and places of worship.

Ground-borne vibration and noise criteria set lower thresholds of significance for frequent than infrequent events, reflecting the importance of multiple events to reports of annoyance. Threshold levels also increase somewhat as the vibration sensitivity of the land-use categories decrease.

Examples of State Noise Guidance

Many states have standards or guidelines relating to noise. Two examples are briefly summarized here.

California

California law requires that county and municipal general plans include a noise element identifying noise sources in the community and describing and mapping current and potential future noise levels. Among the sources of concern are roadways, railways, airports, and industrial plants. The noise element also should define measures for minimizing or abating potential noise problems. These measures may include sound barriers, sound insulation of sensitive buildings, restricted operating hours for stationary sources, compatible use zoning in high-noise areas, or changes in the location of planned noise generators, such as highways. (See California Government Code, Section 65302(f).)

Oregon

The Oregon Department of Environmental Quality (DEQ) sets standards for noise control. (See Oregon Administrative Rules, Chapter 340, Division 35.) The standards apply to motor vehicles, industry and commerce, motor sports, and airports. Maximum noise limits also are established for various kinds of equipment. Criteria and processes are outlined for airport noise abatement programs.

Considerations for Local Noise Regulations

Local noise regulations can approach the problem from two perspectives: (1) reduction of noise at the source and (2) regulation of land use to keep sensitive uses away from noise sources or to require mitigation measures in design and construction. When considering noise regulations, local government officials must bear in mind several considerations.

Federal Preemption

The Constitution reserves to the federal government the power to regulate interstate and foreign commerce. Federal preemption extends to various transportation modes. The courts have ruled, for example, that states and local governments cannot impose direct noise restrictions on aircraft. Federal law also circumscribes the power of local and state governments to impose noise and operational restrictions on airports and railroads.

Rational Basis

A community must have a rational basis for establishing a noise regulation. The public health, safety, or welfare must be promoted in some way by the measure. A careful review of the research literature on noise effects is an indispensable part of this effort. A noise element in a comprehensive plan should provide a helpful factual foundation for this determination.

Reasonable Relationship

The regulation itself should be clearly related to its purpose. If the regulation is intended to reduce sleep disruption caused by nighttime industrial process noise in residential areas, for example, the regulation should avoid restricting daytime noise and should set a noise limit that is related to an awakenings threshold.

Monitoring and Enforcement

A community must determine how it will monitor and enforce the regulation. Regulation of noise from industrial and commercial activities or outdoor concerts will require at least periodic noise monitoring with proper equipment and trained personnel. Several technical issues must be considered in the acquisition, maintenance, and use of noise monitoring equipment. The equipment:

- Should be able to save a data log and, in some cases, an audio recording of the sound;
- Should be able to produce the necessary noise metrics and statistical summaries of the data;
- Should include all the accessories needed to ensure accuracy, such as windscreens, bird spikes, and tripods for the microphones;
- Must be professionally inspected and calibrated periodically; and
- Must be operated and cared for by trained technicians.

For many communities, retaining a qualified acoustical consultant may be a more reliable and economical way of providing the required noise monitoring services.

Land-Use Regulations for Noise Mitigation

Land-use planning and regulation may be used to keep noise-sensitive uses from being developed in areas of significant noise exposure. This requires:

- Defining the noise levels that are incompatible with various noise-sensitive land uses,
- Mapping noise levels associated with high-noise land uses, such as airports and highways,
- Assessing the potential for noise-sensitive uses to be zoned out of the high-noise areas, reserving those areas for the development of noise-compatible land uses, and
- Requiring mitigation measures in site design and construction where it is necessary to allow noise-sensitive uses to be built in high-noise areas.

Developing Noise and Land Use Compatibility Standards

In developing noise and land-use compatibility standards, planners should consult federal agency guidelines, review state agency guidance and regulations, and review the regulations of other local communities. Noise levels of DNL 65 dBA or higher are frequently considered to be incompatible with housing and other noise-sensitive uses, such as group homes and schools. Some states and local communities consider noise levels down to DNL 55 dBA to be problematic.

GROUND-BORNE VIBRATION AND NOISE IMPACT CRITERIA

LAND-USE CATEGORY	GROUND-BORNE VIBRATION IMPACT LEVELS (VdB) 1 MICRO INCH/SEC		GROUND-BORNE NOISE LEVELS (dBA)	
	Frequent Events[1]	Infrequent Events[1]	Frequent Events[1]	Infrequent Events[1]
Vibration Category 1	65[2]	65[2]	N.A.[3]	N.A.[3]
Vibration Category 2	72	80	35	43
Vibration Category 3	75	83	40	48

Notes:
1. "Frequent events" is defined as more than 70 vibration events per day.
2. This criterion is based on levels that are acceptable for most moderately sensitive equipment such as optical microscopes.
3. Vibration-sensitive equipment is not sensitive to ground-borne noise.
Source: Transit Noise and Vibration Impact Assessment Guidance Manual (DOT-T-95-16; 1995).

Mark R. Johnson, AICP, Landrum and Brown, Overland Park, Kansas

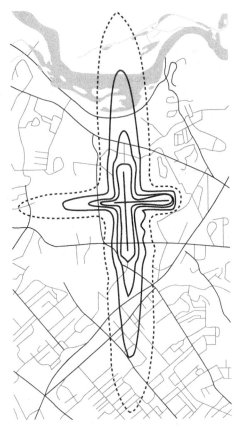

- - - DNL Noise Contour, Marginal Impact
—— DNL Noise Contour, Significant Impact

This noise exposure map for Albany (NY) International Airport shows noise contours for 2003. Contours are mapped at intervals of DNL 5 dBA. The outer dashed contour line represents DNL 60, the inner contour DNL 75.

AIRPORT NOISE EXPOSURE MAP

Source: Albany County Airport Authority, 2003. Albany International Airport, Final Part 150 Noise Compatibility Study Update, Volume I.

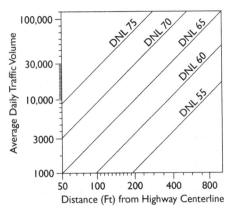

Calculations are based on these assumptions: (1) 10% heavy truck traffic; (2) 55 MPH speed; (3) 15% of traffic at night (from 10 p.m. to 7 a.m.); (4) less than 2% grade. *Note: Distances to noise contours will change as assumptions change.*

ESTIMATING DISTANCES TO HIGHWAY NOISE CONTOURS

Source: Naval Facilities Engineering Command. 1985. "Architectural Acoustics: Functional Requirements Design & Technology," Design Manual 1.03, p. 1.03-14.

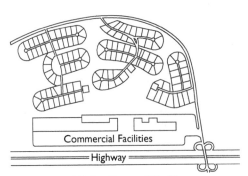

Placement of Noise Compatible Uses Near a Highway in a Mixed-Use Development

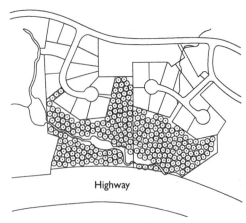

Open Space Placed Near a Highway in a Cluster Development

The left example shows a mixed-use development with the commercial buildings placed between the highway and the homes, buffering the homes from the highway noise. The right example shows an expanse of wooded open space between the highway and the homes. Dense stands of trees can be effective noise barriers, but they must be quite thick and present a continuous barrier from the ground to the treetops. Their effectiveness is substantially reduced, however, when the trees drop their leaves in the fall and winter.

SITE DESIGN FOR NOISE ABATEMENT

Source: Department of Housing and Urban Development 1985.

Mapping of Noise Levels

Noise mapping is a highly technical undertaking usually done with the aid of computer models. Consult with state highway officials and local airport officials to see if noise maps of those facilities are available. Noise mapping should take into account potential increases in traffic or planned facility development that could change noise levels in the future.

Noise contour maps can also be developed along heavy or light rail lines and railroads. With the aid of qualified acoustical engineers, a system of charts can be developed to estimate noise levels along busy streets and highways. Planners can determine an approximate distance from a roadway centerline to a given DNL noise contour, for example, which could provide a basis for defining building setback requirements for noise-sensitive uses along those streets and highways.

Restricting the Development of Noise-Sensitive Land Uses

While land-use compatibility standards might indicate the need to prohibit new housing or other noise-sensitive land uses in a noise-impacted area, local planners must consider other community goals before reaching that conclusion. In some communities, the availability of affordable housing is a substantial problem. Reducing the amount of developable residential land might aggravate the problem. In other communities, the noise-impacted land may have no realistic alternative use than residential, and zoning the land to prohibit housing would invite a successful takings claim.

Noise Mitigation Techniques

If housing and other noise-sensitive uses must be permitted in high noise areas, mitigation of the noise impact becomes important. Noise generally travels by line of sight and dissipates over distance. Thus, noise-sensitive uses should be built as far as possible from the noise source, and, where possible, obstructions should be placed between the noise-sensitive uses and the source.

Barriers can be effective in reducing noise exposure by blocking the line-of-sight between the noise source and the receiver. To be fully effective, barriers must be solid, relatively non-reflective, and long and

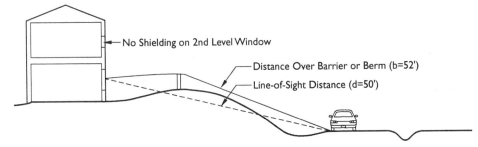

Assumption: receiver is at center of window or 5' high. Noise sources include cars (0' above pavement), trucks (8' above pavement), mechanical (top of equipment) and diesel train (15' above track).

PRINCIPLES OF NOISE BARRIER DESIGN

Source: Department of Housing and Urban Development 1985.

Mark R. Johnson, AICP, Landrum and Brown, Overland Park, Kansas

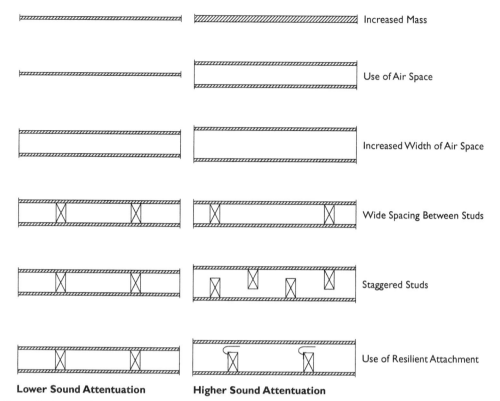

Increased Mass

Use of Air Space

Increased Width of Air Space

Wide Spacing Between Studs

Staggered Studs

Use of Resilient Attachment

Lower Sound Attenuation   **Higher Sound Attentuation**

Factors that improve the sound attenuation properties of a wall section include greater mass, increased air space between inner and outer walls, and techniques to dampen vibration, including wider spacing between studs, staggered studs, and the use of resilient attachments to fasten wallboard to studs.

FACTORS WHICH INFLUENCE SOUND ATTENUATION OF WALLS

Source: Department of Housing and Urban Development. 1985. The Noise Guidebook, p. 33.

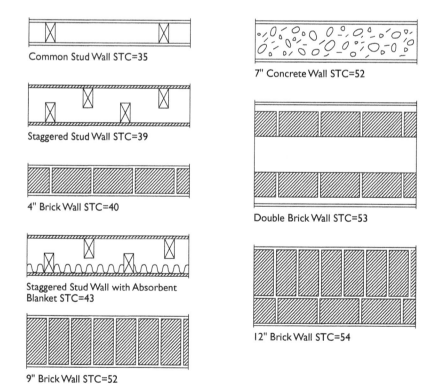

Common Stud Wall STC=35

Staggered Stud Wall STC=39

4" Brick Wall STC=40

Staggered Stud Wall with Absorbent Blanket STC=43

9" Brick Wall STC=52

7" Concrete Wall STC=52

Double Brick Wall STC=53

12" Brick Wall STC=54

Sound transmission class (STC) ratings for different wall sections. STC is a method of rating the sound attenuation capabilities of a structure or building component. The higher the STC rating, the greater the sound attenuation.

SOUND ATTENUATION PROPERTIES OF DIFFERENT WALL SECTIONS

Source: Department of Housing and Urban Development 1985.

high enough to prevent noise from diffracting around the edges to the receiver.

If airport noise is the concern, site design is less effective. Noise from airborne aircraft will bypass noise walls, earthen berms, or other barriers. Barriers and site design can be effective, however, if the airport noise of concern occurs on the ground, from engine run-ups, power-up at the start of the takeoff roll, or reverse thrust on landing.

In areas exposed to airport noise where new housing or other noise-sensitive uses must be permitted, sound insulation is often used for noise mitigation. Typical housing construction is assumed to provide an outdoor-to-indoor noise level reduction of approximately 25 dBA, although this can vary considerably in different parts of the country. This assumes that windows and doors are closed. Special sound insulation can increase the noise level reduction by 5 to 15 dBA, depending on the techniques applied. These techniques include the installation of additional wall and ceiling insulation; special acoustical windows and doors; careful sealing of wall joints and around windows, doors, and vents; the baffling of vents; extra-thick outdoor wall sections; attachment of wallboards to studs with resilient fasteners; and installation of year-round, closed window fresh air ventilation systems (or central air and heating).

Local governments often link special sound insulation requirements to a noise overlay zoning district. New noise-sensitive are permitted within the overlay district, provided that sound insulation to achieve a given noise level reduction is installed. Some communities establish this level as a performance standard with which the builder must demonstrate compliance before an occupancy permit is issued. Others establish specific construction standards in their building codes describing the requirements that must be met to achieve a given noise level reduction.

RESOURCES

Department of Defense. 2002. *Joint Land Use Study Program Guidance Manual.* Office of Economic Adjustment.

Department of Housing and Urban Development. 1985. *The Noise Guidebook.* Environmental Planning Division, Office of Environment and Energy.

http://www.hud.gov/offices/cpd/energyenviron/environment/resources/guidebooks/noise/index.cfm

Federal Aviation Administration. *Land Use Compatibility Planning Toolkit.* www.aee.faa.gov/noise/lupitoolkit.htm

Federal Interagency Committee on Urban Noise. 1980. *Guidelines for Considering Noise in Land Use Planning and Control.*

U.S. Environmental Protection Agency. 1974. *Information on Levels of Noise Requisite to Protect the Public Health and Welfare with an Adequate Margin of Safety.*

U.S. Environmental Protection Agency. 1981. *Noise Effects Handbook: A Desk Reference to Health and Welfare Effects of Noise.* EPA 550-9-82-106. Office of the Scientific Assistant, Office of Noise Abatement and Control.

Mark R. Johnson, AICP, Landrum and Brown, Overland Park, Kansas

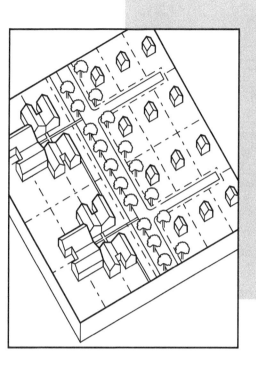

STRUCTURES

Part 3

BUILDING TYPES

RESIDENTIAL TYPES

The design and planning of residential development is a significant component of any planning or urban design effort. Typically provided by private developers, residential development is primarily market-driven, with the housing types in a particular market dictated by a number of factors. Economic factors, such as cost of living, employment base, and disposable income, play a major role. Residential types will also vary greatly between regional markets,

and often they will vary within a single municipal jurisdiction. Housing types acceptable in one locale may not be economically viable a short distance away.

In addition to economic factors, architectural style is perhaps the next greatest determinant in residential planning. Regional vernaculars, stylistic trends, climate, geography, local traditions, and other factors all affect the type of residential development proposed for a particular site.

ROLE OF HOUSING IN PLANNING AND URBAN DESIGN

Residential development creates a core citizenry around which communities are structured. Housing defines a population base that determines the location of schools, employment centers, and community facilities. Planners must be able to project long-term residential growth trends to provide adequate public services.

Planners also need to understand trends in housing development. Due to continued advances in housing types, there is greater variety from which to create plans. The successful planner and urban designer will understand and support a wide range of residential development typologies.

COMMON TERMS

Because residential development is such a broad topic, it is important to have a common set of terms and classifications so as to avoid confusion. The five basic attributes of residential development are building type, style, density, project size, and location.

Building Type

Building type refers to the arrangement of individual dwelling units and their placement next to, above, or below each other. "Single-family detached" and "multifamily attached" are examples of residential building types. Basic residential building types are described elsewhere in more detail in this section of this book.

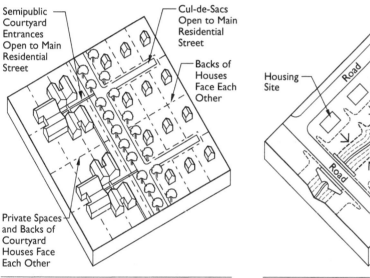

DEFINING PUBLIC AND PRIVATE SPACE

Source: American Planning Association.

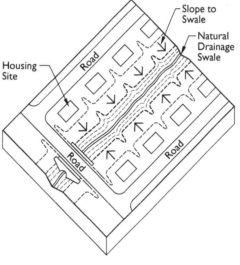

DESIGN WITH NATURAL SYSTEMS

Source: American Planning Association.

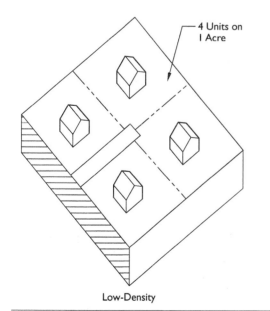

Low-Density

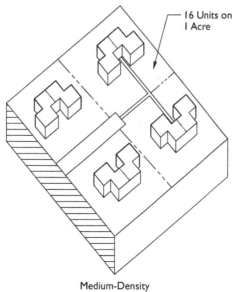

Medium-Density

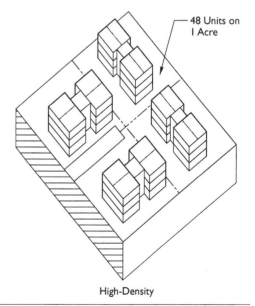

High-Density

COMPARATIVE DENSITIES

Source: American Planning Association.

Peter J. Kindel, AIA ASLA Skidmore, Owings & Merrill LLP, Chicago, Illinois

Style

Style refers to the architectural design of the dwelling unit. It is a subjective and qualitative attribute. "Contemporary," "colonial," and "prairie," for example, are styles.

Density

Density refers to the number of housing units per area of land. The most common measure of residential density is dwelling units per acre (du/ac). Particularly for dense urban projects, density may be measured in floor-area ratio (FAR), which is the ratio of the gross building floor area to the net lot area of the building site. Density is commonly tied to location: densities are typically lower the further one moves from the city center. However, there are often variations in this pattern. New trends, for example, have seen relatively low-density urban infill projects replace obsolete higher-density multifamily housing, and relatively high-density, transit-based projects replacing large-lot residential development in the suburbs. Density is addressed in more detail in another section of this book.

Project Size

Project size refers to the land area of the project. This can range from a single-lot, 2,000-square-foot urban infill project to a 3,000-acre new community. Planners and designers must be conversant with the basic requirements of differing sizes of development.

Location

Location refers to the context of the project. This can range from rural greenfield sites to projects in established suburbs. It can also include urban brownfield sites, projects in well-established transit-based communities, and urban high-rises in a city center.

OTHER TERMS

Planners use other common terms to describe residential development:

> **Total project acreage:** The total land area of a project
>
> **Net developable area:** Total project acreage, minus open space and infrastructure acreage
>
> **Gross density:** Number of residential units/total project acreage
>
> **Net density:** Number of residential units/net developable area

RESIDENTIAL TYPES

Residential types can be classified into five basic categories:

> **Single-family detached.** Single-family detached dwelling units are physically separated from the units immediately adjacent to them.
>
> **Single-family attached.** Single-family attached dwelling units share common walls with units laterally adjacent to them.
>
> **Multifamily low-rise.** Multifamily low-rise developments have dwelling units that share common walls with the units that are laterally

and vertically adjacent. They typically range from two to four levels in height, with multiple service cores and either structured or surface parking.

> **Multifamily mid-rise.** Multifamily mid-rise dwelling units share common walls with the units that are laterally and vertically adjacent. They are generally 5 to 12 levels in height, with a common core. They sometimes include structured parking.
>
> **Multifamily high-rise.** Multifamily high-rise dwelling units share common walls with the units that are laterally and vertically adjacent. They are generally 12 to 50 or more levels in height, with a common core, and often include structured parking.

SITE PLANNING CONSIDERATIONS

Zoning Classification

Zoning typically determines the density of residential development. In addition to density, zoning may also dictate height limits, required planted area, massing criteria, and allowable ancillary uses. Planners must know the zoning under which a plan is to be evaluated or created and the relevant zoning constraints.

Infrastructure Design

A major component of a residential development is infrastructure. This primarily includes roads, utility easements, and other rights-of-way, but also may include other elements such as accommodations for public structures. Infrastructure may use 10 to 30 percent of a project's gross land area.

Open Space

Open space includes parks, plazas, greenways, stormwater management areas, and any other unpaved or undeveloped areas. Open space may use 10 to 30 percent of a project's gross land area. Where conservation is a goal, this percentage may increase.

Setbacks

Often contained within the zoning code, and closely linked to density and massing considerations, setbacks include front, rear, and side-yard setbacks. When density is higher, setbacks are typically smaller. Urban conditions may not require setbacks.

Allowed Density

Density is often the primary determinant in the physical layout and appearance of a project. It will influence the housing type and perhaps the style of the project. Densities are calculated in dwelling units per acre (du/ac), and can range from 1 du/10 ac for

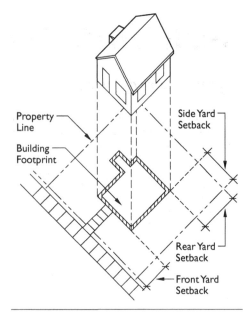

YARDS AND SETBACKS
Source: American Planning Association.

a rural lot to 100 du/ac for an urban high-rise. Typical densities range from 1 du/ac for single-family detached homes to 20 du/ac for townhomes.

Parking

For many residential projects, parking must be provided within or adjacent to each dwelling unit. For higher-density projects (above 20 du/ac), common parking facilities are created adjacent to the residential structure. The number of parking spaces per unit is driven either by regulatory requirements or by market desires. The number of parking spaces required per dwelling unit significantly affects site planning with important economic and design consequences. Planners and developers should carefully examine the standards used to determine the appropriate number of parking spaces for a use; practice has been to require too much parking in many cases.

Restrictions on Ancillary Structures

Zoning may dictate restrictions on ancillary structures, such as garages or dwelling units. Recent practice has indicated a trend of accessory living units near or attached to the main structure. Codes that do not allow ancillary units should be revised to accommodate them to provide affordable housing alternatives and "aging in place."

FOCUS AREAS FOR DIFFERENT SCALES OF RESIDENTIAL DEVELOPMENT

	SMALL SCALE	MEDIUM SCALE	LARGE SCALE
Area	0-10 acres	10-50 acres	Above 50 acres
Density	5-50 units	50-500 units	Above 500 units
Areas of Primary Concern	Building Massing Architectural Details Front Doors/Access Parking Areas Service Areas	Landscape Design Public Space Roadway Widths Traffic Flow Location of Density	Stormwater Management Creating a Center Transit Access Road Framework Mix of Density

Peter J. Kindel, AIA ASLA Skidmore, Owings & Merrill LLP, Chicago, Illinois

BUILDING PLANNING CONSIDERATIONS

Orientation

The direction in which a residential unit or project is oriented should be considered. This will affect potential solar gain. It also affects light penetration into units, as well as solar exposure for outdoor areas such as patios and courtyards.

Entry

Clear access to and identity of primary building entries must be carefully considered. Buildings and units should have a distinct main point of entry, usually identifiable from a public way. Avoid primary entrances from parking structures or other ancillary elements.

Massing

The size and shape of residential structures individually and their arrangement relative to each other are primary urban design considerations. Massing is a major consideration in determining how a building or group of buildings will relate to the surrounding context. Zoning regulations (height and bulk) and design guidelines can be used to address problems related to development mass that is out of scale with neighborhood or community character.

Design Guidelines

Traditionally, design guidelines have been "use-based," dictating acceptable uses and densities. While this approach is still appropriate in some instances, increasingly design guidelines have become "form-based," concentrating more on aesthetic and form issues.

PLANNING AND DESIGN SEQUENCE

The planning and design sequence for residential development follows this general process:

1. *Code delineation*. Research and document all relevant plans and codes, and their effect on gross densities, open-space requirements, setbacks, and design.

2. *Programming*. Clarify the number of units, typical square footage of units, and sizes of other physical elements of the project.

3. *Opportunities and constraints*. Delineate all physical opportunities and constraints present on the site, especially qualitative constraints, such as views, natural features, and adjacent uses.

4. *Site plan testing*. Delineate all development program elements, overlaid with code and site constraints. Reconcile incompatibilities.

5. *Plan development*. Develop project plans that reconcile all code and development program issues for review by municipal officials.

6. *Final platting*. Coordinate and create, typically with a civil engineer, lot configuration and project design for the final site plan.

7. *Implementation*. Create construction documents, obtain building permits, and initiate construction.

Peter J. Kindel, AIA ASLA Skidmore, Owings & Merrill LLP, Chicago, Illinois

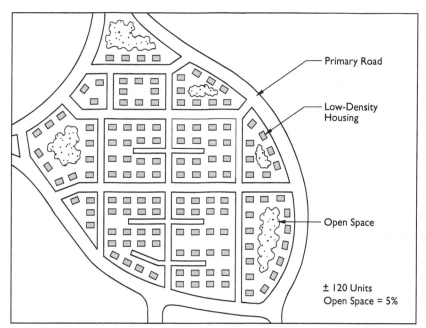

Noncluster Development

± 120 Units
Open Space = 5%

Primary Road
Low-Density Housing
Open Space

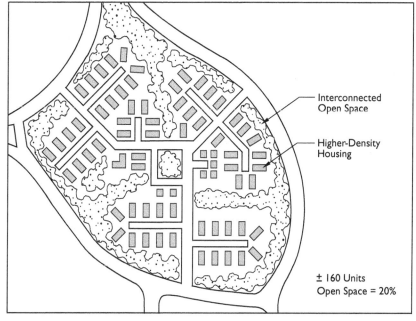

Cluster Development

± 160 Units
Open Space = 20%

Interconnected Open Space
Higher-Density Housing

CLUSTER DEVELOPMENT COMPARED TO NONCLUSTER DEVELOPMENT

Source: Skidmore, Owings & Merrill LLP.

BEST PRACTICE PRINCIPLES

Regional Vernacular

Residential development should be sensitive to regional issues, including climate, materials and methods, and regional styles and traditions. Residential style often reflects the region in which it is constructed.

Mixed-Use

Mixed-use development includes a variety of uses within a project, such as neighborhood commercial retail in portions of a residential project. Mixed-use development also helps provide basic services (e.g., dry cleaners; food store; drug store) to residents, increases design options, and creates opportunities for pedestrian-oriented design.

Transit-Oriented Development

Recent planning trends include a return to higher-density housing located adjacent to transit lines, which increases transportation alternatives for residents and allows for reduced automobile dependency and parking requirements.

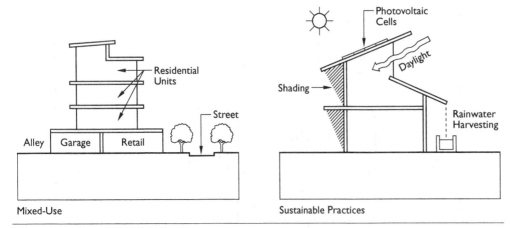

Mixed-Use

Sustainable Practices

RESIDENTIAL BEST PRACTICES

Source: Skidmore, Owings & Merrill LLP.

RESIDENTIAL HOUSING TYPES COMPARISON

TYPE	SUBTYPES	APPROXIMATE PARCEL SIZE (SF)	APPROXIMATE DENSITY RANGE (DU/AC)	TYPICAL HEIGHT	PARKING
Single-Family Detached	2 ac.	85,000	.5	1-2 Levels	Adjacent Garage
	1 ac.	44,000	1	1-2 Levels	Adjacent Garage
	1/2 ac.	22,000	2	1-2 Levels	Adjacent Garage
	1/3 ac.	15,000	3	1-2 Levels	Adjacent Garage
	1/4 ac.	10,000	4	2-3 Levels	Adjacent Garage
	1/8 ac.	5,500	8	2-3 Levels	Adjacent Garage
Single-Family Attached	Row House Subtype 1	3,500	10-15	2-3 Levels	Behind Building
	Row House Subtype 2	1,500	15-30	3-4 Levels	Below Building
Multifamily Low-Rise	Stacked Flats Subtype 1	20,000–170,000	20-40	2-3 Levels	Adjacent to Building
	Stacked Flats Subtype 2	20,000–170,000	30-50	3-4 Levels	Adjacent to Building
Multifamily Mid-Rise	Point Tower, Courtyard, or Slab	20,000–170,000+	40-80	5-12 Levels	Adjacent Parking Structure or within Building
Multifamily High-Rise	Point Tower or Slab	20,000–170,000	80+	12+	Levels Adjacent Parking Structure or within Building

Conservation of Ecologically Sensitive Areas

Development should preserve any areas of ecological value on the site, including streams, lakes, wetlands, mature trees, and known habitat areas. Owners may be compensated for lost development by "transferring" density from some portions of the project site to others to protect a site's ecology.

Open-Space Design

Location, design, and development of open spaces should be considered simultaneous with or in advance of residential development. When creating open spaces, make every effort to connect them into a network or system, such as a greenway, to provide expanded recreational opportunities and allow contiguous wildlife habitat and integration of natural systems.

Stormwater Management

Residential developments typically must accommodate stormwater management on-site. These areas have great potential to be designed as positive contributors to the overall hydrological character of the site. Stormwater management areas should be designed to mimic natural wetland ecology, providing expanded habitat for flora and fauna, recreational opportunities for residents, and greater aesthetic value to the project.

Green Buildings

"Smart" houses, with integrated lighting and mechanical systems controls; solar roofs with photovoltaic cells integrated within roof materials; and regionally appropriate building materials are now practical. The U.S. Green Building Council is one resource for information on green building technology.

See also:
Housing Needs Assessment
Housing Plans
Scale and Density
Transit-Oriented Development
Zoning Regulation

Peter J. Kindel, AIA ASLA Skidmore, Owings & Merrill LLP, Chicago, Illinois

SINGLE-FAMILY DETACHED

COMMON SUBTYPES

Single-family detached units come in many forms. The most prevalent subtype is the stand-alone house. Another subtype is zero-lot line housing, where there is no setback from the property line and the structures do not share common walls.

PROJECT SIZE

Lot sizes typically vary from 1/8-acre (0.5-hectare) lots (approx. 5,500 square feet) to 2-acre (0.81-hectare) or larger lots.

ASPECT RATIO

Typical single-family lots will have a width-to-depth ratio of 1:2. Lot widths are typically multiples of 10 feet (3.1 meters), and can range from 30 feet (9.3 meters) to 100 feet (30.48 meters).

SETBACKS

Setback requirements are typical for single-family detached lots and will apply to front, rear, and side yards. Typical setbacks range from 5 feet (1.55 meters) to 20 feet (6.2 meters), with front-yard setbacks greater than side-yard setbacks by a ratio of 2:1. Rear-yard setbacks are typically similar to side-yard setbacks, but may be reduced if an alley condition exists.

VEHICULAR ACCESS

While vehicular access is often from the front of the lot, recent trends encourage planners and developers to consider alleys for vehicular access, where possible.

COVERAGE

Some zoning classifications may place restrictions on the percentage of the site area that can be covered by the building footprint.

MASS AND VOLUME

Some zoning classifications may restrict the height and bulk of structures. Design guidelines or historic overlay districts may restrict the volume and shape of the structure.

ORIENTATION

Structures should be oriented to take advantage of solar exposure and prevailing winds, and toward the primary street on which they are situated.

PARKING

Parking is commonly provided within the lot, typically in garages accessed from rear alleys or streets.

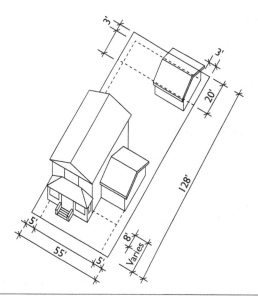

AXONOMETRIC: SINGLE-FAMILY DETACHED
Source: Skidmore, Owings & Merrill LLP.

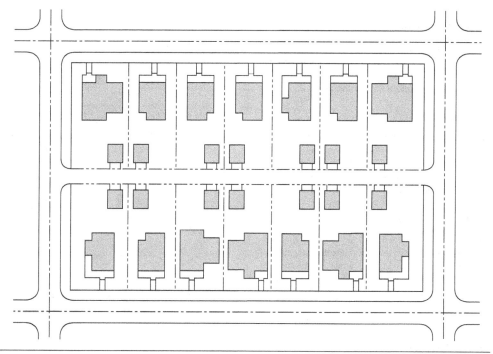

PLAN: SINGLE-FAMILY DETACHED
Source: Skidmore, Owings & Merrill LLP.

Peter J. Kindel, AIA ASLA Skidmore, Owings & Merrill LLP, Chicago, Illinois

BUILDING TYPES

SINGLE-FAMILY ATTACHED

COMMON SUBTYPES

Single-family attached units come in many forms, including duplexes and townhomes. Many town-home variations have emerged as a result of market forces and regional vernacular styles.

PROJECT SIZE

Project sizes vary from 1/12-acre lots (approx 3,500 square feet or 325 square meters) to 1/5-acre lots (approximately 8,000 square feet or 743 square meters).

ASPECT RATIO

Typical single-family attached lots will have a width-to-depth ratio of 1:4. Lot widths are typically multiples of 5 feet (1.5 meters), and can range from 20 feet (6.1 meters) to 40 feet (12.2 meters).

SETBACKS

Setback requirements are typical for the front and rear of single-family attached lots. Typical setbacks range from 5 feet (1.5 meters) to 20 feet (6.1 meters). Rear-yard setbacks are similar to front-yard setbacks, but may be reduced if an alley condition exists. For duplex structures, the setback on the side yard that is not attached will vary.

VEHICULAR ACCESS

For single-family attached housing, vehicular access to the garage is typically from alleys at the rear of the lot. In suburban conditions, some attached homes have garages in front or side of the unit.

COVERAGE

This type of housing will typically have a higher degree of site coverage than single-family detached. Restrictions may still be placed on the overall site coverage of an individual lot, and projectwide provisions may need to be made for stormwater management.

MASS AND VOLUME

This type of housing will typically be taller than single-family detached units, due to smaller lots, parking underneath, or other factors. While most units are two or three levels, occasionally four- and even five-levels units are in use. For taller structures an elevator may be provided in the unit. Some zoning classifications may restrict height and massing of structures.

ORIENTATION

Structures should be oriented to take advantage of solar exposure and prevailing winds, and toward the primary street on which they are situated. More than any other type of housing, single-family attached structures should also be oriented to enhance privacy between units, especially on dense urban lots.

PARKING

Single-family attached units are often provided with an attached garage immediately adjacent or under the dwelling unit, or may have adjacent surface parking.

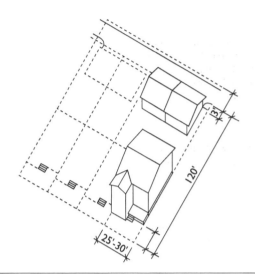

AXONOMETRIC: SINGLE-FAMILY ATTACHED

Source: Skidmore, Owings & Merrill LLP.

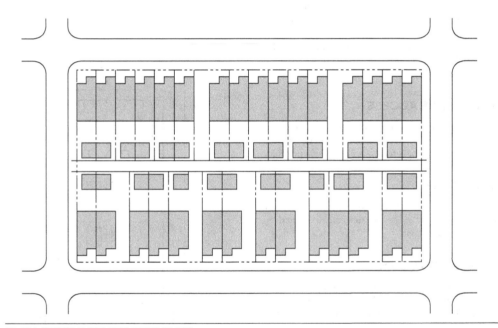

PLAN: SINGLE-FAMILY ATTACHED

Source: Skidmore, Owings & Merrill LLP.

Peter J. Kindel, AIA ASLA Skidmore, Owings & Merrill LLP, Chicago, Illinois

MULTIFAMILY LOW-RISE

COMMON SUBTYPES

Multifamily low-rise is perhaps the most diverse housing type. Subtypes include garden apartments and courtyard apartments.

PROJECT SIZE

Multiunit buildings typically occupy one lot, collectively controlled through condominium ownership or by a single property owner. The number of units and zoning regulations determine the overall building size.

ASPECT RATIO

Multifamily residential development projects are extremely flexible in terms of lot configuration and proportion. They may occupy relatively narrow, deep lots, or shallow, wide lots. Due to the inherent flexibility of unit configurations, building designs can adjust to many parcel variations.

SETBACKS

While setbacks for this type of residential use can vary greatly depending on the urban context, multifamily low-rise buildings are often subject to greater setbacks than lower-density housing because of larger building footprints and three- to four-level building heights. Zoning restrictions dictate specific setbacks.

VEHICULAR ACCESS

Principal access may be from a major public street or from streets and driveways internal to the development. Access to parking can occur from the front, rear, or side yards. Drop-off areas for principal entries should be oriented to the primary addressing street.

COVERAGE

This type will typically have a higher degree of site coverage than single-family attached. Restrictions may still be placed on the overall building site coverage, and projectwide provisions may be required for stormwater management and open space.

MASS AND VOLUME

This type will vary from two to four stories in height. Flexible unit configurations allow corresponding flexibility in massing and volumetric configurations. This type allows a great variety of massing solutions.

ORIENTATION

Orientation of this type is primarily dictated by site configuration and access to primary streets, though solar orientation may be a consideration. Due to larger building footprints, there may be orientation constraints on steep or hilly terrain.

PARKING

Parking is provided either within or immediately adjacent to the structure. In urban conditions, a parking structure may be provided beneath or next to the building.

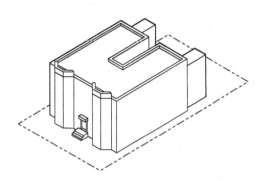

AXONOMETRIC: MULTIFAMILY LOW-RISE
Source: Skidmore, Owings & Merrill LLP.

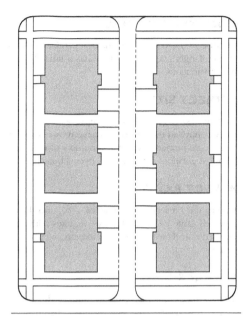

PLAN: MULTIFAMILY LOW-RISE
Source: Skidmore, Owings & Merrill LLP.

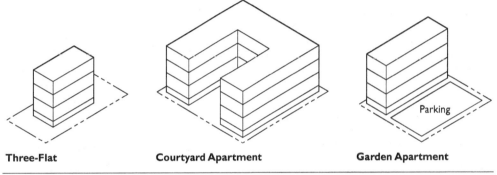

Three-Flat   Courtyard Apartment   Garden Apartment

MULTIFAMILY LOW-RISE SUBTYPES
Source: Skidmore, Owings & Merrill LLP.

Peter J. Kindel, AIA ASLA Skidmore, Owings & Merrill LLP, Chicago, Illinois

MULTIFAMILY MID-RISE

COMMON SUBTYPES

Because of the vertically oriented, repetitive qualities of multifamily mid-rise, this type has a limited number of variations.

PROJECT SIZE

Multiunit buildings typically occupy one lot, collectively controlled through condominium ownership or by a single property owner. The number of units and zoning regulations determine the overall building size.

ASPECT RATIO

Due to the presence of a building core, and thus a relatively large footprint, this type requires fairly regularized parcels with an aspect ratio ranging from 1:1 to 1:2.

SETBACKS

While setbacks for this type vary greatly depending on the urban context, because of larger building footprints and 5- to 12-level building heights, multifamily mid-rise buildings may be subject to greater building setbacks than lower-density housing. Zoning regulations will dictate specific setbacks.

VEHICULAR ACCESS

Principal access may be from a major public street or from streets and driveways internal to the development. Access to parking can occur from the front, rear, or side yards. Drop-off areas should be oriented to the primary addressing street.

COVERAGE

This type will typically have a site coverage range of 40 to 60 percent, though this may increase to 80 to 90 percent in urban conditions. Zoning will dictate the specific site coverage of a building, and projectwide provisions may be required for stormwater management and open space.

MASS AND VOLUME

This type will vary from 5 to 12 stories in height. Repetitive floor configurations with a building core will drive overall massing. Variations in building shape and form can be obtained through volumetric variations and manipulation of external cores and unit configurations.

ORIENTATION

Orientation of this type is primarily dictated by site configuration and access to primary streets, though solar orientation may be a consideration. Due to larger building footprints, there will be some orientation constraints on steep or hilly terrain.

PARKING

Parking is provided either within or immediately adjacent to the structure. Due to the number of units in the building, a parking structure is typically required.

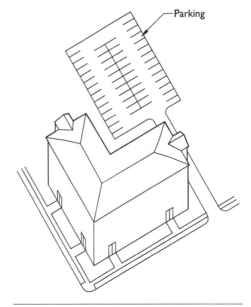

AXONOMETRIC: MULTIFAMILY MID-RISE

Source: Skidmore, Owings & Merrill LLP.

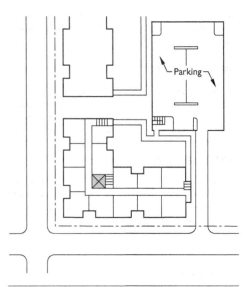

PLAN: MULTIFAMILY MID-RISE

Source: Skidmore, Owings & Merrill LLP.

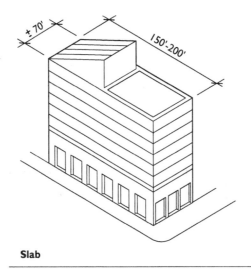

Slab

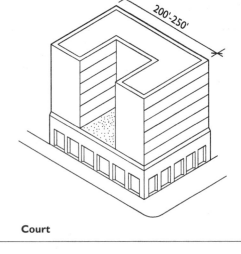

Court

MULTIFAMILY MID-RISE SUBTYPES

Source: Skidmore, Owings & Merrill LLP.

Peter J. Kindel, AIA ASLA Skidmore, Owings & Merrill LLP, Chicago, Illinois

MULTIFAMILY HIGH-RISE

COMMON SUBTYPES

Because of the vertically oriented, repetitive qualities of the multifamily high-rise, this type has a limited number of variations.

PROJECT SIZE

Multiunit buildings typically occupy one lot, collectively controlled through condominium ownership or by a single property owner. The number of units and zoning regulations determine the overall building size.

ASPECT RATIO

Due to the presence of a building core, and thus a relatively large footprint, this type requires regularized, rectangular or square parcels with an aspect ratio ranging from 1:1 to 1:2.

SETBACKS

While setbacks for this type can vary greatly depending on the urban context, multifamily high-rise buildings may be subject to greater building setbacks than lower-density housing because of larger building footprints and 12- to 50-plus-level building heights. Zoning will dictate specific setbacks.

VEHICULAR ACCESS

Principal access may be from a major public street or from streets and driveways internal to the development. Access to parking can occur from the front, rear or side yards. Drop-off areas and building front door should be oriented to the primary addressing street.

COVERAGE

This type will typically have a site coverage range of 40 to 60 percent, though this may increase to 80 to 90 percent in urban conditions. Zoning will dictate the specific site coverage of a building, and projectwide provisions may be required for stormwater management.

MASS AND VOLUME

This type will vary from 12 to 50-plus stories in height. Repetitive floor configurations with a building core will drive overall massing. Variations in building shape and form will typically be in façade manipulation, though some volumetric variations can be obtained through core and unit manipulation. Tower floorplates may decrease in size as building height increases.

ORIENTATION

Orientation of this type is primarily dictated by site configuration and access to primary streets, though solar orientation may be a consideration. Due to larger building footprints, there will be some orientation constraints on steep or hilly terrain.

PARKING

Parking is provided either within or immediately adjacent to the structure. Due to the number of units in the building, a parking structure will almost always be required. Reduced or shared parking is increasingly common.

Peter J. Kindel, AIA ASLA Skidmore, Owings & Merrill LLP, Chicago, Illinois

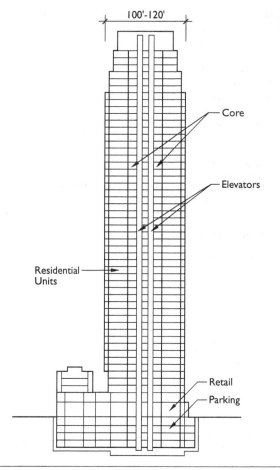

SECTION: RESIDENTIAL HIGH-RISE

Source: Skidmore, Owings & Merrill LLP.

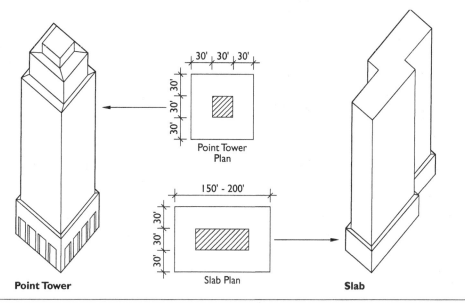

MULTIFAMILY HIGH-RISE SUBTYPES

Source: Skidmore, Owings & Merrill LLP.

MANUFACTURED HOUSING

Factory-built housing describes any structure designed as a residential dwelling that is built primarily off-site from the building site. Factory-built housing consists of three main types: manufactured homes, modular homes, and mobile homes. Panelized and precut homes can also be included in this category.

Nearly 25 percent of all new single-family housing starts are manufactured homes. Affordability is a key factor in the growth of manufactured housing. Manufactured housing can cost from 10 to 35 percent less than traditional site-built housing, due in part to the factory-built process. Manufactured homes are constructed with the same materials as any other site-built residential structure; therefore, the durability of these dwellings is equal to those constructed on-site.

MANUFACTURED HOME TYPES

There are two basic types of manufactured homes, single-section and multisection. The number of units in the structure also defines them.

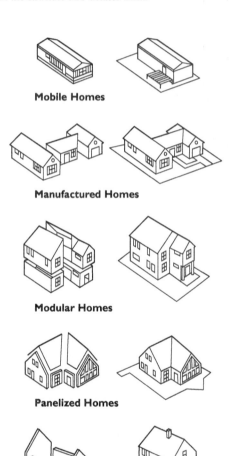

Mobile Homes

Manufactured Homes

Modular Homes

Panelized Homes

Precut Homes

FIVE TYPES OF FACTORY-BUILT HOUSING

Source: Metropolitan Design Center, University of Minnesota.

FACTORY-BUILT HOUSING TYPES

Manufactured Homes	Structures built entirely in a factory to federal performance standards established by the HUD Code.
Modular Homes	Modules are transported to site and installed. Structures must meet local, state, or regional codes.
Mobile Homes	Term used for manufactured homes built prior to 1976 passage of the HUD Code. Homes built to voluntary industry standards.
Panelized Homes	Whole wall panels (including windows, doors, wiring, etc.) are transported to the site and assembled. Structures must meet state or local building codes.
Precut Homes	Building materials are factory-cut to design specifications, transported to the site and assembled. Examples include kit, log, and dome homes. Structures must meet local, state, or regional building codes.

Source: Manufactured Housing Institute.

Single-Section Homes

Single-section homes are structurally complete once they leave a manufacturing facility. They can be one- or two-story structures.

Multisection Homes

Multisection homes consist of two or more sections that are assembled or completed at the building site. Multisection homes are used in two-story designs.

Multiunit Configurations

In addition to multistory configurations, manufactured homes can also be used in multiunit configurations. These units consist of a number of different manufactured sections that are then assembled on-site as duplexes, fourplexes, or townhomes.

REGULATION

Unlike other site-built structures, manufactured home construction is regulated at the federal level.

HUD Code

All manufactured homes are built to the Federal Manufactured Home Construction and Safety Standards. Commonly referred to as the HUD Code, it is the only federally regulated national building code. The HUD Code sets standards for heating, plumbing, air conditioning, thermal and electrical systems, structural design, construction, transportation, energy efficiency, and fire safety. Originally enacted in 1976, the code was revised in the early 1990s to enhance energy efficiency, ventilation standards, and wind resistance. Every manufactured home is issued a label, after inspection, certifying that it was built in compliance with the HUD Code.

The Manufactured Housing Improvement Act, adopted in 2000, provides for more timely updates to the HUD Code. It also requires each state to establish an installation program. On-site additions, such as garages or porches, are not regulated by the HUD Code and must be built to local, state, or regional building codes.

State and Local Regulation

Although federal law regulates how manufactured homes are built, state and local laws still govern where manufactured homes can be sited. Local regulation of manufactured homes is based on state law. State laws regulating manufactured homes vary widely, from failure to address the issue at all to man-dating that the structures be allowed as a matter of right on any land zoned for single-family housing.

SITE CONSIDERATIONS

It is essential that access to the building site be unobstructed, because manufactured homes are transported in large, oversized components. Narrow streets, utility lines, trees, fences, and steep terrain can all impose challenges. Advances in installation equipment and technology have made previously difficult sites more accessible, however.

Manufactured homes are typically placed relatively close to the ground. This type of siting involves excavation within the foundation walls to make room for the steel and wood floor assembly. Care should be exercised to make sure that the site drains properly, including from within the foundation walls. In some cases, the architectural context may require a different type of siting, if additional vertical mass is preferable.

DESIGN CONSIDERATIONS

When constructing or modifying a home, regardless of the type of construction, evaluate the physical surroundings into which the home will be incorporated. Once known primarily for providing rural housing, manufactured homes have evolved with new architectural styles that blend into most neighborhoods. Exterior designs make these homes virtually indistinguishable from site-built homes. Technology advancements now allow for interior ceiling heights to reach up to 9 feet. Also, new "hinged-roof" systems have made it possible to produce homes with pitched roofs like their site-built counterparts. The single most important advancement in the industry in recent years has been the development of two-story models.

An increasing number of jurisdictions are permitting manufactured homes by right in existing communities when certain unit design and siting specifications are met. Essential characteristics and appearance standards include roof material and pitch, siding, shape and orientation of home, elevation, foundation, entrance, and landscape design. In order to achieve true visual compatibility with existing neighborhoods, many manufactured homes are modified or enhanced on-site. Consider such upgrades carefully and equitably so as not to affect affordability of homes or favor one type of construction over another.

Thayer Long, Manufactured Housing Institute, Arlington, Virginia

MANUFACTURED HOUSING DEVELOPMENTS

Manufactured home developments are usually either fee-simple subdivisions or land-lease developments. The major distinction between the two types of developments is ownership of the land.

Manufactured Housing Subdivisions

A manufactured housing subdivision is a tract of lots with manufactured homes that will be sold as individual parcels. In most cases, a manufactured housing subdivision is subject to the same land development standards as a subdivision of site-built homes, and lots are sold in the same manner. Approximately 65 percent of manufactured homes are sited in subdivisions.

Land-Lease Developments

A land-lease development or community is a parcel of land under single ownership on which two or more manufactured homes are sited. Home sites within the community are leased to individual homeowners, who retain customary leasehold rights. Approximately 35 percent of manufactured homes are sited in land-lease developments.

Infill Opportunities

Manufactured homes are increasingly being used in urban areas. Scattered-site manufactured homes can be used to revitalize communities and rejuvenate housing markets. Manufactured homes on infill sites are subject to the same development standards regarding setbacks, access, and parking as site-built homes, and they are sold in the same manner.

See also:
Federal Legislation
Housing Plans
Infill Development
Residential Types

Thayer Long, Manufactured Housing Institute, Arlington, Virginia

OFFICE BUILDINGS

Office buildings are structures designed primarily as places for work, commerce, or research, and characterized by the following attributes:

- Regularized, repetitive floorplate
- Open and flexible floor plan
- Segmented and systematized exterior wall
- A core containing elevators, building mechanical systems, and other common elements

Office buildings may range in height from 1 level to 50 or more levels, with a floorplate ranging from 10,000 to 50,000 square feet. Population density, lease span, daylight requirements, and cost of land all influence building form. Building shape and size is dictated primarily by commercial forces, architectural design, and zoning constraints.

Because of the prevalence of office buildings throughout the world and the relatively common design parameters that influence their form, the office building is one of the most thoroughly understood building types. The economics of planning, constructing, and owning office buildings have been extensively documented and analyzed, creating commonly accepted precedents for their design and construction.

BASIC OFFICE BUILDING TYPES

Office buildings are primarily of two economic types: speculative, where the end user is not defined, and build-to-suit, where the end user is known. For planning purposes, office buildings can be divided into three categories: low-rise, mid-rise, and high-rise.

Low-Rise Office

- One- to three-level structure.
- Suited for large, flat sites and low development densities.
- Used often for research and development or industrial applications.
- Often purpose-built for a known end user.
- Large floorplates and roof areas make them well suited for skylights, rainwater capture, and other sustainable concepts.

Mid-Rise Office

- Four- to 12-level structure.
- Found in urban and suburban conditions.
- Most prevalent of office building types.
- Adaptable to varied site configurations and sizes.
- Typically served by structured parking.

High-Rise Office

- Thirteen to 50 or more levels.
- Found primarily in dense urban conditions.
- Due to economic constraints, high-rise buildings rarely are exclusively for office uses.

Special Types

In addition to the basic types, there are many specialized office building types that have evolved to meet specific functional requirements.

> **Research and development (R&D)/high-tech.** Typically a low-rise office building dedicated to research and development of various types.

> **Medical office.** Typically a mid-rise office building with an above-average (30,000 to 50,000 square feet) floorplate, dedicated to medical-related functions. It may require specialized equipment, including wet risers (vertical shafts or chases), extensive lab equipment, and waste disposal.

> **Exhibition/trading.** Typically located within the base of a larger building, but occasionally a distinct building unto itself. This type has a very expansive (40,000 to 80,000 square feet) floorplate and open floor plan, and is used for functions requiring large open areas. Cores are located at the perimeter of the space.

BUILDING PLANNING CONSIDERATIONS

The architectural organization of office buildings consists of three components:

- Core: Contains most mechanical, electrical, elevator, and service functions
- Shell: Exterior wall
- Floorplate: Determines the leaseable area

The variation of configurations of these three elements can be extensive.

Core Location

There are three common core configurations:

- Center: The core is near the center of the floorplate. This is the most common.
- Side: The core is at the edge of the floorplate. Also called "perimeter."
- Multiple: Several cores arranged at logical intervals across the floorplate.

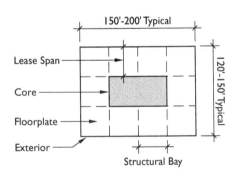

DIAGRAM OF BASIC OFFICE COMPONENTS

Source: Skidmore, Owings & Merrill LLP.

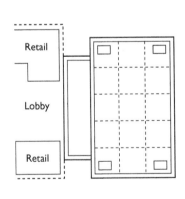

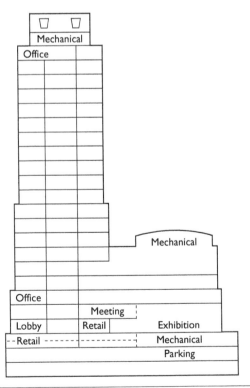

HIGH-RISE OFFICE TOWER WITH MIXED-USE BASE

Source: Skidmore, Owings & Merrill LLP.

Peter J. Kindel, AIA ASLA, Skidmore, Owings & Merrill LLP, Chicago, Illinois

Planning Module

The planning module of an office building is 5 feet. This can be either multiplied to achieve general building dimensions or subdivided to determine detailed dimensions.

Floorplate

A typical floorplate in the United States is approximately 20,000 square feet, but can range up to 50,000 square feet. Special conditions, such as trading floors, can increase this dimension even further. If natural light requirements apply, smaller floorplates may result.

Lease Spans

The lease span is the distance from the edge of the core to the exterior wall. Typical U.S. lease spans, which are defined in multiples of 5 feet, include:

- 20 to 25 feet: Rare in new construction; seen in older city centers without large sites
- 30 feet: Seen in older city centers without large sites
- 35 feet: Small multiple-tenant floors
- 40 feet: Most common
- 45 feet: Desirable for tenants requiring large floor areas
- 50 to 55 feet: Extra deep, but not uncommon

Elevator

Elevators are ubiquitous features of office buildings. Smaller buildings may have three to four elevators, while office towers may have 20 to 40 elevators. Taller buildings often have "zoned" elevators that serve particular zones or groups of floors, expediting travel.

General criteria include:

- One elevator per 50,000 square feet of building area
- Capacity to handle 10 to 15 percent of total building population in five minutes or less

Floor-to-Floor Height

Dictated primarily by economics, and secondarily by functional and aesthetic issues, floor-to-floor height affects the square footage of exterior wall, which affects overall costs.

- Typical office: 9 to 12 feet
- Trading floor: 12 to 18 feet

DESIGN GUIDELINES

Design guidelines can positively affect the aesthetic and functional aspects of a building or series of buildings. Most useful on urban sites or in office parks, design guidelines can provide control for building height, entry location, service locations, building materials, and other aesthetic concerns.

Urban and Suburban Office Buildings

Office buildings are found in both urban and suburban locations. Urban office buildings typically occupy sites ranging from 20,000 to 60,000 square feet (1,858 to 5,574 square meters; or 0.5 to 1.5 acres; or 0.2 to 0.6 hectares). They can be serviced from alleys, if they are present, discrete loading docks adjacent to the street, or underground service areas. Parking is usually underground or on the lower levels of the building.

Peter J. Kindel, AIA ASLA, Skidmore, Owings & Merrill LLP, Chicago, Illinois

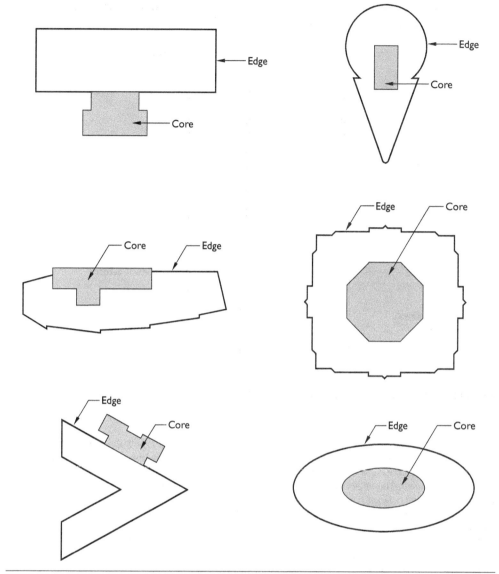

VARIATIONS IN OFFICE FLOORPLATES

Source: Skidmore, Owings & Merrill LLP.

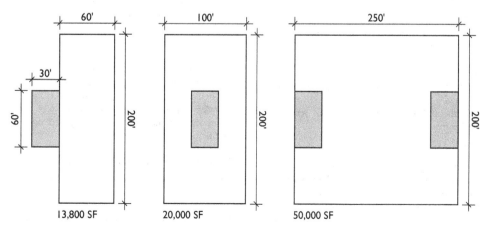

Note: Dimensions shown are for comparison purposes only. Refer to the table and other diagrams for specific recommendations on dimensions and floorplates.

COMPARISON OF FLOORPLATE AREAS

Source: Skidmore, Owings & Merrill LLP.

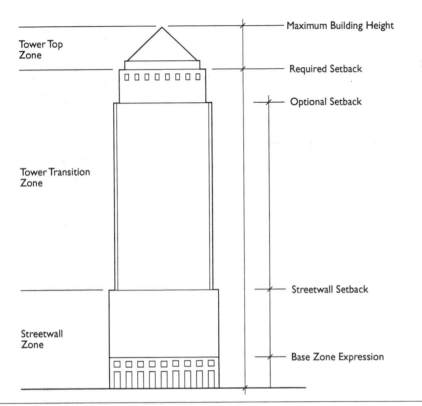

ELEMENTS FOR DESIGN GUIDELINE CONTROL

Source: Skidmore, Owings & Merrill LLP.

Suburban office buildings typically occupy larger sites, ranging from 80,000 to 400,000 square feet (7,432 to 37,161 square meters; or 2 to 10 acres; or 0.81 to 4.04 hectares). The larger site allows more landscape planted areas, larger service areas, and surface parking. Some moderate-density suburban office buildings may have two to three levels of structured parking. One suburban application of the office building is in groupings of multiple buildings, commonly known as office parks, which are usually developed and controlled by one entity. Office parks are addressed elsewhere in this book.

SITE PLANNING CONSIDERATIONS

Zoning

Zoning will control overall site development, including density, height, and setbacks.

Site Constraints

Site constraints include easements, height limits, density limits, road access, curb-cuts, wetlands, floodplains, and any other elements that reduce or otherwise modify buildable area.

Density

Commonly measured in floor-area ratio (FAR), which is the total square footage of the building divided by the total square footage of the site, density determines the overall square footage allowed. Below-grade area, parking, and some mechanical areas typically do not count against allowable FAR.

Site Organization

For a typical suburban condition, planners should estimate one-half of the site for surface parking, one-

fourth of the site for the building footprint, and one-fourth of the site for landscape. As the density of the development increases, the percentage of the site devoted to parking and landscape planting decreases.

Circulation

Circulation includes three primary considerations: site entry and building drop-off, parking ingress and egress, and service access.

Parking

Parking is typically calculated as a number of parking spaces per 1,000 square feet of building area. Check applicable zoning and parking regulations to determine specific requirements. Parking credits may be given for transit-oriented development.

Service

Service access is typically located under, within, or immediately adjacent to the building. Due to the types of activities in an office building, service requirements are relatively minimal. Service areas typically require about 5,000 square feet (464.5 square meters), thought this will vary depending on specific uses and building size.

Planted Areas and Open Space

Planted areas and open space serve two primary functions for an office building site:

• Increase the aesthetic appeal of the development.
• Provide areas for stormwater management.

Planted areas can also screen the building from adjacent uses, and provide some recreational benefit to the building occupants. Local regulations will dictate

the precise amount of open space required on a particular site, which can be as high as 40 to 50 percent of total site area.

PLANNING AND DESIGN SEQUENCE

The general planning and design sequence for office buildings is as follows:

1. *Code delineation.* Research and document all relevant codes and their effect on the buildable area, height, and density allowed, and required open space.
2. *Programming.* Clarify desired square footage and sizes of physical elements of the project. Clarify functional goals and planning module dimensions.
3. *Opportunities and constraints.* Delineate all physical opportunities and constraints present on the site, especially qualitative constraints such as views, natural features, and adjacent uses.
4. *Site plan testing.* Delineate all program elements, overlaid with code and site constraints. Reconcile programmatic incompatibilities.
5. *Plan development.* Create site and building plans that reconcile all code and program issues, for review by municipal officials.
6. *Implementation.* Create construction documents, obtain building permits, and initiate construction.

BEST PRACTICE PRINCIPLES

Mixed Uses

Office buildings work best in a larger urban environment when they are combined with other commercial uses. This allows the population of the office buildings to access neighboring commercial uses. If possible, locate office buildings within close proximity to residential uses, to reduce commuting times.

Green Buildings

Increasingly, office buildings are being constructed according to green building design practices, which take into consideration a building's structure and systems as a whole and examines how these systems work best together to save energy and reduce environmental impact.

Existing office buildings can also become "green" through increased energy efficiency and the incorporation of innovative building materials into renovation. The Natural Resources Defense Council's offices are prime examples of both renovated and new construction "green" office buildings.

Transit-Oriented

Whenever possible, office buildings should be planned for sites served by transit. This provides access opportunities for the greatest number of potential workers, while reducing automobile trips.

Stormwater Management

Office building sites should be planned to preserve and contain stormwater runoff on-site. This is most effectively done through the creation of natural-appearing stormwater management areas that use native wetlands plantings to filter and slow runoff.

Peter J. Kindel, AIA ASLA, Skidmore, Owings & Merrill LLP, Chicago, Illinois

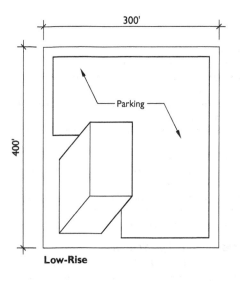

Low-Rise

Low-Rise: 120,000 SF Site
75% Surface Parking

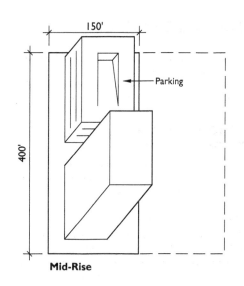

Mid-Rise

Mid-Rise: 60,000 SF Site
Structured Parking

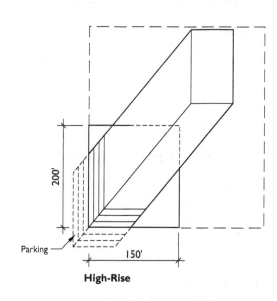

High-Rise

High-Rise: 30,000 SF Site
Underground Parking

SITE UTILIZATION COMPARISON

Source: Skidmore, Owings & Merrill LLP.

OFFICE BUILDING TYPE COMPARISON

	LOW-RISE	MID-RISE	HIGH-RISE
Definition	An office building typically found in low-density conditions, not exceeding three levels in height.	An office building typically found in medium- to high-density conditions, between 4 to 12 levels in height.	An office building typically found very high-density conditions, up to 50-plus levels in height.
Number of Levels	1 to 3	4 to 12	13 to 50-plus
Floor/Area Ratio Range	.25 to 1	1 to 5	5 to 50
Typical Core Location	Multiple, Side or Center	Center or Side	Center
Typical Core Dimension	30' × 30'	30' × 60'	60' × 60'
Typical Exterior Dimensions[1]	120' width; 200' length	120' width; 200' length	150' width; 150' length
Typical Floorplate Area	24,000 sq. ft.	24,000 sq. ft.	22,500 sq. ft.
Total Building Area, Range[2]	24,000 to 100,000 sq. ft.	100,000 to 250,000 sq. ft.	250,000 to 2 million sq. ft.
Elevator Organization	Minimum elevators; no elevator zoning	Fully served by elevators; elevators may be zoned	Completely served by multiple elevator banks; elevators always zoned
Typical Parking Arrangement	Surface parking adjacent to building	Structured parking adjacent to or within building footprint	Structured parking within building footprint
Loading	Adjacent to building	Adjacent or within building	Within building

Source: Skidmore, Owings & Merrill LLP.

1. *Exterior width dimension varies, depending upon core width and lease span width. Typical dimensions are shown here. Exterior width may be reduced slightly, to provide for natural light. For example, the mid-rise floorplate may be reduced to as narrow as 20,000 square feet, based on a 100-foot exterior width.*

2. *Total building area is a product of the floorplate and the number of floors. The ranges shown here are typical approximations for each building type.*

Core Location

Flexibility in core arrangement and location allows great variety in building form. Side cores in particular allow greater daylight to reach the workspaces and allow creative site organization.

See also:

*Leadership in Energy and Environmental
    Design—LEED*
Medical Facilities
Mixed-Use Development
Office Parks
Scale and Density
Stormwater Runoff and Recharge

Peter J. Kindel, AIA ASLA, Skidmore, Owings & Merrill LLP, Chicago, Illinois

ELEMENTARY, MIDDLE, AND HIGH SCHOOLS

The primary purpose of a school is to provide a place conducive to the learning experiences of the youth who attend the school. Placing schools close to the heart of the communities they serve decreases automobile usage and commuting time. Schools built within a community can also leverage opportunities to enter into partnerships with local libraries, theaters, arts centers, and recreational facilities.

BUILDING CONFIGURATIONS

Elementary schools in the United States do not have a standard building configuration by grade level; almost any sequential combination of grades may occur. Configurations might include several grades collected in one building. For example, prekindergarten to second-grade buildings might be followed by third- to fifth-grade buildings and sixth- to eighth-grade buildings. Individual school districts determine building configurations and can be based on many factors, including the determination of how best to meet the individual needs of the students in the district.

Middle and high schools may also be configured in a variety of arrangements. Most common perhaps are middle schools with sixth to eighth grades and high schools with ninth to twelfth grades; however, sixth to twelfth grades, tenth to twelfth grades, and other configurations can be found. Magnet programs, alternative schools, and schools with a special curricular focus can all influence the configuration of grades with the building.

SITE SELECTION

Siting a school facility is an important community decision and should be consistent with the community's adopted comprehensive plan.

When selecting a new school site, preference should be given to in-town sites to maximize the proportion of students who can use safe routes to school on foot or by bicycle. Apart from demographic considerations of population and proximity to other facilities, consideration must also be given to the following:

- Size and available building area
- Shape of the site (rectangular sites are usually easier to plan)
- District standards on school size
- Noise and other potential externalities that could affect the site
- Soil conditions or environmental damage that may require remediation
- Land availability
- Purchase and site modification costs
- Utilities availability
- Geographical area served
- Access to roadways and public transportation
- How students will travel to the site (on foot; by bicycle, school bus, or public transportation, or automobile drop-off)
- Community components (partnerships) to be included, such as medical or police facilities
- Community use of the facilities, such as the library or gymnasium
- Curricular focus and after-school programs

Selection criteria for middle and high school sites may be broadened by the need to house larger populations, exterior sports field requirements, and a commuting population that may drive to school.

SCHOOL GROUNDS PROGRAMMING

School grounds are an important part of a school's educational experience. They should be as carefully considered as the building plan.

Elementary Schools

For elementary schools, the exterior program is a critical part of the school facility's success. A comprehensive listing of suggested requirements can be found in *The School Site Planner* by the Public Schools of North Carolina, State Board of Education, Department of Public Instruction. An understanding of the school's curriculum helps to determine the appropriate types of outdoor learning opportunities and plan for them as an integral part of the site. Include the identified spaces during programming and predesign, and integrate them with the pragmatic requirements of security, access, environmental, and utility design needs.

Outdoor learning opportunities for elementary schools may include the following elements:

- Pathways
- Playgrounds and play structures
- Secure and observable bike park areas
- Free play hard surface space—rectangular or square areas free of equipment and including a range of game markings
- Soft surface areas, such as sandboxes or aquatic features
- Quiet areas with fixed seating for conversation, teaching, reading, or other forms of individual and group interaction
- Loud areas for dramatic, musical, or other similar types of play, such as amphitheaters, covered pavilions, or open-air porches

Middle and High Schools

Middle and high school sites may include features that require some authorities to determine the widest and best use of the available site area. The following possible uses may need to be ranked by importance:

- Sport and play fields (e.g., football, soccer, and tennis)
- On-site pedestrian pathways that connect other community features
- Facilities constructed in partnership with other municipal or private organizations
- Expanded on-site parking and bus access
- Wooded or naturally preserved areas for environmental protection or study

			Site Planning Criteria										
			Public Access and Entrance	Located Near Parking	Located Near Transit Access	Located for Easy Recognition by Visitors	Located Near Service Entrance	Exit Directly to Outdoors (See Note 1)	Direct Access to Playground (See Note 1)	Has Solar and Site Orientation as a Priority	Located in a Private Zone	Located in a Moderately Quiet Zone	Can be Located in a Noisy Zone
Planning Areas	①	Student Assembly Space		○	○			◐	◐	●	●		
	②	Administrative and Staff Space	●	◐	●	●	○	◐		○	◐	●	
	③	Community and Stakeholder Space	●	●	●	●	●	●	●		○	◐	●
	④	Media Center Space (See Note 2)	○			○				●	◐	◐	
	⑤	Fitness and Wellness Space (See Note 2)	◐	○		●	◐	◐				●	●
	⑥	Performing and Visual Art Space (See Note 2)	◐	●	●	●	●	○		◐	●	●	
	⑦	Facility Management and Support Space					●	●				◐	●

● Primary Importance
◐ Secondary Importance
○ Optional but Not Necessary

Seven major building components are shown here in relation to their importance of proximity to exterior functions. The relationship priority of these areas depends on the type of school and the specific program requirements of the project. Relationship of some areas to public access may vary, based on community partnerships. For example, a joint-use school/public library needs a clear and accessible public entry from the exterior.

BUILDING RELATIONSHIPS TO EXTERIOR AREAS

Source: Perkins and Will.

Raymond Bordwell, AIA, CSO Architects, Indianapolis, Indiana

All of these spaces should be planned to include possible expansion of the site or the facilities, to reserve land for other community facilities and to ensure the security and safety of children, school staff, and visitors.

BUILDING DESIGN

The organization of building components can be divided into the following seven generalized space categories:

- Student assembly (classrooms and small group rooms)
- Administrative and staff
- Community and stakeholders (cafeterias and public lobbies)
- Media center
- Fitness and wellness (gymnasiums, pools, and locker rooms)
- Performing and visual arts (theaters, music rooms, and art rooms)
- Facility management and support (central plant, maintenance, and shipping/receiving)

By cataloging space this way, exploration of design solutions for specific and distinct program areas of the facility can occur. It also provides an organized system of "parts" with which to organize the plan of the building, ensuring the proper relationships among program elements and maximizing the use of shared facilities. Determining what is the most important of these components may vary based on the age of the students being served, curriculum or district needs, the opportunities presented by the selected site, and other site selection factors mentioned earlier. In some cases there are state-mandated space standards, although these are often out of date and require more land than is necessary. Check with the state educational facilities entity to determine what is required.

Multistory solutions with more standardized and flexible space are common practice for schools in higher-density areas. These buildings are designed to change over time to meet the dynamic nature of the district or neighborhood the school serves. Proper organization of the components will maximize the use and efficiency of the building.

SITE DESIGN

Playgrounds, covered porches, and hard surface exterior spaces are all widely used at elementary schools. In locating the playground on the site, it is important to understand the curriculum and how the exterior facilities can support learning. Consider locations with the following characteristics:

- Good views
- A combination of sunny and shaded space
- Protection from noisy roads
- Easy access from the building interior
- Fences and protection from off-site intrusion
- Protection from winter wind, and exposure to summer breezes
- Access to other types of outdoor activities

When planning a "tight" school site, the building can define the site boundary or edge. Some additional design considerations for such sites include the following:

- Place the bus drop-off area at the curb or in a public right-of-way. It should be connected to the building entries by wide, well-lit open walkways.
- Make the building envelope sensitive to the proximity of pedestrian walkways.
- Consider factors such as window size and location, and access to the roof.
- Create rectilinear exterior play areas and open spaces, with a minimum of blind spots.
- Include clear signage to indicate public entries with easily controllable entry lobbies.

Larger sites may require additional parking and circulation guidelines relating to play fields and vehicular use. These include providing separate areas for the following:

- Bus drop-off (from other vehicular traffic)
- Student, staff, and community parking areas (from each other)
- Pedestrian site circulation flow (from roadways)

SECURITY AND SAFETY

Building Safety

Follow these guidelines when planning building security features:

- Avoid creating blind spots, unnecessary corners, and corridor recesses greater than 12 inches.
- Locate administrative and teacher preparation areas or offices with good visual contact of major circulation areas, such as corridors, cafeteria, bus drop-off, and parking.
- Locate actively programmed elements around the periphery of the school building so that there is "natural surveillance" from within the school to outdoor areas, such as parking lots and playgrounds.
- Minimize windowless, blank walls at the periphery of the building, particularly when these uses face residential areas, play areas, and parking lots.
- Plan spatial relationships for natural transitions from one location to another.

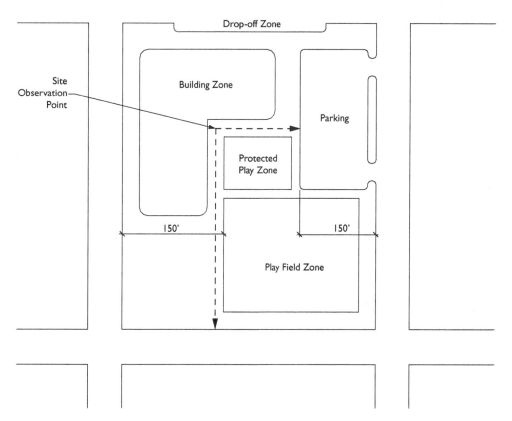

Note: Fencing to define public and private areas.

The diagram illustrates key concepts in developing a well-planned and visually observable site. Setbacks shown are optimal, which cannot always be followed. On tight sites, the building itself may form one or more edges of the site. Key concepts include: proper building zoning for controlled access before, during, and after school hours; maintaining a clear visual path at the perimeter of the building with minimal building relief to reduce the opportunity of individuals to conceal themselves around corners or behind landscape features; and a single point of visual control of exterior play space protected from adjacent streets by a distance of 150 feet. If site clearances cannot be maintained at these distances, consider a site wall or fence to separate on-site activities from the general public.

SITE PLANNING AND PASSIVE SECURITY CONCEPTS

Source: URS Corporation.

Raymond Bordwell, AIA, CSO Architects, Indianapolis, Indiana

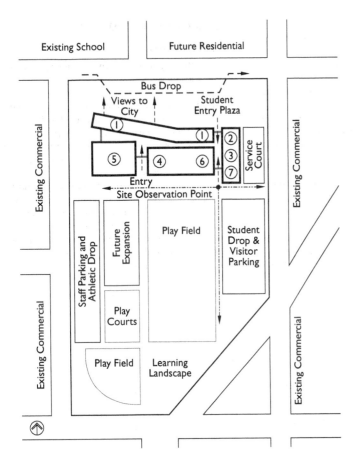

Adapted from Hector Garcia Middle School, Dallas Independent School District. The larger volume spaces of a middle school are used to buffer the classroom block from the adjacent light industrial area and orient the view toward the city skyline, relating the smaller building unit of classrooms to the residential community to the north. The site is zoned for easy vehicular and pedestrian access, to support a wide range of times the building will be used. Its orientation considers the hot climate in which it is planned by orienting classrooms to the north, and keeps student play areas away from major boulevards.

MIDDLE SCHOOL

Source: Perkins and Will.

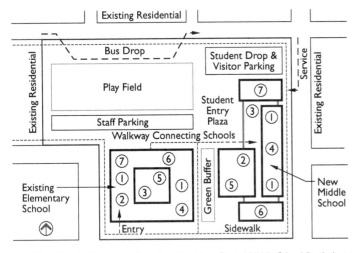

Adapted from Lincoln Elementary School and the New Central Middle School, Bartholomew Consolidated School Corporation, Columbus, Indiana. Already supporting the elementary school, the site reinforces the edge of the residential community, provides easy access between facilities, consolidates vehicular drop-off and pickup zones, and organizes safe and secure exterior play space.

ELEMENTARY AND MIDDLE SCHOOL, SHARED-USE SITE

Source: Perkins and Will/CSO Architects.

Raymond Bordwell, AIA, CSO Architects, Indianapolis, Indiana

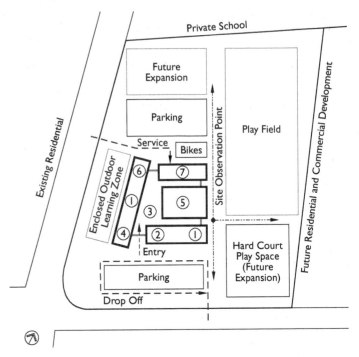

Adapted from Concordia Shanghai International School, Shanghai, China, the illustration shows a 300-student high school on a small urban site. Key concepts include reinforcement of the perimeter edge adjacent to the existing residential community, zoned facility design and parking for visitor use of facilities during nonschool hours, future expansion of elementary and middle school components, and a clear play zone adjacent to indoor athletic facilities.

SMALL HIGH SCHOOL WITH PLANNED EXPANSION

Source: Perkins and Will.

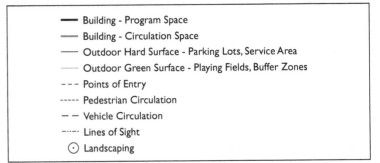

━━━	Building - Program Space
━━━	Building - Circulation Space
───	Outdoor Hard Surface - Parking Lots, Service Area
───	Outdoor Green Surface - Playing Fields, Buffer Zones
- - -	Points of Entry
-----	Pedestrian Circulation
─ ─	Vehicle Circulation
-----	Lines of Sight
⊙	Landscaping

KEY FOR SITE DIAGRAMS

- Locate restrooms in close proximity to classrooms.
- Locate areas likely to have significant after-school use close to parking and where these areas can be closed off from the rest of the building.
- Provide for natural integration of students and staff during class changes.

Site Safety

Expanded hours of use, community use, and nontraditional schedules may require increased security attention. A clear set of use guidelines should be established for each project. Review Crime Prevention Through Environmental Design (CPTED) principles prior to beginning site design or when undertaking site plan review. In general, key site planning strategies include the following:

- Minimize vehicle access points to those required for operation and life safety.
- Provide a means for vehicle speed reduction that is parallel to the building.
- Eliminate the need for students to cross roadways to access playgrounds or other campus facilities.
- Locate playgrounds and exterior learning environments with visibility from the building interior. If the facilities are to be open to the public when the facility is closed, allow for visibility by security personnel during off-hours.
- Provide adequate site lighting to discourage vandalism.
- Provide fencing around play areas, especially elementary school playgrounds, to enhance a sense of security.
- Allow the maximum practical distance from inhabited buildings to major roadways and vehicular access points.
- Keep trash containers away from direct contact with inhabited buildings.
- Where possible, allow 50 feet from inhabited buildings to parking areas (excluding drop-offs).
- Allow 35 feet of unobstructed space around buildings to make it possible to observe persons or unusual objects next to the building. Avoid low landscaping within this zone.
- Avoid large recesses in the perimeter wall that can be used for hiding.

LANDSCAPE PLANTING AND LIGHTING

Landscape planting enhances the learning experience by providing environmental study opportunities and improved aesthetics. Follow these guidelines to help to provide such amenities while addressing security-related site concerns.

- Use high trees and bushes less than 3 feet high to deter hiding.
- Provide aesthetically pleasing fencing around the site perimeter.
- Incorporate site signage into the building design to add clarity for visitors and reduce site impact.
- Place buildings along the site perimeter to protect on-site open space.
- Provide general, nonintrusive site lighting for all parking, pedestrian, and entry areas.
- Include security lighting at selected building and parking lots with photocell timer with on/off capacity.

ENVIRONMENTAL AND SUSTAINABILITY ISSUES

In some situations, school facilities can be constructed on previously developed property, also known as brownfield sites. This decision can be controversial and should be done only after a long period of community engagement to address community concerns about environmental issues.

Environmentally sensitive design is a factor in responsible citizenship and can provide excellent learning opportunities. Environmental learning can be enhanced by site amenities that integrate the experience of those using the site. These could include the following:

- Water gardens
- Outdoor laboratories
- Preservation of soil that can support native vegetation
- Formal and informal opportunities to interact with the site

In general the following guidelines related to site design should be explored thoroughly:

- Carefully design stormwater management during construction and after completion.
- Avoid development of inappropriate sites and reduce the environmental impact of locating the building on the site.
- Orient the building to relate to exterior amenities.
- Maximize the availability of solar orientation, prevailing winds, and views.
- Protect the site from noise or other externalities.
- Provide site access for vehicular, pedestrian, and public transportation.

The U.S. Green Building Council's LEED Green Building Rating System provides guidelines on environmentally sensitive development.

REFERENCES

Public Schools of North Carolina, State Board of Education, Department of Public Instruction. 1998. *School Site Planner, The Land for Learning*. Raleigh, NC: North Carolina Division of School Support, School Planning.

U.S. Green Building Council. 2002. LEED (Leadership in Energy and Environmental Design) Green Building Rating System. Washington, DC: USGBC.

See also:
Brownfields
Playgrounds
Safety

Raymond Bordwell, AIA, CSO Architects, Indianapolis, Indiana

MEDICAL FACILITIES

TYPES OF FACILITIES

There are four general categories of medical facilities: general hospitals, specialty care facilities, ambulatory care, and senior living facilities. When sited together, they are often configured in a medical campus setting.

General Hospitals

General hospitals provide care to the sick or injured. The care is not specific to one illness or patient type.

Specialty Care Facilities

Speciality care facilities provide care for a single or restricted patient cohort. There are three types:

Rehabilitation. Provide long-term recovery of severely physically debilitated patients.

Psychiatric: Provide treatment of patients suffering from mental illness or substance addiction.

Hospice: Offer respite palliative care for terminally ill patients.

Ambulatory Care and Medical Office

Ambulatory care and medical offices can range from typical office buildings for doctors to special treatment or diagnostic facilities.

Senior Living Facilities

Senior living facilities provide medical care or assistance to the elderly for daily living. There are four primary types of senior living facilities:

Skilled nursing facilities. Provide skilled nursing care in a long-term setting.

Assisted living. These residential facilities provide assistance with daily activities for the elderly.

Independent living. These residential facilities in multifamily configurations provide varying levels of services, often including meals. When skilled nursing, assisted living, and independent living units are grouped into a single complex, they form a *continuing care retirement community* (CCRC).

Alzheimer's and related dementia care. Provide continuous care and management of patients suffering from Alzheimer's or related dementia.

Medical Campus

A medical campus contains one or more of the facilities described above, arranged in a campus configuration, with multiple buildings and pedestrian and vehicular entries.

PARKING REQUIREMENTS

The parking requirements for these facilities are generally based on building gross square footage (BGSF). Residential senior living facilities have low parking needs; special senior zoning overlays typically call for

PARKING REQUIREMENTS*

FACILITY TYPE	NUMBER OF SPACES
General Hospital	1.75 to 2.5 spaces/1,000 BGSF
Specialty Care Facility	1.75 to 2.5 spaces/1,000 BGSF
Ambulatory Care/ Medical Office	4.0 to 5.0 spaces/1,000 BGSF
Senior: Skilled Nursing Facility	1.75 to 2.5 spaces/1,000 BGSF
Senior: Residential Types	0.5 spaces/1,000 BGSF plus employee parking

Parking requirements are based on actual projects, not on number of beds. The amount of parking depends upon level of outpatient services. Consult local regulations for parking requirements.

half the total number of spaces required for other multifamily uses. Upscale independent living communities sometimes offer covered parking or garages. Local parking requirements may not take into account the facility's proximity to public transportation. Developers might be able to negotiate lower requirements if proof can be offered of accessibility through other means.

SITE CIRCULATION AND BUILDING ENTRY

On-campus circulation should be self-contained and not rely on adjacent public roadways.

Separate the public (nonsecured) zones and private (secured) zones. When applicable, locate patient intake and outdoor recreational areas in the private zone. Provide appropriate access for emergency and firefighting vehicles as required by local building and safety codes.

Ambulatory Patient/Outpatient Entrance

This entrance serves patients coming and leaving in the same day and so should be adequate and convenient. It may be combined with the public and visitor's entrance, unless privacy is a concern.

Emergency

This entrance offers direct access to the emergency department for both ambulatory and ambulance patients, which, ideally, will be provided with separate doors. The emergency entrances should be easily visible when entering the campus, and a direct, unen-

		Facility Type			
		General Hospital	Specialty Care Facility	Ambulatory Care/Medical Office	Senior Living Facilities
Entry Type	Ambulatory Patient/ Outpatient	x	x	x*	
	Emergency	x			
	Inpatient Processing Entry		x		
	Patient/ Discharge	x		x	
	Physician Office			x	
	Public and Visitor	x	x	x*	x*
	Resident				x*
	Service	x	x	x	x
	Staff/ Physician	x	x	x	x

Note:
* = May be the same entrance.

ENTRY TYPE BY FACILITY

Source: Perkins and Will.

Richard Herring, AIA LEED AP, Perkins and Will, Atlanta, Georgia; Jones Lindgren, Perkins and Will, Atlanta, Georgia

cumbered vehicular route is required. If possible, avoid designing for left-hand turns within the campus.

Inpatient Processing Entry

The inpatient area is where patients may receive various diagnostic, treatment, or evaluation services prior to admission. The entrance to this area should accommodate special patient transport vehicles and security concerns. A vehicle sallyport may be included.

Patient Discharge

An area for discharging patients after treatment should be provided. Privacy and separation from main public areas are important, and accommodation for the disabled is required.

Physician Offices

Direct access to physician offices should be provided when an integrated building configuration is used.

Public and Visitor's Entrance

The entrance for the public and visitors should be easy to find and convenient to the public parking area, with disabled persons accommodation.

Resident

Independent senior living facilities may require a separate resident entrance.

Service

The service entrance is located away from public and patient entrances. It provides access for mate-rial delivery and a pick-up point for trash and other materials leaving the facility. It must be accessible for a variety of vehicle types, depending on facility needs.

Staff/Physician

The staff/physician entrance is separated from public areas and convenient to staff parking to ensure privacy and security.

GENERAL HOSPITALS

There are four basic building configurations for general hospitals:

- Horizontal
- Mall
- Vertical/high-rise
- Tower and pancake

Facility Growth Considerations

Hospitals change and grow throughout their existence, thus sites and buildings should be configured to allow for incremental growth without disrupting major public entrances, operations, or primary circulation paths.

Security

Buildings should be planned to allow only one or two points of entry after hours. Combining all public entrances into one location, except the emergency department, is an effective way to control access into the building even during core operating hours.

Amenities

Access to green space, water, and nature plays a critical role in the healing process. Hospitals should be carefully planned so that patients have views and access to gardens and green spaces for therapeutic purposes. In dense urban environments, roof gardens, water fountains, and other creative methods can be employed to provide positive distractions.

Campus Considerations

Most general hospitals are located on medical campuses, which, in addition to the hospital, comprise some combination of each type of facility defined in this section. The general hospital will almost always be the primary driver of the campus development and planning, but it must relate to the other facilities. Other facilities should be located close enough to the hospital to foster convenient passage between the two, but not so close that future growth of any facility is hampered by proximity of other buildings. The general hospital usually assumes a central location in a medical campus, although this is not true in all cases.

In planning new medical campuses, significant attention should be paid to potential future growth in order to ensure that sufficient property is available, that the utility infrastructure can accommodate future development, and that the locations of initial facilities do not compromise the ability of the campus to grow and change in future years.

Vehicular circulation must be arranged so that access to emergency facilities is clear and direct for both ambulances and individuals.

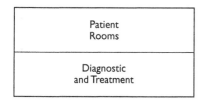

Usually one or two stories, this configuration is ideally suited for smaller hospitals where land is readily available.

HORIZONTAL HOSPITAL CONFIGURATION

Source: Perkins and Will.

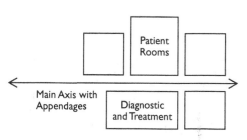

This configuration features a central public circulation spine with building appendages.

MALL HOSPITAL CONFIGURATION

Source: Perkins and Will.

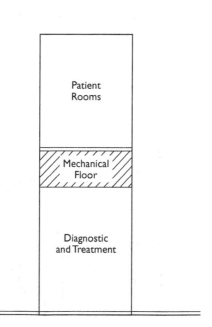

This configuration is best for dense/urban sites or those with high land costs.

VERTICAL/HIGH-RISE HOSPITAL CONFIGURATION

Source: Perkins and Will.

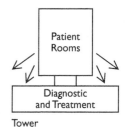

Tower

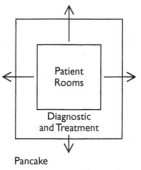

Pancake

Tower configuration allows patients to receive natural light, but they look down on the building. Pancake configuration allows the diagnostic and treatment function to expand around the perimeter.

TOWER AND PANCAKE HOSPITAL CONFIGURATION

Source: Perkins and Will.

Richard Herring, AIA LEED AP, Perkins and Will, Atlanta, Georgia; Jones Lindgren, Perkins and Will, Atlanta, Georgia

SPECIALTY CARE FACILITIES

There are three basic building configurations for specialty care facilities:

- Cluster
- Hub and Spoke
- Village or Campus

Facility Growth Considerations

Growth may occur incrementally or through major building programs.

Incremental growth. Plan "soft" areas adjacent to key programs and services. Over time, these areas are absorbed to accommodate key program growth.

Open-ended designs. Accommodate building additions easily.

The site should have sufficient space to allow for additions and related increased parking.

Campus Considerations

If a psychiatric or rehabilitative facility is located in a campus environment with other types of medical facilities, the overall campus zoning should consider the specific needs of the patient populations. It should be located in a relatively quiet zone and away from primary vehicular and pedestrian circulation paths. Access to secure outdoor areas for patients is also important.

Security

Security is a major concern for patients and staff. Psychiatric patients may pose a threat to themselves as well as staff and visitors; rehabilitative patients, due to cognitive impairments, may pose a threat to themselves. Building designs must be scrutinized to ensure that staff observation is possible in all areas where patients are present.

Amenities

Patients may have lengths of stay that may span weeks or months. Therefore, access to gardens, protected outdoor plazas, informal social gathering areas, and educational resource areas is important to the overall treatment regimen. Staff requires lounges and outdoor areas, as well, for their own respite while on duty.

AMBULATORY CARE AND MEDICAL OFFICE FACILITIES

There are three basic building configurations for ambulatory care and medical office facilities:

- Freestanding
- Attached
- Integrated

Medical office buildings are generally freestanding or integrated with ambulatory care facilities.

Facility Growth Considerations

Consolidation of multiple outpatient services offers critical mass for an ambulatory care facility by increasing patient activity at the planned facility. Generally a site is selected to maximize patient con-

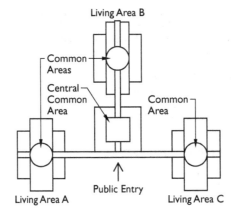

Patients of a similar treatment or security type are grouped together. These clusters may be self-contained with specific treatment areas and/or common spaces.

CLUSTER CONFIGURATION

Source: Perkins and Will.

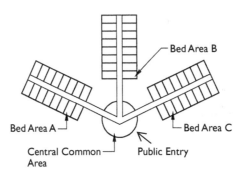

Inpatient bed areas are connected to a central gathering place containing commonly used services and amenities.

HUB AND SPOKE CONFIGURATION

Source: Perkins and Will.

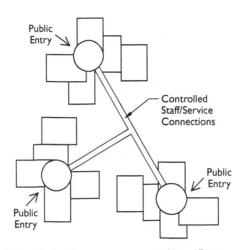

Various treatment programs are separated into different buildings, which may be connected in various ways dependent upon climate conditions.

VILLAGE OR CAMPUS CONFIGURATION

Source: Perkins and Will.

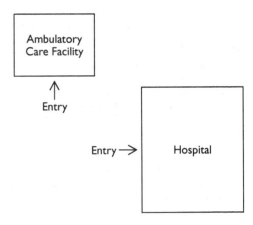

This type of structure may be adjacent to or remote from a hospital.

FREESTANDING FACILITY

Source: Perkins and Will.

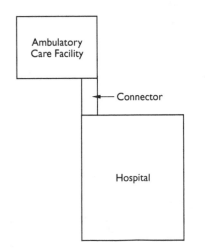

This type of structure is physically attached to a hospital facility.

ATTACHED FACILITY

Source: Perkins and Will.

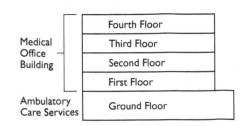

This facility combines ambulatory care services and physician office space.

INTEGRATED FACILITY

Source: Perkins and Will.

Richard Herring, AIA LEED AP, Perkins and Will, Atlanta, Georgia; Jones Lindgren, Perkins and Will, Atlanta, Georgia

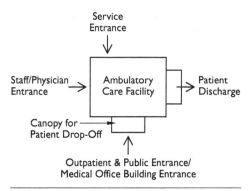

AMBULATORY CARE FACILITY ACCESS POINTS

Source: Perkins and Will.

venience and access. Outpatient surgery and outpatient diagnostic imaging areas will need to be planned with clearly identified expansion zones. Adequate acreage should be acquired to accommodate anticipated future expansion and the associated increased parking demand.

Campus Considerations

The relationship of the services provided in the medical office or ambulatory building to other on-campus medical facility buildings is important when they are all on the same campus. Physician and patient convenience must be balanced from the perspective of campus entry, connectivity to any acute care facility, and parking. Physician tenants value visibility of the buildings from public streets and convenience of entry for their patients. Patients value convenient parking and proximity to other buildings they may be required to enter during a single visit. In a campus configuration, some modification of parking requirements for a single building is sometimes appropriate,

but parking should be generally considered in the broader context of the aggregate need of the campus to avoid parking overcapacity.

Security

Ingress and egress for patient, public, and medical office building entrances should be monitored. In addition to interior and building-related security controls, security cameras for the parking areas and building entrances may be used.

Amenities

Ease of access and patient convenience are essential, beginning with site selection. Dedicated physician parking is necessary when the ambulatory care facility is remote from the physicians' primary place of business. Planning for extended-stay surgical patients who remain beyond business hours will be necessary. In medical office buildings, the parking-to-entry distance should be minimized. In integrated configurations, there should be direct access between the medical office building and the ambulatory care facility.

SENIOR LIVING FACILITIES

Basic Building Configurations

Small buildings are often organized as single-story radial wings extending from a central support/staff work core. Larger congregate care residential communities (CCRCs) may be mid- or high-rise buildings but are best planned to minimize walking distances for residents traveling from their individual rooms to community spaces, such as the dining room. Alzheimer's and related dementia care (ARD) units are laid out to ensure that visual supervision of the residents is possible from staff areas.

Facility Growth Considerations

Senior living facilities typically change over time by expanding square footage and the range of services

offered to suit the advancing age of residents; that is, independent living often becomes de facto assisted living. Construction and occupancy types should be carefully chosen to facilitate future conversion, especially if the project may change from residential care to healthcare.

Campus Considerations

Multiple subtypes of senior living facilities are frequently arranged in campus configurations, known as CCRCs. CCRCs typically contain independent living units or apartments, assisted living facilities, and skilled nursing facilities. More specialized facilities such as adult day care, Alzheimer's care, and rehab and wellness facilities are commonly located on a medical campus focusing on senior care. When different subtypes are combined on a campus, it is important to collocate as many support functions as possible, while maintaining separate identities for each component.

Facilities and vehicular circulation should be designed to encourage residents to use the outdoor campus space. Residents who drive their own automobiles need to have parking located close to entrances.

Security

Controlling building entry is both important and difficult in residential facilities because individual living units often have doors opening directly to the exterior.

Security is particularly crucial for Alzheimer and related dementia (ARD) facilities, which should be designed with safe exterior gardens surrounded by enclosures, and made accessible to residents on a 24-hour basis. Ideally, the gardens are part of wandering loops that continue through the buildings to provide therapeutic activity for active victims of dementia. Access to ARD units for families and the public must be carefully controlled to protect residents.

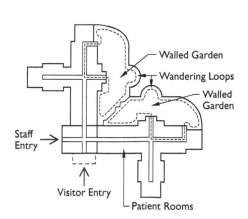

ALZHEIMER'S AND RELATED DEMENTIA CARE FACILITY

Source: Perkins and Will.

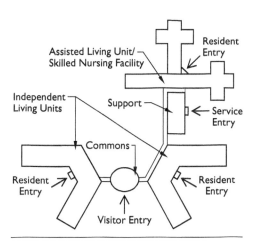

CONGREGATE CARE RESIDENTIAL COMMUNITY

Source: Perkins and Will.

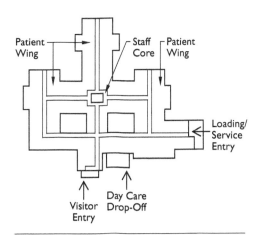

SKILLED NURSING FACILITY

Source: Perkins and Will.

Richard Herring, AIA LEED AP, Perkins and Will, Atlanta, Georgia; Jones Lindgren, Perkins and Will, Atlanta, Georgia

Amenities

CCRCs often have a variety of shared resident spaces grouped into a commons and located near the plan core

- Multiple dining options: public and private dining rooms, ice cream bars, bistros, eat-in country kitchens
- Wellness components: lap and aerobic pools, exercise and equipment rooms, locker rooms, walking tracks through the site
- Business centers: equipped with up-to-date office equipment
- Assembly spaces: meditation rooms or chapels, theaters, club rooms, libraries
- Activity rooms: craft rooms, demonstration kitchens, greenhouses

Features in common spaces and inside individual rooms that emphasize the buildings' residential aspect, contribute to resident independence, and encourage family participation are most successful.

See also:
Office Buildings

Richard Herring, AIA LEED AP, Perkins and Will, Atlanta, Georgia; Jones Lindgren, Perkins and Will, Atlanta, Georgia

TRANSPORTATION

SIDEWALKS

The ADA Accessibility Guidelines for Buildings and Facilities (ADAAG) is the national standard for pedestrian access and travel. ADAAG provides the minimum standards for all public and private facilities. The American Association of State Highway and Transportation Officials (AASHTO) also provides guidelines for public rights-of-way. *A Policy on Geometric Design of Highways and Streets*, commonly referred to as the *AASHTO Green Book*, focuses primarily on vehicle use, whereas ADAAG emphasizes accessible design for pedestrians. Other organizations, such as the Institute of Transportation Engineers and the Federal Highway Administration, have also developed sidewalk and curb ramp design recommendations. The information here is from *Designing Sidewalks and Trails for Access, Part I of II: Review of Existing Guidelines and Practices* (Federal Highway Administration 1999).

SIDEWALK DESIGN CHARACTERISTICS

Sidewalk design is characterized by the elements that affect usability and accessibility:

- Grade
- Cross-slope
- Width
- Passing space
- Vertical clearance
- Changes in level
- Grates and gaps
- Obstacles and protruding objects
- Surface

Grade

Grade is defined as the slope parallel to the direction of travel. It is calculated by dividing the vertical change in elevation by the horizontal distance covered. Running grade is the average grade along a contiguous grade. The *AASHTO Green Book* recommends the running grade of sidewalks be consistent with the running grade of adjacent roadways.

Maximum grade is a limited section of path that exceeds the typical running grade. In the pedestrian environment, maximum grade should be measured over 24-inch intervals, which represent the approximate length of a wheelchair wheelbase or a single walking pace. When measuring sidewalk grade, both running grade and maximum grade should be determined so that small steep sections may be detected.

The rate of change of grade is the change in grade over a given distance. It is determined by measuring the grade and the distance over which it occurs for each segment of the overall distance. Rate of change of grade is measured over 24-inch (61-centimeter) intervals.

Cross-Slope

Cross-slope is the slope measured perpendicular to the direction of travel. Unlike grade, cross-slope can be measured only at specific points. Cross-slope is determined by taking measurements at intervals throughout a section of sidewalk and then averaging the values.

Running cross-slope is the average cross-slope of a contiguous section of sidewalk. Often within a typical running cross-slope there are inaccessible maximum cross-slopes that exceed the running cross-slope. The distance over which a maximum cross-slope occurs significantly influences how difficult a section of sidewalk is to negotiate. Rate of change of cross-slope is the change in cross-slope over a given distance. It can be measured by placing a digital level a specified distance before and after a maximum cross-slope. The specified distance should be about 24 inches (61 centimeters) to represent the approximate stride of a pedestrian or the wheelbase of a wheelchair.

Most sidewalks are built with some degree of cross-slope to prevent water from collecting on the path by allowing water to drain into the street. Water puddles pose a slipping hazard to sidewalk users and are even more difficult to negotiate when frozen.

Width

Sidewalk widths affect pedestrian usability and determine the types of access and other pedestrian elements that can be installed. For example, a 5-foot- (1.5-meter)-wide sidewalk is probably wide enough to accommodate pedestrian traffic in a residential area, but a much wider sidewalk would be necessary to include amenities, such as street furniture or newspaper stands. The specifications for a sidewalk's width is called its design width. Design width extends from the curb or planting strip to any buildings or plantings that form the opposite borders of the sidewalk.

The minimum clearance width is the narrowest point on a sidewalk. If the clearance width is reduced by obstacles, such as utility poles, protruding into the sidewalk, the design width is reduced. A reduction in the design width could also create a minimum clearance width. Although most guidelines require

sidewalk design widths to be at least 5 feet (1.5 meters) wide, larger design widths can accommodate more pedestrians and improve ease of access.

The width of the sidewalk is also affected by pedestrian travel tendencies. Pedestrians tend to travel in the center of sidewalks to separate themselves from the rush of traffic, avoid street furniture, vertical obstructions, and other pedestrians entering and exiting buildings. Pedestrians avoid the edge of the sidewalk close to the street because it often contains utility poles, bus shelters, parking meters, sign poles, and other street furniture. Pedestrians also avoid traveling in the 24 inches (61 centimeters) of the sidewalk closest to buildings because of such obstacles as retaining walls, street furniture, and fences. The sidewalk area pedestrians tend to avoid is referred to as the "shy distance." Taking into account the shy distance, only the center 6 feet (1.83 meters) of a 10-foot (3.05-meter) sidewalk is used by pedestrians for travel. This space is called the "effective width."

Passing Space

Passing space is a section of path wide enough to allow two wheelchair users to pass one another or travel abreast. The passing space provided should

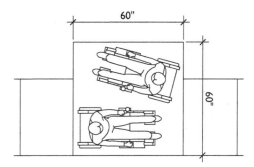

Passing spaces should be included at intervals on narrow sidewalks to allow wheelchair users to pass one another.

PASSING SPACE

Source: Federal Highway Administration 1999.

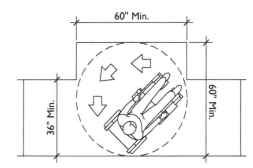

Wheelchair users require 60 inches by 60 inches to maneuver in a complete circle.

TURNING SPACE

Source: Federal Highway Administration 1999.

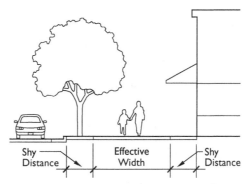

Most pedestrians prefer to travel in the center, or effective width, of the sidewalk.

SHY DISTANCE AND EFFECTIVE WIDTH

Source: Federal Highway Administration 1999.

Federal Highway Administration, Washington, DC

TRANSPORTATION

also be designed to allow one wheelchair user to turn in a complete circle. The passing space interval is the distance between passing spaces. Passing spaces should be provided when the sidewalk width is narrow for a prolonged extent because of a narrow design width or continuous obstacles. ADAAG specifies that accessible routes with fewer than 5 feet (1.5 meters) of clear width must provide passing spaces at least 5 feet (1.5 meters) wide at reasonable intervals not exceeding 200 feet (61 meters). If turning or maneuvering is necessary, a turning space of 5 square feet (0.47 square meters) should be provided.

Vertical Clearance

Vertical clearance is the minimum unobstructed vertical passage space required along a sidewalk. Obstacles such as building overhangs, tree branches, signs, and awnings often limit vertical clearance. ADAAG states that circulation spaces, such as corridors, should have at least 80 inches (203 centimeters) of headroom. ADAAG further specifies that if the vertical clearance of an area next to a circulation route is less than 80 inches (203 centimeters), a barrier must be constructed to visually disabled or blind people about the elements projecting into the circulation space.

Changes in Level

Changes in level are defined as vertical height transitions between adjacent surfaces or along the surface of a path. In the sidewalk environment, curbs without curb ramps, cracks, and dislocations in the surface material are common examples of changes in level. Changes in level can also occur at expansion joints between elements, such as curb ramps and gutters. The following conditions cause changes in level:

- Buckled bricks
- Cracks
- Curbs without ramps
- Drainage grates
- Grooves in concrete
- Heaving and settlement due to frost
- Lips at curb ramp frames
- Railroad tracks
- Roots
- Small steps
- Tree grates
- Uneven transitions between streets, gutters, and ramps

Changes in level can cause ambulatory pedestrians to trip or can catch the casters of a manual wheelchair, causing the chair to come to an abrupt stop. People who are blind or who have poor vision might not anticipate changes in level..

Grates and Gaps

A grate is a framework of latticed or parallel bars that prevents large objects from falling through a drainage inlet but still allows water and some debris to fall through the slots. A gap is a single channel embedded in the travel surface of a path. Gaps are often found at intersections where railroad tracks are embedded into the road surface. ADAAG specifies that grates located in walking surfaces should have spaces no greater than 0.5 inches (1.27 centimeters) wide in one direction. It also states that gratings with elongated openings should be oriented so that the long dimension is perpendicular to the dominant direction of travel.

Obstacles and Protruding Objects

Obstacles in the pedestrian environment are objects that limit the vertical passage space, protrude into the circulation route, or reduce the clearance width of the sidewalk. The full width of the circulation path should be free of protruding objects. Obstacles that reduce the minimum clearance width can create significant barriers for wheelchair or walker users.

The following objects can make a sidewalk difficult for some users to traverse if they protrude into the pathway or reduce the vertical or horizontal clear space:

- Awnings
- Bike racks
- Bollards
- Drinking fountains
- Fire hydrants
- Grates
- Guy wires
- Mailboxes
- Newspaper vending machines
- Parking meters
- Planters
- Public telephones and telephone booths
- Puddles and snow
- Signage and poles
- Signal control and utility boxes
- Street furniture
- Street vendors' carts
- Street sculptures
- Telephone/utility poles and their stabilizing wires
- Transit shelters
- Trash receptacles
- Tree, bush, and shrub branches

Surface

The surface is the material on which a person walks or wheels in the pedestrian environment. The type of surface often determines how difficult an area is to negotiate. For example, most people can traverse wood floors without much difficulty, while a gravel surface can be impossible for some people, especially wheelchair users, to cross. Surfaces in sidewalk environments are generally concrete or asphalt but commonly include tile, stone, and brick.

Firm and stable surfaces resist deformation, especially by indentation or the movement of objects. For example, a firm and stable surface, such as concrete, resists indentation from the forces applied by a walking person's feet and reduces the rolling resistance experienced by a wheelchair. When a pedestrian or wheelchair user crosses a surface that is not firm or stable, energy that would otherwise cause forward motion deforms or displaces the surface instead. A slip-resistant surface provides enough frictional counterforce to the forces exerted in ambulation to permit effective travel. For example, a slip-resistant surface prevents a person's shoes, crutch tips, or tires from sliding across the surface while bearing weight. A broom finish is used on many concrete sidewalks to provide sufficient slip resistance for pedestrians.

SIDEWALK ELEMENTS

Curb Ramps

Curb ramps are most commonly found at intersections, but they may also be used at midblock crossings and medians. Curb ramps should be designed to min-

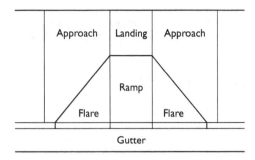

COMPONENTS OF A CURB RAMP

Source: Federal Highway Administration 1999.

imize the grade, cross-slope, and changes in level experienced by users. Although there are a variety of curb ramp designs, each type of curb ramp comprises some or all of the following elements:

> **Landing.** Level area of sidewalk at the top of a curb ramp facing the ramp path.

> **Approach.** Section of the accessible route flanking the landing of a curb ramp. The approach may be slightly graded if the landing level is below the elevation of the adjoining sidewalk.

> **Flare.** Sloped transition between the curb ramp and the sidewalk. The path along the flare has a significant cross-slope and is not considered an accessible path of travel. When the sidewalk is set back from the street, returned curbs often replace flares.

> **Ramp.** Sloped transition between the street and the sidewalk where the grade is constant and the cross-slope is at a minimum (preferably less than 2 percent).

> **Gutter.** Trough or dip used for drainage purposes that runs along the edge of the street and the curb or curb ramp.

Curb ramp widths should depend on the volume of pedestrian traffic at the specified intersection. The *AASHTO Green Book* states that curb ramps that are a minimum of 39 inches wide or of the same width as the approach sidewalk should be provided at crosswalks. Although ramp widths are permitted to vary, they must always be wide enough for comfortable use by wheelchair users. Curb ramps provide critical access between the sidewalk and the street for people with mobility impairments. ADAAG specifies that curb ramps should be at least 3 feet (0.91 meters) wide, not including the width of the flared sides.

Gutters

The slopes of adjacent gutters and streets significantly affect the overall accessibility of curb ramps. Any amount of height transition between the curb ramp and the gutter can compound the difficulties caused by rapidly changing grades. According to ADAAG, the slope of the road or gutter surface immediately adjacent to the curb ramp should not exceed 5 percent, and the transition between the ramp and the gutter should be smooth.

Landings

Landings allow people with mobility impairments to move completely off the curb ramp and onto the

Federal Highway Administration, Washington, DC

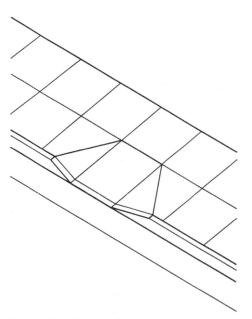

Flares provide a sloped transition between the ramp and the surrounding sidewalk and are designed to prevent pedestrians from tripping.

FLARES

Source: Federal Highway Administration 1999.

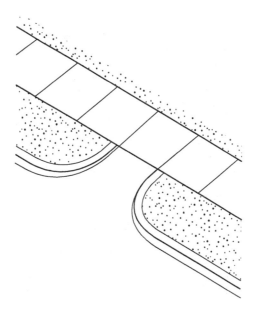

Returned curbs may be used when the curb ramp is located outside the pedestrian walkway, such as in a planting strip.

RETURNED CURBS

Source: Federal Highway Administration 1999.

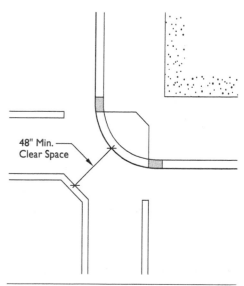

DIAGONAL CURB RAMP

Source: Federal Highway Administration 1999.

sidewalk. Curb ramps without landings force wheelchair users entering the ramp from the street, as well as people turning the corner, to travel on the ramp flares. According to ADAAG, the landing should be a level surface at least 3 feet (0.91 meters) wide to prevent pedestrians from having to cross the curb ramp flare. ADAAG recommends a 4-foot (1.22-meter) landing for perpendicular curb ramps and a 5-foot (1.5-meter) landing for parallel curb ramps.

Flares

The flared sides of curb ramps provide a graded transition between the ramp and the surrounding sidewalk. Flares are not considered an accessible path of travel because they are generally steeper than the ramp and often feature significant cross-slopes with excessive rate of change of cross-slope. Flares may be replaced with returned curbs if the curb ramp is located where a pedestrian does not have to walk across the ramp or if guardrails or handrails protect the sides.

CURB RAMP TYPES

Curb ramps can be configured in a variety of patterns, depending on the location, type of street, and existing design constraints. Curb ramps are often categorized by their position relative to the curb line. Many sidewalk characteristics, including width, elevation of buildings, and position of street furniture, can affect the curb ramp design chosen. The four most common configurations are perpendicular, parallel, diagonal, and built-up ramps.

Perpendicular Curb Ramps

Perpendicular curb ramps are often installed in pairs at a corner. For new construction, two perpendicular

curb ramps with level landings should be provided at street crossings. The path of travel along a perpendicular curb ramp is oriented at a 90-degree angle to the curb face. When the sidewalk is narrow, it can be costly to purchase additional right-of-way necessary to accommodate a landing for perpendicular curb ramps. An alternative to purchasing more land is to extend the corner into the parking lane with a curb extension, also known as a "bulbout."

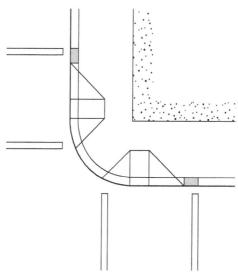

Two perpendicular curb ramps with level landings maximize access for pedestrians at intersections.

PERPENDICULAR CURB RAMPS

Source: Federal Highway Administration 1999.

Diagonal Curb Ramps

Diagonal curb ramps are single curb ramps installed at the apex of a corner. They force pedestrians descending the ramp to proceed into the intersection before turning to the left or right to cross the street. This puts them in danger of being hit by turning cars. A marked clear space of 4 feet (1.22 meters) at the base of diagonal curb ramps is necessary to allow ramp users in wheelchairs enough room to maneuver into the crosswalk.

In many situations, diagonal curb ramps are less costly to install than two perpendicular curb ramps. While these ramps might save money, they create potential safety and mobility problems for pedestrians, including reduced maneuverability and

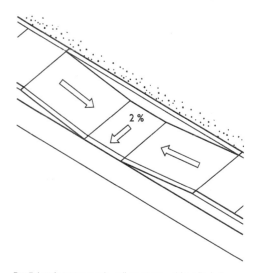

Parallel curb ramps work well on narrow sidewalks but require users continuing on the pathway to negotiate two ramp grades.

PARALLEL CURB RAMP

Source: Federal Highway Administration 1999.

Federal Highway Administration, Washington, DC

TRANSPORTATION

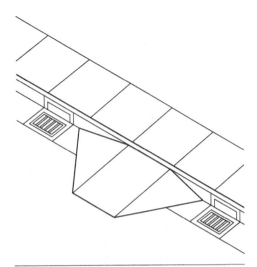

BUILT-UP CURB RAMP WITH DRAINAGE INLETS

Source: Federal Highway Administration 1999.

increased interaction with turning vehicles, particularly in areas with high traffic volumes. Diagonal curb ramps are not desirable in new construction, but might be effective when retrofitting is being done and there is not enough space for two accessible perpendicular curb ramps.

Parallel Curb Ramps

The path of travel along a parallel curb ramp is a continuation of the sidewalk, as parallel curb ramps provide an accessible transition to the street on narrow sidewalks. If the landing on parallel curb ramps is not sloped toward the gutter (no more than 2 percent), however, water and debris can pool there and obstruct passage along the sidewalk.

Built-up Curb Ramps

Built-up curb ramps are oriented in the same direction as perpendicular curb ramps but project out from the curb. For this reason, built-up curb ramps can be installed on narrow sidewalks but are most often installed in parking lots. Built-up curb ramps should not extend into a vehicular traffic lane or bicycle lanes. Built-up curb ramps have additional drainage requirements because they block the gutter. Possible solutions include providing drainage inlets or placing a drainage pipe under the curb ramp.

CURB RAMP PLACEMENT

In addition to specifying curb ramp designs, most transportation agencies provide specifications for their placement. Curb ramp placement can be especially complicated in retrofit situations. In retrofit situations in which sidewalk width is limited, parallel curb ramps might provide more gradual slopes and landings.

Curb ramps that force users to cross storm drain inlets often present hidden risks to pedestrians. The grates covering such inlets can catch the casters of wheelchairs or the tips of canes and walkers, causing falls and injuries. Water at the base of curb ramps can obscure the transition from the ramp to the gutter and cause pedestrians to misjudge the terrain. Puddles at

the base of curb ramps can freeze and cause users to slip. Therefore, locate drain inlets uphill from curb ramps to reduce the amount of water that collects at the base.

Curb ramps ending in parking spaces are not usable when blocked by parked vehicles. This situation can be prevented through parking enforcement and warning signs, but perhaps more effectively through the use of curb extensions. At corners with larger turning radii, the curb ramp cannot always point in the direction of the crosswalk and be perpendicular to the curb face. In some cities, designers align curb ramps parallel to the crosswalk, causing the ramp face to be skewed.

DRIVEWAY CROSSINGS

Driveway crossings permit cars to cross the sidewalk and enter the street. They consist of the same components found in curb ramps. It is the driver's responsibility to yield to the pedestrian at the driveway/sidewalk interface. Intersections of driveways and sidewalks are the most common locations of severe cross-slopes for sidewalk users. Some inaccessible driveway crossings have cross-slopes that match the grade of the driveway because a level area is not provided for the crossing pedestrian. Rapid changes in cross-slope usually occur at driveway flares and are most problematic when they occur over a distance of less than 2 feet (0.61 meters). Well-designed driveway crossings eliminate severe cross-slope along the path of travel. Driveway crossings designed along setback sidewalks can easily be made accessible because the setback permits designers to maintain a level path of travel along the sidewalk. The driveway ramp then resumes sloping at the setback

Wide sidewalks can be designed similar to sidewalks with a setback if the upper portion of the sidewalk is leveled for pedestrians and the bottom portion is sloped for automobiles. A level landing area can be achieved on narrow sidewalks if the side-

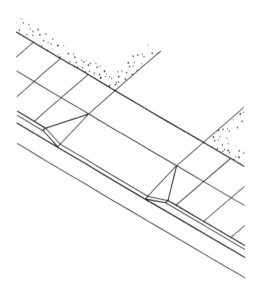

On wide sidewalks, there is enough room to provide a ramp for drivers and retain a level landing for pedestrians.

DRIVEWAY CROSSING WITH WIDE SIDEWALK

Source: Federal Highway Administration 1999.

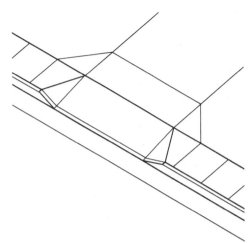

Jogging the sidewalk back from the street provides a level landing for pedestrians on narrow sidewalks.

DRIVEWAY CROSSING WITH JOGGED-BACK SIDEWALK

Source: Federal Highway Administration 1999.

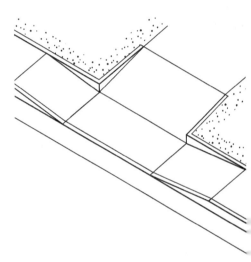

Although parallel driveway crossings provide users with level landings, users continuing on the sidewalk are forced to negotiate two ramps.

DRIVEWAY CROSSING WITH PARALLEL SIDEWALK

Source: Federal Highway Administration 1999.

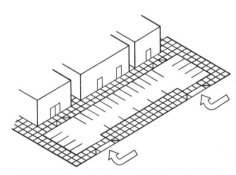

Improve accessibility by combining parking lots and reducing the number of individual entrances and exits.

PARKING LOT ENTRY WITH SIDEWALK ACCESS

Source: Federal Highway Administration 1999.

Federal Highway Administration, Washington, DC

PART 3   STRUCTURES

walk is jogged back from the street as it crosses the driveway. Similar to a parallel curb ramp, a parallel driveway crossing provides a level landing by lowering the sidewalk to the grade of the street. This design is preferable to the severe cross-slopes at some driveway crossings, but it is not as easy to negotiate as setback and wide sidewalk designs.

Commercial districts with front parking are often designed with a series of lots with individual entrances and exits. This design increases the number of driveway crossings and forces pedestrians to encounter automobiles repeatedly. To improve access for pedestrians, including pedestrians with mobility disabilities, individual parking lots should be combined to reduce the number of entrances and exits. The remaining driveway crossings should be retrofitted to include level landings.

CROSSWALKS

Crosswalks are a critical part of the pedestrian network. A crosswalk is that part of the roadway designated for the use of pedestrians in crossing the street. Crosswalks may be either marked or unmarked. Marked crosswalks are most effective when motorists can identify them easily; pedestrians, too, especially those with low vision, benefit from clearly marked crosswalks.

Most state departments of transportation follow the *Manual of Uniform Traffic Control Devices* (MUTCD) guidelines for marking crosswalks. Although the *MUTCD* does permit some variations for additional visibility, the basic specifications call for solid white lines not less than 6 inches (15.24 centimeters) marking both edges of the crosswalk and spaced at least 72 inches (183 centimeters) apart.

Crossing Times

An individual's starting pace and walking pace vary depending on their personal situation. Older pedestrians might require longer starting times to verify that cars have stopped. They also might have slower reaction times and walking speeds. Powered wheelchair

users and manual wheelchair users on level or downhill slopes might travel faster than other pedestrians; but on uphill slopes, manual wheelchair users might have slower travel speeds. At intersections without audible pedestrian signals, people with visual impairments generally require longer starting times because they rely on the sound of traffic for signal-timing information.

The *AASHTO Green Book* suggests an average walking speed in the range of 3.3 feet/second (1 meter/second) to 5.9 feet/second (1.8 meters/second), whereas the *MUTCD* assumes an average walking speed of 4 feet/second (1.22 meters/second). For older pedestrians, the *AASHTO Green Book* suggests a walking rate of 3.28 feet/second (approximately 1 meter/second). However, research on pedestrian walking speeds has demonstrated that more than 60 percent of pedestrians walk more slowly than the speeds suggested by both the *AASHTO Green Book* and the *MUTCD*. In fact, 15 percent of pedestrians walk at less than 3.5 feet/second (1.07 meters/second).

Pedestrians of all mobility levels need to cross intersections, and when crossing times accommodate only those who walk at or above the average walking speed, intersections become unusable for people who walk at a slower pace. To accommodate the slower walking speeds of some pedestrians, transportation agencies should consider extending their pedestrian signal cycles. Signal timing should be determined on a case-by-case basis, although extended signal cycles are strongly recommended at busy intersections that are unusually long or difficult to negotiate.

Midblock Crossings

Midblock crossings are pedestrian crossing points not at intersections. They are often installed to provide more frequent crossing opportunities in areas with heavy pedestrian traffic. For midblock crossings to be accessible to people with mobility impairments, a curb ramp needs to be installed at both ends of the crossing along a direct line of travel. Where the curb

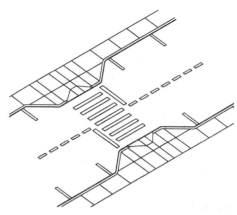

Curb extensions at midblock crossings help to reduce crossing distance.

CURB EXTENSIONS AT MIDBLOCK CROSSING

Source: Federal Highway Administration 1999.

ramps are offset, pedestrians who rely on the curb ramps are forced to travel in the street.

Midblock crossings spanning multiple lanes can be difficult for some pedestrians to negotiate. In these situations, curb extensions can be effective in reducing crossing times and increasing visibility between pedestrians and motorists. A median is another effective method to reduce crossing distances.

SIGHT DISTANCES

Sight distance is the distance one can view along an unobstructed line of sight. Adequate sight distances between pedestrians and motorists increase pedestrian safety. Motorists also need appropriate sight distances to see traffic signals. In particular, vertical sight distance can be important for drivers of high vehicles, such as SUVs, trucks, and buses, whose sight lines might be blocked by trees or signs.

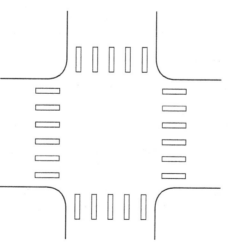

Two horizontal lines are the most common crosswalk markings.

CROSSWALK WITH HORIZONTAL MARKINGS

Source: Federal Highway Administration 1999.

Research has shown the ladder design to be the most visible type of pedestrian crosswalk marking.

CROSSWALK WITH LADDER DESIGN MARKINGS

Source: Federal Highway Administration 1999.

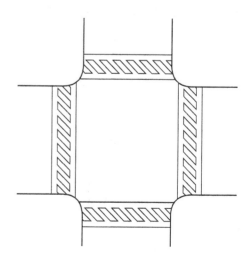

Diagonal crosswalk markings can enhance visibility.

CROSSWALK WITH DIAGONAL MARKINGS

Source: Federal Highway Administration 1999.

Federal Highway Administration, Washington, DC

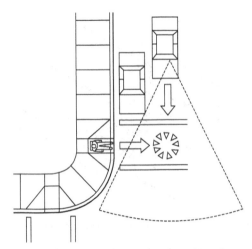

Sight lines obstructed by parked cars prevent drivers from seeing pedestrians starting to cross the street.

OBSTRUCTED SIGHT LINES

Source: Federal Highway Administration 1999.

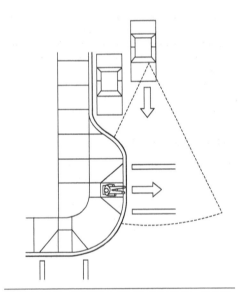

IMPROVED SIGHT LINES: PARTIAL CURB EXTENSION

Source: Federal Highway Administration 1999.

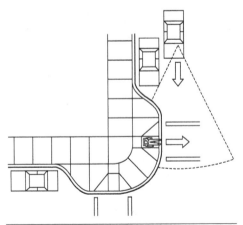

IMPROVED SIGHT LINES: FULL CURB EXTENSION

Source: Federal Highway Administration 1999.

Federal Highway Administration, Washington, DC

PART 3   STRUCTURES

Although bollards, landscaping, parking, benches, or bus shelters make pedestrian areas more inviting by calming traffic and providing amenities, they can also clutter the environment and block sight lines between motorists and pedestrians waiting to cross the intersection. Trimming vegetation, relocating signs, and hanging more than one sign or traffic signal on one arm pole where permitted by the *MUTCD* can improve sight distances at corners.

Parked cars near the intersection or midblock crossing can also reduce sight distances. Installing curb extensions physically deters parking at intersection corners and improves the visibility of pedestrians. Curb extensions can also increase the angle at which pedestrians meet motor vehicles, improving the visibility of both. In addition, curb extensions shorten crossing distances and provide sidewalk space for curb ramps with landings.

GRADE-SEPARATED CROSSINGS

Grade-separated crossings are facilities allowing pedestrians and motor vehicles to cross at different levels. Examples of grade-separated crossings include overpasses and underpasses. Overpasses might be bridges, elevated walkways, skywalks, or skyways. Underpasses are pedestrian tunnels and below-grade pedestrian networks.

Some grade-separated crossings are very steep and difficult for people with mobility impairments to negotiate. In addition, grade-separated crossings are extremely costly to construct and are often not considered pedestrian-friendly because pedestrians are forced to travel out of their way to use the underpass or overpass. The effectiveness of a grade-separated crossing depends on whether pedestrians perceive it as easier to use than a street crossing.

The needs of pedestrians should be a high priority at grade-separated crossings. If designed correctly, grade-separated crossings can reduce pedestrian-vehicle conflicts and potential accidents by allowing pedestrians to avoid crossing the path of traffic. They can also limit vehicle delay, increase highway capacity, and reduce vehicle accidents when appropriately located and designed. Grade-separated crossings are most efficient in areas where pedestrian attractions such as shopping centers, large schools, recreational facilities, parking garages, and other activity centers are separated from pedestrian generators by high volume and/or high-speed arterial streets.

Well-designed grade-separated crossings minimize slopes, feel open and safe, and are well lit. Minimizing the slope of a grade-separated crossing is often difficult because a significant rise, generally from 14 to 18 feet (4.27 to 5.49 meters), must be accommodated. Underpasses might invite crime if insufficiently lit and are seldom traveled. Underpasses can also be more expensive to install than other pedestrian facilities because a tunnel must be dug and utility lines relocated. Tunnels are more inviting to use when they are brightened with skylights or artificial lighting and are wide and high enough to feel open and airy.

MEDIANS AND ISLANDS

Medians and islands help pedestrians cross streets by providing refuge areas physically separated from the automobile path of travel. A median separates opposing lanes of traffic. An island is a protected spot

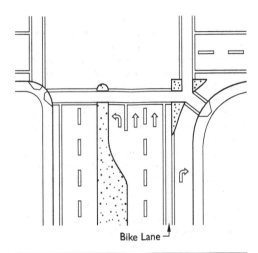

Bike Lane

CUT-THROUGH CORNER ISLAND AND CENTER MEDIAN

Source: Federal Highway Administration 1999.

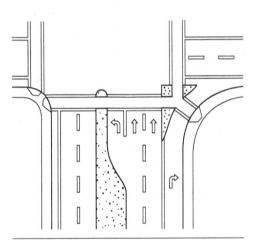

RAMPED CORNER ISLAND AND CUT-THROUGH MEDIAN

Source: Federal Highway Administration 1999.

within a crosswalk for pedestrians to wait to continue crossing the street or to board transit. Medians and islands are useful at irregularly shaped intersections, such as where two roads converge into one.

Medians and islands reduce the crossing distance from the curb and allow pedestrians to cross during smaller gaps in traffic. They are useful to pedestrians who are unable to judge distances accurately and to those who walk slowly. Because medians and islands separate traffic into channels going in specific directions, they require crossing pedestrians to watch for traffic coming in only one direction.

SIGNAGE

Objective signage provides users with information to help them make informed choices about their travel routes. Most agencies rely on the *MUTCD* for sign guidelines. Pedestrian signs should not be placed in locations where they obstruct the minimum clearance width or protrude into the pathway. In the sidewalk environment, signage should be supplemented with audible or tactile information so that it is accessible to people with visual impairments. Braille and raised lettering are not addressed in the *MUTCD*.

The majority of signs in the public right-of-way are directed at the motorist. Although these signs often affect pedestrians, they are usually not intended for or positioned to be seen by them. For example, the street name signs on many large arterials are hung in the center of the intersection, making them essentially invisible to pedestrians traveling along the sidewalk. Pedestrians might even be put in danger because important safety information, such as yield signage, is not easily visible.

Targeting more signs toward pedestrians would improve safety and permit them to identify routes requiring the least effort for travel. Warning signs similar to standard traffic warning signs would provide information on sidewalk characteristics, such as steep grades. To date, these types of signs have not been introduced to the *MUTCD*.

DRAINAGE

Sidewalks provide the main conduit for draining the walking surface, adjacent properties, and, in some cases, the roadway. Therefore, sidewalks and sidewalk elements, such as curb ramps and driveway crossings, must be designed to provide efficient drainage as well as good access. The *AASHTO Green Book*, adopted by most states, provides slope ranges based on street type.

Local topography and weather conditions also affect how steeply sidewalks, gutters, and roads should be sloped to provide adequate drainage. According to the *AASHTO Green Book*, a cross-slope between 1.5 to 2 percent provides effective drainage on paved surfaces in most weather conditions. Gutters are generally sloped more steeply than the roadway to increase runoff velocity.

The *AASHTO Green Book* suggests gutters have a cross-slope ranging from 5 to 8 percent, whereas ADAAG specifies a maximum 5 percent slope. The ADAAG provision is designed to prevent wheelchair users from hitting their footrests on the ramp or gutter and potentially being thrown forward out of their wheelchairs. A wider gutter can be used to drain larger volumes of water without increasing the slope experienced by curb ramp users. However, widening the gutter might require the purchase of additional right-of-way. According to the *AASHTO Green Book*, gutters formed in combination with curbs should range from 12 inches (30.48 centimeters) to 71 inches (180.34 centimeters) wide.

Storm drains and catch basins are normally placed where they will intercept surface water runoff. Installing a curb ramp at a point of strategic runoff interception can compromise effective drainage. Regrading the section of road or curb ramp location to alter drainage patterns can resolve some situations in which drainage concerns conflict with accessibility requirements.

Ideally, inlets should be placed uphill of crossings or curb ramps to drain water before it can puddle where pedestrians are crossing. In locations with heavy rainfall, more frequent drainage inlets, more strategic placement of inlets, and basin pickups will also reduce the frequency of puddles.

MAINTENANCE

Sidewalks are prone to damage caused by environmental conditions. Maintaining sidewalk elements in good condition is an essential part of providing access to public rights-of-way. Sidewalks in poor repair can limit access and threaten the health and safety of pedestrians. If sidewalks are in poor condition or nonexistent, pedestrians may be forced to travel in the street. Maintenance problems are usually identified by pedestrians who report the location to the municipal authorities. Identification of locations requiring maintenance may be done in conjunction with a city's accessibility improvement program. Effective maintenance programs are quick to identify conditions that can impede access and respond with repairs.

Assessing sidewalks for accessibility should be an integral part of maintenance survey programs. Some cities survey and repair all sidewalks in regular cycles. Other cities make or enforce repairs only if a complaint is filed. Cities also might have pavement management programs and personnel devoted entirely to inspecting and repairing damaged access routes. Sidewalk inspectors typically look for conditions that are likely to inhibit access or cause pedestrians to injure themselves. These include: step separation, badly cracked concrete, settled areas that trap water, tree root damage, and noncompliant driveway flares.

Although sidewalks are elements of the public right-of-way, many city charters assign the owner of the adjacent property with responsibility for sidewalk upkeep. It is common for city charters to specify that the city cannot be held liable for any accident or injury due to sidewalk conditions. Homeowners are commonly allowed to decide whether to hire a contractor, perform repairs on their own, or have the city do the repair. The homeowners' associations in some neighborhoods address right-of-way maintenance to minimize the cost to individual members. Some cities subsidize property owners for repairing sidewalks. Local laws also might dictate whether a homeowner must engage a professional contractor to undertake sidewalk repair. If municipal inspectors review and approve sidewalk repairs, the finished sidewalks are more likely to meet pedestrian access needs.

REFERENCES

American Association of State Highway and Transportation Officials.1995. *A Policy on Geometric Design of Highways and Streets: 1994 (The Green Book)*. Washington, DC.

Federal Highway Administration. 1999. *Designing Sidewalks and Trails for Access, Part I of II: Review of Existing Guidelines and Practices*. Washington, D.C.: U.S. Department of Transportation.

U.S. Department of Transportation. 2003. *Manual on Uniform Traffic Control Devices (MUTCD)*. Washington, D.C.

See also:
Federal Legislation
Hierarchy of Streets and Roads
Pedestrian-Friendly Streets
Street Networks and Street Connectivity
Traffic Calming
Walkability

GRADE, CROSS-SLOPE, AND CURB HEIGHT GUIDELINES BY FUNCTIONAL CLASS OF ROADWAY*

ROAD TYPE	MAXIMUM GRADE (%)[1] LEVEL/ROLLING/ MOUNTAIN	CROSS-SLOPE[3] (%)	CURB HEIGHT (MM)	SIDEWALK COVERAGE
Urban local	Consistent with terrain	1.5–6.0[4]	100–225	Commercial—both sides
	<15.0/<8.0[2]			Residential—at least one side
Rural local	8.0/11.0/16.0	1.5–6.0[4]	n/a	n/a[5]
Urban collector	9.0/12.0/14.0	1.5–3.0	150–225	Same as Urban local
Rural collector	7.0/10.0/12.0	1.5–3.0	n/a	n/a[5]
Urban arterial	8.0/9.0/11.0	1.5–3.0	150–225	n/a[5]
Rural arterial	5.0/6.0/8.0	1.5–2.0	n/a	n/a[5]
Recreational	8.0/12.0/18.0	n/a	n/a	n/a[5]

Source: Data based on AASHTO Green Book 1995.

*Chart does not include figures for freeways or divided arterials, which are not designed for pedestrians and are not built with sidewalks.

1. The lower the maximum speed permitted on the road, the steeper the grade is permitted to be. The numbers listed in the chart represent the lowest road speeds indicated in the AASHTO Green Book.

2. Residential/commercial or industrial.

3. The numbers listed in the chart indicate what the cross-slope should generally be for proper drainage.

4. Cross-slopes ranging from 3.0 to 6.0 percent should be used only for low surface types such as gravel, loose earth, and crushed stone.

5. Sidewalks are still needed, even though the AASHTO Green Book does not specify guidelines for sidewalk coverage along this road.

HIERARCHY OF STREETS AND ROADS

FUNCTIONAL CLASSIFICATION SYSTEM FOR URBAN STREETS

The functional classification system developed by the Federal Highway Administration (FHWA) in 1962 is widely used to define the traffic-carrying function of streets. For urban streets, there are four classifications: principal arterials, minor arterials, collector streets, and local streets.

Principal Arterials

Principal arterials provide long-distance "trunk-line" continuous routes within and between urban areas. Typically, but with some important exceptions, they carry high volumes of traffic at high speeds. Freeways, including interstates, are principal arterials.

Minor Arterials

The backbone of the urban street network, minor arterials are continuous routes through urban areas. They are frequently designated as touring (i.e., U.S. or state-numbered) routes. Accounting for only 10 percent of street mileage, they carry more than half of all vehicle miles of travel. They may be state, county, or city streets.

Most trips include arterial streets. They contain most of a city's commercial and institutional uses. The traffic function of minor arterial streets is challenged because of their attractiveness as business addresses, an attractiveness fostered by the traffic function of the street itself.

Collector Streets

With continuity over short segments (one-fourth to one-half mile; 0.4 to 0.8 kilometers), collector streets are minor tributaries, gathering traffic from numerous smaller (local) streets and delivering it to and from minor arterials. Seldom designated as numbered touring routes, collectors are usually city or county streets. Most collectors are bordered by properties (both business and residential) with driveways to the street.

Local Streets

Local streets include all streets not on a "higher" system. They comprise 90 percent of street mileage but carry less than 10 percent of the total vehicle miles of travel. These streets may be short in length or frequently interrupted by traffic control devices (stop signs or signals). Travel distance on local streets is short, typically to the nearest collector street. Speeds are low (20 to 30 mph; 32.2 to 48.3 kilometers/hour). Usually, local streets are city streets, and seldom are part of a numbered touring route. Local streets often have numerous driveways, as they are the addresses for most homes, as well as many nonresidential land uses (professional office, small industrial, churches) not requiring visibility to large numbers of passing motorists.

ACCESS AND MOBILITY

All urban streets provide some mixture of mobility and access. Mobility is the movement of through traffic with neither origin nor destination in the

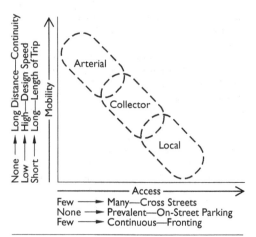

ACCESS, MOBILITY, AND RELATIONSHIP TO FUNCTIONAL CLASS

Source: Walter Kulash.

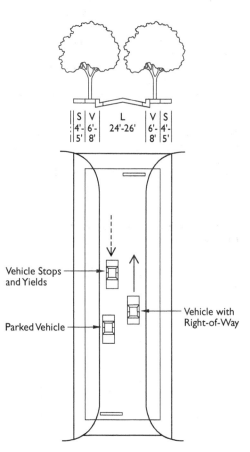

The single-lane yield street, the preferred design for residential streets (new and existing) in neighborhoods throughout the United States, allows for parking on both sides of the street and a single lane of moving traffic, in both directions, in the center of the street. At parked cars, motorists in opposite directions are not able to pass, and one driver yields right-of-way (usually by stopping at vacant curb space). When the intensity of parking prevents this yield flow, parking can be prohibited on one side, assuring an open lane for traffic in each direction.

SINGLE-LANE YIELD STREET

Source: Walter Kulash.

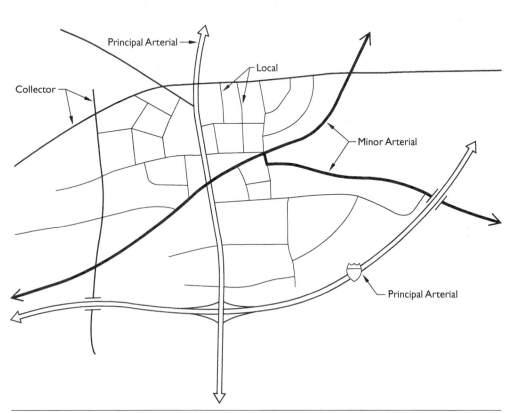

FUNCTIONAL CLASSIFICATIONS AND THEIR RELATIONSHIPS

Source: Walter Kulash.

Walter Kulash, P.E., Glatting Jackson Kercher Anglin Lopez Rinehart, Inc., Orlando, Florida

PART 3   STRUCTURES

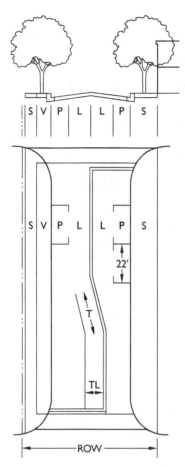

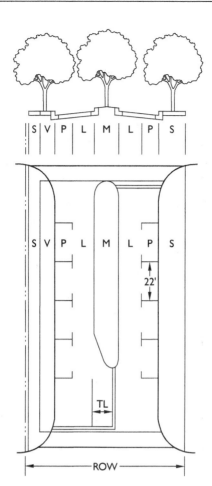

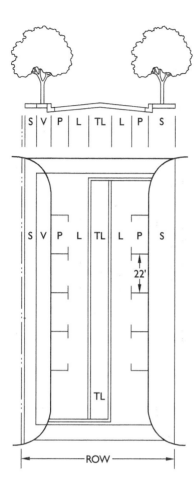

Important options for the two-lane street are on-street parking and left-turn lanes at major intersections. The left-turn lane is provided, without widening the street, by restricting parking as necessary.

Important options for the two-lane divided street are on-street parking and left-turn lanes at major intersections. The left-turn lane occupies the space otherwise used for the median.

The three-lane street, appropriate where large numbers of driveways and cross streets are present, accommodates left turns in a center two-way left-turn lane.

TWO-LANE STREET, UNDIVIDED

Source: Walter Kulash.

TWO-LANE STREET, DIVIDED

Source: Walter Kulash.

THREE-LANE STREET

Source: Walter Kulash.

STREET DIMENSIONS AND CROSS-SECTION ELEMENTS

DESIGN ELEMENT		FUNCTIONAL CLASS (IN FEET)		
		Arterial	Collector	Local
L	Traffic Lane	12	11	10
TL	Turning Lane	12	11	10
P	Parking Lane	8 to 10	8	7
M	Median	12 to 16	10 to 16	10 to 16
V	Verge (Planting Strip)	8 to 12	8 to 12	6 to 8
S	Sidewalk (Business)	12 to 18	12 to 18	12 to 18
S	Sidewalk (Residential)	5 to 6	4 to 5	4 to 5
T	Taper Length	60	40	30
R	Curb Radius	25	20	15 to 20

Walter Kulash, P.E., Glatting Jackson Kercher Anglin Lopez Rinehart, Inc., Orlando, Florida

TRANSPORTATION

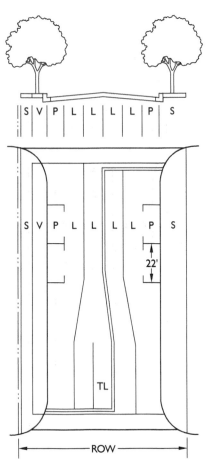

Multilane (four lanes or more) streets can accommodate left turns, at major intersections, by restricting parking at the intersection approach.

MULTILANE STREET, UNDIVIDED

Source: Walter Kulash.

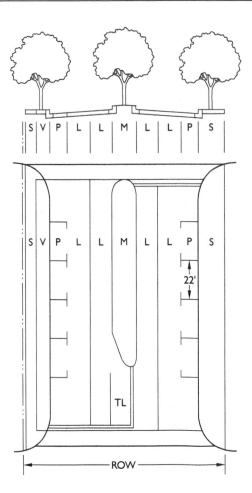

On multilane (four lanes or more) divided streets, the left turn occupies space otherwise used by the median.

MULTILANE STREET, DIVIDED

Source: Walter Kulash.

immediate area. Access is the connection to immediately fronting properties. Arterial streets, located at the mobility end of the mobility/access spectrum, provide large amounts of service to through traffic, but little or no access to surrounding land. Local streets, located at the access end of the spectrum, provide unlimited access to adjacent properties, but little service to through travel. Collector streets are in the midrange of the spectrum. They provide property access with mobility appropriate for connecting local streets to the higher-speed arterials.

EMERGING ISSUES

There are several ongoing initiatives to combine the traffic functional classification of streets with their adjacent land uses to yield a more comprehensive array of streets. The *Lexicon of the New Urbanism* proposes a structure for accomplishing this. The context-sensitive design initiative, sponsored by the Federal Highway Administration, urges state departments of transportation to make the road context an important part of road design.

REFERENCES

Duany Plater-Zyberk & Company. 1998. *Lexicon of the New Urbanism*. Miami, FL: Duany, Plater-Zyberk & Co.

U.S. Department of Transportation, Federal Highway Administration. 1998. *Flexibility in Highway Design*. Washington, DC: USDOT/FHWA.

See also:
Pedestrian-Friendly Streets
Sidewalks
Street Networks and Street Connectivity

Walter Kulash, P.E., Glatting Jackson Kercher Anglin Lopez Rinehart, Inc., Orlando, Florida

STREET NETWORKS AND STREET CONNECTIVITY

COMPONENTS OF STREET NETWORKS

With respect to their traffic function, there are four functional classifications of urban streets:

- Principal arterials
- Minor arterials
- Collector streets
- Local streets

Further descriptions of these street types can be found in Hierarchy of Streets and Roads. The information here focuses on their relationship to each other as part of larger street systems and in terms of their connectivity.

STREET SPACING GUIDELINES

Principal arterials should be located every three to four miles (4.83 to 6.44 kilometers) in urban areas. Minor arterials should be spaced at around one-mile (1.61-kilometer) intervals from other arterials (principal or minor).

Collector streets should be spaced roughly one-half mile (0.8 kilometers) from arterials. Local

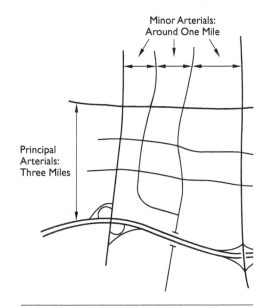

SPACING CRITERIA, PRINCIPAL ARTERIAL STREETS
Source: Walter Kulash.

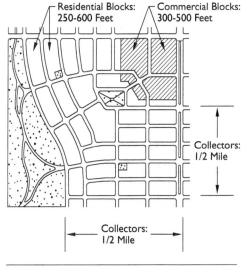

SPACING CRITERIA, COLLECTOR AND LOCAL STREETS
Source: Walter Kulash.

streets complete the network, with a block spacing appropriate to the land use—typically 300 to 500 feet (91.4 to 152.4 meters) in business districts and 250 to 600 feet (76.2 to 182.9 meters) in residential neighborhoods.

LOCAL STREET PATTERNS

The functions of local streets—to provide address and immediate access—can be accomplished equally well under a wide variety of network patterns. Typical street patterns include:

- Grid
- Grid and squares
- Web
- Radial
- Curvilinear
- Irregular

Regardless of pattern, the factors most important for traffic are connectivity and legibility.

STREET CONNECTIVITY

Street connectivity can be defined as the quantity and quality of connections in the street network. The purpose of the street network is to connect one place to another. The design of the street network determines how direct or indirect the connections are and governs the number of different paths that connect two places. A traditional rectilinear street grid provides relatively direct connections and multiple routes and thus has high connectivity. In contrast, the curvilinear networks dominated by cul-de-sacs that are more typical of modern suburban subdivisions often provide relatively indirect connections and few routes and thus have low connectivity.

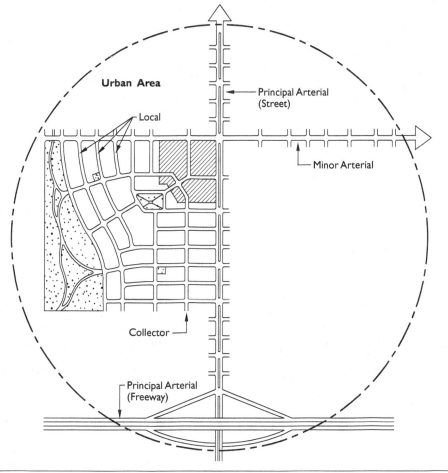

STREET TYPES AND THEIR RELATIONSHIPS
Source: Walter Kulash.

Walter Kulash, P.E., Glatting Jackson Kercher Anglin Lopez Rinehart, Inc., Orlando, Florida; Susan Handy, Ph.D., University of California at Davis, Davis, California

TRANSPORTATION

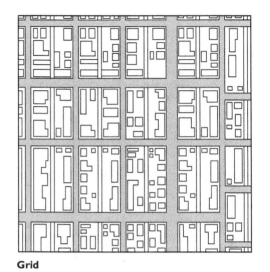

Grid

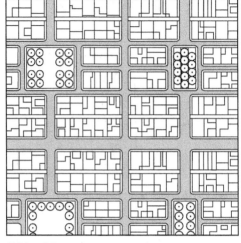

Grid and Squares

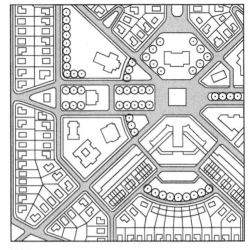

Web

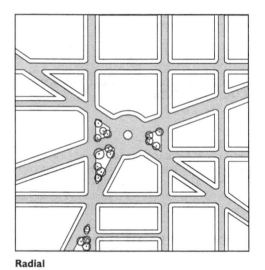

Radial

Curvilinear

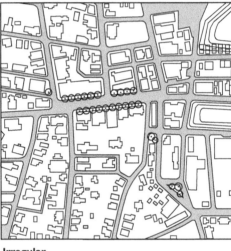

Irregular

TYPICAL STREET NETWORK PATTERNS

Source: Walter Kulash.

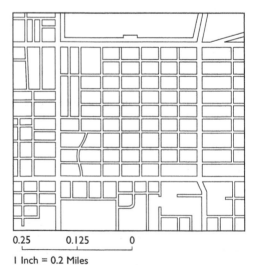

0.25   0.125   0

1 Inch = 0.2 Miles

A traditional rectilinear street grid provides relatively direct connections and multiple routes, thus has high connectivity.

HIGH-CONNECTIVITY NETWORK

Source: Handy, Paterson, and Butler 2003.

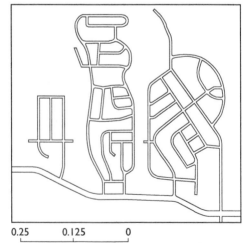

0.25   0.125   0

1 Inch = 0.2 Miles

Curvilinear networks dominated by cul-de-sacs often provide relatively indirect connections and few routes, thus have low connectivity.

LOW-CONNECTIVITY NETWORK

Source: Handy, Paterson, and Butler 2003.

Street connectivity has important implications for travel choices and emergency access. The distance from one point to another, as determined by the directness of the route through the street network, influences the choice to travel to that destination and by what mode. Longer distances reduce the likelihood that an individual will travel to that destination or will choose to walk or bike. For that reason, planners and public health officials have expressed concern that networks with low connectivity discourage walking and biking, thereby increasing vehicle travel and reducing physical activity. Emergency service providers have also expressed concern over low-connectivity networks, which may contribute to longer response times and limit the number of routes for emergency access or evacuation.

Range of Connectivity of Local Streets

In traditional American towns, both historical and neotraditional, all local streets were connected. In a number of cities, the requirement for connectivity now focuses on connection in major compass directions, rather than on connection of all local streets. Connectivity at the collector street level can be main-

Walter Kulash, P.E., Glatting Jackson Kercher Anglin Lopez Rinehart, Inc., Orlando, Florida; Susan Handy, Ph.D., University of California at Davis, Davis, California

PART 3   STRUCTURES

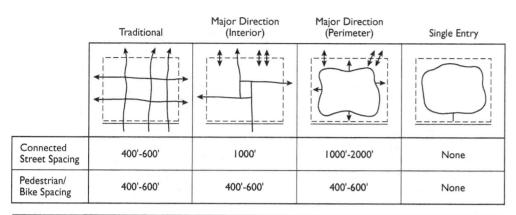

	Traditional	Major Direction (Interior)	Major Direction (Perimeter)	Single Entry
Connected Street Spacing	400'-600'	1000'	1000'-2000'	None
Pedestrian/ Bike Spacing	400'-600'	400'-600'	400'-600'	None

RANGE OF STREET CONNECTIVITY

Source: Walter Kulash.

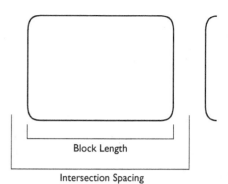

Block Length

Intersection Spacing

Block lengths are usually measured as the distance from curb face to curb face of intersecting streets; intersection spacing is measured as the distance between centerlines for intersecting streets.

MEASURING BLOCK LENGTH AND INTERSECTION SPACING

Source: Handy, Paterson, and Butler 2003.

tained even with inward-turned residential subdivisions. The unconnected subdivision with a single access point, a major contributor to arterial street congestion, is not advisable and is now precluded by a growing number of local land development regulations.

Connectivity Standards

The design of the street network is determined by standard practices and by local land development codes. Many cities specify minimum block lengths and otherwise encourage street networks that discourage through traffic by minimizing connectivity. However, a growing number of cities in the United States have adopted street connectivity standards that encourage greater connectivity in the street network (Handy et al. 2003). These cities have used one of two techniques to establish street connectivity standards: block length requirements or connectivity indexes.

Block Length Standards

By establishing a block length standard, cities control the spacing between local streets. These requirements can take the form of a maximum allowed block length or a maximum allowed intersection spacing. The two forms are essentially equivalent, although the exact measurements may

vary depending on the widths of streets and rights-of-way. Block lengths are usually measured as the distance from curb face to curb face of intersecting streets, while intersection spacing is measured as the distance between centerlines for intersecting streets.

Maximum block length requirements typically fall into the range of 300 to 600 feet (91.4 to 182.9 meters). A variation on this approach is to restrict block size, measured as width by length, number of acres, or block perimeter. Block length standards are usually coupled with significant restrictions on cul-de-sacs, with lengths limited to 200 to 300 feet (61 to 91.4 meters) and use limited to places where street connections would be impractical.

Connectivity Index

A connectivity index is the ratio of the number of links to the number of nodes in the network. Links are street segments, while nodes are intersections. A higher connectivity index reflects a greater number of street segments entering each intersection and thus a higher level of connectivity for the network. Cities have established different rules for counting nodes and links at the boundary of the area of interest. These different rules lead to slightly different values of the index for the same network. Minimum standards for connectivity indexes typi-

cally fall into the range of 1.2 to 1.4. Cities using a connectivity index usually do not restrict the use of cul-de-sacs, as long as the minimum connectivity standard is met.

Connectivity in Practice

Street connectivity standards are often accompanied by other standards that affect the street network. Some cities have adopted connectivity standards that apply specifically to connections between residential areas and arterials. More commonly, cities incorporate requirements for street stubs and the mapping of future streets into their connectivity requirements as a way of ensuring connectivity with future streets. Most cities with connectivity standards have adopted narrower street standards to avoid a net increase in the amount of paving associated with the street network and to discourage the use of residential streets for through traffic. Cities often couple restrictions on gated communities with connectivity standards, and many cities have adopted separate standards for bicycle and pedestrian connections as well. Cities have adopted different packages of standards depending on local conditions and objectives.

EXAMPLES OF STREET CONNECTIVITY STANDARDS

CITY	CONNECTIVITY STANDARD FOR LOCAL STREETS	MAXIMUM INTERSECTION SPACING FOR ARTERIALS (FEET)	STREET STUBS REQUIRED	CUL-DE-SACS ALLOWED	MAXIMUM CUL-DE-SAC LENGTH (FEET)	MAXIMUM SPACING BETWEEN BIKE/PEDESTRIAN CONNECTIONS (FEET)	LOCAL STREET WIDTHS (FEET)	GATED STREETS ALLOWED
Portland, OR	530 feet maximum intersection spacing	530	Yes	No	200	330	Sufficient to accommodate expected users	No
Fort Collins, CO	Maximum block size 7 to 12 acres	660 to 1320	Yes	Limited	660	700	24 to 36	No
Raleigh, NC	660 feet maximum intersection spacing in mixed-use centers	n/a	Yes	Yes	400 to 800	n/a	26	Discouraged
Cary, NC	Connectivity index = 1.2	1,250 to 1,500	Yes	Yes	900	If index waived	27	No
Orlando, FL	Connectivity index = 1.4	n/a	Yes	Yes	700	n/a	24	No

Source: Adapted from Handy, Paterson, and Butler 2003.

Walter Kulash, P.E., Glatting Jackson Kercher Anglin Lopez Rinehart, Inc., Orlando, Florida; Susan Handy, Ph.D., University of California at Davis, Davis, California

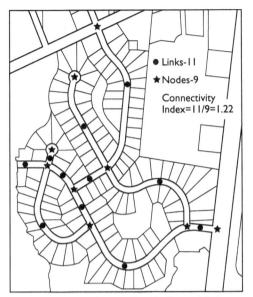

Include Nodes with Arterials But No External Links

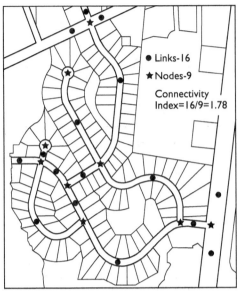

Include Nodes with Arterials and One Link Beyond
Last Node

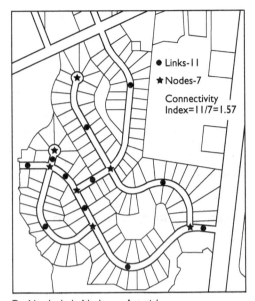

Do Not Include Nodes on Arterials

Cities have established different rules for counting nodes and links at the boundary of the area of interest, and
these different rules lead to slightly different values of the index for the same network, as shown in the illustration.

COMPARISON OF RULES FOR CONNECTING NODES AND LINKS

Source: Handy, Paterson, and Butler 2003.

ISSUES

Connectivity standards are relatively new, and many
questions about their use and effectiveness remain to
be answered. The issues to be resolved include the
following:

- Defining what is the most appropriate way to
  measure connectivity.
- Determining how much connectivity is the right
  amount.

- Identifying what is the best network design for
  achieving the desired level of connectivity.
- Understanding what street connectivity means for
  modes other than the automobile.
- Learning how can connectivity in commercial areas
  be improved.
- Finding ways that cities can increase connectivity in
  existing street networks.

As more cities adopt standards for street connectivity,
the answers to these questions should become clearer.

REFERENCE

Handy, Susan, Robert G. Paterson, and Kent Butler.
2003. *Planning for Street Connectivity: Getting from
Here to There*. Planning Advisory Service Report No.
515. Chicago: American Planning Association.

See also:
Hierarchy of Streets and Roads
Pedestrian-Friendly Streets
Walkability

*Walter Kulash, P.E., Glatting Jackson Kercher Anglin Lopez Rinehart, Inc., Orlando, Florida; Susan Handy, Ph.D., University of California at Davis,
Davis, California*

VEHICLE TURNING RADII

DESIGN VEHICLES FOR URBAN STREETS

The vehicle to be accommodated—the design vehicle—is an important control in the design of urban streets. The most important characteristic of the design vehicle, its turning radius, dictates intersection design. For urban streets, four design vehicles are defined in the American Association of State Highway and Transportation Officials (AASHTO) *Green Book*.

> **Passenger Vehicle (P):** Includes automobiles, vans, SUVs, and light trucks.
>
> **Single-Unit Truck (SU-30):** Used for most local commercial and home deliveries and municipal services.
>
> **Conventional School Bus (S-BUS-36):** The standard school bus.
>
> **Tractor-Trailer (WB-50):** In increasing use for delivery to businesses.

SELECTING THE APPROPRIATE DESIGN VEHICLE

Design vehicles are selected according to the intended traffic use or functional classification of the street. A design for a small vehicle (for example, Passenger Vehicle, "P") does not preclude a street's use by larger vehicles, but may require that larger vehicles encroach into other lanes or directions of traffic while making intersection-turning movements.

Vehicle Turning Radii

Important elements of turning radii are the wheel paths, which define the needed width of pavement, and the front overhang, which is the zone beyond the pavement edge that must be clear of obstructions above curb height. The turning movement templates are shown for a right turn, typically the most constricted on urban streets. For left turns, the turning template is simply the reverse of those shown.

Encroachment by Design Vehicles at Intersections

All intersections must accommodate the P template without encroachment on either the approach or departure leg. Large vehicles, operating on streets designed for smaller vehicles, can encroach into other lanes, in both the same and opposite directions of travel.

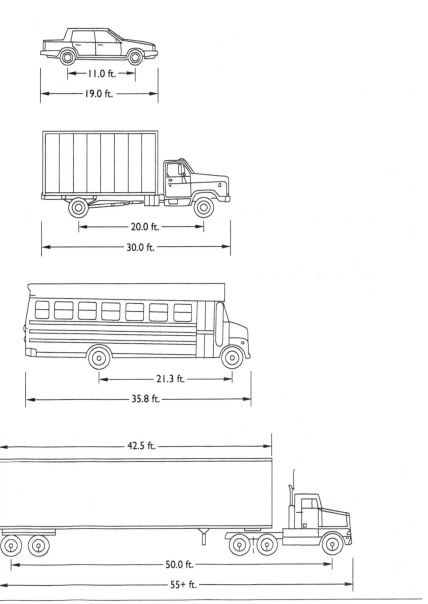

DESIGN VEHICLES FOR URBAN STREETS

Source: Walter Kulash.

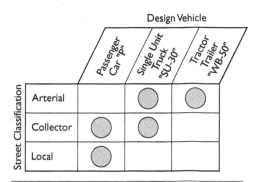

DESIGN VEHICLE AND FUNCTIONAL CLASSIFICATION OF STREET

Source: Walter Kulash.

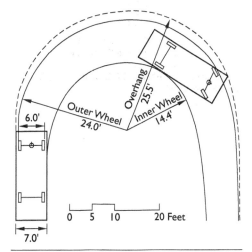

PASSENGER CAR (P) TURNING RADIUS

Source: Walter Kulash.

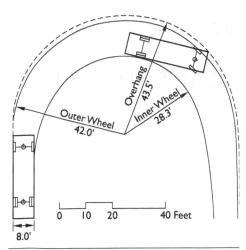

SINGLE-UNIT TRUCK (SU-30) TURNING RADIUS

Source: Walter Kulash.

Walter Kulash, P.E., Glatting Jackson Kercher Anglin Lopez Rinehart, Inc., Orlando, Florida

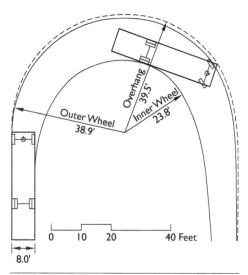

CONVENTIONAL SCHOOL BUS (S-BUS-36) TURNING RADIUS

Source: Walter Kulash.

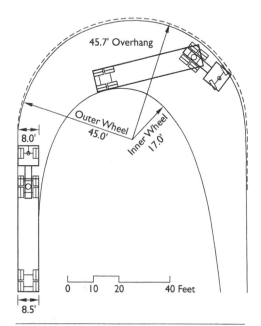

TRACTOR-TRAILER (WB-50) TURNING RADIUS

Source: Walter Kulash.

Use Full Departure Leg

Use Full Approach and Departure Leg

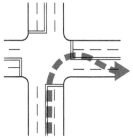

Encroach across Departure Centerline

Encroach across Approach and Departure Centerline

PERMISSIBLE ENCROACHMENTS AT INTERSECTION

Source: Walter Kulash.

PERMISSIBLE ENCROACHMENTS

Approach Street	DEPARTURE STREET		
	Arterial	Collector	Local
Arterial	1	2	3
Collector	2	3	4
Local	2	4	4

Note:
1 = Use full departure leg.
2 = Use full approach and departure leg.
3 = Encroach across departure centerline.
4 = Encroach across approach and departure centerline.

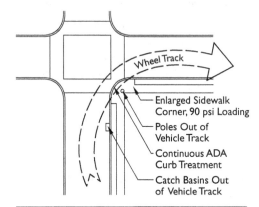

REAR WHEEL TRACK ACROSS CURB AT INTERSECTION

Source: Walter Kulash.

On very narrow streets, large vehicles, in particular the WB-50 vehicles, may be accommodated at intersections by permitting the rear wheel of the trailer to track across the sidewalk.

Additional Information

Vehicle turning radii, as established by AASHTO, are based on broad categories of vehicle types, each of which encompasses a wide variety of actual vehicles on the road. Information on passenger vehicle dimensions for parking design, provided elsewhere in this section, provides a more detailed breakdown of vehicle types within the various categories. For off-street design applications, such as parking and driveways, the more detailed versions are appropriate. For public streets, the AASHTO templates provided here are definitive.

REFERENCE

American Association of State Highway and Transportation Officials 2001. *A Policy on Geometric Design of Highways and Streets (the "Green Book")*. Washington, DC: AASHTO.

See also:
Hierarchy of Streets and Roads

Walter Kulash, P.E., Glatting Jackson Kercher Anglin Lopez Rinehart, Inc., Orlando, Florida

TRAFFIC CALMING

The Institute of Transportation Engineers (ITE) defines traffic calming as the combination of mainly physical measures that reduce the negative effects of motor vehicle use, alter driver behavior, and improve conditions for nonmotorized street users (*ITE Journal,* July 1997). The American Planning Association describes it as a form of traffic planning that seeks to equalize the use of streets among automobiles, pedestrians, bicyclists, and playing children (Hoyle 1995). However it is defined, traffic calming is part of a nationwide change in how we are building our transportation system.

Traffic calming measures have been used primarily on residential streets but are sometimes used on collectors and arterials. Communities are increasingly using center medians in roadways, along with other traffic calming measures to create boulevards and parkways as alternatives to standard arterial streets.

TRAFFIC CALMING TOOLS

A variety of devices and techniques are used to help reduce traffic speed and volume. Detailed information on engineering and aesthetic issues, legal authority and liability, emergency response, and other issues can be found in *Traffic Calming: State of the Practice,* published by ITE in cooperation with the Federal Highway Administration (FHWA) (Ewing 1999).

Traffic calming measures impact both vehicle speed and volume on roadways. The ITE publication classifies traffic calming measures according to their dominant effect. Combinations of various measures can dramatically affect both speed and volume when properly applied. Illustrations shown here provide examples of traffic calming devices and applications, divided into categories based on the ITE model.

Traffic Calming Program Models

Many communities use traffic calming programs that include the "three Es"—education, enforcement, and engineering. These programs involve major campaigns to educate the public and increase enforcement in problem areas, in addition to implementing traffic calming programs.

In traffic calming programs, the most important elements are public involvement and procedures for selection of appropriate traffic calming devices. Poor public input processes can result in a failed traffic calming program.

Public Input Processes

Traffic calming programs are either in reaction to citizen requests for action or a result of staff identifying problems and initiating action. Traffic calming can be

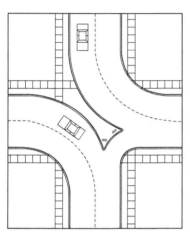

Forced Turns
Traffic islands or other barriers installed at intersections force turning movements and prevent through traffic.

Source: Appleyard 1980.

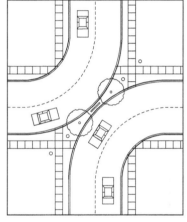

Diagonal Diverters
Raised islands or other barriers are used to block through movement at intersections.

Source: Appleyard 1980.

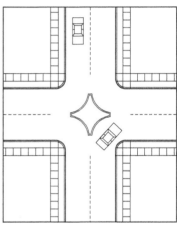

Star Diverter
A star diverter is a barrier placed at intersections to prevent through movement.

Source: Appleyard 1980.

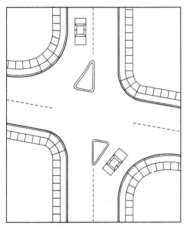

Forced-Turn Islands
Raised islands placed at intersections force turning movements and prevent through traffic.

Source: Ewing 1999.

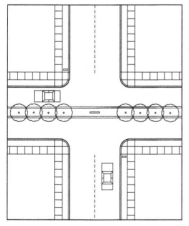

Median Barriers
Raised islands installed along the centerline of a street intersection block through and left-turn movements.

Source: Appleyard 1980.

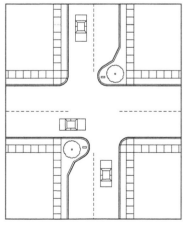

Half Closures or Semidiverters
These barriers placed at intersections block only half of a street and are used to make travel through a neighborhood circuitous.

Source: Appleyard 1980.

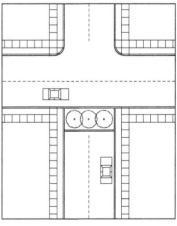

Street Closures and Cul-de-sacs
These barriers, placed at an intersection or midblock, prevent through traffic.

Source: Appleyard 1980.

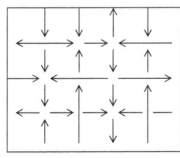

One-Way Maze
One-way streets can be used to control travel through a neighborhood.

Source: Appleyard 1980.

VOLUME CONTROL DEVICES

Cynthia L. Hoyle, AICP, Urbana, Illinois

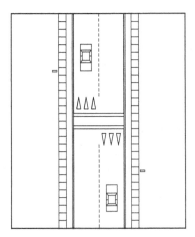

Speed Humps

Speed humps are raised humps extending across the road. ITE guidelines recommend they be 12 feet long, 3 to 4 inches high, and parabolic in shape, with a design speed of 15 to 20 mph.

Source: Appleyard 1980.

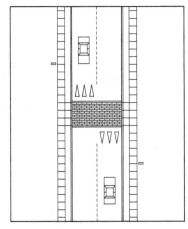

Raised Crosswalks

Raised crosswalks are speed humps with flat tops marked for pedestrian crossings. They bring the street up to the sidewalk level, increasing pedestrian visibility and safety.

Source: Appleyard 1980.

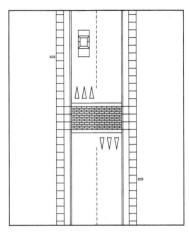

Speed Tables

A speed table is a flat-topped, raised platform that is long enough for both wheels of a car to be on top of the table at the same time. Most speed tables are 3 to 4 inches high and 22 feet long in the direction of travel.

Source: Appleyard 1980.

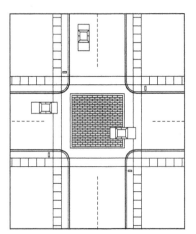

Raised Intersections

A raised intersection is a flat-topped area that covers the entire intersection. They are usually raised to sidewalk level, approximately 6 inches. Approach ramps should not exceed a gradient of 16 percent.

Source: Ewing 1999.

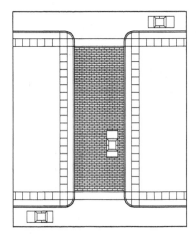

Textured Surfaces

Textured surfaces are usually used in conjunction with other traffic calming devices, but may be used alone.

Source: Appleyard 1980.

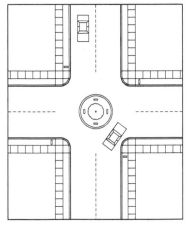

Traffic Circles

A traffic circle is a raised island located at an intersection around which traffic has to circulate. Yield signs are often placed on all four approaches. Traffic circles are used on residential streets in lieu of four-way stop signs.

Source: Appleyard 1980.

SPEED CONTROL DEVICES

Cynthia L. Hoyle, AICP, Urbana, Illinois

PART 3   STRUCTURES

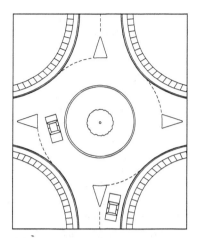

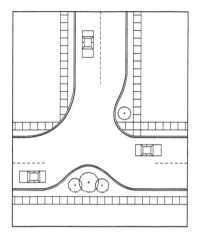

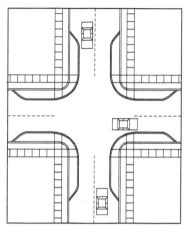

Roundabouts

Roundabouts are circular raised islands installed at intersections on higher-volume streets such as collectors and arterials and are often used in place of traffic signals or four-way stops. They require yield-at-entry design and must be well marked and visible. Roundabouts have been found to have significantly lower accident rates than signalized intersections with equivalent speed limits.

Source: Ewing 1999.

Realigned Intersections

Used at T-intersections, these realign the straight approach into a curving street to slow drivers.

Source: Ewing 1999.

Neckdowns

Neckdowns are curb extensions at intersections used to reduce the roadway width. They are also called bulbouts, curb extensions, or intersection narrowings.

Source: Appleyard 1980.

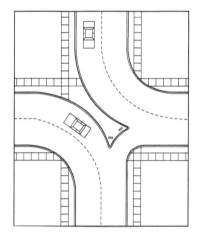

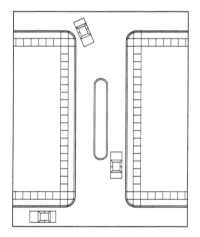

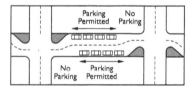

Chicanes

Chicanes are streets on which curb extensions alternate from one side of the street to the other, thereby creating S-shaped curves. They reduce both speed and volume. Design must prevent cut-through driving down the centerline. European manuals recommend shifts in alignment of at least one lane width.

Source: Appleyard 1980.

Chokers

Chokers are narrowing devices similar to neckdowns. They are used at midblock to narrow the street and slow drivers.

Source: Ewing 1999.

Center Island Narrowings

Raised islands located along the centerline of the street narrow the travel lanes and slow drivers.

Source: Ewing 1999.

SPEED CONTROL DEVICES *(continued)*

Cynthia L. Hoyle, AICP, Urbana, Illinois

applied to only one problem area, or it may involve study and implementation of an areawide program. Some communities have used warrants for traffic calming programs. Warrants are minimum requirements that should be met before a device is installed. Warrants are used in most communities for installation of traffic signals and stop signs (Ewing 1999).

In most communities, local officials have found that, for a traffic calming program to achieve success, a majority of the local residents must be in favor of it. Many communities require that 60 to 70 percent of the affected property owners agree to the proposed program through a petition signature or vote. Neighborhood workshops and charrettes are two techniques that can be used to gain community input and support.

The basic steps in most traffic calming programs are to:

1. identify the problem by residents or staff;
2. analyze the problem to verify and define it;
3. identify alternatives and techniques to address the problem;
4. select a plan or program with public input;
5. approve the plan by the majority of residents in the neighborhood and official governing body;

6. design, construct, and implement the plan; and
7. monitor, modify, and evaluate the results.

COMMON ISSUES

Local officials and staff have concerns about how traffic calming affects liability, safety, emergency response, and service vehicle access. Bicyclists have raised concerns about safety with traffic calming devices, such as traffic circles. In response to these concerns, the FHWA launched a national traffic calming technical assistance project in partnership with ITE. The report *Traffic Calming: State of the Practice* was published as a result of this program and provides extensive information on each of the issues raised (Ewing 1999).

Local officials have to coordinate traffic calming programs with other service providers. Prior to installing a traffic calming device, officials must notify local emergency response providers, including fire, police, and ambulance, and the local transit and school systems. Some communities use traffic cones to demarcate proposed traffic circles and other devices and conduct tests using fire trucks and buses. Installation of temporary devices and collection of traffic data before and

after installation is sometimes used to ensure that the correct device and design have been selected prior to the expense of a permanent installation.

REFERENCES

Appleyard, Donald. 1980. *State of the Art: Residential Traffic Management.* Washington, DC: Federal Highway Administration.

Ewing, Reid. 1999. *Traffic Calming: State of the Practice.* Washington, DC: Institute of Transportation Engineers and U.S. Department of Transportation, Federal Highway Administration.

Lockwood, Ian M. July 1997. "ITE Street Calming Definition," *ITE Journal.* 67, no. 7:22–24.

Hoyle, Cynthia. 1995. *Traffic Calming.* Planning Advisory Service Report No. 456. Chicago, IL: American Planning Association.

See also:
Pedestrian-Friendly Streets
Sidewalks
Walkability

Cynthia L. Hoyle, AICP, Urbana, Illinois

PEDESTRIAN-FRIENDLY STREETS

Pedestrian-friendly streets are designed to be more accommodating to pedestrian traffic than are conventionally designed streets. Pedestrian traffic here includes bicyclists, the physically handicapped, transit users, and those of all ages on foot. Pedestrian-friendly streets include yield or queuing streets along with narrower vehicular traffic lanes. Yield streets require that one vehicle yield to another as they pass. Parking density works in part to control that type of movement.

Pedestrian-friendly streets are becoming a popular design strategy for creating walkable neighborhoods, new or retrofitted. This trend is associated with smart growth, context-sensitive design, new urbanism, and other current land development approaches.

Efforts to calm traffic in walkable environments through street design have demonstrated a reduction in accident severity, accident frequency, and environmental impact. Both pedestrian and vehicular accident severity is reduced when vehicles are traveling at slower speeds. When designed properly, narrower streets have design speeds either equal to or less than 20 miles per hour. The Abbreviated Injury Scale (AIS) indicates that when vehicles travel above 20 miles an hour, the potential for serious injury increases greatly.

SCALE AND CONTEXT

Context is the single most important variable in determining the suitable width for a pedestrian-friendly street. The dimensions of the street will vary depending on several factors, including but not limited to:

- parking configuration;
- building use;
- degree/type of nonmotorist activity;
- truck traffic percentage;
- Americans with Disabilities Act (ADA) requirements;
- location within the urban fabric; and
- transit use.

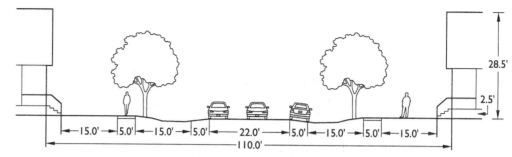

This street type is appropriate at the urban edge in a more rural condition. It may also have open space on one side that defines the edge of the neighborhood. Open drainage, ornamental tree species, and low-density residential land use are typical. Average daily trip (ADT) ranges of up to 250 are common; under special circumstances this may be extended to 400. The recommended building separation to height ratio is 4:1, although 5:1 may be used depending on urban context.

LOW ADT YIELD STREET

Source: Peter Swift.

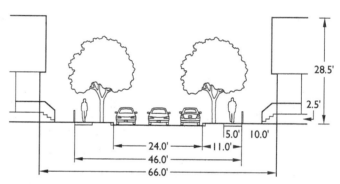

This street type belongs on short blocks and between the edge and center of a neighborhood. Average daily trips (ADT) should not be more than 250 vehicles per day. Single-family detached building types should predominate. The recommended building separation to height ratio is 3:1, although 4:1 may be used depending on urban context.

EDGE YIELD STREET

Source: Peter Swift.

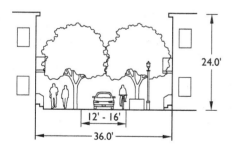

This is the narrowest of the urban street types. Residential building types and live-work units should front a woonerf. It is a pedestrian-dominant street that meanders through a portion of the neighborhood. The ratio of building separation to building height should be at 1.5 or less. Planters, trees, benches, bike racks, and other nonvehicle-oriented elements should be introduced in the street environment. Most of the area between the buildings is paved with the traveled way (12 to 16 feet wide; 3.7 to 4.9 meters) of a different material. Bollards are useful to define the vehicle path.

WOONERF

Source: Peter Swift.

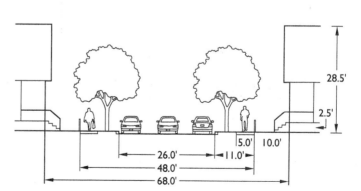

This is a typical residential street. Parking density must be evaluated to accommodate emergency vehicle access and operation. It is framed by one species of tree, closed drainage, offset sidewalks (at least 5 feet (1.5 meters) wide), and a building-separation-to-height ratio of 3:1.

AASHTO RECOMMENDED RESIDENTIAL STREET

Source: Peter Swift.

Peter Swift, P.E., Swift Associates, Longmont, Colorado

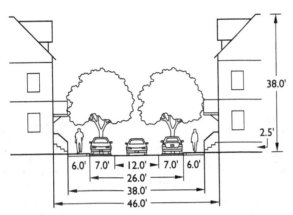

This modification of the AASHTO-recommended residential street places the street trees within the parking lane. This application is used within areas of relatively low parking density, to slow vehicular speeds. The recommended building-separation-to-height ratio is 3:1.

MODIFIED AASHTO RESIDENTIAL STREET

Source: Peter Swift.

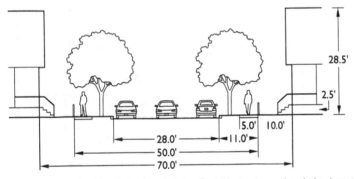

Detached residential and attached residential and mixed-use buildings front this street type, though the character of the street is still predominantly residential. Sidewalks generally are detached (5-foot (1.5-meter) minimum), but in areas of higher density the sidewalks can be attached and at least 10 feet wide. A retail condition may require 12- to 15-foot (3.7- to 4.6-meter) wide sidewalks. The building-separation-to-height ratio of 3:1 should be maintained.

YIELD STREET

Source: Peter Swift.

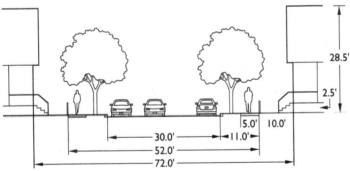

This street type is not a yield condition, but the travel lanes should be narrower than conventional types in a walkable environment. It would therefore be classified as a narrow street. It contains both attached and detached residential in addition to commercial, retail, and mixed-use buildings. The curb face width with parallel parking may be as much as 34 feet (10.4 meters) in an area that includes truck traffic, multistory buildings, and mix of land use. If diagonal parking is used, the width will increase. It is important to use narrower lanes that range from 9 to 11 feet (2.7 to 3.4 meters) in walkable urban conditions. If the street exists in primarily mixed-use conditions, an 8-foot parking lane will be required, for an overall width of 36 feet (11 meters). Building-separation-to-building height ratios should be 3:1 maximum.

NONYIELD STREET

Source: Peter Swift.

Peter Swift, P.E., Swift Associates, Longmont, Colorado

PART 3   STRUCTURES

The street should have parking allowed on both sides as a minimum in all circumstances. This helps reduce speeds, keeps the driver alert, and accommodates activity between the public and private realm.

Context is also relevant to federal, state, and local authorities for both infill and new development projects in urban areas. Federal funding mechanisms for thoroughfare projects require certain criteria be met for the project to qualify, such as the funding of street improvements for redevelopment or new development along state highways. A number of design techniques at the federal level recognize the importance of narrower lanes, wider sidewalks, and transit and access design criteria for pedestrians, bicyclists, and the physically handicapped. There are similar design techniques supported on state and local levels.

STANDARDS

Conventional thoroughfare design standards are based primarily on *A Policy on the Geometric Design of Highways and Streets* (AASHTO 2001) and previous editions. Thoroughfare types include arterial, collector, and local streets, in urban and rural contexts. They are described in terms of vehicle mobility and access; arterial streets are almost exclusively dedicated to vehicular mobility. However, the language used to define these thoroughfare types is not complex enough to properly describe a walkable environment. For about 50 years, transportation design literature has described pedestrians as "friction" or "interference." This further supports vehicle dominance in many traffic design techniques.

Recent design publications from recognized national engineering organizations, including the American Association of State Highway and Transportation (AASHTO), Institute of Transportation Engineers (ITE), Transportation Research Board (TRB), and others, have begun to focus more attention on the nonmotorist and to develop evolving walkability design strategies. Local and state departments of transportation have also begun to develop context-sensitive design approaches.

LAW AND REGULATION

When working with nonstandard design guidelines, liability of the owner of thoroughfares must be considered. Governmental immunity is preserved through the adoption and enforcement of design guidelines. Therefore, jurisdictions should adopt standards by law for pedestrian-friendly streets. If the design is approved as an exception to adopted regulations, there may be some liability exposure, even if there are substantial citations and cases referenced. If the jurisdiction has a single development that needs pedestrian-friendly street design standards, in most cases the adopted ordinance can have provisions exclusive to that development. It is also important to refer to state law when making these decisions.

If the street is in private ownership, the reviewing jurisdiction's scrutiny can address only the operation and maintenance of public utilities, along with emergency and public vehicle access. Because streets must accommodate the needs of utilities and emergency responders, the jurisdiction can have some limited influence in the design of the street, which could create a legally confusing situation. For example, if an accident victim on a narrower street sues the private owner and the public entity, both parties can be at a disadvantage. A clear establishment of the public right-of-way as public property, along with design criteria adopted by ordinance, may avoid these ambiguities and potential legal battles.

DESIGN ELEMENTS

Narrow, pedestrian-friendly streets are best suited to mixed-use, walkable neighborhoods. Therefore, it is important to understand the elements that inform street design.

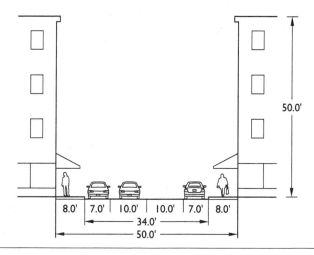

1:1 RATIO
Source: Peter Swift.

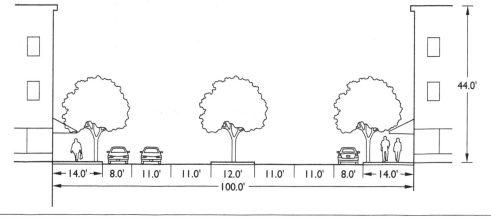

2:1 RATIO
Source: Peter Swift.

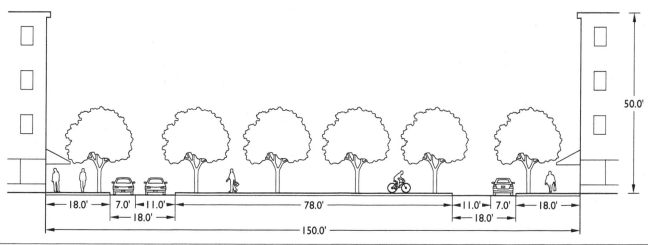

3:1 RATIO
Source: Peter Swift.

Building Enclosure

Building enclosure—the relationship of street and buildings—defines urban space. Analysis of enclosure and urban space is important for achieving a certain aesthetic for the scale, comfort, character, and use of the street as a public room.

The aesthetic of a pedestrian-friendly street relies partly on how the public space is defined by buildings. Building enclosure is defined by the ratio of building separation to building height. For example, a building 50 feet (15.2 meters) high that is 150 feet (45.7 meters) from the building across the street has a ratio of 3:1. Building ratios of 1:1 to 4:1 generally require narrower streets. Ratios approaching 6:1 may lose a perceptible sense of enclosure and should be avoided.

Amenities

The walkability of a street also relies on comfort and safety. Street trees, awnings, arcades, and conditions where at least one side of the street is in shade in the summer all help protect pedestrians from the sun and elements. Because narrower streets have slower vehicular traffic, noise, accident frequency, and accident severity are reduced.

Streets that are accommodating to pedestrians enhance overall street liveliness. Shoppers are attracted to stores when vehicles travel slower and their occupants can look into the windows; thus, economic vitality is enhanced as well.

When choosing to include pedestrian-friendly streets in a design, establish a connected network of streets. This helps disperse traffic and still gives emergency vehicles a number of ways to respond to an incident. Narrower streets are not recommended for cul-de-sac and branchlike thoroughfare patterns.

REFERENCE

American Association of State Highway and Transportation Officials. 2001. *A Policy on the Geometric Design of Highways and Streets*. Washington, DC: AASHTO.

See also:
Hierarchy of Streets and Roads
Sidewalks
Street Networks and Street Connectivity
Traffic Calming
Walkability

Peter Swift, P.E., Swift Associates, Longmont, Colorado

PARKING LOT DESIGN

Parking lots should offer direct and easy access for people walking between their vehicles and the building entrances. Pedestrians usually walk in the aisles behind parked vehicles; aisles perpendicular to the building face allow pedestrians to walk to and from the building without squeezing between parked cars. Walking areas should be graded to prevent standing water.

Where possible, parking lots should be designed to have reduced paved areas, to minimize runoff problems, and to provide areas for trees and other vegetation.

Provide access for fire rescue and transit vehicles as well as safe and efficient circulation routes. Accessible design requires designating parking spaces and curb ramps near building entrances. See information on sidewalks elsewhere in this section for accessible ramp design criteria.

REFERENCE

CHANCE Management Advisors 1991. *Alternative Parking Development Scenarios.* Philadelphia, Pennsylvania.

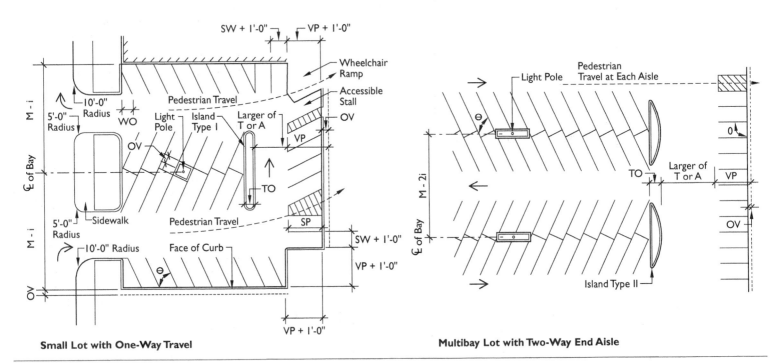

Small Lot with One-Way Travel

Multibay Lot with Two-Way End Aisle

LOT DESIGNS WITH ISLANDS

Source: Architectural Graphic Standards, 10th edition 2000.

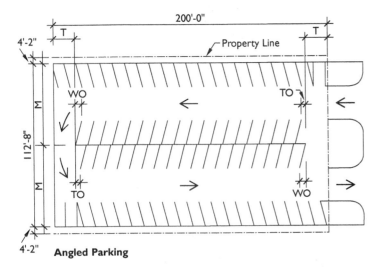

Angled Parking

Notes:
1. GPA = 200 ft × 56.33 ft × 2 = 22,532 sq ft
2. Capacity = 80 vehicles
3. Efficiency = 22,532 sq ft/80 vehicles = 281.7 sq ft/space

90° Parking

Notes:
1. GPA = 200 ft × 60.5 ft × 2 = 24,200 sq ft
2. Capacity = 80 vehicles
3. Efficiency = 24,200 sq ft/80 vehicles = 302.5 sq ft/space

SMALL LOT DESIGNS

Source: Architectural Graphic Standards, 10th edition 2000.

Mary S. Smith, P.E., Walker Parking Consultants, Indianapolis, Indiana

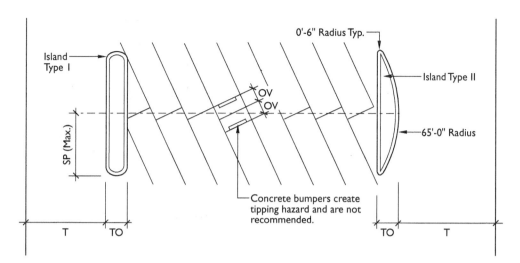

Key to Drawings

Abbreviation	Term
Θ	Angle of Park
A	Aisle Width
i	Interlock Reduction
GPA	Gross Parking Area
M	Module
OV	Overhang
R	Radius
SP	Stripe Protection
SW	Stall Width
T	Turning Bay
VP	Vehicle Projection
WO	Wall Offset
TO	Turning Bay Offset

TYPICAL PARKING BAY WITH ISLAND TYPES

Source: Architectural Graphic Standards, 10th edition 2000.

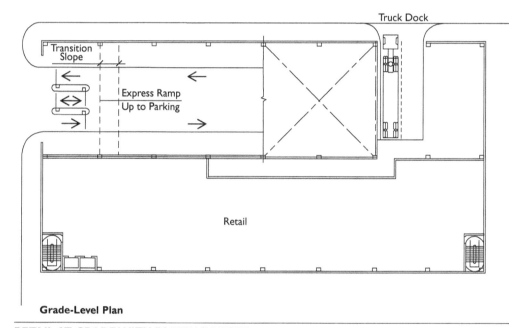

Grade-Level Plan

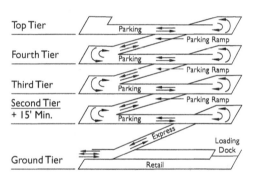

Isometric

RETAIL AT GRADE WITH PARKING ABOVE

Source: Mary Smith.

Mary S. Smith, P.E., Walker Parking Consultants, Indianapolis, Indiana

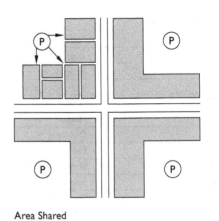

Area Shared

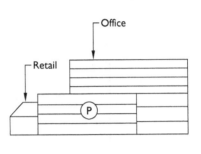

Destination Shared

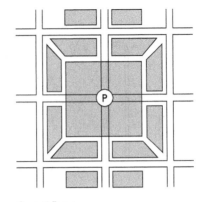

Central Focus

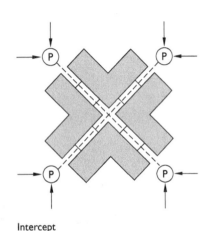

Intercept

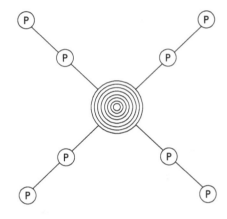

Regional Intercept

Notes:

Area-shared facility: Provides parking for essentially all uses within a reasonable walking distance.

Destination-shared facility: Targets a specific project or several uses in proximity to each other. May be private development or a public/private venture.

Central focus facility: Satisfies parking demand in a facility in the center of activity, with pedestrian system that emanates out to the various destinations.

Intercept facility: Provides parking at the perimeter of the activity center. May involve pedestrian ways or, in larger communities, a shuttle system to various destinations.

Regional intercept facility: Like the intercept facility model, provides parking outside the core activity area. Key to this model's success is a regional transportation system that provides convenient access to the activity center.

PARKING DEVELOPMENT OPTIONS

Source: Walker Parking Consultants. 1992. Downtown Denver Parking Strategy. Indianapolis, IN.

		Short-Term Parking					
		Laissez Faire	Area Shared	Destination Shared	Central	Intercept CBD	Intercept Regional
Long-Term Parking	Laissez Faire	●	◐	●	◐	◐	◐
	Area Shared	○	○	●	◐	◐	◐
	Destination Shared	○	◐	●	◐	◐	◐
	Central	◐	◐	◐	◐	◐	◐
	Intercept CBD	○	○	●	◐	◐	◐
	Intercept Regional	○	○	●	◐	◐	◐

Key:

● Scenario worthy of further analysis.

◐ Scenario has disadvantages that outweigh advantages.

○ Scenario does not support goals.

MATCHING LONG- AND SHORT-TERM PARKING STRATEGIES

Source: Mary Smith.

Mary S. Smith, P.E., Walker Parking Consultants, Indianapolis, Indiana

PART 3   STRUCTURES

Goals	Laissez Faire (ST) Laissez Faire (LT)	Destination-Shared (ST) Laissez Faire (LT)	Destination-Shared (ST) Area Shared (LT)	Destination-Shared (ST) Destination-Shared (LT)	Destination-Shared (ST) CBD-Intercept (LT)	Destination-Shared (ST) Regional-Intercept (LT)
1. To facilitate access to downtown while meeting air quality goals, including strategies to promote transit ridesharing.	■	■	○	■	○	√
2. To coordinate parking facility development with transportation systems (vehicular and pedestrian) to and within downtown.	■	■	√	■	√	√
3. To coordinate parking facility development with the development or redevelopment of other downtown property and desired density patterns.	■	■	√	○	√	√
4. To develop parking facilities that serve shared parking needs.	■	○	√	√	○	○
5. To integrate appropriately designed parking (structure and surface) as a suitable land use (permanent or temporary).	■	■	√	○	○	√
6. To create mechanisms to assure that the appropriate amount of storage is provided for various classifications of vehicles (short-term parkers, long-term parkers, HOV, buses, etc.) that enter downtown.	■	■	√	√	√	√
7. To provide a financially self-supporting parking system.	■	○	○	√	○	○
8. To minimize impact on residential areas from parking generated by commercial land uses.	■	■	■	■	○	√

Key: √ Supports Goal   ■ Opposes Goal   ○ Neither Supports nor Opposes Goal

ALTERNATIVE PARKING DEVELOPMENT SCENARIOS

Source: CHANCE Management Advisors, Inc. 1991.

See also:
Sidewalks

Mary S. Smith, P.E., Walker Parking Consultants, Indianapolis, Indiana

TRANSPORTATION

ON-STREET BIKEWAYS

On-street bikeways bring enormous benefits to both the cycling and noncycling public. Bikeways create opportunities to incorporate exercise into one's daily routine, and bring air, noise, and water quality benefits. They use public dollars efficiently by reducing road maintenance costs and increasing the carrying capacity of the transportation system. Bikeways improve safety for all users; bicyclists feel they have a safe space on the road and tend to be more law-abiding, and motorists are placed at greater ease knowing where bicyclists are apt to be. Bikeways also help motorists to be aware of the presence of bicyclists and their right to be on the road.

Bikeway planning and implementation can be relatively simple and inexpensive, as when a public works agency includes bikeways as part of new roadways or restripes a roadway with bicycle lanes during a routine resurfacing. Bikeways can also be complicated and costly, particularly in built urban environments with space constraints. Moreover, the installation of bikeways may not always be desirable from the public's perspective—for example, if parking has to be removed to install bicycle lanes or if traffic must be diverted to create a bicycle boulevard.

National guidelines for the planning and design of on-street bikeways are provided through the American Association of State Highway Transportation Officials (AASHTO). Standards for signing and striping of on-street bikeways are found in the *Manual on Uniform Traffic Control Devices* (U.S. Department of Transportation/FHWA 2003); and many states and local jurisdictions have their own standards and guidelines. In addition, many localities are developing new innovations in on-street bikeway design, such as shared lane markings (San Francisco; Gainesville, Florida; Denver), bicycle-only traffic signals (Davis, California), colored bicycle lanes at intersections (Portland, Oregon), and innovative bicycle boulevard treatments (Berkeley, California). The Association of Pedestrian and Bicycle Professionals (APBP) provides information on emerging on-street bikeway designs.

Specific issues need to be addressed in the design of on-street bikeways:

- Sight lines and topography
- Lane widths for all travel modes
- Intersection design
- Signing, markings, and striping
- Design of drainage inlet grates
- Pavement conditions
- Specific design for pinch points, driveways, railroad crossings, and other challenging areas
- Integration with off-street shared-use trails/paths

TYPES OF BIKEWAYS

Bicycle Lane

A bicycle lane is that portion of the roadway designated by 6- to 8-inch (15.24- to 20.32-centimeter) striping and bicycle pavement markings for the exclusive or preferential use of bicycles. Bicycle lanes are typically provided on collector and arterial streets. Bicycle lanes can be implemented by:

- narrowing existing travel lanes;
- removing a travel lane;

- removing parking; and
- widening a roadway or paving a shoulder.

Bicycle lanes may be implemented through standalone bikeway projects, roadway construction or reconstruction, and routine roadway resurfacing.

Some streets have circumstances that make bicycle lane installation difficult. These circumstances include:

- harm to the natural environment or character of the natural environment due to additional pavement;
- severe topographical constraint;
- economic or aesthetic necessity of retaining parking on one or both sides of the street; and
- unmanageable levels of traffic congestion that

would result from eliminating travel lanes or reducing lane widths.

If bicycle lanes are deemed unfeasible, alternative improvements may be substituted, examples of which are described below. Other potential treatments include providing a bicycle lane in only one direction, such as in the uphill direction on a steep slope; using shared lane markings, as cities like San Francisco are doing; or directing cyclists to a parallel bikeway.

Bike Route

A bike route, also called a shoulder bikeway, is a street upon which the paved shoulder, separated by a 4-inch (10.2-centimeter) stripe, is usable by bicycles, although

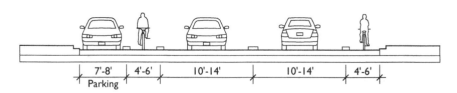

BICYCLE AND TRAVEL LANE DIMENSIONS

Source: Alta Planning & Design 2004.

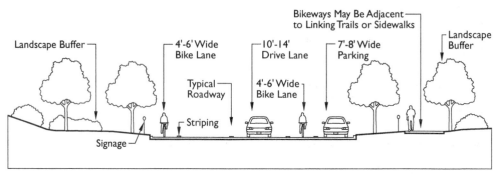

Bike lanes are often found along urban road sections, where maneuvering space is limited and a defined lane is needed for rider safety.

BIKE LANE

Source: Brauer & Associates, Ltd. 2004.

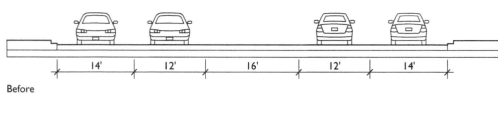

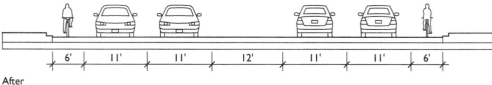

INTEGRATING BICYCLE LANES INTO EXISTING TRAVEL LANES

Source: Oregon Department of Transportation 1995.

Mia Birk, Alta Planning & Design, Portland, Oregon

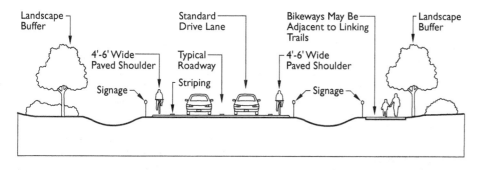

Bike routes, also called shoulder bikeways, are often constructed along rural road sections with no curb and gutter.

BIKE ROUTE

Source: Brauer & Associates, Ltd. 2004.

auto parking may also be allowed on it. These bikeways are typically provided on rural roadways.

Signed Shared Roadway

Signed shared roadways are bikeways without separated bicycle lanes. Bicyclists and motorists are expected to share the outside lane. There are three variations: extra-wide curb lane, bicycle boulevard, and signed bike route.

Extra-Wide Curb Lane

An extra-wide curb lane is a wider-than-normal curbside travel lane provided to give extra room for bicycle operation where there is insufficient space for a bicycle lane or shoulder bicycle lane. Wide curb lanes have proven to be as safe as bicycle lanes; however, they often do not attract bicycle users, particularly novice or family bicyclists, and thus do little to increase bicycle use in a community.

Bicycle Boulevard

On a bicycle boulevard, bicycles and motor vehicles share the space, which does not have marked bicycle lanes. The through movement of bicycles is given priority over motor vehicle travel on a local street. Traffic calming devices are used to control traffic speeds and discourage through trips by motor vehicles. Traffic control devices are designed to limit conflicts between automobiles and bicycles, and favor bicycle movement on the boulevard street. Typically, bicycle boulevard treatments are designed for local or collector roadways with relatively low volumes of traffic.

Bicycle boulevard design treatments continue to emerge and are highly complementary to traffic calming programs and projects, safe routes to school projects, and other neighborhood desires. However, the impact on through-traffic movement from traffic calming devices can be a point of controversy.

Signed Bike Route

A signed bike route is a bikeway upon which guide signing is placed to direct bicyclists to a destination or another bikeway. Signed connections are used on local, low-traffic streets where bicycle lanes or bicycle boulevards are not needed and on and around major recreational cycling destinations. They should not be used as a substitute for appropriate treatments on collectors and arterials but may work well for short connections and in coordination with a comprehensive bikeway network.

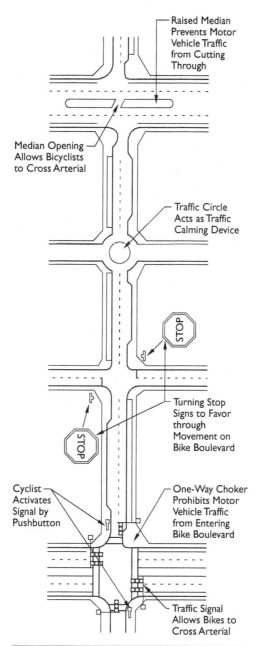

TYPICAL BICYCLE BOULEVARD FEATURES

Source: Oregon Department of Transportation 1995.

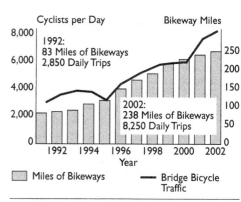

BICYCLE USE TRENDS: PORTLAND, OREGON

Source: City of Portland, Oregon.

BIKEWAY SELECTION AND NETWORK DEVELOPMENT

The appropriate treatment for on-street bikeways depends on motor vehicle traffic volumes, speeds, street width, topography, presence and use of on-street parking, and type of traffic (e.g., presence of freight traffic.) The selection approach varies considerably from jurisdiction to jurisdiction; for example, communities, such as Corvallis, Oregon, provide on-street marked bicycle lanes on all collector and arterial streets, and a few communities use only wide curb lanes and signage. Guidance on methodologies to select appropriate bikeway types is provided in *Bicycle Facility Selection: A Comparison of Approaches* (King, 2002) available through the National Bicycle and Pedestrian Information Clearinghouse.

A number of communities (e.g., San Francisco; Cambridge, Massachusetts; Chicago; and Gainesville, Florida) strive to provide a comprehensive bikeway network through a combination of bicycle lanes, neighborhood bicycle boulevards/routes, and off-street shared paths, as developed through a bicycle master planning process. This is clearly the most effective way to increase bicycle use and improve safety. For example, Portland, Oregon, has implemented an extensive network of more than 180 miles (290 kilometers) of on-street bicycle lanes and boulevards. As a result, bicycle use has increased more than 200 percent on its downtown bridges, and bicycle commuting has more than doubled, according to local counts and the 2000 U.S. census. Some of Portland's neighborhoods have bicycle commute mode shares of more than 4 percent. The increase in bicycle usage has been in lockstep with the increase in bikeway facility mileage, while the number of bicycle-motor vehicle crashes has remained flat.

REFERENCES

King, Michael. 2002. *Bicycle Facility Selection: A Comparison of Approaches.* Chapel Hill, NC: Pedestrian and Bicycle Information Center, Highway Safety Research Center, University of North Carolina at Chapel Hill.

U.S. Department of Transportation/FHWA. 2003. *Manual on Uniform Traffic Control Devices* (MUTCD). Washington, DC: USDOT/FHWA.

See also:
Multiuser Trails
Traffic Calming

Mia Birk, Alta Planning & Design, Portland, Oregon

TRANSPORTATION

MULTIUSER TRAILS

Contemporary trail planning at the local and regional levels focuses on creating integrated trail systems that accommodate a range of users, including walkers, hikers, bicyclists, and inline skaters. Trails that accommodate these most common uses are the focus here.

On a more limited basis, mountain bike, equestrian, and off-leash dog trails are also provided in local and regional trail systems. In northern climates, winter-use trails for cross-country skiing, dog sledding, and skijoring are also common. Off-highway vehicle trails and snowmobile trails are specialized trails common to state-level trail systems. Although not specifically considered here, planners should consider these important types of trails when planning trail systems at the local and regional levels.

FACTORS IN TRAIL PLANNING

Recreational Value

Contemporary trail system planning places great emphasis on the recreational "value" of an individual trail and the trail system as a whole. Preference studies clearly indicate that the vast majority of trail users are seeking a recreational experience while using trails; fitness, transportation, and commuting are secondary concerns. Trails offering a high-quality recreational experience are those that:

- are visually appealing and located in a pleasant, natural open space or linear park corridor that is away from traffic and the built environment;
- provide a continuous experience that takes users from their neighborhood to a variety of destinations (and is a destination unto itself);
- offer continuity with limited interruptions and impediments to travel;
- are not too difficult of a grade; and
- are safe for a family to use, as well as those with limited technical skills.

The notion of a trail's recreational value inherently affects community planning and development. Planning for trails following greenways through private developments and public open spaces is considerably different from planning for trails that follow a roadway right-of-way. Whereas greenway-based trails may be more difficult to implement, the value of those trails to the community far exceeds the challenges they present. Communities with success in integrating these types of trails into their system plan often advertise them as key aspects of the city's built form and quality of life.

Skill Level

One of the important factors in developing a trail system plan is recognizing the broad needs and skill levels of individual trail users. This is especially the case with bicyclists, in which the skill level varies considerably, as follows:

Experienced riders. Generally use their bicycles for fitness or transportation. Speed, convenience, and directness are important factors in route selection. Although they are comfortable riding in traffic, adequate operating space is important to safe riding and avoiding confrontations with motor vehicle operators.

Recreational riders. Typically use their bicycles for recreation and fitness, less so for transportation. These riders tend to avoid busy roads with higher traffic speeds, unless there is a defined area for bicyclists, such as a wide shoulder or a designated bikeway. These riders are generally comfortable riding on local streets and busier trails.

Youth and children. Tend to be slower and less confident than adults. Children use trails for recreation and getting to key destinations in the community, such as schools, convenience stores, parks, and recreational facilities. Residential streets with low motor vehicle speeds are acceptable, but trails are preferred by this group (and their parents).

Trail systems should be planned to accommodate the least skilled bicyclists while still being of interest to the most skilled. Also, trails that are designed to accommodate bicyclists will also be suitable for walkers and inline skaters.

Accessibility

The level of accessibility varies between trail types. In general, the level of accessibility should be consistent with the user expectation, as well as applicable law. In application, this means that multiuse hard-surfaced trails, as classified here, should be accessible to the majority of the population wherever possible. This typically means grades of less than 5 percent.

Accessibility as it relates to nature trails focuses on creating "like experiences" over uniform accessibility. There is often an expectation by the public that these trails will range from easy and accessible to difficult and strenuous. Trail opportunities within each trail system should be planned for the majority of citizens, recognizing that not all trails will be accessible to all people. Clearly marked trailhead and trail signage is critical to users selecting trails that suit their needs and abilities.

TRAIL CLASSIFICATIONS

The distinction between trail types, or classifications, is as much about their location and recreational value as it is about technical design considerations. The user experience and skill level associated with different types of trails greatly affects the value of the system to residents and the degree to which a trail or system of trails will be used. The classifications purposefully correlate with desired user experience, with emphasis on the quality of experience.

The classifications are meant to be guidelines, not rigid standards. Each community must refine and apply them to suit their specific needs. The following provides an overview of the classifications for the most common trail use associated with a typical local and regional trail system.

Destination Trail

This type of trail is often a destination unto itself due to its location and recreational appeal. Destination trails are located within a greenway, natural area, parkway, or designated trail corridor and typically accommodate walkers, bicyclists, and inline skaters.

In areas of low- to modest-use levels, a shared use trail is common. In higher-use areas, separating walkers from bicyclists and inline skaters is also common.

The essential characteristics of a destination trail emphasize harmony with a natural, sometimes park-like setting and the user's recreational experience. The trail allows for relatively uninterrupted pedestrian movement to and through a natural area, the community, or larger park and open-space system. Destination trails also separate trail users both physically and psychologically from vehicular traffic and are, therefore, suitable for all skill levels.

General Design Characteristics

Creating a compelling recreational experience that includes a variety of landscapes and community settings is a design priority in the design of destination trail. Providing an interesting sequence of visual experiences is often as important as the length of the trail to many users.

Asphalt/bituminous is a common surfacing material for destination trails and can be used in most climates. Crushed compacted aggregate surfacing is also acceptable for less traveled trails or those in a natural setting. Concrete surfacing is suitable where long term durability and/or patterned textures are desired. Concrete is not as well suited in climates where freeze-thaw cycles can create problems with expansion and contraction of crack control joints, which can make for a much rougher ride.

Trail width varies considerably depending on the anticipated level of use, length, and setting. Local trails within a neighborhood are typically a minimum of 8 feet (2.4 meters) wide. A 10-foot-wide (3-meter-wide) trail is the desired minimum for primary corridors that traverse through a community or region following a major greenway, parkway, or designated trail corridor. A 12-foot-wide (3.7-meter-wide) trail is becoming more common for regional facilities in a metropolitan area where use levels are high.

One-way directional trails are becoming more common along major greenway or parkway corridors in large urban areas. These trails are used to increase capacity, improve safety, and provide a more pleasant visitor experience. Each directional trail is a minimum of 8 feet (2.4 meters) wide, with 10 feet (3 meters) preferred. A 10-foot (3-meter) minimum green boulevard between trails is typical, with 20 feet (6 meters) or 30 feet (9 meters) preferred.

The design speed varies from 10 to 15 mph (16.1 to 24.1 kph) in a neighborhood setting up to around 20 mph (32.2 kph) for major trails. Most riders pedal at around 12 to 16 mph (19.3 to 25.8 kph), with elite recreational riders maintaining as high as 22 to 25 mph (35.4 to 40.2 kph). Generally, trails should be designed for around 20 mph (32.2 kph) to accommodate most riders. Any higher design speed can encourage riders to go too fast, and then be unable to react to others on the trail. (Most accidents are caused by collisions with other trail users, not trail design.)

Sight distances on all trails should be a minimum of 50 feet (15.2 meters), with 100 feet (30.5 meters) or more preferred. Longer sight distances may be required when trails traverse long open stretches or encounter steeper gradients where higher riding speeds occur.

Jeffrey Schoenbauer, Brauer & Associates, Ltd., Edina, Minnesota

Trail gradients should average less than 5 percent to be considered an accessible trail, with 3 percent preferred. Eight to 10 percent gradients are acceptable for moderate distances. Grades in excess of 10 percent should be avoided.

The cross-slope on a trail should be around 1.5 percent. Excessive cross-slope (beyond 2 percent) is too noticeable and an annoyance to walkers. Super-elevating trails greater than 3 percent can cause accessibility issues and are generally not recommended.

Overhead clearance on trails should be a minimum of 10 feet (3 meters). A shoulder area of grass or compacted gravel should be a minimum of 2 feet (0.6 meters) on each side, with 4 feet (1.2 meters) being desirable prior to grade changes or physical impediments.

Other design characteristics include:

- roadway crossing must be at safe locations as determined in the field;

- trail amenities, such as benches, signage, picnic areas, drinking fountains, and emergency shelters, should be provided at appropriate locations;
- trail lighting is usually provided at intersections and for security. Occasionally, lighting of an entire trail occurs, as in popular walking areas in urban areas; and
- access for general public safety and maintenance vehicles is an important site-specific factor.

Linking Trail

The significant difference between linking (connector) and destination trails is their location, which significantly affects their recreational value. Whereas destination trails emphasize a recreational experience in a natural open space or parklike setting, linking trails emphasize safe travel for pedestrians to and from parks and around the community. In general, linking trails are located within road right-of-ways and utility easements. Once a linking trail enters a park, it technically becomes a destination trail, due to

the setting and higher recreational value. Linking trails still provide notable recreational value, but significantly less than destination trails, due to vehicular traffic (safety, noise, distraction) and a less visually attractive setting. Like destination trails, linking trails are suitable for all skill levels.

General Design Characteristics

Providing a safe connection between specific destinations is a design priority. Recreational value remains important, but the setting is generally less compelling than that of a destination trail. Asphalt/bituminous is a common surfacing material for linking trails, though crushed compacted aggregate surfacing is also acceptable. Concrete surfacing is suitable where long term durability and/or patterned textures are desired. Concrete is not as well suited in climates where freeze-thaw cycles can create problems with expansion and contraction of crack control joints, which can make for a much rougher ride.

Trail width varies considerably depending on the anticipated level of use. Local trails along a roadway are typically a minimum of 8 feet (2.4 meters) wide. A 10-foot-wide (3-meter-wide) trail is the desired minimum for primary corridors where parks, schools, public facilities, and business districts are located.

Along busy thoroughfares with extensive trail destinations, a trail along both sides of the road is more common.

The design speed for linking trails is fairly consistent with destination trails. Ten to 15 mph (16.1 to 24.1 kph) is suitable for a neighborhood setting, and up to around 20 mph (32.2 kph) for trails along major thoroughfares. Overall trail speeds are often lower than destination trails due to the number of roadway crossings and driveways, which force bicyclists to slow down. Generally, trails should be designed to a similar standard as destination trails.

Sight distances on all trails should be a minimum of 50 feet (15.2 meters), with 100 feet (30.5 meters) or more preferred. Longer sight distances may be required when trails traverse long open stretches or encounter steeper gradients where higher riding speeds occur.

Trail gradients should average less than 5 percent to be considered an accessible trail, with 3 percent preferred. Eight to 10 percent gradients are acceptable for moderate distances. Grades in excess of 10 percent should be avoided.

The cross-slope on a trail should be around 1.5 percent. Excessive cross-slope (beyond 2 percent) is too noticeable and an annoyance to walkers. Super-elevating trails greater than 3 percent can cause accessibility issues and are not recommended.

Overhead clearance on trails should be a minimum of 10 feet (3 meters). A shoulder area of grass or compacted gravel should be a minimum of 2 feet (0.6 meters) on each side, with 4 feet (1.2 meters) desirable prior to grade changes or physical impediments. A 10-foot (3-meter) minimum boulevard should be provided between the trail and roadway. More space is preferred where right-of-way space allows.

Other design characteristics include:

- roadway crossings must be at safe locations, as determined in the field;
- trail amenities, such as benches, signage, and drinking fountains, should be provided;
- trail lighting is usually provided at intersections and for security; and

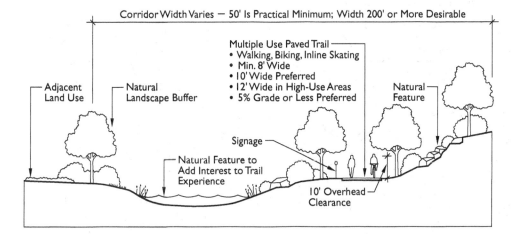

Destination trails emphasize recreational experience in a natural open space or parklike setting. They are located within a greenway, natural area, parkway, or designated trail corridor and typically accommodate walkers, bicyclists, and inline skaters.

DESTINATION TRAIL

Source: Brauer & Associates, Ltd.

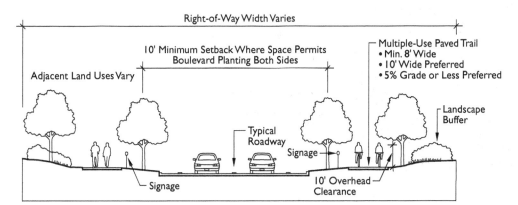

Linking trails emphasize safe travel for pedestrians to and from parks and around the community. They are generally located within road right-of-ways or utility easements, but can also be through parkland.

LINKING TRAIL

Source: Brauer & Associates, Ltd.

Jeffrey Schoenbauer, Brauer & Associates, Ltd., Edina, Minnesota

• access for general public safety and maintenance vehicles, which is an important site-specific design factor.

Nature Trail

Nature trails are located in greenways or natural resource-based parks and open spaces where experiencing the natural environment is the primary objective, along with exercise and quiet space. The character, length, and level of difficulty of nature trails can vary significantly from open prairie and woodlands to mountainous terrain.

General Design Characteristics

The overarching design theme for nature trails is simple and intimate, in keeping with the setting. Also key is to provide "like" experiences for people of varying physical abilities. Shaping the trail layout to conform to the landscape and creating a sequence of visual experiences is critical to creating a successful nature trail. Notable landscape features, topographic

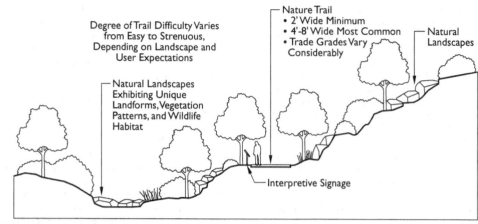

Nature trails are located in greenways or natural resource-based parks and open spaces where experiencing the natural environment is the primary objective, along with exercise and quiet space. They are typically unpaved.

NATURE TRAIL

Source: Brauer & Associates, Ltd.

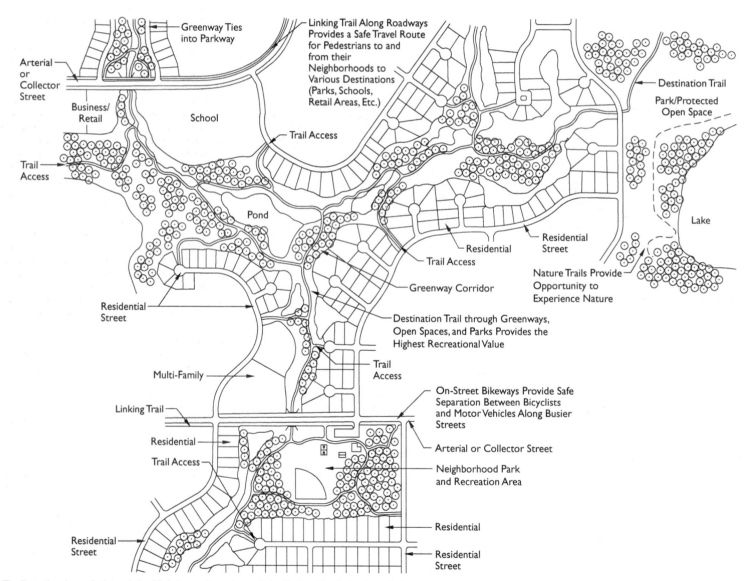

The illustration shows the interrelationship between the various trail classifications. The destination trails form the backbone of a typical trail system, with linking trails primarily used to tie the system together.

TRAIL RELATIONSHIPS

Source: Brauer & Associates, Ltd.

Jeffrey Schoenbauer, Brauer & Associates, Ltd., Edina, Minnesota

PART 3   STRUCTURES

changes, and vegetation patterns are all used to create appealing visual experiences that engage the trail user and cause them to linger and return.

Nature trails are generally surfaced with natural soils, turf, crushed aggregate, or other selected natural material. Grades on nature trails will vary, perhaps considerably. Ruggedness and strenuous trails are often part of the desired experience: easy trails have gradients of 3 to 5 percent; moderate trails have gradients of 8 to 10 percent; steep and strenuous gradients are often over 10 percent.

Sustainability of nature trails is a major design concern. Gradients, soil erosion, and compaction all affect trail stability and sustainability. "Rolling grade" design techniques that factor in alignments, tread grades, sideslopes, tread crests and dips, and erosion prevention are commonly used to create sustainable nature trails.

Trail width varies considerably depending on the anticipated level of use, length, and setting. Remote trails are often footpaths a couple of feet wide. Trail widths of 4 to 8 feet (1.2 to 2.4 meters) are common in local and regional park settings.

Additional design characteristics include:

- overhead clearance on trails should be a minimum of 8 feet. Heavy brush is typically cleared away a minimum of 2 feet on either side of the trail;
- trail amenities, such as benches, interpretive signage, and observation areas, should be provided;
- small trailside shelters for protection from storms or sun; and
- trail lighting, which is usually provided at the entrance to the trails and within adjoining parking lots.

TECHNICAL DESIGN STANDARDS

These classifications are general guidelines to be used for trail system planning. Technical design and development of each type of trail requires site-specific technical evaluation and engineering to ensure public safety.

See also:
Greenways and Trails
On-Street Bikeways

Jeffrey Schoenbauer, Brauer & Associates, Ltd., Edina, Minnesota

TRANSPORTATION

TRANSIT SYSTEMS

The transit planning process can be condensed into four primary elements of a continuous feedback and review cycle: systems planning, service planning, service implementation, and performance measurement.

1. *Systems planning.* Systems planning estimates total regional transit travel demand based on the analysis of regional land uses and activity center special trip generators, assesses the transit market by distributing trips across the region, and differentiates the transit market by defining trips according to their type and length.
2. *Service planning.* Trips are assigned to the mode best suited to serve specific trip types. Service is optimized for frequency, passenger capacity, and service quality.
3. *Service implementation.* Service implementation requires knowledge of two specific capital elements: vehicle fleet and facilities. Fleet requirements are determined by the peak number of vehicles required to operate the given service plus the number of vehicles needed to accommo-

date regular maintenance schedules and to cover vehicles unexpectedly taken out of service. Transit facilities generally include fleet storage and maintenance as well as passenger facilities.

4. *Performance measurement.* Performance measurement is required for regular input to the service planning element to accommodate regular service adjustments to meet customer demands. In addition, periodic performance input is required for the systems planning element of the process.

MARKET DEMAND, ASSESSMENT, AND DIFFERENTIATION

Metropolitan planning organizations (MPO) estimate total travel demand. Demand is based on the evaluation of land uses and accepted trip generation rates.

Following estimation of total transit market demand, transit trips are distributed across the region connecting suburban nodes, regional activity centers, and the urban core.

Based on this market assessment, trips can be differentiated as follows:

- Local circulation within nodes, major activity centers, and the urban core
- Internodal trips connecting nodes, activity centers, and the core
- Regional trips traversing multiple nodes, activity centers, or the urban core

MODE SELECTION/MODAL TOOLBOX

Applying the proper service to each market segment requires an understanding of the operating characteristics of the available modes and their fit within the transportation system. Transit modes are differentiated by average speed, carrying capacity, availability as measured by average distance between stops (called stop spacing), and the level to which exclusive rights-of-way are required to realize optimum operations from each mode.

BUS TRANSIT

Bus transit involves using rubber-tired vehicles that, for the most part, operate on fixed schedules and routes on a roadway. According to the American Public Transportation Association, buses comprise the majority of the total U.S. public transportation fleet. For many communities, bus transit is the only fixed-route transit option available. Diesel, gasoline, battery, or alternative fuel-powered engines contained within the vehicles power them.

TYPES OF SERVICE

There are three primary types of bus service: local, express, and limited-stop. These services can be used alone or in combination with other transit modes.

Local Service

With local service bus transit the vehicles stop every block or two along the route. This is the most common type of bus transit service.

Express Services

Express services connect a number of areas with the central business district (CBD) or other major destinations. These services typically operate during the morning and afternoon-evening peak travel hours. Express routes often use freeways or major arterials and make fewer stops along the way to make more predictable, faster trips.

Limited-Stop Service

Limited stop service is a combination of local and express service. The stops may be several blocks to a mile or more apart.

Bus Rapid Transit

Bus rapid transit (BRT) is a type of limited-stop service. It provides high-speed bus service regardless of traffic conditions and frequently operates in a dedicated right-of-way. BRT combines the advantages of rail transit with the flexibility and lower capital cost of bus service. BRT systems often make use of transit signal priority systems to minimize delays at signalized intersections. BRT is addressed in more detail elsewhere in this book.

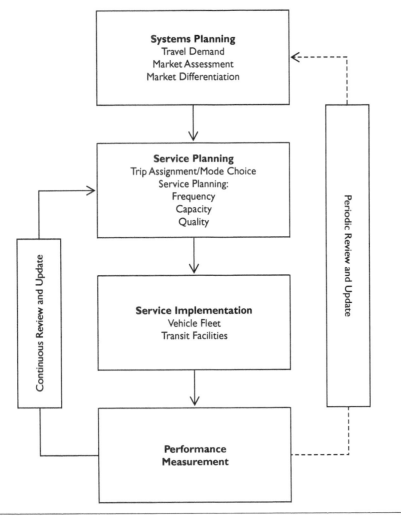

TRANSIT PLANNING PROCESS

Source: Greg Walker.

Gregory A. Walker, AICP, Washington Metropolitan Area Transit Authority, Washington, DC

BUS RAPID TRANSIT

Bus rapid transit (BRT) is a flexible, rubber-tired rapid transit mode that combines stations, vehicles, service, running-ways, and intelligent transportation system (ITS) elements into an integrated system with a positive identity and a unique image. In many respects, BRT is "rubber-tired" light-rail transit, but it has greater operating flexibility and potentially lower capital and operating costs than light rail.

BRT can be especially desirable in large cities, where passenger flows warrant frequent service, and there is a sufficient presence of buses to justify dedicated running ways. To support ridership, this normally requires an urban population in the United States that exceeds 750,000 and a downtown employment base of at least 50,000 to 75,000.

The common types of BRT service are conventional radial routes between a city center and outlying areas (as in Pittsburgh), extension of a rail rapid transit line (as in Miami), and a mostly peak-period commuter express operation (as in Houston).

BRT Features

The primary features of BRT are:

- dedicated running ways;
- accessible, safe, secure, attractive stations;
- easy-to-board, attractive, environmentally friendly vehicles;
- intelligent transportation system (ITS) applications to provide real-time passenger information, signal priority, and service command/control;
- frequent, all-day service; and
- efficient (i.e., off-vehicle) fare collection.

Few existing systems have all six BRT features, although many have several. Exclusive running ways (bus lanes or busways) are the most common feature; off-vehicle fare collection is the least common.

RAIL TRANSIT

Rail transit technology includes a wide range of options. The American Public Transportation Association (APTA) categorizes rail transit into three general groups:

- Commuter rail
- Heavy rail
- Light rail (including streetcars and trams)

Here, light rail and streetcar/tram systems are defined and discussed separately.

These various rail technologies differ as to:

Location. They can operate on exclusive right-of-way, semiexclusive right-of-way (tracks that cross streets at grade), or on shared right-of-way (tracks embedded in a roadway).

Speed. Vehicles on shared right-of-way travel with the speed of the rest of traffic; vehicles in exclusive right-of-way can operate at higher speeds.

Passenger volume. The number of passengers per hour a system can carry is a function of the size and number of vehicles and the frequency of trips.

Cost. The cost of a system is a function of infrastructure and facility costs.

Unlike the universal acceptance of the AASHTO *"Green Book"* for highway design, there is no corresponding national standard for transit. Most transit agencies have agency-specific or even project-specific transit system design criteria. When planning for transit, become familiar with local standards.

COMMUTER RAIL

Also called regional rail, suburban rail, or metropolitan rail, commuter rail typically provides service between a central city and the surrounding suburban areas for short-distance travel. The engines are typically electric or diesel-powered, and the cars are hauled by a locomotive or are self-propelled. Specific station-to-station fares and only one or two stations in the central city characterize these systems.

HEAVY RAIL

These systems use high-speed and rapid-acceleration passenger rail cars that operate singly or in multicar trains on fixed rails. They run on rights-of-way separate from all other vehicular and foot traffic. High-platform loading is used, and these systems have capacity for a heavy volume of traffic, making them well suited for high-volume commuter trips. Sophisticated signaling systems are often in use.

LIGHT RAIL

Light rail transit (LRT) is an electric railway system characterized by its capability to operate single cars

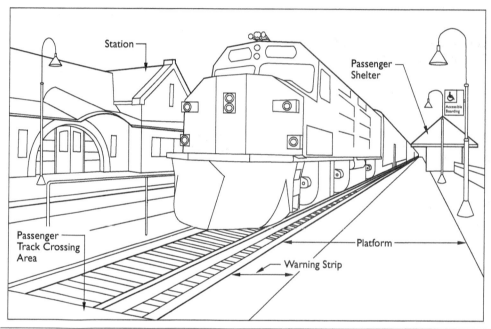

COMMUTER RAIL: CHICAGO, ILLINOIS, METRA SYSTEM, GLENVIEW STATION
Source: Ron Goodson, 2003.

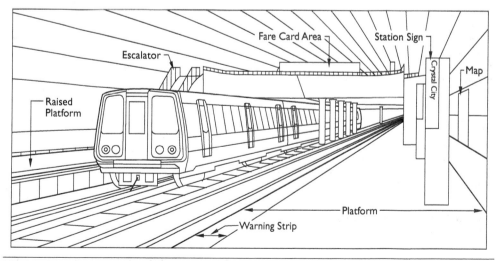

HEAVY RAIL: WASHINGTON, DC, METRORAIL
Source: Professor Jon Bell, Presbyterian College, Clinton, South Carolina, 2001.

Gregory A. Walker, AICP, Washington Metropolitan Area Transit Authority, Washington, DC

or short trains along exclusive rights-of-way at ground level, on aerial structures, in subways, or, occasionally, in streets. LRT systems board and discharge passengers at low-level platforms located either at track or car-floor level. They operate in medium- to high-volume commuter corridors.

STREETCAR/TRAM

Streetcars are metropolitan electric railway vehicles designed to fit the scale and traffic patterns of the neighborhoods through which they travel. Streetcar vehicles are narrower and shorter than other rail cars typically seen in service in the United States. They run in mixed traffic and, except at stops, accommodate existing curbside parking and loading. These systems serve as medium- to high-volume circulator services and often serve as collectors and distributors for regional transit systems.

INTERMODAL AND MULTIMODAL TRANSIT FACILITIES

Intermodal facilities allow for transfer between transportation modes. Multimodal facilities also provide transfer opportunities but, in addition, serve each mode independently, often functioning as a transportation hub for major components of the system. Intermodal and multimodal facilities help a community achieve a balanced transportation system, one that supports all transportation needs.

MODES SERVED

Public transit generally consists of bus and rail technology serving a variety of local and regional trip types. Presented in ranked order in consideration of frequency of stops and carrying capacity, the following are relevant to the discussion of intermodal and multimodal facilities:

- Circulators
- Local bus
- Express bus
- Limited-stop service bus
- Bus rapid transit (BRT)
- Intercity buses
- Streetcars
- Light rail transit (LRT)
- Heavy rail
- Commuter rail
- Water transport: ferries and water taxis
- Intercity rail

Details on bus transit and rail transit are included elsewhere in this section of this book. While not applicable to urban transit, intercity bus lines (e.g., Greyhound) and intercity rail lines (e.g., Amtrak) often interface with local transit and therefore are significant to the discussion of intermodal and multimodal facilities.

ADJACENT COMMUNITY CHARACTER AND FORM

When planning new or expanding existing intermodal and multimodal facilities, community character and form must also be taken into account. In relatively high-density urban environments, intermodal

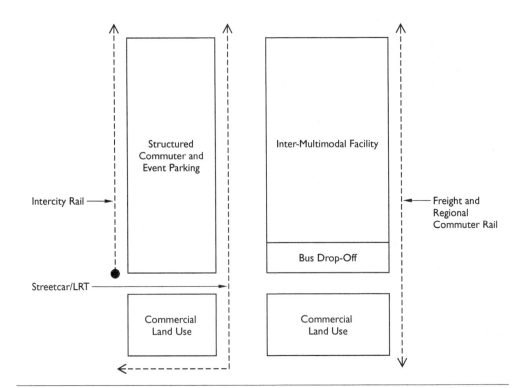

ADAPTIVE JOINT-USE INTERMODAL AND MULTIMODAL FACILITY: FREIGHTHOUSE SQUARE, TACOMA, WASHINGTON

Source: Gregory Walker.

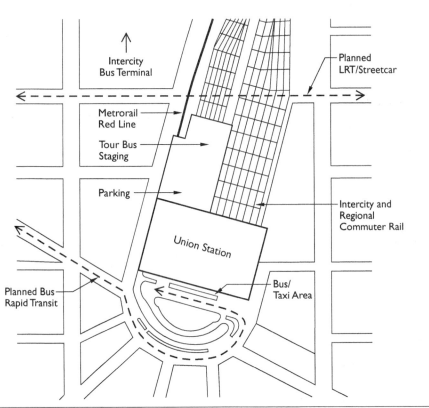

REGIONAL INTERMODAL AND MULTIMODAL FACILITY: UNION STATION, WASHINGTON, DC

Source: Gregory Walker.

Gregory A. Walker, AICP, Washington Metropolitan Area Transit Authority, Washington, DC

and multimodal facilities generally serve as a transfer point between radial trunk services and local distribution modes. Many are developed as mixed-use facilities. In Tacoma, Washington, SoundTransit and the City of Tacoma converted a former freight transfer facility into a regional intermodal and multimodal station. Light rail, commuter rail, and two bus lines serve the facility. Amtrak and Greyhound also have facilities nearby.

A large-scale urban intermodal and multimodal facility is Union Station in Washington, DC, one of the busiest surface transportation passenger facilities in the world. Union Station provides connections to Washington DC's Metrorail, Virginia, and Maryland commuter rail services, Amtrak, intercity buses, tour services, local buses, and taxis. In addition, the facility is a regional shopping and entertainment center, featuring more than 100 shops, restaurants, and bars, and a movie theater.

In suburban environments, it is particularly important to consider adjacent land uses when planning for an intermodal and multimodal transit facility. The level of traffic and noise generated from high-activity facilities may be more compatible with commercial uses than with residential uses.

FACILITY TYPES

In their most basic form, intermodal and multimodal facilities usually provide for passenger transfer between two or three modes. The suburban park-and-ride serves as a centralized access point for bus or rail commuter service. In low-density areas, it is more cost-effective for the transit agency to provide high-frequency service from a central location. In areas of moderate density or where sufficient land is not available for commuter parking, high-capacity transit services rely on a system of feeder buses and passenger drop-off as the primary means of system access.

High-density urban environments usually accommodate a varied mix of facilities, each designed to serve a specific function. Union Station in Washington, DC, includes nearly every mode and trip type. Also in Washington, DC, L'Enfant Plaza allows commuter rail passengers to transfer to either bus or heavy rail, and heavy rail passengers are able to transfer between lines.

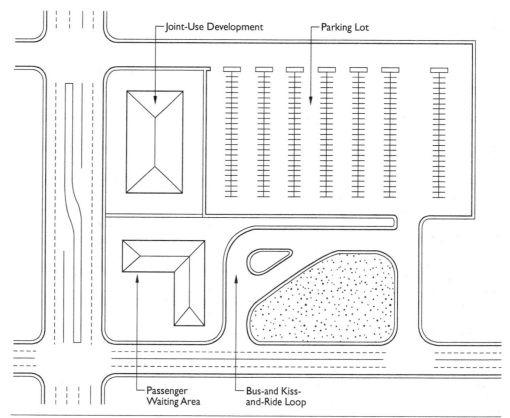

SUBURBAN PARK-AND-RIDE

Source: Gregory Walker.

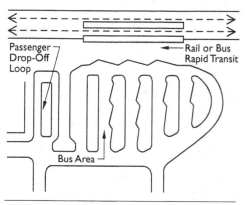

MODERATE-DENSITY INTERMODAL AND MULTIMODAL FACILITY

Source: Gregory Walker.

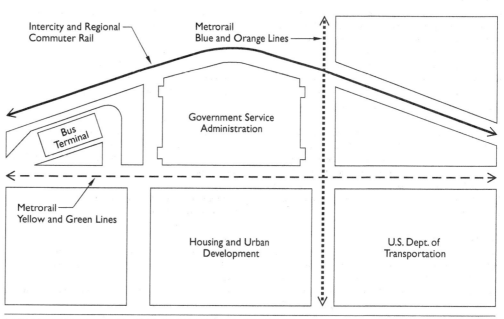

URBAN INTERMODAL AND MULTIMODAL FACILITY

Source: Gregory Walker.

Gregory A. Walker, AICP, Washington Metropolitan Area Transit Authority, Washington, DC

TRANSPORTATION

AIRPORT AND LAND-USE INTERFACE

The airport/land-use interface includes ground transportation linkages, planning and zoning for airport-related business, planning and zoning for airport-compatible uses, and intergovernmental coordination. The majority of the information here addresses airport land-use compatibility planning. The other dimensions of the airport/land-use interface, relating to transportation and economic development planning and inter-governmental coordination, are also touched upon.

Effective transportation linkages between the airport and the community must recognize the needs of different constituencies, including airline passengers, cargo shippers, and airport employees.

Noise Compatibility

Airport noise and land-use compatibility planning is one aspect of the airport land-use interface with widely recognized guidelines and criteria, and with a sizeable body of experience. For the reader not familiar with noise descriptors and interested in the effects of noise, see the section of this book on noise for more information.

Considerations for Local Noise Compatibility Planning

Any local government participating in a Part 150 program or undertaking an independent noise compatibility planning effort must consider at least three factors of fundamental importance to a well-reasoned planning and regulatory framework:

- The airport master plan
- The appropriate noise level threshold for defining noncompatible uses; and
- The appropriate set of noise contours to use for planning and regulaton.

Airport Master Plan. Airport operators must prepare master plans and aviation activity forecasts as a condition of eligibility for federal airport improvement grants. Master plans have information vital for noise compatibility planning, including flight activity forecasts, plans for new or lengthened runways or runway closures, and plans for other improvements intended to create a major change in the airport's role, such as significantly increasing the number of flights, changing the type of aircraft expected to use the airport, or increasing the number of nighttime flights.

Determining a noise compatibility threshold depends perhaps most importantly on the local values of the community. In some communities, people may place a premium on quiet. In communities with aviation-based economies, for example, people may have a more favorable view of aircraft activity and be more willing to accept higher levels of noise.

Safety Compatibility Zones

Accident location data are the starting point in considering how to configure safety compatibility zones around an airport. The decreasing density of accident locations, as distance from the airport and the runway centerline increases, can be reflected through different safety zones, with less restrictive standards as the accident risk declines. Land-use standards for safety areas should reasonably restrict:

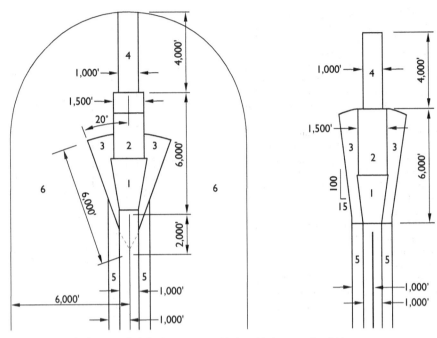

A general aviation airport is shown on the left; a large commercial airport is shown on the right.

CIVIL AIRPORT SAFETY ZONES

Source: California Department of Transportation 2002.

- building densities or lot coverage (to provide opportunities for safe, forced landings);
- land uses attracting large numbers of people (to reduce the risk of harm from accidents to people on the ground);
- hazardous land uses, such as the storage of hazardous chemicals, explosives, or flammable materials (that could greatly increase the harm from an accident);
- uses that can obscure visibility and compromise low-altitude air navigation, such as those attracting birds or producing large quantities of smoke or water vapor; and
- critical public utilities or facilities (that could compromise public safety if they were severely damaged or destroyed in an aircraft accident).

The configuration of safety zones should relate to the patterns in the accident location data but must be adjusted as necessary to reflect local airport operational variables and the local terrain. Some of these considerations include:

- common approach and departure paths;
- local traffic pattern;
- variations in the type of aircraft using particular runways;
- aircraft activity forecasts, especially if the character of traffic using a runway is expected to change over time;
- the Airport Master Plan, especially if new runways or runway extensions are planned; and
- topography in the airport environs, especially if it influences aircraft flight routes or rises significantly under predominant flight tracks.

INTERGOVERNMENTAL COORDINATION

Many airports are at the edges of municipal or county boundaries, and more than a few are near state borders, creating the need for intergovernmental coordination for successful airport vicinity land-use planning and zoning.

Mandated Coordination

State legislation mandating intergovernmental coordination on issues of regional significance, including airports, and providing a structured policy framework within which to make planning and development decisions can help to overcome barriers to coordination. Oregon's Land Conservation and Development Commission (LCDC), the body empowered to adopt and enforce statewide planning goals, requires intergovernmental coordination in the enactment of comprehensive plans. The LCDC has also enacted a rule under Statewide Planning Goal 12 (Transportation) mandating local planning for airport facilities and land-use compatibility.

Extraterritorial Zoning

An approach used in several states is to empower the airport operator, if it is a governmental entity, to enact extraterritorial zoning throughout the area impacted by the airport. This permits the jurisdiction operating the airport to regulate land use, within specified limits, even if the property is in another jurisdiction. Typically the extraterritorial zoning power can only be exercised for airport land-use compatibility purposes. Frequently, this power is limited to regulating structure height.

Gregory A. Walker, AICP, Washington Metropolitan Area Transit Authority, Washington, DC

Joint Airport Zoning Boards

Some states allow for the creation of joint airport zoning boards. They are formed by the communities operating the airport and affected by airport impacts . Each community appoints representatives to the airport zoning board, and the board enacts a special airport zoning ordinance and is empowered to enforce it. The authority of these bodies is often limited to dealing with airport land-use compatibility planning and zoning.

Voluntary Cooperation

Some communities have resolved these obstacles through programs of voluntary cooperation. Tucson and Pima County, Arizona, offer an example of such cooperation resulting in a reasonably strong and consistent program of airport compatibility regulations.

Regional planning commissions often serve as the metropolitan planning organizations for ground transportation planning. They are well positioned to facilitate the coordination of planning among local counties and municipalities on other issues of regional importance, including airport vicinity planning. Two agencies that have had some degree of success in promoting airport vicinity planning are the Mid-Ohio Regional Planning Commission in Columbus (http://www.morpc.org/MORPC.htm) and the Capital District Regional Planning Commission in Albany, New York (http://cdrpc.org/index.shtml).

REFERENCES

California Department of Transportation. 2002. *California Airport Land Use Planning Handbook.* Prepared by Shutt Moen Associates for the California Department of Transportation, Division of Aeronautics. Available online at www.dot.ca.gov/hq/planning/aeronaut/htmlfile/landuse.php.

Denver Regional Council of Governments. 1998. *Airport Compatible Land Use Design Handbook.*

Federal Aviation Administration. 1987. *A Model Ordinance to Limit Height of Objects Around Airports.* Advisory Circular 150/5190-4A. Washington, D.C.: U.S. Department of Transportation.

——. 2002. *Airport Design Handbook.* Advisory Circular 150/5300-13, Change 7. October. Washington, D.C.: U.S. Department of Transportation.

——. *Land Use Compatibility Planning Toolkit.*

Federal Interagency Committee on Urban Noise. 1980. *Guidelines for Considering Noise in Land Use Planning and Control.*

Finegold, L.S., et al. 1994. "Updated Criteria for Assessing the Impacts of General Transportation Noise on People," *Noise Control Engineering Journal.* 42, no. 1.

Florida Department of Transportation. 1994. *Airport Compatible Land Use Guidance for Florida Communities.* Office of Public Transportation, Aviation Office. www.dot.state.fl.us/aviation/compland.htm

Oregon Department of Aviation. 2003. *Oregon Airport Land Use Compatibility Guidebook.* Prepared by Mead & Hunt, Inc. and Satre, Associates, P.C. for the Oregon Department of Aviation. www.aviation.state.or.us/resources.shtml

Papsidero, Vince. 1992. *Airport Noise Regulations.* PAS Report No. 437. Chicago: American Planning Association.

Schultz, T.J. 1978. "Synthesis of Social Surveys on Noise Annoyance." *Journal of the Acoustical Society of America.* 64, no. 2.

See also:
Noise and Vibration

Gregory A. Walker, AICP, Washington Metropolitan Area Transit Authority, Washington, DC

UTILITIES

WASTE MANAGEMENT

Solid waste is regulated under Subtitle D of the Resource Conservation and Recovery Act (RCRA). The primary goal of RCRA is to encourage solid waste management practices that promote environmentally sound disposal methods and maximize the use of materials recovered from waste and foster resource conservation. The U.S. Environmental Protection Agency (U.S. EPA) implements RCRA.

RCRA Subtitle D strongly encourages states to develop and adopt statewide solid waste management plans that attempt to assess solid waste generation and management within the state and describe the state's anticipated direction toward managing its waste during a specific time period. The U.S. EPA's role has been limited to setting the minimum regulatory requirements that states must follow in designing their plans and to approving plans that comply with these requirements. The development of state plans is voluntary. The great majority of rules that regulate municipal waste are state environmental agency rules adopted under enabling laws that address solid waste. RCRA has resulted in a significant decrease in the number of landfills and an increase in recycling since the 1970s.

ROLES AND RESPONSIBILITIES

Decision makers must develop the best possible alternatives for local solid waste management by ensuring that all local, state, and federal legislative factors, as well as private enterprise and concerned members of the larger community, are accounted for in the planning process. Considering the complexity and legal requirements of solid waste management, it is important to clarify the roles and responsibilities of government units, the private sector, and citizens in managing the country's solid waste.

Municipal Government

Municipal governments historically have had the responsibility to coordinate, provide, or otherwise ensure that a collection system for refuse, recyclables, and landscape waste is in place for municipal residents. Municipal governments: offer a range of public services, from curbside collection to drop-off services; contract for services partially or entirely to nonprofit or for-profit service organizations; or have residents privately arrange for services. Four common types of contractual arrangements typically used for collection within municipalities exist:

Municipal service. Municipal employees collect waste with municipally owned equipment.

Municipal contract. One or more private haulers operate under contract to the municipality. The municipality collects fees or taxes, then pays the waste hauler(s) for contracted services.

Franchise contract. The municipality grants or sells hauling privileges (franchises) to one or more private haulers for waste collection services

in the municipality. The fees are collected directly from the customer by the waste hauler(s).

Private contract. Under private contract collection, the individual resident or business contracts directly with the private waste hauler for waste collection services. The only involvement by the municipality is the possible licensing of solid waste haulers.

In order to effectively manage collection programs, municipal governments may want to develop and adopt local ordinances to encourage or facilitate specific solid waste programs. For example, St. Louis County, Missouri, encouraged municipalities to incorporate recycling in their contracts with local haulers by developing a model bid specification that included recycling in the base contract agreement. Nationwide, a number of municipalities and counties require haulers to provide recycling and incorporate "pay-as-you throw" pricing.

Municipal governments should work in partnership with other units of government, industry, and citizens to effectively plan and implement an integrated waste management system consistent with the county, regional, or municipal solid waste (MSW) management plan. An integrated program includes recycling, landscape waste management (e.g., composting), special pickups, household hazardous waste management, public education regarding waste disposal and diversion options, direct or transfer waste hauling for disposed material, and final disposal at landfills or incinerators.

State Government

A number of states provide assistance in developing and implementing a county or municipal integrated waste management program by providing technical and financial assistance, issuing regulations, and developing education programs. The state agencies, such as the state environmental protection agency, pollution control agency, or department of environmental quality, may provide technical assistance on collection, hauling, processing, marketing, disposal, or procurement. The agencies may also encourage certain types of local waste management practices by making solid waste grant funding available. For example, the Illinois EPA made funds available to counties for solid waste planning studies in the mid-1990s. Other state agencies established recycling grant programs that address local recycling needs.

Federal Government

The federal government, through the U.S. EPA, takes a role in waste management by establishing national goals, developing education programs, providing technical and financial assistance, and issuing regulations. The agency also has a role in establishing a framework for state and local planning; setting minimum standards for solid waste facilities; and encouraging the manufacturing industry to design products and packaging for effective waste management, as well as to use secondary materials in

manufacturing. Areas where federal action is likely to occur include interstate transport of waste and a national materials usage policy.

Private Enterprise

Waste management companies, including local haulers, recyclers, processors, end markets, and disposal facilities, have a responsibility for planning and implementing waste management systems consistent with their local solid waste management plan. Private enterprise should work in partnership with units of government, industry, and citizens to effectively plan and implement integrated waste management systems and to educate the public.

Citizens

Citizens, as well as private and public entities, have a responsibility to learn how their purchase, usage, handling, and disposal of products and materials affect the waste management system. Citizens should assume responsibility for the waste they create and attempt to recognize the true costs of disposing of their waste. Citizens should strive to stay apprised of local solid waste management initiatives; provide input throughout the planning and implementation process; and make educated decisions regarding the local management of solid waste.

INTEGRATED WASTE MANAGEMENT

The U.S. EPA's integrated waste management hierarchy includes the following three components, listed in order of preference:

- Source reduction, including reuse of products, changing operations that generate less waste, and backyard composting
- Recycling, including on-site, curbside, and drop-off recycling, and the use of compost facilities
- Disposal, including combustion with energy recovery and landfilling

The strategy is: first generate as little waste as possible, then recycle as much of the waste as possible, and, finally, properly dispose what is left over.

Source Reduction

Source reduction is the practice of generating less waste. It includes numerous practices:

- Reducing the size and weight of packaging
- Purchasing in bulk to reduce package waste
- Making products last longer, such as tires that last 60,000 miles rather than 20,000 miles
- Using a mulching mower
- Changing processes in manufacturing or commercial operations to reduce the amount of waste generated that would require recycling or disposal, such as installing electric hand driers in restrooms, which reduces the amount of paper towel waste.

Chris Burger, Patrick Engineering, Inc., Springfield, Illinois

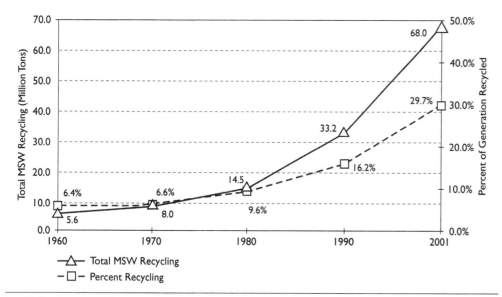

MUNICIPAL SOLID WASTE RECYCLING RATES, 1960-2001

Source: U.S. EPA 2003.

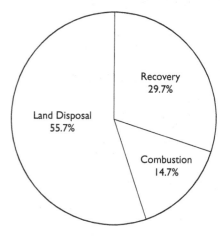

Municipal solid waste recovered for recycling, including composting, and disposed of by combusting and landfilling in 2001.

MANAGEMENT OF MUNICIPAL SOLID WASTE IN THE UNITED STATES, 2001

Source: U.S. EPA 2003.

Recycling

Recycling includes methods of capturing residential, commercial, and industrial materials that are then subsequently remanufactured into new products. This includes recycling paper, glass, aluminum, and other materials commonly considered recycling, but also includes the amount composted by composting facilities. According to the U.S. EPA, in 2001, the United States recycled and composted between 25 and 30 percent of the solid waste generated.

Landfills

Landfills are engineered ground vaults with a controlled method to encapsulate waste that prevents leachate and other pollutants from escaping into the environment. Landfilling is the predominant method of disposing waste in the United States, accounting for about 55 percent of the total waste generated.

Incineration

Incineration is the burning of refuse to reduce its volume and weight. The U.S. EPA estimates that the volume of waste is reduced by 90 percent and the weight of waste is reduced by 75 percent with incineration. Combustion accounted for about 15 percent of the total waste generated in the United States in 2001.

Transfer Stations

Transfer stations are facilities where waste from smaller vehicles, such as garbage trucks that pick up in neighborhoods and at businesses, is consolidated and placed on larger vehicles, such as trains, semitrailers or barges. Because many remaining landfills are located several miles from a number of population sources, waste is more cost-effectively transferred in larger vehicles than in smaller packer trucks.

WASTE MANAGEMENT PLANS

Waste management plans prepared by units of government generally include the recommended ingredients of source reduction, recycling, waste to energy, and landfilling. Plans are developed that include special studies on a region's current and future waste generation and established management goals. Waste planning studies typically include a state or local government's waste reduction goals, as well as the methods to achieve those goals through recycling, composting, and state and local legislation to encourage or mandate recycling. Special studies are often performed, such as household weekly waste setout quantities, burn barrel usage, food waste generation, construction and demolition debris generation, commercial recycling opportunities, and impacts of hauler ordinance changes.

See also:
Federal Legislation

Chris Burger, Patrick Engineering, Inc., Springfield, Illinois

WASTEWATER

Wastewater is potable water that has been used within a community for various purposes.

DOMESTIC WASTEWATER

Wastewater for residential uses, such as showers, sinks, washing machines, and sanitary facilities (including those in commercial buildings and institutions), is domestic wastewater. It is readily treated within a standard wastewater treatment facility.

INDUSTRIAL WASTEWATER

Industrial wastewater is water that has been used for manufacturing purposes and may have specific contaminants related to the source industry. These contaminants, which may be organic compounds, inorganic compounds, or metals, make industrial wastewater difficult to treat using domestic treatment processes.

Municipal officials and regulatory agencies evaluate each industry prior to allowing discharge of its wastes to the treatment plant. A municipality may require the industry to pretreat the waste to remove components that may inhibit or interfere with biological processes at the wastewater treatment plant. In some cases, a municipality may not allow the waste to be discharged to the municipal system even after pretreatment if the waste is hazardous. The industry will then have to contract with a hazardous waste facility for hauling and treating that waste. This can be an expensive proposition. It is important to determine whether the wastewater treatment facility has the capability to treat the waste from a proposed industrial site, prior to any development.

INFLOW AND INFILTRATION

Inflow and infiltration (I&I) is water that enters the collection system (sewer pipes) through various direct and indirect methods. Infiltration is groundwater entering through open joints or cracks in pipes. Inflow is rainwater that enters the system through roof leaders, basement sump pumps, or other access points. I&I may exceed the capacity of a wastewater treatment plant and collection system. It should be reduced or eliminated to the extent possible and cost-effective.

Frequent in-line television (TV) camera inspection can evaluate infiltration and determine the location of open joints and cracked or broken pipes. These can then be repaired by injecting grout into the joints and cracks, replacing the portion of broken sewer, or lining the pipe with a plastic or resin material. These processes are effective but can be costly and must be evaluated on the basis of cost/benefit.

Smoke testing can easily identify inflow. The technician places a smoke bomb in the sanitary sewer and then watches where the smoke exists through roof leaders, basements, and other areas where sump pumps might be connected to the sanitary sewer system. The municipality then notifies the property owner to redirect the flow to a storm sewer. It is important to understand the adverse effect of stormwater entering a separate sanitary sewer system.

TYPICAL WASTEWATER FLOW RATES, URBAN RESIDENTIAL SOURCES, IN THE UNITED STATES

HOUSEHOLD SIZE, NUMBER OF PERSONS	FLOW RATE, GAL/CAPITA-D	
	RANGE	TYPICAL
1	75-130	97
2	63-81	76
3	54-70	66
4	41-71	53
5	40-68	51
6	39-67	50
7	37-64	48
8	36-62	46

Source: Adapted from Metcalf and Eddy, Inc. Wastewater Engineering: Treatment, Disposal and Reuse, 4th Edition, 2003, McGraw-Hill. Material reproduced with permission of The McGraw-Hill Companies.

TYPICAL WASTEWATER FLOW RATES, INSTITUTIONAL SOURCES, IN THE UNITED STATES

SOURCE	FLOW RATE, GAL/UNIT-D		
	UNIT	RANGE	TYPICAL
Assembly hall	Guest	3-5	4
Hospital	Bed	175-400	250
	Employee	5-15	10
Institutions other than hospitals	Bed	75-125	100
	Employee	5-15	10
Prison	Inmate	80-150	120
	Employee	5-15	10
School, day, with cafeteria, gym, and showers	Student	15-30	25
School, day, with cafeteria only	Student	10-20	15
School, boarding	Student	75-100	85

Source: Adapted from Metcalf and Eddy, Inc. Wastewater Engineering: Treatment, Disposal and Reuse, 4th Edition, 2003, McGraw-Hill. Material reproduced with permission of The McGraw-Hill Companies.

TYPICAL WASTEWATER FLOW RATES, COMMERCIAL SOURCES, IN THE UNITED STATES

SOURCE	FLOW RATE, GAL/UNIT-D		
	UNIT	RANGE	TYPICAL
Airport	Passenger	3-5	4
Apartment	Bedroom	100-150	120
Automobile service station	Vehicles served	8-15	10
	Employee	9-15	13
Bar/cocktail lounge	Seat	12-25	20
	Employee	10-16	13
Boarding house	Person	25-65	45
Conference center	Person	6-10	8
Department store	Toilet Room	350-600	400
	Employee	8-15	10
Hotel	Guest	65-75	70
	Employee	8-15	10
Industrial building (sanitary waste only)	Employee	15-35	20
Laundry (self-service)	Machine	400-550	450
	Customer	45-55	50
Mobile home park	Unit	125-150	140
Motel (with kitchen)	Guest	55-90	60
Motel (without kitchen)	Guest	50-75	55
Office	Employee	7-16	13
Public lavatory	User	3-5	4
Restaurant, conventional	Customer	7-10	8
Restaurant, with bar/cocktail lounge	Customer	9-12	10
Shopping center	Employee	7-13	10
	Parking space	1-3	2
Theater (indoor)	Seat	2-4	3

Source: Adapted from Metcalf and Eddy, Inc. Wastewater Engineering: Treatment, Disposal and Reuse, 4th Edition, 2003, McGraw-Hill. Material reproduced with permission of The McGraw-Hill Companies.

Jeanette Brown, P.E., D.E.E., City of Stamford Water Pollution Control Authority, Stamford, Connecticut

QUANTITIES AND FLOW RATES

For residential wastewater sources, quantities are typically determined on the basis of population. For planning purposes, a two-person household is expected to use between 63 and 81 gallons per capita per day, and a six-person household is expected to use between 39 and 67 gallons per capita per day. Flow rates for a particular community depend on the availability and cost of supplied water, and the economic and social climate of that locale.

Flow rates from commercial, institutional, and industrial facilities are based on a variety of factors. For example, the flow rate from a hotel is typically based on a volume of water per guest; and for an apartment it is typically based on a volume of water per bedroom.

Various flow rates must be evaluated to ensure that both the collection system and treatment process will have sufficient capacity. A development could possibly be delayed or disapproved if the flow rate is greater than either the capacity of the treatment plant or collection system. If a sewer line or a pumping station is too small in the immediate area of the proposed project, developers sometimes pay or share the costs of increasing the size of the line or capacity at the station.

CHARACTERISTICS AND TESTING

Wastewater has physical, chemical, and biological characteristics that must be understood and monitored. The relationship and magnitude of wastewater characteristics are community-specific and depend mainly on the geographical location, commercial and industrial makeup, and the source of potable water.

Physical characteristics include solids, turbidity, and temperature. Chemical components include pH, chloride concentration (especially for coastal communities), nitrogen, phosphorus, sulfur, metals of various types, and a variety of inorganic and organic compounds. Biological characteristics include microorganisms, such as bacteria, protozoa, and fungi.

Wastewater treatment plants should monitor influent characteristics on a daily basis. This is typically required by permit, but it is also the only way a treatment plant can be successfully operated.

Biochemical Oxygen Demand Test

Organic (carbon-containing) constituents are measured by the biochemical oxygen demand (BOD) test. BOD measures quantity of oxygen used in the biochemical oxidation of organic matter in a specified time and temperature (20°C). This test mimics what occurs in a modern wastewater treatment plant and in natural water systems. The typical time for a BOD test is five days—the notation for that test is BOD_5. Some BOD tests will be run for 20 days, and are noted as BOD_{20}. For scientific purposes, some BOD tests extend beyond 20 days, referred to as the ultimate BOD (BOD_U).

BOD measurements are required by a plant's operating permit and are used to permit and monitor industrial discharges to a treatment facility. BOD represents the oxygen demand from both carbonaceous and nitrogenous compounds. Some states use carbonaceous BOD as the permit requirement.

TOTAL NITROGEN (TN) TMDL FOR NEWPORT BAY, EXPRESSED AS ALLOWABLE DISCHARGE TO NEWPORT BAY

	ANNUAL (LBS)	OCTOBER 1 – MARCH 31 (LBS) NONSTORM DISCHARGES[1]	APRIL 1 – SEPTEMBER 30 (LBS)
TMDL (Loading capacity)	298,225	144,364	153,861
Waste Load Allocation (WLA)			
Urban Runoff	72,070	55,442	16,628
Other NPDES Discharges	39,311	13,640	25,671
Total WLA	111,381	69,082	42,299
Load Allocation (LA)			
Nurseries[2]	85,646	23,060	62,586
Agricultural Discharges	49,764	38,283	11,481
Undefined Sources	51,434	13,939	37,495
Total LA	186,844	75,282	111,562

Note: The U.S. EPA established a nutrient TMDL for Newport Bay watershed based on scientific data and computer-aided models. The table shows the components of the TMDL for nitrogen and the waste load allocated to each source.

1. The load limits do not apply on days on which the mean daily flow rate in San Diego Creek at Campus Drive exceeds 50 cubic feet per second (cfs) as a result of precipitation events.

2. Includes nurseries currently regulated by the Regional Board and nurseries currently not regulated by the Regional Board.

Source: U.S. EPA, Region 9.

Carbonaceous BOD (CBOD) is always less than the total BOD.

Chemical Oxygen Demand Test

Another test used to measure organic components is chemical oxygen demand (COD), which is a quantitative measure of the amount of oxygen required for the chemical oxidation of carbonaceous (organic) material in wastewater. This test takes two hours to perform and is more useful for monitoring and control than the BOD test.

Solids Testing

Both inorganic and organic solids are also measured. They are typically classified as total solids (TS), volatile solids (VS), total suspended solids (TSS), and volatile suspended solids (VSS).

REGULATIONS

Clean Water Act

The 1972 Federal Water Pollution Control Act Amendments (the Clean Water Act) has had the greatest impact on wastewater treatment and receiving water quality. The goal of this act was to make the waters of the nation "swimable and fishable." To accomplish this, the act established the National Pollutant Discharge Elimination System (NPDES), which is a permitting program for all dischargers based on uniform minimum categorical standards. In most cases, authorized states issue NPDES permits. The act was amended in 1987 to strengthen the water quality regulations by providing changes in permitting, adding substantial financial penalties for violations and emphasizing identification and regulation of toxic pollutants in sewage sludge. NPDES permits take into account the capability of a stream to assimilate discharges.

Sewage Sludge Regulations

Sewage sludge is the by-product of the wastewater treatment process. This material can have significant contaminants and a negative impact on the environment if not treated and disposed of properly. In 1993, sewage sludge regulations (40 CFR Part 503) were passed, which established national standards for pathogen, vector attraction, and metal concentration reduction for sludge (biosolids), which could be used as a fertilizer or soil amendment. This regulation defines two classes of biosolids, A and B. Class A can be used for all land application, including home use as a fertilizer. Land application of Class B biosolids is strictly regulated, and they cannot be used for home application.

Total Maximum Daily Load

The U.S. EPA put the Total Maximum Daily Load (TMDL) rule into effect in 2002. A TMDL is the maximum amount of a pollutant that a water body can receive without negatively affecting the water quality to below the standard set for that body. States, territories, and tribes set water quality standards. They identify the uses for each water body, such as drinking water supply, recreation, and fishing, and determine the scientific criteria to support that use.

A TMDL is the sum of the allowable loads of a single pollutant from all discharges into that specific body of water, including individual wastewater treatment plants, surface runoff, industrial discharges, and aerial deposition. The calculation must include a margin of safety to ensure the water body can be used for the purposes the state has designated. The calculation must also account for seasonal variation in water quality.

Through the TMDL program, regulators establish a waste load allocation for the individual dischargers of that pollutant. The TMDL program enables effluent credit-trading programs, such as the nitrogen credit-trading program in Connecticut. Information on the Connecticut program is available on the state's Web site

REFERENCES

Metcalf and Eddy, Inc. 2003. *Wastewater Engineering Treatment and Reuse.* 4th ed. New York: McGraw-Hill.

See also:
Federal Legislation

Jeanette Brown, P.E., D.E.E., City of Stamford Water Pollution Control Authority, Stamford, Connecticut

STORMWATER RUNOFF AND RECHARGE

Stormwater management encompasses the broad field of managing runoff from precipitation events to control or mitigate a range of issues:

- Conveyance or drainage of runoff from one location to another
- Treatment of runoff to capture and remove a variety of pollutants prior to discharge to receiving water
- Recharge of precipitation into underlying groundwater to maintain supplies for drinking water, irrigation, and dry-weather flow to streams, wetlands, and ponds
- Mitigation of accelerated overland and stream channel erosion caused by either a disruption in hydrology, sediment supply, or both
- Reuse of precipitation for a range of beneficial uses such as drinking water and irrigation
- Control or management of large precipitation events to reduce the risk of downstream flooding

The information here focuses on the issues of recharge of precipitation to groundwater and treatment of runoff to reduce pollutant load delivery to receiving waters.

STORMWATER AND WATER QUALITY

Stormwater runoff, particularly from urban land uses, is widely viewed as one of most significant contributors to water quality impairment (Burton and Pitt 2002). Many believe the cause of impairment is a result of pollutant delivery to receiving waters. While pollutants in stormwater runoff are certainly ubiquitous and frequently at concentrations that do contribute to water quality impairment, the impact on water quality from reduced groundwater recharge, accelerated stream channel erosion, and increased flooding is also part of the stormwater problem.

PRINCIPLES OF STORMWATER MANAGEMENT

Two fundamental principles must be understood in order to gain a grasp of the wide topic of stormwater management. The first is how the basic water balance changes as a result of altered land use. The second is that precipitation varies widely, and the probability of a given precipitation event governs how that event can be effectively managed.

Water Balance

In relatively undeveloped or rural areas, total precipitation is divided into three principal components: evapotranspiration, infiltration, and runoff. The quantity of each of these variables depends on the amount of precipitation, climate, vegetative cover, soils, land slope, amount of impervious area, and the characteristics of precipitation events, such as intensity of rainfall. As land is altered from less intensive to more intensive uses, impervious cover increases, and the relative balance of these three variables is changed. The most dramatic effect is that runoff volume increases and infiltration decreases.

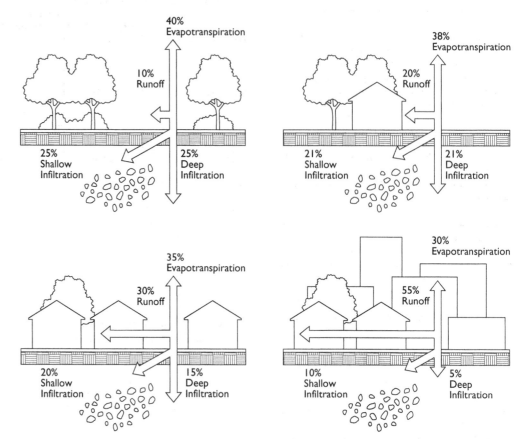

As the percent of impervious land cover increases, the water balance shifts away from infiltration and evapotranspiration, and toward increased runoff.

IMPACT OF IMPERVIOUS COVER ON DISRUPTION TO THE NATURAL WATER BALANCE

Source: Prince Georges County, Maryland, Department of Environmental Resources (PGDER) 1999.

The consequence of more runoff occurring more frequently is an acceleration of overland and channel erosion, increased pollutant washoff from the land to receiving waters, and increased flooding frequency, leading to property damage and potential threats to public safety. Decreased infiltration reduces the amount of groundwater recharge and leads to a loss of total water volume to supply streams, wetlands, ponds, and lakes during dry weather. In many regions, streams that were perennial under more rural conditions become intermittent as a watershed develops. An assessment of the distribution of precipitation characteristics must be the initial step in developing any stormwater management approach.

Precipitation Conversion to Runoff

It is also important to understand how precipitation is converted to runoff. Many models and methods exist to describe this phenomenon; the basic variables include the amount and intensity of precipitation and the infiltrative characteristics of the land surface. More intense rainfall, more impermeable land surface, and steeper land surface all will generate more runoff. In nearly all conditions, the smallest storms do not produce any runoff. Even a parking lot can absorb a small amount of precipitation before runoff occurs. Referred to as the initial abstraction, this is the volume

of storage contained within the land surface prior to runoff occurring.

The runoff frequency spectrum depicts only runoff-producing events, or those precipitation events greater than a given amount, usually between 0.1 inches and 0.2 inches. When addressing stormwater, the main concerns are usually the amount and rate of runoff. The distribution and magnitude of the runoff frequency spectrum vary as a function of long-term climate and rainfall characteristics. Regions that receive little total rainfall or, conversely, a disproportionate number of tropical storms will each have a different curve. To effectively manage stormwater runoff across this broad spectrum, different curves must be produced for different regions. Once the runoff frequency distribution is calculated and understood, criteria can be applied to address the various issues identified above.

STORMWATER RUNOFF RECHARGE

Recharge is the volume of precipitation that infiltrates into underlying soils, which supports and maintains groundwater levels, and is not either directly released as evapotranspiration or conveyed downstream as runoff or interflow. Interflow is an "in-between" category in the water balance, where precipitation is

Richard Claytor, P.E., Horsley Witten Group, Sandwich, Massachusetts

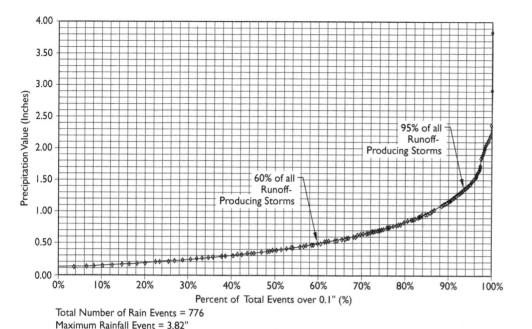

Total Number of Rain Events = 776
Maximum Rainfall Event = 3.82"

A typical runoff frequency spectrum over a period of record of approximately 10 years. The percent of time a precipitation event exceeds a given value is represented on the x-axis, and the magnitude of precipitation is represented on the y-axis. For this example, approximately 60 percent of all precipitation events are less than 0.5 inches, and only 5 percent of all storms exceeded 1.5 inches.

RUNOFF FREQUENCY SPECTRUM

Source: Richard Claytor.

initially infiltrated below the surface but then flows more laterally toward a stream, river, or lake at a much slower rate than direct runoff. Some interflow may ultimately become runoff, evapotranspiration, or recharge.

Simplifications of complex conditions in the natural environment often must be developed and applied to understand stormwater movement. However, it must be recognized that some of the time, conditions will vary. For example, those events that produce little or no runoff and also occur most frequently may contribute to recharge or may support evapotranspiration, depending on the time of year. In colder climates, evapotranspiration is dramatically reduced during the winter months. A small rainfall event occurring in November will likely contribute to recharge, whereas the same-sized rainfall event in June or July will often be transpired directly by vegetation and never reach the groundwater.

Recharge across the Runoff Frequency Spectrum

The amount of recharge needed to mimic natural conditions varies. The best approach is to rely on what occurs naturally and derive criteria to meet that condition. If the natural rate of recharge is 50 percent of the precipitation volume, strive to infiltrate half the total precipitation volume. This is accomplished by setting a design criterion to ensure that half the total long-term precipitation is directed back into the ground.

If practices are sized to capture and infiltrate a 0.4-inch precipitation event, as shown in the illustration, then slightly more than half of the total long-term precipitation will be recharged. All rainfall will infiltrate for storms up to 0.4 inches. This comprises approximately 25 percent of the total long-term precipitation volume. A correspondingly smaller percentage of each storm larger than 0.4 inches will be infiltrated. For example, storms that are between 0.7 and 0.8 inches will recharge only about 60 percent. If in an average year 3.3 inches of precipitation falls from storms in this range, only about 2.1 inches of this would be infiltrated by a practice designed to infiltrate 0.4 inches. Adding all of these together, the total annual average infiltration volume would be approximately 20.9 inches, which is approximately 54 percent of the total annual average precipitation and slightly more than the 50 percent target.

Unfortunately, data on the amount of annual recharge that occurs at a given location are not always available; more importantly, natural recharge varies dramatically as a function of soil

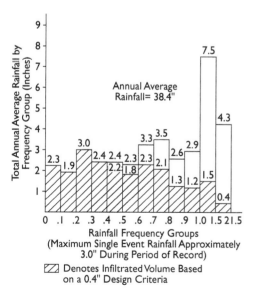

Based on five years of record from Washington, DC, National Airport.

DERIVATION OF RECHARGE CRITERION

Source: Richard Claytor.

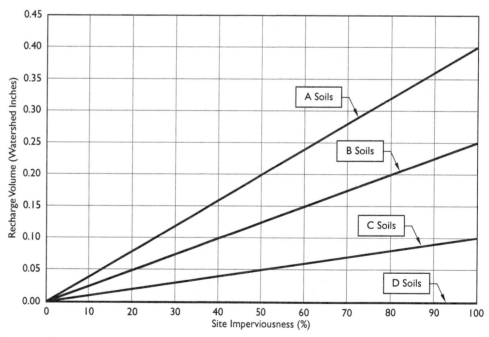

Illustration is for a region receiving 44 inches of annual average rainfall.

RECHARGE VOLUME AS A FUNCTION OF SITE IMPERVIOUS COVER

Source: Center for Watershed Protection 2002.

Richard Claytor, P.E., Horsley Witten Group, Sandwich, Massachusetts

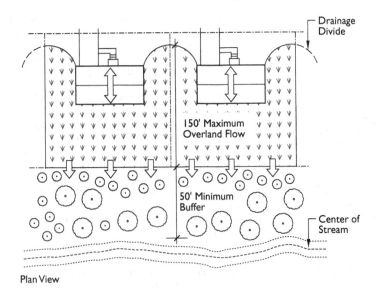

Plan View

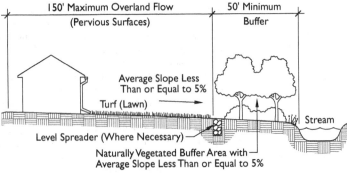

Section

Stream Buffer Credit

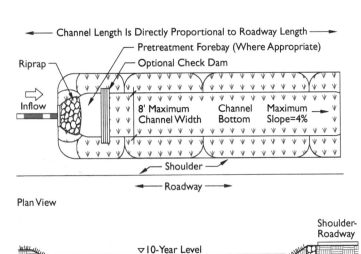

Plan View

Section

Grass Channel

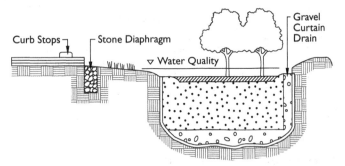

Plan View

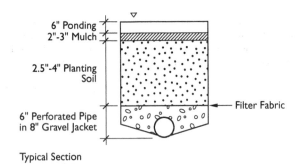

Profile

Typical Section

Bioretention

VARIOUS RECHARGE TECHNIQUES

Source: Center for Watershed Protection 2002.

Richard Claytor, P.E., Horsley Witten Group, Sandwich, Massachusetts

PART 3   STRUCTURES

type. Clay soils have far less recharge capabilities than sandy soils. Consequently, some management programs use a soil-type recharge criterion. The approach involves determining the average annual recharge rate based on the prevailing hydrologic soil group (HSG) present at a project site from the Natural Resources Conservation Service (NRCS) Soil Surveys. HSG is an NRCS designation given to different soil types to reflect their relative surface permeability and infiltrative capability (U.S. Department of Agriculture, Natural Resources Conservation Service 1986).

Group A Soils: Low runoff potential and high infiltration rates. They consist chiefly of deep, well-drained sands or gravels with infiltration rates greater than 0.3 inches/hour.

Group B Soils: Moderate infiltration rates (0.15 to 0.30 inches/hour). They consist chiefly of soils with fine to coarse textures.

Group C Soils: Low infiltration rates (0.05 to 0.15 inches/hour). They have fine textures that impede the downward movement of water.

Group D Soils: High runoff potential with very low infiltration rates (0.0 to 0.05 inches/hour). They consist chiefly of clay soils.

The method was developed based on the amount of annual recharge that occurs as a function of HSG type and uses the following predevelopment recharge percentages to be assigned based on NRCS soil types.

Hydrologic Soil Group	Annual Recharge (percent of annual precipitation)
A	41 percent
B	27 percent
C	14 percent
D	7 percent

The objective of the criterion is to mimic the average annual recharge rate for the prevailing hydrologic soil group(s) at a new development project. Therefore, the recharge volume can be determined as a function of annual predevelopment recharge for a given soil group, average annual rainfall volume, and amount of proposed impervious cover.

GUIDELINES FOR APPLYING A STORMWATER RECHARGE CRITERION

Several constraints and opportunities must be considered when implementing a recharge strategy. These include understanding the array of physical limitations, identifying some cautions on infiltration of runoff from certain land uses, and having a firm understanding of the methods and techniques used to foster infiltration of stormwater runoff. The most current federal, state, and local regulations regarding the introduction of stormwater into groundwater must be reviewed. Some methods are classified as underground injection wells, which require different permits from typical stormwater management approvals.

Physical Limitations

Physical stormwater recharge limitations include the following:

- Extremely fine-grained soils that exhibit very slow infiltration rates
- Shallow depth to groundwater
- Larger drainage areas where runoff volumes become modest to large
- Steeper slopes where runoff velocities exceed 4 to 5 feet per second
- Cold winter climates where large quantities of sand/salt are applied to road surfaces

Land-Use Limitations

Land uses with the potential to generate high concentrations of soluble pollutants that can threaten groundwater quality, if infiltrated directly, include the following:

- Vehicle salvage yards and recycling facilities
- Vehicle repair and refueling stations
- Vehicle and equipment cleaning facilities
- Fleet storage areas (such as buses and trucks)
- Marina service and maintenance facilities
- Public works storage areas
- Certain industrial sites that manufacture, store, or transport toxic soluble pollutants

Carefully evaluate these threats prior to employing groundwater recharge techniques. In many instances, complex pretreatment measures can be used to reduce and/or remove pollutant and then safely apply recharging techniques.

RECHARGE TECHNIQUES

There are a variety of stormwater practices that meet the recharge objectives:

- Infiltration practices (basins, trenches, vaults, and chambers)
- Soil-based filtration systems (bioretention facilities, rain gardens, sand filters, and peat-sand and compost filters)
- Open vegetative channels and swales
- Filter strips and aquatic buffers
- Preservation of natural undisturbed areas
- Disconnection of rooftop runoff

REFERENCES

Burton, G.A., and R.E. Pitt. 2002. *Stormwater Effects Handbook: A Toolbox for Watershed Managers, Scientists, and Engineers.* Boca Raton, FL: Lewis Publishers.

Claytor, R. and R. Ohrel. 1995. *Environmental Indicators to Assess the Effectiveness of Municipal and Industrial Stormwater Control Programs: Profile Sheets.* Silver Spring, MD: Center for Watershed Protection, US EPA Office of Wastewater Management.

Horsley & Witten, Inc. 1997. *Tools for Watershed Protection —A Workshop for Local Governments.* Sponsored by the U.S. EPA. Office of Wetlands, Oceans and Watershed. Washington, D.C.: U.S. EPA.

U.S. Department of Agriculture, Natural Resources Conservation Service. 1986. *Urban Hydrology for Small Watersheds.* Technical Release 55 (TR-55). Washington, D.C.: USDA.

Winer, R. 2002. National Pollutant Removal Performance Database for Stormwater Treatment Practices, 2nd ed. Ellicott City, MD: Center for Watershed Protection.

See also:
Soils Classification and Mechanics
Watersheds

Richard Claytor, P.E., Horsley Witten Group, Sandwich, Massachusetts

WATER SUPPLY

A water supply system consists of one or more of the following components, from initial supply source to delivery:

- Water supply source, either surface water or groundwater
- Piped conduit or open channel to deliver water from source to the water treatment plant if treatment plant is not located at the source
- Water treatment plant
- Transmission line from water treatment plant to the distribution system (Pipe diameters can range from 24 to more than 96 inches.)
- Distribution pipelines located in the streets fronting the businesses and homes (Pipe diameters are typically sized from 6 to 16 inches in diameter.)
- Service lines from the distribution pipeline to the building
- Water meter on service line
- Other miscellaneous facilities including air relief valves, pressure-reducing valves, and backflow prevention devices
- Water reservoirs or tanks

SOURCES OF SUPPLY

Surface Water

Surface water is the water source most commonly used by large cities. Different surface water resources function in various ways.

- *Rivers.* Water is typically pumped from a river to a water treatment plant.
- *Reservoirs and lakes.* Water is retained behind impoundment structures and released into the system. In many cases, the stored water is used during the summer period when there is insufficient flow from the river feeding the lake to provide adequate supply.
- *Ocean.* Several large coastal communities have begun exploring the desalination of ocean water for municipal purposes. This is still emerging as a water supply source.
- *Wastewater reclamation.* Current use of reclaimed wastewater is primarily for grass and landscape irrigation.

When determining the types of surface water sources to be used, public perception is a critical component to consider. Pollution in rivers, multiple uses of lakes and rivers, the ability to desalinate the ocean, and perception issues regarding the potability of reclaimed wastewater are all issues of concern. When considering a new surface water source, conducting an extensive education and public involvement program is often necessary to gain acceptance.

Groundwater

Groundwater is an extremely important water supply source. It is the principal source for approximately 48 percent of the U.S. population (AWWA 1995). Groundwater sources can be relatively simple to develop and often require little or no treatment. They can also be found within the community area and require no more land than a site for the well and pump house, often less than a 50-foot-by-50-foot piece of land. If groundwater wells are located within an urbanized area, a wellhead protection zone should be adopted to protect the well field from contamination. Business and industrial activities located within the groundwater protection zone can be regulated to prevent activities that could contaminate the well field.

One variation of groundwater is aquifer storage and recovery (ASR). ASR involves the injection of domestic water into drilled wells, either modified existing wells or newly developed wells, and then withdrawn during the high-demand season. ASR wells serve as giant reservoirs below the ground and allow a community area to balance the winter and summer flows without construction of reservoirs and pipelines to support the high summer demands.

WATER DEMAND

Several factors influence water demand, including climate, community size and density, types of customers (residential, commercial, industrial), fire flow, cost of water, and level of water conservation.

Demand Averages

The national average daily demand is 160 gallons per capita per day (Merritt et al. 2003).

Water demand is calculated using computer models that take into account variables such as average demand by types of customers, community size and density, and climate variations. For individual developments, the developer typically informs the water agency what their estimated water use will be. Another approach is to look at historical usage and project that forward.

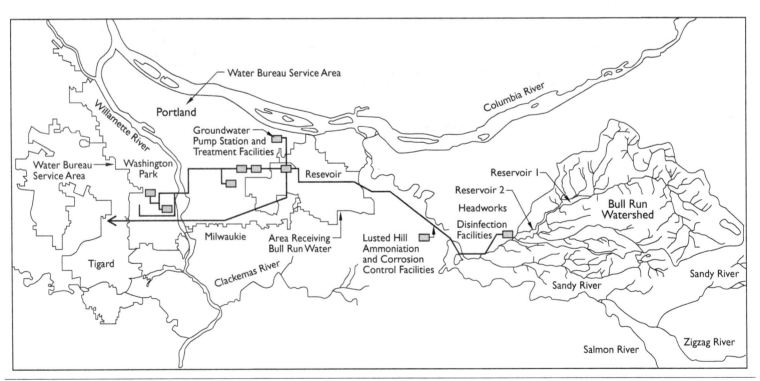

WATER SUPPLY SYSTEM, PORTLAND, OREGON

Source: City of Portland, Oregon, Water Bureau.

Greg DiLoreto, P.E., Tualatin Valley Water District, Beaverton, Oregon

Peaks

Water demand varies over the course of a day, month, and year. The amount of water used on the highest consumption day of the year is known as the peaking factor. A peaking factor is applied to determine maximum daily demands. Typical peaking factors range from 1.1 for communities that are heavily industrialized, have high density, little outside summer water usage, and a strong water conservation program, to more than 2.0 for suburban areas with large lots and mostly residential services. In hot climates with extensive outdoor irrigation, the peaking factor may exceed 2.5.

Fire Flow

The Insurance Services Office (ISO) classifies a community for insurance rating purposes on the basis of a maximum fire flow credit of 3,500 gallons per minute (gpm) flow from the water system. Fire flow requirements are set for various building types, and water systems need to meet those demands. In general, overall water systems are evaluated for fire flow capability assuming fire flows of 3,500 gpm for commercial and industrial areas, and 1,500 gpm for residential areas.

WATER QUALITY REGULATIONS

Federal

All U.S. public water systems serving at least 15 connections or 25 people must comply with the Safe Drinking Water Act (SDWA) of 1974 and its 1986 and 1996 amendments. The SDWA defines a contaminant as any physical, chemical, biological, or radiological substance or matter in water. Maximum contaminant levels (MCL) state the maximum permissible level of a contaminant in water delivered to any user of a public water system.

State and Local

Some states and municipalities have adopted standards and water quality goals for the water they serve their customers that are more stringent than the SDWA. However, no state or municipality may adopt a standard less stringent than those required by the SDWA.

Many statutes are adopted by states to both implement the Safe Drinking Water Act and to address other issues such as the Uniform Fire Code (UFC). The UFC describes the fire flow requirements for various dwelling types.

DEVELOPMENT STANDARDS

Most water providers have adopted development standards that prescribe the required sizing, type, location, and materials to be used in the development of water systems. Typically, the local governing body from which compliance is required adopts these standards.

WATER RIGHTS

To be able to access a source, a water provider must hold water rights to that source. There are two basic systems of water rights in the United States:

- Riparian doctrine, commonly used in the eastern United States
- Doctrine of prior appropriation, used in the more arid western United States

Riparian Doctrine

In the riparian doctrine, the theory is that those owning land adjacent to a body of water should share the water. This represents a sharing concept, as opposed to a right to a specific amount of water.

Doctrine of Prior Appropriation

The doctrine of prior appropriation states "first in time, first in right." A permit is granted for a specific amount of water, and the water right is based on the date of the permit or when the use first occurred. The doctrine follows two basic principles: priority use and beneficial use.

- *Priority use.* When stream flows are less than demand, use is prioritized, assigning those with the oldest permits the most seniority.
- *Beneficial use.* Water can only be used if it can be put to beneficial use, which includes water being used for municipal and agriculture demands.

NEW WATER SUPPLY SOURCES

Developing new surface water sources for urban water supply is a complex process. Involving the public, securing all necessary state and federal permits, securing funding, designing and constructing facilities, and implementing the system can take 10 years or longer. Development and population growth projections are necessary to help best determine the next increment of supply to meet estimated future demand.

REFERENCES

Grady, R. Patrick, and Peter C. Karalekas Jr., editors, with the *Journal of the New England Water Works Association.* 1995. *Water Sources, Principles and Practices of Water Supply Operations.* 2nd edition, 3rd ed. Denver, CO: AWWA.

Merritt, Frederick S., Jonathan T. Ricketts, and M. Kent Loftin. 2003. *Standard Handbook for Civil Engineers.* New York: McGraw-Hill.

See also:
*Adequate Public Facilities and Concurrency
  Management
Aquifers*

Greg DiLoreto, P.E., Tualatin Valley Water District, Beaverton, Oregon

WIRELESS INFRASTRUCTURE

Wireless infrastructure includes the towers, antennas, radio equipment, and associated structures that establish a wireless communications network. Currently, more than 50 percent of U.S. households use mobile phones, and, by 2007, that number will have increased to 80 percent.

Wireless carriers establish and expand their service by constructing base stations or by contracting with an infrastructure company to construct base stations or install their antennas on an existing structure.

DEMAND FOR WIRELESS SERVICE

The demand for more and better wireless service is on the rise. To meet this demand, wireless carriers must try to achieve coverage throughout the community, including residential areas. The challenge facing municipalities throughout the country is twofold: to enable wireless deployment in a responsible way, and to develop zoning regulations and comprehensive plans to accommodate this rapidly changing environment. Because of the continual changes to this technology, municipalities should periodically review their telecommunications regulations to ensure that they meet current and future community demand for wireless services.

COMPONENTS OF WIRELESS INFRASTRUCTURE

The components of wireless infrastructure are essentially the wireless handset, a specialized radio set commonly referred to as a mobile, or "cell," phone, and a base station, a transmission facility in a fixed location designed to communicate with the wired telephone network or with mobile or portable communications devices. Although appearance varies widely, generally, base stations contain the following components:

An **antenna** may be directional, such as a panel or dish antenna, or omnidirectional, such as a whip antenna.

An **antenna support structure** is either a vertical structure built for the express purpose of supporting wireless telecommunications equipment, such as a tower, monopole, or monopine, or a vertical structure normally intended for another purpose but which can also support wireless telecommunications equipment, such as transmission towers, building rooftops, and water towers.

Obstruction lighting comprises either steady or strobe lights mounted on those antenna support structures located in navigable airspace for air traffic safety.

Computerized radio equipment includes the radio receivers, transmitters, and telephone switching gear at the core of the base station operation.

An **equipment shed or cabinet** is a structure used to house the computerized radio equipment.

Cabling is the means by which the antennas connect to the radio equipment.

A **T1 land line and utility connection** are conduits to the telephone network or other portable communications devices and to the power grid.

Emergency generators or an array of batteries serve as backups to enable uninterrupted service during a power outage.

In addition, where appropriate or applicable, base stations may have access roads or driveways; fencing around the compound, to deter public access; landscape planting or screening to mitigate visual impacts; and signage containing contact information, as well as the antenna structure registration (ASR) number if the structure is registered with the Federal Communications Commission (FCC).

REGULATIONS

The construction, siting, and design of wireless infrastructure are regulated on the federal, state, and local levels. Typically the regulated elements include the following:

- Tower height
- Lighting and marking
- Placement
- Frequencies and power levels
- Type and size of associated equipment structures
- Fencing
- Signage
- Landscape planting

Federal Regulations

Several federal laws and agencies have jurisdiction over issues related to telecommunications.

The Telecommunications Act of 1996. The main purposes of this act are to clarify the level of regulation that local governments can apply to service providers and to provide for industry-wide competition.

The Federal Communications Commission (FCC). The FCC regulates operational aspects of wireless services, including antenna frequencies, operating powers, and radio frequency emissions. The FCC also regulates towers with antennas through the antenna structure registration (ASR) program.

The National Environmental Policy Act of 1969 (NEPA). All antenna structures must comply with NEPA. In many instances, applicants must conduct an environmental assessment (EA) to investigate all potential environmental impacts and disclose any significant effects that would result. If the EA determines that significant adverse impacts would result, the FCC places all such proposals on public notice for a 30-day public comment period.

The National Historic Preservation Act of 1966 (NHPA). Infrastructure providers must ensure that structures do not have an adverse effect on historic properties, including buildings, districts, structures, objects, or Native American burial grounds. If there is a potential for impacts

on such a resource, the tower applicant must work with the State Historic Preservation Officer (SHPO) to identify actions to mitigate impacts.

The Federal Aviation Administration (FAA). The FAA regulates structures within navigable airspace. Towers above a certain height or within a certain distance of an airport must be registered with the FAA and possibly be marked with lighting or painting. Tower companies submit project proposals to the FAA for evaluation for a determination of "no hazard to air navigation."

The Occupational Safety and Health Administration (OSHA). OSHA provides regulations to protect the workers who construct, service, or work on or around towers.

State Regulations

On the state level, wireless facility regulations vary, with most states deferring wireless infrastructure siting controls to local governments. However, a few states have enacted legislation that supersedes local regulatory authority to ensure that certain state public policy objectives are met. For example, Washington requires its communities to allow wireless service providers to place antenna sites in public rights-of-way, and Connecticut has a state-level siting council that reviews applications for antenna sites throughout the state. In addition, some state occupational safety agencies have safety standards that supplement the federal requirements, and many state departments of environmental protection provide regulations that protect wetlands and habitat areas from tower construction impacts.

Local Regulations

Zoning

Nearly all local governments have zoning authority over antenna and associated infrastructure siting. Zoning regulations typically identify which zoning districts allow for these facilities and establish standards for the size, height, and type of facility, its placement on the property, and any buffering and screening required to mitigate visual intrusion.

Permitting

Wireless facilities siting typically follows a local government's permit review process, including any requirements for site plan submission and approval. The review process, which is usually a prerequisite for building permit issuance, evaluates the plans to ensure the facility meets all prescribed safety and structural/building code standards.

WIRELESS FACILITIES SITING

In addition to following local zoning regulations, applicants should select sites that are safe, effective, and as visually unobtrusive as possible. Site selection typically involves the applicant identifying the geographic area, or search ring, that will enable the carrier to meet the desired coverage objective while integrating with any existing or planned neighboring sites. The coverage objective is generally based on market demand for new services, enhanced quality, or increased system capacity.

PICA — The Wireless Infrastructure Association, Alexandria, Virginia

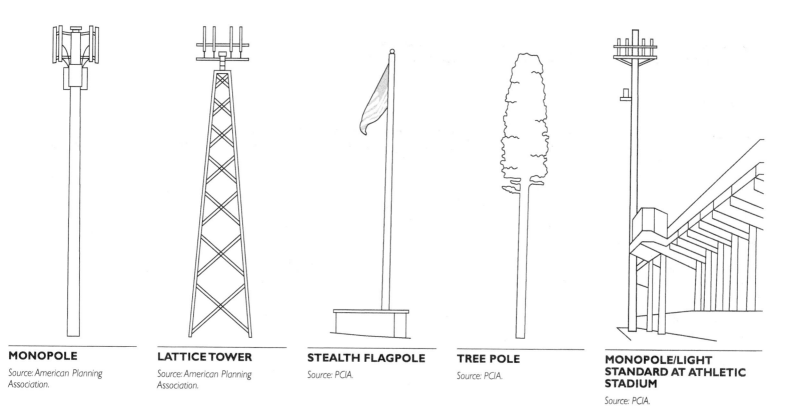

MONOPOLE

Source: *American Planning
Association.*

LATTICE TOWER

Source: *American Planning
Association.*

STEALTH FLAGPOLE

Source: *PCIA.*

TREE POLE

Source: *PCIA.*

**MONOPOLE/LIGHT
STANDARD AT ATHLETIC
STADIUM**

Source: *PCIA.*

Site selection is often a process of elimination. When looking for coverage, there is usually more than one site that is suitable. However, as the demand for more and better wireless services continues to escalate, particularly in residential areas, the number of sites narrows considerably. This is called capacity. Accordingly, companies select those sites that are most likely to:

- meet federal regulations;
- comply with local siting requirements;
- be acceptable to the community;
- provide the highest-quality wireless service; and
- result in the minimum number of sites required overall to meet the service needs of the market.

Zoning Review and Approval

In most communities, local governments have jurisdiction over wireless telecommunications siting decisions. The Telecommunications Act of 1996 preserves this authority. However, local government zoning decisions about wireless telecommunications facilities must satisfy certain conditions:

- No discriminating among providers
- No passing of laws or taking actions that prohibit or have the effect of prohibiting wireless service
- No regulating of wireless based on environmental concerns about radio frequency emissions if the facility will operate within FCC standards
- Acting on siting requests in a reasonable period of time
- Issuing zoning denials in writing, supported by substantial evidence and findings contained in a written record

The act also allows applicants to request expedited appeals of zoning denials to both state and federal courts.

MITIGATING IMPACTS OF WIRELESS TELECOMMUNICATIONS FACILITIES

Several steps can be taken to reduce the impact that towers have on a community:

- Locate facilities in or around areas of mature vegetation that screen all or part of the facility, thereby reducing its visual impact.
- To the extent permitting by federal regulations that govern marking schemes, color the structure to blend in with the surrounding vegetation or skyline.
- Plant vegetative cover or constructing fencing at the base of the facility to screen the ground equipment.
- Pursue "stealth" options, such as designing the tower or monopole to look like a tree, silo, or a flagpole.
- Require low-profile or slim-lined structures where the antennas are installed more closely to the tower, thereby reducing the physical profile of the facility.

See also:
Federal Legislation

PARKS AND OPEN SPACE

TYPES OF PARKS

Contemporary parks and open-space planning focuses on creating systems that respond to local values, needs, and circumstances. The region of the country, physical setting, landscape features, demographics, and socioeconomic characteristics are all determining factors in the form that a community's park and open-space system will take. In each system, parks and open spaces are defined under various classifications that function individually and collectively to create a cohesive and balanced system.

Successful parks and open-space systems are often planned around distinguishing landscape features or local themes that exhibit the unique qualities of a community. The "city as a park" concept is a common theme, whereby parks and open spaces are key factors in shaping the built form and character of a community. Perpetuating an interconnected latticework of parks, natural open spaces, and trails throughout the community is another theme. Common to all systems is the notion of creating a high-quality living environment through the provision of parks, open spaces, trails, and recreational amenities.

With such a broad spectrum of potential applications, the classifications for parks and open space are necessarily flexible and adaptable to the unique circumstances to which they are applied. The extent to which one type of park versus another is found within a system is determined by local needs and circumstances. In a metropolitan system, emphasis on neighborhood parks, parkways, and large urban parks is common in response to the urban form and distinctiveness of individual neighborhoods. In an outer-ring suburban area rich in natural resources, creating an interconnected system of greenways, parks, and trails may be the desired vision.

PARK AND OPEN-SPACE CLASSIFICATIONS

A typical park and open-space system consists of a variety of parks and open spaces defined under various classifications. The classifications presented here are based on consolidating generally accepted professional practices used across the country. They are meant to be guidelines, not rigid standards. Each community must refine and apply them to suit its specific needs. The table provides an overview of the classifications for a typical local park system. Additional references for park and open-space classifications include the *National Park, Recreation, Open Space and Greenway Guidelines*, published by the National Recreation and Park Association (1995).

CUMULATIVE PARK SYSTEM ACREAGE STANDARDS

Historically, acreage standards (i.e., optimal number of acres of parkland per 1,000 population) were used, in part, to determine the overall land area necessary to meet community parks and open-space needs. Since the mid-1990s, this broad-brush approach has been deemphasized because it was found to be too

PARKS AND GREENWAYS CLASSIFICATIONS

CLASSIFICATION	GENERAL DESCRIPTION	SIZE AND SERVICE AREA CRITERIA
Neighborhood Park	Neighborhood parks are the basic units of the park system and serve a recreational and social purpose. Focus is on informal recreation.	Typically 5 acres or more; 8 to 10 acres preferred, with 3 acres the desired minimum size. Service area is one-fourth to one-half mile uninterrupted by major roads and other physical barriers.
Community Park	Serves a broader purpose than neighborhood parks. Focus is on meeting community-based recreational needs, as well as preserving unique landscapes and open spaces.	Varies, depending on function. A minimum of 20 acres is preferred, with 40 or more acres optimal. Service area can be communitywide or several neighborhoods in given area of the community.
Large Urban Park	Large urban parks are generally associated with larger urban centers with large populations. Focus is on meeting wide-ranging community needs and preserving unique and sometimes extensive landscapes and open spaces.	Varies depending on circumstances. A typical minimum size is 50 acres (20.2 hectares), with hundreds of acres not uncommon, such as Central Park in New York City.
Youth Athletic Complex/Facility	Consolidates programmed youth athletic fields and associated facilities to fewer strategically located sites throughout the community. Also can provide some neighborhood use functions.	Varies, with 20 acres or more desirable, but not absolute. Optimal size is 40 to 80 acres (16.2 to 32.4 hectares).
Community Athletic Complex/Facility	Consolidates programmed adult and youth athletic fields and associated facilities to a limited number of sites. Tournament-level facilities are appropriate.	Varies, with 20 acres (8.1 hectares) or more desirable, but not absolute. Optimal size is 40 to 80 acres (16.2 to 32.4 hectares).
Greenway	Lands set aside for preserving natural resources, remnant landscapes, and open space, and providing visual aesthetics/buffering. Also provides passive-use opportunities. Ecological resource stewardship and wildlife protection are high priorities. Suitable for ecologically sensitive trail corridors.	Varies, depending on opportunity and general character of natural systems within the community.
Parkway	Linear parklike transportation corridors between public parks, monuments, institutions, and sometimes business centers. Can be maintained green space or natural in character.	Varies.
Special Use	Covers a broad range of parks and recreation facilities oriented toward single-purpose uses, such as a nature center, historic sites, plazas, urban squares, aquatic centers, campgrounds, and golf courses.	Varies, depending on need.
Park-School	School sites that are used in concert with, or in lieu of, other types of parks to meet community park and recreation needs. School sites often provide the majority of indoor recreational facilities within a community.	Varies, depending on specific site opportunities.
Private Park/Recreation Facility	Parks and recreation facilities that are privately owned, yet contribute to the public park and recreation system.	Varies.
Regional Parks and Park Reserves	Larger-scale, regionally based parks and open spaces that focus on natural resource preservation and stewardship.	Typically a minimum of 500 acres (202.3 hectares) and up to several thousand acres or several hundred hectares. Service area is regional, which generally encompasses several cities.

arbitrary and not reflective enough of the nuances of park and open-space opportunities and needs associated with individual communities.

The current standard is for each community to develop a park and open-space system plan based on an assessment of its own unique park and open-space system needs and opportunities. A comparison analysis against like cities is still often justifiable, but only as part of larger needs assessment to ensure that a well-balanced system plan emerges based on local circumstances.

NEIGHBORHOOD PARK

Neighborhood parks are the basic unit of the park system and serve a recreational and social purpose. Development focuses on informal recreation. Programmed activities are typically limited to youth sports practices and occasionally games.

General Characteristics

- In new developments, typically 5 acres (2 hectares) or more, 8 to 10 acres (3.2 to 4 hectares) preferred, with 3 acres (1.2 hectares) the minimum size. In existing cities, parks are often one acre or smaller.
- Service area radius of between one-fourth and one-half mile (0.4 to 0.8 kilometers) and uninterrupted by major roads or physical barriers, such as wetlands and lakes. A reasonable walking distance is critical to a person's propensity to use the park.
- Centrally located within the neighborhood it serves.
- Site exhibits suitable physical and aesthetic characteristics, with a balance between developable open space and natural areas. Lowlands and other lands not suitable for development are also not suitable for a neighborhood park.
- Connected to neighborhoods via trails or sidewalks. The less convenient the access, the less use a park is likely to receive.

Jeffrey Schoenbauer, Brauer & Associates, Ltd., Edina, Minnesota

- Where feasible, connected to a greenway or open-space system to expand the sense of open space at the neighborhood level.

In situations where neighborhood parks are integrated into a larger greenway system with interlinking trails, the distance between parks can be expanded to one-half to three-fourths mile (0.8 to 12. kilometers) because greenways and trails provide easy access and these corridors are perceived to be part of the park experience by the user.

Development Parameters

The design for each park is uniquely tailored to the neighborhood it serves, rather than the generalized needs of the overall community. The common objective of all neighborhood parks is to bring people together to recreate and socialize close to home. Active, nonprogrammed recreation remains a mainstay of these parks, although contemporary design emphasizes providing a balanced set of amenities that appeal to a broad range of individuals to increase park usage.

The general palette of amenities typically found within a neighborhood park includes the following:

- Play area for multiple age groups
- Accessible trail loop internal to the park, with a connection to the community trail system and local streets
- Open maintained green space for informal use (2 to 3 acres optimal)
- Basketball halfcourt, volleyball court, hardcourt area (for games such as hopscotch and four-square), or tennis court
- Ice skating (on limited basis consistent with overall communitywide program)
- General site amenities, such as benches, picnic tables, trash containers, and security lighting

- Picnic shelter and picnic area (for larger neighborhood parks)
- Aesthetic improvements and architectural elements—arbor structure with benches and ornamental fencing, for example (The importance of this design feature should not be underestimated. Aesthetically appealing parks are far more likely to be used.)
- Ornamental landscape planting near active use areas
- Natural landscape planting and natural-based stormwater infiltration systems
- Parking, on a limited on-demand-only basis. Frequently parking can be provided on street.
- Controlled-glare security lighting

COMMUNITY AND LARGE URBAN PARKS

Community and large urban parks are considerably larger in scale and serve a broader purpose than neighborhood parks. The main difference between a community and large urban park is that the latter is often associated with urban settings with large populations. Large urban parks also tend to be larger than community parks in order to provide more park space in a denser populated urban setting. They are especially prevalent in urban areas with limited natural open spaces, such as New York City's Central Park.

The focus of both types of parks is on meeting wide-ranging community recreation and social needs. The facilities found within these parks are entirely based on meeting defined community needs. Development focuses on both active and passive recreation, with a wide array of programmed activities often being accommodated. Special-use facilities are routinely located within these parks.

This type of park also encompasses unique and extensive landscape features indicative of the region.

Providing respite from the built form is also a major objective of these parks.

General Characteristics

- Size varies for community parks, with 20 acres (8.1 hectares) being the typical minimum. Parks of 40 acres (16.2 hectares) or more are preferred, although smaller ones offering unique features with communitywide appeal are not uncommon.
- Service area ranges from several neighborhoods to community and even regionwide.
- A variety of landscapes are desirable, ranging from natural open space to maintained active recreation areas. Large urban parks tend to have a more manicured character than community parks. The overall character of this type of park responds to the unique qualities of the community. There is significant latitude in the definition of a community or large urban park across the country, given the variety of settings in which they are located.
- Good road access is important.
- Connection to the larger community and neighborhoods via trails or sidewalks is desirable. These parks are often the terminus point for trail systems.
- Direct connection to a greenway system is desirable to expand the sense of open space associated with the park.

Development Parameters

The design for each type of park is a reflection of the community. The common objective of community and large urban parks is to bring people together to recreate, socialize, and find quiet space. Active, programmed recreation is appropriate in these parks as long as it does not unduly interfere with other activities. As with neighborhood parks, contemporary design emphasizes providing a balanced set of amenities that appeal to a broad range of individuals to increase park usage. The general palette of amenities typically found within these two classes of park includes the following:

- Amenities common to a neighborhood park, albeit at a larger scale
- Group picnic facilities—smaller and large-scale
- Extensive looped internal trails, often serving multiple purposes
- Larger open spaces for passive and active use
- Modest level of athletic facilities (formal and informal) that blend into the character of the park (An athletic complex character is not typically desirable.)
- Open maintained green space
- Winter activities, such as ice skating, sledding, and cross-country skiing
- Special-use facilities that serve a specific recreational purpose (i.e., beaches, aquatic centers, ice arenas, campgrounds, dog parks, skateboard parks, and marinas)
- Adequate parking

YOUTH AND COMMUNITY ATHLETIC COMPLEXES

Youth and community athletic complexes consolidate athletic facilities to strategic locations within a community to take advantage of programming efficiencies and economies of scale. Consolidation of athletic facilities also allows for a closer association

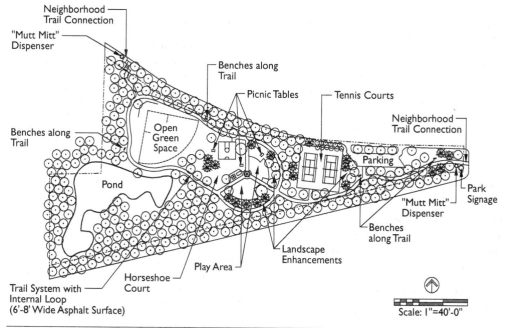

NEIGHBORHOOD PARK, MINNETONKA, MINNESOTA

Source: Brauer and Associates, Ltd.

Scale: 1"=40'-0"

Jeffrey Schoenbauer, Brauer & Associates, Ltd., Edina, Minnesota

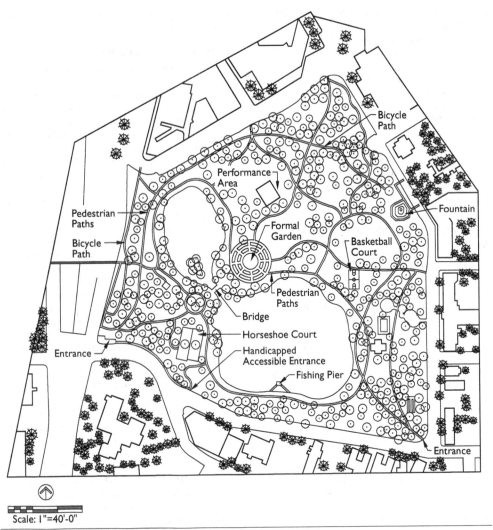

Scale: 1"=40'-0"

COMMUNITY PARK, MINNEAPOLIS, MINNESOTA

Source: Brauer and Associates, Ltd.

between players, parents, and coaches when at scheduled events. Larger and fewer sites also provide greater conveniences, such as parking, restrooms, and concessions, and the capacity to generate revenue to offset operational and maintenance costs.

Community athletic complexes are most common and serve both youth and adult athletic programs. Youth athletic complexes are more common in larger metropolitan areas where there is enough participation in youth sports to warrant a stand-alone complex. In most cases, athletic complexes are heavily programmed with facilities to maximize land uses and operational efficiency. The type of facilities found within these parks is entirely based on meeting defined community athletic program needs. With ever-changing recreational trends, greater emphasis is being placed on designing athletic complexes to be as flexible as possible without unduly compromising specific uses. As an example, "athletic greens" that can accommodate a variety of field games have replaced single-use facilities. This is largely accomplished through site grading and field lighting placement.

General Characteristics

- Size varies for athletic complexes, with 20 acres (8.1 hectares) or more being desirable. Optimal size is 40 to 80 acres (16.2 to 32.4 hectares).

- Service area ranges from numerous strategic locations throughout a large metropolitan area to one centrally located complex that serves an entire community.
- A relatively flat, open parcel of property is most desirable. The topography across the site should be adequate for field drainage and stormwater management.
- Access from major thoroughfares is important.
- Connection to the larger community and neighborhoods via trails or sidewalks is desirable.
- Adequate buffering of residential areas from lighting, noise, traffic, parking, and other impacts should be designed.

Development Parameters

The facilities provided at athletic complexes are entirely driven by demand. In communities where the population is not very diverse, a common set of traditional facilities is often appropriate. In larger, more diverse cities, the facility mix can vary widely. In both cases, due diligence is required to ensure the right mix of facilities are provided at a given site.

Facility quality tends to be highest at athletic complexes to accommodate competitive recreational leagues and tournament play. The facilities and amenities often found at athletic complexes include

fields and courts for softball, baseball, soccer, football, lacrosse, basketball, tennis, and volleyball. Regional facilities like hockey rinks are also provided where demand warrants. A greater sensitivity toward providing athletic facilities associated with new immigrant populations is also warranted in many regions of the country.

A variety of support amenities are also appropriate at athletic complexes, including restrooms, concession stands, spectator sitting areas, play areas for children, and picnic areas with shelters. Adequate parking and internal trails are also ancillary requirements. Special-use facilities that serve a specific recreational purpose (i.e., aquatic centers, ice arenas, and skateboard parks) can also be located on athletic complex sites.

GREENWAYS

Greenways are lands set aside for preservation of natural resources, remnant landscapes, open space, and visual aesthetics/buffering. Greenways also provide passive-use opportunities, most often in the form of trails and, occasionally, nature centers. The key focus is on protecting ecological resources and providing wildlife corridors.

Greenways can take various forms. In the broadest application, greenways form a network of interconnected natural areas throughout a community. They function as part of a borderless system that links together parks, natural open spaces, and trail corridors into a latticework of public space. In this context, the line between greenways, parks, trails, and the built environment is purposefully blurred, fostering the "city as a park" concept. Establishing an extensive continuous greenway system requires a close collaborative relationship between the city and development community in order to set aside the land for this purpose.

Greenways can also take the form of a stand-alone land parcel dedicated to open-space preservation. These are often referred to as nature preserves or nature parks and often serve the same basic function as other forms of greenways.

General Characteristics

The baseline criterion for defining greenways is to preserve the highest-quality and most unique landscape features of the city. This most often includes lakes, wetlands, creek corridors, bluff lines, and remnant, relatively undisturbed natural areas exhibiting vegetative communities common to the area. Ecological buffers, which provide physical separation between sensitive or vulnerable natural resources and the built environment, are often integrated into the greenway system as part of the land development process.

Restored landscape, such as an agriculture field transformed back into a prairie, can also be integrated into the greenway system. This most commonly occurs as part of a development plan in which restored natural areas are part of an ecologically based stormwater management system.

The width of linear greenways can vary considerably. See Greenways and Trails elsewhere in this book for width information.

Development Parameters

Development within greenways is typically limited to trails, sitting areas, observation areas, and interpretive/directional signage. In some cases, nature centers

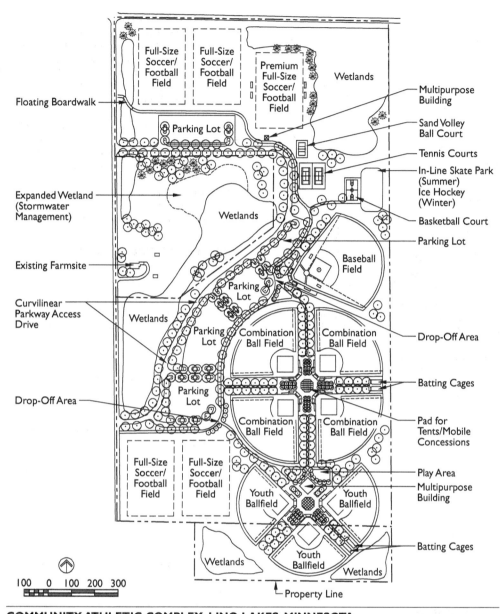

COMMUNITY ATHLETIC COMPLEX, LINO LAKES, MINNESOTA

Source: Brauer and Associates, Ltd.

dated in parkways. Roadway and trailside signage is important.

SPECIAL-USE PARKS

The special-use classification covers a broad range of parks and recreation facilities oriented toward single-purpose or specialized use:

- Nature and cultural/performing arts centers
- Historic sites: downtowns, plazas, cemeteries, historic landscapes, churches, and monuments
- Recreation facilities: aquatic centers, campgrounds, ice arenas, fitness centers, community centers, skateboard parks, and stadiums
- Public gathering areas: amphitheaters, community commons, town centers, and urban squares

In some systems, certain types of special uses are defined under their own classifications when those occurrences are frequent enough to warrant doing so. For example, an urban square classification is sometimes used in major urban communities to accommodate public plazas, courtyards, and formal sitting areas.

General Characteristics and Development Parameters

The development of special-use facilities is driven by local demand and specific circumstances.

PARK-SCHOOL

The park-school classification pertains to school sites used in concert with, or in lieu of, other classes of parks to meet community park and recreation needs. In most cases, these sites are best suited for youth athletic facilities for both school district and community-based recreational programs. Park-school sites also often provide the majority of indoor recreational facilities within a community.

To a lesser degree, school sites can also be used to service neighborhood park needs. The limiting factor is that most of these sites are heavily programmed for active uses and school buildings. This often leaves little space to accommodate neighborhood-focused amenities and create an aesthetically appealing setting that would draw families into the site.

General Characteristics

- For new development, size varies for park-school sites, with 20 acres (8.1 hectares) being the typical minimum. Sites of 40 acres (16.2 hectares) or more are preferred because the school buildings and parking can consume considerable space. Acreage can be reduced considerably in already developed areas through the use of multi-story schools and on-street parking.
- Service area ranges from several neighborhoods to communitywide, depending on the facilities provided. The location is almost always determined by the school district, especially in cases where the district boundaries encompass more than one community.
- A variety of landscape planting is desirable, although these sites tend to be inherently utilitarian in character.
- Good road access is important.
- Connection to the larger community and neighborhoods via trails or sidewalks is desirable.

or arboretums are integrated into larger greenways. A combination of multiuse hard-surfaced trails for biking, walking, and in-line skating and nature trails for hiking are found within most greenway systems. In select instances, no development is allowed and the site is set aside for wildlife and community viewing from the periphery.

PARKWAYS

Parkways are best characterized as linear parks that also serve as transportation corridors between public parks, historic features, monuments, institutions, and business centers. They often follow a notable landscape feature, such as a creek or river.

General Characteristics

The length of a parkway ranges from less than a mile to a complete loop around a major metropolitan area. Their width can vary considerably, with 200 feet being the practical minimum, and widths of 1,000 feet or more being common along major parkways.

Landscape planting and ornamental site amenities (i.e., street lighting, site furnishings and other architectural elements) provide the visual cues that distinguish parkways from other thoroughfares. A broad, tree-lined boulevard is a common image of a parkway, as is a linear park along a major river. In keeping with the setting, heavy truck traffic is often, but not exclusively, prohibited along parkways.

Landscape planting can range from a maintained, ornamental character to one that is more natural, or a combination of both.

Development Parameters

Development within parkways is typically limited to roadways and pedestrian trails. Sitting areas and overlooks often augment trails to view a natural or human-made feature. Occasionally, picnic shelters and other standalone park features are accommo-

Jeffrey Schoenbauer, Brauer & Associates, Ltd., Edina, Minnesota

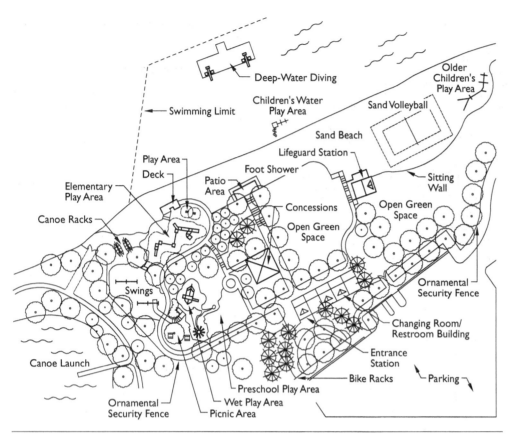

SPECIAL-USE PARK, MINNEAPOLIS, MINNESOTA

Source: Brauer and Associates, Ltd.

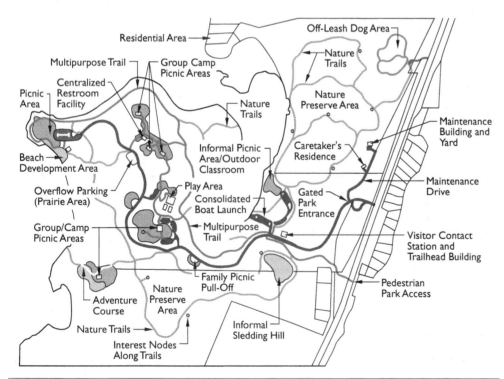

REGIONAL PARK, CARVER COUNTY, MINNESOTA

Source: Brauer and Associates, Ltd.

Jeffrey Schoenbauer, Brauer & Associates, Ltd., Edina, Minnesota

Development Parameters

The design for park-school sites is driven first by the needs of the school district, with most of the facilities designed to accommodate physical education and sports programs. The facilities provided at school sites are most often consistent with the youth athletic complex and neighborhood park classifications. Local cities often partner with local school districts to avoid duplication of facilities and to leverage public capital investments. In many cases, the school district provides the land and basic facilities, and the local community funds improvements to the quality of the facilities.

Well-defined joint use agreements between the community and school district are essential to making these partnerships mutually successful.

PRIVATE PARK/RECREATION FACILITY

The private park/recreation facility classification covers a broad range of nonpublic parks and recreation facilities. This includes facilities such as golf courses, fitness clubs, museums, private courtyards, amphitheaters, horse-riding stables, water parks, and miniature golf courses.

This classification is provided as a means to acknowledge the contribution that a given private facility has to the public parks and open-space system within a community.

General Characteristics and Development Parameters

The development of private parks and recreation facilities is driven by local demand and business opportunities.

REGIONAL PARKS

The definition of a regional park varies considerably across the country. The common distinguishing feature is that regional parks typically service multiple cities and cross political jurisdictions. In many cases, a separate regional park authority is established to manage a series of regional parks.

In some areas of the country, developers of regional parks focus on setting aside larger tracts of land to preserve natural resources, remnant landscapes, and open space. A key objective is protecting ecological resources and providing wildlife habitat. Passive uses, such as hiking, canoeing, and nature viewing, are most common forms of activities. The primary distinction between this type of regional parks and greenways is scale and service area. Regional parks are typically at a much larger scale (in land area) than greenways.

In other areas of the country, regional parks are an extension of the large urban park classification. In addition to preserving natural resources and open space, these parks also provide active recreational areas, gardens, picnic facilities, and other forms of special use. In parts of the country, regional parks include major national monuments and historic landscapes.

General Characteristics

• Size varies for regional parks, with several thousand acres (several hundred hectares) being common. A size of less than 100 acres (40.5 hectares) is uncommon.

- Major natural resource and landscape features typically form the basis for regional parks. Service area is typically several cities.
- The overall character of this type of park responds to the unique qualities of the region that the park serves. There is significant latitude in the definition of a regional park across the country, given the variety of settings in which they are located.

- Good road access is important.
- Connection to the adjoining cities and region via trails is desirable. Regional parks are often the terminus point for trail systems.
- Direct connection to a greenway system is desirable to expand the sense of open space associated with the park.

Development Parameters

The design for regional parks is a reflection of the open-space, recreational, and social needs of the region they serve. The level of development is driven by regional standards and needs.

See also:

Greenways and Trails
Parks and Open-Space Plans
Parks, Recreation, and Open-Space Needs Assessment

Jeffrey Schoenbauer, Brauer & Associates, Ltd., Edina, Minnesota

PARKS AND OPEN SPACE

GREENWAYS AND TRAILS

Greenways are "a linear open space established along either a natural corridor, such as a riverfront, stream valley, or ridgeline, or overland along a railroad right-of-way converted to recreational use, a canal, a scenic road, or other route" (Little 1990). Greenways should be thought of as corridors. Trails can often be found within a greenway, but not all greenways contain trails. Some greenways serve as conservation corridors for plants and animals and do not permit human use.

Land-based greenway systems are normally composed of trails that traverse a variety of terrestrial-based landscapes. Water-based greenway systems use streams, rivers, lakes, and larger bodies of navigable water, including inland seas and sounds.

TYPES OF GREENWAYS

Greenway and trail systems vary in size, scope, and function. They can include:

- local systems within a neighborhood;
- communitywide systems;
- regional systems covering multiple counties; and
- statewide, multistate, and national systems.

Greenway systems also vary by location. They can include urban, suburban, rural, regional, and state greenways.

Greenways and trails have become two of the most popular products of the outdoor conservation movement, largely because they meet the needs of different constituent groups. Successful greenways and trails offer a wide range of benefits, including recreation, health and wellness, transportation, economic, and education.

PLANNING AND DESIGN ELEMENTS

Several factors go into the development of functional and successful greenways systems are described in the following sections.

Accommodating the User

Most greenways should serve the interests of a wide range of users, including people who want to walk, bike, or view wildlife. Some greenways will be developed to serve conservation needs, including habitat, floodplain, or water quality protection. Greenways with trails should be designed and constructed to be accessible to all persons, regardless of their abilities. An excellent guide on this subject is *Designing Sidewalks and Trails for Access: Part 2, Best Practices Design Guide* (Beneficial Designs 2001).

Connectivity

The most successful greenways link people to popular destinations. Each segment of a system should have logical and functional endpoints. Greenways with trails that serve as links throughout a community are the most popular for users. Sometimes greenways will end abruptly, however, especially in urban areas. Greenways should be linked to other trails, conservation areas, parks, and to an on-road network of bicycle facilities and sidewalks, where appropriate.

Connectivity is especially important for plants and animals. In this manner, greenways serve as "geneways," offering the opportunity for migration. Gene-ways are becoming important to the survival of plant and animal species worldwide due to fluctuations in temperature, rainfall, and food source.

Multiuser Conflict

Multiuser conflict is regarded as the most serious safety concern for greenways and trails. Conflicts between cyclists and pedestrians are the most prevalent and are usually caused by reckless and unsafe behavior, incompatible use values, or by overcrowding. The most effective remedies begin with design and management. Trails can and should be designed to reduce conflict by widening the trail tread or by separating the trail tread for different users. The "tread" is the surface area used by trail users. Single-tread, multiuse trails can also be managed to reduce conflicts, sometimes by separating users under a time-of-use or zoning policy.

Involving user groups in the design of a trail is the best way to both understand local needs and resolve the potential for multiuse conflict. It is also important to post trails with a trail use ordinance and provide educational materials on how to use the trail.

Fitting Greenways to the Environment

The most enjoyable greenways celebrate the natural landscapes and native environments they traverse. This is one of the most popular reasons why outdoor advocates choose to use greenways. Greenways should have rhythm and syncopation, and flow

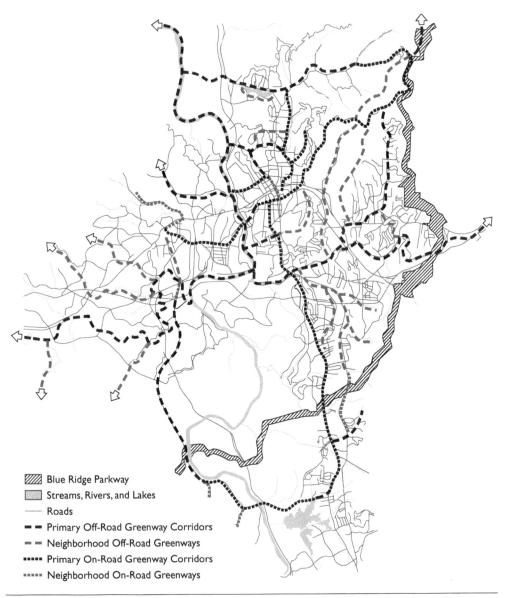

Blue Ridge Parkway
Streams, Rivers, and Lakes
Roads
■ ■ Primary Off-Road Greenway Corridors
■ ■ Neighborhood Off-Road Greenways
■■■■■ Primary On-Road Greenway Corridors
■■■■■ Neighborhood On-Road Greenways

PRIMARY AND NEIGHBORHOOD GREENWAY ROUTE SYSTEM, ASHEVILLE, NORTH CAROLINA

Source: *Greenways, Inc. 1998.*

Charles A. Flink, FASLA, Greenways, Inc., Cary, North Carolina

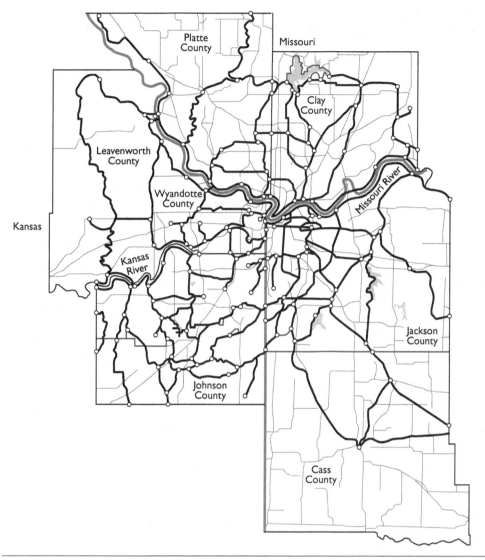

REGIONAL GREENWAY SYSTEM

Source: Mid-America Regional Council, Kansas City, Missouri, 2004.

LARGEST GREENWAY SYSTEMS IN THE UNITED STATES (MILES OF TRAIL)

CITY	MILES OF GREENWAY PLANNED	MILES OF GREENWAY COMPLETE	FEATURED GREENWAY
Denver Metro	900	250	Cherry Creek Greenway
Minneapolis Metro	1,000	200	Cedar Lake Trail
Chicago Metro	4,300	700	Grand Illinois Trail
Portland Metro	950	250	Willamette River Greenway
Boston Metro	800	450	Bay Circuit Trail
San Francisco Metro	2,000	300	Contra Costa Canal Trail

Source: Information compiled by Greenways, Inc. 2004.

Note: Most local governments do not maintain statistics for their greenway systems, so this information is compiled from a variety of sources and represents the best estimation of total planned and completed miles.

within their surroundings so that they captivate users. Greenways should follow the natural contours of the land and take advantage of native landscape features, such as water, groupings of vegetation, scenic views, and interesting built features.

Integrating Greenways into the Built Environment

Greenways should also celebrate the built landscapes they traverse. Planners and designers often try to hide

views deemed unpleasant. This may not always be a good idea. For greenways designed to be used by people, it is much better to keep viewsheds open. Trails through urban landscapes provide an opportunity to interpret the surrounding environment. Great care must also be taken to successfully fit a new greenway and trail into the urban fabric. For example, the conversion of abandoned railroad corridors has been a growing resource for new urban trails in the past 20 years. But this practice presents challenges for

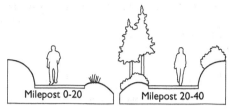

Single-Tread for Multiple-Use Zoning

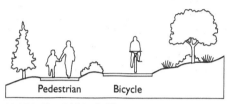

Multiple-Tread, Multiple-Use

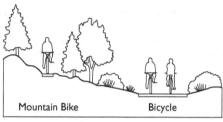

Multiple-Tread, Single-Use

TYPES OF TRAIL TREADS

Source: From Greenways, by Charles A. Flink and Robert M. Searns. Copyright 1993 by The Conservation Fund. Reproduced with permission of Island Press, Washington, D.C.

trail designers because these corridors supported a different type of transportation activity. Creating new intersections between roads and converted rail-trails is the greatest challenge for these urban trails. It is important that intersections be designed to clearly determine who has the right-of-way. Intersections should also be very clearly marked for all groups to delineate crossing zones for trail users. Pavement markings, signage, lighting, and texture pavement can all be used to make intersections safer.

GREENWAY AND TRAIL WIDTHS

Greenway Widths

Greenways will vary in width depending on the amount of land available to support their intended use. Trail-based greenways may be quite narrow, with the sole purpose to support a hiking or biking trail. For metro or urban systems, urban trail greenway corridors should range in minimum width from 50 to 100 feet (15.2 to 30.5 meters). When urban greenway widths are less than 50 feet (15.2 meters), problems will occur with separation from adjacent land uses, maintenance and operations, and enjoyment of use. For suburban greenways and rural greenways where other functions are to be included, such as stormwater management, flood abatement, wildlife preservation, or historic interpretation, minimum widths should begin at 100 feet (30.5 meters) and may extend beyond 300 feet (91.4 meters).

Charles A. Flink, FASLA, Greenways, Inc., Cary, North Carolina

MINIMUM RECOMMENDED TREAD WIDTHS FOR MULTIUSE TRAILS (IN FEET)

TREAD TYPE	URBAN	SUBURBAN	RURAL
Single-tread, multiple-use			
Pedestrian/nonmotorized	12	10	10
Pedestrian/saddle and pack animal	16	12	10
Pedestrian/motorized	22	22	16
Motorized/saddle and pack animal (not recommended for simultaneous use)			
Motorized/nonmotorized	22	16	16
Multiple-tread, multiple-use (each tread)			
Pedestrian only, two-way travel	8	8	6
Nonmotorized only, dual travel	10	10	10
Saddle and pack animal, dual travel	8	8	8
Motorized use only, dual travel	16	16	6

Source: Flink and Searns 1993.

Note: These minimum tread widths do not apply to wilderness and ecologically sensitive lands.

The width for a specific greenway project can and should vary according to the different requirements encountered. In some areas, extra land may need to be protected to support ecosystem preservation; in other areas of the project, a minimum width may be desirable to support through-passage of trail users.

Trail Widths

For multiuse trails within a greenway, the American Association of State Highway Transportation Officials (AASHTO) recommends a minimum width of 10 feet (3 meters). This width, required for projects that use federal transportation funds, is necessary to accommodate two-way bicycle and pedestrian traffic on the prepared trail tread.

To accommodate heavy traffic in urban areas, it may be necessary to increase the width to 12, 14, or even 20 feet (3.7, 4.3, or 6.1 meters). In some cases, it may be desirable to divide the trail into "wheeled" and "nonwheeled" treads if the right-of-way and landscape can support separate treads. Wheeled trails support users who bicycle or use other mechanical, human-powered means, including rollerblades, to navigate a trail. Wheeled trail treads should be 10 feet (3 meters) wide. Nonwheeled users are pedestrians, and normally include people with disabilities who use a wheelchair to navigate a trail. Nonwheeled trail treads can be 6 or 8 feet (1.8 or 2.4 meters) in width.

For greenways not funded by transportation dollars, and that do not intend to accommodate multiple user groups, it may be possible to develop a trail tread that is 6 or 8 feet (1.8 or 2.4 meters) wide. Generally this is done for single-user groups, such as pedestrians or equestrians. Even in these cases, maintenance and public safety accommodations may require a wider tread.

PUBLIC INVOLVEMENT IN GREENWAY AND TRAIL DESIGN

Incorporating public input into the design of a greenway and trail system, or segment, is an important consideration. The manner in which public input is received and used will go a long way toward gaining acceptance and buy-in for the project. Finding the most appropriate method for involving the public in the process is important. There are different ways to involve the public, including meeting with individual landowners, forming citizens' advisory committees, hosting public workshops, and conducting a public survey. Regardless of which techniques are used, all public input should be recorded and made part of a permanent record of the greenway or trail project.

Greenways often traverse landscapes that have historically been regarded as the back door or backyard for residential, commercial, office, and retail lands. Having a public right-of-way in front of and behind a home or business often raises safety and security concerns for property owners. The best strategy to address these concerns is to collect and disseminate factual information about the greenway project. It may be necessary to provide examples of where successful projects have been developed in nearby communities or neighborhoods. When facing opposition, it is important to emphasize that masses of greenways and trails have been successfully open to public use over the past 20 years.

PROJECT DEVELOPMENT

The actual development of a greenway or trail project depends on the availability of land and money. Adequate right-of-way is required to support the multiple purposes of a greenway. Appropriate land is also required to support the intended trail experience. One of the greatest shortcomings in greenway and trail planning is the inability of local communities to conserve and protect adequate land for a greenway or trail project. Some land corridors are too narrow to achieve intended results.

Factors that affect project costs include grading of terrain, drainage, and subsurface construction. These costs can be lowered through the use of volunteer labor, donation of materials, and below-market services from local contractors and manufacturers. Numerous projects throughout the United States have used these techniques to reduce project costs. They can also help reduce maintenance costs.

Some of the most important issues to address and resolve in developing a greenway or trail include the following:

- Adequate drainage of water away from the trail surface
- Public access points, spaced no more than one-quarter mile (0.4 kilometers) apart
- Signage systems
- Appropriate inspection of greenway and trail landscapes to correct deficiencies
- Treatment of intersections with roadways and utilities
- Maintenance and public safety

EMERGING ISSUES

The U.S. greenway and trails movement has been influenced by a variety of trends and special interests. Greenway and trail development has adapted to concerns over adequate recreation, an interconnected transportation network, and the protection of floodplains. Currently, the dominant concerns include health and wellness and water quality.

Health and Wellness

An active community is a healthy community. Numerous studies affirm that sedentary lives and prolonged periods of inactivity are major deterrents to healthfulness. Communities can help combat sedentary lifestyles by developing and providing better access to landscapes that encourage people to venture

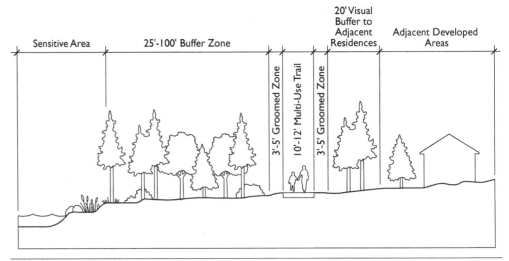

Sensitive Area   25'-100' Buffer Zone   3'-5' Groomed Zone   10'-12' Multi-Use Trail   3'-5' Groomed Zone   20' Visual Buffer to Adjacent Residences   Adjacent Developed Areas

GREENWAYS AS BUFFERS

Source: Greenways, Inc.

Charles A. Flink, FASLA, Greenways, Inc., Cary, North Carolina

outside and enjoy the outdoors, which includes greenways and trails. When these landscapes are incorporated as a system within the fabric of development, they become even more valuable to health and wellness pursuits. The result is an interconnected environment that supports a range of outdoor activities and encourages community residents to incorporate physical activity and exercise into their daily lives.

Water Quality

Greenways can serve as filter strips for overland runoff, trapping harmful pollutants before they enter creeks, streams, rivers, and lakes. The key is to establish a system of greenways that mirrors the native hydrology of a local landscape. When these greenways are properly sized, they can be very effective in protecting source waters from degradation and may also be used to clean and restore degraded waters.

COMPLEXITY OF GREENWAYS

Greenway development is often a reflection of community values and the commitment to balancing conservation and land-use development. Greenway and trail development is a complex undertaking. It requires understanding the opportunities and constraints of the natural and human-made environments, and accounting for the interests and needs of diverse user groups. Defining a logical process for planning and designing each and every greenway and trail system, or segment, is one way to ensure that all factors influencing development have been appropriately addressed and resolved.

REFERENCES

Beneficial Designs. 2001. *Designing Sidewalks and Trails for Access, Part 2, Best Practices Design Guide.* Washington, DC: U.S. Department of Transportation.

Flink, Charles, and Robert Searns. 1993. *Greenways: A Guide to Planning, Design and Development.* Washington, DC: Island Press.

Little, Charles. 1990. *Greenways for America.* Baltimore, MD: Johns Hopkins University Press.

See also:
Multiuser Trails
Types of Parks

Charles A. Flink, FASLA, Greenways, Inc., Cary, North Carolina

CONSERVATION AREAS

Conservation areas are important natural environments that are integrated with human recreation uses. They are important components of worldwide conservation planning. When planning for conservation areas, a variety of methods and tools to identify lands critical for ecosystem protection are used. Fundamental to this is an understanding of the ecological processes and functions that maintain the viability of living systems, including human societies.

CONSERVATION PLANNING GENERALLY

Planning for conservation areas requires an approach to ecosystem protection and management that integrates the concept of sustainable use with human needs and uses into ecosystem management so that the needs and aspirations of future generations are not compromised by those of the present. Conservation areas represent the leading edge of an opportunity to manage protected lands in a way that educates and inspires us while maintaining capacity for future generations.

Conservation planning requires going beyond geopolitical boundaries. For example, the overlap of potential uses for a freshwater lake—water supply, fishing, habitat protection, recreation, tourism, travel—triggers the involvement of multiple regulatory agencies with differing and often conflicting agendas.

Acceleration of ecosystem degradation due to climate change, incursion of invasive species, unsustainable consumption, and inappropriate development will require a reassessment of our lifestyle practices, as well as assessment of the adequacy of our protected areas. Conservation planning requires active, adaptive management to identify new threats and flexible strategies for action.

GLOBAL CONSERVATION PLANNING

In countries such as Australia, the United Kingdom, and Canada, specifically named conservation parks are implemented at both "state" and federal levels. Most nations, under the leadership of the International Union for the Protection of Nature (IUCN)/World Conservation Union, have implemented a system of national parks, biological reserves, wildlife refuges, and conservation areas that incorporate permitted recreation types within the main objective of ecosystem conservation.

IUCN notes that current management structures for parks are not necessarily able to adapt to the pressures of significant and rapid environmental change. New networks, learning institutions, and flexible approaches to open-space management are necessary for increasing our capacity for conservation planning. The multidimensional approach that is being adopted for conservation parks worldwide focuses on several goals:

- Address gaps in national protected-area systems.
- Promote connectivity at landscape and seascape levels.
- Enhance public support for conservation parks and protected open space.
- Recognize the importance of a range of governance types as a means to strengthen management and expand the world's protected areas.

- Strengthen the relationship between people and the land, freshwater, and the sea.

COMPONENTS OF CONSERVATION PLANNING

Based upon a sound understanding of ecological systems, conservation requirements, and community needs, planning for conservation parks and open space should do the following:

- *Reconcile public use with environmental concerns.* Identify and plan for the compatible and sustainable human use of an area within the goals of conservation. Conservation parks often suffer from the same abuse as traditional parks with off-trail hiking, illegal hunting, damage from wheeled vehicles and speedboats, vandalism, and dumping.
- *Provide for public education and awareness.* Conservation planning requires public participation, education, and high levels of communication

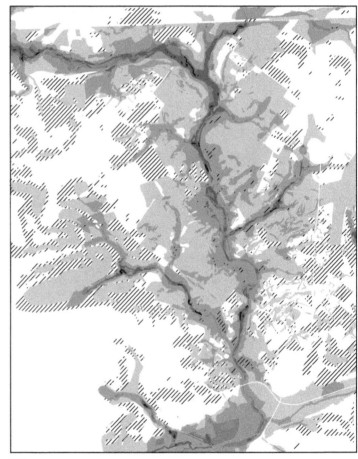

- [ ] Urbanized
- [/] Limited Environmental Value
- [ ]
- [ ]
- [ ]
- [ ]
- [■] Critical Environmental Value (Most Environmentally Sensitive–Preservation Target)

Environmental value is calculated through a geographic information systems (GIS) suitability analysis model. The components of the landscape that represent the critical framework (or structure) of healthy, functioning ecosystems are identified, in addition to areas that respond poorly to development conditions. The model consists of a numerical overlay of all the component layers. Primary components, those items with high conservation value, are equally weighted (e.g., if a point in space contains a wetland and is in the floodplain, it receives one "point" for each). The secondary components are valued at 50 percent (half a point), because they are not as critical. The resultant map indicates areas that have the greatest *coincidence* of landscape components deemed important for ecological function. This does not mean that areas without high valuing on this map should be ignored; it simply provides a baseline for field investigation and verification of areas representing potentially important preservation/restoration targets.

ENVIRONMENTAL VALUE

Source: Andropogon Associates, Ltd. 2004.

Teresa Durkin, ASLA, Andropogon Associates, Philadelphia, Pennsylvania; Merita Roos, ASLA, Andropogon Associates, Philadelphia, Pennsylvania

with the community. Conservation parks provide important opportunities for research and education programs at many levels: local schools and universities, training classes and workshops for young professionals, practitioners and public officials, and visitors to use these lands for long-term investigations.

- *Identify partners for collaboration.* Environmental issues, such as flood control, water quality, coastal erosion prevention, and biodiversity conservation, are not confined to property boundaries and are most effectively addressed through collaboration.

IDENTIFYING AND EVALUATING LANDS FOR CONSERVATION

Conservation and restoration are interrelated. To identify and evaluate lands for conservation parks, a planner must consider land acquisition, the ability to increase habitat and create new habitat from urban land, restore linear connections, and protect riparian and migratory corridors. In addition to natural lands, industrial lands, derelict lands, and brownfields can be regarded as good candidates for conservation parks for their capability to contribute to the elimination of sources of disturbance and pollution.

Consider the identification and evaluation of lands in order of priority, highest to lowest:

- Protect undeveloped properties with significant natural values within a region..
- Conserve properties that could serve to join together existing conserved properties.
- Protect land alongside riparian corridors to develop and maintain a contiguous corridor.
- Preserve or restore riparian communities, and preclude development in floodplains.
- Manage croplands and recreation areas as buffer lands for conservation parks.
- Maintain opportunities to create trail links.
- Assess underutilized or abandoned properties for conservation potential.

INVENTORY AND ANALYSIS STUDIES

The planning process for conservation parks includes studies that identify and evaluate lands along the lines of the natural patterns of the landscape, natural drainage ways and flood retention areas, surface water and groundwater quality, historic and rural landscapes, and vegetation and wildlife diversity. Technological advances are now available to planners and design professionals that include geographic information systems (GIS) and advanced modeling tools to map and analyze vast quantities of data. Geographic data, which are important for analysis and mapping, are available from cities and counties, water districts, and utility providers in digital format. At a minimum, an inventory and analysis dataset for a conservation park includes the following:

I. Environmental Value
- Forested areas
- Stream channel
- Wetlands
- Floodplain areas
- Steep slopes: greater than 12 percent
- Moderate slopes
- Hydrologic soils: D (saturated floodplain soils)
- Stream channel buffer: 30 to 90 feet
- Key species habitats

II. Hydrology
- Physiography
- Watershed subbasins and floodplains
- Tributaries and stream orders
- Land cover: pervious/impervious surfaces

III. Vegetation
- Vegetation cover types, such as forest, open woodland, savannah, prairie, oldfield, turf
- Existing natural plant communities

Legend
- ☐ Urbanized
- ▨ Woodland Edge Restoration
- ⠇ Meadow Restoration
- ▨ Riparian Edge Reforestation
- ▨ Forest Gap Reforestation
- ▨ Existing Forest
- ⩔ Wetland
- ■ Pond or Watercourse

A regional approach to the best possible preservation and restoration conservation lands requires a land management strategy. This map illustrates a strategy for extensive reforestation of riparian edges, particularly in the first- and second-order tributaries. Meadow restoration should be expanded upon, to provide greater sustainability to the interior. Gaps in the existing upland forest should be reforested. Finally, southwest-facing edges of existing high-quality forests should be restored to further resist invasive species migration.

LARGE-SCALE RESTORATION STRATEGY

Source: Andropogon Associates, Ltd. 2004.

CONSERVATION PLAN

A conservation plan uses the inventory maps as an analytical tool to establish degree of protection, permitted uses, and the relationships between resource areas. Composite overlay maps are created as the next planning step in order to outline priorities for further acquisition, park management, and guidelines for permitted uses.

Teresa Durkin, ASLA, Andropogon Associates, Philadelphia, Pennsylvania; Merita Roos, ASLA, Andropogon Associates, Philadelphia, Pennsylvania

Conservation Strategies Maps

High-Priority Conservation/Acquisition Areas

- Important watersheds associated with protection of water quality and water supply
- Habitats or potential habitats of endangered or declining species
- Riparian and coastal areas associated with wildlife, water conservation, and shoreline protection
- Wetlands associated with flooding protection, wildlife, and water conservation
- Geologic features or soil types that contain rare minerals or potential for unique habitat

Medium-Priority Conservation/Acquisition Areas

- Areas of less significant habitat or natural features that can be managed for limited public access for environmental education, tourism, and low-impact recreational uses
- Areas that can be used to test management prescriptions for higher-quality areas

Lower-Priority Conservation/Acquisition Areas

- Areas that can be managed for sustainable use to serve as buffer areas between developed areas and conservation parks. Examples of activities that might be permitted include controlled hunting, organic agriculture and pasturing, and sustainable harvesting.

Restoration Strategies Maps

High-Priority Restoration Areas

- Potential high-quality habitat areas for restoration
- Areas of medium or low disturbance for restoration
- Areas for potential large-scale restoration strategies
- Riparian corridors that can be reforested
- Forest gaps that can be filled to create continuous forest canopy and forest interior
- Woodland edges of mixed plant species
- Savannah and meadow areas

MANAGEMENT AND MONITORING

Conservation areas require both a land management and a monitoring plan/program. The character and quality of the landscape depends directly on how it is managed over time. Land management for conservation parks involves several approaches:

- Control, manage, and, preferably, eliminate invasive, nonnative species.
- Maintain the population density of fauna (such as white-tailed deer) that threaten the natural regeneration of native plant species.
- Replant with species native to the region.
- Reintroduce extirpated native species.
- Maintain habitat diversity, especially high-priority ecosystems, such as interior forest, expansive grasslands, and riparian woodlands.

Stewardship, the long-term management of the land, must balance the maintenance resources of a site between property management (i.e., maintenance programs) and ecological management (i.e., long-range planning, restoration, research, and monitoring). The stewardship staff must simultaneously set priorities for property management, which are largely recurrent and predictable, and ecological management, which require a greater degree of seasonal planning and guidelines that are appropriate for the site.

Controlling invasive species is the most difficult environmental degradation to reverse in a conservation park. The Nature Conservancy has adopted a strategy that gives highest priority to preventing new infestations and to controlling existing, fast-growing, disruptive infestations that affect the most highly valued areas of the preserve.

Continuous scientific monitoring of interventions in the landscape is crucial to the success of future landscapes and to cost-effective actions. Monitoring provides the information to judge the effectiveness of actions and revise poor management decisions—ensuring that chronic problems are resolved, not exacerbated.

See also:

Biodiversity Protection
Environmental Management Overview
Regions

Teresa Durkin, ASLA, Andropogon Associates, Philadelphia, Pennsylvania; Merita Roos, ASLA, Andropogon Associates, Philadelphia, Pennsylvania

PLAYGROUNDS

Playgrounds are important elements of healthy neighborhoods and communities. Successful playgrounds provide safe and challenging environments for children to learn about the world around them and about themselves.

TYPES OF PLAYGROUNDS

Playgrounds fall into three primary categories: neighborhood, school, and regional. A neighborhood playground serves a local community. School playgrounds are areas designated for use by the student body of a specific school. A regional playground serves a wider area, such as a group of neighborhoods or an entire metropolitan area. Regional playgrounds are often elements within a larger outdoor development that includes public parks or athletic fields. Each type of playground offers a unique set of characteristics that affect its design and the activities appropriate for inclusion.

LOCATION

Consider the following when selecting a playground location:

- Locate playgrounds in safe proximities to roadways to reduce the possibility that a child could run into the street or that a distracted driver or car collision could propel an automobile into the play area.
- Place bike paths beyond the immediate perimeter of a playground to prevent children from running into the path of cyclists.
- Locate playgrounds within sight of adult activity areas, such as picnic areas, so that the adults can provide a level of security and supervision. However, provide appropriate distances so that playground noise is not disturbing to other areas.
- Site playgrounds on the same sides of a roadway as support facilities, such as restrooms, picnic areas, concession stands, or ball fields. As children run from one to the other, they may not watch for oncoming traffic.
- For neighborhood playgrounds, a rule of thumb is to assume a playground is accessible to walking children within a one-quarter-mile (0.4-kilometer) radius of the playground.
- Minimize site development costs by selecting relatively level land that is not densely vegetated.

SIZE

To determine the amount of space for a playground, first determine the average number of children expected to be playing on the playground at the same time. As the amount of square footage provided per child increases, the number of injuries has been

found to decrease. The table indicates varying levels of quality based on the amount of square footage provided per child. These guidelines include the minimum 6-foot (1.8-meter) recommended safety zone around the perimeter of all play equipment.

PLAYGROUND ZONES

Current trends in playground design acknowledge that children choose to play in many different ways. This should be reflected in playground design. Include a variety of areas that feature different play activities. Today's playgrounds should seek to incorporate a variety of activities or zones. Depending on factors such as playground type or the level of supervision anticipated, some zones will be appropriate for some playgrounds and inappropriate for others. One zone may be more developed or emphasized on some playgrounds than on others. For some playgrounds certain zones may be inappropriate.

The following list of zones is an inventory of potential activities to be considered for inclusion on a playground. This list can be used during programming to discuss the appropriateness and means of inclusion of each selected activity.

Entry

The playground entry area is a definitive and recognizable transitional space. It may be a transition from the inside of a building to the outdoor play space, or it may be a transition from one type of open space, such as a picnic area, to the play area. The entry area allows a child to assess the playground environment and the other children who may already be engaged in play activities and to decide about the manner and time in which he or she wants to integrate. The entry area may be defined simply by an open area or further distinguished with an entry gate or arch.

Water Play

The introduction of water play provides a unique play experience each time the child comes to the playground. Water enlivens a child's imagination and serves as a natural interactive activity, responding immediately to a child's actions. It can be a simple water table that is filled and drained at the end of each day, allowing a child to interact with hands and arms, or a water feature that allows a child to become totally wet. Water features can be manufactured products or naturally occurring streams. Lockable hose bibbs, useful for washing off hard surfaces or watering the landscape, can also provide water play by serving as a means for filling buckets and combining water and sand play.

When considering the inclusion of water play, factor in the type of playground being developed and the degree of supervision anticipated. School playgrounds used only when adult supervision is present are more valid for the inclusion of water play features because of the increased amount of supervision. Even in this case, the water feature should be located so that it is highly visible. Providing water play activities in neighborhood and regional playgrounds where supervision may not be present at all times should receive serious consideration as to the safety and legal issues involved.

Sand Play

Like water, sand provides a child with a unique experience with every visit to the playground. It is an especially favored activity of young children. It can be enjoyed alone or with other children, making a sand play area very adaptable to a child's level of social development. Sand play has also been found useful in developing fine motor skills that translate to a young child's ability to hold pencils and crayons and manipulate scissors.

Include devices to shade the sand area during the hottest part of the day and storage for toys to be used in the sand box. The sand should be either covered nightly or inspected at the start of each day to keep the area free from litter, debris, and animal feces.

Dramatic Play

Dramatic play areas encompass a wide variety of activities. Foremost is the act of role-playing, an especially favored method of play among four- to six-year-olds. Imitating adults as they play House or Store gives children a script of sorts and a framework for interaction. The structures that promote and support this type of play can be abstract in shape, allowing children to use their imaginations, or they can be more definitive in appearance, such as a playhouse or a store. This area also offers opportunities to include activities and components that reflect important aspects of the community where the playground is located, giving the playground a unique character.

On supervised playgrounds, providing props such as dress-up clothes, empty food boxes, and tables and chairs can further enhance the richness of this play experience. However, provide a means of lockable storage nearby for such items.

This area may also include events that feature music, art, and theater-related themes. For example, a small stage or chalk wall, or a set of hanging chimes or cymbals may be provided. When musical or noise-making activities are provided, locate these activities so that the noise will not be disruptive to other activities occurring on the playground.

Structures built to enhance dramatic play should have an open design and be easily monitored and accessible to children and caretakers.

Hard Surfaces

Some activities, such bouncing or dribbling a ball, riding tricycles, or pushing wheeled toys, require a hard surface. They can be in more than one location on the playground and can double as a circulation system through the playground. However, "roadways" should be laid out in such a way as not to create a potential conflict with an active play area of the playground. In addition, do not locate hard surface areas under or within the "fall zone" for play equipment.

Hard surfaces can be constructed of packed earth, concrete, or asphalt. Each material has advantages and disadvantages. Packed earth maintains a natural look, and when children fall it is less likely to scuff up knees and elbows. However, it can become muddy, making areas of the playground unusable until they dry out or drain. Concrete provides surfaces that can be painted with sidewalk games or used for sidewalk chalk art. It is also durable and

LEVEL OF QUALITY BASED ON SQUARE FOOTAGE

QUALITY	SQUARE FEET PER CHILD
Substandard	60
Good (Minimum)	75
Better	100
Generous	200

Linda Cain Ruth, AIA, College of Architecture, Design & Construction, Auburn University, Auburn, Alabama

sheds rainwater quickly. However, falls onto concrete can result in scraped knees and elbows. Asphalt, although typically less expensive, retains heat during the hot summer months. Environmentally sensitive alternatives include pervious concrete products that allow rainwater to drain through them.

Big Loose Parts

The big loose parts area features large elements that children can manipulate and configure in an infinite number of ways, creating their own unique play experiences and structures. This zone requires an open area of safety surfacing supplied with wood boards and planks, crates, and large boxes that have been checked for safety hazards, such as splinters, nails, and staples. There are also manufactured big loose parts systems available that, while more expensive, offer a higher degree of safety and durability.

This area requires supervision to prevent children from constructing dangerous situations. It may not be appropriate for inclusion on playgrounds in which children may play unattended. Adequate storage is also needed within close proximity to store the materials between uses.

Gross Motor Play

Gross motor play includes the types of activities most commonly associated with playgrounds. Today's playgrounds are typically furnished with a large manufactured or custom-built play structure that features slides and monkey bars, bridges, and tunnels.

When selecting play activities to be included in the gross motor zone, create a balance of activities that will exercise both the upper and lower body. In addition, play equipment for this area may be intended for use by children ages five to twelve, or in the case of a school playground, grades one to six. Provide activities that offer varying levels of challenge because the range of physical abilities of children within these age groups varies greatly.

The play structure should be manufactured and built according to the safety standards recommended by the Consumer Product Safety Commission (CPSC) and the American Society for Testing and Materials (ASTM) and be designed to meet the requirements of the Americans with Disabilities Act Accessibility Guidelines (ADAAG) for play areas.

Swings

Swings can be a traditional type that move back and forth, or a piece of equipment that pivots from a single point, such as a tire swing. Swings are one of the most favored activities and one of the most used pieces of equipment on a playground. They are well liked by children and adults alike. However, swings are also one of the top causes of playground accidents. A major source of swing-related injuries is children running into the path of a moving swing. Both the CPSC and ASTM recommend that swing areas be located away from other pieces of equipment or activities.

In addition to the recommended safety zone around swings, install barriers along the edges of the safety zone parallel to the supports of the equipment and along one end. This technique is especially helpful on compact playground sites or on playgrounds where the swing zone is centrally located. These barriers can be hard materials, such as fencing, or natural barriers, such as dense landscape planting. Barriers

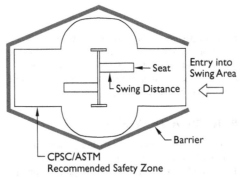

The swings area can be made safer by installing barriers along both of the long sides and at one end of the safety zone. This forces children to enter the area parallel with the movement of the swings, instead of approaching from the side and accidentally running into the path of a moving swing. It also prevents children from running through the area to get to another part of the playground.

SWING BARRIERS

Source: Linda Cain Ruth.

along the sides of the swing area force entry into the swing area in line with the path of the swings, eliminating the possibility of running into the path of a moving swing. A barrier along one end of the swing zone eliminates the potential of a child running through the swing zone.

Social Spaces

Social spaces are spots located throughout a playground that encourage and support social interaction between children and between children and adults. These spaces should be of various sizes to accommodate small and large groups. School playgrounds may even have an area that accommodates an entire class. Social spaces should also feature a variety of character. One may overlook the playground from an elevated platform, while another may be a quiet, shady nook next to a tree. When furnished with strategically placed benches, some can double as locations from which adults can monitor the playground.

Natural Elements

Integrate natural objects and settings into the playground to add to the aesthetic and functional success of the playground. Currently, there is an influential movement in design that encourages making natural elements the prominent focus of the playground in order to create places that provide for play, learning, and environmental education for children.

Natural elements may include trees that provide shade and social spaces, and large boulders children can climb and sit on. An open field for running and playing games, such as kickball and tag, is invaluable. Creeks provide a unique and rich outdoor experience. They may be incorporated into playgrounds that will be closely supervised when in use. Raised vegetated beds can deter children from running through and harming growing plants, and the perimeter of the planter can provide seating.

When planning to incorporate natural elements into a playground, consider how, by whom, and how often these elements will be maintained, so that their nature and heartiness will correspond to the level of

care and maintenance. The installation of an underground irrigation system may also be considered as part of the maintenance program of these areas. It may also be necessary to provide storage for any maintenance equipment.

Safety Amenities

Several safety amenities and issues need to be considered and incorporated throughout all areas of the playground.

Barriers

Placed around the perimeter of a playground, a barrier is advantageous for several reasons. Perhaps most obvious, it keeps children, especially young children, from wandering away from the playground area into surrounding developments. A barrier also establishes a point of entry into the playground, creating a sense of place and providing supervisors with an easier means of monitoring who is coming and going from the playground. Within the playground, using barriers can increase the safety within the swing area and can effectively separate toddler play areas from those of older children.

The physical nature of the barriers, both around the perimeter and inside the playground, may vary depending on the degree of separation desired. For the perimeters and the swing zone, an impenetrable barrier such as an impassable fence or dense landscape planting is appropriate. Around the toddler play area, the barrier may be less formidable. It may consist simply of a wide strip of landscape planting or a small mound. However, for playgrounds featuring a toddler play area, many caretakers of children playing in the toddler area may also have children playing in the larger play area. Therefore, the barrier should not obstruct or eliminate visibility between the two.

Surfacing

One of the most critical components of a safe play environment is the surfacing beneath and around play equipment. There are two types of surfacing that meet recommended safety standards: loose fill materials and unitary materials. Loose fill materials include sand, gravel, shredded wood products, and shredded tires. Unitary materials include rubber mats and poured-in-place rubberlike products.

The Consumer Products Safety Commission's *Handbook for Playground Safety* recommends depths of various surfacing materials depending on the critical height anticipated on the playground. A critical height is the approximation of the fall height below which a life-threatening head injury would not be expected to occur. For a playground, the critical height is the height slightly above the highest point from which a child might fall from a piece of equipment onto the ground. When using unitary materials as a playground surface, request test data from the manufacturer that identifies the critical height of the material because different materials in this category have differing shock-absorbing properties.

Signage

Provide a sign that communicates the hours of operation, the level of supervision provided, the age appropriateness for different areas and pieces of equipment on the playground, and any other rules regarding expected behavior while using the playground. Locate the sign in an obvious and highly

Linda Cain Ruth, AIA, College of Architecture, Design & Construction, Auburn University, Auburn, Alabama

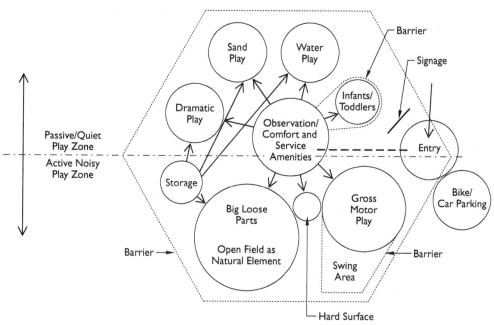

Diagrammatic relationships of the various activity areas and elements that may be included in the design of a playground. Social spaces should be located throughout the play area.

RELATIONSHIP OF PLAYGROUND ACTIVITY AREAS AND ELEMENTS

Source: Linda Cain Ruth.

CRITICAL HEIGHTS OF TESTED SURFACING MATERIALS (IN FEET)

MATERIAL	UNCOMPRESSED DEPTH		COMPRESSED DEPTH	
	6-INCH	9-INCH	12-INCH	9-INCH
Wood Chips	7	10	11	10
Double Shredded Bark Mulch	6	10	11	7
Engineered Wood Fibers	6	7	>12	6
Fine Sand	5	5	9	5
Coarse Sand	5	5	6	4
Fine Gravel	6	7	10	6
Medium Gravel	5	5	6	5
Shredded Tires	10–12*	Not Tested	Not Tested	Not Tested
Unitary Materials	Consult Manufacturer			

*Contact supplier for specific product data.

Source: Consumer Products Safety Commission, Handbook for Playground Safety, 1997.

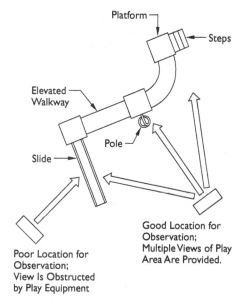

Sight lines should be considered when placing seating throughout the playground so that they can function effectively as points from which to monitor and supervise play.

PLAYGROUND SIGHT LINES

Source: Linda Cain Ruth.

visible location of the playground, such as the entry zone. Information about whom to contact should unsafe situations occur may also be listed.

Observation Points

Provide locations throughout the playground that allow those monitoring the play environment to do so effectively and comfortably. Often simply strategically placed benches, these areas can also serve as social spaces for adults and children to interact. Seating should be placed in such a way as to allow unobstructed views into and around the various pieces of equipment. This feature can be further enhanced by siting play structures in such a way as to maximize the sight lines from observation points to the play equipment.

Lighting

Provide lighting to extend the playground's usable hours, but be aware that doing so can raise additional safety concerns. Therefore, ensure light levels ample enough to make all areas and play components fully visible, without dark spots that may obscure parts of play equipment such as ladder rungs and handholds.

If lighting is not provided, post signage stating that the playground closes either at a certain time or dusk, and continuing to play past that time is at one's own risk. Bury electrical service lines for lighting underground.

Communications

Install a means of communication, such as a telephone or an emergency call box, on or near the playground so that medical services can be reached in the event of an emergency. This may be especially appropriate for neighborhood playgrounds on which children may often play unsupervised by adults. Bury electrical service lines underground.

Comfort Amenities

It is essential to provide for the physical comfort of both the children using the playground and those supervising. This will add to the enjoyment and amount of time spent at the playground.

Tables

Tables provide places for picnic lunches and card and board games. For school playgrounds, tables offer a place for students to do schoolwork outside. If desired, enough tables could be set up to accommodate an entire class, thereby allowing the playground to function as an outdoor classroom.

Water Fountains

Provide water fountains for drinking water because the playground will typically be used during the hottest parts of the day. Water-misting equipment has become a common method to cool off playground users.

Shade

Provide shade, through shade trees, umbrellas, awnings, or gazebos, as a cost-effective and valued means of creating cool areas. Many manufacturers of playground equipment also offer shading devices that can be attached directly to play structures, providing cool spots for children in the active play area.

Restrooms

Restrooms are perhaps the most often used and requested amenity of playground users. Including restroom facilities on or near the playground depends on the type of playground, as well as the plans for maintenance. Playgrounds located near buildings, such as schools, may not need to provide separate facilities on the playground if the distance and path from the playground to the building can be easily monitored. For larger, regional playgrounds, restrooms are highly recommended. Often these restrooms will serve additional areas around the playground, such as picnic areas and ball fields.

Locate the restrooms as close to the playground as possible. Never require a child to cross roadways to access them. It is helpful to those supervising more

Linda Cain Ruth, AIA, College of Architecture, Design & Construction, Auburn University, Auburn, Alabama

than one child if the path to and into the restrooms is clearly visible from the playground. This allows older children to be visually monitored as they go to the restrooms without assistance. If providing restrooms on neighborhood playgrounds that may not be monitored or used continuously, address maintenance and security issues because the playground may be more susceptible to vandalism.

Service Amenities

Storage

Depending on the type of playground, activities provided, and maintenance arrangements, on-site storage may be required. Typically, playgrounds that are supervised during use, such as school playgrounds, benefit from on-site, easily accessible storage. Storage may be required for items and toys used in the water play and sand play zones, props for the dramatic play zone, and materials for the big loose parts zone. Balls, jump ropes, Frisbees, sidewalk chalk, and other miscellaneous toys may also be stored. Gardening tools for use in garden areas maintained by the children should be stored. Brooms and rakes may also be available to allow children to contribute to playground maintenance. First-aid kits, bug sprays, and sunscreens may also be stored on supervised playgrounds. Storage areas for playground equipment should be secured when the playground is not in use.

If maintenance equipment is to be stored on the site, it should be stored separately from the playground equipment. Maintenance storage areas should remain locked except when the playground is being maintained.

Trash

Trash receptacles should be located throughout the playground. They should be convenient to areas most likely to generate trash, such as the entry, table, and seating areas. Playground maintenance should include trash disposal as often as needed to reduce litter, odors, and insects.

Bike/Car Parking

The manner in which people will be arriving at the playground should be considered and provided for accordingly. For neighborhood playgrounds accessed mostly by walkers and bicycles, sidewalks and paths should lead to the entrance of the playground. Bicycle parking racks should be provided. School playgrounds typically do not require car or bike parking unless they serve as neighborhood playgrounds during nonschool hours. Regional playgrounds do require car-parking areas, which should be designed to minimize the potential of a child entering the path of a moving car while running between the car and the playground.

Electrical Power

Depending on the anticipated activities, convenient access to electrical power may be desirable. For school and regional playgrounds, electrical service may allow for outdoor activities that use projection or microphone systems.

Bury electrical service lines underground to prevent the possibility of a sagging or downed power line lying near the play area, and to eliminate a power pole that some children might use as a climb-

ing device. Use weatherproofed and lockable exterior electrical outlets. Make them inaccessible to children.

Maintenance

Many playground injuries result from a lack of maintenance of playground facilities. The design of the playground should include a maintenance process for the playground and its components and materials. This information will influence the selection of playground activities and materials. A document delineating required maintenance procedures and time frames for products or systems used on the playground should be developed during the design phase for use by the client upon completion of construction.

Age-Appropriate Playground Areas

The manner in which children play and the types of activities enjoyed depends greatly on their ages. Therefore, on playgrounds where toddlers and older children will be playing, separate play areas should be developed for both age groups. This is a function of safety and a means of providing age-appropriate activities and appropriately sized equipment for each age group. Programming a toddler area should proceed similarly to programming a playground for older children. Each area listed above should be discussed as to its appropriateness and, if included, developed at a level suitable to this age group. The less active play activities and the dramatic play events take a more prominent role in the toddler playground. These areas also serve as transitional activities for young children between the toddler playground and the main playground.

If a large number of teens will use the play area, consider providing play opportunities that reflect the activity interests of that age group. Consider providing an increased number of places for socializing. Facilities for "extreme sports," such as rollerblading, skateboarding, and freestyle biking, may also be considered. However, barriers should separate these areas from the playground areas.

PLAYGROUND ZONES ADJACENCIES

When designing a playground that has a variety of different play experiences, consider the noise level and type of play each area generates when deciding on the proximity and adjacencies of the different zones. For example, sand, water, and dramatic play activities are typically quieter forms of play than those taking place in the gross motor play area. Locate playground zones so that active play does not interfere with other areas of the playground.

ACCESSIBILITY

The Architectural and Transportation Barriers Compliance Board, often referred to as the "Access Board," has developed accessibility guidelines for newly constructed and altered play areas. The play area guidelines are a supplement to the Americans with Disabilities Act Accessibility Guidelines (ADAAG) and were adopted in July 2004. All newly constructed and altered play areas covered by the ADA are required to comply with these guidelines. The guidelines, as well as helpful sites to assist in the understanding and application of the guidelines, may be obtained from the Access Board's Web site.

ESTIMATING COSTS

The cost of developing a playground depends on many factors. Site development costs are typically a substantial portion of the budget. Therefore, it is beneficial to begin with a fairly flat site on which a 1 to 2 percent slope can be obtained with minimal earthwork. While sites with mature trees and shrubs offer the opportunity to incorporate these into the playground design, avoid sites with extremely dense vegetation to reduce site-clearing costs.

> Cost of playground equipment (x)
> + Cost of installation (.30x)
> + Cost of surfacing (.12x)
> + Cost of design fees, grading, landscaping, and other expenses (.10x)
> _____
> = Total project cost or budget

Therefore,

$$1.52x = \text{Total project cost or budget}$$

The number and types of play structures and zones included on the playground and the type of safety surfacing installed also affect the project's budget. The following formula, proposed by Jay Beckwith, a leader in modern playground design, can be used in determining a programmatic budget for playground design and construction. He suggests that project funds for playground equipment be allocated to the various activity areas within a playground in this way:

For playgrounds serving children over age five:

40 percent for active play areas
15 percent for constructive play areas
20 percent for social play
25 percent to enhance accessibility and accessible play events throughout the playground

For playgrounds serving children ages two to five (toddler areas):

25 percent for active play areas
30 percent for constructive play areas
30 percent for social play
15 percent to enhance accessibility and accessible play events throughout the playground

Community Build

A large portion of a playground's budget is spent on the installation of the playground equipment, including the large play structure in the gross motor play area. To help with this cost, many playground manufacturers and designers work with organizations and communities to conduct community build projects in which volunteers install the equipment. This process can reduce the cost of a project up to 30 percent.

The point at which community volunteers or playground designers become involved in the process of developing a playground can vary. Most playground manufacturers, when given a site, can design and construct a playground with little to no input from a community organization or user group. However, this typically leads to playgrounds that consist of only manufactured play equipment. Speed of delivery is

Linda Cain Ruth, AIA, College of Architecture, Design & Construction, Auburn University, Auburn, Alabama

exchanged for a sense of ownership and a variety of play opportunities on the playground.

Another option is for a community group or organization to plan a playground that designates an area for the gross motor play equipment. Manufacturers can then be sent a drawing indicating the size of the area from which they can propose possible play structure designs, which will become part of the overall playground development. These structures can be installed in one of three ways: solely by the playground manufacturer, by volunteer labor with a supervisor provided by the manufacturer, or by volunteer labor only.

An increasingly popular source of playground design and construction services is the design firm that specializes in community-built playgrounds.

These firms become part of the process from the inception of the project; they lead a community group or organization through activities that result in a unique playground designed specifically for a particular locale. Often these playgrounds feature custom-designed gross motor play activities and incorporate little to no manufactured play equipment. The design firm then assists the community group in organizing the construction of the facility through volunteer labor. While this can be a time-intensive experience for an organization to undertake, the result is a playground unique to the community and one in which the community takes greater responsibility for its upkeep and maintenance because of the high level of civic pride in what was accomplished.

REFERENCES

Architectural Barriers and Compliance Board. 2000. Americans with Disabilities Act (ADA) *Accessibility Guidelines for Building and Facilities: Play Areas.* Available online at: http://www.access-board.gov/play/finalrule.htm.

Consumer Product Safety Commission. 1997. *Handbook for Public Playground Safety.* Available online at: www.cpsc.gov/cpscpub/pubs/325.pdf.

See also:

Safety
Types of Parks

Linda Cain Ruth, AIA, College of Architecture, Design & Construction, Auburn University, Auburn, Alabama

FARMING AND FORESTRY

FARMS

A farm consists of land and buildings used in the production of crops and livestock. The U.S. Department of Agriculture's Census of Agriculture defines a farm as generating at least $1,000 a year in the sale of crops or livestock. According to this definition, in 2002, there were approximately 2.1 million farms in the United States, and 938 million acres of land in farms. The average farm size is 441 acres. A commercial farm is a full-time or part-time operation that produces at least $10,000 a year in gross sales.

Farms are found in every state, and nearly all are family-owned and -operated. They typically consist of a farmstead, which includes a farmhouse and buildings used to shelter livestock and store crops, livestock feed, and farming equipment, and land used to grow crops or pasture to graze livestock. Farms today can include both the classic white farmhouse and red barn and more industrial complexes with modern barns and storage sheds that are primarily functional.

Most local governments do not regulate the construction and design of farm buildings. The regulatory responsibility of local governments over farms typically covers issuing building permits and requiring farm buildings to be set back a certain distance from property lines. However, some activities related to farm operations can have impacts beyond the farm. Confined animal feeding operations (CAFOs) can generate extensive noise and odor. Also, certain nonfarm businesses may be located in farm buildings, generating traffic or sewage that cannot be adequately handled on the farm. These businesses might be more appropriately located in a commercial zoning district off the farm.

FARM SIZES

Farms vary considerably in their size and buildings. Small farms—those smaller than 50 acres (20.2 hectares) and selling less than $100,000 a year in farm products—usually produce specialty crops, such as fruits and vegetables or horticultural nursery stock for landscape planting. Typical buildings on small farms

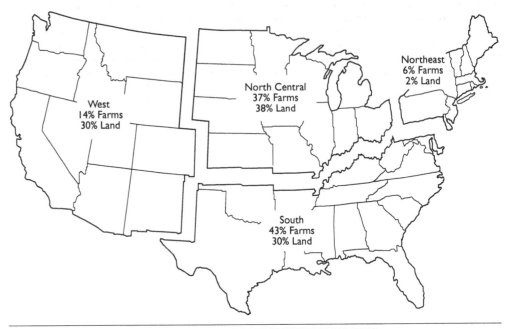

DISTRIBUTION OF FARMS AND LAND IN FARMS BY REGION, 2002

Source: U.S. Department of Agriculture, National Agricultural Statistical Service 2003.

include greenhouses, small machinery and storage sheds, and roadside stands for direct sales to consumers. Specialty livestock farms, especially horse farms, are fairly common. Horse farms have barns for boarding horses and often have an indoor riding ring for training horses.

Row crops, such as corn, soybeans, wheat, and cotton, are usually grown on medium and large farms. Barns, grain bins, and commodity sheds are common on medium to large farms. In the past 30 years, many livestock farms have added large numbers of animals. Many of the hogs and chickens produced today are raised in CAFOs, with thousands of animals in a single building.

Farm size can also vary by geographic location. Farms in the Northeast tend to be small to medium-sized. In the Midwest and South, most farms are medium- to large-sized. In the West, farms are often large, more than 500 acres, for dairy, cattle, or fruits and vegetables.

FARMSTEAD

The area encompassing the farmhouse, barns, and other outbuildings is called the farmstead. Many farmsteads still have an older wooden barn, but modern livestock and production buildings are often the center of the farming operation. These structures are low and long and cover more land area than barns in the past did. Specialty buildings, such as machinery sheds and grain bins, built out of corrugated metal, are also found on farmsteads. In order to support frequent truck traffic, farmsteads often have significant amounts of pavement.

FARMHOUSES

The main farmhouse is where the owner and the owner's family usually live. It can vary in style and age, sometimes dating as far back as to the early eighteenth century in some parts of the eastern United States, or be of more modern construction and style. Some farms may have additional dwellings for other members of the family to live.

Tenant houses provide a place for full-time hired help to live. These houses can also vary in their style

PERCENT OF FARMS AND MARKET VALUE OF FARM PRODUCTS SOLD, 2002

VALUE OF SALES	TOTAL FARMS (NO.)	TOTAL FARMS (%)	VALUE OF SALES (%)
Less than $10,000	1,263,052	59	1.4
$10,000 to $99,999	554,542	26	9.8
$100,000 to $499,999	240,746	11	26.9
$500,000 or more	70,642	3	61.9

Source: U.S. Department of Agriculture, 2002 Census of Agriculture.

FARM SIZES, TOTAL AND AS A PERCENTAGE OF ALL FARMS, 2002

	SMALL	MEDIUM	LARGE
Definition	Less than 50 Acres	50 to 499 Acres	500 or more acres
Number of Farms	743,118	1,047,322	338,542
Percent of Total	34.9	49.2	15.9

Source: U.S. Department of Agriculture, 2002 Census of Agriculture.

Thomas L. Daniels, Ph.D. AICP, University of Pennsylvania, Philadelphia, Pennsylvania

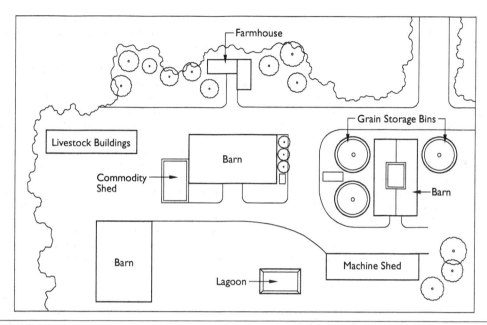

FARMSTEAD

Source: U.S. Department of Agriculture.

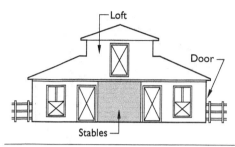

HORSE BARN

Source: American Planning Association.

and construction, but are usually one or two stories high and can be permanent or temporary, sometimes including mobile homes. In the West and parts of the South, temporary housing for migrant labor is often found. This housing, which is meant to shelter several people, often resembles a small barrack.

Barns

A barn is used to shelter animals and store farming equipment and feed for animals. The traditional wooden barn is typically 5,000 square feet (50 feet by 100 feet; approximately 464.5 square meters or 15.2 meters by 30.5 meters) and 60 feet (18.3 meters) high. In recent years, specialty barns have replaced the traditional style. Specialty barns have become popular because of the greater number of livestock raised on farms. Such barns are often dedicated to one type of livestock. For hogs and chickens, there is also the need to provide a barn closed off from the outdoors to minimize the possible spread of diseases.

Dairy Barn

A dairy barn consists of two main parts, the milking parlor and the loafing barn. The portion of the barn that contains the milking parlor and other support areas may be approximately 2,000 square feet (185.8 square meters). The size of the milking parlor depends on the size of the herd. A large dairy farm may have a double-30 "parlor," which has two rows of milking stations, 30 stations in each row, to milk 60 cows simultaneously.

A loafing barn is where the cows sleep, eat, and feed. In modern milking operations, cows are not let out to pasture but are kept inside the loafing barn in stalls. The size of the loafing barn may vary. For example, a loafing barn with 105 stalls, passageways, and holding areas, may be 8,000 square feet (40 feet by 200 feet; approximately 743.2 square meters or 12.2 meters by 61 meters). The loafing barn is attached to the milking parlor, providing the cows with a short walking distance to the parlor. Silos containing corn

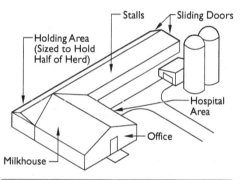

DAIRY BARN

Source: American Planning Association.

silage and other buildings storing hay and animal feed are typically located close to the loafing barn.

Hog Barn

A hog barn is a large, long, low rectangular building, usually constructed of corrugated metal, that sits on a concrete slab and is equipped with large fans to regulate temperature. Some hog barns also have slat systems to collect manure. A typical hog barn is 8,000 square feet (50 feet by 160 feet; approximately 743.2 square meters or 15.2 meters by 48.8 meters). A hog barn can house several hundred to a few thousand hogs. Larger hog farms have a number of hog barns, along with large manure and grain storage facilities and farm machinery sheds.

Chicken Barn

A chicken barn (also referred to as a chicken house) is also a long, low rectangular building that sits on a concrete slab. A typical chicken barn is 15,000 square feet (50 feet by 300 feet; approximately 1,395.5 square meters or 15.2 meters by 91.4 meters). The roof and sides are often constructed of corrugated metal or plastic. A chicken barn may be used for lay-

ers, which produce eggs, or to raise broilers for eating. Although chicken barns contain thousands of chickens, it is fairly common to see more than one chicken barn on a farm.

Horse Barn

A horse barn is likely to be constructed of wood. Older barns can be adapted to house horses, or a new barn can be built. A horse barn features stalls for the horses and storage areas for hay and grain, and may include a loft. A typical horse barn may be 1,440 square feet (36 feet by 40 feet; approximately 133.8 square meters or 11 meters by 12.2 meters), which allows for two stalls on either side of a 16-foot- (4.9-meter) wide alley, a feed area, and a tack area. A typical stall is 144 square feet (13.4 square meters), and the feed and tack areas may be of similar dimensions.

Manure Storage

Livestock farms with large numbers of animals typically store manure for several months before pumping it out and using it to fertilize cropland. There are three main types of manure storage facilities: manure pits, lagoons, and slurry systems. A manure pit is an in-ground concrete-lined cylinder. A manure pit is typically approximately 12 feet (3.7 meters) deep and 100 feet (30.5 meters) in diameter. A lagoon is fairly shallow and open to the air, resembling a large swimming pool, and may have earthen sides or concrete. Lagoons, however, have been banned in some states because their sides may rupture, or the lagoon may overflow during a major rainfall. A slurry system is a large aboveground metal tank.

Silos and Grain Storage Structures

A silo is a common structure on farms with livestock, especially dairy farms. Silos are used to store corn silage or chopped hay (known as haylage) that is fed

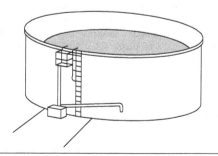

MANURE STORAGE PIT

Source: American Planning Association.

Thomas L. Daniels, Ph.D. AICP, University of Pennsylvania, Philadelphia, Pennsylvania

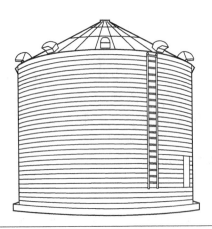

GRAIN STORAGE BIN

Source: American Planning Association.

to farm animals. Silos are either vertical or horizontal in their construction. The tall, cylindrical silo, which has a rounded dome and is often located close to a barn, is the most common. These silos are typically 20 feet (6.1 meters) in diameter and 80 feet (24.4 meters) high. Horizontal concrete bunker silos are often used on large dairy farms, feedlots, and in parts of the United States with low rainfall. A bunker silo is often covered with a plastic tarp, held in place with temporary fixtures (such as old tires).

Farmers store grain to feed to their livestock and to sell on the open market. Older barns often have small grain storage bins inside. A grain bin is usually 25 feet (7.6 meters) in diameter and 35 feet (10.7 meters) high. Some midwestern farms still have corn cribs, which are metal buildings that resemble oversized birdcages stuffed with corn on the cob. Modern farms often need larger structures to store grain. Common storage buildings today are round, corrugated metal bins with a funnel top. Pipes, called grain legs, connect the grain storage bins to a central loading and unloading point.

Machinery Sheds

Machinery sheds are specialty buildings for storing machinery and other farm equipment. They vary in size and often are made of corrugated metal or plastic. These sheds are quick and easy to build. A typical machinery shed is 3,200 square feet (40 feet by 80 feet; approximately 297.3 square meters or 12.2 meters by 24.4 meters) and 20 feet (6.1 meters) high.

Commodity Sheds

Commodity sheds are specialty buildings for storing feed that does not need to be covered, such as cottonseed. They typically have a number of storage bays that offer easy access to bucket loaders or for shoveling. A commodity shed may be constructed of metal or wood with plastic sides. A typical commodity shed is 600 square feet (15 feet by 40 feet; approximately 55.7 square meters or 4.6 meters by 12.2 meters) and 15 feet (4.6 meters) high.

FARM-BASED BUSINESSES

Many farm families supplement their farm income with other businesses conducted on the farm. In some cases, these businesses can be operated within existing farm structures. In others, farm buildings may need to be remodeled. And sometimes completely new buildings are built. Permitted farm-based businesses should be described in the local zoning ordinance.

Typical farm-based businesses include machinery repair and storage, bed and breakfast operations, woodworking shops, beauty salons, limited food processing, and farm stands, among others.

Roadside Stands

Direct marketing of crops, arts, and crafts produced on the farm to consumers has recently grown in popularity. Roadside stands are usually seasonal buildings that cater to consumers arriving via automobile. The stands are typically located close to the road and should have adequate parking space for safety. The local zoning ordinance should define the maximum size of roadside stands allowed. Most of the goods sold from roadside stands should be produced on the farm.

Roadside Markets and Garden Centers

Some communities have allowed farm stands to expand into year-round commercial operations that sell many products not grown or made on the farm. A roadside market features food and fiber products. A garden center typically combines a nursery operation with the sale of mulch and fertilizers to the general public.

Key issues with roadside markets and garden centers are parking and whether the operation should be moved to a commercial zone off the farm.

SITING OF FARM BUILDINGS

The siting of farm buildings has grown in importance, especially as more residential and other nonagricultural development occurs in the countryside adjacent to active farms and as livestock farms increase their number of animals. The local zoning ordinance should establish siting standards to protect health and safety. New farm buildings should be set back a certain distance from property lines to minimize the spillover of noise and odors onto neighboring properties. In the case of farms with livestock, setbacks can vary from a few hundred feet or meters for crop-producing farms with storage buildings to more than 1,000 feet (304.8 meters) for CAFOs.

ENVIRONMENTAL ISSUES

Agriculture is often cited as a major source of water pollution. Rain and wind cause soil erosion from farm fields, which contribute sediment to rivers, streams, and lakes. The increased turbidity can adversely affect drinking water and fish populations. Soil particles often bond with manure and nitrogen fertilizers, carrying nutrients into waterways that can produce algae blooms and reduce water quality. Herbicides and pesticides also can be washed into waterways and seep into groundwater.

Air pollution, especially from large hog operations, has recently become a major concern. The issue of farm odors, mainly from the spreading of manure on fields, also has become contentious in some areas.

Noise from farm machinery operating early in the morning or late at night may raise complaints from neighbors.

Natural Resources Conservation Service Conservation Plans

The Natural Resources Conservation Service (NRCS), formerly the Soil Conservation Service, provides technical, educational, and financial assistance to individuals, groups, and units of government to protect, conserve, and enhance natural resources, including soil, water, air, plants, and animals. The Environmental Quality Incentives Program (EQIP), a voluntary program of NRCS, provides financial assistance to address natural resources concerns on land that remains in agricultural production.

A requirement of the EQIP is the submission of a conservation plan, prepared according to 7 CFR Part 1466.6. The contents of a conservation plan include the following:

- A description of the prevailing farm or ranch enterprises and operations that may be relevant to conserving and enhancing soil, water, or related natural resources
- A description of relevant natural resources, including soil types and characteristics, rangeland types and conditions, proximity to water bodies, wildlife habitat, or other relevant characteristics related to the conservation and environmental objectives of the plan
- A description of the participant's specific conservation and environmental objectives to be achieved
- To the extent practicable, the quantitative or qualitative goals for achieving the participant's conservation and environmental objectives
- A description of one or more conservation practices in the conservation management system to be implemented to achieve the conservation and environmental objectives
- A description of the schedule for implementing the conservation practices, including timing and sequence
- Information that will enable evaluation of the effectiveness of the plan in achieving the conservation and environmental objectives

A conservation plan may be developed as a single plan that incorporates any or all other federal, state, tribal, or local government programs or regulatory requirements.

Natural Resources Conservation Service Conservation Programs

The NRCS also administers the Conservation Reserve Program, which, since 1985, has paid farmers an annual rental fee for setting aside highly erodible land from plowing for 10 years, and the Wetlands Reserve Program, which is a voluntary program to protect, restore, and enhance wetlands through a long-term conservation program. As of 2004, more than 33 million acres were enrolled in the Conservation Reserve Program or Wetlands Reserve Program.

See also:
Feedlots

Thomas L. Daniels, Ph.D. AICP, University of Pennsylvania, Philadelphia, Pennsylvania

FEEDLOTS

Feedlots are large livestock operations that generally involve some type of confinement. The most common feedlot type today is a concentrated animal feeding operation (CAFO), where animals are fed in close quarters in climate-controlled buildings. The U.S. Environmental Protection Agency defines what constitutes a CAFO, as shown in the table. Operations are regulated on the basis of achieving any one of these thresholds for a particular type of livestock. Any smaller operations they may have in addition to the medium or large operation must comply with the rules applying to that medium or large operation.

CAFOs have become the dominant mode of production in the poultry and hog industries, and have made substantial inroads elsewhere. Their presence results in effects on surrounding land uses that must be anticipated and addressed through an adequate regulatory framework.

ENVIRONMENTAL ISSUES

CAFOs cause noticeable environmental and health-related impacts primarily from odors, air pollution, and water pollution. These externalities can raise significant health concerns, such as groundwater contamination, eutrophic conditions in surface waters, which can reduce fish populations, and respiratory problems.

Odors

Swine operations appear to have the most significant odors. The chemical composition of hog manure differs from that of cattle or other livestock. Also, most organic odor control relies on using certain absorbent materials calibrated to react favorably with odorous compounds. The odor from hog manure comes from a mix of approximately 150 compounds, making it difficult to find an effective treatment to mask or remediate odors.

Odors can be mitigated through three basic storage methods: underground containment, steel tanks, and manure lagoons. Underground containment, in

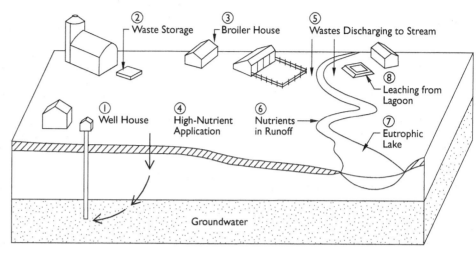

Animal waste can have numerous points of impact on environmental quality.

Notes:
1. Bacteria and nitrates can leach through the soil and contaminate well water.
2. Waste storage structures can contain poisonous and explosive gases.
3. If structures are not properly ventilated, ammonia and other gases can cause respiratory and eye problems in animals and corrosion in buildings.
4. High application of wastes can cause nitrate toxicity and other nitrogen-related diseases in grazing cattle. It can also leach into soil, fractured rock, and sinkholes.
5. Lagoons, feedlots, and livestock that discharge wastes to water bodies can increase organic matter levels and cause low dissolved oxygen in streams, create toxic levels of ammonia for fish, and create eutrophic conditions.
6. Livestock waste runoff from fields can also increase levels of nutrients in streams and lakes, also causing eutrophication.
7. When nutrient levels are increased in water bodies (from inputs such as items 5 and 6), weeds and algae in streams grow to excess, and fish can have nitrate poisoning.
8. Poorly sealed lagoons may leach nutrients and bacteria into groundwater or enter the stream.

POTENTIAL SOURCES OF GROUNDWATER CONTAMINATION FROM FEEDLOTS

Source: Idaho Association of Soil Conservation Districts 2002.

which hog feces and urine fall through floor grates into a pit beneath the confinement building, is more expensive but serves effectively to contain odors belowground. The pit is typically 6 to 8 feet (1.8 to 2.4 meters) deep, depending on the size of the operation and the amount of storage needed, and the waste is channeled belowground through fairly simple drainage devices. The disadvantage is that the pigs live with the odor to a greater degree than when

the manure is moved outdoors to a lagoon. They are also exposed to the gases emitted from the pits, which include hydrogen sulfide, ammonia, carbon dioxide, and methane. Moving the waste to metal tanks can provide containment of the odors.

Lagoons, in contrast, expose hog odors to the outdoor environment; thus, operations using lagoon storage seem to produce more odor complaints. The larger the surface area of the lagoon, the greater the quantity of liquid exposed to the air, with a resulting increase in odor detection downwind. The most effective solutions appear to involve covering lagoons or tanks, such as with industrial-grade plastic sheeting supported by polystyrene floats. These are more expensive than straw but more durable and do not clog the bottom of the lagoon with residue.

Manure application on fields is the other prime source of complaints about odors. The waste is typically applied through sprayers attached to trucks. The faster the ground absorbs the nutrients, the lower the threshold for odor complaints will be. Manure application on frozen ground results in poor and delayed absorption, increasing the strength and longevity of the odors that neighbors may experience. During the summer, the heat may increase the volatility of odors from a heavily filled lagoon. Feedlots need enough storage capacity to hold the manure until there are more favorable weather conditions.

Wind heavily influences odor distribution. Strong odors can be transported at least a mile (1.6 kilometers) away. It is important to examine prevailing wind patterns to determine how they may cause odors to affect downwind properties, so as to situate odor-gen-

U.S. EPA SUMMARY OF CAFO SIZE THRESHOLDS FOR ALL SECTORS, 2003

SECTOR	LARGE (AT LEAST)	MEDIUM[1]	SMALL (LESS THAN)[2]
Cattle or cow/calf pairs	1,000	300-999	300
Mature dairy cattle	700	200-699	200
Veal calves	1,000	300-999	300
Swine (more than 55 pounds)	2,500	750-2,499	750
Swine (less than 55 pounds)	10,000	3,000-9,999	3,000
Horses	500	150-499	150
Sheep or lambs	10,000	3,000-9,999	3,000
Turkeys	55,000	16,500-54,999	16,500
Laying hens or broilers[3]	30,000	9,000-29,999	9,000
Chickens other than laying hens[4]	125,000	37,500-124,999	37,500
Laying hens[4]	82,000	25,000-81,999	25,000
Ducks[4]	30,000	10,000-29,999	10,000
Ducks[3]	5,000	1,500-4,999	1,500

Notes:
1. Must also meet one of two "method of discharge" criteria to be defined as a CAFO, or may be designated.
2. Never a CAFO by regulatory definition, but may be designated as a CAFO on a case-by-case basis.
3. Liquid manure handling system.
4. Other than a liquid manure handling system.

The table provides the U.S. EPA's size thresholds for all livestock sectors, as published at 68 FR 7191. Some state statutes and local land-use ordinances invoke other standards and offer definitions of animal unit equivalencies.

Source: U.S. EPA CAFO Final Rule, 68 FR 7176, February 12, 2003.

James C. Schwab, AICP, American Planning Association, Chicago, Illinois

erating aspects of the facility within the property to reduce the off-property impacts to the extent possible.

Air Pollution

Indoor and outdoor air pollution are both concerns. Indoor air pollution largely affects workers, who breathe dust particles, at least half of which are believed to be respirable. In regard to outdoor air pollution, planners should obtain an assessment of the air quality effects neighboring residents and landowners can expect from a proposed facility. The principal gases of concern include ammonia, carbon dioxide, hydrogen sulfide, and methane.

Water Pollution

The Clean Water Act identifies CAFOs as point sources for water pollution. Surface water contamination can occur from major spills or recurring leaks and accidents, and has produced major public health problems. Water-borne pathogens, such as *Pfisteria piscicida* and *Cryptosporidium*, pose threats to drinking water, recreation, fishing, and tourism.

Lagoon seepage into groundwater can occur as a result of inadequate containment structures, usually clay walls that line the bottom and sides of the lagoon. Groundwater contamination has become a major public health problem in rural America. *Methemoglobinemia*, or blue-baby syndrome, chokes off the oxygen supply in infants' bloodstreams when they consume water tainted with excessive nitrate loadings.

Lagoon overflows are mostly the result of exceeding the lagoon's storage capacity. To avoid possible contamination from overflows, lagoons should not be sited in or near floodplains, wetlands, and other environmentally sensitive or hazardous areas. In the largest CAFOs, spacing of multiple lagoons may require close examination.

CAFOs require significant amounts of water; the drinking water needed for several thousand hogs may be the same as for a city with several times that number of humans. Water is also used for cooling the animals and for flushing waste. CAFOs may draw down groundwater supplies to the point of drying up the working wells of neighbors.

RIGHT TO FARM AND CAFOS

All states, in one form or another, have had right-to-farm statutes, which protect farmers from nuisance suits by neighbors when they are adhering to conventional farming practices. The idea has been that neighbors should expect some odors, noise, and other impacts from ordinary farm activities if they choose to live in rural areas adjacent to farms. However, a 1998 Iowa Supreme Court decision, *Borman v. Board of Supervisors for Kossuth County* (584 N.W.2d 309), may have signaled the beginning of a judicial retreat on this topic by invalidating the state's right-to-farm law for farmers organized in agricultural districts as an unconstitutional taking of neighboring property through an involuntary easement. It remains to be seen whether other state courts will eventually follow Iowa's lead, but such a trend could markedly affect the legal protections for CAFOs because their impacts are already more substantial and controversial than those of smaller operations.

ZONING

In many states, agricultural activities are exempted from zoning ordinances, an exemption designed to make life easier for family farmers. However, courts have typically interpreted that exemption to include CAFOs, despite attempts to reclassify them as industrial uses. Consequently, in many states, large, new corporate confinement operations have been able to develop and expand their operations without the required public review through zoning permit applications.

Public health and environmental regulations have sometimes substituted for zoning, either because the jurisdiction lacked zoning authority over the CAFOs or because those regulations provided more important controls. Air quality regulations are examples of a local environmental regulatory response to the presence of CAFOs.

Legal Authority

Legislators passing state zoning-enabling laws in the 1940s and 1950s could not have envisioned feedlots in their definitions of agriculture. To address this now, some states are attempting to have CAFOs defined as an industrial use, which the livestock industry is resisting. The result is a patchwork of laws and granting of authority to counties on this use. State laws can clearly grant authority (e.g., Minnesota), be somewhat ambiguous (e.g., Kansas), or clearly forbid county zoning power over CAFOs (e.g., Iowa).

Many of the newer state laws and regulations include distancing requirements for the operations within a CAFO to minimize odors and pollution, similar to those included in many local zoning regulations. However, these state requirements do not obviate the value of local zoning, which addresses where in the community such facilities should be allowed to locate.

Technical Capacity

Many rural communities lack the technical capacity to review site plans and enforce regulatory provisions. Also, rural counties often have not enacted zoning ordinances, either because they have sparse populations—and do not feel the pressure to zone—or they lack funds to hire planning staff and zoning administrators to implement them. Therefore, many rural communities that adopt comprehensive plans and zoning ordinances use outside consultants to assist in drafting them.

Communities that want to use zoning to control the siting of CAFOs need to assess their ability to implement the regulations. If the task cannot be handled with existing staff, outside sources of technical and regulatory assistance must be available, and local decision makers need to dedicate resources to ensure that implementation is effective. Counties or townships that have the authority could use impact or other fees to cover the cost of inspections, infrastructure upgrades, or other necessary actions. The industry response will likely be to locate elsewhere.

Regulating CAFOs as industrial uses allows for including performance standards with regard to potential noxious impacts within the zoning ordinance, much as other communities do for other industrial operations, but communities still need to maintain the necessary training and skills for zoning enforcement staff to regulate such uses effectively. For example, odor controls, if enacted as perform-

ance standards, require certain kinds of monitoring equipment, which cost money and staff training.

ZONING STRATEGIES

Districts

Districts serve to separate uses, which function in part to keep people from coming to the nuisance, a problem particularly apparent with agriculture today. Suburban residential encroachment on farm districts is part of the current debate over farmland preservation and urban sprawl. It is also important relative to the debate over odors and other complaints concerning feedlots.

Separation Standards

Separation standards may provide additional restrictions beyond the basic underlying zoning. For animal agriculture, separation standards would be tied to environmental considerations. Many ordinances that use industrial performance standards or address concerns tied to potentially hazardous industrial uses, such as manufacturers of fireworks, use environmentally based separation standards.

Setbacks

Setbacks can be applied to certain activities, such as spraying of animal waste on fields. This should be established as a uniform distance without reference to the size of the operation, such as 500 feet (152.4 meters) from residences, wells used for human consumption, nursing homes, child care centers, office buildings, and similar uses.

Conditional Uses

Conditional uses have been used in some communities to examine the plans for CAFOs before they receive a permit. The ordinance should state the conditions clearly to avoid creating controversy in the permitting process.

Performance Standards

Performance standards have been applied rarely to agriculture uses in local zoning ordinances, but the CAFO situation may be compared to the historical experience with industrial uses. Odors, air quality, and water quality are all viable topics for performance standards for feedlots. While research is evolving quickly, it does not always provide adequate, quantified information on the ideal solutions to all these problems. However, if communities can be receptive to industry innovation and incorporate new best management practices over time, they may be able to use performance standards effectively.

Moratoriums

Moratoriums on permitting for CAFOs can allow communities to put proposals on hold until the communities can complete the planning necessary to draft appropriate regulations. However, in some states, counties and townships do not have the legal authority to enact a moratorium. Moreover, a moratorium cannot be used to avoid confronting the issue entirely or as a way of indirectly banning CAFOs.

See also:
Farms
Federal Legislation
Stormwater Runoff and Recharge

James C. Schwab, AICP, American Planning Association, Chicago, Illinois

FORESTRY

Forestry is often defined as the science and art of growing trees to meet a landowner's objective. Trees are often viewed as an agricultural crop with a long-term commitment of land, which represents a substantial investment. Trees provide many benefits in the short term: clean air and water, wildlife and habitat, hunting and other recreation, as well as economic benefits generated from hunting leases, recreation fees, and forest products, such as pine straw, firewood, pine cones, berries, mushrooms, and even Christmas trees.

REGULATORY SYSTEM

Federal

The two primary federal agencies that manage federal forestland are the U.S. Forest Service and the Bureau of Land Management. Both agencies have legislation that gives specific guidance and direction to planning activities. The National Forest Management Act of 1976 governs the planning process of the U.S. Forest Service. The Federal Land Policy and Management Act directs the planning of resources on Bureau of Land Management lands. In addition, as with all federal agencies, both have to comply with the National Environmental Policy Act of 1969 (NEPA) to analyze environmental impacts of federally funded projects and to ensure the planning process is open and responsive to public participation.

Other federal agencies that manage forestland and produce timber from them include the Department of Defense, the U.S. Army Corps of Engineers, and the U.S. Fish and Wildlife Service. The National Park Service has forestland that remains in preservation.

State

Individual states regulate and provide direction for forest management and forest planning, generally through state agencies, such as departments of natural resources or departments of environmental protection. Departmental regulations and policy, rather than state statutes, govern forestry practices and standards on the state level.

STATUS OF FORESTRY IN THE UNITED STATES

The United States, like many nations, has a history of forest exploitation. Since the 1950s, however, more trees have been planted annually in this country than are harvested. Annual net growth of growing stock has exceeded removals by roughly 50 percent for the last 30 years, despite a nationwide trend of urbanization and sprawl. Public lands (federal and state), which once produced the majority of the nation's timber, now contribute only 3 to 6 percent of the nation's timber supply. The majority of timber comes from forest industry-owned lands and private, nonindustrial landowners.

Most forestland in the United States was cut-over during the Industrial Age, resulting in what is termed "second-growth" forests. Given time, second-growth forests can develop into mature forests, retaining the natural complement of flora and fauna. Lands under continual forest management, however, experience cycles of harvest and regeneration and have attributes

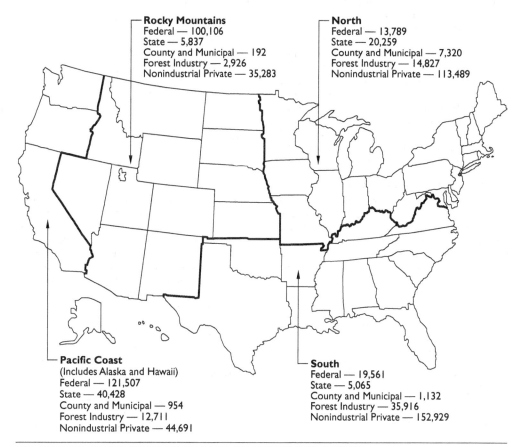

Rocky Mountains
Federal — 100,106
State — 5,837
County and Municipal — 192
Forest Industry — 2,926
Nonindustrial Private — 35,283

North
Federal — 13,789
State — 20,259
County and Municipal — 7,320
Forest Industry — 14,827
Nonindustrial Private — 113,489

Pacific Coast
(Includes Alaska and Hawaii)
Federal — 121,507
State — 40,428
County and Municipal — 954
Forest Industry — 12,711
Nonindustrial Private — 44,691

South
Federal — 19,561
State — 5,065
County and Municipal — 1,132
Forest Industry — 35,916
Nonindustrial Private — 152,929

U.S. FOREST OWNERSHIP BY REGION (IN THOUSAND ACRES)
Source: USDA Forest Service 2002.

that make them appear different from natural forests. Lands that have been cleared, plowed, and planted, as in an abandoned agricultural field, often lack the full complement of vegetative species once found there. For the landowner, commercial plantations or tree farms represent a trade-off between economic efficiency and naturalness; forest management seeks to balance the two and sustain ecosystem health and function.

Planning and design considerations for forestry-related activities center on reducing physical impacts to soil, water, and vegetation; controlling erosion; enhancing visual quality; and enhancing wildlife habitat. Planting, thinning, harvesting, and road building all have technical standards and guidelines, many of which relate specifically to the growing and tending of trees, called silviculture. Some of these techniques are useful to municipal and community planners and are applied in urban settings. These primarily include silvicultural practices, firebreak construction, and fuel reduction activities.

ROAD CONSTRUCTION

Roads provide access to a forested area for resource management, extractive activities, research, or recreation. Many of the existing roads on public lands were originally constructed to reach natural resources: timber, minerals, and grazing lands. Roads

are often constructed for timber harvesting because hauling timber out by truck is cheaper than logging by helicopter and quicker than logging with horses.

Road construction can impact the soil, vegetation, and wildlife of the immediate area. Vegetation is removed from the roadbed and shoulders. Soil is compacted by heavy equipment, and other materials, such as gravel or limestone, are often added for stability. Some wildlife species may lose habitat, cover, or food supplies if the vegetation is removed.

These effects can be reversed if the roadbed is restored and closed to use after timber harvest. If temporary logging roads are not reseeded or restored, they can continue to provide benefits through access to the forest, an increased amount of edge for wildlife, and as a wildlife travel corridor. A proliferation of permanent roads, however, can result in the fragmentation of wildlife habitat, impairing some species' ability to disperse, travel, or forage.

SILVICULTURAL BEST MANAGEMENT PRACTICES

An outgrowth of the Federal Clean Water Act of 1972, best management practices (BMPs) were developed in the 1970s to protect and maintain water quality and to control potential source pollution during forestry activities. BMPs are developed at the state level, and each state has its own BMPs tailored to its terrain,

Haven B. Cook, USDA Forest Service, Tallahassee, Florida

watersheds, habitat associations, and ecosystems. State-level divisions of forestry, departments of natural resources, and departments of environmental protection are all resources for BMP standards.

BMPs exist for several purposes: silvicultural activities and timber harvest, fireline construction, pesticide and fertilizer use, and even cattle grazing. Silvicultural BMPs were developed specifically for forestry-related activities and are not intended to apply to land being cleared for development. Nevertheless, community planners and developers can use these BMPs as guidelines for retaining and protecting natural water features, controlling pollution, and enhancing visual quality.

Streamside Management Zones

Silvicultural BMPs focus on protecting stream corridors and limiting stream crossings during thinning and harvesting activities. A key concept is the streamside management zone (SMZ), a corridor or area of land associated with a stream, creek, wetland, or other water body where silvicultural activities are

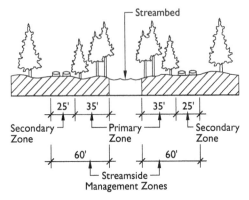

An example of a primary zone where activities are restricted on either side of a stream.

SAMPLE PRIMARY AND SECONDARY STREAMSIDE ZONE MANAGEMENT

Source: Florida Division of Forestry.

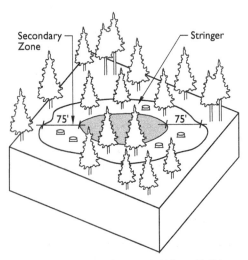

In the example, the secondary zone is 75 feet wide. This width varies based on local conditions.

SECONDARY ZONE AND STRINGER

Source: Florida Division of Forestry.

Haven B. Cook, USDA Forest Service, Tallahassee, Florida

SILVICULTURAL ACTIVITIES PERMITTED IN PRIMARY AND SECONDARY ZONES

PRIMARY ZONE	SECONDARY ZONE
No clear-cutting	No mechanical site preparation
Selective harvesting or thinning must leave at least 50% of the primary zone fully stocked	No fertilization permitted
Landings and loading docks prohibited	Landing and loading docks prohibited
No road construction except for stream crossings	No road construction except for stream crossings
No site prep burning on slopes greater than 20%	No site prep burning on slopes greater than 20%
No trees will be harvested in stream channels or on immediate streambank	
Retain very large trees, dead snags, trees with cavities for wildlife, and trees whose canopy overhangs the water	
No mechanical site preparation	
No aerial application of pesticide	

restricted or eliminated, thereby controlling soil erosion, nutrient runoff, sedimentation of water bodies, and reducing logging debris in streams. SMZs are similar to setbacks required in urban settings.

In an SMZ, a primary zone immediately surrounding a water body is designated, where activities are significantly restricted or prohibited. The width of the primary zone may vary from 25 feet (7.6 meters) to 200 feet (61 meters). The width depends on the terrain, vegetation, and erodibility of soils, among other factors. They are best identified on a state-specific level, and each state has different standards. Planners should consult their State Division of Forestry, Department of Natural Resources, or Department of Environmental Protection for their BMP standards.

In addition to primary zones, secondary zones that extend further out than the primary zone may also be defined. Secondary zones are often designated for intermittent streams, lakes, sinkholes, or wetlands. They are composed of a stringer (the trees immediately in the stream bank) and a zone extending an additional 30 to 35 feet (9.1 to 10.7 meters) on each side of a primary zone, or around the circumference of sinkholes, ponds, or lakes. Secondary zones can extend to as much as 300 feet (91.4 meters) or more, depending on the type of water body or wetland, slope, and soils.

Harvesting

Besides soil erosion and water quality impacts, BMPs can mitigate the visual impacts of harvesting. The size, shape, and location of a final harvest can be designed so that adjacent landowners and residents are not exposed to large clear-cuts. Buffers or strips of trees along roadsides can soften the visual impacts of harvesting. Landings or loading decks should be located adjacent to side roads to reduce the amount of forested area that needs to be cleared.

Planting

Practices common to agricultural activities are also used in forestry to control erosion and sedimentation in streams. Rows can be planted on contours and perpendicular to streams and creeks. Buffer strips along roadsides can also function to minimize the "row" effect of commercial plantations.

Firebreak Construction

Firebreaks are crucial both for prescribed fires and for suppressing wildfires. Plowed lines should be minimized, however. Natural barriers, such as roads and wetlands, should be incorporated as much as possible. Harrowing, light-disking, or permanent grass may be preferable to plowing. Plowed firelines ori-

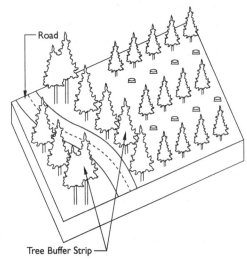

Buffer strip of trees along a roadway can lessen the visual impact of a harvesting operation and soften the "row effect" of a young plantation.

BUFFER STRIPS ALONG ROADWAY TO OBSCURE RECENT THINNING ACTIVITY AND SOFTEN ROW EFFECT OF PLANTATION

Source: Haven Cook.

ented along contours and water bars can slow runoff. Avoid wetlands and SMZs. When a road or fireline must cross a stream, it should cross at right angles to minimize erosion and impacts to the streambank.

Fuel Reduction

Ultimately, forest management is aimed at maintaining healthy forests and ecosystems. This includes the introduction of fire to reduce the amount of dead, dying, and diseased material and to control competing vegetation. Removing these reduces the potential for a wildfire to build into a catastrophic event; thus, prescribed fire is one of the most widely used methods to maintain forest health.

THE WILDLAND-URBAN INTERFACE

More people are choosing to live where they can experience nature as a daily part of their lives. This has brought development into the forest, which includes "in-holdings," private lands within a forest's boundary, and more recently a phenomenon referred to as the wildland-urban interface (WUI), which addresses more broadly the intersection of public and private lands. This latest trend brings new challenges to planners and municipalities. Land is often bought piecemeal by individual landowners, resulting in unplanned communities. Infrastructure and services are stretched as they outgrow a city's capability to provide them. Homeowners who live in the WUI risk losing their home in a wildfire due to the catastrophic nature of wildfires burning in areas with high fuels.

Defensible Space

Defensible space is the creation of an area around homes in the WUI that has limited or no vegetation to reduce the risk of wildfire destroying them. It can also apply to urban dwellings. By reducing the amount of vegetation within a 30-foot (9.1-meter) area around a home, a homeowner can lessen the risk of fire spreading from vegetation to the home. It also allows for space for fire trucks and emergency vehicles to maneuver.

Homeowners should remove trees that grow immediately next to a house or structure or that severely overhang the house. Ornamental and landscape vegetation should be chosen for its capability to resist fire or not burn well. Especially flammable species that contain high amounts of resin, such as pine, yaupon, or gamble oak should not be planted near homes. Following are other general guidelines for creating a defensible space.

- Thin out trees and bushes within 30 feet (9.1 meters) of home:
  - If home is on the crest of a hill, thin fuels at least 100 feet (30.5 meters) below the crest.
  - Reduce the density of the surrounding forest at least 100 feet (30.5 meters) out from the home.
  - Maintain outer edge of tree crowns at least 10 to 12 feet (3 to 3.7 meters) apart.
  - Separate small patches of shrubs separated by at least 10 feet (3 meters) of clear areas of grass or noncombustible material.
  - Stack firewood uphill and at least 15 feet (4.6 meters) from the house.

- Dispose of all debris from thinning and landscape planting:
  - Lop and scatter limbs and twigs.
  - Pile and burn woody debris.
  - Chip woody debris and use as landscape mulch.
  - Clean gutter and roof of pine needles and leaves, especially during hot, dry weather.

- Remove dead limbs, leaves, and ground litter:
  - Regularly prune dead branches from trees within the 30-foot (9.1-meter) zone, to a height of 10 feet (3 meters) aboveground.
  - Remove branches and limbs that are within 15 feet (4.6 meters) of a chimney.
  - Do not use pine straw, wood chips, or cypress mulch directly next to house.
  - Remove shrubs, small trees, or other potential fuels from beneath large trees to prevent the "ladder effect" of a ground fire moving up to the crown of trees.

WILDLIFE MANAGEMENT

Forest management plays a large role in providing habitat for a variety of species of reptiles, mammals, and birds. Forestry activities can create and enhance wildlife habitat. For example, a number of species use the edges of a forest stand, where tree and shrub heights vary and species composition is generally more diverse than within a stand. Meandering harvest unit boundaries can create more edge effect.

Other techniques to create habitat include: planting multiple small stands with asymmetrical borders, prescribed burning to control understory growth, piling logging debris in windows to provide habitat for small mammals and reptiles, and retaining dead trees for cavity-nesting wildlife species.

URBANIZATION

Expansion of urban areas into forests is an issue planners cannot ignore. The wildland-urban interface is growing, and with it the potential fire risk to homeowners and increased constraints on forest landowners to manage fuels. Urbanization and sprawl poses the most immediate and direct effect on forestlands. As people move into forested areas, more limitations are imposed on management options necessary to maintain healthy and productive forests.

As urbanization increases, green space decreases. Planners have long recognized the need and provided for green space within cities; now they must acknowledge that the adjacent forests, whether publicly or privately owned, which offer benefits of open space, clean air, clean water, watchable wildlife, and recreational opportunities, need to be protected. Private lands are becoming less available, and opportunities for recreational experiences are diminishing for urban dwellers. It is becoming crucial to retain and design green space in areas undergoing the transition from forest to urban interface.

SUSTAINABILITY AND THE CERTIFICATION PROCESS

The idea of certifying management practices that can sustain healthy forests for the future grew out of the 1992 Earth Summit in Rio de Janeiro. Standards for forest management and harvest needed to be established and certified in order to be able verify to consumers that the wood they buy has been grown and managed in a sustainable, environmentally friendly manner. The certification process ensures that BMPs are followed during harvesting to protect water quality and to ensure wet weather harvesting impacts are mitigated, nonforested wetlands are protected, wildlife habitat is enhanced, visual impacts of harvesting are minimized, and forests are protected from wildfire, pests, and disease. Lumber and other wood products from the harvested trees typically bear a symbol or mark certifying the wood has been grown sustainably. Such sustainably produced lumber can command a higher price in the marketplace. Like other "green" products, consumers are willing to pay more for certified lumber if they know the environment was not harmed in producing the wood.

The certification process is still in its infancy. A key concern is that there are many different types of certification processes being used. Some companies use internal audit procedures to grade themselves on their procedures. Other companies hire a third party to audit their growing and harvesting operations; still others use a combination of internal review and third-party inspectors. The Sustainable Forestry Initiative developed by the American Forest and Paper Association may emerge as the most widely used set of certification standards. But until the certification process is standardized and finds widespread acceptance, and consumers feel confident they know what it means, demand for certified wood will be low.

INVASIVE EXOTIC SPECIES

Many nonnative plants and trees are used in landscaping, erosion control, and ornamental use. Many have been purposively introduced, and more than a few were "hitchhikers" on other cargo. Without the natural biological controls of their native ecosystems to keep them in check, some plant species are aggressively outcompeting native vegetation. The current rate of introduction and spread of nonnative invasives threatens to replace entire forest and grassland communities. Along with the loss of native plant communities, invasives reduce stability of watersheds and soils, decrease habitat for wildlife by changing plant species composition and structure, and displace plant species important as wildlife food.

The threat of invasive exotics has implications not only for farmers, who spend roughly $8 billion annually to control weeds, but for planners who may end up facing extensive and costly control measures to prevent impairment of water quality, water quantity, and loss of native vegetative communities or landscapes. From spotted knapweed, leafy spurge, and cheatgrass in the West to kudzu, Brazilian pepper tree, and cogongrass in the East, these hardy species are spreading fast. Disturbed areas such as right-of-ways, fencerows, roadsides, and areas severely burned by wildfires are especially vulnerable to invading exotics.

Three strategies exist for dealing with invasive exotics: prevention, control, and eradication. Nonnative plants that have the potential to be invasive should not be permitted. Measures requiring the use of certified weed-free hay or livestock feed can help prevent the introduction of weed seeds or spores. Removing invasive species from adjacent lands will eliminate potential sources of seeds or parent plants.

There are scores of invasive exotics, hence specific control measures will vary. County Cooperative Extension agents can provide the best information and suggestions on controlling these pest plants. Mechanical removal of plant material is possible but may not be feasible or cost-effective over large areas. Trimmed material and plant parts must be disposed of carefully. Stumps of invasive trees should be treated with herbicide to prevent resprouting. Some invasives may require repeat application of herbicides or prescribed fire, or a combination of both. The third alternative, eradication, may be the most difficult of the three measures but should always be considered a viable alternative. In view of the long-term effects invasive exotics can have on an ecosystem, planners should consider eradicating any population of invasive exotics in a project area.

See also:
Open-Space Preservation Techniques
Wildfires

Haven B. Cook, USDA Forest Service, Tallahassee, Florida

PLACES AND PLACEMAKING

Part 4

REGIONS

REGIONS

Regions are areas that have a characteristic or group of characteristics that distinguish them from other areas. These characteristics can be defined in terms of political, physical, biological, social, economic, cultural, or other factors. The structural and functional organization of these factors varies from place to place.

Governmental agencies and others use the term "region" to delineate multijurisdictional areas, such as those composed of more than one town, city, county, state, or nation. Environmental scientists identify regions in reference to parts of the surface of Earth, such as drainage basins, physiographic provinces, climatic zones, or faunal areas. Geographers define a region as an uninterrupted area possessing some kind of homogeneity in its core, but without clearly defined limits. It is important to understand that different types of regions exist, and that the idea of regions presents an important concept for planning and urban design.

TYPES OF REGIONS

For planning and urban design purposes, regions may be defined by political, biophysical, ecological, sociocultural, or economic boundaries. One particular type of region, the metropolitan region, often covers several of these types, because they can serve several purposes. The discussion here focuses on state-level regions and then addresses metropolitan regions.

Maps representing regional boundaries differ among various academic disciplines and government agencies. Because of these variations, the information provided here is not an exhaustive listing of all the types of regions that impact planning; rather, it is provided as a starting point for identifying various regions and regional influences that play a role in planning and urban design.

Political Regions

Political regions are civil divisions of areas. They may be defined at scales that are easily recognized, such as state, county, and township boundaries. These types of regions, known also as governmental jurisdictions, define areas that possess certain legislative and regulatory functions, important to planners and designers.

Political regions may also be groupings of areas, such as multistate regions, that are defined by political entities to serve certain regulatory, policy, and information delivery purposes from the federal level. The U.S. Environmental Protection Agency (EPA), the Census Bureau, and other federal level agencies define the United States according to specific regional criteria, often following state boundaries.

Biophysical Regions

Biophysical regions may be described as the pattern of interacting biological and physical phenomena present in a given area. Perhaps the most commonly

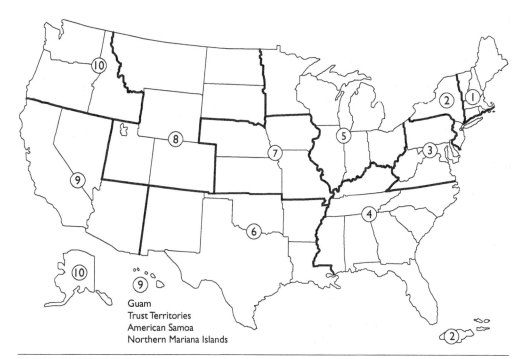

U.S. EPA REGIONS

Source: U.S. EPA.

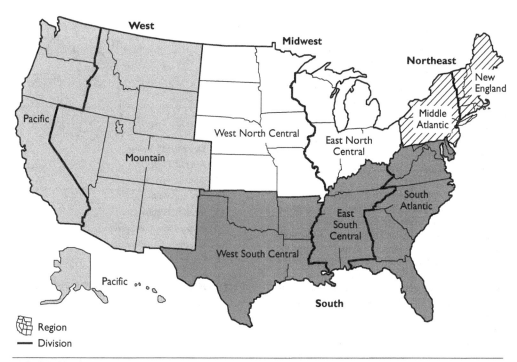

U.S. CENSUS BUREAU REGIONS

Source: U.S. Census Bureau.

Frederick R. Steiner, Ph.D. FASLA, University of Texas at Austin identified type of biophysical region used in planning is the watershed. For example, since the 1930s, the U.S. Department of Agriculture (USDA) has used watersheds for conservation and flood-control planning. Likewise, the U.S. EPA promotes watersheds for regional planning and maintains a "Surf Your Watershed" website (www.epa.gov/surf). Watersheds are important to define for numerous purposes, such as protecting drinking water supplies and identifying wetlands mitigation sites.

Purely physical and more complex ecological regions can be mapped. For example, watersheds are mapped by following drainage patterns, which are relatively easy to trace on a topographic map. Physiographic regions are based on terrain texture, rock type, and geologic structure and history.

Ecological Regions

Ecological regions are delineated through the mapping of physical information, such as elevation, slope aspect, and climate, plus the distribution of plant and animal species. The U.S. EPA defines ecoregions as areas of relative homogeneity in ecological systems and their components. Drawing on the work of Robert Bailey and others, the U.S. EPA uses climate, geology, physiography, soils, and vegetation to designate ecoregions.

Bailey (1998, 7) contends that climate plays a primary role in defining ecoregions: "Climate, as a source of energy and water, acts as the primary control for ecosystems distribution. As climate changes, so do ecosystems...." As a result, weather patterns play an important role in ecosystem mapping as well as for planning and natural resource management. For example, watersheds can be used for flood-control management as well as water-quality planning. For both purposes, charting the amount of precipitation falling in a watershed, where it falls, and how it flows assists in the understanding of flooding patterns and water pollution levels.

Sociocultural Regions

Sociocultural regions represent a type of region that is elusive to delineate and to map. They may be defined as territories of interest to people that have one or more distinctive traits that provide the basis for their identities. Sociocultural regions may span several states, such as the Midwest, the Pacific Northwest, or New England; they may also be smaller areas that may span across a political boundary. For example, the general area of northern Indiana and southern Michigan is commonly referred to as "Michiana."

Unlike many phenomena that constitute biophysical regions, people with widely varying social characteristics can occupy a sociocultural region. In addition, human movement in response to seasons means that different populations may occupy the same space at different times of the year. For example, an Idaho rancher will move livestock out of the high country in the autumn to lower elevations with warmer temperatures. In winter, the same Idaho mountains attract skiers from settlements located at lower elevations.

Wilbur Zelinsky (1980), a Pennsylvania State University geographer, promoted a wider use of vernacular regions to describe social and cultural components of regions. Basically, a vernacular, or a commonly known, region represents the spatial per-

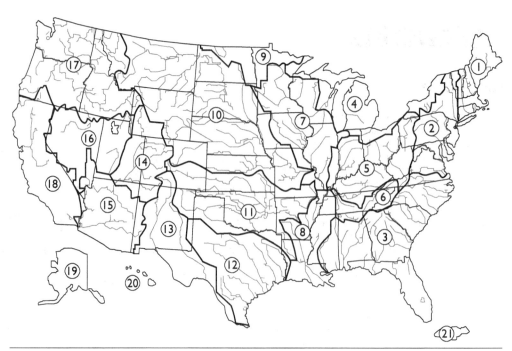

WATER RESOURCE REGIONS OF THE UNITED STATES

Source: USGS.

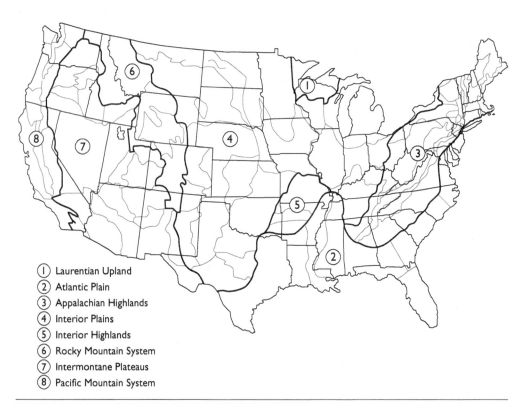

1. Laurentian Upland
2. Atlantic Plain
3. Appalachian Highlands
4. Interior Plains
5. Interior Highlands
6. Rocky Mountain System
7. Intermontane Plateaus
8. Pacific Mountain System

PHYSIOGRAPHIC REGIONS OF THE UNITED STATES

Source: USGS.

Frederick R. Steiner, Ph.D. FASLA, University of Texas at Austin

Agricultural regions are another common delineation of this type; they are often a synthesis of all regional types. The basic resources of agriculture encompass the biophysical factors of soil, water, and plants; and the sociocultural factor of people, with climate providing a linkage, a measure of coincidence for the production of food and fiber. Frequently, labels from agriculture substitute as synonyms for more incorporative regional types: for example, Cotton Belt for the southeastern United States and Corn Belt for the Midwest, or, even more specific, the Napa Valley of California and the Kentucky Bluegrass region. The U.S. Department of Agriculture has defined new farm resource regions, which break away from following state boundaries to more accurately portray the geographic distribution of U.S. farm production. The intent is to help analysts and policymakers better understand economic and resource issues affecting agriculture.

METROPOLITAN REGIONS

Throughout the United States, metropolitan areas have organized political bodies that address multiple planning issues, including transportation, economic development, housing, air quality, water quality, and open-space systems. These organizations encompass more than one political jurisdiction.

Metropolitan planning organizations (MPOs) are responsible for planning, programming, and coordinating federal highway and transit investments. In addition to MPOs, other regional entities with planning responsibility include councils of government, planning commissions, and development districts.

There are more than 450 regional councils of governments in the United States. These are multijurisdictional public organizations created by local governments to respond to federal and state programs. A board of elected officials and other community leaders typically governs regional councils. Further information on regional entities is available through the National Association of Regional Councils and the Association of Metropolitan Planning Organizations.

For example, the Portland, Oregon, Metro guides regional growth through the coordination of land-use and transportation plans. As an elected regional government entity, Metro provides such a platform for the Portland metropolitan region of 3 counties, 24 cities, and 1.3 million people. Metro's capability to guide growth derives from Oregon's planning law that requires comprehensive plans with housing and land-use goals as well as urban growth boundaries.

Another example is the Metropolitan Council of the Twin Cities, which has coordinated control over transit and transportation, sewers, transit, land use, airports, and housing policy (Orfield, 1997). A regional planning council since the 1970s, Metro Council was strengthened through the Metropolitan Reorganization Act to address regional concerns regarding affordable housing, land-use planning, and economic disparity, among other issues.

CHALLENGES TO DEFINING REGIONS

A region forges a complex entity that involves many phenomena and processes. Information about these phenomena and processes must be ordered. This

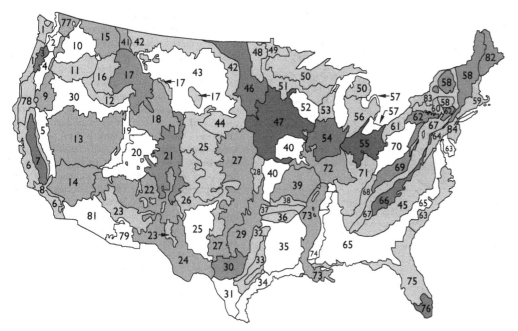

1. Coast Range
2. Puget Lowlands
3. Willamette Valley
4. Cascades
5. Sierra Nevada
6. Southern and Central California Chaparral and Oak Woodlands
7. Central California Valley
8. Southern California Mountains
9. Eastern Cascade Slopes and Foothills
10. Columbia Plateau
11. Blue Mountains
12. Snake River Plain
13. Central Basin and Range
14. Mojave Basin and Range
15. Northern Rockies
16. Idaho Batholith
17. Middle Rockies
18. Wyoming Basin
19. Wasatch and Uinta Mountains
20. Colorado Plateaus
21. Southern Rockies
22. Arizona/New Mexico Plateau
23. Arizona/New Mexico Mountains
24. Chihuahuan Deserts
25. Western High Plains
26. Southwestern Tablelands
27. Central Great Plains
28. Flint Hills

29. Central Oklahoma/Texas Plains
30. Edwards Plateau
31. Southern Texas Plains
32. Texas Blackland Prairies
33. East Central Texas Plains
34. Western Gulf Coastal Plain
35. South Central Plains
36. Ouachita Moutains
37. Arkansas Valley
38. Boston Mountains
39. Ozark Highlands
40. Central Irregular Plains
41. Canadian Rockies
42. Northwestern Glaciated Plains
43. Northwestern Great Plains
44. Nebraska Sandhills
45. Piedmont
46. Northern Glaciated Plains
47. Western Corn Belt Plains
48. Lake Agassiz Plain
49. Northern Minnesota Wetlands
50. Northern Lakes and Forests
51. North Central Hardwood Forests
52. Driftless Area
53. Southeastern Wisconsin Till Plains
54. Central Corn Belt Plains
55. Eastern Corn Belt Plains
56. Southern Michigan/Northern Indiana Drift Plains

57. Huron/Erie Lake Plain
58. Northeastern Highlands
59. Northeastern Coastal Zone
60. Northern Appalachian Plateau and Uplands
61. Erie Drift Plains
62. North Central Appalachians
63. Middle Atlantic Coastal Plain
64. Northern Piedmont
65. Southeastern Plains
66. Blue Ridge
67. Ridge and Valley
68. Southwestern Appalachians
69. Central Appalachians
70. Western Allegheny Plateau
71. Interior Plateau
72. Interior River Valleys and Hills
73. Mississippi Alluvial Plain
74. Mississippi Valley Loess Plains
75. Southern Coastal Plain
76. Southern Florida Coastal Plain
77. North Cascades
78. Klamath Mountains
79. Madrean Archipelago
80. Northern Basin and Range
81. Sonoran Basin and Range
82. Laurentian Plains and Hills
83. Eastern Great Lakes and Hudson Lowlands
84. Atlantic Coastal Pine Barrens

ECOREGIONS OF THE CONTERMINOUS UNITED STATES

Source: U.S. EPA 2003.

ception of indigenous people. Because vernacular regions are commonly known and evolved locally through time, they can be described as "popular" regions. Zelinsky advises that regional, ethnic, and historical questions may be answered by exploring vernacular regions. While not widely recognized in the United States, a few American writers have suggested popular regions, such as Ernest Callenbach's "ecotopia" (1975) from the San Francisco Bay area north to Alaska, and Joel Garreau's "nine nations of North America" (1981).

ECONOMIC REGIONS

Functionally, economic regions overlap sociocultural regions. Economic processes often dominate our view of social processes in regions. For example, daily trips to work, newspaper circulation areas, housing markets, and sports teams may define economic regions. Regions may be branded based on their economic health, such as the Rust Belt in industrial decline in the northeastern United States, and the robust Sun Belt in the South and the West.

Frederick R. Steiner, Ph.D. FASLA, University of Texas at Austin

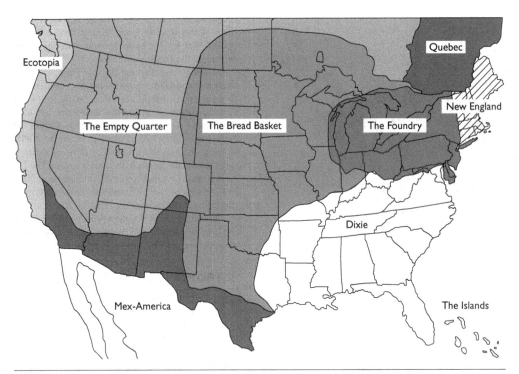

NINE NATIONS OF NORTH AMERICA

Source: Garreau 1981.

involves establishing cores and boundaries, hierarchical classifications, and interrelationships.

On a map, regional boundary lines—be they watersheds, jurisdictions, or newspaper circulation areas—can be carefully rendered. Such boundaries can tend to appear more real than the zones they symbolize and divert attention from actual connections and separations. Boundaries are most often determined for planning purposes through the political process. Goals can be established for planning in a variety of ways, and these goals result in irregular boundaries, a well-recognized problem of regional (and other levels of) planning. A significant difficulty in preparing, and especially in effecting, regional plans is that most "real" units rarely coincide with governmental jurisdictions. The boundaries of metropolitan areas enclose other municipalities and overlap with additional authorities. Watersheds seldom occur entirely within a single state or province, and many of them cross international borders. Although challenging jurisdictionally, watersheds are often advocated as an ideal unit for regional planning.

REFERENCES

Bailey, Robert. 1998. *Ecoregions: The Ecosystem Geography of the Oceans and the Continents.* New York: Springer-Verlag.

Callenbach, Ernest. 1975. *Ecotopia.* Berkeley, CA: Banyan Tree.

Garreau, Joel. 1981. *The Nine Nations of North America.* Boston: Houghton Mifflin.

Orfield, Myron. 1997. *Metropolitics: A Regional Agenda for Community and Stability* (rev. ed.). Washington, DC: Brookings Institution Press.

Zelinsky, William. 1980. "North America's Vernacular Regions." *Annals of the Association of American Geographers* 70:1–16.

See also:
Regional Plans
Transportation Plans
Watersheds

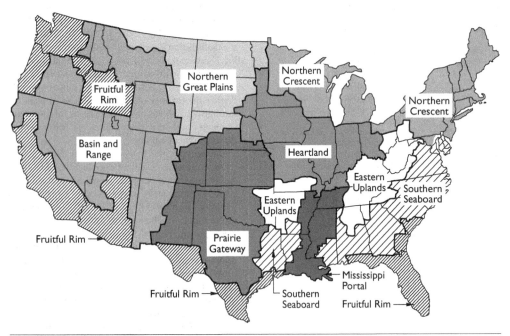

U.S. FARM RESOURCE REGIONS

Source: USDA.

Frederick R. Steiner, Ph.D, FASLA, University of Texas at Austin

PLACES AND DISTRICTS

NEIGHBORHOODS

Neighborhoods have long been a focus within the planning field, and neighborhood-based planning is an area that continues to grow. Among other purposes, such an approach is increasingly seen as an essential part of a comprehensive planning process to inform citywide policy and to gain input, clarify priorities, and garner support for the neighborhood-level details of such plans (Martz 1995; Rohe and Gates 1985). Defining neighborhood for programmatic ends in any given case is problematic, however, because selecting and defining target neighborhoods is a highly political and negotiable process.

DEFINING NEIGHBORHOODS

There is no universal way of defining the neighborhood as a unit. When engaging in neighborhood collaborative planning, the process of neighborhood identification and definition should be considered as a heuristic process, guided by programmatic aims, a theoretical understanding of "neighborhood," and descriptive information on the ecological, demographic, social, institutional, economic, cultural, and political context in which the area exists.

There are three dimensions to this heuristic:

- Program goals and strategies
- Neighborhood characteristics
- Contextual influences

Their consideration should be an iterative process, each stage of which is informed by the preceding stage(s), and in the aggregate providing the basis for an informed choice of neighborhood boundaries and an operational definition of neighborhood for given programmatic ends.

Framing the consideration of these dimensions is a set of general propositions that inform the process of neighborhood definition in any programmatic context:

- Match the place to the intervention.
- Identify the relevant stakeholders.
- Determine the appropriate change agent(s).
- Determine the necessary capacity to foster and sustain change.

A range of criteria is available that might be used to define particular neighborhoods for given programmatic ends. The process of neighborhood definition proposed here involves attention to these criteria through an iterative series of deliberations, beginning with an articulation and clarification of programmatic goals. These goals reflect assumptions about what needs changing. Program strategies reflect hypotheses about how such change might be brought about.

NEIGHBORHOOD SIZE

Consideration of neighborhood size should be related to the strategic intervention, operational focus, and desired impact of a given initiative. Three types of possible neighborhood constructions most useful for guiding neighborhood definition are the face-block, the residential neighborhood, and the institutional neighborhood. These units are nested constructions, each of which provides certain possibilities and constraints for fostering certain kinds of change. (For discussion of the different ways in which neighborhoods are conceptualized as nested constructs, see Chaskin 1997; Warren 1978; Suttles 1972; Hunter 1974; Lynch 1960).

Face-Block

The neighborhood as a face-block is defined as the two sides of one street between intersecting streets. As a planning unit, the face-block focuses on the interpersonal and provides a high level of opportunity for individual participation. Block-level planning will necessarily focus on a small-scale change, because individual blocks command limited resources and are too small in themselves to wield much influence in the broader community.

Residential Neighborhood

This construction focuses on neighborhoods as places to live. As a planning unit, the residential neighborhood provides an opportunity to engage residents in planning through different kinds of local governance mechanisms that can incorporate direct participation and potentially operate as a link to the larger local community. Planning at this level is likely to focus on local issues pertaining to quality of life, including housing, parks, commercial amenities, and transportation access. By itself, the residential neighborhood is less likely to be an appropriate unit of planning targeting broader systems change, seeking to foster institutional collaboration, or attempting to support economic development.

Institutional Neighborhood

The institutional neighborhood is a larger unit that has some official status as a subarea of the city. The institutional neighborhood provides the opportunity to focus on organizational and institutional collaboration and may require the construction of formal mechanisms for citizen participation if individual residents are to be directly represented.

NEIGHBORHOOD ELEMENTS AND CHARACTERISTICS

The consideration of scale of operation has implications for whether particular kinds of neighborhood elements are to be incorporated within the boundaries of a target neighborhood. It is clear that some such characteristics may be more important for the accomplishment of some programmatic goals than others.

Informal Networks of Association

While the existence of or potential for informal networks is clearly central to initiatives seeking to develop or strengthen the social organization of a neighborhood, they are also of implied importance in any neighborhood-based endeavor. The informal social organization of a neighborhood, including neighbor relations, activity patterns, and informal service provision, differs across neighborhoods and for different populations (Lee, Campbell, and Miller 1991; Wellman and Wortley 1990) and may provide mechanisms for agency and social support overlooked in more formal approaches to neighborhood.

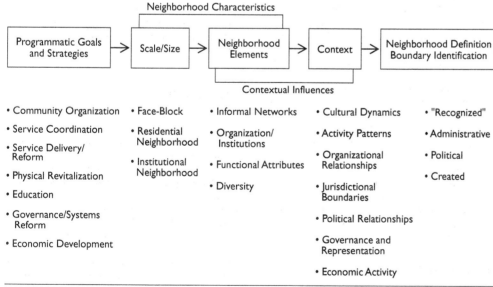

NEIGHBORHOOD DEFINITION PROCESS

Source: Robert Chaskin.

Adapted from Chaskin, Robert J. 1998. "Defining Neighborhoods." Growing Smart Working Paper. Chicago: American Planning Association.

Robert J. Chaskin, University of Chicago, Chicago, Illinois

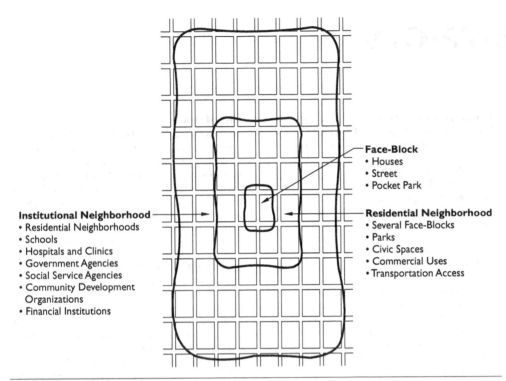

Institutional Neighborhood
• Residential Neighborhoods
• Schools
• Hospitals and Clinics
• Government Agencies
• Social Service Agencies
• Community Development
  Organizations
• Financial Institutions

Face-Block
• Houses
• Street
• Pocket Park

Residential Neighborhood
• Several Face-Blocks
• Parks
• Civic Spaces
• Commercial Uses
• Transportation Access

NESTED NEIGHBORHOOD UNITS

Source: American Planning Association.

Formal Organizations

The availability of neighborhood organizational resources and their use also differs across contexts (Furstenberg 1993). The inclusion of formal organizations is especially important when initiative goals focus on systems change, service provision, or economic development. Because one assumption behind neighborhood-based work is that it provides the opportunity for greater access by and accountability to residents, neighborhood definition should take into account relationships among organizations and between organizations and residents.

Functional Attributes

Functional attributes include those elements necessary for day-to-day living, such as the existence of commercial activities, employment opportunities, recreational facilities, educational opportunities, and health and social services (Warren 1978). The existence of each of these elements represents a portion of the neighborhood's capacity to sustain certain kinds of activities and promote certain kinds of change (Chaskin et al. 2001).

Population Diversity

The relative importance of population diversity or homogeneity depends greatly on an initiative's particular goals. From an organizing perspective, homogeneity is likely to be beneficial, because it provides a clear basis for identity construction and mobilization of residents—particularly in smaller, residential neighborhoods. In larger neighborhoods and where fostering links to the larger community is desired, diversity may be valuable. This is in part a political issue, offering an opportunity to build coalitions across a broader range of constituencies. It may

also be an ideological issue, in which promoting diversity is seen as a virtue in its own right.

NEIGHBORHOOD CONTEXT

Neighborhoods exist in specific contexts, and grounded information about these contexts is essential to any planning process. In addition to socioeconomic and demographic data, other tools such as community assessments, community inventories, and techniques for mapping neighborhood assets can provide valuable information on organizations, available facilities, and resident skills and priorities (Kretzman and McKnight 1993; Bruner et al. 1993). While much information is available through the U.S. Census and various administrative sources, a great deal of (often qualitative) data may not be readily available.

The relational dynamics among these elements within the neighborhood, for example, and with actors beyond the neighborhood may be important for both the definition of neighborhood in given programmatic cases and for ongoing planning and implementation. Identifying and determining the most useful boundaries of particular target neighborhoods for programmatic purposes is much enhanced by the ability to map such relationships, and the ability to inform an interpretation of the impact of such relationships through a qualitative understanding of their dynamics.

BOUNDARY IDENTIFICATION

The criteria for boundary selection should reflect the goals and strategies of a given initiative, consider contextual influences, and examine the sets of choices

made regarding appropriate neighborhood scale and the relative importance of various neighborhood elements. The typology of possible neighborhood definitions implies certain guidelines regarding boundary identification: the face-block is bounded by the first streets that separate a resident's home from the aggregation of homes beyond; the residential neighborhood implies some consensus regarding boundaries on the part of residents; and the boundaries of an institutional neighborhood have been in some way made official, codified and recognized by certain organizations and institutions.

"Recognized" Boundaries

Consistent with the assumptions behind the residential neighborhood, "recognized" boundaries imply the existence of some degree of neighborhood identity and provide the basis for fostering a sense of community. To the extent that the larger local community also recognizes such neighborhood definition, it may help residents and neighborhood groups to advocate their causes with government and other extra-local entities.

Administrative and Political Boundaries

Administrative or political boundaries tend to define larger areas. Given a more systems-oriented or institutionally based approach, the use of such boundaries to define the target neighborhood may be appropriate. However, rarely do administrative and political boundaries coincide with each other, nor do they reflect the social organizational aspects of neighborhoods. The choice of a set of administrative boundaries to define neighborhood may be most useful for sector-bound, institutionally based interventions.

Created Boundaries

Institutional neighborhoods may be officially defined without functioning as an administrative unit. However, because such neighborhoods have no single administrative structure and are rarely recognized as political units, issues of management and long-term representation should be examined. The creation of a neighborhood governance structure that can coordinate constituent neighborhood priorities and activities, as well as represent the neighborhood to the larger community, may help to increase the long-term impact and sustainability of neighborhood-based work.

CONCLUSION

While these guidelines can help direct a process of neighborhood definition, they do not constitute a definitive blueprint for action. The act of defining a neighborhood is a product of both the social and spatial context of the area and subject to several factors, including the purpose for defining the neighborhood, the function that the neighborhood is expected to perform, and the presence of existing neighborhood organizations. Further, the delineation of boundaries is a negotiated process; it is a product of individual cognition, collective perceptions, and organized attempts to codify boundaries to serve political or instrumental aims. The attempt to define neighborhood boundaries for any given program or initiative is thus often a highly political process. These and other factors have to be considered during the plan-

Robert J. Chaskin, University of Chicago, Chicago, Illinois

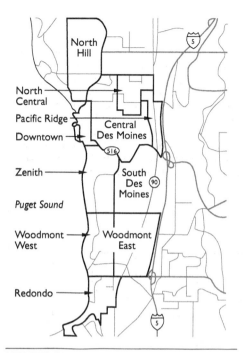

NEIGHBORHOOD PLANNING AREAS, DES MOINES, WASHINGTON

Source: Des Moines, Washington, Community Development Department 2002.

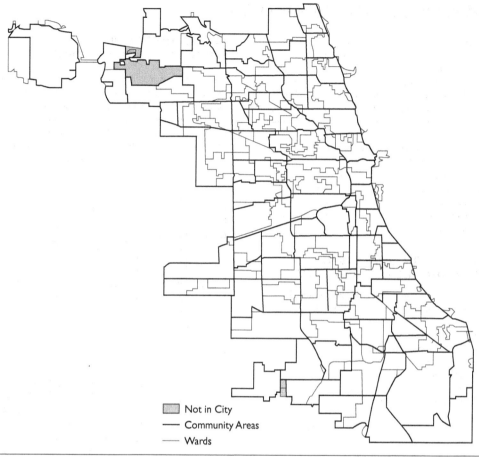

Not in City
— Community Areas
— Wards

COMMUNITIES AND WARDS, CHICAGO

Source: Robert Chaskin.

ning process, which will be conditioned by the existence of enduring tensions between strategic choices that must be made and by the need for meaningful participation, sound information, and the mechanisms and tools to use them both.

REFERENCES

Bruner, C., K. Bell, C. Brindis, H. Chang, and W. Scarbrough. 1993. *Charting a Course:Assessing a Community's Strengths and Needs.* New York: National Center for Service Integration.

Chaskin, R.J., P. Brown, S. Venkatesh, and A. Vidal. 2001. *Building Community Capacity.* New York: Aldine de Gruyter.

———. 1997 Perspectives on Neighborhood and Community: A Review of the Literature." *Social Service Review.* 71, no. 4:521–547.

Furstenberg, F. 1993. "How Families Manage Risk and Opportunity in Dangerous Neighborhoods." In *Sociology and the Public Agenda.* W.J. Wilson (ed.). Newbury Park, CA: Sage Publications.

Hunter, A. 1974. *Symbolic Communities: The Persistence and Changes of Chicago's Local Communities.* Chicago: University of Chicago Press.

Kretzman J., and J. L. McKnight. 1993. *Building Community from the Inside Out: A Path Toward Finding and Mobilizing Community Assets.* Evanston, IL: Northwestern University Center for Urban Affairs and Policy Research.

Lee, B.A., K.E. Campbell, and O. Miller. 1991. "Racial differences in Urban Neighboring." *Sociological Forum.* 6, no. 3:525–550.

Lynch, K. *Image of the City.* 1960. Cambridge, MA: The Technology Press—Harvard University Press.

Martz, W.A. 1995. *Neighborhood-Based Planning:*

Five Case Studies. Planning Advisory Service Report No. 455. Chicago: American Planning Association.

Rohe, W.M., and L.B. Gates 1985. *Planning with Neighborhoods.* Chapel Hill, NC: University of North Carolina Press.

Suttles, G. D. 1972. *The Social Construction of Communities.* Chicago: University of Chicago Press.

Wellman, B., and S. Wortley. 1990. "Different Strokes from Different Folks: Community Ties and Social Support." *American Journal of Sociology.* 96, no. 3:558–588.

See also:
Neighborhood Plans

Robert J. Chaskin, University of Chicago, Chicago, Illinois

NEIGHBORHOOD CENTERS

Neighborhood centers are the areas of more intensive urban uses within a neighborhood. They provide the most localized availability of goods and services needed daily by area residents. A center provides the social and operational focus of a neighborhood. Residential uses and neighborhood-oriented, mixed-use development are inherent to neighborhood centers.

Centers can be retained, preserved, revived, or created. They can be planned in new communities, converted from suburban malls, or restored from distressed inner-city neighborhood business districts. Neighborhood centers play an important role in restoring neighborhoods as the building blocks of community.

COMMUNITY GOALS AND PLANNING CONSIDERATIONS

When planning for a neighborhood center, the community may identify several goals for the center:

- Expand lifestyle choices for residents.
- Increase range of housing types.
- Provide transportation options.
- Create new venues for local employment.
- Provide better access to public services.
- Increase recreation opportunities.
- Improve environmental quality.
- Increase ethnic and economic diversity.
- Bring neighbors together.
- Make the neighborhood safer.
- Increase civic participation.

These goals are then translated into planning considerations:

- Creating greater residential density to increase fiscal and market capacity for enhanced public and private services.
- Addressing housing for seniors, mixed-age, mixed-income, and special-needs populations where their needs can best be met.
- Providing retail convenience for both better variety and capacity to meet local consumer desires.
- Increasing localized consumer demand to create new opportunities to employ youth and attract independent businesses.
- Promoting mixed-use development for lifestyle convenience and efficient service delivery of urban services.
- Attracting growth with public realm amenities, such as public art, street furniture, covered sidewalks, street trees, and parks.
- Creating community by providing public gathering places such as libraries, schools, parks, squares, and sidewalk cafes.
- Providing alternative transportation options including transit, bike lanes, and pathways.
- Preserving the character of the residential neighborhood through compatible design and scale of structures.
- Creating a pedestrian-friendly environment.

WALKABILITY AND NEIGHBORHOOD CENTERS

The viability of a neighborhood center depends on the degree of dependency that can be established between the uses in the center and the neighborhood population. This is a function of the number of people that are within a walkable distance of the center. This walkable population must be of sufficient size to provide a consistent source of demand for the center's retail goods and services. Local market conditions, such as per capita disposable income and regional competition, will generate different population thresholds for this demand. However, the average population density that is within the walkable distance to the center must be several times the density of the neighborhood outside the center, called the "background" density. In traditional low-density neighborhoods, the background density is typically around 15 people per net acre (6 du/acre ×

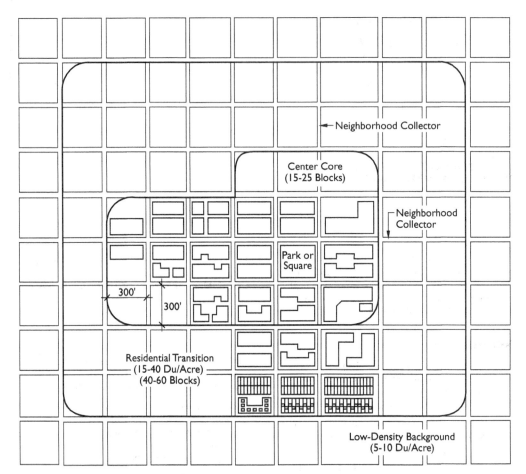

The three elements of a neighborhood center are shown here. The center core covers typically 15 to 25 blocks, with each block approximately 2 acres. A collector street bisects the center core. The residential transition area is approximately 40 to 60 blocks, with a density of 15 to 40 du/acre. The background neighborhood that surrounds the center is of a lower density, between 5 to 10 acres, can be considered in terms of maximum height, lot size, density, land use, structure type, and lot type within each development environment. Section demonstrates the principles of transition and form compatibility.

NEIGHBORHOOD CENTER FORM AND SCALE

Source: Christopher Hugo.

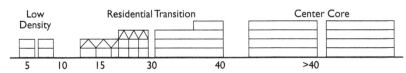

Densities are shown as a gradient, from low-density residential in the background neighborhood to densities of 40 du/acre and higher in the center core.

MINIMUM NEIGHBORHOOD CENTER RESIDENTIAL DENSITIES

Source: Christopher Hugo.

Christopher Hugo, Department of Community Development, Bremerton, Washington

2.5 pp/du). For the center, an average density of 45 people per net acre (30 du/acre × 1.5 pp/du) should be the target, with a somewhat lower density near the edges and higher in the middle of the center.

PLANNING GUIDELINES

The following are planning guidelines that can serve as a basis upon which to start identifying potential sites for a neighborhood center. The criteria included below assume typical urban residential densities of 5 to 10 dwelling units/acre. Criteria should be modified to suit the particular conditions of a community.

- One center serves as the focus of a neighborhood.
- At least 1 mile between centers, to isolate market demand for each center's retail and service uses.
- Mixed-use center core of 15 to 25 blocks (each at 300 feet × 300 feet = 2 acres).
- Core located at the intersection of neighborhood collectors, along one side of a major arterial that serves as a boundary for the area, or focused on the primary quadrant of any existing neighborhood shopping district intersected by arterials.
- Center perimeter defined as a 1/4-mile walking distance from the core, or approximately 40 to 60 blocks in area.
- Area within perimeter outside the mixed-use center core provides a range of housing types and densities, for approximately 3,000 to 4,000 residents.

Even at a relatively low net density of 6 units per acre, a typical 1-square-mile detached, single-family neighborhood has a resident population of around 7,000 people. A neighborhood center that accommodates 2,000 to 3,000 additional residents increases neighborhood demand for goods and services by approximately 25 to over 40 percent. The added convenience of proximity increases the rate of patronage of the center's residents, raising the market capture of center businesses even more.

PROGRAM GUIDELINES

The program that directs the composition of a neighborhood center can be defined according to either conventional zoning or form-based zoning. Conventional zoning will define a finite list of acceptable and prohibited uses, and often has to rely on imperfect information about current needs and future markets. Form-based zoning focuses more on providing a defined set of compatibility and operational standards, and assumes that anything that "fits" the neighborhood setting is appropriate. While more flexible, this approach has to rely on potentially imperfect assessment of the impacts that proposed uses may have. In either case, a development framework should set some minimum expectations for center composition.

When looking at the overall composition of a neighborhood center, the following ratios can generally be applied to the division of land uses, expressed in gross aggregate site area:

- Between 40 and (preferably) 60 percent in higher-density residential use
- Between 20 and 30 percent in mixed-use retail and service uses, with residential above
- The remaining 10 to 40 percent (depending upon the composition of residential and commercial chosen) in public uses, such as a park, library, school or other public gathering spaces

A range of housing types in a variety of densities is essential to create transitions in use intensity and to respond to changes in markets and lifestyles.

Neighborhood Center Features

The specific amount and mix of commercial uses in the center depend upon local conditions and are determined by a subarea or neighborhood planning process involving community stakeholders. A sample list of commercial uses includes the following:

- Retail: grocery, books/music/videos, culinary, flowers, gifts, clothes, art/office supply (some with size limitations)
- Professional office: medical and financial (may be desirable to limit drive-through access)
- Personal services: salon/barber, counseling
- Eating and drinking establishments (with size limitations)
- Entertainment and culture (theaters limited to one or two screens, for example)
- Winery and microbreweries
- Public facilities: elementary school, branch library, fire and police stations, branch post office
- Religious facilities

Other features that should be included in every neighborhood center include sheltered transit stops along a primary street; defined pedestrian routes connecting the greater neighborhood to the center; a focal point, such as a square or public facility, for example, a library; and imageability, which considers architectural compatibility, preserved history, consistent signing, controlled lighting, distinct street furniture, and other elements that add to the neighborhood's identity as a distinct place.

FORM GUIDELINES

Neighborhood centers proposed for already-established neighborhoods need to be compatible with the current residents' perception of "fit" and attractiveness. Form guidelines should be developed to create a center that is well integrated into the existing neighborhood fabric, respects existing residences, and advances the community's planning considerations. The following are examples of such guidelines; again, the specific guidelines to be used should be developed based upon local conditions and community desires.

Blocks, Street Pattern, and Arterials

- Maintain a 300-foot maximum block length for circulation and increased business frontages. Longer blocks may be used for traffic control if fronting higher-volume arterials.
- Create or maintain a grid street pattern for circulation, ease of orientation, pedestrian safety, and street connectivity to all portions of the neighborhood.
- Reduce street curb-to-curb width to operational minimums. For example, a 2-lane street with parking on both sides can be designed to have a 32- to 36-foot maximum width.
- Avoid one-way arterials.
- Orient the core of the center on the intersection of neighborhood collector arterials; avoid spanning minor or principal arterials.

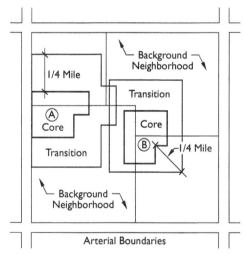

General area size for two center core options within a 1-square-mile neighborhood. The transition area represents the 1/4-mile walkable radius for each center core. Center A fronts on an arterial street and connects to the interior of the area. Arterial traffic supports retail and services. Center B is focused on the intersection of collectors. It is centrally located to serve the neighborhood, and is largely dependent on local market demand for its activity.

NEIGHBORHOOD CENTER SITING OPTIONS

Source: Christopher Hugo.

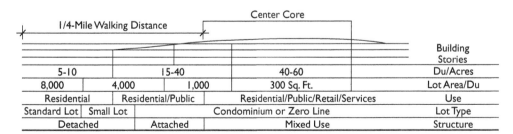

1/4-Mile Walking Distance			Center Core		Building Stories
5-10		15-40		40-60	Du/Acres
8,000	4,000	1,000	300 Sq. Ft.		Lot Area/Du
Residential	Residential/Public		Residential/Public/Retail/Services		Use
Standard Lot	Small Lot	Condominium or Zero Line			Lot Type
Detached	Attached		Mixed Use		Structure

Elements of a neighborhood center shown in terms of density, lot size, land uses, lot types, and structure types within each development environment. Section demonstrates the principles of transition and form compatibility.

NEIGHBORHOOD CENTER DEVELOPMENT, IN SECTION VIEW

Source: Christopher Hugo.

Christopher Hugo, Department of Community Development, Bremerton, Washington

Center Core

- Nonresidential use total aggregate floor area: 200,000 square feet maximum.
- Single nonresidential use floor area: 30,000 square feet maximum.
- Average residential density: minimum of 20 du/acre for any project; maximum determined by floor area ratio, height limits, or other form/bulk standards.
- Building height: three to four stories, which can be even greater in more dense urban neighborhoods, transitioning to two stories at edge.
- Site coverage: up to 100 percent in the core, transitioning down at the edges to blend with the lower site coverage of existing residential uses.
- Reserve street-level use for retail, services, and public spaces, including cultural facilities. Office and residential uses should be located on upper floors

- Establish building set-to lines for nonresidential uses on primary street frontages, and orient uses to the street.
- Set back upper floors facing commercial streets for residential privacy.
- Wider sidewalks (minimum six-foot-wide clear space) with all-weather cover on primary streets.
- Place parking underground, "hidden" in mixed-use structures, or on interior surface lots screened by frontage buildings.

Operational Guidelines

- Apply low traffic level of service (even "F" for pedestrian safety and "active" streets).
- Apply high transit level of service (15- minute or less headways during peaks; 30 minutes otherwise).

- Connect centers to downtown and activity nodes via transit and pathways.
- Include public safety facilities for lower EMT, fire, and police response times.
- Reduce parking standards for all uses as multimodal systems develop.
- Maintain residential speed limits throughout center.
- Control noise levels by urban design and ordinances to attract attached and mixed-use residential demand.
- Control visibility and visual character of nonresidential signing to minimize impacts on residences.

See also:

Innovations in Local Zoning Regulation
Main Streets
Neighborhoods

Christopher Hugo, Department of Community Development, Bremerton, Washington

HISTORIC DISTRICTS

Historic districts are groupings of buildings and structures, noteworthy for their age, architectural integrity, or aesthetic unity. Downtowns, residential neighborhoods, and rural areas that have retained their historic character often receive official historic district designation. Historic district designation is an important tool for preservation-based revitalization, including downtown and neighborhood revival, with federal and state historic preservation tax credits often used to rehabilitate income-producing properties in these districts.

There are two distinct types of historic districts: those that meet standards of the National Register of Historic Places, and local districts established by municipal ordinance, which are administered by a local review board. Although these two types of districts often possess identical geographic boundaries, there are significant differences in the nature of protection and financial incentives each can offer to a community.

NATIONAL REGISTER HISTORIC DISTRICTS

Established by the National Historic Preservation Act of 1966, the National Register of Historic Places is the federal government's official list of cultural resources worthy of preservation. This nationwide program coordinates and supports public and private efforts to identify, evaluate, and protect historic properties and archeological sites. Listed properties include both districts and individual sites, consisting principally of architecturally significant neighborhoods and buildings. In 2004, there were 12,500 listed National Register Historic districts containing more than 1 million contributing buildings and structures.

All National Register properties have been documented and evaluated according to uniform standards established by the National Park Service (NPS), which administers this program. However, most nominations originate at the state level under the auspices of a state historic preservation officer (SHPO). Guidance for preparing such nominations is found in a number of how-to publications directly available from the National Park Service. The establishment of a National Register district involves submitting completed nomination forms and a narrative description of the proposed district to a statewide review panel, which must endorse it prior to its receipt by the National Park Service for final approval.

National Register Evaluation Criteria

The Code of Federal Regulations (36 CFR Part 60, National Register of Historic Places) contains evaluation criteria focusing on districts, sites, and buildings that possess integrity of location, design, setting, and workmanship. While some districts are associated with significant events in American history, or are directly associated with the lives of prominent individuals, it is more often the case that National Register districts embody residential neighborhoods or downtowns unified by distinctive architecture, in which most buildings were constructed more than 50 years ago. Broadly worded evaluation criteria have resulted in a wide diversity in the type and geographical

extent of National Register districts found across the United States.

Districts, sites, buildings, and structures may meet criteria for inclusion in the National Register of Historic Places if they:

- are associated with events that have made a significant contribution to the broad patterns of our nation's history;
- are associated with the lives of persons significant in our nation's past;
- embody the distinctive characteristics of a type, period, or method of construction, or that represent the work of a master, or that possess high artistic values, or that represent a significant and distinguishable entity whose components may lack individual distinction; or
- have yielded, or may be likely to yield, information important in prehistory or history.

Planning and Urban Design Implications

The National Register's utility as a planning tool is derived from the National Historic Preservation Act, which requires federal agencies to consider the effects of their undertakings on historic properties, commonly known as a Section 106 Review. An undertaking is defined as "a project, activity, or program funded in whole or in part under the direct or indirect jurisdiction of a federal agency, including those carried out by or on behalf of a federal agency; those carried out with federal financial assistance; those requiring a federal permit, license, or approval; and those subject to state or local regulation administered pursuant to a delegation or approval by a federal agency." At the local government level, the receipt of community development block grant (CDBG) funds or federal dollars to install a water main or replace a municipally owned bridge would trigger a Section 106 review.

Owners of private structures listed only in the National Register (and not otherwise part of a local historic district) are free to maintain or dispose of their property as they deem appropriate, provided that their actions require no federal license, permit, or funding—there is no obligation to restore or even maintain a federally listed historic property. But

because mapped boundaries of a National Register district are often identical to those of a local historic district, governing rules for the latter can provide a greater degree of protection than that offered under federal law.

At times, property owner opposition can foil the establishment of a local historic district and the creation of its associated review board, as even the most ardent preservation advocates cannot deny that this will add an additional layer to a development oversight process that may also require approvals from a planning board or zoning board. However, the guidance and rules these other boards must follow seldom focus on architectural or aesthetic features of a structure, or consider the extent to which its alteration or demolition would impact a neighborhood's historic character. In the absence of a local historic district architectural review process, the composition of established neighborhoods and business districts risks erosion, and visual character of a community may be irreparably altered.

Financial Incentives for Historic Preservation

Jointly managed by the National Park Service and the Internal Revenue Service, in partnership with State Historic Preservation Offices, the federal historic preservation tax incentives program rewards private sector rehabilitation of historic buildings. The certification process for this program is outlined in the Code of Federal Regulations at 36 CFR Part 67. Properties individually listed in the National Register or those located in a National Register district and certified by a SHPO as being of historic significance are eligible.

Since 1976, these federal tax credits have stimulated more than $18 billion in private investment, and have contributed to the rehabilitation of more than 27,000 historic properties containing more than 30,000 units of low- and moderate-income housing. However, eligibility requirements for federal historic preservation tax credits provide that such properties must be income-producing and be rehabilitated according to architectural design standards set by the Secretary of the Interior. Properties receiving federal tax credits may be used for offices, for commercial,

FINANCIAL INCENTIVES FOR HISTORIC PRESERVATION

DESCRIPTION	BENEFITS
Certified local government grants for local preservation planning	10% of each state's National Historic Preservation Fund allocation is directed toward designated CLG communities.
Federal Historic Preservation Tax Credit program, administered by the National Park Service and Internal Revenue Service (36 CFR Part 67, Historic Preservation Certifications)	20% tax credit for rehabilitation of income producing structures listed in the National Register. 10% tax credit for rehabilitation of nonhistoric, nonresidential buildings constructed before 1936.
State or local homeowner and business owner tax credits (Not obtainable in all states; check with SHPO as to availability.)	Tax credit programs designed to complement, and often used in conjunction with, Federal Historic Preservation Tax Credits, focusing on exterior renovations.
Historical or Local Preservation Loan Funds (Not obtainable in all states; check with SHPO as to availability.)	State or locally administered revolving loans, with interest rates lower than conventional financing.
Community development block grants, designed to address blight or improve low- and moderate-income housing	CDBG monies can be used for improvements to privately-owned residences, multifamily dwellings, sign or façade improvements for businesses, and to fund historic resources surveys.
FHWA Transportation Enhancement Program	Federal grant funds administered through state transportation departments, used for streetscape improvements or renovations to historic transportation-related structures.

William R. Haase IV, AICP, Town of Westerly, Rhode Island

industrial, or agricultural enterprises, or for rental housing, but they may not serve exclusively as a private residence.

A number of additional financial incentives are available to assist communities undertaking historic surveys, or help out property owners willing to restore their buildings in a historically appropriate fashion. A key thread running through virtually all these programs is the need to adhere to the Secretary of the Interior's Standards for Rehabilitation and the requirement that properties be individually listed on the National Register of Historic Places or located within a National Register district.

LOCAL HISTORIC DISTRICTS

Charleston, South Carolina, established America's first local historic district in 1931. Today, it is one of the country's largest, encompassing 3 square miles and nearly 4,200 contributing structures. Fueled partly by federal involvement in historic preservation beginning in the 1960s, every state has enacted legislation authorizing local preservation ordinances, enabling creation of historic districts and local boards or commissions charged with the review and approval of development activities taking place within these districts. Common to virtually all local historic districts are administrative rules intended to preserve a structure's exterior appearance and setting relative to the historical architecture and settlement pattern characteristics of the neighborhood. These rules are typically expressed in a historic preservation ordinance and administered by a locally created review board.

Certified Local Government (CLG) programs allow municipalities to participate more directly in state and federal historic preservation programs. To become a CLG, a local government must enact a local preservation ordinance that meets federal standards and establishes three basic items:

- A local historic preservation commission
- A process to designate historic properties
- A method for reviewing changes to those properties

Benefits of becoming a CLG include special grants, professional legal and technical assistance, training, and membership in the national historic preservation network.

HISTORIC RESOURCES SURVEYS

Conducting a historic resources survey is the first step in both federal and local historic district designation. This survey identifies and evaluates all contributing structures within a proposed historic district. Extensive documentation is required, including a field inventory to visually evaluate buildings and structures, and research in libraries, newspaper archives, and municipal records. Key elements of a completed historic resources survey are described here.

Structure Inventory Forms

Structure inventory forms describe a building's architectural style, level of detailing and craftsmanship, and integrity or alterations to its original character.

Photographs

Photographs of a building's exterior elevations, generally of archival print quality, are included.

Maps

Maps depict the exterior boundary of the historic district and locations of all contributing structures, cross-referenced to each structure inventory form. The map should be capable of yielding a written description of the historic district boundary. Fire insurance maps from the nineteenth and early twentieth centuries can help establish relative dates of neighborhood development.

Narrative Report

The narrative report describes the methods used to determine the boundary and conduct the survey, the district's historical development, the relationship of contributing structures to one another, and buildings that are noteworthy for important personages or architectural significance. This report should also list primary and secondary written materials encountered during the research. It is appropriate to identify potential threats to a neighborhood, such as deteriorating buildings neglected by their owners, architecturally intrusive noncontributing structures, and income-producing properties that may be eligible for federal tax incentives for rehabilitation.

Request for Qualifications

These survey elements can be embodied into a Request for Qualifications, used to solicit proposals from historians, architects, or architectural historians whose education and training meet the Secretary of the Interior's Minimum Professional Qualifications Standards (36 CFR Part 61, Appendix A). A SHPO should be able to provide a prequalified list of acceptable consultants meeting these standards, which are requisite for preparing nominations to the National Register of Historic Places.

LOCAL HISTORIC PRESERVATION ORDINANCE

An ordinance is necessary to identify procedures for creating local historic districts and administering the review of building renovations or alterations to properties located within the district. It should reference the legislative intent of the state enabling act, which grants municipal authority to establish historic districts. The ordinance should require a survey to identify and evaluate all contributing structures, and the preparation of a map depicting district boundaries. It typically establishes a historic district commission or architectural review board that is charged with the review of development proposals within historic districts.

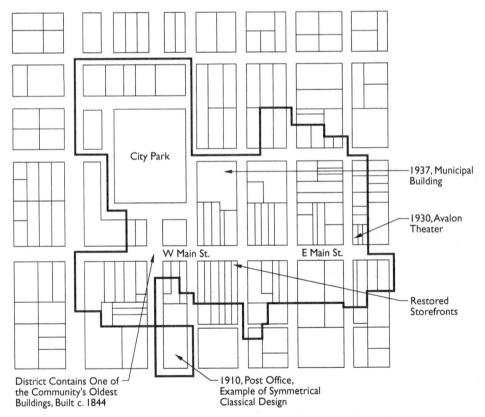

City Park

W Main St.   E Main St.

1937, Municipal Building

1930, Avalon Theater

Restored Storefronts

District Contains One of the Community's Oldest Buildings, Built c. 1844

1910, Post Office, Example of Symmetrical Classical Design

The map shown is of the Main Street Historic District in Platteville, Wisconsin. It is representative of a historic district map, indicating the district's boundary. Labels are added to provide information on historic resources located within the district. Photos may be used to show specific properties. A certificate of appropriateness is required for any modifications to be made to the exterior of buildings and properties located in the district.

SAMPLE HISTORIC DISTRICT MAP

Source: City of Platteville, Wisconsin.

William R. Haase IV, AICP, Town of Westerly, Rhode Island

HISTORIC PRESERVATION ORDINANCE CONTENT

Some states require a vote of approval by a majority, or even two-thirds, of the residents of a proposed local historic district. In other states, a city or town council is empowered to establish a local historic district after conducting a public hearing.

Historic District Commission/Architectural Review Board

A local historic district commission, which may be known as a heritage preservation commission or an architectural review board, depending on the nature of the ordinance, administers a process sometimes referred to as "historic district zoning." These boards are distinct and separate from planning or zoning commissions. They have their own rules of procedure and issue their own approvals, known as certificates of appropriateness, when approving construction plans. The historic district commission's actions do restrict what a person can do with their property; however, there is a significant body of case law that supports the right of a community to regulate a building's visual and historic character.

The review board's jurisdiction typically includes exterior renovations, building demolition, and new construction. The board may also be responsible for approving façade improvements and signage in order to protect and enhance the visual character and encourage economic development in commercial neighborhoods. Some communities allow "minor work" such as repair or replacement of exterior materials with identical or similar materials to be reviewed by staff, with an appeal to the full board if necessary.

When creating a historic district commission, the local governing body should appoint members who have a background in history or architecture. These qualifications are necessary to meet National Park Service criteria for a certified local government (CLG).

Certificate of Appropriateness

The architectural review process begins when a property owner applies for a building permit for repairs or alternations to structures located within a local historic district. The historic district commission or architectural review board grants a certificate of appropriateness prior to the issuance of the building permit or certificate of occupancy. Each commission develops its own written procedures and standards guiding modifications to historic buildings, but the most commonly used measure is known as the Secretary of the Interior's Standards for Rehabilitation (36 CFR Part 67, Historic Preservation Certifications), which is also used to administer the federal historic preservation tax credit program.

William R. Haase IV, AICP, Town of Westerly, Rhode Island

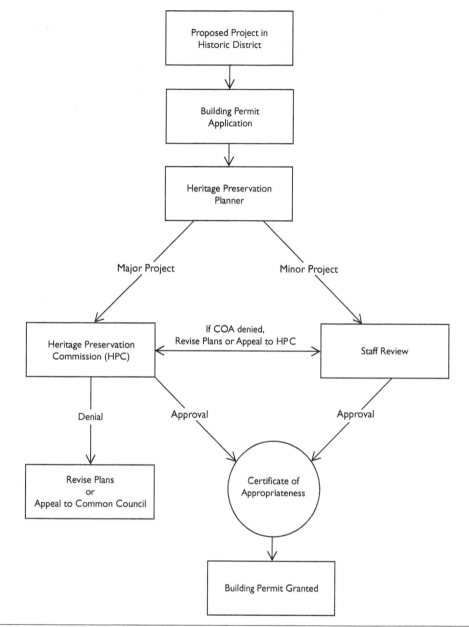

BUILDING PERMIT PROCESS FOR PROJECTS IN HISTORIC DISTRICTS

Source: URS Corporation.

Appeals

Local preservation ordinances should also contain a provision for property owners to appeal the decision of a historic district commission, with such appeal directed toward an existing entity such as a zoning board of review. When considering appeals, the zoning board of review should not substitute its own judgment for that of the historic district commission, but rather consider the issue upon the findings and record of that commission

CHALLENGES TO HISTORIC DISTRICT DESIGNATION

Planners should be aware of arguments used by opponents to historic district designation, who may raise concerns about added construction costs or excessive regulation.

One ongoing debate is that historic district commissions "fossilize" neighborhoods by imposing very narrow or personal definitions of appropriateness that discourage architectural creativity and diversity. Others argue that compliance with architectural design codes restrict the ability of businesses—particularly national franchises—to adjust to market conditions, or are beyond a homeowner's financial capacity to carry out needed exterior renovations. Indeed, blight becomes an issue when property owners fear or resent an additional layer of bureaucracy, or cannot afford historically appropriate building improvements.

To prevent individual board members from becoming arbiters of "good taste," historic district commissions from the outset must have clearly written specifications to determine what constitutes appropriate construction or renovation, and what will add or detract from a historic streetscape. This is why local boards are encouraged to rely on the nationally accepted Secretary of the Interior's Standards for Rehabilitation, possibly supplementing these with more detailed guidelines that are specific to a particular district. Proper documentation will elevate the review process above personal preference or bias, and thus provide a consistency of decision making.

It is recommended that historic district commissions prepare an informational pamphlet that addresses the concerns of property owners, builders, and architects. Pamphlets should summarize the historic preservation ordinance's guiding principles and procedures, list which actions are exempt from design review, and provide graphic illustrations of the types of improvements that would be granted a certificate of appropriateness.

A final challenge is "demolition by neglect," which is defined as the destruction of a building through abandonment or lack of maintenance. This problem is attributable to impoverished owners, difficulties arising from unsettled estates, or uncaring absentee landlords. It is important, therefore, that property owners be made aware of financial incentives that can assist in rehabilitation.

See also:

Historic Structures

William R. Haase IV, AICP, Town of Westerly, Rhode Island

WATERFRONTS

Current interest in the water's edge and the flourishing of public spaces on waterfronts across the United States is the result of a process going back for decades. Once places of trade, military, or industrial advantage, or even places of neglect, waterfronts are increasingly seen as economic and social assets to their communities.

STANDARDS AND REGULATIONS

When contemplating new waterfront projects, take into account the specific standards enforced by federal and state regulatory systems. The following agencies have a role in the regulation of our coastal ecosystems.

Federal Agencies (for Navigable Waterways and Connected Wetlands)

U.S. Environmental Protection Agency (EPA)

U.S. Army Corps of Engineers

National Oceanic and Atmosphere Administration (NOAA)

The Department of Homeland Security (especially the Federal Emergency Management Agency (FEMA) and the U.S. Coast Guard)

U.S. Fish and Wildlife Service

State and Local Authorities

Coastal commissions

Special waterfront agencies

Port authorities

Waterfront transportation authorities

Planning departments and redevelopment agencies

State or local public trust managers

MORPHOLOGICAL ANALYSIS

To understand a waterfront, study its evolution. Consider the shoreline's various stages of development. Create a series of diagrams analyzing the historic and current conditions of the water edge, which will be critical in designing its future uses. In addition, understanding the sectional analysis of a coastline is important when planning a new use on the water and its connections to the built fabric of the city.

Natural Edge

A natural edge diagram describes the undisturbed conditions of the shoreline's ecosystem and its often rich variety of species. Such natural conditions might be used as a benchmark for waterfront restoration.

Productive Edge

A diagram of the waterfront's historic productive uses can be helpful when planning new uses on the water. Maintaining productive waterfront uses is often a priority. Elsewhere, historic artifacts might be incorporated in a new design as cultural and perhaps functional features, such as old gantries, working piers, and cranes. Historic interpretation can be important for the new design by creating a strong identity of a place rooted in the region's past.

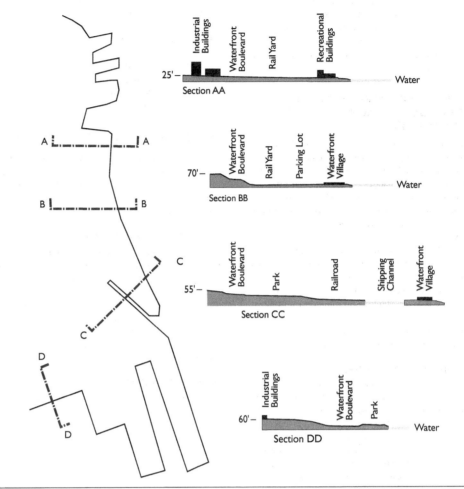

SECTIONAL ANALYSIS

Source: SMWM 2005.

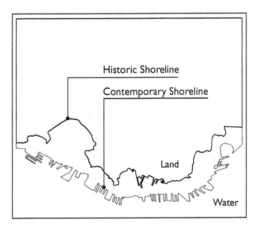

Natural Edge

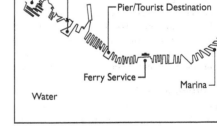

Productive Edge

WATER EDGE TYPES

Source: SMWM 2005.

Ilaria Salvadori, SMWM, San Francisco, California; Sharon Priest, AICP, SMWM, San Francisco, California

Public Life: Placemaking on the Water

Renewed interest in waterfronts has resulted in the conversion of major areas of industrial, shipping, and transportation uses to more public uses. Identify on a diagram potential economic anchors such as large civic or commercial buildings, which can attract more uses over time.

ANALYSIS OF ENVIRONMENTAL AND ECOLOGICAL WATERFRONT CONDITIONS

Pollution and deterioration of the coastal environment often requires major investment in its restoration, considerably increasing a project's total cost. Pollution mitigation, remediation, stormwater management, stream and wetland restoration, and habitat protection are some of the basic aspects of waterfront restoration and development.

Environmental education is a key component in successful waterfront revitalization. Include design elements and signage that provide information about the historic uses of the waterfront area and its current environmental status. Consider alliances that involve local citizens and institutions in long-term restoration efforts. Inform the local community about the health hazards of activities along the new waterfront, such as fishing and swimming, if there is potential for danger.

Ecology of the Water Edge

Investigate ecological conditions at the shoreline to determine the type of cleanup and the subsequent appropriate ecological system when designing the waterfront. Often, this process can inspire the designer to incorporate ecological elements, both aquatic and terrestrial, into the new design, turning them into opportunities to educate and inform the public about the natural history of the shoreline.

Transportation and Connections

Abandoned or active rail lines, freeway structures, neglected culverts, chain-link fences, walls, or even private gates can be obstructions to accessing the waterfront. Take into account their presence and potential for relocation when redesigning new waterfront destinations.

Land Use

Many land uses can be found on the waterfront, depending on its economic and social function. Land uses can include industrial production, commercial development, transportation nodes, recreational uses, public infrastructure, institutional and educational structures, and new residential areas. Successful waterfront development will include several coexisting uses, providing urban vitality and activity at the water's edge.

Environmental Factors

Given the heavy industrial uses that occurred on the shorelines in the past, cleanup processes and programs play a fundamental role and are a key step in the redevelopment process of sites along the waterfronts. Soil analysis is a basic step in the challenging process of cleanup and restoration of a waterfront area. Cleanup costs can be substantial and can add to the total cost of a waterfront redevelopment project.

Because of contamination in the ground, in buildings and other structures, and possibly in groundwater or adjacent surface water, state and federal environmental agencies and financial institutions often require considerable remediation or cleanup before redevelopment can occur, or as part of the redevelopment process. Of particular concern are any anticipated changes to a structure's configuration. A brownfield, as defined by U.S. EPA, is a polluted property that in order to be redeveloped needs to undergo such cleanup process. Also, many jurisdictions prohibit additional fill or require mitigation measures to replace open water.

WATERFRONT DESIGN PROCESS

Because of the often controversial and political nature of waterfront projects, their development is a complex process involving many different state and federal authorities as well as grassroots organizations and community stakeholders.

Community Involvement

Involve the community from the beginning in waterfront redevelopment projects. Educating and informing the community about the challenges ahead will create a strong foundation on which to draft a long-term vision for a new, inclusive waterfront. Environmental monitoring and education are effective tools to build a large community constituency, together with effective visioning tools such as community workshops and charrettes.

Remediation Plan

A remediation plan is necessary when high toxicity levels are found on-site. The intensity and thoroughness of the cleanup process differs with the specific uses planned for the site: a residential area, for example, requires a much higher level of remediation than an area for a parking structure.

Conceptual Framework Design

When designing a waterfront, issues of scale play a major role. A framework plan often builds on previous studies and has the overall planning of the area as a main goal. A comprehensive framework plan allows flexibility and leaves room for future land-use decisions regarding the waterfront. This type of plan ensures a cohesive allocation of investments, connects the new sites to the rest of the urban or rural developments, and supports appropriate uses on the water.

Detailed Design

A detailed plan finds its place within a strong framework and usually focuses on the appropriate specific program for an area. A detailed plan for a waterfront calls for new and reinterpreted uses and creates new places and destinations through the implementation of solid design guidelines.

WATERFRONT TYPES

Different waterfronts encourage different types of activities. River waterfronts promote activities enhancing connections across the two riverbanks: physical and visual connections are equally important in this kind of waterfront. Waterfronts by the ocean or the bay connect the urban fabric to activity nodes along

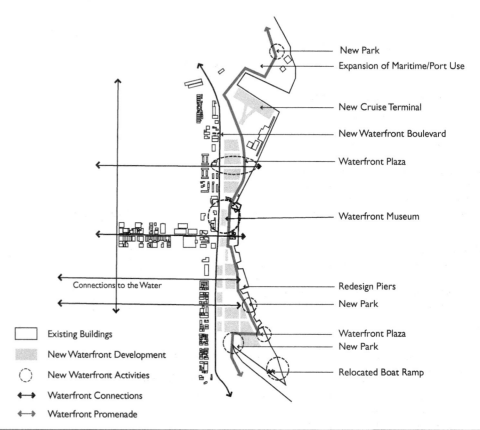

New Park
Expansion of Maritime/Port Use

New Cruise Terminal

New Waterfront Boulevard

Waterfront Plaza

Waterfront Museum

Redesign Piers
New Park

Waterfront Plaza
New Park

Relocated Boat Ramp

Connections to the Water

☐ Existing Buildings

▨ New Waterfront Development

◌ New Waterfront Activities

↔ Waterfront Connections

↔ Waterfront Promenade

COORDINATED FRAMEWORK PLAN

Source: SMWM 2005.

Ilaria Salvadori, SMWM, San Francisco, California; Sharon Priest, AICP, SMWM, San Francisco, California

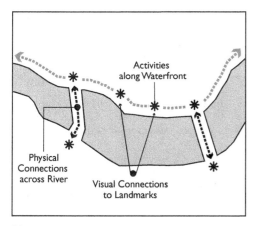

River

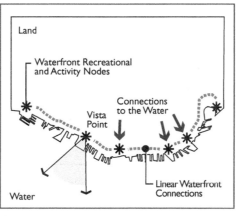

Ocean and Bay

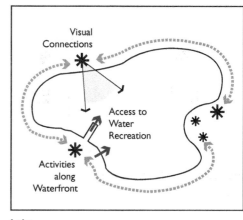

Lake

WATERFRONT TYPES

Source: SMWM 2005.

the water and promote the use of piers for recreational activities. Finally, a body of water such as a lake or a reservoir promotes activities around the edge, invites points of activity along the shore, and is a great setting for water-related sports.

WATERFRONT DESIGN COMPONENTS

Waterfront projects can have different scales, from a plaza to a greenway, and different character, from container port to wetland. Waterfront components can be a series of open-space elements, a system of connections to the inner core of the city, a new development on the water, or a strategy for sustainability.

Design Strategies

Consider the following overall strategies for the design of a successful waterfront area.

> **Continuity:** A continuous waterfront system for walking, jogging, biking, and rollerblading.

> **Sequence:** A sequence of recurring open spaces at significant points along the water. Such places might have a special view or might be directly aligned with major city streets.

> **Variety:** Multiple uses along the water create successful synergies and accommodate different users.

> **Connection:** Visually and physically connect spaces along the waterfront and from the new waterfront to the bay (with views and piers) and to the city (through access points and pedestrian circulation links).

Design Elements

Open Space
Plazas: Waterfront plazas are often part of larger waterfront developments, such as commercial and recreational buildings along the water. They are often hard-surfaced areas with seating, shaded areas, and prime views of the water. In larger developments, plazas can be designed to

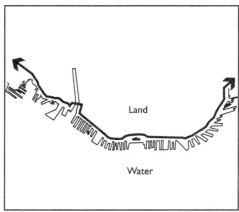

Continuity

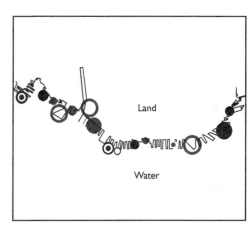

Variety

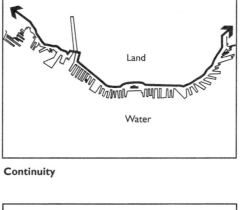

Sequence

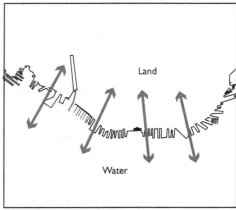

Connections

DESIGN STRATEGIES FOR WATERFRONTS

Source: SMWM 2005.

Ilaria Salvadori, SMWM, San Francisco, California; Sharon Priest, AICP, SMWM, San Francisco, California

End

Edge

Interior

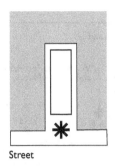
Street

PIER ACTIVITY LOCATIONS
Source: SMWM 2005.

allow for large recreational gathering structures such as amphitheaters or stage areas where local civic events can be held. They also offer great opportunity for displaying the historic memory of the waterfront through interpretive features or art installations.

Parks: Along the water, parks can be hard-paved areas or more natural soft areas. A new park can also be connected to a local ecosystem, such as a wetland, and to larger natural areas, such as greenways along the shoreline.

Piers: Piers can be interesting components in the redesign of waterfronts. They can reinterpret history, provide views, and promote recreation such as fishing. Incorporate safety elements such as lighting and railings, as well as sitting areas with benches to rest and enjoy the view. Focal elements such as art installations or small commercial buildings can be included at the end of a pier to make walking and strolling along its length a more exciting activity.

Connections
Paths: Biking and jogging are among the more iconic uses of a recreational waterfront. Water views and linear, often unobstructed, connections along the water make these activities especially pleasant. Design paths to accommodate these activities. Use smooth paving materials in areas for bikes, and ensure that path widths accommodate bikers and walkers alike, possibly with separate rights-of-way.

Promenades: A promenade can connect spaces along the water or be a destination in itself, offering recreational opportunities for strollers, joggers, bikers, and in-line skaters. Depending on the specific character of the waterfront, promenades can be constructed and sophisticated urban places or natural and understated linear connections. Design elements such as paving materials or light fixtures can vary according to such character. Accommodate biking and jogging activities with materials that can withstand the effects of the moist microclimate.

Water connections for tourists: Tourism can be an economic engine driving the waterfront redevelopment process. Water taxis and ferries can be tourist attractions, as well as interpretive tools of an area's productive past.

Water connections as mode of transportation: When waterfronts are more developed and can support a high number of residential buildings, water connections can become an effective mode of transportation, making the link between residence and work place an easy and interesting transit alternative.

Development
Working waterfronts: In the past, waterfronts were the exclusive realm of harbors, fishing fleets, shipbuilding, warehouses, and manufacturing plants. Changing technology made some of these uses obsolete, and rising land prices connected to the rediscovery of the water edge have endangered many local maritime enterprises. These enterprises can add to the local economy and to the city's character. Consider retaining and promoting existing maritime uses when possible, and integrate their needs with the overall plan of the new waterfront.

For large working ports, container handling, shoreline configuration, updated equipment, regional distribution networks, and environmental impacts are key planning issues. Planning efforts at many ports seek to designate safe and inviting locations for the public to view port activities.

Infill and adaptive use: Infill development can be a catalyst for change in forgotten areas of a waterfront. Adaptive use of historic buildings can be a powerful redevelopment strategy to create new destinations and to reinterpret the waterfront's past in new ways. Successful renovations can generate dynamic synergies that can boost local economies and provide a sense of place.

Recreation and tourist destinations: The number of tourists it attracts is often the measure of a waterfront's success. Promote tourism in the early phases of waterfront redevelopment to encourage investment. Educational, recreational, and interpretive features and activities are often found in the public areas of a waterfront, where visitors exploring the character of the region can readily appreciate a new identity anchored in the past.

New mixed-use development: After the initial success of a waterfront redevelopment, larger developments often follow. All uses benefit from the prime location and the recreational opportunities a new waterfront offers. Some jurisdictions invite residential uses along the water, to bring density and vitality to the area. Be sensitive when locating residential uses at the edge, to ensure public access is maintained.

Art: Public areas along waterfronts offer great opportunities for education and art appreciation.

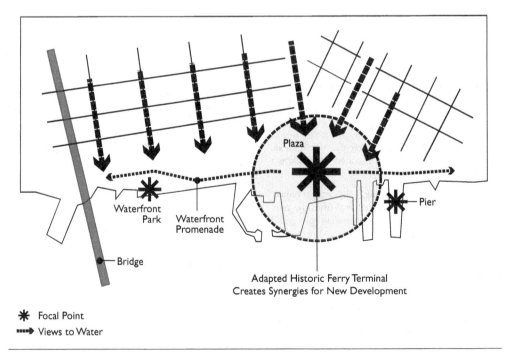

Plaza

Waterfront Park

Waterfront Promenade

Pier

Bridge

Adapted Historic Ferry Terminal Creates Synergies for New Development

✳ Focal Point
➡ Views to Water

ADAPTIVE REUSE
Source: SMWM 2005.

Ilaria Salvadori, SMWM, San Francisco, California; Sharon Priest, AICP, SMWM, San Francisco, California

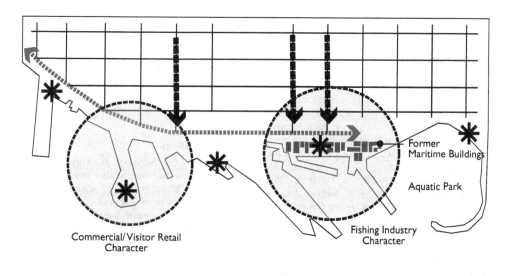

Connections to the Water

✳ Waterfront Activities and Focal Points

▪▪▪▪ Waterfront Promenade

TOURIST DESTINATION

Source: SMWM 2005.

In particular, the rich social and cultural heritage of these sites encourages artists and a municipality to collaborate in often striking public art projects that foster a sense of place. Allow flexibility in waterfront plans to ensure that art interventions and programs can be incorporated.

Sustainability

Ecological preservation: Every waterfront is part of a watershed. Consider sensitive habitats and floodplains during the design process.

Ecological design: Natural conditions of waterbodies and the edge conditions are increasingly seen as opportunities to inspire design and suggest uses along the water. Many new developments incorporate ecological design principles as powerful elements of the design concept. Ideas such as wetland restoration, native vegetation preservation, and stormwater management have created a new design vocabulary in waterfront planning.

See also:

Beach and Dune Systems
Brownfields
Environmental Planning and Management
Estuaries, Flats, and Marshes
Flood Hazards
Infill Development
Mixed-Use Development

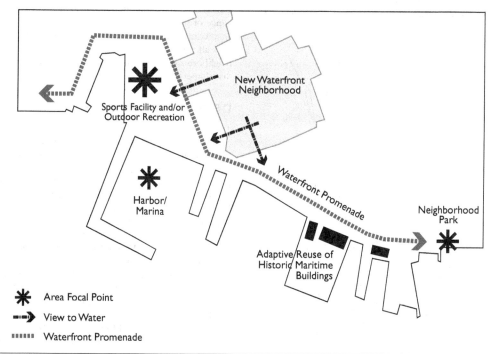

✳ Area Focal Point

■▶ View to Water

▪▪▪▪▪ Waterfront Promenade

NEW WATERFRONT DEVELOPMENT

Source: SMWM 2005.

Ilaria Salvadori, SMWM, San Francisco, California; Sharon Priest, AICP, SMWM, San Francisco, California

PLACES AND DISTRICTS

ARTS DISTRICTS

An arts district is a recognized mixed-use area of a community in which high concentrations of cultural facilities serve as economic and cultural anchors. An area usually less than 100 blocks geographically delineates an arts district, but the defining characteristic is the prevalence of cultural facilities, arts organizations, individual artists, and arts-based businesses. Arts districts attract and retain arts and culture, engage the community in cultural life, and have a positive economic impact. More than 100 communities in the United States have arts districts.

TYPES OF ARTS DISTRICTS

Five types of arts districts are common in the United States: cultural compounds, major cultural institutions, arts and entertainment districts, downtown arts districts, and cultural production-based areas.

Cultural Compounds

The oldest arts districts are cultural compounds, established in many cities prior to the 1930s. Cultural compounds are different from contemporary districts in that their noncultural land uses tend to be limited to parks, medical centers, and housing, with little commercial space. Forest Park in St. Louis is an example of a cultural compound.

Major Cultural Institutions

Major cultural institutions, such as large concert halls, playhouses, libraries, and museums, anchor some arts districts. These districts are typically located close to central business districts and near convention centers or other large tourism sites. Some districts focus on a specific cultural genre, such as Houston's theater district.

Arts and Entertainment Districts

Arts and entertainment districts focus on popular attractions and often have a more bohemian feel than more established districts. Small theaters, private galleries, restaurants, and other entertainment venues are common attractions. Miami Beach's Art Deco District is an example of a district with an arts and entertainment focus.

Downtown Arts Districts

Similarly, some arts districts encompass the entire downtown area of a city. This designation is often closely tied to a tourism focus and is common in small cities with walkable downtowns. Hartford, Connecticut's, downtown area is a designated arts district.

Cultural Production Districts

Cultural production is a focus of some districts. Production spaces such as specialized studios, arts centers, classrooms, and media facilities characterize these areas. Cultural production districts tend to put priority on the cultural life of the neighborhood, rather than on tourist attraction or business development, and often take advantage of areas with affordable housing and commercial space.

DESIGN ELEMENTS

New and renovated cultural facilities, designed public spaces, and public art are among the common strategies in the development of any type of arts district.

Americans for the Arts, Washington, DC

Cultural Facility

A cultural facility is a building used primarily for the production, presentation, or exhibition of cultural disciplines such as music, dance, theater, literature, and visual arts. Most artists and cultural organizations are dependent upon facilities to pursue their creative work. The design of such facilities must also accommodate the highly specialized technical needs of the performing and visual arts.

Funding for cultural facilities is locally specific. Partnerships that combine public support through taxes and private sector resources are common and result in facilities owned and operated by a mix of commercial and nonprofit real estate interests, local arts organizations, or public agencies.

Adaptive reuse of existing structures is a common approach to creating cultural facilities. An example is the 307-acre district in Pawtucket, Rhode Island, where former cotton mills have become homes and studios for more than 300 artists. The Rhode Island General Assembly established the arts district in 1998, and renovation projects are supported and coordinated through the City of Pawtucket Department of Planning and Redevelopment.

Infill development is another approach to creating cultural facilities in an arts district. Areas of a community where structures are beyond feasible rehabilitation, or where vacant parcels can be assembled, are among the types of available infill

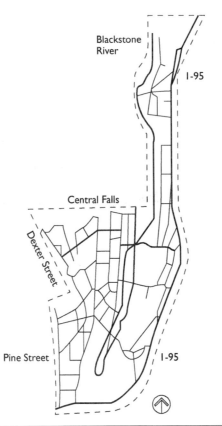

PAWTUCKET, RHODE ISLAND, ARTS AND ENTERTAINMENT DISTRICT

Source: City of Pawtucket, Rhode Island, Department of Planning and Development.

opportunities. An example of this is in the Gateway Arts District in Prince George's County, Maryland. A new facility for 44 artists and their families is being constructed by assembling several parcels that will also include arts-oriented retail on the street level.

Public Spaces

The design of public spaces in an arts district should provide a thematic thread that highlights the local character. Walking paths and seating areas should invite residents to inhabit and enjoy the neighborhood. Distinctive signage, murals, and sculpture help attract visitors. A designed environment that supports cultural activities—exhibitions, festivals, craft fairs, parades, and outdoor events—may include designated performance spaces, accommodations for large groups, and opportunities to promote cultural events in innovative ways.

Public Art

Most arts districts feature public art, including murals on public and private buildings, freestanding works in plazas and corporate lobbies, and temporary installations. Public art may be funded through private developers or public agencies. It is increasingly common for arts districts to employ a "percent-for-art" program in which a portion of construction costs is set aside for the acquisition, installation, and maintenance of public art. There are more than 350 public art programs in the United States. Artists and public art staff often work with planners, developers, and neighborhood organizations to create public spaces that shape arts districts.

DESIGNATING AN ARTS DISTRICT

The process for designating an arts district varies by community. There is no national standard for formal designation. Arts districts may be designated by a private development group, promotional bureau, planning authority, or officially through local or state legislation. Arts districts can also have informal boundaries, such as a former warehouse district that becomes a focal point for the arts.

Arts districts officially designated at the state or local level may also be funded in part through tax revenues and tax incentives to artists and arts-based businesses within the district boundary. An example is Denver's Scientific and Cultural Facilities District (SCFD), a special tax district that receives funds from a 0.1 percent retail sales tax within a seven-county area. State and municipal funds may also be used to fund local arts agencies that coordinate and promote the arts district.

ECONOMIC BENEFITS

Neighborhood revitalization and economic development are among the primary motivations for creating an arts district. Residents and visitors of arts districts support associated businesses such as restaurants, lodging, and retail. The presence of the arts can enhance property values, the profitability of surrounding businesses, and the tax base of the region. The arts can also attract an educated workforce, commonly referred to as the "creative class," which may be a key incentive for new and relocating businesses. Americans for the Arts (2002) estimates that the arts and their audiences have a $134 billion economic impact, annually supporting 4.85 million jobs and producing $89.4 billion in household income. Arts districts leverage this impact to support the economic and cultural growth of a particular region.

For example, three years after establishing the Tucson Arts District, 26 of the 112 businesses in the arts district were new, 54 percent had increased their sales volume, and 53 percent made renovations, with an average cost of $105,272 each. Within four years, the retail vacancy rate declined by 50 percent, and city sales tax revenues in the arts district increased 11.7 percent, compared to a citywide increase of 7.4 percent.

PLANNING CONSIDERATIONS

Structural considerations within or near the district, community leadership, and long-term commitment all influence the planning of an arts district and the type of district that results.

A need for revitalization, as well as the ability to leverage existing investment or interest may be a motivating factor for a district designation. Preexisting cultural assets—including individual artists—as well as other tourism sites will also affect the opportunity. Current and potential development of housing, retail, and office space must be evaluated in comparison to property values and availability in nearby areas. In many districts, the planning and zoning environment will allow or disallow certain approaches to development.

Equally important to district siting and development are the organization and political clout of stakeholders. Typically, arts districts are created through partnerships among four major groups: the arts community (artists, arts organizations, and local arts councils or commissions), government agencies, development authorities, and the business community. Representatives from school districts, universities, local foundations, and other nonprofits may also be involved.

The creation of an art district can result in significant debates about the development projects themselves and other civic issues. Planning stakeholders often have to address complex and competing priorities, such as artistic approaches, community needs, functional uses, and funding realities. Among the planning issues commonly raised are parking and traffic, signage and lighting, buildings and landscape, public art, and the relationship of commercial to residential areas.

CONCLUSION

Arts districts involve long-term vision, planning, and commitment. Each district should respond to the specific cultural, social, and economic needs of the community, and be based on regional assets. Planning for an arts district is best achieved in the context of cultural planning for the broader city or region, and should strive for the widest possible accessibility for both residents and visitors. Arts districts require careful coordination among many interests, and may require specialized management to be developed and maintained. Existing and new arts districts should incorporate evaluation in the earliest stages of planning. Using certain measurement points, such as economic development and cultural vitality, can help identify the impact of cultural districts on community and quality of life.

REFERENCES

Americans for the Arts. 2002. *Arts and Economic Prosperity: The Economic Impact of Nonprofit Arts Organizations and Their Audiences.* Washington, DC: Americans for the Arts.

Americans for the Arts, Washington, DC

INDUSTRIAL PARKS

Industrial parks are areas within a community designated for activities associated with industrial development, which can include materials processing, materials assembly, product manufacturing, and storage of finished products. Uses can include manufacturing facilities, warehouse distribution centers, and truck terminals.

Industrial parks can be stand-alone developments within a community, or they can be adjacent to or part of a larger regional industrial district spanning a number of contiguous jurisdictions. Industrial parks rely on the availability of large tracts of land, efficient transportation systems, and sufficient infrastructure for their success and for their ability to integrate into the larger community.

SITING PARAMETERS

Transportation

Industrial parks should be located in close proximity to major transportation systems, including regional and interstate highway systems, with an efficient system of local roadways between the industrial park and the highway system. Access to other types of transportation systems, such as rail, port, and air-freight, should be available, if they are characteristic of the region and in demand by the industry.

Utilities and Infrastructure

Industrial parks require dependable utility systems. Sufficient supplies of water for domestic fire protection and for use in industrial processes should be available, and sanitary sewer systems need sufficient capacity to support waste generated in the park. Adequate supplies of natural gas and electricity also are necessary.

Consideration should be given to developing regional stormwater management facilities to support the industrial park. Best management practices for stormwater quality and quantity are ideally developed on a district or regionwide basis, based on the watershed of the area. If this approach is not possible, on-site stormwater management facilities need to be provided. Open stormwater management facilities should be allowed within perimeter buffer areas and planted areas, to preserve other land areas for industrial development.

Industrial park developers must also take into account telecommunications utility infrastructure.

Land Area

The land area needed for an industrial park can range from 20 acres to hundreds of acres. An area between 50 and 100 acres in size allows for flexibility for parcels, planting, and internal transportation and parking systems. Large, rectangular tracts of land that are available for development at competitive prices in the region should be considered as sites. Land should have minimal impediments to development, to make it competitive in the marketplace. Conditions such as steep topography, exposed bedrock, wetlands, sensitive environmental areas, and irregularly shaped parcels can contribute to site development costs and inefficient use of the land.

Labor Force

Development of the industrial park will be directly related to the ability to attract labor from proximate areas to the park to serve the industry within the facility. The available labor force is directly related to the

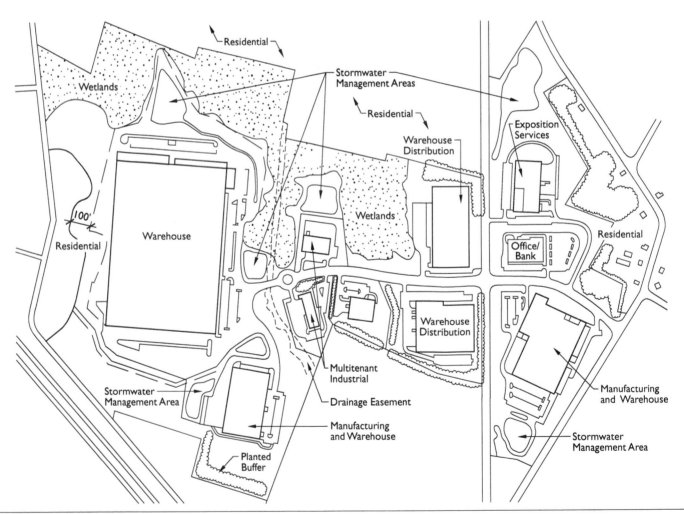

REPRESENTATIVE INDUSTRIAL PARK

Source: Cubellis, Inc.

Zenia Kotval, Ph.D. AICP, Michigan State University, East Lansing, Michigan; John R. Mullin, Ph.D. FAICP, University of Massachusetts, Amherst, Massachusetts; Don Springhetti, Cubellis Associates, Inc., Braintree, Massachusetts; Richard Hurwitz, Cubellis Associates, Inc., Boston, Massachusetts; Larry McClennan, Cubellis Associates, Inc., Boston, Massachusetts; Sheila Vertino, National Association of Industrial and Office Properties, Herndon, Virginia

type of industry that can be attracted and the likely success of the park. Among the labor force considerations to assess are the following:

- Location of the labor force
- Characteristics of the labor force (skilled or unskilled)
- Relative cost of labor in the region
- Transportation systems available to bring the labor force to the industrial park

SITE DESIGN CONSIDERATIONS

Organizational Systems

Industrial parks tend to be organized according to a grid system, to optimize flexibility in parcel shape and size. Internal street patterns also follow a grid, to accommodate heavy truck traffic. Newer industrial parks, which often include office space and require less excessive truck use, may use more curvilinear road systems that follow the natural contours of the land. Parcel sizes often vary, to capture changing market conditions. Most parcels are between 200 and 300 feet deep and allow for land to be resubdivided to create larger lots, if desired.

Circulation and Parking

Traffic, road, and parking standards depend on the uses allowed in the industrial park. Institute of Transportation Engineers (ITE) standards should be reviewed when developing the circulation and parking system for the area. These standards include road width and bearing capacity, truck loading and turning requirements, traffic generation guidelines, and parking requirements based on type of use. Major access points should not conflict with pedestrian movement or adjacent residential areas, and local traffic flow should not be disrupted as a result of truck movement.

Buffers and Open Space

Most industrial parks require planted buffers to separate them from residential uses. They also require sites to be planted and to retain tree cover. Modern industrial parks are often lower in density than older industrial areas; some require between 70 and 80 percent open space. Height and bulk standards, floor area ratios, and other density standards for structures should be compatible with competing industrial areas throughout the region, yet provide for land to be set aside for buffer zones, greenbelts, and protection of environmentally sensitive areas.

Structural Elements

While utilitarian industrial parks with inexpensive structures and minimum site improvements are often required for competitive reasons, enhanced design adds value to the industrial park, the community, the owners, and the employees. Among the elements of enhanced industrial park design are underground util-

ities, architecturally harmonious structures, planted areas, and road systems that allow for safe and efficient movement.

POTENTIAL IMPACTS

The compatibility of industrial uses with adjacent uses will depend highly on the type of industry that locates in the area. When considering an industrial park, the following are among the types of typical impacts from industrial uses:

- *Transportation*: Increased traffic volume and overall impacts on local and regional transportation systems
- *Community services*: Increased demand for community services, including utilities; police, fire and rescue; emergency services; and medical facilities
- *Pollution*: Specifically, air pollution generated from increased traffic and/or processes carried out throughout the industrial park; may also include light pollution, water quality impacts, and noise
- *Aesthetics*: Ensuring compatibility of the design and operation of the industrial park with the character of the community

Performance Standards

Industrial parks are increasingly governed by performance standards. In addition to the typical setbacks, buffers, and landscape planting requirements, these standards govern light and glare, noise, vibration, air pollution, odor, heat and humidity, electric interference, radiation, outdoor storage and waste disposal, traffic, fire and explosive hazards, and toxic and hazardous materials. Consult local regulations or published materials on industrial performance standards to develop specific standards.

Park Covenants

In addition to zoning regulations, covenants can also be used to guide industrial park development. Such covenants can describe the type and character of industry allowed within the industrial park, general guidelines for building construction, environmental considerations, buffer zones, and overall general aesthetics. These assure potential users that their investment will be protected by similar development within the industrial park. Covenants can also be written so that existing users within the park have input into the approval of future users locating within the park. Like zoning regulations, park covenants should be clear and result in a positive conclusion when all conditions are complied with.

EMERGING TRENDS

Mixed Uses

Industrial parks of the past were typically confined to industrial-related uses; today, related uses such as manufacturing support facilities, office and office

support, and research-related uses should be allowed in them. There are even circumstances where hotels and small retail activities can be sited in the industrial park. If they are desired, these uses should be placed on the periphery of the industrial park or in places that enable traffic to easily flow without intermingling with the core activities of the industrial park. Office uses, showrooms, and other ancillary or support functions such as conference and hotel facilities may be placed in the more visible areas of the park.

Eco-Industrial Parks

Eco-industrial parks are industrial parks in which tenants seek to minimize or eliminate waste generation, energy use, and other environmental impacts through symbiotic arrangements with other facilities in the park. Because of the interrelationships among the tenants, eco-industrial parks often require a more sophisticated management and support system than traditional industrial parks. Several eco-industrial parks are in operation in the United States, including Cape Charles, Virginia, and Londonderry, New Hampshire. Because of the reduced impacts of these facilities, they may be more compatible with nonindustrial uses than conventional industrial parks.

Eco-industrial parks can be described as generally having the following characteristics:

- *Energy*: They use existing energy sources efficiently, use waste energy from other facilities, and use renewable energy sources such as wind and solar energy.
- *Material reuse*: Waste generated by one facility becomes input material for other facilities in the park or is marketed elsewhere. Water used by one facility may be reused by another, with pretreatment conducted as needed. Stormwater runoff can be captured and used for certain facility needs. All the facilities work to optimize use of all input materials and to minimize toxic materials use.
- *Natural systems*: Facility and park design minimizes environmental impacts and reduces operating costs by using natural drainage systems, native plantings, and low-impact construction materials.
- *Design and construction*: Buildings and infrastructure are designed to be energy-efficient; minimize pollution generation; and be durable, easily maintained, and flexible in their use. Established standards such as Leadership in Energy and Environmental Design (LEED) and ISO14000 can be used to design and develop structures within industrial parks that are more sustainable in their construction and operation.

See also:
Leadership in Energy and Environmental Design—LEED
Mixed-Use Development
Office Parks
Transportation

Zenia Kotval, Ph.D. AICP, Michigan State University, East Lansing, Michigan; John R. Mullin, Ph.D. FAICP, University of Massachusetts, Amherst, Massachusetts; Don Springhetti, Cubellis Associates, Inc., Braintree, Massachusetts; Richard Hurwitz, Cubellis Associates, Inc., Boston, Massachusetts; Larry McClennan, Cubellis Associates, Inc., Boston, Massachusetts; Sheila Vertino, National Association of Industrial and Office Properties, Herndon, Virginia

OFFICE PARKS

An office park is designed specifically to serve the office space needs of a wide variety of businesses. Office parks often include both multitenant office buildings owned by an investor, such as the developer, and properties built to suit the particular needs of a company. Office parks have evolved as master-planned, mixed-use developments incorporating a variety of ancillary uses such as residential, retail, entertainment, and recreational components. Developers of office parks often consider including neighborhood-type elements, such as retail establishments, entertainment and recreational options, green spaces, and, in some instances, residential development, along with other commercial uses such as light industrial buildings and medical office buildings. The overall goal is to create a vibrant, self-contained business community that is more than just a place in which to work.

TYPES OF OFFICE PARKS

Two of the most common types of developments today are campus-style office parks and urban-style office parks.

Campus Style

The campus-style park, typically a large, relatively self-contained development that could cover several hundred acres, is the more traditional type. To make the parks attractive to office space users, developers often add retail uses such as convenience stores, restaurants, and dry cleaners. Residential development, including for-sale and rental housing, is increasingly integrated into campus-style office parks. These types of office parks are more likely to be constructed in communities where there is an abundant supply of undeveloped land.

Urban Style

An urban-style office park is typically located within a more developed area of a community, where developable land is at a premium. Because of high land costs, these types of office parks are more likely to require higher-density development, including high-rise office buildings, to make them economically feasible. Increasingly, urban-style office parks are being built based on traditional neighborhood development (TND) or new urbanist principles, creating places where people can "live, work, and play" in the same setting. For-sale and rental residential housing, along with entertainment, retail, restaurants, coffee shops, hotels, and outdoor recreational amenities is among the variety of mixed-use components developers use to make urban-style office parks attractive places in which to do business.

SITE LOCATION PARAMETERS

Location is the primary component of a successful office park development. Highly competitive market conditions and high land costs make it imperative to choose a site that contains all the necessary features and has a need for such development.

Site Size

Office parks are built over many acres—project sizes can range from 20 acres or more for an urban-style

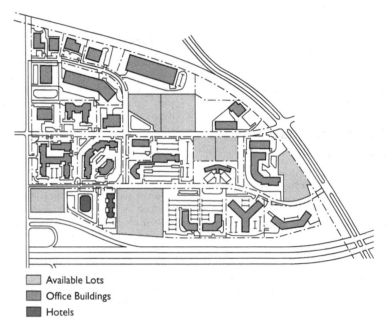

Available Lots
Office Buildings
Hotels

The Mendota Heights Business Park, on land held by United Properties since the 1950s, is centrally located near the airport and freeways that connect the park to both downtown Minneapolis and downtown St. Paul. This master-planned, 230-acre park contains a number of build-to-suit and speculative office and industrial buildings, now totaling almost 2 million square feet.

CAMPUS-STYLE OFFICE PARK

Source: United Properties 2004.

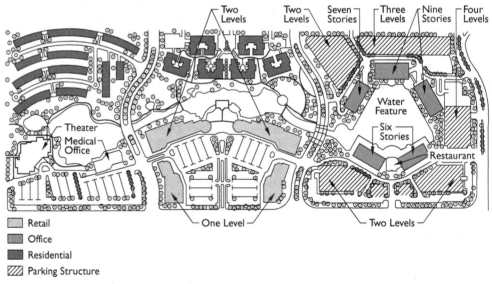

Retail
Office
Residential
Parking Structure

The Centennial Lakes mixed-use office park development includes 100 acres of office, retail, residential, and city-operated parkland. United Properties developed the park over a 13-year period in a close partnership with the City of Edina, Minnesota.

URBAN-STYLE OFFICE PARK

Source: United Properties 2004.

office park to several hundred acres for a campus-style office park. An adequate amount of space is needed to accommodate all the uses for which an office park is intended and to create a unique environment that appeals to the end users. Office parks often serve as anchors for a new town center development that encompasses a substantial quantity of land.

Access and Transportation

Convenient highway access is typically a critical factor in locating a campus-style office park. The local street system must be able to handle the increased flow of vehicle traffic that an office park will generate so that the customer can quickly get to a destination. Access to local and regional transit systems is also an increasingly important aspect of office park development. Because of the concentrated number of people in a park, office parks can provide a community with an opportunity to enhance its overall transit system, through the development or expansion of a regional transit hub adjacent to the development.

Visibility

Visibility is one of the key factors that business space users rely on when choosing a site location for their company. An office park needs to stand out both physically and visually as a readily identifiable feature of the local business landscape and a recognizable component of a community. Some of the ways to accomplish this could be a recognizable building or tenant name, monument signage, or a unique landscape or art form.

Demographics and Trends

Part of the location selection process is researching the community to determine the likelihood of attracting enough business users to make the park successful. This includes understanding the demographic makeup and trends that exist in the local and regional business community. Rather than waiting for the market to respond when a new project is launched, office park developers often seek to create value and generate substantial revenues from the project in as short a period as possible, to recoup initial investments and cover ongoing land, investment, and development costs. For this reason, developers favor providing a mixed-use development, which allows the developer more quickly to absorb the land and put it into productive use.

SITE DESIGN

Specific site design issues will depend upon the number and type of tenants that will occupy the park. Local regulations also provide minimum standards required for each design issue. A planned unit development can give a developer an opportunity to create a unique environment with more design flexibility relative to standard regulations. Below are some of the commonly addressed site design issues.

Circulation

Employees, vendors, and customers must be able to travel to and from their destinations within the office park in a convenient and timely manner. The sidewalk, path, and street network should be designed to facilitate efficient movement patterns.

Parking

Parking requirements will vary depending upon the number and size of buildings and the types of uses included in the office park. Facilities with access to transit, organized carpooling, and other options that may reduce vehicle trips require fewer parking spaces than those where such options are not available. When creating a mixed-use office park, shared parking opportunities may be available. An example is a movie theater located next to an office building: these two facilities could share a parking area because the hours of operation of each are different

and rarely conflict. Local regulations should be consulted to determine actual parking requirements.

Building Height and Massing

Office space is changing from its past configuration. The average ratio of office space per employee is shrinking from 250 feet to 150 feet per employee, and companies are increasingly locating as many employees on the same floor or on contiguous floors as possible, to minimize disruption in business operations. Floorplates for office buildings, which previously were between 22,000 to 26,000 square feet, are now much larger, up to 45,000 square feet. Therefore, there are more employees, requiring more parking needs.

Utility Systems

Office parks require utility systems that support all of the necessary operations within the buildings, and adhere to building and fire codes. Utility factors deemed critical by business space users today include underground utility connections, redundant electrical power sources, state-of-the-art fiber-optic connections, and access to satellite-based communications.

Urban office parks often have double and triple power redundancy and access to multiple data "pipe" supplies. Campus-style office parks are more likely to rely on a generator for power backup.

Electricity

Electrical requirements should be determined based on the use of the building. However, most large facilities now require that standby generators be provided on-site to supplement public supplies, should an outage occur.

Natural Gas

A source of natural gas is generally required for heating and air conditioning, as is a source of emergency power to operate the building during power outages or as a backup source of power to computer systems.

Sanitary Sewer

Office parks require either the service of municipal sewer systems, in order to serve the buildings, or sufficient land area for the on-site disposal of wastewater. Local and state codes should be referenced prior to siting an office park to determine the feasibility of on-site wastewater treatment and disposal, based on the quantity of wastewater generated.

Water Supply

Office parks will need access to a water supply, typically provided by a municipal water authority.

Stormwater Management

Runoff from paved areas, especially parking lots, has the potential to create stormwater management issues. Sufficient land area must be available to provide on-site stormwater collection, and management facilities must meet Clean Water Act best management practices and local regulations.

Aesthetics

Among the elements used to address the aesthetic elements of office parks are standards for building

materials and uses, overall architectural design, vegetation, signage, and lighting. These elements help provide a specific identity for the office park, which is important to the developer's marketing efforts and to park tenants. Most business parks have protective covenants for this purpose.

Open Space

Office parks often include significant amounts of open space. In addition to publicly accessible vegetated areas, common open-space amenities include walking trails, ponds, lakes, flower gardens, putting greens—sometimes even a golf course—and other features. If such amenities are not preexisting on the site, the developer may be required to build them.

LOCAL REGULATORY ISSUES

The supply of prime undeveloped, commercially zoned land has shrunk in many suburban communities. As a result, developers often have to combine different parcels of land to obtain the acreage needed for their developments. This process typically involves purchasing land from a variety of owners, making it quite time-consuming and costly for the developer. Occasionally, developers request the local governing body to intervene to assist the land acquisition process, often through a partnership with the local regulatory authority.

In addition to zoning regulations, office park development may be guided by protective covenants and deed restrictions. Such covenants can describe the type and character of uses allowed within the park, general guidelines for building construction, environmental considerations, buffer zones, and overall general aesthetics. This assures potential users that their investment will be protected by similar development within the park.

EMERGING TRENDS

Office parks of the past are being replaced by master-planned, mixed-use developments that create a sense of community. Communities, regulatory agencies, and future tenants are all increasingly seeking these new types of office parks. Companies want to attract and retain younger, creative employees who drive economic growth. Those employees in return want to work in an urbanlike, amenity-rich environment. They often want pedestrian- and transit-friendly developments that offer affordably priced housing, restaurants and night life, shopping and dining, and entertainment and recreational opportunities, all within easy reach of their workplace.

See also:
Financial Planning and Analysis: The Pro Forma
Industrial Parks
Office Buildings
Stormwater Runoff and Recharge
Wastewater
Water Supply

Dale Glowa, United Properties, Bloomington, Minnesota

MAIN STREETS

Main Street is often thought of as the heart of the community, occupying an iconic position within the typical American small town. The form of a main street is typically a local commercial corridor along the main thoroughfare through town, with buildings organized in storefront blocks and parking on the street.

During the 1960s, as cities expanded outward, automobile use increased, and retail stores were reconfigured to depend almost exclusively on automobile access, main streets declined.

In the late-1970s, many older main streets began to reemerge as vital centers and, today, many communities across the United States have seen significant revitalization of their main streets. In addition, many suburban communities that never had a traditional main street are seeking to create one by developing a new greenfield town center or redesigning a commercial strip.

IMPORTANCE OF MAIN STREETS

A successful main street helps define a unique identity for a community within the larger regional context, while providing opportunities for small businesses to become established. A walkable main street can also help decrease the number of single-purpose automobile trips.

MAIN STREET FEATURES

Main streets flourish when they provide a variety of goods and services, a pleasant community environment, and convenient access for their users. Design and physical appearance contribute directly to livability and economic success. Main street should be a visually stimulating area that encourages people to linger and explore. The following components should be addressed when designing a new main street or revitalizing an existing one:

- Building form
- Streetscape design
- Parking
- Traffic
- Pedestrians
- Bicycles
- Transit

Building Form

Along main streets, the impact of the built environment is influenced by several elements, such as storefronts, height and bulk, setbacks, door and window openings, and roof shape and profile.

Storefront Buildings

Traditional storefront buildings, with large display windows on the ground floor and one or more stories above, are the basic units of main streets. Storefront buildings are designed to facilitate retail activity. Large expanses of glass in the ground-floor façade allow pedestrians to look into shops and see displayed merchandise.

The long, narrow shapes of storefront buildings make it possible to group a large number of shops on one block. In turn, these stores can display a wide

variety of goods and services to shoppers as they walk down the street. Storage spaces in the rear of the buildings allow delivery of goods from alleys and secondary streets.

Storefront buildings were designed for commercial activity, and their physical shape and characteristics reinforce this purpose. The rhythm of storefront openings along the street creates a powerful visual image that consumers recognize and associate with commercial activity.

New buildings should be compatible with surrounding buildings and the entire block. The patterns

of storefronts, upper façades, and cornices and their repetition from one building to the next along a street give the whole streetscape visual cohesiveness and generate a physical rhythm that provides orientation to pedestrians and motorists. Building improvements that take place on a main street should be compatible with the design characteristics of the overall streetscape, as well as with those of the specific building.

Height and Bulk

The height of most buildings within a main street should be relatively constant, although maintaining

New Façade Fills Opening

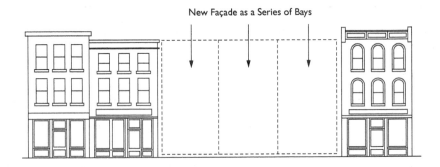

New Façade as a Series of Bays

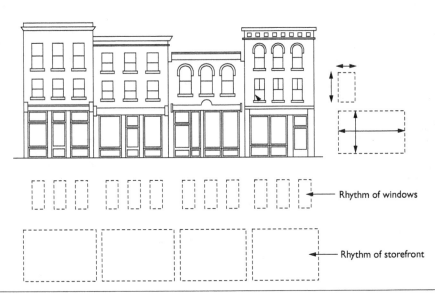

Rhythm of windows

Rhythm of storefront

DESIGN PRINCIPLES FOR MAIN STREET INFILL DEVELOPMENT

Source: Adapted from City of Lake City Downtown Preservation Manual, Thomas R. Zahn & Associates 1999.

Suzanne Sutro Rhees, AICP, URS Corporation, Minneapolis, Minnesota; Karen K. Lindblad, Associate AIA, Chicago, Illinois

the typical minimum height of two or three stories is more critical than establishing a maximum height. Building scale and proportions should also be consistent. Wide buildings should usually be divided into separate bays consistent with the prevailing storefront rhythm.

Setback

Buildings should be flush with the sidewalk, except for small setbacks for entries, courtyards, or outdoor seating areas, to engage pedestrian activity and encourage drivers to slow down and watch for pedestrians and parking cars.

Door and Window Openings

The typical storefront has a high proportion of transparency from ground-level display windows and doors, and this should be maintained in newer buildings. The proportions of door and window openings in traditional main street buildings tend to be relatively constant. Keep proportions and height of upper-floor window placement consistent with the existing pattern, to reinforce a strong horizontal relationship between upper-story windows along the block.

Roof Shape or Profile

Roof profiles are usually consistent throughout the main street. Whether most buildings have the typical flat roofs, mansard roofs, or another shape, maintain consistent profiles.

Streetscape Design

There are numerous streetscape elements and design details that are desirable for main streets. These elements create a visually rich and inviting environment and provide visual cues and signals for motorists that they are entering a pedestrian-dominated district.

Street Trees

Street trees are effective visual signals. Along with the overall building density and scale, they can help define the main street district. As they mature, they create a canopy over the street, providing shade and aesthetic appeal.

Lighting

Lighting along the corridor should be geared toward pedestrians, to encourage main street activity into the evening hours. To have a significant effect on the appearance and sense of safety of the area at night, lampposts should be between 10 and 12 feet high. They can be installed in addition to, or in place of, taller road-illuminating fixtures.

Wayfinding Systems

Wayfinding signs can be used to direct visitors to the main street from regional highways and assist them in navigating within the district and other parts of the community. Such signs also promote the area's identity and sense of place. Businesses can use this identification system for cooperative district advertising and event sponsorship.

Open Spaces

Public or semipublic spaces such as plazas and pocket parks are important main street elements. Relatively small areas adjacent to a sidewalk can bring life to the street and nearby businesses. Open spaces should be highly visible, adjacent to or bisected by the main stream of pedestrian flow; provide ample seating, shade, and weather protection; and offer a focal point, such as a fountain or gazebo.

Other Elements

Other visual signals that may be used in a main street area include hanging planters and window boxes. Space should be provided on sidewalks for display boards, benches, trash receptacles, drinking fountains, and bike racks.

Parking

Main street parking must meet the needs of customers, merchants, employees, visitors, and residents. It should be regulated, to encourage turnover of customer spaces and to discourage abuse by long-term parkers, and it should be accessible to handicapped visitors.

There are many ways to create parking areas that meet these objectives without adversely impacting the character of the main street.

On-Street Parking

On-street parking spaces usually turn over most rapidly. Parking in these spaces is generally limited to two hours or less, as they are intended for use by customers making short trips. These spaces can be angled or parallel. The traffic movements involved in on-street parking help to calm traffic, while the parking itself creates the perception of a narrower street.

Parking Lots

Parking lots tend to accommodate long-term parkers, such as employees, more effectively than on-street spaces. Shared parking in a convenient location can also create a "park once" environment for the visitor. Parking lots can be located behind the main street storefronts with alley access, on an adjacent block near the main street core, or, in the busiest locations, in satellite locations served by shuttles. In general, parking lots should not be located in the typical commercial strip configuration, between the street and a building's front door. Small parking lots between buildings may be acceptable if no alternatives exist, but should continue the street wall by means of an attractive fence, masonry wall, or hedge.

Structured Parking

Structured parking may be publicly or privately owned and operated. Constructing a parking structure is significantly more expensive than surface parking spaces. In main street areas that have a parking shortage, however, constructing a parking structure in an unobtrusive location is often preferable to demolishing buildings to create new surface

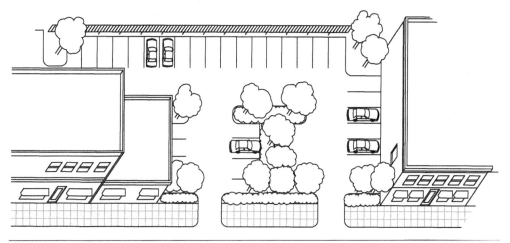

PARKING LOT

Source: URS Corporation.

PARKING STRUCTURE

Source: URS Corporation.

Suzanne Sutro Rhees, AICP, URS Corporation, Minneapolis, Minnesota; Karen K. Lindblad, Associate AIA, Chicago, Illinois

PLACES AND DISTRICTS

THE NATIONAL TRUST MAIN STREET CENTER

Established in 1980, the National Main Street Center of the National Trust for Historic Preservation serves as a resource to communities interested in revitalizing their traditional commercial districts. A nonprofit organization, the center provides information, offers technical assistance, sponsors conferences and workshops, and conducts research and lobbying on critical revitalization issues.

The Main Street Approach

The National Trust Main Street Center developed the Main Street Approach® to downtown and commercial district revitalization to combine historic preservation with economic development in a grassroots setting. This approach has been used in more than 1,200 communities, from rural small towns to urban neighborhoods.

The Main Street approach is a comprehensive strategy to commercial district revitalization, addressing all the areas in which action must take place. Design improvements alone will not bring about meaningful change. Effective marketing, a strong organizational base and solid economic development strategies are all necessary to reverse the cycle of decay from which many downtowns suffer and to sustain preservation activity.

The Main Street Approach is based on four points:

- *Improving the commercial district's image by enhancing its physical appearance*. This includes not just the appearance of buildings, but also that of streetlights, window displays, parking areas, signs, sidewalks, promotional materials, and all other elements that convey a visual message about the downtown and what it has to offer.

- *Building consensus and cooperation among the groups that play roles in the commercial district.* Many individuals and organizations in the community have a stake in the economic viability of the district, including bankers, property owners, city and county officials, merchants, downtown/district residents, professionals, chamber of commerce representatives, local industries, civic groups, historical societies, schools, consumers, real estate agents, and local media.

- *Marketing the commercial district's unique characteristics to shoppers, investors, new businesses, tourists, and others.* Effective promotion creates a positive image of the downtown through coordinated retail promotional activity, special events, and ongoing programs to build positive perceptions of the district.

- *Strengthening the existing economic base of the downtown or commercial district while diversifying it.* Economic restructuring activities include helping existing businesses expand, recruiting new businesses to provide a balanced mix, converting unused space into productive property, and sharpening the competitiveness of downtown merchants. By strengthening the downtown's economy, communities are able to support the ongoing use of historic commercial buildings, preserving unique community assets.

By carefully integrating all four areas into a practical downtown management strategy, the Main Street approach produces fundamental changes in the downtown's economic base, making it economically feasible to put historic commercial buildings to productive use again.

Source: National Main Street Center of the National Trust for Historic Preservation

---

lots. Parking structures can be combined with "liner" storefronts around their perimeter, and even with residential uses on upper floors.

Traffic

Traffic is a critical element of a busy, vital main street, and should be managed so that it is an asset. This can be done through controlling the speed through the corridor and the nature of the trip.

Many urban main streets are designed to accommodate traffic at 25 mph, but many suburban main streets are on arterials designed for 45 mph traffic. Sometimes, the main street is also a state highway, carrying a heavy volume of regional traffic. The on-street parking and streetscape improvements mentioned above, as well as physical traffic-calming devices such as curb extension, can be used to slow traffic and improve pedestrian safety.

Pedestrian Connections

Sidewalks are a common element in older or urban main streets, but are lacking or appear only sporadically in many newer suburban districts. Sidewalks should always be provided, to define a pedestrian space where there is no threat from moving cars; they should ideally be at least 10 feet wide to provide room for intense pedestrian activity as well as streetscape elements.

Pedestrian connections among uses can be as important as the traditional sidewalk route along the street. Walkways from rear parking areas are important for pedestrian wayfinding and safety. In suburban settings where some buildings may be set back from the street, a secondary pedestrian system between parking lots and in front of buildings can improve pedestrian circulation.

Bicycles

Cyclists are often overlooked as potential customers. Provide bicycle parking and dedicated bike routes to make the main street safe and convenient for cyclists, thus encouraging people to mix errands and exercise and expanding the customer base.

Transit

Many main street areas are served by transit systems. Comfortable accommodations for transit riders, including seating, transit shelters, and signage for transit stops, will encourage them to linger and shop.

PUBLIC/PRIVATE PARTNERSHIPS

When considering main street enhancements or improvements, public and private investments need to be linked. A key public investment often will attract additional private investment. Joint facilities, such as public parking lots, may allow private lots to be turned into buildings or open space. Street improvements, when combined with pedestrian improvements, can improve both traffic and pedestrian activity within the main street area. It is essential to involve all public and private partners when developing and maintaining a successful main street.

See also:
Neighborhoods
Neighborhood Centers
Streetscape
Traffic Calming

Suzanne Sutro Rhees, AICP, URS Corporation, Minneapolis, Minnesota; Karen K. Lindblad, Associate AIA, Chicago, Illinois

DEVELOPMENT TYPES

MIXED-USE DEVELOPMENT

Mixed-use developments create vibrant urban environments that bring compatible land uses, public amenities, and utilities together at various scales. These developments seek to create pedestrian-friendly environments, higher-density development, and a variety of uses that enable people to live, work, play, and shop in one place, which can become a destination.

TYPES OF MIXED-USE DEVELOPMENT

Mixed-use development can take many forms but is typically categorized as vertical mixed-use buildings, horizontal mixed-use sites, or mixed-use walkable areas.

Vertical Mixed-Use Buildings

Vertical mixed-use development combines different uses in the same building. The lower floors generally have more public uses, with private uses on the upper levels. Examples include residential space over commercial establishments, street-level retail with an office tower above, residential and hotel uses in the same building, and retail and parking structure with multiple uses above. Vertical mixed-use development can have any number of revenue-producing and mutually supportive uses in the same building.

Horizontal Mixed-Use Sites

Horizontal mixed-use development combines single-use buildings on distinct parcels in a range of land uses in one planned development project. This approach avoids the financing and code complexities of vertical layered uses while achieving the goal of place making that is made possible by bringing together complementary uses in one place.

Mixed-Use Walkable Areas

These developments combine both vertical and horizontal mix of uses in an area ideally within a 10-minute walking distance or a .25-mile radius of a core of activities.

MIXED-USE COMPONENTS

Included here are diagrams showing various possibilities of mixes. These are not meant to be exhaustive but rather suggestive of the many ways one can consider mixing uses.

OBJECTIVES OF MIXED-USE DEVELOPMENT

Mixed-use developments contribute to the creation of places that enliven urban districts while meeting the everyday needs of the community. They offer many advantages over single-use districts in fostering better urban environments, some of which are described below.

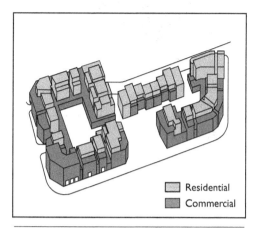

VERTICAL MIXED USE
Source: Howard M. Blackson III.

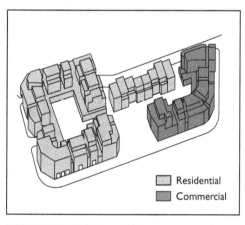

HORIZONTAL MIXED USE
Source: Howard M. Blackson III.

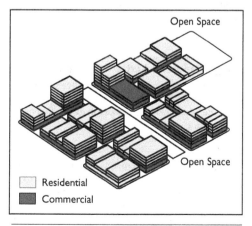

MIXED-USE WALKABLE AREA
Source: SMWM.

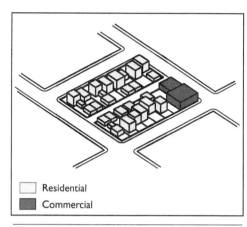

NEIGHBORHOOD COMMERCIAL
Source: SMWM.

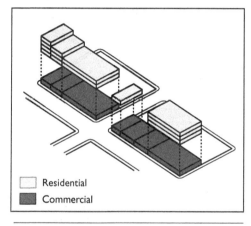

MAIN STREET RESIDENTIAL/COMMERCIAL
Source: SMWM.

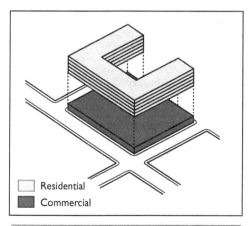

URBAN RESIDENTIAL/COMMERCIAL
Source: SMWM.

Geeti Silwal, SMWM, San Francisco, California; Sharon Priest, AICP, SMWM, San Francisco, California

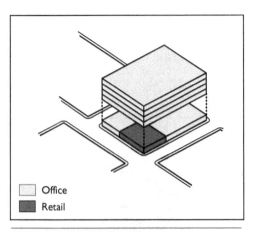

Office
Retail

OFFICE CONVENIENCE

Source: SMWM.

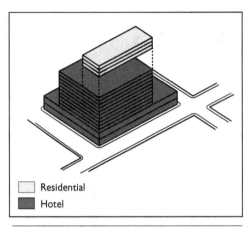

Residential
Hotel

HOTEL/RESIDENTIAL

Source: SMWM.

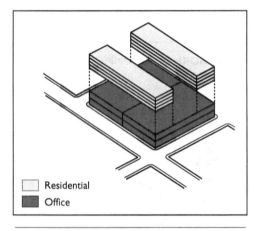

Residential
Office

OFFICE/RESIDENTIAL

Source: SMWM.

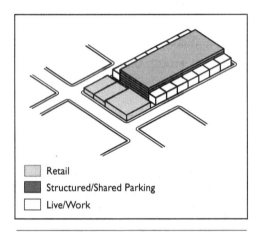

Retail
Structured/Shared Parking
Live/Work

WRAPPED PARKING STRUCTURE

Source: SMWM.

Vitality

Place making has been one of the greatest achievements of mixed-use development. By revitalizing and diversifying urban areas such as downtowns, waterfronts, transit nodes, and infill sites, these developments become community destinations.

Sustainability

Mixing uses and allowing for higher development intensities creates more efficient and less consumptive buildings and spaces, which can be less of a burden on the environment.

Sense of Community

Mixed-use developments cater to a diversity of people and uses in one place, thus providing opportunities for community interaction.

Convenient Access

The proximity of diverse uses makes it possible to reduce vehicle trips and encourage transit ridership. Mixed-use developments can support higher transit use and may be a catalyst for siting transit facilities in the area.

Pedestrian-Friendly Environment

Mixed-use developments provide more opportunities for convenient and safe pedestrian access.

Sharing of Utilities and Amenities

Mixed-use development can result in more efficient use of land and infrastructure. For example, retail uses can share parking facilities with residential uses, because their peak hours for parking do not overlap substantially; thus, the cumulative parking requirement could be appreciably reduced. Similarly, stormwater facilities; sewer; common area maintenance; and central heating, ventilation, and air conditioning can be shared among various uses.

Longer Hours of Active Street Life

The range of uses can be active at different times of the day or on different days of the week, which activates the place for longer hours than is possible for any one single use.

Safety

Mixing residential, commercial, and professional activities within a compact area ensures activity throughout the day and evening, creating a sense of safety. For example, the presence of people living in apartments above stores helps reduce the potential for vandalism during off-hours, because, for all intents and purposes, there are no off-hours.

Historic Renovation and Adaptive Reuse of Structures

Renovating historic buildings and using them in new ways helps preserve the older urban fabric while providing architectural diversity in mixed-use developments.

DEVELOPMENT PARTNERSHIPS

Mixed-use development often involves both private and public sectors, and thus benefits from the efforts of the partnership. The two sectors generally have a few differing objectives, however. The private developer generally has financial gains to pursue, whereas the public sector is concerned with social gains for the community at large. Sharing the risk between the public and private sectors can also be beneficial.

CHALLENGES TO MIXED-USE DEVELOPMENT

Each community may present a set of challenges to creating mixed-use development. The following is a discussion of the obstacles typically faced.

Zoning Ordinances

In many communities, zoning ordinances favor single-use districts, making it difficult to implement mixed-use development. Conventional zoning typically allows for one single quality or function in an area at the exclusion of all others; some communities do allow for cumulative zoning, however, where uses with lesser impacts are allowed in higher-impact zones (e.g., residential allowed in commercial zones). At the district, neighborhood, and town center scale, one dominant building function, use, or type creates a less vibrant and engaging experience. Mixed-use developments can be made possible by modifying the zoning ordinance to accommodate a broader range of compatible uses. For example, consider changing a single-use district to either a planned unit development (PUD) district or an overlay district to allow for a mixed-use development.

Financing

Private sector investment and subsidies for mixed-use development are often more complicated and more difficult to obtain than conventional developments because mixed-use projects are not as commonly pursued; therefore, there are fewer established programs for them. Heavier up-front costs often further deter financing institutions from lending money for mixed-use developments. Developers of mixed-use projects often have to be creative in assembling the necessary financing. A partnership with a public agency may make public funding sources available to increase project feasibility or offer support in the early stages.

Layering

Layering uses, as in vertical mixed-use development, increase the development cost and the associated risk. Mixed-use developments can cause planning and management complexities that might not otherwise exist in a single-use project. Developers need to be aware and well informed of the timeline and cost implications from the onset of the project, to help reduce the complexities that would evolve otherwise. Up-front efforts to inform local code officials of the

Geeti Silwal, SMWM, San Francisco, California; Sharon Priest, AICP, SMWM, San Francisco, California

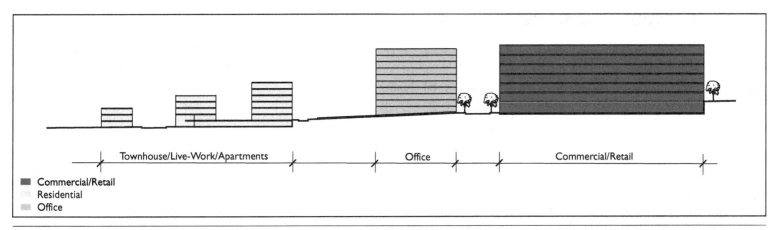

Legend:
- Commercial/Retail
- Residential
- Office

Zones: Townhouse/Live-Work/Apartments | Office | Commercial/Retail

SECTION OF A HORIZONTAL MIXED-USE SITE

Source: SMWM.

Approval Process

The diversity of uses can make the project's approval process more complex, as it involves representatives from numerous agencies and departments. Stakeholders need to engage zoning board members and other agencies in designing possible successful scenarios and case studies in order to help modify methods and conditions for mixed-use project review can be beneficial.

existing approval methods and lead to a more efficient approval process.

Collaboration

Mixed-use developments require collaboration across numerous professions to obtain the optimal mix of uses for a successful project within a community's economic, social, and political requirements. All parties involved—landowner, public sector, and developer—should understand each other's objectives from the beginning of the process and program to achieve maximum benefits.

See also:
Infill Development
Innovations in Local Zoning Regulations
Planned Unit Development
Scale and Density
Transit-Oriented Development
Urban Analysis
Zoning Regulation

Geeti Silwal, SMWM, San Francisco, California; Sharon Priest, AICP, SMWM, San Francisco, California

TRANSIT-ORIENTED DEVELOPMENT

Transit-oriented development (TOD) is generally defined as development that is located within a 10-minute walk, or approximately .5 mile, from a light rail, heavy rail, or commuter rail station. It also includes development along heavily used bus and bus rapid transit corridors. In some communities, waterborne transit supports TOD.

A mix of uses, including housing, retail, office, research, civic, and others, characterizes TOD projects. TOD also involves development at higher densities than typical, to take advantage of transit proximity and planning and design elements that encourage walkability and create pedestrian-friendly connections to the surrounding community. TOD projects range widely in size, from infill loft developments to mixed-use centers to entire new communities.

Many communities have limited opportunities for TOD, because land areas within the half-mile radius have already been developed, transit is not yet an available transportation option, or potential development sites are not of a suitable size for TOD. Most TOD projects contain at least 100,000 square feet (or 60 to 80 housing units), and many are far larger. TOD can be developed at a smaller scale, but such projects often have more difficulty absorbing the costs of creating a pedestrian-friendly public realm. That said, economic benefits often accrue from reduced parking requirements and increased densities. When potential TOD sites become available, communities should be ready to take advantage of the unique potential they offer.

BENEFITS OF TRANSIT-ORIENTED DEVELOPMENT

Certain benefits of TOD make it distinct from conventional development approaches. These benefits are numerous and include quality of life, public health, economic development, community character, environmental quality, and transit use.

Quality of Life

Transit-oriented development can result in many quality-of-life benefits, including reducing automobile dependency; increasing the range of housing options, both the types of housing and the range of affordability available to a community; and enhancing the vitality of neighborhood main streets and centers.

Public Health

Because transit-oriented development reduces automobile dependency, residents can take advantage of a more walkable environment. Reduced vehicle trips also result in improved air quality.

Economic Development

Transit-oriented development provides affordable access to jobs for people without automobiles or with fewer automobiles per household, attracts employers to locate around station areas, and broadens the overall tax base.

Community Character

The increased density in TOD projects provides opportunities to create public spaces and well-designed buildings that give identity and vitality to those spaces.

Environmental Quality

In addition to the public health benefits, transit-oriented development provides a design alternative to sprawl, and is an opportunity to pursue environmentally sensitive site planning and "green" architecture.

Transit Use

Increased ridership and the potential for additional funding sources for new transit facilities are among the transit benefits of TOD.

SITE PROGRAMMING

When developing an overall site program for a transit-oriented development, four principles for achieving optimal use and function of the site should be considered:

- Build densely.
- Mix uses.
- Mix housing types and prices.
- Reduce parking requirements.

Build Densely

One of the primary characteristics of transit-oriented development is an increased level of density as compared to conventional development. Building to a higher density lets one take advantage of reduced auto dependency, make efficient use of TOD sites, support pedestrian-friendly shops, and create lively, people-filled environments. Locating between 1,500 and 2,500 housing units within walking distance can support a new block of "main street" retail space, according to a 2002 study by Goody Clancy and the real estate firm of Byrne McKinney.

Some representative TOD densities include the following:

- *Massachusetts*: TOD guidelines include floor area ratios (FAR) that exceed conventional standards in Massachusetts by 33 to 50 percent—at least 1.0 for suburban communities, 2.0 in smaller cities and urban neighborhoods, 2.5 to 4.0 on urban sites, and greater than 4.0 in downtowns.
- *Arlington, Virginia*: More than 15 million square feet of office space and 18,000 housing units have been built along two transit lines; FARs for development near stations ranges between 6 and 10, similar to traditional downtown densities.
- *Seattle, Washington, and Addison, Texas*: Both Metropolitan Place in the Seattle region and Addison Circle in Addison, Texas, reach or exceed 50 to 100 units per acre in areas where conventional housing densities are far lower.

Mix Uses

Along with higher densities, transit-oriented development can also be characterized by the emphasis on a mixed-use environment. To create such a dynamic, enliven sidewalks and public spaces with as much retail as the market will support, provide tax revenue-generating and job-producing commercial development, and provide opportunities for residential to be located adjacent to or above such uses. This intentional programming can reinforce the vitality of town centers and main streets, where transit stations are often located. The decision to include residential above or adjacent to commercial and office uses will depend upon economic feasibility, market forces, local preferences, or other factors.

Examples of variety in mixed-use projects include the following:

- *Denver, Colorado*: Market Square, located in downtown Denver near the transit mall, consists primarily of office and retail uses.
- *Atlanta, Georgia*: The proposed Lindberg City Center, which includes a MARTA transit station, will include more than 2 million square feet of office space, in addition to more than 800 housing units.
- *Willow Springs, Illinois*: The Willow Springs Village Center includes a new town hall, 52,000 square feet of retail and office, and 274 town houses and condominiums adjacent to a new commuter rail station.
- *Arlington County, Virginia*: This area seeks a fifty-fifty mix of residential and commercial development over time for its TOD. As a result, the county has received a significant boost to the tax base, with 6 percent of the land generating 50 percent of the county's tax revenue.
- *San Francisco, California*: Mission Bay, a new mixed-use district with 6,000 new housing units, 5 million square feet of research and office space, a medical research campus of the University of California San Francisco, 250,000 square feet of retail and hotel space, and 50 acres of new open space is rapidly growing around a transit node of commuter rail, multiple light rail lines, long-distance rail, and water transportation.

Mix Housing Types and Prices

Take advantage of creating housing at higher densities to increase the diversity of housing in the community, including affordable housing. According to the Urban Land Institute (ULI), the share of households with children looking for housing will drop significantly by 2025, producing demand for a wider range of housing options.

Reduce Parking Requirements

One of the most important outcomes of transit-oriented development is increased transit use. Lower parking requirements and dedicated bicycle paths and bicycle parking are among the actions that can be taken to achieve this. The higher density and land values of TOD often make it feasible to construct structured parking or below-grade parking in place of surface lots. Lower parking ratios reduce overall project costs. Mixed-use projects can further reduce parking requirements by enabling shared parking, such as office workers during weekdays and residents during evenings and weekends.

Here are some representative TOD parking ratios in different parts of the United States:

- *Massachusetts*: At least 33 percent below comparable project levels.
- *Portland, Oregon*: Orenco Station, located outside Portland, has approximately one space per 1,000

David Dixon, FAIA, Goody Clancy, Boston, Massachusetts; Anne Tate, Office for Commonwealth Development, Boston, Massachusetts

square feet, which is at least 50 percent below regional norms.

- *Boulder, Colorado:* The mixed-use Steelyards project also has approximately one space per 1,000 square feet, which is rapidly becoming a standard for TOD areas, and at times is a maximum allowed in "transit first" areas.

SITE DESIGN

Within a transit-oriented development site, the following design features should be emphasized in the site planning process.

Pedestrian Access

Provide convenient, direct, and public pedestrian access to transit through TOD projects. Create continuity with local streets, and locate retail and other pedestrian-friendly uses to encourage pedestrian flow to nearby commercial districts and main streets.

Public Spaces

Create new public spaces, including lively streets, squares, and parks, that enhance nearby commercial districts. Take advantage of the increased pedestrian activity generated by both transit and TOD. Relate the new spaces to public and semipublic uses that may also cluster at TOD locations.

Sense of Place

Create a sense of place by orienting buildings and public spaces to create a strong sense of identity for the development, and by using buildings to frame public spaces. Consider design guidelines or standards that celebrate these places.

Pedestrian Experience

Foster an enriched and invigorated pedestrian experience. Include retail and other pedestrian-friendly uses. Maximize windows and entries to build a sense of connection between pedestrians and activities within buildings. When surface parking is needed, locate it on the side or rear of buildings. Visually screen parking areas with vegetation or create urban blocks that allow for screening of parking structures with residential units or retail on the street level.

Character and Quality

Enhance the quality and character of surrounding communities. Allow for well-designed buildings that emphasize place making. Orient buildings to new and existing streets and squares. Use transitions in height and massing to respect, but not mimic, the fabric of nearby districts.

Architecture

Encourage architecture that reflects transit's civic importance, creating buildings that, regardless of architectural style, employ materials and design that convey a sense of quality, permanence, and community-enriching character.

Sustainability

The combination of transit use and intense development around transit stations is one of planning's most powerful policies for long-term sustainability. Plans, guidelines, and development approaches should work to reinforce this use and intensity. On a building or project scale, build for sustainability, including

site and building design, which reflects a commitment to environmental responsibility. This should include the following:

- Green site design that reflects environmental issues such as minimizing impervious surfaces and maximizing sunlight on public spaces.
- Green building design that uses materials and design principles that minimize the use of nonrenewable resources and maximize energy conservation.

PUBLIC/PRIVATE PARTNERSHIPS

TOD often involves public/private partnerships. Involvement of the public sector implies greater responsibility to create projects that promote community goals. In many cases, the public sector must make initial investments to create a site adjacent to a transit station, contribute publicly owned parking lots, or invest in new local access to the TOD site. Where the private sector controls a TOD site, it is often necessary to collaborate on planning and design to create appropriate connections between development and transit.

Transit proximity often increases real estate values, and TOD projects often can afford the cost of public benefits. Studies show that property values within .25 miles of DART stations in Dallas were roughly 25 to 50 percent higher than comparable properties. Arlington County, Virginia, has used density bonuses, often 15 to 25 percent, to fund increased affordable housing and other benefits adjacent to transit. Massachusetts and other states have taken this concept a step further and have proposed that transit-oriented developments help fund new transit initiatives.

IMPLEMENTING TOD

TOD sites often have complex programs, hence require significant planning. It is often the lack of planning, rather than the lack of market demand, that slows or blocks a transit-oriented development. Several mechanisms can be used to address this.

Partnerships

Create effective planning partnerships that include the transit agency, local government, other appropriate public agencies, the community, and the development team.

Planning Study

Conduct a planning study to determine how the TOD should be physically, socially, economically, and culturally integrated into a community. Resolve issues such as parking, site access, relationship to existing neighborhoods and commercial districts, and similar concerns. Identify initial public investments in land acquisition or infrastructure that need to precede significant private investment. The study should also identify zoning and other regulatory hurdles that need to be resolved.

Participation

Establish an effective community participation process that reflects the major role that TOD can play in shaping a community's future and TOD's unique civic dimension.

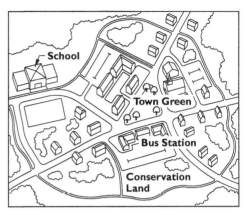

Rural TOD

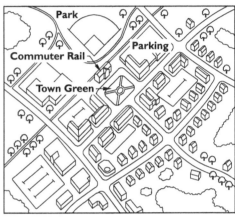

Suburban TOD

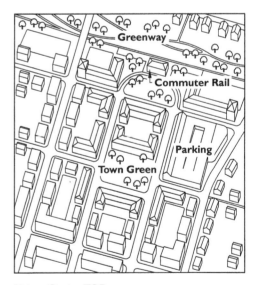

Urban Center TOD

TYPES OF TRANSIT-ORIENTED DEVELOPMENT

Source: Goody Clancy.

David Dixon, FAIA, Goody Clancy, Boston, Massachusetts; Anne Tate, Office for Commonwealth Development, Boston, Massachusetts

DEVELOPMENT TYPES

Design Guidelines

Given the civic nature of TOD, design guidelines and ongoing planning and design review are quite important. If such review processes are not in place, consider establishing review procedures that reinforce these places through massing, materials, lighting, and similar design features.

REFERENCES

Goody Clancy and Byrne McKinney & Associates. 2002. *Density Myth and* Reality. Presentation, Boston, MA.

The Urban Land Institute (ULI). 1994. *Transit-Oriented Design*. Washington, DC: ULI.

See also:
Mixed-Use Development
Scale and Density
Sidewalks
Street Networks and Street Connectivity
Transportation
Walkability

David Dixon, FAIA, Goody Clancy, Boston, Massachusetts; Anne Tate, Office for Commonwealth Development, Boston, Massachusetts

CONSERVATION DEVELOPMENT

When a property is developed as a residential subdivision, an opportunity exists to add land to a communitywide network of open space. Conservation development focuses development on each parcel as it is being planned so at least 50 percent of the buildable land is set aside as open space. The same number of homes can be built in a less land-consumptive manner, allowing the balance of the property to be permanently protected and added to an interconnected network of community green spaces. This "density-neutral" approach provides a fair and equitable way to balance conservation and development objectives.

CONSERVATION DEVELOPMENT APPROACH

Communities protect open space for numerous reasons, such as to protect streams and water quality, provide habitat for plants and animals, preserve rural

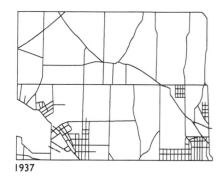

1937

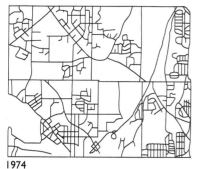

1974

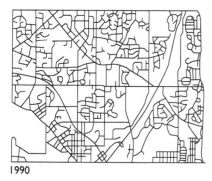

1990

The pattern of wall-to-wall subdivisions that evolves over time with conventional zoning and subdivision ordinances.

WALL-TO-WALL SUBDIVISIONS

Source: Natural Lands Trust 1997.

"atmosphere," provide access to nature and recreational areas, protect home values, and reduce costs of municipal services. To achieve these and other goals of open-space protection, the conservation development process involves three steps:

1. Assess current community development trends.
2. Identify primary and secondary conservation areas.
3. Employ conservation subdivision design steps.

Community Assessments

The community assessment process helps local officials and residents see the ultimate result of continuing to implement current land-use policies. The process helps start discussions about how current trends can be modified to ensure a "greener" future.

Most local ordinances allow or encourage standardized layouts of "wall-to-wall" house lots. Over a period of decades, this process produces a broader pattern of wall-to-wall subdivisions. In many cases, this leads to the conversion of every unprotected acre of buildable land into developed uses.

Municipalities can perform community assessments to "see the future," enabling them to judge whether a midcourse correction is needed. An assessment entails the following:

1. Analyzing growth projections, both in terms of number of dwelling units and number of acres that are likely to be converted to development under present regulations.
2. Evaluating adopted land-use regulations, identifying their strengths and weaknesses, and offering constructive recommendations about how they can incorporate conservation techniques. This should also include a realistic appraisal of the extent to which private conservation efforts are likely to succeed in protecting lands from development through various nonregulatory approaches.
3. Mapping future development patterns for the entire municipality, based upon the data collected in the previous two steps.

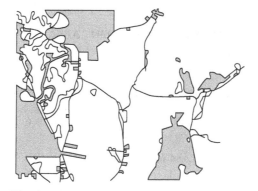

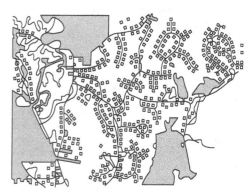

Taken from an actual buildout map, the illustration shows existing conditions on the left, primarily undeveloped land, and the potential development pattern on the right, created through conventional zoning and subdivision regulations.

HYPOTHETICAL BUILD-OUT MAP

Source: Natural Lands Trust 1997.

Open-Space Conservation Areas

Many communities have adopted comprehensive plans or open-space plans that contain detailed inventories of natural and historic resources. In order to create an interconnected network of open space, communities should draw a map of potential conservation lands. This map serves as the tool that guides decisions regarding which land to protect in order for the network to eventually take form and have substance.

A map of potential conservation lands starts with information contained in the community's existing planning documents. The next task is to identify two kinds of resource areas, primary and secondary conservation areas.

Primary Conservation Areas

Primary conservation areas comprise only the most severely constrained lands, where development is typically restricted under current codes and laws, such as wetlands, floodplains, and slopes exceeding 25 percent.

Secondary Conservation Areas

Secondary conservation areas include all other locally noteworthy or significant features of the natural or cultural landscape:

- Mature woodlands
- Hedgerows and freestanding trees or tree groups
- Wildlife habitats and travel corridors
- Prime farmland
- Groundwater recharge areas
- Greenways and trails
- River and stream corridors
- Historic sites and buildings
- Scenic viewsheds

Local residents should be directly involved in the identification of secondary conservation areas. These resource areas are typically unprotected and are often zoned for some type of development.

Randall G. Arendt, FRTPI ASLA (Hon.), Greener Prospects, Narragansett, Rhode Island; Natural Lands Trust, Media, Pennsylvania

Creating a map of potential conservation areas gives clear guidance to landowners and developers where development is encouraged and where conservation areas exist in relation to property boundaries. Overlaying conservation areas on tax parcel maps is one way of showing this information.

POTENTIAL CONSERVATION LANDS

Source: Natural Lands Trust 1997.

Conservation Area Mapping

The primary conservation areas first are identified on a base map that includes lands that are already protected, such as parks, land trust preserves, and properties under conservation easement. Each kind of secondary conservation area is then laid on top of the base map, using clear acetate sheets or a geographic information system (GIS), in an order that reflects the community's preservation priorities, as determined through public discussion.

This overlay process will reveal certain situations where two or more conservation features appear together, such as woodlands and wildlife habitats, or farmland and scenic viewsheds. It will also reveal gaps where no features appear.

This exercise is not an exact science; nevertheless it frequently helps local officials and residents visualize how various kinds of resource areas are connected to one another. It also enables them to tentatively identify both broad swaths and narrow corridors of resource land that could be protected in a variety of ways.

CONSERVATION SUBDIVISION DESIGN

Conservation subdivision design devotes at least 50 percent of the buildable land area within a residential development to undivided permanent open space. The most important step in designing a conservation subdivision is to identify the land to be preserved. The communitywide map of potential conservation lands can be used as a template for the layout and design of conservation areas within new subdivisions, helping to create an interconnected network of open space spanning the entire municipality.

In order to design subdivisions around the central organizing principle of land conservation, ordinances need clear standards that guide the conservation design process. The approach described below reverses the traditional sequence of steps in laying out subdivisions. By requiring 50 to 70 percent open space as a precondition for achieving full density,

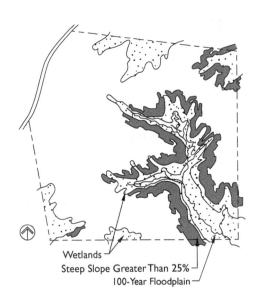

Wetlands
Steep Slope Greater Than 25%
100-Year Floodplain

Primary conservation areas include all constrained land areas, typically wetlands, steep slopes, and floodplains. Other critical and sensitive areas, if present, may be included as part of the primary conservation areas.

PRIMARY CONSERVATION AREAS

Source: Natural Lands Trust 1997.

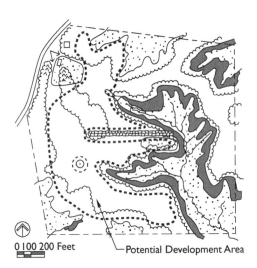

0 100 200 Feet — Potential Development Area

After eliminating the primary and secondary conservation areas, the area for development can be identified.

POTENTIAL DEVELOPMENT AREA

Source: Natural Lands Trust 1997.

officials can effectively encourage conservation subdivision design. The protected land in each new subdivision would then add new acreage to the communitywide open-space networks.

Identify Land for Permanent Protection

Areas identified on the communitywide map of potential conservation lands are incorporated into the map of the potential development area. Primary conservation areas are identified first, followed by secondary conservation areas. Before incorporating these areas onto the map, a detailed site analysis should be conducted in order to precisely locate fea-

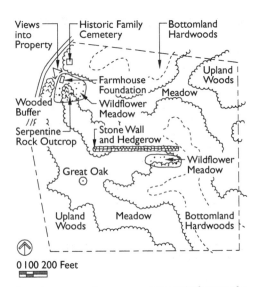

Views into Property — Historic Family Cemetery — Bottomland Hardwoods — Upland Woods — Meadow — Farmhouse Foundation — Wildflower Meadow — Wooded Buffer — Serpentine Rock Outcrop — Stone Wall and Hedgerow — Wildflower Meadow — Great Oak — Upland Woods — Meadow — Bottomland Hardwoods

0 100 200 Feet

Secondary conservation areas are noteworthy features of a property that are typically unprotected under local ordinances and thus are vulnerable to change. These can include woodlands, greenways and trails, river and stream corridors, prime farmland, wildlife habitats and travel corridors, historic sites, and viewsheds, among other features.

SECONDARY CONSERVATION AREAS

Source: Natural Lands Trust 1997.

House Sites

0 100 200 Feet

Locate houses to maximize views. Actual number of houses permitted will be determined by local regulations.

HOUSE SITES

Source: Natural Lands Trust 1997.

tures to be conserved. After "greenlining" these conservation elements, the remaining part of the property becomes the potential development area.

Locate House Sites

Locate sites of individual houses within the potential development area to maximize their views of open space. The number of houses is a function of the density permitted within the zoning district, as shown on a yield plan. In unsewered areas, officials should require a 10 percent sample of the most questionable lots—which they would select—to be tested for septic suitability. Any lots that fail would be deducted,

Randall G. Arendt, FRTPI ASLA (Hon.), Greener Prospects, Narragansett, Rhode Island; Natural Lands Trust, Media, Pennsylvania

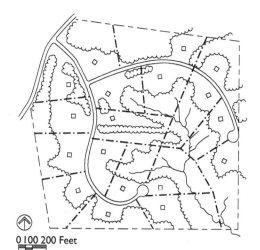

Typical subdivisions often define lot boundaries without regard to the special features of the site. In the plan shown, housing placement avoids the primary conservation areas but disregards the secondary conservation areas. Creating a yield plan is useful to estimate a site's capacity to accommodate new houses at the base density allowed under zoning, and to show how a conventional subdivision could potentially impact the site's conservation areas.

YIELD PLAN

Source: Natural Lands Trust 1997.

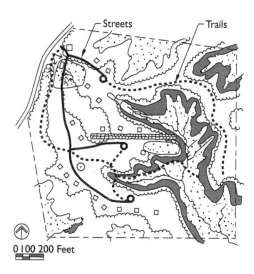

STREETS AND TRAILS

Source: Natural Lands Trust 1997.

LOT LINES

Source: Natural Lands Trust 1997.

and the applicant would have to perform a second 10 percent sample.

Connect Sites and Define Lots

The final step involves "connecting the dots" with streets and informal trails, and drawing in the lot lines.

OPEN-SPACE PROTECTION AND OWNERSHIP

A wide array of open-space protection tools are available for the areas *not* to be developed in a conservation development. The most effective way to ensure they will remain undeveloped is to place a permanent conservation easement on the land. Land trusts and units of government typically hold easements. Other tools, such as deed restrictions and covenants, are not as effective as easements in protecting land in perpetuity, and they are not recommended for this use.

The ownership of the conservation land may occur as one of four options:

- Individual landowner retains ownership of a certain percentage of the area for private use.
- Homeowner's association owns and manages the conservation land.
- Land trusts retain ownership, such as when an area of particular value is part of the conservation area.
- Municipality or other governmental agency owns the land, such as when it is part of a community trail network.

REFERENCE

Arendt, Randall G. 1997. *Growing Greener: Putting Conservation into Local Codes.* Media, PA: Natural Lands Trust, Inc. with funding from Pennsylvania Department of Conservation and Natural Resources, The William Penn Foundation, and The Alexander Stewart, M.D. Foundation.

See also:
Environmental Planning and Management
Open-Space Preservation Techniques

Randall G. Arendt, FRTPI ASLA (Hon.), Greener Prospects, Narragansett, Rhode Island; Natural Lands Trust, Media, Pennsylvania

INFILL DEVELOPMENT

Infill development occurs on vacant or underused lots in otherwise built-up sites or areas. Infill projects can take several forms, such as a small addition in a residential backyard, a single-lot development, a brownfield development, or multiparcel projects in urban downtowns.

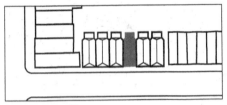

Single-Lot Infill

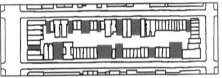

Multiple-Lot Infill

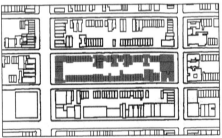

Block Infill

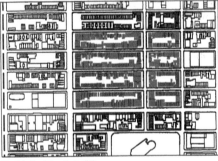

Multiple-Block Infill

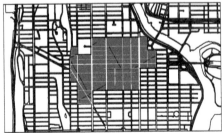

Downtown Area Infill

Infill projects can range significantly in form and size, from single- or multiple-lot development in a neighborhood to entire blocks or districts.

EXAMPLES OF INFILL

Source: SMWM.

GOALS AND BENEFITS OF INFILL

Infill strategies have many benefits. They can:

- preserve open space, agricultural land, and forests by reducing development pressures on greenfield sites;
- provide opportunities to revitalize a neighborhood or downtown;
- increase the tax base for a jurisdiction by creating or renewing a property's value;
- make efficient use of abandoned, vacant, or unused sites;
- enhance sustainability by making efficient use of existing community amenities and infrastructure;
- promote compact development and increase density; and
- create a mixture of uses.

ISSUES TO ADDRESS FOR INFILL PROJECTS

Among the issues to address when considering infill are the existing zoning regulations for the area, the condition of the infrastructure, site acquisition and development financing, parking requirements, and community concerns.

Existing Zoning

A preexisting neighborhood is typically regulated by an existing zoning ordinance and other codes. These regulations may be restrictive or permissive toward creating infill development. Check with local planning departments to identify regulations that may be in conflict with infill projects or, conversely, those that might facilitate such development. Successful infill projects work within the existing regulatory framework and demonstrate how to provide alternatives that fully use the zoning allowances.

Infrastructure Condition

Developers of infill projects often face deteriorating infrastructure or capacity limitations in older areas of a community, and infrastructure upgrade or replacement can be expensive. Thoroughly inspect the existing infrastructure to ensure the project's budget can support the required upgrades.

Acquisition and Development Financing

Concerns over the financial feasibility of infill development can sometimes halt a project. Funding redevelopment in urban areas can be complex when it involves elements of mixed-use development and different building scales within an area. Banks may be reluctant to lend money, and developers may experience high land costs and potential environmental cleanup costs, especially on sites in older communities that have had several uses over the years.

An infill project's strength lies in the potential to increase the market value of an existing area. Infill projects that receive adequate funding are typically the ones that:

- demonstrate the value of an existing neighborhood in terms of its context, safety, and growth potential;

- prelease a percentage of the project;
- include experienced team members, such as developers who have completed similar projects successfully;
- identify any special benefits that may be required during entitlement, such as affordable housing or jobs; and
- demonstrate the city's support for the type of infill development through adopted policies and other incentives for the developer.

Parking

Understand the parking requirements for the area. Often, new parking requirements within an already developed area are difficult to satisfy with infill projects, due to limited land availability. Ensuring a project meets the parking requirements without burdening the streets with additional demand for on-street parking can also be an issue. There are a number of strategies to overcome parking issues:

- Encouraging shared parking between uses and institutions.
- Reducing parking requirements in mixed-use or transit-oriented areas.
- Incorporating transit programs into the development.
- Implementing a day/night use of parking, such as allowing parking for businesses in the daytime, than in the evenings for local entertainment venues or residents.

Community Concerns

Local opposition may pose challenges for infill development. The level and type of opposition depends on the neighborhood's character and history, among other factors. A common concern raised by surrounding residents is that an infill project may adversely affect their property values and may increase burdens on local resources such as streets, parking, schools, and other public amenities. One of the ways to address this situation is to involve the community in the design process through workshops and other public outreach programs.

ANALYSIS OF SITE CONTEXT

The following are various elements of the existing conditions to address when planning for infill development. For a more thorough discussion of these types of analyses, please see Urban Analysis in this part of this book.

Neighborhood Character

Successful infill projects create harmonious relationships between the proposed and existing surroundings, enhancing the unique qualities of the neighborhood through functional and visual relationships. Carefully plan uses within a neighborhood to avoid clashes of incompatible activities, and study existing façades and streets to create guidelines that enhance those elements. Infill projects may also include rehabilitation of historic buildings and preservation of landmarks or significant public squares, which also preserve and enhance the special character of an area.

Hendra Bong, SMWM, San Francisco, California; Sharon Priest, AICP, SMWM, San Francisco, California

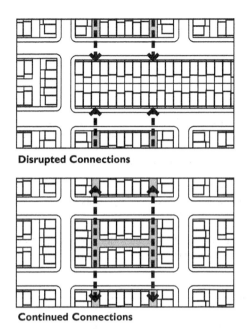

Disrupted Connections

Continued Connections

Allow streets and alleys to continue within an infill project, to avoid disrupting existing connections.

CONNECTIONS
Source: SMWM.

Patterns

Take into account the block patterns of an existing neighborhood when creating infill projects. Patterns of a neighborhood include the streets and alleys and other connections used by residents. Consider the fabric of the neighborhood by studying the size of each block. By respecting the existing neighborhood's scale and urban fabric, an infill project will integrate more successfully and create continuity, which in turns promotes community harmony.

Connections

Integrate an infill project with the existing land-use patterns through street networks, open-space systems, and other connections. Work to connect neighborhoods at multiple scales, from local pedestrian paths to regional patterns of transportation and open space. Because an infill project occurs within an existing area, it can either enhance or disrupt existing connections. Allow streets and alleys to continue, and avoid disrupting existing vital connections.

Amenities

To further integrate infill development into a neighborhood, identify and make use of important existing amenities, such as transit nodes, retail zones, and other public resources. Increase neighborhood value by building on existing amenities, such as open space, transit centers, and other amenities.

STRATEGIES FOR INFILL DEVELOPMENT

Diversity

Promote a mix of uses, including housing, retail, and commercial uses, both horizontally and vertically. Blend housing with other uses to create neighborhoods and districts where people are present at all hours, a key element of public safety and community liveliness.

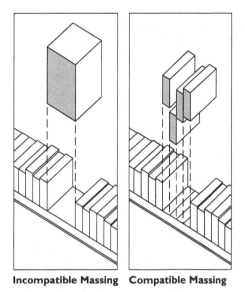

Incompatible Massing   Compatible Massing

Articulate massing to ensure the façade is compatible with surrounding buildings.

INFILL MASSING
Source: SMWM.

Density

Successful infill development is often dense enough to make transit viable and support walkable retail districts. Higher densities create the sense of a strong, residential enclave, and can help to deliver the critical mass of residents essential to support commercial and retail uses, whether existing or part of the infill development.

Transit

Transit, when available, is key to infill development. To achieve strong ridership, transit systems need significant densities. Infill projects can increase ridership on existing systems and make transit an even more viable option. Create infill development that responds to existing transit lines, supports a walkable environment, and makes local services accessible to and from transit stops.

Scale

Take into account the grain and scale of existing frontages, sidewalks, streets, and building façades, and the massing of the surrounding area. Infill projects that take this approach often create a coherent neighborhood that responds to various scales of living, from the pedestrian to the larger, more public scales, such as major retail or commercial corridors. Replicating surrounding structures is not required, but, often, compatibility must be demonstrated.

Massing and Articulation

Consider the relationship of the infill project's massing to that of the existing area to ensure minimal impacts to solar access, wind conditions, and other factors. Strategies to address this include articulation in massing and materials to create interest and break the monotony of a larger façade. Successful massing strategies promote interaction between the sidewalk pedestrian and the building by creating a street frontage that is appropriate at the ground level. Maintaining a consistent urban edge is also an important massing consideration.

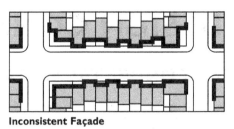

Inconsistent Façade

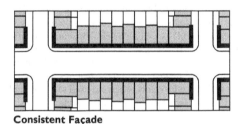

Consistent Façade

Maintain ground-floor façade within an infill project to define a consistent street edge.

STREET EDGE
Source: SMWM.

INFILL PLANNING FRAMEWORK

Among the key elements of the infill planning framework are phasing, community involvement, and design guidelines.

Phasing

For large-scale infill projects, phasing allows projects to be built in multiple steps. It promotes incremental growth, so that the additional population will not unduly strain the community's ability to provide public facilities and services. It also provides the time and capacity necessary to absorb growth into the overall neighborhood. A carefully planned phased development allows the real estate market to adjust to it and expose the new projects to surrounding potential users.

Community Involvement

Public participation is often critical to the success of an infill project. Involve the public early in the development process to help guide projects and make the intent and goals of the project clear to them. Often, most critical are sketches that illustrate before-and-after conditions, and traffic analyses that provide methods to mitigate adverse impacts. Engage residents, civic leaders, and local institutions throughout the process of planning change for a neighborhood.

Design Guidelines

Where appropriate, develop design guidelines to serve as a guide for future development and ensure predictable and desirable growth.

See also:
Mixed-Use Development
Scale and Density
Transit-Oriented Development
Urban Analysis
Zoning Regulation

Hendra Bong, SMWM, San Francisco, California; Sharon Priest, AICP, SMWM, San Francisco, California

DESIGN CONSIDERATIONS

ENVIRONMENTAL SITE ANALYSIS

Site analysis involves understanding the opportunities and constraints of a specific parcel of land for potential new uses. The process links a program for proposed uses with a site inventory of its key features through a site suitability analysis. Planners and urban designers use the site analysis process both to design specific parcels as well as to help implement land-use regulations. The typical components of site analysis are consideration of physical, biological, and cultural features. Information about these features is collected through a site inventory. Maps are used to record and to display site attributes from this inventory.

PHYSICAL FEATURES

The physical features of a site include its geology, physiography, hydrology, microclimate, and soils.

Geology

A geological map provides a graphic representation of the rock units and geological features that are exposed on the surface of the Earth. In addition to showing different types and ages, most geological maps depict features such as faults and folds. Geological information is helpful to determine the capability of the land to support various uses such as building foundations and roadways. In addition, geologic hazards can be revealed.

Physiography

Physiography deals with the physical conditions of the land surface. Elevation and slope are important physiographic features for site analysis. U.S. Geological Survey (USGS) topographic maps can be used to depict elevation changes across a site and to determine different slopes. Steeper slopes will present greater challenges for building than flat areas.

Hydrology

Hydrology includes both groundwater and surface water features. The hydrologic cycle helps planners to understand the balance of water in its various forms in the air, on the land, and in waterbodies such as rivers, lakes, and the sea. Groundwater fills all the unlocked pores of materials lying beneath the surface. Depth to the water table, water quality, aquifer yields, direction of flow movement, and the location of wells are important groundwater factors for site inventories. Surface water flows above the ground. Some surface water characteristics are useful for site inventories:

- Drainage flows
- Stream, lake, estuary, coastline, and wetland locations
- Stream volumes
- Lake and tide levels
- Floodplains and flood-hazard areas
- Sediment loads and waterbody temperatures
- Chemical water-quality characteristics
- Bacteriological water-quality characteristics
- Eutrophication (the process of building up the rich-

ness of nutrient minerals and organisms and the loss of oxygen)
- Water supply systems
- Sewage treatment systems

Often, local land-use and environmental regulations require specific mapped information for a site, such as the location of floodplains.

Microclimate

Microclimate involves small-scale variations in temperature brought about by changes in slope and orientation of the ground surface; soil type and moisture; variations in rock, vegetation type, and height; and human-made features. Some microclimate inventory elements for site analysis include the following:

- Ventilation
- Fog and frost frequency and location
- First and last frosts
- Solar radiation
- Surface condition albedos (level of reflected light) and temperatures
- Vegetation changes

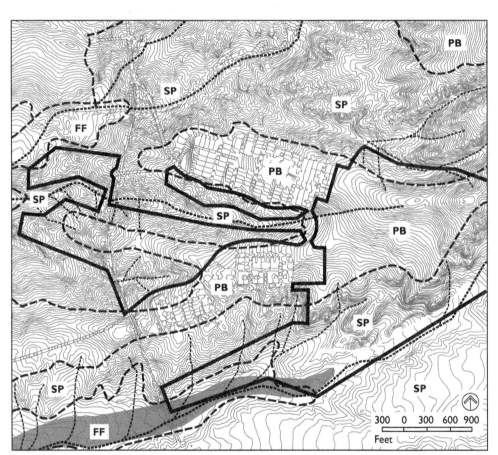

FF	Five Mile Loam Soil Classification - Not Suitable for Building
SP	Silver Pojoaque Soil Classification - Not Suitable for Building
PB	Panky Fine Sandy Loam Soil Classification - Suitable for Building
▬	Master Plan Area Boundary
– –	Soil Classification Boundaries
----	Major Drainages
—	Existing Contour Lines 1' and 4', 1' in Master Plan Area, 4' Around Perimeter of Master Plan Area
▨	FEMA Flood Zone

A physical features map illustrates the most important physical aspects of a site. The map shown here focuses on soil classifications, steep slopes, drainage areas, and the FEMA-classified flood zone.

PHYSICAL FEATURES MAP

Source: Design Workshop 2004.

Frederick R. Steiner, Ph.D, FASLA, University of Texas at Austin, Austin, Texas

Urban heat islands are important concerns in many places; a site analysis can help to mitigate the negative climatic impacts of new land uses. For example, black asphalt will heat up an area more than trees.

Soils

Soils occupy a transition zone that links the biotic and abiotic environments. Soil is a natural three-dimensional body on the surface of the Earth that is capable of supporting plants. Its properties result from the integrated effect of climate and living matter acting upon parent material, as conditioned by relief over time. The Natural Resources Conservation Service (NRCS) of the U.S. Department of Agriculture has mapped most soils and has made them available in published soil surveys as well as in digital formats. NRCS soil surveys contain special information helpful for site analysis including: permeability, texture, erosion potential, drainage potential, soil associations,

cation and anion exchange, and acidity-alkalinity. This information is helpful to determine the capability of soils to support various uses, such as roads, parks, buildings, and farms.

BIOLOGICAL FEATURES

Various plants and animals occupy each site. Vegetation refers to plant life—trees, shrubs, cacti, herbs, and grasses. Plant associations and communities; vegetative units; wildfire susceptibility; and rare, endangered, and threatened plant species can be mapped in a site inventory. In addition, lists of species, including their composition and distribution, can be compiled. For some sites, drawings of physiognomic profiles, as well as ecotone and edge profiles, can be used to illustrate site-specific vegetation. Physiognomic profiles show the structure of plant communities in profile relative to their location

on a slope. Ecotones are transitional areas between two ecological communities, generally of greater richness than either of the communities they separate.

Broadly, wildlife is considered to be animals that are neither human nor domesticated. The potential habitat of wildlife species and its relative value can be mapped. As with vegetation, lists of animal species, including their composition and distribution, can be created. Understanding the plants and animals of the site can help planners and urban designers to protect other living creatures. In addition, plants and animals provide amenities for some land uses.

CULTURAL FEATURES

- Land use and land users
- Settlement patterns
- Historical use
- Property ownership
- Building and open-space types
- Plot, lot, and street arrangement
- Utility lines and easements
- Visual resources

Existing land use refers to the physical arrangement of space utilized by humans. A specific parcel of land can be used for a variety of purposes, and a particular person in a given location may use many parcels of land.

An important component of site analysis is an understanding of both past and existing use. The history of a place can be gathered from various sources, including interviews with older residents and research in community and academic libraries. The past history of a site might be a legal requirement if the property was used for a purpose resulting in pollution or contamination. Understanding a history of a place can reveal how and why its settlement patterns have evolved. One purpose of site analysis is to make new uses compatible with existing settlements. Such settlements are composed of buildings and open spaces with specific arrangements of plots, lots, and streets. A figure-ground map can help illustrate the relationships between buildings and open space.

Site inventories often involve an evaluation of visual quality. This can focus on potential users' preferences for site amenities. The best views from various locations on a site can be mapped. Planners and urban designers can use these vistas to locate uses to optimize those views. Site analysis can also help planners protect visual qualities. Unseen site characteristics can be important as well, such as the location of utility lines and easements.

SITE SUITABILITY ANALYSIS

Land suitability is the process of determining the fitness, or the appropriateness, of a given tract of land for a specific use. It is based on the site inventory as well as the program for future potential uses. Suitability analysis balances opportunities for those uses with site constraints. There are seven steps in suitability analysis:

1. Identify potential land uses and define needs for each use.
2. Relate land-use needs to physical, biological, and cultural site factors collected during the inventory.

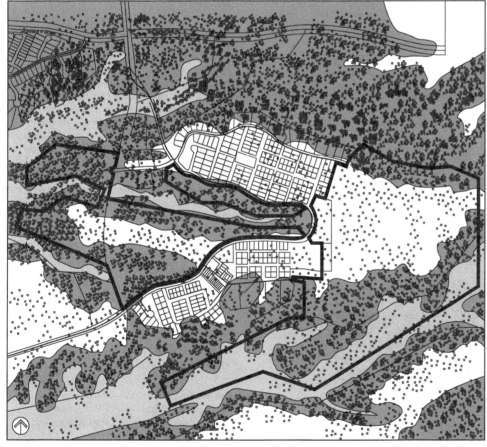

▬ Master Plan Area Boundary
☐ Subclimax Grama-Galleta Grasslands
▨ Pinon Juniper Association
▨ Arroyo Grasslands
ᐧᐧ Existing Trees

A biological features map illustrates the most important biological features of a site. In addition to helping professional planners, such a map can assist elected officials, planning commissioners, and citizens to understand the value of plants and animals. The map shown here focuses on existing trees and land-cover types.

BIOLOGICAL FEATURES MAP

Source: Design Workshop 2004.

Frederick R. Steiner, Ph.D. FASLA, University of Texas at Austin, Austin, Texas

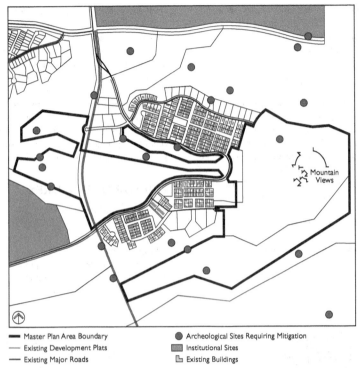

Several cultural elements can be displayed on a single map. Such a map helps show the most important site-specific cultural features. These features may include constraints to future uses—for example, a historical structure. The map here includes archaeological sites requiring mitigation and mountain views.

CULTURAL FEATURES MAP

Source: Design Workshop 2004.

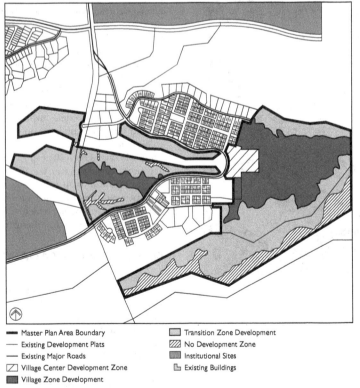

A site suitability map is a composite site map of the most suitable locations for various land uses.

SITE SUITABILITY MAP

Source: Design Workshop 2004.

Frederick R. Steiner, Ph.D. FASLA, University of Texas at Austin, Austin, Texas

3. Identify the relationship between specific mapped phenomena for the site concerning the biophysical environment and land-use needs.
4. Map the congruencies of desired phenomena and formulate ranking criteria to express a gradient of suitability. This step should result in maps of land-use opportunities.
5. Identify the constraints between potential land uses and biophysical processes. Constraints are environmentally or culturally sensitive areas that should be preempted from development because of threats to human health, safety, or welfare or of rare or unique natural or cultural attributes.
6. Overlay maps of constraints and opportunities to identify intrinsic suitabilities for each land use.
7. Develop a composite site map of the highest suitabilities of the various land uses.

Geographic information systems (GIS) can assist planners and urban designers in the site inventory mapping and suitability analysis processes. A GIS allows planners and urban designers to consider multiple rankings of mapped information for site suitability.

SITE ANALYSIS IN PLANNING AND URBAN DESIGN

Planners and urban designers use site analysis for a broad range of purposes. It can be used to change the use of a parcel from farming to housing or a shopping center. It can assist in siting transportation facilities as well as for the layout of conservation areas. Site analysis can also be utilized in existing built-up areas to determine new uses. The nature of the proposed land use and the site will determine the specific features to be inventoried and mapped.

An issue planners often face in site analysis is the availability and the scale of mapped information. Important site-specific data for a proposed land use may be lacking or available at an unusable scale. In such cases, planners will need to create new information, which can be costly. Improved GIS, Web-source information, and remote-sensed imagery help overcome this issue. Continued emerging technologies are likely to improve site analysis techniques further.

Site analysis is a fundamental component of site planning. A thorough analysis of a place enables the planner to link conservation and development goals to site-specific characteristics.

See also:
Environmental Planning and Management
U.S. Geological Survey Topographic Maps
Urban Analysis

URBAN ANALYSIS

Urban analysis links an understanding of a place and its context with generally acceptable urban design concepts and strategies. Whether the place in question is a specific site, a city street, a neighborhood, downtown, or a region, a thorough understanding of the place helps guide the choice of the most appropriate type of project.

The type of analysis chosen should help to better understand a project's location and context; it should not be used to support a desired outcome or predetermined design. Any type of urban analysis needs to begin with the project goals. Understanding the goals and what the client, the city, the developer, or the citizens hope to achieve through the project can help determine the most appropriate type of analysis for ascertaining the project's potential for success.

The process of analyzing the physical environment in urban, suburban, and rural areas can be performed on many scales. Projects can be proposed for a range of sizes, from an individual building site to entire regional areas. The size of the proposed project or study area should dictate the scale of analysis. For example, a single-site project would warrant an analysis of the surrounding neighborhood, while a plan or project for a large, multisite area would involve analyzing the surrounding neighborhoods or larger regional area.

STANDARDS AND REGULATIONS

Several individuals have developed nationally recognized guidelines for urban analysis, including Kevin Lynch, Christopher Alexander, Colin Rowe, and William Morrish, among others. Architects or urban designers developed the majority of these individually created guidelines, so they tend to present simplified categories that focus on the physical character of a place. For a more accurate and balanced understanding of a site, include a wider range of factors, among them economic data, environmental issues, and transportation concerns.

On the federal level, there are two key nationally recognized standards regulating the types of urban analysis undertaken for a particular project. First, there are standard requirements for nominating a place for the National Register of Historic Places, which the National Park Service administers. Second, the National Environmental Policy Act (NEPA) has standards that require certain types of analysis as part of an environmental review process. (See Historic Districts, Environmental Impact Assessment, Legislation, and Other Federal Laws in this book for more information.)

ELEMENTS OF URBAN ANALYSIS

There are many types of analysis that can be performed, but they can be organized into six general categories: community, regulations and ownership, continuity, character, connections, and economics and market setting. Each category includes several different elements that can be examined, including the key reasons to study each element and the best way to perform the analysis.

Community

Key elements of the community to explore include census information, previous planning efforts, and public processes.

Census Information

Although U.S. Census data do not include individual or collective values, they do provide an overview of the demographic character of the residents in a particular community. Statistics available for analysis include age, employment, income, household size and tenure, and commute distance. Census information (available online at www.census.gov) can be analyzed through a series of summary charts and/or bar charts. In addition, many municipalities provide demographic summaries of their communities on their websites.

Previous Planning Efforts

Previous plans may also be a resource to investigate. Understanding why previous plans were or were not successful, as well as what kind of public support they garnered, can help guide future projects and may help in establishing community values.

Previous plans can be analyzed by reading through draft and final reports, interviewing the previous project's or plan's client, city officials or city staff, or planning and design consultants who prepared the plan. The plans can be summarized through a series of maps, with annotations of key improvements and key obstacles to implementation of the plan.

Public Process

A community's perception regarding itself and its environment is an important element to gauge. No matter what the physical or economic analyses say about a place, for a project to be successful, it needs the support of people who live, work, and play there.

Decision makers and citizens often have specific goals and desires for projects, so it is critical to meet with them individually before a project commences. Local decision makers have more direct sway over the success of an individual project, but, today, individual citizens can effectively halt almost any project, so it is important to invite all relevant stakeholders to the table to help ensure a successful project.

Various types of interactive public processes can be used to solicit the public's ideas and viewpoints regarding their community. Two commonly used tools are visual preference analysis, whereby the public identifies what they like and do not like about images of places, and interactive mapping exercises, whereby people use different "game pieces" that represent land uses or other physical elements to map suggestions and improvements for an area. (See Public Meetings in Part 1 of this book for more information and examples.)

Regulations and Ownership
Zoning and Land Use

Documenting the zoning classifications both within and surrounding a project area or site will define the existing potentials for use, along with the building envelope and densities within which those uses can be built.

A record and analysis of zoning regulations is supported by a variety of drawing techniques, starting with a plan drawing that indicates the allowable land uses and densities within and surrounding a site. Plans or section diagrams are useful for illustrating allowable development characteristics such as building heights, floor area ratio (FAR), allowable residential densities, building setbacks, and parking requirements. A map of existing land uses should be independently prepared and compared to the uses allowed by zoning. (See Zoning Regulation in Part 6 of this book for more information.)

Design Guidelines

As a supplement to zoning codes, many municipalities have established design guidelines to shape the architectural character of their communities. Design guidelines that clarify and recommend elements such as windows and doors, private plantings, building and roof shapes, and signage are an appropriate starting point for the definition of character in a proposed development.

Design guidelines are typically represented through drawings and photographs of buildings (both within the community and from outside) that describe the appropriate type of building for a particular site, street, or community. A summary map or memo can illustrate the implications of such guidelines for a particular site or area.

Property Ownership

The type and character of buildings in a place contribute to many important aspects of a community, and in some cases may be a direct result of the patterns of property ownership. Property lines, property ownership, and the shape, pattern, and size of parcels are key factors in the built environment's appearance. The patterns of land ownership—such as public versus private owners, multiple owners for multiple properties, single owners for multiple properties, and small-scale lots versus larger "super blocks"—can be a strong indicator of the likely pattern of urban form.

Multiple ownership projects, including public/private partnerships, are becoming more common. Therefore, documenting all the relevant property lines and ownership is important to identify the contribution of various parties and guide the balance of development funding and investment returns.

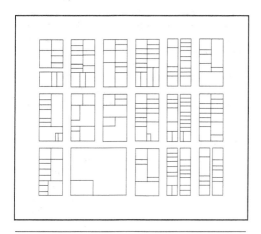

PARCEL MAPS AND PROPERTY LINES

Source: SMWM.

David Schellinger, SMWM, San Francisco, California; Sharon Priest, AICP, SMWM, San Francisco, California

DESIGN CONSIDERATIONS

Property lines and ownership can be analyzed through parcel maps. Much of this information can be found in Sanborn fire insurance maps (www.sanborn.com/Services/Traditional/OrderForm.htm), city planning departments, subdivision plat files, county land and tax records, and even historic maps. This information is not always readily available in digital format, however, or if it is, it may be from scans of original hard copies, which may have limited enlargement capability for diagramming purposes. Some communities keep this information in a geographic information system (GIS) database that ties property lines to property ownership, which can be easily used as a base for diagramming.

Continuity

Key elements of the continuity of a place to explore include history and patterns of development.

History

How a community has changed or remained consistent in physical patterns can reveal a lot about its character and its susceptibility for change. In addition to recognized historic areas, broaden the perspective to study the patterns of building, roads, and landscape features over time to understand how and why communities developed the way they did. Refer to state and federal guidelines for historic analysis of districts as a useful structure for such an analysis.

Mapping changes in the landforms and topography over time can indicate the location of historic shorelines and wetlands or former agricultural lands, sensitive landscape features that have been lost, and remaining natural features that may merit preservation.

Patterns of Development

As communities develop over time, they often create unique patterns in the type, scale, and location of buildings.

Figure ground diagrams, where buildings are dark shapes on a white background, and block pattern diagrams, where blocks of developable property are dark on top of a white street pattern, for different periods of time or different part of a community can help guide the scale, pattern, and even logical locations for future development. Similar in nature to a figure ground diagram, a Nolli Map, named for Giambattista Nolli's groundbreaking map of 1748 Rome, is a useful tool for exploring the continuity of the perceived public space in a community. Whereas a figure ground diagram denotes the difference between built and unbuilt space, Nolli maps denote the public space both outside and inside buildings, such that the interiors of schools, city halls, and community centers, for example, read as part of the overall network of public space. This type of analysis can be helpful in understanding the use of ground floors of buildings to augment the public realm, providing guidance for future developments.

Character

There are several key elements of the character of a place to explore, including urban form, topography, views, open space, activity nodes, architectural character, streetscape, and the natural environment. Aerial photography is often a useful tool in providing a visual overview of the urban form and can be combined with line work over the aerial photograph as a successful diagramming technique for many of the elements described below.

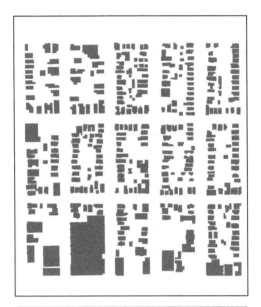

FIGURE GROUND
Source: SMWM.

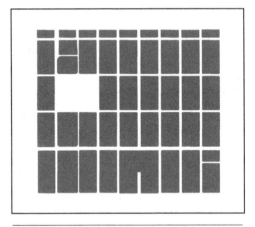

BLOCK PATTERNS
Source: SMWM.

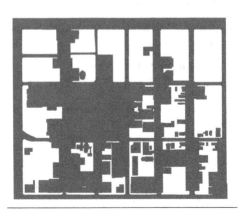

NOLLI MAP
Source: SMWM.

Urban Form

Taken collectively, the scale and character of individual buildings and the topography of a place create an overall urban/built form. Analysis of urban form can highlight patterns ranging from the general shape of development to the integration with the larger natural environment.

Figure ground drawings and block pattern diagrams are useful tools in understanding the general scale and grain of development in a particular built environment.

Topography

Topographic features such as slopes or the presence of a floodplain can limit the type of development allowed in a place. A thorough understanding of the overall topography of a place is also useful for understanding original settlement patterns and locating new development appropriately.

Analysis of the overall landform can be achieved with topographic maps that identify specific landforms that limit development, such as hills or bodies of water, or areas that are suitable for development, such as areas of flat land. Such information should be supplemented with other environmental data, such as the location of aquifer recharge areas. (See Environmental Site Analysis in this part of the book for further information.)

Views

The process of building cities and suburbs simultaneously frames views of the natural environment and creates a multitude of human-made views, from city skylines to residential tree-lined streets. Understanding which views are important, whether they are point views (views toward a single object or group of objects), panoramic viewsheds, or linear views can help guide the scale of development.

Important views in a community can be indicated on aerial photographs or base maps of a community, highlighting the different kinds of views and the subject of the view. Views and viewsheds can also be

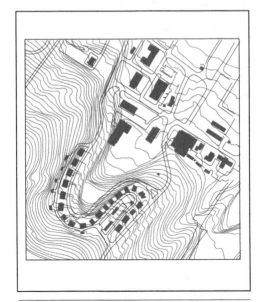

TOPOGRAPHY
Source: SMWM.

David Schellinger, SMWM, San Francisco, California; Sharon Priest, AICP, SMWM, San Francisco, California

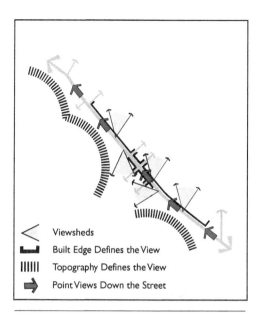

VIEWS

Source: SMWM.

analyzed through section drawings, showing how street edges frame particular views and how the scale of development or the placement of buildings on a particular site can allow or block views to the surrounding landforms.

Open Space

The number of parks and other recreational and non-recreational open spaces is often a useful gauge for the number of residents a community can comfortably support. Various methods can be used for such an assessment. Diagramming the system of existing

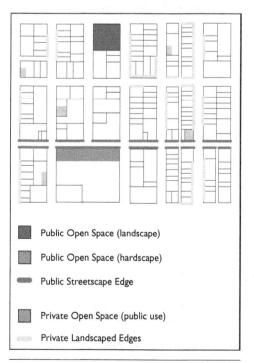

OPEN-SPACE SYSTEMS AND OWNERSHIP

Source: SMWM.

open spaces in a community can help guide the location of new parks and open spaces in a community. Open space can also be analyzed to document the ownership of open space in a community to ascertain if there is an appropriate balance between public and private ownership.

A plan drawing, indicating the different types of open spaces and ownership, is the most common type of diagram used to understand the open-space system in a community.

Activity Nodes

The pattern of land uses can help identify major activity centers. While quiet residential neighborhoods are often considered the backbone of the American city, recent interest has focused on major mixed-use activity centers, from the main street to the reinvented mixed-use shopping centers. Patterns and locations of existing activity nodes can be useful to guide locations of future activity nodes, either as expansions of existing nodes or creation of entirely new, and possibly competing, activity nodes.

In addition to zoning maps, plan diagrams can be used to document individual activity generators, and the larger area from which activity nodes draw or could draw population. Annotations on these plans can also indicate publicly versus privately owned activity nodes.

Architectural Character

Analyzing a community's architectural character can identify significant buildings, provide insight on a community's values, and help determine the types of buildings residents would like to see in the future. Usually, a few individual buildings are more memorable within a particular community. These buildings often have some historic or architectural significance and are given landmark status, although in some instances they are simply buildings that are important to residents and are considered for protection under local criteria. In addition, a collection of architecturally or historically significant buildings in a

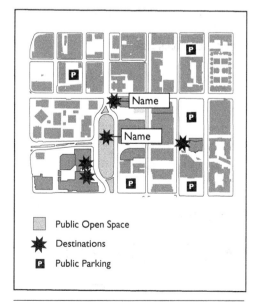

ACTIVITY NODES

Source: SMWM.

neighborhood or district often provides more information about the desired architectural character of a community than a single historic structure.

Axonometric sketches of typical building types and elevation drawings of typical street façades or individual building façades can be used to document a community's architectural character.

Streetscape

Street character is established by the width of streets, the regular or irregular pattern of buildings facing those streets, the tree planting along those streets and specific design features such as lighting, paving, and street furniture. Mapping more or less consistent characteristics of street design, often along with patterns of open space, is an important component for public realm analysis. Streetscape and public realm standards or guidelines may also be available to guide the type of streetscape elements for future development projects.

Analysis of streetscapes is usually presented through plans and sections of streets and sidewalks, indicating the type and location of amenities. (See Streetscape in this part of this book for more information.)

Environmental Concerns

Document the environmental aspects of a community, which will likely include both natural areas for protection and conservation and built areas where new development may involve cleanup and restoration. Consult recent environmental studies at a local, state, or federal level for issues that are citywide or in the vicinity of a site under analysis. Also be aware that jurisdictions may have adopted environmental protection or cleanup plans. For redevelopment or infill sites, remediation is often required before development can occur. This is particularly relevant in military base redevelopment projects and industrial areas such as former rail yards.

Plan diagrams can be used to document sensitive environmental sites, such as riparian zones or wildlife habitats that need to be protected and sites that require environmental remediation.

Connections

An urban analysis must address all relevant components of an area's or site's access characteristics in order to assess the available service to the site, to see how the area is linked to other essential parts of the community, and to understand where a new proposal might serve to fill the gaps or enable access by more alternative modes. A similar analysis is needed to assess the capacity and availability of needed utilities and services.

Included here are checklists of items that should be considered for mapping and capacity, to help identify the opportunities and constraints for the site or area in question. (More detailed information on many of these topics is available in the transportation section in Part 3 of this book.)

Street Network and Rights-of-Way
- Street types
- Pattern and capacity of the street network
- Rights-of-way recorded for the area, showing ownership of streets and sidewalks and often indicating potential for changes and/or expansion of roadways within that ownership
- Local, community, and regional connections, both existing and needed

David Schellinger, SMWM, San Francisco, California; Sharon Priest, AICP, SMWM, San Francisco, California

DESIGN CONSIDERATIONS

Traffic Parking and Collision Data
- Record of traffic flow and current levels of service (LOS)
- Capacity of roadway segments
- Collision data as an indicator of existing problems in design or operations
- Parking facilities (on-street and off-street), usage and capacity
- Parking standards and guidelines for the area, including location, size, and ratios
- Record of parking issues and complaints in terms of adverse impacts, as well as transit-first policies that may limit parking provision in dense urban areas
- Planned improvements to roadway network
- Local community policies in relation to street standards, such as acceptable levels of service and policies encouraging walkable neighborhoods and affecting street and sidewalk widths

Refer to local traffic analysis models for further information on the potential effects of planning or development initiatives.

Transit Modes and Services
- Identification of all available and planned modes of public transportation including the following:
  - Commuter, regional, and interstate rail access
  - Light rail
  - Local and regional bus service
  - Fixed guideway buses
  - Special shuttle bus services
  - Water transportation such as ferries and water taxis
  - Where appropriate, a record of ridership data, location of transit stops, service headways, and potential for expansion

Bicycles and Pedestrians
- Bicycle routes, by classification, and existing or required bike lanes that may require added street right-of-way, both commuter and recreational routes
- Pedestrian network, including sidewalks and special pathways needed to accommodate handicapped access
- Desired pedestrian paths of travel

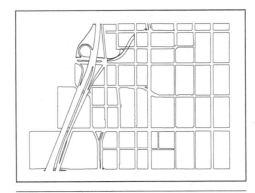

STREET NETWORKS

Source: SMWM.

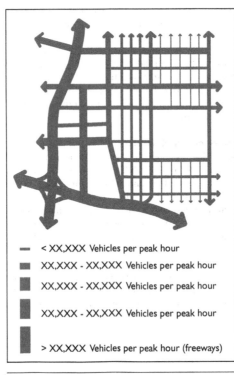

- — < XX,XXX Vehicles per peak hour
- ▬ XX,XXX - XX,XXX Vehicles per peak hour
- ▬ XX,XXX - XX,XXX Vehicles per peak hour
- ▬ XX,XXX - XX,XXX Vehicles per peak hour
- ▬ > XX,XXX Vehicles per peak hour (freeways)

TRAFFIC VOLUMES

Source: SMWM.

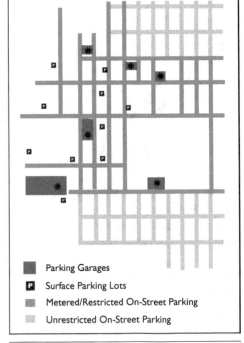

- ■ Parking Garages
- P Surface Parking Lots
- ■ Metered/Restricted On-Street Parking
- ■ Unrestricted On-Street Parking

PARKING LOCATIONS

Source: SMWM.

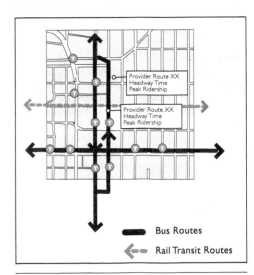

- ▬ Bus Routes
- ←-- Rail Transit Routes

TRANSIT ROUTES

Source: SMWM.

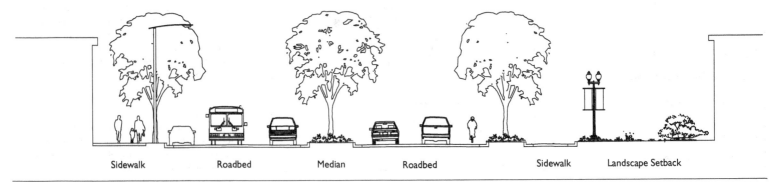

Sidewalk   Roadbed   Median   Roadbed   Sidewalk   Landscape Setback

RIGHT-OF-WAY

Source: SMWM.

David Schellinger, SMWM, San Francisco, California; Sharon Priest, AICP, SMWM, San Francisco, California

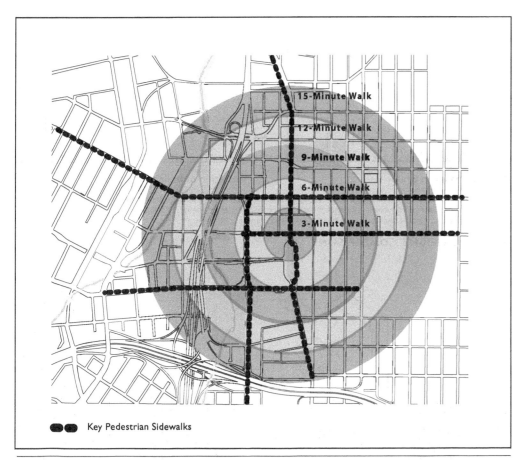

PEDESTRIAN WALKING DISTANCES AND MAJOR PEDESTRIAN SIDEWALKS

Source: SMWM.

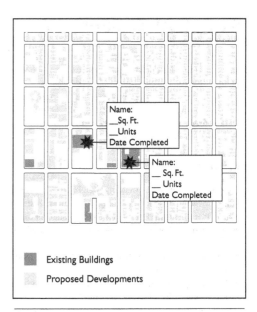

FUTURE DEVELOPMENT

Source: SMWM.

Utilities and Services

- Location, capacity, and planned network changes as relevant for essential utilities and services, including the following:
  - Water
  - Sewer
  - Power
  - Communications
- Community facilities and services, such as libraries, schools, government services, day care, recreational centers, and other key community services

ECONOMIC AND MARKET SETTING

An urban analysis may engage economic and market issues in a variety of ways, including the real estate economics that support new development proposals; an assessment of market demand, including unmet needs for residential, retail, office, or other land uses and specific building types; and fiscal analysis, by which a community judges its ability to provide the services needed for a new planned district or site development or public use proposal. Job creation potential may also be important to a community.

Census data can provide a general overview of income levels in a particular community, but it is highly recommended to work with an economist to help ascertain the economic health of a community. This analysis can suggest locations where the community can support additional land uses and services, such as housing or commercial development.

Thorough economic analysis should include identification of all projects or improvements that are currently under construction or that have been given approval to proceed. Any proposed changes to the existing economic base may affect the community's ability to support future development.

An economic capacity analysis includes a clear understanding of the budget for the project in question. This extends to the sources of funding available for projects, whether they are financed publicly, privately, through public/private partnerships, or through grants, because the available funding often strongly influences the type, scale, and location of development.

CONCLUSION

The findings of research initiatives; a comprehensive review and comparison of these findings to each other; and a comparison of these findings with established community goals, plans, standards, and guidelines conclude a site or area analysis. Maps, diagrams, and spreadsheets should be used to record and display information, summarize findings, and draw conclusions.

In general terms, most urban analyses conclude with a summary of defined constraints and identified opportunities. Findings can be summarized by the physical parameters for construction on-site and off-site, the use program, existing capacities and needed future services, and likely demands on the surrounding area. It may also conclude with identifying gaps in the information that need more study.

The following questions ought to be asked when considering a project:

- Is there a distinctive urban form or pattern that will set the parameters for new development?
- Do key views tell you that there should be set height limits or establishment of a view corridor for a specific site?
- Do traffic patterns indicate places where the street system could handle additional capacity, or, conversely, would be severely impacted by new development?
- Are there sensitive natural areas or built environments that need protection?
- Does the economic analysis support a specific type of land use?

Consider creating summary maps and diagrams to synthesize the analysis. A comprehensive collection of annotated diagrams that include key findings can help guide choices for the project.

See also:

Census Data and Demographic Mapping
Environmental Impact Assessment
Environmental Site Analysis
Mixed-Use Development
On-Street Bikeways
Parks and Open-Space Plans
Public Meetings
Scale and Density
Streetscape
Transit-Oriented Development
Transportation
Viewshed Protection
Zoning Regulation

David Schellinger, SMWM, San Francisco, California; Sharon Priest, AICP, SMWM, San Francisco, California

SCALE AND DENSITY

Scale is a qualitative measure of the relative height and massing of buildings and spaces. Density is a quantitative measure of the number of units on a particular area of land, often expressed as the number of people, number of housing units, or amount of square feet of development per land area, typically expressed in acres or square miles.

SCALE

Presented in terms of building height and massing, scale presents distinct planning and urban design issues. Planners and designers are often called upon to address issues of scale in a variety of situations when:

- creating economically feasible development plans or urban design frameworks;
- developing zoning for a new district or to guide development in a historic downtown;
- evaluating shadow, wind, and other potential impacts of a proposal; or
- reviewing proposals for consistency with community goals or compatibility with adjacent buildings or open space.

New construction technologies have made it possible to build at much greater scales than those prevalent before the middle twentieth century. These earlier buildings provide the traditional scale familiar to many Americans. Starting in the 1950s, the larger buildings constructed provide a contrast of scale that is both exciting and jarring, uplifting and dehumanizing.

HEIGHT

Attitudes toward height vary from community to community. In Chicago and New York, height is valued; in San Francisco, it is resisted. In Providence, Rhode Island, heights increase closer to the downtown riverfront, but in downtown Boston, just 50 miles away, building heights decline toward the waterfront. Such local cultural differences influence decisions about appropriate building heights, as do other objective and subjective considerations, described in the following paragraphs.

Pedestrian Friendliness

Determining how height looks to pedestrians is not an objective measure, yet many zoning codes establish quantifiable limits, such as requiring tall buildings to be set back a prescribed distance at a fixed point above street level, in an effort to make the public realm more hospitable to pedestrians. Several large cities embrace height, and require no setbacks, as long as the public realm meets other standards of pedestrian friendliness.

Height in Relation to Street Width

Building height that is roughly equal to the width of the street the building faces will generally be viewed as reasonable. When height reaches twice the width of the street, many people classify the building as tall.

Framing Public Space

How a building's height relates to the space it frames shapes perceptions of appropriateness. The concept

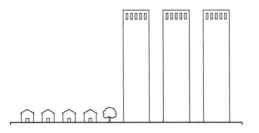

Abrupt Change in Scale

Transition of Building Heights

An abrupt change in building scale creates an inharmonious environment that maximizes the negative effects of tall buildings on adjacent uses, such as loss of sunlight and strengthened wind currents. A transition of building heights from residential neighborhoods to dense commercial districts minimizes these negative impacts

BUILDING HEIGHT COMPARISONS

Source: Goody Clancy.

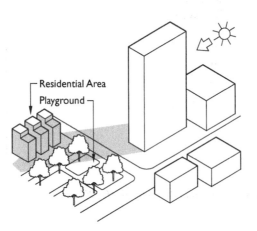

Blocked Solar Exposure

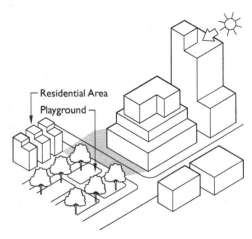

Improved Solar Exposure

When poorly sited, tall buildings can block the sun exposure for sensitive areas, such as parks and neighborhoods. Problematic shadows can be avoided by using careful massing and stepbacks in the building profile.

SOLAR EXPOSURE

Source: Goody Clancy.

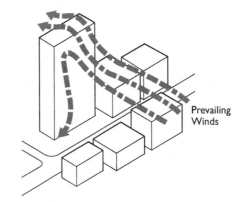

Wind Downwash

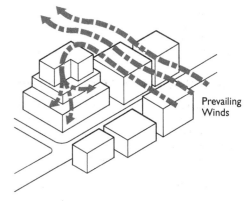

Wind Diffusion

Tall buildings with large, unbroken profiles tend to draw wind down to the ground level. The taller the building, the higher the wind pressure, because wind speed normally increases with height. Lower pressures below cause a descending flow on the building's windward face, called "downwash." Because wind force increases at a square of its speed, pedestrians can experience an extreme increase in wind force. Shorter buildings of equal volume, with a stepped profile, will diffuse wind before it reaches the ground.

WIND EFFECTS

Source: Goody Clancy.

David Dixon, FAIA, Goody Clancy, Boston, Massachusetts; David Spillane, Goody Clancy, Boston, Massachusetts

of a "public room" is often used to envision the positive qualities of a public space that is framed by buildings of similar or compatible heights, or an ensemble of buildings that works with the size, solar orientation, wind conditions, and design potentials of a public park, plaza, or varied civic space.

Symbolism and Identity

A tall building can impart a strong sense of identity, and many communities take pride in their tall structures for this reason. Context and use also play a role, however, calling for use of greater height and distinctive shape and design to signify buildings and uses of importance to a community. In each city or community there is a role for imageable buildings that give identity and for background buildings that establish a context.

Context

In every community, a set of heights—often growing out of tradition—will seem right for a neighborhood, a district, even a city itself. For most of the twentieth century, an informal agreement in Philadelphia limited buildings to 33 stories, a number chosen to maintain the prominence of the statue of William Penn atop City Hall. Today, the two structures that comprise Liberty Place—both higher than City Hall—now define the skyline of Center City Philadelphia. A tower in a neighborhood of three-story houses would strike most observers as out of scale. Within downtown, however, the same building would likely be embraced as a welcome addition to the streetscape and skyline.

Economics

Height can markedly alter project costs, adding to construction cost per square foot as requirements for structural and life safety systems change, for example, but conferring economies of scale on others elements, such as overall land cost per square foot of a new building. In some instances—residential projects in particular—height can contribute significantly to project value. To a lesser degree, height adds value for class A office space but has not been shown to add value to either class B or C office space. (According to the Urban Land Institute's *Office Development Handbook*, class A office space is the most desirable in terms of location, design, building systems, amenities, and management, among other features. Class B office space is in good locations and has good management, and was constructed well; it is generally of a generation earlier than class A space. Class C office space is substantially older than A or B and has not been modernized.) Attractive views combined with height, however, almost always add value. Also, height has been found generally not to add value to research-oriented development; in fact, beyond 10 to 12 stories, it begins to add significantly to mechanical costs.

Environmental Considerations

Sun, wind, and shadow concerns assume extra significance when structures reach 12 to 15 stories or more. Designs for buildings at these heights should incorporate measures to mitigate the building's impact on the public realm. Breaking the building mass into smaller units can diminish wind forces around the base. Towers should be designed to minimize the casting of shadows on parks and public squares for a pronounced length of time—although framing public spaces with prominent urban scale structures may be essential to create handsome,

imageable places of civic importance. Some municipalities have written such a prohibition into the zoning code: for example, in Boston, there are strict limitations on new shadows that might be cast on the city's public garden. For tall buildings, wind tunnel tests should be required, so that pedestrian level effects can be evaluated.

MASSING

Members of the public will often turn to height as a proxy for problems they perceive in scale; but, frequently, it is massing that determines whether a building's scale feels appropriate. Massing refers to the organization of the building's overall volume: Is it

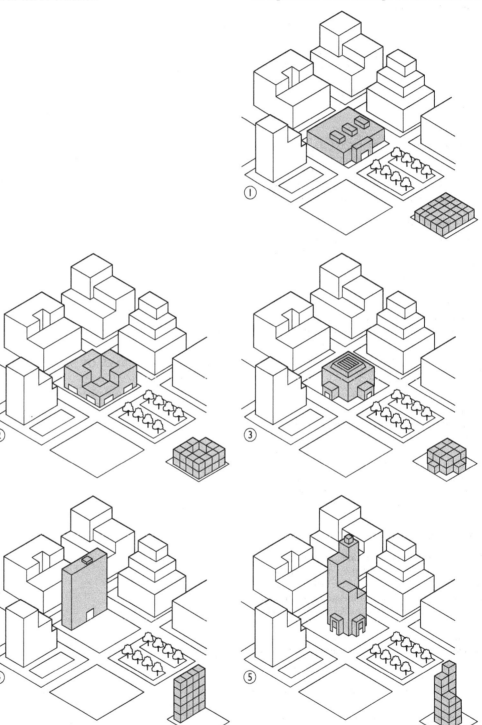

An equal amount of built volume can be "massed" in a variety of ways to achieve certain ends: (1) Create a large, enclosed floor space, such as an exhibit hall. (2) Place mass around the perimeter of a block to create a protected internal courtyard. (3) Place a monumental mass in the center of a site, to create a civic focal point. (4) Collect all the building mass on one edge of the site to allow for a park or plaza. (5) Draw all the mass into a single iconic tower to accent the city skyline.

MASSING ALTERNATIVES

Source: Goody Clancy.

David Dixon, FAIA, Goody Clancy, Boston, Massachusetts; David Spillane, Goody Clancy, Boston, Massachusetts

DESIGN CONSIDERATIONS

a slender tower, a low box, or a combination of elements of varying heights, organized to reflect internal functions or external conditions? Many of the same considerations that help define appropriate heights determine whether a building's massing seems appropriate.

Pedestrian Friendliness

A building's massing should contribute positively to a pedestrian-friendly public realm. Long, unbroken walls feel overwhelming at street level; the same mass, divided into rhythmic blocks, brings the basic design unit of a façade much closer to human scale. Some cities have written such treatments into their zoning codes or into design guidelines.

Context

Structural massing should respect the surrounding context. In particular, the structure should take design cues from the generally smaller and more articulated massing found in structures built before 1950 to help reduce any perceived context issues regarding size.

Symbolism and Identity

A courthouse or municipal building may warrant a far more monumental design expression than a mixed-use building on an urban main street—even if height and square footage are identical.

Economics

Design variety and façade articulation to address massing concerns can add to project costs; however, some communities require such elements. Various markets require a distinct floorplate, or overall size and configuration of each floor:

- Residential projects have a great deal of floorplate configuration and expression flexibility. Using these variations can add value to a project.
- Research/development buildings and office buildings—particularly class A—have been moving toward larger floorplates.
- Retail floorplate needs vary widely, from small mom-and-pop operations to local-destination and strip retail stores to "big-box" retailers.

DENSITY

Gross density includes infrastructure, such as streets and parks, in the overall density measurement. Net density excludes these features and includes just the area devoted specifically to the structure, including all private land areas and ancillary structures. Floor area ratio (FAR) is often used to describe density of commercial structures. It is the ratio of built floor area for all floors to the area of the site. A 2 FAR (or 2:1 FAR) allows for 2 square feet of development for every 1 square foot of site area. FAR is also at times expressed as a percentage or a fraction (.50 or 50 percent).

Depending on scale, the same density may look and feel quite different. Perceptions of inappropriate density can trigger strong reactions from the public, with concerns about increased traffic congestion and concentrated poverty. Good design employs scale as a way to make denser development feel humane and look appealing while capturing the benefits it brings to the public realm.

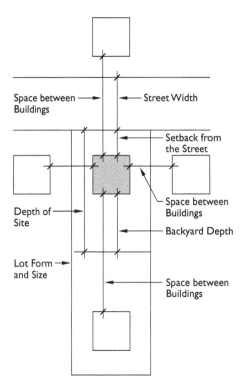

Site coverage of a building, also referred to as the building footprint, is a factor of the setback distances from adjacent structures, lot lines and streets, and the lot form and size. Combinations of different structure sizes and heights can result in a variety of densities with the same overall lot coverage.

PHYSICAL VARIABLES OF SITE COVERAGE

Source: Alexander and Reed, with Murphy 1988.

Regional-Level Density

Achieving the smart growth ideal of balancing economic development with environmental protection requires directing new jobs, housing, and other growth to developed areas or areas targeted for concentrated development within a region. A 2002 study by the Lincoln Institute for Land Policy projected a $40 billion savings over 25 years if the public sector in the Northeast were to encourage "more compact" development—an essential tactic for maintaining regional economic competitiveness. Density also addresses energy consumption. Denser regions such as the metropolitan areas of New York, San Francisco, and Portland, Oregon, consume far less energy per capita than less-dense regions such as Atlanta and Phoenix.

Community-Level Density

From San Diego, California, to Providence, Rhode Island, cities are encouraging new housing in downtowns and older neighborhood centers to attract "knowledge industry" employees, who often prefer lively, walkable, mixed-use neighborhoods. An accumulating body of evidence suggests that higher-density, walkable neighborhoods enhance public health; a recent study that compared a denser city to a less-dense city found that raising density had a more positive impact on health indicators than did increasing income by 50 percent. Compact development also increases transportation options. Walkable neighborhoods that combine housing, schools, jobs, and other uses reduce automobile dependence and broaden the market for public transit.

Neighborhood-Level Density

Density provides the people and disposable incomes required to revitalize older urban neighborhoods. A 2002 study by Goody Clancy suggests that 1,500 to 2,500 new housing units within walking distance are

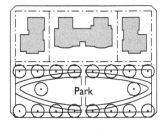
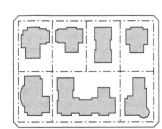
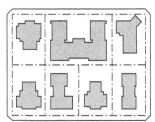
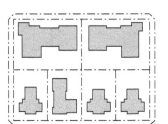
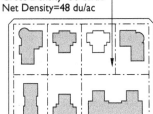

Gross density of the site includes a proportional amount of the street and park area; the net density excludes these features. In this example, gross density is assumed to be approximately 75 percent of net density.

GROSS AND NET DENSITY

Source: Goody Clancy.

David Dixon, FAIA, Goody Clancy, Boston, Massachusetts; David Spillane, Goody Clancy, Boston, Massachusetts

required to sustain a new block of main street retail. As public financial resources shrink, adding density is often critical to paying for parks, street trees, community services, and other "building blocks" of livability. Similarly, increased densities, accompanied by internal subsidies from market-rate units, are one mechanism for providing affordable housing. Increasing densities promotes diversity by supporting a wider range of housing types within a neighborhood.

Comparative Densities

A given density within the same area can take dramatically different forms. Single-family housing developed at 8 to 12 units per acre can resemble a crowded suburb or a classic village neighborhood. A mix of single-family and multifamily housing at 15 to 25 units per acre can resemble an unremarkable apartment complex within a parking lot or Washington, DC's Dupont Circle neighborhood. At 30 to 50 units per acre—the density of traditional urban neighborhoods—a development can take the form of isolated high-rise apartment buildings or the architectural rhythms of Chicago's Lincoln Park. *Boston Globe* architecture critic Robert Campbell has pointed out that Paris is almost four times as dense as Boston, with few complaints.

PLANNING AND DESIGN CONSIDERATIONS

Many communities support a range of densities; it is not uncommon for urban neighborhoods to comprise 100 or more units per acre, with a broad mix of housing types and heights.

TYPICAL DENSITIES OF SELECT HOUSING TYPES

HOUSING TYPES	TYPICAL GROSS DENSITY RANGE (UNITS/ACRE, INCLUDING STREETS)
Single-family detached (generally 1- to 2-story)	4 to 10
Single-family rowhouses (2- to 3-story)	8 to 20
Three- to six-family houses (3- to 4-story)	8 to 25
Multifamily rowhouses (3- to 4-story)	20 to 40
Low-rise multifamily (2- to 5-story)	15 to 50
Lofts	25 to 50
Midrise multifamily	100 to 150
High-rise multistory	60 to 200+

Design can help a project capture the benefits of greater density while giving it a scale that feels appropriate. Extend the surrounding neighborhood fabric into the site by employing similar materials, maintaining continuity along the street, designing comparable rooflines and floor-to-floor heights, and making transitions in scale that reflect nearby buildings.

A wide range of densities within a mix of land uses should also be considered. A single new housing development can mix rowhouses, lofts, and midrise and high-rise apartments. Older single-use retail centers have been successfully redeveloped with housing on upper floors. Office and research facilities can achieve significantly greater densities if parking is located below grade. Hotels and retail can be successfully integrated with housing and other uses.

When determining the appropriate density of a site, take into account several factors, including the site context, the aspirations and goals of the community, the economics of development, and the building's or project's civic role. When scale and density are considered together, they can help developers create public spaces, new buildings, and neighborhoods that respect the past while pointing toward the future.

REFERENCES

Alexander, Ernest R., and K. David Reed with Peter Murphy. 1988. *Density Measures and Their Relation to Urban Form.* PAM91-0746. University of Wisconsin at Milwaukee, School of Architecture and Urban Planning. Milwaukee, WI: University of Wisconsin at Milwaukee.

Campbell, Robert. "Density's Darling." *Boston Globe,* May 25, 2003.

Campoli, Julie, and Alex MacLean. 2002. *Visualizing Density.* Cambridge, MA: Lincoln Institute of Land Policy.

Gause, Jo Allen, et al. 1998. *Office Development Handbook.* 2nd Edition. Washington, D.C.: ULI-the Urban Land Institute.

Goody Clancy. 2002. *Eastern Cambridge Planning Study.* Commissioned by City of Cambridge, Massachusetts.

See also:
Mixed-Use Development
Office Buildings

David Dixon, FAIA, Goody Clancy, Boston, Massachusetts; David Spillane, Goody Clancy, Boston, Massachusetts

DESIGN CONSIDERATIONS

SAFETY

Crimes such as vandalism, terrorism, burglary, shoplifting, employee theft, assault, and espionage endanger lives and threaten the built environment. Increasingly, planners and urban designers are being called upon to address security and crime concerns in site and building design. The growth in the demand for security design poses challenges for planners and designers in determining essential security requirements, knowing security technology, and understanding the site and building design implications.

Security design is more than bars on windows, a security guard booth, a camera, or a wall. It is a systematic integration of design, technology, and operation for the protection of three critical assets: people, information, and property. Protection of these assets is a concern for all building types and should be considered throughout the planning, design, and construction processes.

Designing a site without security in mind can lead to expensive retrofitting with security equipment and increased security personnel. If not properly integrated, security equipment can distort key design elements and inhibit building function. Most important, planning without security can lead to successful legal claims against owners, architects, and building managers.

CRIME PREVENTION THROUGH ENVIRONMENTAL DESIGN GENERALLY

The process of designing security into planning and urban design is known as crime prevention through environmental design (CPTED). It involves designing the built environment to reduce the opportunity for, and fear of, stranger-to-stranger predatory crime. This approach to security design recognizes the intended use of space in a building. It is different from traditional crime prevention practice, which focuses on denying access to a crime target with barrier techniques such as locks, alarms, fences, and gates. CPTED takes advantage of opportunities for natural access control, surveillance, and territorial reinforcement. It is possible for natural and normal uses of the environment to meet the same security goals as physical and technical protection methods.

CPTED strategies are implemented three ways:

- *Electronic methods*: mechanical security products, target-hardening techniques, locks, alarms, closed circuit television (CCTV), and gadgets
- *Design methods*: building design and layout, site planning, planting, signage, and circulation control
- *Organizational methods*: manpower, police, security guards, receptionists, doormen, and business block watches

CPTED CONCEPTS

Concepts involved in crime prevention through environmental design are described below.

Defensible Space

Oscar Newman coined the expression "defensible space" to cover a range of mechanisms, real and symbolic barriers, strongly defined areas of influence, and improved opportunities for surveillance that combine to bring the environment under the control of its residents.

Natural Access Control

Natural access control involves decreasing opportunities for crime by denying access to crime targets and creating a perception of risk in offenders. It is accomplished by designing streets, sidewalks, building entrances, and neighborhood gateways to mark public routes and by using structural elements to discourage access to private areas.

Natural Surveillance

A design concept intended to make intruders easily observable, natural surveillance is promoted by features that maximize visibility of people, parking areas, and building entrances. Examples are doors and windows that look onto streets and parking areas, pedestrian-friendly sidewalks and streets, front porches, and adequate nighttime lighting.

Territorial Reinforcement

Physical design can create or extend a sphere of influence. In this setting, users develop a sense of territorial control, while potential offenders perceive this control and are discouraged from their criminal intentions. Territorial reinforcement is promoted by features that define property lines and distinguish private spaces from public spaces such as landscape plantings, pavement design, gateway treatments, and fences.

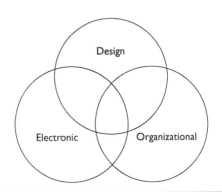

CPTED STRATEGIES

Source: Architectural Graphic Standards, 10th edition 2000.

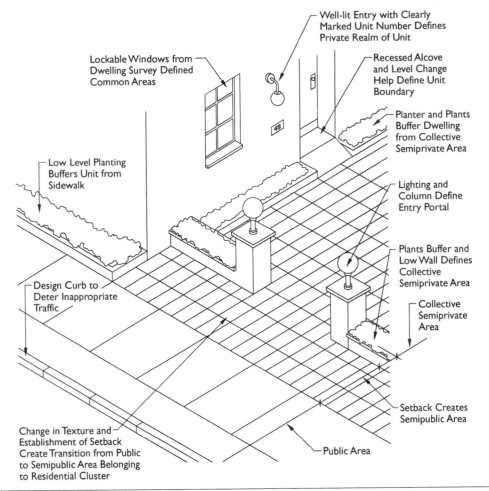

Well-lit Entry with Clearly Marked Unit Number Defines Private Realm of Unit

Lockable Windows from Dwelling Survey Defined Common Areas

Recessed Alcove and Level Change Help Define Unit Boundary

Planter and Plants Buffer Dwelling from Collective Semiprivate Area

Low Level Planting Buffers Unit from Sidewalk

Lighting and Column Define Entry Portal

Plants Buffer and Low Wall Defines Collective Semiprivate Area

Design Curb to Deter Inappropriate Traffic

Collective Semiprivate Area

Change in Texture and Establishment of Setback Create Transition from Public to Semipublic Area Belonging to Residential Cluster

Setback Creates Semipublic Area

Public Area

SECURITY LAYERING OF SPACES

Source: Architectural Graphic Standards, 10th edition 2000.

Randall I. Atlas, Ph.D. AIA CPP, Atlas Safety & Security Design, Inc., Miami, Florida

Management and Maintenance

Operational and management concepts that maintain buildings and facilities in good working order and that maintain a standard of care consistent with national and local standards contribute to the security effort. Equipment and materials used in a facility should be designed or selected with safety and security in mind.

Legitimate Activity Support

Legitimate activity for a space or building is encouraged through use of natural surveillance and lighting and architectural design that clearly defines the purpose of the structure or space. Crime prevention and design strategies can discourage illegal activity and protect a property from chronic problem activity.

CPTED AND COMMUNITY DESIGN

CPTED strategies related to the design of the planned environment on the community scale include the following:

- *Provide clear border definition of controlled space.* The intention of a potential offender is to commit an act without detection or risk of being recognized. The defining of boundaries declares an ownership of space and recognition of public versus private space. The declared space may then reach a point of becoming defensible.
- *Provide clearly marked transitional zones.* Transitional zones are a form of boundary definition and access control. They are areas where the user is made more clearly aware through the design of the environment that a change of ownership is taking place. The effort made to mark the entrance into the space reduces the range of excuses for improper behavior.
- *Relocate gathering areas.* The relocation of gathering spaces to areas with good natural surveillance and access control enables those spaces to become more active and likely to support activity.
- *Place safe activities in unsafe locations.* Safe activities bring safe users to a site, where they can serve as factors to control behavior. That said, the unsafe location must be within reason with respect to the activity pursued. A critical density of users must be reached to change the acceptability of behavior patterns.
- *Place unsafe activities in safe locations.* Vulnerable activities placed in areas with good natural surveillance and controlled space increases potential offenders' perception of risk. The controlled atmosphere maintains a level of accountability for the offender and provides security to those attempting to act in accordance.
- *Redesignate the use of space to provide natural barriers.* Define the boundaries of ownership through distance, natural terrain, and planted barriers, through site planning and landscape design. This process often results in a lower general cost to the owner and may create spaces in harmony with the natural environment.
- *Improve scheduling of space.* The effective use of space lowers risk, because the density of the space may be regulated for optimum physical and social features. Activities create a sense of place and control behavior through recognition of the intended user. Proper scheduling legitimizes various users to

achieve their individual goals while in accordance with the structure of the community.

- *Redesign space to increase the perception of natural surveillance.* An offender perceives risk only when he or she can be observed; thus, removing hiding places and incorporating improved natural and human-made site lines increases the risk of detection, deterring the presence of offenders. The redesign of space must also serve the nature of users, so as to increase the capability of the space to support more legitimate users.

Walls and objects to provide protection must support natural surveillance. Opaque walls define ownership, but they may also provide a hiding place or barrier from protection on the outside. Walls can also become obstacles for the legitimate users, such as police and rescue personnel. Open space lowers the cost of construction and improves natural surveillance of the environment.

SITE EVALUATION FOR THREATS AND VULNERABILITY

The CPTED and security analysis process can identify measures to address any identified security deficiencies that a site may present. Consider on- and off-site conditions, including topography, vegetation, adjacent land uses, circulation patterns, sight lines, potential areas for refuge or concealment, existing lighting conditions, and the types and locations of utilities, including their vulnerability to tampering or sabotage. Also consider off-site pedestrian and vehicular circulation, access points for service vehicles and personnel, employee access and circulation, and visitor access and circulation.

SECURITY LAYERING

Once the risks, threats, and vulnerabilities of a project have been assessed, analyze the potential security measures that could be used. The choices fall into the three CPTED strategy areas: organizational (people strategies), electronic (technology and hardware),

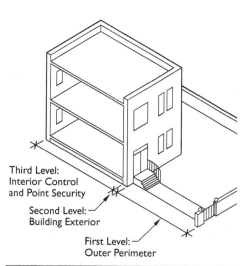

Third Level:
Interior Control
and Point Security

Second Level:
Building Exterior

First Level:
Outer Perimeter

CLASSIFICATIONS FOR VARIOUS LEVELS OF DEFENSE

Source: Architectural Graphic Standards, 10th edition 2000.

and design (design and circulation patterns). These classifications should be considered for each level of defense or security layer:

- First level: outer perimeter and site
- Second level: building exterior
- Third level: interior control and point security

In defensible space, these security layers are defined as public, semipublic, semiprivate, and private spaces.

LIGHTING FOR SECURITY

Security lighting does not prevent or stop crime, but it can help owners protect people and property. Good pedestrian lighting offers the natural surveillance people need to feel comfortable walking ahead or across a parking lot to their cars. Lighting can prevent surprises from "jump-out" criminals, or give pedestrians the opportunity to request assistance, to turn and go another way, or to retreat.

Security lighting goals should be to achieve a uniform, consistent level of light on both pedestrian and vehicular paths of travel. Lighting is critical for the illumination of street and building names and numbers for effective response by police, fire, and emergency personnel. Design lighting to avoid light intrusion into residential settings.

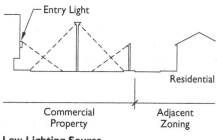

Low Lighting Source

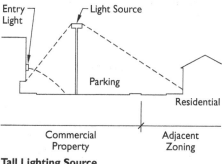

Tall Lighting Source

1. Proper beam control saves a system from glare, loss of light energy, and light intrusion.

2. Fixtures should be installed to cast a light pattern over a broad horizontal area rather than a tall vertical area.

3. Light surfaces reflect light more efficiently than dark surfaces.

4. Keep in mind the line of sight between the location of a light fixture and objects that may cast a shadow. Careful placement will avoid dark corners behind doors, trashcans, and other features.

SECURITY LIGHTING FOR COMMERCIAL PROPERTY

Source: Architectural Graphic Standards, 10th edition 2000.

Randall I. Atlas, Ph.D. AIA CPP, Atlas Safety & Security Design, Inc., Miami, Florida

RECOMMENDED LIGHTING LEVELS BY BUILDING TYPE (IN LUMENS)

SITE FEATURE	COMMERCIAL	INDUSTRIAL	RESIDENTIAL
Entrances	10	5	5
Public spaces	30	30	—
Private spaces	20	20	20
Self-parking	1.0	1.0	1.0
Attendant parking	2.0	2.0	2.0
Sidewalks	0.9	0.6	0.2

The quality of lighting may be an important security feature. Prevention of glare is essential, requiring the use of full or partial cutoff luminaires. True-color, full-spectrum light rendition can help with identification of vehicles and persons. Car lots and gas stations are examples of building types where metal halide luminaires are used for full-spectrum light rendition.

COMMERCIAL, OFFICE, AND INDUSTRIAL SECURITY STRATEGIES

Designing safe stores, shopping areas, office buildings, and industrial structures is critical to ensuring strong business draw and retention.

Commercial Structures

Commercial security measures and design must protect the patrons, property, and business information of a commercial business.

Commercial Storefronts
Natural Access Control
- Clearly mark public paths.
- Use signs to direct patrons to parking and entrances.
- Prevent easy access to the roof.
- Provide shops with rear parking lots with rear entrances.

Natural Surveillance
- Plan for good visibility. Rear parking lots should have building windows looking out onto them for easy surveillance. Signs in windows should cover no more than 15 percent of the window area. Unobstructed views should be available from the store to the street, sidewalk, parking areas, and passing vehicles.

- Light the building exterior well, but control glare.
- Avoid creating hiding spaces in loading areas.
- Create stormwater management areas to be visual amenities, such as a pond or smaller waterway, rather than a fenced area, but make them visible from nearby buildings and streets, for security.
- Provide visual or electronic surveillance for all entrances.

Territorial Reinforcement
- Where possible, mark property boundaries with hedges, low fences, or gates.
- Distinguish private areas from public spaces.
- Identify shops with wall signs for those parking in the rear.
- Specify awnings over rear doors and windows.

Commercial Shopping Areas
Natural Access Control
- Use signs to mark public entrances clearly.
- Clearly mark sidewalks and public areas with special paving and/or planting.
- Separate loading zones from public parking zones; designate limited delivery hours.
- Prevent exterior access from parking garages to adjacent rooftops.

Natural Surveillance
- Light parking areas well. Use high-intensity lighting using special cutoff luminaires in parking garages to minimize hiding places. In addition, make all levels of the parking garage visible from the street or ground floor.
- Avoid creating loading areas with dead-end alleys or blind spots.

Territorial Reinforcement
- Define property perimeters with planting, post-and-pillar fencing, and gates.
- Keep the number of entrances as low as possible and make them obvious and celebrated.

Management
- Assign close-in parking for nighttime employees.
- Help business associations work together to promote shopper and business safety.

Commercial Drive-Throughs
Natural Surveillance
- Locate ATMs in bank vestibules accessed by ATM cards and facing main roads, or as a drive-through in the drive-in teller lanes.
- Place the ordering station for a restaurant within sight of the restaurant interior.

Office Buildings

Office building security focuses on the safety and security of people, goods, and services. Office building security can assume a high or low profile based on the type and number of building users.

Natural Access Control
- Clearly define public entrances with walkways and signs.
- Accentuate building entrances with architectural elements, lighting, and planting or paving stones.

Natural Surveillance
- Well-light all exterior doors, hallways, parking areas, and walkways.
- Avoid Dumpster placement that creates blind spots or hiding places.
- Make all windows and exterior doors visible from the street or to neighbors.
- Provide windows on all four façades.
- Do not obstruct windows with signs.
- Assign parking spaces to each employee and visitor.
- Make parking areas visible from the windows; make side parking areas visible from the street.
- Keep shrubbery below 3 feet and tree branches at least 10 feet above the ground for good visibility.

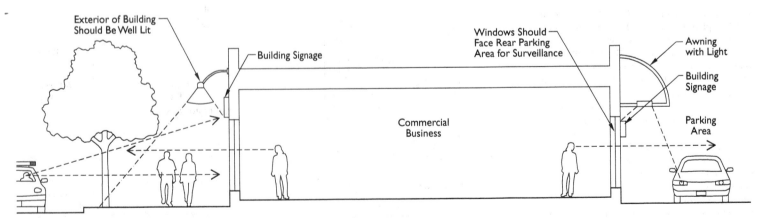

Note: Clear visibility should be maintained from store to sidewalk, street, parking areas, and passing vehicles. Window signs should cover no more than 15 percent of any window area.

NATURAL SURVEILLANCE FOR COMMERCIAL PROPERTY

Source: Architectural Graphic Standards, *10th edition 2000.*

Randall I. Atlas, Ph.D. AIA CPP, Atlas Safety & Security Design, Inc., Miami, Florida

Territorial Reinforcement

- Define the perimeter with planting or fencing.
- Design fences to permit visibility from the street.
- Make exterior private areas easily distinguishable from public areas.
- Position a security or a reception area to screen all entrances.

Industrial Buildings

Industrial enterprises need to protect the assets in their facilities. Special security consideration must be given to receiving and outgoing areas, to reduce theft. Individual building tenants should have security technology availability for continuous monitoring and supervision of their space.

Natural Access Control

- Avoid creating dead-end spaces.
- Make site entrances easy to secure.
- Control entrances to parking areas with fences, gates, or an attendant's booth.
- Assign parking by shifts and ensure that late workers have the close-in spaces.
- Restrict access to railroad tracks.
- Plan storage yards for vehicular access by patrol car.
- Avoid access to roofs via Dumpsters, loading docks, poles, or stacked items, for example.
- Keep delivery entrances separate; make sure they are well marked and monitored.
- Place employee entrances close to employee parking and work areas.
- Separate nighttime parking areas from service entrances.
- Avoid providing access from one part of the building into other areas.

Natural Surveillance

- Ensure all entrances are well lit, well defined, and visible to public and patrol vehicles.
- Design parking areas to be visible to patrol cars, pedestrians, parking attendants, and/or building personnel.
- Position the parking attendant for maximum visibility of the property.
- Give reception areas a view of parking areas.
- Use walls only when necessary.
- Avoid creating blind alleys, storage yards, and other out-of-the-way places with hiding places.

RESIDENTIAL SITE SECURITY STRATEGIES

Designing CPTED and security features into residential buildings and neighborhoods can reduce opportunities for, and vulnerability to, criminal behavior and help create a sense of community. The goal in residential design is to create safe dwelling places through limited access to properties, good surveillance, and a sense of ownership and responsibility.

Single-Family Dwellings
Natural Access Control and Surveillance

- Use walkways and landscaping to direct visitors to the proper entrance and away from private areas.
- Well-light all doorways that open to the outside, sidewalks, and all areas of the yard.
- Make the front door at least partially visible from the street and clearly visible from the driveway.

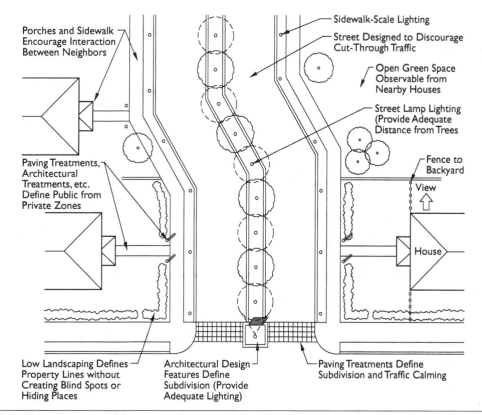

CRIME PREVENTION THROUGH ENVIRONMENTAL DESIGN—PLANNING FOR SUBDIVISIONS

Source: Architectural Graphic Standards, 10th edition 2000.

- Install windows on all sides of the house with full views of the property. The driveway should be visible from the front or back door and from at least one window.
- Properly maintain planting to provide good views to and from the house.

Territorial Reinforcement

- Provide front porches or stoops to create a transitional area between the street and the house.
- Define property lines and private areas with plantings, pavement treatments, or fences.
- Make the street address clearly visible from the street.

Subdivisions
Natural Access Control

- Provide paving treatments, plantings, and design features, such as columned gateways, to guide visitors away from private areas.
- Locate walkways where they can direct pedestrian traffic and remain unobscured.

Natural Surveillance

- Maintain planting to avoid creating blind spots or hiding places.
- Locate parks, open spaces, and recreational areas so they can be observed from nearby houses.

Territorial Reinforcement

- Design lots, streets, and houses to encourage interaction between neighbors.
- Accent entrances with changes in street elevation,

different paving materials, and other design features.
- Clearly identify residences with street address numbers.
- Define property lines with post-and-pillar fencing, gates, and plantings to direct pedestrian traffic.

Multifamily Dwellings
Natural Access Control

- Avoid constructing balcony railings of a solid, opaque material. Railings should be no more than 42 inches high.
- Define parking lot entrances with curbs, planting, or structural design features; block dead-end areas with a fence or gate.
- Well-light hallways, and centrally locate elevators and stairs.
- Provide common building entrances with locks that automatically engage when the door closes.
- Limit access to the building to no more than two points. No more than four units should share the same entrance.

Natural Surveillance

- Make exterior doors visible to the street or neighbors, and ensure they are well lighted.
- Provide windows on all four building façades. Orient buildings so the windows and doors of one unit are visible from those of other units.
- Well-light all parking areas and walkways.
- Make parks, open spaces, and recreational areas visible from a multitude of windows and doors.
- Avoid Dumpster placement that creates blind spots or hiding places.

Randall I. Atlas, Ph.D. AIA CPP, Atlas Safety & Security Design, Inc., Miami, Florida

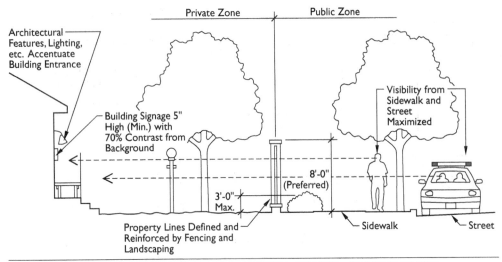

CRIME PREVENTION THROUGH ENVIRONMENTAL DESIGN—PLANNING FOR RESIDENTIAL PROPERTY

Source:Architectural Graphic Standards, 10th edition 2000.

- Make elevators and stairwells clearly visible from windows and doors. In addition, they should be well lighted and open to view.
- For clear visibility, maintain shrubbery to be no more than 3 feet high and tree canopies not lower than 8.5 feet.

Territorial Reinforcement

- Define property lines with planting or post-and-pillar fencing, but keep shrubbery and fences low to allow visibility from the street.
- Accent building entrances with architectural elements and lighting or landscape features.
- Install doorknobs 40 inches from windowpanes.
- Clearly identify all buildings and residential units with well-lighted address numbers.
- Provide common doorways with windows that are key-controlled by residents.
- Locate mailboxes next to the appropriate residences.

Site Security Planning for Terrorism

Security planning processes for the twenty-first century will require a holistic approach that includes social and physical planning concerns and acts of terror. Terrorism has impacts on major functions of infrastructure within the planning realm, such as transportation, communications, utilities, and delivery of public services.

While planning has addressed both natural and human-made disasters through the area of disaster planning and hazards mitigation, concerns regarding terrorism have increased, with an amplified emphasis on the security implications of evacuation routes and traffic flows. In addition, built environment features such as gated communities, walled neighborhoods, cul-de-sacs, service alleys, building setbacks, and mixed-use development can have significant security considerations.

The safety and security of a building, its site, and its users are important design criteria. Increased threats to people and property from acts of terrorism, workplace violence, and street crime make it important to identify security issues and establish a plan to manage the risks.

SECURITY ASSESSMENT

An assessment of the security requirements should be made as early as possible before the design phase of a project. Determining the security requirements is mainly a matter of managing the perceived risks. Although the assessment is the owner's responsibility, planners should review the impact of growth and development to address overall security and safety issues. Failure to identify security issues will surely result in design changes, delays, and project cost increases.

A security assessment should answer four questions:

- What are the assets—persons, places, information, and property—that require security protection?
- What are the criminal or other threats—street crime, workplace violence, terrorism, and sabotage—against which the assets must be protected? Are the threats highly probable, possible, or unlikely?
- How vulnerable are the assets to the threats (e.g., if workplace violence is identified as a threat, can

unauthorized persons enter private workspaces unchallenged)?
- What countermeasures are required to mitigate the threat (e.g., is the circulation pattern designed to channel visitors through controlled site-access portals)?

The cost of achieving the correct level of site-based protection may be high, depending on the nature of the protected assets and the perceived threat to them. After the recommended countermeasures have been identified, organize them according to their priority and ask the owner to select those that are prudent and cost-effective for the project. In the case of federal projects (and many state and local government projects as well), the assessment results in the assignment of a defined level of protection (LOP), with specific countermeasures attached to each level.

Risk assessment and security design are especially relevant in schools, hospitals, airports, office buildings, and multifamily apartment buildings. In recent years, terrorists have targeted such buildings because of their "architectural vulnerability," so it is clearly important to address security issues in their site planning and design.

SECURITY LAYERING

One way to think about security requirements is as a layering process. The first layer, the site perimeter of the property, is the first line of defense. The U.S. Department of State seeks setbacks of at least 100 feet for new buildings; and even at that distance, securing the perimeter is difficult in most urban settings. The building skin of the structure is the next layer. Sensitive areas within a building are deeper layers requiring protection. Finally, at the center of all the layers, are the particular persons, information, or property that may require point protection.

SITE SECURITY DESIGN STANDARDS

In response to recent terrorism events, several organizations have developed design guidelines or standards to help mitigate the potential for impacts to structures. No single set of standards or codes has been developed, however, to address both public and

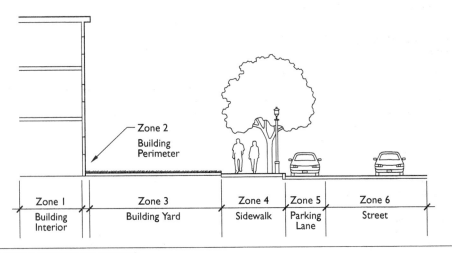

BUILDING SECURITY ZONES

Source: Courtesy of the National Capital Planning Commission.

Randall I. Atlas, Ph.D. AIA CPP, Atlas Safety & Security Design, Inc., Miami, Florida

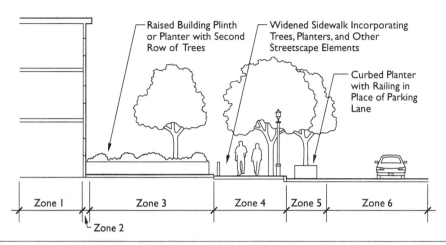

Raised Building Plinth or Planter with Second Row of Trees

Widened Sidewalk Incorporating Trees, Planters, and Other Streetscape Elements

Curbed Planter with Railing in Place of Parking Lane

Zone 1 | Zone 2 | Zone 3 | Zone 4 | Zone 5 | Zone 6

SECURITY ELEMENTS IN BUILDING SECURITY ZONES

Source: Courtesy of the National Capital Planning Commission.

private sector buildings. Among the guidance produced to date are the following:

- American Planning Association, *Policy Guide on Security* (2005) www.planning.org/policyguides/pdf/security.pdf
- Interagency Security Committee (ISC), *Security Design Criteria for New Federal Office Buildings and Major Modernization Projects: A Review and Commentary* (2004)
- General Services Administration (GSA), *Facility Standards for the Public Building Service* (2003)
- Federal Emergency Management Agency (FEMA) 426, *Manual to Mitigate Potential Terrorism Attacks Against Buildings* (2003)

- GSA, *Progressive Collapse Analysis and Design Guidelines for New Federal Office Buildings and Major Modernization Projects* (2003)
- National Capital Planning Commission (NCPC), *Designing for Security in the Nation's Capital* (2001)

For any project, conduct a project-specific risk assessment to determine which approaches should be applied or which standards should be used. Determine at the onset of a project the level of security that is desired. Design features and elements should be used in a manner that enhances a building's security without compromising its aesthetics and functionality.

In an urban setting, planners and designers will likely have to make trade-offs, to achieve a balance between security and design. Among the elements to consider are pedestrian and vehicular access points, feasible building setback distances, parking and loading security, and exterior design features and elements, including site lighting, site signage, landscape planting, and bollards.

RESOURCES

Federal Emergency Management Agency (FEMA) 426. 2003. *Manual to Mitigate Potential Terrorist Attacks Against Buildings.* Washington, D.C.: Federal Emergency Management Agency. www.fema.gov/pdf/fima/426/fema426.pdf

General Services Administration. 2003. *Facility Standards for the Public Building Service.* Washington, D.C.: Government Printing Office.

General Services Administration. 2003. *Progressive Collapse Analysis and Design Guidelines for New Federal Office Buildings and Major Modernization Projects.* Washington, D.C.: Government Printing Office.

Interagency Security Committee. 2004. *Security Design Criteria for New Federal Office Buildings and Major Modernization Projects: A Review and Commentary.* Washington, D.C.: National Academies Press.

National Capital Planning Commission Interagency Task Force. 2001. *Designing for Security in the Nation's Capital.* Washington, D.C.: National Capital Planning Commission.

See also:
Streetscape

Randall I. Atlas, Ph.D. AIA CPP, Atlas Safety & Security Design, Inc., Miami, Florida

DESIGN CONSIDERATIONS

WALKABILITY

Walking is the most basic mode of transportation available to human beings. It has been a factor in the design of communities from the earliest human settlements. More recently, however, the terms "walkable" and "walkability" have been given new meaning as a result of efforts to address the multiple problems caused by designing communities primarily for motorized travel. Concern over the negative health impacts of sedentary lifestyles has also focused greater attention on walkability and the role of walking in promoting the health, safety, and welfare of residents.

In that context, "walkable" and "walkability" refer to the broad range of community design features that support walking. At the macroscale, planners and urban designers must consider the mix of land uses along with issues related to site and roadway network design. At the microscale, walkability requires careful attention to detail and to the design of sidewalks, crosswalks, building façades, benches, and other elements of human-scale design.

A walkable community is ultimately a place in which residents of all ages and abilities feel that it is safe, comfortable, convenient, efficient, and welcoming to walk, not only for recreation but also for utility and transportation.

WALKING SPEEDS AND DISTANCES

The average adult walks 3.0 to 4.0 feet per second, or 2.05 to 2.73 mph. Transportation planners use 4.0 feet per second as the amount of time pedestrians need to cross a street. However, children, seniors, and people with disabilities may walk only 2.0 or 2.5 feet per second. There is a possibility that the standard may be reduced to 3.5 feet per second, in recognition of the overall aging of the population.

The speed at which people walk is the critical measure that helps define the size of a walkable community or neighborhood. Most residents typically walk to destinations that are five minutes from their homes (Untermann, 1984). If the distance is greater, people with access to an automobile are more likely to use it, unless the quality of the walking experience is high or there are constraints on driving such as traffic congestion, limited parking, or parking charges, for example. At 3.0 feet per second, a person can walk from 1/6 to 1/3 of a mile in 5 to 10 minutes. At 4.0 feet per second, a person can reach a destination of 1/4 mile in 5.5 minutes. Using the 1/4-mile walk as the standard, a walkable neighborhood covers approximately 125 acres.

WIDTH NEEDS FOR WALKING

An average-sized person requires 1.5 to 2.0 feet of width while standing. A person walking needs approximately 3 to 4 feet of width, to allow for swaying or carrying a bag or briefcase. Since walking is often a social activity, a minimum of 5.0 feet of clear unobstructed space for two individuals to walk side by side is required. When a sidewalk is adjacent to a wall, building, or fence, an additional 1.0 to 2.0 feet of "shy" distance should be provided.

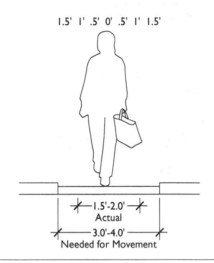

WALKING SPACE FOR ONE PERSON

Source: Dan Burden, Walkable Communities.

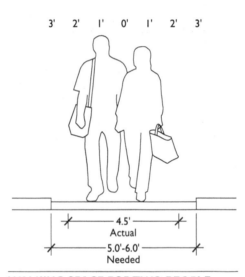

WALKING SPACE FOR TWO PEOPLE

Source: Dan Burden, Walkable Communities.

SIDEWALK DESIGN

Well-designed sidewalks provide the necessary comfort, safety, and sense of welcome to support walking. Sidewalks should be designed with a buffer between the sidewalk and the street. In commercial areas, the buffer is often the "furniture zone" where utility poles, trees, hydrants, signs, benches, transit shelters, and planters should be placed. The furniture zone in a low-density commercial zone should be a minimum of 4.0 feet wide, and commonly is 5.0 to 8.0 feet wide.

In residential areas, a continuous landscape planted strip or parkway is strongly recommended to create a "detached" or "setback" sidewalk. Trees in the planted strip create a tree canopy that shades the street and sidewalk. Ideally, the planted area should be a minimum of 6.0 feet for healthy tree growth.

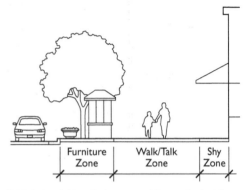

Well-designed sidewalks in commercial areas clearly delineate the three different zones.

COMMERCIAL SIDEWALK ZONES

Source: Dan Burden, Walkable Communities.

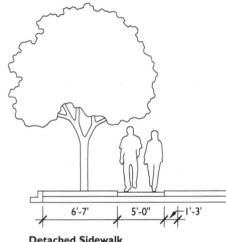

Detached Sidewalk

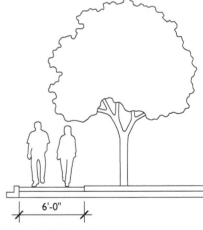

Attached Sidewalk

Detached sidewalks should be at least 5 feet wide. Attached sidewalks should be at least 6 feet wide.

MINIMUM WIDTHS FOR SIDEWALKS

Source: Dan Burden, Walkable Communities.

Paul Zykofsky, AICP, Local Government Commission, Sacramento, California; Dan Burden, Walkable Communities, High Springs, Florida

Even in constrained situations, a narrower planting strip should be included. The planted strip buffers pedestrians from motor vehicles and helps accommodate curb-cuts without having to slope the sidewalk, which otherwise may result in a violation of the Americans with Disabilities Act (ADA) requirements for cross-slopes.

If a planted strip cannot be accommodated due to space limitations, and the sidewalk must be attached to the curb, provide an extra 1.0 to 2.0 feet in width as an added buffer. Rolled curbs should be avoided, because they typically result in drivers parking up on the sidewalk and intruding on the pedestrian realm. (See *Sidewalks* in Part 3 of this book for further details on sidewalk design.)

STREET DESIGN

The design of the street itself strongly influences whether individuals feel safe or comfortable walking. Pedestrians stay away from streets with high speeds and high volumes (Appleyard, 1980). To encourage people to walk, residential streets need to be designed to maintain speeds below 25 mph. Busier avenues should be designed to maintain speeds below 35 mph. In residential areas, this usually translates into narrow streets with short blocks and compact intersections on which motorists feel uncomfortable traveling faster than the 25 mph "design speed."

CROSSWALK DESIGN

Pedestrians are exposed to the greatest danger when they cross the street; thus careful attention should be given to designing safe, well-marked crosswalks. Slower vehicle speeds and shorter crossing distances help improve safety. For streets with on-street park-

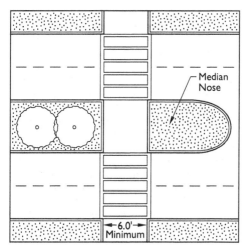

A median refuge provides added protection for pedestrians on wide streets.

MEDIAN REFUGE

Source: Dan Burden, Walkable Communities.

ing, curb extensions—also called "neckdowns" or "bulb-outs"—located at intersections and midblock crossing locations provide multiple benefits: they help slow traffic entering and exiting the street, reduce the crossing distance, and make it easier to see and be seen by motorists.

In commercial areas, crosswalks should be at least 12 feet wide to allow people to flow in both directions. On wide streets, median refuges or islands with a median "nose" can provide added protection for pedestrians. Ideally, the clear path for pedestrians through the median island should be 6.0 feet. Countdown signals that let pedestrians know how much time they have left to cross are also helpful.

At midblock crossing locations, refuge islands are strongly recommended. An innovative design for median refuges angles the crossing area by 45 degrees, which forces pedestrians to look in the direction of oncoming traffic. In-pavement flashing lights that warn motorists when a person is crossing the street can provide an added measure of safety.

LAND-USE MIX

At the macroscale, the mix of land uses is key to ensuring that there are nearby destinations to which people can walk. Walkable community design is based on the patterns of traditional neighborhoods that include retail, civic, educational, and recreational uses in close proximity to residential uses. A "pedestrian shed" is the area within the 1/4-mile to 1/2-mile radius that people will walk. At appropriate density levels, a pedestrian shed can typically support a neighborhood commercial center or school. This mix of uses not only provides a wealth of destinations in close enough proximity to entice people to walk, but can help provide security through more "eyes on the street" at different times of the day and night.

ROUTE CONNECTIVITY

Walkable communities require multiple route connections so that pedestrians do not have to take lengthy detours to reach their destinations. A detour of 200 feet, which is imperceptible to a motorist, adds an additional minute of travel in each direction for a pedestrian. Small blocks, typically less than 300 feet long, with multiple connections, are critical to supporting walkability.

Most pedestrians will not walk more than 150 to 200 feet out of their way to cross the street at an intersection. As a result, in areas with a high volume of pedestrians, blocks that are longer than 400 feet should provide carefully designed midblock crossings with curb extensions, median refuges, and other features to ensure pedestrian safety. Where the street network is interrupted, due to topographical features, to prevent through-traffic, or for other reasons, safe trail connections should be provided for pedestrians and bicyclists.

A road network with high connectivity also helps to prevent funneling large volumes of motor vehicle traffic onto high-speed, high-capacity arterials. These roadways are typically not accommodating to pedestrians and pose a significant barrier to walkability.

SITE PLANNING CONSIDERATIONS

Locate automobile-oriented elements, such as driveways, garages, parking lots, and drive-through establishments, away from sidewalks and the pedestrian realm to the extent possible. In residential neighborhoods, garages should be either set back or accessed through alleys, where possible. Windows and porches should be provided on the front of residential structures.

In commercial districts, buildings should provide a continuous street wall with activated spaces and transparency at the ground-floor level to draw pedestrians along the street. Blank walls should be avoided, and parking lots should be placed behind buildings. Front entrances should face the street with secondary access from parking lots, if necessary. The placement of buildings close to the property line, with windows looking out on the sidewalk, improves safety and surveillance and helps create the sense of enclosure that human beings find more comfortable.

HUMAN-SCALE DESIGN

At the microscale, designing walkable communities requires a greater attention to detail than designing for the motorist. Pedestrians traveling at 3.5 feet per second notice the details on a building's façade, items in

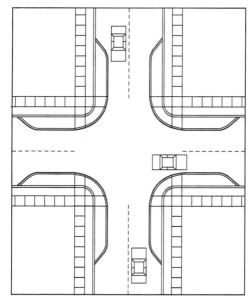

Curb extensions such as neckdowns and chokers help slow traffic, reduce crossing distance, and improve visibility of pedestrians.

NECKDOWNS

Source: Appleyard 1980.

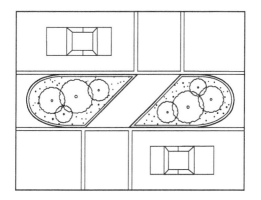

The angled crossing area forces pedestrians to look in the direction of oncoming traffic.

ANGLED CROSSWALK

Source: Dan Burden, Walkable Communities.

Paul Zykofsky, AICP, Local Government Commission, Sacramento, California; Dan Burden, Walkable Communities, High Springs, Florida

a display window, the slope of a sidewalk, or the quality of a bench. Urban designers and planners need to work closely with architects and traffic engineers to ensure that the multiple details that comprise the street and sidewalk are carefully considered. Human-scale design can help make the pedestrian feel welcome.

IMPLEMENTATION

Planners and urban designers should strive to create walkable-scale communities with a mix of land uses, a well-connected network of short blocks, and slow, quiet streets. On-street parking, landscape planted strips and vertical curbs provide a buffer for pedestrians and a tree canopy. Sidewalks should be at least 5 feet wide, and homes and businesses should enclose the street and provide for natural surveillance through front porches, windows, and storefronts.

Retrofitting Older Communities

Most neighborhoods built in the United States prior to World War II contain many of the land-use and community design features associated with walkability. Where these communities have deteriorated due to high volumes of drive-through traffic or high vehicle speeds, steps should be taken to implement traffic-calming programs and related revitalization strategies to bring back safe and walkable areas.

Single-use suburban neighborhoods present a specific walkability challenge. Streets are often wide and unfriendly to pedestrians. Traffic-calming measures can often help, but additional steps are likely necessary to address overly wide streets and lack of connectivity. One approach is a "road diet," where excess lanes are removed to add parking, bicycle lanes, or turning lanes, and to slow vehicle speeds to safer levels. Most road diets involve reducing four-lane roads to two travel lanes, with a central turning lane or median, and adding bicycle lanes or parking. Generally, roadway capacity often remains unchanged, but vehicle speeds drop, safety improves, and walking increases. Other approaches that can be taken include adding midblock crosswalks and pedestrian linkages and connections when opportunities arise.

CONCLUSION

Creating walkable, livable neighborhoods requires careful coordination between different disciplines and attention to detail. Planners need to consider the importance of providing a good mix of land uses and connectivity. Along with traffic engineers, planners must also consider the need for a high degree of street and route connectivity and for the proper design of slow, safe streets and compact intersections with well-designed crosswalks. Planners, urban designers, architects, and landscape architects need to carefully consider where to locate buildings, building entrances, and parking on the site, and how to design human-scale, visually engaging places to encourage walking.

REFERENCES

Appleyard, Donald. 1980. *Livable Streets*. Berkeley, CA: University of California Press.

Burden, Dan. 1999. *Street Design Guidelines for Healthy Neighborhoods*. Sacramento: Local Government Commission.

Untermann, Richard K. 1984. *Accommodating the Pedestrian — Adapting Towns and Neighborhoods for Walking and Bicycling*. New York: Van Nostrand Reinhold.

See also:
Pedestrian-Friendly Streets
Sidewalks
Streetscape
Street Networks and Street Connectivity
Traffic Calming

Paul Zykofsky, AICP, Local Government Commission, Sacramento, California; Dan Burden, Walkable Communities, High Springs, Florida

LEADERSHIP IN ENERGY AND ENVIRONMENTAL DESIGN—LEED

The Leadership in Energy and Environmental Design (LEED) Green Building Rating System® is a voluntary standard for developing high-performance, sustainable buildings. Members of the U.S. Green Building Council (USGBC), representing all segments of the building industry, developed LEED and continue to contribute to its evolution. The USGBC works to promote buildings that are environmentally responsible, profitable, and healthy places to live and work.

LEED standards are currently available for the following:

- New commercial construction and major renovation projects (LEED-NC)
- Existing building operations (LEED-EB)
- Commercial interiors projects (LEED-CI)

Standards are under development for:

- core and shell projects (LEED-CS);
- neighborhood developments (LEED-ND); and
- homes (LEED-H) (in development).

According to the USGBC, LEED was created to:

- define "green building" by establishing a common standard of measurement;
- promote integrated, whole-building design practices;
- recognize environmental leadership in the building industry;
- stimulate green competition;
- raise consumer awareness of green building benefits; and
- transform the building market.

LEED CERTIFICATION

LEED defines a quantifiable threshold for green buildings and provides a tool to promote and guide comprehensive and integrated building design. LEED is self-evaluating and self-documenting, but not self-certifying. Certification is done solely by the USGBC. The LEED Green Building Rating System® for new commercial construction and major renovation projects (LEED-NC) has four levels of certification, based upon the number of points achieved by a project, out of a total of 69 possible:

LEED certified: 26 to 32 points, or 40 percent of base points

Silver level: 33 to 38 points, or 50 percent of base points

LEED™ Scorecard

0	0	0	Total Project Score		Possible Points	69
			Certified 26 to 32 Points Silver 33 to 38 Points Gold 39 to 51 Points Platinum 52 or More Points			

0	0	0	Sustainable Sites		Possible Points	14
Y	?	N				
Y			Prereq 1	Erosion and Sedimentation Control		0
			Credit 1	Site Selection		1
			Credit 2	Urban Redevelopment		1
			Credit 3	Brownfield Redevelopment		1
			Credit 4.1	Alternative Transportation, Public Transportation Access		1
			Credit 4.2	Alternative Transportation, Bicycle Storage, and Changing Rooms		1
			Credit 4.3	Alternative Transportation, Alternative Fuel Refueling Stations		1
			Credit 4.4	Alternative Transportation, Parking Capacity		1
			Credit 5.1	Reduced Site Disturbance, Protect or Restore Open Space		1
			Credit 5.2	Reduced Site Disturbance, Development Footprint		1
			Credit 6.1	Stormwater Management, Rate, and Quantity		1
			Credit 6.2	Stormwater Management, Treatment		1
			Credit 7.1	Landscape and Exterior Design to Reduce Heat Islands, Nonroof		1
			Credit 7.2	Landscape and Exterior Design to Reduce Heat Islands, Roof		1
			Credit 8	Light Pollution Reduction		1

0	0	0	Water Efficiency		Possible Points	5
Y	?	N				
			Credit 1.1	Water-Efficient Landscaping, Reduce by 50%		1
			Credit 1.2	Water-Efficient Landscaping, No Potable Use or No Irrigation		1
			Credit 2	Innovative Wastewater Technologies		1
			Credit 3.1	Water-Use Reduction, 20% Reduction		1
			Credit 3.2	Water-Use Reduction, 30% Reduction		1

0	0	0	Energy and Atmosphere		Possible Points	17
Y	?	N				
Y			Prereq 1	Fundamental Building Systems Commissioning		0
Y			Prereq 2	Minimum Energy Performance		0
Y			Prereq 3	CFC Reduction in HVAC&R Equipment		0
			Credit 1.1	Optimize Energy Performance, 20% New/10% Existing		2
			Credit 1.2	Optimize Energy Performance, 30% New/20% Existing		2
			Credit 1.3	Optimize Energy Performance, 40% New/30% Existing		2
			Credit 1.4	Optimize Energy Performance, 50% New/40% Existing		2
			Credit 1.5	Optimize Energy Performance, 60% New/50% Existing		2
			Credit 2.1	Renewable Energy, 5%		1
			Credit 2.2	Renewable Energy, 10%		1
			Credit 2.3	Renewable Energy, 20%		1
			Credit 3	Additional Commissioning		1
			Credit 4	Ozone Depletion		1
			Credit 5	Measurement and Verification		1
			Credit 6	Green Power		1

0	0	0	Materials and Resources		Possible Points	13
Y	?	N				
Y			Prereq 1	Storage and Collection of Recyclables		0
			Credit 1.1	Building Reuse, Maintain 75% of Existing Shell		1
			Credit 1.2	Building Reuse, Maintain 100% of Existing Shell		1
			Credit 1.3	Building Reuse, Maintain 100% of Shell and 50% Nonshell		1
			Credit 2.1	Construction Waste Management, Divert 50%		1
			Credit 2.2	Construction Waste Management, Divert 75%		1
			Credit 3.1	Resource Reuse, Specify 5%		1
			Credit 3.2	Resource Reuse, Specify 10%		1
			Credit 4.1	Resource Reuse, Specify 25%		1
			Credit 4.2	Resource Reuse, Specify 50%		1
			Credit 5.1	Local/Regional Materials, 20% Manufactured Locally		1
			Credit 5.2	Local/Regional Materials, of 20% Above, 50% Harvested Locally		1
			Credit 6	Rapidly Renewable Materials		1
			Credit 7	Certified Wood		1

0	0	0	Indoor Environmental Quality		Possible Points	15
Y	?	N				
Y			Prereq 1	Minimum IAQ Performance		0
Y			Prereq 2	Environmental Tobacco Smoke (ETS) Control		0
			Credit 1	Carbon Dioxide (CO_2) Monitoring		1
			Credit 2	Increase Ventilation Effectiveness		1
			Credit 3.1	Construction IAQ Management Plan, During Construction		1
			Credit 3.2	Construction IAQ Management Plan, Before Occupancy		1
			Credit 4.1	Low-Emitting Materials, Adhesives, and Sealants		1
			Credit 4.2	Low-Emitting Materials, Paints		1
			Credit 4.3	Low-Emitting Materials, Carpet		1
			Credit 4.4	Low-Emitting Materials, Composite Wood		1
			Credit 5	Indoor Chemical and Pollutant Source Control		1
			Credit 6.1	Controllability of Systems, Perimeter		1
			Credit 6.2	Controllability of Systems, Nonperimeter		1
			Credit 7.1	Thermal Comfort, Comply with ASHRAE 55-1992		1
			Credit 7.2	Thermal Comfort, Permanent Monitoring System		1
			Credit 8.1	Daylight and Views, Daylight 75% of Space		1
			Credit 8.2	Daylight and Views, Views for 90% of Space		1

0	0	0	Innovation and Design Process		Possible Points	5
Y	?	N				
			Credit 1.1	Innovation in Design: Specific Title		1
			Credit 1.2	Innovation in Design: Specific Title		1
			Credit 1.3	Innovation in Design: Specific Title		1
			Credit 1.4	Innovation in Design: Specific Title		1
			Credit 2	LEED™-Accredited Professional		1

LEED PROJECT CHECKLIST

Source: U.S. Green Building Council 2003.

Lee Fithian, AIA, Benham, Oklahoma City, Oklahoma

DESIGN CONSIDERATIONS

Gold level: 39 to 51 points, or 60 percent of base points

Platinum level: 52-plus points, or 80 percent of base points

As of February 2005, there were LEED-certified or -registered projects in all 50 states and in 14 countries. There were a total of 167 certified projects and 1,8381635 registered projects (projects must be registered before they can be considered for LEED certification). To achieve LEED certification, each project must meet the sustainable design and performance criteria set forth in the LEED Green Building Rating System® and submit a complete application with the required documentation to the USGBC for review.

LEED PROJECT CHECKLIST

The rating system consists of six broad categories for achieving points: sustainable sites, water efficiency, energy and atmosphere, materials and resources, indoor environmental quality, and innovation and design process. Projects earn one or more points toward certification by meeting or exceeding each credit's technical requirements.

Sustainable Sites

The sustainable sites category has a total of 14 possible points. Of the six LEED categories, this category has perhaps the most significant planning implications. The points that can be awarded support infill development, brownfields redevelopment, historic preservation, transit-oriented development, land conservation, and biodiversity protection, among other goals. Not all the credits can be described here, but the three examples that follow are representative of the areas addressed:

- *Site selection credit.* Requires that buildings, roads, and parking areas are not developed on portions of sites that meet any one of the following criteria: prime farmland, as defined by the U.S. Department of Agriculture; land whose elevation is lower than 5 feet above the 100-year flood elevation, as defined by the Federal Emergency Management Agency (FEMA); land that is specifically identified as habitat for any species on federal or state threatened or endangered lists; land that is within 100 feet of any water, including wetlands; and land that prior to acquisition for the project was public parkland, unless land of equal or greater value as parkland is accepted in trade by the public landowner.
- *Development density credit.* Is intended to direct development to areas with existing infrastructure, protect greenfields, and preserve habitat and natural resources. It requires that developments increase localized density to conform to existing or desired density goals by using sites located within an existing minimum development density of 60,000 square feet per acre.
- *Brownfields development credit.* Encourages the use of sites that have been either classified contaminated through a Phase II environmental site assessment or classified as a brownfield by a local, state, or federal government agency. The alternative transportation credit awards a point for locating development within a half-mile of a commuter rail,

light rail, or subway/heavy rail station, or one-quarter mile of two or more bus lines. Additional points can be awarded for supporting cyclists and alternative means of transportation.

Water Efficiency

A total of 5 points can be achieved through water efficiency. This LEED area focuses on strategies to increase water conservation for both the facility and its site. Points are awarded for water-efficient fixtures and reduced irrigation requirements, as well as innovative wastewater technologies. Water-efficient landscaping includes reducing irrigation requirements by 50 percent, not using potable water for irrigation, or not installing a permanent irrigation system. Innovative wastewater technologies include reducing potable water use for wastewater treatment or using alternative on-site wastewater treatment systems. Water-use reduction involves reducing water use by 20 percent as compared to the baseline for the building, with an additional point if consumption is reduced by 30 percent. Strategies to achieve these points, while reducing potable water usage and treatment, will require coordination with code and permitting officials.

Energy and Atmosphere

Of the total 69 points that can be achieved, the majority (17) are in this section. Emphasis is placed on quality control in the built environment, envelope and mechanical systems performance, reduction in chlorofluorocarbons (CFCs) in equipment, and support for alternative energy, including renewable energy sources. The green power credit involves providing at least 50 percent of the building's electricity from renewable sources by entering in a minimum two-year renewable energy contract. However, renewable energy technologies may not be available to all regions of the country, thereby reducing the number of points available.

Materials and Resources

A total of 13 points can be achieved here. The materials and resources category focuses on life-cycle analysis, including design for deconstruction and adaptability, certified wood sources, and environmentally preferable materials. A number of points are available to support preserving historic and cultural resources. Several points are given to divert waste from landfills through construction waste management. Additional points are awarded for using local/regional materials, where "local" is defined as within 500 miles. While this serves to reduce transportation pollutants and support regionalized development, some rural areas may be disenfranchised by the 500-mile limitation.

Indoor Environmental Quality

Recognizing that the most valuable asset to a facility owner are the occupants, LEED devotes 15 points to indoor environmental quality. Focus is placed on low or no volatile organic compounds (VOC) materials, universal design elements, systems integration, and statistically proven productivity enhancements through daylighting and controllability of systems. Urban designers should be aware of and plan for balancing daylighting principles with infill development and development densities. This is important

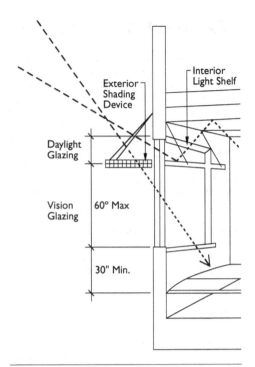

DAYLIGHT AND VIEWS

Source: Lee Fithian.

to note particularly in anticipation of design guidelines where sustainability will be incorporated, because lot spacing and pedestrian/vehicular pathways will be developed to respond to these criteria.

Innovation in Design

The remaining five points available to LEED reward innovation in design to achieve performance above the requirements set by the rating system and through the inclusion of a LEED™-accredited professional as a principal participant in the project team.

IMPACT ON ASSET VALUES

Buildings that have been constructed to LEED standards tend to have increased asset values. Using the income-capitalization method, where asset value equals net operating income (NOI) divided by the capitalization rate, if the capitalization rate is 10 percent, multiplying the reduction in annual operating costs by 10 can be used to calculate the probable increase in the building's asset value.

MUNICIPAL GREENING BUILDING CODES AND GUIDELINES

Among the members of the USGBC is the International Code Council (ICC), which together have approved plans for USGBC and ICC to develop a strategic alliance that will foster technical cooperation and resource exchange. This is intended giving green building a stronger voice in the building regulatory community.

A number of cities have already adopted municipal green building guidelines or LEED-based criteria, including Austin, Texas; Portland, Oregon; New York, New York; Seattle, Washington; Fairfax County,

Virginia; Boulder, Colorado; Chicago, Illinois; and, in California, Long Beach, San Francisco, San Jose, Santa Monica, San Mateo County, and Los Angeles.

EMERGING AREAS FOR LEED STANDARDS

LEED for Neighborhood Developments (LEED-ND)

The USGBC, the Congress for the New Urbanism (CNU) and the Natural Resources Defense Council (NRDC) have initiated the development of LEED-ND standards that integrate green building and smart growth princi-ples. The scope will be guided by the Smart Growth Network's 10 principles of smart growth and will include density, proximity to transit, mixed use, mixed housing type, and pedestrian/bicycle-friendly design among the areas where points may be acquired.

LEED for Homes (LEED-H)

The LEED for Homes (LEED-H) standards are being synchronized with LEED-ND to avoid duplication of efforts. Where LEED-ND focuses on multiple uses, buildings, and parcels, LEED-H covers individual struc-tures on individual sites, single-family detached homes, duplexes, rowhouses, town homes, and multifamily projects up to three stories. Projects larger than three stories are covered by the LEED-NC rating system.

REFERENCE

U.S. Green Building Council. Revised March 2003. *Green Building Rating System for New Construction and Major Renovations (LEED-NC) Version 2.1.* www.usgbc.org/Docs/LEEDdocs/LEED_RS_v2-1.pdf

See also:

Environmental Planning Considerations
Forestry

Lee Fithian, AIA, Benham, Oklahoma City, Oklahoma

STREETSCAPE

Streetscape design in the broadest sense refers to the design of a street, including the roadbed, sidewalks, landscape planting, and character of the adjacent building façade or planted setback. Each of these individual parts is important in successful streetscape design. Information on streets and street design is included in Part 3 of this book; this section focuses primarily on the pedestrian realm of the sidewalk.

Memorable sidewalks and streets that are oriented toward the pedestrian experience characterize excellence in streetscape design. Special attention to streetscape with a consistent focus on implementation can establish a new and welcoming character for a whole city or neighborhood.

Several individual elements can be used to shape the character of sidewalks and overall street elements, including street furniture, landscape planting, lighting, and other amenities. Successful streetscape design balances the desire for pedestrian amenities, such as benches and street trees, with an understanding of the functional aspects of streets and sidewalks.

Planners, designers, and developers can design and implement streetscapes at a variety of scales:

• The sidewalk in front of an individual property
• Individual streets
• Larger street networks in neighborhoods and districts
• Entire communities and municipalities

SIDEWALK ZONES AND DIMENSIONS

An important characteristic of sidewalks is the pedestrian "path of travel." A typical sidewalk has three zones: the building zone, the path of travel, and the curb zone. Successful streetscape designs accommodate a clear path of travel, typically in the center of the sidewalk. The curb zone, on the outer edge of the sidewalk, is typically the location of streetscape amenities.

All sidewalks should comply with the Americans with Disabilities Act (ADA) requirements to accommodate a clear path of travel. When including streetscape amenities, such as street furniture or landscape planting, provide increased sidewalk width in addition to the path of travel. For example, sidewalks with street trees typically require a 10-foot-wide sidewalk, to accommodate a six-foot pedestrian path and the four-foot-wide tree bed.

PEDESTRIAN LEVELS OF SERVICE

Similar to traffic levels of service on roads and freeways, pedestrian levels of service (LOS) classifications exist for sidewalks. These range from A (completely unimpeded movement) to F (complete congestion). The LOS calculation is based on average sidewalk width and the total volume of pedestrians in a given period of time. Wide sidewalks in conjunction with a high pedestrian LOS can seem empty and uninviting; narrow sidewalks with several streetscape elements can result in both physical and visual clutter and a low pedestrian LOS.

Identify the current pedestrian level of service and the level the community would like as a basis for

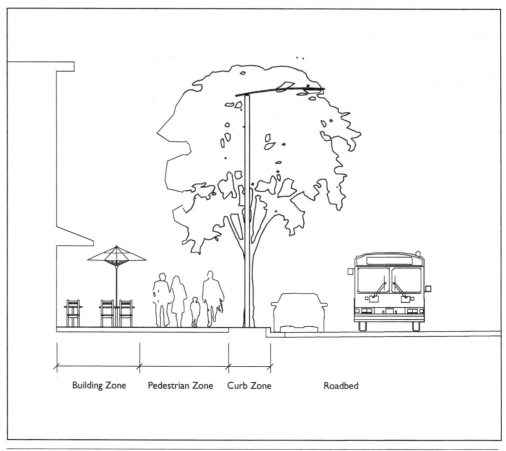

SIDEWALK ZONES

Source: SMWM.

determining the amount of pedestrian amenities that can be accommodated comfortably on any given sidewalk.

LOCATION OF STREETSCAPE AMENITIES

The majority of public streetscape amenities are located in the curb zone of the sidewalk, often clustered at intersections. In some communities, the sidewalk is enlarged at the intersection, referred to as a "bulb-out." Bulb-outs can accommodate more streetscape elements, such as trees and benches, and can serve as a traffic-calming measure.

STANDARDS AND REGULATIONS

Streetscape design and implementation is regulated at the local level. Specific requirements and regulations likely will vary for each community. Consult local regulations before planning streetscape improvements or modifications. Consult applicable local codes and ordinances for appropriate plant material and buffer guidelines, which are often contained within landscape regulations.

Typically, within each community there are multiple agencies that govern specific aspects of streetscape design and implementation. These agencies can include planning departments for planning

and design; public works departments for utilities, road maintenance, and dimensions requirements; park and recreation departments or forestry departments for recommended street trees and plantings; and economic development agencies for working with the owners of private properties to control the location of private street furniture and displays.

On the federal level, the ADA requirements with regard to streetscapes focus on the width of a clear path of travel on sidewalks, to allow two wheelchairs to pass each other unimpeded, and the slope and location of special curb treatments.

STREETSCAPE ELEMENTS

The following section provides an overview of five key categories of streetscape elements:

• Paving
• Landscape planting
• Street lighting
• Street furniture
• Public facilities and private streetscape amenities

This section provides a brief introduction to each element, its typical placement on sidewalks, and the available types of design and construction. Specific street furniture design and vendors can be found in trade publications and on the Internet.

David Schellinger, SMWM, San Francisco, California; Sharon Priest, AICP, SMWM, San Francisco, California

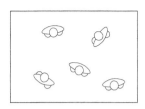

LEVEL OF SERVICE A
Average Pedestrian Density: 13 sq ft/person or more
Average Space between People : 4 ft, or more
Description: Standing and free circulation is possible without disturbing others.

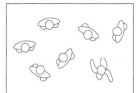

LEVEL OF SERVICE B
Average Pedestrian Density: 10 to 13 sq ft/person
Average Space between People: 3.5 to 4 ft
Description: Standing and partially restricted circulation to avoid disturbing others
Is possible.

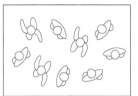

LEVEL OF SERVICE C
Average Pedestrian Density: 7 to 10 sq ft/person
Average Space between People: 3 to 3.5 ft
Description: Standing and restricted circulation to avoid disturbing others is
possible; this density is within the range of personal comfort.

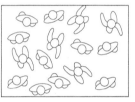

LEVEL OF SERVICE D
Average Pedestrian Density: 3 to 7 sq ft/person
Average Space between People: 2 to 3 ft
Description: Standing without touching is possible; circulation is severely
restricted and forward movement is only possible as a group;
long-term waiting at this density is discomforting.

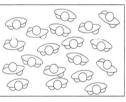

LEVEL OF SERVICE E
Average Pedestrian Density: 2 to 3 sq ft/person
Average Space between People: 2 ft or less
Description: Standing in physical contact with others is unavoidable; circulation
is not possible; movement can only be sustained for a short period without
serious discomfort.

LEVEL OF SERVICE F
Average Pedestrian Density: 2 sq ft/person or less
Average Space between People: Close contact with persons
Description: Virtually all persons are standing in direct physical contact with
those surrounding them; this density is extremely discomforting; no movement
is possible.

source :: www.walksf.org/pedestrianLOS.html

PEDESTRIAN LEVELS OF SERVICE

Source: Reprinted courtesy of Walk San Francisco.

Paving

Paving material is perhaps the most visually prominent streetscape element. Choice of paving material often depends on the scale of the sidewalk, the overall character and design intent of the street, and local climate conditions. For cities in colder weather climates, use more durable materials that allow for expansion and contraction in extreme temperatures and that can withstand the use of salt and other melting agents. For locations that receive higher levels of rainfall throughout the year, use materials with more surface texture, as they will provide greater traction. In some extreme cold weather climates, communities have added electric heating coils embedded beneath the paving to melt snow and ice. Long-term maintenance and replacement should be considered throughout the design process.

The most common and economical choice of material is scored concrete. Dyes can be added to concrete to add color and character to the pavement and retain its cost and maintenance benefits. Stone or brick pavers are a more expensive paving material, hence are often reserved for more ceremonial or special streets, such as a main street. Some harder stones, such as granite, which can hold up under the pressures of everyday use of the sidewalks, can be used as curbs. Because special paving materials are often more expensive, economical solutions can be derived by combining concrete and special pavers in a variety of interesting patterns along the sidewalk.

Special paving can also be used in crosswalks or entire intersections as a design element or a traffic-calming measure. Colored concrete or pavers in a crosswalk provide a visual clue to changes in the

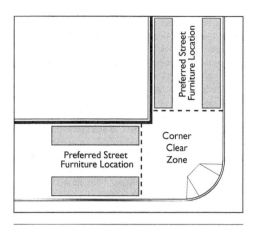

TYPICAL LOCATION OF STREETSCAPE AMENITIES

Source: SMWM.

character of the street, and raised crosswalks make drivers more cognizant of driving through a pedestrian zone.

Landscape Planting

Street trees and other plant material add four-season color, visual interest, and living and ever-changing texture to a streetscape. Landscape planting can soften the hard surfaces of sidewalks and help improve air quality. Unlike most streetscape elements, street trees and plantings change over time, require continual maintenance, and can cause problems such as roots cracking sidewalks and leaves clogging sewer grates. Even with the potential problems, street landscape planting is often a first choice for many communities when seeking to improve street character. This section describes a variety of street planting types, general planting and location guidelines, and a few rules of thumb to consider when selecting and installing landscape planting along streets.

Street Trees

The most visually prominent of all street planting is the street tree. Street tree selection should include consideration of numerous factors, including the community's recommended tree list, its overall aesthetic desire, climatic concerns, potential for disease and pests, maintenance requirements, the space available for root growth, and the size of a mature tree crown and canopy.

The total volume of soil in which trees are planted will affect the size of the mature tree. Greater room for roots to grow allows for larger trees with more expansive tree canopies.

Residential Streets

Street trees on residential streets are typically located in a planted strip between the sidewalk and the curb. When selecting a tree species, consider the size of the individual mature tree canopy and root system, so that trees will not compete for light and nutrients.

Commercial Streets

Street trees on more commercial streets are often in containers or in linear planting strips in the sidewalk. The tree species selected may depend on the desires

David Schellinger, SMWM, San Francisco, California; Sharon Priest, AICP, SMWM, San Francisco, California

of adjacent business and property owners, because they are often concerned about trees blocking their storefront windows. Smaller, more ornamental trees or trees with higher or lighter canopies are often chosen for commercial streets.

On many commercial streets, especially in more recent developments, street trees often compete with underground utilities for space, which can limit the number and location of trees. Wider commercial sidewalks often provide enough room to accommodate both underground utilities in the pedestrian path of travel and street trees in the curb zone. Narrower commercial sidewalks can be more limited in their capability to do so.

Trees in Medians

On commercial and larger residential streets, trees can be planted in medians, either in the center of the street or in the area separating through-lanes from local traffic and parking lanes, which are found on many boulevards. Medians typically need to be at least 6 to 10 feet wide (excluding the curb dimension), depending upon local regulations, to accommodate a mature street tree. Medians wider than 10 feet can also include strips of special paving along the curb, to provide maintenance access. Also of note are median planting programs that install ornamental plantings and perennial garden planting, which require yearly maintenance.

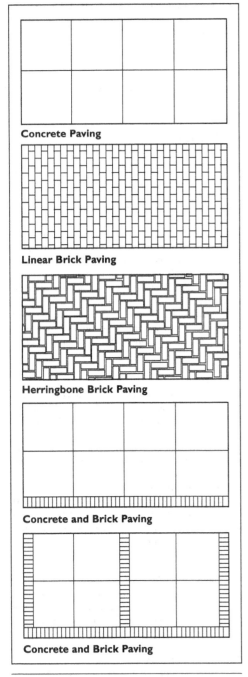

Concrete Paving

Linear Brick Paving

Herringbone Brick Paving

Concrete and Brick Paving

Concrete and Brick Paving

PAVING PATTERNS

Source: SMWM.

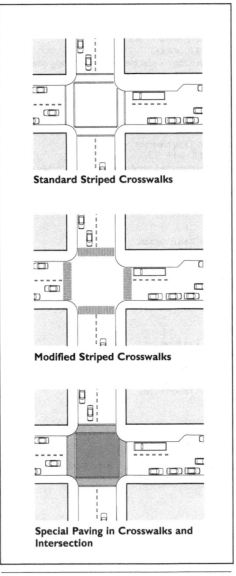

Standard Striped Crosswalks

Modified Striped Crosswalks

Special Paving in Crosswalks and Intersection

CROSSWALKS

Source: SMWM.

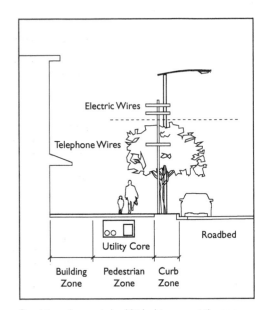

Street tree placement should take into account the presence of any utilities underneath the sidewalk or electric wires overhead. Street trees should be selected such that mature tree height is less than the height of any wires, or the tree should be pruned to below wires.

STREET TREES AND UTILITIES

Source: SMWM.

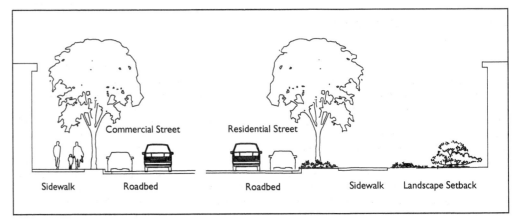

Commercial street trees are typically planted in the sidewalk, and residential street trees are typically planted in the planted strip between the sidewalk and the roadbed.

TREE PLACEMENT ON COMMERCIAL AND RESIDENTIAL STREETS

Source: SMWM.

David Schellinger, SMWM, San Francisco, California; Sharon Priest, AICP, SMWM, San Francisco, California

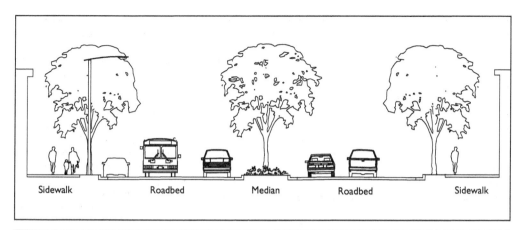

TREES IN MEDIAN

Source: SMWM.

Tree Base Covers

When trees are located within the sidewalk, the base of the tree is typically covered by some form of water-permeable materials, which can range from metal tree grates to stone or brick pavers, decomposed granite, or other crushed stones. The selected covering should be stable enough for pedestrians to walk on it. In some cases, metal tree grates can be acceptable for use within the ADA-accessible path of travel. Most types of tree base covering are designed to allow for the continual growth of the tree trunk. Brick or stone pavers can often be removed; some metal tree grates include radial links that can also be removed; and materials such as decomposed granite can be moved aside as the tree trunk grows.

Tree Guards

Most street trees are fairly small when planted and require wooden stakes or more elaborate metal tree guards to help support and or protect them as they

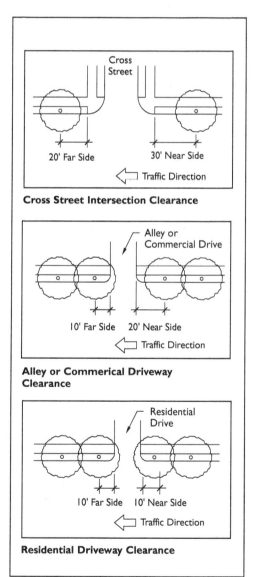

TREE PLANTING CLEARANCE AT TYPICAL INTERSECTIONS

Source: SMWM.

Distance Standards

Most communities have established standards for the distance between street trees and intersections, alleys, and curb-cuts, to avoid obstructing the view of cross traffic and pedestrians waiting at the corners. Check with the governing agency (typically the city or state department of transportation) to determine local requirements. Many communities seek a 25- to 30-foot distance between street trees on urban residential or mixed-use streets.

Tree Crown

On streets with buildings located adjacent to the property line, regardless of the type of land use, when selecting the tree species to plant, consider the mature shape of the tree crown, to prevent the tree canopy from growing into the building wall and potentially requiring severe pruning over time.

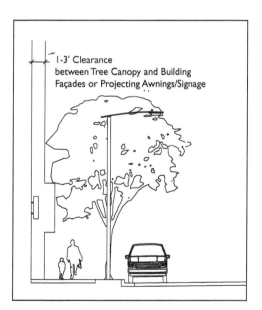

TREE CANOPY CLEARANCE

Source: SMWM.

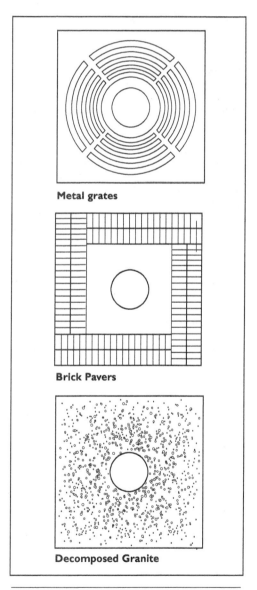

TREE GRATES

Source: SMWM.

David Schellinger, SMWM, San Francisco, California; Sharon Priest, AICP, SMWM, San Francisco, California

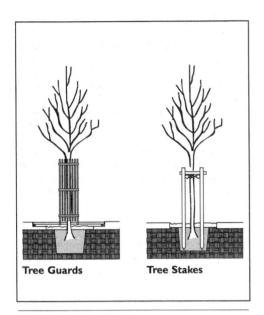

Tree Guards   **Tree Stakes**

TREE PROTECTION

Source: SMWM.

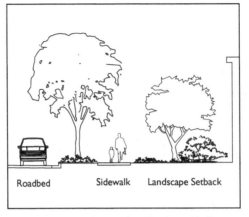

Roadbed   Sidewalk   Landscape Setback

Planting in adjacent private yards and landscaped buffers add to the landscape character of the street.

BORROWED LANDSCAPES

Source: SMWM.

become established. Wooden stakes are a temporary solution; metal tree guards are more permanent and should be sized to accommodate the diameter of the mature tree trunk to avoid hindering the growth of the tree.

Small-Scale Landscape Planting

Other landscape elements of the streetscape include planted beds in the ground or raised planters, hanging planters attached to light fixtures or buildings, and plantings in medians. Any landscape planting within the sidewalk needs to allow a clear path of pedestrian travel, and as such is typically found in the curb zone or in private planters within the building zone, if the width of the sidewalk permits.

Medians between 2 and 6 feet wide, excluding curb dimensions, can easily accommodate small-scale planting, such as grasses and bushes.

Borrowed Landscapes

Though not located within the public right-of-way, planting on adjacent private property often plays an

integral role in the overall landscape character of a street. These landscape elements are referred to as "borrowed" landscapes. Take into account the type, scale, and location of private landscape planting when designing an overall street planting plan.

In addition, private landscape planting can provide a visual buffer and natural transition between a street and adjacent land uses, or between different land uses. Also, depending on plant types and density, they may provide physical barriers and noise reduction from street traffic.

Preparation and Planting

Time the implementation of planting and landscape plans so that landscape materials are planted in the

appropriate season for the species. In general, transplanting is not recommended during the summer and winter months, unless climate conditions allow.

Prepare the soil or planting bed for the specific type of plant material. If more than one type of plant material is to be installed, address proper planting conditions for all plants. Many newer streets also include irrigation systems planned as an integral part of the streetscape, to facilitate ongoing watering.

If required, topsoil in planters and in the ground can be improved through special soil and fertilizer mixtures to provide optimum growing conditions for the specific plant species. Minimum soil depth in a planter varies with the plant type: for large trees, the soil should be 36 inches deep, or 6 inches deeper than the root ball; for small trees, 30 inches deep; for shrubs, 24 inches deep; and for lawns, 12 inches deep (10 inches if irrigated).

Choose plant species carefully. Consider the ultimate maturity of the plant species when determining the size of the plant bed or planter. Different species require different volumes of soil to reach maturity. Sources for determining the appropriate species for the volume of soil available to support landscaping on the street include the community's arborist, landscape maintenance staff, the parks department, or private nurseries.

As mentioned above, avoid underground utilities, if possible. If utilities are located where root interference may be an issue, especially for street trees, implement special planting procedures or root barriers that control root growth.

Planter materials such as wood or concrete can affect soil temperatures in planters, so they should be considered when specifying appropriate planting species. Cold or heat can cause severe root damage in certain plant species. Proper drainage helps alleviate this condition. Irrigation, mulches, and moisture-holding soil help reduce moisture loss from the wind and sun. Most planters do not require insulation, but in colder climates, planters with small soil volumes located over heated structures may require

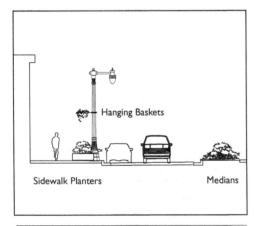

Hanging Baskets

Sidewalk Planters   Medians

SMALL-SCALE PLANTING LOCATIONS

Source: SMWM.

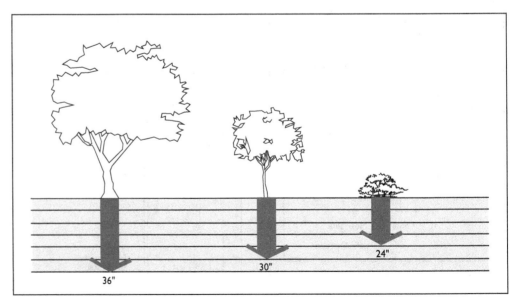

36"   30"   24"

Note: Not to scale.

REQUIRED SOIL DEPTH

Source: SMWM.

David Schellinger, SMWM, San Francisco, California; Sharon Priest, AICP, SMWM, San Francisco, California

insulation. Consult local sources for a list of cold-hardy plants, and select planter materials that best suit local conditions.

Street Lighting

Exterior street lighting provides general illumination for safety and wayfinding purposes for both pedestrians and motorists. Lighting is used to illuminate buildings, landscapes, roadways, parking areas, signs, and other outdoor areas, as well as advertising in certain instances. In addition to being a practical consideration, the choice of light fixtures, type of lighting source, and illumination patterns are also design elements.

Illumination Levels

Most communities have requirements for minimum levels of illumination on their streets. Lighting should be designed to attain the recommended light level, distribution, and glare control, and should also address the aesthetic impact of the illumination.

Illumination levels are measured in footcandles (lumens per square foot) and lux (lumens per square meter). A footcandle is the unit of illumination lighting a surface, all points of which are 1 foot from a uniform light source, equivalent to one candle in brightness or illumination. Recommended illumination levels may be found in the Illumination Engineering Society of North America (IESNA) *Lighting Handbook* and other IESNA publications.

Most street-lighting manufacturers can provide photometric studies to determine the resulting illumination levels for specific designs and applications. Computerized point-by-point calculations are recommended for more accurate results.

Luminaires or lamps for street and parking lot lighting are categorized according to the lighting patterns they create on the ground, ranging from Type I to V. While many communities have requirements for roadway illumination levels, fewer communities have requirements for sidewalks and other pedestrian areas. A general rule of thumb for sidewalks and bikeways is 0.2 footcandles in residential areas, 1.0 footcandles in commercial areas, and 5.0 footcandles near building entrances.

Location of Streetlights

Streetlights are typically located in the curb zone of the sidewalk. Spacing of streetlights should be uniform, with the distance depending on the minimum illumination levels required. Regular spacing is often broken by curb-cuts along the street, so the placement of light fixtures requires some level of flexibility. If the sidewalk includes street trees, locate streetlights between the trees so that the tree canopy does not interfere with illumination coverage. Average distance of shade trees from streetlights is 40 feet on center and 15 feet on center for smaller ornamental trees. Pedestrian lighting fixtures may be required to supplement the street lighting or in plazas and parks. Additional lighting for security purposes is often located near building entrances and in parking garages. Require such lighting to be placed to control glare.

Streetlight Types

There are three broad classes of lights on streets: those that illuminate the roadway, those that light the sidewalk and the pedestrian realm, and other ancillary light fixtures such as bollards and fixtures mounted on the façades of buildings and security lighting. Standard roadway lights, often called cobra-heads, are usually mounted to a mast arm and suspended over the roadway at heights of 25 to 40 feet. Cobrahead lights are typically mounted on simple aluminum poles and are frequently used on highways and other major traffic thoroughfares. They may not always control glare.

On more important or intimate streets, many communities opt for more ornamental street poles and lighting fixtures, often with a particular theme or design that the community has selected. These lights fixtures are usually mounted on ornate poles less than 25 feet high. Many of these types of light fixtures also include the option of a pedestrian-scale light fixture, usually mounted around 12 to 15 feet above the sidewalk. Note that with light fixtures mounted at this level, it is difficult to control glare and achieve proper illumination levels. Light fixtures often include an option for brackets (either single- or double-sided) to attach banners and other temporary graphic elements between the pedestrian fixture and the street-level fixture.

Private street lighting comes in a variety of shapes and sizes and is typically mounted to the façade of the building or located on smaller-scale poles in private landscape planted buffers.

Lighting as Security

Sufficient lighting increases security and decreases opportunities for criminal activity. The overall perception of safety is greatly affected by lighting. Both sufficient lighting levels and proper glare control are critical to preserving visibility and helping pedestrians and drivers see potential dangerous situations. Streetlight levels should permit faces to be identified at 50 feet. The use of multiple light sources is preferable to fewer, brighter light fixtures. Insufficient or uneven lighting can cast shadows where an assailant might hide. Too much light can also be a problem, creating an unattractive image or a nuisance to residents.

Lighting fixtures require maintenance. Lamps diminish in brightness as they age, trees may block

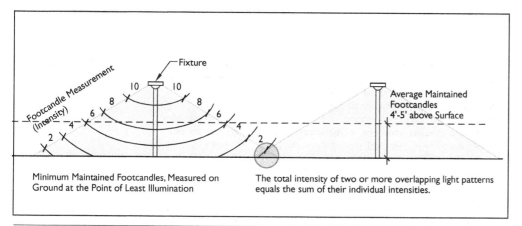

FOOTCANDLE MEASUREMENT

Source: SMWM.

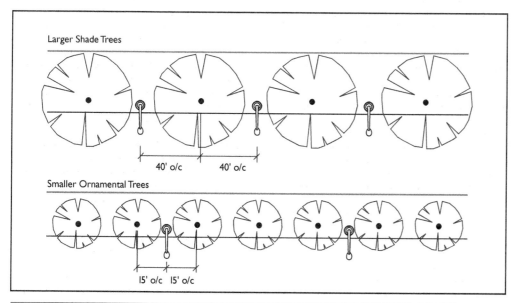

STREETLIGHTS AND STREET TREES

Source: SMWM.

David Schellinger, SMWM, San Francisco, California; Sharon Priest, AICP, SMWM, San Francisco, California

DESIGN CONSIDERATIONS

Roadway Light Fixtures (25-40' Tall)   Pedestrian Light Fixtures (12-15' Tall)

LIGHT FIXTURES

Source: SMWM.

illumination, and broken fixtures create dark areas. Select light fixtures that are durable and easily maintained. Consider any special conditions that may affect lighting. For example, a senior citizen's residential complex may require increased illumination for night lighting.

Increased lighting levels at outdoor uses such as gas stations and car lots often serves a combination of security and advertising purposes, as the lights are used to both draw in customers and illuminate the products for sale. Excessive lighting in such instances, however, can cause nearby areas to seem "dark" even if properly illuminated.

Lighting Considerations

The color of the light that is cast is often an important consideration in streetscape design. Light sources such as high-pressure sodium that have poor color retention can create a yellowish glow on the street, which should be avoided. White-light sources such as metal halide, fluorescent, and compact fluorescent luminaries are recommended for sidewalks and other pedestrian areas and situations requiring color discrimination.

Choose fixtures that are physically strong and resistant to vandals, weather, and the environment. Also, choose light sources that have a longer lamp life to minimize repeated replacement of lamps. Fixtures should be able to start and operate at the lowest anticipated temperature on a site. Consult an individual fixture's specifications to determine if the color rendering, lamp life, and starting temperatures are appropriate for the street being designed.

Light Pollution

Light pollution is light with no useful purpose. Inefficient light sources and certain types of light fixtures cause this energy waste. Some communities have developed outdoor lighting ordinances that regulate a variety of types of light pollution. When specifying the type and location of street light fixtures, address the different types of light pollution

and available design and manufacturing solutions.

The International Dark Sky Association (IDA) in Tucson, Arizona, has developed a model outdoor lighting ordinance. The ordinance addresses the reasonable use of outdoor lighting for general illumination and safety purposes, to minimize light pollution, conserve energy, and protect the natural nighttime visual environment. Lighting zones have been established to identify different uses and characteristics, from very dark to high light-level applications.

Street Furniture

Street furniture includes the smaller-scale amenities located on sidewalks that add scale, functionality, and a human element to the streetscape. Types of street furniture include benches, tables and chairs, trash receptacles, bicycle racks, drinking fountains, and other items as desired. Street furniture is typically fixed in place, with removable elements as required, such as trash receptacle liners. Durability and ease of maintenance are important factor is the selection of permanent street furniture.

The placement of street furniture is based on function and need and may be included as part of communitywide streetscape requirements. The most common location for street furniture is within the curb zone of the sidewalk. Street furniture is often clustered near intersections, where pedestrians wait while crossing the street. An area of at least 10 feet immediately adjacent to the intersection should be kept clear.

When selecting street furniture, create a palette of materials and pieces that work together in color, style, and character. Some communities have developed and implemented a palette of appropriate streetscape elements, including street furniture, which provides an easy first step in selecting pieces for a project. Coordination of city services is required, especially for items such as fountains and features requiring electrical power. Review local codes and ordinances for any street furniture location requirements or restrictions.

The most common elements of street furniture include the following:

- Benches
- Trash receptacles
- Newspaper racks
- Bike racks
- Bollards
- Kiosks
- Transit shelters
- Signage
- Public utilities and other public amenities
- Private amenities

Benches

Benches are essential to making a sidewalk pedestrian-friendly. Benches are available in a wide array of shapes, materials, and styles, including those with arms and backs and those that are simply a seat bottom. Benches can include a center or intermediate arm that can discourage loitering or sleeping on the bench. Benches are often located in high-use or high-pedestrian traffic areas and are typically fastened to the pavement for security purposes. Benches are typically placed parallel to the sidewalk and may face in either direction. Typically, if located in the curb zone, they face either a building or the street; if placed in the building zone, they face the street. Benches may also be placed perpendicular to the sidewalk when placed in bulb-outs at intersections. Bench location should be coordinated with transit services to be compatible with stops and waiting areas.

Trash Receptacles

Trash receptacles are among the most ubiquitous elements of a streetscape. They come in a variety of types and materials, ranging from more modern concrete square containers to more traditional metal or wood-slatted round containers. Many styles can also include an attached receptacle, often on the top of the container, for recyclable materials. Some communities are starting to include separate receptacles for recyclable materials.

David Schellinger, SMWM, San Francisco, California; Sharon Priest, AICP, SMWM, San Francisco, California

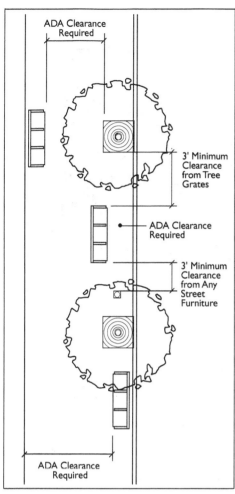

Benches can be located in either the building or the curb zone, facing in either direction such that there is adequate ADA clearance in front of the bench.

BENCH PLACEMENT

Source: SMWM.

Primary placement of public trash receptacles is in the curb zone. Private trash receptacles are typically located in the building zone.

TRASH RECEPTACLE PLACEMENT

Source: SMWM.

Provide trash receptacles at frequent-enough intervals so that their use is convenient and that they are well-maintained. Publicly maintained trash receptacles are typically located in the curb zone; privately maintained receptacles are located in the building zone, often adjacent to building entrances.

Bike Racks

As more communities seek to make their streets bicycle-friendly, it is critical to provide adequate bike racks throughout major activity centers. Bike racks can be modern in their styling, ranging from vertical metal slats on a flat base to continuous sinuous curving pieces of metal, or more artistic shapes. In addition to formal bike racks, many bicycle riders often lock their bikes to street sign poles when there is no formal bike rack available.

Newspaper Racks

Newspaper racks serve an important function in the community, and are protected by the First Amendment, but improperly placed newspaper racks and too many different newspaper racks crammed onto small sidewalks can be both an eyesore and a safety hazard. To control the design aesthetic of newspaper racks, many communities are installing larger-scale, single newspaper racks with multiple containers inside. Although these multiple containers are an increased expense to the municipality (individual racks are paid for by the individual publication), they establish a cleaner and more coherent streetscape environment. Some communities are exploring the use of a single structure that includes both multiple newspaper racks and a space for utility boxes, further streamlining the sidewalk character.

Bollards

Bollards are streetscape elements of concrete or steel that typically prevent traffic from encroaching in pedestrian areas. Besides being a necessary functional element, bollards can be an attractive, well-designed component of the overall streetscape. They are typically located along the curb edge of a sidewalk, but bollards can also be used to protect pedestrians on traffic islands and medians and to protect standpipes, streetlights, street trees, public art, and other sidewalk elements. Bollards have been used as a security element around sensitive buildings and important sites. They come in a multitude of styles, from fixtures reminiscent of hitching posts to sleek steel posts.

Kiosks

Kiosks provide a central location for information on community events and other announcements. Well-designed and -located sidewalk kiosks can help establish the design tone for an individual street or even a larger community. Kiosks can be designed to include amenities such as newspaper racks, maps, public phones, and signage. When deciding whether kiosks may be appropriate, consider sidewalk width, pedestrian volume, the proposed design, and long-term maintenance, to ensure that the kiosk provides a benefit to the community. Kiosk design can range from more elaborate or traditional types to more modern or contemporary concrete, wooden, or metal designs. Often, kiosk design can be incorporated into a public art program, resulting in a collection of unique artistic pieces throughout a community. Like

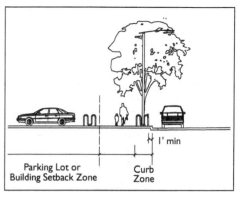

Bike racks should be located in the curb zone with a 3-foot minimum clearance between bicycles parked at racks and any other street furniture or, if possible, in an adjacent parking lot or setback zone.

BIKE RACK PLACEMENT

Source: SMWM.

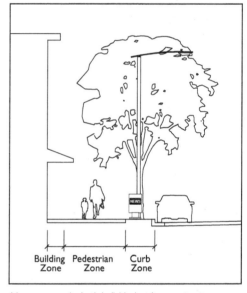

Newspaper racks, both individual and group structures, should be located in the curb zone, opening towards the pedestrian zone.

NEWSPAPER RACK PLACEMENT

Source: SMWM.

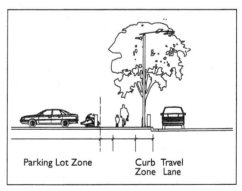

Bollards are typically located in the curb zone to buffer pedestrians from moving vehicles or in parking lots adjacent to a sidewalk.

BOLLARD PLACEMENT

Source: SMWM.

David Schellinger, SMWM, San Francisco, California; Sharon Priest, AICP, SMWM, San Francisco, California

DESIGN CONSIDERATIONS

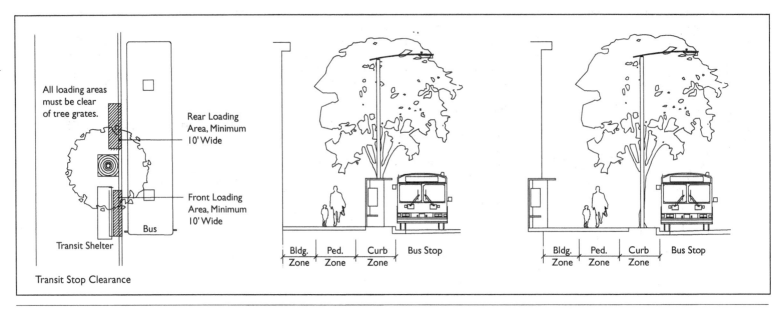

TRANSIT STOP LOCATIONS

Source: SMWM.

most street furniture, kiosks, especially due to their size, should be located within the curb zone and only in sidewalks with sufficient width. Sidewalk bulb-outs at intersections are prime locations for kiosks.

Transit Stops and Shelters

Integrate transit stops and associated transit amenities into the overall streetscape plan. Transit stops can range from a sign identifying the stop and route number or name to a bench or to a partially enclosed transit shelter that protects waiting passengers from the elements. Other elements often included are route maps, route schedules, and, more recently, electronic tracking displays to show the time of the next arrival. Transit shelters may include benches or individual seats that need to be flipped down to sit on, to prevent sleeping in the shelters.

Transit shelters come in a variety of shapes and designs. Basic shelters have a roof and a panel on the back side, for wind protection. In colder climates, shelters may be enclosed on three or four sides, with an opening for ingress and egress. Also in colder climates, shelters can include heating lamps that can be turned on by waiting passengers or lighting that is sensitive to light levels, turning on at sundown. Designs can range from traditionally detailed shelters to sleeker and more modern structures. Materials are typically steel or some other metal for the frame, with strengthened glass for the side panels. Often, the surface of the glass includes etching or other graphic elements to visually identify the glass and prevent people from walking into the glass. The glass needs to be shatterproof to prevent injury if the glass is broken or vandalized.

Transit stops are typically located adjacent to intersections, either before or after the stoplight. Buses have flexibility in changing lanes, so stops can be accommodated on sidewalks by having the bus pull into the parking or curb lane. Consider the location of street trees and other street furniture when locating transit stops, to ensure that there are no obstructions to the front and back doors for passengers entering and disembarking.

Some communities have implemented cutouts into wider sidewalks to allow buses to pull out of the traffic flow. Buses in dedicated transit lanes and rail transit have less flexibility. Many of these types of transit run in center lanes, which require transit islands in the middle of the road. Special care should be taken to ensure that these traffic islands are comfortable and safe. See Transporation in Part 3 of this book for more information on planning for various forms of transit.

Signage

The shape, color, and graphic design of most traffic and directional signage are federally controlled. Community-oriented signs can be designed as an integral part of the streetscape plan. Street signs can be designed as simple, flat metal panel faces attached to aluminum or other metal poles or more elaborate signs with two legs and multiple spots for removable signs. These signs can include gateway features, monument signs, directional signage to public parking locations, and other community-focused signs. Most street signs are located in the curb zone of the sidewalk.

Public Utilities and Private Streetscape Amenities

There are four main types of secondary streetscape elements that a community has slightly less control over than street furniture: utility-related structures, ATMs and public phones, parking meters, and private streetscape amenities.

Utility-Related Structures

Utilities are the often-hidden systems that keep our cities running smoothly. The most visually prominent element on many streets are overhead electrical and telecommunication wires. Although telecommunication wires do not pose any serious danger, live electrical wires, even those that are coated, need to be kept clear of all obstructions, which typically means street trees. Trees located below electrical lines

will need to be pruned to allow a clear space around the wires. Many newer communities have located these wires in utility corridors underneath the sidewalk, and some older communities have followed suit, undergrounding wires as part of redevelopment plans and streetscape improvements.

Utility cabinets, a necessary element in most city streets, house equipment to operate traffic signals, light rail systems, and telecommunications or utility company systems. For existing streets, there is little that can be done to move the existing cabinets unless

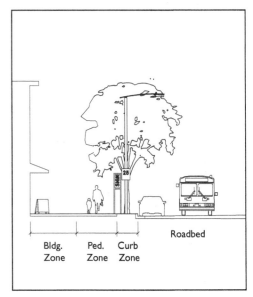

Most public signs are located in the curb zone, either attached to existing poles or on self-supporting structures. Temporary private signage is typically located in the building zone, but can sometimes be found in the curb zone.

SIGNAGE PLACEMENT

Source: SMWM.

David Schellinger, SMWM, San Francisco, California; Sharon Priest, AICP, SMWM, San Francisco, California

major utility work is being done. For newly planned streets, the challenge is to locate these components in a manner that meets operational requirements while making the sidewalk more inviting and safe for pedestrians. This typically means placing utility cabinets in the curb zone.

ATMS and Public Phones

Public phones are becoming less common, and ATMs are gradually being added to the streetscape environment; nevertheless, it is useful to plan for and locate these elements accordingly. Pay phones are often located in either the curb zone or the building zone, whereas ATMs are almost always located in the building zone and are often recessed into the façade of the building.

Parking Meters

On most commercial streets, parking meters are a common site. Located within the curb zone of the sidewalk, parking meters range from the more traditional manually operated meters to more modern and elaborate electric meters that work with debit card systems. Multiple meters are rapidly replacing single-space or double-space meters.

Private Streetscape Amenities

On many commercial streets, private business owners want to use the space outside their stores to place tables and chairs, display wares, or place temporary

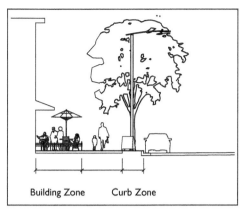

Private streetscape amenities such as chairs, tables, and displays are typically located in the building zone. Temporary easel signs can often be located in the curb zone.

PRIVATE STREETSCAPE AMENITIES

Source: SMWM.

signs. The cost and maintenance for these private amenities are covered by the individual property owners, but the community has a stake in controlling the type and location of these amenities, to ensure a clear and safe path of travel. Communities typically control the placement of private amenities through zoning permits, specifying the height of elements and how far they can extend into the sidewalk, which depends on the overall sidewalk width.

IMPLEMENTATION

Streetscape plans can be implemented at one time or phased in. For one-time construction projects, streetscape plans require a set of construction drawings, typically prepared by an urban designer or licensed landscape architect. Phased approaches or streetscape plans that rely on private implementation on an incremental basis typically require both construction drawings and streetscape design guidelines/summary charts of the allowable streetscape elements.

In many communities, the local government funds some of the cost through a business improvement fee paid by businesses along the street. Funding for streetscape improvements in conjunction with other street improvements is sometimes available through the National Main Streets Center of the National Trust for Historic Preservation or federal legislation such as ISTEA.

See also:

On-Street Bikeways
Pedestrian-Friendly Streets
Sidewalks
Street Networks and Street Connectivity
Traffic Calming
Transit Systems
Walkability

David Schellinger, SMWM, San Francisco, California; Sharon Priest, AICP, SMWM, San Francisco, California

DESIGN CONSIDERATIONS

ANALYSIS TECHNIQUES

Projections and Demand Analysis

Impact Assessment

Mapping

Visualization

Part 5

PROJECTIONS AND DEMAND ANALYSIS

POPULATION PROJECTIONS

Projecting population is a skill central to planning. Comprehensive plans rely on projections for forecasting land use, housing, and transportation. State and local governments use projections for sizing and timing major public facilities such as water and wastewater treatment plants, water and sewer lines, and designing new roads.

Projections may be employed in needs analyses for schools, park facilities, hospitals, social service agencies, and libraries. Assumptions about future household size are incorporated into cost-revenue and other impact analyses of proposed developments. Finally, the private sector draws upon projections in making business decisions, such as through market analyses for shopping centers and housing.

Knowing the detailed characteristics of future populations, such as growth in preschool or elderly populations, permits an analyst to determine whether, for example, there is a market for more nursery schools or more nursing homes.

PROJECTIONS VERSUS FORECASTS

A population projection is a prediction of a future demographic conditions that will occur if the assumptions inherent in the projection technique prove true. In contrast, a population forecast makes judgments about the likelihood of assumptions behind the projection. Thus, it is common to see in comprehensive plans a range of projections (i.e., high, medium, and low), with the plan's authors selecting a particular set as the official forecast to drive other analyses and decisions, such as the determination of need for additional urbanized land.

BIRTHS, DEATHS, AND MIGRATION

Population projections incorporate three components: births, deaths, and migration. Depending on the projection technique, these components may be calculated in detail, so that their relationships can be understood, or merged into a single set of numbers.

Births

Births are the product of the number of women in their childbearing years (ages 15 to 44) multiplied by either a general or age-specific fertility rate. The rate may be obtained from state or county health departments, and it may vary depending on age, race, and socioeconomic status. For example, college-educated women may be more likely to postpone giving birth until their late twenties or early thirties, or even beyond. In contrast, in a region of the country where cultural or religious norms favor large families, births may occur early and frequently in a woman's childbearing years.

Deaths

Deaths are influenced by access to and quality of health care, income (which determines how much health care one can afford), and use of preventive medicine. The death rate—the number of deaths in a

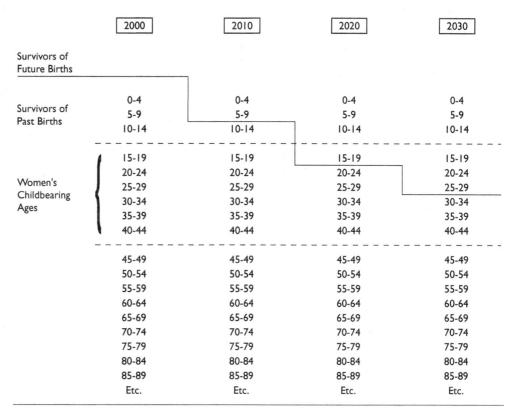

	2000	2010	2020	2030
Survivors of Future Births				
Survivors of Past Births	0-4	0-4	0-4	0-4
	5-9	5-9	5-9	5-9
	10-14	10-14	10-14	10-14
Women's Childbearing Ages	15-19	15-19	15-19	15-19
	20-24	20-24	20-24	20-24
	25-29	25-29	25-29	25-29
	30-34	30-34	30-34	30-34
	35-39	35-39	35-39	35-39
	40-44	40-44	40-44	40-44
	45-49	45-49	45-49	45-49
	50-54	50-54	50-54	50-54
	55-59	55-59	55-59	55-59
	60-64	60-64	60-64	60-64
	65-69	65-69	65-69	65-69
	70-74	70-74	70-74	70-74
	75-79	75-79	75-79	75-79
	80-84	80-84	80-84	80-84
	85-89	85-89	85-89	85-89
	Etc.	Etc.	Etc.	Etc.

RELATIONSHIP OF FUTURE AGE GROUPS TO POPULATION, ENUMERATED IN 2000: ASSUMING NO MIGRATION

Adapted from Principles and Practice of Urban Planning *by W.I. Goodman and E.C. Freund. Copyright © 1968. Reprinted with permission of the International City/County Management Association.*

time period divided by the population in the middle of the time period—is fairly stable in Western countries. The survival rate is one minus the death rate. The excess of births over deaths is called "natural increase."

Migration

Migration is the number of persons moving into an area, less the number of persons moving out. It is the hardest component to calculate, and most projections break down here, even in sophisticated models. Regional economic differences, cost and availability of housing, and level of public services influence migration. Real job and wage growth over time should result in a positive migration number. However, an area's natural amenities, which make a community attractive to retirees or to second-home purchasers, can also be a factor in migration, absent strong economic growth in an area's basic, or export-oriented, industries.

Federal policy on immigration affects migration to certain communities, especially those that traditionally have served as a port of first entry for the foreign born. These gateway metropolitan areas historically have included New York, Los Angeles, San Francisco,

Miami, and Chicago. These five areas correlate to the U.S. Census Bureau's six gateway states for foreign-born migration: California, New York, Texas, Florida, Illinois, and New Jersey. Recent studies have found significant amounts of internal migration of foreign-born people out of four of these states—California, New York, Illinois, and New Jersey—to other states. The highest rates of internal migration have been to Nevada, North Carolina, Georgia, and Arkansas.

SPECIAL POPULATIONS

Special populations include people associated with military bases, tourists, prisons, and colleges and universities. The size of a special population may have no connection to the general trends affecting the area. A special population can be stable for long periods of time, balloon quickly, and deflate, or, in the case of military bases, disappear rapidly through a closure program. It is best to develop a detailed understanding of the nature of the special population and set out the projection for it separately. For example, for a college or university population, contact the administrators to determine if there are plans to expand or contract enrollment.

Stuart Meck, FAICP, American Planning Association, Chicago, Illinois

PROJECTION TECHNIQUES

Population projection techniques can be simple and straightforward or exotic and complex. Most techniques described here can be conducted on computer spreadsheets, using built-in functions, such as transformation of raw numbers into logarithms for nonlinear curve-fitting models. These functions allow for quick analysis and for recalculation of alternate projections. The charting capability of spreadsheets permits a visual representation of past trends, which can be helpful when selecting the type of curve to use, and projections and their elements, such as population pyramids showing age and sex cohorts.

Linear Model

A linear model assumes that population growth or decline is a constant amount over time. It is represented by a curve that is a plotted straight line. If a community's population has grown by 2,000 persons per decade over the past three decades, and there is no likelihood for change on the horizon, a linear projection model will show the same pattern of growth for the future. Thus, a linear projection model is appropriate for communities and regions in which the pattern of growth or decline is relatively stable.

Exponential Curve

An exponential, or nonlinear, projection technique assumes that population growth or decline will occur at a constant rate over time. For example, if a community has grown at 10 percent per decade over the past three decades, the exponential approach assumes that rate will continue into the future. The exponential model is valid only for very limited periods when a particular rate can be maintained.

PROJECTIONS IN GROWTH-CONSTRAINED AREAS

Growth is constrained by the amount of land, either vacant or redevelopable, for housing, public facilities, and other resources. Unless the local government expands its boundaries through annexation, shifts vacant land-use allocation from one category to another, such as from industrial to residential, increases densities in its development regulations, or promotes redevelopment, population growth will begin to taper off. As Richard Klosterman comments in *Community Analysis and Planning Techniques*, even population decline has a floor: "Declining communities rarely disappear entirely; rather they decline only until they reach population and employment levels appropriate to their current position in the regional or national economy."

A variety of nonlinear curve-fitting techniques recognize the existence of a constraint posed by local government land-use policies. These models are useful for growing communities where the land-use policies are relatively established and are unlikely to change much over time, and where community boundaries are fixed.

Modified Exponential Curve

A modified exponential curve shows population growth increasing at a decreasing rate, as it approaches an upper limit. It can also show population decreasing, at a decreasing rate, as it approaches a lower limit. When plotted on a graph, the population curve begins to flatten out over time. The limit

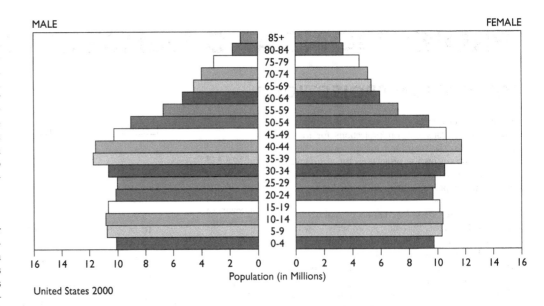

United States 2000

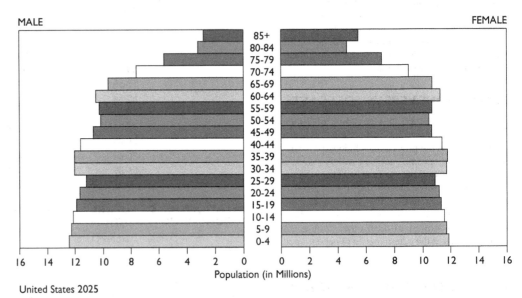

United States 2025

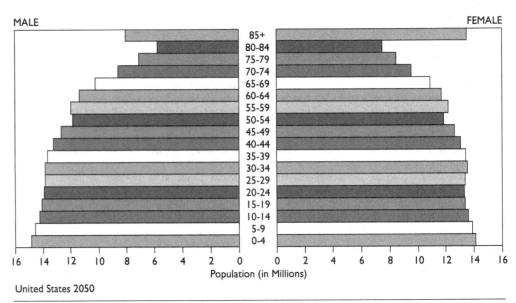

United States 2050

POPULATION PYRAMID SUMMARY FOR THE UNITED STATES

Source: U.S. Census Bureau.

Stuart Meck, FAICP, American Planning Association, Chicago, Illinois

that is being reached is called the asymptote. Other asymptotic projection techniques include Gompertz and logistic curves.

Gompertz Curve

The Gompertz curve, named after its inventor, is similar to the modified exponential curve. When plotted on a graph, it resembles an S and describes a growth pattern that is initially quite slow, increases for a period, and then flattens out as it approaches its limit.

Logistic Curve

A logistic curve is similar to the modified exponential and Gompertz curves in appearance. Also S-shaped, it shows small initial growth increments followed by rapid growth, then increasingly slower growth as the curve approaches the upper (or lower) limit.

POPULATION DENSITY MODEL

An innovative approach developed by demographer Donald Newling and described in *Local Population and Employment Projections* is a population density model. It assumes that past growth rates and population density, measured in persons/square mile, affect population changes. At different stages in a community's life cycle, maxi-

mum population density changes, and growth or decline results.

Under this model, communities progress through stages of adolescence, maturity, and decline, which are each represented by mathematically derived critical density ceilings. The model is calibrated using statewide data from counties and regression analysis to determine the growth/density categories.

Because its output is expressed in persons per square mile, and population is established by multiplying that figure with the current area of the community, the model can account for annexations or other boundary changes. It also allows a what-if analysis that produces different results depending on where a community is in its life cycle and how the analyst categorizes the community with calculated projected parameters.

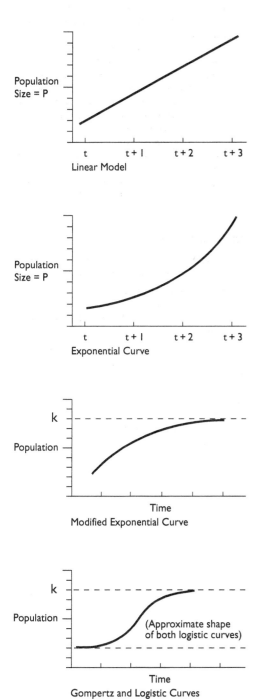

POPULATION PROJECTION STRATEGIES

Adapted from Principles and Practice of Urban Planning by W.I. Goodman and E.C. Freund. Copyright © 1968. Reprinted with permission of the International City/County Management Association.

Stuart Meck, FAICP, American Planning Association, Chicago, Illinois

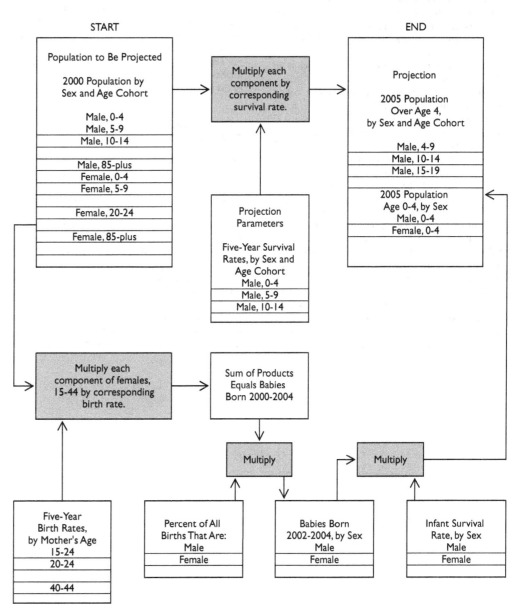

THE COHORT-SURVIVAL APPROACH (EXCLUDING MIGRATION)

Adapted from Principles and Practice of Urban Planning by W.I. Goodman and E.C. Freund. Copyright © 1968. Reprinted with permission of the International City/County Management Association.

COMMUNITY PROJECTIONS

One approach sometimes used is the adjustment of a series of individual community projections by a control projection total developed by an external planning agency. For example, three communities in a county may have individually prepared projections that show the county total to be 120,000 persons at a point in time. However, a state planning agency, using another type of model—one that takes into consideration likely regional economic changes—determines that the population will be only 100,000. Consequently, the individual community projections are all scaled back proportionally by the same ratio.

Cohort-Survival

The most detailed community projection technique, and one commonly taught in planning schools, is cohort-survival or cohort-component. This technique relies on data from the U.S. Census Bureau and local and state health department records. The technique focuses on individual age and sex cohorts (and sometimes race), such as ages 5 to 9, 10 to 14, and so on, and the effects of births, deaths, and migration on them over time.

Survival rates are applied to an existing cohort group, to estimate how many will be alive at the beginning of the next cycle. For example, if a 0.95 survival rate were applied to a male cohort of 1,000 persons aged 5 to 9 from 2000 to 2004, the result would show 950 persons to be alive at the beginning of 2005, the next five-year cycle, when the cohort members would be 10 to 14 years in age.

Births are calculated separately by applying a fertility rate to women in their childbearing years and are further divided into male and female components. Rates of survival are applied to the cohort of babies born in the initial five-year projection period as well. Sometimes alternate survival and fertility assumptions are employed.

A variety of approaches may be employed to compute net migration. Residual net migration calculates net migration from two census counts as the difference between total change and natural increase. Using it assumes that rates of in- and out-migration

will continue forward in time. Another approach, weighting migration rates, gives more emphasis to more recent trends, such as in the previous five years.

The results of the cohort calculations are then summed to give a total for the projection areas. The cohort survival technique, which produces a detailed picture of what is going to happen to population, is particularly useful when a planner wants projections that will assist in the planning of facilities, such as hospitals and schools, that depend on the age of the likely users. The private sector may use this same information to determine the future market for its products; if a cohort projection shows a bulge in the 15-to-19 cohort for a region, at some point that bulge may produce a demand for entry-level housing as households form when the cohort reaches its twenties.

Economic-Based Models

Typically housed in university research institutes or in state planning offices, economic-based models link job growth with population by looking at the relationships of total employment and labor force to population in a given year and using them to adjust migration rates on the theory that job or wage growth or decline will affect net migration.

POPULATION PROJECTION OUTCOMES

Projections have technical and political dimensions, and it is the political dimensions that are often the most difficult to address. Projections may conflict with a local government's or its residents' aspirations about its future.

A planner working for a county planning agency whose projections show the central city of the county in continued decline may find the projections challenged even though they reflect the near-term reality. Projections that anticipate exponential growth for a suburban government that sits astride an interchange may come under fire from slow- or no-growth advocates living there who view them as self-fulfilling prophecies. Alternately, a state transportation department may favor an "enhanced" projection to support

a road-widening project. A positive projection may represent economic progress or a corresponding decline in quality of life.

POPULATION PROJECTIONS ISSUES FOR POLICY MAKERS

The following are a sample of the types of issues that may be faced by decision makers when conducting or using population projections:

- What do changes in the economic fabric of the region or local government portend for population growth or decline?
- Are the projections aspirations or goals?
- What is happening to household size?
- What population-based standards are appropriate?
- Is demand for the planning activities for which the projections are to be used strictly population-based, or do other factors come into play, such as income or changes in tastes or preferences?
- How does the age composition of the population affect demand, as in the case of schools and hospitals?
- Are projections technically reliable and replicable? Will more exotic projection models produce a superior result?

REFERENCES

Goodman, W.I., and E.C. Freund. 1968. *Principles and Practice of Urban Planning*. Washington, DC: ICMA.

Greenberg, Michael R., Donald A. Krueckeberg, and Connie O. Michaelson. 1978. *Local Population and Employment Projection Techniques*. New Brunswick, NJ: Center for Urban Policy Research.

Klosterman, Richard E. 1990. *Community Analysis and Planning Techniques*. Savage, MD: Rowman & Littlefield.

See also:
Comprehensive Plans
Economic Development Plans
Impact Assessment

Stuart Meck, FAICP, American Planning Association, Chicago, Illinois

ECONOMIC BASE AND ECONOMETRIC PROJECTIONS

Economic projections are a necessary element of comprehensive planning for the purpose of forecasting future land-use needs. In turn, future land-use allocations drive transportation models for metropolitan areas. In addition, economic projections by the industrial sector can help identify the kinds of jobs and related skill sets a region will need in the future. Moreover, by analyzing the relationship between employment growth and housing unit needs, local governments can ensure that housing production keeps up with job creation. Two models are described here: economic base projections and econometric models.

ECONOMIC BASE ANALYSIS

Economic base analysis can be used as a technique to project local or regional employment by relating it to national or state employment projections, which are often prepared by state agencies and private forecasting firms. It assumes that the local economy can be divided into two sectors: the basic (or nonlocal) sector and the nonbasic (or local) sector.

Basic Sector

A basic sector supports the local economy by exporting goods whose purchase brings new money into the local economy. Manufacturing, agriculture, and mining were traditionally assumed to be the primary basic sectors. Current thinking includes any sector that brings money to the local economy as basic, which could include tourism and federal and state government activities.

Nonbasic Sector

The nonbasic sector consists of activities such as retail trade, services, and local government expenditures that provide goods and services primarily to local residents and which are therefore largely dependent on local economic conditions. In some situations, where retail trade has no competition within a large area or is unique (such as a retail outlet mall), retail trade can function as an export-oriented or basic industry because it brings in revenue from outside the region. For the most part, however, retail trade will fall into the nonbasic category.

Economic Base Analysis Assumptions

The economic base analysis technique assumes that the basic sector is the prime mover of the local economy; that is, the local economy will grow and prosper primarily because the basic sector exports goods and brings in additional money. Some of this money remains in the local economy, increasing the demand for goods and services provided by the nonbasic sector. That money then stimulates both nonbasic and additional basic economic activity as it cycles through the economy. The cycling of economic activity is referred to as the multiplier effect; input-output models estimate sector-specific multipliers.

Location Quotients

The first step in an economic base study is identifying the basic and nonbasic sectors. A simple way to do this is to use location quotients, which is the "ratio of ratios" that compares an industry's share of the local employment to its share of the national employment. The location quotient formula is as follows:

> Location quotient for industry i = (Regional employment in industry i) Total regional employment)) (National employment in industry i) Total national employment)

The numerator in the location quotient formula is the industry's share of the total regional employment; it is the portion of the local employment that is attributable to industry i. The denominator is the industry's share of the national employment; it is the portion of the national employment that is attributable to industry i. If the location quotient is greater than 1, the industry's local employment share is greater than its national employment share. The inference from a location quotient greater than 1 is that the region has more employment in this industry than is needed to support the local economy and creates a surplus for export, which means that the industry is a basic industry. Conversely, if the location quotient is less than 1, the local employment share is less than its national employment share, and it is assumed to be a nonbasic industry.

Example Location Quotient Calculation

Assume the following data for a particular year for a hypothetical region:

> Local employment in electrical equipment manufacturing = 28,080
> Total local employment = 328,580
> National employment in electrical equipment manufacturing = 1,943,300
> Total national employment = 66,713,000

Insert the data into the location quotient equation to yield the following:

> (28,080) 328,580)) (1,943,300) 66,713,000) – 2.93

In this example, the location quotient for electrical equipment manufacturing is 2.93, suggesting local specialization, surplus, export, and classification as a basic industry. Changes in the location quotient should be tracked over time. If the ratio drops, it may indicate some type of weakness in the export-oriented nature of the business within the region (Klosterman 1990).

Basic-Sector Employee Estimates

The location quotient can also be used to estimate the number of basic-sector employees in an industry, using the following formula:

> X_i) Total local employment = National employment in industry i)Total national employment
>
> Where X_i is local employment in industry i

This equation assumes that the industry's share of the local employment (the ratio on the left-hand side of the equation) is exactly equal to its share of the national employment (the ratio on the right-hand side of the equation)—the location quotient is assumed to be 1. The number of local employees in industry i (X_i) can be assumed to be nonbasic; it is just enough to serve the local demand. Any employment the area has beyond this minimum can be assumed to be basic; in other words, it serves the export market. If the local employment is less than this minimum, it can be assumed that the local employment is not enough to serve the local demand and all employment is nonbasic.

Example Basic-Sector Employee Calculation

Using the data from the location quotient example, the number of basic-sector employees can be calculated.

> X_i) 328,580 = 1,943,300) 66,713,000
> 66,713,000 × X_i = 1,943,300 × 328,580
> X_i = (1,943,300 × 328,580)) 66,713,000 = 9,571

This employment figure is assumed to be just enough to serve local demand for electrical equipment manufacturing. Any employment the region has in addition to this can be assumed to be basic, serving the export market. From the previous example, given that the region has a total of 28,080 employees in electrical equipment manufacturing, the difference (28,080 minus 9,571, or 18,509) can be assumed to be basic. So of the 28,080 jobs in the electrical equipment category, 65.9 percent are basic, and 34.1 percent are nonbasic.

ECONOMIC BASE PROJECTIONS

This projection technique involves multiplying the projected total basic-sector employment by a base multiplier, computed from historical data. This procedure assumes that the various sectors of the local economy will grow by the projected national or state growth rate; that is, the local economy will retain a constant share of the state or national employment in all industries. A more sophisticated shift-and-share projection technique accounts for the fact that a region's industries may grow more rapidly or more slowly than they do for the state or nation.

Using Economic Base Projections

There are five steps in building an economic base projection:

1. Obtain subnational or state employment projections, by sector (see table for sample state employment projections).
2. Calculate the projected state growth rates.
3. Use state growth rate to project the basic employment by sector and for the entire local economy (see table of projected basic employment by sector).
4. Calculate the base multiplier (BM) for the base year.
5. Project total local employment for the future year.

Stuart Meck, FAICP, American Planning Association, Chicago, Illinois; Richard Klosterman, Ph.D., The University of Akron, Akron, Ohio; James D. Ebenhoh, AICP, ECONorthwest, Eugene, Oregon; Terry Moore, FAICP, ECONorthwest, Eugene, Oregon

PROJECTIONS AND DEMAND ANALYSIS

SAMPLE STATE EMPLOYMENT PROJECTIONS BY SECTOR

SECTOR	STATE EMPLOYMENT 2000	PROJECTED STATE EMPLOYMENT 2010	GROWTH RATE 2000-2010
Agriculture	133,400	125,400	-0.06
Manufacturing	130,900	158,400	0.21
Transportation	226,100	269,100	0.19
Services	234,000	311,900	0.33

Source: Adapted from Klosterman 1990.

PROJECTED BASIC EMPLOYMENT BY SECTOR

SECTOR	2000 TOTAL LOCAL EMPLOYMENT	2000 BASIC INDUSTRY	GROWTH RATE 2000-2010	PROJECTED BASIC EMPLOYMENT
Agriculture	5,240	2,807	-0.06	2,639
Manufacturing	2,398	1,929	0.21	2,334
Transportation	612	510	0.19	607
Services	2,996	9	0.33	12
Total	11,246	5,255	—	5,592

Source: Adapted from Klosterman 1990.

Example Economic Base Projection

Using agriculture as the economic sector, the following is an example of an economic base projection:

1. Obtain subnational or state employment projections for agriculture from the table:

$$= 125,400$$

2. Calculate the projected state growth rate for agriculture:

Growth rate for 2000-2010 = (Projected employment in 2010 − Observed employment in 2000) ÷ Observed employment in 2000) = (125,400 − 133,400) 4 133,400 = -0.06

3. Use state growth rate to project the basic employment for agriculture and for the entire local economy:

Basic employment in Agriculture in 2010 = Basic employment in Agriculture in 2000 × (1 + Growth rate for 2000 to 2010) = 2,807 × (1.0 + -0.06) = 2,639

The projected basic employment in all sectors can be added to determine the total projected basic employment, which for this example is 5,592 (see the table).

4. Calculate the base multiplier (BM) for the base year, 2000.

BM = Total local employment for 2000
Total basic employment for 2000
= 11,246
5,255
= 2.14

5. Project total local employment for the future year, 2010:

Total local
employment in 2010 = Basic employment in 2010 × BM
= 5,592 × 2.14
= 11,967

ECONOMETRIC PROJECTION MODELS

Econometrics is the application of economic theory, mathematics, and statistical techniques for the purpose of testing hypotheses and forecasting economic phenomena, such as income and employment. Econometrics uses regression analysis, which relates dependent variables to one or more independent or explanatory variables. Sophisticated multivariate models (multiple dependent variables) use extensive historical data so that the model's predicted time path can be compared with the historical time path.

Using Econometric Projection Models

There are five steps in econometric model building:

1. A decision is made on the outputs or dependent variables to be modeled or forecasted.
2. A causal model is hypothesized that uses economic theory to identify the variables and relationships assumed to be related to the dependent variables.
3. The coefficients of the causal model are estimated from past data for the causal model and the output variables.
4. The regression coefficients are then used to forecast the possible effects of manipulating various controllable inputs, which are the policy variables.
5. A set of simulations of policy effects is built from a series of tests of the policy variables.

Typically, regional models are linked to national macroeconomic models, in order to apply national forecasts of economic changes to the local level as part of the time-series analysis.

Planning Applications of Econometric Modeling

Regional planning agencies in the United States often employ econometric modeling to predict job growth, which is then used in comprehensive planning and, in particular, transportation planning (Dick Conway and Associates, 2002). A forecast of employment is made for the regional level and then disaggregated to the local government level. For transportation planning, it is disaggregated to traffic analysis zones, which are the unit of analysis for modeling future vehicular trip generation.

REFERENCES

Dick Conway and Associates. September 2002. *Regional Economic and Demographic Data Base, Modeling and Forecasting.* Prepared for the Puget Sound Regional Council. Seattle, WA. Website: www.psrc.org/datapubs/pubs/step2002.pdf, accessed February 16, 2005.

Klosterman, Richard E. 1990. *Community Planning and Analysis Techniques.* Savage, MD: Rowman and Littlefield.

See also:
Comprehensive Plans
Transportation Plans

Stuart Meck, FAICP, American Planning Association, Chicago, Illinois; Richard Klosterman, Ph.D., The University of Akron, Akron, Ohio; James D. Ebenhoh, AICP, ECONorthwest, Eugene, Oregon; Terry Moore, FAICP, ECONorthwest, Eugene, Oregon

HOUSING NEEDS ASSESSMENT

A housing needs assessment is an inventory and analysis of existing housing needs and needs anticipated as a result of planned growth over a planning period. It evaluates the extent to which the existing and projected market can provide housing at various costs and for various rental levels. It involves quantitative techniques, such as forecasting; qualitative techniques, such as citizen surveys and site-specific surveys of housing conditions; and citizen involvement techniques, to identify goals, objectives, and priorities for housing programs. A housing needs assessment is used to prepare local comprehensive plans and for other governmental and private sector purposes.

PURPOSES OF A HOUSING NEEDS ASSESSMENT

A housing needs assessment may be prepared for the following purposes:

- As support for a housing element of a local comprehensive plan.
- As a prerequisite to receiving Community Development Block Grant (CDBG), HOME, and Emergency Shelter Grant funds from the U.S. Department of Housing and Urban Development. The 1990 National Affordable Housing Act, which HUD administers, requires a housing needs assessment in preparation of the "consolidated plan," the document that serves as the comprehensive housing assistance strategy for the purposes of the CDBG program.
- To assist local government task forces and commissions studying the problem of housing affordability.
- To assist the private and nonprofit sectors in making decisions about individual housing projects.

USES OF HOUSING NEEDS ASSESSMENTS

Typical uses of housing needs assessments include the following:

- Basis for economic development efforts
- Compliance with federal or state legislative or administrative requirements
- Defining budget priorities for expenditure of housing funds
- Descriptions and evaluations of the local housing situation
- Fund-raising
- Housing advocacy and community awareness
- Housing database development
- Housing information and referral
- Litigation
- Meeting requirements of private and public lenders

DETERMINING HOUSING NEED

One approach to determining housing need involves examining the choices householders make when selecting their next home. The first choice they face is tenure—whether to rent or own. Then they determine how much they can afford to pay for

housing—total monthly rent and expenses for renting or the purchase price and operating costs for owning. Finally, they decide on the preferred type of housing. Housing need can be considered met when a mix of housing units exists that satisfies these three choices for all households in the study area. A thorough housing needs assessment must account for tenure, income/price, and housing type projections that reflect the needs and preferences of the population to be housed.

The market- or demand-driven approach commonly used to define housing "needs" for an area may not address the true housing needs of that area's population. Local housing markets are frequently imperfect, and "demand" or supply may not be in equilibrium with actual needs. In many regions, new housing supply is a function of what local builders are inclined or able to produce, which may not be what the households in the region actually need or desire and can afford.

TYPICAL HOUSING NEEDS ASSESSMENT STEPS

The table here lists the typical steps involved when a governmental unit undertakes a housing needs analysis.

HOUSING FORECASTING

A housing forecast projects the number of housing units that will be needed at some future time. The analysis includes a study of how many housing units currently exist, and an estimate of how many are likely to be removed from supply and will thereby need replacement. For example, if high-rise public housing is scheduled to be removed during the analysis period, it will need to be replaced by other forms of subsidized housing. The analysis then projects how many households will want housing.

Need components are introduced as part of the demand forecast. For example, if it is concluded that 25 percent of the existing public housing units are inadequate and will need to be replaced, then this number may be added to the supply requirement. (A

governmental entity will be responsible for demolishing and replacing these units, either through a public housing authority or some other vehicle.) Similarly, if an analysis of census data and other sources determines that 20 percent of the households are paying in excess of 30 percent of their gross income on housing, this can be identified as the number of units that need to be supported by subsidies, either by the provision of Section 8 vouchers, or by the construction of housing that is affordable and subject to long-term affordability restrictions.

Housing Forecast Steps

A housing forecast for planning purposes involves the following two steps:

1. Defining the relevant housing region or the market area, which can be a local government, county, or a metropolitan area.
2. Identifying the components of change, which include the change in the number and composition of households, in the number of vacant units, and in the existing supply of housing.

Assuming that the analysis is begun sometime in the middle of the decade, a general and simple format for a five-year housing projection for 2006 to 2010 would be as shown in the table here. Note that this analysis does not further break down the housing demand by tenure choices or need into a variety of income subgroups.

IMPACT OF DATA ASSUMPTIONS

Assumptions about economic and population forecasts, household size (which can change over time), and the vacancy rate are key to the housing projections. Altering the assumptions of the forecasts will vary the outcomes. For example, increasing the desired vacancy rate raises the number of units that need to be produced. Changing the rate of economic and population growth also has an effect on the outcomes. In addition, if one has data for the first three or four years of a decade, that data may be arithmetically extrapolated to get to the middle of the decade.

STEPS IN THE HOUSING NEEDS ASSESSMENT AND STRATEGIC PLANNING PROCESS

STEP	DESCRIPTION
1. Initiate the process.	Develop an inclusive list of participants from which to select housing task force members. Plan for community awareness through the local media, housing tours, and public hearings.
2. Identify the problem.	Use quantitative and qualitative data sources and techniques to describe the housing concerns of the community. Select key addressable public policy issues, then prepare and circulate the preliminary mission statement.
3. Develop the community housing profile.	Assemble community population data, including housing demand, changes in the inventory, and the local housing delivery system. Use existing federal, state, and local data.
4. Assess local housing needs.	Select research methodologies to collect original data on housing needs and conditions of specific populations or neighborhoods. Interpret these relative, expressed, and perceived housing needs data against explicit housing standards.
5. Set public policy goals and objectives.	Given the political realities and economic situation of the communities, select and finalize broad goals to be accomplished. Use the housing needs assessment to shape a few community-specific objectives that are measurable and achievable.
6. Prepare community housing strategies and action plans.	State the accomplishments to be achieved, including their rationale(s). Prepare housing strategies and action plans, including new or revised policies, within the context of wider community planning initiatives.
7. Implement, monitor, and evaluate progress.	Present the strategies to obtain favorable public opinion of planned activities.

Source: Adapted from White, Jensen, and Cook 1992.

Stuart Meck, FAICP, American Planning Association, Chicago, Illinois; Richard Bjelland, Oregon Housing and Community Services, Salem, Oregon; Betty Jo White, Ph.D., Kansas State University, Manhattan, Kansas

EXAMPLE FIVE-YEAR HOUSING PROJECTION, 2006-2010

STEPS	2000 CENSUS	2005 ESTIMATE	2010 PROJECTION
Step 1: Collect and analyze population data.			
a. Population	250,000	285,000	325,000
b. Group population	20,000	23,000	25,000
c. Household population (a-b)	230,000	262,000	300,000
d. Average household size	2.8	2.7	2.6
e. Number of households (c/d)	82,100	97,000	115,400
Step 2: Collect and analyze housing data.			
f. Total housing units	85,000	101,000	121,500
g. Occupied housing units	82,100	97,000	115,400
h. Vacant units (f-g)	2,900	4,000	6,100
i. Vacancy rate ((h/f) × 100)	3.4%	4.0%	5.0%
Step 3: Determine housing demand.			
j. Change in number of households (e for 2010-e for 2000)	33,300		
k. Change in number of vacant units (h for 2010-h for 2000)	3,200		
l. Units lost that must be replaced (m+n+o)	8,500		
m. Units lost to disaster	800		
n. Units lost to conversion	1,000		
o. Units lost to demolition	6,700		
p. Total number of units needed 2000 to 2010 (j+k +l)	45,000		
q. Housing starts, 2000-2005	19,000		
r. Housing demand, 2006- 2010	26,000		

Source: Adapted from Lieder 1988.

CALCULATING THE NUMBER OF AFFORDABLE HOUSING UNITS IN A JURISDICTION

As part of a housing needs assessment, one must calculate the number of existing dwelling units that constitute affordable housing, owner- and renter-occupied, vacant, and for sale or for rent. The U.S. Department of Housing and Urban Development (HUD) definitions of "affordable housing," as used in the regulations for the Consolidated Plan (24 CFR 91.5 Definitions), include:

> **Moderate-income housing:** housing that is affordable to households with incomes between 50 and 80 percent of the median income for county or primary metropolitan statistical area.

> **Low-income housing:** housing affordable to households with incomes between 30 and 50 percent of the median income.

> **Extremely low-income housing:** housing affordable to households with incomes less than 30 percent of the median income.

Note, however, that HUD regulations on these definitions vary by federal program, and other federal programs may use different definitions.

As a general rule, housing for low-income and extremely low-income households is hard to achieve without governmental subsidies.

The affordability of housing is calculated as a maximum percentage of household income. In the case of dwelling units for sale, housing that is affordable is that in which the mortgage, amortization, taxes, and insurance constitute no more than 30 percent of the gross annual household income. In the case of dwelling units for rent, housing that is affordable is that for which the rent and utilities constitute no more than 30 percent of the gross annual household income.

Data on median income may be obtained from two sources: the U.S. Census Bureau for the year 2000, which includes median reported household income from 1999; and HUD, which periodically publishes median family income data as well as monthly fair market rents for nonmetropolitan counties and primary metropolitan statistical areas, adjusted by household size (HUD 2002).

Typical Calculation Steps

The method below identifies and counts owner-occupied and rental units that are within the means of a household earning 80 percent or less of the area's median household income for such a household. It then determines whether the number of such units will satisfy a state-established or local-established goal of having at least 10 percent of the local year-round housing stock as affordable housing. This method is adapted from the Report on Affordable Housing Planning and Appeal Act, Public Act 93-595, as amended by Public Act 93-678, prepared by the University of Illinois Building Research Council for the Illinois Housing Development Finance Authority in 2004.

1. Determine the maximum monthly payment for affordable owner-occupied and rental housing. For either rental or ownership, this is a product of the median household income multiplied by the median income affordability level multiplied by the maximum share of income to spend on housing divided by 12 months. Note that by varying the specific affordability level (30, 60, or 80 percent are

typical levels) one can identify low- or extremely low-income payment levels.

2. Determine the maximum house value corresponding to the maximum monthly payment for owner-occupied and for-sale units.

For dwelling units for sale, detailed U.S. Census data on house value are available within the Summary File 3 (SF3) in Table H84, Value for All Owner-Occupied Housing Units, and Table H87, Price Asked for Specified Vacant-for-Sale-Only Housing Units. In this step, the maximum affordable monthly housing payment is converted to a corresponding house value, so that these detailed census data may be used.

Mortgage and amortization are the monthly principal and interest payments required as part of an amortized mortgage. The maximum monthly affordable housing payment and data on mortgage costs, including principal and interest payment, taxes, and insurance, are translated to a housing value for the hypothetical local government.

Insurance costs, which in this method are independent of housing value, are subtracted from the maximum affordable monthly payment. Next, data related to the housing price, including tax rate, mortgage interest rate and term, and down-payment size, are used to calculate the maximum affordable housing price using equations. The equations work in the same manner as mortgage calculators used on many websites, including that of Fannie Mae, and produce identical results.

3. Count the number of affordable units. The decennial census provides extensive data on house value and rental costs for each municipality, including the number of units in each price category for owner-occupied housing and for units that are vacant and for sale, and the number of units in various cost ranges for rental costs for renter occupied units, and vacant units.

These data can be compared directly to the maximum affordable monthly payment. Data for vacant for-rent units are provided on "asking rent." For the vast majority of rental units, gross rent, which includes utilities, is used to determine affordability. For owner-occupied units, the number of units at or below the maximum affordable house price is determined using census data on house value or price asked.

To determine the number of affordable rental units, count the number of units in each municipality and county at or below the maximum affordable monthly payment using census data on gross rent.

Census 2000 provides the number of units that fall into either one of 24 different sales price ranges or one of 21 different rent ranges. The number of affordable housing units is the number of units that have sales price or rent less than a cut-off value, calculated as described above. For the range that includes a cut-off value, a straight-line interpolation of the boundary values in the sales price or rent range is used under the assumption that the cut-off value lies on the left side of the peak point on a normal distribution curve. Since a normal distribution curve tends to place over a straight line on the left side of its peak point, the method may be slightly conservative.

Stuart Meck, FAICP, American Planning Association, Chicago, Illinois; Richard Bjelland, Oregon Housing and Community Services, Salem, Oregon; Betty Jo White, Ph.D., Kansas State University, Manhattan, Kansas

4. Calculate the percentage of affordable units to the statewide goal of 10 percent. To determine the percentage of the housing stock that is affordable, use the following formula:

Percentage of housing units that are affordable = [[affordable rental units that are occupied or for rent] + [affordable owner-occupied and for-sale units] ÷ [total year-round units for which affordability is determined]] × 100

GROUPS WITH SPECIAL HOUSING NEEDS

The Comprehensive Housing Affordability Strategy (CHAS), a component of the consolidated plan that is submitted to HUD, requires a housing needs assessment of persons with special needs. Persons in the following groups may or may not be low-income, but each one faces special housing problems that should be addressed by any complete community housing assessment:

- At-risk youth, homeless and/or runaways
- Elderly, frail
- Families, large (with more than five members)
- Farmworkers
- Homeless or at risk of homelessness
- Households, single-parent
- Persons released from correctional institutions
- Persons infected with AIDS-HIV
- Persons recovering from drug/alcohol abuse
- Persons with developmental disabilities
- Persons with physical disabilities
- Persons with psychiatric disabilities
- Teen parents
- Victims of domestic violence/other abuse

Accurate information on these populations can help decision makers focus on those groups that most need assistance. This information will be very useful in determining groups with a severe need for assistance. The facts can be used to educate others and advocate for support. Once the housing study is complete, use this information to prioritize a community's affordable housing efforts.

REFERENCES

Lieder, Constance. 1988. "Planning for Housing," in Chapter 12 of *The Practice of Local Government Planning*, 2d ed. Frank S. So and Judith Getzels, eds. Washington, DC: International City Management Association, 388-391.

U.S. Department of Housing and Urban Development. 2002. *Guide to PD&R Data Sets*. Washington, DC: HUD Office of Policy Development and Research.

University of Illinois, Building Research Council. June 232004. *Report on Affordable Housing Planning and Appeal Act Public Act 93-595, as Amended by Public Act 93-678*. Champaign, IL: University of Illinois Building Research Council.

White, Betty Jo, Marjorie Jensen, and Christine Cook. 1992. *Developing Community Housing Needs Assessments and Strategies: A Self-Help Guidebook for Nonmetropolitan Communities*. Prepared with the assistance of the Kansas Center for Rural Initiatives and distributed by American Association of Housing Educators (AAHE). Manhattan, KS: AAHE.

See also:
Comprehensive Plans
Housing Plans
Residential Types

Stuart Meck, FAICP, American Planning Association, Chicago, Illinois; Richard Bjelland, Oregon Housing and Community Services, Salem, Oregon; Betty Jo White, Ph.D., Kansas State University, Manhattan, Kansas

PARKS, RECREATION, AND OPEN-SPACE NEEDS ASSESSMENT

Parks, recreation, and open-space needs assessments are used to determine community needs or gaps between existing and ideal conditions, including parks, recreation facilities, programs, operations, and maintenance. Such needs assessments should be conducted to form the basis for decisions such as the location and size of needed parks and open spaces; the types of recreation facilities and programs that should be provided; phasing priorities; and funding/implementation strategies.

APPLICATIONS

Findings from a parks, recreation and open-space needs assessment are most commonly used to determine the following:

- level of resident satisfaction with existing facilities, programs, and services;
- community needs, priorities, and preferences for various types of parks, facilities, and/or programs; and
- willingness and/or preferences of residents to fund needed improvements, facilities, and/or programs.

COMPONENTS

Typical components of a parks, recreation, and open-space needs assessment include the following:

- identification of target constituents or populations;
- determination of the techniques most likely to generate credible, meaningful results in a cost-effective manner;
- development of instruments such as workshop exercises, survey questionnaires, interview discussion points, and other tools to be used as part of the assessment;
- tabulation, interpretation, and summary of the findings; and
- identification of the consensus-building process, such as deciding who will review and approve the findings.

OUTCOMES

When designing a needs assessment process, first clarify the desired outcomes. Among the questions to consider:

- Who does the agency want to reach?
- How will the information be used?
- Who will review and approve the findings?

The true test of a needs assessment is whether the affected stakeholders believe in the credibility of the results and support actions proposed as a result of the process.

TECHNIQUES

A variety of techniques are commonly used in parks, recreation, and open-space needs assessments. When selecting the techniques that are most appropriate for a given situation, the concept of triangulation—

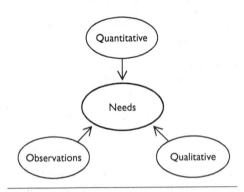

TRIANGULATION FOR NEEDS ASSESSMENT

Source: Glatting Jackson 2004.

approaching needs from at least three different vantage points—becomes particularly useful. An assessment conducted solely from the vantage point of organized sports leagues, for example, may indicate that additional sports fields are the highest priority in a community. In reality, safe bikeways and quiet sitting areas may be more important than sports fields to most residents. Thus, the practice of triangulation helps ensure a more accurate assessment of community needs.

Most types of assessment tools fall into one three categories: anecdotal, qualitative, and quantitative techniques. Not all of the techniques listed below need to be used, but at least two or three techniques should be selected from each category to ensure that the needs assessment process is objective.

Anecdotal

Anecdotal techniques are sometimes the most valid assessment tools, although they are the least scientific. These techniques can be used to form the "first tier" of a needs assessment, if properly recorded and documented:

- Site visits and photographs
- Phone calls and/or personal conversations with facility/program participants
- Personal observations
- Informal discussions with parks and recreation staff

Qualitative

Qualitative techniques involve talking with a cross section of community stakeholders to identify common themes, needs, and interests. While not as scientific and objective as quantitative techniques, qualitative techniques can provide insight into community issues, hidden agendas, and emotions. First identify the community stakeholders to be included in the process, and then select the appropriate techniques for each. For instance, the top 100 community leaders might be selected for phone interviews.

Qualitative techniques include the following:

- Staff interviews and workshops
- Interviews with elected officials and community leaders
- Interviews with representatives of public school

boards, nonprofit organizations, and other parks and recreation providers
- Focus group meetings
- Workshops with various stakeholders

Quantitative

Quantitative techniques are scientifically based and are often considered to have the greatest level of credibility; however, numbers, too, can be manipulated to support various positions. Therefore, quantitative techniques should never be used alone to determine community needs and priorities.

Typical quantitative techniques include the following:

- Measuring acreage level of service (acres per 1,000 population).
- Measuring facilities' level of service (number of facilities per 1,000 population).
- Mapping park and recreation facility service areas (geographic distance served by various facilities).
- Benchmarking against other communities of a similar size and demographic (including acreage, facilities, staff, and budget, for example).
- Measuring existing capacity versus demand for various facilities and programs.
- Measuring per capita investment in parks by planning or political district.
- Conducting a telephone or mail survey.

Most of these quantitative techniques are *comparison exercises,* designed to reveal any gaps between existing and ideal circumstances. Of all of the quantitative techniques, the telephone survey is the most accurate and reliable. If conducted correctly, using a qualified statistician/professional researcher who can determine the appropriate sample size and design the most effective survey tool, the telephone survey can yield results that most closely reflect the opinions and feelings of community residents.

STANDARDS AND GUIDELINES GENERALLY

Relying on state or federal standards to determine community needs can be time-efficient and cost-effective; that said, this approach is problematic. Standards and guidelines developed at the federal level cannot address the conditions present in individual communities. State guidelines are intended to address conditions only in that state or region and may not be applicable elsewhere in the country. For example, Florida's Statewide Comprehensive Outdoor Recreation Plan (SCORP) contains population guidelines for various types of recreation facilities but encourages local jurisdictions to develop their own guidelines to better reflect local conditions.

NATIONAL RECREATION AND PARK ASSOCIATION GUIDELINES

The National Recreation and Park Association's (NRPA) *Park, Recreation, Open Space and Greenway Guidelines* provides a framework for park system planning. It also includes an approach to developing

David L. Barth, ASLA AICP CPRP, Glatting Jackson Kercher Anglin Lopez Rinehart, Inc., West Palm Beach, Florida

a level-of-service (LOS) standard for local communities, based on estimates of local supply and demand. There are eight basic steps in this demand analysis:

1. Determine park classifications.
2. Determine recreation activity menus.
3. Determine open-space standards.
4. Determine present supply.
5. Determine expressed demand.
6. Determine minimum population service requirements.
7. Determine individual LOS for each park class.
8. Determine total LOS for the entire parks system.

FINDINGS

Once a needs assessment has been completed, document the results so that common themes, issues, and priorities can be easily identified. The top priorities of a community tend to consistently appear as a top priority, regardless of the technique used. Planners may wish to weight some techniques more than others; for example, a 500-person telephone survey may carry more weight than a public workshop attended by only three residents.

Present the findings of the needs assessment to several stakeholder groups to build consensus regarding interpretation of the findings and to discuss preliminary recommendations and actions. The needs assessment process can be considered successful only when there is broad-based acceptance of the findings and support for the proposed resultant actions.

REFERENCES

Florida Department of Environmental Protection. 2002. *Outdoor Recreation in Florida 2000: Florida's Statewide Comprehensive Outdoor Recreation Plan (SCORP)*. Tallahassee, FL.

Mertes, James D., and James R. Hall. 1996. *Park, Recreation, Open Space and Greenway Guidelines*. Alexandria, VA: National Recreation and Park Association.

See also:
Parks and Open-Space Plans
Types of Parks

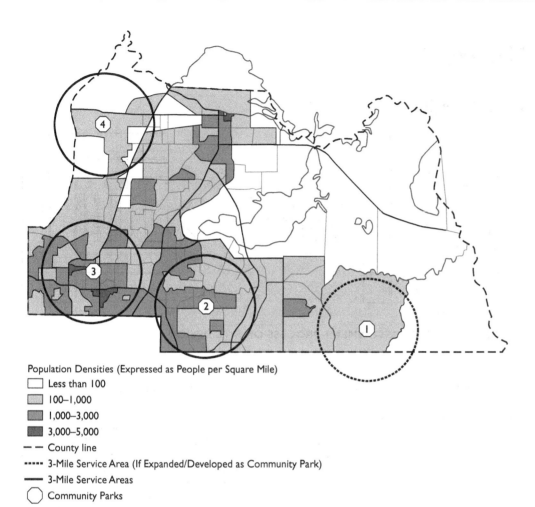

Population Densities (Expressed as People per Square Mile)

☐ Less than 100
▨ 100–1,000
▨ 1,000–3,000
▨ 3,000–5,000
– – County line
····· 3-Mile Service Area (If Expanded/Developed as Community Park)
— 3-Mile Service Areas
⬡ Community Parks

TYPICAL SERVICE AREA MAP

Source: Adapted from Glatting Jackson service area map for Seminole County, Florida.

SAMPLE COUNTY-LEVEL PARK ACREAGE LOS GUIDELINES FROM STATE SCORP

	2000	2005	2010	2015	2020
Total County Population	198,143	222,140	245,542	265,185	286,400
Acreage of Community Parks (2000)	217	217	217	217	217
Acres Needed for Total Population (according to SCORP standards)	396	444	491	530	573
Surplus/Deficit	-179	-227	-274	-313	-356
Acres Needed for Total Population (according to comprehensive plan)	991	1111	1228	1326	1432
Surplus/Deficit	-774	-894	-1011	-1109	-1215

David L. Barth, ASLA AICP CPRP, Glatting Jackson Kercher Anglin Lopez Rinehart, Inc., West Palm Beach, Florida

IMPACT ASSESSMENT

ENVIRONMENTAL IMPACT ASSESSMENT

Environmental impact assessment involves systematically identifying, evaluating, discussing, and documenting the potential beneficial and adverse consequences of implementing a project, development, or program. An effective, balanced impact assessment process considers a broad range of community and natural resources and uses these insights to help shape project design. Impact assessment considers the long-term outcomes associated with a project and its operation, and the short-term effects of project implementation, as a result of construction activities.

The scope of the impact assessment depends on the nature and magnitude of the proposed project, as well as the characteristics of the project site and adjacent area. It may consider ecological features and communities, combined with economic, cultural, aesthetic, health, safety, and neighborhood impacts, and identify the potential trade-offs across these resources. This comprehensive consideration of project effects early in project development can make the difference between successful project implementation and a project that cannot be realized.

Critical elements in the environmental impact assessment process are identifying possible measures to avoid, reducing potentially adverse impacts, and maximizing the project or program's beneficial effects. The most effective environmental impact assessment processes include proactive and inclusive collaboration with a wide range of potential stakeholders, including agencies with jurisdiction over the proposed activity or affected resources, and the potentially affected public. Through this collaboration, combined with an understanding of the potential effects of different courses of action, project sponsors can most effectively steer the project development process and ensure responsiveness to a wide range of values and perspectives while meeting project objectives.

ROLE OF ENVIRONMENTAL IMPACT ASSESSMENT IN PROJECT PLANNING

In its most basic form, environmental impact assessment provides a basis for informed, sound decision making during project design and development. It consists of understanding existing and future conditions in sufficient detail to predict how the implementation of a proposed project might alter these conditions.

Depending on the nature of the potential consequences revealed, project design can be altered to enhance positive effects on the natural and human environment or to avoid or reduce potentially adverse impacts. Environmental impact assessment ensures that potential problems are identified and addressed in the early stages of project planning and design through a systematic technical process, combined with open public discussion and disclosure. The earlier in the project planning process the potential effects are identified and evaluated, the greater

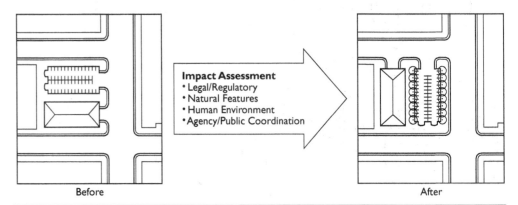

EFFECT OF IMPACT ASSESSMENT PROCESS ON SITE DESIGN

Source: Diana Mendes.

the potential to increase the project's "fit" into the community context in a manner that promotes sustainable development by respecting natural, social, and economic resources.

In addition to ensuring compliance with pertinent environmental laws, regulations, and requirements, there are other potential benefits of early impact assessment:

- Increased environmental quality
- Improved community design
- Reduced project costs
- Reductions in the time required to implement projects
- Increased community support

ENVIRONMENTAL IMPACT ASSESSMENT CONSIDERATIONS

In preparing to identify and analyze a project's likely outcomes, comprehensively consider the scope of the impact assessment and how resources can be effectively allocated to focus on those issues most relevant to decision making. Scoping should be based on a description of the project with respect to the legal and regulatory context, natural environment, human environment, and agency and public coordination issues.

Legal and Regulatory Context

Environmental laws and regulations provide important foundations governing environmental impact assessment. Early consultation and understanding of these laws and regulations are important, as they can define and influence the:

- process to follow;
- resources to include;
- breadth of the technical analysis to conduct;
- methods and analytical techniques to employ;
- types and format of the documentation to prepare; and

- extent to which coordination with agencies and the public is necessary

Projects with federal funds are required to comply with the National Environmental Policy Act (NEPA). Several states have enacted statutes similar to NEPA that apply to state-sponsored projects irrespective of federal funding.

In addition, there are also specific laws and regulations at the federal, state, and local levels governing particular resources, such as coastal zones, floodplains, wetlands, endangered species, and forests. These specific statutes and regulations relate to both natural resources and elements of the human environment, including land use, housing, noise, contaminated materials, civil rights, and protected populations such as minority and low-income communities.

The Natural Environment

The natural environment includes air, land, water, and other biological resources that could be affected by implementation of a project or program. (See Part 2 of this book for a more in-depth of discussion of these resources.)

The Human Environment

The analysis of a project's effects on the human environment should include land use and development, communities and neighborhoods, historic and archaeological resources, transportation systems, and economic impacts.

Land Use and Development

The impact assessment should focus on the proposed project's compatibility in terms of density, scale, and intensity of use with existing and planned land-use activities on and adjacent to the project site, and compatibility with the existing and planned character of adjacent land uses and development. An important element of the analysis is the degree to which the project might support or discourage land-use conver-

Diana C. Mendes, AICP, DMJM+Harris Planning, Fairfax, Virginia

sions, and the extent to which these conversions are consistent with longer-term community goals and objectives.

Communities and Neighborhoods

Community and neighborhood impact assessment is an iterative process that focuses on the character of the area combined with the aspects of the social environment that area residents value and that contribute to their quality of life. Analyses should address the following:

- Demographic and socioeconomic characteristics and trends
- Effects on growth, decline, or redevelopment
- Propensity to support neighborhood transitions or encourage stability
- Impacts on community cohesion
- Property values
- Displacement of residents and businesses
- Tax-base implications
- Increases or decreases in employment
- Noise
- Aesthetics
- Safety
- Demands on public facilities and services, among others

To complete the impact assessment process successfully and develop a project that responds to community needs, affected communities must be consulted and residents must be involved proactively in discussing and understanding the potential benefits and negative consequences of the project. In addition, impacts to utilities can cause significant community disruption associated with the need to physically relocate the utility, disruptions to service, or the need to add capacity.

Historic and Archaeological Resources

Historic and archaeological resources are important for their cultural value, are often distinguishing characteristics of the community fabric, and help to shape community identity. These resources are protected by a variety of federal, state, and local laws and regulations that govern the assessment of the effects of a project on the resources in terms of both the resource itself as well as the context.

Transportation Impacts

Transportation system impacts associated with a proposed project can include increases in demand for existing infrastructure, effects on level of service on affected roadways and at intersections, enhancements or limitations on access and mobility, changes in pedestrian and vehicular circulation patterns, and effects on safety. These impacts can cause the need for additional improvements to transportation infrastructure as a condition of implementing the project, or the payment of fees in lieu of improvements.

Economic Impacts

Economic impacts include assessment of project costs and benefits. These costs and benefits can be assessed at both the regional and site-specific scales. Fiscal impacts associated with the project, as well as who pays and who benefits, should be addressed.

Agency and Public Coordination Issues

Maintain open and continuous coordination and communication with advisory, resource, and regulatory agencies with jurisdiction over the project area and with the affected public to complete an environmental impact assessment successfully. When effectively conducted, the impact assessment process can be a forum for collaborative problem solving. Agency contacts and community leaders can be valuable resources in iden-

tifying and verifying potential issues and concerns, and how those concerns might be most effectively addressed. Build and maintain solid working relationships with agencies and the public over the process of the impact assessment to generate support for the findings of the analysis; resolve misunderstandings as early as possible; and avoid late-stage surprises that can delay the conclusions of the impact assessment, undermine support for the project, increase project costs, or cause delays in project completion.

ENVIRONMENTAL IMPACT ASSESSMENT PROCESS

There are seven typical steps in an environmental impact assessment process:

1. Establish boundaries relating to the project, study area, limits of potential effects, and process participants.
2. Identify environmental and community resources that could be affected by the project.
3. Define legal requirements, including laws, regulations, ordinances, and public notification.
4. Initiate coordination with local governments, resource and regulatory agencies, affected communities, and the general public, as well as any groups with special interest or jurisdiction.
5. Establish impact assessment methodologies, including assumptions, technical protocols, and review processes.
6. Analyze and document potential effects, and widely communicate and disseminate the findings to appropriate parties.
7. Collaborate with project designers and sponsors to refine and finalize the project program and design, and to identify modifications that reduce potential adverse impacts and incorporate beneficial features.

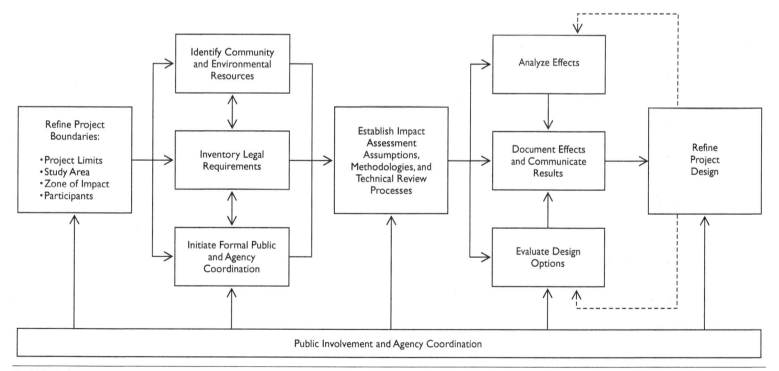

TYPICAL STEPS IN ENVIRONMENTAL IMPACT ASSESSMENT

Source: Diana Mendes.

Diana C. Mendes, AICP, DMJM+Harris Planning, Fairfax, Virginia

IMPACT ASSESSMENT

This approach enables project sponsors to identify potential issues and take control of uncertainties associated with potential impacts and the public perception of those impacts. The process culminates in documenting the project's evolution by considering effects on the natural and human environment through open public discussion, and developing a project that responds to local needs and conditions.

Key Goals of the Process

- Raise potential project issues early in the impact assessment process for discussion and resolution.
- Conserve project resources by concentrating on the issues most relevant to project decision making.
- Limit the potential for unexpected cost increases or schedule delays during subsequent project phases as a result of environmental uncertainties or unresolved issues.

- Reduce the risk of future project opposition or legal challenges by providing objective, factual information regarding potential project effects and by cultivating consensus for the results.
- Proactively identify and pursue opportunities to modify project design to avoid and minimize impacts to important social, economic, and environmental resources, including mitigation.
- Establish a defensible public record documenting findings, results, conclusions, and the public and agency coordination process used to review this information.

Typical challenges faced in conducting a successful environmental impact assessment include effectively balancing the needs of the project or project sponsor with those of affected resources or communities; resolving differences of opinion on the

appropriate level of analysis to be undertaken; ensuring the reliability of the data available to conduct the analysis; and providing participation throughout the process that is broad and inclusive.

Establish Boundaries and Identify Interested Parties

Give particular care to establishing the definition and limits of the project and the scope of the proposed analysis of potential impacts. This includes defining both the study area and the appropriate boundaries to be applied to conduct the impact assessment. The area of potential project effects may vary from resource to resource, and different interests may well perceive different limits of analysis as appropriate. Consequently, as part of this initial phase, all parties with a potential interest in the results of the impact assessment must be con-

Consideration or Factor	Alternative A	Alternative B	Alternative C	Alternative D
Natural Environment				
Wetlands				
Acres Impacted	2	6	1	0
Functions Affected	Water Quality	Habitat and Water Quality	Water Quality	None
Floodplains				
Acres Impacted	3	10	1	0
Fill Required (Cubic Yards)	50,000	150,000	25,000	0
Detracts from Floodplain Values	Yes	Yes	No	No
Violations of National Ambient Air Quality Standards				
Carbon Monoxide (Number of Receptors)	0	0	0	2
Human Environment				
Potential for Community Disruption	Low	Low	Medium	High
Visual Impacts	Low	Low	Medium	High
Cultural Resources				
Historic Structures Demolished	0	0	2	6
Archaeological Sites Disturbed	1	2	0	0
Parklands				
Number of Parklands Affected	0	0	1	2
Total Acreage Impacted	0	0	10	5
Facilities Disrupted	None	None	3 Ballfields	Trails System
Transportation Impacts				
Number of Intersections with Level of Service F	1	1	1	5
Increased Potential for Cut-Through Traffic	Low	Low	Low	High
Disruption to Pedestrian Circulation	No	No	Yes	Yes
Noise and Vibration				
Number of Sensitive Receptors Affected	2	5	2	10
Land Use				
Compatibility with Existing Uses	Yes	No	Yes	No
Compatibility with Future Plans	No	Yes	Yes	Yes
Residential Units Displaced	0	0	2	15
Businesses Displaced	0	0	2	4

SAMPLE COMPARATIVE IMPACT ASSESSMENT MATRIX

Source: Diana Mendes.

Diana C. Mendes, AICP, DMJM+Harris Planning, Fairfax, Virginia

sulted in developing the physical and analytical "scope" of the impact assessment.

Identify Environmental and Community Resources

Identifying all the resources that the project could affect involves locating the best available data sources, including current aerial photography. Conduct a survey of the project and study area through field visits. Based on these activities, create databases and maps for future analysis using either manual methods or, if available, a geographic information system (GIS). Verify the resources and conditions identified in consultation with those having jurisdiction over the resource or those who are potentially affected by the project.

Define Legal Requirements

A comprehensive search of applicable laws, regulations, and guidance can provide the background needed to initiate an impact assessment process. Equally important to the procedural, technical, or documentation requirements articulated in these sources are the public notification and comment requirements. In reviewing these requirements, identify opportunities for streamlining the impact assessment process through consolidating similar requirements, such as data collection. Note that some resources or impacts that are of concern to affected parties many not be formally protected by a specific statute or regulations. Consequently, for most projects, it is not sufficient to limit the impact assessment only to those resources that are afforded legal protection.

Initiate Coordination

Local governments, agencies with jurisdiction over affected resources, communities, and residents who must live with the outcomes of a proposed project need to understand how the project might affect them. Information on the project, including decisions that have been made, should be presented and discussed with affected governments, agencies, and communities early in project planning, before project decisions are finalized, and when changes are easier to make.

Establish Impact Assessment Methodologies

Agree upon and document the assumptions, technical protocols, and review processes associated with the impact assessment process. Consensus must be reached on the methodologies prior to conducting the actual impact assessment, to maintain the integrity of the process and manage the expenditure of resources.

Most impact assessment processes involve the use of both quantitative and qualitative measures. The potential impacts on many resources are sometimes best understood through a combination of both quantitative and qualitative measures. For example, in assessing the potential visual effects of a project, it might be appropriate to understand the number of residents who might experience either a quantitative (percent of obstruction) or qualitative (subjective interpretation) change or both.

Analyze, Document, and Communicate Potential Effects

Analyze potential effects clearly and concisely and document those findings to meet the needs of a broad range of interests. Documentation can be highly technical to satisfy the requirements of a specific resource agency or take the form of nontechnical narrative and graphics, designed to communicate to the lay reader. When conducting the analysis and completing the documentation, consider the audiences who need to assimilate the information, and decide on a course of action.

The analysis and documentation should address both long-term (operational) and short-term (construction) effects, for both adverse and beneficial impacts. The analysis should cover direct, indirect, secondary, and cumulative impacts:

- Direct impacts result from physical intrusion into or use of a resource.
- Indirect impacts occur as a result of adjacency, absent physical occupation.
- Secondary impacts are induced as a result of the project, but are not associated with the specific physical components or elements of the project.
- Cumulative impacts result when a particular resource or area is subject to multiple, simultaneous, or sequential impacts that limit or weaken its capability to assimilate or recover from the effects.

Collaborate to Refine the Project

One of the most difficult but critical tasks associated with environmental impact assessment is to interpret and translate the findings into meaningful recommendations. This is an iterative, multidisciplinary process that can involve reevaluating the initial impact assessment as the project design evolves to the final program, design, and configuration.

ROLE OF MITIGATION IN IMPACT ASSESSMENT

Mitigation measures can avoid or reduce potential impacts on the human and natural environment. The identification of potential mitigation measures should evolve during impact assessment and inform project design. This process typically occurs in close consultation with appropriate advisory, resource, and regulatory agencies, as well as interested citizens. An essential component of impact assessment is to understand which impacts might warrant mitigation; the extent of likely mitigation required; the potential opportunities or difficulties associated with mitigation efforts; and the effects of mitigation on project costs, schedule, and implementation.

Mitigation actions typically include the following:

- Considering alternative project designs that avoid the resource, either by selecting one site over another, altering the site program, or modifying the facilities configuration so that development can avoid a specific resource or avoid a conflict with an adjacent land use.
- Incorporating features that buffer the resource from potential impact, or otherwise minimize the extent of the impacts (if avoidance is not possible), such as constructing noise walls to shield a community from the potential increases in noise associated with highway construction, or incorporating landscape planting into a site plan to preserve or screen views.
- Replacing a resource or facility that may be lost or altered with an in-kind replacement of the lost resource, facility, or associated values. Replacement should occur in proximity to the location of impact, so that the benefits of mitigation can accrue to the people, community, or natural systems that experience the loss or potentially adverse effects of the project.
- Documenting the resources to be impacted or lost. For example, for projects involving demolition of historic buildings, it is common to prepare measured drawings and archival quality photographs of the structure, along with a narrative regarding its historical significance.
- Enhancing the remaining resources, such as restoring or rehabilitating a historic structure, adding supplemental planting in a natural area such as a forest or floodplain to increase habitat values, or cleaning up and remediating an area known to contain contaminants.
- Contributing to mitigation banks, which can either be actual replacement of the resource, or a cash contributions in lieu of replacement. This mitigation technique is used most frequently for resources such as wetlands. In some areas, systems have been established to support monetary compensation as an offset to a potential impact through a financial contribution to an established fund or mitigation bank.

See also:
Environmental Management Overview
Federal Legislation
Historic Districts
Participation
State Enabling Legislation

Diana C. Mendes, AICP, DMJM+Harris Planning, Fairfax, Virginia

FISCAL IMPACT ANALYSIS

Fiscal impact analysis compares local government costs against local government revenues associated with land-use policies and specific development projects. It projects net cash flow to the public sector resulting from development. The analysis indicates if and when a community could face budget deficits. Local governments are then able to weigh land-use policy decisions, acceptable levels of public services, plans for capital investments, and long-term borrowing needs, in addition to prompting local officials to evaluate current and future revenue sources.

FISCAL IMPACT ANALYSIS STEPS

There are four basic steps common to all fiscal impact analysis, regardless of methodology:

1. Determine the relevant demand base(s). These demand bases are generated by the land-use change, development project, or growth scenario alternative being analyzed. They usually include number and types of housing units, population, school-age children, nonresidential building area, employment, and similar data.
2. Estimate the public sector costs to serve these demand bases.
3. Estimate the public sector revenue generated by these demand bases.
4. Compare the resulting costs to revenue.

TYPES OF FISCAL IMPACT ANALYSIS

The majority of fiscal impact analyses conducted throughout the country fall into one of three categories:

- Land-use analysis
- Project analysis
- Areawide analysis

Land-Use Analysis

In this type of analysis the characteristics of various residential and nonresidential "prototypes" are defined; the annual costs and revenues are then determined for each land use to understand the generalized impacts each land use independently has on a local government budget. The factors used to define these prototypes typically include persons per household, employment per 1,000 square feet, vehicle trips, assessed value, and other factors. The table "Residential Prototypes" shows an example of inputs used in defining residential land-use prototypes.

Project Analysis

Local governments conduct this type of fiscal analysis most commonly. Whereas a prototype land-use fiscal impact analysis evaluates the impact of individual land uses, a project analysis evaluates the overall fiscal impacts of all land uses combined, usually over a specific time frame. However, because most project-level analyses are prepared in conjunction with development proposals, this type of analysis is incremental: it addresses the impacts of only one development project at a time, typically in isolation.

Areawide Analysis

An areawide analysis can be applied to a neighborhood, several contiguous neighborhoods, or an entire city, county, or region. This type of analysis is cumulative: it evaluates the fiscal impacts of all anticipated development within the analysis area over a defined period, usually between 10 and 20 years. It is common for this type of analysis to evaluate different development scenarios, which can include variations in absorption schedules, comparison of alternative land-use plans, or a comparison of alternative development patterns. The table "Scenario 2: Totals" shows an example of annual scenario projections for residential and nonresidential land uses.

FISCAL IMPACT ANALYSIS APPLICATIONS

A fiscal impact analysis has many applications that are of benefit to both planners and budget personnel. From a planning perspective, a fiscal impact analysis directly links proposed zoning and land uses with projected population and employment growth related to residential and nonresidential development, bringing a realistic sense of the cost of growth into public discussion. From a budget and finance perspective, a fiscal impact analysis provides a link between land-use and budget considerations. The following examples indicate how fiscal analysis can be an effective tool for land-use and financial planning.

Land-Use Policies

Suppose a jurisdiction is considering whether to encourage higher-density land uses or allow an overlay district in a certain subarea. If costs, as well as other factors, are to be considered, then a fiscal impact evaluation can provide valuable information to aid the decision-making process.

Rezonings

A rezoning changes the density or type of use for a parcel; it may also signal a change in development policy. Too often, significant rezoning cases are not sufficiently evaluated from a fiscal perspective. In many cases, the outputs from a fiscal analysis can be helpful in local government-developer negotiations.

Annexations

Annexations are often attractive to a city because of the potential for realizing instant revenues from property taxes and, in many cases, sales and income taxes. Costs are rarely considered, because it takes longer to ascertain the costs of increased demands for services and extension of infrastructure. As shown in the graph here, a fiscal impact analysis quantifies the net surplus or deficit resulting from an annexation.

Capital Improvement Programming

Capital improvement planning takes on an extra dimension with the use of fiscal analysis, which enables a local government to forecast the need for additional capital facilities, given projected increases in population or employment. Fiscal analysis also clarifies the timing of infrastructure improvements by incorporating the demand for capital facilities in the near as well as the longer term. This approach can also be used to calculate the cost and timing for replacing existing infrastructure.

Revenue Forecasting

A forecast of projected changes in revenues due to land-use or demographic changes in the community is one of the results of a fiscal impact analysis.

Fiscal Planning

Fiscal planning is different from budget planning because fiscal planning focuses on changes and uses in the 2- to 10-year time frame. Fiscal planning provides a long-term perspective on the costs and revenues associated with each department and activity of a local government, offering local officials the opportunity to reconsider plans and policies.

RESIDENTIAL PROTOTYPES

PROTOTYPE	PERSONS PER UNIT (1)	EQUIVALENT DWELLINGS PER UNIT	UNIT CONSTRUCTION COST (2)	VEHICLE TRIPS (3)
Low-Density, Single-Family	2.77	1.00	$337,500	9.57
Moderate-Density, Single-Family	2.51	0.91	$280,000	9.57
Low-Density, Multifamily	2.01	0.73	$250,000	5.86
High-Density, Multifamily				
Owner-Occupied	1.65	0.60	$120,000	4.18
Rental Unit	2.01	0.73	$120,000	4.18
Duplex	2.13	0.77	$150,000	5.86

1. Based on 1990 U.S. Census data.
2. Based on building validation data provided by the city.
3. Based on ITE Trip Generation, 6th ed.

SCENARIO 2: TOTALS

	FY2001	FY2002	FY2003	FY2004	FY2005	FY2006	FY2007	FY2008	FY2009
Office Square Feet	0	158,000	183,000	225,000	0	112,500	225,000	112,500	225,000
Retail Square Feet	75,000	47,000	0	0	0	0	0	0	0
Industrial Square Feet	0	0	0	0	0	0	0	0	0
Other Square Feet	0	0	0	0	0	0	0	0	0
MF Units	398	398	152	0	0	0	0	0	0
SFA Units	360	319	0	0	0	0	0	0	0
SFD Units	114	150	0	0	0	0	0	0	0

L. Carson Bise II, AICP, TischlerBise, Bethesda, Maryland

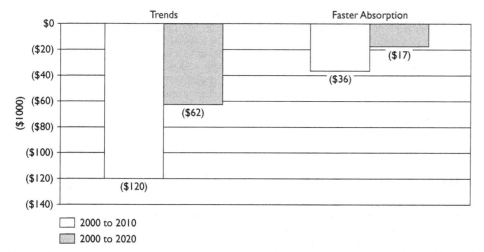

Source: L. Carson Bise 2004.

In this example, two scenarios were evaluated for this proposed annexation area. As the chart illustrates, the net deficits under both scenarios are greater over the short term (2000 to 2010) than they are over the long term (2000 to 2020). This is due to the need to "upfront" the infrastructure necessary for the subarea.

AVERAGE ANNUAL RESULTS, ANNEXATION SUBAREA B

Level-of-Service Changes

A growing number of local governments are finding it useful to focus policy discussions on the basic levels of public services that citizens want and are willing to pay for. Quantifying existing levels of service and the costs of different service levels can help lead to more constructive discussions regarding acceptable levels of service.

METHODS

There are three primary methodologies used in fiscal impact analyses:

- Average cost
- Case study-marginal
- Econometric

How the fiscal impact analysis will be used should play a large part in determining the method that will be employed. Therefore, for those communities contemplating the use of fiscal impact analysis, methodology is the most important consideration, particularly as the methodology selected has a direct bearing on how cost and revenue factors are derived, as well as impacts the political acceptability.

Average Cost

The average cost approach is the simplest and most popular method. Costs and revenues are calculated on the average cost per unit of service, often per capita or per employee. This method, which assumes the current average cost of serving existing residents, workers, students, or other population group, is the best estimate of the cost to serve new residents, workers, students, or other population groups. The major weaknesses of this methodology are that: it does not reflect how both costs and revenues generated by new development can differ significantly from those of the existing development base; it does not consider available public service and capital capacities; and usually it does not consider the geographic location of new development.

Case Study-Marginal

The case study-marginal methodology is the most realistic method for evaluating fiscal impacts. This methodology takes site- or geographic-specific information into consideration. Therefore, any unique demographic or locational characteristics of new development are accounted for, as well as the extent to which a particular infrastructure or service operates under, over, or close to capacity. This methodology is more labor-intensive than the average cost method, because of its more specific data needs.

Econometric

The econometric approach is the least used of the three primary fiscal impact analysis methodologies. It attempts to reflect the dynamic nature of a jurisdiction's economic, land-use, and demographic characteristics over time. Whereas the average cost and case study-marginal methodologies assume a "snapshot in time" analysis, the econometric method assumes that as new development occurs, a jurisdiction's service levels, service expenditures per demand unit, and revenue parameters (rate and base) will change throughout the course of the analysis period. Because of the considerable setup time and the number of assumptions that must be made related to the future, this method requires substantial data collection, expertise, and time. Therefore, it is the most expensive and least used of the three methodologies.

Comparison among Methods

Through the example of schools, the basic difference among the three methods can be shown. The average cost method would divide the school board's budget by current enrollment to obtain a cost per student—$3,300 is used here as an example. This cost would be incurred regardless of the nature of the development or its location relative to attendance boundaries.

The case study-marginal method would involve discussions with key school board personnel about the current enrollment to ultimate school capacity by individual school and attendance area. If the schools

impacted by a particular development have sufficient capacity, there would be no need to construct additional student space. Therefore, the only costs incurred would be operating costs related to additional teachers (possibly) and student materials. However, if there were not sufficient capacity, additional capacity would be added in form of either an addition or a new school, with associated operating costs for teachers, materials, and administrative staff incurred.

The econometric approach starts with the average cost per student of $3,300 but modifies this cost over time as new development in the short term interacts with the existing development base and new development that will occur over the long term. The change in the cost per person could go up or down, for example, if one assumes more/fewer students are being generated by existing and new development.

FACTORS THAT INFLUENCE FISCAL IMPACT RESULTS

From a fiscal perspective, several factors may influence whether new development pays its own way:

- Local revenue structure
- Levels of service
- Existing infrastructure capacity
- Spatial and demographic characteristics
- Assessed value of new construction

Local Revenue Structure

The key determinant in the calculation of the net fiscal results generated by new development is the local revenue structure, which affects the fiscal findings through its composition and revenue distribution/collection formulas. Every community has at least one predominant revenue source, and in some cases, several on which it relies. Common examples include property tax, local sales tax, and local income (payroll) tax.

An important component of the revenue structure is the distribution/collection formulas used for the various sources. With the exception of property tax, the distribution/collection formulas for commonly found revenues can vary greatly from state to state. For example, in states where sales tax is collected, some allow communities to exact a local option sales tax, which is usually collected on a *situs*-basis (point of sale). Other states collect sales tax at the state level and distribute the revenue to communities using a population-based formula. The same situation exists with income tax, where some states allow a local income, or "piggyback," tax on top of the state income tax.

Level of Service

Another important factor in the fiscal equation is the level of service currently being provided in a community. The existing level of service is generally defined as the facility or service standard currently being funded through the budget. Examples of level-of-service standards are pupil-teacher ratios and parkland per capita. The existing levels of service are important factors as they generally vary from community to community.

Existing Infrastructure Capacity

The capacity of existing infrastructure in a community also has a bearing on the fiscal sustainability of new development. For example, a community may have the capacity to absorb a large number of additional vehicle trips on its existing road network, or may be significantly under capacity with regard to high school enrollment. In both of these situations, a community with excess capacity could absorb substantially higher growth over time without making additional infrastructure investments than a community without these capacities. This excess capacity would result in lower capital costs over time. This is an important factor in the fiscal equation, because the highest costs associated with capital facilities are the *annual* operating costs, which typically account for approximately 80 percent of a community's budget.

Spatial and Demographic Characteristics

Next to a community's revenue structure, no other factor has as great an impact on the fiscal results as the demographic and market characteristics of new development. Examples of demographic and market variables for residential development include average household sizes, pupil generation rates, assessed value of housing units, trip generation rates, density per acre, and average household income. Important

demographic and market characteristics for nonresidential development include square feet per employee, trip generation rates, assessed value per square foot, income by type of job, sales per square foot (retail), and floor area ratio.

The relative importance of the various demographic and market factors depends on a community's revenue structure. For example, if payroll tax is the largest source of revenue in a community, office and industrial development will generate better results than retail development.

CUSTOMIZING THE ANALYSIS

Residential and nonresidential land uses should not be viewed in a vacuum, as each locality has unique revenue structures. Each community is also unique in its socioeconomic characteristics, infrastructure capacity, and levels of service, all of which are important factors in the fiscal equation. Fiscal issues are only one concern when evaluating land uses, because virtually all communities will have contributors and recipients. Nonfiscal issues, such as the

environment, housing affordability, jobs/housing balance, and quality of life, must also be considered. The emphasis should be on achieving an appropriate mix of land uses.

From determining whether a new development proposal will create a financial burden on a local government to assessing the impact of a proposed comprehensive plan amendment, a fiscal impact analysis can help bring a realistic sense of the cost of growth into the public discussion. By linking land-use decisions with budgetary and financial concerns, a fiscal impact analysis can facilitate discussions related to acceptable levels of service and revenue enhancement. For example, if an analysis indicates a shortfall, several what-if scenarios could be tested that include new revenue sources such as impact fees or special assessment district.

See also:

Capital Improvement Plans
Environmental Impact Assessment
Growth Management
Parks, Recreation, and Open-Space Needs Assessment

L. Carson Bise II, AICP, TischlerBise, Bethesda, Maryland

TRAFFIC IMPACT STUDIES

A traffic impact study assesses the effects that a particular development's traffic will have on the surrounding transportation network. A traffic impact study will vary in range and complexity, depending on the type and size of the proposed development. In many urban and suburban jurisdictions, traffic impact studies are an established part of the development process.

Before a traffic impact study is authorized to begin, the reviewing agency should have the following assurances:

- The area covered by the traffic impact study is within an area planned for development.
- Roadway cross sections and alignments are generally adequate within the traffic impact study area.
- Existing arterial spacing meets existing and proposed land-use requirements.
- Residential and nonresidential land uses will remain in balance.

Traffic impact studies do not normally lead to the large-scale transportation improvements that are most likely to be needed if these assurances are not met. A corridor or an areawide transportation study, or a comprehensive plan update, may be necessary.

A jurisdiction that typically requires traffic impact studies should officially adopt procedural guidelines that cover every major step in the preparation, review, and approval of the study. The guidelines should also list the names of the state and local agencies that typically would assist the planning agency in the review of the study.

The actual list of reviewing agencies may vary, depending on the transportation facilities that would potentially be affected by the proposed development. Especially when state highways may be affected by a proposed new development, state highway agency representatives should be invited to participate in the development and review of traffic impact studies.

Public works and street departments, and city and traffic engineering agencies should also play a direct role, with coordination to be maintained by the planning agency staff. As much as possible, close coordination should also be maintained among all of the city and county governments that may be affected by a proposed new development.

SCOPING SESSION AND SCOPE OF WORK

Before a traffic study is conducted, a scoping session should be organized, to establish the procedural schedule and to review any special circumstances that might affect the study. Both the entity that will prepare the study and the agency that will review the study should attend the scoping session. It would also be helpful for stakeholders, including state and local transportation agencies, as well as citizen and neighborhood groups, to participate in the scoping session.

Following the scoping session, the reviewing agency issues the scope of work, which describes the study requirements, a list of resources available to the preparer, and the schedule for study completion. The scope should also specify the study area boundaries and the horizon year to be used. (These concepts are

described in more detail below.) The traffic study should not begin until the scope has been finalized.

Use the scope of work as a checklist after the traffic impact study has been submitted, to determine whether the study complies with the scope. If the traffic study is approved, and as the development proceeds, put in place a process for monitoring the actual traffic impacts in relation to the traffic impact study findings.

THRESHOLDS AND STANDARDS

To have a measurable impact, a proposed development must be anticipated to generate a significant amount of traffic. Typical thresholds for "significant amount" include the amount of traffic that would be generated by 150 single-family dwelling units, 15,500 square feet of leasable retail space, or 55,000 square feet of leasable general office space. Actual thresholds may vary widely from this, depending upon the context.

Any traffic study should be consistent with the most current editions of the following reference manuals:

- *Trip Generation* (Institute of Transportation Engineers)
- *Highway Capacity Manual* (Transportation Research Board)
- *Manual on Uniform Traffic Control Devices* (Federal Highway Administration)
- *A Policy on Geometric Design of Streets and Highways,* generally referred to as the *AASHTO Green Book* (American Association of State Highway and Transportation Officials)

Other standards and methods may be preferable in certain situations. In such cases, the use of alternate standards and methods should be approved by the reviewing agency in advance.

The entity responsible for preparing the study should be experienced and qualified, either as a professional transportation planner or as a transportation engineer. If a traffic impact study is to be used for the design of specific transportation improvements, the traffic impact study should be signed and sealed by a registered professional engineer (PE) who can attest to his or her expertise in traffic operations or transportation facility design.

TRAFFIC IMPACT STUDY CONSIDERATIONS

Preparing a traffic impact study requires the consideration of several issues:

- Impact study area
- Horizon year
- Analysis periods
- Existing conditions
- Planned and previously funded transportation projects
- Methods for forecasting background traffic
- Trip generation rates
- Distribution and assignment of site-generated traffic
- Capacity analyses for background and buildout conditions

- Site plan review
- Typically recommended improvements
- Funding

Impact Study Area

The traffic impact study should cover those intersections and roadway segments whose measurable capacities might be affected if the proposed development were approved. The study should also cover driveway entrances to the proposed development. Typically, larger developments will require larger study areas.

Horizon Year

The horizon year is the year in which the proposed development is expected to have its maximum potential traffic impact. The selection of a horizon year should be based on documented market absorption rates for a given region, community, or corridor within a community. The reviewing agency should concur with the selected horizon year before beginning any technical analyses.

Analysis Periods

Within the horizon year, the days and time periods selected for analysis should reflect the times and days when the proposed development would have its greatest potential traffic impact. Generally, the greatest impact occurs during the morning and evening peak hours for work trips on a typical weekday. For retail developments, the peak hour of travel may occur on a Saturday, although overall travel volumes are generally highest on days when schools and businesses are both open.

Existing Conditions

The text of the traffic impact study report should begin with a general description of existing land uses, development trends, and roadway and traffic conditions within the traffic impact study area. The land-use description should include descriptions of ongoing development trends and development potential, existing land uses and zoning, and a description of the existing topography of the traffic impact study area. This section of the study report should set a framework for the technical analyses that will follow.

The overview of existing roadway and traffic conditions should include descriptions of any intersection or roadway deficiencies that may affect existing safety or capacity. The functional classifications of existing roadways should also be described. Existing daily traffic counts and peak-hour turning movement counts should be shown on a schematic diagram of roadways and major intersections.

In order to conduct an intersection capacity analysis using an accepted methodology, the volume of vehicles approaching each leg of an intersection must be broken down into left turns, right turns, and through movements per hour. To determine the maximum potential impact of a proposed new development, the "peak hours," those hours that have the highest approach volumes, are the hours that must be analyzed. These peak hours should be identified before the scope of work is finalized.

Stephen Tocknell, AICP, Reynolds, Smith and Hills Inc., Jacksonville, Florida

Planned and Previously Funded Transportation Projects

The study should include a description of any planned or previously funded projects that may affect intersection or roadway capacities within the traffic impact study area. In addition to a general description of the project and its effect upon safety and capacity, the narrative or tabulated description should include the project limits, its funding status, and the name of the agency or party responsible for completing the project.

Methods for Forecasting Background Traffic

The preparer and the reviewing agency should agree on the methods to be used to modify existing traffic counts to reflect background traffic conditions in the horizon year. These methods may include the application of growth factors to existing traffic counts, along with consideration for traffic to or from approved but uncompleted new developments that may add traffic to major intersections or roadways within the designated traffic impact study area. The growth factors used can be based upon historical traffic trends, or upon output from an approved transportation systems planning model.

Trip Generation Rates

To estimate the amount of traffic that will flow in and out of a proposed development, a published trip generation rate can be multiplied by the proposed number of new dwelling units, or by the square footage of proposed nonresidential development. Different trip generation rates have been determined for a large number of different land use types. The most widely used source of published trip generation rates is *Trip Generation*, published by the Institute of Transportation Engineers. The use of localized trip generation rates would be preferable, as long as the rates are reliable, well documented, and agreed upon in advance. Procedures for developing trip generation forecasts are described in more detail in *Trip Generation, Volume 1*.

Distribution and Assignment of Site-Generated Traffic

After background traffic levels and trip generation estimates have been determined for the proposed development, the next task is the distribution and assignment of site-generated traffic. This step can be simple or elaborate. Different trip distribution percentages may be developed for different land uses within the same development, or for different times of day.

For some small-scale developments, existing turning movement counts at existing intersections may be used as a guide for the development of trip distribution estimates. But for larger developments, or where existing traffic patterns are likely to change, some other method should be used. A systems planning software package, such as QRSII, Tranplan, or TransCAD, can be used for this purpose; or the output from a recently completed corridor or regional transportation planning study can be modified for use in a traffic impact study. In such cases, either the preparer or the reviewing agency may require some assistance from the staff of either a metropolitan planning organization (MPO) or a state highway agency.

Capacity Analyses for Background and Buildout Conditions

The background capacity analyses show how roads and intersections will work if the development is not built; the buildout capacity analyses show directly comparable results if approval is granted and the development is completed as proposed. These analyses are the heart of the traffic impact study.

The most generally accepted method for describing highway and intersection capacities is the level-of-service (LOS) concept. Although commonly used, the LOS concept is not meant to be a rigorous standard. Procedures for determining levels of service, for various types of intersections and highways, are documented in the Transportation Research Board's *Highway Capacity Manual*. The "Level of Service" illustration offers a brief informal description of the meaning of different levels of service.

Many roadways and intersections are designed to operate at a level of service C, but in other cases a level of service D is used as a more cost-effective design standard. In most built-up areas, drivers routinely encounter traffic conditions that would be described as either a level of service E or F. The level of service E is the theoretical maximum capacity of a roadway. Beyond a level of service E, the capacity of a roadway declines sharply.

There are problems with using the LOS concept to determine roadway or intersection capacity. Critics have suggested that an overemphasis on LOS standards can promote sprawl and overreliance on motor vehicles, to the exclusion of walking and other forms of transportation. Additionally, in some cases, an acceptable level of service can only be demonstrated in a traffic impact study by using unrealistic signal timings that would be unsafe if put into operation.

New methods for level-of-service analyses have been developed that are more mode-neutral, so that transit and highway alternatives can be evaluated in relation to each other within a given corridor. These new methods are documented in the Year 2000 edition of the *Highway Capacity Manual*.

For transit and for other nonhighway modes, new "quality-of-service" standards are now being developed and introduced. Quality-of-service standards were introduced in the 2000 edition of the *Highway Capacity Manual*, and the second edition of the *Transit Capacity and Quality of Service Manual* (TC/QSM) was published by the Transit Cooperative Research Program (TCRP) in 2004.

But for minimizing sprawl, the best performance standards measure cumulative delays, such as vehicle hours of travel per capita, rather than congestion at individual locations.

The results of detailed level-of-service analyses may rest on variables, such as signal timings and cycle lengths, which cannot be predicted reliably at the time that a traffic impact study is conducted. In these cases, it is preferable to use the *Highway Capacity Manual* quick estimation procedures for signalized intersections.

Many software packages allow their users to carry out the procedures outlined in the *Highway Capacity Manual* with great ease and precision. Some of these packages are specifically set up for use in traffic impact studies.

Site Plan Review

A site plan review should be part of every traffic impact study; that said, it need not be overly technical or elaborate unless there is a potential safety risk. The site plan should show the following:

- Adequate access for emergency vehicles, delivery trucks, and service vehicles

TYPICAL TRIP GENERATION RATES

USE	UNIT	TRIP RATE PER UNIT	FOR PERIOD[1]
Office			
Office Building	Employee	0.49	Weekday—AM Peak Hour
Office Building	Employee	0.46	Weekday—PM Peak Hour
Office Building	1,000 ft² GFA[2]	1.55	Weekday—AM Peak Hour
Office Building	1,000 ft² GFA	1.49	Weekday—PM Peak Hour
Medical-Dental Office	1,000 ft² GFA	3.62	Weekday—AM Peak Hour
Medical-Dental Office	1,000 ft² GFA	4.45	Weekday—PM Peak Hour
Residential			
Single-Family Detached	Dwelling Unit	0.77	Weekday—AM Peak Hour
Single-Family Detached	Dwelling Unit	1.02	Weekday—PM Peak Hour
Apartment	Dwelling Unit	0.55	Weekday—AM Peak Hour
Apartment	Dwelling Unit	0.67	Weekday—PM Peak Hour
Retail			
Shopping Center	1,000 ft² GLA[3]	1.03	Weekday—AM Peak Hour
Shopping Center	1,000 ft² GLA	3.75	Weekday—PM Peak Hour
Shopping Center	1,000 ft² GLA	4.90	Saturday—Peak Hour
24-Hour Market	1,000 ft² GFA[2]	73.10	Weekday—AM Peak Hour
24-Hour Market	1,000 ft² GFA	53.42	Weekday—PM Peak Hour
Supermarket	1,000 ft² GFA	12.02	Weekday—PM Peak Hour
Restaurant			
Quality Restaurant	Seat	0.33	Saturday—Peak Hour
Sit-Down Restaurant	Seat	0.88	Saturday—Peak Hour
Bagel Shop	Seat	6.33	Saturday—Peak Hour
Church	Seat	0.63	Sunday—Peak Hour

Notes:
1. Peak hours vary by use.
2. GFA = Gross Floor Area
3. GLA = Gross Leasable Area

Source: ITE Trip Generation, 7th Edition, 2003.

Stephen Tocknell, AICP, Reynolds, Smith and Hills Inc., Jacksonville, Florida

Level of Service		Description
A		Free Flow: Low volumes and no delays.
B		Stable Flow: Speeds restricted by travel conditions, minor delays.
C		Stable Flow: Speed and maneuverability closely controlled due to higher volumes.
D		Stable Flow: Speeds considerably affected by change in opening conditions. High-density traffic restricts maneuverability; volume near capacity.
E		Unstable Flow: Low speeds, considerable delay; volume at slightly over capacity.
F		Forced Flow: Very low speeds; volumes exceed capacity; long delays with stop-and-go traffic.

LEVEL OF SERVICE

Source: Bucher, Willis & Ratliff Corporation.

- Adequate parking, including shared and on-street parking
- Conditions that are conducive to transit, bicycle, and pedestrian access
- Connectivity to the surrounding street network
- Good driver orientation
- Multiple access points

Typically Recommended Improvements— On- and Off-Site

Typically recommended capacity improvements may include new traffic signals or major improvements to existing traffic signals, including coordinated traffic signal systems. Larger-scale improvements may require new turn lanes, the addition of through travel lanes on affected roadways, new bridges or grade separations at major intersections, and even entirely new roadways.

Where capacity analyses indicate that new traffic signals or left-turn lanes are required, the traffic impact study should also include a signal warrant analysis or a turn lane warrant analysis, in order to show that such improvements will be feasible and safe. Procedures for traffic signal warrant analyses are documented in the *Manual on Uniform Traffic Control Devices.*

Typically, a state highway agency must review and approve any proposal for the installation of a new or modified traffic signal that would be located along any state-owned or -operated highway. State highway agencies also have the authority to approve or reject proposals to add travel lanes or turning lanes that may be recommended pursuant to a traffic impact study. Ideally, state highway agency representatives should be invited to participate in the development and review of traffic impact studies.

Where trip reduction strategies are proposed as part of a solution to anticipated traffic capacity problems, the traffic impact study should include a realistic plan for the implementation of these strategies, including a staffing and operations plan, and a timetable for plan implementation.

Funding

Funding issues should be addressed within the traffic impact study when cost factors might influence whether a recommended capacity improvement is actually built. If the developer is expecting that pub-lic or other private parties may be asked to participate in the financing of a proposed improvement, the traffic impact study should include a reasonable and verifiable set of cost estimates for all such recommended improvements.

For the purposes of a traffic impact study, the estimated cost of a recommended improvement can be based on unit or per-mile cost estimates derived from similar projects that have recently been bid or built within the vicinity of the proposed development.

Where impact fees have been enacted, the traffic study should show how these fees might be generated and applied if the proposed development were approved. The exaction or proffer process is more erratic and subjective. But even in these cases, a traffic impact study can be a useful deliberative guide for developers as well as for decision makers.

For financial reasons affecting the developer, it often becomes necessary to consider a limiting threshold for a new development. Before the approved development can proceed beyond that threshold, a list of specified improvements must be completed or, at least, the funding must be in place. This consideration may make it necessary for the traffic impact study to include capacity analyses and recommendations for intermediate phases of a proposed development.

REFERENCES

American Association of State Highway and Transportation Officials. 1995. *A Policy on Geometric Design of Highways and Streets: 1994 (The Green Book).* Washington, DC: AASHTO.

Institute of Transportation Engineers. 2003. *Trip Generation,* 7th ed. Washington, DC: ITE.

Stover, Vergil G., and Frank J. Koepke. 2002. *Transportation and Land Development,* 2nd ed. Washington DC: Institute of Transportation Engineers.

Transportation Research Board. 2000. *Highway Capacity Manual.* TRP A3A10. Washington, DC: Transportation Research Board.

U.S. Department of Transportation. 2003. *Manual on Uniform Traffic Control Devices.* Washington, DC: U.S. Department of Transportation, Federal Highway Administration.

See also:
Transit Systems

Stephen Tocknell, AICP, Reynolds, Smith and Hills Inc., Jacksonville, Florida

MAPPING

MAPPING DATA OVERVIEW

Maps are a representation of a place at a particular point in time to convey particular ideas or pieces of information. Maps are a fundamental source of information for planning and design activities.

This section of the book contains information on specific types of maps and data sources commonly used by planners and designers. It is not intended to provide an exhaustive list, but rather a sampling of the some of the most common maps used. Many of the map concepts described here that are widely used, such as topographic maps and geographic information systems, are described in greater detail; other map types that have more specific applications are also included.

TYPICAL MAP ELEMENTS

- Titles, including main titles and descriptive headings above the map key or legend
- Map legend, or key, to any system used to identify map features (colors, grayscale, or patterns).
- North arrow
- Scale (representative or bar)
- Projection
- Labels, either by kind of item, name, or attribute
- Sources and credits
- Insets, used to place a main map in a larger geographic context
- Borders and neatlines (Neatlines, also called clipping lines, indicate exactly where the area of a map begins and ends. The border is the outer neatline of a map.)
- Accompanying graphics, such as charts, tables, and images

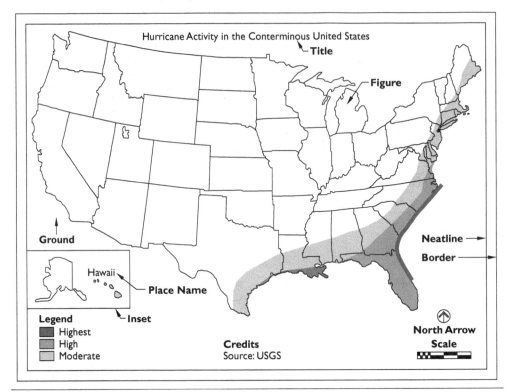

MAP ELEMENTS

Source: American Planning Association.

U.S. GEOLOGICAL SURVEY (USGS) MAP SCALES

SERIES	SCALE	1 INCH REPRESENTS APPROXIMATELY	1 CENTIMETER REPRESENTS	STANDARD QUADRANGLE SIZE (LATITUDE BY LONGITUDE)	QUADRANGLE AREA (SQUARE MILES)
Puerto Rico					
7.5 minute	1:20,000	1,667 feet	200 meters	7.5 by 7.5 minute	71
7.5 minute	1:24,000	2,000 feet (exact)	240 meters	7.5 by 7.5 minute	49 to 70
7.5 minute	1:25,000	2,083 feet	250 meters	7.5 by 7.5 minute	49 to 70
7.5 by 15 minute	1:25,000	2,083 feet	250 meters	7.5 by 15 minute	98 to 140
USGS-DMA 15 minute	1:50,000	4,166 feet	500 meters	15 by 15 minute	197 to 282
15 minute*	1:62,500	1 mile	625 meters	15 by 15 minute	197 to 282
Alaska Maps	1:63,360	1 mile (exact)	633.6 meters	15 by 20 to 36 minute	207 to 281
County Maps	1:50,000	4,166 feet	500 meters	County area	Varies
County Maps	1:100,000	1.6 miles	1 kilometer	County area	Varies
30 by 60 minute	1:100,000	1.6 miles	1 kilometer	30 by 60 minute	1,568 to 2,240
30 minute*	1:125,000	2 miles	1.25 kilometers	30 by 30 minute	786 to 1,124
1° by 2° or 3°	1:250,000	4 miles	2.5 kilometers	1° by 2° or 3°	4,580 to 8,669
State Maps	1:500,000	8 miles	5 kilometers	State area	Varies
State Maps	1:1,000,000	16 miles	10 kilometers	State area	Varies
U.S. Sectional Maps	1:2,000,000	32 miles	20 kilometers	State groups	Varies
Antarctica Maps	1:250,000	4 miles	2.5 kilometers	1° by 3° to 15°	4,089 to 8,336
Antarctica Maps	1:500,000	8 miles	5 kilometers	2° by 7.5°	28,174 to 30,462

*Abandoned map series, but still available for ordering as black-and-white photographic reproductions.

Source: USGS 2004.

Ann-Margaret Esnard, Ph.D., Cornell University, Ithaca, New York

MAP SCALE

Scale is the relationship between distance on the map and distance on the ground. Large-scale maps (e.g., 1 inch = 100 feet) show a small land area in considerable detail. Small-scale maps (e.g., 1 inch = 1,000,000 feet) show less detail but a larger land area. In mapping, scale is presented either as a representative scale or a graphical scale.

Representative Scale

A representative scale is given as a fraction or a ratio—1/10,000 or 1:10,000. The first number, the 1, is the map distance. It is always shown as 1, and typically represents 1 inch or 1 centimeter. The second number, in this instance 10,000, is the ground distance. This number varies for different map scales—the larger the second number, the smaller the scale of the map.

The representative fraction scale means that the unit of measurement on the map represents the actual ground distance shown in the scale. For this example, 1 inch on the map represents 10,000 inches on the ground, or approximately 833 feet.

Graphical Scale

A graphical scale, also called a bar scale, presents a scale that represents a certain length, with the units of measurement provided, typically feet or miles. It is typically represented as 1 inch = 500 feet, for example. A graphical scale can be easily enlarged or reduced without affecting the accuracy of the scale, assuming the reproduction is enlarged or reduced by the same factor in both horizontal and vertical directions.

Relationship of Scale to Detail and Use

When choosing a map, the scale to be used must be considered, because it will affect the content and detail in the map. For example, when working on a site plan, a highly detailed map at a large scale, such as 1:600, may be needed to draw features such as streets and structures to scale. For a project that will cover a greater area, a topographic map at a scale of 1:24,000 may be needed to identify steep slopes, locate transportation networks, protect critical environmental areas, and locate power and water lines.

As scale increases, detail is reduced. Maps at scales of 1:50,000 to 1:100,000 show increasingly less detail, but they cover large areas. Such maps are often used for larger-scale land management and planning. Maps at scales of 1:250,000 to 1:1,000,000 cover quite large areas of land; they are frequently used for regional and statewide planning. Details in maps at these scales are limited to features such as major boundaries, parks, airports, major roads, railroads, and surface water bodies.

MAP PROJECTIONS

Map projections allow features of the Earth, which is a curved surface, to be represented on a map, a flat surface. Various mathematical formulas have been developed to allow this transformation. All map projections distort shape, area, distance, or direction to some extent. But for data layers to be together on one map, they need to have the same map projection to avoid errors in measurement and to conduct analysis across different data layers.

APPROACHES TO MAP CREATION

When creating maps, there are certain protocols to keep in mind:

- Follow cartographic conventions. For example, reserve italic type to represent streams, rivers, lakes, oceans, and other hydrologic features.
- Avoid an excessive variety of typefaces and other visual distractions.
- Understand the impacts, intended or not, of subjective map titles, such as "high-crime neighborhood."
- Use symbols and color schemes based on professional standards.
- Use data that are created at a resolution appropriate for the level of study. For example, parcel-level studies should not use information created for a statewide analysis.

BASE LAYER

When starting a mapping project, often the first step is to establish a base map or layer. The features of a base layer are called base data. The mission or purpose of the study dictates the elements in the base layer. These elements may be one or more of the map layer elements described below.

MAP LAYERS

Map layers can include a variety of data types. The following are various examples of the types of data to include on a map layer.

- Natural features, such as topographic contours, elevation, and steep slopes; surface water features; vegetative cover, including tree locations; soil characteristics and types; and floodplains, wetlands, and other critical and sensitive areas
- Built environment features, such as paved and unpaved roads and parking areas, walls and fences, major streets and other transportation features, land use, building footprints, and parks, open space, and recreational facilities
- Political boundaries, such as state, county, city, and town boundaries; census boundaries; tax parcels; and zoning

MAPPING DATA CONSIDERATIONS

Keep track of map resources and the dates they were created, to allow for good judgment in using maps for various planning and design tasks. Updating maps and map information is a constant challenge. Information can come from subdivision plans, plats and new surveys, building permits, and the wide suite of digital products such as digital orthophoto quadrangles. Organization is an important element to a mapping system.

Metadata are the specific parameters under which the data were created and the description of their intended use. More information on metadata is included in "Geographic Information Systems" in this section of this book.

See also:
Aerial Photographs and Digital Orthophoto Quadrangles
Census Data and Demographic Mapping
Geographic Information Systems
Property Maps in Modern Cadastres
U.S. Geological Survey Topographic Maps

Ann-Margaret Esnard, Ph.D., Cornell University, Ithaca, New York

AERIAL PHOTOGRAPHS AND DIGITAL ORTHOPHOTO QUADRANGLES

Aerial photographs are typically low-altitude photographs of the Earth's surface, taken from aircraft. Digital orthophoto quadrangles are computer-generated images of aerial photographs, with the image displacement caused by terrain relief and camera tilts removed. They combine the image characteristics of photographs with the geometric qualities of a map.

AERIAL PHOTOGRAPHS GENERALLY

Aerial photographs are important tools for planners, designers, developers, and others who need detailed and timely site data. Among the uses of aerial photographs are to:

- provide information on vegetation types, soil conditions, lakes and waterbody boundaries, and other features;
- in combination with on-the-ground observations, guide the creation of sketch maps of the planning and design area to show certain features;
- serve as useful tools to study the Earth's environmental and developmental changes over time; and
- facilitate the identification of critical and sensitive resources, such as wetlands.

READING AERIAL PHOTOGRAPHS

Aerial photographs are available either in black-and-white or in color infrared (CIR). Choice of film type depends on the purpose for which the photograph is to be used. Black-and-white photography is suggested for large areas, because it is less expensive. However, CIR is often preferred for land cover mapping. To read aerial photographs correctly—they seldom have legends—one must understand how the two photo types capture parts of the electromagnetic spectrum to generate the various colors or shades.

Color Infrared Images

Color infrared film, also called false color, presents images through both visible and invisible parts of the electromagnetic spectrum. Near-infrared light, which is invisible to the human eye, is added to aerial images, creating color-infrared photography. Objects appear as one of four colors: black, blue, green, or red. The color shown is the color reflected from the surface:

- Waterbodies appear as shades of blue, varying from nearly black to pale blue.
- Densely vegetated areas appear red.
- Less densely vegetated areas and urbanized areas appear light red.
- Unhealthy vegetation appears as shades of greens.
- Bare soils appear as shades of white, blue, or green. The more moist the soil, the darker the shade of that particular soil color.

Black-and-White Images

Black-and-white film records the reflected radiation in tones of gray, with vegetated areas appearing darker and paved areas appearing lighter.

This illustration shows a comparison of black and white (panchromatic), color, and color infrared data from aerial photographic sensors. Color infrared is particularly useful for differentiating water and vegetation types.

AERIAL PHOTOGRAPHY SENSOR COMPARISON

Source: Futurity, Inc. 2005.

SOURCES FOR AERIAL PHOTOGRAPHS

The U.S. Geological Survey (USGS) maintains a database of aerial photograph coverage from the 1940s to the present for the United States and its territories. The information covers photo projects from the USGS, other federal, state, and local government agencies, and commercial firms.

Images from the USGS are available through the National Aerial Photography Program (NAPP), which provides a standardized set of cloud-free aerial photographs covering the conterminous United States over five-to-seven-year cycles. Each photo is centered on one-quarter section of a 7.5-minute USGS quadrangle and covers approximately a 5.5-mile by 5.5-mile area. Taken at an altitude of 20,000 feet, photographs are available in either black-and-white or color infrared, depending on location and date.

In addition to the USGS, TerraServerUSA and GlobeXplorer are two online sources of digital aerial photographs. Also, decommissioned U2 photos, taken in the 1960s and 1970s, are a source of historic images, which can be used when analyzing land-cover changes.

DIGITAL ORTHOPHOTO QUADRANGLES

Aerial photographs display a high degree of radial distortion. Before information on features such as roads, vegetation, and waterbodies can be gathered in a way that is useful in geographic information systems, that distortion must be removed from the image. This process is called orthorectification. Without this process, direct measurements of distances, angles, positions, and areas cannot be made.

Digital orthophoto quadrangles (DOQs) are rectified and projected digital aerial photographs. Unlike a standard aerial photograph, relief displacement in orthophotos has been removed so that ground features are displayed in their true ground position. This allows for the direct measurement of distance, areas, angles, and positions.

DOQs produced by the USGS are grayscale, natural color, or color infrared images with 1-meter ground resolution. They cover an area measuring 3.75 minutes longitude by 3.75 minutes latitude, or an area 7.5 minutes longitude by 7.5 minutes latitude.

A DOQ can be incorporated into any geographic information system (GIS) that can manipulate raster images. It can function as a cartographic base for displaying, generating, and modifying associated digital planimetric data. Other planning applications include vegetation and timber management, habitat analysis, environmental impact assessments, flood analysis, soil erosion assessment, facility management, and groundwater and watershed analysis. DOQ accuracy and detail allows users to evaluate data for accuracy and completeness, make real-time data modifications, and generate new files.

DOQ files are available from the USGS; however, coverage is not yet available for all areas in the United States.

See also:
Geographic Information Systems

Ann-Margaret Esnard, Ph.D., Cornell University, Ithaca, New York

U.S. GEOLOGICAL SURVEY TOPOGRAPHIC MAPS

A topographic map provides a representation of the Earth's surface through contour lines. Contours are imaginary lines that join points of equal elevation on the surface of the land above or below a reference surface, such as mean sea level. Contours make it possible to measure height, depth, and slope steepness. In addition to contours, a topographic map includes symbols that represent features such as streets, buildings, streams, and woods.

The most widely known forms of geographic base information for the United States are the U.S. Geological Survey (USGS) primary series topographic maps. These maps are produced at the following scales: 1:24,000; 1:25,000; and 1:63,360.

The USGS has also produced provisional maps, which were established to expedite completion of the remaining large-scale topographic quadrangles of the conterminous United States. They contain essentially the same level of information as the primary series maps, but some symbols and lettering are handdrawn. This series can be easily recognized by the title "Provisional Edition" in the lower right-hand corner.

Most USGS map series divide the United States into quadrangles bounded by two lines of latitude and two lines of longitude. For example, a 7.5-minute map shows an area that spans 7.5 minutes of latitude and 7.5 minutes of longitude. The map is usually named after the most prominent feature in the quadrangle. Understand how much area is covered by these quadrangles so that the most appropriate map is obtained to correspond with specific needs.

APPLICATIONS

Planners and urban designers can use topographic maps to represent elevation and contours, and to generate slope data as part of site analyses. Topographic maps are also used for:

- identifying suitable locations for placing buildings and roads;
- providing reference information for names of prominent natural and cultural features;
- surveying and mapping of archaeological sites;
- extracting information related to stormwater runoff and drainage basins; and
- providing reference information for review and approval of subdivision plans.

SOURCES FOR TOPOGRAPHIC MAPS

The USGS is the main resource for topographic maps. Its website, www.usgs.gov, and private sector business partners are both sources for topographic maps.

MAP CONTENT AND SYMBOLS

Topographic maps typically contain the following types of information, which are identified using standard symbols or line types:

- *Elevation*: Contours, and control data and monuments
- *Boundaries*: State, county, and incorporated city boundaries, and land survey lines
- *Land surface features*: Vegetation, mines and caves, and other surface features
- *Water features*: Shorelines; coastal features; rivers, lakes, and canals; wetlands; and other water features
- *Buildings and related features*: Buildings, schools, built-up areas, airports, cemeteries, and other built features
- *Roads, railroads and other features*: Roads, railroads, bridges, tunnels, transmissions lines, telephone lines, pipelines, and other linear features.

The USGS-established topographic map symbols and colors represent these map elements. However, within the same series, maps may have slightly different symbols for the same feature. Examples of symbols that have changed over time include built-up areas, roads, intermittent drainage, and some type styles.

READING TOPOGRAPHIC MAPS

When using topographic maps, the first step is to interpret the colored lines, areas, and other symbols. Features are shown as points, lines, or areas, depending on their size and extent. For example, individual houses may be shown as small black squares. For larger buildings, the actual shapes are mapped. In densely built-up areas, most individual buildings are omitted and an area tint is shown. On some maps, post offices, churches, city halls, and other landmark buildings are shown within the tinted area.

Color-Related Features

The first features usually noticed on a topographic map are area features such as vegetation (green), water (blue), information added during update (purple), and densely built-up areas (gray or red).

Lines that are straight, curved, solid, dashed, dotted, or in a combination indicate many features. Line colors typically indicate similar kinds or classes of information: topographic contours (brown); lakes,

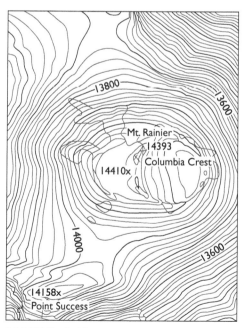

1:24,000-Scale Map

1:100,000-Scale Map

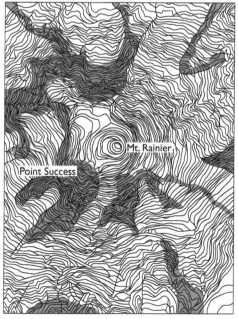

1:250,000-Scale Map

TOPOGRAPHIC MAPS AT VARIOUS SCALES

Source: USGS.

Megan S. Lewis, AICP, American Planning Association, Chicago, Illinois

MAPPING

Control Data and Monuments

Aerial Photograph Roll and Frame Number*	3-20

Horizontal Control

Third Order or Better, Permanent Mark	Neace △ Neace ⟁
With Third Order or Better Elevation	BM △ 45.1 ⟁ Pike BM 45.1
Checked Spot Elevation	△ 19.5
Coincident with Section Corner	△– Cactus ⟁– Cactus
Unmonumented*	+

Vertical Control

Third Order or Better, with Tablet	BM × 16.3
Third Order or Better, Recoverable Mark	× 120.0
Benchmark at Found Section Corner	BM ⊥ 18.6
Spot Elevation	× 5.3

Boundary Monument

With Tablet	BM ○ 21.6 BM ⊞ 21.6
Without Tablet	○ 171.3
With Number and Elevation	67 ○ 301.1
U.S. Mineral or Location Monument	▲

Contours

Topographic

Intermediate [1]	⌣
Index [1]	⌣
Supplementary [1]	⌣
Depression	⬭
Cut; Fill	⨏⨏

Bathymetric

Intermediate [1]	
Index [1]	
Primary [1]	
Index Primary [1]	
Supplementary [1]	

*Provisional Edition maps only. Provisional Edition maps were established to expedite completion of the remaining large-scale topographic quadrangles of the conterminous United States. They contain essentially the same level of information as the standard series maps. This series can be easily recognized by the title "Provisional Edition" in the lower right hand corner.

[1] These symbols are differentiated by color on USGS topographic maps. To view these images in color, go to http://erg.usgs.gov/isb/pubs/booklets/symbols/elevation.html.

Elevation

Boundaries

National	— – –
State or Territorial	— – –
County or Equivalent	— – –
Civil Township or Equivalent	– — –
Incorporated City or Equivalent	— · – · –
Park, Reservation, or Monument [1]	— · — ▬
Small Park	– – – – – –

Land Survey Systems [1]

U.S. Public Land Survey System

Township or Range Line	▬▬
Location Doubtful	– – – –
Section Line	▬▬
Location Doubtful	– – – –
Found Section Corner; Found Closing Corner	–+–⊥–
Witness Corner; Meander Corner	WC + ⊣ MC

Other Land Surveys

Township or Range Line	··············
Section Line	············
Land Grant or Mining Claim; Monument	··· — ○
Fence Line	– – – – – –

[1] These symbols are differentiated by color on USGS topographic maps. To view these images in color, go to http://erg.usgs.gov/isb/pubs/booklets/symbols/boundaries.html.

Boundaries

TOPOGRAPHIC MAP SYMBOLS

Source: USGS.

Megan S. Lewis, AICP, American Planning Association, Chicago, Illinois

Surface Features[1]

Levee	
Send or Mud Area, Dunes, or Shifting Sand	
Intricate Surface Area	
Gravel Beach or Glacial Moraine	
Tailings Pond	

Mines and Caves

Quarry or Open-Pit Mine	
Gravel, Sand, Clay, or Borrow Pit	
Mine Tunnel or Cave Entrance	
Prospect; Mine Shaft	
Mine Dump[1]	
Tailings[1]	

Vegetation[1]

Woods	
Scrub	
Orchard	
Vineyard	
Mangrove	

Glaciers and Permanent Snowfields[1]

Contours and Limits	
Form Lines	

[1] These symbols are differentiated by color on USGS topographic maps. To view these images in color, go to http://erg.usgs.gov/isb/pubs/booklets/symbols/landsurface.html.

Land Surface Features

Roads and Related Features

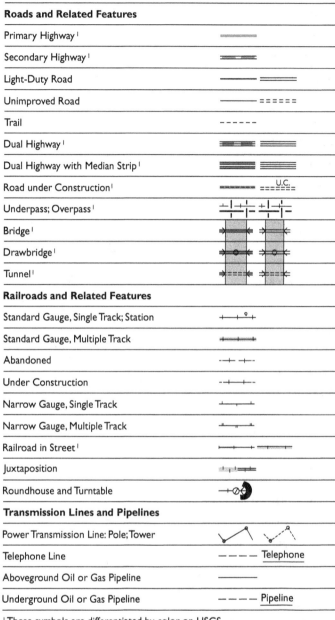

Primary Highway[1]	
Secondary Highway[1]	
Light-Duty Road	
Unimproved Road	
Trail	
Dual Highway[1]	
Dual Highway with Median Strip[1]	
Road under Construction[1]	
Underpass; Overpass[1]	
Bridge[1]	
Drawbridge[1]	
Tunnel[1]	

Railroads and Related Features

Standard Gauge, Single Track; Station	
Standard Gauge, Multiple Track	
Abandoned	
Under Construction	
Narrow Gauge, Single Track	
Narrow Gauge, Multiple Track	
Railroad in Street[1]	
Juxtaposition	
Roundhouse and Turntable	

Transmission Lines and Pipelines

Power Transmission Line: Pole; Tower	
Telephone Line	
Aboveground Oil or Gas Pipeline	
Underground Oil or Gas Pipeline	

[1] These symbols are differentiated by color on USGS topographic maps. To view these images in color, go to http://erg.usgs.gov/isb/pubs/booklets/symbols/roads.html.

Roads, Railroads, and Other Features

TOPOGRAPHIC MAP SYMBOLS *(continued)*

Source: USGS.

Megan S. Lewis, AICP, American Planning Association, Chicago, Illinois

MAPPING

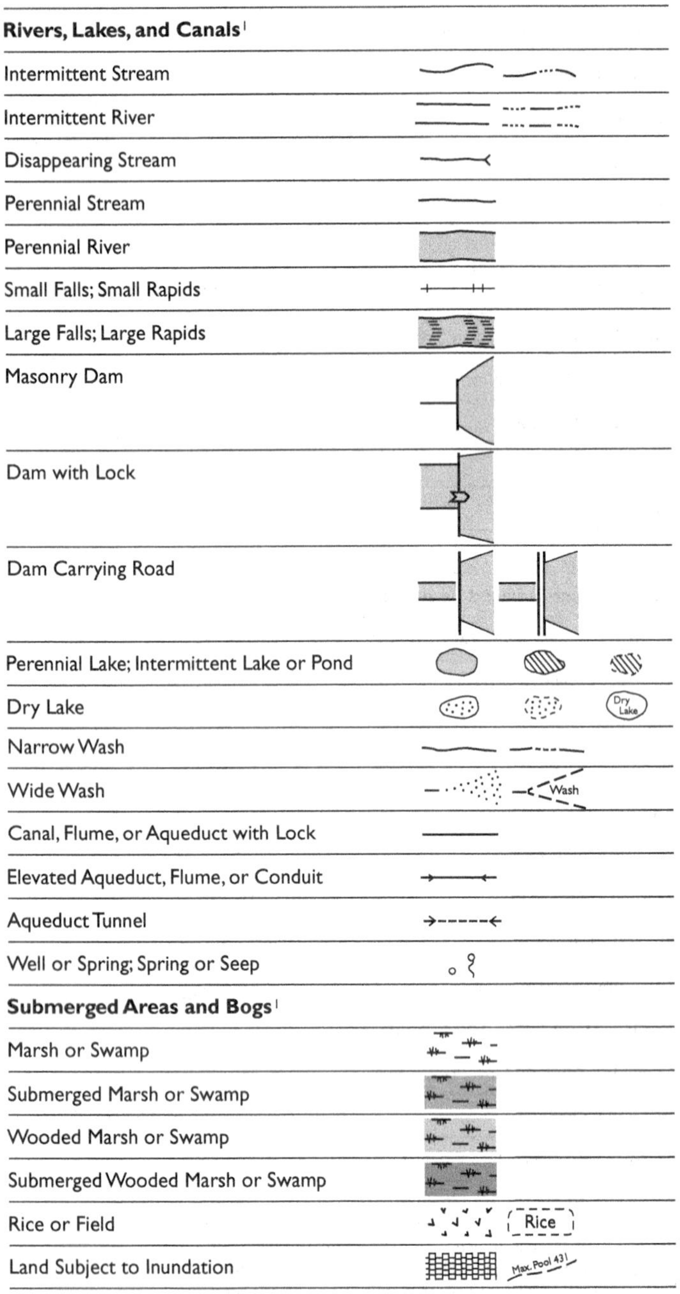

Rivers, Lakes, and Canals [1]

Intermittent Stream	
Intermittent River	
Disappearing Stream	
Perennial Stream	
Perennial River	
Small Falls; Small Rapids	
Large Falls; Large Rapids	
Masonry Dam	
Dam with Lock	
Dam Carrying Road	
Perennial Lake; Intermittent Lake or Pond	
Dry Lake	
Narrow Wash	
Wide Wash	
Canal, Flume, or Aqueduct with Lock	
Elevated Aqueduct, Flume, or Conduit	
Aqueduct Tunnel	
Well or Spring; Spring or Seep	

Submerged Areas and Bogs [1]

Marsh or Swamp	
Submerged Marsh or Swamp	
Wooded Marsh or Swamp	
Submerged Wooded Marsh or Swamp	
Rice or Field	
Land Subject to Inundation	

[1] These symbols are differentiated by color on USGS topographic maps. To view these images in color, go to http://erg.usgs.gov/isb/pubs/booklets/symbols/water.html.

Water Features

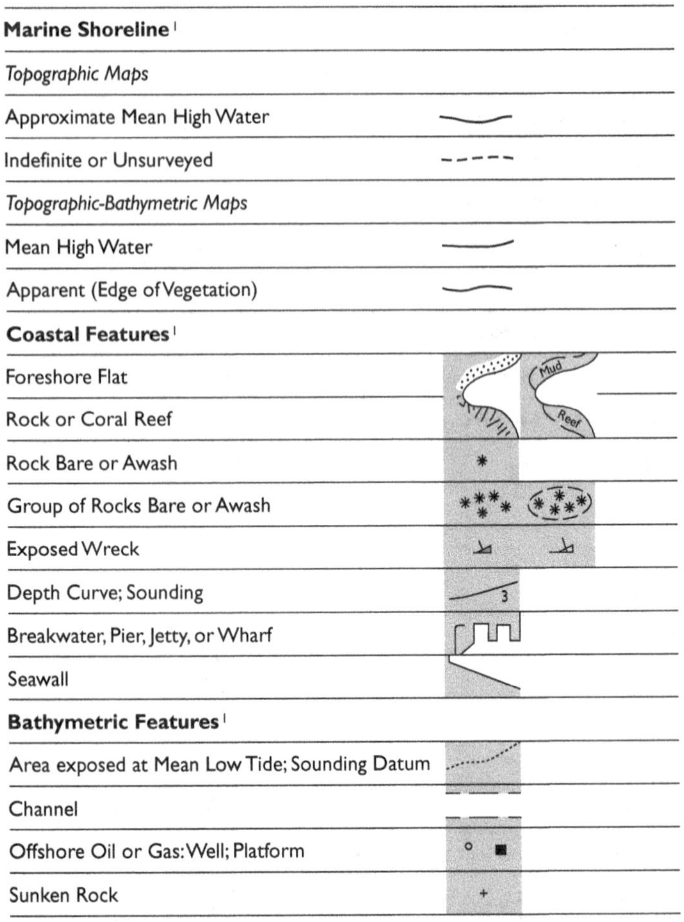

Marine Shoreline [1]

Topographic Maps

Approximate Mean High Water	
Indefinite or Unsurveyed	

Topographic-Bathymetric Maps

Mean High Water	
Apparent (Edge of Vegetation)	

Coastal Features [1]

Foreshore Flat	
Rock or Coral Reef	
Rock Bare or Awash	
Group of Rocks Bare or Awash	
Exposed Wreck	
Depth Curve; Sounding	
Breakwater, Pier, Jetty, or Wharf	
Seawall	

Bathymetric Features [1]

Area exposed at Mean Low Tide; Sounding Datum	
Channel	
Offshore Oil or Gas: Well; Platform	
Sunken Rock	

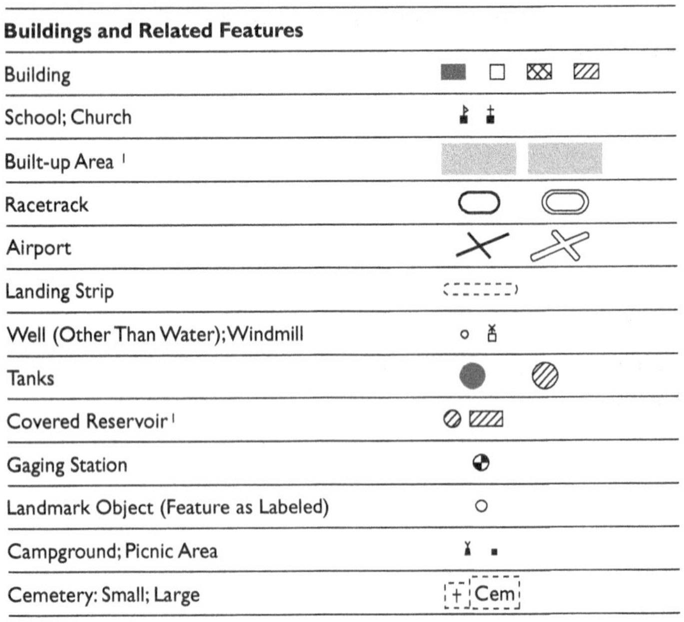

Buildings and Related Features

Building	
School; Church	
Built-up Area [1]	
Racetrack	
Airport	
Landing Strip	
Well (Other Than Water); Windmill	
Tanks	
Covered Reservoir [1]	
Gaging Station	
Landmark Object (Feature as Labeled)	
Campground; Picnic Area	
Cemetery: Small; Large	

[1] These symbols are differentiated by color on USGS topographic maps. To view these images in color, go to http://erg.usgs.gov/isb/pubs/booklets/symbols/buildings.html.

Building and Related Features

TOPOGRAPHIC MAP SYMBOLS (continued)

Source: USGS.

Megan S. Lewis, AICP, American Planning Association, Chicago, Illinois

streams, irrigation ditches, and other water features (blue); land grids and important roads (red); other roads and trails, railroads, and boundaries (black); and features that have been updated using aerial photography, but not field-verified (purple).

Names of places and features also are shown in a color corresponding to the type of feature, and are often are identified by labels such as "Substation" or "Golf Course."

Symbol-Related Features

Various point symbols are used to depict features such as buildings, campgrounds, springs, water tanks, mines, survey control points, and wells. These are also often shown in a corresponding color.

Contours

Topographic contours are shown in brown, by lines of different widths. Each contour is a line of equal elevation; therefore, contours never cross. They show the general shape of the terrain. To help the user determine elevations, index contours (usually every fourth or fifth contour) are wider. The narrower intermediate and supplementary contours found between the index contours help to show more details of the land surface shape. Contours that are close together represent steep slopes. Widely spaced contours, or the absence of contours, means that the ground slope is relatively level.

The contour interval is the elevation difference between adjacent contour lines. The interval used is selected to best show the general shape of the terrain. A map of a relatively flat area may have a contour interval of 10 feet or less. Maps in mountainous areas may have contour intervals of 100 feet or more. Elevation values are shown at frequent intervals on the index contour lines to facilitate their identification and to allow the user to interpolate the values of adjacent contours.

Bathymetric Contours and Depth Curves

Bathymetric contours show the shape and slope of the ocean bottom and are shown in blue or black. Bathymetric contours, which are shown in meters at intervals appropriate to map scale and coastal profile, should not be confused with depth curves.

Depth curves are shown along coastlines and on inland bodies of water where the data are available from hydrographic charts or other reliable sources. Depth figures, shown in blue along the curves, are in feet on older USGS maps and in meters on newer maps. Soundings, which are individual depth values, may also be shown.

DIGITAL RASTER GRAPHICS

A digital raster graphic (DRG) is a scanned image of a USGS topographic map. Between 1995 and 1998, the USGS produced DRGs of the 1:20,000- (Puerto Rico), 1:24,000-,1:25,000-, 1:30,000- (Caribbean Islands), 1:63,360- (Alaska), 1:100,000-, and 1:250,000-scale topographic map series. DRGs are available from the USGS.

The USGS has continued to make new DRGs since 1998, to replace data found to contain errors, and to make new DRGs of revised maps. Approximately 1,000 replacement and new-version DRGs have been produced each year since 1998.

In addition to the standard topographic quadrangles, many DRGs have been made for other areas, such as national parks maps, maps of Antarctica, and geologic and hydrologic maps. A USGS DRG has a standard color palette of 13 colors, intended to model the line-drawing nature of the source graphic.

Uses of a Digital Raster Graphic

DRGs are used as base maps onto which other digital data can be overlaid. The USGS uses DRGs for collecting and validating digital line graph (DLG) data, which are digital representations of cartographic information. They are digital vectors converted from maps and related sources. USGS DLG data are classified as large, intermediate, and small scale:

- Large-scale DLGs are derived from 1:20,000-, 1:24,000-, and 1:25,000-scale 7.5-minute topographic quadrangle maps.
- Intermediate-scale DLGs are derived from USGS 1:100,000-scale 30- by 60- minute quadrangle maps.
- Small-scale DLGs are derived from USGS 1:2,000,000-scale sectional maps of the National Atlas of the United States.

DRGs can also help assess the completeness of digital data from other mapping agencies, and they can be used to produce "hybrid" products from other data sources, such as creating shaded-relief maps.

THE NATIONAL MAP

The USGS is developing the National Map, which will provide real-time geographic base information, available on the Internet and in the public domain. The goal is to minimize the amount of time and effort necessary to find, develop, integrate, and maintain geographic base information each time data are needed.

Types of Information

The National Map will provide data and operational capabilities that include the following:

- High-resolution digital orthorectified imagery that will provide some of the feature information content now symbolized on topographic maps
- High-resolution surface elevation data, including bathymetry, to derive contours for primary series topographic maps and to support production of accurate orthorectified imagery
- Vector feature data for hydrography, transportation (roads, railways, and waterways), structures, government unit boundaries, and publicly owned lands boundaries
- Geographic names for physical and cultural features to support the U.S. Board on Geographic Names and other names, such as those for highways and streets
- Land-cover data that classify the land surface into categories such as open water and high-density residential

Data Customization and Consistency

Data will allow users to extract information for irregular geographic areas, such as counties or watersheds, and to analyze the information. Data resolution and completeness will vary depending on geographic area and need. For example, the National Map will contain higher-resolution elevation data in areas of subtle relief variation, such as river floodplains, to support hydrographic modeling.

Users will also be able to create their own maps by defining a geographic area of interest, selecting unique combinations of data, and printing their maps at home or at other locations. All content of the National Map will be documented by metadata that comply with Federal Geographic Data Committee standards.

See also:
Slope, Relief, and Aspect

Megan S. Lewis, AICP, American Planning Association, Chicago, Illinois

MAPPING

PROPERTY MAPS IN MODERN CADASTRES

Cadastral refers to maps and records showing boundaries, ownership, and attributes of real property. Cadastral maps depict land ownership information, typically used for purposes of taxation, planning, zoning, assessment, and permit granting. The modern cadastre is an integrated database of land description, value, ownership, and socioeconomic data. Surveyors create parcel footprints for property ownership maps with additional data input from planning, architecture, archaeology, real estate appraisal, and applied statistics. The Bureau of Land Management (BLM) has extensive historical and current information about land ownership and the use of public lands in the United States.

APPLICATIONS

- Determining the radius around a property to notify neighbors of proposed actions.
- Conducting a land survey to inventory land use and improvements.
- Determining the location of a right-of-way.
- Serving as base maps for land titles, registration, and property ownership identification.
- Verifying and updating metes and bounds.
- Creating a snapshot of spatial relationships between land, either objects or improvements.
- Identifying environmental and geographic spatial relationships affecting property values.
- Providing a basis for competitive market, or spatial analysis, within real estate sectors.

MAP CONTENT

The International Association of Assessing Officers (IAAO) suggests that the following elements be shown on all digital and printed cadastral maps:

- Parcel boundaries, dimensions, and areas
- Parcel identifiers
- Subdivision areas or plat boundaries, including lot and block numbers
- Nonparcel specific-municipal and political boundaries, which list the names of political subdivisions, including counties, towns, and municipalities
- Geographic subdivision boundaries and names, including sections, townships, land districts, and land lots
- Geographic elements showing names and locations of transportation networks, including streets, highways, alleys, railroads, lakes, rivers, and other geographic features
- Fundamental map elements including map number, title block, map scale, legend, north arrow, date, author, key or link to adjoining maps, use disclaimer, and metadata

MAP DEVELOPMENT

Cadastral base maps are usually created from paper map scanning, digitizing, and digital orthophotography and coordinate geometry (COGO) data capture methods. Source maps can be obtained from munic-

ipal tax assessment departments at various scales (e.g., 1:200, 1:2,400, or 1:4,800).

Train all personnel involved in creating and maintaining these maps appropriately with regard to understanding topology and surveying for boundary creation and legal principles of boundary and title law, among other areas.

SOURCE INFORMATION

When creating a new or updating an existing cadastral map, assemble all the relevant information first. The IAAO recommends the following information be included:

- List of the parcels in the area to be mapped
- Taxing district and municipal boundary maps
- Geodetic control network information
- All Government Land Office and Bureau of Land Management cadastral survey plats and field notes (for areas covered by the U.S. Public Land Survey System (PLSS) of township, range, and sections)
- Surveys for railroads, highways, and, if needed, utility routes
- Subdivision, town site, and town plats and surveys
- Private land surveys and associated corner records
- Current orthophotographic imagery of the area
- Deed descriptions for unplatted parcels and for parcels that vary from lot and block boundaries
- Court decisions for relevant parcels
- Applicable base map data, such as edge of pavement, street and railroad centerlines, water features, fence and field lines
- Rights-of-way information, whether dedicated by plat, purchased in fee, vacated, abandoned, or unopened and, if required, held as an easement

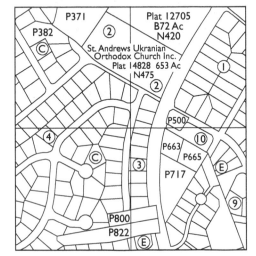

Note: This excerpt is from a larger property base map that was approximately one-third the size of the original 1:2,400-scale map.

SAMPLE PROPERTY BASE MAP

Source: Montgomery County, MD, GIS Department.

- Information on utility easements, if required
- Previously produced maps on various media (vellum, paper, drafting film, and in digital form)
- Other imagery of the area, from nonorthophotographic or historical photographic sources
- Highway maps, street name databases, and other information sources for official names of roads
- USGS topographic maps and geographic name databases for additional feature names

MULTIPURPOSE CADASTRES

Multipurpose cadastres are integrated databases that contain information on the physical, legal, economic, demographic, and fiscal aspects of all parcels. They can be used from local to national levels to address issues of economic development, sprawl, poverty, land policy, and sustainable development, among other applications.

STANDARDS AND GUIDELINES

The Federal Geographic Data Committee (FGDC) and its Subcommittee for Cadastral Data have published several versions of the *Cadastral Data Content Standard for the National Spatial Data Infrastructure*. The Urban and Regional Information Systems Association (URISA) and IAAO have published standards and guidelines that reflect advancements in information technology. Planners and urban designers should also become familiar with mass appraisal valuation processes and other related standards employed for land taxation, land registration, and physical building inventory and construction. Specifically, modern assessment valuation models can vary by region and do not always adhere to theoretical residential (hedonic) models for estimating value. Understand the constraints and opportunities of using assessed versus market value in developing strategic and economic planning initiatives.

EMERGING ISSUES

Ongoing efforts to create national cadastres must ensure consistent development and application of modern and multipurpose cadastres, and can benefit from multidisciplinary standards. At the heart of this endeavor is the property ownership map that drives the process of public and private land investment in both urban and rural contexts.

REFERENCES

Federal Geographic Data Committee. 2003. *Cadastral Data Content Standard for the National Spatial Data Infrastructure, Version 1.3*. Washington, DC: Subcommittee on Cadastral Data.

See also:
Aerial Photographs and Digital Orthophoto Quadrangles
Subdivision Regulation

Ann-Margaret Esnard, Ph.D., Cornell University, Ithaca, New York; Michelle M. Thompson, Ph.D., Cornell University, Ithaca, New York

CENSUS DATA AND DEMOGRAPHIC MAPPING

The U.S. Census Bureau is the primary source of U.S. socioeconomic data, which includes population, median income, and employment, among other data. Socioeconomic data are commonly represented in the following types of thematic maps:

Choropleth maps. Different colors or shades of gray show different values. Data are often grouped into ranges, and each range has a different color or shade.

Dot maps. Data as shown as dots, with each dot representing a unit of value (e.g., one dot = 100 people). Depending on the type of data and the intended use of the map, other more intuitive symbols can be used, such as symbols of people.

Proportional symbol maps. Symbols such as circles or squares are used to represent data, with a larger-size symbol representing a larger data set. This technique is not recommended to show density of distribution.

The U.S. Census Bureau has developed various products and interactive online services that allow users to display different thematic maps using data from the decennial census, economic census, and the American Community Survey (ACS). The ACS annually disseminates surveys to a random sample of 3 million households throughout the country and Puerto Rico to gather data on a range of social, economic, housing, and demographic issues. In 2010, the ACS is slated to replace the decennial census "long form," which is sent out to a sample population (approximately one in every six households). The long form, which is compared to the "short form" that is received by each household, has additional questions on population and housing.

TYPES OF SOCIOECONOMIC VARIABLES

Among the types of information available from the Census Bureau are boundaries, line features, and landmarks, and socioeconomic variables.

Boundaries, Line Features, and Landmarks

These data are provided by TIGER®/Line files, which are extracted from the Census Bureau's TIGER (Topologically Integrated Geographic Encoding and Referencing) database:

- Political boundaries (state, county, metropolitan area, and congressional district, for example)
- Statistical area boundaries for Census Bureau purposes (blocks, block groups, and tracts)
- Corridors, including roads, railroads, and rivers

Socioeconomic Variables

- Population
- Housing and homeownership
- Income
- Educational attainment
- Gender
- Age
- Race

Consult the Census Bureau website for available and downloadable extraction programs that allow socioeconomic data to be aggregated by zip codes or other meaningful spatial boundaries.

SUMMARY FILES

Summary files are statistics for a large number of geographic areas that are designed to show subject matter detail in tabular form. Data users should understand the content and completeness of Summary Files 1 to 4, and the file-naming conventions used by the Census Bureau, as these are the four main summary files produced from the data collected during Census 2000:

Summary File 1 (SF 1). Presents 100 percent population and housing figures for the total population, for 63 race categories, and for many other race and Hispanic or Latino categories. Data include age, sex, households, household relationship, housing units, and tenure (whether the residence is owned or rented).

Summary File 2 (SF 2). Presents data similar to the information included in SF 1. These data are shown down to the census tract level for 250 race, Hispanic or Latino, and American Indian and Alaska Native tribe categories.

Summary File 3 (SF 3). Presents data on the population and housing long-form census subjects, such as income and education. It includes population totals for ancestry groups and selected characteristics for a limited number of race and Hispanic or Latino categories.

Summary File 4 (SF 4). Presents data similar to the information included in SF 3. These data are shown down to the census tract level for 336 race, Hispanic or Latino, American Indian and Alaska Native tribe, and ancestry categories.

CREATING THEMATIC MAPS

To best and most accurately represent socioeconomic data on a map, understand the underlying principles of map classifications and the color and symbol schemes published by experts and professional

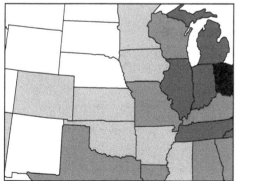

Population per Square Mile (1990 Data)
- ☐ 1-29
- ☐ 30-59
- ☐ 60-113
- ☐ 114-232
- ☐ 233-9187

CHOROPLETH MAP

Source: Ann-Margaret Esnard.

▪▫ 1 Dot = 200,000
(Based on 1990 Population Data)

When a GIS creates a dot density map, the GIS randomly spreads points over the area, rather than being associated with specific population centers. This should be taken into account when using the mapping technique.

DOT DENSITY MAP

Source: Ann-Margaret Esnard.

- ° 100,000
- ◎ 1,000,000
- ◯ 10,000,000
  (Based on 1990 Population Data)

PROPORTIONAL SYMBOL MAP

Source: Ann-Margaret Esnard.

Ann-Margaret Esnard, Ph.D., Cornell University, Ithaca, New York

organizations. And be aware that the default classifications and colors created by existing GIS software products are not always the best way to represent the data, so attention to this is especially important when creating such maps in a GIS.

For example, use choropleth maps to show the intensity of numerical data, such as densities, means, rates, ratios, percentages, and percent rates, by grouping numerical data into classes through several classification methods, such as natural breaks and equal intervals, and shading each class on a map where the shading/pattern is used to reflect hierarchy (e.g., low to high ranks).

NORMALIZED DATA

Normalized data show the relationship between raw count data, such as population and area, to obtain new information, for example, population density. Planners must understand how to normalize data against meaningful common denominators, to avoid confusing or misleading the map reader. The table here shows other examples of normalizing pairs.

APPLICATIONS

Socioeconomic variables can be mapped at different levels of political and census statistical area boundaries. This allows for a wide range of applications. Special-purpose maps, such as population characteristics, are often overlaid with other data sets as part of a more comprehensive, multipurpose GIS. Socioeconomic data can be used to do a number of things:

- Show decadal changes in population density, house values, and median income for growth management studies.
- Provide a snapshot of the extent of urbanization

EXAMPLES OF NORMALIZING PAIRS

CENSUS VARIABLE	NORMALIZE BY
Age, gender, race	Total population (persons)
Labor force, employment	Population age 16 and older
Educational attainment (years of school completed)	Population age 25 and older
Household income	Total households
Occupancy status (occupied, vacant, seasonal units)	Total housing units
Housing tenure (owner vs. renter)	Total households
Contract rent	Renter-occupied housing units

Source: Adapted from Dailey 2000.

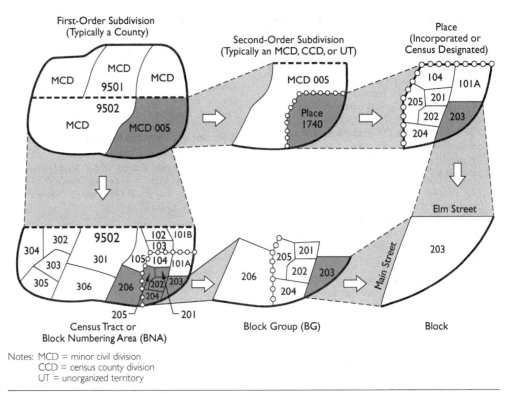

CENSUS SMALL-AREA GEOGRAPHY

Source: U.S. Census Bureau.

Notes: MCD = minor civil division
CCD = census county division
UT = unorganized territory

using population density thresholds of 1,000 persons per square mile.
- Show location and concentrations of specific age groups as input to land-use planning, recreational planning, school facilities planning, and provision of social services, for example.
- Maps at-risk persons, using age and income proxies, as input to disaster planning and emergency management activities. For example, mapping low-income elderly populations would be important in planning for local government responses to heat emergencies.

When selecting a data source and method of representation, consider the following questions:

- What is the best unit of analysis or geography at which to represent this data?
- Does sample data represent the phenomena being studied or mapped?

- What is the most accurate way to realign census boundaries across decades, and how are these discrepancies initially identified?

OTHER CONSIDERATIONS

By law, no one is permitted to reveal information from the census and associated surveys that could be used to identify any specific person, household, or business. Census data remain confidential for 72 years, after which they are released publicly.

REFERENCES

Dailey, George. 2000. "Normalizing Census Data in ArcView GIS." *ArcUser,* October-December: 44–45.

See also:
Geographic Information Systems
Mapping Data Overview

Ann-Margaret Esnard, Ph.D., Cornell University, Ithaca, New York

REMOTE SENSING AND SATELLITE IMAGE CLASSIFICATION

Remote sensing refers to collecting information about an object without coming into contact with that object. The field of remote sensing encompasses many activities, including sensor design and function, data processing and storage, and image classification. Image classification is the area most commonly encountered by planners.

Satellite imagery is typically analyzed to produce land cover maps and statistics. Planners use these data to study many conditions such as urban sprawl, open space, species habitat, and impervious cover.

Image classification is the process of assigning the pixels of an image to a specific class or category to identify ground features. Examples of classes include woodlands, prairie, roof cover, pavement, and maintained turf.

INTRODUCTION TO IMAGE CLASSIFICATION

Earth sensing satellites record the sun's energy as it is reflected by the surface of the Earth. A satellite image is composed of thousands of pixels with different spectral values, which represent surface reflectance. The classification process attempts to interpret raw pixel values, called spectral information, into specific classes of information, called thematic information.

Highly specialized software has been developed to import, enhance, and analyze remotely sensed data. In most cases, satellite images are delivered in a raw format and must be imported into the image processing software. This process converts the image into that program's image format (e.g., .hdf converted to .img). A number of corrections, such as radiometric correction, geometric correction, and noise removal, can then be applied to alleviate spectral or geometric distortions in the image. Finally, enhancements are used to alter the image to facilitate a particular analysis. Examples of enhancements include spectral enhancement, spatial enhancement, and radiometric enhancement.

Classification Schemes

Image pixels are sorted based on their spectral value and assigned to a category. The categories represent a specific theme or condition in the study area. The U.S. Geological Survey system, also called the Anderson system, is a widely accepted land-cover classification scheme with several levels of detail. The chosen scheme depends on the spatial resolution of the data and the goal of the analysis. For example, for low-resolution imagery (30-meter resolution) from the Landsat satellite, a land-cover class might be "urban;" for high-resolution imagery (4-meter resolution) from the Ikonos satellite, a land-cover class might be "pavement."

TYPES OF IMAGE CLASSIFICATION

Different end users require different information. Understand what users want to achieve to ensure that the proper and most useful classes are identified. End users need to understand the limitations of the classification process and appropriate applications for data. There are two general types of classification: unsupervised and supervised.

WORKING WITH END USERS

End users need to understand the limitations of the classification process, in particular spatial resolution of data, land-cover classes, and accuracy. This is best accomplished through a close working relationship with users where the following are discussed or developed:

- The classification process
- Key terms and standards
- Limitations and potential of data
- Ground-truth data
- Classification scheme
- Appropriate end uses for land-cover data

This process of engagement results in greater acceptance and use of data, a more advanced understanding of land-cover conditions, and a willingness to be involved in future mapping and planning efforts.

Unsupervised Classification

An unsupervised classification is the process of letting the computer sort image pixels into classes based on their spectral patterns. The analyst sets the number of classes desired, and the software determines classes by grouping pixels with similar reflectance values. For example, if the analyst sets the number of classes at five, the image-processing program will categorize each pixel into one of five classes. An unsupervised classification results in a thematic image with any number of classes. The user must determine what ground condition each class represents.

Unsupervised classification simplifies the classification task for the analyst because few parameters need to be set and detailed knowledge of the data is not required to run the classification. However, classes may not be meaningful, because they are based purely on reflectance. The analyst must decipher the meaning, which requires an interpretation of the spectral groupings. Unsupervised classification does not work as well as supervised classification in heterogeneous land-cover areas, but it is good base for a supervised classification because it can provide an initial set of signatures to improve upon.

Supervised Classification

With supervised classification, an analyst selects areas of an image with similar spectral response characteristics that are recognized as a specific ground cover or feature. The supervised classification process "trains" the software to look for other groups of pixels with similar reflectance, also called spectral signature. Additional data sets, such as aerial photographs and GIS data, can be used to assist in signature collection and to improve the classification result.

The spectral signatures of different training samples are then evaluated to ensure that there is minimal overlap between different classes. There are two types of evaluation: visual and statistical. Visual evaluations include checking histogram overlap; classifying "to screen," which displays general class assignment; or assessing signature mean plots to see which signatures overlap in a specific image band. Statistical evaluations determine the separability of the signatures using statistics such as separability cell arrays, covariance calculations, and signature means.

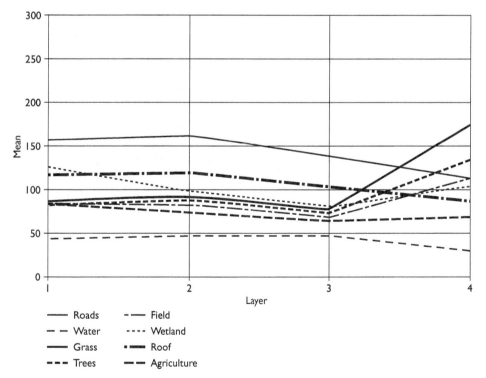

Signature mean plots allow the user to evaluate the separability of the signatures for a supervised classification.

SPECTRAL SIGNATURES

Source: Futurity, Inc.

David C. Bier, Futurity, Inc., Chicago, Illinois; Jessica M. Braden, Futurity, Inc., Chicago, Illinois

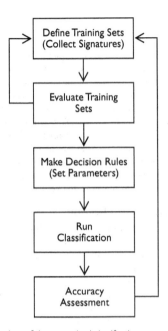

An overview of the supervised classification process

SUPERVISED CLASSIFICATION PROCESS

Source: Futurity, Inc.

ACCURACY ASSESSMENT

An accuracy assessment is the process of randomly selecting pixels and comparing them to actual land-cover conditions, provided by ground-truth information, with the land-cover class assigned by classification model. Perform an accuracy assessment to determine whether pixels have been misclassified and to see if the classification result is acceptable.

The output of an accuracy assessment is a report or series of reports that typically include the following:

- Overview of classes that might be misclassified.
- Comparison of assigned classes to actual land cover provided by ground-truth information.
- Percentage statistics that illustrate how "true" the classification results are when compared to a random assignment of classes. Typically, an accuracy assessment of 85 percent or higher is considered acceptable.

GROUND-TRUTH INFORMATION

Ground-truth information is defined as accurate information about land-cover conditions at a particular location. This location can be a point or a small area, such as a 30-meter diameter circle. Information recorded electronically or as field notes includes location, land-cover conditions, observer, and date. The process used to collect information and the data itself must be both accessible and repeatable.

Ground-truth information is used to complete a supervised classification and to evaluate accuracy. Collection and organization of ground-truth information can be a significant part of the classification process. While the number of ground-truth locations required varies with the size of the study area and number of land-cover classes, there must be enough to complete both the classification and accuracy assessment during which locations are randomly selected from a pool.

PRODUCTS

Land-cover raster data can be used to create map compositions or in a GIS program for further analysis. Raster data can also be converted to a vector layer and imported into a GIS for further analysis. In addition to the land-cover data, a number of statistics can be generated to quantify areas of land cover.

Metadata

Metadata documents the data product and the process of preparing the data. This includes information about resolution, data sources, classification process, contact names, and purpose. Metadata helps a secondary user understand the proper use of the land-cover/land-use product based on factors such as time of year, scale, and methodology used. Creating metadata can be time-consuming, even with templates; nevertheless, it is extremely important that future users understand the methodology behind a data set. The Federal Geographic Data Committee (FGDC) has developed a standard metadata format, which can be obtained at www.fgdc.gov.

GENERAL CONSIDERATIONS

When using remote sensing and satellite image classification tools, consider the following:

- A classification is a snapshot of conditions at a point in time. To assess change over time, additional images must be used. For example, in order to assess land-cover change every five years, a new image must be purchased every five years.
- A single image cannot be used for all analyses. For example, if the goal is to map tree canopy and impervious cover, the analyst needs two images: one with leaf-on to map tree canopy and one with leaf-off to map impervious cover.
- In many cases, imagery will need to be enhanced before classification, because of phenomena such as shadows or haze.
- Every image/study area has its own set of issues. It is difficult to predict the time required to complete supervised classification. Image enhancement techniques may be needed to improve the quality of the image. It is also difficult to predict the number of times the classification will need to be refined in order to attain an acceptable level of accuracy.
- Classifications are complicated and require advanced skills. An analyst must understand the parameters that need to be set and their effect on the final product.
- Image classification requires advanced image processing software; software and upgrades are often expensive.

EMERGING ISSUES

Images with one-meter resolution are available at relatively low prices. However, pixel-based classifications do not work as well for high-resolution data because the images are so detailed that they often have a distracting "salt-and-pepper" appearance. A new classification approach—object-based classification—has been developed, which is designed specifically for high-resolution imagery. Instead of classifying the image pixel by pixel, objects are created by merging contiguous pixels of similar spectral response.

REFERENCES

Federal Geographic Data Committee. 1998. *Content Standard for Digital Geospatial Metadata*. FGDC-STD-001-1998. Washington, DC: Federal Geographic Data Committee: www.fgdc.gov/metadata/csdgm/.

See also:

Geographic Information Systems

David C. Bier, Futurity, Inc., Chicago, Illinois; Jessica M. Braden, Futurity, Inc., Chicago, Illinois

GEOGRAPHIC INFORMATION SYSTEMS

A geographic information system (GIS) is a tool that connects databases to maps. It combines layers of information about where things are located with descriptive data about those things and their surroundings. Information such as where a point is located on a map, the length of a road, the size of a parcel, and the number of square miles a community occupies can all be stored in digital format in layers, also called themes, of the GIS. By combining a range of spatially referenced data and analytic tools, GIS technology enables people to prioritize issues, understand them, consider alternatives, and reach viable conclusions.

The capability of a GIS to link data sets together by common location information facilitates the sharing of information, such as interdepartmentally within an organization or via the Internet with the public. Participatory GIS efforts involve partnerships among GIS technical professionals, planners, and community members to ensure adequate neutrality, confidentiality, and objectiveness of information, as well as adequate grounding in community perspectives to explore all possible scenarios that may apply during any planning process.

GIS COMPONENTS

The main components of a GIS are hardware, software, data sources, including metadata, and data structure types.

Hardware

The hardware consists of a computer that meets the software system requirements and other equipment, such as printers, scanners, or digitizers. Check with the particular software vendor to make sure that the equipment being purchased has the specifications that the software needs. Unlike in the past, when there were cost issues regarding the most appropriate hardware, today many systems have increased technological capacity at decreased cost.

Software

GIS software provides the functions and tools necessary for storing, analyzing, and displaying spatial information. These include a graphical user interface, a database management system, tools for entering and manipulating geographic information, and query functions.

Data Sources

To determine the type of data needed, one needs to first determine the types of products a GIS will produce. Data can come from existing sources, such as spreadsheets, relational databases, images, or computer-assisted drawing (CAD) files; paper or mylar maps that are scanned and digitized; field-collected data using global positioning systems (GPS); and remotely sensed information, such as satellite imagery, aerial photography, digital elevation models (DEMs), and orthophotos.

Metadata

Metadata are perhaps the most critical part of a GIS, and often the most neglected. Metadata provide specific information about a data set, such as its creation

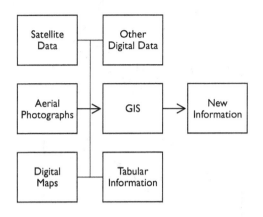

DATA INTEGRATION

Source: USGS 2005.

SAMPLE METADATA CONTENT

TITLE	2000 CENSUS TRACTS
Location	www.census.gov/geo/www/cob/tr2000.html
Geography	Each State, D.C., American Samoa, Guam, N. Mariana Islands, Puerto Rico, Virgin Islands
Vintage	January 1, 2000
Formats	ARC/INFO Export (.e00), Arcview Shapefile, and ARC/INFO Ungenerate (ASCII)
Projection	Geographic (Lat/Lon)
Datum	NAD83
Distributor	Department of Commerce, Census Bureau, Geography Division
Originator	Department of Commerce, Census Bureau, Geography Division

Source: www.census.gov/geo/www/cob/tr_metadata.html#meta, April 22, 2005.

date, scale, projection, resolution, and accuracy. This information is necessary to make sure the data can be accurately used for the analysis. The Federal Geographic Data Committee (FGDC) metadata standard provides guidance on required content, particularly for posting data sets on Internet-based data clearinghouses. In addition, each state has metadata rules that should be consulted.

Data Types

There are two types of data: vector data and raster data. A GIS will integrate both types of data.

Vector Data

Vector data contain information about points, lines, or polygons, which are stored as x and y coordinates. Below are examples of the types of data that would be represented as points, lines, or polygons:

- Points: trees, benches, street lights, fire hydrant locations
- Lines: streets, water and sewer lines, electrical networks
- Polygons: census tracts, parcels, building footprints, building layouts, and landscape planted areas

Raster Data

Raster data are values assigned to evenly spaced cells in an image. They contain information about the Earth's geographic features that is stored in cells

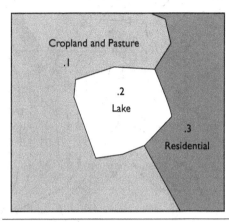

VECTOR DATA FILE STRUCTURE

Source: USGS 2005.

RASTER DATA FILE STRUCTURE

Source: USGS 2005.

within a grid or matrix. Each cell stores a single numeric value representing data, such as land use, vegetation, slope, elevation, or aspect.

GIS FUNCTIONALITY

Some of the various GIS software functions commonly used by planners and designers are described here.

Query by Location

A query by location can be a search on a point within a polygon, or a radius search from a specific point. For example, a query to identify all parcels less than 0.5 acres in size.

Query by Attribute

A query by attribute searches on data stored in the table; for example, a query to identify all parcels owned by people with the last name Smith.

Boolean Queries

Boolean queries are a combination of location queries and attribute queries. They specify relationships between fields and values using common operators such as "and" (both expressions are true)

Ann-Margaret Esnard, Ph.D., Cornell University, Ithaca, New York; Nancy Sappington, ESRI, Redlands, California; Milton R. Ospina, ESRI, Redlands, California

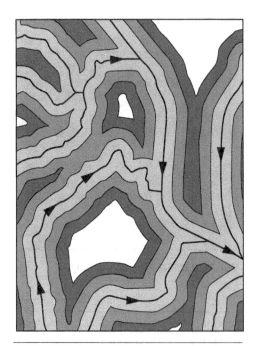

THREE 200-METER STREAM BUFFERS

Source: USGS 2005.

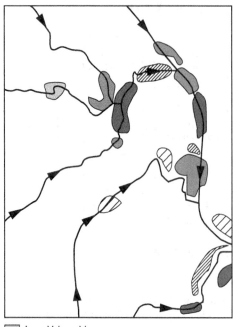

☐ Least Vulnerable
▨ Low Vulnerability
▩ Medium Vulnerability
▨ High Vulnerability
▱ Very High Vulnerability

VULNERABILITY TO POLLUTION, BASED ON A COMBINATION OF FACTORS

Source: USGS 2005.

User Needs Assessment

A comprehensive needs assessment serves as a blueprint for implementing an integrated suite of GIS applications. Typically, a needs assessment involves analyzing all work processes with an organization to study current and future workflows and data requirements. The assessment also identifies opportunities for implementing best practices and defines which GIS applications will support that work. The information for the survey can be summarized in a matrix, which helps prioritize needs and identify which software tools to develop first. The following questions suggest which factors an analyst will need to consider:

* Which business processes would benefit from GIS?
* What data are needed for the necessary products?
* Which software will produce the desired outcome?
* What hardware is required to support the software?
* How will existing workflows be changed by the GIS?

Data Inventory and Evaluation

Building the data is often the most expensive component of a GIS. It is generally estimated that 80 percent of the total cost of creating a GIS is for building and maintaining data. Therefore, before hiring someone to build data, find out what data are already available within your agency or organization. Five important factors need to be considered:

* Required data format, scale, and resolution
* Whether integration with other data sets and applications is possible
* Who will maintain the data
* Verification that there are legal rights to use the data
* Identification of missing data through a gap analysis

System Design and Implementation Plan

This step ties in with the needs assessment—determining what you want to do with the GIS drives what is purchased. In an ideal situation, this is all done beforehand to determine which products or services to buy. The elements covered in the system design and implementation plan include the following:

* Hardware and software configuration
* Database and application software design
* Staff training program
* Implementation costs
* Phased implementation plan

Pilot Project

Before fully implementing the GIS, perform a test of the system, to refine the requirements and identify any other data gaps. Among the items to test are the following:

* Hardware and data communications
* Data automation procedures
* Database design and data model
* Application software

Implementation

This final step is where the GIS is put through its final tests, and where it becomes integrated into day-to-day operations. This stage may reveal that greater speed or storage capacity is needed, or that a different product is required. The following are the tasks completed here:

---

and "or" (at least one expression is true). For example, a Boolean query could involve searching for all parcels that are less than 0.5 acres in size and are owned by people with the last name Smith.

Buffers

A buffer is a region around a geographic feature or phenomenon. Buffers can be one ring or multiple rings. Also called proximity analysis, buffer analysis can be used to depict spheres of influence, areas that are more significantly impacted by a given phenomenon than those on the outside, and zones of protection, areas that are protected from impacts from a given phenomenon.

Address Matching

This process matches the location of an event, recorded as a street address, latitude and longitude position, or milepost locations along a route in a table, to a street centerline, zip code, or other administrative zone. The common result is a GIS layer with points corresponding to these events. A common use for this is taking name and address information collected at a public meeting and correlating this with the GIS database.

Address matches are often imperfect, because of inconsistencies between the address table and the digital street map, and errors such as misspellings or other data entry errors. Most software packages can do rematching when partial or unmatched records result. Depending on the sensitivity of the planning analysis, there might be a need to balance specificity with confidentiality. Offsetting points, matching to more generalized boundaries such as a zip code or raster-based density mapping might be necessary.

Measuring Distance

Distance can be measured as Euclidean distance, which is the distance of straight or curved paths, to indicate how far apart things are; and cost distance,

which is the distance measured that involves the least effort in moving across a surface.

Overlays

The overlay operation is central to many GIS applications. It is one of the original motivations for creating GIS software technology. An overlay uses a geometric process to associate all the attributes at each location and then uses a rule to combine these attributes.

Suitability Analyses

Suitability analysis is commonly used for finding optimum locations for a project, based on a combination of map layers. For example, suitability analysis can be used to locate the most suitable location for a new park or school. This technique offers the opportunity to use GIS in conjunction with public participation, bringing together stakeholders to solve a community problem.

Often, some objectives and their related data layers have more importance to the overall suitability model. To account for this, one can rank and weight the data sets. Ranking and weighting are subjective processes, which differ based on the analyst's background, expertise, and preferences.

GIS IMPLEMENTATION

A successful GIS implementation requires both management and user support. Use a team approach to involve all potential users. Emphasize how the GIS will help facilitate planning functions and tasks and improve the planning business workflow. Clearly define expectations to ensure the success of the GIS and keep the budget on track.

Ann-Margaret Esnard, Ph.D., Cornell University, Ithaca, New York; Nancy Sappington, ESRI, Redlands, California; Milton R. Ospina, ESRI, Redlands, California

- Final hardware and software configuration
- Database construction
- Staff training
- Software application development

ETHICAL GUIDELINES

In the spirit of providing full, clear, and accurate information on planning issues, use codes and guidelines specific to the use of GIS and information technologies to complement the AICP Code of Ethics and Professional Conduct. The GIS Code of Ethics, approved in April 2003 by the Urban and Regional Information Systems Association (URISA) board, provides a basis for making appropriate and ethical choices and for evaluating an analyst's work from an ethical point of view.

STANDARDS

The following organizations set GIS standards:

The International Standards Organization (ISO): www.iso.org

Open Geospatial Consortium (OGC): www.opengeospatial.org

Federal Geographic Data Committee (FGDC): www.fgdc.org

Open Mobile Alliance: www.openmobilealliance.org

Web Services Interoperability Organization: www.ws-i.org

Organization for the Advancement of Structured Information Standards (OASIS): www.oasis-open.org/home/index.php

World Wide Web Consortium (W3C): www.w3.org

Internet Engineering Task Force (IETF): www.ietf.org

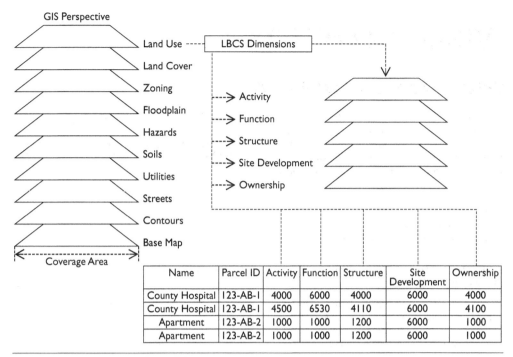

Name	Parcel ID	Activity	Function	Structure	Site Development	Ownership
County Hospital	123-AB-1	4000	6000	4000	6000	4000
County Hospital	123-AB-1	4500	6530	4110	6000	4100
Apartment	123-AB-2	1000	1000	1200	6000	1000
Apartment	123-AB-2	1000	1000	1200	6000	1000

LAYERS OF DATA IN LBCS MODEL

Source: American Planning Association.

LAND-BASED CLASSIFICATION STANDARDS

The Land-Based Classification Standards (LBCS) include a set of color codes that may be used as a standard convention for top-level land-use categories. The American Planning Association website provides information on preparing GIS maps using LBCS classifications. In addition, ask the selected GIS software vendor whether they have developed functionality to incorporate LBCS color-coding. See "Land-Based Classification Systems" in an appendix to this book for more information.

See also:
Mapping Data Overview

Ann-Margaret Esnard, Ph.D., Cornell University, Ithaca, New York; Nancy Sappington, ESRI, Redlands, California; Milton R. Ospina, ESRI, Redlands, California

MAPPING

VISUALIZATION

VISUALIZATION OVERVIEW

Visualization is the process of taking abstract ideas or data and translating them into easily understood and interpreted images to enhance planning, urban design, and decision-making processes. This section of the book discusses three specific visualization techniques:

- Visual preference
- Montage visualization
- Three-dimensional (3-D) visualization

VISUALIZATION TECHNIQUES AT VARIOUS PROCESS STAGES

VISUALIZATION TECHNIQUE	STAGE OF PROCESS			
	ENGAGE STAKEHOLDERS	EXPLORE DESIGN OPTIONS	PRIORITIZE PLANS	ASSESS IMPACTS
Visual Preference	X	X		
Montage Visualization	X	X	X	X
3-D Visualization	X	X	X	X

Source: PlaceMatters.com.

VISUALIZATION TOOLS AND TECHNIQUES

Visualization tools and techniques show what the built environment might look like under different design and development scenarios, over time. These tools and techniques allow planners, urban designers, citizens, and decision makers to experience design alternatives that are otherwise difficult or impossible to see in raw data form. They can also help overcome communication difficulties caused by the use of planning jargon and technical terms.

Visualization tools take advantage of the human capacity to process visual information. Individual interpretations are transformed into a shared understanding of both the aesthetic and functional qualities of a plan or design. Discussions move away from the abstract, where everyone might have a different notion about what could happen, to the concrete, where everyone is responding to the same realistic image of possible futures. Because of this, visualization tools can elevate the debate from rhetoric to what a development project will actually look like and what it will take to make the development successful. For example, when a realistic image of infill development is shown, it is not uncommon for people who were opposed to it to change their minds and to launch into discussions about transit, mixed-use development, and other necessary components of a mixed-use project.

Visualization tools draw people into a planning process and provide a venue for immediate feedback on the quality and appeal of different design choices. They allow citizens to become active participants in an iterative decision-making process. With the integration of relational databases, some visualization tools provide visual information coupled with analysis capabilities. This integration allows for a better understanding of the potential implications of visual preferences on the environment, community and economic development, housing, and equity, for example. Informed discussions can occur about these complicated interrelationships, and better decisions can be made about the future of a neighborhood, city, or region.

APPLICATIONS

Visualization tools and techniques can be applied at a variety of scales, from small, site-specific projects to regional areas. In addition to educating and motivating the public to become involved in the future of their community, visualization tools and techniques can be used in a variety of capacities:

- To present and evaluate development impact on vacant lots.
- To design and evaluate a transportation corridor.
- To choose the appropriate trees and lampposts on a city street.

Visualization tools and techniques are commonly used in the early stages of a community development or design process, to help identify a community vision, educate the public about a specific design concept, and obtain feedback on planning and design alternatives, for example. Visualization is also valuable at other stages of the planning process, from engaging stakeholders to assessing impacts. It can be used during development review, comprehensive planning, and reviews of zoning codes and regulations.

Though these techniques may at times be interrelated, each is independent and can play a different

TOOLS FOR COMMUNITY DESIGN AND DECISION MAKING

Visualization techniques are part of a broader suite of tools for community design and decision making. They help communities make better plans for the future by ensuring the integration of good data, comprehensive analysis, and strong civic engagement processes. These tools and techniques fit into four categories of decision support that reflect critical phases of a community development process.

- *Visualization tools and techniques* allow stakeholders to more easily see how choices will look in the built environment.
- *Impact analysis tools* assess the past, present, and future economic and environmental impacts for a wide range of development projects and policies. They provide quantitative and visual outputs for a variety of scenarios, making it easier to understand trade-offs between alternative development approaches and public policy decisions.
- *Geographic information systems (GIS) and modeling techniques* simulate how the natural and built environments, as well as the social and economic systems of a community, relate to each other on dif-

ferent scales and at different times. GIS-generated maps and charts can also help community members without technical backgrounds to spatially visualize land uses, environmental hazards, transportation access, and other relevant information.

- *Community process tools* allow greater numbers of people to be involved in a more effective and efficient process.
  - Websites provide an opportunity for hosting meetings and sharing documents, calendars, and important event information.
  - Electronic meeting systems, such as keypad voting, can facilitate effective large-scale meetings.
  - Databases help communities gather and share important data and information to promote better communication.

Tools for community design and decision making can range from low-tech tools that use cardboard and scissors to high-tech computer-based tools. Whether using high- or low-tech tools, once the community is clear about what they do and do not want, other community design and decision-making tools can be used to provide analysis of their choices and inform them about the benefits and trade-offs of each possible scenario.

Julie Herman, PlaceMatters.com, a Division of the Orton Family Foundation, Denver, Colorado; Ken Snyder, PlaceMatters.com, a Division of the Orton Family Foundation, Denver, Colorado

role during the planning process. For example, when engaging stakeholders, the visual preference technique can gauge the public's current opinions about specific design choices, and three-dimensional visualization can help the public visualize an entire project.

SELECTING A VISUALIZATION TOOL

A community's particular character, issues, and processes should be the driving forces to determine which tools will be the best fit. A community should do the following before choosing any tool:

- Identify the planning issue it is exploring.
- Clarify the goal and desired outcomes of the planning process.
- Identify what needs to be assessed, evaluated, or designed.

- Understand the types of processes/analyses that may be required to achieve those goals.
- Keep an eye on the budget. Though powerful graphic imaging tools can play a useful role, if funds are not available to support implementation, all efforts can be lost and important relationships built throughout the process strained.

ISSUES TO CONSIDER

- The development of visualization tools is taking place at a rapid pace, often making it challenging to remain current with new tools and advancements in existing tools.
- The pace of technological development is typically faster than the development of standards and

guidelines, also making it challenging to keep up with technology.
- Communities have various standards or guidelines that require developers to demonstrate how a new plan will look in the landscape, yet there is no single set of standards to guide the methods required to portray those designs, which can ultimately lead to inconsistent decision making.

See also:
Community Visioning
Computer-Based Public Participation
Environmental Impact Assessment
Fiscal Impact Assessment
Geographic Information Systems
Montage Visualization
Three-Dimensional Visualization
Visual Preference Techniques

Julie Herman, PlaceMatters.com, a Division of the Orton Family Foundation, Denver, Colorado; Ken Snyder, PlaceMatters.com, a Division of the Orton Family Foundation, Denver, Colorado

VISUALIZATION

MONTAGE VISUALIZATION

Montage portrays changes to a place by overlaying images of potential new design elements, such as transit, retail, or pedestrian features, on an image of an existing location, such as a street. Montage can visually portray how planning and urban design changes can alter the look and function of a place, and can clearly demonstrate complicated interrelating components that are otherwise difficult to convey. It can help take the guesswork and ambiguity out of decision making so that informed discussions can take place about the best plan or design for a community's future.

CREATING PHOTOMONTAGE

Montage can be created using prints, digital photos, or illustrations. When digital photos and computers are used to create montage visualizations, it is often referred to as photomontage, photo simulation, or digital reimaging. Montage images are directly compared with existing site images, either side by side or sequentially, and can be presented as side-by-side prints, in a slide-show presentation, or in combination with PowerPoint.

The level of sophistication required for computer-generated montage can range from a digital camera and basic photo-editing software to the integration of three-dimensional software with digital images that create realistic details, such as shadows and lighting.

APPLICATIONS

Educating and Engaging the Public

Montage can be an effective technique to educate the public about planning concepts that are often controversial, such as density and mixed-use development. Once the public sees realistic images, often they are more open to these concepts, and even supportive of them. Thus, montage can be particularly effective in public meetings and other public venues.

Internet

Photomontage images can also be posted on the Internet, to inform the general public about planning and design issues. For example, the Sierra Club uses photomontage images on its website to demonstrate what smart growth can look like. Several photos show the difference between existing sprawl and potential smart growth solutions.

Visual Preference

Montage can also be used to obtain feedback on planning and design alternatives. With this technique, known as a visual preference survey, people view different images and vote on their preferred choice or the concepts they would like to see applied to a specific project. See "Visual Preference Techniques" elsewhere in this section for more information.

Understanding Benefits and Trade-Offs

In addition to showing the visual appeal and functionality of choices, realistic-looking design alternatives also allow planners and designers to discuss the costs, benefits, and trade-offs of those

Existing Conditions

Potential Solutions
Photomontage was used as an educational tool in Silicon Valley, California, where light rail was going to significantly change the infrastructure in several communities. Residents were presented with photomontage images of light rail community design projects. In this example, participants could compare an existing site in Silicon Valley with what a neighborhood light rail stop might look like. The use of this technique fostered a healthy discussion about the issues surrounding transit and land use and helped residents clarify their own vision for the future of light rail in their communities.

PHOTOMONTAGE AS AN EDUCATIONAL TOOL

Source: Steve Price.

choices, so the public and decision makers can make more informed decisions as they choose their preferred solution. Information on costs, benefits, and trade-offs should be made available along with the images of the proposed alternatives.

Demonstrating Impacts of Buildout Analysis

Montage is also a powerful technique for demonstrating what complete buildout under a community's current zoning ordinances might look like. Actually seeing specific buildout scenarios that could occur under existing outmoded codes and regulations is often a powerful motivator for people to become involved in their reform. This is particularly true for preserving agricultural land or environmental areas.

Public-Private Partnerships

From a developer's perspective, photomontage can be a useful tool to help foster critical public/private partnerships and to interest a community in investing in public improvements. It can help demonstrate the potential that investing in smart growth approaches has to urban revitalization, for example, with images at both the large and small scale.

PLANNING APPLICATIONS

Montage is commonly used during the early stages of a community development or design process, to show specific design concepts. This technique also works well later in the design process, to develop and explore the impacts of realistic alternative design

Julie Herman, PlaceMatters.com, a Division of the Orton Family Foundation, Denver, Colorado; Ken Snyder, PlaceMatters.com, a Division of the Orton Family Foundation, Denver, Colorado

Existing Conditions

Alternative A

Alternative B

Alternative C

The Jefferson Planning District Commission in Charlottesville, Virginia, used photomontage images to discuss the costs, benefits, and trade offs of alternative improvements along the U.S. 29 corridor and Hydraulic Road so the public and decision makers could make more informed decisions as they choose their preferred solution.

PHOTOMONTAGE FOR ALTERNATIVES ANALYSIS

Source: Steve Price.

Julie Herman, PlaceMatters.com, a Division of the Orton Family Foundation, Denver, Colorado; Ken Snyder, PlaceMatters.com, a Division of the Orton Family Foundation, Denver, Colorado

choices. In addition, montage can be used to present a final plan to a design review board, or sell a concept to investors or developers.

Montage can work well when applied to smaller-scale urban design projects, such as infill projects, streetscape improvements, or downtown redevelopment intitiatives, where extensive details create realistic-looking design alternatives. Montage can also be used on a larger scale to show the regional implications of buildout, for example.

ISSUES TO CONSIDER

- Montage can be time-consuming and expensive. Ensure that the techniques chosen to create montage images are appropriate for the overall goals and budget of the project.
- Because photomontage looks real, users must be careful not to set unrealistic expectations about what a community can build on a site. For example, when mature trees are put into montage, the public could be disappointed when the new streetscape is lined with small, immature trees that will take a long time before they look anything like the montage image.
- Consider alternative methods of input for those with visual impairments.
- The Internet is an extremely valuable resource, but use it as a complement to face-to-face meetings, not in place of them.
- Be aware of the biases that can result from photos used to create the montage. For example, a photo of a building taken on a sunny day will look significantly more attractive than one taken on a cloudy day.

See also:
Visual Preference Techniques

THREE-DIMENSIONAL VISUALIZATION

Three-dimensional (3-D) visualization tools show proposed buildings in the context of their actual surroundings. These tools can communicate the potential impacts of a development more clearly than two-dimensional plans or written reports. Representing development concepts in three dimensions can make relationships among different design components, such as housing, transportation, land use, and the environment, easier to understand, and consensus building can be more effective.

GENERAL APPLICATIONS

Three-dimensional visualization is typically used after alternative solutions have been identified and designers and planners start to explore and understand the implications of these options. Designers and planners then bring realistic alternatives back to stakeholders, either for more discussion and input or for final approval. However, 3-D visualization tools can be integrated throughout the entire planning and design process, including the engagement of stakeholders and the formation of a conceptual design. When these tools are utilized early in the process, design decisions can be made more effectively from the beginning, rather than waiting until after critical decisions have been made.

HIGH-TECH APPLICATIONS

Computer-based 3-D visualization tools range from simple three-dimensional blocklike images to those with realistic textures, photo images, and lighting. Some tools provide static views of a design from different vantage points, while others can simulate motion. Animation tools can create highly detailed and realistic three-dimensional environments that can be prerecorded through a rendering process and then played back to an audience.

Real-time 3-D tools offer a fully interactive three-dimensional environment, allowing users to, for example, "walk" or "fly" to any location in the model. While real-time three-dimensional tools can look relatively realistic by incorporating aerial photographs draped over the topographic landscape and applying images and textures to buildings, they tend to be less detailed than three-dimensional scenes created from animation tools. Real-time applications of visualization tools are a growing niche in planning. They give users the ability to quickly add new buildings or change existing ones and observe how that affects a development's look, feel, and impact.

The integration of 3-D visualization tools with geographic information systems (GIS) tools that have impact analysis functionality has made it possible to take decision making to a new level of sophistication. For example, users can add a new building to a three-dimensional scene and immediately see how the proposed change affects land consumed or infrastructure costs, or determine the implications for value-based indices, such as job-housing balance, environmental quality, or pedestrian friendliness.

LOW-TECH APPLICATIONS

Low-tech three-dimensional tools can also be effective to demonstrate a concept. They create an opportunity for the public to engage in hands-on exercises about the future of their community. Box City, a design exercise conducted by the Center for Understanding the Built Environment, is one example. Its low-tech aspect is one of the reasons it works well. Basic art supplies—box, paper, scissors, paste, and markers—allow participants of all ages to understand design. Box City becomes a platform from which to discuss where neighborhoods are today and how residents want them to be in the future.

COMPUTER-BASED THREE-DIMENSIONAL TOOLS

Computer-based three-dimensional tools are becoming an increasingly popular tool for understanding how a specific project will look and function in a landscape. These tools can support an iterative process between the look of a design and its impacts. In addition, 3-D GIS tools make it possible

Street Level View

Aerial View
Xtra-Spatial Productions, LLC, used World Construction set to create this three-dimensional visualization of a site design for a condominium complex in Calabash, North Carolina.

3-D ANIMATION EXAMPLE
Source: Xtra-Spatial Productions, LLC and VR Marketing, Inc.

Julie Herman, PlaceMatters.com, a Division of the Orton Family Foundation, Denver, Colorado; Ken Snyder, PlaceMatters.com, a Division of the Orton Family Foundation, Denver, Colorado

Existing Conditions

Three-Dimensional Model

Project Under Construction
Vail, Colorado, requires developers to submit a three-dimensional model, preferably a virtual model, for design review. The virtual model is then placed into a three-dimensional model of the mountains, roads, and ground plain, to explore the impacts of new buildings in the context of their surroundings.

THREE-DIMENSIONAL VISUALIZATION IN DESIGN REVIEW

Source: Architecture by Odell Architects.

Julie Herman, PlaceMatters.com, a Division of the Orton Family Foundation, Denver, Colorado; Ken Snyder, PlaceMatters.com, a Division of the Orton Family Foundation, Denver, Colorado

to integrate spatial impact analysis into three-dimensional visualization.

There are four categories of computer-based three-dimensional visualization tools:

- Design software
- Three-dimensional animation
- Real-time three-dimensional visualization
- Three-dimensional GIS

Understanding the strengths and weaknesses of each category can help users choose the best tool for their application. (Note: Some of the tools mentioned here fall under more than one category.)

Design Software

Three-dimensional design tools assist in creating a 3-D image of a single building or object. Once the object is completed, it can usually be imported into other programs to create a compilation of tools placed in a three-dimensional landscape.

3-D Animation

Animation tools involve a rendering process that takes the frame of a designed object and applies texture, images, and lighting to develop viewing screens or walk-throughs. Because rendering is done in advance of creating a visual walk-through, these animation tools can be more powerful in their capability to show the finer details of a development. These tools can present design alternatives from predefined views and prerecorded walkthroughs. Most applications do not provide real-time interaction, however.

Real-Time Three-Dimensional Visualization

Real-time 3-D tools offer the ability to explore a three-dimensional scene from multiple viewpoints immediately. Similar to a video game, real-time three-dimensional modeling enables a more interactive, 3-D environment that allows users to "walk" or "fly" to any location within the model.

Three-Dimensional GIS

Applications can be used to create three-dimensional massing models of a place directly from GIS information, for analysis in both two and three dimensions. Some allow the placement of models into the landscape from a library of three-dimensional symbols. Others allow georeferencing based on latitude and longitude coordinates. Still others can be integrated with a GIS, making it possible to add GIS spatial analysis to a project.

ISSUES TO CONSIDER

- Using three-dimensional visualization can be time-consuming and expensive. Therefore, ensure that the techniques chosen to create the images are appropriate in context of the overall goals and budget of the project.
- Because three-dimensional images with photo façades or realistic textures can look quite real, be careful not to set unrealistic expectations about what a community can build or how it will look.
- When choosing the level of detail to display, consider the goals and objectives of the presentation. The level of detail should be sufficient to convey the appropriate context issues, and not be distracting to the viewer.
- Consider alternative methods of input for those with visual impairments.

See also:
Geographic Information Systems

VISUAL PREFERENCE TECHNIQUES

Visual preference techniques allow people to choose their preferences among images used to illustrate various options applicable to a project. The visual preference technique has been a popular method since the early 1990s to educate the public about specific design concepts and to obtain feedback on planning and design alternatives. With this technique, people express their likes or dislikes for a number of images featuring community design elements and characteristics. Visual preference methods are valuable because they translate feelings and emotions into objective desires and preferences.

APPLICATIONS

Typical uses for the visual preference survey include helping a community define its vision and identify preferred architectural styles, signs, streetscapes, and other design elements. Using the visual preference method, planners and designers can obtain immediate feedback on specific alternatives for a particular project, or acquire a sense of the types of solutions the public would like to see applied to a specific project.

In addition to collecting information, the visual preference technique can also be integrated into efforts to educate the public about design choices and create a format for discussion about general costs and benefits associated with each preference. It can help build support for a project and address easily misunderstood concepts, such as increasing density with multifamily housing or how transit might integrate into an existing street corridor.

METHODS

There are several approaches to gathering visual preference data. One method is to show two images of different design elements and ask participants to vote for the one they prefer. Another strategy is to use a sliding scale so that participants can vote on each individual image.

TECHNICAL APPLICATIONS

Visual preference techniques can be created using low-tech strategies, such as sketches or 35 mm slides/prints, or through high-tech approaches using digital photos, a computer, and photo-imaging software. Whereas prints and slides can be a simple and affordable method of creating a visual preference study, computer-generated images can be manipulated to show how different design choices will look on an existing site. This technique, known as photomontage, takes a digital image of an existing site and uses photo-imaging software and other three-dimensional software to overlay alternative design solutions directly onto the image of the existing site. (See "Montage Visualization" in this section for more information.)

Computer images can also be manipulated to account for biases generated by viewing prints and slides. For example, the weather conditions when a photo is taken can affect how people will vote their preference. The ability to create or adjust digital images helps ensure that people stay focused on the design elements.

Existing Conditions

Tree Alternative A

Tree Alternative B

Photomontage images must be created or doctored to account for potential biases that occur when, for example, one image has a gray sky and the other a blue one. People tend to vote for sunny weather rather than the design elements being compared. In this example, details such as the sky and shadows remain the same; only the trees are changed.

VISUAL PREFERENCE USING PHOTOMONTAGE

Source: Steve Price.

Julie Herman, PlaceMatters.com, a Division of the Orton Family Foundation, Denver, Colorado; Ken Snyder, PlaceMatters.com, a Division of the Orton Family Foundation, Denver, Colorado

STRATEGIES FOR GATHERING PREFERENCES

Meeting-Based Strategies

Visual preferences can be gathered in small meetings with low-tech tools, such as a slide show and a show of hands to vote on images, or in larger meetings with more high-tech tools, such as computerized keypads and software. Keypad technologies, combined with software, help gather feedback and tabulate the results from individuals and table discussions while participants are still present to view and respond to them. Gathering preferences in meetings where the public is able see how their opinions help shape real plans can be an extremely valuable exercise in public participation and gaining buy-in into a project.

Strategies to Supplement the Face-to-Face Meeting

For those unable to attend a main face-to-face meeting, there are additional strategies for collecting visual preferences. Low-tech options include putting together picture books or wall displays that can be brought to public events, or creating a video that people can check out and return.

High-tech options include using the Internet, where the public can view and vote on images online. Such surveys can be designed to be relatively brief (30 minutes) and present a range of potential development scenarios.

In addition to the Internet, there are other strategies that take advantage of computer technologies to solicit the public's input on design choices or aesthetic preferences. For example, computer kiosks can be placed in public locations, such as libraries and cafes, to allow passersby to stop and choose their preferences.

PLANNING APPLICATIONS

Visual preference techniques are typically used in the early stages of a planning process, to help guide design and planning choices. Visual preference techniques can assist planners and agencies in the public

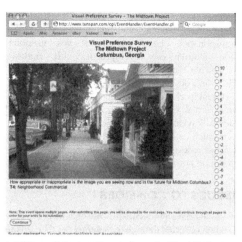

In Midtown Columbus, Georgia, the online Visual Preference Survey™ was used in conjunction with a face-to-face workshop to gather visual preferences as a foundation for guiding the future planning recommendations for their master plan.

ONLINE PREFERENCE GATHERING

Source: A. Nelessen Associates.

Arch Bridge

Cable-Stayed Bridge

Girder Bridge

Truss Bridge

In Contra Costa County, California, city planners asked residents to voice their opinion on four alternative pedestrian bridge designs for the Iron Horse Trail Overcrossing of Treat Boulevard. The visual preference survey was conducted at community meetings as well as posted online. More than 550 individuals indicated their preference.

VISUAL PREFERENCE FOR DESIGN ALTERNATIVE

Source: Images produced by MacDonald Architects Bridge Designers and ARUP for the Iron Horse Trail Overcrossing Community Design Program, Pleasant Hill, CA. November 2002.

Julie Herman, PlaceMatters.com, a Division of the Orton Family Foundation, Denver, Colorado; Ken Snyder, PlaceMatters.com, a Division of the Orton Family Foundation, Denver, Colorado

participation component of various efforts, such as choosing community and urban design features, transportation subarea or corridor studies, transportation alternatives developments and analysis, large-scale regional planning efforts, visioning exercises, and design charrettes.

Visual preference techniques can be used on a small scale, such as choosing building heights and sidewalk widths, or for larger-scale urban design projects, such as identifying a specific planning strategy for the redevelopment of a shopping mall or transportation corridor.

ISSUES TO CONSIDER

- Visual preference techniques are extremely valuable when collected through the Internet or other remote methods; however, nothing can replace the importance of face-to-face meetings where the public can see for themselves how their preferences can be translated into changes in their community.
- For segments of the population that cannot access the Internet or do not feel comfortable using a high-tech vehicle such as a computer kiosk, make the visual preference survey available in a format that is comfortable to them.
- When working with a multicultural population, have the survey available in more than one language.
- Take the bias out of photographs whenever possible to ensure that people are voting on the design elements being discussed and are not being influenced by other factors, such as weather conditions.
- Give attention to language used in the design of the survey, so that wording does not influence the results.
- Visual preference surveys can be time-consuming and expensive. Ensure that the techniques chosen to implement a visual preference survey are appropriate within the context of the overall goals and budget of the project.
- Consider alternative methods of input for those with visual impairments.
- The influence of the mass media leads the public to have high expectations for the quality of images. People may dismiss visual content if they perceive the quality is not comparable with their expectations. Conversely, detailed and sophisticated images, such as those using photomontage, can raise false expectations about how an area will change.
- Apply visual and planning preferences identified in one planning arena to other local projects.

See also:
Montage Visualization

Julie Herman, PlaceMatters.com, a Division of the Orton Family Foundation, Denver, Colorado; Ken Snyder, PlaceMatters.com, a Division of the Orton Family Foundation, Denver, Colorado

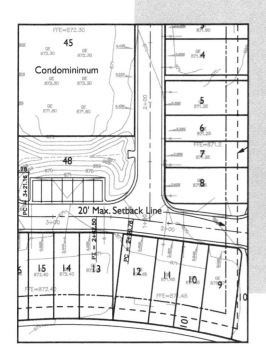

IMPLEMENTATION TECHNIQUES

Legal Foundations

Growth Management

Preservation, Conservation, and Reuse

Economic and Real Estate Development

Part 6

LEGAL FOUNDATIONS

PLANNING LAW OVERVIEW

Several mechanisms implement plan objectives and policies, including: zoning, subdivision regulations, capital improvement programs design review, historic preservation controls, sign regulations, voluntary agreements (contracts), and others. These mechanisms are controlled by three aspects of the law: federal and state constitutional law; federal or state statutory law; and the common law, principally that of nuisance.

CONSTITUTIONAL LAW

The U.S. Constitution contains several important provisions that influence land-use development regulation, as shown in the table.

State constitutions commonly contain the same or similar provisions, though they may vary in some significant ways or be interpreted differently. In addition, state constitutions increasingly include provisions specific to protecting property rights, limiting taxes or limiting government spending, which often influence land-use planning and regulation.

STATUTORY LAW

No comprehensive federal land-use statutes exist, though federal statutes increasingly influence land-use development and environmental decisions, either indirectly, such as through housing, transportation, taxation, and environmental statutes, or directly, through, for example, the Religious Land Use and Institutionalized Persons Act (RLUIPA). State statutes largely control land-use planning and regulation in the United States, principally those statutes authorizing local governments to adopt and implement local statutes governing land use and development. These local statutes are generally called ordinances or bylaws. This enabling legislation delegates the state's police power to local governments and sets the framework within which local governments must operate.

Enabling legislation for planning, and managing development in most states derives from two model statutes drafted and promoted by the federal government in the 1920s. Those model statutes focused on planning and zoning as the concerns of local urban governments.

Since the 1920s, enabling legislation in most states has evolved considerably, to reflect a greater scope and variety of community concerns, environmental impacts, a more active citizenry, and the regional and intergovernmental dimensions involved in managing land use and development. More and more states are considering and enacting substantial reforms to enabling legislation, with some mandating the scope, objectives, and procedures for local planning, development review, and environmental impact assessment.

COMMON LAW

Before states began enacting planning and zoning statutes, land was controlled by the common law, principally nuisance law. Nuisance law forbids the unreasonable use of one's property in a manner that seriously interferes with another's interest in the use or enjoyment of his or her property, called a private nuisance, or with the health, safety, peace, comfort, or convenience of the general community, called a public nuisance. Nuisance law was the basis for original statutory zoning laws, and is relied on to interpret land-use regulations and to deal with issues not yet addressed by land-use regulations.

CURRENCY OF THE LAW

The discussions of federal and state laws presented in this section are based on the most current information available at press time. However, laws, especially those on the federal level, are often undergoing revision and reinterpretation. The American Planning Association has created an online clearinghouse to provide the most up-to-date information on the laws covered in this section. The clearinghouse can be accessed at www.planning.org.

See also:
Due Process and Equal Protection
Eminent Domain, Takings, and Exactions
Freedom of Religion and Expression
Innovations in Local Zoning Regulations
Planned Unit Development
Property Rights, Police Power, Nuisance, and Vested Rights
State Enabling Legislation
Subdivision Regulation
Zoning Regulation

U.S. CONSTITUTION PROVISIONS RELATED TO LAND-USE REGULATION

First Amendment: Freedom of Speech*	"Congress shall make no law ... abridging the freedom of speech..."	Freedom of speech is most commonly an important issue when regulating signs and adult uses.
First Amendment: Freedom of Religion*	"Congress shall make no law respecting an establishment of religion, or prohibiting the free exercise thereof..."	Freedom of religion issues are raised when regulating places of worship and other religious institutions.
Fifth Amendment: Takings*	"...nor shall private property be taken for public use, without just compensation."	This provision governs the use of eminent domain and the extent to which land-use regulations may burden property use.
Fifth and Fourteenth Amendments: Due Process	"...nor shall any person... be deprived of ... property, without due process of law..."	Due process concerns both how land-use laws are enacted and enforced, as well as to why they are enacted and enforced.
Ninth Amendment	"The enumeration in the Constitution of certain rights shall not be construed to deny or disparage others retained by the people."	The Bill of Rights does not list all rights that may be protected from government interference, though courts have been reluctant to identify such unlisted rights.
Tenth Amendment: States' Rights	"The powers not delegated to the United States by the Constitution, nor prohibited by it to the States, are reserved to the States respectively, or to the people."	This provision recognizes reserved powers such as regulation of local government, in-state commerce, and family concerns, and is sometimes cited as limiting federal powers to regulate state activities.
Fourteenth Amendment: Equal Protection	"...nor shall any state... deny to any person within its jurisdiction the equal protection of the laws."	Equal protection issues arise with any land-use action involving classification of people for different benefits or burdens.

*Although the First and Fifth Amendment protections apply only to actions of the federal government, the Fourteenth Amendment's due process provision has been deemed to apply those protections to state and local government actions.

Stephen G. Sizemore, AICP, American Planning Association, Chicago, Illinois; Stuart Meck, FAICP, American Planning Association, Chicago, Illinois

PROPERTY RIGHTS, POLICE POWER, NUISANCE, AND VESTED RIGHTS

PROPERTY RIGHTS

The collective property rights held by individuals and entities to own and use land are often referred to as a "bundle of rights." The bundle is the sum total of the rights pertaining to property ownership. In the case of real property (e.g., land and buildings), it embraces the following rights:

- Quiet enjoyment of the property.
- Occupy the property and exclude others.
- Sell, lease, donate, or bequeath the property.
- Mortgage the property or grant easements.
- Subdivide the property or build and remove improvements.
- Control the property's use within the law.

The bundle also embraces public rights to tax or assess the property, to control its use and development, and to acquire it for public use (with just compensation).

Land-use regulations restrict private property rights to protect the public's health, safety, morals, and general welfare. Hence, land-use regulation always involves a balance—and often conflicts—both between private and public property rights and among private rights.

POLICE POWER

The rights of government to establish laws and ordinances to preserve public order and tranquility and to promote the public health, safety, morals, and general welfare are called police powers. Police powers are reserved to the states. The states, in turn, grant police power to local governments through charters and enabling statutes. A government exercises its police power by imposing rules and regulations on individuals and on a property owner's use of privately owned land. Both stop signs and zoning regulations are examples of the government's exercise of its police power.

It is under the police power that a local government adopts zoning regulations that prohibit the operation of industry and other noisy or noxious businesses next to schools and neighborhoods. Local governments also have the right to legitimately use the police power to make or a keep a city beautiful, as well as healthy. It is in accordance with that principle that cities today now regulate community appearance, including using zoning and land development regulations to control signs, billboards, planting, and the appearance of buildings; and to preserve and protect historic landmarks and sites.

The police power must be used reasonably and fairly. Regulations must be tied to a valid public purpose (substantive due process) and be enacted and implemented so those directly affected have a meaningful opportunity to participate (procedural due process).

Delegation of Power

For planning and land use, delegation of power has two contexts: (1) the state government's delegation of police power authority to local government; and (2) a legislative body's delegation of power to an administrative body.

Statutes or enabling legislation confer the state's police power authority upon local governments or other regulating entities and establish the procedures and standards for exercising that authority. Generally, each state has delegated to local governments the power to plan, zone property, control the subdivision of land, regulate the construction of buildings, and exercise other land-use controls. However, state enabling legislation varies in detail, procedure, and the role of state oversight. Local governments may also have additional authority to regulate land use through a more general delegation of the police power, sometimes through other general statutory authority or a home rule provision for municipal governments in the state constitution.

In the second context, local legislative bodies may not give up their legislative or policy-making power to administrative agencies. However, legislatures may delegate substantial discretion to such agencies, as long as this delegation is accompanied by clear-cut

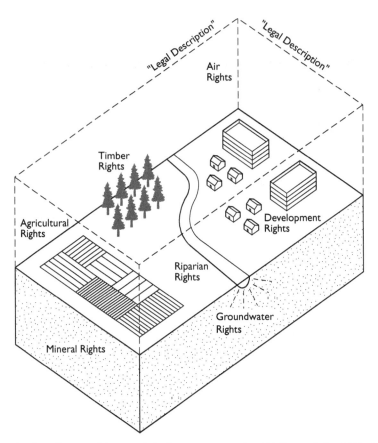

Property rights may be viewed in terms of the separate land resources or uses to which they apply: the right to cut timber; to farm; to extract minerals from its surface or subsurface; to use its surface waters or groundwaters; to build and develop improvements; and to use or control overhead airspace.

BUNDLE OF RIGHTS

Source: American Planning Association.

ELEMENTS OF PROPERTY RIGHTS

Source: American Planning Association.

Stephen G. Sizemore, AICP, American Planning Association, Chicago, Illinois; Stuart Meck, FAICP, American Planning Association, Chicago, Illinois; Alan C. Weinstein, Cleveland Marshall College of Law, Cleveland State University, Cleveland, Ohio; Brian W. Blaesser, Robinson & Cole LLP, Boston, Massachusetts

policy guidelines or standards to control the discretion, particularly when the regulation potentially affects fundamental rights such as those protected by the First Amendment.

NUISANCE

The term nuisance refers to the use of one's property in a manner that seriously interferes with another's use or enjoyment of his or her property (a private nuisance) or is injurious to the community at large (a public nuisance). In a private nuisance action, the land use that is claimed to be a nuisance is usually adjacent or close to the property of the claimant, who seeks to prohibit the use by injunction and obtain monetary damages for injuries suffered.

Zoning was originally based, in part, on nuisance avoidance, and thus consisted of a comprehensive scheme for separating incompatible land uses into mapped zones of districts. Because of the adoption of zoning in most communities, landowners use private nuisance suits less frequently to resolve land-use disputes. However, a land use permitted by a zoning ordinance may still be operated in a way to constitute a nuisance. For example, while a zoning ordinance may allow farming uses, a large-scale concentrated animal feeding operation may result in odors that affect a large area of the community due to improper control or disposal of animal waste, and therefore could be both a private and a public nuisance.

VESTED RIGHTS

A vested right is the right to use property in some way that the government may not limit or extinguish, such as by the adoption of new or modified regulations. Common law, statute, or both, establish vested rights.

Under common law, a vested right generally exists if a developer has made substantial or extensive expenditures in reasonable reliance on governmental action. Whether such a vested right exists involves determining what constitutes sufficient governmental action to trigger reasonable reliance, whether expenditures were made in reliance on the action, and whether the expenditures are substantial or extensive. For example, a favorable statement or recommendation of a zoning official by itself may not be insufficient to support reasonable reliance. Final plan approval and issuance of permits generally would suffice.

Most often, only postaction expenditures count toward substantial expenditures. Expenditures made before the triggering governmental action, such as for preparing site plans or transportation studies for an application, cannot be said to have been made in reliance on the action. Sometimes expenditures are viewed in relative terms. Whereas spending $50,000 on grading and foundation work for a permitted house will almost certainly be deemed "substantial expenditure," spending the same amount for a large permitted planned unit development or a shopping mall may not.

Because of the difficulties in making these determinations on a case-by-case basis, many states have enacted statutes that define how a vested right may be established. They generally focus on identifying the particular step in a development approval process that establishes a vested right. That "trigger" may be issuance of a building permit, issuance of a zoning permit, approval of a site plan, approval of a preliminary subdivision plat, or even approval of a master plan for a large planned development. Vested right statutes may also provide that developers are not protected against certain regulations intended to address substantial public safety concerns.

Plans and policies usually do not carry the force of law and thus are not deemed to establish vested rights. The zoning of property generally does not confer a vested right protection against its subsequent rezoning. Furthermore, a vested right may be lost if the permit issuance or approval that established it was based on an intentional misrepresentation of information about the development, or if the development creates a hazard to the public health, safety, morals, or welfare.

See also:
State Enabling Legislation

Stephen G. Sizemore, AICP, American Planning Association, Chicago, Illinois; Stuart Meck, FAICP, American Planning Association, Chicago, Illinois; Alan C. Weinstein, Cleveland Marshall College of Law, Cleveland State University, Cleveland, Ohio; Brian W. Blaesser, Robinson & Cole LLP, Boston, Massachusetts

DUE PROCESS AND EQUAL PROTECTION

The Fourteenth Amendment provides "[no] state shall ... deprive any person of life, liberty, or property, without due process of law; nor deny to any person within its jurisdiction the equal protection of the laws." The amendment plays a unique dual role in contemporary planning and land-use law. Its reiteration of the Fifth Amendment's due process clause has been interpreted by the courts as a pass-through for applying the First Amendment rights to free speech and religion and the Fifth Amendment limitation on takings to states and their political subdivisions—that is, local governments. It also directly prohibits states and local governments from denying any person equal protection of the laws.

DUE PROCESS

The U.S. Constitution includes two due process clauses: the Fifth Amendment clause applies to the federal government, and the Fourteenth Amendment clause applies to state and local governments. Both prohibit the government from taking a person's life, liberty, or property without due process of law.

There are two types of due process: procedural due process and substantive due process, which might be viewed, respectively, as involving how and why laws and regulations are enacted and applied.

Procedural Due Process

When laws affect a person's life, liberty, or property, procedural due process requires that there be some orderly procedure allowing the person to meaningfully participate in and contest the means by which the law is enacted and applied. The type of procedure appropriate to land-use decision making will vary with the importance of the individual or property interest at stake, the extent to which certain procedures are needed to reduce the possibility of erroneous decision making, and the governmental interest in avoiding administrative and fiscal burdens. For legislative land-use actions, where policies of communitywide application are set and soliciting public opinion is the paramount concern, procedural due process merely requires such actions to be dealt with in an open, orderly, and fair manner.

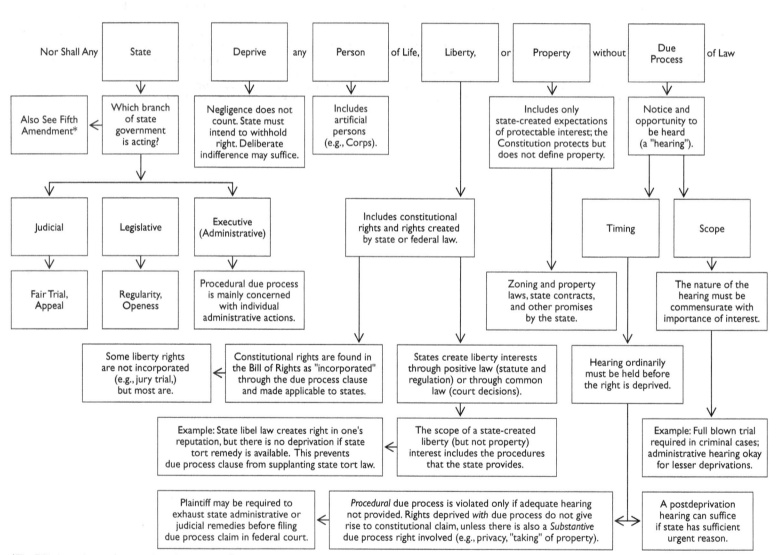

*The Fifth Amendment also contains a due process clause, which protects individuals against federal action.

Note: The Fourteenth Amendment due process clause has both procedural and substantive components. The first (shown here) protects against arbitrary governmental action. The second prohibits certain outcomes, no matter how fairly arrived at.

PROCEDURAL DUE PROCESS

Source: Professor Karl Manheim, Loyola Law School–Los Angeles.

Stephen G. Sizemore, AICP, American Planning Association, Chicago, Illinois; Stuart Meck, FAICP, American Planning Association, Chicago, Illinois; Alan C. Weinstein, Cleveland Marshall College of Law, Cleveland State University; Brian W. Blaesser, Robinson & Cole LLP, Boston, Massachusetts

For administrative land-use actions, and especially quasi-judicial land-use actions, which involve fact finding and discretion, where already-established standards are applied to particular properties and situations, the property rights of specific individuals are directly affected, hence procedural due process requires more to protect those rights. The basic aspects of procedural due process for quasi-judicial land-use actions typically involve the following:

- Sufficient notice to apprise interested parties of the pending action, enable them to determine what is being proposed, and afford them an opportunity to present objections
- Some form of hearing, to provide affected persons an opportunity to be heard—in the case of quasi-judicial actions, a formal hearing
- An impartial decision maker, free of bias or conflicts of interest
- With quasi-judicial actions, the opportunity for affected persons to present evidence or witnesses and cross-examine opposing witnesses or evidence
- A decision based on the record, supported by reasons and finding of fact

Substantive Due Process

Substantive due process is meant to ensure that a person's life, liberty, or property cannot be taken without appropriate governmental justification. The right to substantive due process does not depend on the fairness of procedures, but on whether the goal of the government action constitutes a valid state interest, and whether there is sufficient relationship between that goal and the means being used to achieve it.

For example, a local government may adopt an ordinance requiring design review of all new development. The ordinance raises a substantive due process question because a court must determine whether the aesthetic purposes alone advanced by design review are legitimate. A point of confusion at times is that the U.S. Supreme Court and some state courts consider the governmental purposes advanced by land-use regulation when they consider whether the regulation is a taking of property.

There are different tests for substantive due process, depending on whether fundamental rights are involved. If the government action impairs a "fundamental right," such as First Amendment rights, it is subject to "strict scrutiny": the objective being pursued by the government must be compelling and the means chosen to achieve the objective must be necessary and narrowly tailored; that is, there must be an extremely tight "fit" between the means, and there must not be any less restrictive means that would achieve the objective just as well. If no fundamental right is involved, the government action will be upheld if there is a legitimate objective and the means is rationally related to that objective.

In examining alleged violations of substantive due process, courts generally presume the constitutionality of locally enacted ordinances and actions. Thus the person challenging the constitutionality of an ordinance or action has the burden—a heavy one—of presenting evidence sufficient to overturn the presumption in favor of its constitutionality. This presumption cannot be overcome by evidence that merely raises questions about which people could reasonably differ. This judicial rule is known as the fairly debatable rule.

Federal due process requirements only apply where there is a property interest. Landowners are frequently said to have an entitlement to a property interest if they have a vested right in a particular use of the land, or if they apply for a permit or request approval of a use or development for which the deciding official has no discretion to deny the application or request.

EQUAL PROTECTION

The Fourteenth Amendment prohibits any state or its political subdivisions, local governments, from denying any person equal protection of the laws. Although this equal protection clause does not apply to the federal government, the Fifth Amendment's due process clause has been interpreted as prohibiting equal protection violations by the federal government. Equal protection requires that all persons under like circumstances be treated equally and be equally secure in their life, their liberty, and their property, and bear no greater burdens than are imposed on others under like circumstances. Equal protection issues arise when the government allows people in one classification to do something it denies to people in another classification.

Because land-use regulation involves the characterization of land uses through the drawing of zoning district lines and the imposition of use standards, such classifications can raise questions of equal protection. Equal protection in the land-use context means there must be a legitimate governmental purpose for the classifications and use restrictions applied to properties, and there must be a rational justification for the disparate treatment of similarly situated properties.

Three standards are used to examine government action involving the classification of persons:

- If the classification involves a "suspect class," such as race, religion, or national origin, or impairs a "fundamental right," like First Amendment rights, it is subject to "strict scrutiny" and will be upheld only if proven to be necessary to achieve a compelling governmental interest.
- If the classification involves a "quasi-suspect class," such as gender or illegitimacy, intermediate scrutiny is applied and the classification will be upheld only if proven to be substantially related to achieving an important governmental interest.
- Any other classification will be upheld if there is a minimally rational relationship to achieving a legitimate government interest. Most classifications in land-use regulations raise this mere rationality standard because, although some basic property rights are deemed "fundamental rights," the right to develop land for a profit has not been so deemed.

See also:

Freedom of Religion and Expression
Zoning Regulation

Stephen G. Sizemore, AICP, American Planning Association, Chicago, Illinois; Stuart Meck, FAICP, American Planning Association, Chicago, Illinois; Alan C. Weinstein, Cleveland Marshall College of Law, Cleveland State University; Brian W. Blaesser, Robinson & Cole LLP, Boston, Massachusetts

LEGAL FOUNDATIONS

FREEDOM OF RELIGION AND EXPRESSION

The First Amendment of the U.S. Constitution states, "Congress shall make no law respecting an establishment of religion, or prohibiting the free exercise thereof; or abridging the freedom of speech, or of the press; or the right of the people peaceably to assemble, and to petition the Government for a redress of grievances." The rights to freedom of speech and the press, and to assembly and petition, together make up what is commonly referred to as the "freedom of expression."

The First Amendment has been interpreted by the courts as applying to all federal laws and, through the

Fourteenth Amendment's due process clause, to all state and local governments. State constitutional provisions regarding freedom of religion and expression may provide more protection than the federal constitution.

FREEDOM OF RELIGION

The First Amendment's establishment clause prohibits the government from sponsoring, supporting, or actively involving itself with a particular religion or religion in general. The free exercise clause prohibits

the government from encroaching on the free exercise of religion.

The establishment clause has been interpreted to require a separation between church and state. To be constitutional, a government law or program with a religious component must: (1) reflect a clearly secular purpose; (2) have a primary secular effect that neither hinders nor advances religion; and (3) avoid excessive government entanglement with religion. If the law or program fails to satisfy all three of these tests, it will be found to be unconstitutional. The free

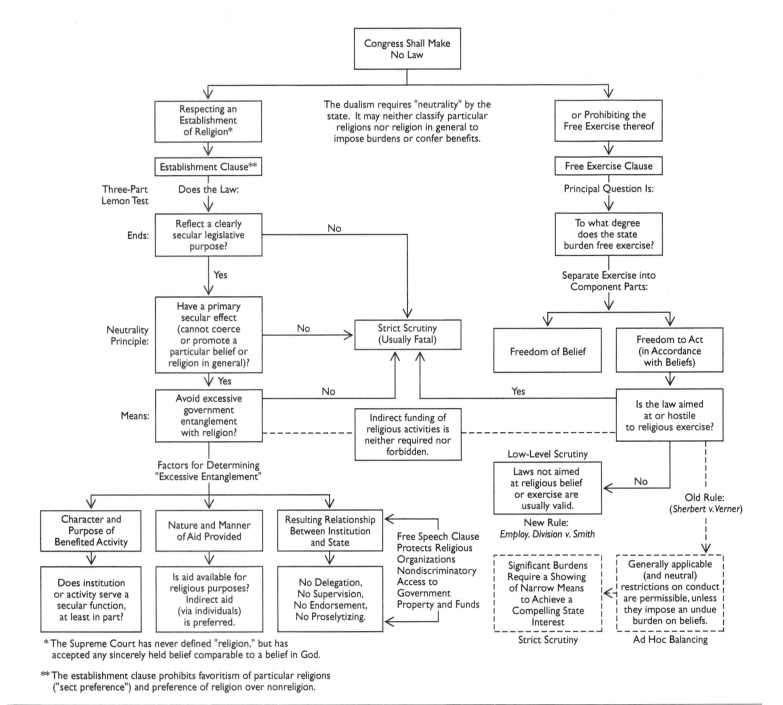

* The Supreme Court has never defined "religion," but has accepted any sincerely held belief comparable to a belief in God.

** The establishment clause prohibits favoritism of particular religions ("sect preference") and preference of religion over nonreligion.

FREEDOM OF RELIGION

Source: Professor Karl Manheim, Loyola Law School–Los Angeles.

Stephen G. Sizemore, AICP, American Planning Association, Chicago, Illinois; Stuart Meck, FAICP, American Planning Association, Chicago, Illinois; Alan C. Weinstein, Cleveland Marshall College of Law, Cleveland State University, Cleveland, Ohio; Brian W. Blaesser, Robinson & Cole LLP, Boston, Massachusetts

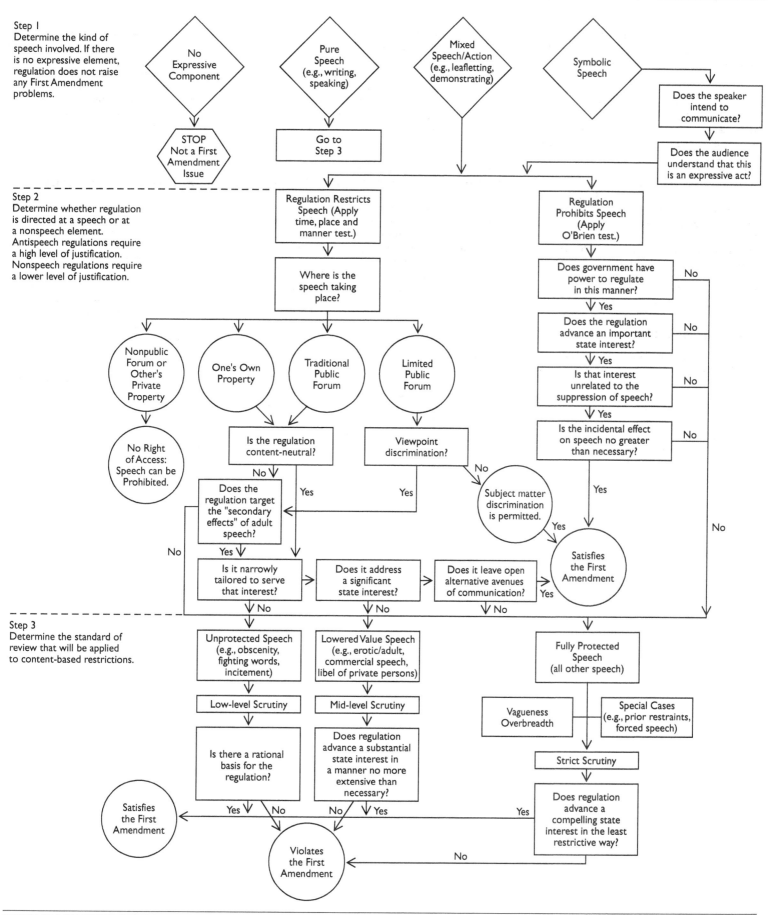

Step 1
Determine the kind of speech involved. If there is no expressive element, regulation does not raise any First Amendment problems.

Step 2
Determine whether regulation is directed at a speech or at a nonspeech element. Antispeech regulations require a high level of justification. Nonspeech regulations require a lower level of justification.

Step 3
Determine the standard of review that will be applied to content-based restrictions.

FREEDOM OF EXPRESSION

Source: Professor Karl Manheim, Loyola Law School–Los Angeles.

Stephen G. Sizemore, AICP, American Planning Association, Chicago, Illinois; Stuart Meck, FAICP, American Planning Association, Chicago, Illinois; Alan C. Weinstein, Cleveland Marshall College of Law, Cleveland State University, Cleveland, Ohio; Brian W. Blaesser, Robinson & Cole LLP, Boston, Massachusetts

LEGAL FOUNDATIONS

exercise clause protects sincerely held beliefs of any kind, whether or not those beliefs are part of an organized religion or include a belief in a deity.

When courts first began applying the First Amendment to zoning or church uses, they used variations of a test balancing the government interest in regulating nonreligious conduct against the regulation's burden on the practice of religious beliefs. If the burden was significant, the regulation was subject to strict scrutiny. In 1990, the U.S. Supreme Court ruled that "neutral laws of general application," like zoning regulations, that do not single out religion for unfair treatment are subject to a rational basis test rather than strict scrutiny. This decision prompted congressional efforts to reinstate a strict scrutiny standard, first by enacting the Religious Freedom Restoration Act (RFRA) in 1993 (which was ruled unconstitutional), then by enacting the more narrowly focused Religious Land Use and Institutional Persons Act (RLUIPA) in 2000. The constitutionality of RLUIPA currently is being litigated.

FREEDOM OF EXPRESSION

Freedom of speech protects expression from governmental suppression. Therefore, it is critical to determine whether an activity being regulated has an expressive component. In the context of planning-related regulations, freedom of expression concerns most commonly arise with the regulation of signs, sexually oriented businesses, and newspaper racks. Concerns also arise with regulation of the use of public spaces for demonstrations, parading, picketing, and leafleting.

Although the First Amendment uses absolute terms in referring to the right to free expression, not all types of expression are protected absolutely, or to the same degree. Most expression is fully protected, with any regulation of it subject to strict scrutiny. If the regulation involves a *prior restraint* (e.g., permitting or licensing schemes giving the issuing officials substantial discretion over expressive content), there is a heavy presumption against its constitutional validity. Regulations of commercial speech and those types of expression that only marginally satisfy First Amendment principles (e.g., erotic expression) are subject to less than strict scrutiny, but greater than a rational basis test. Regulations of those types of expression that fail to advance any First Amendment purposes (e.g., obscenity, incitement) are unprotected, subject to mere rational basis analysis.

If a regulation prohibits an activity with an expressive component, it is subject to the *O'Brien* test:

- Does it advance an important state interest?
- Is that interest unrelated to suppressing expression?
- Is the incidental effect on expression no greater than necessary?

If the answer to any of these questions is no, the regulation is subject to strict scrutiny (or to the lesser level of scrutiny appropriate to the lesser protected types of expression).

If a regulation limits but does not prohibit an activity with an expressive component, it is subject to the *time, place, and manner* test. The first focus of this test is on whether the regulation is content-based (directed at the activity's expressive components) or content-neutral (directed at the activity's nonexpressive components). If content-based, it must pass strict scrutiny or the lesser level of scrutiny appropriate to the lesser protected types of expression. If content-neutral, it must be narrowly tailored to serve a significant state interest and leave open alternative avenues of communication.

OVERBREADTH AND VAGUENESS

Because they involve the most fundamental rights guaranteed by the U.S. Constitution, regulations that affect freedom of religion and expression are particularly subject to the concerns about their overbreadth and vagueness. Overbreadth applies when a regulation is broader than necessary to achieve the state interest and encompasses matter or conduct that is constitutionally protected. Courts will invalidate such a regulation. Courts will also invalidate a regulation if its terms are so unclear or ambiguous that a person of normal intelligence must guess what the regulation prohibits (a violation of procedural due rights), or if the regulation invites arbitrary and discriminatory enforcement (which may indicate prior restraint).

See also:
Due Process and Equal Protection
Zoning Regulation

Stephen G. Sizemore, AICP, American Planning Association, Chicago, Illinois; Stuart Meck, FAICP, American Planning Association, Chicago, Illinois; Alan C. Weinstein, Cleveland Marshall College of Law, Cleveland State University, Cleveland, Ohio; Brian W. Blaesser, Robinson & Cole LLP, Boston, Massachusetts

EMINENT DOMAIN, TAKINGS, AND EXACTIONS

Eminent domain is the power of the government to take property for public use with just compensation; it is one of several powers fundamental to a functioning government. Although eminent domain has traditionally referred to government action that directly appropriates private property, most commonly through a condemnation process, the courts more recently have recognized it as applicable when government adoption of police power regulations may restrict a property's use to an extent tantamount to appropriation. These indirect appropriations of property are called "regulatory takings" or "inverse condemnation" and have been the focus of many court decisions in recent years. A special regulatory takings issue involves situations where the govern-

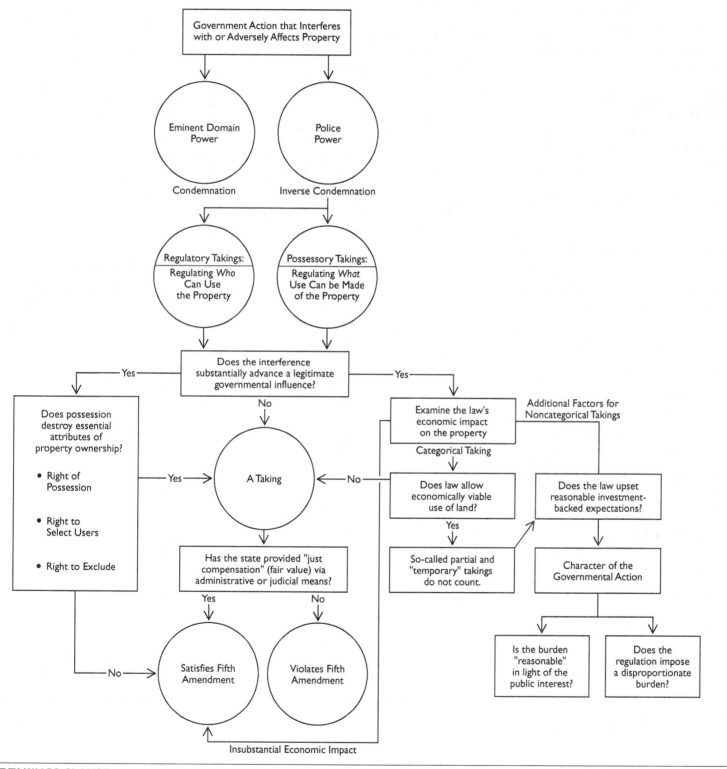

THE TAKINGS CLAUSE

Source: Professor Karl Manheim, Loyola Law School–Los Angeles.

Stephen G. Sizemore, AICP, American Planning Association, Chicago, Illinois; Stuart Meck, FAICP, American Planning Association, Chicago, Illinois; Alan C. Weinstein, Cleveland Marshall College of Law, Cleveland State University, Cleveland, Ohio; Brian W. Blaesser, Robinson & Cole LLP, Boston, Massachusetts

ment approves a development on the condition that the developer provide, dedicate land for, or contribute money for improvements to public facilities and services.

The Fifth Amendment provides that "private property [shall not] be taken for public use, without just compensation." This provision limits the federal government's inherent power of eminent domain to require that it justly compensate the owner of property taken. The Fourteenth Amendment has been read to apply the same requirement to state and local governments, and most state constitutions have similar, or even more restrictive, limits on the power of eminent domain.

EMINENT DOMAIN OR CONDEMNATION

In addition to constitutional limits, the direct use of eminent domain is also governed by statutes that typically set forth the process by which the government may take or condemn property and determine what just compensation is due the property owner. Local governments most commonly exercise their powers of eminent domain to acquire land for schools, roads, public buildings, and for redevelopment of blighted areas. States use eminent domain to acquire property for roads and other public uses as well. The federal government may acquire property for only those purposes authorized by the U.S. Constitution. State constitutions and statutes may similarly limit the purposes for which eminent domain may be used.

Challenges to the use of eminent domain center around two issues: (1) whether the government objective is a "public use," and (2) how to determine the amount of just compensation due. In recent years, governments have broadened the scope of what they deem a public use, particularly in the context of redevelopment proposals that involve transfer of acquired property to private owners for their use and development. Just compensation has been accepted as meaning the fair market value of the property taken. Calculating fair market value can be contentious and is complicated by the fact that many condemnations involve taking only part of a property for public uses that may add value to the remaining property.

REGULATORY TAKINGS

If a government regulation absolutely and permanently denies a property owner exclusive possession or other fundamental attributes of property, such as by a permanent physical invasion, a per se, or categorical, taking has occurred, irrespective of the regulation's affect on the property's use or value. If a regulation permanently deprives the owner of all economical or productive use of the property as a whole, again a per se, or categorical, taking has occurred, irrespective of the importance of the public interest served by the regulation.

Land-use regulations falling into these categories, however, are relatively rare. More common are land-use regulations that restrict a property's use or

development so as to substantially reduce—but not eliminate—its economic or productive use. Whether such regulations result in a taking is an issue that has dominated court review of land-use regulation in recent years and resulted in some considerable confusion about which "tests" apply to particular circumstances.

Considerations identified by the courts as relevant to whether a government action constitutes a taking include the economic impact on the property, the extent of interference with reasonable investment-backed expectations, and the character of the government action. But the courts have provided little guidance on how to apply these considerations. States are increasingly adopting statutes that seek to define when regulations go too far and constitute a taking.

When a property owner believes a government regulation has "taken" his or her property, and the government has not exercised any formal eminent domain or condemnation proceedings, the owner may institute a legal action challenging the validity of the regulation or seeking just compensation. These are called "inverse condemnation actions." Originally, courts finding a regulatory taking merely invalidated the regulation because it had been imposed without compensation. More recently, courts have ruled that

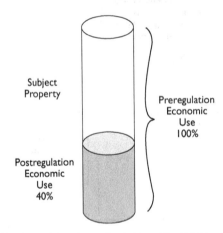

The diagram is based upon the decision of the U. S. Court of Appeals for Federal Claims in *Florida Rock Indus., Inc. v. United States*, 18 F. 3d 1560, 1568 (Fed. Cir. 1994). Since the Lucas case, the Supreme Court has stated that where, as in *Penn Central*, a regulation is deemed to have effected less than a Lucas "total taking," that is, a "partial taking," but is alleged to have denied the claimant economically viable use of his or her land ("a partial regulatory taking" according to Justice O'Connor in *Palazzolo v. Rhode Island* 533 U.S. 606, 121 S. Ct. 2466 (2001) (O'Connor, J., concurring), the reviewing court should use the *Penn Central* three-pronged balancing test to determine whether a partial taking has in fact occurred. *Tahoe-Sierra Preservation Council, Inc. v. Tahoe Regional Planning Agency*, 535 U.S. 302, 122 S. Ct. 1465. See J. Delaney, S. Abrams, and F. Schnidman, "Land Use Practice and Forms, Handling The Land-Use Case," Sec. 32:5 (West, 2d Ed.) for a further discussion of what is to be taken into account in such an analysis.

PARTIAL TAKING CONCEPT

Source: Reprinted with permission from Land Development *© 1995.*

governments may also be required to pay compensation for a regulatory taking.

GIVINGS

Although land-use regulations are often seen as adversely affecting private property values, such regulations and related government actions often also benefit private property values. Regulations requiring preservation of floodplains and sensitive natural areas, or reservation of recreation areas, create protections and amenities that can significantly increase the value of nearby properties. Water and sewer lines may be extended into the area by the government, or new roads may be constructed into the area. By making area properties more developable and accessible, these government actions significantly increase their value.

To the extent that these "givings" benefit certain areas more than the community as a whole, some might argue that it is appropriate to incorporate them into any consideration of a takings claim based on the adverse effects of regulation on an area property. Although givings are generally considered in eminent domain proceedings (as offsets), they have yet to find a place in regulatory takings law.

DEVELOPMENT EXACTIONS

Land-use regulations commonly condition approval of new developments on the developer making some contribution (e.g., construction, dedication, or money payment) to providing or improving public

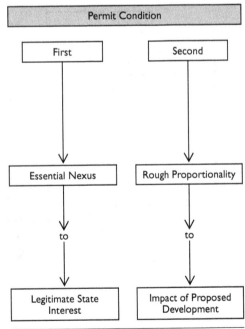

NOLLAN/DOLAN DOUBLE NEXUS TEST

Source: Reprinted with permission from Land Development *© 1995.*

Stephen G. Sizemore, AICP, American Planning Association, Chicago, Illinois; Stuart Meck, FAICP, American Planning Association, Chicago, Illinois; Alan C. Weinstein, Cleveland Marshall College of Law, Cleveland State University, Cleveland, Ohio; Brian W. Blaesser, Robinson & Cole LLP, Boston, Massachusetts

facilities or services associated with serving needs created by the development. Similar issues arise with regulations requiring developers to pay fees to compensate for their developments' impacts on public facilities and services.

The courts have developed two tests to determine whether such an exaction constitutes a taking: whether there is an "essential nexus" between the condition and the legitimate public interests that justify the regulation; and whether the burden imposed by the condition is "roughly proportionate" to the impact created by the proposed development. Some states have codified these tests, or some variation of them, and a number of states have enabling legislation that defines or limits the types of exactions local governments may make.

REFERENCE

Delaney, John J. 1995. "Lucas and Dollan: Two Different Routes to the Regulatory Takings End Zone." *Land Development* 8, no. 1 (Spring/Summer): 17-21.

See also:

Development Impact Fees

Stephen G. Sizemore, AICP, American Planning Association, Chicago, Illinois; Stuart Meck, FAICP, American Planning Association, Chicago, Illinois; Alan C. Weinstein, Cleveland Marshall College of Law, Cleveland State University, Cleveland, Ohio; Brian W. Blaesser, Robinson & Cole LLP, Boston, Massachusetts

FEDERAL LEGISLATION

The federal government has passed numerous environmental laws protective of the public health and environmental quality that create both opportunities and constraints for planning practice at federal, state, and local levels. It is important for planners to familiarize themselves with these laws and their implementing regulations to be effective in planning practice. This discussion begins by briefly summarizing a number of the major federal environmental and planning-related statutes. It concludes with suggested sources to learn more and to stay abreast of changes in federal environmental law impacting planning practice.

CLEAN AIR ACT

The Clean Air Act (CAA) of 1970 and its subsequent amendments set goals and standards for improving and maintaining air quality for the public health and environmental protection by regulating area (e.g., agriculture and resource extractive activities), stationary (e.g., factories and power plants), and mobile (e.g., trucks and autos) sources of air pollution. The U.S. Environmental Protection Agency's (EPA) primary vehicle for air quality improvement is enforcement of the National Ambient Air Quality Standards (NAAQS) for six priority pollutants: lead, carbon monoxide, nitrogen oxide, ozone, particulates, and sulfur oxides. All regions of the United States must ensure that ambient levels of these pollutants remain below the NAAQS. The 1990 amendments to the Clean Air Act were intended to reinvigorate efforts to improve national air quality by addressing several additional unmet concerns, including acid rain, ground-level ozone, stratospheric ozone depletion, and air toxics (Bell et al., 2005).

The United States is divided into 247 Air Quality Control Regions (AQCRs), where shared air quality monitoring by the U.S. EPA and the states allows classification of all airsheds as being either in "attainment" or in "nonattainment" for each of the six priority pollutants. All states must prepare a *state implementation plan* (SIP) that describes how they will bring nonattainment AQCRs back into attainment (through air quality permitting of point sources, and other control efforts on area and mobile sources), along with measures they will undertake to maintain the air quality found in AQCRs meeting the NAAQs. The U.S. EPA reviews and approves SIPs based on CAA criteria. If a state SIP is found to be noncompliant, the EPA may create a *federal implementation plan* (FIP) and take over CAA enforcement in that state, impose fines on major polluters, and stop any new development that would make air quality worse for priority pollutant(s) of concern. The more seriously out-of-attainment an airshed is for certain priority pollutants, the more restrictive the measures and sanctions the EPA and the states may impose on a region. Those regions found to be in-attainment are classified as "prevention of significant deterioration" airsheds and are monitored to prevent backsliding into nonattainment (Mayer, 1993).

Another important element of the CAA is the National Emissions Standards for Hazardous Air Pollutants (NESHAPs), which strive to control air toxics that are anticipated to result in either an increase in mortality or an increase in serious irreversible or incapacitating (but reversible) illness. The 1990 amendments directed EPA to establish technology-based standards for 189 hazardous substances based on the use of "maximum achievable control technology" (MACT). The California Air Quality Resources Board (CAQRB) recently released suggested land-use planning guidelines to protect the public health from air toxics typically emitted by various mobile and areas sources located in urbanizing areas (CAQRB, 2005).

THE NATIONAL ENVIRONMENTAL POLICY ACT

The National Environmental Policy Act (NEPA), often referred to as the "magna carta" of all U.S. environmental laws, declares it a national policy to encourage harmony between man and the environment, and to prevent damage to ecological systems and natural resources important to the nation. To that end, NEPA requires that all branches of the federal government give proper consideration to "environment impacts" prior to any major federal action that may significantly affect the environment before funding or implementing a proposed action. Actions encompass new and continuing activities, including projects or programs entirely or partly financed by federal agencies, new or revised agency rules, regulations, plans, policies, permits or procedures, and legislative proposals. Environmental information on "expected impacts" must be available to public officials and citizens, to aid agency decisions (in a manner consistent with the Federal Administrative Procedures Act), and to inform federal actions. The "lead" federal agency proposing the "action" is responsible for meeting the requirements of NEPA, although federal, state, tribal, and local cooperating agencies may be invited to participate as well, due to regulatory jurisdiction under other federal environmental statutes or because they may offer other forms of special expertise that would be useful for the environmental review. The environmental review process centers on two key questions: Is a "major federal action" proposed? If so, will that action "significantly affect the quality of the human environment?" If an action is not major or federal, then no environmental review is required. If it is federal but is clearly not a major action, then it is likely to be excluded from further environmental review because the action is a predefined "categorical exclusion" under NEPA (e.g., repairing existing fences on Bureau of Land Management lands).

Each federal agency has its own guidelines and categorical exclusions published in the code of federal regulations to streamline the NEPA review process. If the action is both federal and major, but it is unclear whether it will significantly affect the quality of the environment, then the agency must undertake an *environmental assessment* (EA) study to determine whether the impacts are likely to be significant. At the conclusion of the EA study and report, the federal agency either issues a "finding of no significant impacts" (FONSI) (also possibly called a "mitigated FONSI," which, due to mitigation measures, reduces anticipated environmental impacts below significance levels), and this ends the EA process; or the federal agency reports that significant impacts are likely and it begins a full-scale *environmental impact study* (EIS).

An EIS is a comprehensive study and report that typically takes between one and three years to complete. It must describe in detail:

- The environmental impact of the proposed action
- Any adverse environmental effects that cannot be avoided if the proposal is implemented
- Alternatives to the proposed action and their environmental impacts
- The relationship between local short-term uses of the environment and the maintenance and enhancement of long-term productivity
- Any irreversible and irretrievable commitments of resources that would be involved in the proposed action (Bass et al., 2001).

The EIS is presented to the U.S. EPA, policy decision makers, and the public in draft form, after which revisions are made in light of substantive comments from U.S. EPA, cooperating agencies, policy decision makers within the lead agency, interest groups, and the general public. When the final EIS is completed, a record of decision (ROD) is issued, which details the rational for the action chosen from among the alternatives (including the no-action alternative as a possibility) and any mitigation measures that are proposed to be undertaken to reduce environmental impacts. Should there be any disagreement between the lead and cooperating agencies on a proposed federal action, the President's Council on Environmental Quality mediates the disputes. The President's Council on Environmental Quality is also charged with providing guidance to federal agencies to implement NEPA review processes.

THE ENDANGERED SPECIES ACT

The Endangered Species Act (ESA) of 1973 strengthened and expanded federal efforts to conserve threatened and endangered species, to plan for the recovery of endangered species within the territory of the United States, and to conserve the ecosystems upon which they depend. The ESA prohibits any "action" by any person (i.e., a public or private entity or person) that results in a "taking" of a listed endangered or threatened species, or that adversely affects its habitat. To "take" a protected species encompasses killing, collecting, removing, harassing, as well as importing or exporting an endangered or threatened species without a permit from the Secretary of the Department of the Interior (DOI). The DOI's Fish & Wildlife Service (FWS) is charged with listing species, recovery planning, critical habitat designation, and enforcement for terrestrial and freshwater species, while the National Marine Fisheries Service (NMFS) in the U.S. Department of Commerce (DOC) manages the same functions for protected marine species. As with many federal environmental statutes, many mini ESA or state-level ESA statutes exist, and cooperative agreements have been created to share in the planning, management, and enforcement of species protection (Bell et al, 2005).

The ESA defines an endangered species as one that is in "danger of extinction throughout all or a signifi-

Robert Paterson, Ph.D., University of Texas at Austin

cant portion of its range," and a threatened species as one that is "likely to become endangered in the foreseeable future." Decisions on species listing for protection are based solely on biological and commerce information, without any consideration of possible economic or other effects. The FWS or NMFS consult with states affected by a listing decision, but the Secretary of Interior or Commerce makes the final listing decision. The Secretaries of Interior and Commerce must periodically update the endangered and threatened species lists and develop and implement "recovery plans" for the conservation and survival of the endangered and threatened species. Whenever prudent and feasible, "critical habitat" is designated, along with the listing of an endangered or threatened species.

The ESA requires all federal agencies to ensure that their actions (or actions approved, funded, or permitted by the agency) are not likely to jeopardize the survival of any endangered or threatened species or cause the degradation of habitat critical to the survival of the species. The federal agencies engage in a biological opinion consultation process with the FWS or NMFS to determine whether proposed actions will constitute jeopardy for listed species. In the rare circumstances where a federal agency may continue to propose an action that would jeopardize the survival of a listed species, a cabinet-level exemption review process is used (comprised of six federal officials and a representative of each affected state). This so-called God Squad can only allow an exemption when it finds there is (1) no "reasonable and prudent" alternatives to the proposed activity, and (2) the benefits of the action outweigh the future harm to the species (Bell et al., 2005).

In 1982, the ESA was amended to allow for the use of single or *multispecies habitat conservation plans* (HCPs), which, when approved by the Secretary of the Department of the Interior, would allow private landowners, corporations, state or local governments, or other nonfederal landowners to obtain an "incidental take" permit. Under an HCP, parties to the negotiated HCP are allowed to continue activities on their land that might incidentally harm (or "take") protected species, provided that landowners meet the mitigation conditions and other compensatory requirements stipulated by the HCP and permit. The FWS's 2000 edition of the *Habitat Conservation Planning Handbook* can be downloaded from http://www.fws.gov/endangered/hcp/hcpbook.html.

THE CLEAN WATER ACT

The Clean Water Act (CWA) was first known as the Federal Water Pollution Control Act of 1972, but after amendments to the law in 1977, it became commonly known as the Clean Water Act. The CWA and its subsequent amendments make it the goal of the United States, and the responsibility of the U.S. EPA, to maintain and restore the chemical, physical, and biological integrity of navigable waters, which are broadly defined as all waters of the United States (this includes territorial seas and larger bodies of water, lakes, streams, wetlands, rivers, ponds, and other small water bodies, if they affect interstate commerce). The U.S. EPA attempts to accomplish this mission by (1) working with the states to designate beneficial uses for all surface waters (beneficial uses include drinking water supply, fishing, swimming,

boating, wildlife habitat, and shellfish harvesting); (2) adopting numerical or narrative water quality criteria supportive of those beneficial uses; (3) enforcing a discharge permit program that translates those uses and water quality criteria into enforceable "technology-based" limits; (4) loaning publicly-owned water treatment plants construction funds to meet discharge limits; and (5) implementing antidegradation provisions to maintain existing beneficial uses and water quality. Most states are delegated authority to implement the CWA provisions under EPA supervision. All major point sources of water pollution (e.g., factories and wastewater treatment plants) must maintain a National Pollution Discharge Elimination System (NPDES) permit from the state regulatory agency that specifies the pollution control technology used to control the concentration of pollutants discharged (as well as the testing and reporting of water quality to the state agency to demonstrate continuing compliance) (CRS, 2005). When either an existing or new industrial facility discharges "toxic pollutants," more stringent controls are required.

Under the CWA's Section 303(d) provisions, states must identify waters that are threatened or not meeting their water quality standards despite the use of NPDES permitting. States must then undertake watershed studies and planning to establish the total maximum daily loads (TMDLs) of pollutants that "impaired waters" can assimilate and still be supportive of their designated beneficial uses. TMDLs take into account wasteloads from all point and nonpoint sources of pollution, natural background sources of pollutants, surface water withdrawals, and a "margin of safety" to take into account problems with uncertainty. The TMDL water quality improvement study then provides guidelines to reduce wasteloads across point and nonpoint sources to meet the designated beneficial uses of the impaired water body.

Section 404 of the CWA establishes a program to regulate the discharge of dredged or fill material into waters of the United States, including wetlands. Discharge or fill activities include fill for land development, water resource projects (such as dams and levees), infrastructure (such as highways), and mining projects. Section 404 requires a permit issued by the U.S. Army Corps of Engineers before dredged or fill material can be discharged into waters of the United States (unless specifically exempted, e.g., certain forestry activities). The U.S. Army Corps of Engineers and the EPA jointly define Section 404 jurisdictional wetlands based on the presence of hydrophytic vegetation, hydric soils, and hydrology as delineated in the *Corps of Engineers Wetlands Delineation Manual* (1987).

The basic premise of the Section 404 program is that no discharge of dredged or fill material may be permitted if (1) a practicable alternative exists that is less damaging to the aquatic environment, or (2) the nation's waters would be significantly degraded. Before a permit may be issued, the applicant must demonstrate to the extent practicable that (1) steps have been taken to avoid wetland impacts; (2) efforts have been made to minimize adverse impacts on wetlands; and (3) where unavoidable impacts remain, compensatory measures will be undertaken.

Where commonly occurring actions are likely to have a minor noncumulative impact, a "general permit" may suffice, provided applicants agree to use the mitigation conditions associated with this expedited

permit. An individual permit, which requires more detailed study, is required for potentially significant impacts. Individual permits are reviewed by the U.S. Army Corps of Engineers and are subject to veto authority by the U.S. EPA. Federal agencies are also required, under Executive Order 11990 (a.k.a. the "no net loss of wetlands" rule), to "minimize the destruction, loss or degradation of wetlands and to preserve and enhance the natural and beneficial values of wetlands." To meet these objectives, federal agencies must, in planning their activities, consider alternatives to wetland sites and limit potential damage if an activity affecting a wetland cannot be avoided.

THE COMPREHENSIVE ENVIRONMENTAL RESPONSE, COMPENSATION, AND LIABILITY ACT

The Comprehensive Environmental Response, Compensation, and Liability Act of 1980 (CERCLA; also known as the Superfund) was enacted in response to a growing national concern about the release of hazardous substances from abandoned industrial facilities and waste disposal sites. The U.S. EPA is charged with ensuring the cleanup of seriously contaminated property and hazardous waste sites through four programs (CRS, 1999):

The $1.6 billion Hazardous Substance Response Trust Fund. Supported by an excise tax on chemicals and petroleum (later increased by an additional $8.5 billion through the Superfund Amendments and Reauthorization Act, SARA, of 1987), this program allows the EPA to undertake short-term and long-term cleanups when public health concerns require immediate action or when parties responsible for the contamination cannot be found.

Threat or use of litigation under the Superfund's "strict, joint, and several" liability scheme. This program can require a single party or multiple parties responsible for contamination to either clean up or pay for the cleanup of contaminated sites. Parties that fight EPA Superfund enforcement lawsuits and lose may be held liable for treble the actual cleanup costs.

Creation of a National Contingency Plan (NCP). This provides the EPA with guidelines to screen and rank hazardous waste sites to determine the appropriate response action (e.g., those requiring immediate action and those that can be contained until litigation and negotiation with the parties that caused the contamination can be completed).

A brownfield program. This program offers liability relief and technical assistance for cleanup and reuse of lesser contaminated properties that are unlikely to rise to a federal or state superfund action, but nevertheless are passed over by the real estate industry because of fear of Superfund liability or other forms of environmental liability.

As noted, the National Contingency Plan (NCP) establishes the criteria and procedures the EPA uses to determine which sites have priority for long-term evaluation and cleanup response. Reported sites are evaluated based on the EPA's hazard ranking system,

Robert Paterson, Ph.D., University of Texas at Austin

and if posing a serious enough risk to public health and the environment are listed on the National Priorities List (NPL) for further evaluation and eventual remediation. Most states have equivalent state-level superfund laws and state priority lists. However, some 30,000 low to moderate contamination properties have been delisted from the federal Superfund database, and these are typically properties that the U.S. EPA and state voluntary cleanup programs target as brownfields suitable for redevelopment. The 2002 brownfield amendments to CERCLA's owner/operator liability provisions made it easier for a person to purchase or lease contaminated properties without being held potentially liable for Superfund liability. State voluntary cleanup programs often assist potential purchasers and redevelopers of brownfield sites with technical support for site assessments and cleanup plans. Upon completion of the cleanup, "certificates" are issued that convey the Superfund liability release (so banks and other lending institutions will provide loans for new development projects) (Bell et al., 2005).

In 1986, Congress provided further precaution to public health hazards from hazardous waste and toxic material release by enacting the Emergency Planning and Community Right-to-Know Act (EPCRA) amendments to CERCLA. The law requires companies to disclose information about the types and amounts of toxic chemicals they produce as well as release into the air, water, and land. The law was enacted in the aftermath of the Bhopal, India, disaster where more than 2,000 people died or suffered serious injury from the accidental release of methyl isocyanate by an industrial plant. Industrial facilities and other users of toxic substances must notify local emergency planning districts about the materials stored and possibly subject to release from their facilities. Local government emergency planning districts must prepare plans to deal with accidental releases or spills of hazardous substances within their jurisdiction. A related federal provision is Executive Order 12856 (the Federal Compliance with Right-to-Know Laws and Pollution Prevention Requirements), which directs federal agencies and their facilities to comply with all provisions of EPCRA.

RESOURCE CONSERVATION AND RECOVERY ACT

The Resource Conservation and Recovery Act (RCRA) of 1976 and its subsequent amendments aim to curtail the legacy of contaminated industrial facilities and hazardous waste dumps that are the subject of Superfund cleanups, as well as to ensure environmentally sound disposal of nonhazardous wastes. RCRA empowers the U.S. EPA to accomplish these efforts through three major programs: (1) the manifest tracking system that ensures the proper identification, permitting, storage, transport, and disposal of hazardous wastes from the "cradle to the grave; (2) the municipal solid waste (MSW) landfill program, which regulates the permitting, operation, and closure of MSW facilities; and (3) the underground storage tank program, which regulates the manufacture of tanks used to store hazardous materials or petroleum products below grade, the requirements for upgrading existing tanks, and the requirements for leak prevention and cleanup of existing or abandoned underground storage tanks.

The purpose of the manifest tracking system is to ensure accountability for the production and movement of hazardous wastes. Hazardous waste generators must maintain records and report hazardous waste management activity, including the amount of hazardous waste produced, the transporters of their wastes, and the disposal facilities in possession of their hazardous wastes for three years from date the waste was created. Any movement of hazardous wastes by air, rail, highway, or water triggers RCRA transporter reporting and tracking requirements. Owners and operators of hazardous waste management facilities must meet strict EPA design, operation, and closure regulations, as well as record-keeping requirements, to ensure the long-term safety of the public from disposed hazardous wastes (Bell et al., 2005).

State environmental agencies typically take the lead role in implementing the MSW programs by reviewing state or regional solid waste management plans for consistency with federal and state minimum MSW standards. The U.S. EPA promulgated the minimum national criteria for all municipal solid waste landfill (MSWLF) units in terms of design (e.g., siting and liner requirements), operation (e.g., leachate collection and groundwater/gas-monitoring requirements), and closure requirements.

The underground storage tank regulations were created to deal with the estimated hundreds of thousands of leaking underground storage tanks (LUSTs) in the United States that contained petroleum or hazardous substances, as well as the hundreds of thousands of LUSTs that were nearing the end of their design life (and which would require removal and replacement). In addition to regulations governing the manufacture, removal, construction, and operation of LUSTs, the EPA also received a $1.9 billion trust fund appropriation to clean up UST releases where the owner or operator does not or is unable to clean up a site (CRS, 1999). The LUST Trust Fund money is used primarily by the EPA, and states that have entered into cooperative agreements with the EPA, to oversee and enforce UST corrective actions. As in the Superfund, the U.S. EPA and the states also have authority to take cost recovery legal action against parties that fail to respond to a UST enforcement order.

SAFE DRINKING WATER ACT

Congress passed the Safe Drinking Water Act (SDWA) in 1974 to protect the public health by setting national drinking water standards for public water systems, and for related reasons, regulates underground injection to protect groundwater resources. The SDWA required the EPA to establish National Primary Drinking Water Regulations (NPDWRs) for contaminants that may cause adverse public health effects. These regulations generally include numerical standards to limit the amount of a contaminant that may be present in drinking water. When it is not economically or technically feasible to measure a contaminant at very low concentrations, the EPA establishes a treatment technology in lieu of a standard. Some 91 drinking water contaminants are now regulated. In setting the drinking water standards, the EPA first sets health goals based on best scientific information on the maximum contaminant levels (MCLs) for each contaminant, and then an enforceable MCL is set as close to a health-based standard as

possible, taking into account pollutant detection limits and costs. The primary drinking water standards apply to drinking water "at the tap" as delivered by public water supply systems that regularly serve at least 25 people. The U.S. EPA sets the national drinking water standards, and most states are delegated primary enforcement and implementation authority (with U.S. EPA oversight) (CRS, 1999).

OTHER FEDERAL ENVIRONMENTAL AND PLANNING STATUTES

Beyond the major environmental statutes and programs described, planners also need to be aware of other important federal and state programs encompassing housing policy, transportation policy and disaster preparedness, mitigation, and recovery planning. This section briefly describes additional statutes and policies with which planners should familiarize themselves in order to be more effective in planning practice.

The U.S. Department of Housing and Urban Development (HUD) has myriad laws that cover its mission to promote home ownership, to increase the production of affordable housing, to assist low-income renters, to protect against discrimination in housing, and to promote overall community development. The primary vehicles to coordinate these grant and regulatory programs at the state and local levels are the five-year consolidated housing plan and annual action plans that detail how Community Development Block Grants, Emergency Shelter, Home Investment Partnership funds, and Housing Opportunities for People with Aids grant funds will be used. The consolidated plan must be based on a participatory planning process that creates a shared vision of the community development goals and clearly delineates an affordability strategy and shows how funds will be distributed across program needs. A performance measurement system is also necessary, to track results.

The Intermodal Surface Transportation Efficiency Act (ISTEA) of 1991 and its subsequent amendments provide the framework for current state and regional transportation planning in the United States. The law redefined federal, state, and regional roles in transportation planning by providing greater flexibility in use of federal transportation funds between highways and transit; allowed for use of those funds for non-highway activities such as trails and other environmental enhancements; emphasized stronger collaboration between state departments of transportation and metropolitan regional planning organizations (MPOs); and required stronger linkages between transportation and regional planning as the basis for transportation fund allocations. Under ISTEA, MPOs (which serve communities with populations over 50,000) develop long-range transportation plans (LRTPs) that project needs and a regional transportation vision for the next 20 years. MPOs then submit transportation improvement programs (TIPs) that spell out the short-term priority projects needed to implement the 20-year vision. Both LRTPs and TIPs must be developed in a manner that is consistent with the state's SIP under the CAA provision to make sure mobile source emissions do not violate NAAQs in AQCRs (see the CAA section above).

Federal disaster laws encompass planning, regulatory, and grant programs to enable states and localities to prepare, mitigate, respond to, and recover from natural and technological disasters. The U.S.

Robert Paterson, Ph.D., University of Texas at Austin

Department of Homeland Security's Federal Emergency Management Agency (FEMA) is the lead federal agency for disaster mitigation planning and relief efforts. Two of the most important laws for planning practice in this area are the Flood Disaster Protection Act (FDPA) of 1973 and the Robert T. Stafford Disaster Relief and Emergency Assistance Act of 1988. The FDPA improved the planning and regulatory requirements of the National Flood Insurance Program to ensure that localities take appropriate measures to reduce flood risks in high hazard zones through floodplain management and floodplain development regulations that meet minimum national standards. Amendments to the FDPA in 1990 created the Community Rating System, which allows communities to earn flood insurance premium reductions by enhancing flood loss reduction capacity according to a ranking system created by FEMA. The Robert T. Stafford Act formalized the cost-sharing and public assistance grant programs for federal disaster declarations, and reemphasized FEMA's commitment to hazard mitigation efforts to reduce escalating losses from natural disasters. The 2000 amendments offered for the first time hazard mitigation grants for state and local planning. However, to be eligible for predisaster mitigation funds and to redirect postdisaster relief funds toward mitigation, states and localities must have submitted and have FEMA-approved hazard mitigation plans in place by 2005.

Finally, there are a number of federal special-issue laws that are beyond the scope of this discussion but that planners should take time to learn more about for effective planning practice. These include the Religious Land Use and Institutionalized Persons Act of 2000, which addresses restrictions that local governments can and cannot place on places of religious worship and assembly; the Telecommunications Act of 1966, which creates some restrictions on local government regulation of mobile phone cell towers, satellite dishes, and TV antennas; the Americans with Disabilities Act of 1990, which affirms planners' responsibilities to ensure that site planning, parking, and building codes respect the rights of disabled persons in the enjoyment of the built environment and in employment; the Highway Beautification Act of 1965, which requires the control of billboards, outdoor advertising signs, and other displays within 660 feet of interstate and primary highways; and the National Historic Preservation Act, which requires all federal agencies to consider historic and cultural resource preservation in their activities, and provides for mitigation for any adverse effects that might result from a federal undertaking in consultation with the State Historic Preservation Officer.

To stay abreast of important changes and issues in federal environmental law, planners should consult the following online resources:

- The National Council for Science and Environment (www.ncseonline.org/NLE), in a cooperative arrangement with the U.S. Congressional Research Service (CRS), posts virtually all of the CRS's briefings to Congress on federal environmental matters in PDF format for download. These are invaluable for staying current on proposed and recent changes to the major federal environmental statutes.
- The Environmental Law Institute has published the Environmental Law Reporter (www.elistore.org) for more than 10 years. It is a reliable resource for environmental, health and safety, toxic tort, natural resource, and land-use professionals. The institute also publishes a number of working papers in PDF format that summarize existing and proposed changes to major environmental laws.
- Pace Law School (www.virtualref.com/abs/469.htm) maintains an extensive link system on environmental law matters through its virtual environmental law library.

REFERENCES

Bass, Ronald E., Albert I. Herson, and Kenneth M. Bogdan. 2001. *The NEPA Book,* Point Arena, CA: Solano Press.

Bell, Christopher, and others. 2005. *Environmental Law Handbook,* 18th edition, Washington DC: Government Institutes.

California Air Quality Resources Board. 2005. *Air Quality and Land Use Handbook: A Community Health Perspective* (April), Sacramento, CA: CARB.

Congressional Research Service. 1999. Summaries of Environmental Laws Administered by the EPA, Congressional Research Service Report RL30022, Web Accessed on December 15th, 2005, at http://www.ncseonline.org/nle/crsreports/briefingbooks/laws/e.cfm.

Mayer, Susan L. 1993. Air Quality: State Plans and Sanctions, U.S. Congressional Research Service Report, 93-1062 ENR, Washington DC, Web Accessed on December 15th, 2005, at http://www.ncseonline.org/nle/crsreports/air/air-5.cfm.

U.S. Army Corps of Engineers. 1987. *Corps of Engineers Wetland Delineation Manual.* Technical Report Y-87-1. January 1987.

See also:
Environmental impact Assessment
Environmental Planning and Management
Participation

Robert Paterson, Ph.D., University of Texas at Austin

STATE ENABLING LEGISLATION

Enabling legislation is a mechanism by which a state delegates police power, which includes the power to plan and to zone, to local government. It permits the local governments to "do something," but in a certain way and through certain mechanisms.

All states have planning and zoning enabling legislation. Such legislation will include definitions, a grant of authority, an organizational framework, a set of procedures, and, often, a set of duties that accompanies the delegation. Municipal charters, which may have different procedures and institutional structures from state legislation, and which are adopted under home rule authority or by action of the state legislature, may govern in lieu of state legislation.

Several model enabling acts have been developed for possible adoption by states:

- U.S. Department of Commerce's Standard State Zoning and City Planning Enabling Acts
- American Law Institute's Model Land Development Code
- American Planning Association's Growing Smart Legislative Guidebook

THE STANDARD ACTS

Two standard state enabling acts published by the U.S. Department of Commerce in the 1920s laid the basic foundation for zoning and for planning in the United States. For many states, the standard acts still supply the institutional structure, although some procedural and substantive components may have changed. In 1921, a federal advisory committee on zoning and then Secretary of Commerce Herbert Hoover developed the Standard State Zoning Enabling Act (SZEA). The Government Printing Office published the first edition in May 1924. The SZEA had nine sections. It includes a grant of power, a provision that the legislative body could divide the local government's territory into districts, a statement of purpose for the zoning regulations, and procedures for establishing and amending the zoning regulations. A legislative body was required to establish a zoning commission to advise it on the initial development of zoning regulations. The U.S. Department of Commerce tracked the SZEA's progress. It was adopted by all 50 states and is still in effect, in modified form, in 47 states.

In 1928, the Standard City Planning Enabling Act (SCPEA) was published. The SCPEA covered six subjects: (1) the organization and power of the planning commission, which was directed to prepare and adopt a master plan; (2) the content of the master plan for the physical development of the territory; (3) provision for adoption of a master street plan by the governing body; (4) provision for approval of all public improvements by the planning commission; (5) control of private subdivision of land; and (6) provision for the establishment of a regional planning commission and a regional plan. The SCPEA was not as popular as the SZEA, perhaps because there was less pressure to authorize planning institutions and more pressure to allow and implement zoning.

AMERICAN LAW INSTITUTE'S MODEL LAND DEVELOPMENT CODE

The American Law Institute's (ALI) *A Model Land Development Code*, published in 1976 after 11 years of work, represented a critical rethinking of American planning and zoning law. The code was not intended to replace the standards acts, but to serve as a source of various statutory models to address specific development concerns by either local or state government. The code allocates responsibility for planning and land-use decision making between the state and local governments in three alternative ways. Under one model, for example, the local government retains control over its planning and development regulation, subject to state supervision and policy guidance.

A widely cited method of allocating state and local authority found in the ALI code was the designation, planning, and management of areas of critical state concern, for which plans would be developed by either local or state agencies, but under state guidelines, and management would remain subject to state oversight or direct supervision. A number of states adopted the code's proposals for state regulation of areas of critical state concern. Most notably, Florida adopted its state land-use statutes based on the ALI code. Other states adopted portions of the code, but they mostly avoided the approaches recommended and proceeded to enact growth management legislation and other specific initiatives addressing such problems as housing affordability.

GROWING SMART LEGISLATIVE GUIDEBOOK

The *Growing Smart Legislative Guidebook Model Statutes for Planning and the Management of Change*, 2002 edition, was published by the American Planning Association in January of that year. The result of seven years of work, it is intended to update both the Standard Acts and the ALI Code, described above. *Growing Smart Legislative Guidebook* contains model statutes and commentary. There are 15 chapters covering local planning for a wide array of contexts and purposes, as well as local, regional, and state land-use regulation. A widely used set of provisions of the *Guidebook* is found in Chapter 10, which provides for the integration of all local land development regulations into a single ordinance and explains the concept of a development permit, very broadly applied.

STATE ENVIRONMENTAL POLICY ACTS

When a project requires a discretionary decision, or "action," by administrative agencies of the federal government, the obligations set forth in the National Environmental Policy Act of 1969 (NEPA) may be triggered. Moreover, 16 states, the District of Columbia, Puerto Rico, and the City of New York have enacted environmental policy acts that are largely modeled on NEPA and may create additional obligations for projects in those jurisdictions. These environmental laws are collectively referred to as "little NEPAs."

Like NEPA, little NEPAs require administrative agencies of state governments making discretionary decisions to consider the potential adverse environmental effects of their actions. Although little NEPAs are modeled on their "parent" NEPA, there remain numerous exceptions that exist on a state-by-state basis.

That said, most state courts apply the same general standard of judicial review of decisions under little NEPAs as do federal courts under NEPA: the agency must identify the relevant areas of concern, take a hard look at them, and provide a reasoned elaboration of the basis for its decision.

Procedural versus Substantive Statutes

NEPA is a procedural statute: it requires federal agencies to take procedural steps, such as preparation of an Environmental Impact Statement (EIS), but does not require the agencies to select the environmentally preferable alternative after review of the environmental impacts identified in the EIS. The EIS procedures under little NEPAs are generally comparable to that under the federal NEPA:

- Preparation of a draft EIS
- Public comment period (often with the opportunity for a public hearing)
- Preparation of a final EIS that addresses comments on the draft EIS
- Decisional document
- Actions that trigger a little NEPA environmental review

STATE ENVIRONMENTAL POLICY ACTS: BEST PRACTICE CHECKLIST

For states that have enacted an environmental policy act or are proposing one:

- Determine the extent to which the act's requirements apply to current or future actions.
- If the act applies, study the environmental review process and requirements, and develop standard procedures and formats for notifying potentially affected parties, soliciting needed information and evaluation input, preparing required environmental impact evaluations and publishing them for review and comment, assessing and responding to comments, and making and publishing decisions.
- If the act does not apply, become familiar with the environmental review process, find out which covered actions are being proposed in your area, and actively participate in all stages of the review process, from a definition of the proposed action through analysis to review and comment.

Kent S. Butler, Ph.D., University of Texas at Austin

As with NEPA, little NEPAs generally are activated by an action of a governmental unit. The critical issue is which government units are covered and which actions of such units trigger the obligation to conduct an environmental review. Most little NEPAs cover all state "agencies," and some define the term. Check the specific state statute to determine which agencies are covered.

Most little NEPAs cover a broad scope of state action, so that any proposed project requiring discretionary acts by the state/local administrative agency will likely trigger environmental review. Little NEPAs sometimes limit application to projects that are "major" actions, requiring environmental review only for actions that *significantly* affect the human environment or its quality.

REFERENCES

Advisory Committee on Planning and Zoning, U.S. Department of Commerce. 1928. A Standard City Planning Enabling Act. Washington, DC: U.S. GPO.

————. Advisory Committee on Zoning, U.S. Department of Commerce. 1926. A Standard State Zoning Enabling Act (rev. ed.). Washington, DC: U.S. GPO.

American Law Institute (ALI). 1976. *A Model Land Development Code: Complete Text and Commentary.* Philadelphia, PA: ALI.

Mandelker, Daniel R. Fall 2003. "Model Legislation for Land Use Decisions," *The Urban Lawyer,* 35(4): 635–669.

Meck, Stuart, gen. ed. 2002. *Growing Smart Legislative Guidebook: Model Statutes for Planning and the Management of Change.* Chicago: American Planning Association.

See also:
Comprehensive Plans
Environmental Impact Assessment
Federal Legislation
Fiscal Impact Assessment
Subdivision Regulation
Zoning Regulation

Kent S. Butler, Ph.D., University of Texas at Austin

ZONING REGULATION

A zoning ordinance divides a local government's jurisdiction into districts or zones. For each district or zone, the zoning ordinance regulates the following:

- Types of land uses allowed
- Intensity or density of development
- Height, bulk, and placement of structures
- Amount and design of parking
- A number of other aspects of land-use and development activity

Zoning ordinances also contain standards common to all districts and a set of procedures for applying, administering, and enforcing its regulations. Finally, the ordinance will contain a map or series of maps that show precise boundaries for the various zoning districts.

BACKGROUND

Zoning in the United States derived from nineteenth-century German zoning laws. In the 1920s, the U.S. Department of Commerce produced the Standard Zoning Enabling Act, model zoning enabling legislation, which laid the foundation for zoning laws in most of the country. The act reflects an interest in protecting the value of private investment by separating incompatible land uses and assuring the availability of light and air circulation through height and bulk controls.

Since the 1950s, zoning districts have traditionally been defined in terms of land use, with various residential districts distinguished by type (e.g., single-family, multifamily) and maximum density, plus similarly distinguished commercial districts (e.g., central business, general business, highway business, shopping center, office, and institutional) and industrial districts (e.g., light industrial, heavy industrial). Over the years, many communities added agricultural districts, conservation districts, and institutional (e.g., campus) districts, as well as mixed-use districts that allow a blend of uses. Many zoning ordinances also include special-purpose districts that address flood hazard areas, historic properties, and other specialized uses. Such districts are commonly applied as overlay districts, where a special set of standards is applied in addition to the standards applicable in the underlying general zoning district.

TYPICAL ELEMENTS

Although zoning ordinances vary greatly in their organization and content, and the nature of zoning regulation is currently undergoing substantial change in many areas, most zoning ordinances are still organized according to some variation of the following:

- General provisions
- Use standards
- Intensity and density standards
- Dimensional standards
- General development standards
- Development standards for hazard areas or sensitive lands
- Nonconformity standards
- Development review procedures

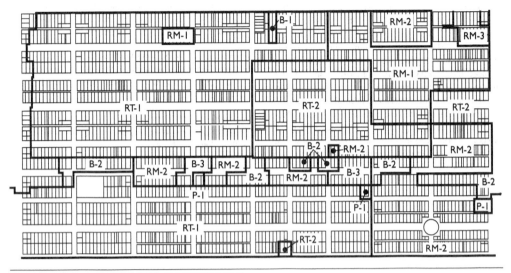

EXAMPLE OF AN OFFICIAL ZONING MAP

Source: URS Corporation.

- Appeal and variance provisions
- Enforcement provisions
- Amendment provisions

Zoning ordinances are composed of two primary components: the ordinance text and the official map or series of maps. The official zoning map(s) apply the zoning district classifications established by the zoning ordinance text to specific land areas within the community's zoning jurisdiction. It depicts the boundaries of zoning districts, including general-use districts and any special or overlay districts established or authorized by the ordinance. Regulations affecting any single land parcel may be linked to one or more maps. Changing the zoning district classification applicable to any land area requires a zoning map amendment (rezoning). Such changes are deemed amendments of the zoning ordinance and must be enacted in accord with procedures prescribed by the ordinance.

General Provisions

Zoning ordinance general provisions are usually applicable across all districts. They typically include the following:

- *Statement of purposes,* which clearly expresses what the jurisdiction seeks to accomplish with the ordinance. It may refer to community values, goals, objectives, and policies set forth in a comprehensive plan. Courts will often examine an ordinance's purpose statements when assessing its constitutionality or its applicability to a particular development.
- *Applicability provisions,* which identify the types of situations or activities intended to be regulated by or exempted from the ordinance and the geographic reach of the regulations. This may include "extraterritorial jurisdiction" extending beyond the local jurisdiction's political boundaries where authorized by statute.

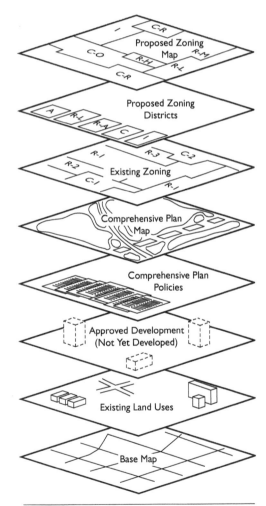

FACTORS CONTRIBUTING TO THE ZONING MAP

Source: Lerable 1985.

Stephen G. Sizemore, AICP, American Planning Association, Chicago, Illinois

- *Definitions,* which attach specific meanings to words and concepts used in the ordinance, many of which are unique to zoning.
- *Zoning map provisions,* which establish procedures for creating, updating, and copying the official zoning map(s).
- *Administrative provisions,* which describe the duties of the various entities involved in administering the zoning regulations. Such entities typically include:
  - The governing body, which decides on proposals to amend the ordinance (including rezonings).
  - The planning commission, which generally serves as an advisor to the governing body on zoning matters and may conduct site plan reviews.
  - The zoning board (board of zoning appeals, board of adjustment), which hears administrative appeals and requests for hardship variances from zoning standards, and may decide applications for conditional or special-use permits.
  - The zoning administrator and other staff, who coordinate review processes, review and recommend action on applications and proposals (and may decide applications for minor development), and enforce permit compliance.

Some communities may have special boards such as historic preservation commissions, appearance commissions, or wetland commissions.

Use Standards

Use standards identify the land uses and the restrictions or limitations specific to each permitted use for each zoning district. Uses are typically classified according to several criteria:

- *Permitted "by right" uses:* Permitted as long as they comply with other applicable standards.
- *Permitted conditional or special uses:* May be compatible with the district's permitted uses, but are subject to discretionary review and supplemental standards intended to ensure that the particular proposed use is compatible with other uses permitted in the district.
- *Permitted accessory uses:* Incidental or subordinate to the district's permitted "principal" uses.
- *Prohibited uses:* Specifically declared as not allowed in the district, or not allowed there in specific circumstances. Zoning ordinances generally state that all uses not specifically listed as permitted are prohibited, but may list prohibited uses to clarify that certain uses are not included as part of some general listed permitted use.

Intensity and Density Standards

These standards regulate the overall intensity of development and may be linked to the single map or to additional maps. For each zoning district they typically include one or more of the following standards:

- *Maximum density:* Typically expressed as a number of dwelling units per acre. Generally used for multifamily and planned unit development.
- *Minimum lot size:* The inverse of maximum density; lot size may be converted to density (dwelling units per acre) by dividing lot size into the number of square feet in an acre. Generally used for single-family and two-family (duplex) dwellings.

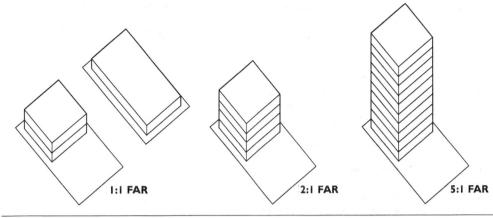

EXAMPLE OF FLOOR AREA RATIO

Source: URS Corporation.

- *Maximum floor area ratio (FAR):* The maximum ratio of building floor area to land area. FAR is more commonly applied to nonresidential development.

Dimensional Standards

These standards address the bulk and scale of development and may be linked to the single map or to additional maps. For each zoning district, they typically include one or more of the following standards:

- *Maximum building height:* Commonly expressed as number of feet, but sometimes expressed as the number of stories. It typically varies among districts in relation to the types of uses allowed and in proportion to the maximum density/intensity allowed, commonly starting at 30 to 35 feet in single-family residential districts.
- *Minimum yard depth or minimum building setback (in feet):* Used to preserve open space or

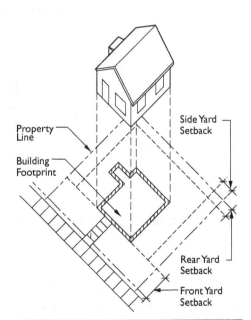

Property Line

Building Footprint

Side Yard Setback

Rear Yard Setback

Front Yard Setback

DIMENSIONAL STANDARDS

Source: URS Corporation.

separation between buildings and lot boundaries and between neighboring buildings; generally varies among districts in proportion to the maximum intensity/density allowed.

- *Maximum front or side setbacks (in feet):* Used to bring buildings closer to the street or to each other, thereby creating more pedestrian-friendly design.
- *Maximum building coverage:* Usually expressed as a percentage of lot area; it limits the size of the building "footprint."
- *Maximum impervious surface (percentage):* Limits the percentage of a site's land area that may be covered or paved (including buildings, paving, and decks); it is used to limit rainfall runoff and, thus, stormwater impacts and facilities. Typical standards can range from 100 percent in downtown districts to 80 percent in suburban commercial districts to 50 percent for multifamily residential or industrial districts to 25 percent or less in single-family residential districts.
- *Maximum building size or building envelope standards:* Controls the scale of buildings in designated neighborhoods or zoning districts.

General Development Standards

General development standards address the design of various aspects of development in general:

- *Parking and loading standards:* Dictate how much off-street parking space should be provided for the loading and unloading of trucks. This information is typically provided in a table that lists parking spaces for various categories of land use, based on some measurement of the use's intensity (e.g., 1 space per 250 square feet of floor area for retail uses) Increasingly, local governments are establishing maximum as well as minimum parking requirements in order to control the scale and impact of parking areas.
- *Landscape planting standards:* Typically require some portion of development sites, or at least parking lots, to be landscaped, to soften the visual effect of the development or parking lot and reduce heat generation. Landscape planting standards generally specify the amount of landscaping and its location, type(s) of vegetation, size of planting areas, and maintenance.

Stephen G. Sizemore, AICP, American Planning Association, Chicago, Illinois

Development Standards for Hazard Areas or Sensitive Lands

Standards for natural hazard areas and critical or environmentally sensitive lands most commonly address flood hazard areas. Increasingly, zoning ordinances include special development standards designed to protect wetlands, aquifer recharge areas, water supply watersheds, steep slopes, and other environmentally sensitive areas from the adverse impacts of development. These standards are typically linked to maps for each hazard or each type of sensitive area.

Nonconformity Standards

Nonconformity standards address how to treat a land use, structure, or other feature of development that was legal when established, but would not be allowed under current zoning regulations. These standards usually "grandfather" nonconformities—allow them to continue without having to conform to new regulations—while prohibiting or strictly limiting the expansion, renovation, or reconstruction of the nonconformity. Nonconformity standards may also "amortize" nonconformities by requiring them to either conform to current regulations or cease within a certain time period. This controversial method is often limited to nonconformities involving minimal capital investment (e.g., signs).

Development Review Procedures

This set of procedures identifies the approvals and permits required by the ordinance. Development review procedures also define the steps to be followed in applying for, reviewing, and deciding the approvals and permits required. These vary by state; check with state statutes to determine specific required approvals. There are eight types of development review:

- Comprehensive plans or plan amendments
- Specific plans
- Rezoning
- Conditional or special-use permit (or special exception)
- Site plan
- Zoning compliance permit or approval
- Building permits and certificates of occupancy
- Development agreements

Appeal and Variance Provisions

This set of provisions sets forth the processes by which aggrieved parties may appeal alleged errors in administrative decisions, including interpretations, to the zoning board, and by which the board may relax normally applicable standards in certain conditions.

Enforcement Provisions

Enforcement provisions identify actions that will constitute a violation of the zoning ordinance, for instance, construction without the requisite permit, work contrary to the terms and conditions of a permit, or use of land or a building contrary to use standards. These provisions also identify enforcement actions that may be taken in case of a violation, and they describe procedures used in taking enforcement actions, usually providing for a hearing on permit revocation and appeal of permit withholding.

Amendment Provisions

This set of provisions set forth the procedures by which the text of the zoning regulations and the zoning map may be changed. As legislative amendments to the zoning ordinance, such changes generally must be enacted by the same entity (usually the governing body) and procedures (e.g., noticed public hearing) required to enact the zoning ordinance in the first place.

TYPES OF ZONING DECISIONS

TYPE OF DECISION	CLASSIFICATION		
	LEGISLATIVE	QUASI-JUDICIAL	MINISTERIAL
Comprehensive Plan or Plan Amendment	X		
Specific Plan	X		
Rezoning	X		
Conditional/Special-Use Permit		X	
Site Plan		X	X
Zoning Compliance Permit			X
Building Permit and Certificate of Occupancy			X
Development Agreements	X		
Variance		X	
Appeal		X	

Source: Mark White, 2005.

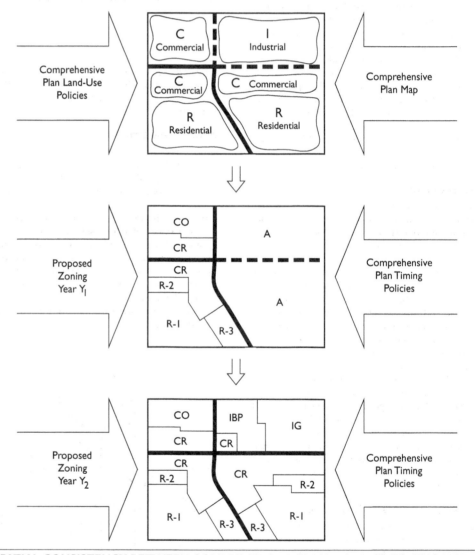

SPATIAL CONSISTENCY BETWEEN COMPREHENSIVE PLAN MAP AND ZONING MAP

Source: Lerable 1985.

FROM COMPREHENSIVE PLAN TO ZONING MAP

Preparing a zoning map is one of the most demanding steps in developing a zoning code. Drawing zoning districts is not as simple as tracing over the

Stephen G. Sizemore, AICP, American Planning Association, Chicago, Illinois comprehensive plan map, nor is it as exacting. There are important differences that must be understood before this process begins. Consider these differences before preparing a new zoning code and map, and ideally before preparing a comprehensive plan.

Variations in Detail

Zoning maps must be specific in order to perform a regulatory function. Comprehensive plan maps are typically quite general, with their application to individual parcels being less specific. Avoid overlapping purposes between zoning maps and comprehensive plan maps; policy and regulation should be separate and clearly distinguishable functions. Keep parcel-specific details out of the comprehensive plan to maintain the long-term integrity of the plan and make it less likely the plan map will need to be amended each time there is a rezoning.

Spatial and Temporal Differences

The comprehensive plan map is a spatial depiction of future land uses; the plan's policies may decide when such land uses are allowed, but the zoning makes the decision operative. The comprehensive plan map often depicts land for future development, including its type and general distribution, with no indication when such development should be allowed. Plan policies determine when development is appropriate, if at all.

Zoning is for the short term. Land should not be prematurely zoned for long-term intended uses. One option is to temporarily zone such land for interim uses. The availability of infrastructure or the surplus of existing developable land may be the plan's triggering mechanisms that allow interim zoning to change to zoning that would allow development consistent with the long-term land-use pattern envisioned by the plan map. Actual zoning will evolve over time based on the comprehensive plan's timing, and policies with each development phase will be directed by the plan's long-term timing policies.

Comprehensive plan maps typically show broad categories of land uses. For each land use category there may be several zoning districts so that, for example, the comprehensive plan's commercial cate-gory may result in retail, highway commercial, office, and downtown zoning districts. The number of zoning districts will depend on local circumstances and policies in the comprehensive plan. These zoning districts, in turn, may be subject to additional divisions with the application of overlay districts.

REFERENCE

Lerable, Charles A. 1995. *Preparing a Conventional Zoning Ordinance.* Planning Advisory Service Report No. 460. Chicago: American Planning Association.

See also:

Critical and Sensitive Areas Plans
Flood Hazards
Innovations in Local Zoning Regulations
Planned Unit Development
State Enabling Legislation
Subdivision Regulation

Stephen G. Sizemore, AICP, American Planning Association, Chicago, Illinois

SUBDIVISION REGULATION

A subdivision ordinance controls the division of a tract of land for building and development purposes. It includes standards for the design and layout of lots, streets, utilities, and other public improvements, as well as procedures and requirements to ensure that public improvements are available when it is time to build on the lots.

BACKGROUND

The initial purpose of subdivision regulation was to provide a more efficient method of conveying land than through deeds and their metes and bounds descriptions. The Standard City Planning Enabling Act of 1928 laid the foundation for subdivision regulation in the United States. In accord with that model legislation, subdivision regulation in most states is principally

the responsibility of a local government's planning commission, and is largely a technical exercise involving a determination that proposed subdivision plans comply with technical standards for street and utility design. Increasingly, environmental requirements must also be satisfied.

ELEMENTS

Although the procedures and standards in subdivision ordinances vary among states (and among local governments within a state), most subdivision ordinances contain the following elements:

- General provisions
- Review procedures
- Performance guarantees

- Vested right provisions
- Development standards

General Provisions

- *Statement of purposes*: Expresses what the jurisdiction seeks to accomplish with the ordinance, which generally focuses on efficient lot, street, and utility layout, and, increasingly, on integration with the site's natural features and neighboring development.

- *Applicability provisions*: Identify the geographic reach of the regulations (which may include "extra-territorial jurisdiction" extending beyond the local jurisdiction's political boundaries), and which divisions of land are exempt from subdivision regulation or review. Typically exempt are divisions requiring no public improvements and

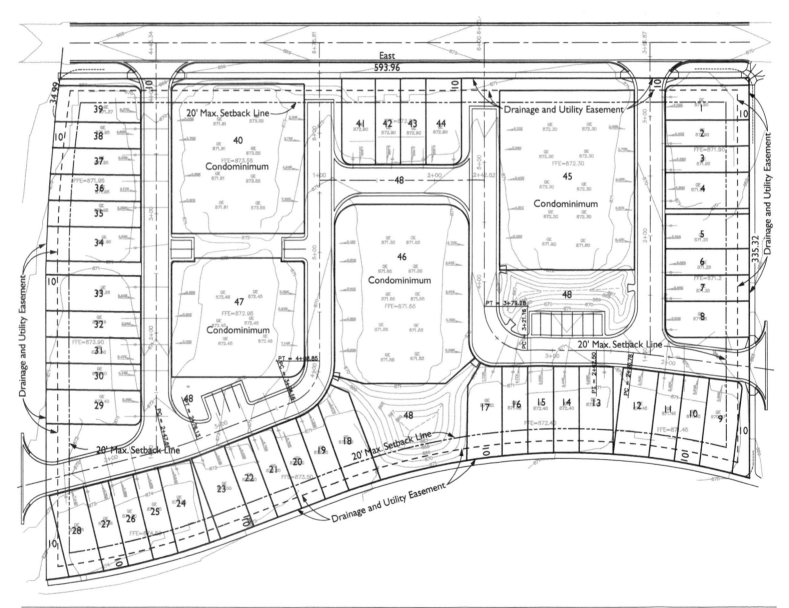

SUBDIVISION PLAT

Source: URS Corporation.

Stephen G. Sizemore, AICP, American Planning Association, Chicago, Illinois

creating only a few lots (or merely recombining existing lots).

- *Definitions*: Attach specific meaning to words and concepts used in the ordinance, many of which are unique to subdivision regulation (and may differ from those used in the zoning ordinance).
- *A bar on subdivisions by deed*: The use of deeded conveyances to achieve parcel divisions that are subject to the subdivision ordinance.

Review Procedures

Review procedures typically consist of at least two steps: preliminary plat review and final plat review. Some ordinances precede preliminary plan review with an informal review of a sketch or concept plan showing the proposed general layout of lots and streets and treatment of sensitive lands.

Preliminary Plat

A preliminary plat typically shows:

- site features (such as topography, streams and ponds, and flood hazard areas);
- the layout and dimensions of lots and street rights-of-way;
- the type and dimensions of streets; and
- the type, size, and placement of utilities and other public improvements.

Generally, staff and the planning commission review the preliminary plat for compliance with the ordinance's specific standards. Because review is largely technical, most commissions do not hold public hearings on subdivision proposals. The review is generally considered ministerial; that is, if the plat meets all applicable standards, it must be approved. If the plat is approved, the developer may seek final plat approval for the subdivision (or phases thereof). Under some ordinances, the developer may also begin to construct approved public improvements after obtaining staff approval of detailed engineering and construction plans.

Final Plat

A final plat is a surveyor's precise drawing that fixes the locations and boundaries of lots and streets and, when recorded in the county land records, serves as the means by which public improvements are dedicated and lots are sold. It may be submitted for the whole subdivision or for individual phases. If the ordinance does not provide for prior approval of construction plans for public improvements, a final plat will be accompanied by such plans. Final plats may be approved by the staff, or by the planning commission, or by the governing body (particularly where only the governing body can accept public improvements).

With the widespread use of geographic information systems (GIS), digital submission of plats in a form compatible with a municipality's own system is increasingly common. It improves both efficiency of processing by staff and accuracy of the submissions.

Many subdivision ordinances distinguish between minor and major subdivisions (usually based on the extent of required public improvements and number of lots) and provide a simpler review process for minor subdivisions that involve more basic plans and staff review only. Also, most state enabling legislation and subdivision ordinances do not provide for administrative appeal; appeals generally go straight to court.

Performance Guarantees

Performance guarantees generally take the form of a bond or letter of credit. Such guarantees for public improvements are usually required to be posted before construction of the improvements is approved or the final plat is recorded. When the public improvements have been completed and become the accepted responsibility of the local government or other public entity, the local government releases the performance guarantee back to the developer. Should the developer fail to complete the improvements, the local government may use the guarantee to pay to complete them.

Vested Right Provisions

These provisions are generally found in subdivision ordinances because of the multistep review process and the long time often involved in the phased development of subdivisions. They generally vest a subdivider with preliminary plat approval with the right to complete subdivision review and subdivision development in accord with the approved preliminary plat, irrespective of subsequent changes to subdivision regulations—provided the subdivider applies for final plat approval within a certain time (often, two years).

Development Standards

Development standards address the layout and design of lots, streets, and other public improvements:

- *Lot standards*: Define lot size and width requirements (usually by reference to standards in the zoning ordinance) and limit irregular lot shapes ("flag" lots) and arrangements (double frontage lots).
- *Block standards*: Define the minimum and maximum width and length of blocks (which affects street layout).
- *Street standards*: Define, for various classifications of streets, requirements for right-of-way width, roadway design (e.g., width, grade and curvature, base and surface materials, curb and gutter), intersection design, and sidewalk provision and design.
- *Utility standards*: Identify the water distribution and sewage collection facilities that are required, prescribe their size and location, and provide for utility easements necessary to ensure their future maintenance.
- *Stormwater management standards*: Typically require facilities to handle drainage from streets, call for on-site retention or detention of peak stormwater runoff from a storm of a certain frequency and duration, and provide for drainage easements to ensure maintenance of natural drainageways and stormwater pipes.
- *Open space standards*: Require a certain amount of land to be reserved for recreational use of future subdivision residents, or require land in natural hazard areas or other sensitive environmental areas to be set aside as open space.

CLUSTER SUBDIVISIONS

Many subdivision ordinances authorize "cluster subdivisions," where lot sizes may be reduced a certain extent below those normally required in return for using the "saved" land area as part of set-aside permanent open space. Some ordinances limit the number of lots to that allowed for a "conventional" subdivision of the site, while others encourage cluster subdivisions by allowing increased lot numbers resulting from more efficient lot layout or by providing a density bonus.

See also:
Conservation Development
Innovations in Local Zoning Regulations
Planned Unit Development
Residential Types
Zoning Regulation

Stephen G. Sizemore, AICP, American Planning Association, Chicago, Illinois

PLANNED UNIT DEVELOPMENT

Planned unit development (PUD) regulations typically merge zoning and subdivision controls, allowing developers to plan and develop a large area as a single entity, with the design flexibility to mix land uses, housing types, and densities, and to phase large developments over a number of years.

PUD emerged as an alternative to the residential subdivision and lot-by-lot development practices associated with the post-World War II period. Early PUD development was sometimes referred to as planned residential development (PRD). These early examples typically were single planned units of residential development consisting of variable housing or lot types on large parcels of land, together with accessory common open space and community and recreation facilities.

PUD offers the advantage of a diversity of units and use types. It also provides a way to customize development standards to the specific land under consideration, thereby minimizing environmental disturbance and alteration of existing topography, particularly in comparison with conventional forms of development. Also, because PUD development is often liberated from the rigid standards of base zoning districts, including density and dimensional requirements, development and construction costs related to infrastructure can be minimized.

NATURE OF THE PUD ORDINANCE

PUD zoning provisions—and the parameters of the process for their approval—must be added to an existing zoning ordinance in order to use the PUD development technique. In most cases, a municipality will amend the text of its zoning ordinance to establish and define the process and circumstances in which approval of a PUD development can be authorized.

Many PUD regulations first require rezoning to a PUD district. This legislative action is followed by review and approval of a specific PUD project's details by a planning commission or planning board, which is a separate, administrative action. Those drafting initial PUD regulations need to carefully assess applicable state law to determine the scope of PUD approval authority and which part(s) of the process may be determined as legislative versus administrative.

Municipalities considering implementing PUD regulations need to determine whether such regulations should be established as a floating zone, overlay district, or separate base district, or whether PUD should be authorized as a conditional use or special permit. This determination will often depend on how widespread the municipality sees its future use of the PUD tool.

BASIC ELEMENTS OF A PUD ORDINANCE

Basic elements of a PUD ordinance typically include the following:

- Purpose or intent statement
- Eligible zoning districts and permissible uses: Some PUD ordinances permit most or all of the uses in the base zoning districts; others allow greater use flexibility, including uses not typically permitted in the base districts.
- Development standards (density, dimensional, and open-space standards): Some PUD ordinances have few predetermined standards, although others have minimum parcel size standards.
- Development plan approval steps
- Concept plan, preliminary plan, and final plan, including plan form and content standards: Final plans are typically similar to final site plans and include final building envelope and site development details such as drainage, grading, and landscape planting.
- Amendments or changes to the plan

PUD zoning, because of its flexibility, is being used for a variety of purposes throughout the United States. Today, master planned communities of all types are being approved as PUD developments. Although initially used to permit residential development with an array of unit types on undeveloped sites, today, urban settings are also using PUD zoning to approve mixed-use development. Additionally, PUD zoning is being used to reclaim and redevelop brownfield sites.

STATES WITH PUD DEFINITIONS

A number of states currently provide definitions of PUD in their state statutes, including Colorado, Massachusetts, Nebraska, Nevada, and New Jersey. Most of these definitions reflect that the purpose of PUD is to permit a unified plan for development with an array of dwelling units and land uses not always corresponding to the otherwise applicable zoning standards, such as use and dimensional requirements. Some states, such as New York, specifically authorize the use of PUDs through state statutes,

PUD AND FLOATING ZONES

Some PUD development is implemented through a floating zone process, with the boundaries of the development not determined in advance on the zoning map. Because there are few predetermined development standards in a PUD ordinance, and because overall density is often negotiated for each separate project, some PUD development is attacked as a kind of unlawful contract or spot zoning device. Early challenges regarding PUD zoning not being authorized by relevant state zoning legislation, or on the basis that it conflicted with the uniformity requirements of zoning enabling legislation, have generally not prevailed. Court decisions have reinforced that the legislative purposes of zoning are advanced by this technique.

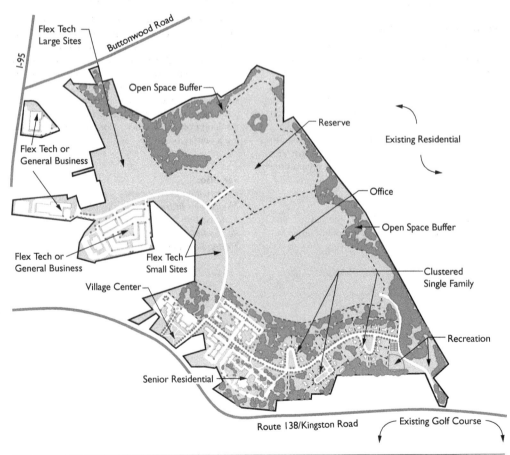

REPRESENTATIVE PLANNED UNIT DEVELOPMENT

Source: Vanasse Hangen Brustlin, Inc.

Terry S. Szold, Massachusetts Institute of Technology, Cambridge, Massachusetts

EMERGING ISSUES AND FUTURE CHALLENGES FOR PUDS

A variety of issues sometimes limit the use of PUD as a development and planning tool. Despite the fact that a development project may be given more flexibility within the density, dimensional, or use requirements of the existing base zoning district, developers sometimes perceive using PUD regulations as an arduous process. Developers often make changes to PUD site plans or concept plans over time, and may find themselves at odds with the regulating authority. To minimize conflict, ordinances need to clearly delineate how to distinguish between and act upon changes that are deemed minor in nature versus those that are more significant. A natural tension also exists between those proponents of PUD development who wish to maintain limited predetermined project standards and those who seek greater predictability about how the tool may be used and applied.

Nonetheless, because PUD is a flexible tool that can be adjusted based on emerging needs, it is likely to survive and flourish in an array of forms, and as an important tool for managing and guiding land development.

See also:

Innovations in Local Zoning Regulations

Terry S. Szold, Massachusetts Institute of Technology, Cambridge, Massachusetts

INNOVATIONS IN LOCAL ZONING REGULATIONS

Over the years, planners have become aware of the deficiencies of regulating development through traditional ("Euclidean") zoning, particularly of the single-use district variety, and stand-alone subdivision regulations. Particular shortcomings include their inflexibility, their failure to allow for mixed-use and mixed-housing development, their disconnect from growth management issues, their exclusionary nature, and their inability to address design issues. Described here are some of the more common variations from traditional zoning, including flexible zoning approaches, unified development codes, and inclusionary zoning. Also discussed here are regulations developed to support new urbanism development approaches.

FLEXIBLE ZONING

Beginning as early as the 1950s, planners began modifying conventional zoning regulations to provide relief from their rigid predetermination of which land uses and development standards were appropriate to zoned land. Known as "flexible zoning," some of these techniques seek to tie approval of unconventional uses to review of specific development plans:

Conditional-Use or Special-Use Permits

These permits provide a way to allow a land use that would not normally be allowed in a particular zoning district, but might be compatible with the district's character if controlled through additional standards and discretionary review that ensure the appropriateness of a particular development proposal at a particular location in the district.

Overlay Zoning Districts

These districts are superimposed on top of portions of one or more underlying general use-based zoning districts that allow application of additional standards

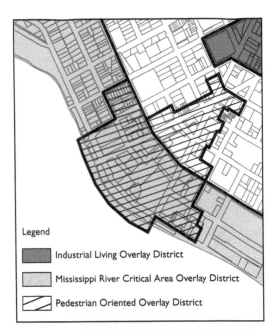

Legend

▦ Industrial Living Overlay District

▧ Mississippi River Critical Area Overlay District

▨ Pedestrian Oriented Overlay District

OVERLAY ZONE

Source: URS Corporation.

addressing a special purpose (such as historic preservation or floodplain protection).

Floating Zones

These are unmapped zoning districts whose standards are described in the text of the zoning ordinance but are applied to land only through a rezoning approval of a proposed development meeting the district's standards.

Planned Unit Development

A planned unit development (PUD) is generally a large area of land under unified control that is planned and developed as a whole through a single development operation or programmed series of development phases, in accord with a master plan. PUDs are discussed in more detail elsewhere in this section of the book.

Other alternative regulatory techniques seek to simply add flexibility to development standards or emphasize a development's environmental impacts rather than its compliance with predetermined, or "prescriptive," use and development standards.

Cluster Development or Conservation Design

Most commonly shown in the form of cluster subdivisions, these development approaches apply density limitations (as set directly, or indirectly through lot size standards) to the development site as a whole and provide flexibility in the lot size, setback, and other standards that apply to individual house lots. They provide considerable flexibility in locating building sites and associated roads and utilities, allowing them to be concentrated in parts of the site, with the remaining land used for agriculture, recreation, preservation of sensitive areas, or other open-space purposes. (See *Conservation Development* in Part 4 of this book for more information.)

Performance Standards

These standards, which were initially used to control industrial uses, try to control the external effects of development through standards directly related to its operational characteristics. General categories of industrial use are allowed subject to performance standards that set limits on externalities such as noise, odor, smoke, dust, noxious gases, vibration, heat, and glare. Performance standards may be used instead of use restrictions to control physical, traffic, and fiscal impacts of all types of development.

Performance Zoning

Performance zoning defines the character of a zoning district according to the allowable intensity of development rather than use, relying on measures such as floor area ratio and impervious surface coverage.

Point Rating Systems

These systems evaluate and rate proposed development by whether it meets prescribed criteria and standards, requiring minimum point thresholds (and sometimes additional thresholds for higher development intensities) before the development is allowed. The criteria and standards are generally performance-based, but are often expanded to address broad compatibility issues.

Incentive Zoning

With incentive zoning, developers are awarded additional development capacity in exchange for a public benefit, such as provision for low- or moderate-income housing, or amenity, such as additional open space.

Of the above techniques, PUDs probably have had the greatest impact on more recent regulatory innovations. In requiring the integration of zoning and subdivision regulations, they pointed the way toward the increased development of unified development codes. And in allowing mixed-use development and flexible design standards, PUDs accommodated early experimentation with traditional neighborhood development and other new urbanist forms of development that have emerged in recent years as an increasingly popular alternative to conventional zoning.

UNIFIED DEVELOPMENT CODES

As the purposes behind regulating development have become more complex and comprehensive, it has become more and more difficult to rely on separate zoning and subdivision regulations. They often end up with duplicative or conflicting standards and review procedures that are administered by different personnel and boards. A unified development code (UDC) consolidates development-related regulations into a single unified development code that represents a more consistent, logical, integrated, and efficient means of controlling development. The UDC can provide greater predictability for all involved in the development process, because it is organized to track that process.

UDC development standards may include the following:

- *Circulation standards* that address how vehicles and pedestrians will move onto and through the site so as to limit conflicts between them and ensure safe ingress/egress, efficient traffic flow, adequate service access (e.g., garbage pickup), and adequate emergency access to buildings (by fire trucks).
- *Utility standards* that identify the water distribution and sewage collection facilities that are required, prescribe their size and location, and provide for utility easements necessary to ensure their future maintenance.
- *Stormwater management standards* that typically call for on-site retention or detention of peak stormwater runoff from a storm of a certain frequency and duration, and provide for drainage easements to ensure maintenance of natural drainageways and stormwater pipes.

INCLUSIONARY ZONING

Communities have used incentive zoning and mandatory set-aside provisions to address shortages in the availability of housing affordable to low- and moderate-income families. These approaches either encourage or require developers to make a portion (e.g., 15 to 20 percent) of the housing units in a new development available and affordable to low- and

Stephen G. Sizemore, AICP, American Planning Association, Chicago, Illinois

moderate-income households. Where used, mandatory set-aside programs have been successful. Their use is likely to grow as housing affordability problems become more acute.

TRADITIONAL NEIGHBORHOOD DEVELOPMENT AND NEW URBANISM-SUPPORTIVE REGULATIONS

New urbanism is defined as the process of reintegrating the components of modern life—housing, workplace, shopping, and recreation—into compact, pedestrian-friendly, mixed-use neighborhoods and set in a larger metropolitan framework providing open space and transit. Several forms of new urbanist development have been enabled or required through development regulations.

Traditional Neighborhood Development (TND)

Also referred to as "neotraditional" development, TND is a style of development that works to emulate many of the features of urban neighborhoods of 50 to 100 years ago. It stresses a walkable scale, an integration of different housing types and commercial uses, and the building of true neighborhood centers with civic uses. TNDs were the first new urbanist forms to be recognized by development regulations, most commonly through enactment of a TND ordinance, a floating zone, or a special zoning district with mixed-use standards, extensive street and building design standards intended to establish pedestrian-friendly streetscapes, and its own plan review process.

Transit-Oriented Development (TOD)

TOD is essentially a compact development built around transit stops, especially rail transit. The same attributes that define a TND—higher density, walkable scale, and mix of uses—are good generators of transit usage. The concept includes neighborhood and community levels of TODs to accommodate different land-use mixes and development intensities in conjunction with different transit types. TOD regulations are generally enacted as overlay or special zoning districts with mixed-use standards and pedestrian-oriented street and building design standards that focus on a central transit stop. (See *Transit-Oriented Development* in in Part IV of this book for more information.)

Form-Based Zoning

This approach seeks to regulate building form rather than, or in addition to, land use. It establishes zones of building type based on pedestrian accessibility and the scale and character of surrounding development, but largely allows building owners to determine how the buildings will be used. Form-based codes typically contain a regulating plan that identifies which building envelope standards apply to which block frontages; building envelope standards that set basic parameters for building height, setbacks, roof design, and fenestration; and architectural and streetscape standards.

Transect-Based Code

This approach is based on a series of habitats, or "ecozones," on a continuum from wilderness to

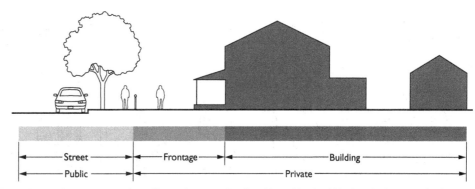

Three urban typologies comprise the public to private transition found in traditional neighborhoods: the street, the frontage, and the building. The frontage is the semi-public private area between the public street and the private building.

FRONTAGE-BASED CODE EXAMPLE

Source: Peter J. Musty, CharretteCenter Town Design, Minneapolis.

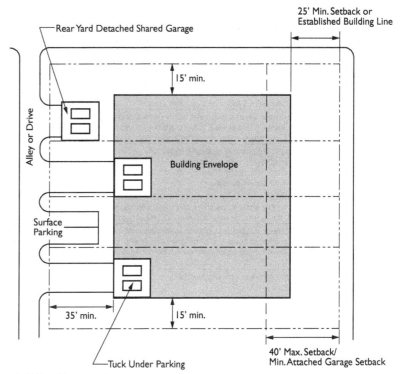

Building Placement

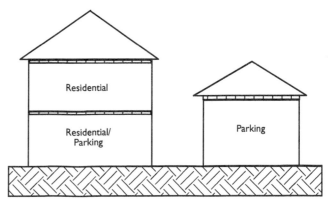

Building Use and Height

EXAMPLE OF FORM-BASED CODE, SINGLE-FAMILY ATTACHED

Source: URS Corporation.

Stephen G. Sizemore, AICP, American Planning Association, Chicago, Illinois

DIAGRAM OF THE TRANSECT SYSTEM

Reprinted with permission from Journal of the American Planning Association, copyright Summer 2002 by the American Planning Association, Suite 1600, 122 S. Michigan Avenue, Chicago, IL 60603-6107.

MAIN CHARACTERISTICS OF TRANSECT ZONES

TRANSECT ZONE	MAIN CHARACTERISTICS
T1: Rural Preserve	Open space legally protected from development in perpetuity. Includes surface water bodies, protected wetlands, public open space, and conservation easements.
T2: Rural Reserve	Open space not yet protected from development but should be. Includes open space identified by public acquisition and areas identified as transfer of development rights (TDR) sending areas. May include floodplains, steep slopes, and aquifer recharge areas.
T3: Sub-Urban	The most naturalistic, least dense, most residential habitat of a community. Buildings consist of single-family, detached houses. Office and retail buildings are permitted on a restricted basis. Buildings are a maximum of two stories. Open space is rural in character. Highways and rural roads are prohibited.
T4: General Urban	The generalized, but primarily residential, habitat of a community. Buildings consist of single-family, detached houses and rowhouses on small and medium-sized lots. Limited office buildings and lodging are permitted. Retail is confined to designated lots, typically at corners. Buildings are a maximum of three stories. Open space consists of greens and squares.
T5: Urban Center	The denser, fully mixed-use habitat of a community. Buildings consist of rowhouses, flex houses, apartment houses, and offices above shops. Office and retail buildings and lodging are permitted. Buildings are a maximum of five stories. Open space consists of squares and plazas.
T6: Urban Core	The densest residential, business, cultural, and entertainment concentration of a region. Buildings consist of rowhouses, apartment houses, office buildings, and department stores. Buildings are disposed on a wide range of lot sizes. Surface parking lots are not permitted on frontages. Open space consists of squares and plazas.

Reprinted with permission from Journal of the American Planning Association, copyright Summer 2002 by the American Planning Association, Suite 1600, 122 S. Michigan Avenue, Chicago, IL 60603-6107.

urban core. The ecozones are distinguished by varying density and character of the built environment. Development in each is regulated by design standards for building setbacks, height, and façade treatment, as well as for parking location, street design, and creation of a public realm. Regulation of uses is limited, principally to encourage mixed-use development.

SUMMARY

American communities are in the middle of an extraordinary era of regulatory reform, unmatched since the advent of zoning in the 1920s. Innovations in local development regulations will continue to evolve, and new innovations are sure to arise. What makes the newest innovations special is the context in which they are being developed—not just as variations of conventional development controls, but reflective of new and increasingly accepted concepts about how neighborhoods and communities should be shaped and function.

REFERENCE

Duany, Andrés, and Emily Talen. 2002. "Transect Planning." *Journal of the American Planning Association.* 68, no. 3:245–266. Chicago: American Planning Association.

See also:
Conservation Development
Planned Unit Development
Transit-Oriented Development

Stephen G. Sizemore, AICP, American Planning Association, Chicago, Illinois

SIGN REGULATION

Signs are a form of speech and expression and, as such, are entitled to protection under the First Amendment. This distinguishes their regulation from other land-use regulations. In the leading case on sign regulation, *Metromedia v. City of San Diego*, the U.S. Supreme Court struck down the city's sign ordinance that had permitted on-premise commercial signs but forbade all off-premise signs (i.e., billboards), with numerous exceptions. In invalidating the city's approach, the court noted that most noncommercial messages (e.g., a campaign sign or a political viewpoint painted on a placard) do not have a "premises" and thus were effectively banned by the ordinance. Such a ban gave preferential treatment to commercial messages over noncommercial messages. The court did not rule that the ordinance was invalid on the basis of its treatment of commercial speech. Rather it ruled that noncommercial speech is entitled to a higher degree of First Amendment protection than commercial speech. The solution to this problem for regulators is to include a clause in the sign ordinance stating that any noncommercial message may be substituted for the message on any commercial sign permitted by the ordinance, and that signs with noncommercial messages may be modified to contain any other noncommercial message.

Since *Metromedia*, courts have gradually moved toward affording commercial speech the same level of protection that noncommercial speech enjoys. This is largely due to the difficulty, in some instances, of differentiating between the two, and the realization that the distinction may not do anything to further the objectives of an ordinance, such as protecting and enhancing community aesthetics or ensuring traffic safety. (That said, despite the need for a regulator to make a content-based distinction to do so, courts have continued to allow local governments to distinguish between on-premise business signs and off-premise billboards.)

The safest regulatory approach for a municipality is to apply content-neutral, time, place, and manner regulations to all forms of signs. The table displays content-neutral, time, place, and manner provisions common to most sign ordinances.

Despite decades of litigation, sign law is still rife with complexities and contradictory opinions in the case law. As a result, it is common for applicants whose sign permits are denied or subject to modifications to meet ordinance standards to sue the municipality. Most claimants argue that their First Amendment rights have been violated and that the denial or restrictions will cause economic hardship. In determining whether restrictions on commercial speech are a reasonable exercise of the police power, courts have used a four-prong test established in *Central Hudson Gas and Electric v. Public Service Commission (Central Hudson Gas & Elec. Corp. v. Public Service Comm'n*, 447 U.S.557 (1980)).

The form of speech:

…at least must concern lawful activity and not be misleading. Next, we ask whether the asserted governmental interest is substantial. If both inquiries yield positive answers, we must determine whether the regulation directly advances the government interest asserted, and whether it is not more extensive than is necessary to serve that interest.

When answered in the affirmative, the first part of the *Central Hudson* test—assessing whether the speech concerns a lawful activity—determines that the speech is protected by the First Amendment. Part two of the test—whether the asserted government interest is substantial—must be established by the municipality through statements of purpose in the sign ordinance and, ideally, through local plan policies, all of which the court would consider. The third and fourth prongs, dealing with whether the regulation directly advances the governments interest and is no more extensive than necessary to serve it—is how courts measure the validity of time, place, and manner regulations.

Many local sign ordinances contain provisions that violate the content neutrality rule. Such violations commonly occur when an ordinance provides numerous content-based exemptions from the regulations for certain sign types. In its ruling invalidating the city's ordinance, the court in *North Olmsted Camber of Commerce v. City of North Olmsted*, 86 F. Supp. 2d 770 (N.D. Ohio 2000), identified at least a dozen content-based distinctions among commercial signs, including exemptions or special rules for holiday decorations, which "despite their size, aesthetic sensibility, and use of flashing or moving parts, are 'exempt for customary periods of time'" under the ordinance. And signs associated with "a charity drive or political signs advocating election of a candidate or passage or disapproval or an issue are exempt from the ordinance, while others are not." In describing how the ordinance had failed the third and fourth prongs of the *Central Hudson* test, the court said the City of North Olmsted "has provided no evidence that they would support the contention that the content-based restrictions … directly and materially contribute to safety and aesthetics" nor do they "materially advance the City's interest in safety and aesthetics."

While courts have shown high tolerance for content-neutral, time, place, and manner regulations, there are cases where ordinances have been invalidated on the basis of the municipalities' inability to demonstrate how the regulations advance the government's interest. In the mid-1990s, Long Hill Township, New Jersey's sign ordinance included a communitywide ban on the use of exposed neon lighting. The township had prosecuted three business owners who had violated the ordinance by displaying neon signs. The township's sign ordinance had read: "Commercial signs are regulated as to size, placement, lighting source, and degree of illumination to prevent the look of 'highway commercial signage.'"

The defendants sued on numerous grounds, and their convictions were overturned by the New Jersey Superior Court. In *State of New Jersey v. Calabria*, 301 N.J. Super. 96; 693 A.2d 949, the court ruling noted the ordinance language was content-neutral but the township had not provided evidence that a ban on exposed neon—while other types of illumination were readily permitted—would do anything to advance the township's desire to avoid the look of "highway commercial signage." The court concluded:

Certainly, it is for Long Hill to determine that it should be beautiful and should maintain a non-highway commercial appearance.This court is mindful of the principle that legislative enactments are presumed to be valid and the burden to prove invalidity is a heavy one. . . . However, there must be shown a factual basis for a particular regulatory scheme, namely, a reason for a total municipal-wide ban. A record cannot be devoid of evidence of how a ban advances the interest of aesthetics. This record is.

The record is devoid of evidence, facts or analysis why the mere existence of neon is offensive to that goal. There is no evidence that there are unusual problems in the use of neon that cannot otherwise be regulated as other forms of lighting, specifically, as to degree of illumination; amount of light used within a given space or size of structure; direction of the light; times when the light may be used; or number of lights used on the interior of the store.

It is apparent that the appearance of the commercial district may be enhanced by limiting forms of lighting, but it is not apparent as a matter of experience—or of fact—that a complete elimination of one form of lighting has any impact on the undesirable "highway" look of the town. There is no evidence that neon is, in and of itself, inconsistent with careful design or tasteful presentation of advertisements, the general goal of aesthetic restrictions [citations omitted].

PRIOR RESTRAINT

Prior restraint is a separate constitutional issue that arises in sign regulation. Prior restraint is a requirement for discretionary government approval based

TIME, PLACE, OR MANNER REGULATIONS

SIGN CHARACTERISTIC	PERMISSIBLE REGULATIONS
Dimensions	Maximum size, height, degree of projection, measurement of sign area, and number per lot or building
Type	Freestanding, monument, pole, wall, projecting, portable, temporary, electronic reader boards, and so on
Location	Setbacks from street, sidewalk, placement on buildings, prohibited areas, rules for corner lots
Lighting and Illumination	Allowing or prohibiting internal lighting, external lighting, flashing signs, neon, electronic reader by animation or neon
Sign materials/colors	Allowing or prohibiting cabinet signs, wood signs, metals, colors, gold leaf

Marya Morris, AICP, American Planning Association, Chicago, Illinois

LEADING CASES IN SIGN REGULATION

Metromedia, Inc. v. City of San Diego, 453 U.S. 490 (1981)

Key outcomes: Seven justices of the Supreme Court agreed that San Diego's interest in avoiding visual clutter was sufficient to justify a complete prohibition of commercial off-premises signs. Seven members of the court also agreed that San Diego could prohibit "commercial" billboards but not "noncommercial" billboards, a distinction that has clouded the issue of when it is appropriate or inappropriate for a sign ordinance to distinguish between the two types of messages. Several decades later, some courts still allow the distinction, while others have ruled that there can be no such distinction.

Members of the City Council v. Taxpayers for Vincent, 466 U.S. 789 (1984)

Key outcome: The U.S. Supreme Court upheld a ban on posting signs on public property.

City of Ladue v. Gilleo, 512 U.S. 43 (1994)

Key outcome: The Supreme Court ruled unanimously that an ordinance banning all residential signs, except for those categories of signs falling within 10 exemptions, violated homeowners' First Amendment rights because it precluded any opportunity for them to display political, religious, or personal messages on their own property.

Central Hudson Gas & Elec. Corp. v. Public Service Comm'n, 447 U.S.557 (1980)

Key outcome: The Supreme Court offered a four-part test to determine when government regulation of commercial speech was valid. (1) The court must ask whether the commercial speech at issue concerned "lawful activity" and was not "misleading." If so, it was protected by the First Amendment. (2) The court must ask if the government interest served by the regulation was substantial. (3) If the answer to the first two questions was yes, then the court "must determine (3) whether the regulation directly advances the governmental interest asserted, and (4) whether it is not more extensive than necessary to serve that interest" (447 U.S. at 566).

North Olmsted Chamber of Commerce v. City of North Olmsted, 86 F.Supp.2d 755, (N.D. Ohio 2000)

Key outcome: A federal trial court ruled that a sign ordinance that classifies signs by their use (e.g., "identification sign," "information sign," etc.) is content-based and therefore is unconstitutional.

United States v. O'Brien, 391 U.S. 367 (1968)

Key outcome: The U.S. Supreme Court created a four-part test to balance the government's interest in regulating the noncommunicative aspect of speech against any incidental restriction on freedom of expression. The *O'Brien* test permits a government regulation that incidentally restricts speech if: (1) such regulation is within the constitutional power of government; (2) it furthers an important or substantial government interest; (3) the government interest is unrelated to the suppression of free expression; and (4) the incidental restriction goes no further than what is essential to the furtherance of that interest.

on subjective judgments prior to "speaking." The sign industry and business groups have long argued that a requirement to receive a permit prior to displaying a sign that contains protected speech is a prior restraint. To avoid prior restraint problems in sign cases, municipalities must: "Provide clear standards to guide the discretion of the official; the local official must decide on the permit within a specific and brief period, during which the status quo must be preserved; and the regulation must state and express and prompt judicial review procedure in the case of a denial" (Stroud 2001).

REFERENCE

Stroud, Nancy. 2001. "Some concluding thoughts on the effect of the First Amendment in Land Use Law." In *Protection Free Speech and Expression: The First Amendment and Land Use Law*. Daniel R. Mandelker and Rebecca L. Rubin. Eds., Chicago: American Bar Association, Section of State and Local Government Law.

See also:
Federal Legislation

Marya Morris, AICP, American Planning Association, Chicago, Illinois

GROWTH MANAGEMENT

ADEQUATE PUBLIC FACILITIES AND CONCURRENCY MANAGEMENT

An adequate public facilities or concurrency management ordinance ties or conditions the approval of developments to the availability and adequacy of public facilities. The purpose is to ensure that the local government's public facility or system of facilities has sufficient available capacity to serve development at a predetermined service level. A development is determined to be in compliance with the ordinance if its impacts do not exceed the capability of public facilities to accommodate those impacts at the specified service level. If the proposed development cannot be supported by the existing system at the required service level, the developer must either install or pay for the required infrastructure improvements or postpone part or all of the development until the local government provides the needed public facilities. Alternatively, the local government can elect to move up the priorities of constructing new or expanded facilities.

CONCURRENCY

The term concurrency derives from Florida, whose growth management act has incorporated such a standard and requires that needed facilities be available concurrent with development. The Florida Department of Community Affairs has adopted an administrative rule regarding concurrency that is part of a longer rule on criteria for state review of local comprehensive plans. The rule requires each local government to adopt objectives, policies, and service-level standards for a concurrency management system as a component of its comprehensive plan. It identifies the categories and facilities that are subject to the concurrency rule. The rule also requires a system for monitoring and ensuring adherence to the adopted service-level standards, the schedule of capital improvements, and the availability of public facilities capacity.

In addition, the rule provides that the local government must adopt land development regulations that implement the concurrency management system. The rule states that, under the concurrency management system, the latest point in the application process for determining concurrency is prior to the approval of an application for a development order or permit that contains a specific plan for development. The concurrency rule requires the adoption of service-level standards for roads, sanitary sewer, solid waste, drainage, potable water, parks and recreation, and, if applicable, mass transit. Local governments may also impose concurrency standards for public schools, but, in order to do so, the concurrency system must be countywide in nature (rather than involving individual jurisdictions), must enter into interlocal agreements, and must adopt public school facilities elements to their comprehensive plans.

Washington State also requires concurrency as part of its growth management act, but only for transportation. Once a local government has adopted a plan, it must adopt and enforce ordinances that prohibit development approval if the development causes the level of services on a locally owned (not state-owned) transportation facility to decline below the standards adopted in the transportation element of the comprehensive plan, unless transportation improvements or strategies to accommodate the impacts of development are made concurrent with the development. The strategies can be noninfrastructure-related activities, such as increased public transportation service, ride-sharing, and demand management. Under the statute, "concurrent with the development" is defined as meaning that "the improvements or strategies are in place at the time of development, or that a financial commitment is in place to complete the improvements or strategies within six years," which is also the time span of the required capital facilities element under the growth management act. The state issues administrative rules interpreting the concurrency requirements, but, unlike Florida, they are guidelines rather than directives.

Several other states have concurrency or adequate public facilities requirements. Other local governments, including those in California and Colorado, have adopted such requirements absent specific state authorization. Maryland and New Hampshire both authorize, but do not require, adequate public facilities ordinances. In contrast to Florida and Washington, neither state issues administrative rules describing minimum elements of concurrency.

ADEQUATE PUBLIC FACILITIES

Adequate public facilities ordinances are in one sense self-administering. As noted, a community adopts a service-level standard for each type of facility, and development applications are denied if the service demands of a project cannot be accommodated at the adopted service level by existing or planned facilities. In practice, however, adequate public facilities systems are not nearly as simple as they might seem. If planned facilities are included in the capacity analysis, the timing of completion of those facilities must be related to the buildout of the project. On the demand side, development approvals must be tracked to estimate the already committed capacity, so that the local government does not allocate capacity twice. Nonetheless, these are technical tasks, and, once established, can be administered with periodic reviews.

POTENTIAL PITFALLS

Concurrency and adequate public facilities systems pose the problem of building planned facilities in a timely fashion. In order to make such systems work, planned facilities must be constructed so that additional capacity is available when the need arises. If the local government is responsible for the facility expansion, such as construction of a new wastewater treatment plant, but fails to construct it as planned, then the goal of concurrency for that particular public service will not be satisfied, and service shortfalls will be experienced.

Another difficult problem is the nature of public services that are open systems, such as highways. Interstate highway systems and state highways that cross numerous local government boundaries pose the problem of open public facility systems. One local government cannot adopt a relaxed service level for an arterial road segment that runs through another jurisdiction with tougher requirements. Local governments are not able to internalize traffic impacts in their communities because they cannot control access to roads that cross jurisdictional boundaries. Thus, local governments cannot control traffic congestion through the development review process as successfully as they can control adequacy of water and sewer service, for example, which involve closed systems.

Still another potential drawback is that concurrency or adequate public facility ordinances can lead to urban sprawl. If a suburban community has no more sewage treatment capacity, but an exurban community does, development denied in the suburban community may go to the exurban community.

PROGRAM ELEMENTS

To establish an adequate public facilities or concurrency management program, the following components are needed:

- A current comprehensive plan with transportation and public facilities elements for water supply, treatment, and distribution; wastewater treatment and sanitary sewerage; and solid waste, roads, and other public facilities, as necessary
- A capital improvement program (CIP) and capital budget for the first year of the CIP, both of which are updated annually
- Service-level standards for each facility subject to the adequate public facility requirements
- An evaluation of the public facilities for which service-level standards have been set to determine whether or not they meet them and by what degree
- An adequate public facilities ordinance that contains:
  - Procedures and assignment of responsibility regarding the issuance of development permits consistent with the standards in the ordinance
  - A list of the types and categories of development and land use that are exempt from the adequate public facilities ordinance because they have no impact on facilities (e.g., storage sheds)
  - Steps for ensuring adherence to service-level standards that are stated in the ordinance and for monitoring the capacity of existing public facilities so that it can be determined at any point how much of that capacity is being used, or has otherwise been reserved
  - A process for allocating facility capacity to determine whether a proposed development can be

Stuart Meck, FAICP, American Planning Association, Chicago, Illinois; Arthur C. Nelson, Ph.D. FAICP, Virginia Polytechnic Institute and State University, Alexandria, Virginia

accommodated within the existing and proposed public facilities

- A means for reserving public facility capacity for a proposed development for a maximum period of time
- Procedures for administrative appeals of determinations on development permits
- Mechanisms to ensure that a developer or the public sector will pay for public facilities necessary to support development consistent with the level-of-service standards, to include developer agreements, impact fees, special assessments, and general obligation or revenue bonds

GUIDELINES

Concurrency and adequate public facilities ordinances need to be guided by several considerations:

- *Project future development needs accurately.* "Projections" and "accuracy" may seem to be mutually exclusive terms but some reasonable effort must be made to anticipate the nature and level of development demand. Far too many communities make no projections, and many of those that do are not refined enough to anticipate such basic land-use needs as office, retail, industry, and single- and multifamily development.
- *Be serious about a capital improvement program.* CIP must be designed to meet long-term development needs and must be followed to ensure the facilities are actually provided in a timely manner.
- *Be flexible.* If a development proposal might result in some development occurring in advance of new or expanded facilities that are planned based on a CIP, it may be better to allow it than to have it displaced. The community might be better off incurring some short-term congestion or inconveniences in exchange for achieving development patterns that maximize the use of facilities based on the community's overall vision.
- *Be proactive.* For many communities, facility needs outpace the ability to pay for them. A variety of funding approaches should be used to help finance facilities such as improvement districts, impact fees, user fees, latecomer fees (where a developer may build some facilities, such as an oversized sewer line, and be reimbursed by the local government or from future development using the same facilities), and leveraging local funds for additional state and federal resources, where they are available.

See also:
Capital Improvement Plans
Comprehensive Plans

Stuart Meck, FAICP, American Planning Association, Chicago, Illinois; Arthur C. Nelson, Ph.D. FAICP, Virginia Polytechnic Institute and State University, Alexandria, Virginia

URBAN GROWTH AREAS

An urban growth area (UGA) is an area delineated in a comprehensive plan within which urban development is encouraged and outside of which urban development is discouraged. UGAs are a regional land-use planning tool used to influence the development pattern within a region and the communities within it. They are devices to achieve or ensure urban containment by promoting planned, compact, and orderly development patterns. These are patterns that can be efficiently served by public services and that preserve open space, agricultural land, and environmentally sensitive areas that may not be suitable for development.

The important detail of an urban growth area is that land-use regulations applied to land within it must allow existing or proposed land uses at densities and intensities sufficient to permit urban growth that is projected for a specified period. In addition, services and facilities adequate to support that urban growth must either exist or be planned. If either of these conditions is not met, then compact, contiguous development of the type contemplated within the UGA will not occur, or will be substantially hindered.

A subcategory of the urban growth area is the urban service area. This is an area within which urban services will be provided and outside of which such services will not be extended. Urban service areas are generally located within urban growth areas. They can be derived by comparing the various maps of service areas, such as those for sewer, water, and transit, and taking into account the desired level of service and available funding for system expansion. By contrast, urban growth areas have a broader purpose than service provision. The primary issue is that a sufficient quantity of land be available within the specified boundaries to accommodate long-range population and economic growth, and at appropriate densities, intensities, and uses.

STATES WITH URBAN GROWTH AREA LAWS

Several states either require or authorize urban growth area planning in various ways.

Washington State

In Washington, all counties that are required or choose to plan under the state growth management must designate urban growth areas within the county comprehensive plan. Municipalities in such counties must include the county-designated UGA in their comprehensives plans as well.

Maine

Maine requires local comprehensive plans to identify both growth areas, those areas suitable for orderly residential, commercial, and industrial development forecast over a 10-year period; and rural areas, areas where protection is to be provided for agricultural, forest, open space, and scenic lands.

Maryland

A "smart growth" act passed here in 1997 called for directing new development in "priority funding areas" that are automatically designated in the statute or that a county may designate on its own initiative. County-designated areas must meet specified use, water and sewer service, and residential criteria. The statute requires the state to give priority in funding projects with state money in those growth areas as well as in existing municipalities (which the statute designates as priority funding areas) and industrial areas. Here the intention to use the state power of investment to channel growth into areas that are suited for growth and limit development in rural areas by not extending sewers or making transportation improvements that would spur growth.

Tennessee

A 1998 law intended to create a comprehensive growth policy for the state requires counties, with the participation of municipalities and other government and private entities, to create a growth plan for the county. The growth plan must include urban growth areas, which form an envelope for municipal annexation; planned growth areas, which are like UGAs but are outside of UGAs and in unincorporated areas; and rural areas, which are intended to be used for the next 20 years for agriculture, forestry, wildlife preservation, recreation, and other low-density uses.

Oregon

The best-known system incorporating UGAs is Oregon's statewide system, which has been in effect since 1973. In Oregon, a combination of state statutes and administrative rules require all cities in the state to establish UGAs to separate urbanizable land from rural land for a 20-year planning period. Under state housing goals, the urban growth area boundaries are drawn and amended based on a series of factors in the state's adopted planning goals that relate to urbanization. Local governments must inventory buildable lands—urban and urbanizable lands that are suitable, available, and necessary for residential use. Local plans are to encourage the availability of adequate numbers of needed housing units at price ranges and rent levels that are commensurate with financial capabilities of Oregon households.

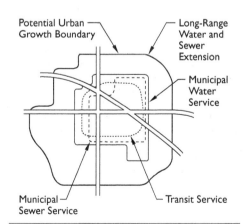

URBAN SERVICE AREA
Source: Easley 1992.

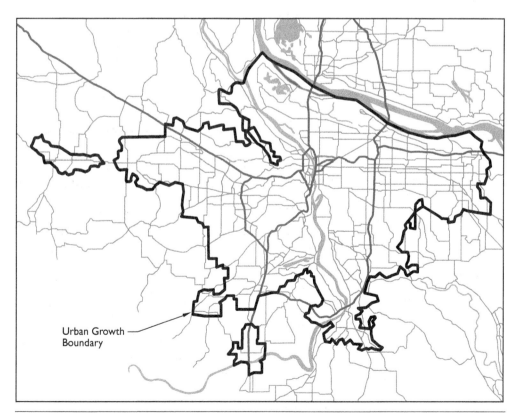

GROWTH BOUNDARY MAP, PORTLAND, OREGON
Source: Portland Metro 2002.

Gerrit J. Knaap, Ph.D., National Center for Smart Growth Research and Education, University of Maryland, College Park, Maryland; Stuart Meck, FAICP, American Planning Association, Chicago, Illinois

In some places in the United States, UGAs have been established without the benefit of a statewide framework. These include Boulder, Colorado; Sacramento, California; Larimer County, Colorado; and Lexington-Fayette County, Kentucky.

DELINEATING URBAN GROWTH BOUNDARIES

In order to delineate urban growth areas, the following steps should be followed.

1. *Develop a population and employment forecast for the urban area or region.* The process of delineating urban growth area boundaries begins by developing a population and employment forecast for the entire urban area. At a minimum, population forecasts must be disaggregated by household size, and employment forecasts must be disaggregated into commercial and industrial sectors. The regional planning agency can develop the forecasts itself or may obtain them from state agencies or national forecasting firms. In preparing or obtaining the forecasts, the agency should ensure that they are consistent with larger supraregional economic and demographic forecasts.

2. *Develop regional density targets or estimates and public service standards.* The regional urban growth boundary must be based on carefully chosen targets or estimates for residential and employment densities and standards for public service. Regional residential density targets or estimates (measured in terms of dwelling units per acre), for example, must be based on housing plans or assumptions about housing development that provide for a range of housing alternatives. Commercial and industrial employment density targets (measured in terms of the number of employees per acre) must reflect carefully considered plans for regional economic development. Public service standards may be expressed through such measures as acres of parks and open space per capita, minimum sizes for or acreage per capita of schools, fire and police stations and health care facilities, and miles of road network per acre. Alternately, they may also be expressed as a percentage of total urban land.

3. *Estimate residential and nonresidential land required to accommodate future urban growth.* This is done by conducting a series of calculations to show how land requirements can be determined using regional population and employment density targets and infrastructure service standards. These calculations use generalized standards to show how the formulas work; thus, to determine the needs in your community, use standards defined by your community's existing conditions and projected needs. The following is one example of such calculations, for residential land.

Assume that, over a period of 20 years, the population of a hypothetical region is projected to rise from 200,000 to 225,000 persons, an increase of 25,000, or 12.5 percent. Projected occupancy is 2.5 persons per dwelling unit on the average for the period. If the density target or minimum for the urban growth area in the regional comprehensive plan is set at six dwelling units per net acre, the land for residential purposes that would need to be set aside would be calculated as follows:

EXPANDING THE URBAN GROWTH AREA AS AN INVENTORY PROBLEM

Related to the issue of projecting land-use needs for urban growth areas is the question of how often to revisit the size of the growth area.

Time-Driven Expansion

One approach is to revisit the area at specified periods, say every five years, in order to maintain a supply of buildable land sufficient to accommodate development needs for a certain time span, such as 20 years, and to add a "market factor," or additional percentage on top of the projections to account for the uncertainty of forecasting. The problem with this approach is that it does not take into account the "lumpy" nature of land-use planning and the large, indivisible investments of public infrastructure, as well as the swings in the local land development market. Thus it can lead to either greatly undersizing the urban growth area, when the economy is brisk, or oversizing it and increasing the prospect that growth will spread out, unless steps are taken to make it more compact, such as establishing minimum densities or land-use intensities (Knaap and Hopkins 2001).

Event-Driven Expansion

An alternative method of monitoring and reevaluating the extent of urban growth areas is to treat the decision as an inventory problem, in which the quantity of land is held for some future demand. In contrast to the time-drive system, a UGA in an event-driven system of inventory control is expanded not at predetermined times but when the number of buildable acres inside the growth boundary reaches a predetermined trigger level. If urban growth occurs at the same constant rate, and similar rules are followed regarding the size of UGA expansions, then the pattern of inventory over time would be the same in time-driven and event-driven systems. If the rate of urban growth varies, however, the intervals between and the sizes of UGA expansion will vary as well (Knaap and Hopkins 2001).

Components of Growth Area Expansion "Trigger"

The reorder trigger for expanding the urban growth area should contain three components:

1. *Lead-time inventory,* which is needed to accommodate expected growth between the decision to expand the UGA and the time additional land is ready to develop. If there is no lead time between the placement of a new order for land and the replenishment of the land inventory (assuming the buildable acres become immediately available after the decision to expand the UGA), then the lead-time inventory equals zero. If buildable acres cannot be increased instantaneously, and there is no uncertainty over the rate of urban growth, then the lead-time inventory equals the number of acres needed to accommodate demand over the period between

the decision to expand the UGS and the time land is ready for development (by, for example, installing public infrastructure)

2. *Safety-stock inventory,* which is needed in case growth is faster than expected after the decision to expand but before additional land is reading. If the rate of urban growth is not certain, but variable, then the inventory of buildable acres may be depleted faster than expected. If the rate of urban growth varies widely or the reorder lead time is long (for example, the time it takes to study and debate the expansion), a large safety stock is needed; if the growth rate varies narrowly or the lead time is short, only a small safety stock is needed. The optimal safety stock therefore depends on: (a) the variation in the urban growth rate around its expected value; (b) the lead time between the decision to expand the UGA and the time land is read for development; and (c) the acceptable level of risk of inventory exhaustion.

3. *Market-factor inventory,* which is needed to assure consumer choice and prevent monopoly pricing by owners of the few remaining parcels of buildable but undeveloped land. Again, this will be a judgment about which level is appropriate (Knaap and Hopkins 2001).

Cost of Expansion

In addition to the components of the reorder trigger level, another factor to consider is the total cost of the expansion, which comprises the sum of the order costs (i.e., expansion costs per unit) and the costs of holding inventory. In a standard inventory problem, order costs fall with the size of the order because quantity discounts are possible when making large orders. Holding costs rise with order size because the average inventory rises with the order size, holding the reorder level constant. Thus, under typical assumptions, total costs fall, then rise with the cost of the order (Knaap and Hopkins 2001).

For example, assume a sewage treatment plant treats 5 million gallons per day, the planned gross density of a development (including all residential and nonresidential land uses) is 1 acre per household, and a typical household and its multipliers generate 400 gallons of wastewater per day. In this case, the urban service area for the plant and, thus, the urban growth area should expand by 12,500 acres when a new sewage treatment plant is built (5,000,000 ÷ 400) ÷ 1. Here, the size of the UGA expansion reflects the size of the new sewage treatment plant. The order cost is the net present value of capital costs plus operating costs over the life of the plant. The order costs per unit of capacity falls with plant size (order size) because of economies of scale in construction and operation. The holding costs increase with plant size because of the greater time during which the plant will be underutilized until buildout of its service area (Knaap and Hopkins 2001).

Gerrit J. Knaap, Ph.D., National Center for Smart Growth Research and Education, University of Maryland, College Park, Maryland; Stuart Meck, FAICP, American Planning Association, Chicago, Illinois

(25,000 persons projected population growth) ÷
(2.5 persons per dwelling unit) ÷
(6 dwelling units per net acre) =
1,667 net residential acres

As illustrated in the equation, residential land requirements depend critically on the target or minimum for residential density. If the net density target were increased to 10 units per net acre, the amount of residential land necessary for the 20-year period would drop to 1,000 acres, a reduction of about 40 percent.

4. *Identify potential for infill and redevelopment within existing urbanized areas.* Encouraging infill and redevelopment is critical for successful urban containment planning. Identifying potential for infill and redevelopment within existing urbanized areas requires a detailed analysis of land use and land-use potential within each jurisdiction in the region. At a minimum, such analysis requires the identification of vacant developable land. The potential of such land can be determined by examining the proposed use of the land in local comprehensive plans. Vacant land zoned for residential use, for example, should be considered as potential for accommodating future residential growth. The assessment of redevelopment potential requires a similar but more difficult process. Specifically, it requires identifying land that is currently in one use but planned for a more intensive use. Land currently in single-family use but zoned for multiple-family use, for example, should also be considered as suitable for accommodating future residential growth.

5. *Identify environmentally sensitive and undevelopable land both inside and outside existing urbanized areas.* Before demarcating areas for future urban growth, the regional planning agency must identify those areas that should not be designated for urban use or intensive development. These lands include environmentally sensitive areas, such as wetlands, threatened and endangered species habitats, and shorelands; and resource areas, such as prime agricultural land. These also include areas that are difficult to develop due to physical attributes, such as steep slope or natural hazards (e.g., potential for landslides or flooding). These areas, however, may be used to satisfy park and open-space requirements.

6. *Identify areas for future urban growth.* Once the technical tasks of estimating land necessary to accommodate future urban growth and identifying areas where growth can be accommodated are done, the potentially difficult task of selecting areas for future urban growth begins. Three outcomes are possible:

- In the unlikely event that estimated land requirements equal land available for development and redevelopment within existing urban areas, and that planned densities in local comprehensive plans meet regional density targets or minimums, the urban growth area boundary can simply be drawn around the area contained in the local comprehensive plans.
- If land available for development or redevelopment exceeds estimated land requirements, local governments can designate less land for urban use or experience idle land use within the planning period.
- In the most likely event that estimated land requirements exceed land available for development or redevelopment, growth will have to be accommodated by increasing planned densities or intensities, by expanding the area of urban development, or by some combination of both.

CAVEATS

UGAs are controversial because of their potential for land-price inflation, which occurs when demand for urban land outstrips available supply, and the prospect that owners of land within the UGA will benefit from the financial windfall of designation.

Once they are established, the local government must monitor the supply of land through a land market monitoring system. In addition, the local government must periodically review—at least on a five-year basis—the UGA and consider amendments to the UGA. Or the local government must make modifications to land-use designations that control use, density, and intensity, to ensure there is an adequate supply of buildable land, so that there is always sufficient number of acres for the number of years of land inventory for the time horizon of the UGA.

Finally, municipal government actions must occur in the context of the county or region in which the municipality is located, and take into account changes in the regional job, housing, and real estate markets. Absent such a framework, a municipality initiating UGAs on its own will result in a situation where growth is simply shifted away from one part of one community in the urban area to another community in the area, or where growth simply bypasses the enacting municipality and jumps outward to the next tier of vacant, but developable land.

REFERENCES

Easley, Gail. 1992. *Staying Inside the Lines: Urban Growth Boundaries*. Planning Advisory Service Report No. 440. Chicago: American Planning Association.

Knaap, Gerrit J., and Lewis D. Hopkins. Summer 2001. "The Inventory Approach to Urban Growth Boundaries." *Journal of the American Planning Association*. 67, no. 3:314–326.

See also:
Comprehensive Plans
Critical and Sensitive Areas Plans
Farmland Preservation
Population Projections
Regional Plans
Regions

Gerrit J. Knaap, Ph.D., National Center for Smart Growth Research and Education, University of Maryland, College Park, Maryland; Stuart Meck, FAICP, American Planning Association, Chicago, Illinois

DEVELOPMENT IMPACT FEES

A development impact fee is a one-time fee or charge on new development projects imposed by local governments to cover capital expenditures by the governmental unit on the infrastructure required to serve the new development. Impact fee ordinances define what kinds of capital expenditures may be supported by impact fees, procedures, and standards for assessing and collecting the fee, either in money or in kind (for example, provision of the facility by the developer), and other necessary parameters. Local governments may enact such ordinances as a consequence of state enabling legislation or by virtue of home rule powers.

Impact fees are intended to pay for the provision of new facilities and the expansion of existing facilities. They are not for the maintenance of existing facilities used wholly by existing development, nor are they intended to cover operating expenses. Once the development project has paid for the additional facilities it requires, the regular assessment of taxes on all development, old and new, should fund the ongoing operation of all public facilities.

An impact fee provision is not the same as a requirement in a subdivision or site plan ordinance that a developer will provide certain facilities, such as streets, sidewalks, and utilities, within the development project itself. Impact fees are to be expended on capital facilities that are generally not on the premises of the development project but that are necessitated by it. These may include roads, schools, parks and recreation facilities, and utilities. The need for a new facility may be created by more than one development project, in which case, each project should pay a fee that covers its share of the facility.

PROS AND CONS OF IMPACT FEES

As the name suggests, the purpose of an impact fee is to require new development to pay for the impact it makes upon the infrastructure of the local government, rather than have the cost be paid by the taxpayers in general.

In economics, "externalities" are costs or benefits that are not accrued directly to the parties involved. Theoretically, decisions made in a free market lead to the most efficient use of resources, because costs and benefits balance when every market participant is trying to minimize costs and maximize benefits. However, the existence of externalities means that some decisions do not result in the most efficient outcome, because those receiving the benefits are not bearing all the costs of their decision. "Internalizing" externalities—making a decision maker bear the full cost of his or her decision—should therefore result in a more efficient use of resources. If there is no impact fee, the local government and its taxpayers pay part of the costs created by a new development: the additional infrastructure needed to serve the new development.

On the other hand, impact fees may be set disproportionately high with the intent of excluding all development or some classes of development. For example, the impact fee could make affordable housing development unprofitable, and thus not built, while luxury developments are still profitable. Or the

fee may be set higher than the infrastructure capital costs because the existing officials and residents see it as a way to keep taxes low by passing on government expenses (in excess of the impact of new development) to the new residents and businesses who do not yet have a voice in the community. When this occurs, the impact fee is generating surplus revenue that is not directly connected to the impact of the development, and thus the entire set of relationships on which the impact fee is built may be called into question. If the impact fee raises the cost of the development above the level of similar developments in the neighboring communities, thus making the project noncompetitive, then the developer may consider not undertaking the project.

ESSENTIAL ELEMENTS OF IMPACT FEE PROGRAMS

The structure of impact fee programs can vary, depending on the state or the needs of the local government, but the following are considered to be the essential elements:

- There must be enabling legislation for impact fees, although in some states municipalities may be able to enact impact fees on the basis of home rule powers.
- There must be a local comprehensive plan from which land-use assumptions, including land-use density and intensity, as well as use, can be established in order to project facilities' needs.
- There must be a capital budget and a multiyear capital improvements program, so that the local government makes an assessment of its existing capital facilities, their capacity, planned or projected demand from new development, and planned capital facilities to meet that demand. Monies from the impact fees go toward the construction of capital facilities.
- The imposition of a fee must be based on a "rational nexus" that must exist between the regulatory fee and the activity being regulated. Among the states, the nature of the linkage differs, but generally the impact fee must meet a three-part constitutional test:
  - The need for new facilities must be created by new development.
  - The amount of fee charged must not exceed a proportionate share of the cost to serve new development.
  - All fee revenues must be spent within a reasonable period of time and in proximity to the fee-paying development.
  Thus, prior to enacting an impact fee ordinance, a study must be carried out to document the rational nexus relationship and establish the per-dwelling-unit or per-square-foot charge, in the case of nonresidential development. This study must be updated periodically, as capital facilities and other costs change and planned projects are built.
- A fee cannot be imposed to address existing deficiencies except where they are exacerbated by new development.

- Funds received under such a program must be segregated from the general fund of the local government and used solely for the purposes for which the fee is established.
- The fees collected must be encumbered or expended within a reasonable time frame, typically not to exceed five years, to ensure that needed improvements are implemented.
- The fee assessed cannot exceed the cost of the improvements, and credits must be given for outside funding sources (such as federal and state grants, and developer-initiated improvements for impacts related to new development) and local tax payments, which fund capital improvements, for example.
- The fee cannot be used to cover normal operation and maintenance or personnel costs, but must be used for capital improvements or, under some linkage programs, for affordable housing, job training, or child care—assuming a nexus can be demonstrated.
- The impact fee ordinance must permit refunds for development that are not constructed, since no impact will have manifested. Similarly, if the local government fails to construct the planned capital project in a reasonable period of time, the impact fee ordinance should also provide a refund to those who paid for the permit, such as a homeowner.
- Impact fee payments are typically required as a condition of approval of the development, either at the time the building or occupancy permit is issued.

Some impact fee programs contain waivers or exemptions. Affordable housing projects are often exempted from impact fee requirements. In addition, impact fees are not necessary for all types of development. Storage sheds or other accessory dwelling units would be an example of a development that would not require a fee.

Certain jurisdictions face initial problems in gaining developer and builder acceptance of impact fees. Problems have also occasionally arisen from technical difficulties associated with the newness of the technique, such as determining demand levels, calculating construction costs and accurate fee levels, and implementing proper accounting methods.

Because the structure of impact fees is determined in advance of development, they provide predictability for the public and private sectors and general acceptability due to the linkage with the needs of new development. For the private sector, they eliminate the negotiation over paying the costs of public improvements that often accompanies local government decisions to approve a development. Their limitations include that: they do not fund operating costs; they depend on construction cycles to generate revenues; and, because the fees are usually not a stable revenue source required by the bond market, they do not lend them to bonding capability.

See also:
Capital Improvement Plans
Comprehensive Plans
State Enabling Legislation

James Duncan, FAICP, Duncan Associates, Austin, Texas; Stuart Meck, FAICP, American Planning Association, Chicago, Illinois; Arthur C. Nelson, Ph.D. FAICP, Virginia Polytechnic Institute and State University, Alexandria, Virginia

TRANSFER AND PURCHASE OF DEVELOPMENT RIGHTS

Transfer of development rights (TDR) is the yielding of some or all of the right to develop or use a parcel of land in exchange for a right to develop or use another parcel of land, or another portion of the same parcel of land, more intensively. In TDR programs, a local or regional government that wishes to preserve land in an undeveloped or less-developed state may do so without payment of cash compensation to the owner of the land, if the governmental agency is willing to accept higher densities or more intensive uses elsewhere. Purchase of development rights (PDR) allows owners of land meeting certain criteria to sell the right to develop their property. A conservation easement is then placed on the land, limiting its future use to agriculture or open space and prohibiting further development.

TRANSFER OF DEVELOPMENT RIGHTS PROGRAMS

TDR programs are typically instituted to preserve open space or ecologically sensitive areas, such as wetlands, agricultural or forest uses, or historic buildings or landmarks. In each case, the purpose is to protect the underlying resource while compensating the owner of the resource for its use. Detaching development rights from agricultural land means that such land cannot be developed or could only be developed at a very low intensity. When TDR is applied to historic buildings located in high-value areas, those buildings are preserved, because development pressure that would otherwise result in a building's demolition and replacement is alleviated.

TDR Administration

There are two primary ways that TDR can be administered. The first involves overlay districts, where specific districts are zoned as sending or receiving parcels. A sending district provides development rights that are transferred to a receiving district. The second involves identifying sending and receiving districts in the text of the zoning ordinance itself, rather than through a separate amendment of the zoning ordinance on a case-by-case basis.

Process of Transferring Rights

There must be a process by which a local government official, such as a zoning administrator, determines the specific number of development rights for a sending parcel in terms of dwelling units per net acre or square feet of nonresidential floor area (for commercial and industrial parcels) and issues a certificate to the transferor. Development rights are legally severed from the sending parcel through instruments of transfer and attached to the receiving parcel. Once the transaction is recorded, the owner of the receiving parcel can use the development rights. It is important that the use of the development rights in receiving areas be planned carefully. The receiving area must have adequate public facilities and services to accommodate the increased development the TDRs bring.

In some cases, receiving districts may not be necessary. The local government or a nonprofit organization may purchase the development rights, hold them, and offer them for sale at a later date. Alternately, the development rights could be permanently retired. Often, local governments establish a TDR bank, which buys and receives donations of development rights, holds them, and then may sell or convey them. The bank may be funded by tax or fee revenue or by donations with local legislative approval, and it is expected to use the revenue from the sale of development rights to fund future purchases.

PURCHASE OF DEVELOPMENT RIGHTS

When local governments or nonprofit organizations purchase development rights, with or without a TDR program, the land stays in private ownership. The price may be less than the fee-simple price of the land, and the purchaser may be relieved of the responsibilities of maintenance, depending on the nature of the restriction. (See Open-Space Preservation Techniques for more information on fee-simple).

The restriction on the use of property from which the development rights have been purchased takes the form of a conservation easement or similar legal instrument. A conservation easement is an example of a negative easement, whereby the owner of the burdened estate is bound not to engage in development activities that he or she would otherwise have a right to perform. A conservation easement can prohibit all future development, or it can specify particular development activities that are prohibited. Because the conservation easement decreases the monetary value of the land it affects, property taxes will be lower, and it is likely that capital gains resulting from the sale of the restricted land also will be lower.

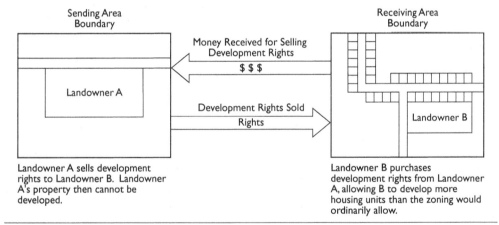

TRANSFER OF DEVELOPMENT RIGHTS

Source: Adapted from Dane County, Wisconsin, Planning and Development Department 1998.

See also:

Farmland Preservation
Innovations in Local Zoning Regulations
Open-Space Preservation Techniques

Stuart Meck, FAICP, American Planning Association, Chicago, Illinois

PRESERVATION, CONSERVATION, AND REUSE

OPEN-SPACE PRESERVATION TECHNIQUES

The preservation of open space in America has increased significantly since the 1980s. The preservation of open space is essentially a voluntary process, involving a landowner who is willing to sell or donate land or an interest in land to a government agency or a qualified private organization.

Open space broadly includes woodlands, fields, wetlands, streambanks, floodplains, and unique geologic formations. Open space differs from working landscapes of farms and forestry operations. (See *Farmland Preservation* for information on techniques to preserve that landscape type.)

BENEFITS OF PRESERVING OPEN SPACE

There are numerous benefits from preserving open space from development, including biodiversity protection, stormwater management, scenic value, and smart growth.

Biodiversity Protection

In many parts of the United States, land-use regulations alone have been unable to protect environmental quality or to maintain the amount of open space that the public desires. Biodiversity—the number and variety of plant and animal species—is an indicator of the overall health of an ecosystem. Preserving open space, especially woodlands and wetlands, can protect valuable wildlife habitats and thus sustain a healthy number of plants and animals and maintain environmental processes such as the recycling of nutrients.

Stormwater Management

Stormwater runoff from impervious surfaces, such as buildings, roads, and parking lots, is a major source of water pollution. Impervious surfaces can also cause flood events to become more intense. They also block rain and melting snow from percolating down into aquifers to recharge groundwater supplies. Open spaces, such as woodlands and wetlands, filter and absorb stormwater runoff and allow water to seep into the soil and replenish groundwater supplies.

Scenic Value

Open space offers scenic vistas that translate into higher real estate values. A house or land next to preserved open space will have a higher market value because of the scenic amenity and access to recreational activities that the open space provides. Open space can be used for walking, hiking, hunting, bird watching, horseback riding, mountain biking, and, in the winter, snowshoeing, snowmobiling, and cross-country skiing.

Smart Growth

The preservation of open space is a key ingredient in smart growth efforts. The preservation of open space in the countryside helps to curb sprawl and channel development toward areas where development can be served by central sewer and water systems in compact settlements. Within cities and suburbs, the preservation of open land provides parkland, trails, and greenways that can be linked together in a system of green infrastructure. This green infrastructure is also an important asset for economic development in the information age economy where highly educated workers put a premium on environmental quality.

TECHNIQUES TO PRESERVE OPEN SPACE

The preservation of open space has been a major focus of land trusts and a number of government programs. Often, private interests and governments work together to preserve open space. There are several ways these groups work to preserve open space; five of the most common are described here.

Fee-Simple Acquisition

Land ownership in America means owning a bundle of rights to land. These rights include water rights, mineral rights, air rights, the right to use land, the right to sell or lease land, the right to pass land to heirs, and the right to develop land. The entire bundle of rights is known as the "fee simple." If a goal is to actively manage open space for recreational, ecological, or educational purposes, fee-simple acquisition and ownership is recommended.

Land Trust

A land trust is a private nonprofit organization that has received a designation from the Internal Revenue Service as a 501(c) (3) corporation involved in charitable and educational activities. Land trusts may receive donations of land, interests in land known as conservation easements (described below), stock, bonds, and cash. Donors may use these gifts as charitable deductions for federal income tax purposes. Some land trusts acquire open space in fee simple, either through donation or purchase. A land trust may opt to manage the open space it owns as a nature preserve with some public access for limited recreational and educational uses.

It is a common practice for land trusts, especially the larger ones such as The Nature Conservancy and the Trust for Public Land, to purchase open space and then sell it to local and state governments for parkland.

According to the Land Trust Alliance, a national organization devoted to promoting the creation and development of land trusts, there are more than 1,300 land trusts in the United States, with at least one in every state.

Land and Water Conservation Fund

The primary federal program for preserving open space is the Land and Water Conservation Fund (LWCF), created by Congress in 1965. LWCF receives royalties from federal offshore oil and gas leases. The annual allocation of LWCF is 40 percent for federal land acquisition and 60 percent for state projects. The federal government has used LWCF funds to add almost seven million acres to the national parks, national forests, and the National Wildlife Refuge System.

To receive LWCF funds, a state must draft a State Comprehensive Outdoor Recreation Plan (SCORP) for approval by the Department of the Interior describing how the state will spend the federal money to meet its outdoor recreation needs. The federal funds may be used to cover half the cost of purchasing or improving recreational land, and must be matched by funds from state and local governments and nonprofit groups. Land acquired with LWCF funds must remain forever in outdoor recreation use. Much of the money to states has gone to expand state parks.

State Programs

Several states operate open-space preservation programs, through their departments of natural resources, environment, or parks. Maryland's Program Open Space has preserved more than 300,000 acres, mainly for parkland, since 1969. New York State's Open Space Conservation Plan directs the acquisition of land by the state; the program is funded through real estate transfer taxes. Cities, counties, and townships have used a variety of funding sources, such as bonds, sales taxes, and property taxes, to purchase local open space for parks, greenways, and trails.

Conservation Easements

A conservation easement is an interest in real estate less than the fee simple. It is a legally binding contract in which a landowner voluntarily restricts the rights to use and develop land, as well as the right to sell or convey mineral rights. For instance, a conservation easement could limit activities allowed on the land to open-space uses, such as wildlife habitat and watershed protection. A conservation easement may exist in perpetuity or for a specific time spelled out in the easement document. The large majority of conservation easements are in perpetuity.

Compensation

A landowner may choose to sell or donate a conservation easement to a land trust or government agency. The landowner may receive cash for selling a conservation easement, or tax benefits from donating an easement. Also, a landowner may make a bargain sale of an easement, receiving part cash and part tax benefits on the donation portion. After a conservation easement has been sold or donated, the land remains private property, and public access may or may not be allowed.

Transaction and Monitoring

The landowner and the land trust or government agency sign a conservation easement, which is recorded at the county courthouse. The easement

Thomas L. Daniels, Ph.D., University of Pennsylvania, Philadelphia, Pennsylvania

"runs with the land," meaning that it also applies to future landowners. The land trust or government agency that holds the conservation easement has a legal responsibility to monitor the property and enforce the terms of the easement. Monitoring typically consists of an annual on-site visit and written report.

Appraisal Value

A professional appraiser determines the value of a conservation easement in a written appraisal. The value is the difference between the estimated fair market value of the property if it were sold today and the estimated value of the property subject to the restrictions of the conservation easement.

DETERMINING THE VALUE OF A DONATION OF A CONSERVATION EASEMENT

As an example, assume there are 90 acres of natural area in open land, forest, and wetland:

$450,000 appraised fair market value − $180,000 appraised value restricted to open space and wildlife habitat = $270,000 appraised conservation easement value

Income Tax Savings

Landowner's adjusted gross income (AGI) = $80,000

Thirty percent of AGI is the maximum deduction for one year, but the landowner can spread the donation over six years. Depending on income, a landowner may not be able to use the entire donation as an income tax deduction.

$24,000 = Maximum one-year deduction

Assuming a constant income of $80,000 a year, $24,000 × 6 = $144,000 maximum deduction over six years. (Note: The landowner cannot use $126,000 of the donation and it is lost.)

Total income tax savings = approximately $50,000

Estate Tax Savings

Estate value reduction = $270,000

Actual estate tax savings will depend on size of the landowner's estate and year of settlement.

Property Tax Savings

Property tax savings vary from state to state, and even community to community. In some cases, there may be no property tax savings.

Tax Benefits

There are several potential tax benefits from donating a permanent conservation easement. The landowner may use the value of the easement as an income tax deduction, subject to certain limits defined in Section 170(h) of the Internal Revenue Code. There may be estate tax benefits, depending on the size of the landowner's estate. A few states offer state income tax credits for people who donate a conservation easement on their land. In some states, the landowner may receive a reduction in the assessed value of the property for property tax purposes.

Scenic Easements

Scenic easements are a subset of conservation easements. A scenic easement is voluntary and may be sold or donated or transferred in a bargain sale. Unlike the typical conservation easement, a scenic easement usually does not apply to an entire property. Scenic easements mostly apply to a land within a few hundred yards of a highway, to maintain a greenbelt of undeveloped and thus protect scenic vistas. Wisconsin pioneered the use of scenic easements in the late 1940s and early 1950s to protect the views along the Great River Road beside the shores of the Mississippi River.

Purchase and Transfer of Development Rights

The purchase of development rights (PDR) and the purchase of a conservation easement are the same thing. By convention, however, the purchase of development rights refers to the purchase of a conservation easement by a government agency, whereas the acquisition of conservation easements is done by private land trusts. Purchase of development rights also tends to refer to the preservation of active farm and forestlands.

The purchase of a conservation easement and PDR involve retiring development rights so that they cannot be used again. Transfer of development rights (TDR) features moving development potential from a property targeted for preservation to a property planned for development. The owner of the first property receives cash compensation from a developer or local government. (See *Transfer and Purchase of Development Rights* for more information.)

Mandatory Dedication and Cluster Development

Many communities have subdivision regulations that include the mandatory dedication of parkland and open space to maintain open space when allowing development on greenfield sites. Ideally, the amount of required open space should be described in the regulations, but in practice the size of the dedicated land is often negotiated.

Cluster development involves arranging building lots on a portion of a parcel and while retaining a certain percentage of the parcel as open space. For example, a cluster zoning ordinance might require a subdivision that creates five or more lots to set aside 40 percent of the land area as permanent open space. A cluster zoning ordinance can require a developer to donate a conservation easement on the open space to a land trust or the local government to ensure that it stays undeveloped.

CONCLUSIONS

A number of techniques are available to preserve open space. Fee-simple acquisition is recommended when the goal is to actively manage the property for wildlife habitat, recreation, or educational purposes. The purchase of conservation easements is attractive because the cost is often much less than fee-simple purchase. Scenic easements are useful in maintaining scenic vistas, especially along highways. Mandatory dedication can be used to enable a community to acquire public open space. Cluster development can be used to create private preserved open space when the open space is required to be restricted by a conservation easement held by a land trust or government agency.

See also:
Biodiversity Protection
Farmland Preservation
Property Rights, Police Power, Nuisance, and Vested Rights
Transfer and Purchase of Development Rights
Viewshed Protection

Thomas L. Daniels, Ph.D., University of Pennsylvania, Philadelphia, Pennsylvania

FARMLAND PRESERVATION

Farmland preservation describes both the short- to medium-term protection of high-quality farmland, through land-use regulations and financial incentives, and the more permanent protection of farmland through voluntary programs that enable governments and land trusts to acquire the right to develop farmland. Because it often has gentle slope and deep, well-drained soils, prime farmland is often the easiest land to develop. But farmland provides a variety of environmental services, such as aesthetically pleasing open space, wildlife habitat, water recharge, and air filtering, which are especially important in metropolitan areas, where most farmland preservation programs are found.

Farming is a $200 billion industry nationwide and an important sector of many local economies. About 940 million acres is dedicated to farming and ranching uses, but only about 230 million acres are actually in crop production. Each year more than one million acres of farmland are converted to other uses, mainly in metropolitan areas. Metro counties produce most of the nation's fruits, vegetables, and milk, and about one-quarter of all farm output. These counties are anticipated to absorb most of the nation's population growth in the twenty-first century. Thus, farmland preservation is an essential growth management element.

Farmland is vulnerable to price competition from two types of development, large-scale urban and suburban expansion, and scattered housing, office, and store construction into rural areas. Development of farmland to nonagricultural uses may have significant consequences for food production throughout the United States. In addition, farming as practiced today is largely not compatible with suburban residential and commercial development. Hence, separating growth areas from good farming areas is important for the continuation of farming in a community.

Many states have enacted farmland protection programs and allow local governments to use an array of financial incentives and land-use regulations to minimize land-use conflicts between farmers and newcomers. Local governments can use these techniques to implement a comprehensive plan that identifies farmland and agriculture as valuable resources that should be maintained within the community. A local government ideally should try to preserve a critical mass of farms and farmland, both to manage development and to enable the farm-support businesses to remain profitable and maintain agriculture as a local industry.

FARMLAND PRESERVATION TOOLS

There are a variety of financial incentives, laws, and regulatory tools available for farmland preservation. These tools work to preserve farmland for the short, medium, or long term, and are available to varying degrees across the country. Planners should consult state statutes and local regulations to determine availability, or consider adopting policies where they do not exist.

Agricultural Districts

An agricultural district is an area where farming is the preferred land use, and no land-use restrictions are imposed on the farmers. Instead, landowners receive

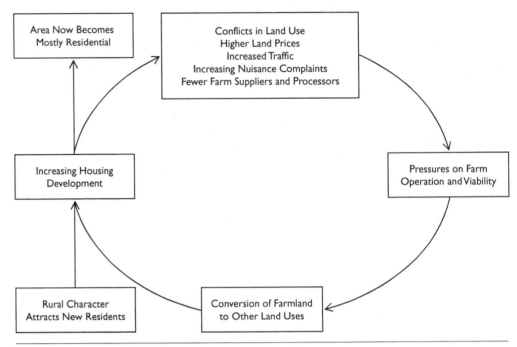

CYCLE OF FARMLAND CONVERSION

Excerpted from Holding Our Ground: Protecting America's Farms and Farmland, by Tom Daniels and Deborah Bowers. Copyright © 1997 Island Press. Reprinted with permission of Island Press, Washington, DC.

FARMLAND PRESERVATION TOOLS

TOOLS	DURATION	
	SHORT TO MEDIUM TERM	**LONG TERM**
Agricultural Districts		X
Differential Assessment	X	
Right-to-Farm Law		X
Agricultural Zoning		X
Urban Growth Boundary	X	
Donation of Development Rights		X
Purchase of Development Rights		X
Transfer of Development Rights		X

a number of benefits that vary from state to state. They may include exemption from sewer and water assessments, greater protection against eminent domain, use-value taxation, and eligibility to sell development rights. In return for these benefits, landowners usually agree not to develop their land for a certain number of years. Currently, more than 20 states allow farmers to form voluntary agricultural districts.

Differential Assessment

Differential assessment involves determining the value of farmland for property tax purposes, based on its use value for farming, rather than on its "highest and best" use for potential development. Every state has some form of differential assessment for farmland. There are three types of differential assessment: preferential assessment, deferred taxation, and restrictive agreement.

Preferential Assessment

Preferential assessment gives farmland owners a reduced assessment if they meet standards for a certain minimum number of acres and value of farm output. If the farmland owner sells the farm for development, the owner is not required to pay back the taxes that would have been due if the farmland had been taxed at its "highest and best" use. Preferential assessment is used mainly in the southern United States. It does little to preserve farmland in the long run, especially where the value of farmland is greater for development.

Deferred Taxation

Deferred taxation provides a reduced assessment, but if a landowner sells farmland for development, then the landowner must pay back at least some of the tax benefits, along with an interest penalty.

Restrictive Agreement

A restrictive agreement is a contract between the landowner and local government under which the landowner agrees not to sell the farm for development for a certain number of years in return for a preferential use-value assessment.

Thomas L. Daniels, Ph.D., University of Pennsylvania, Philadelphia, Pennsylvania

Right-to-Farm Law

Farming can generate noise, dust, animal odors, and chemical sprays that spill onto neighboring properties. A right-to-farm law is a state law that protects farmers against nuisance lawsuits from neighbors if the farmers are using standard farming practices. The law may also prevent local governments from enacting nuisance ordinances that prohibit standard farming practices.

Agricultural Zoning

Agricultural zoning is designed to protect farmland from incompatible nonfarm uses. It is the most widely implemented land-use regulation to protect farmland from development. There are several types of agricultural zoning. Exclusive agricultural zoning allows only farm-related uses, and is found in Hawaii and parts of California. Nonexclusive agricultural zoning varies according to the nonfarm uses allowed, the minimum farm size allowed, the number of nonfarm dwellings allowed, and the size of setbacks or buffer areas between farms and nonfarm properties.

There are three basic types of nonexclusive agricultural zoning: large minimum lot size, fixed area ratio, and sliding scale.

Large Minimum Lot Size

For large minimum lot size, the minimum lot size should reflect the minimum-size viable farm, which varies by the type of agriculture. For example, in Oregon, minimum lot sizes range from 40 acres in the Willamette Valley, where fruit and vegetable production is common, to 320 acres in the rangeland of eastern Oregon. The larger the minimum lot size, the less likely nonfarmers will be interested in buying the land. The price of the land will tend to reflect a value affordable to farmers.

Fixed Area Ratio Zoning

Fixed area ratio zoning allows one dwelling at a density standard. Townships in Lancaster County, Pennsylvania, for example, use a fixed area ratio of one nonfarm dwelling per 25 acres, but the maximum building lot is two acres. For a 100-acre farm, a maximum of four lots totaling eight acres could be subdivided off the farm; 92 acres would remain in farm use.

Sliding Scale Zoning

Sliding scale zoning allows more nonfarm dwellings to be subdivided off smaller farm parcels. It is designed to appease owners of small parcels within agricultural zones and tends to result in more nonfarm dwellings than large minimum lot size or fixed area ratio zoning.

Other Elements of Agricultural Zoning

Many communities use smaller minimum lot sizes, such as one house per five acres, for agricultural zoning. In actuality, this is rural residential zoning and will not maintain agricultural operations. Related to this, the clustering of houses on a part of a farm in most cases will maintain some open space or cropland, but not sustain a commercially viable farm.

Setbacks in the agricultural zoning ordinance describe the distance required to locate a farm building from a road, property line, or other building. Setbacks vary according to the type of agriculture.

FUNDING SOURCES FOR PURCHASE OF DEVELOPMENT RIGHTS PROGRAMS

STATE AND FEDERAL GOVERNMENT	LOCAL GOVERNMENT AND PRIVATE NONPROFITS
State Bonds	Local Bonds
State General Fund	Local General Fund
State Cigarette Taxes	Local Sales Taxes
State Lottery Proceeds	Local Property Transfer Tax
Federal Farmland Preservation Funds	Nonprofit Land Trusts
Federal Wetlands Reserve Program	Fundraising
Federal Grassland Reserve Program	Foundations

Livestock, for example, requires setbacks between a few hundred feet and a few thousand feet, depending on the number of animals, because of the intensity of animal odors.

Growth Boundary

A growth boundary is a line on a map agreed upon by a city and county, a village and county, or a village and township within which there is enough land to accommodate urban expansion, typically up to 20 years. The governments agree not to extend urban-type services, especially public sewer and water, beyond the growth boundary. This encourages development inside the boundary and reduces the likelihood of development onto nearby farmland. Growth boundaries can be expanded over time as needed.

Local governments that decide to use growth boundaries must clearly demonstrate that the boundary is serving a public purpose, otherwise, a boundary could be ruled a "taking" of private property or an "arbitrary and capricious" act by the government.

The first American growth boundary was put into place around Lexington, Kentucky, in 1958 through an agreement between the city and Fayette County. Outside the boundary is the famous Kentucky blue grass country of horse breeding farms. In 1995, the Lexington-Fayette Urban County Planning Commission approved expanding the urban service area by 5,700 acres.

Donation of Development Rights

The right to develop land is one of several rights that come with landownership. This right may be sold or given away separately from the other rights. If it is removed, the land remains private property, but the allowed uses are limited, typically to farming and open space. Landowners who donate development rights, such as to a private, nonprofit land trust, may use the value of the donation as an income tax deduction and possibly as an estate tax deduction, depending on the size of the estate.

Purchase of Development Rights

The purchase of development rights (PDR) involves the voluntary sale by a landowner of the right to develop a property to a government agency or private nonprofit land trust. The landowner receives a cash payment in return for signing a legally binding agreement, a deed of easement, that restricts the use of the land, usually in perpetuity, to farming and open space. The land remains private property with no right of public access.

Twenty-five states, dozens of local governments, and even the federal government have raised money to purchase development rights on farmland. State

and local governments have relied primarily on the sale of bonds to finance the purchase. The sale of development rights lowers the value of the farm for estate tax purposes, aiding in the transfer of the farm to the next generation. The price of the development rights is determined by an appraisal. Although future generations that farm a preserved farm will not have development rights to sell, the farm will retain a value for farming, and the land can be sold to someone else to farm.

When development rights are purchased from several contiguous farms, development can be more effectively directed away from the farming area, allowing farm owners to invest in their farms without complaints from nonfarm neighbors. Approximately a dozen counties, mainly in Maryland, Pennsylvania, and California, have preserved more than 30,000 acres with the purchase of development rights.

Transfer of Development Rights

The transfer of development rights (TDR) means that the development right can be moved to another site to develop that other property at a higher density than would normally be allowed. The first step is for a local government to establish a TDR market. This includes identifying a sending area, from which TDRs will be sent, and a receiving area, where developers use the TDRs to build at a higher density. For farmland preservation purposes, after the development rights are transferred, the sending area is then restricted to farming.

The two leading TDR programs for preserving farmland are in Montgomery County, Maryland, and in the New Jersey Pinelands. Purchase of development rights has been far more popular than the transfer of development rights, however, partly because of the controversy in identifying sending and receiving areas.

PACKAGE OF FARMLAND PRESERVATION TECHNIQUES

No single farmland preservation technique can succeed alone. Local governments should have a coordinated package of financial incentives and land-use regulations. The leading counties in farmland preservation use at least six techniques: a comprehensive plan, differential assessment, right-to-farm laws, agricultural zoning, purchase or transfer of development rights, and urban growth boundaries.

The comprehensive plan presents an inventory of the importance of farming and farmland to the community. It also identifies where the good farmland is located, and where farmland should remain largely undeveloped.

Differential assessment reflects that the farmland is zoned for agriculture and hence should be taxed as

Thomas L. Daniels, Ph.D., University of Pennsylvania, Philadelphia, Pennsylvania

agricultural land. The state right-to-farm law indicates that farmers will be allowed to continue standard farming practices, even if nonfarmers settle in the agricultural zone.

The agricultural zoning serves two other purposes. It complements the urban growth boundary to ensure that large residential and commercial developments do not leapfrog over the growth boundary into agricultural areas. It also provides a buffer to farms preserved by PDR, TDR, and through the donation of development rights. In places with only rural residential zoning, preserved farms can act as magnets for development, providing a preserved view. Agricultural zoning helps to keep nonfarm development away from preserved farms.

Currently, Lancaster County, Pennsylvania, is the only local government intentionally purchasing development rights to farmland to create parts of urban growth boundaries. The county is trying to channel development away from the best farming areas and in directions where the development has access to adequate infrastructure. Leapfrog development over the growth boundaries will probably not occur, except for a few scattered nonfarm residences, because the farmland is zoned at one house per 25 acres.

IMPLICATIONS FOR PLANNERS

There is a need to look at farmland preservation as part of an initiative to preserve working agricultural landscapes, to maintain food and fiber production, and for growth management. This regional perspective requires a county level of government or higher as the most effective entity to plan for farmland preservation. However, farmland preservation makes sense only if there is a viable agricultural industry to preserve. Farmland preservation is not identical to the preservation of open space. If a community or county can preserve enough farmland to maintain an agricultural industry, however, it may preserve enough open space to satisfy the public.

REFERENCE

Daniels, Tom, and Deborah Bowers. 1997. *Holding Our Ground: Protecting America's Farms and Farmland.* Washington, D.C.: Island Press.

See also:
Conservation Development
Farms
Land Evaluation and Site Assessment
Open-Space Preservation Techniques
Transfer and Purchase of Development Rights
Zoning Regulation

Thomas L. Daniels, Ph.D., University of Pennsylvania, Philadelphia, Pennsylvania

LAND EVALUATION AND SITE ASSESSMENT

The Land Evaluation and Site Assessment (LESA) system is a two-part process developed in the early 1980s by the U.S. Department of Agriculture as a way for local governments to assess the suitability of one or more parcels of farmland for continued agricultural use. Agricultural suitability includes soil quality, agricultural productivity, development pressure, and other factors. Local planners can use the LESA system to plan and manage growth, or to implement a farmland or ranchland preservation program.

The land evaluation criteria rate the quality of the soils for farming and development potential. Soils rated Class I and II by the Natural Resources Conservation Service (NRCS) are considered prime farmland. Class III soils are of statewide importance, and certain Class IV soils are unique or of local importance. Class V through VIII soils have very limited potential for farming or nonfarm development.

The site assessment criteria rate the surrounding economic, social, and geographic features that indicate development pressures on the farm and farm viability. When the LESA points are totaled, they produce a total score for a farm. Those operating the LESA system should set a threshold level of points above which a farm should remain in farming and below which the farmland should be allowed to be developed.

For a 150-acre farm with 50 acres of Class I soils, 80 acres of Class II soils, and 20 acres of Class III soils, the land evaluation score would be:

50 acres × 100 rating = 5000 +
80 acres × 88 rating = 7040 +
20 acres × 75 rating = 1500 =
13540
13,540 points divided by 150 acres = 90.26 Total
Land Evaluation Score

The LESA system is objective, numerically based, and flexible. Some trial and error is often involved in selecting point scores and the overall weighting of factors. In the example in Site Assessment Score table, farmland quality is weighted one-third of the total potential 300 points; development potential makes up two-thirds. However, a different weighting on farmland quality, such as 150 points out of 300 total points, could lead planners and local officials to preserve more farmland and permit rather little development.

In 2003, 10 states and 177 county and municipal governments were using the LESA system as part of their land planning or farmland protection efforts. The Delaware Department of Agriculture, for example, has created a LESA map for the entire state. The map has five colors that indicate the current or potential use of land. Light green and dark green areas show the best farming regions, defined as areas with good soils, access to farm services, and low development pressure. Light yellow and dark yellow areas indicate cities or developed areas. Blue areas have some farming along with moderate development pressures.

SOIL CAPABILITY RATINGS

SOILS CLASS	GENERAL SLOPE	EROSION FACTOR	USE LIMITATIONS
Class I	Slight	Slight	Few
Class II	3%-8%	Moderate	Some; conservation practices needed
Class III	8%-15%	High	Many; special conservation practices needed
Class IV	15%-25%	Severe	Many; careful management required
Class V			Very limited; pasture, range, woodland, and wildlife uses
Class VI			Severe; few crops, pasture, woodland, and wildlife uses
Class VII			Very severe; no crops, only range, pasture, and wildlife uses
Class VIII			Most limited; only for range, woodlands, and wildlife

LAND EVALUATION SCORE BASED ON SOIL PRODUCTIVITY

SOIL CLASS	CORN YIELD IN BUSHELS ACRE FOR SOIL CLASS/ HIGHEST SOIL CLASS YIELD	RATIO	LAND EVALUATION X 100	RATING
I	160/160	1.00	100	100
II	140/160	0.88	100	88
III	120/160	0.75	100	75
IV	100/160	0.66	100	66
V	70/160	0.44	100	44
VI	50/160	0.31	100	31
VII	45/160	0.28	100	28
VIII	0/160	0	100	0

SITE ASSESSMENT SCORE

SITE ASSESSMENT FACTORS	WEIGHT ASSIGNED	X	FARM SCORE	MAXIMUM TOTAL POINTS	MAXIMUM POSSIBLE POINTS
1. Percentage of land in agriculture within 1.5 mile radius	2.0		9	18.0	20
2. Percentage of land in agriculture adjacent to the farm site	1.5		8	12.0	15
3. Percentage of farm site in agriculture	1.5		9	13.5	15
4. Percentage of farm site zoned for agriculture	2.0		10	20.0	20
5. Distance from a city or village	1.5		8	12.0	15
6. Distance to public sewer or water	1.5		5	7.5	15
7. Size of farm vs. average farm size in county	2.5		8	20.0	25
8. Road frontage of site	1.5		8	12.0	15
9. Farm support services available	1.5		8	12.0	15
10. Historic, cultural, and environmental features on farm site	1.0		6	6.0	15
11. Consistency with county plan	1.0		15	15.0	15
12. Consistency with municipal plan	1.0		15	15.0	15
Site Assessment Subtotal	163.0 out of 200 maximum points				
Land Evaluation Subtotal	90.26 out of 100 maximum points				
Total Points Possible	300				
Total Points Scored	253.26				

Source: Adapted from U.S. Department of Agriculture, Soil Conservation Service, National Agricultural Land Evaluation and Site Assessment Handbook, 1983.

The LESA map has facilitated land planning by both the state and its three counties. The map can help identify where to locate infrastructure to serve development and to keep infrastructure away from good farming areas. The LESA map has also been used to identify where the state should purchase development rights to farmland.

See also:

Farmland Preservation
Soils Classification and Mechanics

Thomas L. Daniels, Ph.D., University of Pennsylvania, Philadelphia, Pennsylvania

VIEWSHED PROTECTION

A viewshed is the area visible from a point, a line, or a specific locality. It is the visual equivalent of a watershed. Often defined as the landscape visible from a specific point, a viewshed can also consist of the sum total of the area covered by views along a road or trail, as well as the aggregate of the views vis-ible from a specific area such as a park, city square, or historic landmark. The borders of viewsheds are usually defined by topography, structures, vegetation, or other physical barriers, but in some cases can be limited by distance, changes in land use, or changes in visual character.

REASONS FOR VIEWSHED PROTECTION

Significant viewsheds are often highly valued community resources. Courts have ruled that they contribute to public health safety and welfare, enhance property values, contribute to the economy, and often serve as a foundation of a community's identity and well-being. In the landmark 1954 case *Berman v. Parker*, U.S. Supreme Court Justice William O. Douglas said that values representing the public welfare "are spiritual as well as physical, aesthetic as well as monetary." Viewsheds often represent more than just pretty images; they can become treasured symbols of national and community identity.

A close correlation exists between high visual quality and high environmental quality. Many of the highest rated views of natural scenery feature relatively undisturbed, unpolluted landscapes. Human visual preferences often have a biological base—in this case, a preference for healthy natural settings. Viewshed protection also has strong ties to economic development: it is often motivated by a desire to maintain high property values, enhance tourism, and promote the economy by enhancing the region's quality of life. Equity is inherent in a process that protects access to views for all and prevents the privatization of scenery.

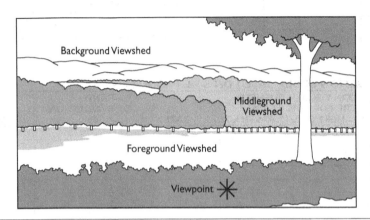

VIEWSHED ELEMENTS

Source: Dodson Associates 2004.

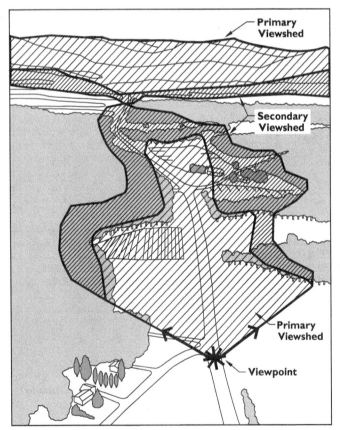

☑ Primary Viewshed — Area Visible Today

☑ Secondary Viewshed — Area Potentially Visible in the Future if Vegetation and Structures Are Removed

RURAL VIEWSHED

Source: Dodson Associates 2004.

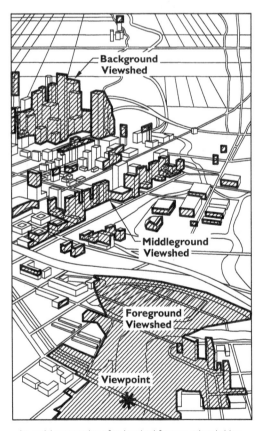

An aerial perspective of a viewshed from an urban bridge (360-degree viewshed).

URBAN VIEWSHED

Source: Dodson Associates 2004.

Harry Dodson, ASLA, Dodson Associates, Ashfield, Massachusetts

EXAMPLES OF VIEWSHED PROTECTION ACTIONS

Viewshed protection has been successfully implemented at a variety of scales, from local to regional. Denver's 1968 Mountain View Ordinance protects views of the Rocky Mountains from the city's squares and parks and applies to specific sites within the urban area. Napa County, California's Viewshed Protection Ordinance applies to specific areas of the entire county. New York State's Hudson River Scenic Areas of Statewide Significance (SASS) covers 12 counties in an area 140 miles long and up to 5 miles wide along this famous scenic river corridor. The California Coastal Commission is responsible for viewshed protection over 800 miles of shoreline. Different methods and techniques are involved, depending on the scale of protection involved, but the goals and end results are similar.

Geographic Variations

Viewshed protection in open regions, such as flat deserts and plains with few visual borders, requires different approaches to inventory and assessment techniques than in more defined landscapes such as mountains, urban areas, or areas with dense vegetation. The greatest variable from region to region is often the changing perceptions and attitudes of the local population, which provide the foundation for viewshed protection.

Settlement Context Variations

Urban, rural, and natural landscapes each have their own unique approaches to inventory, assessment, and implementation due to the different social and economic factors at play in each area. Urban viewshed protection typically applies in a precise manner to the preservation of specific views from specific streets or squares or to the protection of urban neighborhoods through urban design standards. Rural viewshed protection often applies to varied natural, cultural, and working farm and ranchland landscapes, requiring complex assessment and implementation that addresses the requirements of working landscapes.

Multiple Political Jurisdictions

Mutual cooperative agreements between political jurisdictions, often with the help of a higher political authority such as state or federal government, frequently create successful compacts for implementing viewshed protection. In New York State, for example, 12 counties and 26 communities worked under the guidance of the New York State Coastal Management Program to create the Hudson River Scenic Areas of Statewide Significance. The National Park Service has implemented this approach with its Wild and Scenic Rivers program involving visual protection of both public and private lands spanning multiple jurisdictions. The U.S. Department of Transportation's Scenic Byways Program takes a similar multijurisdictional approach, with extensive local involvement.

STANDARDS GOVERNING VIEWSHED PROTECTION

Courts have ruled that aesthetic concerns can be regulated as legitimate community resources if they are based on shared, clearly documented public perceptions of visual significance. Regulations and policies governing visual preservation must be based on methodical public opinion surveys to ensure their legal defensibility. They also must use accurate maps of views and visual zones and include an accurate ranking of visual quality within each zone. Digital mapping and geographic information system (GIS) techniques have brought much greater accuracy to the mapping and analysis of viewsheds. Clear standards are also required to deal with varying visual conditions in different seasons and for potential future alterations to structures, vegetation, or topography that could alter viewsheds.

Three elements are crucial for effective and enforceable viewshed protection:

• A master plan or enabling document that states the community's support for viewshed protection

• An accurate visual inventory and assessment process
• A methodical testing of public opinions and perceptions regarding scenic issues

PLANNING ISSUES RELATED TO VIEWSHED PROTECTION

Viewshed protection is intertwined with a number of planning issues, including zoning and land use, building massing regulations, public access, public participation, environmental protection, protection of community character, and preservation and enhancement of the quality of life. It is also closely related to tourism, economic development, and public health and safety issues, which provide the foundation for many planning policies.

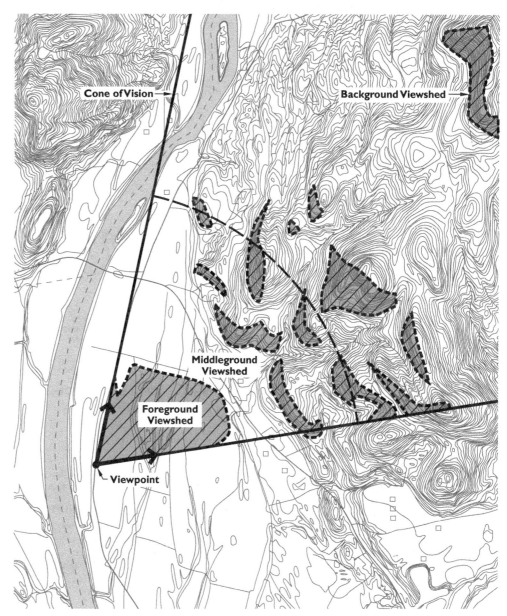

The view shown here would be framed by buildings or trees, down a corridor such as a road or river, or framed by a window.

VIEWSHED FROM A SINGLE POINT (45 DEGREES)
Source: Dodson Associates 2004.

Harry Dodson, ASLA, Dodson Associates, Ashfield, Massachusetts

Public Participation

The value of the viewshed to be protected must be established through a methodical public opinion polling process. Respondents are usually asked to rate representative photographs of viewshed landscapes. The results are used to establish a rating system to evaluate the scenic quality of the viewshed. The visual poll can be conducted in meetings or on the Internet. The goal should be to reach at least one percent of the target population.

Viewshed Protection in the Comprehensive Plan

To withstand court challenges, viewshed protection requires enabling legislation at the local or state level. A comprehensive plan can support this enabling legislation by gauging community values and establishing the justification, methodology, and goals of viewshed protection. Aesthetic regulations stand up in most courts if based on widely held community values as defined and expressed in a comprehensive plan.

Viewshed Protection and Other Plans

Viewshed protection can be implemented as a stand-alone ordinance, or it can be incorporated in other plans, such as a community's zoning regulations as an overlay zone or a modification to existing zones. Subdivision regulations and engineering codes, vegetation management regulations, wetlands regulations, floodplain regulations, height and dimensional ordinances, open-space plans, park and recreation plans, and historic district regulations and other codes can also be adapted for viewshed protection purposes. Visual issues are often an important element in critical area plans that combine environmental and visual concerns.

VIEWSHED PROTECTION IN URBAN AREAS

In urban areas, viewshed protection often focuses on the preservation of views to key landmarks and on the protection of views down important streets, squares, and parks toward more distant visual features such as mountains and waterbodies. Urban viewsheds are usually very precisely defined by buildings, streets, and very specific vistas. Key preservation measures include height limitation, building setbacks, and sign controls. Denver, Colorado, Charleston, South Carolina, and Scottsdale, Arizona, have preserved viewshed and view corridors in their downtowns with strong urban design controls.

Urban Design Elements and Viewshed Protection

Many basic urban design elements can be used to create viewshed protection zones. Setbacks, height limitations, architectural and landscape design guidelines, façade controls, and streetscape standards can be incorporated in a successful viewshed protection plan. Additional elements unique to viewsheds include viewshed mapping, visibility studies, digital viewshed modeling, and public visual preference polling. Criteria for implementing viewshed protec-

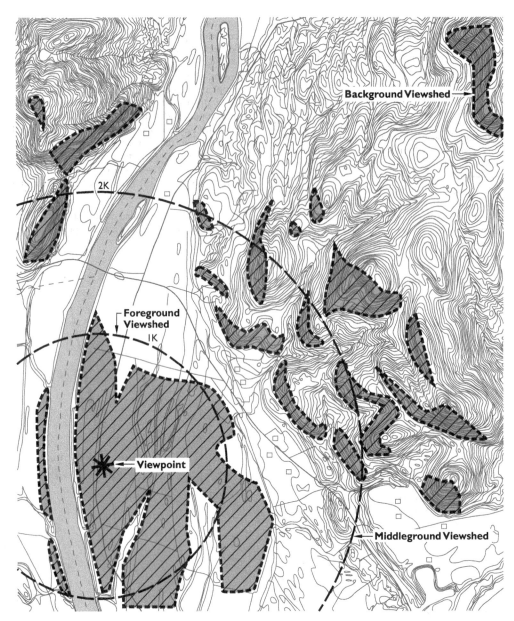

Views would be from a vista point, a road pullout, structure, or overlook.

VIEWSHED FROM A SINGLE POINT (360 DEGREES)

Source: Dodson Associates 2004.

tion plans include design guidelines, design review boards, and precise models showing the potential impacts of proposed changes on the protected views.

Protection of Natural Views and Vistas

Many cities have taken steps to protect their visual link to the surrounding natural landscape. Pittsburgh protects views from the urban core to its rivers; the cities of Denver, Portland, Seattle, and Burlington, Vermont, protect their mountain vistas; and Austin, Texas, protects its hill-country views.

Protection of Focal Buildings

Rochester, New York, protects views of the Eastman Tower; the U.S. National Capital Planning Commission protects views of the major Washington, D.C., monuments; Boston has limited building heights adjacent to the State House.

IMPLEMENTATION

Viewshed protection can be implemented through regulation, donation, purchase, administrative policy,

Harry Dodson, ASLA, Dodson Associates, Ashfield, Massachusetts

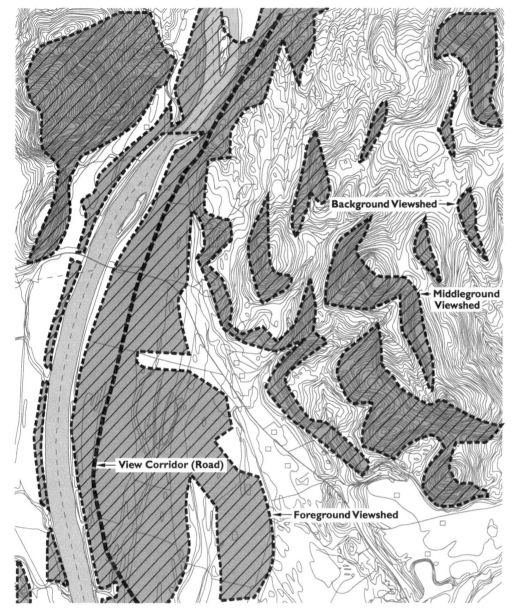

Labels on image: Background Viewshed → · ← Middleground Viewshed · ← View Corridor (Road) · ← Foreground Viewshed

This viewshed would be the sum total of views from a car traveling down the road, a boat traveling down a river, or a person walking along a hiking trail (both directions).

VIEWSHED FROM A CORRIDOR

Source: Dodson Associates 2004.

or through voluntary agreements. It can protect specific views and larger landscapes, as well as urban streets, neighborhoods, and urban vistas. Resources to be protected must be inventoried using a comprehensive process that incorporates public opinion and public perception.

Protection of viewsheds by local, state, or federal government can be achieved through either the regulation of specific views or the incorporation of visual protection measures into general land-use regulations. Land or structures important to a viewshed can be protected by the purchase or donation of conservation restrictions or of fee-simple ownership to be held by the government or a nonprofit conservation group.

Voluntary agreements can also be entered into between property owners and government or nonprofit groups to govern issues such vegetation management, the location of structures, the height of buildings, and other factors affecting the protection of the viewshed.

Administrative policies protect specific viewsheds and scenic areas within the jurisdiction of agencies such as the National Park Service, the Forest Service, Bureau of Land Management or private, nonprofit conservation groups.

OPTIONS FOR VIEWSHED PROTECTION MEASURES

Protections can apply to specific views from specific points or to entire viewshed areas. They can apply to foreground elements only or to the entire visible landscape. Different types of viewsheds can be defined, such as a primary viewshed defining visible areas, and a secondary viewshed defining additional areas that could be made visible by clearing vegetation, demolishing buildings, or grading the land.

Legal and regulatory measures work best for larger viewsheds with complex ownership or jurisdictional patterns. Administrative measures work well for large single land ownerships. Educational and voluntary measures work well in smaller communities. Incentive and financial options are effective in cases involving a relatively small number of landowners with clear financial stakes in the protection of the viewshed.

AGENCIES AND ORGANIZATIONS THAT MANAGE AND ENFORCE VIEWSHED PROTECTION

In addition to state and federal governmental agencies, on the local level, planning agencies, development authorities, historic commissions, transportation authorities, and parks agencies are typically responsible for implementing viewshed protection ordinances. Private nonprofit land conservation groups, as well as some private organizations such as homeowner associations and business owners, can also hold and administer viewshed easements.

LEGAL GOVERNANCE AND ENFORCEMENT

Municipalities have traditionally used their zoning powers, their police powers, and, to a lesser extent, subdivision controls and environmental regulations to protect visual resources. The ability to regulate based on aesthetics varies from state to state. To date, 30 states permit regulation for aesthetic purposes alone, 5 do not, and 15 are undecided or have not considered the issue. Enforcement can be placed in the hands of planning authorities, municipal executive bodies, parks departments, or special commissions.

Legal Tools to Reduce Visual Impacts

Viewshed protection can range from radical measures preventing any alteration of the visual environment to less stringent protections that modify future changes to the landscape in order to reduce visual impacts. Tools to reduce visual impacts include:

- tree-cutting standards;
- eyesore regulations;
- site planning standards to govern the location of buildings, height limitations, and setbacks; and

Harry Dodson, ASLA, Dodson Associates, Ashfield, Massachusetts

PRESERVATION, CONSERVATION, AND REUSE

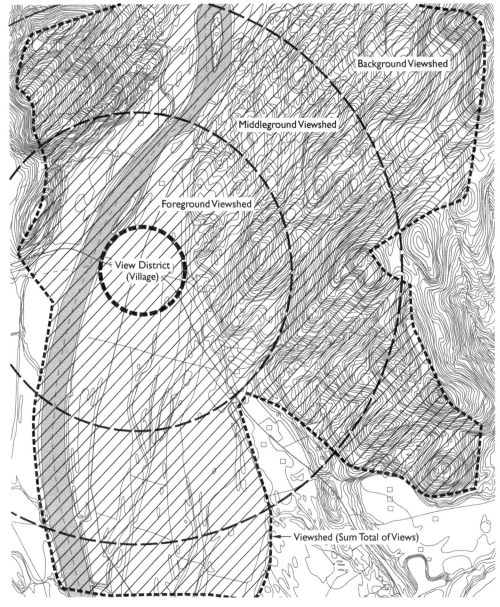

The sum total of all views from an area such as a town, large park, or neighborhood.

VIEWSHED FROM A DISTRICT

Source: Dodson Associates 2004.

- design controls relating to building massing, proportions, materials, and colors.

EMERGING ISSUES IN VIEWSHED PROTECTION

A recent California case has solidified the importance of viewshed protection as an essential element of public health, welfare, and safety. In *Crown Motors vs. City of Redding*, the California Court of Appeals decided that a visually offensive electronic sign proposed for a major gateway to the city would threaten the psychological well-being of the general public. Making a medical link to aesthetic issues strengthens the legal case for viewshed protection. Other emerging issues include new developments in GIS mapping and analysis that bring greater ease and efficiency to the mapping of viewsheds.

See also:
Environmental Site Analysis
Geographic Information Systems
Slope, Relief, and Aspect
Urban Analysis

Harry Dodson, ASLA, Dodson Associates, Ashfield, Massachusetts

HISTORIC STRUCTURES

Historic structures can include any structure of significant character or special historic or aesthetic interest or value as part of the development, heritage, or cultural characteristics of a city, state, nation, or the world. Such structures are recognized as having special status, and worthy of preservation so they are protected from inappropriate alteration.

BACKGROUND

In 1916, Congress created the National Park Service (NPS) in the Department of the Interior to be responsible for monuments as well as national parks, and to conserve, among other things, historic objects. The Historic Sites Act (1935) made the preservation of historic sites, buildings, and objects of national significance for public use a national policy and led to the creation of the National Historic Landmarks program and related programs that record historic buildings, structures, and landscapes. The National Historic Preservation Act (NHPA), which became law in 1966, is the central legislation protecting historic structures across the United States today.

NATIONAL HISTORIC PRESERVATION ACT

The NHPA sets forth preservation as a national policy, authorizes the National Register of Historic Places (National Register), provides for state historic preservation officers (SHPOs), created the Advisory Council on Historic Preservation to advise the president and the Congress on preservation, and provides for certified local government (CLG) historic preservation programs.

NHPA also requires federal agencies to take into account the effects of their undertakings on historic properties. This process is commonly called Section 106 review. The National Environmental Policy Act (NEPA) reinforces historic preservation policy by requiring that environmental impact studies for federal or federally assisted undertakings take into account potential impacts on historic resources. Section 4(f) of the Department of Transportation Act of 1966 prohibits actions by the Secretary of Transportation that require "use" of a historic property, unless there is no feasible and prudent alternative and all possible planning has been undertaken to minimize harm.

State Law and Regulation

Some states, including New York, have a state historic preservation act modeled closely after NHPA. Others have different provisions in their laws. For example, the Antiquities Code of Texas (1969) protects historic buildings on public land and requires state agencies and political subdivisions to notify the Texas Historical Commission of projects involving potential disturbance to historic sites or extensive excavation on public land. State-level environmental policy acts also provide protection to historic resources.

Local Laws and Regulations

At the local level, most historic preservation ordinances provide for the identification and designation of historic properties and districts and for implementing review procedures and design guidelines. The validity of local historic preservation law was upheld in *Penn Central Transport Co. v. New York* (1978), when the U.S. Supreme Court rejected a "takings" claim brought after the New York Landmarks Preservation Commission refused to allow construction of a tower atop Grand Central Terminal. The decision was significant because it weighed the rights of owners to develop a property versus the rights of cities to review and regulate the development of a historic property. For 25 years the ruling has inspired the adoption of more than 2,000 similar ordinances nationwide.

IDENTIFICATION OF HISTORIC STRUCTURES

When planning for the preservation, reuse, or conversion of an older building, it is necessary to know if it is an officially designated historic resource or meets the criteria for such designation and what reviews and approvals may be necessary.

National Register

The National Register lists buildings, sites, and districts of local, state, and national importance. Criteria for inclusion on the National Register are as follows:

The quality of significance in American history, architecture, archaeology, engineering, and culture is present in districts, sites, buildings, structures, and objects that possess integrity of location, design, setting, materials, workmanship, feeling, and association, and:
a. That are associated with events that have made a significant contribution to the broad patterns of our history; or
b. That are associated with the lives of persons significant in our past; or
c. That embody the distinctive characteristics of a type, period, or method of construction, or that represent the work of a master, or that possess high artistic values, or that represent a significant and distinguishable entity whose components may lack individual distinction; or
d. That have yielded or may be likely to yield, information important in prehistory or history.

Under NEPA, federal agencies are required to identify historic structures listed on or eligible for the National Register that may be affected by a proposed undertaking. This requirement has greatly expanded the number of identified historic resources. National Register properties are listed on the NPS Web site (www.cr.nps.gov/places.htm). In addition, SHPOs have information on structures that have been nominated but not yet listed or that have been reviewed for eligibility.

State Registers

States have their own registers or lists of historic structures that they recognize. In many states the criteria for listing on the state register are the same as National Register criteria, while some states may have other but generally similar criteria.

Local Designation

At the local level, a municipality's historic preservation ordinance defines the criteria for designation as a local landmark. For example, New York City's Landmarks Law requires a landmark to be at least 30 years old and possess "a special character or special historical or aesthetic interest or value as part of the development, heritage, or cultural characteristics of the city, state, or nation." Many municipalities also use the National Register criteria. Comprehensive historic site surveys are often the basis of local ordinances and are used by municipalities to identify the potential historic properties that may be worthy of designation and protection.

STANDARDS FOR THE TREATMENT OF HISTORIC STRUCTURES

Section 106 of NHPA requires a federal agency head with jurisdiction over a federal undertaking to consider the effects of the undertaking on properties included in or eligible for the National Register. State historic preservation acts generally provide similar protection for historic structures on state registers. NEPA and state environmental laws also require review of impacts to historic resources. However, a private owner of a building listed on the National Register or a national historic landmark can alter or demolish the structure as he or she sees fit, as long as no other discretionary approvals are required.

The Secretary of the Interior's Standards for the Treatment of Historic Properties provide detailed guidelines for the protection of National Register properties. The specified treatments are preservation, rehabilitation, restoration, and reconstruction, defined as follows:

- *Preservation* places a high premium on the retention of all historic fabric through conservation, maintenance, and repair. It reflects a building's evolution over time, through successive occupancies.
- *Rehabilitation* emphasizes the retention and repair of historic materials, but provides more latitude for replacement of materials because it is assumed the property is more deteriorated prior to the work.

(Both preservation and rehabilitation standards focus attention on the preservation of those materials, features, finishes, spaces, and spatial relationships that, together, give a property its historic character.)

- *Restoration* focuses on the retention of materials from the most significant time in a property's history, while permitting the removal of materials from other periods.
- *Reconstruction* establishes limited opportunities to re-create a nonsurviving site, landscape, building, structure, or object in all new materials.

Federal agencies use these standards in carrying out their historic preservation responsibilities. Adherence is required for federal grant-in-aid funds and Federal Historic Preservation Tax Incentives Program funds.

Anne Locke, AIA, AKRF, Inc., New York, New York; Nathan Riddle, AKRF, Inc., New York, New York; Jennifer Morris, AICP, AKRF, Inc., New York, New York; Andrea Burk, AKRF, Inc., New York, New York

SECRETARY OF THE INTERIOR'S STANDARDS FOR THE TREATMENT OF HISTORIC STRUCTURES

Preservation

1. A property will be used as it was historically, or be given a new use that maximizes the retention of distinctive materials, features, spaces, and spatial relationships. Where a treatment and use have not been identified, a property will be protected and, if necessary, stabilized until additional work may be undertaken.
2. The historic character of a property will be retained and preserved. The replacement of intact or repairable historic materials or alteration of features, spaces, and spatial relationships that characterize a property will be avoided.
3. Each property will be recognized as a physical record of its time, place, and use. Work needed to stabilize, consolidate, and conserve existing historic materials and features will be physically and visually compatible, identifiable upon close inspection, and properly documented for future research.
4. Changes to a property that have acquired historic significance in their own right will be retained and preserved.
5. Distinctive materials, features, finishes, and construction techniques or examples of craftsmanship that characterize a property will be preserved.
6. The existing condition of historic features will be evaluated to determine the appropriate level of intervention needed. Where the severity of deterioration requires repair or limited replacement of a distinctive feature, the new material will match the old in composition, design, color, and texture.
7. Chemical or physical treatments, if appropriate, will be undertaken using the gentlest means possible. Treatments that cause damage to historic materials will not be used.
8. Archeological resources will be protected and preserved in place. If such resources must be disturbed, mitigation measures will be undertaken.

Rehabilitation

1. A property will be used as it was historically or be given a new use that requires minimal change to its distinctive materials, features, spaces, and spatial relationships.
2. The historic character of a property will be retained and preserved. The removal of distinctive materials or alteration of features, spaces, and spatial relationships that characterize a property will be avoided.
3. Each property will be recognized as a physical record of its time, place, and use. Changes that create a false sense of historical development, such as adding conjectural features or elements from other historic properties, will not be undertaken.
4. Changes to a property that have acquired historic significance in their own right will be retained and preserved.
5. Distinctive materials, features, finishes, and construction techniques or examples of craftsmanship that characterize a property will be preserved.
6. Deteriorated historic features will be repaired rather than replaced. Where the severity of deterioration requires replacement of a distinctive feature, the new feature will match the old in design, color, texture, and, where possible, materials. Replacement of missing features will be substantiated by documentary and physical evidence.
7. Chemical or physical treatments, if appropriate, will be undertaken using the gentlest means possible. Treatments that cause damage to historic materials will not be used.
8. Archeological resources will be protected and preserved in place. If such resources must be disturbed, mitigation measures will be undertaken.
9. New additions, exterior alterations, or related new construction will not destroy historic materials, features, and spatial relationships that characterize the property. The new work shall be differentiated from the old and will be compatible with the historic materials, features, size, scale and proportion, and massing to protect the integrity of the property and its environment.
10. New additions and adjacent or related new construction will be undertaken in such a manner that, if removed in the future, the essential form and integrity of the historic property and its environment would be unimpaired.

Restoration

1. A property will be used as it was historically or be given a new use that reflects the property's restoration period.
2. Materials and features from the restoration period will be retained and preserved. The removal of materials or alteration of features, spaces, and spatial relationships that characterize the period will not be undertaken.
3. Each property will be recognized as a physical record of its time, place, and use. Work needed to stabilize, consolidate, and conserve materials and features from the restoration period will be physically and visually compatible, identifiable upon close inspection, and properly documented for future research.
4. Materials, features, spaces, and finishes that characterize other historical periods will be documented prior to their alteration or removal.
5. Distinctive materials, features, finishes, and construction techniques or examples of craftsmanship that characterize the restoration period will be preserved.
6. Deteriorated features from the restoration period will be repaired rather than replaced. Where the severity of deterioration requires replacement of a distinctive feature, the new feature will match the old in design, color, texture, and, where possible, materials.
7. Replacement of missing features from the restoration period will be substantiated by documentary and physical evidence. A false sense of history will not be created by adding conjectural features, features from other properties, or by combining features that never existed together historically.
8. Chemical or physical treatments, if appropriate, will be undertaken using the gentlest means possible. Treatments that cause damage to historic materials will not be used.
9. Archeological resources affected by a project will be protected and preserved in place. If such resources must be disturbed, mitigation measures will be undertaken.
10. Designs that were never executed historically will not be constructed.

Reconstruction

1. Reconstruction will be used to depict vanished or non-surviving portions of a property when documentary and physical evidence is available to permit accurate reconstruction with minimal conjecture, and such reconstruction is essential to the public understanding of the property.
2. Reconstruction of a landscape, building, structure, or object in its historic location will be preceded by a thorough archeological investigation to identify and evaluate those features and artifacts which are essential to an accurate reconstruction. If such resources must be disturbed, mitigation measures will be undertaken.
3. Reconstruction will include measures to preserve any remaining historic materials, features, and spatial relationships.
4. Reconstruction will be based on the accurate duplication of historic features and elements substantiated by documentary or physical evidence rather than on conjectural designs or the availability of different features from other historic properties. A reconstructed property will re-create the appearance of the non-surviving historic property in materials, design, color, and texture.
5. A reconstruction will be clearly identified as a contemporary re-creation.
6. Designs that were never executed historically will not be constructed.

Source: Weeks and Grimmer 1995.

Anne Locke, AIA, AKRF, Inc., New York, New York; Nathan Riddle, AKRF, Inc., New York, New York; Jennifer Morris, AICP, AKRF, Inc., New York, New York; Andrea Burk, AKRF, Inc., New York, New York

State and Local Standards

State officials may use the Secretary of the Interior's standards in reviewing proposals involving historic structures, making funding decisions, and establishing mitigation measures identified in environmental impact assessments. The standards are also used by local preservation and planning commissions across the country.

Protection of historic resources is also provided at the local level, where master plans and zoning ordinances are created and code enforcement occurs. Historic preservation ordinances may be an extension of zoning laws and can be tailored to community character and preservation goals. Most ordinances establish a historic preservation commission to designate and regulate historic properties. Advisory commissions can only make recommendations, whereas regulatory commissions make final decisions on projects that are subject to their review.

FINANCIAL INCENTIVES

Incentives exist at the local, state, and national levels to encourage historic preservation by addressing financial challenges involved.

Tax Credits

The Federal Historic Preservation Tax Incentives Program encourages private investment in income-producing historic properties. Administered by the NPS and IRS in partnership with SHPOs, a tax credit is given for rehabilitating a structure on the National Register or located in a National Register Historic District in compliance with the Secretary of the Interior's Standards. The earned tax credit is 20 percent of the qualified project expense; then the IRS calculates how much of the earned credit can be redeemed. The program also provides for a 10 percent tax credit for the rehabilitation of any income-producing properties built before 1936. "Income-producing" properties include those used for office, commercial, industrial, agriculture, or rental housing, but not as private residences. The success of this program in revitalizing communities has led approximately half of the states and various municipalities to adopt similar programs.

Façade Easements

In general, a façade easement is a legal agreement between a property owner and a historic preservation nonprofit organization granting an easement in perpetuity for the preservation of a historic building's façade. In exchange for maintaining and preserving the façade, the donor receives a federal tax deduction equal to the value of the façade easement. The building must be listed on the National Register or be a contributing structure in a National Register historic district. Subsequent exterior changes require consultation with the involved preservation organization and must comply with the Secretary of the Interior's Standards.

Transfers of Air/Development Rights

This local zoning tool facilitates preservation while encouraging surrounding development. Numerous localities allow property owners to sell air/development rights from historic properties.

Before Restoration

After Restoration

"BEFORE AND AFTER" EXAMPLES OF RESTORATION OF MAIN STREET BUILDINGS

Source: URS Corporation.

Anne Locke, AIA, AKRF, Inc., New York, New York; Nathan Riddle, AKRF, Inc., New York, New York; Jennifer Morris, AICP, AKRF, Inc., New York, New York; Andrea Burk, AKRF, Inc., New York, New York

Grants

In addition to the CLG program, there are a variety of other federal grant programs benefiting historic structures and the people who care for them. Grant funds have been awarded to states, territories, Native American tribes, local governments, and the National Trust for Historic Preservation, to support:

- architectural/historical surveys;
- National Register nominations;
- staff work for historic preservation commissions;
- design guidelines and preservation plans;
- public outreach materials;
- training for commission members and staff; and
- rehabilitation or restoration of National Register-listed properties.

Save America's Treasures grants are administered by the NPS, the National Endowment for the Arts, the National Endowment for the Humanities, and others. These grants may be used for preservation and/or conservation work on nationally significant historic structures. However, they also require a dollar-for-dollar nonfederal match.

Grant and loan programs of the National Trust for Historic Preservation have assisted thousands of preservation projects. In cities across the United States, private preservation organizations also offer aid to worthy projects.

PLANNING FOR INDIVIDUAL STRUCTURES

In determining a use for a historic structure, it is important that the use fit the existing historic form, including the use of the structure's interiors. The Secretary of the Interior's standards specify that a property be used for its original purpose or for a new use that requires minimal change. While some historic commercial or office buildings lend themselves easily to reuse as residential buildings or hotels, other structures are more difficult to use.

Sometimes interiors have been so altered that there is little or nothing to preserve. And whereas federal regulations consider the interiors of buildings as part of the historic resource, local laws may not. For example, the New York City Landmarks Preservation Commission only concerns itself with changes to the interior of a building if it is a designated interior landmark. Nevertheless, the success of the effort often depends on how well the function fits the form.

URBAN DESIGN

Preservation and planning commissions make urban design decisions when they designate historic structures and historic districts and review proposals for alterations of historic properties, new construction in historic districts, and transfers of development rights, for example. The unique circumstances or characteristics of the resources or proposals also guide decisions. The decision to preserve a historic structure is an urban design decision, as are the decisions relating to how its façade looks. A few of the many urban design-related considerations include the following:

- *Use.* To the extent that use affects the way the building looks and relates to the street and sidewalk, it is an urban design consideration. If the Standards for Preservation and Rehabilitation are applied, they generally specify that a property be used as it was historically or for a new use that minimizes alteration.
- *Compatibility.* Additions or alterations of historic structures should be differentiated from the old, but be compatible or contextual or relate harmoniously to the historic structure(s) or fabric. Reconstructions should be clearly identified as reconstructions.
- *Scale.* New structures should relate in scale to the historic structure or context. In some cases, this means the base of a tower, rather than the overall structure, is of the same height as surrounding smaller historic buildings. The setback of the tower above its base is also a factor in how well the new building relates to its context. This is an important consideration for streetscapes.
- *Windows.* New windows in historic buildings are generally required to match the character and visual appearance of the original windows. Windows of similar size and type in new buildings in historic districts may be contextually appropriate. The rhythm (spacing and location) of the window openings in new buildings may also be made to match those in historic structures.
- *Materials.* Replacements for deteriorated features on historic buildings that cannot be repaired may be required to match the old in design, color, texture, and, if possible, materials. New buildings may be required to match the materials of the historic buildings. Using different façade materials may be acceptable in differentiating new construction from old, however.
- *Style.* A new building can be compatible with an adjacent building without imitating its style.

Modern interpretations can blend well with a historic context especially if they are similar in scale and if horizontal elements on the façades, such as cornices or floor heights or window opening shapes) correspond.
- *Street walls.* New buildings are often required to match an existing street wall, both in location and height.
- *Materials.*

TRENDS IN HISTORIC STRUCTURE RECOGNITION

The early historic preservation movement focused on buildings and sites associated with people and events of national significance, such as the homes of presidents, and buildings of outstanding architectural merit. Now, buildings of the Modern movement, once scorned for their plainness and lack of tradition, are now recognized for their merit.

Advocacy efforts also broaden the definition of what is historically significant. Sites and structures associated with more recent historic events are now being recognized, both locally and nationally. For example, in 2004, there were 49 properties in the United States listed on the National Register for their association with the Civil Rights Movement. The World Trade Center Site was determined eligible for listing on the State and National Registers of Historic Places.

Advocacy efforts may result in recognition of properties that have cultural importance for a constituency but may not have architectural merit. For example the Casa Amadeo record store in the Bronx, the oldest Latin music story in New York City, and Bohemian Hall, a Czech social hall and beer garden in Astoria, Queens, were listed on the National Register in 2001 for their associations with the Puerto Rican and Czech communities.

REFERENCE

Weeks, Kay D., and Anne E. Grimmer. 1995. *Guidelines for Preserving, Rehabilitating, Restoring and Reconstructing Historic Buildings.* Washington, DC: U.S. Department of the Interior, National Park Service.

See also:
Environmental Impact Assessment
Historic Districts

Anne Locke, AIA, AKRF, Inc., New York, New York; Nathan Riddle, AKRF, Inc., New York, New York; Jennifer Morris, AICP, AKRF, Inc., New York, New York; Andrea Burk, AKRF, Inc., New York, New York

BROWNFIELDS

A brownfield site is real property, the expansion, redevelopment, or reuse of which may be complicated by the presence or potential presence of a hazardous substance, pollutant, or contaminant. The U.S. Environmental Protection Agency (EPA) estimates that there are between 500,000 and 1 million brownfield sites in the United States.

BACKGROUND ON REGULATION OF CONTAMINATED SITES

Prior to 1980, hazardous and industrial wastes in the United States were largely unregulated. In the 1980s, two federal laws, the Comprehensive Environmental Response, Compensation, and Liability Act (CERCLA) and the Resource Conservation and Recovery Act (RCRA), were passed by Congress and signed into law.

CERCLA, also known as "Superfund," authorized the U.S. EPA to respond to environmental emergencies involving pollution, contaminants, or hazardous wastes. Superfund mostly addresses abandoned properties. Through Superfund, the U.S. EPA created the National Priority List (NPL), which focuses on the most contaminated properties or Superfund sites. RCRA regulates the actions of operating businesses. It endowed the U.S. EPA with corrective action authority, with which it can demand environmental compliance. (See Federal Legislation in this section of this book for more information.)

BROWNFIELDS PROGRAM BACKGROUND

Brownfields differ from Superfund sites in the degree of contamination. Superfund sites may pose a real threat to human health and/or the environment because of their higher levels of contamination. Brownfields may not pose as serious a health or environmental threat; rather, they represent an economic or social threat, because they prevent development.

In 1995, the U.S. EPA developed a brownfields initiative to assist states in addressing the vast majority of contaminated sites through State Voluntary Cleanup Programs. Memorandums of Understanding (MOUs) between U.S. EPA and many states are used to manage brownfields cleanup programs within certain parameters.

State Voluntary Cleanup Programs

Most states have voluntary cleanup programs in place that are based upon assessing and mitigating the risk

to human health and the ecosystem. These risk-based standards consider human and ecological populations at risk; the sources and types of pollution; the pathways to expose these populations to the contaminants; the frequency, duration, intensity, and overlap of the exposures; and the potential effects of the exposures to set standards for various contaminants. (Further information on the State Voluntary Cleanup Program and state-level contacts is available on U.S. EPA's website, www.epa.gov/compliance/cleanup/redevelop/state.html.

RCRA Brownfields Initiative

A potential RCRA brownfield is a RCRA facility that is not in full use, where there is redevelopment potential, and where reuse or redevelopment of that site is slowed due to real or perceived concerns about actual or potential contamination, liability, and RCRA requirements. The U.S. EPA established the RCRA Brownfields Prevention Initiative in 1998 to encourage the reuse of potential RCRA brownfields so that the land better serves the needs of the community, either through more productive commercial or residential development or as greenspace.

BROWNFIELD LOCATIONS

Brownfield sites are found throughout the United States, but are most heavily concentrated in large metropolitan areas with a history of industrial activity. The U.S. EPA, through its EnviroMapper Store Front (available on EPA's website at www.epa.gov/envirofw/html/em/index_bkup_01272005.html), provides an interactive map function to locate brownfield sites, as well to as obtain information on other environmental conditions and features of an area.

IMPETUS FOR BROWNFIELD REUSE

Redevelopment is the driver for brownfield cleanup and reuse. Only sites that pose an imminent danger to health are cleaned up without a redevelopment plan or project driving the effort. A local government, community group, private developer, or end user typically sees redevelopment potential in a site and takes the predevelopment steps needed to create a plan and determine project feasibility by assessing the costs, risks, and benefits of a potential project.

TYPICAL BROWNFIELDS REDEVELOPMENT STAKEHOLDERS

Source: URS Corporation.

Predevelopment Planning

When starting a brownfield redevelopment process, communities need to have the capacity to come to a working consensus regarding future land use; to develop realistic, market-based redevelopment goals; and to create the tools to support redevelopment. Stakeholder involvement is key to laying the foundation for successful redevelopment. Such involvement can require local government to take proactive measures to assess environmental conditions, address ownership issues, create redevelopment incentives, and take other steps that may be unfamiliar to public officials. Typical concerns of community residents and business owners include the potential environmental impact of the cleanup, the new use, or the type of community benefits desired from the redevelopment effort, such as jobs, taxes, or open space.

Predevelopment Steps

Several steps are involved in the predevelopment stage of a brownfield redevelopment project:

1. Site selection and control
2. Development team creation
3. Market analysis
4. Environmental assessment
5. Engineering and traffic assessments
6. Political support
7. Entitlements, such as zoning and regulatory approvals
8. Project design
9. Financial feasibility and incentives

Environmental Assessment

Most of these steps are common to any development project; a brownfields site also must have an environmental assessment conducted, which is described

Planning	Site Preparation	Development
Exit Strategies	Project Funding	Marketing
Market and Financial Analysis	Environmental Remediation	Brokerage
Master Planning	Regulatory Approval	Architectural Design
Community Relations	Demolition	Construction Management
	Infrastructure Design and Installation	

INTEGRATED PROPERTY REDEVELOPMENT PROCESS

Source: URS Corporation.

Donna Ducharme, AICP, Delta Institute, Chicago, Illinois

PRESERVATION, CONSERVATION, AND REUSE

below. In some instances, institutional controls or engineered barriers are used in lieu of cleanup.

Phase I Environmental Assessment. All brownfield sites require a Phase I environmental assessment. This process determines the past and current site ownership and identifies any chemical processes that took place. The American Society for Testing and Materials (ASTM) has issued guidelines for conducting Phase I assessments. These guidelines recommend the following data-gathering tasks:

- Conducting interviews with current and past operators of the property.
- Conducting interviews with governmental officials.
- Searching electronic and paper historical records regarding operations on the property.
- Conducting an on-site inspection of the property.

If the Phase I assessment identifies potential environmental contamination, the investigation proceeds to a Phase II. If not, the investigation stops with the Phase I report.

Phase II Environmental Assessment. The Phase II environmental assessment verifies the contaminants that exist and their location on the site, usually through soil and groundwater sampling and analysis. The scientific sampling and technical review required to conduct a Phase II investigation make it much more expensive than a Phase I. There are no standards for conducting a Phase II, so it is important to work with a qualified consultant.

A Phase II report (sometimes called a Phase III) establishes cleanup goals, identifies future land-use restrictions, determines remediation techniques, identifies remediation risks, and develops a remedial action plan and timeline. The goals and action plan should relate directly to the standards set by the State Voluntary Cleanup Program.

Institutional Controls and Engineered Barriers

Institutional controls and engineered barriers are often used to meet risk-based cleanup standards without fully removing or cleaning the contaminated soil. An example of an institutional control is when a property owner agrees to use a property only for industrial or commercial use, which requires less remediation than a residential use. An example of an engineered barrier is when a building or a parking lot is constructed over a contaminated area to block the pathway for human exposure to the contaminants. Both institutional controls and engineered barriers are only effective at reducing risk if they are properly maintained. Many states are struggling to determine how to monitor the growing number of sites that have used these remedies.

POTENTIAL BARRIERS TO BROWNFIELD REDEVELOPMENT

Among the potential barriers a redevelopment strategy for a brownfield site must take into consideration include the following:

- Barriers to clear title
- Deterioration or obsolescence of any buildings on the property
- Changes in parcelization needed for optimal reuse
- Zoning ordinances
- Market conditions
- Public infrastructure, both available and needed
- Type, level, and location of the environmental contamination
- Costs and risks from both the public and the private sector point of view

In addition, while predevelopment is extremely important, it is often difficult to fund it because of the high risk that a project will not go forward.

Liability Considerations

Liability considerations impact when and how property ownership is transferred, as well as project financing. Municipalities are no longer liable for the environmental contamination on properties they take "involuntarily," such as through foreclosing on tax liens. However, to be considered an "innocent" (not liable) landowner, private owners must conduct a thorough environmental investigation of a site prior to coming into ownership.

Viability

Many brownfield projects require a mix of public incentives and private financing to be viable in the market. This is especially true in communities where land values are relatively low and cannot accommodate nonvalue-added costs, such as environmental cleanup and demolition. Many local, county, and state governments, as well as the federal government, offer a variety of incentives to support the assessment, cleanup, and redevelopment of brownfield sites.

COMMUNITY REVITALIZATION IMPLICATIONS

Brownfields redevelopment can have significant potential benefits to their host communities.

Brownfield sites located near large population clusters, transportation systems, and networks of suppliers and buyers are prime redevelopment areas. Reusing brownfields can generate a sense of momentum and lead to notable community benefits, such as increasing the local tax base, generating job growth, creating community amenities and services, encour-

aging equitable development, reusing existing infrastructure, increasing surrounding property values, protecting human health, improving the environment, and reducing urban sprawl.

A growing number of communities want brownfield redevelopers to ensure that the wide range of potential environmental impacts—from energy and waste, to air, water, and land impacts—of their new use are minimized, and that redevelopment does not cause a new round of environmental problems.

SMALL BUSINESS LIABILITY RELIEF AND BROWNFIELDS REVITALIZATION ACT OF 2002

Brownfields grants will continue to serve as the foundation of the U.S. EPA's brownfields program, but the Small Business Liability Relief and Brownfields Revitalization Act of 2002 (PL 107-118) provides additional tools for the public and private sector to promote sustainable brownfield cleanup and reuse:

- Assessment grants, which provide funding for brownfield inventories, planning, environmental assessments, and community outreach.
- Revolving loan fund grants, which provide funding to capitalize loans that are used to clean up brownfields.
- Cleanup grants, which provide direct funding for cleanup activities.
- Job training grants, which provide environmental training for residents of brownfields communities.
- Training, research, and technical assistance grants, which fund organizations supporting local and national brownfields efforts.
- State and tribal response program grants, which fund the establishment or enhancement of state and tribal response programs.

REFERENCES

American Society for Testing and Materials (ASTM). 2000. *Standard Practice for Environmental Site Assessments: Phase I Environmental Site Assessment.* E-1527-00. West Conshohocken, PA.

American Society for Testing and Materials (ASTM). 1997. *Standard Guide for Environmental Site Assessments: Phase II Environmental Site Assessment Process.* E1903-97. West Conshohocken, PA.

See also:
Federal Legislation

Donna Ducharme, AICP, Delta Institute, Chicago, Illinois

ECONOMIC AND REAL ESTATE DEVELOPMENT

CAPITAL IMPROVEMENT PROGRAMS

Capital planning involves the purchase or construction, major repair, reconstruction, or replacement of capital items, such as buildings, utility systems, roadways, bridges, parks, landfills, and heavy equipment, which are expensive and have a long, useful life. The capital improvement program (CIP) is a five- to six-year schedule of capital projects. The first year of the CIP is the capital budget, which the local government formally adopts and implements, along with the operating budget. The CIP is one of the most powerful tools for implementing a local comprehensive plan.

The careful study of capital project selection and timing can:

- help a planning commission and its staffs provide valuable advice and perspective to the legislative and executive branches of government;
- help coordinate activities of various government departments and agencies; and
- influence the pace and quality of development in a community.

DEFINING A CAPITAL IMPROVEMENT

Capital improvements are projects that involve major, nonrecurring expenditures. They include acquisition or lease of land; projects requiring significant public borrowing for equipment, building, and facilities; studies whose costs exceed a stated dollar amount; and related major equipment, furnishings, and improvements that exceed a stated dollar amount.

Capital expenditures may be further distinguished as being either a capital outlay or a capital project. Capital outlays are: any nonmajor capital expenditure with a certain service life; of a relatively minor dollar value; and not physically dependent on or affixed to a particular stationary fixed asset. Examples include office equipment and vehicles. Capital projects are major capital expenditures exceeding a set dollar value and attached to a particular fixed asset. These projects are separate, discrete improvements that have a specific purpose in developing, upgrading, replacing, or maintaining existing infrastructure. Examples include upgrades to facilities, roads, and sewers.

ROLE OF LEGISLATION

State planning enabling legislation or municipal charters may describe capital improvement roles and responsibilities. For example, New Jersey statutes authorize the governing body to formally designate the planning board as a group that formulates the CIP, coordinating its preparation with municipal officials and the local school board.

In Florida, the local comprehensive plan itself must include a capital improvement element, to be reviewed on an annual basis. The element must contain standards to ensure the availability of public facilities at acceptable levels of public service.

In Nevada, a local government cannot impose impact fees unless it first prepares and updates the CIP at least every three years. This requirement was expressly imposed to ensure that local governments adequately plan for the expenditure of impact fee revenues after they have been collected from developers. The statute requires that such revenues be placed in a separate interest-bearing account that clearly identifies the category of capital improvement within the service area for which the fee was imposed.

Some modern growth management programs link the approval of projects to the presence of adequate public facilities nearby. A developer can choose whether to wait for such facilities to be constructed through the CIP process or to install the facilities ahead of the long-range schedule.

ADVANTAGES OF CAPITAL IMPROVEMENTS PROGRAMMING

Advance planning and scheduling of community facilities may avoid costly mistakes. A systematic, organized approach to planning capital facilities provides a number of practical advantages.

Using Taxpayers Dollars Wisely

Deliberate assessment of the need to repair, replace, or expand existing public works, as well as careful evaluation of the need and timing of new facilities, can provide many savings. Project timing may be improved to make better use of available personnel, expensive equipment, and construction labor by scheduling related major activities over a longer period. Coordinating construction of several projects may affect savings in construction costs—for example, so that streets do not need to be dug up several times. Overbuilding or underbuilding usually can be avoided. Needed land can be purchased at lower cost well in advance of construction.

Focusing on Community Needs and Capabilities

Capital projects should reflect the community's needs, objectives, expected growth, and financial capability. Assuming each community has limitations for funding capital facilities, planning ahead will help assure that high-priority projects will be built first.

Obtaining Community Support

Citizens are more supportive of projects that are part of an overall plan. When the public participates in the planning of community facilities, citizens are better informed about community needs and priorities. Also, when citizens participate in the process, they are often more supportive of bond issues, rate increases, and other funding methods.

Encouraging Economic Development

Typically, a firm considering expansion or relocation is attracted to a community that has well-planned and well-managed facilities in place. A capital improvements program allows private investors to understand a community's tax burdens and service costs, and reflects the fact that the community has done some advance planning to minimize the costs of capital projects.

Increasing Administration Efficiency

Coordinating capital facilities construction, both within a jurisdiction and among city, county, and spe-

IS IT A CAPITAL IMPROVEMENT?

THESE ARE CAPITAL IMPROVEMENTS	THESE MAY BE CAPITAL IMPROVEMENTS	THESE ARE USUALLY OPERATING EXPENSES
City Halls	Fire Trucks	Office Furniture
Courthouses	Road Graders and Similar Equipment	Library Books
Fire and Police Stations	Computer Systems	Fire Hoses
Libraries	Police and Fire Radio System	Lawn Mowers
Park Land and Development	Trash Compactor Trucks	Pothole Repairs
Streets, Roads, and Sidewalks	Minor Building Additions or Remodeling	Electric Typewriters
Parking Lots and Buildings	Parking Meters	Blueprint Machines
Sewer and Water Mains	Police Cars	Road Gravel
Schools	Street and Road Repairs	
Hospitals	Playground Equipment	
Water and Sewage Treatment Plants		
Land Purchases		
Street Lighting Systems		
Storm Sewers		
Major Building Additions and Remodeling		
Airports		
Disposal Sites and Equipment		
Jails		
Recreation Buildings		
Tennis Courts		
Swimming Pools		

Colorado Department of Local Affairs, Denver, Colorado; Stuart Meck, FAICP, American Planning Association, Chicago, Illinois

cial districts, can reduce scheduling problems, conflicts, and overlapping of projects. A capital improvements program allows a community to anticipate lead times necessary to conduct bond elections and bond sales, prepare design work, and receive contract bids.

Maintaining a Stable Financial Program

When construction projects are spaced over a number of years, abrupt changes in the tax structure and bonded indebtedness may be avoided. Major expenditures can be anticipated, resulting in the maintenance of a sound financial standing through a more balanced program of bonded indebtedness. Where there is ample time for planning, the most economical methods of financing each project can be selected in advance. Keeping planned projects within the financial capacity of the community helps to preserve its credit and bond rating and makes the area more attractive to business and industry.

Taking Advantage of Federal and State Grant and Loan Programs

A capital improvements program places the community in a better position to take advantage of federal and state grant programs, because plans can be made far enough in advance to use matching funds, both anticipated and unanticipated. Most federal and state grant and loan programs require prior facilities planning, or favor applications that have conducted such planning.

PROCESS

Local officials must decide how elaborate their approach should be and who will conduct the various steps for their community. There are eight major steps in developing a capital facilities program:

1. Identifying the needs for facilities and the timing, costs, and means of financing for each project.
2. Presenting the relationship of the CIP to the comprehensive plan.
3. Preparing a financial analysis of the jurisdiction's capacity to pay for new facilities.
4. Setting priorities among the proposals.
5. Seeking review and comment by the public on the recommended projects and priorities.
6. Preparing a final capital facilities program showing projects, priorities, schedule of completion, and methods of funding each project.
7. Adopting the capital facilities program by the governing body and adopting first-year projects as a capital budget as part of the annual budget.
8. Reviewing the capital improvements program annually.

	Checklist of Capital Improvement Program Procedures
☐	Appoint a Coordinator and Other Participants, and Define Responsibilities
☐	Inform Citizens
☐	Set Rules/Policies • Define Capital Improvement • Determine Length of Plan
☐	Develop a Priority System
☐	Prepare Inventory List • Include Age, Condition, Replacement Dates • Include Improvements Underway and Current Status
☐	Prepare a Project Request List in Priority Order • Include In-Depth Information on Each (Justification, Future Operation and Maintenance Costs, Relationship to Other Projects)
☐	Review Projects and Develop Project Summary Lists
☐	The Financial Picture • Revenue Trends/Projections • Expenditure Trends/Projections
☐	Alternative Financing Mechanisms
☐	Final Report, Adoption, and Implementation

CHECKLIST OF CAPITAL IMPROVEMENT PROGRAM PROCEDURES

Source: American Planning Association.

Steps in CIP Preparation

Local government practices vary as to how the document is formulated. The chief responsibility for assembling the CIP may be that of the municipal manager's office or the public works or planning department. Typically, planners, working with the finance department and the government's chief executive, request proposals from all operating departments several months before the beginning of the new fiscal year. They evaluate them, determine the local government's ability to pay for new projects based on revenue forecasts, and then organize the projects into a schedule.

The planning commission may be involved in identifying projects that eventually appear in the CIP because of the impact that the projects may have on the community's physical development. Sometimes it may advise elected officials and administrators on general priorities for selecting projects—for example, whether projects that affect health and safety should take precedence over those that stimulate economic development when money is tight.

The commission will review the draft CIP against the backdrop of the comprehensive plan and forward its recommendations to the legislative body. If the legislative body approves the plan for the first year of the CIP, this is adopted by ordinance as the capital budget, along with the annual operating budget, which appropriates monies for personnel, indirect costs such as health insurance and electricity, supplies and equipment (for example, computers and police cars are typically in the operating budget). Public hearings on the draft document are always part of the CIP process. The public hearing may be before the planning commission, or governing body, or both. Once the capital budget is adopted, then governmental departments can begin to spend money on individual projects, contract for architectural and engineering design, and send out requests for construction bids.

Policies

One of the most important steps in preparing a CIP is to have a set of fundamental policies in place. These policies should define a capital improvement, determine the length of the plan, and develop a priority system. A CIP should show at least five years of capital planning. The CIP of projected projects is typically reviewed once a year and updated as necessary. Factors that could positively influence the priority of a project to a funding entity include whether the project:

- involved significant citizen participation in the process;
- is consistent with the comprehensive plan or other goals and priorities;
- receives financing from specific revenue sources (such as user fees and grants);
- is mandated by state and/or federal law;
- is essential to public health or safety;
- results in savings of operating costs;
- generates sufficient revenue to be self-supporting;
- includes capital improvements identified in accordance with the approved CIP;
- requires adoption of a multiyear plan (CIP), updated annually;
- allows the community to maintain all its assets to protect city investments and minimize future maintenance and/or replacement; or
- involves long-term debt financing that matches costs with benefits received by future residents.

See also:
Comprehensive Plans
Development Impact Fees
State Enabling Legislation

Colorado Department of Local Affairs, Denver, Colorado; Stuart Meck, FAICP, American Planning Association, Chicago, Illinois

TAX INCREMENT FINANCING

Tax increment financing (TIF) is a financing technique that allows a local government or redevelopment authority to target a group of contiguous properties for improvement—a TIF district—and earmark any future growth in property tax revenues in the district to pay for initial and ongoing improvements there. This growth in tax revenue is the "tax increment."

Since its inception in the 1950s, TIF has become one of the most popular sources of financing for public-private development projects. In some ways, its popularity stems from the fact that other sources, especially federal ones, have contracted, and that tax and expenditure limits currently restrict the amount of revenue local governments can raise both internally and through the bond market.

TIF offers a means of circumventing these obstacles and has many qualities that distinguish it as an attractive development tool. Unlike the federal categorical programs that preceded it, TIF can be used for most kinds of projects that demonstrate financial feasibility and promise increases in property value. TIF's flexibility has enabled local governments to channel funds to such varied activities as infrastructure improvement, industrial expansion, downtown redevelopment, historic preservation, and military base conversion. Moreover, reducing the up-front costs of development, primarily those related to site preparation, is often more attractive to potential developers than conventional abatements that reduce a developer's tax burden over time.

HOW TIF WORKS

The precise details of TIF enabling legislation differ in each state; however, the underlying design is similar. The process is set in motion when a local government designates an area for improvement. This area must be "blighted," the definition of which can be found in state statutes authorizing the use of TIF and must be confirmed in local ordinances designating the TIF district. In Illinois, for example, state legislation provides a checklist of features that impair values or prevent a normal use or development of property, including the presence of structures that do not meet building codes, obsolete platting of the land, and excessive vacancies or land coverage. The local government and its consultants draft a study to determine whether the proposed area meets the state's definition of blight, documenting the deterioration and declining property values. In some states, nonblighted areas may be designated as TIF districts as long as they serve other legislated goals, such as industrial job creation.

State statutes also require the local government to attest to the fact that redevelopment of the area would not occur "but for" the use of TIF; that is, without public assistance. If the blight and "but for" conditions are met, a TIF district may be formed by ordinance after notice is given and a public hearing is held to discuss the local government's plan for redeveloping the area.

Once the district is designated, local governments and redevelopment authorities are given the power to engage in almost any kind of activity that they believe would encourage private investment and enhance the property tax base of the blighted area.

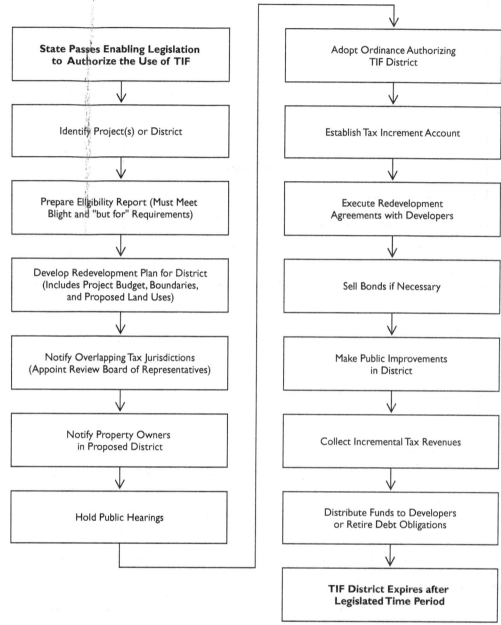

The TIF process can vary from state to state. Check state statutes to determine the specific process that applies.

TIF DESIGNATION AND DISTRIBUTION PROCESS

Source: Rachel Weber.

They may use their powers of land assembly and sale, site clearance, relocation, utility installation, and street repair to improve the district. They may also offer below-market rate financing to make it more attractive to businesses and developers.

If private investment is attracted to the area, the assessed value of property there is expected to rise. The difference between the original assessed value of the properties in their undeveloped state and the new assessed value, as noted above, is the tax increment. Taxes on this incremental value must be channeled back into the TIF district and used to finance any debt accumulated when making improvements.

In most states the lifetime of a TIF district is around 20 years, although some states have no limits on how long a TIF district can be in existence. Therefore, the increase in the property values of the district over the subsequent 20-plus years will pay for the economic development activities, while taxes on the base value of the properties will remain the same and will continue to be paid to all local taxing bodies.

TIF districts do not generate funds for incentives or infrastructure immediately; instead, increments trickle in over the lifespan of the district. The local government, therefore, must find ways of paying for the up-front costs of any initial improvements. In many

Rachel N. Weber, Ph.D., University of Illinois at Chicago, Chicago, Illinois

From Financing Economic Development in the 21st Century, Sammis B. White, Richard Bingham, and Edward W. Hill, editors (Armonk, NY: M.E. Sharpe, 2003). Copyright 2003 M.E. Sharpe, Inc. Reprinted with permission

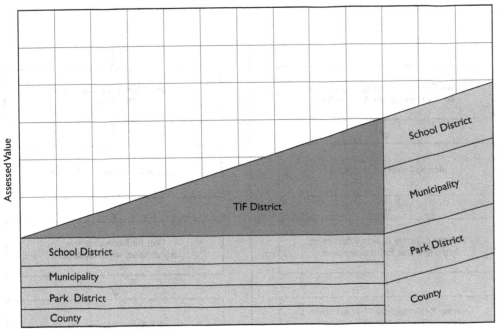

This graph shows the effect of TIF designation on tax revenue allocation over time. Prior to TIF designation, taxes on the base assessed value of all property are allocated among taxing districts. After designation, the added increment of assessed value is taxed, and the revenues pay off bonds or fund other expenses specifically for the TIF district. Base assessed value is unaffected. When the designation expires, the increment of assessed value is added to the base assessed value. This combination is taxed, and revenues are allocated among taxing bodies.

ALLOCATION OF ASSESSED VALUE WITHIN TIF DISTRICT

Source: Rachel Weber.

CALCULATING TAX INCREMENT

The general formula used to calculate increment revenues is:

$$I = r (n - i)$$

Where:

I = the increment revenues
r = the tax rate in the current year
n = the assessed valuation in the current year
i = the assessed valuation in the base year

For example, if the assessed value in the base year was \$25 million, and rose to \$45 million in year 4 of the TIF district designation, and the tax rate in year 4 is 9 mils, then:

I = .009 (\$45,000,000 − \$25,000,000)
= .009 (\$20,000,000)
= \$180,000

That is, in year 4, \$180,000 will be available for the local government or redevelopment agency to make bond payments or fund improvements in the TIF district. If the local government or redevelopment agency wants to use the future increment in the present, this amount needs to be discounted by an appropriate discount rate to determine the present value.

Source: Casella 1984.

cases, the TIF mechanism provides the local government with the legal means and security to borrow against the future property tax revenues for current spending. Local governments float bonds for the public portion of the development costs, dedicating the expected tax increments to pay the debt service. In other cases, the developer initially pays for the costs of the project and is reimbursed by the local government as the incremental property taxes are generated. Because developers require sums of money larger in amount than the increments trickling in, they often turn to banks to pay for costs such as land acquisition.

ELIGIBLE USES FOR TIF FUNDS

State enabling legislation will spell out the eligible uses for TIF funds. These typically include the cost of demolition, parcel assembly, remediation and land preparation, historic rehabilitation and other façade improvements, planning studies, and, occasionally, workforce development and training. Individual developers must apply and be approved for an allocation of increment by the local administration and city council to cover the costs of an eligible use. In many states, part of the TIF district designation process also involves the approval of a "redevelopment plan," a wish list of the future projects in the district written by the local government, development authority, or planning consultant—often in concert with an interested developer. The local government uses this plan to guide its increment allocation strategy, basing its decision to fund specific projects on whether they meet the objectives specified there. The

local government will enter into a redevelopment agreement with the individual developer or business tenant that spells out the details of how TIF funds will be used and the schedule for disbursements.

The decision of a local government to use TIF funds also depends on the degree to which the project promises to increase the value of property in the district. This is why the design of TIF works well with large, expensive projects that promise quick and substantial spikes in the tax increment, such as cases where land uses are up-zoned (i.e., when property moves from less-intensive to more-intensive usage). Government-owned (i.e., tax-exempt) property, abandoned buildings, or derelict sites in appreciating neighborhoods are especially ripe for TIF-financed in-fill development. In these cases, the base value of the property—the value in the year of the TIF designation—is low enough so that when the property values start to grow in subsequent years, a substantial amount of increment can be generated. Even if a project looks like an excellent candidate for TIF funding, however, the local government ultimately has the discretion to make the final determination about projection selection and the magnitude of public investment.

CONTROVERSIES AND RECOMMENDATIONS

TIF is designed so that subsidized development will pay for itself through taxes on the increased property values. TIF can only be considered self-financing, however, if the increases in property values within the district would not have occurred "but for" the

incentive. If property value increases within a district are solely due to the local government's public assistance, the cost to taxpayers is arguably zero. TIF would therefore obviate the need for unpopular tax increases.

If, however, TIF has no effect on the value of property within the district, and property taxes would have increased without its use, either because of inflation or the attractiveness of the particular location, then this mechanism is not really creating new value. When TIF is used in areas that need no stimulus, it becomes a device for capturing revenues in areas rich in appreciating property and redistributing them from overlapping taxing jurisdictions (e.g., school districts and county governments). The potential for redistribution exists because taxes on any increase in the assessed property values of the TIF district go into a separate fund to pay for TIF activities while taxes on the base value of the properties remain the same for the designated lifespan of the TIF.

In order to address this problem, state legislation can be amended to require local governments to demonstrate responsibility for creating the incremental value that is appropriated for economic development. It can, for example, adjust the base value of the property in the TIF district by the inflation rate to allow school districts and other jurisdictions to recapture some of the increment that is not attributable to the new development. Local governments can also reduce opposition from other taxing jurisdictions by involving their representatives from the onset of the TIF designation process. If they can convince other jurisdictions that their projects are legitimate use of tax dollars, there is a greater likelihood that local governments will fund worthwhile development that would not have taken place "but for" the incentive.

Other constituencies may oppose the local government's use of TIF to fund redevelopment. Upward

Rachel N. Weber, Ph.D., University of Illinois at Chicago, Chicago, Illinois

movement in property values is often applauded as a sign of revitalization, but renters, small business tenants, and elderly homeowners may feel threatened by proposals for large-scale TIF-funded developments. If an area is targeted for large and rapid increases in property taxes because it is within a TIF, these groups may not be prepared for the higher tax burden and higher rents. Because TIF districts are intended to lead to a rapid appreciation of property values, the local government should put protections in place for those groups unable to bear the additional burden. Property tax deferral programs for elderly homeowners in TIF districts are one way of ensuring that TIF does not cause displacement of existing residents.

Another concern about TIF relates to a local government's capacity for fiscal management. Local governments speculate on future increases in property taxes, having committed them to developers, banks, and bondholders long before they are actually generated. If subsidized projects do not increase in value, or do not increase rapidly enough, they could jeopardize the fiscal health of sponsoring local governments. The risks inherent in such an arrangement can be expensive for local governments, as bondholders will demand higher interest rates for TIF-backed revenue bonds. Indeed, many TIF-funded development projects—such as convention centers, shopping malls, and mixed-use entertainment complexes—are risky ventures. Minimizing financial exposure may involve traditional strategies such as conducting accurate feasibility studies up front and accessing bond insurance and refinancing.

REFERENCE

Casella, Sam, et al. 1984. *Tax Increment Financing.* Planning Advisory Service Report no. 389. Chicago: American Planning Association.

See also:
State Enabling Legislation

Rachel N. Weber, Ph.D., University of Illinois at Chicago, Chicago, Illinois

FINANCING METHODS AND TECHNIQUES

Real estate finance is inherently complicated. Funds are needed from the moment the developer wants to "tie up" land, through predevelopment approvals, construction, lease-up, or sell out. In a property held for investment, or an operating business, such as a hotel, working capital may also be needed. Providers of funds expect a return, although the level of that return depends on their investment goals, the source of funds, and the level of risk in the project.

The presentation below is a summary and is, of necessity, incomplete in some ways.

DEBT AND EQUITY DEFINED

All funds involved in a deal are either debt or equity (although there are many complexities that sometimes make it hard to tell which is which).

Debt

Debt is funds lent to the developer or development entity. The debt carries an interest rate, has some form of due date or term, repayment expectations, and is an obligation to be paid. The developer must pay taxes and contractors before the debt to protect the lender from tax sales and liens, but must pay the lender before equity investors. Debt is usually secured with a note and a mortgage on the property. Lenders do not own the property.

Equity

Investors provide equity; in turn, they receive an ownership interest in the property. There may be multiple tiers of owners with varying degrees of risk. Owners may be general or limited partners, members of a limited liability company (LLC), a corporate owner, or a sole owner. In many cases, the developer will be a single-purpose entity, to limit liability in the event of a problem.

Owners' funds are at-risk. They are the last to be paid. They may share in available funds after debt on varied bases, but they are owners and take the highest level of financial risk.

VARIATIONS ON DEBT

Mezzanine Debt

Sometimes debt looks like equity. There can be many layers of debt, each one taking a mortgage (second, third, and so on). One common form in development deals is a second layer during construction that reduces the amount and percentage of equity. This type of lender gets paid after the primary lender and often has an interest rate that is contingent on the profit level in the deal. It usually has a cap to meet IRS regulations, but the rate still can be quite high.

Construction Debt

During construction, debt is used to pay construction costs, marketing, and soft costs, such as property taxes, insurance, and a portion of development fee. Construction debt is usually provided on a floating-rate basis tied to prime or to the London Interbank Offering Rate (LIBOR). Construction loans usually are limited to 80 percent or less of construction costs,

although in boom times and for preferred customers or with guarantees, 100 percent loans have been made. The borrower usually must guarantee construction loans, either personally or with other collateral.

Long-Term Debt

In a for-sale project, such as single-family homes, the end buyer takes a mortgage and provides the long-term debt. In investment projects, the developer/owner must obtain a mortgage. This is often called "take-out" financing, because it retires or "takes out" the construction loan. Sometimes the construction lender will require an advance agreement or "forward commitment." Long-term debt usually carries a fixed rate, amortization, and term. The amortization period and term may be different: for example, a loan may amortize over 25 years but be due in 10 years or have its interest reset. Rates depend on overall financial market conditions and are often related to the rates on U.S. treasuries of similar duration.

Other Debt Arrangements

Larger corporate developers will have much more complex financial arrangements, involving major investment houses, bank lines, corporate bonds or other "commercial paper." Similarly, retailers who develop and/or own their own stores may bring a blend of corporate equity (shareholder equity) and corporate debt from credit lines or commercial paper.

CONCEPTS UNDERLYING FINANCIAL STRUCTURE

The blend of debt and equity that applies to a particular project will be determined through negotiation with the lenders and investors. The investor/owner typically wants to maximize debt as long as the expected profit rate is higher than the cost of debt (positive leverage). Whatever amount that the first mortgage cannot cover must be covered by other loans from lenders taking more risk, public economic assistance or subsidies, or equity.

Lenders want to control risk and therefore want a margin of value or cash flow over and above the debt to ensure that they can recover their capital. As a result, their lending will be limited by certain measures. Which one applies and the level will also depend on the nature of the project, the amount of preleasing, the market character, the track record of the borrower, and other factors that contribute to risk. Among the key measures are the following:

> **Loan to value.** Loans will be limited to a percentage of value that is expected to be present upon completion. Value is determined by two of the three appraisal techniques—comparables and cash flow/income approach, but not cost approach (see below). If the project is a build-to-suit to sell, the loan would be based on the contract sale price. Loan to value ratios range from 65 percent to (occasionally) 100 percent during construction. For most types of investment properties, 75 to 80 percent is common.

Loan to cost. A property may cost more or less to build than it is worth. If it appears to be worth more than it costs, the loan may still be limited to a percentage of cost rather than value. This will depend on the nature of the property, the risk, and the borrower.

Debt coverage ratios. The debt coverage ratio is the property's capability to pay its operating expenses and mortgage payments. Available cash flow will be reviewed to determine this ratio. A debt coverage ratio of 1 is breakeven. A coverage ratio of 1:1 to 1:3 is typically applied to determine the amount of cash that can reasonably be applied to pay debt. Again, this will vary based on the type of property, risk, and borrower track record, among other factors. The cash available will be applied as a payment to determine how much debt can be supported at current interest rates and amortization terms.

PRIVATE FINANCIAL SOURCES

There are numerous entities that come in and out of real estate finance, depending on market conditions and strategies. The ones discussed below are among the primary sources of real estate capital; however, this is not an exhaustive list.

Private Equity

Private equity comes from a number of sources. For many smaller projects, the developer or development entity itself provides equity. For larger projects, equity partners are sought. These may be individuals or other companies. Many developers raise equity through private networks of business associates. Others may partner with corporate partners whose primary business is other than real estate. Other equity comes from companies specifically in the business of financing real estate. These companies may also provide loans and mezzanine funds.

Banks

Commercial banks most commonly provide construction period financing, but they may also provide other longer-term funds. Typically, banks are lenders to projects taking a first or second mortgage until the project is complete. In residential for-sale projects, the construction lender may also provide mortgages to buyers.

Credit Companies

Credit companies refer to a group of finance firms that are often engaged in a wide variety of financing activities for equipment leasing as well as real estate. Two of the most prominent at this time are GE Credit and GMAC Mortgage. As their corporate parenthood suggests, the companies' original mission related to industrial and automotive finance, respectively. Credit companies are a potential source for both debt and equity, often providing debt financing for development projects, including "mezzanine" loans that replace equity and earn contingent interest if the project is successful.

Stephen B. Friedman, AICP, CRE, S.B. Friedman & Company, Chicago, Illinois

Investment Banks

Investment banking firms such as Goldman Sachs and Lehman Brothers have become involved in real estate both as development partners and portfolio lenders. In development, there are several examples of investment banks providing equity as joint venturers with developers for both large residential and retail projects. In many cases, the investment bank provides capital during the high-risk periods of pre-development and development. They expect premium yields as a result, often seeking to cash out at the end of the development period.

Pension Funds

Pension funds may be either lenders or providers of equity. They also may act as long-term owners of real estate either as development partners or buyers of completed projects. Pension funds are not in themselves taxable, with taxation deferred until payments are made to the pension recipient. This has an impact on their investment motivation. For example, a pension fund will have a great deal of difficulty taking full advantage of historic tax credits. Conversely, their perspective is often longer term and matched to the expected retirement pattern of those on whose behalf they are investing. Return expectations may also be tempered by tax considerations.

Real Estate Investment Trusts (REITs)

REITs are a special type of investment company required by tax code to pay out 90 percent of their earnings to shareholders to avoid taxation at the corporate level. Stock is generally publicly traded. REITSs may be developers, development financing partners, lenders, or equity investors. Many are long-term holders of real estate.

Life Insurance Companies

Life insurance companies are typically both owners of real estate for their own account and permanent mortgage lenders. They may also be joint-venture financial partners with developers.

PUBLIC SOURCES AND ENRICHMENTS

Provided here are generally available public financing sources and enrichments. Each state and locality may have other specific programs that serve as one form of another of real estate development financing.

Tax Increment Financing

Most states have some form of tax incremental financing (TIF). Under TIF, some or all of the tax revenues generated on increased value within a specified area is dedicated to support the redevelopment of that area. Much of the funding is used for infrastructure. However, in most of the states where it is permitted, TIF funds may also be used for site assembly and land write-down, rehabilitation costs, interest subsidy, or other forms of developer assistance. In exchange, profits are usually limited, and in many cases the locality will share in profits above a specified level.

Special Service and Assessment Areas

Called different things in different states, special taxing districts are often used for infrastructure improvements that would otherwise be the responsibility of either the municipality or the developer. This shifts the burden from existing residents directly to new residents. It is recommended that the developer's economics be reviewed to determine whether such an extra tax is needed or the pricing of the development in the market covers these costs. In rapidly growing areas where the price of housing cannot directly support new infrastructure, this can be a useful tool.

Historic Tax Credits

The federal government allows a 20 percent credit against federal income taxes for qualified rehabilitation costs of a certified historic structure meeting National Park Service standards. The buyers of the credits are usually corporations, which in turn become the equity investors in all or part of the deal. The actual use of the credits is quite complex, and the costs of meeting the standards sometimes call into question the economic utility of the credits. Nonetheless, there are many successful examples of using the credits to restore historic properties. There is also a 10 percent credit for rehabilitation of older structures (1936 and older), subject to various Internal Revenue Service rules. This credit is more likely to be passed through to whomever the investors are to enhance returns rather than attract a different class of investor.

Low-Income Housing Tax Credits (LIHTC)

There is a special tax credit for rental housing affordable to households whose income is below 60 percent of area median income (AMI). Available credits are limited by a dollar amount per capita set by Congress. Credits are obtained by applying to the allocating agency for the jurisdiction (typically the state, except in the case of the City of Chicago, which has its own allocation). Credits are based on approximately 9 percent of qualified development costs and are made for 10 years. A lesser amount of credit based on 4 percent of qualified costs is available for projects using tax-exempt bonds. The credits are sold to investor groups at a discount from face value to generate return to the investor. Proceeds are invested in the project as equity, sometimes covering as much as 60 percent of total costs.

Home Investment Partnership Program (HOME) Funds

The U.S. Department of Housing and Urban Development (HUD) provides funds to local government either by entitlement or through the states for housing development. These funds can be used independently or in tandem with tax credits to support affordable housing developments.

New Markets Tax Credits

A recent addition to the toolkit of real estate finance for job-creating projects are New Markets Tax Credits (NMTC). Administered by the Department of the Treasury, the credits are provided over a period of seven years and enhance the return to the lender or equity provider allowing lower rates of return or interest. They are available for use in qualified census tracts. Some cities have applied for and received allocations. A number of private and not-for-profit organizations such as the Local Initiatives Support Corporation (LISC) have also obtained allocations that can be tapped by multiple developers for projects.

Tax-Exempt Bonds

Tax-exempt bonds can still be used for industrial projects and low-income housing projects. From a real estate finance perspective, they serve as lower-interest lending sources for both construction and permanent financing because the interest on the bonds is exempt from federal income tax. Their use is quite complex and subject to numerous rules; and in periods of low interest, the benefits are more limited than in periods of high interest rates.

FINANCING ISSUES

Planners and public officials are sometimes puzzled by the difficulties developers report in financing projects that meet public goals and follow cutting-edge ideas in planning and urban design. Issues have arisen with regard to mixed-use projects, downtown projects where there are no comparables, new urbanist developments, transit-oriented developments, and virtually any other new idea that has not been successfully built in recent years in that locality. These problems arise from certain structural issues in the financing community, including the following.

Single-Product Orientation

Many lenders and developers specialize in one type of product. The lender may not understand how a mixed-use project works and may be uncomfortable with unique attributes, such as shared parking. For example, the lead developer may not have sufficient experience with retail and office development if its primary experience is residential, causing concern for the lender.

Lack of Comparables

Lenders are limited by value, hence look to appraisers to certify that the likely value at the end of development is sufficient. An innovative project may not have nearby comparables for the appraiser to use in the "sales" approach to value, one of the three required approaches. Other appraisers with specialized expertise and experience may need to be found.

New Design Concepts

There are many examples here, but likely the most common is parking for retail projects. Lenders are accustomed to fields of parking in front of the stores, and have confidence in this configuration. Structured and underground parking, and even counting street spaces toward the ratio, may require a special effort at market and traffic analysis to support the design. Again, examples from elsewhere in the country may help.

Developers or Investors

Most of the real estate industry consists of people who buy, sell, invest in, or manage existing properties. In many communities, these individuals possess the greatest knowledge of the local, existing market. They may be consulted; they may be sought to undertake development projects. Development, however, is quite different from investment only, and it is important to find the right participants and team that includes the

Stephen B. Friedman, AICP, CRE, S.B. Friedman & Company, Chicago, Illinois

developer, the sources of funding (investors), and those who will manage the property in the long term.

CORE DEVELOPMENT FINANCE PRINCIPLES

Development is market-driven and entrepreneurial. It is, therefore, intrinsic to development that new players will emerge, new financial instruments will be offered, and new ideas regarding what constitutes a good project will be offered. These will all require open-minded, but careful, consideration, focusing on the core principles covered here:

- The developer has extensive responsibilities for design and execution, not just the idea.
- The developer does take a great deal of risk, if the deal is properly constructed.
- A financing source is either an owner (equity), and gets paid last, or a lender (debt), and gets paid in some order of priority before the owners.

- Projects can and should be carefully evaluated economically.
- For desired projects, the public sector can often be a financial participant through "public-private partnerships" and in exchange for reducing risk share in profits.
- New ideas that appear promising can often be evaluated and validated from the experience elsewhere.

See also:
Tax Increment Financing

Stephen B. Friedman, AICP, CRE, S.B. Friedman & Company, Chicago, Illinois

PART 6 IMPLEMENTATION TECHNIQUES

FINANCIAL PLANNING AND ANALYSIS: THE PRO FORMA

Financial analysis is essential to planning an economically successful development. All revenues, operating expenses, and development costs must be identified to ensure that the project will be able to cover its costs and generate a reasonable profit and return on investment. For-sale projects, such as single-family homes, townhouses, and condominiums, have a different financial structure from investment properties such as offices, retail complexes, hotels, and rental apartments. However, the commonalities in analyzing the two types are discussed below.

REVENUES AND OPERATING EXPENSES

The market largely determines the revenue levels that any project can attain, whether for sale or for rent. Studies of similar projects can help determine selling prices, rents, rate of absorption, and vacancy rates to use in analysis. Operating expenses are researched using comparable properties and industry studies.

For-Sale Projects

Revenues include base sale prices, upgrades, and parking spaces, depending on the market and property type involved. Sales prices are usually listed per unit; however, analytically it is important to relate prices to total gross square footage to be constructed. Thus, when prices are expressed per square foot, it must be determined whether the salable square footage includes garages, hallways, and other space outside the unit proper.

Ongoing operating expenses of for-sale properties are the responsibility of the end buyers. Expenses accrued during construction are almost entirely development costs; these are discussed below.

For-Rent (Investment) Projects

The primary revenue source of investment properties is rent, whether expressed as room rates (in a hotel), rent per space (for a storefront), monthly (for apartments), or annually by square foot (for most commercial property). Rent is generated on some measure of net-rentable space. In retail spaces, this is called gross leaseable area (GLA). In office buildings, there may be different definitions of gross space, net-rentable, and net-occupiable space. Definitions have become more standardized in recent years, but they still vary by market.

Investment properties have other minor sources of income, including parking rentals, vending, laundry, cable TV, and similar incidental income.

Operating expenses for rental properties include, among others, the following:

- Maintenance
- Security
- Utilities
- Repairs
- Painting and decorating
- Releasing fees
- Insurance
- Management fees
- Taxes
- Tenant improvements (capital)

Many of these costs are passed on to the tenant in the form of common area maintenance (CAM), operating expense pass-throughs, tax pass-throughs, and similar mechanisms included in the lease. Leases may be gross (including all operating costs), net (excluding operating expenses and taxes but not repairs, management fees, and insurance), or triple net (excluding virtually everything). Specifics vary from landlord to landlord and market to market. Even rental apartment leases can vary with regard to payment for utilities, repairs, and maintenance of appliances, for example.

DEVELOPMENT COST PRO FORMA

A development cost pro forma for a community shopping center is included here as an example. Key elements of the pro forma are discussed below.

Land Acquisition

Land acquisition reflects the results of the site assembly process. Depending on the stage of planning, costs here may be the actual cost (often including interest and taxes since purchase) or the contract or option price. Where a specific deal has not been reached, costs may be estimated based on sales of similar properties or appraisals.

In redevelopment projects, costs of relocation, legal fees for condemnation, and other similar costs are typically considered part of land acquisition.

Site Development and Improvement Costs

These costs are always site-specific and are, therefore, difficult to estimate without the help of an architect and engineer. Costs are greater and more unique in environmentally sensitive areas and redevelopment projects.

Demolition

Demolition costs include both removal and disposal.

Site Grading/Preparation

On large sites, this cost category includes mass grading. It also often includes addressing soil conditions that impact the ability to build on the site. These may be soft soils of various kinds; environmental issues, such as wetlands mitigation or floodplains (subject to regulatory approval); or, in redevelopment, addressing rubble and other noncompactable soils. This latter item is a common problem, resulting in part from the intrinsic character of reuse of urban land, but also often the result of improper demolition procedures in which foundations were left in the ground and the rubble of the building dumped in a basement.

Environmental Issues

Remediation costs must be addressed in pro forma estimates. If Phase II environmental studies have been prepared, relatively accurate cost estimates will be available for contamination issues. However, standard rules of thumb for addressing these issues are not available.

Soil-Bearing Capacity Issues

Beyond site preparation, specific engineering measures may be required, such as providing engineered fill under foundations, use of extensive grade beams, or drilling for caissons to reach solid material.

REPRESENTATIVE COMMUNITY SHOPPING CENTER DEVELOPMENT COSTS

DEVELOPMENT COMPONENT	SQUARE FOOTAGE	COST FACTOR	TOTAL COST
Land Acquisition	678,720	$10	$6,787,200
Building Construction Costs			
Supermarket	65,000	$74	$4,829,994
Drugstore	15,000	$84	$1,254,864
Small Retail	89,000	$98	$8,693,751
Parking (Spaces)	680	$3,500	$2,380,000
Total Building Construction Costs	169,680		$17,156,609
Site and Soft Costs			
Other Site Improvements	678,720	$3.00	$2,036,160
Environmental Cleanup		Lump Estimate	$1,000,000
A&E	Hard Cost	4.0%	$807,791
Construction Supervision	Hard Cost	2.5%	$504,869
Permits and Impact Fees		Estimate	$150,000
Real Estate Taxes During Construction			$50,000
Legal	Per Square Foot	$1.00	$169,680
Leasing	Per Square Foot	$6.00	$1,018,080
Contingency	Hard and Soft Costs	5%	$1,144,759
Financing Fees	Construction and Permanent	2%	$545,346
Construction Interest	One-year, Half-Out Method	8%	$1,090,692
Development Fee	Total Development	2.5%	$811,580
Total Site and Soft Costs			$9,328,957
Initial Year Operating Loss After Debt Service			$1,768,113
Total Development Cost			$35,042,879
Per Square Foot			$206.52

Source: S. B. Friedman & Company.

Stephen B. Friedman, AICP CRE, S.B. Friedman & Company, Chicago, Illinois

Site Utilities and Extensions

These costs are specific to the location of connections and the design of the project. Streets, sewer, and water are typically the key utilities of concern. In some jurisdictions, however, there may be charges levied by electric, gas, and telephone companies to extend service to a site.

Parking

Costs vary greatly, depending on the type of parking. Surface parking is least expensive to construct; fully underground parking with ramps is the most expensive. Many residential building types include indoor parking on grade at a moderate cost.

Landscaping

Regulatory and market factors both drive this cost, which can range from trivial to substantial.

Off-Site Costs and Fees

Some developments will require improvements to off-site systems, to provide capacity to hook up sewer or water or relieve transportation bottlenecks, for example. In addition, many jurisdictions impose impact fees that are intended to cover capital costs of schools, parks, transportation facilities, or other public facilities.

Other Costs

Because site conditions and jurisdictions vary so widely, an analyst must think comprehensively to ensure that all relevant costs have been accounted for.

Construction Costs

Construction costs are central to estimating overall development costs as part of the pro forma financial projection. Construction costs are typically estimated several times during the development process, and then confirmed by bids prior to construction. Preliminary estimates can be made based on an outline specification or conceptual design, or, at the most rudimentary level, be based on gross square footage of a type of building. As the architectural design proceeds, increasingly detailed and accurate estimates can be prepared at the stage of schematic design, design development, construction documents, and final bid. The methods of obtaining estimates include the following:

- *Contractor estimates.* In many larger-scale projects, developers work with a general contractor from the beginning. The contractor provides estimates based on experience and records. Many residential developers are vertically integrated and include their own construction capabilities, hence estimate internally.
- *Estimating manuals.* Several companies produce cost-estimating manuals for use by lenders, insurance companies, developers, and others. These manuals are based on research conducted by the company on buildings actually constructed. Two commonly available ones are the *National Building Cost Manual* and *Means Square Foot Costs.* The manuals allow the user to consider the quality and complexity of the building in arriving at a cost estimate. Geographic adjusters are included to reflect costs around the country. The manuals typically include costs at the builder or contractor level, including architects fees, general conditions,

and contractor's profit. Other developer level costs are not included.
- *Architect and construction consultant estimates.* A third way to obtain cost estimates is to engage an independent cost estimator. Some architectural firms provide this service separate from design. There are specialty firms that provide estimates, typically as one of their services. Other services of such a firm can include construction oversight, construction administration, and construction monitoring on behalf of lenders or grantors.

Construction Cost Estimation Factors

No matter which source is used in estimating construction costs, an analyst must consider a number of factors:

- Building types
- Quality levels
- Key systems:
  - HVAC
  - Structural
  - Materials
  - Finish levels
  - Parking types
- Furniture, fixtures, and equipment (for certain property types)
- Tenant improvements

SOFT COSTS AND FEES

The total capital development costs of the project include a wide variety of soft costs. Each of these costs must be carefully researched and calculated to arrive at the total development costs against which returns are measured:

- Architecture and engineering
- Legal and consulting (other professional services)
- Taxes during construction
- Insurance
- Bonds and performance guarantees
- Development fees or general and administrative costs
- Marketing and commissions
- Financing fees
- Construction period interest
- Working capital

Many of these fees are objectively determined; they are what they are. However, several need some elaboration.

Development Fees or General and Administrative Costs

Lenders and investor partners allow these costs as a payment to the developer for the cost of producing and delivering the product. The developer may have given personal guarantees of completion and lease-up or cash flow; these fees help compensate for the value of such guarantees. The level of the fees depends on the complexity of the project, its size, the amount of risk, and the marketplace. A simple build-to-suit drugstore may garner a fee of only 3 percent. In contrast, a complex affordable housing project may provide for a 10 percent fee. The typical level of general and administrative cost for a U.S. homebuilder is 3.5 to 4.5 percent, according to the National Association of Home Builders (NAHB).

Marketing and Commissions

Marketing and commissions is another area of some complexity. Most developers pay outside brokers' commissions in addition to their own marketing costs. Those costs may include advertising, inside salespeople, and models, for example. In addition, inside salespeople may or may not share in general market commissions. Local research is needed to understand specifically how these costs may be incurred.

Financing Fees and Construction Period Interest

Financing fees and construction period interest (CPI) are also areas with great variability. The developer will pay a fee, often expressed as "points," for origination of each type of financing obtained. This may include third-party equity, the construction loan, and the permanent loan in an investment property. Developers often borrow as much of the construction cost as possible, typically 80 percent of peak outflow, but sometimes 100 percent will be borrowed, based on track record or additional collateral.

ECONOMIC FEASIBILITY

Investment Analysis for Rental Property Held for Investment

Once all of the costs have been estimated, the potential return on investment can be analyzed. If return is not sufficient, developers may ask for public assistance through tools such as tax increment financing, tax abatements, free land, or other tools used in a particular locale and at a particular time. It is essential to understand how net operating income, financing terms, and investor expectations interact to result in an economically feasible project.

Developers must provide competitive returns on investment, or investment capital will not be available to them—or they would rationally invest their own funds elsewhere. Real estate investments have many elements of risk, and are not liquid, in contrast to a stock, which can be easily sold. The tax benefits of real estate investment were severely curtailed in 1986, and most investments are evaluated on the basis of their cash returns. Generally, real estate investors look for returns in the upper tier of performance of alternative investments at a given time. There are industry studies that provide information on actual returns on total cost, typically for completed and "seasoned" properties. Return on equity is judged more anecdotally or researched on a case-by-case basis. Typically, real estate returns on equity must match the best-performing stock mutual funds and corporate equity returns to attract capital. There is a premium expected for investing in development deals, as compared to seasoned properties.

Returns on investment real estate are measured in several ways.

Return on Total Cost

In this measure, net operating income (revenues less cash operating expenses) is divided by the total cost of the project to determine the return. (This may also be called cash-on-cash, which is applicable only if the property is not partially financed with debt). The resulting factor is called the income capitalization rate (cap rate). This analysis is conducted two ways: annually after stabilization and discounted over time as an internal rate of return.

Stephen B. Friedman, AICP CRE, S.B. Friedman & Company, Chicago, Illinois

SAMPLE MEANS

Model costs calculated for a three-story building with 10-foot-story height and 22,500 square feet of floor area

			UNIT	UNIT COST	% PERCENT OF COST	PER S.F. SUB-TOTAL
A. SUBSTRUCTURE						
1010	Standard Foundations	Poured concrete; strip and spread footings	S.F. Ground	4.50	1.50	4.8%
1030	Slab on Grade	4" reinforced concrete with vapor barrier and granular base	S.F. Slab	3.65	1.21	
2010	Basement Excavation	Site preparation for slab and trench for foundation wall and footing	S.F. Ground	.14	.05	
2020	Basement Walls	4' foundation wall	l., F., Wall	108	1.11	
B. SHELL						
	B10 Superstructure					
1010	Floor Construction	Open web steel joists, slab form concrete, interior steel columns	S.F. Floor	12.50	8.33	12.5%
1020	Roof Construction	Open web steel joists with rib metal dock, interior steel columns	S.F. Roof	5.55	1.85	
	B20 Exterior Enclosure					
2010	Exterior Walls	Face brick with concrete block backup: 88% of wall	S.F. Wall	17.11	8.03	11.9%
2020	Exterior Windows	Aluminum horizontal sliding: 12% of wall	Each	332	1.41	
2030	Exterior Doors	Aluminum and glass	Each	1219	.21	
	B30 Roofing					
3010	Roof Coverings	Built-up tar and gravel with flashing; perlite/EPS composite Insulation	S.F. Roof	4.26	1.42	1.7%
3020	Roof Openings	N/A				
C. INTERIORS						
1010	Partitions	Gypsum board and sound-deadening board on metal studs	S.F. Part.	4.86	4.32	27.1%
1020	Interior Doors	15% solid core wood, 85% hollow core wood	Each	4.21	5.26	
1030	Fittings	Kitchen cabinets	S.F. Floor	1.92	1.92	
2010	Stair Construction	Concrete-filled metal pan	Flight	53.75	1.19	
3010	Wall Finishes	70% paint, 25% vinyl wall covering, 5% ceramic tiles	S.F. Surface	1.96	1.96	
3020	Floor Finishes	60% carpet, 30% vinyl composition tile, 10% ceramic tiles	S.F. Floor	4.61	4.61	
3030	Ceiling Finishes	Painted gypsum board on resilient channels	S.F. Ceiling	3.00	2.78	
D. SERVICES						
	D10 Conveying					
1010	Elevators and Lifts	One hydraulic passenger elevator	Each	70.200	3.12	3.8%
1020	Escalators and Moving Walks	N/A	—	—	—	
	D20 Plumbing					
2010	Plumbing Fixtures	Kitchen, bathroom and service fixtures, supply and drainage	Each	15.48	7.74	12.7%
2020	Domestic Water Distribution	Gas-fired water heater	S.F. Floor	2.28	2.28	
2040	Rain Water Drainage	Roof drains	S.F. Roof	.84	.28	
	D30 HVAC					
3010	Energy Supply	Oil-fired hot water, baseboard radiation	S.F. Floor	4.88	4.88	13.6%
3020	Heat Generation System	N/A	—	—	—	
3030	Cooling Generation System	Chilled water, air-cooled condenser system	S.F. Floor	6.17	6.17	
3050	Terminal and Package Units	N/A	—	—	—	
3090	Other HVAC Sys. & Equipment	N/A	—	—	—	
	D40 Fire Protection					
4010	Sprinklers	Wet pipe sprinkler system	S.F. Floor	1.98	1.98	2.4%
4020	Standpipes	Standpipe	S.F. Floor	—	—	
	D50 Electrical					
5010	Electrical Ser/Distribution	600 ampere service, panel board and feeders	S.F. Floor	1.67	1.67	9.3%
5020	Lighting and Branch Wiring	Incandescent fixtures receptacles switches A.C. and miscellaneous power	S.F. Floor	5.21	5.21	
5030	Communications and Security	Alarm systems and emergency lighting	S.F. Floor	.55	.55	
5090	Other Electrical Systems	Generator, 11.5KW	S.F. Floor	.16	.16	
E. EQUIPMENT & FURNISHINGS						
1010	Commercial Equipment	N/A	—	—	—	0.0%
1020	Institutional Equipment	N/A	—	—	—	
1030	Vehicular Equipment	N/A	—	—	—	
1090	Other Equipment	N/A	—	—	—	
F. SPECIAL CONSTRUCTION						
1020	Integrated Construction	N/A	—	—	—	0.0%
1040	Special Facilities	N/A	—	—	—	
G. BUILDING SITEWORK						
N/A						
			Subtotal	81.20		100%

CONTRACTOR FEES (General Requirements: 10%, Overhead: 5%, Profit; 10%)			25%	20.33
ARCHITECT FEES			8%	8.12

Total Building Cost 109.65

Source: Reprinted with permission from Means Square Foot Costs, 2004. Copyright Reed Construction Data, Kingston, MA 781-585-7880. All rights reserved.

Stephen B. Friedman, AICP CRE, S.B. Friedman & Company, Chicago, Illinois

The internal rate of return is calculated by:

1. estimating a residual value at the end of a hypothetical holding period;
2. adding that value to the final-year cash flow; and
3. discounting back to the initial year of the project.

The result can then be compared to benchmarks in publications such as the *American Council of Life Insurers Investment Bulletin,* the *RERC Report,* and the *Korpacz Real Estate Investor Survey* from PricewaterhouseCoopers. Interpretations and adjustments must be made for risk, because the core data in these studies tend to focus on existing properties.

Return on Equity

Equity returns are calculated after considering financing that has been arranged or that could reasonably be expected based on market conditions. In this case, debt service is deducted from net operating income to arrive at cash flow after debt service. In many public-private transactions, there may be several layers of debt. Whatever cash is left is available to service equity. The same types of calculations are made as above, but only cash available after debt service and against equity, rather than total cost.

Other Measures

Investors may also measure how quickly their capital is returned. This is valid in restaurant projects, which typically have a shorter lifespan. They may also look at returns without considering residual value, or may argue that the property will have little value at the end of a holding period. This is not typically true, but can be in some high-risk situations.

They may also argue that they are holders, not sellers, and that a hypothetical sale to estimate a value is not relevant. This may be true, but there is still long-term value to be taken into account in arriving at the types of estimates that can be compared to industry benchmarks.

Finally, note that many developers do not hold the property. They "underwrite" their investment by seeking a higher expected return if all goes well, compensating them for their risk. They then often sell to an investor-owner at a favorable price because the risk is lower, with a typical target profit level on the sale of 20 percent.

Profitability Analysis of For-Sale Projects

In for-sale projects, profitability is typically measured as margin on sales. While there is still concern about return on investment by the developer or its investors, profit margin is the benchmark measure. Profit margin is used because return on invested capital is quite volatile and can be greatly impacted by the length of time it takes to sell out a project. Indeed, if it ultimately takes too long, all profit may be consumed by carrying costs. However, the standard of profit margin is relatively easy to use. The National Association of Home Builders has prepared a benchmark study. Key benchmarks include:

- Cost of goods: approximately 75 percent of sales
- General and administrative costs: 3.5 to 4.5 percent of sales
- Net profit, excluding general and administration costs: 5 percent typically; 10 percent for the most successful builders.

These factors apply to the integrated homebuilder. If a project requires multiple layers of builders/contractors/developers, then there may be additional fees.

The table here shows the summary analysis for a typical for-sale housing development.

COMMUNITY SHOPPING CENTER INCOME, EXPENSE, AND RETURNS

Exhibit XX
Community Shopping Center
Income, Expense & Returns

| Internal Rate of Return (RR) | 10% | on Total Cost |
| Internal Rate of Return (RR) | 19% | on Cash Equity |

Assumptions

Project Cost		$35,042,878
Equity	19%	$6,775,589
Mortgage Loan	78%	$27,267,289
TIF	3%	$1,000,000
Check		$35,042,878

Financing Factors

Debt Coverage Ratio	1.25
Supportable Annual Debt Service	$(2,624,063)
Inflation Rate	2%
Cap Rate	10%
Loan Term (years)	20
Interest Rate	7.25%

Operating Income

	Initial Occupancy	Building Area	Lease Rate (Net)	Gross Income	Vacancy Rate	Lease Term	Inflation Factor
Grocery Store	Year 2	65,000	$17.00	$1,105,000	0	10.0	1.2190
Drugstore	Year 2	15,000	$20.00	$300,000	0	10.0	1.2190
Small Stores	Year 3	89,000	$25.00	$2,225,000	5%	5.0	1.1041
Total SF/Operating Income		169,000		$3,630,000			

Operating Costs

		Annual Cost
Management (% of Income)	5%	$181,500
Reserves PSF	$0.20	$33,800
Common Area Maintenance (CAM)	$3.00	$507,000
Property Taxes	$2.00	$338,000
Total Operating Costs		$1,060,300

	Year 1		Year 2	Year 3	Year 4	Year 5	Year 6	Year 7	Year 8	Year 9	Year 10	Year 11
Revenue	Occupancy		47%	97%	97%	97%	97%	97%	97%	97%	97%	97%
Rental Income		Construction	$1,405,000	$3,630,000	$3,630,000	$3,630,000	$3,630,000	$3,861,580	$3,861,580	$3,861,580	$3,861,580	$4,169,267
Vacancy Loss—Small Stores			$ –	$(111,250)	$(111,250)	$(111,250)	$(111,250)	$(111,250)	$(122,829)	$ (122,829)	$(122,829)	$(135,613)
Recoveries		$ –	$400,000	$839,205	$855,989	$873,109	$890,571	$908,382	$926,550	$945,081	$963,983	$983,262
Total Revenue			$1,805,000	$4,357,955	$4,374,739	$4,391,859	$4,409,321	$4,658,712	$4,665,301	$4,683,832	$4,702,734	$5,016,916
Operating Expenses												
Management Fee			$(70,250)	$(181,500)	$(181,500)	$(181,500)	$ (181,500)	$(193,079)	$(193,079)	$(193,079)	$(193,079)	$(208,463)
Reserves		$ –	$(33,800)	$(34,476)	$(35,166)	$(35,869)	$(36,586)	$(37,318)	$(38,064)	$(38,826)	$(39,602)	$40,394
Common Area Maintenance			$(507,000)	$(517,140)	$(527,483)	$(538,032)	$(548,793)	$(559,769)	$(570,964)	$(582,384)	$(594,031)	$(605,912)
Taxes			$(338,000)	$(344,760)	$(351,655)	$(358,688)	$(365,862)	$(373,179)	$(380,643)	$(388,256)	$(396,021)	$(403,941)
Total Expenses		$ –	$(949,050)	$(1,077,876)	$(1,095,804)	$(1,114,090)	$(1,132,741)	$(1,163,345)	$(1,182,751)	$(1,202,544)	$(1,222,733)	$(1,258,711)
Net Operating Income			$855,950	$3,280,079	$3,278,936	$3,277,769	$3,276,580	$3,495,367	$3,482,550	$3,481,288	$3,480,000	$3,758,206
Debt Service		$ –	$(2,624,063)	($2,624,063)	($2,624,063)	($2,624,063)	($2,624,063)	($2,624,063)	($2,624,063)	($2,624,063)	($2,624,063)	($2,624,063)
Equity Investment		$(5,007,476)	$ –	$ –	$ –	$ –	$ –	$ –	$ –	$ –	$ –	$ –
Residual Value		$ –	$ –	$ –	$ –	$ –	$ –	$ –	$ –	$ –	$ –	$21,070,819
IRR on Total Cost	10%	$(35,042,878)	$855,950	$3,280,079	$3,278,936	$3,277,769	$3,276,580	$3,495,367	$3,482,550	$3,481,288	$3,480,000	$44,263,310
IRR on Equity	19%	$(5,007,476)	$(1,768,113)	$656,016	$654,872	$653,706	$652,516	$871,304	$858,487	$857,225	$855,225	$22,204,961

Stephen B. Friedman, AICP CRE, S.B. Friedman & Company, Chicago, Illinois

MIXED-USE CONDOMINIUM DEVELOPMENT FINANCIAL ANALYSIS

ASSUMPTIONS

Residential Units			Parking for Residential	
Number of Units		48	Enclosed Parking Total Area	16,502
Net Liveable Square Feet (Salable)		55,009	Enclosed Parking Spaced	48
Average Unit Size		1,146	Additional Salable Parking Spaces	27
Average Selling Price Per Net Square Foot		$200	Visitor Spaces	5
Average Selling Price/Unit		$229,204	Total Residential Parking	80
Average Selling Price/Unit Including Upgrades	10%	$252,125	Retail/Commercial Parking	146
Retail Space			Total Parking, Residential and Commercial	226
Retail Space (net SF)		15,000		
Restaurant (net SF)		5,000	Construction Costs Per SF	
Commercial (net SF)		9,100	Residential (per net SF)	$110
Total Commercial and Retail		29,100	Retail (per net SF)	$105
			Commercial (per net SF)	$90
Total Net SF, Residential and Commercial		84,109	Restaurant (per net SF)	$105
Gross Building, Residential and Commercial		111,610		

INCOME (Residential Condominiums)				
Condo Sales	$200	PSF, including balconies	$11,001,800	
Net Upgrade Income (25% Margin)	$5,730	per unit	$275,045	
Extra Parking Spaces	$10,000	per space	$270,000	
Net Sales Proceeds			$11,546,845	
Closing Costs	0.6%	of condo sales	($74,000)	
Commissions 6% of condo sales ($676,308)				
TOTAL NET INCOME CONDOS			$10,796,537	
Commercial/Retail Space Value	Based on NPV of Retail			Approx NOI, $20 PSF
	Income		$5,820,000	Separate Pro Forma
TOTAL INCOME CONDOS AND RETAIL			$16,616,537	

PROJECT COSTS			Cost	% TDC
Hard Construction Costs	$118	per net SF	$9,951,990 7	7.08%
Residential Units (including parking)	$110	per net SF	$6,050,990	46.87%
Retail Space	$105	per net SF	$1,575,000 1	2.20%
Commercial	$90	per net SF	$819,000	6.34%
Restaurant	$105	per net SF	$525,000	4.07%
Tenant Improvements	$20	per net SF	$582,000	4.51%
General Conditions			$400,000	3.10%
Site Preparation Costs			$887,001	6.87%
Demolition			$0	0.00%
Relocation			$0	0.00%
Soils			$0	0.00%
Landscaping/Lighting			$391,633	3.03%
Environmental Test and Remediation			$0	0.00%
Sewer/Water/Detention			$105,264	0.82%
Site Improvements			$165,452	1.28%
Street and Parking Lot (including condo lot)			$224,652	1.74%
Soft Costs			$1,116,000	8.64%
Appraisal			$25,000	0.19%
Architecture			$290,000	2.25%
Engineering—All			$75,000	0.58%
Legal			$58,000	0.45%
Survey and Title			$18,000	0.14%
Real Estate Taxes			$150,000	1.16%
Permits			$0	0.00%
Sales and Marketing			$500,000	3.87%
SUBTOTAL DEVELOPMENT COST EXCLUDING LAND			$11,954,991	92.59%

FINANCING FEES				
Construction Period Interest—Half-Out Method (80% of Subtotal DC)				
Subtotal Development Cost	80%		$9,563,993	
Period (Years)			2.5	
Interest Rate	8.0%			
Construction Loan Financing Costs			$956,399	7.41%
TOTAL DEVELOPMENT COST, INCLUDING FINANCING COSTS			$12,911,390	100.00%
TOTAL DEVELOPMENT COST, INCLUDING FINANCING COSTS Per Net SF			$154	% of income
NET PROFIT B/4 Land Cost (Net Total Income Less Total Dev. Cost)			$3,705,147	22.3%
BENCHMARK PROFIT Incl. most Overhead			$2,243,232	13.5%
LAND PRICE/(SUBSIDY) TO ACHIEVE BENCHMARK PROFIT			$1,461,914	8.8%

Source: S. B. Friedman & Company.

Stephen B. Friedman, AICP CRE, S.B. Friedman & Company, Chicago, Illinois

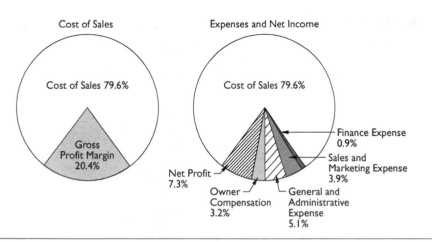

Cost of Sales

Cost of Sales 79.6%

Gross Profit Margin 20.4%

Expenses and Net Income

Cost of Sales 79.6%

Finance Expense 0.9%

Sales and Marketing Expense 3.9%

General and Administrative Expense 5.1%

Owner Compensation 3.2%

Net Profit 7.3%

REFERENCES

American Council of Life Insurers. 2004. *Commercial Mortgage Commitments, Second Quarter 2004.* Washington, D.C.: American Council of Life Insurers.

Innerarity, Dean et al. 2004. *Cost of Doing Business Study, The Business of Building, Measuring Your Success.* Washington, D.C.: National Association of Homebuilders.

Korpacz, Peter. 2004. "Real Estate Investor Survey." *CMBS Insider* 17 (1). Ridgewood, NJ: Price Waterhouse Coopers LLP.

Real Estate Research Corporation, Real Estate Report. 2004. *The Good, the Bad, and the Real Estate Market: Waiting for the Dust to Settle* 33 (2).

BENCHMARKS

Reprinted by permission from the 2004 edition of Cost of Doing Business Study: The Business of Building, *p. 15, © 2004 by BuilderBooks.com, National Association of Homebuilders, Washington, D.C.*

Stephen B. Friedman, AICP CRE, S.B. Friedman & Company, Chicago, Illinois

RESOURCES

PART I: PLANS AND PLAN MAKING

PLAN MAKING

Anderson, Larz T. 1995. *Guidelines for Preparing Urban Plans*. Chicago: Planners Press.

Hopkins, Lewis. 2001. *Urban Development: The Logic of Making Plans*. Washington, DC: Island Press.

Kaiser, Edward J., David R. Godschalk, and F. Stuart Chapin. 1995. *Urban Land Use Planning*, 4th ed. Urbana, IL: University of Illinois Press.

Levy, John M. 2002. *Contemporary Urban Planning*, 6th ed., Englewood Cliffs, NJ: Prentice Hall.

COMPREHENSIVE PLANS

Anderson, Larz. T. 1995. *Guidelines for Preparing Urban Plans*. Chicago: Planners Press.

Kaiser, Edward J., David R. Godschalk, and F. Stuart Chapin, Jr. 1995. *Urban Land Use Planning*, 4th ed. Urbana, IL: University of Illinois Press.

Kelly, Eric Damian, and Barbara Becker. 2000. *Community Planning: An Introduction to the Comprehensive Plan*. Washington, D.C.: Island Press.

Kent, T.J. 1990. *The Urban General Plan*. Chicago: Planners Press (reprint of 1964 edition).

URBAN DESIGN PLANS

Barnett, Jonathan. 2003. *Redesigning Cities: Principles Practice, Implementation*. Chicago: American Planning Association.

Clay, Grady. 1973. *Close-Up: How to Read the American City*. New York: Praeger Publishers.

Cullen, Gordon. 1971. *The Concise Townscape*. New York: Van Nostrand Reinhold Co.

Jacobs, Allan. 1985. *Looking at Cities*. Cambridge, MA: Harvard University Press.

Katz, Peter. 1994. *The New Urbanism: Toward an Architecture of Community*. New York: McGraw-Hill, Inc.

Kelbaugh, Doug (ed.). 1989. *The Pedestrian Pocket Book: A New Suburban Design Strategy*. New York: Princeton Architectural Press.

———. 1997. *Common Place: Toward Neighborhood and Regional Design*. Seattle: University of Washington Press.

Kostof, Spiro. 1999. *The City Shaped: Urban Patterns and Meanings Through History*. London: Thames and Hudson.

Lynch, Kevin. 1975. *The Image of the City*. Cambridge, MA: MIT Press.

———. 1987. *Good City Form*. Cambridge, MA: MIT Press.

Urban Design Associates. 2003. *The Urban Design Handbook: Techniques and Working Methods*. New York: W.W. Norton and Company.

Walters, David, and Linda Luise Brown. 2004. *Design First: Design-Based Planning for Communities*. Oxford: Elsevier.

REGIONAL PLANS

Calthorpe, Peter, and William Fulton. 2001. *The Regional City: Planning for the End of Sprawl*. Washington, DC: Island Press.

Orfield, Myron. 2002. *American Metropolitics: The New Suburban Reality*. Washington, D.C.: Brookings Institution Press.

So, Frank, Irving Hand, and Bruce D. McDowall. 1986. *The Practice of State and Regional Planning*. Washington, DC: American Planning Association, in cooperation with the International City Management Association.

Yaro, Robert D., and Tony Hiss. 1996. *Region at Risk: The Third Regional Plan for the New York-New Jersey-Connecticut Metropolitan Area*. Washington, DC: Island Press, with the Regional Plan Association.

NEIGHBORHOOD PLANS

Brower, Sidney. 2000. *Good Neighborhoods*. Westport, CT: Praeger.

Jones, Bernie. 1990. *Neighborhood Planning*. Chicago: Planners Press.

Martz, Wendelyn. 1995. *Neighborhood-Based Planning*. Planning Advisory Service Report No. 455.Chicago: American Planning Association.

Rue, Harrison Bright. 2000. *Real Towns: Making your Neighborhood Work*. Sacramento, CA: Local Government Commission.

TRANSPORTATION PLANS

Edwards, John D. Jr., P.E. (ed.). 1999. *Transportation Planning Handbook*, 2nd ed. Washington, D.C.: Institute of Transportation Engineers.

National Cooperative Highway Research Program No. 446. 2000. *A Guidebook for Performance -Based Transportation Planning*. Washington, D.C.: National Academy Press.

Pline, James L. (ed.). 1999.*Traffic Engineering Handbook*, 5th ed. Institute of Transportation Engineers.

Stover, Vergil G., and Frank J. Koepke. 2002. *Transportation and Land Development*. Washington, D.C.: Institute of Transportation Engineers.

Wright, Paul H., Norman J. Ashford, and Robert J. Stammer. 2001. *Transportation Engineering: Planning and Design*. Hoboken, NJ: John Wiley & Sons, Inc.

HOUSING PLANS

Katz, Bruce, Margery Austin Turner, Karen Destorel Brown, Mary Cunningham, and Noah Sawyer. 2003. *Rethinking Local Affordable Housing Strategies: Lessons from 70 Years of Policies & Practices*. Washington, DC: The Brookings Institution Center on Urban and Metropolitan Policy.

Massachusetts Citizens' Housing and Planning Association. 2002. "Taking the Initiative: A Guidebook on Creating Local Affordable Housing Strategies."

Meck, Stuart, Rebecca Retzlaff, and Jim Schwab. 2003. *Regional Approaches to Affordable Housing*. Planning Advisory Service Report No. 513/514. Chicago: American Planning Association.

White, S. Mark. 1992. *Affordable Housing: Proactive and Reactive Planning Strategies*. Planning Advisory Service Report No. 441. Chicago: American Planning Association.

ECONOMIC DEVELOPMENT PLANS

Blakely, Edward J. and Ted K. Bradshaw. 2002. *Planning Local Economic Development: Theory and Practice*. 3rd ed. Thousand Oaks, CA: Sage Publications.

Canada, Eric P. 1995. *Economic Development: Marketing for Results*. Wheaton, IL: Blane Canada Ltd.

Klosterman, R.E. 1990. *Community Analysis and Planning Techniques*. Savage, MD: Rowman & Littlefield Publishers, Inc.

Koven, Steven G., and Thomas S. Lyons. 2003. *Economic Development*. Washington, D.C.: International City/County Management Association.

McLean, M.L., and K.P. Voytek. 1992. *Understanding Your Economy: Using Analysis to Guide Local Strategic Planning*. Chicago: Planners Press.

PARKS AND OPEN-SPACE PLANS

Cooper Marcus, Clare, and Carolyn Francis (ed.). 1990. *People Places: Design Guidelines for Urban Open Space*. New York: Van Nostrand Reinhold.

Garvin, Alexander. 2000. *Parks, Recreation, and Open Space: A Twenty-First Century Agenda*. Planning Advisory Service Report No. 497/498. Chicago: American Planning Association.

Hopper, Kim (ed.). 2002. *Local Greenprinting for Growth, Overview,* Volume I. Washington, DC: Trust for Public Land.

Mertes, James D., and James R. Hall. 1996. *Park, Recreation, Open Space and Greenway Guidelines*. Washington, DC: National Recreation and Park Association.

CRITICAL AND SENSITIVE AREAS PLANS

Duerksen, Christopher, and R. Matthew Gobel. 1999. *Aesthetics, Community Character and the Law*. Planning Advisory Service Report No. 489/490. Chicago: American Planning Association.

ROLE OF PARTICIPATION

Burns, J. 1979. *Connections: Ways to Discover and Realize Community Potentials*. New York: McGraw-Hill.

Creighton, J.L. 1994. *Involving Citizens in Community Decision Making: A Guidebook.*. Washington, DC: Program for Community Problem Solving.

Hester, R.T. Jr. 1990. *Community Design Primer*. Mendocino, CA: Ridge Times Press.

Lach, D., and P. Hixson. 1996. "Developing Indicators to Measure Values and Costs of Public Involvement Activities." *Interact: The Journal of Public Participation* 2, 1:51–63.

Moore, C. Nicholas. (ed.) 1997. *Participation Tools for Better Land-Use Planning*. 2nd ed. Sacramento, CA: Center for Livable Communities.

Rosner, J. 1978. "Matching Method to Purpose: The Challenges of Planning Citizen Participation Activities." In *Citizen Participation in America*, edited by S. Langton. New York: Lexington Books.

Sanoff, Henry. 2000. *Community Participation Methods in Design and Planning*. Hoboken, NJ: John Wiley & Sons, Inc.

STAKEHOLDER IDENTIFICATION

Bryson, John. 1988. *Strategic Planning for Public and Nonprofit Organizations*. San Francisco: Jossey-Bass Publishers.

Carlson, Chris. 1999. "Convening." In *Consensus Building Handbook*, edited by L. Susskind, S. McKearnon, and S. Carpenter. Thousand Oaks, CA: Sage Publications.

Chrislip, David D., and Carl E. Larson. 1994. *Collaborative Leadership: How Citizens and Civic Leaders Can Make a Difference*. San Francisco: Jossey-Bass Publishers.

Gray, Barbara. 1989. *Collaborating: Finding Common Ground for Multiparty Problems*. San Francisco: Jossey-Bass Publishers.

Walsh, Mary L. 1997. *Building Citizen Involvement*. Washington, DC: International City/County Management Association.

SURVEYS

Dandekar, Hemalata C. 2003. *Planner's Use of Information*, 2nd ed. Chicago: Planners Press.

Lake, C. C., and Harper, P. C. 1987. *Public Opinion Polling: A Handbook for Public Interest and Citizen*

Advocacy Groups. Washington, DC: Island Press.

Langer, Gary. May/June 2003. "About Response Rates: Some Unresolved Questions" in *Public Perspective*: 16-18.

Rea, Louis M., and Richard A. Parker. 1992. *Designing and Conducting Survey Research: A Comprehensive Guide*. San Francisco: Jossey-Bass.

Salant, Priscilla, and Don A. Dillman. 1994. *How to Conduct your Own Survey*. Hoboken, NJ: John Wiley & Sons, Inc.

Survey Research Center. 1983. *Interviewer's Manual*. Ann Arbor, MI: University of Michigan Press.

Swanbrow, Diane. October 2002. "When to Trust the Polls." *The University Record Online*. University of Michigan News Service.

COMMUNITY VISIONING

Ames, Steven C. (ed.). 1998. *A Guide to Community Visioning: Hands-On Information for Local Communities*. Portland, OR: Oregon Visions Project, Oregon Chapter of the American Planning Association.

Green, Gary, Anna Haines, and Stephen Halebsky. 2000. *Building Our Future: A Guide to Community Visioning*. UW-Extension Publication G3708. Madison, WI: University of Wisconsin-Extension.

Okubo, Derek. 2000. *The Community Visioning and Strategic Planning Handbook*, 3rd ed. Denver: National Civic League Press.

Weisbord, Marvin R., and Sandra Janoff. 2000. *Future Search: An Action Guide to Finding Common Ground in Organizations and Communities*, 2nd ed. San Francisco: Berrett-Koehler.

CHARRETTES

Burden, Dan. 2003. *Community Guide to Conducting a Successful Charrette*. Orlando, FL: Walkable Communities.

Lennertz, Bill, and Aarin Lutzenhiser. 2003. "Charrettes 101: Dynamic Planning for Community Change." *BuildingBlocks* 4 (1): 3-11.

National Charrette Institute. 2005. *NCI Charrette Start Up Kit* 2nd ed. CD-ROM. Portland, OR: National Charrette Institute.

Straus, David. 2002. *How to Make Collaboration Work: Powerful Ways to Build Consensus, Solve Problems, and Make Decisions*. San Francisco: Berrett-Koehler.

PUBLIC MEETINGS

Cogan, Arnold, Sumner Sharpe, and Joe Hertzberg. 1986. "Citizen Participation." *The Practice of State and Regional Planning*. Chicago: American Planning Association/International City Management Association.

Cogan, Elaine. 2000. *Successful Public Meetings, A Practical Guide*. 2nd ed. Chicago: American Planning Association.

Dandekar, Hemalata C. (ed.). 2003. *The Planner's Use of Information*. Chicago: American Planning Association.

Jones, Bernie. 1990. *Neighborhood Planning*. Chicago: Planners Press.

PUBLIC HEARINGS

Carpenter, Susan L., and Kennedy, W.J.D. 1988. *Managing Public Disputes: A Practical Guide to Handling Conflict and Reaching Agreements*. San Francisco: Jossey-Bass.

Cogan and Associates. 1977. *Techniques of Public Involvement*. Washington, DC: Council of State Planning Agencies.

Cogan, Elaine. 2000. *Successful Public Meetings, A Practical Guide*. 2nd ed. Chicago: American Planning Association.

Mater, Jean. 1984. *Public Hearings Procedures and Strategies: A Guide to Influencing Public Decisions*. Englewood Cliffs, NJ: Prentice-Hall.

COMPUTER-BASED PUBLIC PARTICIPATION

Langendorf, Richard. 1995. "Towards an Improved Information Utilization in Design Decision-Making: A Case Study of the Hurricane Andrew Recovery Efforts." Environment and Planning B: Planning and Design, Vol. 22, No. 3: 315-330.

Moughtin, J.C., Rafael Cuesta, Christine Sarris, and Paola Signoretta. 2003. *Urban Design: Methods and Techniques,* 2nd ed. Oxford: Elsevier Press.

Obermeyer, Nancy J. 1998. "The Evolution of Public Participation GIS." *Cartography and Geographic Information Systems*. Vol. 25, No.2: 65-66.

Pietsch, Susan M. 2000. "Computer Visualization in the Design Control of Urban Environments: A Literature Review." *Environment and Planning B: Planning and Design*, Vol. 27, No. 4: 521-536.

PART 2: ENVIRONMENTAL PLANNING AND MANAGEMENT

ENVIRONMENTAL PLANNING CONSIDERATIONS

Daniels, Tom, and Katherine Daniels. 2003. *The Environmental Planning Handbook for Sustainable Communities and Regions*. Chicago: Planners Press.

Groves, Craig R. 2003. *Drafting a Conservation Blueprint: A Practitioner's Guide to Planning for Biodiversity*. Washington, DC: Island Press.

McHarg, Ian. 1969. Reprinted 1995. *Design with Nature*. Garden City, NY: Natural History Press. New York: John Wiley & Sons, Inc.

RESOURCES

Niebanck, Paul. 1993. "The Shape of Environmental Planning Education." *Environment and Planning B: Planning and Design*. Vol. 20, pp. 511-518.

Randolph, John. 2004. *Environmental Land Use Planning and Management*. Washington, DC: Island Press.

Steiner, Frederick. 2000. *The Living Landscape: An Ecological Approach to Landscape Planning*, 2nd ed. New York: McGraw Hill.

Yaro, Robert, and Tony Hiss. 1996. *Region at Risk: The Third Regional Plan for the New York-New Jersey-Connecticut Metropolitan Area*. Washington, DC: Island Press.

AIR QUALITY

Daniels, Tom, and Katherine Daniels. 2003. "Planning for Sustainable Air Quality," in *The Environmental Planning Handbook for Sustainable Communities and Regions*. Chicago: Planners Press.

U.S. Environmental Protection Agency, Office of Air and Radiation. 2001. *Improving Air Quality Through Land Use Activities*. EPA-420-R-01-001.

Washington State Department of Ecology. 2003. *Focus on Linking Land Use, Air Quality, and Transportation Planning*. www.ecy.wa.gov/pubs/0302015.pdf. Last accessed June 27, 2005.

Winkelman, Steve, Greg Dierkers, Erin Silsbe, Mac Wubben, and Shayna Stott. 2005. *Air Quality and Smart Growth: Planning for Cleaner Air*. Coral Gables, FL: Funders' Network for Smart Growth and Livable Communities.

AIR SHEDS

Arya, S. Pal. 1999. *Air Pollution Meteorology and Dispersion*. New York: Oxford University Press.

Sokhi, Ranjeet S., and John G. Bartzis (eds). 2002. *Urban Air Quality—Recent Advances*. Dordrecht, Netherlands: Kluwer Academic Publishers.

Turner, D. Bruce. 1994. *Workbook of Atmospheric Dispersion Estimates: An Introduction to Dispersion Modeling*, 2nd ed. Boca Raton, FL: CRC Press.

Wark, Kenneth, Cecil F. Warner, and Wayne T. Davis. 1997. *Air Pollution: Its Origin and Control*, 3rd ed. Englewood Cliffs, NJ: Prentice Hall.

HEAT ISLANDS

Akbari, H., S. Davis, S. Dorsano, J. Huang, and S. Winnett (eds). 1992. *Cooling Our Communities: A Guidebook on Tree Planting and Light-Colored Surfacing*. U.S. Environmental Protection Agency, Office of Policy Analysis, Climate Change Division. Lawrence Berkeley National Laboratory Report No. LBL-31587.

Estes, Maurice G., Jr., Dr. Dale Quattrochi, Dr. Jeffrey Luvall, and Virginia Gorsevski. May 2000. "Urban Heat Islands: Mitigation Strategies for Planners." *PAS Memo*. Chicago: American Planning Association.

Nowak, D. J., and J. F. Dwyer. 2000. "Understanding the Benefits and Costs of Urban Forest Ecosystems." *Handbook of Urban and Community Forestry in the Northeast*. J. E. Kuser, editor. New York: Kluwer Academic/Plenum Publishers: 11–25.

Stone, Brian Jr., and Michael O. Rodgers. 2001. "Urban Form and Thermal Efficiency: How the Design of Cities Influences the Urban Heat Island Effect." *Journal of the American Planning Association*. Vol. 67, No. 2. Chicago: American Planning Association. Pp.186-198.

Wilson, A., and M.R. Pelletier. 2001. "A Garden Overhead: The Benefits and Challenges of Green Roofs." *Environmental Building News*: 1, 10–18.

WATERSHEDS

Center for Watershed Protection. 1998. *Rapid Watershed Planning Handbook: A Comprehensive Guide for Managing Urbanizing Watersheds*. Ellicott City, MD: Center for Watershed Protection.

Clements, J.T., C. S. Creager, A. R. Beach, J. B. Butcher, M.D. Marcus, and T. R. Schueler. 1996. *Framework for a Watershed Management Program*. Alexandria, VA: Water Environment Research Foundation.

Schueler, Thomas R., and Heather K. Holland, editors. 2000. *The Practice of Watershed Protection: Techniques for Protecting and Restoring Urban Watersheds*. Ellicott City, MD: Center for Watershed Protection.

Shoemaker, L., M. Lahlou, M. Bryer, D. Kumar, and K. Kratt. 1997. *Compendium of Tools for Watershed Assessment and TMDL Development*. EPA 841-B-97-006. Washington, DC: Tetra Tech, Inc. and U.S. EPA Office of Wetlands, Oceans, and Watersheds.

AQUIFERS

U.S. Environmental Protection Agency, Office of Groundwater Protection. 1988. *Model Assessments for Delineating Wellhead Protection Areas*. Washington, DC: EPA, OGWP.

U.S. Geological Survey. 1984. U.S. Geological Survey Open File Report 84-475.

Witten, Jon, and Scott Horsley. 1995. A Guide to Wellhead Protection. PAS Report No. 457/458. Chicago: American Planning Association.

RIVERS AND STREAMS

Brookes, A. 1988. *Channelized Rivers*. Chichester, England: John Wiley & Sons, Inc.

Dunne, Thomas, and Luna B. Leopold. 1978. *Water in Environmental Planning*. New York: W.H. Freeman.

Federal Interagency Stream Restoration Working Group. 1998. *Stream Corridor Restoration: Principles, Processes, Practices*. Washington, DC: Government Printing Office.

MacBroom, James. 1998. *The River Book: The Nature and Management of Streams in Glaciated Terrains*. Hartford, CT: Connecticut Department of Environmental Protection.

FLOODPLAINS AND RIPARIAN CORRIDORS

Committee on Riparian Zone Functioning and Strategies for Management, editor. 2002. *Riparian Areas*. Washington, DC: National Academy Press.

Federal Interagency Stream Restoration Working Group. 1998. *Stream Corridor Restoration: Principles, Processes, Practices*. Washington, DC: Government Printing Office.

MacBroom, James. 1998. *The River Book: The Nature and Management of Streams in Glaciated Terrains*. Hartford, CT: Connecticut Department of Environmental Protection.

Mitigation Success Stories in the United States. 2000. Madison, WI: Association of State Floodplain Managers.

Otto, Betsy, Kathleen McCormick, and Michael Leccese. 2004. *Ecological Riverfront Design: Restoring Rivers, Connecting Communities*. Planning Advisory Service Report No. 518/519. Chicago: American Planning Association.

Schueler, T.R. 1996. "The Architecture of Urban Stream Buffers." *Watershed Protection Techniques* 1, no. 4.

WETLANDS

Dennison, Mark S., and James F. Berry (eds). 1993. *Wetlands: Guide to Science, Law and Technology*. Park Ridge, NJ: Noyes Publications.

France, Robert L. 2003. *Wetland Design: Principles and Practices for Landscape Architects and Land Use Planners*. New York: Norton.

Mitsch, William J., and James G. Gosselink. 2000. *Wetlands*, 3rd ed. Hoboken, NJ: John Wiley & Sons, Inc.

Want, William L. 2003. *Law of Wetlands Regulation*. St. Paul, MN: West Group.

BEACH AND DUNE SYSTEMS

Beatley, Timothy, David J. Brower, and Anna K. Schwab. 2002. *An Introduction to Coastal Zone Management*. Washington, DC: Island Press.

Bird, Eric C.F. 1996. *Beach Management*. Hoboken, NJ: John Wiley & Sons, Inc.

Bush, David, Orrin H. Pilkey, and William Neal, 1996. *Living by the Rules of the Sea*. Durham, NC: Duke University Press.

Psuty, Norbert P., and Douglas D. Ofiara. 2002. *Coastal Hazard Management: Lessons and Future Directions from New Jersey*. New Brunswick, NJ: Rutgers University Press.

Rogers, Spencer, and David Nash, 2003. *The Dune Book*. Raleigh, NC: North Carolina Sea Grant.

Virginia Marine Resources Commission. 1993. *Coastal Primary Sand Dunes/Beach Guidelines: Guidelines for the Permitting of Activities Which Encroach into Coastal Primary Sand Dunes/Beaches*. Newport News, VA.

ESTUARIES, FLATS, AND MARSHES

Beatley, Timothy, David J. Brower, and Anna K. Schwab. 2002. *An Introduction to Coastal Zone Management*, Washington, DC: Island Press.

Davis, Richard A. 1994. *The Evolving Coast*. New York: Freeman and Company

Horton, Tom. 1991. *Turning the Tide: Saving the Chesapeake Bay*, Washington, DC: Island Press.

National Oceanic and Atmospheric Administration. 2002. *Strategic Plan, National Estuaries Research Reserve System, 2003–2008*, Washington, DC: NOAA.

SLOPE, RELIEF, AND ASPECT

Landphair, Harlow C., and John L. Motloch. 1985. *Site Reconnaissance and Engineering*. New York: Elsevier.

Smoltczyk, Ulrich. 2002. *Geotechnical Engineering Handbook, Volume 1: Fundamentals*. Berlin: Ernst & Sohn.

SOILS CLASSIFICATION AND MECHANICS

McCarthy, David F. 1993. *Essentials of Soil Mechanics and Foundations: Basic Geotechnics*, 4th ed. Englewood Cliffs, NJ: Regents/Prentice-Hall.

Soil Survey Division Staff, U.S. Department of Agriculture. 1993. *Soil Survey Manual*. Washington, DC: U.S. Government Print Office.

HABITAT PATCHES, CORRIDORS, AND MATRIX

Adams, Lowell W. 1989. *Wildlife Reserves and Corridors in the Urban Environment: A Guide to Ecological Landscape Planning and Resource Conservation*. Columbia, MD: National Institute for Urban Wildlife.

Carr, E. 1998. *Wilderness by Design: Landscape Architecture and the National Park Service*. Lincoln, NB: University of Nebraska Press.

Convis, C.L. (ed.). 2001. *Conservation Geography*. Rollands, CA: ESRI Press.

Dramstad, Wenche E., James D. Olson, and Richard T. T. Forman. 1997. *Landscape Ecology: Principles in Landscape Architecture and Land-Use Planning* Washington, D.C.: Island Press.

Meffe, G.K., L.A. Nielsen, R.L. Knight, and D.A. Schenborn. 2002. *Ecosystems Management: Adaptive, Community-Based Conservation*. Washington, DC: Island Press.

BIODIVERSITY PROTECTION

Elzinga, C.L., D.W. Salzer, J.W. Willoughby, and J.P. Gibbs. 2001. *Monitoring Plant and Animal Populations.* New York: Blackwell Science.

Defenders of Wildlife. 2003. *Integrating Land Use Planning and Biodiversity.* Washington, DC: Defenders of Wildlife.

Groves, Craig R. 2003. *Drafting a Conservation Blueprint: A Practitioner's Guide to Planning for Biodiversity.* Washington, D.C.: Island Press.

Meffe, G.K., L.A. Nielsen, R.L. Knight, and D.A. Schenborn. 2002. *Ecosystems Management: Adaptive, Community-Based Conservation.* Washington, DC: Island Press.

FLOOD HAZARDS

Federal Emergency Management Agency. 1995. *CRS Coordinator's Manual.* Washington, DC: FEMA.

Interagency Floodplain Management Review Committee. 1994. *Sharing the Challenge: Floodplain Management into the 21st Century.* Washington, DC: Executive Office of the President.

L.R. Johnston Associates. 1992. *Floodplain Management in the United States: An Assessment Report, Vol. 2; Full Report.* Washington, DC: Federal Interagency Floodplain Management Task Force.

Morris, Marya. 1997. *Subdivision Design in Flood Hazard Areas.* PAS Report No. 473. Chicago: American Planning Association.

EROSION AND SEDIMENTATION

Bush, D.M., O.H. Pilkey, and W.J. Neal. 1996. *Living by the Rules of the Sea.* Durham, NC: Duke University Press.

Clark, J.R. 1995. *Coastal Zone Management Handbook.* Boca Raton, FL: Lewis Publishers.

Dennison, Mark S. 1995. S*torm Water Discharges: Regulatory Compliance and Best Management Practices.* Boca Raton, FL: Lewis Publishers.

Indiana Department of Natural Resources. nd. *Small Site Erosion and Sediment Control Guidance.* Indianapolis, IN: Indiana Department of Natural Resources.

Johnson, Carolyn. 1999. *Erosion Control for Home Builders.* Madison, WI: University of Wisconsin Extension Service and Wisconsin Department of Natural Resources.

Erosion Hazards Steering Committee, H. John Heinz III Center for Science, Economics, and the Environment. 2000. *Evaluation of Erosion Hazards.* Washington, DC: The H. John Heinz III Center for Science, Economics, and the Environment.

Steiner, Frederick R. 1990. *Soil Conservation in the United States: Policy and Planning.* Baltimore, MD: Johns Hopkins University Press.

HURRICANES AND COASTAL STORMS

Federal Emergency Management Agency. May 2000. *Coastal Construction Manual: Principles and Practices of Planning, Siting, Designing, Constructing, and Maintaining Residential Buildings in Coastal Areas.* FEMA 55, 3rd ed. Washington, DC: FEMA. (Also available on CD.)

Godschalk, David R., David J. Brower, and Timothy Beatley. 1989. *Catastrophic Coastal Storms: Hazard Mitigation and Development Management.* Durham, NC: Duke University Press.

H. John Heinz Center for Science, Economics, and the Environment. 2000. *Hidden Costs of Coastal Hazards: Implications for Risk Assessment and Mitigation.* Washington, DC: Island Press.

National Research Council (Panel on the Assessment of Wind Engineering in the United States). 1993. *Wind and the Built Environment: U.S. Needs in Wind Engineering and Hazard Mitigation.* Washington, DC: National Academy Press.

Schwab, Jim, Robert E. Deyle, Charles C. Eadie, Richard A. Smith, and Kenneth C. Topping. 1998. *Planning for Post-Disaster Recovery and Reconstruction.* Planning Advisory Service Report No. 483/484. Chicago: American Planning Association.

LANDSLIDES

American Planning Association. 2003. *Landslide Hazards and Planning.* Available at www.planning.org/landslides/docs/main.html. Last accessed June 27, 2005.

Dikau, Richard, Denys Brunsden, Lothar Schrott, and Maïa-Laura Ibsen. 1996. *Landslide Recognition: Identification, Movement, and Causes.* Hoboken, NJ: John Wiley & Sons, Inc.

McInnes, Robin. 2000. *Managing Ground Instability in Urban Areas: A Guide to Best Practice.* Centre for the Coastal Environment, Isle of Wight Council, United Kingdom, Cross Publishing, Walpen Manor, Chale, Isle of Wight.

Olshansky, Robert B. 1996. *Planning for Hillside Development.* Planning Advisory Service Report No. 466. Chicago: American Planning Association.

Turner, A. Keith, and Robert L. Schuster (eds). 1996. *Landslides: Investigation and Mitigation.* Transportation Research Board, Special Report 247. Washington, DC: National Academy Press.

USGS National Landslide Information Center. landslides.usgs.gov/html_files/nlicsun.html. Last accessed June 27, 2005.

Wold, Robert L., Jr., and Candace L. Jochim. 1989. *Landslide Loss Reduction: A Guide for State and Local Government Planning.* Denver, CO: Colorado Geological Survey.

SINKHOLES AND SUBSISTENCE

Beck, Barry, editor. 1989. *Engineering and Environmental Impacts of Sinkholes and Karst.* Rotterdam, Netherlands: Balkema Press.

Dinger, James S., and James R. Rebmann. 1986. "Ordinance for the Control of Urban Development in Sinkhole Areas in the Bluegrass Karst Region, Lexington, Kentucky." In *Environmental Problems in Karst Terranes and Their Solutions.* Conference Proceedings. Dublin, OH: National Water Well Association.

Dougherty, Percy H. 1989. "Land Use Regulations in the Lehigh Valley: Zoning and Subdivision Ordinances in an Environmentally Sensitive Karst Region." In *Engineering and Environmental Impacts of Sinkholes and Karst,* edited by Barry Beck. Rotterdam, Netherlands: Balkema Press.

Fisher, Joseph A., and Hermia Lechner, 1989. "A Karst Ordinance-Clinton Township, New Jersey." In *Engineering and Environmental Impacts of Sinkholes and Karst,* edited by Barry Beck. Rotterdam, Netherlands: Balkema Press.

Kemmerly, Phillip R. 1993. "Sinkhole Hazards and Risk Assessment in a Planning Context." *Journal of the American Planning Association* 59, 2; 221–227. Chicago: American Planning Association.

———. 1981. "The Need for Recognition and Implementation of a Sinkhole-Floodplain Hazard Designation in Urban Karst Terrains." *Environmental Geology and Water Sciences* 3, 281–292.

Newton, John G. 1987. *Development of Sinkholes Resulting from Man's Activities in the Eastern United States.* U.S. Geological Survey Circular 968. Reston, VA: U.S. Geological Survey.

Quinlan, James F. 1986. "Legal Aspectes of Sinkhole Development and Flooding in Karst Terranes" 1: Review and Synthesis. *Environmental Geology and Water Sciences* 8, no. 1: 41-61.

EARTHQUAKES

Berke, Philip R. 1992. *Planning for Earthquakes.* Baltimore, MD: Johns Hopkins University Press.

Building Seismic Safety Council. 2000. *NEHRP Recommended Provisions for Seismic Regulations for New Buildings and Other Structures.* Washington, DC: FEMA.

Geschwind, Carl-Henry. 2001. *California Earthquakes: Science, Risk, and the Politics of Hazard Mitigation.* Baltimore, MD: Johns Hopkins University Press.

Governor's Office of Emergency Services. 1992. *Seismic Retrofit Incentive Programs: A Handbook for Local Governments.* Sacramento, CA: Office of Emergency Services, State of California.

Spangle Associates. 2002. *Redevelopment After Earthquakes.* Portola Valley, CA: Spangle Associates.

WILDFIRES

Cohen, Jack, Nan Johnson, and Lincoln Walther. May 2001. "Saving Homes from Wildfires: Regulating the Home Ignition Zone." *Zoning News.* Chicago: American Planning Association.

Dennis, F.C. 2003. "Creating Wildfire-Defensible Zones." Fact Sheet No. 6.302. Fort Collins, CO: Colorado State University Extension Service. As found on the Colorado State University Cooperative Extension Website, www.ext.colostate.edu/pubs/natres/06302.html. Last accessed June 27, 2005.

International Code Council. 2003. *International Urban-Wildland Interface Code.* Country Club Hills, IL: International Code Council.

National Fire Protection Association. 2002. NFPA 1144: Standard for Protection of Life and Property from Wildfire. Quincy, MA: NFPA.

Pyne, Stephen J. *Fire in America: A Cultural History of Wildland and Rural Fire*. 1982. Seattle, WA: University of Washington Press.

Schwab, Jim, and Stuart Meck. 2005. *Planning for Wildfires*. Planning Advisory Service Report, No. 529/530. Chicago: American Planning Association.

State of California. 2003. *Fire Hazard Planning: General Plan Technical Advice Series*, Sacramento, CA: Governor's Office of Planning and Research.

HAZARDOUS MATERIALS

Federal Emergency Management Agency, U.S. Department of Transportation, and U.S. Environmental Protection Agency. No date. *Handbook of Chemical Hazard Analysis Procedures*. Washington, DC: U.S. Government Printing Office.

Lesak, D.M. 1999. *Hazardous Materials: Strategies and Tactics*. Upper Saddle River, NJ: Prentice-Hall.

Lindell, M.K., and R. W. Perry. 1992. *Behavioral Foundations of Community Emergency Planning*. Washington, DC: Hemisphere Press.

———. 2004. *Communicating Environmental Risk in Multiethnic Communities*. Thousand Oaks, CA: Sage Publications.

National Response Team. 1987. *Hazardous Materials Emergency Planning Guide*. Washington DC: U.S. Environmental Protection Agency, Federal Emergency Management Agency, and U.S. Department of Transportation.

U.S. Department of Transportation, Transport Canada, and Secretariat of Transport and Communications of Mexico. 2000. *Emergency Response Guidebook*. Washington DC: U.S. Department of

Transportation, Transport Canada, and Secretariat of Transport and Communications of Mexico.

U.S. Environmental Protection Agency, Federal Emergency Management Agency, and U.S. Department of Transportation. 1987. *Technical Guidance for Hazards Analysis*. Washington DC: U.S. Environmental Protection Agency, Federal Emergency Management Agency, and U.S. Department of Transportation.

TSUNAMIS AND SEICHES

Federal Emergency Management Agency. 2000. *Coastal Construction Manual: Principles and Practices of Planning, Siting, Designing, Constructing, and Maintaining Residential Buildings in Coastal Areas*, 3rd ed. (FEMA 55). Washington, DC: FEMA.

National Tsunami Hazard Mitigation Program. March 2001. *Designing for Tsunamis: Background Papers*. Washington, DC: National Oceanographic and Atmospheric Administration.

National Tsunami Hazard Mitigation Program. March 2001. *Designing for Tsunamis: Seven Principles for Planning and Designing for Tsunami Hazards*. Washington, DC: National Oceanographic and Atmospheric Administration.

Oregon Department of Land Conservation and Development. July 2000. *Planning for Coastal Hazards Technical Resource Guide*. Salem, OR: Oregon Department of Land Conservation and Development.

NOISE AND VIBRATION

Department of Defense. 2002. *Joint Land Use Study Program Guidance Manual*. Washington, D.C.: Office of Economic Adjustment.

Department of Housing and Urban Development, Environmental Planning Division, Office of Environment and Energy. 1985. *The Noise Guidebook*. Washington, D.C.: U.S. Department of Housing and Urban Development. www.hud.gov/offices/cpd/energyenviron/environment/resources/guidebooks/noise/index.cfm. Last accessed June 28, 2005.

Federal Aviation Administration. *Land Use Compatibility Planning Toolkit*. www.faa.gov/about/office_org/headquarters_offices/aep/planning_toolkit. Last accessed June 28, 2005.

Federal Interagency Committee on Urban Noise. 1980. *Guidelines for Considering Noise in Land Use Planning and Control*. Washington, D.C.: U.S. Department of Transportation, Department of Defense, Environmental Protection Agency, Veterans Administration, and Department of Housing and Urban Development.

Finegold, L.S. 1994. "Updated Criteria for Assessing the Impacts of General Transportation Noise on People." *Noise Control Engineering Journal*. Vol. 42, No. 1.

Schultz, T.J. 1978. "Synthesis of Social Surveys on Noise Annoyance." *Journal of the Acoustical Society of America*. Vol. 64, No. 2. pp.377-405.

U.S. Environmental Protection Agency. 1974. *Information on Levels of Noise Requisite to Protect the Public Health and Welfare with an Adequate Margin of Safety*. Washington, D.C.: U.S EPA.

U.S. Environmental Protection Agency. 1981. *Noise Effects Handbook: A Desk Reference to Health and Welfare Effects of Noise*. EPA 550-9-82-106. Office of the Scientific Assistant, Office of Noise Abatement and Control.

PART 3: STRUCTURES

RESIDENTIAL TYPES

De Chiara, Joseph, and Julius Panero. 1995. *Time-Saver Standards for Housing and Residential Development*. New York: McGraw-Hill.

Jones, Tom, William Pettus, and Michael Pyatok. 1996. *Good Neighbors: Affordable Family Housing*. New York: McGraw-Hill.

Schmitz, Adrienne, editor. 2000. *Multi-Family Housing Development Handbook*. Washington, DC: The Urban Land Institute.

Schmitz, Adrienne, editor. 2004. *Residential Development Handbook*. 3rd ed. Washington, DC: Urban Land Institute.

Shewood, Roger. 1981. *Modern Housing Prototypes*. Cambridge, MA: Harvard University Press.

Van Vliet, Willem. 1998. *Encyclopedia of Housing*. Thousand Oaks, CA: Sage.

MANUFACTURED HOUSING

Alley, David I., and Donald C. Westphal. 2002. *Navigating the Manufactured Housing Zoning Process*. Arlington, VA: Manufactured Housing Institute.

Hullibarger, Steve. 2001. *Developing with*

Manufactured Homes. Arlington, VA: Manufactured Housing Institute.

National Association of Home Builders Research Center. 2000. *Homebuilders' Guide to Manufactured Housing*. Washington, DC: Partnership for Advancing Technology in Housing, U.S. Department of Housing and Urban Development.

Sanders, Welford. 1998. *Manufactured Housing: Regulation, Design Innovations, and Development Options*. Planning Advisory Service Report No. 478. Chicago, IL: American Planning Association.

OFFICE BUILDINGS

De Chiara, Joseph, and Michael J. Crosbie. 2001. *Time-Saver Standards for Building Types*, 4th ed. New York: McGraw-Hill.

Hascher, Rainer, Simone Jeska, and Birgit Klauck. 2002. *A Design Manual: Office Buildings*. Berlin: Birkhauser.

Kohn, A. Eugene, and Paul Katz. 2002. *Building Type Basics for Office Buildings*. Hoboken, NJ: John Wiley & Sons, Inc.

Urban Land Institute. 1998. *Office Development Handbook*. 2nd ed. Washington, DC: Urban Land Institute.

ELEMENTARY, MIDDLE, AND HIGH SCHOOLS

Council of Educational Facility Planners International (CEFPI). 2004. *Creating Connections: The CEFPI Guide for Educational Facility Planning*. Scottsdale, AZ: CEFPI.

National Crime Prevention Council (NCPC). 2003. *School Safety and Security Toolkit*. Washington, DC: NCPC.

Public Schools of North Carolina, State Board of Education, Department of Public Instruction. 1998. *School Site Planner, The: Land for Learning*. Raleigh, NC: North Carolina Division of School Support, School Planning.

Simril, Renata. 2002. *A New Strategy for Building Better Neighborhoods*. Los Angeles, CA: New Schools, Better Neighborhoods.

MEDICAL FACILITIES

Carpman, Janet R., and Myron A. Grant. 2001. *Design That Cares: Planning Health Facilities for Patients and Visitors*. 2nd ed. New York: Jossey-Bass.

Gregory, Michelle. March 1994. "Planning and Zoning for Medical Districts." *Zoning News*. Chicago: American Planning Association.

Miller, Richard L., and Earl S. Swensson. 2002. *Hospital and Healthcare Facility Design*. 2nd ed. New York: W. W. Norton.

SIDEWALKS

American Association of State Highway and Transportation Officials (AASHTO). 2004. *A Policy on Geometric Design of Highways and Streets*, 5th ed. Washington, DC: AASHTO.

Bowman, B.L., J.J. Fruin, and C.V. Zegeer. 1989. *Planning Design and Maintenance of Pedestrian Facilities*. McLean, VA: Federal Highway Administration.

Federal Highway Administration. 1999. *Designing Sidewalks and Trails for Access, Part I of II: Review of Existing Guidelines and Practices*. Washington, DC: U.S. Department of Transportation.

National Highway Traffic Safety Administration. 1998. *Zone Guide for Pedestrian Safety*. Washington, D.C.: U.S. Department of Transportation.

Traffic Engineering Council Committee. 1998. *Design and Safety of Pedestrian Facilities*. Washington, DC: Institute of Transportation Engineers.

U.S. Department of Justice. 1991. *Americans with Disabilities Act (ADA) Accessibility Guidelines for Buildings and Facilities, 36 CFR part 1191*. Washington, D.C.

U.S. Department of Transportation. 2003. *Manual on Uniform Traffic Control Devices*. Washington, D.C.: U.S. Department of Transportation.

HIERARCHY OF STREETS AND ROADS

Duany Plater-Zyberk & Company. 1998. *Lexicon of the New Urbanism*. Miami, FL: Duany, Plater-Zyberk & Co.

U.S. Department of Transportation, Federal Highway Administration. 1998. *Flexibility in Highway Design*. Washington, DC: USDOT/FHWA.

STREET NETWORKS AND STREET CONNECTIVITY

Ewing, Reid. 1996. *Best Development Practices: Doing the Right Thing and Making Money at the Same Time*. Chicago: American Planning Association.

Handy, Susan, Robert G. Paterson, and Kent Butler. 2003. *Planning for Street Connectivity: Getting from Here to There*. Planning Advisory Service Report No. 515. Chicago: American Planning Association.

Southworth, Michael, and Eran Ben-Joseph. 2003. *Streets and the Shaping of Towns and Cities*, 2nd ed. Washington, DC: Island Press.

VEHICLE TURNING RADII

American Association of State Highway and Transportation Officials (AASHTO). 2004. *A Policy on Geometric Design of Highways and Streets*. 5th ed. ("The Green Book"). Washington, DC: AASHTO.

Institute of Transportation Engineers (ITE). 2000. *Turning Vehicle Templates, A Transportation Design Aid*. Washington, DC: ITE.

TRAFFIC CALMING

Appleyard, Donald. 1980. *State of the Art: Residential Traffic Management*. Washington, DC: Federal Highway Administration.

———. 1981. *Livable Streets*. Berkeley, CA: University of California Press.

Burden, Dan. 2000. *Streets and Sidewalks, People and Cars: The Citizens' Guide to Traffic Calming*. Sacramento, CA: Local Government Commission Center for Livable Communities.

Ewing, Reid. 1999. "Traffic Calming: State of the Practice." Washington, DC: Institute of Transportation Engineers.

Hoyle, Cynthia. 1995. *Traffic Calming*. Planning Advisory Service Report No. 456. Chicago: American Planning Association.

Lockwood, Ian M. July 1997. "ITE Traffic Calming Definition." *ITE Journal*. 67, no. 7:22–24.

PEDESTRIAN-FRIENDLY STREETS

American Association of State Highway and Transportation Officials (AASHTO). 2004. *A Policy on the Geometric Design of Highways and Streets*. 5th ed.Washington, DC: AASHTO

Engwicht, David. 1999. *Street Reclaiming: Creating Livable Streets and Vibrant Communities*. Gabriola Island, BC: New Society Publishers.

Ewing, Reid. 1999. *Traffic Calming: State of the Practice*. Washington, DC: Institute of Transportation Engineers.

Institute of Transportation Engineers (ITE). 1999. *Traditional Neighborhood Development Street Design Guidelines*. Washington, DC: ITE.

Kulash, Walter. 2001. *Residential Streets*, 3rd ed. Washington, DC: ULI-The Urban Land Institute.

PARKING LOT DESIGN

National Parking Association and Urban Land Institute. 2000. *The Dimensions of Parking*. 4th ed. Washington, DC: Urban Land Institute.

ON-STREET BIKEWAYS

American Association of State Highway and Transportation Officials. 1999. *Guide for the Development of Bicycle Facilities*. Washington, DC: AASHTO.

Forester, John. 1994. *Bicycle Transportation: A Handbook for Cycling Transportation Engineers*. Cambridge, MA: MIT Press.

King, Michael. 2002. *Bicycle Facility Selection: A Comparison of Approaches*. Chapel Hill, NC: University of North Carolina.

Nabti, Jumana, and Matthew Ridgway. 2002. *Innovative Bicycle Treatments*. Washington, DC: Institute of Transportation Engineers.

Oregon Department of Transportation. 1995. *Oregon Bicycle and Pedestrian Plan*. Salem, OR: Oregon Department of Transportation, Bicycle and Pedestrian Program.

MULTIUSER TRAILS

Flink, Charles A, Kristine Olka, and Robert M. Searns. 2001. *Trails for the Twenty-First Century: Planning, Design, and Management Manual for Multi-Use Trails*. Washington, DC: Island Press.

Flink, Charles A., and Robert M. Searns. 1993. *Greenways: A Guide to Planning, Design, and Development*. Washington, DC: Island Press.

TRANSIT SYSTEMS

Federal Aviation Administration. 1987. *A Model Ordinance to Limit Height of Objects Around Airports*. Advisory Circular 150/5190-4A. Washington, D.C.: U.S. Department of Transportation.

———. 1998. *Land Use Compatibility and Airports: A Guide for Effective Land Use Planning*. Available online at www.faa.gov/about/office_org/headquarters_offices/aep/planning_toolkit. Last accessed June 28, 2005.

———. 2002. *Airport Design Handbook*. Advisory Circular 150/5300-13, Change 7. October. Washington, D.C.: U.S. Department of Transportation.

Federal Transit Administration, National Transit Database. www.ntdprogram.com/NTD/ntdhome.nsf/?Open. Last accessed June 27, 2005.

Fitzpatrick, Kay, T. Urbanik, and R.W. Stokes August 1990. *Guidelines for Planning, Designing, and Operating Bus-Related Street Improvements*. FHWA/TX-90/1225-2F. College Station, TX: Texas Transportation Institute.

Florida Department of Transportation. 1994. *Airport Compatible Land Use Guidance for Florida Communities*. Office of Public Transportation, Aviation Office. Available at www.dot.state.fl.us/aviation/compland.htm. Last accessed June 28, 2005.

Giannopoulos, G. A. 1990. *Bus Planning and Operating in Urban Areas*. Aldershot, England: Avebury Press.

Goodman, Leon, and Jerome L. Martin. 1999. "Transportation Terminals," in *Transportation Planning Handbook*, 2nd ed. Washington, DC: Institute of Transportation Engineers.

Grava, Sigurd. 2003. *Urban Transportation Systems: Choices for Communities*. New York: McGraw-Hill.

Institute for Transportation Engineers (ITE). 1984. *Guidelines for Urban Major Street Design*. Washington, DC: ITE.

Light Rail Transit: Planning, Design, and Implementation. TRB Special Report, No. 195. Washington, DC: Transportation Research Board.

Meyer, Michael D., and Eric J. Miller. 2000. *Urban Transportation Planning*. New York: McGraw-Hill.

Oregon Department of Aviation. 2003. *Oregon Airport Land Use Compatibility Guidebook*. Prepared by Mead & Hunt, Inc., and Satre Associates, P.C. for the Oregon Department of Aviation. Available at egov.oregon.gov/Aviation/landuseguidebook.shtml. Last accessed June 28, 2005.

Papsidero, Vince. 1992. *Airport Noise Regulations*. PAS Report No. 437. Chicago: American Planning Association.

TCRP Report 16. 1996. *Transit and Urban Form*. Transportation Research Board. Washington DC: National Academies of Science.

TCRP Report 17. 1996. *Integration of Light Rail Transit into City Streets*. Transportation Research Board. Washington DC: National Academies of Science.

RESOURCES

TCRP Report 100. 2003. *Transit Capacity and Quality of Service Manual,* 2nd ed. Transportation Research Board. Washington DC: National Academies of Science.

Toole, Jennifer L., and Bettina Zimny. 1999. "Bicycle and Pedestrian Facilities," in *Transportation Planning Handbook,* 2nd ed. Washington, DC: Institute of Transportation Engineers.

Transit Cooperative Research Program. 1998. *Transit-Friendly Streets: Design and Traffic Management Strategies to Support Livable Communities.* TCRP Report No.33. Washington, DC: National Academies Press.

Transportation Research Board (TRB). 2004. "Bus Rapid Transit, Vol. 2: Implementation Guidelines." *Transit Cooperative Research Program Report 90.* Washington, DC: TRB.

Transportation Research Board. 2003. *Transit Capacity and Quality of Service Manual,* 2nd ed. TCRP Report 100. Washington, DC: National Academies of Science.

Transportation Research Board (TRB). 2003. "Bus Rapid Transit, Vol. 1: Case Studies in Bus Rapid Transit." *Transit Cooperative Research Program Report 90.* Washington, DC: TRB.

Vuchic, Vukan R. 1999. *Transportation for Livable Cities.* New Brunswick, NJ: CUPR Press.

Wells, Alexander T. 2004. *Airport Planning and Management.* New York: McGraw-Hill.

WASTE MANAGEMENT

Kreith, Frank. 2002. *Handbook of Solid Waste Management.* 2nd ed. New York: McGraw-Hill.

Qian, Xuede, Robert M. Koerner, and Donald H. Gray. 2002. *Geotechnical Aspects of Landfill Design and Construction.* New York: Prentice-Hall, Inc.

Themelis, Nickolas J., and Scott M Kaufman. April 2004. "State of Garbage in America: Data and Methodology Assessment." *BioCycles.* 45, no. 4 (April): 22.

U.S. Environmental Protection Agency, Office of Solid Waste and Emergency Response. October 2003. *Municipal Solid Waste in the United States: 2001 Facts and Figures.* EPA530-R-01-011.

WASTEWATER

Billings, Bruce R., and C. Vaughn Jones. 1996. *Forecasting Urban Water Demand.* Denver, CO: American Water Works Association Research Foundation.

Mayer, Peter B., William B. DeOreo, Eva M. Opitz, Jack C. Kiefer, William Y. Davis, Benedykt Dziegielewski, and John Olaf Nelson. 1999. *Residential End Uses of Water.* Denver, CO: American Water Works Association Research Foundation.

Metcalf and Eddy, Inc. 2002. *Wastewater Engineering Treatment and Reuse.* 4th ed. New York: McGraw-Hill.

Vesilind, P. Aarne. 2003. *Wastewater Treatment Plan Design.* Alexandria, VA: Water Environment Federation.

Vickers, Amy. 2001. *Handbook of Water Use and Conservation.* Denver, CO: American Water Works Association Research Foundation.

STORMWATER RUNOFF AND RECHARGE

Burton, G.A., and R.E. Pitt. 2002. *Stormwater Effects Handbook: A Toolbox for Watershed Managers, Scientists, and Engineers.* New York: Lewis Publishers.

Center for Watershed Protection. 2002. *Vermont Stormwater Management Manual.* Waterbury, VT: Vermont Agency of Natural Resources.

Claytor, R. and R. Ohrel. 1995. *Environmental Indicators to Assess the Effectiveness of Municipal and Industrial Stormwater Control Programs: Profile Sheets.* Silver Spring, MD: Center for Watershed Protection, US EPA Office of Wastewater Management.

Ferguson, Bruce K. 1994. *Stormwater Infiltration.* New York: Lewis Publishers.

Horsley & Witten, Inc. 1997. *Tools for Watershed Protection – A Workshop for Local Governments.* Sponsored by the U.S. EPA. Office of Wetlands, Oceans and Watershed. Washington, D.C.: U.S. EPA.

Metro. 2002. *Green Streets: Innovative Solutions for Stormwater and Stream Crossings.* Portland, OR: Metro.

Pitt, R.E., M. Lilburn, S.R. Durrans, S. Burian, S. Nix, J. Vorhees, and J. Martinson. 1999. *Guidance Manual for Integrated Wet Weather Flow Collection and Treatment Systems for Newly Urbanized Areas.* Edison, NJ: U.S. Environmental Protection Agency.

Prince Georges County, Maryland, Department of Environmental Resources (PGDER). 1999. *Low-Impact Development Design Strategies, An Integrated Design Approach.* Prince Georges County, MD: PGDER.

Schueler, T.R. 1987. *Controlling Urban Runoff, A Practical Manual for Planning and Designing Urban BMPs.* Washington, DC: Metropolitan Washington Council of Governments.

Schueler, T.R, and R.A. Claytor. 1996. *Design of Stormwater Filtering Systems.* Ellicott City, MD: Center for Watershed Protection.

————. 1997. *Technical Support Document for the State of Maryland Stormwater Design Manual Project.* Baltimore, MD: Maryland Department of the Environment.

U.S. Department of Agriculture, Natural Resource Conservation Service. 1986. *Urban Hydrology for Small Watersheds, Technical Release 55* (TR-55).

Winer, R. 2002. *National Pollutant Removal Performance Database for Stormwater Treatment Practices,* 2nd ed. Ellicott City, MD: Center for Watershed Protection.

WATER SUPPLY

American Water Works Association (AWWA). 1995. *Principles and Practices of Water Supply Operations I: Water Sources,* Denver, CO: AWWA.

Cech, Thomas V. 2003. *Principles of Water Resources: History, Development, Management, and Policy.* Hoboken, NJ: John Wiley & Sons, Inc.

Hillyer, Theodore M., and Germaine A. Hofbauer. 1998. *Water Supply Handbook: A Handbook on Water Supply Planning and Resource Management.* Alexandria, VA: Institute for Water Resources.

Merritt, Frederick S., Jonathan T. Ricketts, and M. Kent Loftin. 2003. "Water Resources." *Standard Handbook for Civil Engineers.* New York: McGraw-Hill.

Prasifka, David W. 1994. *Water Supply Planning.* Malabar, FL: Krieger Publishing.

WIRELESS INFRASTRUCTURE

Duerksen, Christopher A., and Matt Goebel. 1999. *Aesthetics, Community Character, and the Law.* Planning Advisory Service Report No. 489/490. Chicago: American Planning Association.

Heverly, Robert A. November 1996. "Dealing with Towers, Antennas, and Satellite Dishes." *Land Use Law and Zoning Digest.* Chicago: American Planning Association.

Kaylor, Charles H., and Christopher Steins. 2004. "Today's Scheme for Tomorrow's Technology." *Planning* 70, no. 7 (July): 32-36.

Kramer, Jonathan. July 2004. "Seeing the Forest through the Cell Trees." *Public Management* 86, no. 6:23-25. Washington, D.C.: ICMA.

TYPES OF PARKS

Garvin, Alexander. 2000. *Parks, Recreation, and Open Space: A Twenty-First Century Agenda.* Planning Advisory Service Report No. 497/498. Chicago: American Planning Association.

Molnar, Donald J. 1986. *Anatomy of a Park: The Essentials of Recreation Area Planning and Design.* New York: McGraw-Hill.

Phillips, Leonard E. 1996. *Parks: Design and Management.* New York: McGraw-Hill.

GREENWAYS AND TRAILS

Beneficial Designs. 2001. *Designing Sidewalks and Trails for Access, Part 2, Best Practices Design Guide.* Washington, DC: U.S. Department of Transportation.

Flink, Charles, and Robert Searns. 1993. *Greenways: A Guide to Planning, Design and Development.* Washington, DC: Island Press.

Flink, Charles, Robert Searns, and K. Olka. 2001. *Trails for the Twenty-First Century.* Washington, DC: Island Press.

Little, Charles. 1990. *Greenways for America.* Baltimore, MD: Johns Hopkins University Press.

CONSERVATION AREAS

Hockings, Mark, Sue Stolton, and Nigel Dudley. 2002. *Evaluating Effectiveness: A Summary For Park Managers and Policy Makers.* Gland, Switzerland: IUCN and WWF.

McNeely, Jeffrey A., James Thorsell, and Hector Ceballos-Lascuráin. 1992. *Guidelines: Development of National Parks and Protected Areas for Tourism.* Madrid, Spain: World Tourism Organization.

World Parks Congress. 2003. *Recommendations of the 5th IUCN World Parks Congress.* WPCA/World Commission on Protected Areas, and IUCN/The World Conservation Union. Available online at: www.iucn.org/themes/wcpa/wpc2003/pdfs/outputs/wpc/recommendations.pdf. Last accessed June 27, 2005.

PLAYGROUNDS

Architectural Barriers and Compliance Board. 2000. *Americans with Disabilities Act (ADA) Accessibility*

Guidelines for Building and Facilities: Play Areas. Available online at: www.access-board.gov/play/finalrule.htm. Last accessed June 27, 2005.

ASTM F1487-01 Standard Consumer Safety Performance Specification for Playground Equipment.

ASTM F1292-99 Standard Specification for Impact Attenuation of Surface Systems Under and Around Playground Equipment.

Brett, Arlene, Robin C. Moore, and Eugene F. Provenzo, Jr. 1993. *The Complete Playground.* Syracuse, NY: Syracuse University Press.

Consumer Product Safety Commission. 1997. *Handbook for Public Playground Safety.* Available online at: www.cpsc.gov/cpscpub/pubs/325.pdf.

Goltsman, Susan M., Daniel S. Iacofano, and Robin C. Moore. 1987. *Play for All Guidelines.* Berkeley, CA: MIG Communications.

FARMS

Daniels, Tom. 1997. *Holding Our Ground: Protecting America's Farms and Farmland.* Washington, DC: Island Press.

Gibbons, Jim. September 2003. "Regulating Farm Stands." *Zoning News.* Chicago: American Planning Association.

Steiner, Frederick R. 1990. *Soil Conservation in the United States: Policy and Planning.* Baltimore, MD: Johns Hopkins University Press.

U.S. Department of Agriculture, National Agricultural Statistics Service. February 2004. *Farms and Land in Farms.* Washington, DC: USDA.

FEEDLOTS

Schwab, Jim. 1998. *Planning and Zoning for Concentrated Animal Feeding Operations.* Planning Advisory Service Report No. 482. Chicago: American Planning Association.

U.S. Department of Agriculture and U.S. EPA. 1999. *Unified National Strategy for Animal Feeding Operations.* Washington, DC: USDA and U.S. EPA.

U.S. Environmental Protection Agency. February 12, 2003. "National Pollutant Discharge Elimination System Permit Regulation and Effluent Limitation Guidelines and Standards for Concentrated Animal Feeding Operations (CAFOs); Final Rule," *Federal Register* 68, no. 29: 7176.

FORESTRY

Aplet, Gregory H., Nels Johnson, Jeffrey T. Olson, and V. Alaric Sample (eds). 1993. *Defining Sustainable Forestry.* Washington, DC: Island Press.

Collard, Sneed B., III. 1996. *Alien Invaders: The Continuing Threat of Exotic Species.* New York: Franklin Watts.

Heimlich, R.E., and W.D. Anderson. 2001. *Development at the Urban Fringe and Beyond: Impacts on Agriculture and Rural Land.* Economic Research Service, U.S. Department of Agriculture. Agriculture Economic Report No. 803. Washington, D.C.: U.S. Department of Agriculture.

Sharpe, Grant William, John C. Hendee, and Wenonah F. Sharpe. 2003. *Introduction to Forests and Renewable Resources,* 7th ed. New York: McGraw-Hill.

PART 4: PLACES AND PLACEMAKING

REGIONS

Bailey, Robert. 1998. *Ecoregions: The Ecosystem Geography of the Oceans and the Continents.* New York: Springer-Verlag.

Callenbach, Ernest. 1975. *Ecotopia.* Berkeley, CA: Banyan Tree.

Calthorpe, Peter, and William Fulton. 2001. *The Regional City.* Washington, DC: Island Press.

Garreau, Joel. 1981. *The Nine Nations of North America.* Boston: Houghton Mifflin.

Geddes, Patrick. 1915. *Cities in Evolution: An Introduction to Town Planning and to the Study of Cities.* London: Williams & Norgate.

MacKaye, Benton. 1940. "Regional Planning and Ecology." Ecological Monographs 10:349–353.

McHarg, Ian. 1969. *Design with Nature.* Garden City, New York: Natural History Press/Doubleday.

Orfield, Myron. 1997. *Metropolitics: A Regional Agenda for Community and Stability* (rev. ed.). Washington, DC: Brookings Institution Press.

Steiner, Frederick. 2002. *Human Ecology: Following Nature's Lead.* Washington, DC: Island Press.

Zelinsky, William. 1980. "North America's Vernacular Regions." *Annals of the Association of American Geographers* 70:1–16.

NEIGHBORHOODS

Chaskin, R.J., P. Brown, S. Venkatesh, and A. Vidal. 2001. *Building Community Capacity.* New York: Aldine de Gruyter.

Chaskin, R.J. 1998. "Neighborhood as a Unit of Planning and Action: A Heuristic Approach." *The Journal of Planning Literature* 13(1): 11–30.

———. 1997. Perspectives on Neighborhood and Community: A Review of the Literature." *Social Service Review* 71(4): 521–547.

Kretzman J., and J. L. McKnight. 1993. *Building Community from the Inside Out: A Path Toward Finding and Mobilizing Community Assets.* Evanston, IL: Northwestern University Center for Urban Affairs and Policy Research.

Lynch, Kevin. *Image of the City.* 1960. Cambridge, MA: The Technology Press—Harvard University Press.

Martz, W.A. 1995. *Neighborhood-Based Planning: Five Case Studies.* Planning Advisory Service Report No. 455. Chicago: American Planning Association.

Rohe, W.M., and L.B. Gates 1985. *Planning with Neighborhoods.* Chapel Hill, NC: University of North Carolina Press.

Rue, Harrison Bright. 2000. *Real Towns: Making Your Neighborhood Work.* Sacramento, CA: Local Government Commission.

NEIGHBORHOOD CENTERS

Bohl, Charles C. 2002. *Place Making: Developing Town Centers, Main Streets, and Urban Villages.* Washington, DC: Urban Land Institute.

Oldenburg, Ray. 1989. *The Great Good Place: Cafes, Coffee Shops, Community Centers, Beauty Parlors, General Stores, Bars, Hangouts, and How They Get You through the Day.* New York: Paragon House.

HISTORIC DISTRICTS

Cassity, Pratt. 2001. *Maintaining Community Character: How to Establish a Local Historic District.* Washington, DC: National Trust for Historic Preservation.

Cox, Rachel. 1994. *Design Review in Historic Districts.* Washington, DC: National Trust for Historic Preservation.

Roddewig, Richard J. 1983. *Preparing a Historic Preservation Ordinance.* Planning Advisory Service Report No. 374. Chicago: American Planning Association.

Rypkema, Donovan. 1994. *Economics of Rehabilitation: A Community Leader's Guide.* Washington, DC: National Trust for Historic Preservation.

White, Bradford J., and Richard J. Roddewig. 1994. *Preparing a Historic Preservation Plan.* Planning Advisory Service Report No. 450. Chicago: American Planning Association..

Wood, Byrd. 1991. *Basic Preservation Procedures.* Washington, DC: National Trust for Historic Preservation.

WATERFRONTS

Breen, Ann, and Dick Rigby. 1996. *The New Waterfront. A Worldwide Urban Success Story.* New York: McGraw-Hill.

———. 1997. *Waterfronts: Cities Reclaim Their Edge.* Washington, DC: The Waterfront Press.

Gastil, Raymond. 2002. *Beyond the Edge: New York's New Waterfront.* New York: Princeton Architectural Press.

Port of San Francisco. 1997. *Waterfront Design and Access: An Element of the Waterfront Land Use Plan.* San Francisco, CA.

Project for Public Spaces. www.pps.org/info/placemakingtools/issuepapers/issuewaterfronts. Last accessed June 27, 2005.

Remaking the Urban Waterfront. 2004. Washington, DC: Urban Land Institute.

ARTS DISTRICTS

Americans for the Arts. 2002. *Arts and Economic Prosperity: The Economic Impact of Nonprofit Arts Organizations and Their Audiences.* Washington, DC: Americans for the Arts.

———. 2003. *Cultural Development in Creative Communities.* Washington, DC: Americans for the Arts.

RESOURCES

———. 2004. *Public Art: An Essential Component of Creating Communities.* Washington, DC: Americans for the Arts.

Colorado Business Committee for the Arts. 2001. *Economic Impact Study of the Scientific and Cultural Facilities District.* Denver, CO: Colorado Business Committee for the Arts.

Vincent, Christine. 1992. *National Cultural Facilities Study.* New York: Nonprofit Facilities Fund.

INDUSTRIAL PARKS

Derven, Ronald, and Carol Feder (eds). 1986. *Parking for Industrial and Office Parks.* Herndon, VA: National Association of Industrial and Office Parks.

Frej, Anne, and Jo Allen Gause, editors. 2001. *Business Park and Industrial Development Handbook.* 2nd ed. Washington DC: Urban Land Institute.

Institute of Traffic Engineers. 2003. *Trip Generation,* 7th ed. Washington, DC: Institute of Traffic Engineers.

Schwab, Jim. 1993. *Industrial Performance Standards for a New Century.* Planning Advisory Service Report No. 444. Chicago: American Planning Association.

OFFICE PARKS

Frej, Anne, and Jo Allen Gause, editors. 2001. *Business Park and Industrial Development Handbook,,* 2nd ed. Washington, DC: Urban Land Institute.

MAIN STREETS

Fregonese, John, Mary Weber, and Barbara Duncan. 1996. *Main Street Handbook: A User's Guide to Main Streets.* Portland, OR: Metro.

Kemp, Roger L. 2000. *Main Street Renewal: A Handbook for Citizens and Public Officials.* Jefferson, NC: McFarland.

Seidman, Karl F. 2004. *Revitalizing Commerce for American Cities: A Practioner's Guide to Urban Main Street Programs.* Washington, DC: Fannie Mae Foundation.

Smith, Kennedy, Kate Joncas, and Bill Parrish. 1996. *Revitalizing Downtown: The Professional's Guide to the Main Street Approach.* Washington, DC: National Trust for Historic Preservation.

MIXED-USE DEVELOPMENT

Atlanta Regional Commission. n.d. *Quality Growth Toolkit: Mixed-Use Development.* Atlanta, GA: Atlanta Regional Commission.

Jones Lang LaSalle. 2005. *Mixed-Use Development and Investment: Summary Document.* London: British Council for Offices.

Schultz, Jim, Kelly Kline, and Jennifer Gerend. January 2004. "Getting to the Bottom of Mixed-Use." *Planning.* 70, no. 1:16-21.

Schwanke, Dean, editor. 2003. *Mixed-Use Development Handbook,* 2nd ed. Washington, DC: Urban Land Institute.

TRANSIT-ORIENTED DEVELOPMENT

Bernick, Michael, and Robert Cervero. 1997. *Transit Villages in the 21st Century.* New York: McGraw-Hill.

Dittmar, Hank, and Gloria Ohland (eds). 2004. *The New Transit Town: Best Practices in Transit-Oriented Development.* Washington, DC: Island Press.

Goody Clancy and Byrne McKinney & Associates. 2002. *Density Myth and* Reality. Presentation, Boston, MA.

Morris, Marya (ed.). 1996. *Creating Transit-Supportive Land-Use Regulations.* PAS Report No. 468. Chicago: American Planning Association.

The Urban Land Institute (ULI). 1994. *Transit-Oriented Design.* Washington, DC: ULI.

CONSERVATION DEVELOPMENT

Arendt, Randall. 1999. *Growing Greener.* Washington, DC: Island Press.

———. 1994. *Rural by Design.* Chicago: Planners Press.

Arendt, Randall G. 1997. *Growing Greener: Putting Conservation into Local Codes.* Media, PA: Natural Lands Trust, Inc. with funding from Pennsylvania Department of Conservation and Natural Resources, The William Penn Foundation, and The Alexander Stewart, M.D. Foundation.

INFILL DEVELOPMENT

Benefield, F. Kaid, Matthew D. Raimi, and Donald D.T. Chen. 1999. *Once There Were Greenfields.* New York: Natural Resources Defense Council

Bragado, Nancy, editor. 1995. *Building Livable Communities: A Policymaker's Guide to Infill Development.* Sacramento, CA: Center for Livable Communities.

Dunphy, Robert, Deborah Myerson, and Michael Pawlukiewicz. 2003. *Ten Principles for Successful Development around Transit.* Washington, DC: Urban Land Institute.

Fader, Steven, 2000. *Density by Design.* Washington, DC: Urban Land Institute.

Kackar, Adhir, and Ilana Preuss. 2003. *Creating Great Neighborhoods: Density in Your Community.* Sacramento, CA: Local Government Commission.

Northeast-Midwest Institute and Congress for the New Urbanism. 2001. *Strategies for Successful Infill Development.* Washington, DC: Northeast-Midwest Institute.

Paumier, Cy. 2004. *Creating a Vibrant City Center.* Washington, DC: Urban Land Institute.

Porter, Douglas R. 2002. *Making Smart Growth Work.* Washington, DC: Urban Land Institute.

ENVIRONMENTAL SITE ANALYSIS

Arendt, Randall G. 1996. *Conservation Design for Subdivisions: A Practical Guide to Creating Open Space Networks.* Washington, DC: Island Press.

Lynch, Kevin, and Gary Hack. 1984. *Site Planning,* 3rd ed. Cambridge, MA: MIT Press.

McHarg, Ian L. 1969. *Design with Nature.* Garden City, NY: Natural History Press/Doubleday.

Steiner, Frederick R. 2000. *The Living Landscape: An Ecological Approach to Landscape Planning,* 2nd ed. New York: McGraw-Hill.

SCALE AND DENSITY

Alexander, Ernest R., and K. David Reed with Peter Murphy. 1988. *Density Measures and Their Relation to Urban Form.* PAM91-0746. University of Wisconsin at Milwaukee, School of Architecture and Urban Planning. Milwaukee, WI: University of Wisconsin at Milwaukee.

Campoli, Julie, and Alex MacLean. 2002. *Visualizing Density.* Cambridge, MA: Lincoln Institute of Land Policy.

Fader, Steven. 2000. *Density by Design: New Directions in Residential Development.* 2nd ed. Washington, D.C.: Urban Land Institute.

Goody Clancy. 2002. Eastern Cambridge Planning Study. Commissioned by City of Cambridge, Massachusetts.

Jenks, Mike and Elizabeth Burton. 1996. *Compact City. A Sustainable Urban Form.* London: E & FN Spon.

SAFETY

Hopper, Leonard J., and Martha J. Droge. 2005. *Security and Site Design: A Landscape Architectural Approach to Analysis, Assessment, and Design Implementation.* New York: John Wiley & Sons.

Nadel, Barbara A., editor. 2004. *Building Security: Handbook for Architectural Planning and Design.* New York: McGraw-Hill.

Newman, Oscar. 1996. *Creating Defensible Space.* Washington, DC: U.S. Department of Housing and Urban Development.

Zelinka, Al, and Dean Brennan. 2001. *Safescape: Creating Safer, More Livable Communities Through Planning and Design.* Chicago: Planners Press.

WALKABILITY

Appleyard, Donald. 1980. *Livable Streets.* Berkeley, CA: University of California Press.

Burden, Dan. 1999. *Street Design Guidelines for Healthy Neighborhoods.* Sacramento, CA: Local Government Commission.

Untermann, Richard K. 1984. *Accommodating the Pedestrian — Adapting Towns and Neighborhoods for Walking and Bicycling.* New York: Van Nostrand Reinhold.

Vernez Moudon, Anne (ed.). 1987. *Public Streets for Public Use.* New York: Van Nostrand Reinhold.

LEADERSHIP IN ENERGY AND ENVIRONMENTAL DESIGN—LEED

U.S. Green Building Council. Revised March 2003. *Green Building Rating System for New Construction and Major Renovations (LEED-NC) Version 2.1.* www.usgbc.org/Docs/LEEDdocs/LEED_RS_v2-1.pdf. Last accessed June 27, 2005.

STREETSCAPE

Gehl, Jan. 1987. *Life Between Buildings: Using Public Spaces.* New York: Van Nostrand Reinhold.

Getting Back to Place: Using Streets to Rebuild Communities. 1996. New York: Project for Public Spaces.

Jacobs, Allan B. 1993. *Great Streets.* Cambridge, MA: MIT Press.

———. 2002. *The Boulevard Book: History, Evolution, Design of Multiway Boulevards.* Cambridge, MA: MIT Press.

Rudofsky, Bernard. 1969. *Streets for People: A Primer for Americans.* Garden City, NY: Doubleday

PART 5: ANALYSIS TECHNIQUES

POPULATION PROJECTIONS

Goodman, W.I., and E.C. Freund. 1968. *Principles and Practice of Urban Planning.* Washington, DC: ICMA.

Greenberg, Michael R., Donald A. Krueckeberg, and Connie O. Michaelson. 1978. *Local Population and Employment Projection Techniques.* New Brunswick, NJ: Center for Urban Policy Research.

Irwin, Richard. July 1977. *Guide for Local Area Populations.* Washington, DC: U.S. General Printing Office.

Klosterman, Richard E. 1990. *Community Analysis and Planning Techniques.* Savage, MD: Rowman & Littlefield.

Krueckeberg, Donald A., and Arthur L. Silvers. 1974. *Urban Planning Analysis: Methods and Models.* Hoboken, NJ: John Wiley & Sons, Inc.

ECONOMIC BASE AND ECONOMETRIC PROJECTIONS

Dick Conway and Associates. September 2002. *Regional Economic and Demographic Data Base, Modeling and Forecasting.* Prepared for the Puget Sound Regional Council. Seattle, WA. Website: www.psrc.org/datapubs/pubs/step2002.pdf, accessed February 16, 2005.

Gujarati, Damodar. 2003. *Basic Econometrics.* New York: McGraw-Hill.

Hill, R. Carter, William E. Griffths, and George G. Judge. 2000. *Using Excel for Undergraduate Econometrics.* Hoboken, NJ: John Wiley & Sons, Inc.

Klosterman, Richard E. 1990. *Community Planning and Analysis Techniques.* Savage, MD: Rowman and Littlefield.

Krueckeberg, Donald A., and Arthur L. Silvers. 1974. *Urban Planning Analysis: Methods and Models.* Hoboken, NJ: John Wiley & Sons, Inc.

Wilson, A.G., and R.J. Bennett. 1985. *Mathematical Methods in Human Geography and Planning.* Chichester, UK: John Wiley & Sons, Inc.

HOUSING NEEDS ASSESSMENT

Lieder, Constance. 1988. "Planning for Housing," in Chapter 12 of *The Practice of Local Government Planning,* 2nd ed. Frank S. So and Judith Getzels, eds. Washington, DC: International City Management Association.

U.S. Department of Housing and Urban Development. 2002. *Guide to PD&R Data Sets.* Washington, DC: HUD Office of Policy Development and Research.

———. *FHA Techniques of Housing Market Analysis.* Washington, DC: U.S. General Printing Office.

White, Betty Jo, Marjorie Jensen, and Christine Cook. 1992. *Developing Community Housing Needs Assessments and Strategies: A Self-Help Guidebook for Nonmetropolitan Communities.* Prepared with the assistance of the Kansas Center for Rural Initiatives and distributed by American Association of Housing Educators (AAHE). Manhattan, KS: AAHE.

PARKS, RECREATION, AND OPEN SPACE NEEDS ASSESSMENT

Mertes, James D., and James R. Hall. 1996. *Park, Recreation, Open Space and Greenway Guidelines.* Alexandria, VA.: National Recreation and Park Association.

Reviere, Rebecca, Susan Berkowitz, Carolyn C. Carter, and Carolyn Graves Ferguson (eds). 1996. *Needs Assessment: A Creative and Practical Guide for Social Scientists.* Washington, DC: Taylor & Francis.

ENVIRONMENTAL IMPACT ASSESSMENT

Canter, Larry W. 1995. *Environmental Impact Assessment.* New York: McGraw-Hill Science/Engineering/Math.

Gilpin, Alan. 1994. *Environmental Impact Assessment—Cutting Edge for the 21st Century.* Cambridge, England: Cambridge University Press.

Glasson, John, Riki Therivel, and Andrew Chandwick. 1999. *Introduction to Environmental Impact Assessment: Principles, Procedures, Process, Practice, and Prospects.* London: Taylor and Francis.

Marriott, Betty Bowers. 1997. *Impact Assessment: A Practical Guide.* New York: McGraw-Hill Professional.

FISCAL IMPACT ASSESSMENT

Burchell, Robert W., and David Listoken. 1978. *The Fiscal Impact Handbook.* New Brunswick, NJ: Center for Urban Policy Research.

Burchell, Robert W., David Listoken, Lawrence Q. Newton, Susan J. Foxley, Robert M. Rodgers, Jeffrey L. Greene, Larry W. Canter, David J. Minno, Wonsik Shim, and Wansoo Im. 1994. *Development Impact Assessment Handbook,* Washington, DC: The Urban Land Institute.

Holzheimer, Terry. Spring 1998 "Fiscal Impact Analysis in Local Comprehensive Planning," *Planners' Casebook,* No. 26. Chicago: American Planning Association.

Siegel, Michael, Jutka Harris, and Kaid Benfield. 2000. *Developments and Dollars: An Introduction to Fiscal Impact Analysis in Land Use Planning.* New York: Natural Resources Defense Council.

Tischler, Paul S. 1998. "Analyzing the Fiscal Impact of Development," *ICMA MIS Report,* 20 (7). single topic issue

TRAFFIC IMPACT STUDIES

American Association of State Highway and Transportation (AASHTO) Officials. 2004. *A Policy on the Geometric Design of Highways and Streets.* 5th ed.Washington, DC: AASHTO

Forkenbrock, David J. 2001. *Guidebook for Assessing the Social and Economic Effects of Transportation Projects.* Washington, DC: National Academy Press.

Institute of Transportation Engineers. 2003. *Trip Generation,* 7th ed. Washington, DC: ITE.

Stover, Vergil G., and Frank J. Koepke. 2002. *Transportation and Land Development,* 2nd ed. Washington DC: Institute of Transportation Engineers.

Transportation Research Board. 2000. *Highway Capacity Manual.* TRP A3A10. Washington, DC: Transportation Research Board.

MAPPING DATA OVERVIEW

Campbell, John. 1998. *Map Use and Analysis,* 3rd ed. Boston: McGraw-Hill.

Clarke, Kenneth C. 2002. *Getting Started with Geographic Information Systems,* 4th ed. Englewood Cliffs, NJ: Prentice Hall.

Monmonier, Mark. 1993. *Mapping It Out: Expository Cartography for the Humanities and Social Sciences.* Chicago: The University of Chicago Press.

———. 1996. *How to Lie with Maps,* Second Edition. Chicago: University of Illinois Press.

Muehrcke, Phillip C., and Juliana O. Muehrcke. 1992. *Map Use: Reading, Analysis, and Interpretation.* Madison, WI: JP Publications.

AERIAL PHOTOGRAPHS AND DIGITAL ORTHOPHOTO QUADRANGLES

Campbell, J. 1998. *Map Use and Analysis,* 3rd ed. Boston: McGraw-Hill.

Holtz, Robert K. 1985. *The Surveillance Science: Remote Sensing of the Environment.* Hoboken, NJ: John Wiley & Sons, Inc.

U.S. Geological Survey, www.usgs.gov. Last accessed June 27, 2005.

U.S. GEOLOGICAL SURVEY TOPOGRAPHIC MAPS

U.S. Geological Survey, www.usgs.org. Last accessed June 27, 2005.

PROPERTY MAPS IN MODERN CADASTRES

Cowen D.J., and W.J. Craig. Summer 2004. "A Retrospective Look at the Need for a Multipurpose Cadastre." *ArcNews Online.*

Elayachi, M., and E.H. Hassane. October 2-5, 2001. "Digital Cadastre Map: A Multipurpose Tool for Sustainable Development." International Conference on Spatial Information for Sustainable Development, Nairobi, Kenya.

Federal Geographic Data Committee. 2003. *Cadastral Data Content Standard for the National Spatial Data Infrastructure, Version 1.3.* Washington, DC: Subcommittee on Cadastral Data.

International Association of Assessing Officers (IAAO). 2003. *Standard on Cadastral Maps and Parcel Identifiers.* Chicago: International Association of Assessing Officers.

URISA. 1999. *GIS Guidelines for Assessors,* 2nd ed. Chicago: Urban and Regional Systems Association and the International Association of Assessing Officers.

CENSUS DATA AND DEMOGRAPHIC MAPPING

Dailey, George. 2000. "Normalizing Census Data in ArcView GIS." *ArcUser*, October-December: 44–45.

U.S. Census Bureau, www.census.gov. Last accessed June 27, 2005.

REMOTE SENSING AND SATELLITE IMAGE CLASSIFICATION

Bier, David. July 1997. "Planning with Satellite Remote Sensing." *PAS Memo*. Chicago: American Planning Association.

Federal Geographic Data Committee. 1998. *Content Standard for Digital Geospatial Metadata*. FGDC-STD-001-1998. Washington, DC: Federal Geographic Data Committee: www.fgdc.gov/metadata/csdgm/.

Jensen, J.R. 1996. *Introductory Digital Image Processing: A Remote Sensing Perspective*, 2nd ed. Upper Saddle River, NJ: Prentice Hall.

Lillesand, T.M., and R.W. Keifer. 2000. *Remote Sensing and Image Interpretation*, 4th ed. New York: John Wiley & Sons, Inc.

National Aeronautics and Space Administration. November 16, 2004. *On-Line Remote Sensing Tutorial*, http://rst.gsfc.nasa.gov/start.html.

GEOGRAPHIC INFORMATION SYSTEMS

Clarke, K. 2002. *Getting Started with Geographic Information Systems*, 4th ed. Englewood Cliffs, NJ: Prentice Hall.

Hanna, K.C., and R.B. Culpepper. 1998. *GIS in Site Design*. Hoboken, NJ: John Wiley & Sons, Inc.

Kent, R.B., and R.E. Klosterman. 2000. "GIS and Mapping: Pitfalls for Planners." *Journal of the American Planning Association*. 66, no. 2:189–198.

Longley, P.A., M.F. Goodchild, D.J. Maguire, and D. W. Rhind. 2001. *Geographic Information Systems and Science*. Hoboken, NJ: John Wiley & Sons, Inc.

Malczewski, Jacek. 2003. "GIS-Based Land Suitability Analysis: A Critical Overview." *Progress in Planning* 62:1: 3–65.

MassGIS. 2002. *Getting Started with GI: A Guide for Municipalities*. Boston, MA: Massachusetts Executive Office of Environmental Affairs. www.mass.gov/mgis/Getting_Started_With_GIS.pdf, accessed March 24, 2005.

O'Looney, J. 2000. *Beyond Maps: GIS and Decision Making in Local Government*. Redlands, CA: ESRI Press.

Urban and Regional Information Systems Association. *GIS Code of Ethics*. www.urisa.org/ethics/code_of_ethics.htm, accessed March 23, 2005.

VISUALIZATION OVERVIEW

Boyd, Susan, and Roy Chan. 2002. *Placemaking Tools for Community Action*. Washington, DC: CONCERN, Inc. and Environmental Simulation Center. www.placematters.us/Placemaking/Placemaking_v1.pdf, accessed March 9, 2005.

Snyder, Ken, and Julie Herman. November 2003. "Visualization Tools to Improve Community Decision Making." *PAS Memo*. Chicago: American Planning Association.

Snyder, Ken. 2003. "Tools for Community Design and Decision Making." In *Planning Support Systems in Practice*. S. Geertman and John Stillwell, eds. Heidelberg: Springer Verlag.

MONTAGE VISUALIZATION

PlaceMatters.com. www.placematters.us. Last accessed June 27, 2005.

Environmental Simulation Center. www.simcenter.org. Last accessed June 27, 2005.

Snyder, Ken, and Julie Herman. November 2003. "Visualization Tools to Improve Community Decision Making." *PAS Memo*. Chicago: American Planning Association.

THREE-DIMENSIONAL VISUALIZATION

Boyd, Susan, and Roy Chan. 2002. *Placemaking Tools for Community Action*. Washington, DC: CONCERN, Inc. and Environmental Simulation Center. www.placematters.us/Placemaking/Placemaking_v1.pdf, accessed February 17, 2005.

Brail, Richard (ed.). June 2001. *Planning Support Systems: Integrating Geographic Information Systems, Models, and Visualization Tools*. New Brunswick, NJ: Rutgers University Center for Urban Policy Research and ESRI Press.

Longley, Paul A., and Michael Batty (eds). 2003. *Advanced Spatial Analysis: The CASA Book of GIS*, Center for Advanced Spatial Analysis, Redmond, CA: ESRI Press.

Snyder, Ken. November 2001. "Decision Support Tools for Community Planning." *PM: Public Management*. Washington, DC: ICMA. Placematters.us/Documents/RESOURCES/Article for ICMA.pdf, accessed February 17, 2005.

Snyder, Ken, and Julie Herman. November 2003. "Visualization Tools to Improve Community Decision Making." *PAS Memo*. Chicago: American Planning Association.

VISUAL PREFERENCE TECHNIQUES

Environmental Simulation Center. www.simcenter.org. Last accessed June 27, 2005.

PlaceMatters.com. www.placematters.us. Last accessed June 27, 2005.

Snyder, Ken, and Julie Herman. November 2003. "Visualization Tools to Improve Community Decision Making." *PAS Memo*. Chicago: American Planning Association.

PART 6: IMPLEMENTATION TECHNIQUES

PLANNING LAW OVERVIEW

Blaesser, Brian W., and Alan C. Weinstein (eds). 1989. *Land Use and the Constitution: Principles for Planning Practice*. Chicago: Planners Press

Kelly, Eric D. (gen. ed.). 1998. *Rohan, Zoning and Land Use Controls*. New York: LexisNexis Matthew Bender.

Mandelker, Daniel R. 2003 *Land Use Law*, 5th ed. Charlottesville, VA: LexisNexis.

PROPERTY RIGHTS, POLICE POWER, NUISANCE, AND VESTED RIGHTS

Blaesser, Brian, and Alan Weinstein. 1989. *Land Use and the Constitution: Principles for Planning Practice*. Chicago: Planners Press.

Jacobs, Harvey M. 2004. *Private Property in the 21st Century: The Future of an American Ideal*. Northampton, MA: Edward Elgar.

DUE PROCESS AND EQUAL PROTECTION

Blaesser, Brian, and Alan Weinstein. 1989. *Land Use and the Constitution: Principles for Planning Practice*. Chicago: Planners Press.

FREEDOM OF RELIGION AND EXPRESSION

Blaesser, Brian W., and Alan C. Weinstein. 1989. *Land Use and the Constitution: Principles for Planning Practice*. Chicago: Planners Press.

Juergensmeyer, Julian Conrad, and Thomas E. Roberts. 1998. *Land Use Planning and Control Law*, Chapter 10, "Constitutional Limitations on Land Use Controls," Part IV, "First Amendment." St. Paul, MN: West Group.

Kelly, Eric Damian, and Connie Cooper. 2000. "Everything You Always Wanted to Know about Regulating Sex Businesses." Planning Advisory Service Report No. 495/496. Chicago: American Planning Association.

Mandelker, Daniel R., and Rebecca L. Rubin (eds). 2001. *Protecting Free Speech and Expression: The First Amendment and Land Use Law*. Chicago: American Bar Association.

EMINENT DOMAIN, TAKINGS, AND EXACTIONS

Delaney, John J. 1995. "Lucas and Dollan: Two Different Routes to the Regulatory Takings End Zone." *Land Development*. 8, no. 1 (Spring/Summer): 17–21.

Freilich, Robert H.,and David W. Bushek, editors. 1995. *Exactions, Impact Fees, and Dedications: Shaping Land-Use Development and Funding Infrastructure in the Dolan Era*. Chicago: American Bar Association.

Marzulla, Nancie G., and Robert J. Marzulla. 1997. *Property Rights: Understanding Government Takings and Environmental Regulation.* Rockville, MD: Government Institutes.

Roberts, Thomas E. 2002. *Taking Sides on the Taking Issues: Public and Private Perspectives.* Chicago: American Bar Association.

FEDERAL LEGISLATION

Bass, Ronald E., Albert I. Herson, and Kenneth M. Bogdan. 2001. *The NEPA Book,* Point Arena, CA: Solano Press.

Bell, Christopher, and others. 2005. *Environmental Law Handbook,* 18th edition, Washington DC: Government Institutes.

California Air Quality Resources Board. 2005. *Air Quality and Land Use Handbook: A Community Health Perspective* (April), Sacramento, CA: CARB.

Congressional Research Service. 1999. Summaries of Environmental Laws Administered by the EPA, Congressional Research Service Report RL30022, Web Accessed on December 15th, 2005, at http://www.ncseonline.org/nle/crsreports/briefingbooks/laws/e.cfm.

Mayer, Susan L. 1993. Air Quality: State Plans and Sanctions, U.S. Congressional Research Service Report, 93-1062 ENR, Washington DC, Web Accessed on December 15th, 2005, at http://www.ncseonline.org/nle/crsreports/air/air-5.cfm.

U.S. Army Corps of Engineers. 1987. *Corps of Engineers Wetland Delineation Manual.* Technical Report Y-87-1. January 1987.

STATE ENABLING LEGISLATION

Advisory Committee on Planning and Zoning, U.S. Department of Commerce. 1928. *A Standard City Planning Enabling Act.* Washington, DC: U.S. GPO.

———. Advisory Committee on Zoning, U.S. Department of Commerce. 1926. *A Standard State Zoning Enabling Act,* revised ed. Washington, DC: U.S. GPO.

American Law Institute (ALI). 1976. *A Model Land Development Code: Complete Text and Commentary.* Philadelphia, PA: ALI.

Meck, Stuart (gen. ed.). January 2002. *Growing Smart℠ Legislative Guidebook: Model Statutes for Planning and the Management of Change.* Chicago: American Planning Association.

ZONING REGULATION

Lerable, Charles A. 1995. *Preparing a Conventional Zoning Ordinance.* Planning Advisory Service Report No. 460. Chicago: American Planning Association.

Salkin, Patricia E. (ed.). 1981–2004. *Zoning and Planning Law Handbook.* Eagan, MN: West Group.

Salsich, Peter W., Jr., and Timothy J. Trynieki. 2004. *Land Use Regulation: A Legal Analysis & Practical Application of Land Use Law,* 2nd ed. Chicago: American Bar Association Section of Real Property, Probate and Trust Law.

Ziegler, Edward H., Jr. 2001. *Rathkopf's The Law of Zoning and Planning,* 4th ed. Eagan, MN: West Group.

SUBDIVISION REGULATION

Freilich, Robert H., and Michael M. Schultz. 1995. *Model Subdivision Regulations: Planning and Law,* 2nd ed. Chicago: Planners Press.

Kushner, James A. 2002. *Subdivision Law and Growth Management,* 2nd ed. (with cumulative supplement). Eagan, MN: West Group.

Listokin, David, and Carole Walker. 1989. *The Subdivision and Site Plan Handbook.* New Brunswick, NJ: CUPR Press.

PLANNED UNIT DEVELOPMENT

Babcock, Richard. 1979. "Zoning." In *The Practice of Local Government Planning,* Frank S. So and Judith Getzels (eds). Washington, DC: International City Management Association, in cooperation with the American Planning Association: 416–443.

Blaesser, Brian W. 2001. *Discretionary Land Use Controls—Avoiding Invitations to Abuse of Discretion.* Eagan, MN: West Group.

Krasnowiecki, Jan. 1965. *Legal Aspects of Planned Unit Residential Development (with Suggested Legislation).* Technical Bulletin 52. Washington, DC: National Association of Home Builders and Urban Land Institute.

Mandelker, Daniel R., and John M. Payne. 2001. *Planning and Control of Land Development: Cases and Materials,* 5th ed. New York: Lexis Publishing.

Moore, Colleen Grogan. 1985. *PUDs in Practice.* Washington, DC: Urban Land Institute.

INNOVATIONS IN LOCAL ZONING REGULATIONS

Brough, Michael B. 1985. *Unified Development Ordinance.* Chicago: Planners Press.

Congress for the New Urbanism. 2004. *Codifying New Urbanism.* Planning Advisory Service Report No. 526. Chicago: American Planning Association.

Duany, Andrés, and Emily Talen. 2002. "Transect Planning." *Journal of the American Planning Association.* 68, no. 3:245–266.

Kendig, Lane. 1980. *Performance Zoning.* Chicago: Planners Press.

New Urban News. 2003. *New Urbanism: Comprehensive Report & Best Practices Guide.* 3rd ed. Ithaca, NY: New Urban Publications.

Porter, Douglas R., Patrick L. Phillips, and Terry J. Lassar. 1988. *Flexible Zoning: How It Works.* Washington, DC: The Urban Land Institute.

SIGN REGULATION

Goebel, Matt and Christopher Duerksen. 1999. *Aesthetics, Community Character, and the Law.* PAS Report 489/490. Chicago: American Planning Association.

Mandelker, Daniel R., and Rebecca L. Rubin. 2001. *Protecting Free Speech and Expression: The First Amendment and Land Use Law.* Chicago: American Bar Association.

Morris, Marya, Mark Hinshaw, Douglas Mace, and Alan Weinstein. 2002. *Context-Sensitive Signage Design.* Chicago: American Planning Association. Available in electronic format only, from www.planning.org.

ADEQUATE PUBLIC FACILITIES AND CONCURRENCY MANAGEMENT

Morris, Marya, and James Schwab. May 1991. "Adequate Public Facilities Ordinances," *Zoning News.* Chicago: American Planning Association.

Nelson, Arthur C., James B. Duncan, Clancy J. Mullen, and Kirk R. Bishop. 1995. *Growth Management Principles and Practices.* Chicago: Planners Press.

White, S. Mark. 1996. *Adequate Public Facilities Ordinances and Transportation Management,* Planning Advisory Service Report No. 465. Chicago: American Planning Association.

URBAN GROWTH AREAS

Easley, Gail. 1992. *Staying Inside the Lines: Urban Growth Boundaries.* Planning Advisory Service Report No. 440. Chicago: American Planning Association.

Knaap, Gerrit, and Arthur C. Nelson. 1992. *The Regulated Landscape: Lessons on State Land Use Planning from Oregon.* Cambridge, MA: Lincoln Institute of Land Policy.

Knaap, Gerrit J., and Lewis D. Hopkins. Summer 2001. "The Inventory Approach to Urban Growth Boundaries." *Journal of the American Planning Association* 67(3): 314–326.

Meck, Stuart (gen. ed.). 2002. *Growing Smart℠ Legislative Guidebook: Model Statutes for Planning and Management of Change.* Chicago: American Planning Association, Section 6-201.1 (Urban Growth Areas), Note 6B (A Note on Urban Growth Areas and Regional Planning).

Nelson, Arthur C., and Casey J. Dawkins. 2004. *Urban Containment in the United States: History, Models, and Techniques for Regional and Metropolitan Growth Management.* Planning Advisory Service Report No. 520. Chicago: American Planning Association, March.

Nelson, Arthur C., and James B. Duncan, with Clancy J. Mullen and Kirk R. Bishop. 1995. *Growth Management Principles and Practices.* Chicago: Planners Press.

Weitz, Jerry, and Terry Moore. Autumn 1998. "Development Inside Urban Growth Boundaries: Oregon's Evidence of Contiguous Urban Form." *Journal of the American Planning Association* 65(4): 424–440.

DEVELOPMENT IMPACT FEES

Meck, Stuart (gen. ed) 2002. *Growing Smart℠ Legislative Guidebook: Model Statutes for Planning and Management of Change.* Chicago: American Planning Association, Section 8-602 ("Development Impact Fees").

Nelson, Arthur C., and James B. Duncan, with Clancy J. Mullen and Kirk R. Bishop. 1995. *Growth*

Management Principles and Practices. Chicago: American Planning Association.

Nelson, Arthur C. (ed.). 1988. *Development Impact Fees: Policy Rationale, Practice, Theory, and Issues.* Chicago: American Planning Association.

Nicholas, James C. 1988. *The Calculation of Proportionate-Share Impact Fees.* Planning Advisory Service Report No. 408. Chicago: American Planning Association.

TRANSFER AND PURCHASE OF DEVELOPMENT RIGHTS

Barrett, Thomas S., and Stefan Nagel. 1996. *Model Conservation Easement and Historic Preservation Easement, 1996.* Washington DC: Land Trust Alliance.

Costonis, John J. 1974. *Space Adrift: Landmark Preservation and the Marketplace.* Urbana, IL: University of Illinois Press for the National Trust for Historic Preservation.

Gottsegen, Amanda Jones. 1997. *Planning for Transfer of Development Rights: A Handbook for New Jersey Municipalities.* Mount Holly, NJ: Burlington County Board of Chosen Freeholders.

Johnston, Robert A., and Mary E. Madison. Summer 1997. "From Landmarks to Landscapes: A Review of Current Practices in the Transfer of Development Rights," *Journal of the American Planning Association* 63 (3): 365–378.

Pruetz, Rick. 2003. *Beyond Takings and Givings: Saving Natural Areas, Farmland, and Historic Landmarks with Transfer of Development Rights and Density Transfer Charges.* Marina Del Rey, CA: Arje Press.

OPEN-SPACE PRESERVATION TECHNIQUES

Daniels, Tom, and Katherine Daniels. 2003. *The Environmental Planning Handbook for Sustainable Communities and Regions.* Chicago: American Planning Association.

Diehl, Janet, and Thomas Barrett. 1988. *The Conservation Easement Handbook.* San Francisco: The Trust for Public Land; and Alexandria, VA: The Land Trust Exchange.

McQueen, Mike. 2003. *Land Conservation Financing.* Washington, DC: Island Press.

Nolon, John R. 2003. *Open Ground: Effective Local Strategies for Protecting Natural Resources.* Washington, DC: Environmental Law Institute.

Small, Stephen J. 2002. *Preserving Family Lands, III.* Boston, MA: Landowner Planning Center.

———. 2001. *Third Supplement to the Federal Tax Law of Conservation Easements.* Washington, DC: Land Trust Alliance.

FARMLAND PRESERVATION

American Farmland Trust. 1997. *Saving American Farmland: What Works.* Northampton, MA: American Farmland Trust.

Chadbourne, Joseph H. and Mary M. Chadbourne. 2000. *Common Groundwork: A Practical Guide to Protecting Urban and Rural Land,* 3rd ed. Chagrin Falls, OH: Chadbourne & Chadbourne.

Daniels, Tom. 1999. *When City and Country Collide: Managing Growth in the Metropolitan Fringe.* Washington, DC: Island Press.

Daniels, Tom, and Deborah Bowers. 1997. *Holding Our Ground: Protecting America's Farms and Farmland.* Washington, DC: Island Press.

USDA Advisory Committee on Farm and Forest Protection and Land Use. 2001. *Maintaining Farms and Forests in Rapidly Growing Areas.* Washington, DC: U.S. Department of Agriculture.

LAND EVALUATION AND SITE ASSESSMENT

Pease, J.R., and R.E. Coughlin, 1996. *Land Evaluation and Site Assessment: A Guidebook for Rating Agricultural Lands,* 2nd ed. Ankeny, IA: Soil and Water Conservation Society.

Soil and Water Conservation Society. 2003. *Enhancing LESA: Ideas for Improving the Use and Capabilities of the Land Evaluation and Site Assessment System.* Ankeny, IA.

Steiner, Frederick R., Robert E. Coughlin, and James R. Pease. 1994. *A Decade with LESA: The Evolution of Land Evaluation and Site Assessment.* Ankeny, IA: Soil and Water Conservation Society.

VIEWSHED PROTECTION

Smardon, Richard C. 1993. *Legal Landscape: Guidelines for Regulating Environmental and Aesthetic Quality.* New York: Van Nostrand Reinhold.

HISTORIC STRUCTURES

King, Thomas F. 2004.*Cultural Resource Laws & Practice: An Introductory Guide,* 2nd ed. Lanham, MD: Altamira Press.

National Park Service Heritage Preservation Services Web site, www2.cr.nps.gov/index.htm. Last accessed June 27, 2005.

National Register of Historic Places website, www.cr.nps.gov/nr/index.htm. Last accessed June 27, 2005.

Weeks, Kay D., and Anne E. Grimmer. 1995. *Guidelines for Preserving, Rehabilitating, Restoring and Reconstructing Historic Buildings.* Washington, DC: U.S. Department of the Interior, National Park Service.

BROWNFIELDS

American Society for Testing and Materials (ASTM). 1997. *Standard Practice for Environmental Site Assessments: Phase I Environmental Site Assessment.* E-1527-00. West Conshohocken, PA: ASTM.

———. 2002. *Standard Guide for Environmental Site Assessments: Phase II Environmental Site Assessment Process.* E1903-97. West Conshohocken, PA: ASTM.

Council for Urban Economic Development. 1999. *Brownfields Redevelopment Manual.* Washington, DC: Council for Urban Economic Development.

Jenner & Block, and Roy F. Weston. 1997. *The Brownfields Book.* Chicago: Jenner & Block, and Roy F. Weston.

Rafson, Harold J. 1999. *Brownfields: Redeveloping Environmentally Distressed Properties.* New York: McGraw-Hill.

Schilling, Joe. 2002. *Beyond Fences: Brownfields and the Challenges of Land Use Controls.* Washington, DC: International City/County Management Association.

CAPITAL IMPROVEMENT PROGRAMS

Bowyer, Robert A. 1993. *Capital Improvements Programs: Linking Budgeting and Planning.* Planning Advisory Service Report No. 442. Chicago: American Planning Association.

Dalton, Linda C., Charles Hoch, and Frank S. So. 2000. *Practice of Local Government Planning,* 3rd ed. Washington, DC: International City/County Management Association

Developing a Capital Improvement Program. 2002. Colorado Department of Local Affairs.

Vogt, John A. 2004. *Capital Budgeting and Finance: A Guide for Local Governments.* Washington, DC: International City/County Management Association.

TAX INCREMENT FINANCING

Dye, Richard, and David Merriman. 1999. "Does Tax Increment Financing Discourage Economic Development?" *Journal of Urban Economics* 47: 306–328.

Johnson, Craig, and Joyce Man, editors. 2001. *Tax Increment Financing and Economic Development: Uses, Structures, and Impact.* Albany: SUNY Press.

Weber, Rachel. 2003. "Tax Increment Financing in Theory and Practice." In Sammis White, Edward Hill, and Richard Bingham, eds. *Financing Economic Development for the 21st Century.* Armonk, NY: M.E. Sharpe.

FINANCING METHODS AND TECHNIQUES

Brueggeman, William B., and Jeffery D. Fisher. 2001. *Real Estate Finance and Investments,* 11th ed. New York: McGraw-Hill Irwin.

Urban Land Institute (ULI). 2004. Case Study: The Yards. http://207.86.218.154/CaseStudies/C034005.htm, accessed February 17, 2005.

———. 2004. Case Study: American Can Company Apartments. www.casestudies.uli.org/CaseStudies/C034012.htm, accessed February 17, 2005.

———. 2004. Case Study: The Gallup Building. http://207.86.218.154/CaseStudies/C032011.htm, accessed February 17, 2005.

FINANCIAL PLANNING AND ANALYSIS: THE PRO FORMA

American Council of Life Insurers. 2004. *Commercial Mortgage Commitments, Second Quarter 2004.* Washington, DC: American Council of Life Insurers.

Balboni, Barbara, editor. 2004. *RSMeans Square Foot Costs, 25th Annual Edition.* Kingston, MA: Reed Construction Data.

Benshoof, Mike, editor. 2001. *The Business of Building, Measuring Your Success, 2001 Cost of Doing Business Study.* Washington, DC: National Association of Home Builders.

Building Owners & Management Association International. 2004. www.boma.org. Last accessed June 27, 2005.

Institute of Real Estate Management. 2004. www.irem.org. Last accessed June 27, 2005.

NAHB Business Management, IT/NAHB Economics. 2004. *Cost of Doing Business Study, The Business of Building, Measuring Your Success.* Washington, DC: National Association of Homebuilders.

Ogershok, Dave. 2004. *2004 National Building Cost Manual,* 28th ed. Carlsbad, CA: Craftsman Book Company.

PricewaterhouseCoopers. 2004. *Korpacz Real Estate Investor Survey* 17 (1).

Real Estate Research Corporation, Real Estate Report. 2004. *The Good, the Bad, and the Real Estate Market: Waiting for the Dust to Settle* 33 (2).

Urban Land Institute (ULI). 2004. *Dollar & Cents of Shopping Centers.* Washington, DC: ULI.

———. 2003. *Dollar & Cents of Multi-Family Housing 2003: A Survey of Income and Expenses in Rental Apartment Communities.* Washington, DC: ULI.

PLANNING RESOURCES

American Planning Association (APA)

http://www.planning.org

APA is a nonprofit public interest and research organization committed to urban, suburban, regional, and rural planning. APA and its professional institute, the American Institute of Certified Planners, advance the art and science of planning to meet the needs of people and society.1 For more information including a list of divisions, visit the APA web site.[1]

Planning Accreditation Board (PAB)

http://showcase.netins.net/web/pab_fi66/

The Planning Accreditation Board's (PAB) principal mission is to evaluate and reach decisions regarding applications for academic accreditation; and to discuss and propose appropriate policy changes to enhance the role of accreditation in furthering academic excellence. The PAB conducts the planning accreditation program for all planning programs in North America.[2]

American Institute of Certified Planners (AICP)

http://www.planning.org/aicp/

AICP is the American Planning Association's professional institute, providing recognized leadership nationwide in the certification of professional planners, ethics, professional development, planning education, and the standards of planning practice.[3]

Association of Collegiate Schools of Planning (ACSP)

http://www.acsp.org

The Association of Collegiate Schools of Planning (ACSP) is a consortium of university-based programs offering credentials in urban and regional planning. It seeks to strengthen the role of planning education in colleges and universities through publications, conferences, and community engagement as well as through participation in the accreditation process.[4]

Land Based Classification Systems (LBCS)

http://www.planning.org/lbcs/

Land-Based Classification Standards provide a consistent model for classifying land uses according to their characteristics. The standards are based on a multidimensional land-use classification model. LBCS updates the 1965 Standard Land Use Coding Manual (SLUCM), a standard which was widely adopted for land-use classifications. Because many current applications and land-based data depend on SLUCM and its derivatives, this update includes tools and methods to migrate such data.[5]

1 APA web site, http://www.planning.org, 2006.
2 PAB web site, http://showcase.netins.net/web/pab_fi66/, 2006.
3 APA web site, 2006.
4 ACSP web site, http://www.acsp.org, 2006.
5 APA web site, 2006.

GRAPHIC SYMBOLS AND DRAWING ANNOTATIONS

Abbreviations

AS = Asphalt
BR = Brick
BW = Bottom of wall
CL = Centerline
CONC = Concrete
DIA = Diameter
DN = Down
DR = Drain
DU = Dwelling unit
EXP JT = Expansion joint
FF = Finished floor

PL = Property line
RAD = Radius
SS = Stainless steel
ST = Steel
SWM = Stormwater management
TOC = Top of curb
TW = Top of wall
UP = Up
WD = Wood

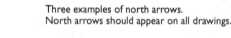

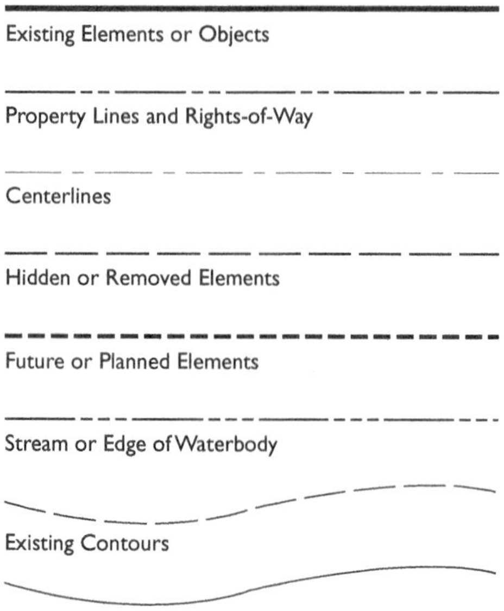

Existing Elements or Objects

Property Lines and Rights-of-Way

Centerlines

Hidden or Removed Elements

Future or Planned Elements

Stream or Edge of Waterbody

Existing Contours

Proposed Contours

Notes:
1. Length of dashes and gaps may vary depending on desired effect of drawing.
2. Lines shown above illustrate relative line weights.

Relative Line Weights:
1 Guidelines or Centerlines
2 Surface Conditions
3 Edges of Three-Dimensional Objects
4 Cuts through Materials or Objects

LINEWORK

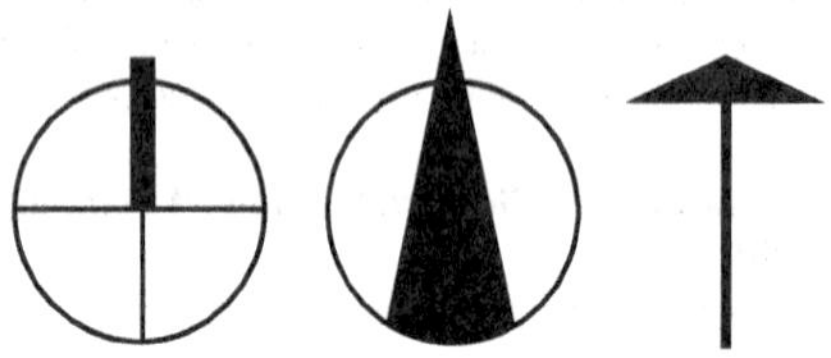

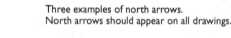

Three examples of north arrows.
North arrows should appear on all drawings.

Scales:
1. Graphic scales should be provided on all drawings, and scale should be legible when drawing is reduced in size.
2. Scale should indicate both multiples and subdivisions of actual scale.

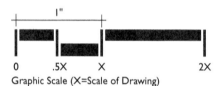

0   .5X   X   2X
Graphic Scale (X=Scale of Drawing)

0   50'   100'   200'
Example: Scale for a Drawing at 1"=100'

SYMBOLS

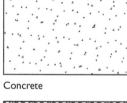

Soil

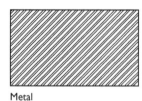

Concrete

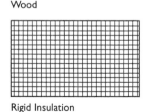

Gravel

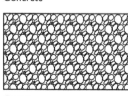

Metal

Wood

Rigid Insulation

Sand

Batt Insulation

Masonry

MATERIALS

Section or Elevation Indication

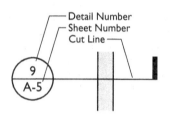

Line of sectional cut. Arrow indicates direction of view, and letter or number identifies section.

Detail Number
Sheet Number
Cut Line

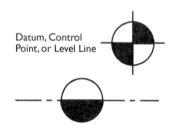

Datum, Control Point, or Level Line

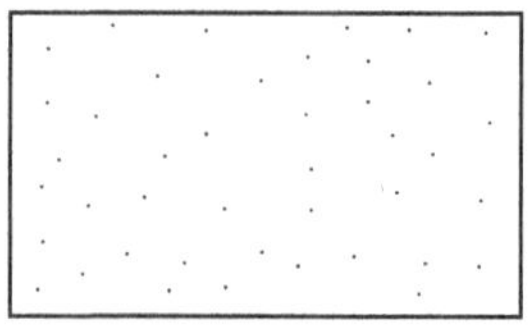

Match line between drawings.
Shaded side indicates side under consideration.

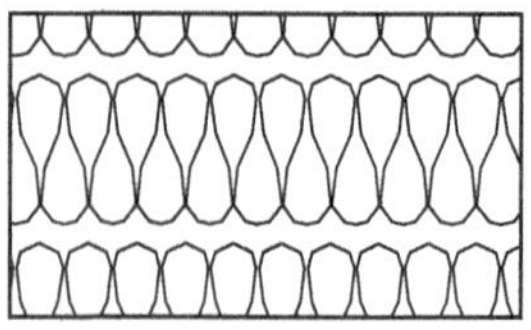

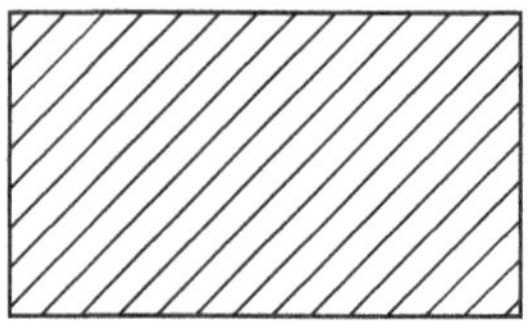

INDEX